A TREATISE

ON

HINDU LAW AND USAGE

A TREATISE

ON

HINDU LAW AND USAGE

JOHN D. MAYNE

GYAN

Published by

Gyan Publishing House
5, Ansari Road
Daryaganj, New Delhi-110002
Phone: 011-47034999, 9811692060
E-mail: books@gyanbooks.com

Distribution Network
gyanbooks.com
India, USA, Canada, UK, Australia

ISBN: 978-93-6920-287-4 (HB)

First Published, 1878

2nd Impression 2025

Printed at: Gyan Press, Delhi.

A TREATISE ON HINDU LAW AND USAGE
Author: JOHN D. MAYNE

A TREATISE

ON

HINDU LAW AND USAGE.

BY

JOHN D. MAYNE,

OF THE INNER TEMPLE, ESQ., BARRISTER-AT-LAW,
FORMERLY OFFICIATING ADVOCATE GENERAL OF MADRAS,
AUTHOR OF "A TREATISE ON DAMAGES," "COMMENTARIES ON THE INDIAN PENAL CODE," ETC.

1892.

PREFACE TO THE FIFTH EDITION.

In preparing this edition the whole of the text has been carefully reconsidered, with reference to later decisions. The most important of these is the ruling of the Privy Council, which establishes that under the Mitakshara law the holder of an impartible Zemindary possesses absolute powers of alienation, which cannot be controlled by his sons. The same tribunal has also enlarged and explained its former decisions in reference to the liability of sons for the debts of their father.

I have again to thank my publishers, Messrs. Higginbotham & Co., for the great care with which they have passed the sheets through the press. To save trouble to those who consult the work I have added a list of cases bearing on the subjects discussed; which have appeared while the edition was passing through the press.

JOHN D. MAYNE.

October, 1892.

PREFACE TO THE THIRD EDITION.

SINCE the publication of the last edition of this work, many new materials for the study of Hindu Law have been placed within the reach of those, who, like myself, are unable to examine the authorities in their original Sanskrit. Professor Max Müller's Series of the Sacred Books of the East has given us translations of the entire texts of Apastamba, Gautama, and Vishnu, by Dr. Bühler and Dr. Jolly. Mr. Narayen Mandlik has supplied us with a translation of the whole of Yajnavalkya, and a new rendering of the Mayukha; while the Sarasvati Vilasa and the Viramitrodaya have been rendered accessible by the labours of Mr. Foulkes and of Golapchandra Sarkar.

Judging from an examination of these works, I doubt whether we need expect to receive much more light upon the existing Hindu Law from the works of the purely legal writers. They seem to me merely to reproduce with slavish fidelity the same texts of the ancient writers, and then to criticise them, as if they were algebraic formulas, without any attempt to show what relation, if any, they have to the actual facts of life. When, for instance, so modern a work as the Viramitrodaya gravely discusses marriages between persons of different castes, or the twelve species of sons, it is impossible to imagine that the author is talking of anything which really existed in his time. Yet he dilates upon all these distinctions with as much apparent faith in their value, as would be exhibited by an English Lawyer in expounding the peculiarities of a bill of exchange. From the extracts given by Mr. Narayen Mandlik, I imagine that the modern writers of Western India are more willing to recognise realities than those of Bengal and Benares. Probably, much that is useful and interesting might be found (amid an infinity of rubbish) in the works on ceremonial law. But what we really want is that well informed Natives of India should take a law book in their hands, and tell us frankly, under each head, how much of the written text is actually recognised and practised as the rule of every-day life. The great value of Mr. Narayen Mandlik's work consists in the extent to which he has adopted this course. His forthcoming work will be looked for with the greatest interest by every student of Hindu Law.

I feel a natural timidity in entering upon the region of volcanic controversy which has sprung up around the works of Mr. J. H. Nelson. It seems a pity that amid so much with which every one must agree, there should be so much more with which no one can agree. When he denies that Manu, Yajnavalkya, and the Mitakshara form the recognised guides of Dravidian, or even of Sudra life, one is willing to accept the statement. But when he goes on to assert that Manu, Yajnavalkya, and the Mitakshara are themselves without authority among Sanskrit lawyers, or have authority only among obscure and limited sects, one is tempted to ask what possible amount of evidence he would consider sufficient to establish the contrary? Can Mr. Nelson put his finger upon any single law book subsequent to the probable dates of Manu and Yajnavalkya in which those sages are not referred to, not only with respect and reverence, but with absolute submission? If the Mitakshara is a work of no authority, how does it happen that every pundit in every part of India except Bengal invariably cites Vijnanesvara in support of his opinion? Mr. Nelson's grotesque suggestion that the Mitakshara dates from the 17th or 18th century is dismissed by *M. Barth,** one of the greatest of living Sanskrit scholars, with the summary remark;—"Every Orientalist who has read Colebrooke will answer, that if that admirable inquirer had found nothing better to write about

* Revue Critique, 1882, p. 165; the article contains a thorough examination of Mr. Nelson's views, and seems to me to be a model of acute, candid, and courteous criticism.

the Mitakshara, he would not have written a line upon the subject." His proposal that every law suit should commence with an exhaustive enquiry as to the legal usages, if any, by which the respective parties considered they were bound, is a sly stroke of humour which cannot be too much admired. Coming from an opponent it might have been considered malicious. I fancy that Mr. Nelson, as a Judge, would be the first to resist the application of his own proposal.

An unusual number of important decisions have been recorded since the publication of the last edition, and it will be seen that several portions of this work have been re-written in consequence. The law as to the liability of a son for his father's debts, and as to the father's power of dealing with family property to liquidate such debts, seems at last to be settling down into an intelligible, if not a very satisfactory, shape. The controversies arising out of the text of the Mitakshara defining stridhanum appear also to be quieted by direct decision, and the conflicting view of woman's rights taken by the Bombay High Court has at last been restricted and defined, and made to rest upon inveterate usage, rather than upon written law. A single decision of the Privy Council has established the heritable right of female Sapindas in Bombay, and recognised the all-important principle, that succession under the Mitakshara law is based upon propinquity, and not upon degrees of religious merit.

JOHN D. MAYNE.

INNER TEMPLE,
January, 1883.

PREFACE.

I HAVE endeavoured in this Work to show, not only what the Hindu Law is, but how it came to be what it is. Probably many of my professional readers may think that the latter part of the enquiry is only a waste of time and trouble, and that in pursuing it I have added to the bulk of the volume without increasing its utility. It might be sufficient to say, that I have aimed at writing a book which should be something different from a mere practitioner's manual.

Hindu Law has the oldest pedigree of any known system of jurisprudence, and even now it shows no signs of decrepitude. At this day it governs races of men, extending from Cashmere to Cape Comorin, who agree in nothing else except their submission to it. No time or trouble can be wasted, which is spent in investigating the origin and development of such a system, and the causes of its influence. I cannot but indulge a hope, that the very parts of this Work which seem of least value to a practising lawyer, may be read with interest by some who never intend to enter a Court. I also hope that the same discussions which appear to have only an antiquarian and theoretical interest, may be found of real service, if not to the counsel who has to win a case, at all events to the judge who has to decide it.

The great difficulty which meets a judge is to choose between the conflicting texts which can be presented to him on almost every question. This difficulty is constantly increased by the labours of those scholars who are yearly opening up fresh sources of information. The works which they have made accessible are, naturally, the works of the very early writers, who had passed into oblivion because the substance of their teaching was embodied in more modern treatises. Many of these early texts are in conflict with each other, and still more are in conflict with the general body of law as it has been administered in our Courts.

An opinion seems to be growing up that we have been going all wrong; that we have been mistaken in taking the law from its more recent interpreters, and that our only safe course is to revert to antiquity, and, wherever it may be necessary, to correct the Mitakshara or the Daya Bhaga by Manu, Gautama, or Vasishtha. Such a view omits to notice that some of these authors are perhaps two thousand years old, and that even the East does change, though slowly. The real task of the lawyer is not to reconcile these contradictions, which is impossible, but to account for them. He will best help a Judge who is pressed, for instance, by a text which forbids a partition, or which makes a father the absolute despot of his family, by showing him that these texts were once literally true, but that the state of society in which they were true has long since passed away. This has been done to a considerable extent by Dr. Mayr in his most valuable work, *Das Indische Erbrecht*. He seems, however, not to have been acquainted with the writers of the Bengal school, and of course had no knowledge of the developments which the law has received through nearly a century of Judicial decisions. I have tried to follow in the course marked out by him, and by Sir H. S. Maine in his well-known writings. It would be presumption to hope that I have done so with complete, or even with any considerable success. But I hope the attempt may lead the way to criticism, which will end in the discovery of truth.

Another, and completely different current of opinion, is that of those who think that Hindu Law, as represented in the

Sanskrit writings, has little application to any but Brahmans, or those who accept the ministrations of Brahmans, and that it has no bearing upon the life of the inferior castes, and of the non-Aryan races. This view has been put forward by Mr. Nelson in his "View of the Hindu Law as administered by the Madras High Court." In much that he says I thoroughly agree with him. I quite agree with him in thinking that rules, founded on the religious doctrines of Brahmanism, cannot be properly applied to tribes who have never received those doctrines, merely upon evidence that they are contained in a Sanskrit law-book. But it seems to me that the influence of Brahmanism upon even the Sanskrit writers has been greatly exaggerated, and that those parts of the Sanskrit law which are of any practical importance are mainly based upon usage, which in substance, though not in detail, is common both to Aryan and non-Aryan tribes. Much of the present Work is devoted to the elucidation of this view. I also think that he has under-estimated the influence which the Sanskrit law has exercised, in moulding to its own model the somewhat similar usages even of non-Aryan races. This influence has been exercised throughout the whole of Southern India during the present century by means of our Courts and Pandits, by Vakils, and officials, both judicial and revenue, almost all of whom till very lately were Brahmans.

That the Dravidian races have any conscious belief that they are following the Mitakshara, I do not at all suppose. Nor has an Englishman any conscious belief that his life is guided by Lord Coke and Lord Mansfield. But it is quite possible that these races may be trying unconsciously to follow the course of life which is adopted by the most respectable, the most intellectual, and the best educated among their neighbours. The result would be exactly the same as if they studied the Mitakshara for themselves. That this really is the case is an opinion which I arrived at, after fifteen years' acquaintance with the litigation of every part of the Madras Presidency. Even in Malabar I have witnessed continued efforts on the part of the natives to cast off their own customs and to deal with their property by partition, alienation, and devise, as if it were governed by the ordinary Hindu Law. These efforts were constantly successful in the provincial Courts, but were invariably foiled on appeal to the Sudder Court at Madras, the objection being frequently taken for the first time by an English barrister. It so happened that during the whole time of this silent revolt the Sudder Court possessed one or more Judges, who were thoroughly acquainted with Malabar customs, and by whom cases from that district were invariably heard. Had the Court been without such special experience, the process would probably have gone on with such rapidity, that by this time every Malabar *tarwad* would have been broken up. The revolt would have been a revolution.

A third class of opinion is that of the common-sense Englishman, whose views are very ably represented by Mr. Cunningham—now a Judge of the Bengal High Court—in the preface to his recent "Digest of Hindu Law." He appears to look upon the entire law with a mixture of wonder and pity. He is amused at the absurdity of the rule which forbids an orphan to be adopted. He is shocked at finding that a man's great-grandson is his immediate heir, while the son of that great-grandson is a very remote heir, and his own sister is hardly an heir at all. He thinks everything would be set right by a short and simple code, which would please everybody, and upon the meaning of which the Judges are not expected to differ. These of course are questions for the legislator, not for the lawyer. I have attempted to offer materials for the discussion by showing how the rules in question originated, and how much would have to be removed if they were altered. The age of miracles has passed, and I hardly expect to see a code of Hindu Law which shall satisfy the trader and the agriculturist, the Punjabi and the Bengali, the pandits of Benares and Ramaiswaram, of Umritsur and of Poona. But I can easily imagine a very beautiful and specious code, which should produce much more dissatisfaction and expense than the law as at present administered.

I cannot conclude without expressing my painful consciousness of the disadvantage under which I have laboured from my ignorance of Sanskrit. This has made me completely dependent on translated works. A really satisfactory treatise on Hindu Law would require its author to be equally learned as a lawyer and an Orientalist. Such a work could have been produced by Mr. Colebrooke, or by the editors of the Bombay Digest, if the Government had not restricted the scope of their labours. Hitherto, unfortunately, those who have possessed the necessary qualifications have wanted either the inclination or the time. The lawyers have not been Orientalists, and the Orientalists have not been lawyers. For the correction of the many mistakes into which my ignorance has led me, I can only most cordially say,—*Exoriare aliquis nostris ex ossibus ultor.*

JOHN D. MAYNE.

INNER TEMPLE,

July, 1878.

ABBREVIATIONS AND REFERENCES.

Agra.	North-West Province High Court, 3 vols., [1866-1868.]
All.	Indian Law Reports, Allahabad Series, [from 1876.]
Amb.	Ambler's Reports, Chancery.
Apast.	Apastamba, Translated by Bühler.
Ap. Ca.	English Law Reports, Appeal Cases.
Atk.	Atkyn's Reports, Chancery, *tempore* Lord Hardwicke, [1736-1754.]
Atsi.	Quoted in Sutherland's Dattaka Mimamsa.
B. and Ald	Barnewall and Alderson, [King's Bench, 1817-1822.]
B. L. R.	Bengal Law Reports, High Court, [1868-1875.]
B. L. R. (Sup. Vol.)	Bengal Law Reports, Supplemental Volume, Full Bench Rulings, in 2 parts, [1862-1868.]
——— a. c. j.	,, ,, Appellate Civil Jurisdiction.
——— app.	,, ,, Appendix.
——— f. b.	,, ,, Full Bench.
——— o. c. j.	,, ,, Original Civil Jurisdiction.
——— p. c.	,, ,, Privy Council.
Baudh.	Baudhayana, cited from translation, by Bühler.
Beav.	Beavan's Reports, Rolls Court, *tempore* Lord Langdale and Sir John Romilly, [1838-1863.]
Bellasis.	Bombay Sudder Dewany Adawlut Reports.
Bom.	Bombay Series of the Indian Law Reports, [from 1876.]
Bom. H. C.	Bombay High Court Reports, [1863-1875.]
——— a. c. j.	,, ,, ,, Appellate Civil Jurisdiction.
——— o. c. j.	,, ,, ,, Original ,, ,,
Bom. Sel. Rep.	Bombay Select Reports, Sudder Dewany Adawlut.
Bor.	Borrodaile's Reports, (Bombay Sudder Adawlut) Folio, 1825. [The references in brackets are to the paging of the edition of 1862.]
Boul.	Boulnois, Calcutta Supreme Court, [1856-1859.]
Bourke.	Calcutta High Court, Original side, 1 vol., [1865.]
Breeks.	Primitive Tribes of the Nilaghiris, by J. W. Breeks, Esq.

Cal.	Indian Law Reports, Calcutta Series, [from 1876.]
C. L. R.	Calcutta Law Reports [from 1877.]
Ch. D.	English Law Reports, Chancery Division.
Cole. Pref.	Colebrook's Prefaces to the Daya Bhaga and the Digest.
——— Essays.	Colebrook's Essays.
Coop. Geo.	Cooper's (George) Reports, Chancery, *tempore* Lord Eldon, [1815.]
Coryton.	Calcutta Reports, High Court, Original side, 1 vol., [1864.]
D. Bh.	Daya Bhaga, by Jimuta Vahana. (Colebrooke.)
D. Ch.	Dattaka Chandrika. (Sutherland.)
Dig.	Jagannatha's Digest. (Colebrooke.) 3 vols., [1801.]
D. K. S.	Daya Krama Sangraha. (Wynch.)
D. M.	Dattaka Mimamsa. (Sutherland.)
Domat.	Domat's Civil Law.
Elb.	Elberling on Inheritance, &c., [1844.]
F. MacN.	Sir F. MacNaghten's Considerations on Hindu Law, [1829.]
Fult.	Fulton's Reports, Supreme Court, Calcutta, [1842-1844.]
Gaut.	Gautama, cited from translation, by Bühler.
Gib.	Gibelin. Etudes sur le Droit civil des Hindous, [1846.]
Goldst.	Goldstücker's Present Administration of Hindu Law. [1871.]
Hay.	Calcutta High Court, Appellate side, 2 vols., [1862-1863.]
Hyde.	Calcutta Reports, High Court, Original side, 2 vols., [1864-1865.]
I. A.	English Law Reports. Indian Appeals, [from 1873.]
I. A. Sup. Vol.	English Reports. Indian Appeals. Supplemental Volume, [1872-1873.]
Ib. or *Ibid.*	The same reference as the one immediately preceding.
In. Jur.	Indian Jurist, 1 vol., Calcutta High Court, Original side, [1860-1863.]
In. Jur.	Indian Jurist, continuation of the Madras Jurist, [from 1877.]
In. Jus. N. S.	Calcutta High Court, Original side, 2 vols., [1866-1867.]
Ind. Wis.	Monier Williams' Indian Wisdom.
Jac. and W.	Jacob and Walker's Reports, Chancery, *tempore* Lord Eldon, [1819-1823.]
John.	Johnson's Reports, Chancery, *before* Sir Page Wood, [1858-1860.]

Jolly. Lect.	Dr. Jolly's Tagore Lectures, 1883.
Kn.	Knapp's Privy Council Cases, [1831-1836.]
Lewin.	Lewin on Trusts, 6th ed., 1875.
L. R. (P. and D.)	English Law Reports, Probate and Divorce.
Mad.	Madras Series of the Indian Law Reports, [from 1876.]
Mad. Dec.	Decisions of the Madras Sudder Court. The selected decisions from 1805-1847 are cited by volumes : the subsequent reports, by years.
Mad. H. C.	Madras High Court Reports, [1862-1876.]
Madhav.	Madhava's Daya Vibhaga. (Burnell,) [1868.]
Mad. Jur.	Madras Jurist, 11 vols., [1866-1876.]
Mad. Law. Rep.	The Madras Law Reporter, one Volume, High Court, [1877.]
——Rev. Reg.	Madras Revenue Register, [1867-1874.]
Manu.	Cited from translation, by Sir William Jones.
Marsh.	Marshall's Cases on Appeal to the High Court of Bengal, [1864.]
Max Müller A. S. L.	Ancient Sanskrit Literature.
Mayr.	Das Indische Erbrecht, [1873.]
McLennan.	Studies in Ancient History, [1876.]
Mit.	Mitakshara. (Colebrooke.)
M. Dig.	Morley's Digest, 2 vols., Calcutta, [1850.]
M. I. A.	Moore's Indian Appeals, [1836-1872.]
Morton.	Decisions of late Supreme Court, Calcutta, 1 vol., [1774-1848.]
Montr.	Montriou's Hindu Law Cases, Calcutta Supreme Court, [1780-1801.]
Morris.	Bombay Sudder Adawlut Reports.
Nar.	Narada, cited from translation, by Bühler, or by Jolly, [London, 1876.]
N. C.	Sir Thomas Strange's Notes of Cases, Madras, [1816.]
Nelson's View.	View of the Hindu Law as administered by High Court of Madras, Nelson, Madras, [1877.]
„ Scientific Study.	A Prospectus of the Scientific Study of the Hindu Law, Nelson, Madras, [1881.]
N.-W. P.	Decisions of the High Court of the N.-W. Provinces, Allahabad, [1869-1875.]
N.-W. P. (S. D.)	Sudder Reports of North-West-Provinces.
P. C.	Privy Council.
Perry. O. C.	Sir Erskine Perry's Oriental Cases, Bombay Supreme Court, [1853.]

Punjab Customs.	Notes on Customary Law as administered in the Courts of the Punjab. Boulnois and Rattigan, 1876.
Punjab Customary Law.	Three Volumes, edited by C. L. Tupper, C. S., Calcutta, [1881.]
P. Williams.	Peere Williams' Reports, Chancery, [1695-1735]
Raghunandana.	The Daya Tattwa of Raghunandana, translated by Golap Chandra Sarkar, Sastry, Calcutta, 1874.
Raj. Sarvadhikari.	Mr. Rajkumar Sarvadhikari's Tagore Lectures, 1880.
S. C.	Same Case.
S. D.	Decisions of the Bengal Sudder Court. The selected decisions from 1791-1848 are cited by volumes, with a double paging, which refers to the original edition, and to that recently published in Calcutta. The subsequent reports are referred to by years.
Sev.	Cases on Appeal to High Court of Bengal in continuation of Marshall, by Sevestre, [1869]
Sm. Ch.	Smriti Chandrika. (Kristnasawmy Iyer), Madras, [1867.]
Spencer.	Principles of Sociology.
Stokes, H. L. B.	Stokes' Hindu Law Books, Vyavahara Mayukha, by Borrodaile; Daya Bhaga and Mitakshara, by Colebrooke; Dattaka Mimamsa, and Dattaka Chandrika, by Sutherland, [Madras, 1865.]
Story.	Equity Jurisprudence.
Stra. H. L.	Sir Thomas Strange's Hindu Law, [1830.]
Stra. Man.	Mr. T. L. Strange's Manual of Hindu Law, 1863.
Suth.	Weekly Reporter, [Calcutta, 1864-1877]
Suth. (A. O. J.)	" " Appeals from the Original Jurisdiction.
Suth. Mis.	" " Miscellaneous Appeals.
Suth. (P. C.)	" " Privy Council Rulings.
Suth. Sp. No.	" " Special Number. Full Bench Rulings, July 1862 to July 1864.
Suth. Syn.	Mr. Sutherland's Synopsis of the Law of Adoption. The paging refers to this work as printed in Mr. Stokes' Hindu Law-Books, Madras, 1865.
T. &. B.	Taylor and Bell. (Supreme Court of Calcutta.)
Teulon.	La Mère. Par A. Girard Teulon. 1867.
Thesawal.	The Thesawaleme; or, Laws and Customs of Jaffna. (H. F. Mutukisna) 1862.
Varad.	Varadrajah's Vyavahara Nirnaya. (Burnell.) 1872.
Vas.	Vasishtha, cited from translation, by Bühler.
V. Darp.	Vyavastha Darpana, by Shamachurn Sircar, 1867.
Ves.	Vesey's (Junior) Reports, Chancery, [1789-1817.]

Ves. Sen.	Vesey's (Senior) Reports, Chancery, *tempore* Lord Hardwicke, [1746-1755.]
Vill. Com.	Maine's Village Communities, [1871.]
Viramit.	The Law of Inheritance as in the Viramitrodaya, of Mitra, by Gopalchandra Misra Sarkar Sastri, Calcutta, 1879.
Vish.	Vishnu, cited from translation by Bühler, or by Jolly.
Viv. Chint.	Vivada Chintamani, by Vachespati Misra. (Prosonno Coomar Tagore.) 1865.
V. May.	Vyavahara Mayukha. (Borrodaile.)
V. N. Mandlik.	The Vyavahara Mayukha and Yajnavalkya, with Introduction and Appendix, by Rao Saheb Vishvanath Narayan Mandlik, Bombay, 1880.
W. & B.	West and Bühler's Digest, Bombay, 3rd ed., 1884.
W. R.	Sutherland's Weekly Reporter. [A few cases have been accidentally cited from these reports under this designation instead of "Suth."]
W. MacN.	W. MacNaghten's Hindu Law, 1829.
Wym.	Wyman's Civil and Criminal Reports, Calcutta.
Yaj.	Yajnavalkya, cited from translation, by Dr. Roer, or Professor Stenzler.

CONTENTS.

*** The references throughout are to paragraphs.*

CHAPTER I.

ON THE NATURE AND ORIGIN OF HINDU LAW.

SOURCES OF HINDU LAW.

CHAPTER II.

TEXTS AND DECISIONS.

CHAPTER III.

CUSTOMARY LAW.

FAMILY RELATIONS.

CHAPTER IV.

MARRIAGE AND SONSHIP.

CHAPTER V.

ADOPTION.

CHAPTER VI.

MINORITY AND GUARDIANSHIP.

FAMILY PROPERTY.

CHAPTER VII.

EARLY LAW OF PROPERTY.

CHAPTER VIII.

THE JOINT FAMILY.

CHAPTER IX.

DEBTS.

CHAPTER X.

ALIENATION.

CHAPTER XI.

WILLS.

CHAPTER XII.

RELIGIOUS AND CHARITABLE ENDOWMENTS.

CHAPTER XIII.

BENAMI TRANSACTIONS.

CHAPTER XIV.

MAINTENANCE.

CHAPTER XV.

PARTITION.

LAW OF INHERITANCE.

CHAPTER XVI.

PRINCIPLES OF SUCCESSION IN CASE OF MALES.

CHAPTER XVII.

PRINCIPLES OF SUCCESSION IN CASE OF FEMALES.

CHAPTER XVIII.

ORDER OF SUCCESSION.

CHAPTER XIX.

EXCLUSION FROM INHERITANCE.

WOMAN'S ESTATE.

CHAPTER XX.

PROPERTY INHERITED FROM MALES.

CHAPTER XXI.

PROPERTY NOT INHERITED FROM MALES.

TABLE OF CASES.

N.B.—In the citation of cases, prefixes, such as Stri, Rajah, Rani, Maharajah, Maharani, and Baboo are omitted, and where the name is long, the latter part is left out. The spelling of the Report from which the case is quoted has always been followed, so that the same name is often spelt in different ways. The references are to paragraphs.

ADDENDA.

Cases upon the following subjects have been decided while this edition was passing through the press.

ADOPTION.—*Shankaran* v. *Kesavan*, 15 Mad. 6; *Virayya* v. *Hanumanta*, 14 Mad. 459; *Chamsukh* v. *Parbati*, 14 All. 53; *Beni Prasad* v. *Hardai Bibi*, 14 All. 67; *Rukhab* v. *Chunlal*, 16 Bom. 347; *Surendra Keshav* v. *Doorgasunderi*, 19 I. A. 108.

ALIENATION by one member of a joint family, *Rangayana* v. *Ganapabhatta*, 15 Bom. 673; *Pem Singh* v. *Partab Singh*, 14 All. 179; *Muhammad Husain* v. *Dip Chand*, ibid. 190.

GUARDIAN AND WARD.—*Jwala Dei* v. *Pirbhu*, 14 All. 35; re *Saithri*, 16 Bom. 307; *Sham Kuar* v. *Mohanunda Sahoy*, 19 Cal. 301; *Indur Chunder* v. *Radhakishore*, 19 I. A. 90.

MAINTENANCE.—Re *Gulabdas Bhaidas*, 16 Bom. 269.

NON-JOINDER OF CO-OWNER.—*Parameswaran* v. *Shangaran*, 14 Mad. 489; *Paramasiva* v. *Krishna*, ibid. 498.

PERSONA DESIGNATA.—*Bireswar* v. *Ardha Chunder*, 19 I. A. 101; *Surendra Keshav* v. *Doorgasunderi*, ib. 108.

WIFE, Custody of—Re *Dhuronidhur Ghose*, 17 Cal. 298.

HINDU LAW AND USAGE.

CHAPTER I.

ON THE NATURE AND ORIGIN OF HINDU LAW.

Authority of Sanskrit lawyers

§ 1. UNTIL very lately, writers upon Hindu Law have assumed, not only that it was recorded exclusively in the Sanskrit texts of the early sages, and the commentaries upon them, but that those sages were the actual originators and founders of that law. The earliest work which attracted European attention was that which is known as the Institutes of Manu. People talk of this as the legislation of Manu; as if it was something which came into force on a particular day, like the Indian Penal Code, and which derived all its authority from being promulgated by him. Even those who are aware that it never had any legislative authority, and that it only described what its author believed to be, or wished to be, the law, seem to imagine that those rules which govern civil rights among Hindus, and which we roughly speak of as Hindu law, are solely of Brahmanical origin. They admit that conflicting customs exist, and must be respected. But these are looked on as local violations of a law which is of general obligation, and which ought to be universally observed; as something to be checked and put down, if possible, and to be apologised for, if the existence of the usage is proved beyond dispute.

not universal.

§ 2. On the other hand, those who derived their knowledge of law not from books, but from acquaintance with Hindus in their own homes, did not admit that the Brahma-

quently, though perhaps unconsciously, answer, before he can decide a case. For instance, it is quite certain that religious efficacy is the test of succession according to Brahmanical principles. If, then, one of two rival claimants appears to be preferable in every respect except that of religious efficacy, the judge will have to determine, whether the system which he is administering is based on Brahmanical principles at all. So as regards adoption. A Brahman tests its necessity and its validity, solely by religious motives. If an adoption is made with an utter absence of religious necessity or motive, a judge would have to decide whether religion was an essential element in the transaction or not.

Sanscrit law based on usage:

§ 5. My view is, that Hindu law is based upon immemorial customs, which existed prior to and independent of Brahmanism. That when the Aryans penetrated into India, they found there a number of usages either the same as, or not wholly unlike, their own. That they accepted these, with or without modifications, rejecting only those which were incapable of being assimilated, such as polyandry, incestuous marriages, and the like. That the latter lived on a merely local life, while the former became incorporated among the customs of the ruling race. That when Brahmanism arose, and the Brahman writers turned their attention to law, they at first simply stated the facts as they found them, without attaching to them any religious significance. That the religious element subsequently grew up, and entwined itself with legal conceptions, and then distorted them in three ways. *First*, by attributing a pious purpose to acts of a purely secular nature. *Secondly*, by clogging those acts with rules and restrictions, suitable to the assumed pious purpose. And, *Thirdly*, by gradually altering the customs themselves, so as to further the special objects of religion, or policy, favoured by Brahmanism.

not on direct authority.

§ 6. I think it is impossible to imagine that any body of usage could have obtained general acceptance throughout

India, merely because it was inculcated by Brahman writers, or even because it was held by the Aryan tribes. In Southern India, at all events, it seems clear that neither Aryans nor Brahmans ever settled in sufficient numbers to produce any such result (*e*). We know the tenacity with which Eastern races cling to their customs, unaffected by the example of those who live near them. We have no reason to suppose that the Aryans in India ever attempted to force their usages upon the conquered races, or that they could have succeeded in doing so, if they had tried. The Brahman treatises themselves negative any such idea. There is not an atom of dogmatism, or controversy, among the old Sutra writers. They appear to be simply recording the usages they observed, and occasionally stop to remark that the practices of some districts, or the opinions of other persons are different (*f*). The greater part of Manu is exclusively addressed to Brahmans, but he takes pains to point out that the laws and customs of districts, classes, and even of families ought to be observed (*g*). Example and influence, coupled with the general progress of society, have largely modified ancient usages; but a wholesale substitution of one set of usages for another appears to me to be equally opposed to philosophy and to facts.

Distinctive features not Brahmanical.

§ 7. The most distinctive features of the Hindu law are the undivided family system, the order of succession, and the practice of adoption. The two latter are at present thoroughly saturated with Brahmanism. Its influence upon the family has only been exerted for the purpose of breaking it up. But in all cases, I think it will be satisfactorily shown, that Brahmanism has had nothing whatever to do with the early history of those branches of the law; that

---

(*e*) See Hunter's Orissa, i. 241-265; Nelson's View, chaps. i. & ii.; Madura Manual, Pt. II., p. 11, Pt. III., chap. ii.

(*f*) See Apast., ii. vi. 14, § 6-9; Gaut., xxviii. § 26, 40. Dr. Jolly, referring to the differences of doctrine among the Sutra writers, says, "It is hardly possible to trace this diversity of doctrine to another cause than the difference of popular usage subsisting between the divers times and countries in which the existing Dharmasutras had originated." (Jolly, § 40.)

(*g*) See *post*, § 40; see M. Müller, A. S. L. 50.

these existed independently of Brahmanism, or even of Aryanism ; and that where the religious element has entered into, and remodelled them, the change in this direction has been absolutely modern. This view will be developed at length in the course of the present work. It will be sufficient here briefly to indicate the nature of the argument.

Joint Family system.

§ 8. The Joint Family is only one phase of that tendency to hold property in community, which, it is now proved, was once the ordinary mode of tenure. The attention of scholars was first drawn to this point by the Sclavonian Village Communities. But it is now placed beyond doubt that joint ownership of a similar character is not limited to Sclavonian, or even to Aryan, races, but is to be found in every part of the world where men have once settled down to an agricultural life (*h*). In India such a corporate system is universally found, either in the shape of Village Communities, or of the simple Joint Family. So far from the system owing its origin to Brahmanism, or even to Aryanism, its most striking instances are found precisely in those provinces where the Brahman and Aryan influence was weakest. As regards the Village Communities, the Punjab and the adjoining districts are the region in which alone they flourish in their primitive vigour. This is the tract which the Aryans must have first traversed on entering India. Yet it seems to have been there that Brahmanism most completely failed to take root. Dr. Muir cites various passages from the *Mahabharata* which establish this. The inhabitants "who dwell between the five rivers which are associated with the Sindhu (Indus) as the sixth," are described as "those impure *Bahikas*, who are outcasts from righteousness." "Let no Arya dwell there even for two days. There dwell degraded Brahmans, contemporary with Prajapati. They have no Veda, no Vedic ceremony, nor any sacrifice." "There a *Bahika*, born a Brahman, becomes afterwards a Kshatriya, a Vaiciya, or a Sudra, and eventually a barber. And again the barber becomes a Brah-

(*h*) See Laveleye Propriété, and Sir H. S. Maine's Works, *passim*.

man. And once again the Brahman there is born a slave. One Brahman alone is born in a family. The other brothers act as they will without restraint" (*i*). And they retain this character to the present day, as we shall see that with them the religious element has never entered into their secular law. Next to the Punjab the strongest traces of the Village Community are found among the Dravidian races of the South. Similarly as regards the Joint Family. It still flourishes in its purest form, not only undivided but indivisible, among the polyandrous castes of Malabar and Canara, over whom Brahmanism has never attempted to cast even the hem of its garment. Next to them, probably, the strictest survival of the undivided family is to be found in Northern Ceylon, among the Tamil emigrants from the South of India. It is only when the family system begins to break up that we can trace the influence of Brahmanism, and then the break up proceeds in the direct ratio of that influence (*k*).

Law of inheritance.

§ 9. The case of inheritance is even more strongly in favour of the same view. The principle that "the right of inheritance, according to Hindu law, is wholly regulated with reference to the spiritual benefits to be conferred on the deceased proprietor," has been laid down on the highest judicial authority as an article of the legal creed, which is universally true, and which it would be heresy to doubt. It is strictly and absolutely true in Bengal. It is not so elsewhere (*l*). Among the Hindus of the Punjab, the order of succession is determined by custom, and not by spiritual considerations (*m*). Throughout the Presidency of Bombay, numerous relations, and especially females, inherit, to whom no ingenuity can ascribe the slightest religious merit. According to the Mitakshara, consanguinity in the male line is the test of heirship, not religious merit. All those

(*i*) Muir, S. T., ii. 482.
(*k*) See *post*, chap. vii. § 237.
(*l*) This was long since pointed out by Professor Wilson. See his Works, v. 14. Sir H. S. Maine has also had the hardihood to hint a disbelief of the doctrine. Village Communities, 53.
(*m*) Punjab Customs, 11. Punjab Customary law, ii. 100-142.

who follow its authority accept agnates to the fourteenth degree, whose religious efficacy is infinitesimal, in preference to cognates, such as a sister's son, whose capacity for offering sacrifices ranks very high. The doctrine that heirs are to be placed in the direct order of their spiritual merit, was announced for the first time by Jimuta Vahana, and has been expanded by his successors. But it rendered necessary a complete remodelling of the order of succession. Cognates are now shuffled in among the agnates, instead of coming after them; and the very definition of cognates is altered, so as to exclude those who are actually named as such by the Mitakshara. The result is a system, whose essence is Brahmanism, and whose logic is faultless, but which is no more the system of early India, or of the rest of India, than the English Statute of Distributions (*n*). In Bengal the inheritance follows the duty of offering sacrifices. Elsewhere the duty follows the inheritance.

Law of adoption.

§ 10. The law of adoption has been even more successfully appropriated by the Brahmans, and in this instance they have almost succeeded in blotting out all trace of a usage existing previous to their own. There can be no doubt that among those Aryan races who have practised ancestor-worship, the existence of a son to offer up the religious rites has always been a matter of primary importance. Where no natural-born son exists, a substituted son takes his place. This naturally leads to the practice of adoption. But apart from all religious considerations, the advantages of having a son to assist a father in his life, to protect him in his old age, and to step into his property after his death, would be equally felt, and are equally felt, by other races. We know that the Sudras practised adoption, for even the Brahmanical writers provide special rules for their case. The inhabitants of the Punjab and North-West Provinces, whether Hindus proper, Jains, Jats, Sikhs, or even Muhammedans, practise adoption, without religious rites, or the slightest reference to religious purposes. The

(*n*) As to the whole of this, see chap. xvi. § 459, *et seq.*

same may be said of the Tamils in Ceylon. Even the Brahmanical works admit that the celebration of the name, and the perpetuation of the lineage, were sufficient reasons for affiliation, without reference to the rescue of the adopter's soul from Hell. In fact some of the very earliest instances mentioned are of the adoption of daughters. This latter practice is followed to the present day by the Bheels, certainly from no motives of piety, and by the Tamils of Ceylon. There can, I think, be no doubt that if the Aryans brought the habit of adoption with them into India, they also found it there already; and that the non-Aryan races, at all events, derive it from their own immemorial usage, and not from Bráhmanical invention. There seems, also, every reason to believe, that even among the Aryan Hindus the importance now ascribed to adoption is comparatively recent. Little is to be found on the subject in the works of any but the most modern writers, and the majority of the ancient authors rank the adopted son very low among the subsidiary sons. The series of elaborate rules, which now limit the choice of a boy, are all the offspring of a metaphor; that he must be the reflection of a son. These rules may be appropriate enough to a system which requires the fiction of actual sonship for the proper performance of religious rites; but they have no bearing whatever upon affiliation, which has not this object in view, and, as we shall find, they are disregarded in many parts of India where the practice of adoption is strongly rooted. Yet the Brahmans have created the belief, that every adoption is intended to rescue the soul of a progenitor from Put, and that it must be judged of solely by its tendency to do so. And our tribunals gravely weigh the amount of religious conviction present to the minds of persons, not one of whom probably connects the idea of religion with the act of adoption, more than with that of procreation (*o*).

(*o*) Manu gives a preference to the eldest son, on the ground that he alone has been begotten from a sense of duty, ix. § 106, 107. See this subject discussed at length, *post*, ch. v. § 92—95.

Limited applicability of Sanskrit law.

§ 11. If I am right in the above views, it would follow that races who are Hindu by name, or even Hindu by religion (*p*), are not necessarily governed by any of the written treatises on law, which are founded upon, and developed from, the *Smritis*. Their usages may be very similar, but may be based on principles so different as to make the developments wholly inapplicable. Possibly all Brahmans, however doubtful their pedigree, may be precluded, by a sort of estoppel, from denying the authority of the Brahmanical writings which are current in their district (*q*). But there can be no pretence for any such estoppel with regard to persons who are not only not Brahmans, but not Aryans. In one instance, a very learned judge, after discussing a question of inheritance among Tamil litigants, on the most technical principles of Sanskrit law, wound up his judgment by saying, "I must be allowed to add that I feel the grotesque absurdity of applying to these *Maravers* the doctrine of Hindu Law. It would be just as reasonable to give them the benefit of the Feudal Law of real property. At this late day it is however impossible to act upon one's consciousness of the absurdity" (*r*). I must own I cannot see the impossibility. In Northern and Western India, the Courts have never considered themselves bound to apply these principles to sects who did not profess submission to the *Smritis*. In the case of the Jains, for instance, research has established that their usages, while closely resembling those of orthodox Hinduism, diverge exactly where they might be expected to do, from being based on secular, and not on religious, principles (*s*). The Bengal Court, as might be anticipated, is less tolerant of heresy. But it is certainly rather startling to find it assumed as a matter of course that the natives of Assam, the rudest of our provinces, are governed by the Hindu law as modified by Jimuta Vahana (*t*). It would be

(*p*) Many of the Dravidian races, who are called Hindus, are worshippers of snakes and devils, and are as indifferent to Vishnu and Siva as are the inhabitants of Whitechapel.

(*q*) See *Gopalayyan* v. *Raghupatiayyan*, 7 Mad. H. C. 255.

(*r*) *Holloway*, J., *Muttu Vizia* v. *Dorasinga*, 6 Mad. H. C. 341.

(*s*) *Post*, § 44.

(*t*) *Deepo Debia* v. *Gobindo Deb*, 16 Suth., 42; S. C. 11 B. L. R. 131.

curious to enquire whether there was any reason whatever for this belief, except the fact that appeals lay to the High Court of Bengal. It is a singular and suggestive circumstance that the Oriya chieftains of Orissa and Ganjam, who are identical in origin, language and religion, are supposed to follow different systems of law; the system ascribed to each being precisely that which is most familiar to the Courts to which they are judicially subject (*u*).

Brahmanism has modified usage.

§ 12. On the other hand, while I think that Brahmanical law has been principally founded on non-Brahmanical customs, so I have little doubt that those customs have been largely modified and supplemented by that law. Where two sets of usage, not wholly reconcilable, are found side by side, that which claims a divine origin has a great advantage in the struggle for existence over the other (*v*). Further, a more highly developed system of law has always a tendency to supplant one which is less developed. A very little law satisfies the wants of rude communities. As they advance in civilization, and new causes of dispute arise, they feel the necessity for new rules. If they have none of their own, they naturally borrow from their neighbours. Where evidence of custom is being given, it is not uncommon to find a native saying, "We observe our own rules. In a case where there is no rule we ask the pundits." Of course the pundit, with much complacency, produces from his Shasters an answer which solves the difficulty. This is first adopted on his authority, and then becomes an accretion to the body of village usage. This process would, of course, be aided by the influence which the Brahmans always carry with them, by means of their intellectual superiority. Dr. Jolly points out that a large number of law Commentaries and Digests have been written either by Indian

(*u*) See as to Orissa, note to *Bishenpirea* v. *Soogunda*, 1 S. D. 37 (49, 51). But in a case reported by Mr. MacNaghten from Orissa, in 1813, the futwah was certainly given according to Mitakshara law. 2 W. MacN. 306. As to Ganjam, see *Raghunadha* v. *Brozo Kishoro*, 3 I. A. 154; S. C. 1 Mad. 69; S. C. 25 Suth., 291.

(*v*) See Maine's Vill. Com. 52.

Kings and Prime Ministers themselves, or under their auspices and by their order (Jolly, Sect. 27). The Hindu Judges were also Brahmans. Both writers and judges would naturally tinge native usages with their own views, and supplement them by their own doctrines. The change must have gone on with great rapidity during the last century, when so many disputes were referred to the decision of our Courts, and settled in those Courts solely in accordance with the opinions of the pundits (*w*).

Practical inferences.

§ 13. The practical result of this discussion, so far as it may turn out to be well founded, seems to be—*First*, that we should be very careful before we apply all the so-called Hindu Law to all the so-called Hindus. *Secondly*, that in considering the applicability of that law, we should not be too strongly influenced by an undoubted similarity of usage. *Thirdly*, that we should be prepared to find that rules, such as rules of inheritance, adoption, and the like, may have been accepted from the Brahmans by classes of persons who never accepted the principles, or motives, from which these rules originally sprung; and, therefore, *lastly*, that we should not rashly infer that a usage which leads to necessary developments, when practised by Brahmans, will lead to the same developments when practised by alien races. It will not do so, unless they have adopted the principle as well as the practice. Without both, the usage is merely a branch severed from the trunk. The sap is wanting, which can alone produce growth (*x*).

(*w*) See *post*, § 38.

(*x*) For a full discussion as to the cases in which Hindu law is made the rule of decision in the Courts of British India, see W. & B. (3rd ed.) 1—7. Where a person fails to establish that he conforms to any religion which carries with it any special form of law, his rights will be dealt with according to "justice, equity and good conscience." *Raj Bahadur* v. *Bishen Dyal*, 4 All. 343.

CHAPTER II.

THE SOURCES OF HINDU LAW.

1. *The Smritis*, § 15.
2. *The Commentators*, § 25.
3. *Schools of Law*, § 33.
4. *Judicial Decisions*, § 38.

§ 14. I PROPOSE in this chapter to examine the sources of Hindu Law, so far as they are to be found in the writings of the early Sanskrit sages and their commentators. A general reference to the accessible authorities on this branch of the subject is given below (*a*). I have not thought it necessary to give special references, unless where the statement in the text was still a matter of controversy; nor have I attempted to make a show of learning, which I do not possess, by referring at length to the works of Hindu writers of whom I know nothing but their names. Under this branch of the subject I shall offer some observations upon those differences of opinion which are generally spoken of as constituting various "schools of law." I shall conclude by making some remarks upon the influence which our judicial system has exercised upon the natural development of Hindu Law. The important subject of Custom will be reserved for the next chapter.

§ 15. I. THE SMRITIS.—The great difficulty which meets us

(*a*) See M. Müller's Ancient Sanskrit Literature; Dr. Bühler's Introduction to the Digest of Hindu Law by West and Bühler; Colebrooke's Prefaces to the Daya Bhaga and the Digest, and his note, 1 Stra. H. L. 315; the Preface to Sir Thomas Strange's Hindu Law; Dr. Burnell's Prefaces to his translations of the Daya Vibhaga and Varadrajah, and the introduction to the first volume of Morley's Digest; Stenzler's Preface to his translation of Yajnavalkya; Dr. Jolly's Preface to Narada; Mayr, Ind. Erbrecht, 1—10, where the conclusions of Professor M. Müller and Dr. Bühler are adopted; Professor Monier Williams' Indian Wisdom. N. Mandlik. Introduction and Appendix I. Dr. Bühler's Introductions to Apastamba and Gautama, Vasishtha and Baudhayana, and Manu: Dr. Jolly's Introduction to Vishnu. Sacred Books of the East, Vols. II, VII, XIV and XXV. R. Sarvadhikari, § 4; Jolly, § 2 and 3.

in the study of Hindu Law, is to ascertain the date to which any particular statement should be referred. Chronology has absolutely no existence among Hindu writers. They deal in a vast, general, way with cycles of fabulous length, which, of course, have no relation to anything real. It is impossible to ascertain when the earliest sages lived, or whether they ever lived. Most of the recorded names are probably purely mythical. Tradition is of no value when it has a fable for its source. Names of indefinite antiquity are assumed by comparatively recent writers, or editors, or collectors, of texts. Even when we can ascertain the sequence of certain works, it is unsafe to assume that any statement of law represented an existing fact. To a Hindu writer every sacred text is equally true. Maxims which have long since ceased to correspond with actual life are reproduced, either without comment, or with a non-natural interpretation. Extinct usages are detailed without a suggestion that they are extinct, from an idea that it is sacrilegious to omit anything that has once found a place in Holy Writ. In short we have exactly the same difficulty in dealing with our materials as a palæontologist would find, if all the archaic organisms which he compares had been discovered, not reposing in their successive strata, but jumbled together in a museum.

Chronology non-existent.

Sruti and *Smriti*.

§ 16. The two great categories of primeval authority are the *Sruti* and the *Smriti*. Somewhere in the order of precedence either in between the *Srutis* and the *Smritis*, or more probably after them, come the Puranas, which, according to Colebrooke, "are reckoned as a supplement to the Scripture, and as such constitute a fifth Veda" (*b*). The *Sruti* is that which was seen or perceived, in a revelation, and includes the four Vedas. The *Smriti* is the recollection handed down by the Rishis, or sages of antiquity (*c*.) The former is of divine, the latter of human, origin. Where the two conflict, if such a conflict is conceivable, the latter

(*b*) *Per Mahmood, J.*, *Ganga Sahai* v. *Lekhraj Singh* 9 All., p 289.
(*c*) Manu, ii. § 9, 10; W. & B. 25.

must give away. Practically, however, the *Sruti* has little, or no, legal value. It contains no statements of law, as such, though its statements of facts are occasionally referred to as conclusive evidence of a legal usage. Rules, as distinct from instances, of conduct are for the first time embodied in the *Smriti*. The *Smriti*, again, are found on examination to fall under two heads, *viz.*, works written in prose, or in prose and verse mixed, and works written wholly in verse. The latter class of writings, being fuller and clearer, are generally meant when the term *Smriti* is used, but it properly includes both classes. To Professor Max Müller we owe the important generalisation, that the former, as a rule, are older than the latter. His views may be summarised as follows (*d*).

§ 17. The first duty of a Brahman was to study the Vedas. These were orally transmitted for many ages before they were committed to writing, and orally taught, as they are even at the present time (*e*). Naturally many various versions of the same Veda arose, and sects, or schools, were formed, headed by distinguished teachers who taught from these various versions. To facilitate their teaching they framed *Sutras* or strings of rules, chiefly in prose, which formed rather a *memoria technica* by which the substance of the oral lessons might be recalled, than a regular treatise on the subject. Every department of the Vedas had its own *Sutras*. Those which related to the rules of practical life, or law, were known as the *Dharma-Sutras*, and these last again were as varied as the sects, or *Charanas*, from which they originated, and bore the names of the teachers by whom they were actually composed, or whose views they were supposed to embody. Thus the *Dharma-Sutras* which bear the name of Apastamba, Baudhayana, Gautama and the like, contain the substance of the rules of law imparted in the *Charanas* which recognized *Sutras.*

(*d*) See his letter to Mr. Morley, 1 M. Dig. Introd. 196; A. S. Lit., pp. 125—134, 260, 377; W. & B. 31.
(*e*) See as to the introduction of writing, A. S. Lit. 497; Ind. Wisdom, 252.

those teachers as their heads, or which had adopted those names. Works of this class are known to have existed more than two hundred years before our era. Professor Max Müller places the *Sutra* period roughly as ranging from B.C. 600-200. But the composition of these works may have continued longer, and it cannot be asserted of any particular *Sutra* now in existence that it is of the age above specified.

Relative age of the Sutras.

§ 18. The *Dharma-Sutras* which bear the names of Gautama, Baudhayana, Apastamba, Vasishtha and Vishnu have been translated, the last named by Dr. Jolly and the others by Dr. Bühler (*f*). As to their relative antiquity Gautama is the oldest of all, being quoted by Baudhayana who ranks next in order of time. He belonged to the school of the Sama Veda. His use of the word Yavana, a term applied in very early Indian parlance to the Greeks, has been supposed to mark his period as not earlier than 300 B.C. The word, however, appears to have had other applications, and Dr. Bühler considers that it would be unsafe to found any opinion upon its use. At present nothing else is known by which the date of Gautama can be even approximately fixed (*g*). Next in point of time is Baudhayana. His Sutras were originally studied by the followers of the Black Yajurveda alone, but subsequently were accepted by all Brahmans as an authority on the Sacred Law. He was probably of Southern origin. Dr. Bühler considers that a period counted by centuries elapsed between his date and that of Apastamba, whom he places before the first century B.C. (*h*). Apastamba was also an inhabitant of Southern India, probably of the Andhra district, and a follower of the same Veda as Baudhayana. He is remarkable for the uncompromising vigour with which he rejects certain practices recognised by the early Hindu law, such as the various species of sons, the Niyoga and the Paisacha form of marriage (*i*).

(*f*) Sacred Books of the East, Vols. II, VII, and XIV.
(*g*) Bühler's Introduction to Gautama, 45, 49, 56.
(*h*) Bühler's Introduction to Baudhayana, 29, 35, and to Apastamba, 18, 22, 40.
(*i*) Bühler's Introduction to Apastamba, 16, 18, 30, 34.

Except from quotations contained in his work there is nothing to show the date of Vasishtha. He knew of Yama, Gautama, Harita, and a Manu, the author of the Manava Sutras. He may perhaps be supposed to have known Baudhayana. Dr. Jolly considers that he quoted from Vishnu, but in this opinion Dr. Bühler differs from him. Vasishtha appears to have been a native of the Northern part of India (*k*). No tradition exists as to the authorship of the Vishnu-Sutra. Dr. Bühler and Dr. Jolly agree in thinking that in its present form it has been recast with additions by those who, ignorant of its origin, wished to attribute it to the God Vishnu. Much of the work, both in style and substance, bears the mark of extreme antiquity, and portions of it are thought by Dr. Jolly to have been borrowed by Vasishtha or even by Baudhayana. He, like Vasishtha, was a follower, of the Black Yajur-veda (*l*). Harita, Hiranyakesin, Uçanas, Yama, Kaçyapa and Çankha, all of whom are quoted in Colebrooke's Digest and by the commentators, are also of the Sutra period. Of these Harita is earlier than Baudhayana, and Hiranyakesin is later than Apastamba. (*m*).

Dharma-Sastras generally more recent.

§ 19. The Dharma-Sastras, which are wholly in verse, Professor Max Müller considers to be merely metrical versions of previously-existing Dharma-Sutras. Dr. Bühler, after pointing out "that almost in every branch of Hindu science, where we find text books in prose and in verse, the latter are only recent redactions of works of the former class," proceeds to say, "This view may be supported by some other general reasons. *Firstly,* if we take off the above-mentioned Introductions, the contents of the poetical Dharma-Sastras agree entirely with those of the Dharma-Sutras, whilst the arrangement of the subject-matter differs only slightly, not more than the Dharma-Sutras differ amongst each other *Secondly,* the language of the poeti-

(*k*) Bühler's Introduction to Vasishtha, 16, 17, 21, 25.
(*l*) Dr. Jolly's Introduction to Vishnu. Lecture, 38. W. & B 35.
(*m*) Bühler's Introduction to Apastamba, 23, 27.

cal Dharma-Sutras and Dharma-Sastras is nearly the same. Both show archaic forms, and in many instances the same *Thirdly*, the poetical Dharma-Sastras contain many of the Slokas or Gathas given in the Dharma-Sutras, and some in an apparently modified form. Instances of the former kind are exceedingly numerous. A comparison of the Gathas from Vasishtha, Baudhayana, Apastamba and Hiranyakesin with the Manu Smriti, shows that more than a hundred of the former are incorporated in the latter." And he goes on to point out other instances in which passages of Manu are only modernised versions of passages now existing in Vasishtha's Sutra. In one case Manu (viii. § 140) quotes Vasishtha on a question of lawful interest, and the passage so quoted is still extant in the Sutras of that author. The result in Dr. Bühler's opinion is that "it would seem probable that Dharma-Sastras, like that ascribed to Manu and Yajnavalkya, are versifications of older Sutras, though they, in their turn, may be older than some of the Sutra works which have come down to our times" (*n*). A third work of a similar class is that known by the name of Narada. All of these are now accessible to English readers (*o*). As to relative age they rank in the order in which they are named. Their actual age is a matter upon which even proximate certainty is unattainable.

Manu.

§ 20. The Code of Manu has always been treated by Hindu sages and commentators, from the earliest times, as being of paramount authority; an opinion, however, which does not prevent them from treating it as obsolete whenever occasion requires (*p*). No better proof could be given of its antiquity. Whether it gained its reputation from its

---

(*n*) W. & B. 42.

(*o*) Yajnavalkya has been wholly translated in German by Professor Stenzler (1849). An English translation of the whole of the 2nd book, and of part of the 1st, has been made by Dr. Roer (Calcutta, 1859). The entire work has lately been translated by Mr. V. N. Mandlik (Bombay, 1880). Vrihaspati, whom Dr. Bühler classes in the same category, is only known by fragments cited by the commentators, and by Jagannatha in his Digest.

(*p*) See Preface by Sir W. Jones, p. 11, and general note at the end, p. 363 (London, 1796). V. N. Mandlik Introduction, 46. *Per curiam*, 14 M. I. A. 570.

intrinsic merits, or from its alleged sacred origin ; or whether its sacred origin was ascribed to it in consequence of its age and reputation, we cannot determine. The personality of its author, as described in the work itself, is upon its face mythical. The sages implore Manu to inform them of the sacred laws, and he, after relating his own birth from Brahma, and giving an account of the creation of the world, states that he received the Code from Brahma, and communicated it to the ten sages, and requests Bhrigu, one of the ten, to repeat it to the other nine, who had apparently forgotten it. The rest of the work is then admittedly recited, not by Manu but by Bhrigu (*q*). Manu, the ancestor of mankind, was not an individual, but simply the impersonal and representative man. What is certain is, that among the Brahmanical schools was one known as the School of the Manavas, and that they used as their text for teaching a series of Sutras, entitled the Manava-Sutras. The Dharma-Sutras of this series are unfortunately lost, but it may be supposed that they were the concentrated essence from which the Manava Dharma-Sastras were distilled. Whether the sect took its name from a real teacher called Manu, or from the mythical being, cannot now be known (*r*).

§ 21. The age of the work in its present form is placed by Sir W. Jones at 1280 B.C.; by Schlegel at about 1000 B.C.; by Mr. Elphinstone at about 900 B.C.; and by Professor M. Williams at about the 5th century B.C., (*s*). Professor Max Müller would apparently place it as a post-Vedic work, at a date not earlier than 200 B.C., (*t*). One of his reasons for this view, *viz.*, that the continuous slokas in which it is written did not come into use until after that date, has been shown not to be beyond doubt, as Professor Goldstücker has established their existence at an earlier period (*u*). In order His age.

(*q*) Manu, i. § 1—60, 119, iii. § 16, viii. § 204, xii. § 1. This fiction of recital by an early sage is a sort of common form in Hindu works of no great antiquity, W. & B. Introd. 24, (2nd ed).

(*r*) A. S. Lit. 532; 1 M. Dig. Introd. 197; Ind. Wisd. 213. Jolly, § 47. Bühler's Introduction to Manu, 14, 40, 91, 57, 63.

(*s*) Ind. Wisd. 215; Elphinstone, 227; Stenz., Pref. to Yajnavalkya, 10.

(*t*) A. S. Lit. 61, 244.

(*u*) W. & B. 42.

to determine the question of age, it is necessary to settle whether the present rescension of Manu is the earliest or the latest of the many which undoubtedly existed. The introduction to Narada states that the work of Manu originally consisted of 1,000 chapters and 100,000 slokas. Narada abridged it to 12,000 slokas, and Sumati again reduced it to 4,000. The treatise which we possess has been supposed to be a third abridgment, as it only extends to 2,685. We also find a *Vriddha*, or old, Manu quoted, as well as a ***Brihant***, or great, Manu (*v*). Further, while the existing Manu quotes from Vasishtha a rule which is actually found in his treatise, Vasishtha in turn quotes from Manu verses, two of which are found still, and two of which are not found, one of these latter being in a metre unknown to our Manu. Obviously, the interval between the Manu quoted by Vasishtha, and the Manu who quotes Vasishtha, must be very considerable. Further, Baudhayana quotes Manu for a proposition exactly the reverse of that now stated by him (ix. § 89). Even in a work so late as the 6th century A.D., verses are cited from Manu which can only be found in part in the existing work. The same fact would be apparent, as a matter of internal evidence, from the contradictions in the code itself. For instance, it is impossible to reconcile the precepts as to eating flesh meat (*w*), or as to the second marriage of women (*x*). Even as regards men, some passages seem to indicate that a man could not marry again during the life of his first wife, while in others second marriages are expressly recognized and regulated (*y*). So the texts which refer to the marriage of a Brahman with a Sudra woman (*z*), and to the procreation of children upon a widow for the benefit of the husband (*a*), are evidently of different periods. In former treatises Dr. Bühler had been disposed

Various versions.

(*v*) Dr. Jolly shows that these epithets have no historical significance, and that in general the authors to whose names they are appended are more recent than those with the same names and without the epithet, § 65.

(*w*) Manu, iv. § 250, v. § 7—57, xi. § 156—159.

(*x*) Manu, v. § 157, § 160—165, ix. § 65, 76, 175, 176, 191.

(*y*) Manu, v. § 167, viii. § 204, ix. § 77—87, 101, 102.

(*z*) Manu, iii. § 13—19, ix. § 148—155, 178, x. § 64—67.

(*a*) Manu, ix. § 56—66, 120, 143, 162—165, 167, 190, 191, 203.

to accept the view that the Manu which we possess was the most recent form of the work. In the introduction to his present translation, he has examined the whole question again, and has reached a different result. While admitting that the Manava-Smriti was based on materials of very much greater antiquity, he arrives at the conclusion "that Bhrigu's Samhita is the first and most ancient recast of a Dharma-Sastra, attributed to Manu, which latter must be identified with the Manava Dharma-Sutra." The age of this version he places between the 2nd century B.C., and the 2nd century A.D. (*b*).

§ 22. Next to Manu in date and authority is Yajnavalkya. Yajnavalkya.
No Sutras corresponding to it have been discovered, and the work is considered by Professor Stenzler to have been founded on that of Manu. It has been the subject of numerous commentaries, the most celebrated of which is the Mitakshara, and is practically the starting point of Hindu law for those provinces which are governed by the latter. Of the actual author nothing is known. A Yajnavalkya is mentioned as the person who received the White Yajur-veda from the Sun, and this mythical personage is apparently put forward as the author of the law-book. Of course the two works are widely distant in point of time, but Dr. Bühler is disposed to think that the Dharma-Sastras, known by the name of Yajnavalkya, may have been based on Sutras which proceeded from the school which followed the Vedic author, or perhaps even from that author himself (*c*). This, of course, is mere conjecture. As in the case of Manu, an "old" and a "great" Yajnavalkya are spoken of, evidencing the existence of several editions of the same work. Its date can only be determined approximately within wide limits. It is undoubtedly much later than Manu, as is shown by references to the worship of Ganesa and the planets, to the use of deeds on metal plates, and the endowment of monasteries, while other pas-

(*b*) Bühler's Introduction to Manu, 92—117. Introduction to Vasishtha, 18—20.

(*c*) Yaj., i. § 1, iii. § 110; A. S. Lit. 329; W. & B. 47.

sages, speaking of bald heads and yellow robes, are supposed to be allusions to the Buddhists (*d*). Professor Wilson points out that "passages taken from it have been found on inscriptions in every part of India, dated in the tenth and eleventh centuries. To have been so widely diffused, and to have then attained a general character as an authority, a considerable time must have elapsed, and the work must date therefore long prior to those inscriptions." He considers that the mention of a coin, Nanaka, which occurs in Yajnavalkya, refers to one of the coins of Kanerki, and therefore establishes a date later than 200 A.D. This inference, however, is considered by Professor Max Müller to be very doubtful. Passages from Yajnavalkya are found in the Panchatantra, which cannot be more modern than the end of the fifth century (*e*), and it is quoted wholesale in the Agni Purana, which is supposed to be earlier than the eighth century (*f*). It seems therefore tolerably certain that the work is more than 1,400 years old, but how much older it is impossible to state (*g*).

His age.

Narada.

§ 23. The last of the complete metrical Dharma-Sastras which we possess is the Narada-Smriti, which has been recently translated by Dr. Jolly. The work, as usual, is ascribed to the divine sage Narada, and purports to have been abstracted by him from the second abridgment of

---

(*d*) Yaj., i. § 270, 271, 272, 284, 318, ii. § 185.

(*e*) Wilson's Works, iv. 89.

(*f*) Wilson's Works, iii. 87, 90. See Stenzler's Preface, 10; A. S. Lit 330.

(*g*) The above conclusions are substantially the same as those arrived at by Mr. V. N. Mandlik, in his Introduction, pp. 48—59. He says, (p. 51) "From an examination of the Yajnavalkya Smriti and its comparison with others, I may roughly state that I consider it to be later than Manu, Vasishtha, Gautama, Çankha, Likhita, and Harita, nearly contemporaneous with Vishnu and prior to Parasara and others. It does not seem to have at any one time formed the distinct basis of the Aryan law, like Manu, Gautama, Çankha, Likhita, and Parasara; but as bearing the impress of the leading exponent of the doctrines of the White Yajur-veda, it formed the principal guide of the fifteen Sakhas of that Veda. These Sakhas, as we find from the Charana Vyaha and other authorities, have chiefly predominated in the countries to the North of the Narmada." At p. 49 he says, "Yajnavalkya himself is only one of the numerous Smritikars, and his authority outside his own Sakha is of no peculiar importance." This latter statement seems inconsistent with the fact that the commentators of every district of India refer to, and rely on, his authority. Dr. Jolly says, "The composition of the metrical Smriti of Yajnavalkya cannot be referred to an earlier date than the first centuries A.D." § 49.

Manu in 4,000 slokas. It differs from Manu, however, in many most important respects, which are enumerated by Dr. Bühler and Dr. Jolly. One point of even greater importance than any mentioned by them, is the rank he gives to the adopted son. Manu places him third in the order of sons, and Narada places him ninth, thereby excluding him from the list of collateral heirs (*h*). It is, of course, possible (and I think probable) that in this respect Narada may be really following what was the original and genuine text of Manu. With this exception, if it be one, the whole of Narada is marked by a modern air as compared with Manu. Some of his rules for procedure in particular, seem to anticipate the English principles of special pleading (*i*). The same mode of comparison also establishes that Narada is more recent than Yajnavalkya. On the other hand, his age is so much greater than that of the Mitakshara, that he is not only quoted throughout that work, but quoted as one of the inspired writers. His views also appear to be of a more ancient character than those announced by Katyayana, Vrihaspati, Yama, and other Smritis referred to by the commentators. The result, according to Dr. Jolly, is, that the Narada-Smriti should be placed about the 5th or 6th century, or perhaps a little later; that is to say, about mid-way between Yajnavalkya and the time when the Smritis ceased to be composed. Dr. Bühler has recently made the interesting discovery of a fragment of a larger rescension of Narada than the one translated by Dr. Jolly. It is evidently the edition which was used by the earliest commentators, as it contains texts ascribed by them to Narada which are not found in the existing and abridged form of the work. Unfortunately the fragment does not extend beyond v. 19. (*k*).

His age.

§ 24. Of still later date than Narada, is a class of Smritis, which are described by Dr. Bühler as "secondary redactions

Secondary *Smritis*.

(*h*) Manu, ix. § 159; Nar. xiii. § 46.
(*i*) See Nar., i. § 50—57.
(*k*) Jolly, § 54.

of metrical Dharma-Sastras." Under this head he enumerates "the various Smritis which go under the names of Angiras, Atri, Daksha, Devala, Prajapati, Yama, Likhita, Vyasa, Sankha, Sankha Likhita, Vriddha-Satatapa. All these works are very small and of little significance. That they are really extracts from, or modern versions of, more extensive treatises, and not simply forgeries, as has been supposed, seems to follow from this, that some of the verses quoted by the older commentators of Yajnavalkya and Manu, such as Vijnanesvara, are actually found in them, whilst they cannot be the original works which those lawyers had before them, because other verses quoted are not found in them. In the case of the Vriddha-Satatapa-Smriti, the author himself states in the beginning that he only gives an extract from the larger work" (*l*). Of course, the texts contained in these works may be very ancient, though the editions which contain them are comparatively modern. Many of the names in the above list are actually enumerated by Yajnavalkya as original sources of law (*m*). They must, therefore, have existed, though not in their present shape, long before his time.

Authority of *Smritis.*

§ 25. II. THE COMMENTATORS.—All the works which come under the head of Smritis agree in this—that they claim, and are admitted to possess, an independent authority. One Smriti occasionally quotes another, as one Judge cites the opinion of another Judge, but every part of the work has the same weight, and is regarded as the utterance of infallible truth. No doubt these Smritis exhibit the greatest difference in their statements, owing to the lapse of time, and, probably, in part to local peculiarities. Parasara, one of the latest of this class, recognized this difference, and its cause, and is recorded as laying down that the Institutes

(*l*) W. & B. 50. For complete list of the Smritis, see *ibid.* 13; 1 Morl. Dig. 193; Stokes, H. L. B. 5; Ind. Wisd. 211. V. N. Mandlik, xiv. Jolly, § 51.

(*m*) "Manu, Atri, Vishnu, Harita, Yajnavalkya, Usanas, Angiras, Yama, Apastamba, Samvarta, Katyayana, Vrihaspati, Parasara, Vyasa, Sankha Likhita, Daksha, Gautama, Satatapa, and Vasishtha, are they who have promulgated Dharma-Sastras." Yaj., i. § 4, 5. See an elaborate examination of these works. V. N. Mandlik, Appx. I.

of Manu were appropriate to the *Krita Yuga,* or first age; those of Gautama to the *Treta,* or second age; those of Sankha and Likhita to the *Dvapara,* or third age; and his own to the *Kali,* or sinful age, which still continues (*n*). Unhappily, the legal portion of his work, which we may imagine was founded on some attempt at historical principles, has disappeared. Later writers assume that the Smritis constitute a single body of law, one part of which supplements the other, and every part of which, if properly understood, is capable of being reconciled with the other (*o*). To a certain extent this may, perhaps, be true, as none of the Dharma-Sutras, or Dharma-Sastras, purport to cover the whole body of law (*p*). But the variances between them are not, and could not in the nature of things be, reconcilable. The unquestioning acceptance of the whole mass of Smritis in bulk, could only arise—*first* when their antiquity had become so great that the real facts which they represented had been forgotten, and that a halo of semi-divinity had encircled their authors; and, *secondly,* when the existing law had come to rest on an independent foundation of belief, so as to be able to maintain itself in defiance of the authorities on which it was based. A direct analogy may be found in modern theology, where systems of the most conflicting nature are all referred to the same documents, which are equally at variance with each other and with the dogmas which they are made to support.

Their antiquity.

Mitakshara.

§ 26. Far the weightiest of all the commentaries is that by Vijnanesvara, known as the Mitakshara (*q*). Its authority is supreme in the City and Province of Benares, and it stands at the head of the works referred to as settling the

(*n*) 1 Stra. H. L. Pref. 12. Manu, as we now possess it, mentions all four ages. i. § 81—86.

(*o*) It seems doubtful whether Manu considered that any texts except those of the Vedas were necessarily true, and therefore reconcilable. See ii. § 14, 15.

(*p*) W. & B. (2nd ed.) Introd. 3, 32; Stenz. Preface, 6.

(*q*) The portion of this work which treats of Inheritance is familiar to students by Mr. Colebrooke's translation. The portion on Judicial Procedure has been translated by Mr. W. MacNaghten, and forms the latter part of the first volume of his work on Hindu law. A table of contents of the entire work will be found at the end of the first volume of Borrodaile's Reports (folio, 1825).

law in the South and West of India. It is the basis of the works which set out the law in Mithila. In Bengal alone it is to a certain extent superseded by the writings of Jimuta Vahana and his followers, while in Guzerat the Mayukha is accepted in preference to it, in the very few points on which they differ (*r*). The age of Vijnanesvara has been fixed by recent research to be the latter part of the eleventh century (*s*). His work is followed, with occasional though slight variances, by the writers to whom special weight is attributed in the other provinces.

Apararka.

Another commentator of little later date than Vijnanesvara, is Apararka, a Sovereign who reigned in the Konkan between 1140 and 1186. His views are very similar to those of the Mitakshara, which, however, he never mentions by name. His work is of paramount authority in Kashmir, and is referred to with respect by many of the later Digests. A portion of it, stating the order of succession, has been translated by Mr. Rajkumar Sarvadhikari (*t*).

Authorities in Southern India.

§ 27. The principal of the supplementary works in Southern India are the Smriti Chandrika, the Daya-Vibhaga, the Sarasvati Vilasa, and the Vyavahara Nirnaya (*u*). The Smriti Chandrika was written by Devanda Bhatta, during the existence of the Vijayanagara dynasty in the Deccan, and his date is stated by Dr. Burnell and by Dr. Jolly, to have been about the middle of the 13th century. Rajkumar Sarvadhikari places him a century earlier. The only translation as yet published is that by Kristnasawmy Iyer; Madras, 1867. Dr. Goldstücker is stated by Dr. Burnell (*v*) to have left an edition and translation ready for the press, but it appears never to have been printed. The Sarasvati-Vilasa was written in the beginning of the 16th, or,

(*r*) Colebrooke's note, 1 Stra. H. L. 317; W. & B. 10, *Krishnaji* v. *Pandurang*, 12 Bom. H. C 65, *Collector of Madura* v. *Moottoo Ramalinga*, 12 M. I. A. 437, S. C. 10 Suth. (P. C.) 17; S. C. 1 B. L. R. (P. C.) 1.

(*s*) W. & B. 17.

(*t*) Sarvadhikari, 426. W. & B. 18. Jolly, § 13.

(*u*) See *Collector of Madura* v. *Moottoo Ramalinga*, *ante*, § 26, note (r).

(*v*) Pref to Varadraja.

according to Mr. Rajkumar Sarvadhikari, early in the 14th, century by Pratapa Ruda Deva one of the kings of Orissa. It has recently been translated by the Rev. Mr. Foulkes (*w*). To Dr. Burnell we owe translations of the two other works above mentioned. The Daya-Vibhaga was written by Madhaviya, who was prime minister of several kings of the Vijayanagara dynasty, and who flourished during the latter half of the 14th century. The Vyavahara-Nirnaya was written by Varadaraja, of whom his editor remarks, "it is impossible to say any more than that he was probably a native of the Tamil country, and lived at the end of the 16th or beginning of the 17th century."

§ 28. The works which supplement the Mitakshara in Western India are the Vyavahara Mayukha, and the Viramitrodaya. Of these, the Mitakshara ranks first and paramount in the Maratha country and in Northern Kanara, and Ratnagiri while in Guzerat, and apparently also in the Island of Bombay, the Mayukha is considered as the overruling authority when there is a different of opinion (*x*). In Ahmednagar, Poona and Khandesh the Mayukha appears to be an authority equal to though not capable of over-ruling the Mitakshara (*y*). The Mayukha has been translated by Mr. Borrodaile, and quite recently by Mr. V. N. Mandlik. It is written by Nilakantha, whose family appears to have been of Mahratta origin, but settled in Benares. He lived about 1600 A.D., and his works came into general use about 1700. The Viramitrodaya was written by Mitra Misra, and, like the Mayukha, follows the Mitakshara in most points. Its composition may be assigned to the beginning of the 17th century (*z*). It has lately (1879) been translated by Golapchandra Sarkar Sastri. Western India.

(*w*) Foulkes' Preface to Sarasvati Vilasa, vii.

(*x*) W. & B. 39, 11, 19, *Krishnaji* v. *Pandurang*, *ante*, § 26, note (r); *Lallubhai* v. *Mankuvarbai*, 2 Bom. 418. *Balkrishna* v. *Lakshman*, 14 Bom. 605. *Janki Bai* v. *Sundra*, *ib*. 612, 623. The Mayukha is also said to be an authority Paramount to the Mitakshara in the North Konkan. *Sakharam* v. *Sitabai*, 3 Bom. 353; *Jankibai* v. *Sundra*, 14 Bom. 624.

(*y*) *Bhagirthi Bhai* v. *Kahnujirav*, 11 Bom. 285, 294.

(*z*) W. & B. 22.

It is rather a Benares than a Bombay authority, and of inferior weight to the Mayukha in Western India (*a*). Other works of authority in Western India are mentioned by Dr. Bühler in his Introduction, but being untranslated I have not referred to them any further.

Mithila.

§ 29. In Mithila (or Tirhut and North Behar) the Mitakshara is also an authority, though the Pundits of that district appear to be in the habit rather of referring to the Vivada Chintamani and Vyavahara Chintamani of Vachespati Misra, whose laws they say "are to this day venerated above all others by the Mithilas," and the Retnakara and the Vivada Chandra (*b*). The date of the first named work is put by Mr. Colebrooke, writing in 1796, as ten or twelve generations previously, that is about the middle of the 15th century. The Vivada Chintamani has been translated by Prossonno Coomar Tagore. Of the other works I only know the name.

Treatises on Adoption.

§ 30. The two special works on adoption, *viz.*, the Dattaka Chandrika and the Dattaka Mimamsa, possess at present an authority over other works on the same subject, which is, perhaps, attributable to the fact that they became early accessible to English lawyers and Judges from being translated by Mr. Sutherland. Mr. W. H. MacNaghten says of them (*c*). "In questions relative to the law of adoption, the Dattaka Mimamsa and Dattaka Chandrika are equally respected all over India; and where they differ, the doctrine of the latter is adhered to in Bengal and by the Southern jurists, while the former is held to be the infallible guide in the provinces of Mithila and Benares." This statement was accepted by the Judicial Committee in the Ramnad case (*d*), and has no doubt largely added to the weight which the works would otherwise have possessed. On the other

(*a*) *Collector of Madura* v. *Moottoo Ramalinga*, 12 M. I. A. 438, 466, *ante*, § 26, note (r), *Dhondu Gurav* v. *Gangabai*, 3 Bom. 369.
(*b*) *Rutcheputty* v. *Rajunder*, 2 M. I. A. 134, 146; Coleb. Pref. to Dig. 19.
(*c*) W. MacN. Preface xxiii. and p. 74.
(*d*) *Collector of Madura* v. *Moottoo Ramalinga*, 12 M. I. A. 437, S. C. 10 Suth. (P. C.) 17; S. C. 1 B. L. R. (P. C.) 1.

hand, Mr. V. N. Mandlik states positively as to the Bombay Presidency, that the Dattaka Mimamsa "was not even known to the people in original for many years after the publication of its translation under the auspices of Government. And now the people are guided by the Nirnaya Sindhu, the Viramitrodaya, the Kaustubha, the Dharma Sindhu, the Mayukhas, and not by the Mimamsa or the Chandrika" (*e*). Mr. W. H. MacNaghten had no special knowledge of Southern India. It is possible that he was equally mistaken as to the acceptance of these works in the Madras Presidency (*f*). Probably his belief that the Dattaka Chandrika was an authority in Southern India arose from his supposing that it was written by Devanda Bhatta, the author of the great southern work the Smriti Chandrika. But there seems strong reason to doubt this. The last verse of the original work expressly states that the author's name was Kuvera, but because the author avowed himself to be the writer of the Smriti Chandrika, which was supposed to be the well known production of Devanda Bhatta, the latter name was substituted by Mr. Sutherland in his translation (*g*). Now Mr. V. N. Mandlik points out (*h*) that there were several works named Smriti Chandrika by different authors, and that there is strong internal evidence for supposing that the Dattaka Chandrika and the Smriti Chandrika of Devanda Bhatta were by different writers, while the influence possessed by the former work in Bengal could only be accounted for by supposing that it was really written by Kuvera, who was a Bengal author.

Nanda Pandita, the author of the Dattaka Mimamsa, was

(*e*) V. N. Mandlik, Introduction 73. See *per Mahmood*, J., 9 All. 322. West and Bühler (11) say that the D. M. & D. Ch. are now treated in Bombay as supplementary, but inferior, authorities. In a Full Bench decision of the Bombay High Court, however, the judges stated that the Dattaka Mimamsa and Dattaka Chandrika were regarded by the Court as the leading authorities on adoption, and they declined to allow the reasonings of Mr. Mandlik to alter the usage of the Court in that respect. *Waman Raghupati* v. *Krishnaji*, 14 Bom., 259.

(*f*) See Nelson's Scientific Study, 87. n. citing a native of Madras on this point.

(*g*) Stokes, H. L. B. 662.

(*h*) V. N. Mandlik, Introduction 73. In this opinion he is supported by Dr. Bühler (W. & B. 10. n.) and by Dr. Jolly, (§ 22).

a member of a Benares family, whose descendants of the ninth generation are stated by Mr. V. N. Mandlik to be still flourishing in upper India. He must, therefore, have lived about 250 or 300 years ago (*i*).

Authorities in Bengal.

§ 31. In Bengal, the Mitakshara and the works which follow it have no authority, except upon points where the law of that province is in harmony with the rest of India. In respect to all the points on which they disagree, the treatise of Jimuta Vahana is the starting point, just as that of Vijnanesvara is elsewhere. Little is known either of his identity or of his age. Many portions of his work are supposed to be a refutation of the Mitakshara, and he is expressly named and followed by Raghunandana, who lived in the beginning of the 16th century. On the other hand he quotes the Commentary of Govindaraja which was written in the 12th century. His date must lie between the 13th and 15th century (*k*). His authority must have been overpowering, as no attempt seems ever to have been made to question his views except in minute details; and the principal works of the Bengal lawyers since his time have consisted in commentaries on his treatise. Particulars of these works will be found in Mr. Colebrooke's Prefaces to the Daya Bhaga and to Jagannatha's Digest. The Dayatatwa by Raghunandana has been translated by Golap Chandra Sarkar. The only other work of the Bengal school which I know of in an English form, is the Daya-Krama-Sangraha by Sri Krishna Tarkalankara, translated by Mr. Wynch. It is very modern, its author having lived in the beginning of the last century, but it is considered as of high authority. It follows, and develops, the peculiarly Brahmanical views of the Daya Bhaga.

§ 32. Before quitting this part of the subject, a few words should be said as regards two digests made under European influence. I mean the *Vivadarnava Setu,* compiled at the

(*i*) V. N. Mandlik, Introduction 72 and p. 488.
(*k*) Jolly, § 22. Sarvadhikari (408).

request of Warren Hastings, and commonly known as Halhed's Gentoo Code, from the name of its translator; and the *Vivada Bhangarnava*, compiled at the instance of Sir William Jones by Jagannatha Terkapunchanana, and translated by Mr. Colebrooke, which is generally spoken of as Jagannatha's, or Colebrooke's, Digest. The former work, in its English garb, is quite worthless. It was translated by Mr. Halhed, not from the original Sanskrit, of which he was ignorant, but from a Persian version supplied to him by his interpreter, which Sir W. Jones describes as "a loose, injudicious, epitome of the original Sanskrit, in which abstract many essential passages are omitted, though several notes of little consequence are interpolated, from a vain idea of elucidating, or improving, the text" (*l*). No such drawback exists in the case of the latter work, which was translated by one who was not only the greatest Sanskrit scholar, but the greatest Sanskrit lawyer, whom England has ever produced. But Mr. Colebrooke himself early hinted a disapproval of Jagannatha's labours as abounding with frivolous disquisitions, and as discussing together the discordant opinions maintained by the lawyers of the several schools, without distinguishing which of them is the received doctrine of each school, or whether any of them actually prevail at present. This feature drew down upon the Digest the criticism of being "the best law-book for a Counsel and the worst for a Judge" (*m*). On the other hand, Mr. Justice Dwarkanath Mitter, who was of the greatest eminence as a Bengal lawyer, lately pronounced a high eulogium upon Jagannatha and his work, of whom he says: "I venture to affirm that, with the exception of the three leading writers of the Bengal school,—namely, the author of the Daya Bhaga, the author of the Dayatatwa, and the author of the Daya-kramasangraha,—the authority of Jagannatha Turkopunchanana, is, so far as that school is concerned, higher

Halhed's Code.

Jagannatha's Digest.

(*l*) Pref. to Colebrooke's Digest, 10.

(*m*) Pref. to Digest, 11; Pref. to Daya Bhaga; 2 Stra. H. L. 176; Pref. to Stra. H. L 18.

than that of any other writer on Hindu law, living or dead, not even excluding Mr. Colebrooke himself" (*n*). It certainly seems to me that Jagannatha's work has fallen into rather undeserved odium. As a repertory of ancient texts, many of which are nowhere else accessible to the English reader, it is simply invaluable. His own Commentary is marked by the minute balancing of conflicting views which is common to all Hindu lawyers. But as he always gives the names of his authorities, a very little trouble will enable the reader to ascertain to what school of law they belong. His own opinion, whenever it can be ascertained, may generally be relied on as representing the orthodox view of the Bengal school.

Only two schools of law.

§ 33. III. DIFFERENT SCHOOLS OF LAW.—The term "school of law," as applied to the different legal opinions prevalent in different parts of India, seems to have been first used by Mr. Colebrooke (*o*). He points out that there really are only two schools marked by a vital difference of opinion, *viz.*, those who follow the Mitakshara, and those who follow the Daya Bhaga. Those who fall under the former head are again divided by minor differences of opinion, but are in principle substantially the same. Of course in every part of India, though governed by practically the same law, the pundits refer by preference to the writers who lived nearest to, and are best known to, themselves; just as English, Irish, and American lawyers refer to their own authorities, when attainable, on any point of general jurisprudence. This has given rise to the idea that there are as many schools of law as there are sets of local writers, and the subdivision has been carried to an extent for which it is impossible to suggest any reason or foundation. For instance, Mr. Morley speaks of a Bengal, a Mithila, a Benares, a Maharashtra, and a Dravida School, and sub-

---

(*n*) *Kery Kolitany* v. *Moneeram*, 13 B. L. R. 50, S. C. 19 Suth. 394.

(*o*) 1 Stra. H. L. 315. As to the mode in which such divergences sprung up, see the remarks of the Judicial Committee in the *Ramnad case*, *Collector of Madura* v. *Moottoo Ramalinga*, 12 M. I. A. 435; S. C. 10 Suth. (P. C.) 17; S.C. 1 B. L. R. (P. C.) 1.

divides the latter into a Dravida, a Karnataka and an Andhra division (*p*). So the Madras High Court and the Judicial Committee distinguish between the Benares and the Dravida schools of law (*q*), and a distinction between an Andhra and a Dravida School has also received a sort of quasi-recognition (*r*). On the other hand, Dr. Burnell ridicules the use of the terms Karnataka and Andhra, which he declares to be wholly destitute of meaning, while the term Dravidian has a very good philological sense, but no legal signification whatever. Practically he agrees with Mr. Colebrooke in thinking that the only distinction of real importance is between the followers of the Mitakshara and the followers of the Daya Bhaga (*s*).

§ 34. In discussing this subject, it seems to me that we must distinguish between differences of law arising from differences of opinion among the Sanskrit writers, and differences of law arising from the fact that their opinions have never been received at all, or only to a limited extent. In the former case there are really different schools of law; in the latter case there are simply no schools. I think it will be found that the differences between the law of Bengal and Benares come under the former head, while the local variances which exist in the Punjab, in Western, and in Southern, India, come under the latter head. Causes of variance.

§ 35. Any one who compares the Daya Bhaga with the Mitakshara will observe that the two works differ in the most vital points, and that they do so from the conscious application of completely different principles. These will be discussed in their appropriate places through this work, but may be shortly summarised here. The Daya Bhaga.

(*p*) 1. M. Dig. Introd. 221. In this he is supported by Mr. Rajkumar Sarvadhikari (p. 409), who (p 334) traces the origin of divergent opinions on questions of law to the teaching of Srikara in the 11th century.

(*q*) See the *Ramnad adoption suit*, 2 Mad. H. C. 206; 12 M. I. A. 397, *supra* note (o).

(*r*) *Narasammal* v. *Balaramacharlu*, 1 Mad. H. C. 420.

(*s*) Pref. to Varadrajah, 5; Nelson's View of Hindu Law, 21: V. N. Mandlik. Introduction, 70 See the remarks of *Mahmood*, J. in *Ganga Sahai* v. *Lekhraj Singh*, 9 All., p. 290.

First; the Daya Bhaga lays down the principle of religious efficacy as the ruling canon in determining the order of succession; consequently it rejects the preference of agnates to cognates, which distinguishes the other systems, and arranges and limits the cognates upon principles peculiar to itself (*t*).

Secondly; it wholly denies the doctrine that property is by birth, which is the corner-stone of the joint family system. Hence it treats the father as the absolute owner of the property, and authorises him to dispose of it at his pleasure. It also refuses to recognize any right in the son to a partition during his father's life (*u*).

Thirdly; it considers the brothers, or other collateral members of the joint family, as holding their shares in quasi-severalty, and consequently recognizes their right to dispose of them at their pleasure, while still undivided (*v*).

Fourthly; whether as a result of the last principle, or upon independent grounds, it recognizes the right of a widow in an undivided family to succeed to her husband's share, if he dies without issue, and to enforce a partition on her own account (*w*).

Factum valet.

It is usual to speak of the doctrine *factum valet* as one of universal application in the Bengal school. But this is a mistake. When it suits Jimuta Vahana, he uses it as a means of getting over a distinct prohibition against alienation by a father without the permission of his sons (*x*). I am not aware of his applying the doctrine in any other case. No Bengal lawyer would admit of any such subterfuge as sanctioning, for instance, the right of an undivided brother to dispose of more than his own share in the family property for his private benefit, or as authorising a widow to adopt without her husband's consent, or a boy to be adopted

---

(*t*) See *post*, § 459, *et seq.*
(*u*) See *post*, § 224, 235.
(*v*) See *post*, § 241.
(*w*) See *post*, § 242, 438.
(*x*) Daya Bhaga, ii. § 30.

after *upanayana,* or marriage. The principle is only applied where a legal precept has been already reduced by independent reasoning to a moral suggestion.

Females in Western India.

§ 36. Now, in all the above points the remaining parts of India agree with each other in disagreeing with Jimuta Vahana and his followers. Their variances *inter se* are comparatively few and slight. Far the most important is the difference which exists between Western India and the other provinces which follow the Mitakshara, as to the right of females to inherit. A sister, for instance, who is nowhere else recognized as an heir, ranks very high in the order of succession in the Bombay Presidency, and many other heiresses are admitted, who would have no *locus standi* elsewhere (*y*). Any reader of Indian history will have observed the public and prominent position assumed by Mahratta Princesses, and it seems probable that the doctrine which prevails in other districts, that women are incapable of inheriting without a special text, has never been received at all in Western India. Women inherit there, not by reason, but in defiance, of the rules which regulate their admission elsewhere. In their case, written law has never superseded immemorial custom (*z*.)

Law of adoption.

§ 37. Another matter as to which there is much variance is the law of adoption. For instance, as regards the right of a widow to adopt a son to her deceased husband. In Mithila no widow can adopt. In Bengal and Benares she can, with her husband's permission. In Southern India, and in the Punjab, she can adopt, even without his permission, by the consent of his sapindas. In Western India she can adopt without any consent (*a*). So as regards the person to be adopted. The adoption of a daughter's, or a sister's, son is forbidden to the higher classes by the Sanskrit writers. It is legal in the Punjab. It is commonly

(*y*) Vyavahara Mayukha, iv. 8, § 19; W. & B. 127—132.
(*z*) See *post*, § 472, 488—490, 513, 541.
(*a*) See *post*, § 101.

practised in the South of India (*b*). In all these cases we may probably trace a survival of ancient practices which existed before adoption had any religious significance, unfettered by the rules which where introduced when it became a religious rite. The similarity of usage on these points between the Punjab and the South of India seems to me strongly to confirm this view. It is quite certain that neither borrowed from the other. It is also certain that in the Punjab adoption is a purely secular arrangement. There seems strong reason to suppose that in Southern India it is nothing more (*c*). But what is of importance with regard to the present discussion is, that these differences find no support in the writings of the early sages, or even of the early commentators. They appear for the first time in treatises which are absolutely modern, or merely in recorded customs. To speak of such variances as arising from different schools of law, would be to invert the relation of cause and effect. We might just as well invent different schools of law for Kent and Middlesex, to account for Gavelkind and the Customs of London. Even Hindu lawyers cannot alter facts. In some instances they try to wrest some holy precept into conformity with the facts (*d*); but in other cases, and especially in Western India, the facts are too stubborn. The more closely we study the works of the different so-called schools of law, other than those of Bengal, the more shall we be convinced that the principles of all are precisely the same. The local usages of the different districts vary. Some of these usages the writers struggle to bring within their rules; others they silently abandon as hopeless. What they cannot account for, they simply ignore (*e*).

(*b*) See *post*, § 123, 124. (*c*) See *post*, § 95.

(*d*) See, for instance, the mode in which four conflicting views as to the right of a widow to adopt have been deduced from a single text of Vasishtha, *Collector of Madura* v. *Moottoo Ramalinga*, 12 M. I. A. 435; S. C. 10 Suth. (P. C.) 17; S. C. 1 B. L. R. (P. C.) 1.

(*e*) For instance, second marriages of widows or wives, which are equally practised in the North, the West, and the South of India, see *post*, § 89.

§ 38. IV. Judicial Decisions.—A great deal has been said, often by no means in a flattering spirit, of the decisions upon Native Law of our Courts, whether presided over by civilian, or by professional, Judges. It seems to be supposed that they imported European notions into the questions discussed before them, and that the divergences between the law which they administered and that which is to be found in the Sanskrit law-books, are to be ascribed to their influence. In one or two remarkable instances, no doubt, this was the case; but those instances are rare. My belief is that their influence was exerted in the opposite direction, and that it rather showed itself in the pedantic maintenance of doctrines whose letter was still existing, but whose spirit was dying away. It could hardly have been otherwise. It seems to be forgotten that upon all disputed points of law, the English Judges were merely the mouthpieces of the pundits who were attached to their Courts, and whom they were bound to consult (*f*). The slightest examination of the earliest reports at a time when all points of law were treated as open questions, will show that the pundits were invariably consulted, wherever a doubt arose, and that their opinions were for a long time implicitly followed. If, then, the decisions were not in accordance with Hindu law, the fault rested with the pundits, and not with the Judges. The tendency of the pundits would naturally be to magnify the authority of their own law-books; and accordingly we find that they invariably quote some text in support of their opinion, even when the text had no bearing whatever upon the point. The tendency of the Judges was even more strongly in the same direction. The pundit, however bigoted he might be, was at all events a Hindu, living amongst Hindus, and advising upon a law which actually governed the every-day lives of himself and his family and his friends. He would torture a sacred text into an authority for his opinion; but his

Influence of English Judges.

The Pundits.

(*f*) The pundits, as official referees of the Courts, were only abolished by Act XI of 1864.

opinion would probably be right, though unsustained by, or even opposed to, his text. With the English Judge there was no such restraining influence. He was sworn to administer Hindu law to the Hindus, and he was determined to do so, however strange or unreasonable it might appear. At first he accepted his law unhesitatingly from the lips of the pundits; and so long as he did so, probably no great harm was done. But knowledge increased, and the fountains were opened up, and he began to enquire into the matter for himself. The pundits were made to quote chapter and verse for their opinions, and it was found that their premises did not warrant their conclusions. Or their opinions upon one point were compared with their opinions upon an analogous point, and found not to harmonise, and logic demanded that they should be brought into conformity with each other. Sometimes the variance between the futwahs and the texts was so great that it was ascribed to ignorance, or to corruption. The fact really was that the law had outgrown the authorities. Native Judges would have recognized the fact. English Judges were unable to do so, or else remarked (to use a phrase which I have often heard from the Bench), "that they were bound to maintain the integrity of the law." This was a matter of less importance in Bengal, where Jimuta Vahana had already burst the fetters. But in Southern India it came to be accepted, that Mitakshara was the last word that could be listened to on Hindu law. The consequence was a state of arrested progress, in which no voices were heard unless they came from the tomb. It was as if a German were to administer English law from the resources of a library furnished with Fleta, Glanville and Bracton, and terminating with Lord Coke (*g*).

Force of usage.

§ 39. In Western and Northern India the differences between the written and the unwritten law were too palpa-

(*g*) The substance of this paragraph was written by me in an Indian journal so long ago as 1863. I mention the fact, lest it should be supposed that I have borrowed, without acknowledgment, from a very interesting passage in Sir H. S. Maine's Village Communities, p. 44.

ble to be passed over. Accordingly in many important cases in Borrodaile's Reports, we find that the Court did not merely ask the opinion of their pundits, but took the evidence of the heads of the castes concerned as to their actual usage. The collection of laws and customs of the Hindu castes, made by Mr. Steele under the orders of Government, was another step in the same direction. It is probable that the laxity, which has been remarked as the characteristic of Hindu law in the Bombay Presidency, would be found equally to exist in many other districts, if the Courts had taken the trouble to look for it. In quite recent times the Courts of the N.-W. Provinces and of the Punjab have acted on the same principle of taking nothing for granted. The result has been the discovery, that while the actual usages existing in those districts are remarkably similar to those which are declared in the Mitakshara and the kindred works, there is a complete absence of those religious principles which are so prominent in Brahmanical law. Consequently the usages themselves have diverged, exactly at the points where they might have been expected to do so (*h*). *Absente causâ, abest et lex.*

(*h*) See Punjab Customs, 5, 11, 78; *Sheo Singh Rai* v. *Mt. Dakho*, 6 N.-W. P. 382: *affd.* 5 I. A. 87; S. C. 1 All. 688; *Chotuy Lall* v. *Chunno Lall*, 6 I. A. 15; S. C. 4 Cal. 744.

CHAPTER III.

THE SOURCES OF HINDU LAW.

Custom.

Custom binding.

§ 40. If I am right in supposing that the great body of existing law consists of ancient usages, more or less modified by Aryan or Brahmanical influence, it would follow that the mere fact that a custom was not in accordance with written law, that is with the Brahmanical code, would be no reason whatever why it should not be binding upon those by whom it was shown to be observed. This is admitted in the strongest terms by the Brahmanical writers themselves. Manu says that "immemorial usage is transcendant law," and that "holy sages, well knowing that law is grounded on immemorial custom, embraced, as the root of all piety, good usages long established" (*a*). And he lays it down that "a king who knows the revealed law, must enquire into the particular laws of classes, the laws or usages of districts, the customs of traders, and the rules of certain families, and establish their peculiar laws" (*b*); to which Kulluka Bhatta adds, as his gloss, "If they (that is, the laws) be not repugnant to the law of God," by which no doubt he means the text of the Vedas as interpreted by the Brahmans. But that Manu contemplated no such restriction is evident by what follows a little after the above passage. "What has been practised by good men and by virtuous Brahmans, if it be not inconsistent with the legal customs of provinces or districts, of classes or families, let

(*a*) Manu, i. § 108, 110.

(*b*) Manu, viii. § 41. See, too, Vrihaspati, cited Vyavahara Mayukha, i. 1, § 13, and Vasishtha and other authorities, cited M. Müller, A. S. Lit. 50.

him establish" (*c*). So Yajnavalkya says (*d*), "Of a newly-subjugated territory, the monarch shall preserve the social and religious usages, also the judicial system, and the state of classes, as they already obtained." And the Mitakshara quotes texts to the effect, that even practices expressly inculcated by the sacred ordinances may become obsolete, and should be abandoned if opposed to public opinion (*e*).

Recognized by modern law.

§ 41. The fullest effect is given to custom both by our Courts and by legislation. The Judicial Committee in the Ramnad case said, "Under the Hindu system of law, clear proof of usage will outweigh the written text of the law" (*f*). And all the recent Acts which provide for the administration of the law dictate a similar reference to usage, unless it is contrary to justice, equity or good conscience, or has been actually declared to be void (*g*).

Records of local customs.

§ 42. It is much to be regretted that so little has been done in the way of collecting authentic records of local customs. The belief that Brahmanism was the law of India was so much fostered by the pundits and Judges, that it came to be admitted conventionally, even by those who knew better. The revenue authorities, who were in daily intercourse with the people, were aware that many rules which were held sacred in the Court, had never been heard of in the cottage. But their local knowledge appears rarely to have been made accessible to, or valued by, the Judicial department. I have already mentioned, as an exception, Mr. Steele's collection of customs in force in the Deccan. In the Punjab and in Oudh most valuable records of village and tribal customs, relating to the succession to, and disposition of, land have been collected under the authority of

(*c*) Manu, viii. § 46. (*d*) Yajnavalkya, i. § 342.

(*e*) Mitakshara, i. 3, § 4. See V. N. Mandlik. Introduction, 48, 70. Raghunandana, i. 33.

(*f*) *Collector of Madura* v. *Moottoo Ramalinga*, 12 M. I. A. 436; S. C. 10 Suth. (P. C.) 17; S. C. 1 B. L. R. (P. C.) 1.

(*g*) See, as to Bombay, Bom. Reg. IV of 1827, s. 26; Act II of 1864, s. 15. As to Burmah, Act XVII of 1875, s. 5. Central Provinces, Act XX of 1875, s. 5. Madras, Act III of 1873, s. 16. Oudh, Act XVIII of 1876, s. 3. Punjab, Act XII of 1878, s. 1. See *Sundar* v. *Khuman Singh*, 1 All. 613.

the settlement officers, and these have been brought into relation with the Judicial system by an enactment that the entries contained in them should be presumed to be true (*h*). Many most interesting peculiarities of Punjab Law will be found in a book to which I shall frequently refer, which gives the substance of these customs, and of the decisions of the Chief Court of Lahore upon them, and in three volumes issued under the authority of the Punjab Government on the same subject (*i*). The special interest of these customs arises from the fact, already noticed (*k*), that Brahmanism seems never to have succeeded in the Punjab. Accordingly, when we find a particular usage common to the Punjab and to Sanskrit law, we may infer that there is nothing necessarily Brahmanical in its origin (*l*). Another work of the greatest interest, which I believe no writer has ever noticed, is the Thesawaleme, or description of the customs of the Tamil inhabitants of Jaffna, on the island of Ceylon. The collection was made in 1707, under the orders of the Dutch Government, and was then submitted to, and approved by, twelve Moodelliars, or leading Natives, and finally promulgated as an authoritative exposition of their usages (*m*). Now, we know that from the earliest times there

Thesawaleme.

(*h*) These records are known by the terms, Wajib-ul-arz (a written representation or petition) and Riwaz-i-am (common practice or custom). See Punjab Customs, 19; Act XXXIII of 1871, s. 61. XVII of 1876, s. 17. *Lekraj Kuar* v. *Mahpal Singh*, 7 I. A. 63; S. C. 5 Cal. 744; *Harbhaj* v. *Gumani*, 2 All. 493; *Isri Singh* v. *Ganga*, *ib.* 876. In the case of *Uman Parshad* v. *Gandharp Singh*, 14 I. A. 127, C. S. 15 Cal. 20, the Judicial Committee called attention to a practice which had grown up in Oudh, of allowing the proprietor to enter his own views upon the Wajib-ul-arz, whereas it ought to be an official record of customs, arrived at by the inquiries of an impartial officer. See too *per curiam*, 12 All. 335 A Wajib-ul-arz which has long stood on record, and been unquestioned by the parties who would be affected by it, is *primâ facie* evidence of custom, though not signed by any landholder in the village. *Rustam Ali* v. *Abbasi*, 13 All. 407.

(*i*) Notes on Customary Law, as administered in the Courts of the Punjab, by Charles Boulnois, Esq., Judge of the Chief Court, and W. H. Rattigan, Esq., Lahore, 1876. I cite it shortly as Punjab Customs. Punjab Customary Law. Edited by C. L. Tupper, C. S. Calcutta, 1881.

(*k*) *Ante*, § 8.

(*l*) Mr. C. L. Tupper says of the Punjab, "The Brahmans are not in the Punjab the depositaries of Customary law. To ascertain it, we must go to the Tribal Council, if there be one, or to the elders of the tribe." "It is not, I think, the custom which has modified the law. It is the Brahmanical law occasionally, and the Muhammedan law more often, which has modified the custom." Punjab Customary Law, II. 82, 86.

(*m*) The edition which I possess was published in 1862, with the decisions of the English Courts, by Mr. H. F. Mutukistna, who gave it to me.

has been a constant stream of emigration of Tamulians into Ceylon, formerly for conquest, and latterly for purposes of commerce. We also know that the influence of Brahmans, or even of Aryans, among the Dravidian races of the South has been of the very slightest, at all events until the English officials introduced their Brahman advisers (*n*). The customs recorded in the Thêsawaleme may, therefore, be taken as very strong evidence of the usages of the Tamil inhabitants of the South of India two or three centuries ago, at a time when it is certain that those usages could not be traced to the Sanskrit writers. Undoubted evidence of the condition of Hindu law at a very much earlier period may also be found in the usages of the Nambudry Brahmans on the West Coast in the Madras Presidency. The tradition is that they were introduced into Malabar as an organised community by king Parasurama, and the evidence tends to show that they must have been settled there about 1200 or 1500 years ago. As they took their place among a community which was governed by a totally different system, it may safely be assumed that the form of Hindu law which prevails among the Nambudries of the present day is that which was universal among the Brahmans of Eastern India at the time of their emigration. Its archaic character exactly accords with such a conclusion (*o*). Many very interesting customs still existing in Southern India will be found in the Madura Manual by Mr. Nelson, and in the Madras Census Report of 1871 by Dr. Cornish. These show what rich materials are available, if they were only sought for.

Various applications of customary law.

§ 43. Questions of usage arise in four different ways in India. *First;* as regards races to whom the so-called Hindu law has never been applied; for instance, the aboriginal Hill tribes, and those who follow the *Marumakatayem* law of Malabar, or the *Alya Santana* law of Canara. *Secondly;* as regards those who profess to follow the Hindu law generally, but who do not admit its theological developments.

(*n*) See *ante*, § 6.
(*o*) *Vasudevan* v. *Secy. of State*, 11 Mad. 160, 181.

Thirdly; as regards races who profess submission to it as a whole; and, *fourthly,* as regards persons formerly bound by Hindu law, but to whom it has become inapplicable.

Cases where religious principles are ignored.

§ 44. The first of the above cases, of course, does not come within the scope of this work at all. The distinction between the second and third classes is most important, as the deceptive similarity between the two is likely to lead to erroneous conclusions in cases where they really differ. For instance, in an old case in Calcutta, where a question of heirship to a Sikh was concerned, this question again turning upon the validity of a Sikh marriage, the Court laid it down generally that "the Sikhs, being a sect of Hindus, must be governed by Hindu law" (*p*). Numerous cases in the Punjab show that the law of the Sikhs differs materially from the Hindu law, in the very points, such as adoption and the like, in which the difference of religion might be expected to cause a difference of usage. Similar differences are found among the Jats (*q*), and even among the orthodox Hindus of the extreme north-west of India (*r*). So, as regards the Jains, it is now well recognized that, though of Hindu origin, and generally adhering to Hindu law, they recognize no divine authority in the Vedas, and do not practise the *Shradhs,* or ceremony for the dead, which is the religious element in the Sanskrit law. Consequently, that the principles which arise out of this element do not bind them, and, therefore, that their usages in many respects are completely different (*s*). I strongly suspect that most of the Dravidian tribes of Southern India come under the same head (*t*).

(*p*) *Juggomohun* v. *Saumcoomar*, 2 M. Dig. 43.

(*q*) The Jats (Sanskrit, Yadava) are the descendants of an aboriginal race. Manning's Ancient India, i. 66.

(*r*) See Punjab Customs, *passim.* As to the effect of the introduction of the Punjab code as creating a *lex loci*, see *Mulkah Do* v. *Mirza Jehan*, 10 M. I. A. 252; S. C. 2 Suth. (P. C.) 55.

(*s*) *Bhagvandas* v. *Rajmal*, 10 Bom. H. C. 241; *Sheo Singh Rai* v. *Mt. Dakho*, 6 N.-W. P. 382, *affd.* 5 I. A. 87; S. C. 1 All. 688. See cases where such difference of usage was held not to be made out, *Lalla Mohabeer* v. *Mt. Kundun*, 8 Suth. 116; *affd. Sub nomine Doorga Pershad* v. *Mt. Kundun*, 1 I. A. 55; S. C. 21 Suth. 214; S. C. 13 B. L. R. 235. *Bachebi* v. *Makhan*, 3 All. 55.

(*t*) See *ante*, § 2, 11.

§ 45. As regards those who profess submission to the Hindu Law as a whole, questions of usage arise, *first*, with a view to determine the particular principles of that law by which they should be governed; and, *secondly*, to determine the validity of any local, tribal, or family exceptions to that law. *Primâ facie*, any Hindu residing in a particular province of India is held to be subject to the particular doctrines of Hindu Law recognized in that province. He would be governed by the Daya Bhaga in Bengal; by the Vivada Chintamani in North Behar and Tirhut; by the Mayukha in Guzerat; and generally by the Mitakshara elsewhere (*u*). But this law is not merely a local law. It becomes the personal law, and a part of the *status* of every family which is governed by it. Consequently, where any such family migrates to another province, governed by another law, it carries its own law with it. (*v*) For instance, a family migrating from a part of India where the Mitakshara, or the Mithila, system prevailed, to Bengal, would not come under the Bengal law from the mere fact of its having taken Bengal as its domicil. And this rule would apply as much to matters of succession to land as to the purely personal relations of the members of the family. In this respect the rule seems an exception to the usual principles, that the *lex loci* governs matters relating to land, and that the law of the domicil governs personal relations. The reason is, that in India there is no *lex loci*, every person being governed by the law of his personal status. The same rule as above would apply to any family which, by legal usage, had acquired any special custom of succession, or the like, peculiar to itself, though differing from that either of its original, or acquired, domicil (*w*).

Disputed applicability of local law.

(*u*) See *ante*, § 26—31. As to Assam and Orissa, which are supposed to be governed by Bengal law, and Ganjam by the law of Madras, see *ante*, § 11.

(*v*) This law will not necessarily be the law now prevailing in the domicil of origin, but that which did prevail there at the time of emigration. *Vasudevan* v. *Secy. of State*, 11 Mad. 157, 162.

(*w*) *Rutcheputty* v. *Rajunder*, 2 M. I. A. 132; *Byjnath* v. *Kopilmon*, 24 Suth. 95, and *per curiam*, *Soorendronath* v. *Mt. Heeramonee*, 12 M. I. A. 91, *infra*. note (x) *Manik Chand* v. *Jagat Settani*, 17 Cal. 518.

Change of personal law.

§ 46. When such an original variance of law is once established, the presumption arises that it continues; and the *onus* of making out their contention lies upon those who assert that it has ceased by conformity to the law of the new domicil (*x*). But this presumption may be rebutted, by showing that the family has conformed in its religious or social usages to the locality in which it has settled; or that, while retaining its religious rites, it has acquiesced in a course of devolution of property, according to the common course of descent of property in that district, among persons of the same class (*y*).

Act of Government.

Of course the mere fact that, by the act of Government, a district which is governed by one system of law is annexed to one which is governed by a different system, cannot raise any presumption that the inhabitants of either district have adopted the usages of the other (*z*).

Evidence of valid custom.

§ 47. The next question is as to the validity of customs differing from the general Hindu law, when practised by persons who admit that they are subject to that law. According to the view of customary law taken by Mr. Austin (*a*), a custom can never be considered binding until it has become a law by some act, legislative or judicial, of the sovereign power. Language pointing to the same view is to be found in one judgment of the Madras High Court (*b*). But such a view cannot now be sustained. It is open to the obvious objection, that, in the absence of legislation, no custom could ever be judicially recognized for the first time. A decision in its favour would assume that it was already binding. The sounder view appears to be that law

(*x*) *Soorendronath* v. *Mt. Heeramonee*, 12 M. I. A. 81; S. C. 1 B. L. R. (P. C.) 26; S. C. 10 Suth. (P. C.) 35; *Obunnessurree* v. *Kishen*, 4 Wym. 226; *Sonatun* v. *Ruttun*, Suth. Sp. 95; *Pirthee Singh* v. *Mt. Sheo*, 8 Suth. 261.

(*y*) *Rajchunder* v. *Goculchund*, 1 S. D. 43 (56); *Chundro* v. *Nobin Soondur*, 2 Suth. 197; *Rambromo* v. *Kaminee*, 6 Suth. 295; S. C. 3 Wym. 8; *Junaruddeen* v. *Nobin Chunder*, Marsh. 232; *per curiam*, *Soorendronath* v. *Mt. Heeramonee*, 12 M. I. A. 96; *Supra*. note (x).

(*z*) *Prithee Singh* v. *Court of Wards*, 23 Suth. 272.

(*a*) Austin, i. 148, ii. 229.

(*b*) *Narasammal* v. *Balaramacharlu*, 1 Mad. H. C. 424.

and usage act, and re-act, upon each other. A belief in the propriety, or the imperative nature, of a particular course of conduct, produces a uniformity of behaviour in following it; and a uniformity of behaviour in following a particular course of conduct, produces a belief that it is imperative, or proper, to do so. When from either cause, or from both causes, a uniform and persistent usage has moulded the life, and regulated the dealings, of a particular class of the community, it becomes a custom, which is a part of their personal law. Such a custom deserves to be recognized and enforced by the Courts, unless it is injurious to the public interests, or is in conflict with any express law of the ruling power (*c*). Hence, where a special usage of succession was set up, the High Court of Madras said, "What the law requires before an alleged custom can receive the recognition of the Court, and so acquire legal force, is satisfactory proof of usage, so long and invariably acted upon in practice, as to show that it has, by common consent, been submitted to as the established governing rule of the particular family, class, or district of country; and the course of practice upon which the custom rests must not be left in doubt, but be proved with certainty" (*d*). This decision was affirmed on appeal, and the Judicial Committee observed (*e*): "Their Lordships are fully sensible of the importance and justice of giving effect to long established usages existing in particular districts and families in India, but it is of the essence of special usages, modifying the ordinary law of succession, that they should be ancient and invariable; and it is further essential that they should be established to be so by clear and unambiguous evidence. It is only by means of

(*c*) See the subject discussed, *Khojah's case*, Perry, O. C. 110; *Howard* v. *Pestonji*, *ib*. 535; *Tara Chand* v. *Reeb Ram*, 3 Mad. H. C 56; *Bhau Nanaji* v. *Sundrabai*, 11 Bom. H. C. 249; *Mathura* v. *Esu*, 4 Bom. 545; Savigny, Droit Rom. i. 33—36, 165—175; Introduction to Punjab Customs.

(*d*) *Sivananjanja* v. *Muttu Ramalinga*, 3 Mad. H. C. 75, 77; affirmed on appeal, *Sub nomine*, *Ramalakshmi* v. *Sivanantha*, *the Oorcad case*, 14 M. I. A., 570; S. C. 12 B. L. R. 396, S. C. 17 Suth. 553. Approved by the Bombay High Court, *Shidhojirav* v. *Naikojirav*, 10 Bom. H. C. 234. See also *Bhujangrav* v. *Malojirav*, 5 Bom. H. C. (A. C. J.) 161.

(*e*) 14 M. I. A. 585.

such evidence that the Courts can be assured of their existence, and that they possess the conditions of antiquity and certainty on which alone their legal title to recognition depends." Accordingly, the Madras High Court, when directing an inquiry as to an alleged custom in the south of India that Brahmans should adopt their sisters' sons, laid it down that: "I. The evidence should be such as to prove the uniformity and continuity of the usage, and the conviction of those following it that they were acting in accordance with law, and this conviction must be inferred from the evidence; II. Evidence of acts of the kind; acquiescence in those acts; decisions of Courts, or even of punchayets, upholding such acts; the statements of experienced and competent persons of their belief that such acts were legal and valid, will all be admissible; but it is obvious that although admissible, evidence of this latter kind will be of little weight if unsupported by actual examples of the usage asserted" (*f*). Finally, the custom set up must be definite, so that its application in any given instance may be clear and certain, and reasonable. (*g*)

§ 48. Where a tribe or family are admittedly governed by Hindu law, but assert the existence of a special custom in derogation of that law, the *onus* of course rests upon those who assert the custom to make it out. For instance, a custom forbidding adoption, or barring inheritance by adoption, might be established, though in a family otherwise subject to Hindu law it would probably require very strong evidence to support it (*h*). But if the tribe or family had been originally non-Hindu, and only adopted Hindu usages in part, the *onus* would be shifted, and the burthen of proof would rest upon the side which alleged that any particular doctrine had become part of the personal law. A case of

---

(*f*) *Gopalayyan* v. *Raghupatiayyan* 7 Mad. H. C. 250, 254. See, too, *per* Markby, J., *Hiranath* v. *Baboo Ram*, 9 B. L. R. 294; S. C. 17 Suth. 316; *Collector of Madura* v. *Moottoo Ramalinga*, 12 M. I. A., 436, S. C. 10 Suth. (P. C.) 17; S. C. 1 B. L. R. (P. C.) 1 and *Hurpurshad* v. *Sheo Dyal*, 3 I. A. 285, S. C. 26 Suth. 55. *Vishnu* v. *Krishnan*, 7 Mad. 3.

(*g*) *Lachman* v. *Akbar*, 1 All. 440; *Lala* v. *Hira*, 2 All. 49.

(*h*) *Bishnath Singh* v. *Ram Churn Mujmodar*, S. D. of 1850, 20.

this sort arose in regard to the Baikantpur family, who were not originally Hindus, but who had in part, though not entirely, adopted Hindu customs. On a question of succession, when the estate was claimed by an adopted son, it was held by the Judicial Committee that the *onus* rested upon those who relied on the adoption to show that this was one of the Hindu customs which had been taken into the family law. If the family was generally governed by Hindu law the claimant might rely on that, and then the *onus* of proving a family custom would be on him who asserted it (*i*).

Custom cannot be created by agreement.

§ 49. It follows from the very nature of the case, that a mere agreement among certain persons to adopt a particular rule, cannot create a new custom binding on others, whatever its effect may be upon themselves (*k*). Nor can a family custom ever be binding where the family, or estate, to which it attaches is so modern as to preclude the very idea of immemorial usage (*l*). Nor does a custom, such as that of primogeniture, which has governed the devolution of an estate in the hands of a particular family, follow it into the hands of another family, by whom it may have been purchased. In other words, it does not run with the land (*m*).

Continuity essential.

§ 50. Continuity is as essential to the validity of a custom as antiquity. In the case of a widely-spread local custom, want of continuity would be evidence that it had never had a legal existence; but it is difficult to imagine that such a custom, once thoroughly established, should come to a sudden end. It is different, however, in the case of family usage, which is founded on the consent of a smaller number of persons. Therefore, where it appeared

---

(*i*) *Fanindra Deb* v. *Rajeswar*, 12 I. A. 72. S. C. 11 Cal. 463.

(*k*) *Per cur.*, *Myna Boyee* v. *Ootaram*, 8 M. I. A. 420, S. C. 2 Suth. (P. C.) 4; *Abraham* v. *Abraham*, 9 M. I. A. 242; S. C. 1 Suth. (P. C.) 1; *Sarupi* v. *Mukh Ram*, 2 N.-W. P. 227. *Bhaoni* v. *Maharaj Singh*, 3 All. 738.

(*l*) *Umrithnath* v. *Goureenath*, 13 M. I. A. 542, 549, S. C. 15 Suth. (P. C.) 10.

(*m*) *Gopal Dass* v. *Nurotum*, 7 S. D. 195 (230).

that the members of a family, interested in an estate in the nature of a Raj, had for twenty years dealt with it as joint family property, as if the ordinary laws of succession governed the descent, the Privy Council held that any impartible character which it had originally possessed, was determined. They said: "Their Lordships cannot find any principle, or authority, for holding that in point of law a manner of descent of an ordinary estate, depending solely on family usage, may not be discontinued, so as to let in the ordinary law of succession. Such family usages are in their nature different from a territorial custom, which is the *lex loci* binding all persons within the local limits in which it prevails. It is of the essence of family usages that they should be certain, invariable, and continuous; and well established discontinuance must be held to destroy them. This would be so when the discontinuance has arisen from accidental causes; and the effect cannot be less when it has been intentionally brought about by the concurrent will of the family. It would lead to much confusion, and abundant litigation, if the law attempted to revive and give effect to usages of this kind after they had been clearly abandoned, and the abandonment had been, as in this case, long acted upon" (*n*).

May be discontinued.

Usage of single family.

§ 51. The above cases settle a question, as to which there was at first some doubt entertained, *viz.*, whether a particular family could have a usage differing from the law of the surrounding district applicable to similar persons (*o*). There is nothing to prevent proof of such a family usage. But in the case of a single family, and especially a family of no great importance, there will of course be very great difficulty in proving that the usage possesses the antiquity and continuousness, and arises from the sense of legal necessity as distinguished from conventional arrangement,

---

(*n*) *Rajkishen* v. *Ramjoy*, 1 Cal. 186, S. C. 19 Suth. 8. See, also, *per cur.*, *Abraham* v. *Abraham*, 9 M. I. A. 243, S. C. 1 Suth. (P. C.) 1.

(*o*) See *Basvantrav* v. *Mantappa*, 1 Bom. H. C. Appx. 42 (2nd ed.); *per cur.*, *Tara Chand* v. *Reeb Ram*, 3 Mad. H. C. 58; *Madhavrav* v. *Balkrishna*, 4 Bom. H. C. (A. C. J.) 113.

that is required to make out a binding usage (*p*). Where the family is a very great one, whose records are capable of being verified for a number of generations, the difficulty disappears. In the case of the Tipperah Raj, a usage has been repeatedly established by which the Raja nominates from amongst the members of his family the Jobraj (young sovereign) and the Bara Thakoor (chief lord), of whom the former succeeds to the Raj on a demise of the Raja, and the second takes the place of Jobraj (*q*). Also a custom in the Raj of Tirhoot, by which the Raja in possession abdicates during his lifetime, and assigns the Raj to his eldest son, or nearest male heir (*r*). Many of the cases of estates descending by primogeniture appear to rest on the nature of the estate itself, as being a sort of sovereignty, which from its constitution is impartible (*s*). But family custom alone will be sufficient, even if the estate is not of the nature of a Raj, provided it is made out (*t*). And where an impartible Raj has been confiscated by government, and then granted out again, either to a stranger, or to a member of the same family, the presumption is that it has been granted with its incidents as a Raj, of which the most prominent are impartibility and descent by primogeniture (*u*). This presumption, however, will not prevail, when the mode of dealing with the Raj after its confiscation, and the mode of its regrant are consistent with an intention that it should for the future possess the ordinary incidents of partibility (*v*).

(*p*) See the subject discussed, *Bhau Nanaji* v. *Sunbdrabai*, 11 Bom. H. C. 269; *Ismail* v. *Fidayat*, 3 All. 723.

(*q*) *Neelkisto Deb* v. *Beerchunder*, 12 M. I. A. 523, S. C. 12 Suth. (P. C.) 21; S. C. 3 B. L. R. (P. C.) 13.

(*r*) *Gunesh* v. *Moheshur* 6 M. I. A. 164, which see in the Court below, 7 S. D. 228 (271); see the *Pachete Raj*, *Gurundnarain* v. *Unund*, 6 S. D. 282 (354), *affd. Sub nomine*, *Anund* v. *Dheraj*, 5 M. I. A. 82.

(*s*) There may, however, be a partible Raj. See *Ghirdharee* v. *Koolahul*, 2 M. I. A. 344, S. C. 6 Suth. (P. C.) 1.

(*t*) *Rawut Urjun* v. *Rawut Ghunsiam*, 5 M. I. A. 169; *Chowdhry Chintamun* v. *Nowlukho*, 2 I. A. 263, S. C. 24 Suth. 255; *Yarlagadda Mallikarjuna* v. *Y. Durga*, 17 I. A. 134, S. C. 13 Mad. 406.

(*u*) *Beer Pertab* v. *Maharajah Rajender*, (*Hunsapore* case) 12 M. I. A. 1, S. C. 9 Suth. (P. C.) 15; *Mutta Vaduganatha* v. *Dorasinga*, 8 I. A. 99, S. C. 3 Mad. 290.

(*v*) *Venkata Narasimha* v. *Narayya*, (*Nuzvid* case), 7 I. A. 38, S. C. 2 Mad. 128. *Mirangi Zamindar* v. *Satrucharla Ramabhadra*, 18 I. A. 45, S. C., 14 Mad. 237.

Immoral usages.

§ 52. Customs which are immoral, or contrary to public policy, will neither be enforced, nor sanctioned (*w*). For instance, prostitution is not only recognized by Indian usage, and honoured in the class of dancing girls, but the relations between the prostitute and her paramour were regulated by law, just as any other species of contract (*x*). Even under English law prostitution is, of course, not illegal, in the sense of being either prohibited, or punishable; and I conceive there can be no reason why the existence of a distinct class of prostitutes in India, with special rules of descent *inter se*, should not be recognized now, and those rules acted on (*y*). But prostitution even according to Hindu views is immoral, and entails degradation from caste (*z*). It is quite clear, therefore, that no English Court would look upon prostitution as a consideration that would support a contract; and it has been held that the English rule will also be enforced to the extent of defeating an action against a prostitute for lodgings, or the like, supplied to her for the express purpose of enabling her to carry on her trade (*a*). So it has been held that the procuring of a minor to be a dancing girl at a pagoda, or the disposing of her as such, is punishable under ss. 372 & 373 of the Indian Penal Code (*b*), and the Bombay High Court went so far as to hold that the adoption of a girl by persons of this class, to be brought up in their profession, cannot be recognised as conferring any rights (*c*). The soundness of any such general rule seems, however, to have been doubted by the

---

(*w*) Manu, viii. § 41; M. Müller, A. S. L. 50. See statutes cited, *ante*, § 41, *note* (g).

(*x*) See Viv. Chint. 101.

(*y*) *Tara Munnee* v. *Motee*, 7 S. D. 273 (325); *Shida* v. *Sunshidapa*, Morris, Pt. I. 137; *Kamakshi* v. *Nagarathnam*, 5 Mad. H. C. 161; and see *per cur.*, *Chalakonda* v. *Ratnachalam*, 2 Mad. H. C. 78.

(*z*) 2 W. MacN. 132. *Sivasungu* v. *Minal*, 12 Mad. 277; *Tara Naikin* v. *Nana Lakshman*, 14 Bom. 90; *Kamalam* v. *Sadagopa Sami*, 1 Mad. 356; *Muttukannu* v. *Paramasami*, 12 Mad. 214.

(*a*) *Goureenath* v. *Modhoomonee*, 18 Suth. 445, S. C. 9 B. L. R. *appx.* 37. See *Sutao* v. *Hurreeram*, Bellasis, 1.

(*b*) *Ex p. Padmavati*, 5 Mad. H. C. 415; *R.* v. *Jaili*, 6 Bom. H. C. (C. C.) 60; *Chinna Ummayi* v. *Tegarai*, 1 Mad. 168. See, however, *Reg.* v. *Ramanna*, 12 Mad. 273.

(*c*) *Mathura* v. *Esu*, 4 Bom. 545.

Bombay Court in a more recent case, and was expressly denied in Madras (*d*). So it has been held in Bombay that caste customs authorising a woman to abandon her husband, and marry again without his consent, were void for immorality (*e*). And it was doubted whether a custom authorising her to marry again, during the lifetime of her husband, and with his consent, would have been valid (*f*). Among the Nairs, as is well known, the marriage relation involves no obligation to chastity on the part of the woman, and gives no rights to the man. But here what the law recognizes is not a custom to break the marriage bond, but the fact that there is no marriage bond at all (*g*). In a case before the Privy Council, a custom was set up as existing on the west coast of India, whereby the trustees of a religious institution were allowed to sell their trust. The Judicial Committee found that no such custom was made out, but intimated that in any case they would have held it to be invalid, as being opposed to public policy (*h*).

Change of family usage.

§ 53. The fourth class of cases mentioned before (§ 43), arises when circumstances occur which make the law, which has previously governed a family, no longer applicable. In one sense any new law which is adopted for the governance of such a family must be wanting, as regards that family, in the element of antiquity necessary to constitute a custom. On the other hand, the law itself which is adopted may be of immemorial character; the only question would be as to the power of the family to adopt it. We have already seen that a family migrating from one part of India to another, may either retain the law of its origin, or adopt that of its domicil (*i*). The same rule applies to a family which has changed its *status*. If the new *status* carries

(*d*) *Tara Naikin* v. *Nana Lakshman*, 14 Bom. 90. *Venku* v. *Mahalinga*, 11 Mad. 393. See *post*, § 183.

(*e*) *R.* v. *Karsan*, 2 Bom. H. C. 124; see *R.* v. *Manohar*, 5 Bom. H. C. (C. C.) 17; *Uji* v. *Hathi*, 7 Bom. H. C. (A. C. J.) 133; *Narayan* v. *Laving*, 2 Bom. 140.

(*f*) *Khemkor* v. *Umiashankar*, 10 Bom. H. C. 381.

(*g*) See *Koraga* v. *Reg.*, 6 Mad. 374.

(*h*) *Rajah Vurmah* v. *Ravi Vurmah*, 4 I A. 76, S. C. 1 Mad. 235.

(*i*) *Ante*, § 46.

with it an obligation to submit to a particular form of law, such form of law is binding upon it. If, however, it carries with it no such obligation, then the family is at liberty, either to retain so much of its old law as is consistent with its change of *status*, or to adopt the usages of any other class with which the new *status* allows it to associate itself.

Conversion to Muhammedanism.

§ 54. Where a Hindu has become converted to Muhammedanism, he accepts a new mode of life, which is governed by a law recognized, and enforced, in India. It has been stated that the property which he was possessed of at the time of his conversion will devolve upon those who were entitled to it at that time, by the Hindu Law, but that the property which he may subsequently acquire will devolve according to Muhammedan law (*k*). The former proposition, however, must, I should think, be limited to cases where by the Hindu law his heirs had acquired an interest which he could not defeat. If he was able to disinherit any of his relations by alienation, or by will, it is difficult to see why he should not disinherit them by adopting a law which gave him a different line of heirs. The latter part of the proposition, however, has been affirmed by the Privy Council, in a case where it was contended that a family which had been converted several generations back to Muhammedanism was still governed by Hindu law. Their Lordships said, "This case is distinguishable from that of *Abraham* v. *Abraham* (*l*). There the parties were native Christians, not having, as such, any law of inheritance defined by statute; and, in the absence of one, this Committee applied the law by which, as the evidence próved, the particular family intended to be governed. But the written law of India has prescribed broadly that in questions of succession and inheritance, the Hindu law is to be applied to Hindus, and the Muhammedan law to Muhammedans; and in the judgment delivered by Lord Kingsdown in *Abraham* v.

(*k*) 2 W. MacN. 131, 132; *Jowala* v. *Dharam*, 10 M. I. A. 537.
(*l*) 9 M. I. A. 195, S. C. 1 Suth. (P. C.) 1.

Abraham, p. 239, it is said that 'this rule must be understood to refer to Hindus and Muhammedans, not by birth merely, but by religion also.' The two cases in W. H. MacNaghten's Principles of Hind. L., vol. ii., pp. 131, 132, which deal with the case of converts from the Hindu to the Muhammedan faith, and rule that the heirs according to Hindu law will take all the property which the deceased had at the time of his conversion, are also authorities for the proposition that this subsequently acquired property is to be governed by the Muhammedan law. Here there is nothing to show conclusively when or how the property was acquired by 'the great ancestor;' there was no conflict as in the cases just referred to, between Hindus and Muhammedans touching the succession to him. Whatever he had is admitted to have passed to his descendants, of whom all, like himself, were Muhammedans; and it seems to be contrary to principle that, as between them, the succession should be governed by any but Muhammedan law. Whether it is competent for a family converted from the Hindu to the Muhammedan faith to retain for several generations Hindu usages and customs, and by virtue of that retention to set up for itself a special and customary law of inheritance, is a question which, so far as their Lordships are aware, has never been decided. It is not absolutely necessary for the determination of this appeal to decide that question in the negative, and their Lordships abstain from doing so. They must, however, observe, that to control the general law, if indeed the Muhammedan law admits of such control, much stronger proof of special usage would be required than has been given in this case" (*m*).

§ 55. These remarks of the Judicial Committee were not necessary for the decision of the case before them, as they held that the plaintiff would equally have failed if the prin- Retention of Hindu usages.

(*m*) *Jowala* v. *Dharum*, 10 M. I. A. 511, 537. See *Hakim Khan* v. *Gool Khan*, 8 Cal. 826, in which the Court, with much reason, doubted the decision in *Rupchund* v. *Latu Chowdhry*, 3 C. L. R. 97, where it was laid down as settled law that with Muhammedans living in a Hindu country, the presumption of joint family and commensality arises. See next paragraph.

ciples of Hindu law had been applied to his claim. Nor did they profess absolutely to decide that a convert to Muhammedanism might not still retain Hindu usages, and they partly rest their view against such retention of usage upon the ground that there was no decision upon the subject. The point, however, has been repeatedly decided the other way in Bombay, with regard to a sect called *Khojahs*. These are a class of persons who were originally Hindus, but who became converts to Muhammedanism about four hundred years ago, retaining however many Hindu usages, amongst others an order of succession opposed to that prescribed by the Koran. A similar sect named the *Memon Cutchees* had a similar history and usage. In 1847, the question was raised in the Supreme Court of Bombay, whether this order of succession could be supported, and Sir Erskine Perry, in an elaborate judgment, decided that it could. His decision has been followed in numerous cases in Bombay, both in the Supreme and High Court, and may be considered as thoroughly established (*n*). It has, however, been held that these decisions did not establish that the Khojas had adopted the entire Hindu family law, and that it could not be assumed without sufficient evidence that they were bound by the law of partition, so far as it allows a son to claim a share of the family property in his father's life time (*o*). But although these cases may probably be taken as settling that an adherence to the religion of the Koran does not necessarily entail an adherence to its civil law, there may be cases in which religion and law are inseparable. In such a case the ruling of the Privy Council would be strictly in point, and would debar any one who had accepted the religion from relying on a custom opposed to the law. For instance, monogamy is an essential part of

(*n*) *Khojah's case*, Perry, O. C. 110; *Gangbai* v. *Thavur*, 1 Bom. H. C. 71, 73; *Mulbai, in the Goods of*, 2 Bom H. C. 292; *Rahimbai, in the Goods of*, 12 Bom. H. C. 294; *Rahimatbai* v. *Hirbai*, 8 Bom. 84; *Suddurtonnessa* v. *Majada*, 3 Cal. 694; Haji Ismail's Will, 6 Bom. 452; *Ashabai* v. *Haji Tyeb*, 9 Bom. 115; *Abdul Cadur* v. *Turner*, *ibid.* 158; *Mahomed Sidick* v. *Haji Ahmed*, 10 Bom. 1; *Re Haroon Mahomed*, 14 Bom. 189.

(*o*) *Ahmedbhoy* v. *Cassumbhoy*, 13 Bom. 534, over-ruling S. C. 12 Bom. 280.

the law of Christianity. A Muhammedan, or Hindu, convert to Christianity could not possibly marry a second wife after his conversion, during the life of his first, and if he did so, the issue by such second marriage would certainly not be legitimate, any Hindu or Muhammedan usage to the contrary notwithstanding (*p*). His conversion would not invalidate marriages celebrated, or affect the legitimacy of issue born before that event. What its effect might be upon issue proceeding from a plurality of wives retained after he became a Christian, would be a very interesting question, which has never arisen.

Case of the Abrahams.

§ 56. The second part of the rule above stated (*q*) is illustrated by the case of *Abraham* v. *Abraham* (*r*), referred to above. There it appeared that there were different classes of native Christians of Hindu origin. Some retained Hindu manners and usages, wholly or chiefly, while others, who were known as East Indians, and who are generally of mixed blood, conformed in all respects to European customs. The founder of the family in question was of pure Hindu blood, and belonged to a class of native Christians which retained native customs. But as he rose in the world and accumulated property, he assumed the dress and usages of Europeans. He married an East Indian wife, and was admitted into, and recognized as a member of, the East Indian community. After his death the question arose whether his property was to be treated as the joint property of an undivided Hindu family, and governed by pure Hindu law; or if not, whether it was to be governed by a law of usage, similar to Hindu or to European law. The former proposition was at once rejected. Their Lordships said (*s*): "It is a question of parcenership and not of heirship. Heirship may be governed by the Hindu law, or by any

(*p*) See *Hyde* v. *Hyde*, L. R. 1. P. & D. 130; *Skinner* v. *Orde*, 14 M. I. A. 309, 324, S. C. 10 B. L. R. 125; S. C. 17 Suth. 77.

(*q*) *Ante*, § 53.

(*r*) 9 M. I. A. 195, S. C. 1 Suth. (P. C,) 1. Native Christians are now governed by the Indian Succession Act. *Ponnusami* v. *Dorasami*, 2 Mad. 209. See *Sarkies* v. *Prosonomoyee*, 6 Cal. 794.

(*s*) 9 M. I. A. 237, S. C. 1 Suth. (P. C.) 5.

other law to which the ancestor may be subject; but parcenership, understood in the sense in which their Lordships here use the term, as expressing the rights and obligations growing out of the *status* of an undivided family, is the creature of, and must be governed by the Hindu law. Considering the case, then, with reference to parcenership, what is the position of a member of a Hindu family who has become a convert to Christianity? He becomes, as their Lordships apprehend, at once severed from the family and regarded by them as an outcast. The tie which bound the family together is, so far as he is concerned, not only loosened but dissolved. The obligations consequent upon, and connected with the tie must, as it seems to their Lordships, be dissolved with it. Parcenership may be put an end to by a severance effected by partition; it must, as their Lordships think, equally be put an end to by severance which the Hindu law recognizes and creates. Their Lordships, therefore, are of opinion that, upon the conversion of a Hindu to Christianity, the Hindu law ceases to have any continuing obligatory force upon the convert. He may renounce the old law by which he was bound, as he has renounced his old religion; or, if he thinks fit, he may abide by the old law, notwithstanding he has renounced the old religion." Their Lordships then reviewed the facts, showing the different usages of different classes of Christians, and the evidence that Abraham had, in fact, passed from one class into another, and proceeded to say (*t*): "That it is not competent to parties to create, as to property, any new law to regulate the succession to it *ab intestato*, their Lordships entertain no doubt; but that is not the question on which this case depends. The question is, whether, when there are different laws as to property applying to different classes, parties ought not to be considered to have adopted the law as to property, whether in respect of succession *ab intestato*, or in other respects, of the class to which they belong. In this parti-

(*t*) 9 M. I. A. 242, 244, S. C. 1 Suth. (P. C.) 6.

cular case the question is, whether the property was bound by the Hindu law of parcenership." "The law has not, so far as their Lordships can see, prohibited a Christian convert from changing his class. The inconvenience resulting from a change of succession consequent on a change of class is no greater than that which often results from a change of domicil. The *argumentum ab inconvenienti* cannot therefore be used against the legality of such a change. If such change takes place in fact, why should it be regarded as non-existing in law? Their Lordships are of opinion, that it was competent for Matthew Abraham, though himself both by origin and actually in his youth a 'native Christian,' following the Hindu laws and customs on matters relating to property, to change his class of Christians, and become of the Christian class to which his wife belonged. His family was managed and lived in all respects like an East Indian family. In such a family the undivided family union, in the sense before mentioned, is unknown."

Illegitimate issue of European.

§ 57. On the same principle, where a European had illegitimate sons by two Hindu women, and they conformed in all respects to Hindu habits and usages, it was held that they must for all purposes be treated as Hindus, and governed by Hindu law as such. "They were not an united Hindu family in the ordinary sense in which that term is used by the text writers on Hindu law; a family of which the father was in his lifetime the head, and the sons in a sense parceners in birth, by an inchoate, though alterable, title; but they were sons of a Christian father by different Hindu mothers, constituting themselves parceners in the enjoyment of their property, after the manner of a Hindu joint family" (*u*). And it was held that their rights of succession *inter se* and to their mother, must be judged by Hindu law, which recognized such rights, and not by Eng-

---

(*u*) *Myna Boyee* v. *Ootaram*, 8 M. I. A. 400, 420, S. C. 2 Suth. (P. C.) 4.

lish law, which denied them (*v*). On the other hand, the vast majority of the class known as East Indians, and referred to in the judgment in *Abraham* v. *Abraham*, have been the illegitimate sons of Europeans by natives or half-caste women, who, from being acknowledged and cared for by their fathers, have adopted European modes of life. These, as already stated, would be governed by European law.

(*v*) Same case, 2 Mad. H. C. 196.

CHAPTER IV.

FAMILY RELATIONS.

Marriage and Sonship.

§ 58. No part of the Hindu Law is more anomalous than that which governs the Family relations. Not only does there appear to be a complete break of continuity between the ancient system and that which now prevails, but the different parts of the ancient system appear in this respect to be in direct conflict with each other. We find a law of inheritance, which assumes the possibility of tracing male ancestors in an unbroken pedigree extending to fourteen generations; while coupled with it is a family law, in which several admitted forms of marriage are only euphemisms for seduction and rape, and in which twelve sorts of sons are recognized, the majority of whom have no blood relationship to their own father. I am not aware that any attempt has hitherto been made to harmonise, or to account for, these apparent inconsistencies. It has been suggested, however, that some of the peculiarities of the system may be referred to the practice of polyandry, which is supposed to have been once universal (*a*). It seems to me that the proved existence of such a practice would not account for the facts. I also doubt whether polyandry, properly so called (*b*),

Anomalies in Family Law.

(*a*) I refer, of course, to the views put forward by Mr. McLennan throughout his Studies in Ancient History, 1876. Also in two articles in the Fortnightly Review, May and June, 1877. McLennan. Patriarchal Theory, 1885.

(*b*) By polyandry, properly so called, I mean a system under which a woman is the legal property of several husbands at once, as among the Todas; or under which a woman, who is legally married to one husband, has the right, which he cannot dispute, to admit other men at her own pleasure, as among the Nairs. I

ever prevailed among the races who were governed by the system now under discussion, while they were governed by it. It is quite possible that it may have prevailed among them at a still earlier stage of their history. But this circumstance would be immaterial, if there is reason to suppose that they had escaped from its influence before the introduction of the Family law, which we find in force at the time of the earliest Sanskrit writings. Still more, if that law can be accounted for on principles which have nothing to do with polyandry. It will be well, however, to clear the ground for the discussion, by enquiring what are the actual facts.

Polyandry among non-Aryan races.

§ 59. Among the non-aryan races of India, both the former and the present existence of polyandry is beyond dispute. It is peculiarly common among the Hill tribes, who are probably aboriginal; but it is also widely diffused among the inhabitants of the plains (*c*). Among the Nairs, the woman remains in her own home after her marriage, and there associates with as many men as she pleases (*d*). The Teehurs of Oude "live together almost indiscriminately in large communities, and even where two people are regarded as married, the tie is but nominal" (*e*). Among the Western Kallans of Madura, "it constantly happens that a woman is the wife of either ten, eight, six, or two husbands, who are held to be the fathers jointly and severally of any children that may be born of her body. And still more curiously, when the children of such a family grow up, they for some unknown reason style themselves the children, not of ten, eight, or six fathers, as the case

exclude cases of mere dissoluteness. No one would apply the term polyandry to the institution of the *cavalier servente* in Italy or Spain. I also exclude cases in which a woman is allowed to offer herself to a man, who claims a sort of semi-divinity, as in the case of the Maharajas of Bombay; and the analogous cases of promiscuous prostitution of married women as a sort of religious rite. See Dubois (ed. 1862), 302; Wilson, Works, i. 263.

(*c*) In the Punjab it is still found existing in Seoraj, Lahoul and Spiti. Punjab Customary Law, II. 186, 187, 191. Here the joint husbands are always brothers.

(*d*) McLennan, 147.

(*e*) Lubbock, Origin of Man (ed. 1870), 73, citing the People of India, by Kaye and Watson, ii. 85.

may be, but of eight and two, or six and two, or four and two fathers" (*f*). Among the Kannuvans of Madura, "a woman may legally marry any number of men in succession, though she may not have two husbands at one and the same time. She, may, however, bestow favours on paramours without hindrance, provided they be of equal caste with her" (*g*). Among the Todas of the Nilgiris, as in Thibet, the wife is the property of all the brothers, and lives in their home (*h*). A similar custom prevails among the Tiyars, or palm cultivators of Malabar and Travancore (*i*). Among the Tottiyars, a caste of Madura, it is the usage for brothers, uncles, nephews and other relations, to hold their wives in common, and their priests compel them to keep up the custom, if they are unwilling; outside the family they are chaste (*k*).

Polyandry among Aryans.

§ 60. It is difficult to believe that polyandry in its lowest form, as authorising the union of women with a plurality of husbands of different family, could ever have been common among the Aryan Hindus. Such a system, as Mr. McLennan points out (*l*), would necessarily produce a system of kinship through females, such as actually exists among the polyandrous tribes of the West Coast of India. Now, the most striking feature in the Aryan Hindu customs is the strictness with which kinship is traced through males. Except in Bengal, where the change is comparatively modern, agnates to the fourteenth degree exclude cognates. This rule is connected with, if it is not based upon, their religious system, the first principle of which was the practice of worshipping deceased male ancestors to the remotest degree (*m*). This, of course, involved the assumption that

(*f*) Madura Manual, Pt. II. 54.
(*g*) *Ibid.* 34.
(*h*) Breeks, Primitive Tribes, 10.
(*i*) Madras Census Report, 162.
(*k*) Dubois, 3; Madura Manual, Pt. II. 82.
(*l*) Studies, 124, 135. Mr. L. H. Morgan's objections (p. 515) to the general proposition stated by Mr. McLennan as to kinship through females, seem not to apply to the limited form of that proposition as stated in the text.
(*m*) Manu, iii. § 81—91, 122—125, 189, 193—231, 282—284; Spencer, i. 304; Appx. 1.; M. Müller, A. S. Lit. 386; Ind. Wisd. 255.

those ancestors could be identified with the most perfect certainty. The female ancestors were only worshipped in conjunction with their deceased husbands. We can be quite certain that this system was one of enormous antiquity, since we find exactly the same practice of religious offerings to the dead prevailing among the Greeks and Romans. We may assert with confidence that a usage common to the three races had previously existed in that ancient stock from which Hindus, Greeks, and Romans, alike proceeded. No doubt, Mr. McLennan points out numerous indications of kinship through females among the Greeks, especially in the case of the Trial of Orestes. But, if I may be allowed to say so, all these instances seem to be less the voice of a living law, than the feeble echoes of one sounding from a past that was dead (*n*). I by no means deny that polyandry of the second, or Toda, type, may have existed among the Hindu Aryans. But I think that at the earliest times of which we have any evidence it had become very rare, and had fallen into complete discredit even where it existed. Also, that everything which we find in the oldest Hindu laws can be accounted for without any reference to it.

Evidences of polyandry.

§ 61. What then is the actual evidence upon the subject? The earliest indication of polyandry of which I am aware, is to be found in a hymn in the Rig-Veda, which is addressed to the two Asvins. "Asvins, your admirable horses bore the car which you have harnessed first to the goal for the sake of honour; and the damsel who was the prize came through affection to you, and acknowledged your husbandship, saying, you are my lords" (*o*). This evidently points to the practice of *Svayamvara*, when a

(*n*) See Teulon, La Mère, 7. "Sous les conquerants Aryas et Sémites s'étend souvent, suivant l'heureuse expression de M. d'Eckstein, un *humus scientifique*. Sous cette couche d'êtres humains, d'autres races ont vécu, obéissant à des lois qui, si elles n'ont été générales, ont régné du moins sur d'immenses étendues. Leurs civilisations reposaient sur *le droit de la mère, &c.*" See also Teulon, 62, 63. "Partout, où les Aryas se sont établis, ils ont introduit avec eux la famille gouvernée par le père."

(*o*) Cited Wheeler, Hist. of India, ii. 502.

maiden of high rank used to offer herself as the prize to the conqueror in a contest of skill, and in this instance became the wife of several suitors at once. It is exactly in conformity with the well-known case of Draupadi, who, as the Mahabharata relates, was won at an archery match by the eldest of the five Pandava princes, and then became the wife of all. As far as I know, this is the only definite instance in which an Aryan woman is recorded to have become the legal permanent wife of several men. Undoubtedly, as Professor Max Müller remarks (*p*) the epic tradition must have been very strong to compel the authors to record a proceeding so violently opposed to Brahmanical law. Yet the very description of the transaction represents it as one which was opposed to public opinion, and which was rather justified by very remote tradition than by existing practice. I take the account of it given by Mr. McLennan (*q*). "The father of Draupadi is represented by the compilers of the epic as shocked at the proposal of the princes to marry his daughter. 'You who know the law,' he is made to say, 'must not commit an unlawful act which is contrary to usage and the Vedas.' The reply is, 'The law, O King, is subtle. We do not know its way. We follow the path which has been trodden by our ancestors in succession.' One of the princes then pleads precedent. 'In an old tradition it is recorded that Iatila, of the family of Gotama, that most excellent of moral women, dwelt with seven saints; and that Varski, the daughter of a Muni, cohabited with ten brothers, all of them called Prachetas, whose souls had been purified with penance.'" Now, upon this statement the alleged ancestral usage appears really to have been non-existent. The only specific instances that could be adduced were certainly not cases of marriage. They were instances of special indulgence allowed to Rishis, who had passed out of the order of married men, and whose greatness of spiritual merit made it impossible for them to commit sin (*r*). It is also to be remembered

Draupadi.

(*p*) A. S. Lit. 46. (*q*) Fort. Rev., May 1877, 698.
(*r*) See Apastamba, ii. vi. 13, § 8—10, and *post*, § 62.

that the Pandava princes were Kshatriyas, to whom greater license was allowed in their dealings with the sex, and for whom the loosest forms of marriage were sanctioned (*s*). If polyandrous practices existed among the aborigines whom they conquered, these would naturally be imitated by them. Just as the English knights who settled beyond the Pale became *Hibernis Hiberniores*. On the other hand, in a passage of the Ramayana (*t*), where the Rakshasa meets Rama and his brother wandering with Sita, the wife of the former, the giant accosts them in language of much moral indignation, saying, "Oh little dwarfs, why do you come with your wife into the forest of Dandaka, clad in the habit of devotees, and armed with arrows, bow and scimitar? Why do you two devotees remain with one woman? Why are you, oh profligate wretches, corrupting the devout sages?" The giant seems to have looked upon polyandry with the same abhorrence as Draupadi's father.

Rama and Sita.

Looseness of marriage tie.

§ 62. Other passages of the Mahabharata are referred to, which seem rather to evidence the greatest grossness, and want of chastity, in the relations between the sexes, than anything like polyandry. It is said that "women were formerly unconfined, and roamed about at their pleasure independent. Though in their youthful innocence they abandoned their husbands, they were guilty of no offence; for such was the rule in early times. This ancient custom is even now the law for creatures born as brutes, which are free from lust and anger. This custom is supported by authority, and is observed by great Rishis, and it is still practised among the northern Kurus." Dr. Muir goes on to add, "A stop was, however, put to the practice by Svetaketu, whose indignation was on one occasion aroused by a Brahman taking his mother by the hand, and inviting her to go away with him, although his father, in

(*s*) Manu, iii. § 26.

(*t*) Cited Wheeler, Hist. India, ii. 241. Mr. V. N. Mandlik (p. 397) says that the original passage contains nothing to show that the giant accused the brothers of having a joint wife.

whose presence this occurred, informed him that there was no reason for his displeasure, as the custom was one which had prevailed from time immemorial. But Svetaketu could not tolerate the practice; and introduced the existing rule. A wife and a husband indulging in promiscuous intercourse were thenceforward guilty of sin" (*u*). So the Gandhara Brahmans of the Punjab are said "to corrupt their own sisters and daughters-in-law, and to offer their wives to others, hiring and selling them like commodities for money. Their women, being thus given up to strangers, are consequently shameless;" as might have been expected (*v*). In exactly the same way, the Koravers of Southern India, who are not polyandrous, sell and mortgage their wives and daughters when they are in want of money (*w*). Of course, delicacy, or chastity, must be utterly unknown in such a state of society. But these very texts seem to show that each wife was appropriated to a single husband, though he was willing to allow her the greatest freedom of action (*x*).

Early Family Law.

§ 63. When we come to the law writers it is quite certain that a woman could never have more than one husband at a time. But we also find that sonship and marriage seem to stand in no relation to each other. A man's son need not have been begotten by his father, nor need he have been produced by his father's wife. How is such a state of the family, which appears to set genealogy at defiance, reconcilable with a system of property which is based upon the strictest ascertainment of pedigree? I believe the answer is simply this—that a son was always assigned in law to the male who was the legal owner of the mother. Further,

Principle of sonship.

(*u*) Muir, A. S. T. ii. 418 (2nd ed.) The first passage is cited by Mr. McLennan, p. 173, n., from the 1st ed. ii. 336. See also other passages from the Mahabharata, cited 2 Dig. 392—394.

(*v*) Muir, A. S. T. ii. 482, 483.

(*w*) Madras Census Report, 167.

(*x*) Mr. V. N. Mandlik says of the passages cited from Dr. Muir "To me the whole chapter shows that the Northern kurus were then what the Nairs in Malabar are now; so that a man did not know his own father." But he admits that these and similar passages "point to times anterior to the compilation of the Vedas. For even in the earliest Veda marriage appears to have become a well established institution," pp. 395—397.

that the filial relation was itself capable of being assigned over by the person to whom the son was subject, or by the son himself if emancipated. If I am right in this view, the theory that the *levirate* is invariably a survival of polyandry will fall to the ground.

Different sorts of sons.

§ 64. The various sorts of sons recognized by the early writers were the following. The legitimate son (*aurasa*), the son of an appointed daughter (*putrika putra*), the son begotten on the wife (*kshetraja*), the son born secretly (*gudhaja*), the damsel's son (*kanina*), the son taken with the bride (*sahodha*), the son of a twice married woman (*paunarbhava*), the son by a Sudra woman (*nishada*), or by a concubine (*parasava*), the adopted son (*dattaka*), the son made (*kritrima*), the son bought (*kritaka*), the son cast off (*apaviddha*), and the son self-given (*svayamdattaka*) (*y*). Of these it will be at once seen that the five last never could be the actual sons of their father, and of the other nine only the first and the last two need be. Of the remaining seven, some necessarily, and others probably, were not begotten by him at all. Further, many of these were not even the offspring of his wife. The problem for solution is, how they came to be considered as his sons? To answer this, we must enquire into the Hindu idea of paternity.

Necessity for sons.

§ 65. In modern times children are a luxury to the rich, an encumbrance to the poor. In early ages female offspring stood in the same position, but male issue was passionately prized. The very existence of a tribe, surrounded by enemies, would depend upon the continual multiplication of its males. The sonless father would find himself without protection or support in sickness or old age, and would see his land passing into other hands, when he became unable to

(*y*) Baudhayana, xvii. 2, § 10—24; Gautama, xxviii. § 32, 33; Vasishtha, xvii. § 9—22; Vishnu, xv. § 1—27; Narada, xiii. § 17—20, 45—47; Manu, ix. § 127—140, 158—184; Devala, 3 Dig. 153; Yama, *ib.* 154; Yajnavalkya, ii. § 128—132; Mit., i. 11. Apastamba stands alone among the earlier writers in only recognizing the legitimate son, ii. vi. 13, § 1—11.

The annexed table shows the order in which the different sons are placed

cultivate it. The necessity for male offspring extended in the case of the Aryan even beyond this world. His hap-

by the various authors.

	Aurasa. Legitimate son.	Kshetraja. Son begotten on wife.	Putrika putra. Son of appointed daughter.	Kanina. Damsel's son.	Gudhaja. Secretly born.	Paunarbhava. Son of twice married woman.	Sahodha. Son of pregnant bride.	Nishada. Son of Sudra woman.	Dattaka. Adopted son	Kritrima. Son made.	Kritaka. Son bought.	Apaviddha. Son cast off.	Svayamdattaka. Self-given son.
Baudhayana, ii. 2, § 10—23 ...	1	3	2	8	6	11	9	13	4	5	10	7	12
Gautama, xxviii. § 32—33 ..	1	2	10*	7	5	9	8	—	3	4	12	6	11
Vasishtha, xvii. § 9—21 / Vishnu, xv. § 1—27 ...	1	2	3	5	6	4	7	12	8	—	9	11	10
Manu, ix. § 158—160 ... / Kalika Purana, 3 Dig. 155	1	2	†	7	5	10	8	12	3	4	9	6	11
Yajnavalkya, ii. § 128—132 ...	1	3	2	5	4	6	11	—	7	9	8	12	10
Narada, xiii. § 45—46	1	2	3	4	6	7	5	—	9	11	10	8	12
Sancha and Lichita, 3 Dig. 151 ...	1	2	3	5	6	4	8	11	9	—	10	7	12
Harita, 3 Dig. 152	1	2	5	4	6	3	10	—	7	12	8	9	11
Devala, 3 Dig. 153 ‡	1	3	2	4	5	8	7	—	9	11	12	6	10
Yama, 3 Dig. 154	1	2	3	5	6	4	8	—	9	10	11	7	12
Vrihaspati, 3 Dig. 162—171 ...	1	8	2	10	12	9	11	7	3	6	5	4	—
Brahma Purana, 3 Dig. 174 ...	1	2	3	7	5	10	8	12	4	—	9	6	11

Vijnanesvara quotes both Yajnavalkya and Manu, but seems to follow the latter as to the order of the sons. Mit., i. 11, § 30, 31.

Jimuta Vahana follows Devala. D. Bh., x. § 7.

The Smriti Chandrika follows Manu, Chap. x.

* Mitakshara (i. 11, § 35) explains the low position assigned by Gautama to the son of an appointed daughter as being relative to one differing in tribe.

† The son of an appointed daughter is not specified in Manu's list of twelve sons. He had been already described, and stated to be equal to an actual son. Manu, ix. § 134—136.

‡ See an explanation offered of Devala's text *Puddo Kumaree* v. *Juggut Kishore*, 5 Cal. 630, post § 153.

piness in the next depended upon his having a continuous line of male descendants, whose duty it would be to make the periodical offerings for the repose of his soul. Hence the works of the Sanskrit sages state it to be the first duty of man to become the possessor of male offspring, and imprecate curses upon those who die without a son (*z*). Where a son was so indispensable, we might expect that every contrivance would be exhausted to procure one. What has been already said about the relations between the sexes in early times would make it certain that neither delicacy, nor sentiment, would stand in the way.

Theory of paternity among Hindus.

§ 66. A frequent subject for discussion in Manu is as to the property in a child. He says: "They consider the male issue of a woman as the son of the lord: but on the subject of that lord, a difference of opinion is mentioned in the Veda; some giving that name to the real procreator of the child, and others applying it to the married possessor of the woman." He argues the point on the analogy of seed sown by a stranger on the land of another, or of flocks impregnated by a strange male. He sums up by declaring: "Thus men who have no marital property in women, but sow in the fields owned by others, may raise up fruit to the husbands, but the procreator can have no advantage from it. Unless there be a special agreement between the owners of the land and of the seed, the fruit belongs clearly to the landowner, for the receptacle is more important than the seed. But the owners of the seed and of the soil may be considered in this world as joint owners of the crop, which they agree by special compact, in consideration of the seed, to divide between them" (*a*). The conflicting opinions referred to by Manu are probably the texts mentioned by the early Sutra writers (*b*). In one of these

(*z*) Vasish., xvii. § 1—5; Vish., xv. § 43—46; Manu, vi. § 36, 37, ix. § 45; Atri. D. M., i. § 3.

(*a*) Manu, ix. § 32—44, 48,—55, 181; x. § 70; Nar., xii. § 56—60. Viramit., p. 104, § 4.

(*b*) Apast., ii. vi. 13, § 6, 7, and note; Baudh., ii. 2, § 25; Vasish., xvii. § 6, 7. Gautama, xviii. § 11.

passages quoted from the Vedas, a husband is reported as announcing, with considerable *naiveté,* that he will not any longer allow his wives to be approached by other men, since he has received an opinion "that a son belongs to him who begot him in the world of Yama." In this world, it is to be observed, there seems to be no doubt entertained that the son begotten by others on his wife would be his own.

Origin of the *Niyoga.*

§ 67. It was upon this principle—*viz.*, that a son, by whomsoever begotten, was the property of the husband of the mother—that the *kshetraja,* or son begotten upon a wife, ranked so high in the list of subsidiary sons. The Mahabharata and Vishnu Purana relate how king Saudasa, being childless, induced Vasishtha to beget for him a son upon his wife Damayanti. So king Kalinga is represented as requesting the old Rishi Dirghatamas to beget offspring for him; and Pandu, when he became a Sunnyasi, accepted, as his own, sons begotten upon his wife by strangers. The same passage of the Mahabharata which relates how Svetaketu put an end to promiscuous intercourse on the part of husbands and wives, also states that a wife, when appointed by her husband to raise up seed to him by connection with another man, is guilty of sin if she refuses (*c*). And so the law-books expressly sanction the begetting of offspring by another on the wife of a man who was impotent, or disordered in mind, or incurably diseased; and the son so begotten belonged to the incapacitated husband (*d*). No rule is laid down that the person employed to beget offspring during the husband's life should be a near relation, or any relation (*e*). In fact, in the instances just mentioned, the procreator, who was called in aid, was not only not of the same family, but was not even of the same caste, the owner

(*c*) Muir. A. S. T. i. 418, 419; Wilson, Works, v. 310; M. Müller, A. S. Lit. 56; 3 Dig. 252.

(*d*) Baudh., ii. 2, § 12; Manu, ix. § 162, 167, 203. § 162 shows that a man might have a son begotten by procuration, and also a son begotten by himself.

(*e*) Apastamba, who is strongly opposed to the *Niyoga*, says (ii. x. 27 § 2) that a husband shall not make over his wife, who occupies the position of a *gentilis*, to others than to his *gentilis* in order to cause children to be begotten for himself. It is probable that this refers to an authority to beget after the husband's death. If not, it is merely a restriction on the old usage.

of the wife being a Kshatriya, and his assistant being a Brahman.

Offspring begotten upon a widow.

§ 68. The begetting of offspring upon the widow of a man who had left no issue is, of course, merely an extension of the practice just discussed (*f*). But there was this difference between the two cases; that in the latter, for the first time, the element of fiction was introduced. In the former case, the husband became the father, not by any fiction of paternity, but by the simple fact that he was the owner of the mother. But after his death the ownership had ceased; unless, indeed, by another fiction, he was considered as still surviving in her (*g*). Therefore, unless the husband had given express directions during his lifetime, the process to be adopted was to be as like as possible to an actual begetting by him, or was to be such a substituted begetting as he would probably have sanctioned. Hence, such a connection was never permitted when the widow had issue already. Nor was it to be continued further than was necessary for the purpose of conception. Nor was it allowable to procreate more than one son, though at one time it was thought that a second might lawfully be produced (*h*). Nor was the widow allowed to consort with any one she pleased, or to do so at all merely of her own free will. The procreator was to be the brother of the deceased if possible, or, if he was not attainable, a near sapinda (*i*). This was either to enhance the fiction of paternity; or, perhaps, still further to exclude any personal feeling on the part of the widow. Further, some authorisation was necessary, though it is not very clearly stated by

(*f*) This alone is the *levirate* referred to by Mr. McLennan, see Fort. Rev., May, 1877. The general usage of begetting a son upon the wife of another on his behalf was known by the term *Niyoga*, (that is, order or commission) of which the *levirate* was only a special instance.

(*g*) Manu, ix, § 45; Vrihaspati, 3 Dig. 458.

(*h*) Manu, ix. § 58—63, 143, 147; Narada, xii. § 62, 80—88; Yama, 2 Dig. 468.

(*i*) Gautama, xviii. § 4—7, xxviii. § 23; Manu, ix. § 59; Narada, xii. § 80—88; Yajnavalkya, ii. § 128. Manu, permits either a brother or another. Yajnavalkya, either a relative or another. Kulluka Bhatta in his gloss adds the word *sapinda* as limiting the vague word *another*.

whom it was to be given. In a legend mentioned in the Mahabharata, Vyasa begets children on both the widows of his brother, at the request of Satyavat, the mother of the deceased (*k*). Gautama asserts that the widow must obtain the permission of her Gurus. Narada speaks of the authorisation as being given to the widow by her spiritual parents, or by her relations. Manu merely speaks of her being authorised, to which Kulluka Bhatta adds *by the husband or spiritual guide.* Yajnavalkya refers to the authority of the latter (*l*). It is quite plain that even the brother could not perform the act without some external authority.

Niyoga not connected with polyandry.

§ 69. If I am right in this view, it is evident that the *levirate,* as practised among the Aryan Hindus, was not a survival of polyandry. The *levir* did not take his brother's widow as his wife. He simply did for his brother, or other near relation, when deceased, what the latter might have authorised him, or any other person, to do during his life-time. And this, of course, explains why the issue so raised belonged to the deceased and not to the begetter. If it were a relic of polyandry, the issue would belong to the surviving polyandrous husband, and the wife would pass over to him as his wife. Such a course would have been natural enough even among Hindus, and, as we shall see presently, the practice actually existed (*m*). But it is something completely different from the Hindu *Niyoga.* And the same explanation which accounts for the origin of the *levirate* accounts, also, for its extinction. As soon as any idea of mutual fidelity, sentiment, or delicacy, arose as an element in the marriage union, the notion of allowing issue to be begotten on a wife would become most repulsive. And as that practice died away, the usage of authorising it in regard to a widow would naturally die away also, though it might continue longer in the latter case than in

(*k*) Ind. Wisd. 376.
(*l*) Gautama, xviii. § 5; Narada, xii. § 80—87; Manu, ix. § 58; Yajnavalkya ii. § 68.
(*m*) *Post* § 70.

the former. We can see that a considerable amount of refinement in the relations between man and wife had already sprung up at the date of our compilation of Manu (*n*); and we can understand how it came about, that texts were interpolated forbidding a practice which the preceding texts had sanctioned and regulated (*o*). The *Niyoga* would also become unpopular, as partition became more common. So long as the family remained undivided, the afterborn son would be merely an additional mouth to feed, accompanied by a pair of hands to work, and he would take upon himself the entire duty of performing the recurring ceremonies to his quasi-father. But as soon as the practice of division sprang up, he would be entitled to claim a share, and to stand generally in his parent's place. At one time, too, it appears that the widow had a right to manage the property of her deceased husband on his behalf (*p*). Naturally the relations would cease to authorise an act which tended to defeat their own rights.

Marriage of widow with husband's brother.

§ 70. The actual marriage of a widow with the brother of her deceased husband is, of course, something quite different from the *levirate*. This was sanctioned by Manu in the single case of a girl who had been left a virgin widow (*q*). The practice still exists in many parts of India. It has been found among the Ideiyars, a pastoral race of Southern India; in Orissa, among the Jat families of the Punjab, both Brahman and Rajputs; and among some of the Rajput class of Central India. In the Punjab such marriages are considered of an inferior class, and do not give the issue full right of inheritance (*r*). Such marriages may in some cases be a relic of polyandry, but they seem to me capable of a much simpler explanation. There is nothing in the usage of itself unnatural and revolting. The

(*n*) Manu, iii. § 45, 55—62, ix. § 101—105.
(*o*) Manu, ix. § 64—68.
(*p*) Manu, ix. § 210, 146, 190.
(*q*) Manu, ix. § 60, 70.
(*r*) Madras Census Rep. 149; Punjab Cust. 94; Lyall, Fort. Rev., Jan. 1877 103; Sarvadhikari, 528, n.

marriage of a woman with two brothers successively is merely the converse of the marriage of a man with two sisters successively, a sort of union which, though illegal, is by no means uncommon in Great Britain, and which is absolutely legal in several of our colonies. Marriage with a deceased wife's sister is believed to be very common among the lower orders, from the simple fact that a sister-in-law very frequently becomes a permanent member of the family during the life of the sister, and continues in it after her death. She naturally takes the place of her sister as mother and wife. Exactly the same facts would lead to the converse result in a Hindu undivided family. On the death of the husband the widow would continue to reside in the same house with her brother-in-law. He would take possession of all the effects of his deceased brother, not as heir, but as manager of the family corporation by virtue of seniority (*s*). At a time when women were regarded merely as chattels (*t*), the wives of the deceased would naturally pass over to the manager, who was bound to support them. To take the illustration from Scandinavian history cited by Mr. McLennan: "Now Bork sets up his abode with Mordissa, and takes his brother's widow to wife with his brother's goods; that was the rule in those days, and wives were heritage like other things." The only difference is, that the Hindu Mordissa would have been living all along in the house with the Hindu Bork, and that on the death of her husband the latter would have become her natural protector and legal guardian. The transition to husband is so natural that it is strange it did not more universally take place.

(*s*) Among some tribes of the Punjab the custom is that the widow should marry not her husband's elder brother but his younger brother. Punjab Customary Law, II. 94.

(*t*) The prohibition against dividing women at a partition (Manu, ix. § 219; Gautama, xxviii. § 45) seems to point to a time when they had been looked upon merely as a part of the family property. Perhaps those curious texts which state the liability of a man who had taken the wife, or widow, of another to pay his debts, may be founded on the same principle (1 Dig. 321—323, 2 Dig. 476; Narada, iii. § 21—26; V. May, v. 4, § 16, 17; Spencer, i. 680; *post*, § 302.) Accordingly Narada says (iii. § 23, 24), "In all the four classes, wives and goods go together; he who takes a man's wives takes his property also." "The wife is considered as the dead man's property."

Son born in secret.

§ 71. The same principle, *viz.*, that the son belongs to the owner of the mother, can be shown with greater ease in the other cases. The secretly born son is described by Vishnu as follows: "The son who is secretly born in the house is the sixth. He belongs to him on whose bed he was born" (*u*). Manu is to the same effect, and the gloss of Kulluka Bhatta shows that the mother is supposed to be a married woman, whose husband's absence makes it certain that he was not the father. Yet the child belongs to him (*v*). In the case of the son of a damsel (*Kanina*) born in her father's house, if she marries, the son belongs to the husband, and inherits to him. If she does not marry, he belongs to, and is the heir of, her father, under whose dominion she remains (*w*). So, "if a pregnant young woman marry, whether her pregnancy be known or unknown, the male child in her womb belongs to the bridegroom, and is called a son received with his bride" (*Sahodha*) (*x*). As regards the sons of twice married women (*paunarbhava*), and of disloyal wives, Narada lays down the same rule. "Their offspring belongs to the begetter, if they have come under his dominion, in consideration of a price he had paid to the husband. But the children of one who has not been sold belong to her husband" (*y*). Of course the children of a woman who had actually been married to a second husband would, *a fortiori*, have belonged to him (*z*).

Son of damsel; or bride; or twice married woman.

Son by a concubine.

§ 72. The same considerations seem to govern the case of a child by a concubine, who is classed by some writers with the child by a Sudra (*a*). The union of a man of the higher classes with a Sudra was, in the later law, though not

(*u*) Vishnu, xv. § 13, 14.
(*v*) Manu, ix. § 170. Viramit., ii. 2, § 5.
(*w*) Vishnu, xv. § 10—12; Vasishtha, xvii. § 14; Narada, xiii. § 17, 18. The Viramitrodaya, p. 113, says that the child belongs to the father of the woman or husband, according as she was affianced or not at the time of birth. This is also the view taken by Nanda Pandita in the Vaijayanti. Jolly, § 152.
(*x*) Manu, ix. § 173; Vishnu, xv. § 15—17; Narada, xiii. § 17.
(*y*) Narada, xii. § 55. For the definition of a "paunarbhava," see Vishnu, xv. § 7—9; Manu, ix. § 175; Narada, xii. § 46—49; Vasishtha, xvii. § 13.
(*z*) Katyayana, 3 Dig. 236.
(*a*) See Baudhayana, ii. 2, § 21, 22; Vishnu, xv. § 27, note.

originally, looked upon as so odious, that the son was only entitled to maintenance, and not to inheritance (*b*). And the position of a son born to him by a concubine was no better (*c*). But the son of a Sudra by a concubine was always entitled to inherit under certain events. The distinction, however, seems to have been taken, that in order to do so, he must have been begotten upon a woman who was under the absolute control of the begetter. Manu speaks of the son begotten by a man of the servile class "on his female slave, or on the female slave of his male slave" (*d*). And so Narada says, "there is no issue if a man has had intercourse with a woman in the house of another man; and it is termed fornication by the learned if a woman has intercourse with a man in the house of a stranger" (*e*). Obviously, because in the latter case the woman is not under his dominion. Her issue would belong to the person who was her owner.

Son of an appointed daughter.

§ 73. The case of the son of the appointed daughter is a little more complicated, but appears to me to be explicable in the same way. She was lawfully married to her husband. Yet her son became the son of her father, if he had no male issue; and he became so, not only by agreement with her husband, but by a mere act of intention on the part of her father, without any consent asked for or obtained. Hence a man was warned not to marry a girl without brothers, lest her father should take her first son as his own (*f*). Now Vasishtha quotes a text of the Vedas as showing that "the girl who has no brother comes back to the males of her own family, to her father and the rest. Returning she becomes their son" (*g*). In her case, therefore, the father seems to have retained his dominion over

---

(*b*) Cf. Manu, iii. § 13—19, ix. § 145—155, 178; Gautama, xxviii. § 39; Devala, 3 Dig. 135, and other authorities cited 3 Dig. 115—133; Yajnavalkya, ii. § 125.
(*c*) Mitakshara, i. 12, § 3.
(*d*) Manu, ix. § 179.
(*e*) Narada, xii. § 61.
(*f*) Gautama, xxviii. § 19, 20; Manu, iii. § 11.
(*g*) Vasishtha, xvii. § 12.

her, to the extent of being able to appropriate her son if he wished it (*h*). The same result of course followed, where the marriage took place with an express agreement that this dominion should be reserved (*i*).

A custom precisely similar to that of the son of an appointed daughter still exists among the Nambudri Brahmans of the Malabar Coast in Madras. They are believed to have emigrated from Eastern India about 1200 or 1500 years ago, bearing with them a system of Hindu law of an archaic character, more nearly representing that of the Sutra writers than the later form to be found in the Mitakshara (*k*). Where a Nambudri has no male issue, he may give his daughter in Sarvasvadhanam marriage. The result of such a marriage is that if a son is born, he inherits to, and is for all purposes the son of, his father-in-law. If there is no male issue, or on failure of such issue, the property of the wife's family does not belong to the husband, but reverts to the family of the father-in-law (*l*).

Adopted sons. § 74. The remaining sons are all adopted sons, and avowedly the original property of their natural parents. Their case will be separately treated in the next chapter. The only matter of remark bearing on the present enquiry is this; that in two of the cases, *viz.*, the son given (*dattaka*) and the son bought (*kritaka*), the boy was a minor, and the right in him was given over by those who had dominion over him, and could be given over by no one else (§ 119). In the case of the son made (*kritrima*), the youth was of full age, and therefore able to dispose of himself; and in the case of the son self given (*svayamdattaka*) or cast off (*apaviddha*) he had been abandoned, or ill treated by his

(*h*) In Russia, a father retains his dominion over his daughter after marriage, and may claim her services at his own home if they are required in case of illness, or by the death of his wife. See an article on Marriage Customs, in the Pall Mall Budget, xix. 249, one of a series on The Russians of to-day.

(*i*) Baudhayana, ii. 2, § 11.

(*k*) *Vasudevan* v. *Secretary of State*, 11 Mad. 157, 160.

(*l*) 11 Mad. 158, 162. *Kumaran* v. *Narayanan*, 9 Mad. 260.

parents, or had lost them. Their dominion had accordingly come to an end (*m*).

§ 75. All of these sons, except the legitimate and the adopted, are long since obsolete (*n*). Possibly traces of the old usage may still linger on in remote districts. Jagannatha says that in Orissa it is still the practice with some people to raise up issue on the wife of a brother, but his own opinion is strongly expressed against the legality of such a proceeding. Mr. Colebrooke states that, in his time, the practice of appointing brothers to raise up male issue to deceased, impotent, or even absent brothers, still prevailed in Orissa. Mr. Rajkumar Sarvadhikari says in reference to this statement,—"From all the enquiries we have made on the subject, it appears that the practice is highly reprobated among the higher classes in Orissa, and if it exists among the lower classes at all, it exists in such a form that it is of no importance whatever from a juridical point of view." He adds, that among some of the rich and noble classes in Orissa, the practice of *Niyoga* has probably assumed the modernised form of marriage with an elder brother's widow (*o*). The same reason which caused the *Kshetraja* son to fall into disrepute, necessarily led to the disappearance of several of the others also. The increasing strictness of the marriage tie made a husband refuse to recognize as his son any issue which was not begotten upon his own wife by himself, or at all events might not be supposed to have been so begotten. This would eliminate from the list of sons the *Kanina*, the *Gudhaja*, and the *Sahodha*, unless, in the latter case, the son

All but two now obsolete.

(*m*) Baudhayana, ii. 2, § 13, 14, 16, 19, 21 ; Vasishtha, xvii. § 17—20 ; Vishnu, xv. § 18—26 ; Manu, ix. § 168, 169, 174, 177 ; *post*, § 94. Similarly in Rome there were two sorts of adoption ; *adoptio*, properly so called of a child who was under the dominion of another, and *adrogatio*, of a person who was *sui juris*.

(*n*) Vrihaspati, 3 Dig. 271 ; Aditya, Purana, *ib*. 272, 288 ; Apararka, cited, Sarvadhikari, 512 ; V. May, iv. 4, § 46 ; Dattaka Mimamsa, i. § 64 ; Smriti Chandrika, x. § 5 ; D. Ch. i. 9 ; 2 Bor. 456 ; *post*, § 94. The mention of them in works so late as the Daya Bhaga cannot be taken as any evidence that they were still recognized at that time. See *ante*, § 15. Sarvadhikari, 519.

(*o*) 3 Dig. 288, 289, 276, note. Sarvadhikari, 528.

conceived before marriage was born after marriage (*p*). When a second marriage came to be forbidden (§ 88), the *Paunarbhava* would follow the same fate (*q*). The practice of appointing a daughter would also fall into disuse, since so long as it lasted there would be a difficulty in finding a husband for a girl who had no brothers. It was probably at this period that the son of a daughter not appointed came to take the high rank which he at present occupies, in the list of heirs (*r*). Among the Nambudris in Malabar, the son of the appointed daughter is still recognised as heir to his maternal grandfather, where the marriage of the daughter has taken place according to the form known as *Sarvasvadhanam*; the formula used being, "I give unto thee this virgin, who has no brother decked with jewels; the son who may be born of her shall be my son" (*s*). In one case the Judicial Committee intimated a doubt whether such a son might not even now be lawfully created in the orthodox parts of India (*t*). It is improbable, however, that this doubt will be found to have any substantial foundation. The cessation of marriage between persons of different classes (§ 84) would similarly put an end to the *Nishada*. The five sorts of adopted sons would alone remain. These are reserved for future discussion (§ 93).

Eight forms of marriage.

§ 76. The above statements will show that in the view of early Hindu law, sonship was not by any means founded on marriage. A consideration of the marriage law itself will show that in ancient times it meant something very different from what it does at present. Eight forms of marriage are described by Manu, and in less detail by Narada and

---

(*p*) See *Collector of Trichinopoly* v. *Lekkamani*, 1 I. A. 283, 293, S. C. 14 B. L. R. 115; S. C. 21 Suth. 358.

(*q*) The Sudder Court of Bengal, however, admitted that by local usage such a son might inherit. In the particular instance, that of the Nagur Brahmans of Benares, the custom was negatived, *Mohun Singh* v. *Chuman Rai*, 1 S. D. A. 28, (37).

(*r*) See *post*, § 483.

(*s*) *Kumaran* v. *Narayan*, 9 Mad. 260.

(*t*) *Thakur Jeebnath Singh* v. *Court of Wards*, 2 I. A. 163; 23 Suth. P. C. 409. S. C. 15 B. L. R. 190.

Yajnavalkya (*u*). "The ceremony of Brahma, of the Devas, of the Rishis, of the Prajapatis, of the Asuras, of the Gandharvas, and of the Rakshasas; the eighth, and basest, is that of the Pisachas. The gift of a daughter, clothed only with a single robe, to a man learned in the Veda, whom her father voluntarily invites, and respectfully receives, is the nuptial rite called Brahma. The rite which sages call Daiva, is the gift of a daughter, whom her father has decked in gay attire, when the sacrifice is already begun, to the officiating priest, who performs that act of religion. When the father gives his daughter away, having received from the bridegroom one pair of kine, or two pairs, for uses prescribed by law, that marriage is termed Arsha. The nuptial rite called Prajapatya, is when the father gives away his daughter with due honour, saying distinctly, 'May both of you perform together your civil and religious duties.' When the bridegroom, having given as much wealth as he can afford to the father and paternal kinsmen, and to the damsel herself, takes her voluntarily as his bride, that marriage is named Asura. The reciprocal connection of a youth and a damsel with mutual desire, is the marriage denominated Gandharva, contracted for the purpose of amorous embraces, and proceeding from sensual inclination. The seizure of a maiden by force from her house, while she weeps and calls for assistance, after her kinsmen and friends have been slain in battle or wounded, and their houses broken open, is the marriage styled Rakshasa. When the lover secretly embraces the damsel, either sleeping or flushed with strong liquor, or disordered in her intellect, that sinful marriage, called Pisacha, is the eighth and the basest."

Different stages of law marked by:

§ 77. It is obvious that these forms are founded upon different views of the marriage relation, that they belong to different stages of society, and that their relative

(*u*) Manu, iii. § 20—42; Narada, xii. 39—45; Yajnavalkya, i. § 58—61; Apastamba, ii. 11 and 12, and Vasishtha, i. 28—36, omit the Prajapatya and Pisacha forms.

antiquity is exactly in the inverse ratio to the order in which they are mentioned. The last three point to a time when the rights of parents over their daughters were unknown or disregarded, and when men procured for themselves women (they can hardly yet be called wives) by force, fraud, or enticement. But even these three show variations of barbarism. The Pisacha form is more like the sudden lust of the ourang-outang than anything human. The first dawning of the conjugal idea cannot have arisen, when the name of marriage could be given to a connection, which it would be an exaggeration to describe as temporary. The Rakshasa form is simply the marriage by capture, the existence of which, coupled with the practice of exogamy, Mr. McLennan has tracked out in the most remote ages and regions. It is at the present day practised among the Meenas, a robber tribe of central India, and among the Gonds of Berar, not as a symbol but a matter of real earnest; as real as any other form of robbery (*v*). The connection between the Rakshasa and the Gandharva forms is evidenced by the fact that both were considered lawful for the warrior tribe (*w*). The latter is an advance beyond the former in this respect, that it assumes a state of society in which a friendly, though perhaps stealthy, intercourse was possible between man and woman before their union, and in which the inclinations of the female were consulted. Both forms admitted of a permanent connection, though there is certainly nothing in the definition to show that permanence was a necessary element in either transaction. The remaining forms of marriage all agree in this, that the dominion of the parents over the daughter was fully recognized, and that the essence of the marriage consisted in a formal transfer of this dominion to the husband.

The Pisacha; The Rakshasa; The Gandharva forms.

The Asura form.

§ 78. The Asura form, or marriage by purchase, which

(*v*) Lyall, Asiatic Studies, 163. V. N. Mandlik, 441. As to survivals of this practice in the Punjab, see Punjab Customary Law, ii. 91.
(*w*) Manu, iii. § 26.

the Sanskrit writers so much contemn (*x*), was probably the next in order of antiquity to those already mentioned. When it became impossible, or inconvenient, to obtain wives by robbery or stealth, and when it was still necessary to obtain them from another tribe (*y*), the only other mode would be to obtain them by purchase. And, of course, the same system would survive even when marriage was permitted within the tribe, though not within the family, if an unmarried girl was a valuable commodity in the hands of her own family, either as a servant, while she remained unmarried, or as a possible wife, where the balance of the sexes rendered it difficult to obtain wives. As delicacy increased in the relation between the sexes, marriage by sale would fall into disrepute from its resemblance to prostitution (*z*). Hence Manu says: "Let no father, who knows the law, receive a gratuity however small for giving his daughter in marriage, since the man who through avarice takes a gratuity for that purpose is a seller of his offspring" (*a*). The Arsha form, which is one of the approved forms, appears to be simply a survival from the Asura, the substantial price paid for the girl having dwindled down to a gift of slight, or nominal, value (*b*). Another mode of preserving the symbol of sale while rejecting the reality, appears to have been the receipt of a gift of real value, such as a chariot and a hundred cows, which was immediately returned to the giver, much in the same way as our Indian officials touch a valuable *nuzzur*, which is at once removed by the servants of the donor. This arrangement is said by Apastamba to have been prescribed by the Vedas "in order to fulfil the law,"—that is, apparently, the ancient law, by which the binding form of marriage was a sale (*c*). The ultimate compromise, however, appears to have been that the present given by the suitor

The Arsha form.

Origin of dowry.

(*x*) Manu, iii. § 41.
(*y*) See as to this necessity, *post*, § 82.
(*z*) See Teulon, 12. *Tusco more tute tibi dotem quœris corpore.*
(*a*) Manu, iii. § 5, ix. § 98, 100.
(*b*) Manu, iii. § 29; Yajuavalkya, i. § 59.
(*c*) Apastamba, ii. vi. 13, § 12. See Mayr, 155, who compares the Roman "Coemptio," and the German "Fraukauf."

was received by the parents for the benefit of the bride, and became her dowry. Manu says: "When money or goods are given to damsels, whose kinsmen receive them not for their own use, it is no sale; it is merely a token of courtesy and affection to the brides" (*d*). This gift, which was called her fee (*çulka*), passed in a peculiar course of devolution to the woman's own brothers; that is, back again into her original family, instead of to her own female heirs. One rendering of the text of Gautama which regulates this succession, even allowed the fee to go to her brothers during her life. In either view, it was evidently considered to be something over which her family had special rights. If they abandoned the possession, they retained the reversion (*e*). This was probably the reason that where a girl, who had been allowed to pass maturity, exercised her right of choosing a husband for herself, the bridegroom was not to give a nuptial present to her father, "since he had lost his dominion over her, by detaining her at a time when she might have been a parent." But, on the other hand, as the reversion was thus lost, she was not allowed to carry with her the ornaments she had received from her own family (*f*). If the girl died before marriage, the gifts made by the bridegroom reverted to him, after deducting any expenses that might have been already incurred (*g*).

Essence of remaining forms is absence of equivalent.

§ 79. The essential difference between the three remaining forms, *viz.*, the Brahma, Daiva and Prajapatya, and those just described, is this; that while on the one hand the girl is voluntarily handed over by her parents, they on the other hand receive no equivalent. The Daiva form is expressly stated to be appropriate to an officiating priest, that is a Brahman. Manu describes the bridegroom in the

Brahma form.

Brahma form as "a man learned in the Vedas," therefore

(*d*) Manu, iii. § 54; Mayr, 157. See a case held to be of this sort in Bombay *In the goods of Nathibai*, 2 Bom. 9. Mr. McGahan mentions an exactly similar usage as prevailing among the Kirghiz. *Campaigning on the Oxus*, 60.

(*e*) Mayr, 170.

(*f*) Manu, ix. § 90—93.

(*g*) Yajnavalkya, ii. § 146; Mitakshara, ii. 11, § 30.

presumably a Brahman also. It is probable that these forms first arose in the case of Brahmans. When mixed marriages were allowed, the great reverence shown to the Brahman would naturally have led to his being accepted upon his own merits, without any payment. In time, the same practice would be adopted, even when he was marrying a girl of his own caste. When these forms came to be universally adopted by the Brahmans, they would be followed by the inferior classes also as a mark of respectability. Just as a marriage in St. George's, Hanover Square, is specially prized by persons who do not happen to have houses in that fashionable district. *Primâ facie* one would imagine that a Brahma marriage, from its very definition, was inadmissible for a Sudra; and Manu certainly seems to contemplate only the last four as applicable to the case of the three lower classes (*h*). But there is no doubt that the Brahma marriage has long since ceased to be the property of any class; and the Madras Sudder Court have held that, in the case of Sudras, the mere fact that the bride is given without the bestowal of any gift by the bridegroom, constitutes the marriage one of the Brahma form (*i*).

Brahma and Asura alone survive.

§ 80. Of these various forms of marriage all but two, the Brahma and the Asura, are now obsolete. Manu treats the first four as the approved forms, and the latter four as disapproved. He permits the Gandharva and the Rakshasa to a military man. Narada forbids the Rakshasa in all cases. Both absolutely forbid the Asura and the Pisacha (*k*). The existence of the disapproved forms, or some of them, at a period much later than Narada, is evidenced by the rules which provide a peculiar descent for the *stridhana* of a woman so married (*l*). It is stated generally, that the Brahma is the only legal form at present, and probably this may be so among the higher classes, to whom the assertion

(*h*) Manu, iii. § 22—26.
(*i*) *Sivarama* v. *Bagavan*, Madras Dec. of 1859, 44.
(*k*) Manu, iii. § 23, 24, 36—41; Narada, xii. § 45.
(*l*) Mitakshara, ii. 11, § 11.

is limited by Mr. Steel (*m*). But there is no doubt that the Asura is still practised; and in Southern India, among the Sudras, it is a very common, if not the prevailing, form (*n*).

Presumption as to form.

Even there, however, and among Sudras, it has been held that the presumption will be against the assertion that a marriage is in a disapproved form, and that it must be proved by those who rely on it for any purpose. The same point has been decided by the High Court in Calcutta, as regards Bengal, and seems to have been assumed by the Judicial Committee in a case from Tirhoot (*o*). In a case in Western India, the Shastras stated that although Asura marriages were forbidden, it had nevertheless been the custom of the world for Brahmans and others to celebrate such marriages, and that no one had ever been expelled from caste for such an act (*p*).

Gandharva form

The validity of a Gandharva marriage between Kshatriyas appears to have been declared by the Bengal Sudder Court in 1817, and to have been assumed both by the District and Sudder Court so late as 1850 and 1853 (*q*). It seems to me, however, that this form belongs to a time when the notion of marriage involved no idea of permanence or exclusiveness. Its definition implies nothing more than fornication. It is difficult to see how such a connection could be treated at present as constituting a marriage, with the incidents and results of such a union. This view was unhesitatingly laid down by

---

(*m*) Gibelin, i. 63; Colebrooke, Essays, 142 (ed. of 1858); Steele, 159. V. N. Mandlik, 301.

(*n*) 3 Dig. 605; 1 Stra. H. L. 43; Mayr, 155. I have often heard the same statement made, *arguendo*, in the Madras Courts by the late Mr. J. W. Branson, a barrister of great local and professional experience, and thoroughly versed in the languages and customs of Southern India. The statement seemed to be accepted by the Bar and the Bench. Jagannatha quotes a text from Yajnavalkya, stating that the Asura ceremony is peculiar to the mercantile and servile classes, which is not to be found in Stenzler's edition. It ought to come in after i. § 61. See 3 Dig. 604; *In the goods of Nathibai*, 2 Bom. 9. Even between Brahmans such a marriage has been held valid in Madras. *Visvanathan* v. *Saminathan*, 13 Mad. 83.

(*o*) *Kaithi* v. *Kulladasi*, Madras Dec. of 1860, 201; *Judoonath* v. *Bussunt Coomar*, 11 B. L. R. 286, 288, S. C., 19 Suth. 264; *Mt. Thakoor* v. *Rai Baluk Ram*, 11 M. I. A. 175, S. C. 10 Suth. (P. C.) 3.

(*p*) *Keshow Rao* v. *Naro*, 2 Bor. 193, [215, 221] and see *Nundlal* v. *Tapeedas*, 1 Bor. 18, [16, 20.]

(*q*) *Hujmu Chul* v. *Ranee Bhadoorun*, cited S. D. of 1846, 340; S. D. 7 B. S. D. 355, 3 Dig. 606; *Jogendro Deb.* v. *Funendro Deb.*, 14 M. I. A. 375.

the Allahabad High Court in a case between Rajputs, when the offspring of such a marriage claimed as, but was held not to be, legitimate (*r*). The Madras High Court considers that a Gandharva marriage would be legal, if celebrated with nuptial rites, of which the *homum* ceremony, or sacrifice by fire is an essential part (*s*). It is obvious that such a ceremonial proceeding is something very different from the unconventional arrangement described by Manu. No doubt the texts referred to in the Judgment of the High Court result from the attempt of later writers to reconcile a respect for ancient usages with the greater formality of modern society.

Power to dispose of girl.

§ 81. As regards the persons who are authorised to dispose of a girl, Narada says: "A father shall give his daughter in marriage himself, or a brother with the father's consent, or a grandfather, maternal uncle, kinsmen, or relatives. In default of all these, the mother, if she is qualified; if she is not, the remoter relations should give a girl in marriage. If there be none of these, the girl shall apply to the king, and having obtained his permission to make her own choice, choose a husband for herself" (*t*). Where a father had abandoned his wife and daughter, the mother would be capable to give away her daughter (*u*). But under no other circumstances would a marriage contract be binding without the father's consent (*v*). And the maternal grandfather has a right of disposal superior to that of the stepmother (*w*). Where the natural guardian is a female, she is not necessarily invested with exclusive authority in the matter, as is clear from the fact that the mother, who ranks next to the father as natural guardian, ranks low in the list of relations for the purpose of dispos-

(*r*) *Bhaoni* v. *Maharaj Singh*, 3 All. 738.

(*s*) *Brindavana* v. *Radhamani*, 12 Mad. 72, *per curiam*, 13 M. I. A. 506.

(*t*) Narada, xii., § 20—22; Yajnavalkya, i. § 63.

(*u*) *Baee Rulyat* v. *Jeychund*, Bellasis, 43, S. C. 1 Mor. (N. S.) 181. *Khushalchand* v. *Bai Mani*, 11 Bom. 247.

(*v*) *Nundlal* v. *Tapeedas*, 1 Bor. 14, [16.] *Nanabhai* v. *Janardhan*, 12 Bom. 110.

(*w*) *Ram Bunsee* v. *Soobh Koonwaree*, 7 Suth. 321; S. C. 3 Wym. 219; S. C. 2 In. Jur. 193.

ing of her daughter in marriage (*x*). But the High Court of Madras refused to allow a divided uncle to dispose of his niece in marriage without consulting her mother. They admitted that the text of Yajnavalkya (i. § 63) could not be limited to the case of a divided family, but they thought that the object of placing the male relations before the mother was merely to supply that protection and advice which the Hindu system considered to be necessary on account of the dependent condition of women. That dependence had now practically ceased to be enforced by the law. Where the mother was at once the guardian of the girl, and the legal possessor of the estate out of which the marriage expenses must be defrayed, they considered that she was entitled to be consulted on the one hand, and the male relations on the other, but that the Court would probably interfere to compel the marriage of a girl to a suitable husband, if chosen by either party, and rejected without reasonable cause by the other (*y*). Where the guardian is about to effect a marriage which is obviously injurious to the girl, the Court has power to interfere especially where his conduct is actuated by improper or interested motives. Such interference, however, would very rarely, and only in extreme cases, be allowed, where the guardian was the father (*z*).

Interference of Court.

§ 81 A. The above rules are of importance so long as the marriage rests in contract, and an attempt to give away a girl in marriage by a person not authorised to do so would be over-ruled by the Court upon a proper application by the person in whom the right was reposed (*a*). A very different question arises where the marriage has actually been celebrated. A very strong case of that sort recently arose in Madras (*b*). There the mother had caused her

(*x*) *Per cur.*, 7 Suth. 323.
(*y*) *Namasevayam* v. *Annamal*, 4 Mad. H. C. 339; *Mt. Ruliyat* v. *Madkowjee*, 2 Bor. 680, [739]; *Kumla Buhoo* v. *Muneeshunkur*, *ib.* 689, [746.]
(*z*) *Shridhar* v. *Hiralal*, 12 Bom. 480.
(*a*) *Per curiam*, 11 Bom. 253.
(*b*) *Venkatacharyulu* v. *Rangacharylu*, 14 Mad. 316.

daughter's marriage to be celebrated without her husband's permission. The Brahman who celebrated the marriage was falsely informed by her that the father's consent had been given. It was found as a fact that the mother acted *bonâ fide* in the interest of her daughter, and, as her natural guardian, desiring to secure her a suitable husband. The father repudiated the marriage. The husband sued for a declaration that the marriage is irrevocable. The High Court decided in his favour. They said, "two propositions of law may be taken to be established beyond controversy, *viz.*, (1) where there is a gift by a legal guardian, and the marriage rite is duly solemnised (*c*) the marriage is irrevocable, and (2) where the girl is abducted by fraud or force and married, and there is no gift either by a natural or legal guardian, there is a fraud upon the policy of the religious ceremony, and there is therefore no valid religious ceremony" (*d*). "The third proposition of law which is material to the case before us is, that when the mother of the girl, acting as her natural guardian, in view to her welfare, and without force or fraud, gives away the girl in marriage, and the marriage rite is duly solemnised, the marriage is not to be set aside. This view is supported by authority (*e*) and is sound in principle."

Persons to be selected.

§ 82. The selection of persons to be married is limited by two rules: *first*, that they must be chosen outside the family; *secondly*, that they must be chosen inside the caste. The first of these rules is only a special instance of that singular prohibition against marriage between persons belonging to the same family, or tribe, which is to be found in almost every part of the world, and to which Mr. McLennan has given the name of Exogamy. According to the Sanskrit writers, persons are forbidden to marry who are related as

Exogamy.

Forbidden affinities.

(*c*) See as to presumption in favour of due performance of a marriage actually celebrated. *Brindabun Chundra* v. *Chundra Kurmokar*, 12 Cal. 140.

(*d*) See *per Norman, J.*, *Aunjona Dasi* v. *Prahlad Chandra*, 6 B. L. R., p. 254.

(*e*) Citing *Bai Ruliyat* v. *Jeychand Rewal*, Bellasis, 43; S. C., 1 Morley N. S. 181. *Modhoosoodhun* v. *Jadub Chunder*, 3 Suth. 194. *Brindabun Chundra* v. *Chundra Kurmokar*, 12 Cal 140. *Khushal Chand* v. *Bai Mani*, 11 Bom. 247.

sapindas. This relationship extends to six degrees where the common ancestor is a male. Where the common ancestor is a female there is a difference of opinion; Manu and Apastamba extending the prohibition in her case also to six degrees, while Gautama, Vishnu, Vasishtha, Sankha, Narada and Yajnavalkya limit it to four degrees. To this restriction some of the above writers add a further rule that the bride and bridegroom must not be of the same *gotra* or *pravara*. That is, that they must not be of the same family, nor invoke the same ancestor (*f*). In counting according to the above rules the person under consideration is to be excluded. That is to say, begin from the bride or bridegroom, and count, exclusive of both, six, or four, degrees upwards according as their relationship with the common ancestor is through the father or the mother respectively, and if the common ancestor is not reached within those degrees on both sides, they are not sapindas, and marriage between them can be solemnised (*g*). In this way 2,121 possible relations are rendered ineligible for marriage; while further complications, rendered more complex by differences of opinion among the commentators, arise in the case of an adopted son, who is excluded from marriage in two families, or where relationship is traced through stepmothers (*h*). On the other hand, the strictness of these rules is relaxed as regards Western and Southern India by writers who recognise the validity of district, or family, custom permitting intermarriages within the forbidden degrees. They expressly refer to marriages between first cousins, such as that of a man with the daughter of his mother's brother, or of his father's sister (*i*).

(*f*) *Manu*, iii, 5, *Apastamba*, ii. v. 11, § 15. 16. *Gautama*, iv. § 2—5, *Vishnu*, xxiv. § 9, 10, *Narada*, xii. § 7. *Yajn*. i. § 52, 53, V. N. Mandlik, 411. It is said that a woman married within the forbidden degrees, though she cannot be the wife of the bridegroom for any conjugal or religious purposes, yet cannot be married by another, and must be maintained by her attempted husband. V. N. Mandlik, 508. See as to the prohibited degrees in the Punjab, Customary Law, II. 120, 174.

(*g*) V. N. Mandlik, 347: Mitakshara, cited W. & B. 121, *post*, § 469. The apparent variance in the authorities quoted above arises from some counting exclusively and others inclusively.

(*h*) See V. N. Mandlik, 352.

(*i*) See the authorities cited by Mr. V. N. Mandlik, 408, 413, 416—424, 448.

Usage, unsupported by direct authority, permits the union of a man with his own sister's daughter (*k*). Marriage with a niece has, however, been held by the Bombay High Court to be incestuous and the Madras High Court, while admitting that the rules among Sudras were not as strict as among Brahmans, and that instances existed of a man marrying his brother's daughter, intimated that such a practice was not warranted by usage (*l*).

§ 83. The restrictive Sanskrit texts which have been referred to above only apply to the twice born classes. Even amongst these it is stated by Mr. V. N. Mandlik that the Kshatriyas and Vaisyas have neither *gotra* nor *pravara*, and that thousands of Brahmans in different parts of the country are in the same position. As regards Sudras, the restraint upon intermarriage must arise from usage, or from voluntary adoption of the Sanskrit rules, not from any inherent efficacy of the rules themselves (*m*). But exactly the same rule against intermarriages between members of the same family has been observed among the Kurumbas of the Nilgiris, the Meenas of Central India, the Kandhs of Orissa, and among the Dravidian races of Southern India (*n*). In Madura, the women of the Chakkili tribe belong to the right-hand faction, and the men to the left-hand (*o*). Evidently a relic of the time when men had to marry women of a different tribe. So the chiefs of the Maravers are accustomed to marry Ahambadyan women, and of the children born of such marriages, the males must marry Ahambadyans, and the females must marry Maravers (*p*). Exactly the opposite rule of Endogamy is found to exist among other tribes in the same district. For instance, among the Kallans, the most proper marriage for a man is with his first cousin, that is

Endogamy.

(*k*) V. N. Mandlik.
(*l*) *Ramangavda* v. *Shivaji* cited V. N. Mandlik, 438; *Vythilinga* v. *Vijiathammal*, 6 Mad. 43.
(*m*) V. N. Mandlik, 412, 431.
(*n*) Breeks, 51; Lyall, Fort. Rev., Jan. 1877, 106; Hunter, Orissa, ii. 81.
(*o*) Mad. Manual, Pt. II. 7.
(*p*) Mad. Manual, Pt. II. 42.

the daughter of his father's sister or brother, and failing her, with his own aunt or niece. Among the Maravers, also, marriage is permitted between the children of brothers (*q*). In ancient times, the incestuous marriages of the Sakya princes with their own sisters, and the similar intercourse of the Gandhara Brahmans with their own sisters and daughters-in-law (*r*), present an illustration of the same curious conflict of principle.

Mixed marriages formerly permitted.

§ 84. The prohibition against marriages between persons of different castes is comparatively modern. Originally, marriages between men of one class and women of a lower, even of the Sudra class, were recognized (*s*), and must have tended strongly to produce that amalgamation of the customs of the Aryans and the aborigines, which I have already suggested as probable (*t*). The sons of such unequal unions were said to rank and to inherit, not equally, but in proportions regulated according to the class of their mother (*u*). Even this rule, however, appears to have been an innovation. Baudhayana lays it down generally, that "in case of a competition of a son born from a wife of equal class, and of one born from a wife of a lower class, the son of the wife of lower class may take the share of the eldest, in case he be possessed of good qualities" (*v*). All the writers allow marriages between a Sudra woman and a Kshatriya or Vaisya, but there is much conflict as to marriages between a Brahman and a Sudra woman. Among the Sutra writers the validity of such marriages seems to be undisputed, but there is much variance as to the position of the offspring. Some texts represent him as sharing with

(*q*) Mad. Manual. Pt. II. 40, 50.

(*r*) Wheeler, Hist. Ind. iii. 102; Muir, A. S. T. ii. 483.

(*s*) Apastamba stands alone among the early writers in not recognising unequal marriages, ii. vi. 13, § 4, 5. It will be remembered that he does not recognize the subsidiary sons either. I cannot account for this difference, unless some passages have fallen out in the text.

(*t*) I take the Sudras as representing the aborigines in early times, but I am aware there is much controversy upon the point. See Muir, A. S. T. i. 140—159, 289—295, ii. 368, 455, 485; Lassen, Ind. Alt. i. 799.

(*u*) Manu, ix. § 149—154.

(*v*) Baudhayana. ii. 2. § 8. See Gautama, xxviii. § 35—38.

the higher sons; others as only inheriting in default of them; others as never taking more than a small fraction of the estate; and others as never entitled to more than maintenance (*w*). The conflict in Manu is still greater, and shows that the present compilation is made up of texts of different periods. Some texts forbid the marriage, some permit it. Some allow the son to inherit, others forbid him to do so (*x*). But perhaps the strongest possible recognition of such marriages is that afforded by Manu himself, when he admits that the offspring resulting from them might in seven generations rise to the highest class (*y*). It seems, however, to have been always admitted that a Sudra man could not lawfully marry a woman of a higher class than his own (*z*).

Mixed marriages obsolete.

§ 85. Marriages between persons of different classes are long since obsolete (*a*). No doubt from the same process of ideas which has split up the whole native community into countless castes, which neither eat, drink, nor marry with each other (*b*). It is impossible now to say when mixed marriages first became extinct. The Mitakshara follows Yajnavalkya in recognizing such marriages, though the phrase, "under the sanction of the law instances do occur," seems to show that they were dying out (*c*). They are also mentioned without disapproval by the Daya Bhaga, Smriti Chandrika, Sarasvati Vilasa, Viramitrodaya, Madhaviya, and Varadrajah (*d*). But in the case of the later authors, at all events, it is probable the discussion was

(*w*) Baudhayana, ii. 2, § 6, 7, 21; Gautama. xxviii. § 39; Vasishtha, xvii. 21, 25.

(*x*) Cf. Manu. iii. § 12—19, ix. § 149—155; Narada, xii. § 4—6; Yajnavalkya, i. § 56, 57; Smriti Chandrika, ii. 2, § 8.

(*y*) Manu, x. § 64; see, too, § 42.

(*z*) Manu, iii § 13, ix. § 157.

(*a*) *Vrihat Naradiya Purana*, 3 Dig 141; D. K. S i. 2, § 7.

(*b*) Marriages between persons in different sub-divisions of the same caste, *e.g.*, of Brahmans or Sudras, have said to be invalid unless sanctioned by local custom. *Melaram* v. *Thanooram*, 9 Suth. 552; *Narain Dhara* v. *Rakhal*, 1 Cal. 1, S. C. 23 Suth. 334. Contra, *Pandaiya Talaver* v. *Puli Talaver*, 1 Mad. H. C. 478; *affd.* 13 M. I. A. 141; S. C. 4 Mad. Jur. 328; S. C. 3 B. L. R. (P. C.) 1; S. C. 12 Suth. (P. C.) 41. *Ramamani* v. *Kulanthai*, 14 M. I. A. 346, 352. *Upoma-Kuchain* v. *Bholaram Dhubi*, 15 Cal. 708.

(*c*) Mitakshara, i. 8, § 2.

(*d*) Daya Bhaga, ix.; Smriti Chandrika, ii. 2, § 6—9; Viramit., p. 101 § 2; Madhaviya, § 24; Varadrajah, 18. Sarasvati Vilasa, § 163—167.

merely introduced to give completeness to the subject, and not because such a practice really subsisted. Illegitimacy is of itself no disqualification for marriage. Where one or both parties to a marriage are illegitimate, it will be valid if they are in fact recognised by their caste men as belonging to the same caste (*e*).

Physical or mental capacity.

§ 86. As the great and primary object of marriage is the procuring of male issue, physical capacity is an essential requisite, so long as mere selection of a bridegroom is concerned; but a marriage with a eunuch is not an absolute nullity as with us (*f*). Mental incapacity stands in the same position. While the matter rested in contract, no Court, I imagine, would treat a promise to marry a lunatic or an idiot as binding; but the marriage, if celebrated, would be valid. The lunatic, or idiot, would be incapable of inheriting; but his issue would receive their shares (*g*). A Hindu marriage is the performance of a religious duty (*h*), not a contract; therefore the consenting mind is not necessary, and its absence, whether from infancy or incapacity, is immaterial (*i*).

Polygamy.

§ 87. The efficacy of the marriage tie, as binding either party to the transaction, is a matter upon which there has been a considerable change in the Hindu law, while its earlier stage was evidently in accordance with usages which we find at present existing among the non-Aryan races. Among the Kandhs, "so long as a woman remains true to her husband, he cannot contract a second marriage, or even keep a concubine, without her permission" (*k*). The same rule prevails among the caste of musicians in Ahmedabad, and in the Vadanagara Nagar caste, (*l*), and seems,

(*e*) *In re* Ram Kumari, 18 Cal. 264.

(*f*) Cf. Narada, xii. § 8—19; Manu, ix. § 79, 203. Jolly, § 280. See as to withdrawal from contract, *post*, § 100. *Kanahi* v. *Biddya*, 1 All. 549.

(*g*) See Gautama, xxviii. § 44; Narada, xiii. § 22; Manu, ix. § 201—203; W. & B. 908; *Dabychurn* v. *Radachurn*, 2 M. Dig. 99.

(*h*) Manu, ii. § 66, 67, vi. § 36, 37. See, however, v. § 159.

(*i*) *Supra*, 2 M. Dig. 99, W. & B. 908, *per curiam*, 5 All. 513.

(*k*) Hunter's Orissa, ii. 84.

(*l*) *Muhashunkur* v. *Mt. Oottum*, 2 Bor. 524. [572.] V. N. Mandlik, 406.

from the evidence of the Thesawaleme, to have been in force among the Tamil emigrants into Ceylon (*m*). One text of Manu seems to indicate that there was a time when a second marriage was only allowed to a man after the death of his former wife (*n*). Another set of texts lays down special grounds which justify a husband in taking a second wife, and except for such causes it appears she could not be superseded without her consent (*o*). Other passages provide for a plurality of wives, even of different classes, without any restriction (*p*). A peculiar sanctity, however, seems to have been attributed to the first marriage, as being that which was contracted from a sense of duty, and not merely for personal gratification. The first married wife had precedence over the others, and her first-born son over his half-brothers (*q*). It is probable that originally the secondary wives were considered as merely a superior class of concubines, like the handmaids of the Jewish patriarchs. It is now quite settled that a Hindu is absolutely without restriction as to the number of his wives, and may marry again without his wife's consent, or any justification except his own wish (*r*). He cannot, however, divorce his wife except by special local usage (*s*); nor does conversion to christianity, with its consequence of expulsion from caste, operate as a dissolution of the union (*t*).

Second marriages of women formerly allowed.

§ 88. The prohibition against second marriages of women, either after divorce, or upon widowhood, has no foundation

(*m*) Thesawaleme, i. § 11.

(*n*) "Having thus kindled sacred fires and performed funeral rites to his wife, who died before him, he may again marry, and again light the nuptial fire." Manu, v. § 168; and see ix. § 101, 102.

(*o*) Manu, ix. § 77—82, Apastamba, ii. v. ii. § 12—13. This seems still to be the usage among some castes of the Deccan. Steele, 30, 168, and in Bengal. *Kally Churn* v. *Dukhee*, 5 Cal., 692.

(*p*) Manu, iii. § 12, viii. § 204, ix. § 85—87.

(*q*) See Manu, iii. § 12, 14, ix. § 107, 122—125; *post*, § 499.

(*r*) Daya Bhaga, ix. § 6, note; 1 Stra. H. L. 56; Steele, 168; *Huree Bhaee* v. *Nuthoo*, 1 Bor. 59 [65]; *Virasvamy* v. *Appasvamy*, 1 Mad. H. C. 375.

(*s*) Such a usage has been affirmed in Assam. *Kudomee* v. *Joteeram*, 3 Cal. 305.

(*t*) *Administrator-General* v. *Anandachari*, 9 Mad. 466. See Act XXI of 1866.

either in early Hindu law or custom. Passages of the Vedas quoted by Dr. Mayr sanction the remarriage of widows (*u*). And the second marriage of women who have left their husbands for justifiable cause, or who have been deserted by them, or whose husbands are dead, is expressly sanctioned by the early writers (*v*). The authority of Manu is strongly on the other side; but I think it is plain that this is one of the many instances in which the existing text has suffered from interpolations and omissions. Manu declares that a man may only marry a virgin, and that a widow may not marry again (*w*). The only exception which he appears to allow, is in the case of a girl whose husband has died before consummation, who may be married again to the brother of the deceased bridegroom (*x*). On the other hand, two other texts appear to recognize and sanction the second marriage, either of a widow, or of a wife forsaken by her husband (*y*). The contradiction appears to arise from the deliberate omission of part of the original text in an earlier portion of the same chapter. At ix. § 76 a wife, whose husband resides abroad, is directed to wait for him eight, six, or three, years according to the reason for his original absence. Nothing is said as to what is to happen at the end of the time. Kulluka Bhatta inserts a gloss:—" after these terms have expired, she must follow him" (*z*). Now if we look to the corresponding part of Narada, who had an earlier text of Manu before him (*a*), we find that he lays down that " there are five cases in which a woman may take another husband; her first husband having perished, or died naturally, or gone abroad, or if he be impotent, or have lost his caste." Then follow the periods during which

Probable omission in present text of Manu.

(*u*) Mayr, 181. It is now restored by Act XV of 1856, see *post*, § 512.

(*v*) Narada, xii. § 97—101; see too § 18, 19, 24, 46—49, 62; Devala, 2 Dig. 470; Baudhayana, ii. § 20; Vasishtha, xvii. § 13; Katyayana, 3 Dig. 236.

(*w*) Manu, viii. § 226, v. § 161—163. See, to the same effect, Apastamba, ii. vi. 13, § 4.

(*x*) Manu, ix. § 69, 70; *ante*, § 70. Vasishtha, xvii. 74, places no restriction on her second choice.

(*y*) Manu, ix. § 175, 176. See 1 Gib. 34, 104.

(*z*) This is apparently founded on a text attributed to Vasishtha, xvii. 75—80, which is to the same effect.

(*a*) See *ante*, § 21; Introd. to Narada.

a woman is to wait for her absent husband, and the whole thing is made into sense by the direction, that when the time has expired she may betake herself to another man (*b*). Nothing is said about her following him, which after such an absence would probably be impossible or useless. If a similar passage had followed § 76 in Manu, the texts at § 175, 176 would be intelligible and consistent. When second marriages were no longer allowed, these passages seem to have been left out, and others of an exactly opposite character were inserted; the texts at § 175, 176 then became unmeaning, but they were retained to explain the phrase, "son of an unmarried woman," which had already appeared in the list of subsidiary sons. It is probable that the change of usage on this point arose from the influence of Brahmanical opinion, marriage coming to be looked upon as a sort of sacrament, the effect of which was indelible. A similar cause has produced that difference of opinion upon the legality of marriage following upon divorce which prevails in Protestant and Roman Catholic countries. If it is asked why the law varied in exactly the opposite direction in regard to second marriages of men, the only answer I can suggest is, that men have always moulded the law of marriage so as to be most agreeable to themselves.

Usage of other tribes.

§ 89. When we examine the usages of the aboriginal races, or of those who have not come under Brahmanical influence, we find a system prevailing exactly like that described by Narada. Among the Jat population of the Punjab, not only a widow, but a wife who has been deserted, or put away, by her husband, may marry again, and will have all the rights of a lawful wife. The same rule exists among the Lingaits of South Canara (*c*). In Western India, the second marriage of a wife or widow (called *Pat* by the Mahrattas, and *Natra* in Guzerat) is allowed among all the lower castes. The cases in which a wife may re-marry are

(*b*) Narada, xii. § 97—101. See also authorities, *ante*, note (*o*).

(*c*) Punjab Customary Law, II. 131, 174, 190, 192, 193. Punjab Cust., 95. *Virasangappa* v. *Rudrappa*, 8 Mad. 440.

stated by Mr. Steele as being, if the husband prove impotent, or the parties continually quarrel; if the marriage were irregularly concluded; if by mutual consent the husband breaks his wife's neck-ornament, and gives her a *chorchittee* (writing of divorcement), or if he has been absent and unheard of for twelve years. Should he afterwards return, she may live with either party at her own option, the person deserted being reimbursed his marriage expenses. A widow's *pat* is considered more honourable than a wife's, but children by *pat* are equally legitimate with those by a first marriage (*d*). The right of a divorce and second marriage has been repeatedly affirmed by the Bombay Courts (*e*). So, in Southern India widow marriage and divorce is common among many of the lower castes, such as the Vellalans of the Palanis, the Maravers (except in the case of the women of the Sambhu Nattan division), the Kallans, the Pallans (*f*), the tank-diggers, the potters, the barbers, and the pariahs generally (*g*). In the better classes, such as the oilmongers, the weavers, and a wandering class of minstrels, called the Bhat Rajahs, who claim to be Kshatriyas, it is found in some localities and not in others (*h*). It is not practised at all among the Brahmans and Kshatriyas, or among the higher classes of Sudras, such as the shepherds, the Komaty caste, the writers, or the five artisan classes, who claim equality with the Brahmans and wear the thread (*i*). Similarly the Bengal High Court has recognised the validity of widow marriage among the

Second marriages and divorce.

(*d*) Steele, 26, 159, 168; W. & B. (2nd ed.) 139 to 146, 162, 163, 167. The futwahs recorded at pp. 112, 114, 139, 141, were evidently given by Shastris, who treated such second marriages as illegal. See to *Huree Bhaee* v. *Nuthoo*, 1 Bor. 59, [65] note.

(*e*) As to divorce, see *Kaseram* v. *Umbaram*, 1 Bor. 387 [429]; *Kasee Dhoollubh* v. *Rutton Baee*, ib. 410 [452]; *Muhashunker* v. *Mt. Oottum*, 2 Bor. 524 [572]; *Dyaram* v. *Baeeumba*, Bellasis, 36. *R.* v. *Karsan*, 2 Bom. H. C. 124, *R.* v. *Sambhu*, 1 Bom. 347, *Government of Bombay* v. *Ganga*, 4 Bom. 330. *Empress* v. *Umi*, 6 Bom. 126. As to widow marriage, *Hurkoonwur* v. *Ruttun Baee*, 1 Bor. 431 [475]; *Treekumjee* v. *Mt. Luro Laroo*, 2 Bor. 361 [397]; *Baee Rutton* v. *Lalla Munnohur*, Bellasis, 86; *Baee Sheo* v. *Ruttonjee*, Morris, Pt. I. 103. See *per curiam*, *Rahi* v. *Govind*, 1 Bom. 114.

(*f*) Mad. Manual, Pt. II. 33, 40, 58; *Kattama Nachiar* v. *Dorasinga Tevar*, 6 Mad. H. C. 329; *Murugayi* v. *Viramakali*, 1 Mad. 226.

(*g*) Madras Census Report, 157, 159, 164, 171.

(*h*) *Ibid.* 141, 143, 155.

(*i*) *Ibid.* 137, 140, 143, 149, 152.

Nomosudras (*k*). The degree in which divorce and widow marriage prevails is probably in the direct ratio to the degree in which the respective castes have imitated Brahman habits. The Thesawaleme treats widow marriage as a matter of course (*l*), and we may fairly assume that it was so originally among all the Tamil races.

§ 90. Marriage is not to be confounded with betrothal. The one is a completed transaction; the other is only a contract. Manu says, "Neither ancients nor moderns who were good men have ever given a damsel in marriage after she had been promised to another man" (*m*). But Narada and Yajnavalkya both admit the right of a father to annul a betrothal to one suitor, if a better match presents himself; and either party to the contract is allowed to withdraw from it, where certain specified defects are discovered (*n*). Narada states that a man who withdraws from his contract without proper cause, may be compelled to marry the girl even against his will. But it is now settled by decision that a contract to marry will not be specifically enforced, and that the only remedy is by an action for damages (*o*). All expenses resulting from the abortive contract would be recoverable in such an action (*p*). Of course, no such claim could be maintained where the contract failed from the wilful, or negligent, conduct of the complaining party (*q*). Probably the real difficulty has often been to distinguish between two things which are sometimes called by the same name, *viz.*, the betrothal, which is only a promise to marry, and the pledging of troth, which forms part of the marriage itself. The former class of betrothal is often celebrated with much ceremony,

Betrothal

is revocable.

Result of breach of contract.

(*k*) *Hurry Churn* v. *Nunai Chand*, 10 Cal. 138.

(*l*) Thesawaleme, i. § 10.

(*m*) Manu, ix. § 99.

(*n*) Narada, xii. § 30—38; Yajnavalkya, i. § 65, 66; Vasishtha, 2 Dig. 487, 490; Katyayana, *ib.* 491; Mitakshara, ii. 11, § 27.

(*o*) Narada, xii. § 35; *Umed* v. *Nagindas*, 7 Bom. H. C. O. C. 122; *Nowbut* v. *Mt. Lad Kooer*, 5 N.-W. P, 102; *re Gunput Narain Singh*, 1 Cal. 74.

(*p*) Mitakshara, ii. 11, § 28. *Mulji Thakersey* v. *Gomti*, 11 Bom. 412.

(*q*) *Divi Virasalingam* v. *Alaturti*, Mad. Dec. of 1860, 274.

but this does not alter its character. So, in the actual marriage there are numerous formalities, and many recitals of holy texts, but the operative part of the transaction consists in the seven steps taken by the bridal pair. On the completion of the last step, the actual marriage has taken place (r). Till then it is imperfect and revocable. Even this proceeding, however, is not absolutely essential. It is a form which, if complied with, is conclusive. But if it is shown that by the custom of the caste, or district, any other form is considered as constituting a marriage, then the adoption of that form, with the intention of thereby completing the marriage union, is sufficient (s). In some communities there is a custom that after the actual marriage has taken place a further ceremony must be performed before cohabitation, and if the man who has gone through the first ceremony declines to perform the second, the girl may lawfully marry again (t). But the legal result of such a custom would appear to be that there is no binding and complete marriage until after the second ceremony. In the absence of any such custom the marriage is complete, even though never followed by consummation, and though, in consequence of the conversion to christianity of one party, the other renounces the obligations of marriage (u).

Septapati.

Irregular marriage:

§ 91. A marriage actually and properly celebrated will be legal and binding, although it has taken place in violation of a previous agreement to marry another person (v); or although it has been performed without the consent of the person whose consent ought to have been obtained (w). For this is one of the cases in which necessity compels the appli-

(r) Manu, ix. § 227; Narada, xii. § 2; Yama, 2 Dig. 488; Viramit., ii. 2. § 4; Coleb. Essays, 128. See cases last cited.

(s) Manu, iii. § 35; see futwah, 2 M. Dig. 45; *Gatha Ram* v. *Moohita Kochin*, 14 B. L. R. 298, S. C. 23 Suth. 179. *Kally Churn* v. *Dukhee*, 5 Cal. 692. V. N. Mandlik, 404. *Hurry Churn* v. *Nimai Chand*, 10 Cal. 138. When the fact of the celebration of marriage is established, it will be presumed, in the absence of evidence to the contrary, that all the necessary ceremonies have been complied with. *Brindabun Chundra* v. *Chundra Kurmokar*, 12 Cal. 140.

(t) *Boolchand* v. *Janokee*, 25 W. R. 386.

(u) *Administrator-General* v. *Anandachari*, 9 Mad. 466.

(v) *Khooshal* v. *Bhugwan Motee*, 1 Bor. 138 [155].

(w) *Baee Rulyat* v. *Jeychund*, Bellasis, 43 S. C. 1 Mor. N. S. 181.

cation of the maxim, *Factum valet quod fieri non debuit.* When the marriage is once completed, if either party refuses to live with the other, the case is no longer one for specific performance of a contract, but for restitution of conjugal rights. It has long since been settled that such a suit would lie between Hindus, but there was much conflict of authority as to the mode in which the decree was to be enforced (*x*). The point has now been settled by s. 260 of the Civil Procedure Code (Act XIV of 1882), which provides that where the party against whom the decree has been made has had an opportunity of obeying it, and has wilfully failed to do so, it may be enforced by imprisonment, or by attachment of property, or by both (*y*). *Primâ facie* the husband is the legal guardian of his wife, and is entitled to require her to live in his house from the moment of the marriage, however young she may be. But this right does not exist, where by custom, or agreement, the wife is to remain in her parents' house, until puberty is established (*z*).

how enforced.

Custody of wife.

(*x*) See *Gatha Ram* v. *Moohita Kochin*, 14 B. L. R. 298 S. C. 23 Suth. 179, *Jogendronundini* v. *Hurry Doss*, 5 Cal. 500. *Pakhandu* v. *Manki*, 3 All. 506. *Dadaji* v. *Rukmabai*, 10 Bom. 301. *Binda* v. *Kaunsilia*, 13 All. 126.

(*y*) Under this Section, as in England, the Court will take into consideration any circumstances which establish a reasonable objection on the part of the wife, and will impose proper conditions upon the husband in reference to such objection. *Paigi* v. *Sheonarrain*, 8 All. 78.

(*z*) *Kateeran* v. *Mt. Gendhenee*, 23 W. R. 178; *Suntosh Ram* v. *Gera Pattuck*, ib. 22. See *post*, § 414.

CHAPTER V.

FAMILY RELATIONS.

Adoption.

Little noticed in early writings.

§ 92. THERE is a singular disproportion between the space necessarily devoted to adoption in the English works on Hindu law, and that which it occupies in the early law-books. One might read through all the texts from the Sutra writers down to the Daya Bhaga without discovering that adoption is a matter of any prominence in the Hindu system. But for the two treatises translated by Mr. Sutherland, it may almost be affirmed that Englishmen would never have discovered the fact at all. Even in Jagannatha's Digest, the subject only takes up thirty-two pages. The fact is that the law of adoption, as at present administered, is a purely modern development from a very few old texts. The very absence of direct authority has caused an immense growth of subtleties and refinements. The effect that every adoption must have upon the devolution of property causes every case that can be disputed to be brought into Court. Fresh rules are imagined, or invented. Notwithstanding the spiritual benefits which are supposed to follow from the practice, it is doubtful whether it would ever be heard of, if an adopted son was not also an heir. Paupers have souls to be saved, but they are not in the habit of adopting.

Importance of sons.

§ 93. I have already (§ 65) pointed out the advantages which all early races would derive from the possession of sons, and the peculiar necessity for male offspring which would press upon the Aryans, on account of their religious system. This want was amply met by the early Hindu law, which provided twelve sorts of sons, all of whom were competent to prevent a failure of obsequies, in the absence of legitimate issue (*a*). For religious purposes, the son of the appointed daughter seems to have been completely equal in efficacy with the natural-born son (*b*), and where any one of several brothers had a son, the latter was considered to be the son of all the brothers; Kulluka Bhatta actually adds a gloss: "So that if such nephew would be the heir, the uncles have no power to adopt a son;" and the same view was maintained by Chandesvara and other commentators (*c*). It is evident, therefore, that in early times the five sorts of adopted sons must have been of very secondary importance. Apastamba expressly states that "the gift or acceptance of a son, and the right to buy or sell a child, is not recognized" (*d*). And Katyayana permits the gift, or sale, of a son during a season of distress, but not otherwise (*e*) The same low estimation of adopted sons is evidenced by the rank which they occupied in the order of sons. A reference to the table which accompanies § 64 will show, that out of fourteen authorities there quoted only five place even the *dattaka* among the first six. Now this is not a mere matter of arrangement, for they all without exception give rights of inheritance to the first six sons which are denied to the remaining six. No doubt Manu is one of the five who thus favours the adopted son. But it may be questioned whether his text has not undergone an alteration in that respect. Both Yajnavalkya and Narada, who were later than Manu, place the adopted among the later six. Narada expressly states that he took Manu as the basis of his work. An examination of the marginal references in Stenzler's Yajnavalkya will establish that he did the same. It will be seen by the table that these two agree much

Comparative inferiority of adopted son.

(*a*) Manu, ix. § 180; cf. § 161, which, as explained by Kulluka Bhatta, seems to be an interpolation, introduced when subsidiary sons had become obsolete. Vrihaspati, Dattaka Chandrika, i. § 8.

(*b*) Vishnu, xv. § 47; Manu, ix. § 127—139.

(*c*) Vasishtha, xvii. § 8; Vishnu, xv. § 42; Manu, ix. § 132; 3 Dig. 266; Dattaka Chandrika, i. § 21.

(*d*) Apastamba, ii. 13, vi. § 11.

(*e*) Dattaka Mimamsa, i. § 7, 8. Mitakshara, i. 11, § 10 refers this prohibition to the giver not the taker of the son. A contrary view was taken by Apararka.

more closely with each other than either does with Manu as it now stands. It is difficult to account for their differing from so high an authority, if they had before them the text which we possess. In any case, the mere fact that differences of opinion did exist on such a point would seem to show that it had not assumed any great prominence.

Diminished number of modes of adoption.

§ 94. When the number of subsidiary sons was diminished from the causes I have already suggested (§ 75), the importance of the adopted sons, who alone were left, would naturally increase. Even where a brother's son existed, though he might procure for his uncle all the required spiritual blessings, still an adoption would be necessary, "for the celebration of name, and the due perpetuation of lineage" (*f*). As partition and self-acquisition became more common, the latter objects would naturally be more desired. It is singular, then, that we should find the same diminution exhibiting itself in the forms of adoption (*g*). The explanation is probably to be found in the growth of Brahmanical influence, and the consequent prominence given to the religious principle. If the primary object of adoption was to gratify the *manes* of the ancestors by annual offerings, it was necessary to delude the *manes*, as it were, into the idea that the offerer really was their descendant. He was to look as much like a real son as possible, and certainly not to be one who could never have been a son. Hence arose that body of rules which were evolved out of the phrase of Çaunaka, that he must be "the reflection of a son" (*h*). He was to be a person whose mother might have

---

(*f*) Dattaka Chandrika, i. § 22; V. Darp. 739.

(*g*) In addition to the general authorities cited, *ante*, § 75, see as to the obsoleteness of the *Krita* form, 1 Stra. H. L. 132; 1. N. C. 72; *Eshan Kishor* v. *Haris Chandra*, 13 B. L. R. Appx. 42, S. C. 21 Suth. 281. As to the Svayamdatta, *Bashetiappa* v. *Shivlingappa*, 10 Bom. H. C. 268. As to a form called *paluk patro*. *Kalee Chunder* v. *Sheeb Chunder*, 2 Suth. 281. Other forms might perhaps be valid, when sanctioned by local custom, as the *Krita* system is said still to exist among the Gosains, 1 W. MacN. 101.

(*h*) Dattaka Mimamsa, v. § 15. It seems possible that this metaphor is itself a mistake. Dr. Bühler translates the verse, "He then should adorn the child, which (now) resembles a son of the receiver's body; that is, which has come to resemble a son by the previous ceremony of giving and receiving. See Journal, As. Soc. Bengal, 1866, art. *Çaunaka-Smriti*.

been married by the adopter (*i*); he was to be of the same class; he was to be so young that his ceremonies might all be performed in the adoptive family; he was to be absolutely severed from his natural family, and to become so completely a part of his new family as to be unable to marry within its limits. His introduction into the family must appear to be a matter of love and free-will, unsullied by every mercenary element. All these restrictions had the effect of eliminating the other forms of adoption, and leaving the *dattaka* alone in force.

Influence of secular motives.

§ 95. It must not be supposed that the religious motive for adoption ever excluded the secular motive. The spiritual theory operated strongly upon the Shastries who invented the rules; but those who followed them were, in all probability, generally unconscious of any other aim than that of securing an heir, on whom to lavish the family affection which is so strong among Hindus. The propriety of this motive was admitted by the Sanskrit writers themselves. In the ceremonial for adoption given by Baudhayana, the adopter receives the child with the words: "I take thee for the fulfilment of religious duties. *I take thee to continue the line of my ancestors*" (*k*). A text which is by some attributed to Manu, states that "a son of any description must be anxiously adopted by one who has none, for the sake of the funeral cake, water and solemn rites, *and for the celebrity of his name*" (*l*). And the author of the Dattaka Chandrika admits that even where no spiritual necessity exists, a son may, and even ought to, be adopted, for "the celebration of name, and the due perpetuation of lineage" (*m*). In fact, the earliest instances of adoption found in Hindu legend are adoptions of daughters (*n*). The Thesawaleme shows that such adoptions

---

(*i*) It will be seen (*post*, § 123) that the origin and scope of this rule is open to much doubt.

(*k*) The whole passage is translated by Dr. Bühler in his article on Çaunaka, Journ. As. Soc. Bengal, 1866.

(*l*) Dattaka Chandrika, i. § 9; 3 Dig. 297. (*m*) *Ibid*. i. § 22.

(*n*) See Dattaka Mimamsa, vii. § 30—38.

were practised among the Tamil races of Southern India (*o*). At the present day the Bheels carry away girls by force for wives, and then, with a zeal for fiction which is interesting among savages, adopt them into one family, that they may marry them into another (*p*). The *Kritrima* form of adoption which is still in force in Mithila, and which in several particulars strongly resembles that which is practised in Jaffna, has no connection with religious ideas, and is wholly non-Brahmanical. Among the tribes who have not come under Brahmanical influence, we find that adoption is equally practised, but without any of those rules which spring from the religious fiction. One Sanskrit purist actually laid it down that Sudras could not adopt, as they were incompetent to perform the proper religious rites (*q*). As a matter of fact they always did adopt, but were expressly freed from the restrictions which fettered the higher classes. They not only might, but ought to, adopt the son of a sister or of a daughter, who was forbidden to others; and they might take as their son a person of any age, and even a married man (*r*); that is to say, they adopted persons who made no pretence to religious fitness, but who were perfectly suitable for all other objects. So in the Punjab, adoption is common to the Jats, Sikhs, and even to the Muhammedans, just as in other parts of India. But with them the object is simply to make an heir. "The religious notion of a mystical second birth is not imported into the transaction." No religious ceremonies are used. There is no exclusion of an only son, or of the son of a daughter, or of a sister, nor is there any limit of age. Of later years, however, a tendency to introduce these Brahmanical rules is showing itself. The explanation given by Mr. Justice Campbell is interesting, as illustrating the way in which the process has often taken place:—"In Sikh times, when the land was of little value, and young men of much value, the introduction of a new boy into the com-

Adoptions among non-Brahmanical races.

(*o*) Thesawaleme, ii. § 4. (*p*) Lyall, Asiatic Studies, 163.
(*q*) Vachespati, cited Dattaka Mimamsa, i. § 26.
(*r*) See *post*, § 124, 129.

munity was probably looked on with satisfaction. But by the time of our regular settlements the value of land was discovered, and the brotherhood would naturally look to the chances of dividing the land of an heirless co-sharer, rather than to the introduction of an extra hand to share in the profits, which had begun to be considerable. Hence the main body of a tribe would be inclined to enter as a custom what they wished should be the custom, and unless there were men with interests to defend, the general wish for the future was entered without protest" (*s*). Among the Jain dissenters, and in the Talabda Koli caste in Western India, adoption is also practised, but without any religious significance attached to it, and consequently with a complete absence of the restrictions arising therefrom (*t*). Among the Ooriya Rajahs of Ganjam, who are Kshatriyas, the exequial rites are always performed by a Brahman official, who is permanently attached to the family, and who is called the son-Brahman (*u*). Yet these Rajahs invariably adopt, as might be expected where an old feudality has to be maintained. In Jaffna, the Tamil people adopt both boys and girls; and so little is there any idea of a new birth into the family, that the adopted son can marry a natural-born daughter of the adopting parents; and where both a boy and girl are adopted, they can intermarry (*v*). The secular character of the transaction is even more forcibly shown by the circumstance that the person who makes the adoption must obtain the consent of his heirs. If they withhold it, their rights of inheritance will be unaffected (*w*). These facts appear to be of much weight in support of the suggestion I have already made

---

(*s*) Punjab Cust., 78—83.

(*t*) *Sheo Singh* v. *Mt. Dakho*, 6 N.-W. P. 382, 392 *affd.* 5 I. A. 87 S. C., 1 All. 688; *Bhala Nahana* v. *Parbhu*, 2 Bom. 67.

(*u*) This usage was frequently proved in cases in which I was counsel. For instance, in the case of the Seerghur succession, and that of the Chinna Kimedy taluq, (*Tammirazu* v. *Pantina*, 6 Mad. H. C. 301; *Raghanadha* v. *Brozokishoro*, 3 I. A. 154 S. C. 1 Mad. 69; S. C. 25 Suth. 291) but the custom has not been noticed in either of the reports. It was fully set out in the evidence. It is stated in a more recent case, 11 Mad., 289.

(*v*) Thesawaleme, ii. § 4. (*w*) *Ibid.* ii. § 1, 5, 6. See *post*, § 117, note.

(§ 10), that the spiritual theory is not the sole object of an adoption, even upon Brahmanical principles, and that it can only be applied with the greatest possible caution in the case of non-Aryan tribes, or such as dissent from orthodox Hinduism. (*x*).

Early texts. § 96. The whole Sanskrit law of adoption is evolved from two texts and a metaphor. The metaphor (if it is not itself a mis-translation) is that of Çaunaka, that the boy to be adopted must be "the reflection of a son" (§ 94 note *h*). The texts are those of Manu and Vasishtha.

Manu says (*y*), "He whom his father or mother gives to another as his son, provided that the donee have no issue, if the boy be of the same class, and affectionately disposed, is considered as a son given, the gift being confirmed by pouring water."

Vasishtha says (*z*), "A son formed of seminal fluids and of blood, proceeds from his father and mother as an effect from its cause. Both parents have power to sell, or to desert him. But let no man give, or accept, an only son, since he must remain to raise up a progeny for the obsequies of ancestors. Nor let a woman give, or accept, a son, unless with the assent of her lord. He who means to adopt a son, must assemble his kinsmen, give humble notice to the king, and then having made an oblation to fire with words from the Veda, in the midst of his dwelling-house he may receive, as his son by adoption, a boy nearly allied to him,

---

(*x*) Where the family, being non-Hindu by origin, has adopted Hinduism in part, though not entirely, the *onus* lies on those who set up an adoption to show that this part of the Hindu law has been incorporated in the family usage. Where a family is governed by Hindu law, it may be possible to make out a usage forbidding adoption. It is evident, however, that it would be very difficult to establish a negative usage of such a nature. (*Fanindra Deb* v. *Rajeswar Das*, 12 I. A. 72; S. C. 11 Cal. 463.)

(*y*) Manu, ix. § 168.

(*z*) 3 Dig. 242. The passage from the Grihyasutra of Baudhayana, translated by Dr. Bühler in the Journal As. Soc. Beng. 1866, art. Çaunaka Smriti, is almost word for word the same, but contains no limitation as to relationship or class. See also the passage from Çaunaka on Adoption, translated in the same article, which is also given, V. May., iv. 5, § 8.

or (on failure of such) even one remotely allied. But if doubt arise, let him treat the remote kinsman as a Sudra. The class ought to be known, for through one son the adopter rescues many ancestors."

These texts only apply to the *Dattaka* form. The *Kritrima*, which prevails in Mithila, but nowhere else, will be treated of subsequently. From this small beginning a body of law has been developed, which will be considered under the following heads:—FIRST, who may take in adoption; SECOND, who may give in adoption (§ 129); THIRD, who may be adopted (§ 123); FOURTH, the ceremonies necessary to an adoption (§ 140); FIFTH, the evidence of adoption (§ 145); SIXTH, the results of adoption (§ 152).

Adopter must be without issue.

§ 97. FIRST, WHO MAY ADOPT.—An adoption may either be made by the man himself, or by his widow on his behalf. But in either case it is a condition precedent that he should be without issue at the time of adoption (*a*). Issue is taken in the wide sense peculiar to the term in Hindu law (§ 498). Accordingly, if a man has a son, grandson, or great-grandson actually alive, he is precluded from adopting. Because any one of such persons is his immediate heir, and is capable of performing his funeral rites with full efficacy (*b*). But the existence of a great-great-grandson, or of a daughter's son, is no bar to an adoption (*c*). Still less the previous existence of issue who are now dead (*d*). Nanda Pandita in discussing this subject suggests, upon the authority of a legend in the Purana, that an adoption might be valid even during the life of a natural-born son, if made with the consent of the latter; and in Bengal the validity of such an adoption has been maintained, and also that of two suc-

Only one son at a time.

(*a*) The same rule prevailed as regards adoption both in Greece and Rome. It is singular that the earliest instance of adoption is that in the Rigveda, where Visvamitra, who had at the time a hundred living sons, adopted Sunahsepa. V. N. Mandlik, 454.

(*b*) Dattaka Mimamsa, i. § 13; Dattaka Chandrika, i. § 6.

(*c*) F. MacN. 149; 1 W. MacN. 66, n.

(*d*) Cankha. Dattaka Mimamsa, i. § 4; Dattaka Chandrika, i. § 4.

cessive adoptions, the latter of which was made while the son first adopted was still alive (*e*). But the contrary rule is now established; and it is settled that a man cannot have two adopted sons at the same time, though of course he may adopt as often as he likes, if at the time of each successive adoption he is without issue (*f*). On the same principle, the simultaneous adoption of two or more sons is invalid as to all (*g*). And where an adoption is invalid by reason of the concurrent existence of a son, natural or adopted, the death of the latter will not give validity to a transaction which was an absolute nullity from the first (*h*). It is suggested by Mr. Sutherland, and assented to by Mr. MacNaghten, that if the son, natural or adopted, became an outcast, and therefore unable to perform the necessary funeral rites, an adoption would be lawful; and a practice to that effect is stated to exist in Bombay (*i*). But since Act XXI of 1850 a son would not forfeit any legal right by loss of caste. Therefore an adopted son could not, by virtue of his adoption, step into his place on the ground that he had lost his caste. If the question were to arise, it is possible the Courts would refuse to recognize an adoption which could confer no civil rights. The question might, however, become of importance on the death of the natural son without issue.

Bachelor or widower.

§ 98. It has been suggested that an adoption by a bachelor, or a widower, would be invalid, either on the ground that such a person was not in the order of *grihastha* (householder or married man), or that the right of adoption was only allowed where the legitimate mode of procreation had failed. But it may now be taken as settled that an adop-

---

(*e*) *Mt. Solukna* v. *Ramdolal*, 1 S. D. 324 (434); *Goureepershad* v. *Mt. Jymala*, 2 S. D. 136 (174); Steele, 45, 183.

(*f*) *Rungama* v. *Atchama*, 4 M. I. A. 1, S. C. 7 Suth. (P. C.) 57. But an adoption will not be invalid because it is made in breach of an agreement to adopt another person, where such agreement has not been carried out. 2 Stra. H. L. 115.

(*g*) *Akhoy Chunder* v. *Kalapar Haji*, 12 I. A. 198; S. C. 12 Cal. 406; *Doorga Sundari* v. *Surendra Keshav*, 12 Cal. 686.

(*h*) *Basoo* v. *Basoo*, Mad. Dec. of 1856, 20.

(*i*) 2 W. MacN. 200; Steele, 42, 181.

tion in either of the above cases would be valid (*k*) In one case the Madras Sudr Court held that an adoption was illegal which had been effected during the pregnancy of the adopter's wife; not on the ground that she afterwards produced a son, which it does not appear that she did, but because it was "of the essence of the power to adopt that the party adopting should be hopeless of having issue" (*l*). This principle, if sound, would preclude a man ever adopting until extreme old age, or until he was on his death-bed. It is also opposed to the rules which provide for the case of a son born after an adoption (§ 155). Accordingly in a later case (1881) where an adoption had been held invalid on the ground that the wife was at the time pregnant, and known to be so by her husband, the Court after an examination of the above decision over-ruled it, and held the adoption to be valid. They pointed out that the logical result of such a rule would be to suspend an adoption during the pregnancy, not only of the adopter's wife, but also of the wives of his sons and grandsons, since the existence of issue in the most extended sense of the word is a bar to an adoption (*m*). **Pregnancy.**

§ 99. Where a person is disqualified from inheriting by any personal disability, such as blindness, impotence, leprosy, or the like, a son whom he may adopt can have no higher rights than himself, and would be entitled to maintenance only (*n*). Mr. Sutherland was of opinion that the adoption itself would be valid, in which case, of course, the adopted son would succeed to the self-acquired or separate property of his adoptive father (*o*). On the other **Adoption by disqualified heir.**

(*k*) Suth. Syn. 664, 671; 3 Dig. 252; 1 W. MacN. 66; 2 W. MacN. 175; *Gunnappa* v. *Sankappa*, Bom. Sel. Rep. 202; *Nagappa* v. *Subba Sastry*, 2 Mad. H. C. 367; *Chandvasekharudu* v, *Bramhanna*, 4 Mad. H. C. 270. *Gopal Anant* v. *Narayan Ganesh*, 12 Bom. 329. *Per Mahmood*, J., 12 All. 352.

(*l*) *Narayana* v. *Vedachala*, Mad. Dec. of 1860, 97. See Steele, 43.

(*m*) *Nagabhushanam* v. *Seshamma*, 3 Mad. 180; acc. *Hanmant Ramchandra* v. *Bhimacharya*, 12 Bom. 105.

(*n*) Dattaka Chandrika, vi. § 81; *Sevachetumbara* v. *Parasucty*, Mad. Dec. of 1857, 210. In the Punjab a man who is blind, impotent, or lame can adopt, though the Brahmans deny the right of one who was always impotent. Punjab Customary Law, II. 154.

(*o*) Suth. Syn., 664, 671.

hand, in two cases which Mr. MacNaghten cites with approbation, the Bengal pundits held that the capacity of a leper to adopt depended upon his having performed the necessary expiation. When he had done so the adoption was valid. When he had not done so, or where the disease was such as to be inexpiable, the adoption was invalid (*p*). This opinion rested on the ground that until expiation he was unable to perform the necessary religious ceremonies. Accordingly, the Bengal High Court decided that an adoption was invalid when effected by a widow who was living in concubinage, as this made her unfit to take part in any religious ceremony (*q*). In Bombay it was contended that an adoption by a widow was invalid, as she had not undergone tonsure, and was therefore impure. It appeared, however, that she had made certain expiatory gifts, which the Shastras, on being consulted previous to the adoption, had pronounced sufficient. The Court refused to allow their opinion to be questioned (*r*). In a case before the Privy Council it was argued, and seems to have been assumed, that an adoption would have been invalid, if it had been made while the adopter was still in a state of pollution (*s*). No decision was given upon the point, as the facts which would have raised it were negatived. When the case arises it will require a previous determination of the question, What religious ceremonies are necessary to an adoption, and who must take part in them (*t*).

Adoption by minor.

§ 100. The law as to the capacity of a minor to adopt, or to authorise an adoption, seems also unsettled. The various acts which constitute Courts of Wards all contain provisions forbidding a disqualified landholder to adopt without the consent of the Court (*u*). It has been held that these

(*p*) 2 W. MacN. 201, acc.; Mitakshara, ii, 10, § 11.
(*q*) *Sayamalal* v. *Saudamini*, 5 B. L. R. 362.
(*r*) *Ravji Vinayakrao* v. *Lakshmibai*, 11 Bom. 381, 392.
(*s*) *Ramalinga* v. *Sadasiva*, 9 M. I. A. 506; S. C. 1 Suth. (P. C.) 25.
(*t*) See as to this, *post*, § 142, 143, and as to the grounds upon which disability to inheritance arises, *post*, chap. xix.
(*u*) Beng. Reg. X of 1793, s. 33; LII of 1803, s. 37 (N.-W. P.); Mad. Reg. V of 1804, s. 25; Act XXXV of 1858, s. 74; Act IV of 1870, s. 74 (B. C.). Act

provisions do not apply at all unless actual possession has been taken by the Courts of Wards; but that where they do apply, they equally forbid the giving of an authority to adopt, and that an adoption made in violation of them is absolutely invalid (*v*). Under Act IX of 1875, (Majority) § 3, minority in the case of Hindus now extends to the end of the 18th year, unless in cases where a guardian has been appointed by a Court of Justice, or where the minor is under the jurisdiction of the Court of Wards, in which case it lasts till the end of the 21st year. It has, however, been held in Bengal and Bombay that both an actual adoption effected by a minor, and an authority to adopt given by him, will be valid, provided he has attained years of discretion, and this opinion appears to have been approved by the Judicial Committee. Mr. Justice *Mitter* said: "Every act done by a minor is not necessarily null and void. Those acts only which are prejudicial to his interest can be questioned and avoided by him after he reaches his majority. But no such prejudicial character can be predicated of adoption in the case of a childless Hindu, and as under the Hindu Shasters a minor who has arrived at the age of discretion is not only competent but bound to perform the religious ceremonies prescribed for his salvation, we cannot hold the adoption made in this case to be invalid, merely because the adoptive father was in the eye of the law a minor" (*w*). The judgment does not state when a Hindu arrives at years of discretion; whether the period is a fixed one, or whether it depends upon the special capacity of

Age of discretion.

IX of 1879 (B. C.) s. 61. This last Act also extends the prohibition to an authority to adopt.

(*v*) *Jumoona* v. *Bamasoonderai*, 3 I. A. 72; S. C. 1 Cal. 289; *Neelkaunt* v. *Anundmoyee*, S. D. of 1855, 218; *Anundmoyee* v. *Sheebchunder*, 9 M. I. A. 287; S. C. 2 Suth. (P. C.) 19. But see *per Pontifex*, J., *Banee Pershad* v. *Moonshee Syud*, 25 Suth. 192, 198. It has been held that the corresponding provision in Bombay, Act II of 1863, s. 6, cl. 2 only applies as between Government and the person claiming as adopted son, and cannot be taken advantage of by third parties for the purpose of invalidating the adoption. *Vasudevanant* v. *Ramkrishna*, 2 Bom. 529.

(*w*) *Rajendro Narain* v. *Saroda*, 15 Suth. 548; *Patel Vandravan Jekisan* v. *Manilal*, 15 Bom. 565; *per curiam*, *Jumoona* v. *Bamasoonderai*, 3 I. A. 83; S. C. 1 Cal. 289; *Mt. Pearee* v. *Mt. Hurbunsee*, 19 Suth. 127; V. Darp. 770, where conflicting opinions are cited.

each individual. In general, the Hindu law-books speak of the age of discretion and majority as convertible terms, and treat each period as being attained at the sixteenth year. But a further subdivision is stated, *viz.*, infancy to the end of the fourth year, boyhood to the end of the ninth, and adolescence to the end of the fifteenth. This distinction, according to Jagannatha, regards penance, expiation, and the like. An opinion is also mentioned by him, that the period of legal capacity may be determined with reference to the degree in which a youth has actually become conversant with affairs (*x*). It may be that Mr. Justice *Mitter* meant, that an adoption would be valid if effected by a boy between the ages of ten and sixteen, who was shown to be capable of understanding the nature of his act (*y*). The actual decision appears to have been as to an authority to adopt given by the minor. Of course he could not authorise an adoption which he could not effect. The converse of the proposition does not seem necessarily to follow. An act done might be valid, though an authority to do it might be invalid.

Adoption by wife.

§ 101. As an adoption is made solely to the husband and for his benefit, he is competent to effect it without his wife's assent, and notwithstanding her dissent (*z*). For the same reason, she can adopt to no one but her husband. An adoption made to herself, except where the *Kritrima* form is allowed, would be wholly invalid (*a*). Nor can she ever adopt to her husband during his lifetime, except with his assent (*b*). Her capacity to adopt to him, after his death, whether with or without his assent, is a point which has given rise to four different opinions, each of which is settled

Adoption by widow.

(*x*) 1 Dig. 291—293; 2 Dig. 115—117; Mitakshara on Loans, cited V. Darp. 770.

(*y*) Act IX of 1875 (Majority) does not settle the point, as s. 2 provides that the Act is not to affect any person in the matter of adoption.

(*z*) Dattaka Mimamsa, i. § 22; *Rungama* v. *Atchama*, 4 M. I. A. 2; S. C. 7 Suth. (P. C.) 57.

(*a*) *Chowdhry Pudum* v. *Koer Oodey*, 12 M. I. A. 356; S. C. 12 Suth. (P. C.) 1; S. C. 2 B. L. R. (P. C.) 101. Adoptions by women of the dancing-girl caste rest on a different footing, see *post*, § 183.

(*b*) Dattaka Mimamsa, i. § 27.

to be law in the province where it prevails. "All the schools accept as authoritative the text of Vasishtha, which says, 'Nor let a woman give or accept a son unless with the assent of her lord' (§ 96.) **Mithila.** But the Mithila school apparently takes this to mean that the assent of the husband must be given at the time of the adoption, and therefore that a widow cannot receive a son in adoption, according to the Dattaka form, at all (*c*). **Bengal.** The Bengal school interprets the text as requiring an express permission given by the husband in his lifetime, but capable of taking effect after his death (*d*); whilst the Mayukha, Kaustubha, and **Mahratta.** other treatises which govern the Mahratta school, explain the text away by saying, "that it applies only to an adoption made in the husband's lifetime, and is not to be taken to restrict the widow's power to do that which the general law prescribes as beneficial to her husband's soul" (*e*). The same interpretation is put upon the text by the Nambudry Brahmans of the West Coast (§ 42) with the same result (*f*). A fourth and intermediate view was established by the Judicial Committee in the case from which this quotation is taken, *viz.*, **Southern India.** that in Southern India the want of the husband's assent may be supplied by that of his sapindas. **Benares.** The doctrine of the Benares school, as it prevails in Northern India, appears to be the same as that of Bengal, as to the necessity for the husband's assent; though upon this point a greater difference of opinion has prevailed, from the circumstance that the Viramitrodaya, which allows the assent of the kinsmen to be sufficient, is an authority in that province (*g*). The result is, that in the case of an adoption

---

(*c*) Dattaka Mimamsa, i. § 16; Vivada Chintamani, 74; 1 W. MacN. 95, 100; *Jai Ram* v. *Musan Dhami*, 5 S. D. 3.

(*d*) 1 W. MacN. 91, 100; 2. W. MacN. 175, 182, 183; *Janki Dibeh* v. *Suda Sheo*, 1 S. D. 197 (262); *Mt. Tara Munee* v. *Dev. Narayun*, 3 S. D. 387 (516).

(*e*) *Per curiam, Collector of Madura* v. *Moottoo Ramalinga*, 12 M. I. A. 435; S. C. 1 B. L. R. (P. C.) 1; S. C. 10 Suth. (P. C.) 17; V. N. Mandlik, 463.

(*f*) 11 Mad. 167, 178, 187.

(*g*) Viramit., ii. 2, § 8; 1 W. MacN. 91, 100; 2 W. MacN. 189; *Shumshere* v. *Dilraj*, 2 S. D. 169 (216); *Haiman* v. *Koomar*, 2 Kn. 203; *Chowdry Padum Singh* v. *Oodey Singh*, 12 M. I. A. 350; *per curiam, Collector of Madura* v. *Moottoo Ramalinga*, 12 M. I. A. 440; S. C. in Court below, 2 Mad. H. C. 216; 2 Stra. H. L. 92. *Tulshi Ram* v. *Behari Lal*, 12 All. (F. B.) 328, where it was also held that the want of proper authority could not be cured on the principle of *Factum valet*. *Semble*, *Lala Parbhu Lal* v. *Mylne*, 14 Cal. 401—415.

by a widow, in Mithila, no consent is sufficient; in Western India no consent is required; in Bengal and Benares the husband's assent is required; in Southern India the consent either of the husband or of the sapindas is sufficient. The cases of Western and Southern India alone require any further discussion. Before examining them it will be well to dispose of the other matters relating to an adoption by a widow upon which the law is uniform.

Nature of authority.

§ 102. No particular form of authority is required. It may be given in writing or in words (*h*), or by will (*i*). It may also be conditional; that is, an authority to adopt upon the happening of a particular event, provided an adoption made when the event happened, would be legal. For instance, an authority to a widow to adopt, in the event of a disagreement between herself and a surviving son, would be invalid, because the father himself could not adopt so long as the son lived (*k*). But an authority to adopt in the event of the death of a son then living would be good, and so it would be if the authority were to adopt several sons in succession, provided one was not to be adopted till the other was dead (*l*).

Must be strictly followed.

§ 103. The authority given must be strictly pursued, and can neither be varied from nor extended. If the widow is directed to adopt a particular boy, she cannot adopt any other, even though he should be unattainable. If she is directed to adopt *a son*, her authority is exhausted as soon as she has made a single adoption; and she cannot adopt a second time, even on the failure of the son first adopted (*m*). Where a man died, leaving his wife pregnant, and

---

(*h*) Futwah, 1 Mad. Dec. 104; *per curiam*, *Soondur Koomaree* v. *Gudadhur*, M. I. A. 64; S. C. 4 Suth. (P. C.) 116.

(*i*) *Saroda* v. *Tincowry*, 1 Hyde, 223.

(*k*) *Mt. Solukna* v. *Ramdolal*, 1 S. D. 324 (434); *Gopee Lall* v. *Mt Chundraolee*, 19 Suth. 12, (a Privy Council case).

(*l*) *Shamchunder* v. *Narayni*, 2 S. D. 209 (279); *Bhoobun Moyee* v. *Ram Kishore*, 10 M. I. A. 279; S. C. 3 Suth. (P. C.) 15; *Jumoona* v. *Bamasoonderai*, 3 I. A. 72; S. C. 1 Cal. 289; *Vellanki* v. *Venkata Rama*, (Guntur case) 4 I. A. 1; S. C. 1 Mad. 174; S. C. 26 Suth. 21.

(*m*) *Per curiam*, *Chowdry Padum* v. *Koer Oodey*, 12 M. I. A. 356; S. C. 12

authorised her to adopt, in case the son to be born should die, and she had a daughter, it was held she could not adopt (*n*). And so it was decided that a direction to a widow to adopt a boy along with a living son, which was illegal and could not be carried out, did not authorise her to adopt after the death of that son (*o*). But an authority to adopt generally, authorises the adoption of any person whose affiliation would be legal (*p*). A direction by a testator that his widow should adopt a son "with the good advice and opinion of the manager," whom he had appointed as a sort of agent, was held only as a direction, and that an adoption made without consulting him was valid (*q*).

Case of Iyah Pillay.

In one case decided at Madras, the authority to the widow was contained in the following words of her husband's will :—"If Iyah Pillay beget a son, beside his present son, you are to keep him to my lineage." At the testator's death, Iyah Pillay had no second son. Sir *Thomas Strange*, decided that the widow was not bound to wait indefinitely, and he affirmed the validity of the adoption by her of another boy (*r*). This decision is canvassed with much vigour by the author of *Considerations on Hindu Law* (*s*), who argues that the authority was specific, that under it no one could be adopted but a son of Iyah Pillay, that the widow was bound to wait till after possibility extinct of further issue by him, and then that the authority would lapse, from the failure of any object, upon whom it could be exercised. Sir *Thomas Strange*, however, construed the document as evidencing a primary desire to be represented by an adopted son, coupled with a subsidiary desire that that son should have been begotten by Iyah

---

Suth. (P. C.); 1 F. MacN. 156, 175; 1 W. MacN. 89, *dub.; Purmanund* v. *Oomakunt*, 4 S. D. 318 (404); *Gournath* v. *Arnapoorna*, S. D. of 1852, 332 *Amirthayyan* v. *Ketharamayyan*, 14 Mad. 65.

(*n*) *Mohendro Lall* v. *Rookinny*, 1 Coryton, 42; cited V. Darp. 814.

(*o*) *Joychundro* v. *Bhyrub*, S. D. of 1849, 41.

(*p*) 1 Mad. Dec. 105.

(*q*) *Surendra Nandan* v. *Sailaja Kant*, 18 Cal. ~~335~~ 385.

(*r*) *Veerapermall* v. *Narain Pillay*, 1 N. C. 91.

(*s*) F. MacN.

Pillay. In this construction he was certainly more liberal than the Courts have been in the other instances just mentioned.

When power of adoption becomes incapable of being exercised.

§ 104. Another limitation to the right of adoption has been laid down by the Privy Council, in some cases which decide, that a widow cannot adopt to her deceased husband where he has left a son, who has himself died, leaving an heir to his estate. The first case in which this point arose was that of *Bhoobun Moyee* v. *Ram Kishore Achari* (*t*). There Gour Kishore died leaving a son Bhowani, and a widow Chundrabullee, to whom he gave an express authority to adopt in the event of his son's death. Bhowani married, attained his majority, and died, leaving a widow but no issue. Chundrabullee then adopted a son Ram Kishore, who sued Bhowani's widow to recover the estate. The Privy Council held that her estate could not be divested by the subsequent adoption. Lord Kingsdown, however, went on to say "that at the time when Chundrabullee professed to exercise it, the power was incapable of execution." Their Lordships admitted that Gour Kishore had fixed no limits to the period during which his power might be acted on by his widow, but, they said, "it is plain that some limits must be assigned. It might well have been that Bhowani had left a son, natural born or adopted, and that such son had died himself, leaving a son, and that such son had attained his majority in the lifetime of Chundrabullee. It could hardly have been intended that after the lapse of several successive heirs a son should be adopted to the great-grandfather of the last taker, when all the spiritual purposes of a son, according to the largest construction of them, would have been satisfied. But whatever may be the intention, would the law allow it to be effected? We rather understand the Judges below to have been of opinion, that if Bhowani Kishore had left a son, or if a son

---

(*t*) 10 M. I. A. 279; S. C. 3 Suth. (P. C.) 15. See this case referred to on another point, § 172.

had been lawfully adopted to him by his wife under a power legally conferred upon her, the power of adoption given to Chundrabullee would have been at an end. But it is difficult to see what reasons could be assigned for such a result which would not equally apply to the case before us." The same question arose again after the deaths of Bhowani's widow and of Chundrabullee. Ram Kishore got into possession of the property left by Gour Kishore and Bhowani. He was sued for its recovery by a more distant relation. It was admitted that he was entitled to hold it, if his adoption was valid, and the High Court of Bengal decided in his favour (*u*). They limited the effect of the Privy Council judgment to that which it had actually decided, *viz.*, that the plaintiff in the suit had no right to the property which he claimed. This decision, however, was in its turn reversed by the Judicial Committee (*v*). They said "the substitution of a new heir for the widow was no doubt the question to be decided, and such substitution might have been disallowed, the adoption being held valid for all other purposes, which is the view the Lower Courts have taken of the judgment, but their Lordships do not think that this was intended. They consider the decision to be that, upon the vesting of the estate in the widow of Bhowani, the power of adoption was at an end, and incapable of execution and if the question had come before them without any previous decision upon it they would have been of that opinion." Both these cases were again considered and followed in a subsequent case from Madras (*w*), when the facts were exactly similar, except that the widow acted upon an authority from her husband's sapindas, given after the death of the natural born son, but during the life of his widow. After her death the distant collaterals sued for, and obtained a declaration that the adoption was wholly invalid, and could not stand in the way of their reversion-

---

(*u*) *Puddo Kumaree* v. *Juggut Kishore*, 5 Cal. 615.

(*v*) *Pudma Coomari* v. *Court of Wards*, 8 I. A. 229.

(*w*) *Thayammal* v. *Venkatrama*, 14 I. A. 67, S. C., 10 Mad. 205; *Tarachurn* v. *Suresh Chunder*, 16 I. A. 166; S. C. 17 Cal. 122.

ary rights. Of course the same doctrine would apply *à fortiori* as against the independent right of a widow in Bombay to adopt to her late husband (*x*).

Further consideration of the rule.

§ 104A. The applicability of this doctrine to cases differing in their facts has been considered in two cases in Bengal. In the first (*y*) a husband had left his widow authority to adopt five sons in succession. She adopted Kristo Churn who died twelve years after his adoption, apparently unmarried. She then adopted another boy, whose right to succeed to the husband's property was disputed by a collateral relation of the husband. Before the High Court, the only point raised was that under the decision in Bhoobun Moyee's case (*z*) the power to the widow to make a second adoption was incapable of execution, inasmuch as Kristo Churn had lived long enough to perform all acts of spiritual benefit for the deceased, and it must be assumed he had performed them. The High Court found that the second adoption was valid. They said that "an adopted son attaining an age of sufficient maturity, and performing the religious services enjoined by the Shasters cannot exhaust the whole of the spiritual benefit which a son is capable of conferring upon the soul of his deceased father. Because these services are enjoined to be repeated at certain stated intervals, and the performance of them on each successive occasion secures fresh spiritual benefit to the soul of the deceased father." As regards Bhoobun Moyee's case, they proceeded to state their opinion that the Privy Council had not meant to hold that the power was incapable of execution for all purposes, but only for the purpose of divesting the widow of Bhowani Kishore of her proprietary rights. This view can no longer be maintained after the more recent decisions of the Judicial Committee. But the case before the High Court differed from the three cases in the Privy Council which followed and

---

(*x*) See W. & B. 987—991. *Keshav Ramkristna* v. *Govind Ganesh*, 9 Bom. 94.
(*y*) *Ram Soondar* v. *Surbanee Dossee*, 22 Suth. 121. (*z*) *Ante*, § 104.

explained Bhoobun Moyee's case (*a*), in this respect that on the death of Kristo Churn the estate vested in no one as his heir, other than the widow who exercised the power of adoption. In this respect the case may well stand along with the four already discussed. In fact it comes within the express words of Lord Kingsdown, when he said (*b*) "If Bhowani Kishore had died unmarried, his mother, Chundrabullee Debia, would have been his heir, and the question of adoption would have stood on quite different grounds. By exercising the power of adoption she would have divested no estate but her own, and this would have brought the case within the ordinary rule."

This *dictum* was the ground of the later decision of the Bengal High Court (*c*). There Jagat Sett died in 1865 leaving an adopted son Gopal Chand and a widow Pran Kumari. Gopal Chand died in 1868, leaving a son Gopi Chand, and he again died unmarried and without issue. On his death Pran Kumari, who was his heir, adopted Jibun Mull. The plaintiff, a distant collateral relation of Gopi Chand, sued for a declaration that he was entitled to succeed to the estate on the death of Pran Kumari, and that the adoption of Jibun Mull was invalid. The High Court appears to have admitted that the adoption would have been invalid if it had been based upon an authority to adopt granted by Jagat Sett. In this case, however, the parties were Jains, and by Jain law a widow can adopt without authority from her husband (*d*). They held that this distinguished the case from that of *Pudma Kumari Debi* v. *The Court of Wards* (*e*), and brought it within the dictum of Lord Kingsdown above quoted. But, although a Jain widow can adopt without any authority from her husband, it is difficult to suppose that she can do what her husband could not have authorised her to do. Both in Madras and Bombay a widow is precluded from adoption

(*a*) 8 I. A. 229; 14 I. A. 67; 16 I.A. 166. (*b*) 10 M. I. A., p. 311.
(*c*) *Manick Chand* v. *Jagat Settani*, 17 Cal. 518, p. 536.
(*d*) *Post*, § 119. (*e*) 8 I. A. 229.

where a prohibition from her husband can be proved or inferred (*f*). Can she be in a better position, where the law would have prohibited her to act upon his directions, if they had been given?

Adoption by minor;

§ 105. A widow, who is duly authorised by her husband, may adopt while she is a minor, because the act is her husband's, and she is only the instrument (*g*). I presume the same rule would apply in cases where an authority by his sapindas is requisite, and is given. In Western India it is stated that a widow under the age of puberty cannot adopt (*h*). I suppose the reason for the difference is that there the adoption is the act of the widow, for which no authority, or consent, is required.

or unchaste widow.

An unchaste widow cannot adopt even with the express authority of her husband, because her dissolute life entails a degradation which renders her unable to perform the necessary ceremonies. This incapacity may, it is said, be removed by performing the penances proper for expiation. But these cannot be performed during pregnancy; therefore, while it lasts an unchaste widow cannot possibly adopt (*i*). In the case of an adoption by a Vaisya widow under authority from her husband it seems to have been considered by the Madras High Court, though it was not necessary to decide the point, that the adoption was bad, being made while the corpse was still in the house, and the widow was therefore in a state of pollution (*k*). Whether this ground of incapacity would apply in the case of Sudras, depends upon the question, whether in their case any religious ceremonies are necessary (*l*).

(*f*) 12 M. I. A., p. 443, *post*, § 110 and § 118.

(*g*) 2 W. MacN. 180; V. Darp. 769; *Mondakini* v. *Adinath*, 18 Cal. 69.

(*h*) Steele, 48.

(*i*) *Thukoo* v. *Ruma*, 2 Bor. 446, 456 [488]; *Sayamalal* v. *Saudamini*, 5 B. L. R. 362, approved by *Mitter*, J., *Kery Kolitany* v. *Moneeram*, 13 B. L. R. 14; S. C. 19 Suth. 367. As to the possibility of removing by penance the results of unchastity, see *per Mitter*, J., S. C. 13 B. L. R. 39.

(*k*) *Ranganayakamma* v. *Alwar Setti*, 13 Mad. p. 222.

(*l*) As to this, see *post*, § 142.

§ 106. Where there are several widows, if a special authority has been given to one of them to adopt, she, of course, can act upon it without the assent of the others, and, I presume, she alone could act upon it (*m*). If the authority has been given the widows severally, the junior may adopt without the consent of the senior, if the latter refuses to adopt (*n*). In Bombay, it is said that where there are several widows, the elder has the right to adopt even without the consent of the junior widow, but that the junior widow cannot adopt without the consent of the elder, unless the latter is leading an irregular life, which would wholly incapacitate her (*o*).

Several widows.

§ 107. It is a curious thing, that while the husband's right is recognized to delegate to his widow an authority to adopt, he can delegate it to no one else (*p*). In cases where the assent of sapindas will supply the place of an authority by the husband, that assent must be sought for and acted upon by the widow. Where no authority is given or required, equally the widow alone can perform the act (*q*). The reason probably is, that she is looked upon, not merely as his agent, but as the surviving half of himself (*r*), and, therefore, exercising an independent discretion, which can neither be supplied, nor controlled, by any one else. It is no doubt upon the same principle, that an express authority, or even direction, by a husband to his widow to adopt is, for all legal purposes, absolutely non-existent until it is acted upon. She cannot be compelled to act upon it unless, and until, she chooses to do so (*s*). If she

Widow alone can adopt for husband.

Her discretion absolute.

(*m*) 2 Stra. H. L. 91.
(*n*) *Mondakini* v. *Adinath*, 18 Cal. 69.
(*o*) Steele, 48, 187; W. & B. 977, 999; *Rakhmabai* v. *Radhabai*, 5 Bom. H. C. (A. C. J.) 181.
(*p*) *E.g.*, A direction by a testator to his son's widow to adopt might authorise an adoption to the son, but not to the testator. *Karsandas* v. *Ladkavahu*, 12 Bom. 185.
(*q*) F. MacN. 202; 2 Stra. H. L. 94; *Veerapermall* v. *Narain Pillay*, 1 N. C., 103; *Bhagvandas* v. *Rajmal*, 10 Bom. H. C. 241.
(*r*) See Vribaspati, 3 Dig. 458.
(*s*) *Dyamoyee* v. *Rasbeharee*, S. D. of 1852, 1013; *Bamundoss* v. *Mt. Tarinee*, 7 M. I. A. 190; *Uma Sunduri* v. *Sourobinee*, 7 Cal. 288.

acts upon it, not voluntarily but under the influence of coercion, physical or moral, the adoption is invalid (*t*). And so it has been held in a case where a widow adopted in ignorance of the legal effect of her acts in divesting her estate (*u*). The Court will not even recognize the authority to the extent of making a declaration as to its validity (*v*). Till she does act, her position is exactly the same as it would be, if the authority had never been given. If she would be the heir to her husband's estate in the absence of a son, she is such heir until she chooses to descend from that position; and she is in of her own right, and not as trustee for any son to be adopted hereafter (*w*). If she is not the heir, she can claim no greater right to interfere with the management of the estate, or to control the persons in possession, than if she had no authority. The only mode of giving it effect is to act upon it (*x*) If a husband directs his widow to adopt a particular boy, or the child of a particular father, she is under no obligation to submit to any conditions which the latter may attempt to impose (*y*). A question has arisen, but not been decided, whether a widow with power to adopt can bind herself not to adopt. The Court refused an *interim* injunction against the adoption but there the matter ended (*z*). Should the case arise again, it might affect the decision to consider the nature of the widow's power; whether she was expressly directed by her husband to adopt or only allowed to do so at her own discretion or whether her husband had been wholly silent on the point, and her authority to adopt arose from consent of sapindas, or, in the West Coast, from her own independent power.

No limit of time.

Nor is there any limit to the time during which a widow may act upon the authority

(*t*) *Ranganayakamma* v. *Alwar Setti*, 13 Mad. 214, 220.

(*u*) *Bayabai* v. *Bala*, 7 Bom. H. Ct. Appx. 1.

(*v*) *Mt. Pearee* v. *Mt. Hurbunsee*, 19 Suth. 127; *Sreemutty Rajcoomaree* v. *Nobocoomar*, 1 Boul. 137; Sev. 641, n.

(*w*) *Bamundoss* v. *Mt. Tarinee*, 7 M. I. A. 169, overruling *Bijaya* v. *Shama*, S. D. of 1848, 762.

(*x*) *Mt. Subudra* v. *Goluknath*, 7 S. D. 143 (166).

(*y*) *Shamavahoo* v. *Dwarkadas*, 12 Bom. 202.

(*z*) *Assar Purshotam* v. *Ratanbai*, 13 Bom. 56.

given to her (*a*). In a Bengal case, an adoption made fifteen years after the husband's death was supported; and in Bombay cases the periods were twenty, twenty-five, fifty-two, and even seventy-one years (*b*).

§ 108. Having now seen the effect of an authority to adopt when given by the husband, it remains to examine the mode in which it may be supplied when wanting. This can only be in Southern and Western India and in some parts of Northern India (§ 101, 110, 119). In Madras the balance of opinion had always been that in the absence of authority from the husband, the assent of sapindas was sufficient. Till lately, however, the point was certainly open to argument. It has now been definitively settled by the judgment of the Privy Council in the case of the Ramnaad Zemindary, and in several other cases which followed, and were founded upon, that decision. **Absence of husband's authority.**

§ 109. In the Ramnaad case (*c*), the adoption in dispute was made by a widow, who had taken as heir to her late husband a Zemindary, which was his separate estate. The adoption was made with the assent, original or subsequent, of a number of sapindas of the last male holder, who were certainly the majority of the whole number then alive, if indeed they did not constitute the entire body of sapindas. The only question, therefore, which required decision was, whether in Southern India any amount of assent on the part of sapindas could give validity to an adoption made by a widow without her husband's consent. The High Court of Madras, after an elaborate examination of all the authorities, came to the conclusion that such an adoption was **Ramnaad case.** **High Court.**

(*a*) F. MacN. 157; 1 N. C. 111; *Ramkishen* v. *Mt. Strimutee*, 3 S. D. 367. (489, 494).

(*b*) Anon. 2 M. Dig. 18; *Bhasker* v. *Narro Ragoonath*, Bom. Sel. Rep. 24; *Brijbhookunjee* v. *Gokoolootsaojee*, 1 Bor. 181; [202] *Nimbalkar* v. *Jayavantrav*, 4 Bom. H. C. (A. C. J.) 191. *Giriowa* v. *Bhimaji Raghunath*, 9 Bom. 58. See *Dukhina* v. *Rash Beharee*, 6 Suth. 221, where it was suggested that a widow could not act upon an authority after twelve years. *Sed quære*.

(*c*) *Collector of Madura* v. *Moottoo Ramalinga*, 2 Mad. H. C. 206; *affd.*, 12 M. I. A. 397. S. C. 1 B. L. R. (P.C.) 1; S. C. 10 Suth. (P. C.) 17.

valid. They relied much on the theory that the law of adoption was founded upon, and a development from, the old principle of actual begetting by a brother or sapinda. Arguing from this analogy, they proceeded to say (*d*), "On the reason of the rule, then, it seems to us that if the requirement of consent is more than a moral precept, and it must never be forgotten that in all Hindu authors, as in the works of all authors who expound a system of positive law, professing to be based upon divine revelation, ethical and jural notions are inextricably intermixed, the assent of any one of the sapindas will suffice. If, however, the sapindas are by a fanciful, rather than a solid, analogy to be treated as a juridical person in which the whole authority of the husband is to be vested, it would be wholly contrary to sound jurisprudence to treat the assent of every individual member as necessary. On the contrary, the will of the majority of individual members must be taken as the will of the body, in any matter not manifestly repugnant to the purpose for which the body was created."

§ 110. The Judicial Committee confirmed this decision upon the ground of positive authority and precedent, while declining to accept the supposed analogy between adoptions according to the *Dattaka* form, and the obsolete practice of raising up issue to the deceased husband by carnal intercourse with the widow. They then proceeded as follows (*e*) :—

Judicial Committee.

"It must, however, be admitted that the doctrine is stated in the old treatises, and even by Mr. Colebrooke, with a degree of vagueness that may occasion considerable difficulties and inconveniences in its practical application. The question who are the kinsmen whose assent will supply the want of positive authority from the deceased husband,

Undivided property.

is the first to suggest itself. Where the husband's family

(*d*) 2 Mad. H. C. 231. I have already suggested my belief that the two things were perfectly independent of each other. See *ante*, § 68, *et seq.*

(*e*) 12 M. I. A. 441. S. C. 1 B. L. R. (P. C.) 1; S. C. 10 Suth. (P. C.) 17.

is in the normal condition of a Hindu family, *i.e.*, undivided, that question is of comparatively easy solution. In such a case, the widow, under the law of all the schools which admit this disputed power of adoption, takes no interest in her husband's share of the joint estate, except a right to maintenance. And though the father of the husband, if alive, might, as the head of the family and the natural guardian of the widow, be competent by his sole assent to authorise an adoption by her, yet, if there be no father, the assent of all the brothers, who, in default of adoption, would take the husband's share, would probably be required, since it would be unjust to allow the widow to defeat their interest by introducing a new co-parcener against their will. Where, however, as in the present case, the widow has taken by inheritance the separate estate of her husband, there is greater difficulty in laying down a rule. The power to adopt, when not actually given by the husband, can only be exercised when a foundation is laid for it in the otherwise neglected observance of religious duty, as understood by Hindus. Their Lordships do not think there is any ground for saying that the consent of every kinsman, however remote, is essential. The assent of kinsmen seems to be required by reason of the presumed incapacity of women for independence, rather than the necessity of procuring the consent of all those whose possible and reversionary interest in the estate would be defeated by the adoption. In such a case, therefore, their Lordships think that the consent of the father-in-law, to whom the law points as the natural guardian and 'venerable protector' of the widow, would be sufficient (*f*). It is not easy to lay down an inflexible rule for the case in which no father-in-law is in existence. Every such case must depend on the circumstances of the family. All that can be said is, that there should be such evidence of the assent of kinsmen as suffices to show that the act is done by the widow in the

Separate estate.

(*f*) So held where the case arose. *Vithoba* v. *Bapu*, 15 Bom. 110.

proper and *bonâ fide* performance of a religious duty, and neither capriciously, nor from a corrupt motive. In this case no issue raises the question that the consents were purchased, and not *bonâ fide* obtained. The rights of an adopted son are not prejudiced by any unauthorised alienation by the widow which precedes the adoption which she makes; and though gifts improperly made to procure assent might be powerful evidence to show no adoption needed, they do not in themselves go to the root of the legality of an adoption.

Express or implied prohibition.

"Again, it appears to their Lordships that, inasmuch as the authorities in favour of the widow's power to adopt with the assent of her husband's kinsmen proceed in a great measure upon the assumption that his assent to this meritorious act is to be implied wherever he has not forbidden it, so the power cannot be inferred when a prohibition by the husband either has been directly expressed by him, or can be reasonably deduced from his disposition of his property, or the existence of a direct line competent to the full performance of religious duties, or from other circumstances of his family, which afford no plea for a supersession of heirs, on the ground of religious obligation to adopt a son in order to complete, or fulfil, defective religious rites" (*g*).

Ramnaad doctrine not to be extended.

§ 111. Of course, in all subsequent instances of adoption by a widow without express authority from her husband, the effort has been to bring the case within, or to exclude it from, some of the above dicta. I say *dicta*, because the only point actually decided was that the assent of the majority of the sapindas was sufficient.

Accordingly, in a Madras case, which followed shortly

(*g*) The practice in the Punjab appears to be exactly the same as that laid down in the *Ramnaad case*. An adoption is there looked upon merely as a mode of transferring, or creating, a title to property. A widow may adopt either with her husband's permission, or by consent of his kinsmen, but in no case against an express prohibition by him. Punjab Cust., 83.

after the decision of the Ramnaad suit, an attempt was made to push that doctrine to the extent of holding that the consent of sapindas was wholly unnecessary, and that the widow might adopt of her own authority. But the Court refused to carry the law further than had been laid down in that judgment, in which "there had been the assent of a majority of the husband's sapindas to the adoption on his behalf" (*h*).

§ 112. The next case arose in the Travancore Courts, where a widow had made an adoption without the consent of her husband's undivided brother, but with the consent of her divided kinsmen. The Court, after weighing the judgments of the High Court and the Privy Council in the *Ramnaad* case, decided against the sufficiency of the authorization. The Chief Judge, after observing that a woman under Hindu law was in a perfect state of tutelage, passing from the control of her father to that of her husband, and after his death to that of the head of his family, pointed out that, in the absence of the father-in-law, the eldest surviving brother must necessarily be that head. He said, "it is clear to me, then, that the kinsman whose assent the law requires for this act is the one who would be liable to support her through her widowhood, and to defray the marriage expenses of her female issue. In the case of divided kinsmen the case may be different, because no one in particular can claim to control her, or is chargeable for her maintenance; but it seems to be clear that, united as the family is, the natural head and venerable protector contemplated by the *Shastras* is the surviving brother, or if there are more than one, the eldest of them. It seems to me impossible to affirm that the liability to maintain the widow, and undertake the other duties of the family, is not coupled with a right to advise and control her act in so important a matter as the introduction of a stranger into

Travancore case.

Head of family must assent.

(*h*) *Arundadi* v. *Kuppammal*, 3 M. H. C. 283; and *per curiam*, *Parasara* v. *Rangaraja*, 2 Mad. 206.

the family, with claims to the family property" (*i*). It will be seen that this reasoning was approved and followed by the Privy Council in the case which follows.

Berhampore case.

§ 113. The next case was one of the class contemplated by the Judicial Committee in their remarks above quoted, and exactly similar to that in the Travancore suit, the family being an undivided family, and the consent of the father-in-law being wanting. In it (*k*) the Zemindar of Chinna Kimedy died, leaving a wife, a brother, and a distant and divided sapinda, the Zemindar of Pedda Kimedy; there were no other sapindas. The deceased and his brother were undivided. Therefore, in default of an adoption, the brother was the heir. The widow adopted the son of the Pedda Kimedy Zemindar, admittedly without the consent of the brother. She alleged a written authority from her husband, but pleaded that even without such authority, she had sufficient assent of sapindas within the meaning of the *Ramnaad* decision. The Lower Court found against her on both points. On appeal, the High Court was inclined to think the authority proved, but reversed the decision of the Lower Court, on the ground that the assent of the Pedda Kimedy Zemindar, evidenced by his giving his son, was sufficient. The Court expressly ruled (*l*) and it was necessary so to rule,—1st. That the consent of one sapinda was sufficient; 2nd. That proximity to the deceased with regard to rights of property was wholly beside the question. In the particular instance the assenting sapinda was not only not the nearest heir, but was not an immediate heir at all, because, being divided, he could not take till after the widow.

High Court.

Judicial Committee.

§ 114. The Judicial Committee, on appeal, held that the written authority was made out. It was therefore unneces-

(*i*) *Ramaswami Iyen* v. *Bhagati Ammal*, 8 Mad. Jur. 58.
(*k*) *Raghunadha* v. *Brozo Kishoro*, 3 I. A. 154; S. C. 1 Mad. 69; S. C. 25 Suth. 291.
(*l*) 7 M. H. C. 301.

sary to go into the question of law. But being of opinion that the views laid down by the High Court were unsound, they proceeded to intimate their dissent from them (*m*).

In the first place, they reiterated their opinion that speculations derived from the practice of begetting a son upon the widow, upon which Mr. Justice *Holloway* had again founded his opinion, were inadmissible as a ground for judicial decision. They also stated that the analogy of that practice would not support the conclusions drawn from it. "Most of the texts speak of 'the appointed' kinsman. By whom appointed? If we are to travel back beyond the *Kali* age, and speculate upon what then took place, we have no reasonable grounds for supposing that a Hindu widow, desirous of raising up seed to her deceased husband, was ever at liberty to invite to her bed any sapinda, however remote, at her own discretion (*n*); and that his consent of itself constituted a sufficient authorization of his act.

"Positive authority, then, does not do more than establish that, according to the law of Madras, which in this respect is something intermediate between the stricter law of Bengal and the wider law of Bombay, a widow, not having her husband's permission, may adopt a son to him, if duly authorized by his kindred. If it were necessary, which in this case it is not, to decide the point, their Lordships would be unwilling to dissent from the principle recognized in the *Travancore* case, viz., that the requisite authority is, in the case of an undivided family, to be sought within that family. The joint and undivided family is the normal condition of Hindu society. An undivided Hindu family is ordinarily joint, not only in estate but in food and worship; therefore, not only all the concerns of the joint property, but whatever relates to their commensality and their religi-

Authority of separate kinsman insufficient.

(*m*) 3 I. A. 190, 192.

(*n*) Gautama expressly declares that "a son begotten on a widow whose husband's brother lives, by another more distant relation, is excluded from inheritance," xxviii. § 23. See *ante*, § 68.

ous duties and observances, must be regulated by its members, or by the manager to whom they have expressly or by implication delegated the task of regulation. The Hindu wife upon her marriage passes into, and becomes a member of, that family. It is upon that family that, as a widow, she has her claim for maintenance. It is in that family that, in the strict contemplation of law, she ought to reside. It is in the members of that family that she must presumably find such counsellors and protectors as the law makes requisite for her. These seem to be strong reasons against the conclusion that for such a purpose as that now under consideration she can at her will travel out of that undivided family, and obtain the authorization required from a separated and remote kinsman of her husband (o).

Conscious exercise of discretion.

"In the present case there is an additional reason against the sufficiency of such an assent. It is admitted on all hands that an authorization by some kinsman of the husband is required. To authorize an act implies the exercise of some discretion whether the act ought or ought not to be done. In the present case there is no trace of such an exercise of discretion. All we know is that the *Mahadevi*, representing herself as having the written permission of her husband to adopt, asked the Rajah of Pedda Kimedy to give her a son in adoption, and succeeded in getting one. There is nothing to show that the Rajah ever supposed that he was giving the authority to adopt which a widow not having her husband's permission would require."

The remarks last quoted would probably make it difficult hereafter for a widow to plead, as she did in this case, *first*, that she had express authority from her husband to adopt, and, *secondly*, that if she had not such authority, the want of it was supplied by authority from kinsmen. Ac-

(o) Where, however, all the branches of the family are divided from the deceased husband and from each other, the Madras High Court has held that the *bonâ fide* consent of one divided member is sufficient, where the assent of the other is withheld from improper motives. *Parasara* v. *Rangaraja*, 2 Mad. 202.

cordingly in a later case decided by the Judicial Committee (*p*), an adoption was set aside (*inter alia*) on the ground that the consent of the managing member of the family, which might in other respects have been sufficient, had been obtained by the widow upon a representation that she had received authority to adopt from her deceased husband, no such authority having been in fact given.

Guntur case.

§ 115. In a case, subsequent to the Berhampore case, one would have imagined that everything had concurred to place the validity of the adoption beyond dispute. The family was divided; all the sapindas had assented, and the persons in possession of the property had no title whatever. But the High Court set the adoption aside on the ground "that it was not made out that there had been such an assent on the part of the widow as to show, to quote the words of the judgment of the Privy Council in the *Ramnaad* case, 'that the act was done by the widow in the proper and *bonâ fide* performance of a religious duty;'" and that there was no appearance of any anxiety or desire on the part of the widow for the proper and *bonâ fide* performance of any religious duty to her husband. Her object appeared to have been to hold the estate till her death, and then continue the line in the person of the plaintiff. This judgment was reversed on appeal. The Privy Council, after pointing out that the facts of the case did not justify the inference drawn from them by the High Court, proceeded to say:—

Religious motive for adoption.

Judicial Committee.

"This being so, is there any ground for the application which the High Court has made of a particular passage in the judgment in the *Ramnaad* case? The passage in question perhaps is not so clear as it might have been made. The Committee, however, was dealing with the nature of the authority of the kinsman that was required. After dealing with the *vexata quæstio* which does not arise

(*p*) *Karunabdhi* v. *Ratnamaiyar*, 7 I. A. 173, S. C. 2 Mad. 270. *Venkatalakshmamma* v. *Narasayya*, 8 Mad. 545.

in this case, whether such an adoption can be made with the assent of one or more sapindas in the case of joint family property, they proceed to consider what assent would be necessary in the case of separate property; and after stating that the authority of the father-in-law would probably be sufficient, they said: 'It is not easy to lay down an inflexible rule for the case in which no father-in-law is in existence. Every such case must depend upon the circumstances of the family. All that can be said is, that there should be such evidence,' not, be it observed, of the widow's motives, but 'of the assent of kinsmen, as suffices to show that the act is done by the widow in the proper and *bonâ fide* performance of a religious duty, and neither capriciously nor from a corrupt motive. In this case no issue raises the question that the consents were purchased and not *bonâ fide* attained.' Their Lordships think it would be very dangerous to introduce into the consideration of these cases of adoption nice questions as to the particular motives operating on the mind of the widow, and that all which this Committee in the former case meant to lay down was, that there should be such proof of assent on the part of the sapindas as should be sufficient to support the inference that the adoption was made by the widow, not from capricious or corrupt motives, or in order to defeat the interest of this or that sapinda, but upon a fair consideration by what may be called a family council, of the expediency of substituting an heir by adoption to the deceased husband. If that be so, there seems to be every reason to suppose that in the present case there was such a consideration, both on the part of the widow and on the part of the sapindas; and their Lordships think that in such a case it must be presumed that she acted from the proper motives which ought to actuate a Hindu female, and that, at all events, such presumption should be made until the contrary is shown" (*q*).

(*q*) *Vellanki* v. *Venkata Rama*, 4 I. A. 1, 13 S. C. 1 Mad. 174, S. C. 26 Suth. 21. In this case the husband had died, leaving a son. The decision established that sapindas had the same power of authorising an adoption in lieu of a son who died, as they would have had if there had never been a son.

§ 116. It does not seem quite clear, even now, whether their Lordships are of opinion that the motive which operates upon the mind of a widow in making an adoption can be material upon the question of its validity, where she has obtained the necessary amount of assent: that is, whether evidence would be admissible which went to show that the widow was indifferent to the religious benefits supposed to flow from an adoption to her husband, or even disbelieved in the efficacy of such an adoption; and that her real and only object in making an adoption was to enhance her own importance and position, and to prevent the property of her late husband from passing away to distant relations. With the greatest deference to any conclusions to the contrary which may be drawn from the above passages, it seems to me that the Judicial Committee did not mean to lay down that such evidence would be material or admissible. The fair result of all their judgments appears to be, that the assent of one or more sapindas is necessary, as a sort of judicial decision that the act of adoption is a proper one. That decision, like any other, may (perhaps) be impeached, by showing that it was procured by fraud or corruption. But if it was arrived at *bonâ fide* by the proper judges, it is conclusive as to the propriety of the adoption. The judgment of the Court cannot be affected by the motives of the suitor. The reasons which influence the widow may be puerile or even malicious. But what the family decide upon is the propriety of her act, not the propriety of her reasons (*r*).

Discussion as to motive.

§ 117. As might have been anticipated, the ingenuity of Hindu litigants was next directed to invalidating the assent of the *sapindas*. Accordingly an adoption by a widow, with the consent of the managing member, and only adult *sapinda* of an undivided family was set aside on the ground (*inter alia*) that his consent was given from inter-

Is religious motive essential?

(*r*) *Acc. Vithoba* v. *Bapu*, 15 Bom. 134; *Patel Vandravân Jekisan* v. *Manilal*, *ibid.* 565.

ested motives (*s*). But where the assent is fair and *boná fide*, I would submit that it could not be objected to on the ground that it did not arise from religious motives. I have already suggested that even according to Brahmanical views, religious grounds were not the only ones for making an adoption, and that among the dissenting sects of Aryans, and all the non-Aryan races, religious motives had absolutely nothing to do with the matter (*t*). But further, when a religious act comes to be indissolubly connected with civil consequences, it follows that the act may be properly performed, either with a view to the religious or the civil results. Not only so, but that if the act is in fact performed, the civil consequences must follow, whatever be the motive of the actor. Marriage is just as much a duty with a Hindu as adoption. It could not be contended that the validity of a marriage, or any of its legal results, could be in the slightest degree affected by the motives of either of the parties to the transaction. When the Test and Corporation Acts rendered it necessary that a candidate for office should have taken the sacrament, it was not material or permissible to enquire, whether the communicant had spiritual or temporal benefits in view.

Western India.

§ 118. In Western India the widow's power of adoption is even greater than in Southern India. The Mayukha, commenting on the same text of Vasishtha, draws from it, as already remarked (§ 101), exactly the opposite conclusion from that arrived at by Nanda Pandita. The latter

(*s*) *Karunabdhi* v. *Ratnamaiyar*, 7 I. A. 173, 2 Mad. 270 and see *Parasara* v. *Rangaraja*, 2 Mad. 202.

(*t*) See *ante*, § 94, 95. I have already stated (§ 95) that among the Tamil inhabitants of Northern Ceylon even the husband, when desirous to adopt, must obtain the consent of his heirs, and they must evidence their assent by dipping their fingers in the saffron water. If such consent is withheld, the rights of the dissenting parties to the inheritance will not be affected. Thesawaleme, ii. 1, 5, 6. Probably this was the original law in Southern India, though it may have passed away when the Brahmanical view of adoption, as a duty and not merely a right, was introduced. But the necessity for obtaining the consent of sapindas to an adoption by a widow, and the sufficiency of such consent, may be a survival from the old law. If so, it would be an additional reason for supposing that religious motives had nothing to do with the adoption itself, or with the consent given to it by kinsmen. See as to the Nambudri Brahmans, 11 Mad. 188.

infers that a widow can never adopt, as she can never obtain her husband's assent; the former infers that the prohibition can only extend to a married woman, as she only can receive such an assent (*u*). The whole of the authorities are collected and reviewed in several cases in the Bombay High Court, which have established, *First*, that in the Mahratta country and in Gujarat, a widow, who is sole or joint heir to her husband's estate, may adopt a son to her deceased husband, without authority from her husband, and without the consent of his kindred, or of the caste, or of the ruling authority. The qualification is added, borrowed from the dictum of the Privy Council in the *Ramnaad* case, provided "the act is done by her in the proper and *bonâ fide* performance of a religious duty, and neither capriciously nor from a corrupt motive" (*v*). *Secondly*, that she cannot do so, where her husband has expressly forbidden an adoption (*w*). *Thirdly*, that she can never adopt during his lifetime, without his assent (*x*). *Fourthly*, that a widow, who has not the estate vested in her, and whose husband was not separated at the time of his death, is not competent to adopt a son to her husband without his authority, or the consent of his undivided co-parceners (*y*). A further qualification is suggested by the Bombay High Court, *viz.*, that where the adoption by a widow would have the effect of divesting an estate already vested in a third person, the consent of that person must be obtained (*z*). This will be considered subsequently under the head of effects of an adoption (*a*). *Fifthly*, that an adoption made

(*u*) V. May., iv. 5, § 17, 18. Dr. Bühler says that the principal argument advanced by the Mahratta writers for this view is a version of the text of Çaunaka, where they read "a woman who is childless, or whose sons have died" (may adopt), instead of "a man," &c. The error of this reading is shown by the fact that in the subsequent verses (13, 14) the adopter is referred to in the masculine gender. See art. *Çaunaka-Smriti*, Journ. As. Soc. Bengal, 1866.

(*v*) *Rakhmabai* v. *Radhabai*, 5 Bom. H. C. (A. C. J.) 181, acc. *per curiam*; *Bhagvandas* v. *Rajmal*, 10 Bom. H. C. 257. *Ramji* v. *Ghaman*, 6 Bom. 498. *Dinkar Sitaram* v. *Ganesh Shivram*, ib. 505. *Giriowa* v. *Bhimaji Raghunath*, 9 Bom. 58. The *onus* of proving such a corrupt motive lies heavily on him who alleges it. *Patel Vandravan Jekisan* v. *Manilal*, 15 Bom. 565.

(*w*) *Bayabai* v. *Bala Venkatesh*, 7 Bom. H. C. Appx. 1.

(*x*) *Narayan* v. *Nana Manohar*, 7 Bom. H. C. (A. C. J.) 153.

(*y*) *Ramji* v. *Ghaman*; *Dinkar* v. *Ganesh*. *ub. sup.*

(*z*) *Rupchund* v. *Rakhmabai*, 8 Bom. H. C. (A. C. J.) 114.

(*a*) See *post*, § 171, *et seq.*

by a widow, which in other respects is valid is not rendered invalid by the fact that the husband to whom she adopted was a minor (*b*).

Jains.

§ 119. Among the Jains a sonless widow has the same power of adoption as her husband would have had, if he chose to exercise it. Neither his sanction, nor that of any other person is necessary (*c*). The Court said of this class:—"They differ particularly from the Brahmanical Hindus in their conduct towards the dead, omitting all obsequies after the corpse is burnt or buried. They also regard the birth of a son as having no effect on the future state of his progenitor, and consequently adoption is a merely temporal arrangement, and has no spiritual objects (*d*)." In the Punjab the custom appears to vary. In Gurgaon a widow can adopt without any consent, if she selects a son from her husband's agnates. She cannot adopt any one else without the consent of such agnates. In Rohtak and several other districts, the husband's consent is necessary. In three cases, the Punjab Courts set aside adoptions by a widow for *want* of her husband's permission. Two of these cases came from Lahore and Delhi respectively. It does not appear where the third case arose (*e*).

Punjab.

Only parents can give.

§ 120. SECOND, WHO MAY GIVE IN ADOPTION.—As the act of adoption has the effect of removing the adopted son from his natural, into the adoptive, family, and thereby most materially and irrevocably affects his prospects in life, and as the ceremony almost invariably takes place when the adoptee is of tender years, and unable to exercise any discretion of his own in the matter, it follows that only those who have dominion over the child have the power of giving him in adoption. According to Vasishtha (*f*), both parents

(*b*) *Patel Vandravan Jekisan* v. *Manilal*, 15 Bom. 565.

(*c*) *Govindnath Ray* v. *Gulal Chand*, 5 S. D. 276 (322); *Sheo Singh* v. *Mt. Dakho*, 6 N.-W. P. 382; affd., 5 I. A. 87, S. C. 1 All., 688; *Lakmi Chand* v. *Gatto Bai*, 8 All. 319; *Manik Chand* v. *Jagat Settani*, 17 Cal. 518.

(*d*) *Per cur.*, 6 N.-W. P. 392.

(*e*) Punjab Customary Law, II. 154, 178, 205; III. 87, 89, 90.

(*f*) 3 Dig 242.

have power to give a son, but a woman cannot give one without the assent of her lord. Manu says (*g*): "He whom his father or mother (with her husband's assent) gives to another, &c., is considered as a son given." The words in parenthesis are the gloss of Kulluka Bhatta. Different explanations have been given to Vasishtha's text (*h*). Some say that the wife's assent is absolutely necessary; others, that if not given, the adopted son remains the son of his natural mother and performs her obsequies; others, that the words mean that either parent has the power to give, but that the wife can only exercise this power during her husband's life with his assent. The last explanation is the one which is now accepted. It is quite settled that the father alone has absolute authority to dispose of his son in adoption, even without the consent of his wife, though her consent is generally sought and obtained (*i*). The wife cannot give away her son while her husband is alive and capable of consenting, without his consent; but she may do so after his death, or when he is permanently absent, as, for instance, an emigrant, or has entered a religious order, or has lost his reason (*k*), provided the husband was legally competent to give away his son, and has not expressly prohibited his being adopted (*l*). But in a Bengal case the pandits laid it down, and it was held accordingly, that an adoption was bad where a widow had given away her only son as *dvyamushyayana* without the express consent of her late husband (*m*). It does not, however, appear from the report whether the decision went upon the ground that the adopted son was an only son, or upon the ground that he was given away without sufficient authority. The former seems

Assent of wife.

(*g*) Manu, ix. 168.

(*h*) 3 Dig 254, 257, 261; V. May., v.; Steele, 45, 183.

(*i*) Dattaka Mimamsa, iv. 13—17; v. 14, n.; 3 Dig. 244; *Alank Manjari* v. *Fakir Chand*, 5 S. D. 356 (418); *Chitko Raghunath* v. *Janaki*, 11 Bom. H. C. 199; Mitakshara, i. 11, § 9.

(*k*) Dattaka Mimamsa, iv. 10—12; Dattaka Chandrika, i 31, 32; Mitakshara, i. 11, § 9. *Arnachellum* v. *Iyasamy*, 1 Mad., Dec. 154; *Huro Soondree* v. *Chundermoney*, Sevest. 938. *Rangubai* v. *Bhagirthibai*, 2 Bom. 377. *Mhalsabai* v. *Vithoba*, 7 Bom. H. C. Appx. 26.

(*l*) *Narayanasami* v. *Kuppusami*, 11 Mad. 113.

(*m*) *Debee Dial* v. *Hur Hor Singh*, 4 S. D. 320, (407).

rather to have been the case. It has been expressly ruled in Bombay, that whether the giving in adoption of an only son by his father is valid or invalid, it is at all events so improper that a widow, without the direct sanction of her husband, cannot be assumed to have authority to give such a son away (*n*). It was evidently the opinion of the High Court that a widow, in giving her son, exercises not an independent but a delegated authority, and that such an authority will be negatived when it is exercised in a manner which it may be supposed the husband would have disapproved. No other relation but the father or mother can give away a boy. For instance, a brother cannot give away his brother (*o*). Nor can the paternal grandfather, or any other person (*p*). Nor can the parents delegate their authority to another person, for instance a son, so as to enable him after their death to give away his brother in adoption, for the act when done must have parental sanction (*q*). And, therefore, an orphan cannot be adopted, because he can neither give himself away, nor be given by any one with authority to do so (*r*). But what the law declines to sanction is the delegation by an authorised person to an unauthorised person of the discretion to give in adoption which is vested solely in the former. Where the necessary sanction has been given by an authorised person, the physical act of giving away in pursuance of that sanction may be delegated to another (*s*).

Conditions imposed by natural parent.

§ 121. The person who is authorised to give away a boy in adoption may make his consent dependent on the fulfilment of certain conditions and it has been held that where

---

(*n*) *Lakshmappa* v. *Ramappa*, 12 Bom. H. C. 364. *Somasekhara* v. *Subadramaji*, 6 Bom. 524.

(*o*) V. Darp., 825; *Mt. Tara Munee* v. *Dev Narayun*, 3 S. D. 387 (516); *Moottoosamy* v. *Lutchmeedavummah*, Mad. Dec. 1852, p. 97. See F. MacN. 228, combating *Veerapermal* v. *Narain Pillay*, 1 N. C. 91.

(*p*) *Collector of Surat* v. *Dhirsingji*, 10 Bom. H. C. 235.

(*q*) *Bashetiappa* v. *Shivlingappa*, 10 Bom. H. C. 268.

(*r*) *Subbaluvammal* v. *Ammakutti*, 2 M. H. C. 129; *Balvantrav* v. *Bayabai*, 6 Bom. H. C. (O. C. J.) 83; *Supra*. 10 Bom. H. C. 268.

(*s*) *Vijiarangam* v. *Lakshuman*, 8 Bom. H. C. (O. C. J.) 244. *Venkata* v. *Subadra*, 7 Mad. 549.

these conditions are not complied with the adoption is invalid. For instance, where a father by letter authorised the giving of his son in adoption, provided the adopting party first obtained the assent of the British Government, an adoption made without such assent was held invalid, though the assent was not in other respects necessary (*t*).

Consent of Government.

§ 122. The consent of the Revenue Board is necessary to an adoption by a person whose estate is under the actual management of the Court of Wards (*u*). It was once supposed that the consent of Government was also necessary in the case of Inamdars, Zemindars, and feudal chieftains whose estates would fall into the hands of the Government in the event of their dying without heirs, and in the time of Lord Dalhousie this principle was frequently acted on. But it seems clear that, though it was customary in such cases to ask for the sanction of the ruling power, and to pay a nuzzur on receiving it, still the sanction was considered to be due as a matter of right, and was not a condition precedent to the validity of the adoption itself, although in some cases the native power, with a high hand, may have refused to allow the adopted son to succeed (*v*).

Origin of restrictions.

§ 123. THIRD, WHO MAY BE TAKEN IN ADOPTION.—The restrictions upon the selection of a person for adoption appear all to be of Brahmanical origin, and to rest upon the theory, that as the object of adoption was the performance of religious rites to deceased ancestors, the fiction of sonship must be as close as possible (§ 94). Hence, in the first place, the nearest male sapinda should be selected, if suitable in other respects, and if possible a brother's son, as he was already in contemplation of law a son to his uncle.

Nearest sapinda.

(*t*) *Rangubai* v. *Bhagirthibai*, 2 Bom. 377. (*u*) See *ante*, § 100.

(*v*) Steele, 183; *Bhasker Bhachajee* v. *Narro Ragonath*, Bom. Sel. Rep. 24; *Ramchandra* v. *Nanaji*, 7 Bom. H. C. (A. C. J.) 26; *Narhar Govind* v. *Narayan*, 1 Bom. 607; *Rangubai* v. *Bhagirthibai*, 2 Bom. 377; Bell's Empire in India, 127; Bell's Indian Policy, 10; Sir C. Jackson's Vindication of Lord Dalhousie, 9. By Lord Canning's proclamation the right to adopt has now been recognized in the case of feudal chiefs and jaghiredars.

If no such near sapinda was available, then one who was more remote; or in default of any such, then one who was of a family which followed the same spiritual guide, or, in the case of Sudras, any member of the caste (*w*). Probably this rule was strengthened by the feeling that it was unjust to the members of the family to introduce a stranger if a near relative was available. Originally it seems to have been a positive precept. Subsequently it sunk to a mere recommendation. It is now settled that the adoption of a stranger is valid, even though near relatives, otherwise suitable, are in existence (*x*). In the second place, no one can be adopted whose mother the adopted could not have legally married (*y*). The origin and binding character of this rule have been criticised with great learning and force by Mr. V. N. Mandlik (*z*). He admits that "the Dattaka Chandrika, the Dattaka Mimamsa, the Samskara Kaustubha, the Dharma Sindhu and the Dattaka Nirnaya contain this prohibition." These authorities base their opinion, *first*, on the text of Çaunaka, that the adopted boy must bear the reflection of a son, to which they append the gloss "that is the capability to have been begotten by the adopter through *niyoga* and so forth" (*a*). Many objections are offered to this gloss by Mr. V. N. Mandlik, and, as I have already pointed out, (§ 94, note) it is possible that the text itself had originally a different meaning. *Secondly*, they rely upon a text which is attributed variously to Çaunaka, Vriddha Gautama, and Narada, which states that a sister's son and a daughter's son may be

One whose mother could have been married.

(*w*) Dattaka Mimamsa, ii. § 2, 28, 29, 67, 74, 76. 80; Dattaka Chandrika, i. § 10, 20. ii. § 11; Mitakshara, i. 11, § 13, 14, 36; V. May., iv. 5, § 9, 16, 19.

(*x*) 1 W. McN. 68; 2 Stra. H. L. 98, 102; *Gocoolanund* v. *Wooma Daee*, 15 B. L. R. 405, S. C. 23 Suth. 340; affd. *sub nomine*, *Uma Deyi*, v. *Gokoolanund*, 5 I. A. 40, S. C. 3 Cal. 587; *Babaji* v. *Bhagirthibai*, 6 Bom. H. C. (A. C. J.) 70; *Darma Dagu* v. *Ramkrishna*, 10 Bom. 80. These authorities must be taken as overruling the case of *Ooman Dut* v. *Kunhia Singh*, 3 S. D. 144 (192), which was also a *Kritrima* adoption.

(*y*) Dattaka Mimamsa, v. § 20.

(*z*) Pages, 478—495, 514. The rule itself was reaffirmed by the High Court of Madras after a full examination of Mr. Mandlik's argument. *Minakshi* v. *Ramanada*, 11 Mad. 49.

(*a*) D'Mimamsa, v. § 15—17. Dattaka Chandrika, ii. § 7, 8. I am unable to refer to the other authorities, but Mr. V. N. Mandlik says that they rely upon the same texts, p. 489.

adopted by Sudras, but not by members of the three higher classes, and upon a text of Çakala which explicitly forbids the adoption by one of the regenerate classes of "a daughter's son, a sister's son, and the son of the mother's sister" (*b*). As to the former text Mr. Mandlik argues that the correct translation is "Sudras should adopt a daughter's son, or a sister's son. A sister's son is in some places not adopted as a son among the three classes beginning with a Brahmana." He points out that the Mayukha as properly rendered interprets the text as meaning that Sudras should adopt only, or primarily, a daughter's or a sister's son, but not as forbidding such adoptions by Brahmans. This view is also supported by the Dvaita Nirnaya, and the Nirnaya Sindhu (*c*). The text of Çakala he disposes of (p. 495) by treating its authority as of no weight in opposition to usage and conflicting authorities. The fact still remains, however, that the five digests above referred to lay down the rule in distinct and positive terms. The rule so laid down was stated by Mr. Sutherland, both the MacNaghtens, and both the Stranges (*d*); and, as limited to the three regenerate classes, it has been affirmed by a singularly strong series of authorities in all parts of India as forbidding the adoption of the son of a daughter, or of a sister, or of an aunt (*e*). On the same ground, it is unlawful to adopt a brother, or stepbrother, or an uncle, whether paternal or maternal (*f*). And it makes no difference that the adopter has himself been removed from his natural family by adoption; for adoption does not remove

---

(*b*) Dattaka Mimamsa, ii. § 32, 74, 107. Dattaka Chandrika, i. § 17, 7.
(*c*) V. May., iv. 5, § 9, 10, V. N. Mandlik, pp. 53—56.
(*d*) Suth. Syn. 664, F. MacN. 150, 1 W. MacN. 67, 1 Stra. H. L. 83, S. M. § 84.
(*e*) *Baee Gunga* v. *Baee Sheokoovur*, Bom. Sel. Rep. 73; *Narasammal* v. *Balarama Charlu*, 1 M. H. C. 420; *Jivani* v. *Jivu*, 2 M. H. C. 462; *Gopalayyan* v. *Raghupatiayyan*, 7 M. H. C. 250; *Ramalinga* v. *Sadasiva*, 9 M. I. A. 506, S. C. 1 Suth. (P. C.) 25, where the side-note calls the parties Vaisyas, though they were really Sudras. See *Supra*. 2 M. H. C. 467; *Kora Shunko* v. *Bebee Munnee*, 2 M. Dig. 32; *Gopal Narhar* v. *Hanmant*, 3 Bom. 273, where all the authorities are examined; *Bhagirthibai* v. *Radhabai*, 3 Bom. 298. *Parbati* v. *Sundar*, 8 All. 1; affd. 16 I. A., 186, S. C. 12 All. 51.
(*f*) Dattaka Mimamsa, v. § 17; *Runjeet Singh* v. *Obhya*, 2 S. D. 245 (315) *Moottoosamy* v. *Lutchmedavummah*, Mad. Dec. of 1852, 96. *Sriramulu* v. *Ramaiyya*, 3 Mad. 15.

the bar of consanguinity which would operate to prevent intermarriage within the prohibited degrees (*g*). This rule must, of course, be understood as excluding only the sons of women whose original relationship to the adopter was such as to render them unfit to be his wives. A man could not lawfully marry his brother's, or nephew's, wife, but a brother's son is the most proper person to be adopted, and so is a grandnephew (*h*). A wife's brother, or his son, may be adopted (*i*), and so may the son of a wife's sister (*k*) or of a maternal aunt's daughter (*l*).

Rules not universal.

§ 124. This rule again appears to be of Brahmanical origin. The same authorities which lay it down as regards the higher classes state that Sudras (*m*), may adopt a daughter's, or a sister's, son. The Mayukha even states that as regards them such a person is the most proper to be adopted (*n*). He is obviously the most natural person to be selected. A mother's sister's son may also be adopted among Sudras (*o*). In the Punjab such adoptions are common among the Jats, and this laxity has spread even to Brahmans, and to the orthodox Hindu inhabitants of towns, such as Delhi (*p*). They are also permitted among the Jains (*q*), and in Southern India even among the Brahmans such adoptions are undoubtedly very common. It was decided so late as 1873 that the practice had not attained the force of a legal custom (*r*). But in 1881, upon a renewed enquiry, the High Court pronounced that in Southern India

---

(*g*) *Moothia* v. *Uppen*, Mad. Dec. of 1858, 117.

(*h*) *Morun Moee* v. *Bejoy*, Suth. Sp. No. 122.

(*i*) *Kristniengar* v. *Vanamamalay*, Mad. Dec. of 1856, 213; *Runganaigum* v. *Namesevoya*, Mad. Dec. of 1857, 94; *Ruree Bhudr* v. *Roopshunker*, 2 Bor. 662 [713]; *Sriramulu* v. *Ramayya*, 3 Mad. 15.

(*k*) *Baee Gunga* v. *Baee Sheokoovur*, Bom. Sel. Rep. 73, 76.

(*l*) *Venkata* v. *Subhadra*, 7 Mad. 549.

(*m*) The Kayasthas in Bengal are Sudras, and may make such adoptions. *Rajcoomar Lall* v. *Bissessur Dyal*, 10 Cal. 688.

(*n*) V. May., iv. 5, § 10, 11.

(*o*) *Chinna Nagayya* v. *Pedda Nagayya*, 1 Mad. 62.

(*p*) Punjab Cust. 79—83. Punjab Customary Law, II. 111, 154, 205, 210.

(*q*) *Sheo Singh* v. *Mt. Dakho*, 6 N.-W. P. 382, *affd.* 5 I. A. 87, S. C. 1 All. 688; *Hassan Ali* v. *Nagamal*, 1 All. 288; *Lakhmi Chand* v. *Datto Bai*, 8 All. 319.

(*r*) *Gopalyyan* v. *Raghupatiayyan*, 7 M. H. C. 250; 2 Stra. H. L. 101; 1 Gibelin, 89, Nelson's view of the Hindu Law, 90.

such adoptions were valid among Brahmans. A similar practice among the Nambudri Brahmans of Malabar has also received judicial sanction (*s*). In Western India also they appear to be permitted. It is also said that in the Deccan a younger brother may be adopted, and though the adoption of uncles is forbidden, a different reason is alleged for the prohibition (*t*).

Extension of rule to son of wife's brother.

§ 125. A singular extension has been given to this rule by Nanda Pandita. He quotes a text of Vriddha Gautama:—"In the three superior tribes a sister's son is nowhere mentioned as a son,"—and says that here a sister's son is inclusive of a brother's son. But as the brother's son is not only not prohibited, but is expressly enjoined, for adoption, he draws the remarkable conclusion that a brother's son must not be adopted by a sister. And this opinion was acted upon in the N.-W. Provinces, where the Court set aside an adoption by a widow, acting under her husband's authority, where she had selected the son of her own brother (*u*). If the adoption had been made by her husband, and not by herself, it would have been perfectly valid (*v*). The same principle seems to have been the ground of a case which is reported, and discussed at much length, by Sir F. MacNaghten (*w*). There a man died leaving three widows, and an authority to them to adopt. As they could not agree, a reference was made to the Master, who reported in favour of a boy who was the son of the second widow's uncle. The next question that arose was, whether the boy could be received in adoption by the second widow. It was argued that this was impossible, because she could not without incest have been the mother of a boy by her own uncle. The pandits differed, and no decision

(*s*) *Vayidinada* v. *Appu*, 9 Mad. 44; *Vishnu* v. *Krishnan*, 7 Mad. 3; *per curiam*, 11 Mad. 55.
(*t*) Steele, 44; *Huebut Rao* v. *Govindrao*, 2 Bor. 85, V. N. Mandlik, 474, 495, W. & B. 887.
(*u*) Dattaka Mimamsa, ii. § 33, 34; *Mt. Battas* v. *Lachman Singh*, 7 N.-W. P. 117.
(*v*) See authorities quoted § 123, notes (*h*) (*i*).
(*w*) *Dagumbaree* v. *Taramonee*, F. MacN. 170, App. 10.

was ever given, the second widow having waived her right in favour of the elder. Sir F. MacNaghten, however, pronounces unhesitatingly in favour of the objection. It seems to me, however, with the greatest respect, that this is introducing into the Hindu theory of adoption a second fiction for which there is no foundation. The real fiction is, that the adopting father had begotten the child upon its natural mother; therefore it is necessary that she should be a person who might lawfully have been his wife. There is no fiction that the natural father had also begotten the child upon the adopting mother. The natural son becomes the son, not merely of the particular wife from whom he is born, but of all the wives; and the authors of the Dattaka Mimamsa and Dattaka Chandrika seem to think that the same result follows in the case of several wives from an adoption (*x*). The fiction can hardly extend to the length of his being conceived by all. In fact it would appear that the Hindu law takes no notice of the wife in reference to adoption. The relation of the adopted son to her arises upon adoption. But the balance of authority and reasoning appears to be opposed to the idea that relationship to her has any effect upon the choice of the boy to be adopted (*y*).

Identity of caste.

§ 126. The adopted son must be of the same class as his adopting father; that is, a Brahman may not adopt a Kshatriya, or *vice versâ*. This rule is probably an innovation upon ancient usage, as Medhatithi and others interpret the words of Manu "being alike" (translated by Sir W. Jones "being of the same class") as meaning merely, possessing suitable qualities, though of a different class (*z*). In the time of Manu a man might have married wives of different class, and the sons of all such wives would have been legitimate, and would have inherited together, though

---

(*x*) Manu, ix. § 183; Dattaka Mimamsa, ii. § 69; Dattaka Chandrika, i. § 28. And so the pandits stated in this case, F. MacN. App. 11.

(*y*) This view was approved by the Madras High Court. *Sriramulu* v. *Ramayya*, 3 Mad. p. 17.

(*z*) Manu, ix. § 168; Mitakshara, i. 11, § 9; V. May., v. 5, § 4; Dattaka Mimamsa, ii. § 23—25; Dattaka Chandrika, i § 12—16.

in different proportions (*a*). Each of such sons must have been competent to perform his father's obsequies, though perhaps with varying merit. It would have been remarkable, therefore, if a man could not have adopted the son of a woman whom he might have married. Baudhayana makes no reference to caste, and Vasishtha merely says, "the class ought to be known" (§ 96), which is natural enough, as determining a preference. The other authors (Katyayana, Çaunaka, Yajnavalkya, and Yaska) who forbid the adoption of one of unequal class, admit that such adoptions do take place, and are effectual as prolonging the line, though not for purposes of oblations. They, therefore, declare that a son so adopted is entitled to receive maintenance (*b*). From this, I presume, they considered that he was effectually severed from his natural family. It is probable, therefore, that as long as mixed marriages were lawful, the adoption of sons of inferior caste was also lawful (*c*). When the former ceased, the latter also ceased. At present, I imagine that the adoption of a Kshatriya by a Brahman would be a mere nullity, and would neither take the boy out of his natural family, nor give him any claim upon the family of the adopter. The case has never occurred, and is quite certain never to occur.

§ 127. As the chief reason for adoption is the performance of funeral ceremonies, it follows that one who, from any personal disqualification would be incapable of performing them, would be an unfit person to be adopted (*d*). Nothing is said upon the point by Hindu law writers. Probably the idea that such an adoption could be made would never have occurred to their minds. As a person so adopted would also be incapable of succeeding to the property of the adopter,

Personal disqualification.

(*a*) Manu, ix. § 148—156.
(*b*) See too D. K. S. vii. § 23, 24, citing Narada.
(*c*) In Northern Ceylon this is the case still. The son, if adopted by a man, passes into his caste. If adopted by a woman, he remains in the caste of his natural father. Thesawaleme, ii. § 7.
(*d*) Suth. Syn. 665; V. Darp. 828, 830.

and so continuing his name and lineage, every object would fail which an adoption is intended to serve.

Limitation from age.

§ 128. A further limitation upon the selection of a son for adoption arises from age, and the previous performance of ceremonies in the natural family (*e*). The leading authority upon this point is a passage from the Kalika-purana, which is relied on by Nanda Pandita, but which is treated as spurious by the author of the Dattaka Chandrika, Nilakanta, and others, and which is admittedly wanting in many copies of that work. It lays down absolutely that a child must not be adopted whose age exceeds five years, or upon whom the ceremony of tonsure has been performed in the natural family (*f*). The result of a lengthened commentary on this passage in the Dattaka Mimamsa appears to be; *first*, that the limit of age as not exceeding five is absolute: *secondly*, that one who has had the tonsure performed ought not to be adopted, as he will at the outside be the son of two fathers: but, *thirdly*, that if no other is procurable, a boy on whom tonsure has been performed may be received. In that case, however, the previous rites must be annulled by the performance of the *putreshti*, or sacrifice for male issue. As regards other rites, those previous to tonsure are immaterial, the performance of the *upanayana* is an absolute bar (*g*).

Dattaka Mimamsa.

Jagannatha.

Jagannatha appears to accept the text as literally binding, and not to recognize the right of performing the tonsure over again. He, therefore, considers an adoption to

---

(*e*) As to the eight ceremonies for a male, see Colebrooke, note to Dattaka Mimamsa, iv. § 23; 3 Dig. 104. Of these, tonsure is the fifth, and *upanayana*, or investiture with the sacred thread, is the eighth. The former is performed in the second or third year after birth, the latter, in the case of Brahmans, in the eighth year from conception. But it may be performed so early as the fifth, or delayed till the sixteenth year. The primary periods for *upanayana* in the case of a Kshatriya are eleven, and of a Vaisya twelve years, but it may be delayed till the ages of twenty-two and twenty-four respectively. For Sudras there is no ceremony but marriage.

(*f*) Dattaka Mimamsa, iv. § 22; Dattaka Chandrika, ii. § 25; V. May, iv. 5. § 20; Mitakshara, i. 11, § 13, note. Jolly, § 161.

(*g*) Dattaka Mimamsa, 30—56; 1 W. MacN. 72. Mr. Sutherland's gloss upon Dattaka Mimamsa § 53 that the words 'a boy five years old' means under

be invalid, if it is made after tonsure, or after the fifth year (*h*).

Dattaka Chandrika.

On the other hand, the author of the Dattaka Chandrika refuses to accept the text of the Kalika-purana as authentic. But even if it should be genuine, he explains it away by the possibility of performing tonsure a second time in the adoptive family. The result he arrives at is, that age is only material as determining the term at which *upanayana* may be performed. So long as this rite in the case of the three higher classes, and marriage in the case of Sudras, can be performed in the family of the adopter, there is no limit of any particular time (*i*).

Mr. W. MacNaghten is of opinion that the rules laid down by the Dattaka Mimamsa and the Dattaka Chandrika should be followed in the Provinces in which they are respectively in force; that is, the Dattaka Mimamsa in Benares, and the Dattaka Chandrika in Bengal and Southern India (*k*). From what has been already stated (§ 30) as to the authorship of the Dattaka Chandrika there seems to be no reason for ascribing to it any special authority in Southern India. The authority of the Dattaka Mimamsa in Benares appears to be equally open to doubt.

Benares law.

§ 129. The only decisions upon this point under Benares law have been given in the Courts of the North-West Provinces. The first of these was in 1868 (*l*), when it was held that under the Dattaka Mimamsa an adoption was valid so long as the boy was below six years. Here the Court accepted the authority of the Dattaka Mimamsa, and of the Kalika-purana on which the rule is based, but fell into a mistake as to the meaning of the rule, in conse-

---

six is a mistake. It means one who has not passed his fifth birth-day. *Per Mahmood*, J., *Ganga Sahai* v. *Lekhraj Singh*, 9 All. 310.

(*h*) 3 Dig. 148, 249—251, 263. See too F. MacN. 139—146, 194.

(*i*) Dattaka Chandrika, ii. § 20—33; 1 W. MacN. 72.

(*k*) 1 W. MacN. 73.

(*l*) *Thakoor Oomrao Singh* v. *Thakooranee Mehtab Koonwer*, N.-W. P., H. C. Rep. 1868, 103*a*. See *per Mahmood*, J., 9 All., p. 312.

quence of the gloss put upon it by Sutherland Mr. (§ 128 *n*). The question arose again in 1886, and was examined in the most elaborate manner by Mr. Justice Mahmood (*m*). The conclusions he arrived at are stated as follows: "I hold that the passage of the Kalika-purana upon which the limitation of five years for adoption is entirely founded, is not proved to be authentic; that even if it be taken to be authentic, the interpretation adopted by Nanda Pandita in his Dattaka Mimamsa is not shown to be universally applicable; that the interpretation may be restricted only to Brahmans intended for priesthood; that this interpretation would bring the Dattaka Mimamsa in accord with the Dattaka Chandrika; that various other plausible interpretations of the passage have been adopted by other authorities; that such authorities may be referred to for the purposes of this question; and that the matter being so dealt with by those authorities, it would be unsafe to set aside the plaintiff's adoption upon the solitary ground that he was older than five years at that time." He then proceeded to express his opinion that, as regards the twice-born classes, age was only material as determining the time at which the *upanayana* may be performed, and that its performance was the ultimate limit for a valid adoption. As regards Sudras adoption could be performed effectually till marriage.

Bengal.

§ 129A. In Bengal and Southern India the decisions are in favour of the view laid down by the Dattaka Chandrika. In some of the earlier Bengal cases, the pandits, while agreeing that the age of five years was not an absolute limit which could not be exceeded, seem to have thought that if tonsure had already been performed in the natural family, and in the name of the natural father, a subsequent adoption would be invalid (*n*). In 1838, however, the Sudder Court Pandit, in reply to a question as to age,

(*m*) *Ganga Sahai* v. *Lekhraj Singh*, 9 All. 253, pp. 316—324, 327, 328.

(*n*) *Kerutnaraen* v. *Mt. Bhobinesree*, 1 S. D. 161 (218) (as to the remark appended to this decision, see 1 W. MacN. 75); 2 W. MacN. 180; *Mt. Dullabh* v. *Manu*, S. D. 50 (61).

answered "that the period fixed for adoption with respect to the three superior tribes, Brahmans, Kshatriyas, and Vaisyas, was prior to their investiture with their respective cords; and with respect to Sudras, prior to their contracting marriage" (*o*). This opinion has been affirmed in several subsequent cases, and may now be treated as beyond doubt (*p*). The same rule has been repeatedly laid down in Madras, both by the Pandits and the Court (*q*). It is also suggested by Mr. Ellis, that even after *upanayana* an adoption would be valid, if the person adopted was of the same *gotra* as his adopter. He bases this view on the ground, that where the *gotra* is different, the *upanayana* is a bar, since by it the person is definitely settled in his natural family, and this renders the performance of the *datta homam* (§ 141) impossible. But where the *gotra* is the same, the performance of the *datta homam*, though proper, is not necessary for an adoption. And this view was adopted by the Travancore Court in a case between Brahmans. There the *upanayana* had been performed previous to adoption. But the Court held the objection to be immaterial, since the person adopted was the son of the adopter's brother (*r*). This ruling was followed by the High Court of Madras after a very full investigation of the authorities, and upon evidence of local usage (*s*). The usage in Pondicherry admits of adoption after the *upanayana* in any case (*t*). **Madras.**

§ 130. This restriction again does not exist where the Brahmanical fiction of an altered paternity is unknown. **Limit of age not universal.**

(*o*) *Bullabakant* v. *Kishenprea*, 6 S. D. 219 (270).

(*p*) *Nitradayee* v. *Bholanath*, S. D. of 1853. 553; *Ramkishore* v. *Bhoobun*, S. D. of 1859, 229, 236; affirmed on review, S. D. of 1860, i. 485, 490; reversed on a different point in the P. C. *Sub Nomine Bhoobun Moyee* v. *Ramkishore*, where, however, the ruling as to the validity of the adoption on the ground of age was not disputed. 10 M. I. A. 279; S. C. 3 Suth. (P. C.) 15.

(*q*) 1 Stra. H. L. 87, 91; 2 Stra. H. L. 87, 110; *Mootoo Vizia Raghoonadha Satooputty, alias Annasamy* v. *Sevagamy Nachiar*, 1 Mad. Dec. 106; affirmed by P. C. on the 28th April 1828, *Chetty Colum Prusunna* v. *Chetty Colum Moodoo*, 1 Mad. Dec. 406; *Sreenevassien* v. *Sashyummal*, Mad. Dec of 1859, 118; *Veerapermall* v. *Narrain Pillay*, 1 N. C. 133; *Vythilinga* v. *Vyiathammal*, 6 Mad. 43. *Pichuvayyan* v. *Subbayyan*, 13 Mad. 128.

(*r*) 2 Stra. H. L. 104; *Ramaswami Iyen* v. *Bhagati Ammal*, 8 Mad. Jur. 58.

(*s*) *Viraragava* v. *Ramalinga*, 9 Mad. 148, overruling *Venkatasaiya* v. *Venkata Charlu*, 3 Mad. H. C. 28.

(*t*) 1 Gibelin, 94.

In the Punjab there is no restriction of age (*u*). Among the Jains the period extends to 32, and it is said by *Holloway*, J., that there is no limit of age (*v*). So in Western India, the author of the Mayukha says, "And my father has said that a married man, who has even had a son born, may become an adopted son" (*w*). In accordance with this *dictum* the pandits of the Surat Sudder Court reported that "the rule that a boy should be adopted under five years related to cases where no relationship exists; but when a relation is to be adopted, no obstacle exists on account of his being of mature age, married and having a family, provided he possesses common ability, and is beloved by the person who adopts him" (*x*). So Mr. Steele states, "the Poona Shastries do not recognize the necessity that adoption should precede *moonj* and marriage." And he gives various statements as to the proper age for adoption ranging from five to fifty, and ending, "there is no limit as to age. The adoptee should not be older than the adopter" (*y*). None of these authorities make any distinction as to the caste of the person adopted. In the Surat case the parties appear to have been Brahmans, or at least Kshatriyas. In some of the cases in which the adoption of a married man has been held valid by the Bombay High Court, the parties happened to be Sudras, but the decision did not turn upon that circumstance (*z*). It has been settled by recent cases, after some doubt, that a married Brahman may be lawfully adopted, and that it makes no difference as to the legality of the transaction whether he belongs to a different or to the same *gotra* as the adopter (*a*).

(*u*) Punjab Cust., 82.

(*v*) *Rithcurn* v. *Soojun*, 9 Mad. Jur. 21, cited in *Sheo Singh* v. *Mt. Dakho*, 6 N.-W. P. 402; *Govindnath* v. *Gulalchund*, 5 S. D. 276 (322).

(*w*) V. May., iv. 5, § 19. His father was Shanker Bhatt, author of the Dvait Nirnaya, a work of special authority in the Deccan. *Nathaji* v. *Hari*, 8 Bom. H. C. (A. C. J.) 70.

(*x*) *Brijbhookunjee* v. *Gokoolootsaojee*, 1 Bor. 195 [217].

(*y*) Steele, 44, 182; V. N. Mandlik, 471; 1 W. MacN. 75 This was also the case in Rome.

(*z*) *Rajo Nimbalkar* v. *Jayavantrav*, 4 Bom. H. C. (A. C. J.) 191; *Nathaji* v. *Hari*, 8 Bom. H. C. (A. C. J.) 67.

(*a*) *Sadashiv* v. *Hari Moneshvar*, 11 Bom. H. C. 190; *Lakshmappa* v. *Ramappa*, 12 Bom. H. C. 364; *Dharma Dagu* v. *Ramkrishna*, 10 Bom. 80. Among the Nambudri Brahmans, (§ 42) the power to adopt a married man appears only to exist when the adoption is of the *Kritrima* form, 11 Mad. p. 176.

§ 131. The prohibition against adopting an only son rests on the texts of Vasishtha, Baudhayana and Çaunaka, (§ 96). "Let no man give or accept an only son, since he must remain for the obsequies of his ancestor" (*b*). So Çaunaka says, "By no man having an only son is the gift of a son to be ever made." From these Nanda Pandita infers a prohibition against accepting also, and says that the offence of extinction of lineage, denounced by Vasishtha, is incurred by both giver and receiver (*c*). This prohibition is by some authorities extended to the adoption of an eldest son, since his merits are specially appropriated in the interests of his own father (*d*). And even to the adoption of one of two sons, since such an act would leave the father with an only son, and thereby subject him to the chance of being left wholly without issue. But this final precept is admittedly only dissuasive, and not peremptory (*e*). And the same decision has lately been given as regards the adoption of an eldest son (*f*). The value to be placed upon these texts according to Hindu rules of interpretation is discussed at length by Mr. V.N. Mandlik. His view is that they are recommendatory only, and not prohibitory, and that a violation of them affects the offender, but does not detract from the validity of the rite (*g*).

Only son.

Eldest son.

§ 132. It seems to be admitted everywhere that there is no objection to the adoption of an only son, when he is taken as *dwyamushyayana*, or the son of two fathers; either by an express agreement that his relationship to his natural family shall continue (*h*), or by the fact that the only son of one

Son of two fathers.

(*b*) So in Rome, the only male of his *gens* could not be adopted, for the *sacra* would in such a case be lost.

(*c*) Dattaka Mimamsa, iv. § 1—6; Dattaka Chandrika, i. § 27, 28; Mitakshara, i. 11, § 11; V. May., iv. 5, § 9, 16; V. N. Mandlik, 502.

(*d*) Mitakshara, i. 11, § 12, citing Manu, ix. § 106; Viramit. ii. 2, § 8; Sarasvati Vilasa, § 368, 369; 2 Stra. H. L. 105; 2 W. MacN., 182; V. May., iv. 5, § 4; *Permaul Naicken* v. *Pottee Ammal*, Mad. Dec. of 1851, 234.

(*e*) Dattaka Mimamsa, iv. § 8; 1 Stra. H. L. 85; 1 W. MacN. 77.

(*f*) *Janokee* v. *Gopaul*, 2 Cal. 365; *Kashibai* v. *Tatia*, 7 Bom. 221; *Jamnabai* v. *Raichand*, ib. 225.

(*g*) V. N. Mandlik, 496—508 where he gives instances of the adoption of only sons from the Vedic ages downwards.

(*h*) 2 W. MacN. 192; 1 Stra. H. L. 86; *futwahs*, 2 Kn. 206; *Shumshere* v. *Dilraj*, 2 S. D. 189 (216); *Joymonee* v. *Sibosoondry*, Fulton, 75.

brother is taken in adoption by another brother, in which case the double relationship appears to be established without any special contract (*i*). But whether in other cases the adoption of an only son is absolutely invalid, or is only sinful, is a point on which a great conflict of opinion exists. In Southern India, the balance of authority is in favour of the validity of the adoption. In Bengal the decisions are almost unanimously opposed to its validity. In Western India there is a conflict of decisions, which appear to have finally settled that such adoptions are invalid. In all the Provinces reliance is placed on the same texts, and no special usage appears to be set up as qualifying them. Whether there is any difference between the law in the different parts of India, is a matter which can now only be settled by a decision of the Privy Council. It will be sufficient for me to furnish the materials on which a decision may be given.

Decisions in Madras.

§ 133. The question came before Sir Thomas Strange, as Recorder of Madras in 1801, in the case of *Veerapermall* v. *Narrain Pillay* (*k*), where the objection was taken to an adoption that the boy was an only son. There was in fact nothing in the objection, for he was the only son by a younger wife, and had an elder brother by another wife living at the time. The Recorder, after citing the text of Vasishtha, and the opinion of Jagannatha (*l*) that such an adoption if made would be valid, proceeded :—

"The opinion of the present pandits of Bengal is, 'that a person who has only one son should not give him away; nor should he give away an elder son: the adoption of an only son indeed is valid, but both giver and receiver are

---

(*i*) Dattaka Mimamsa, ii. 37, 38, vi. § 34—36, 47, 48; Dattaka Chandrika, i. § 27, 28, iii. § 17, v. § 33; 1 Stra. H. L. 86; 2 Stra. H. L. 107; Steele, 45, 183; Sarvadhikari, 535. *Permaul Naicken* v. *Pottee Ammal*, Mad. Dec. of 1851, 234; *per curiam*, *Gocoolanund* v. *Wooma Daee*, 15 B. L. R. 415, S. C. 23 Suth. 340; *Nilmadhub* v. *Bishumber*, 13 M. I. A. 101, S. C. 12 Suth. (P. C.) 29; *Chinna Gaundan* v. *Kumara*, 1 Mad. H. C. 57; *Uma Deyi* v. *Gokoolanund*, 5 I. A. 42, S. C. 3 Cal. 587. V. May., iv. 5, § 21, 22.

(*k*) 1 N. C. 91, 125. (*l*) 3 Dig. 243.

blameable.' This appears to have been settled in the instance of the Rajah of Tanjore. In that important case the person adopted was the only son of his parents; and it is a mistake if any one imagines that the deviation from the rule on that occasion was supported upon any ground of Mahratta custom or policy. The objection appears to have undergone deep consideration, conducted in part through the fortunate medium of Sir W. M. Jones; and certainly in a way to evince the anxiety of Government to be rightly advised. It appears that the pandits of Bengal and Benares in general were of opinion that 'in all countries the affiliation of an only son is valid, although the parent who gives the child, and the adopter, both incur sin by deviating from the ordinances of the *Shaster*, which declare the giving or taking of an only son in adoption to be improper.' Ramavana indeed, and the other pandits who sign with him, state 'that an only son could not be given to the Rajah to adopt as his son.' But it appears that they rather mean that the act could not be done consistently with the ordinances of the *Shaster*, than that the adoption was invalid, for they expressly state that 'several usages had been adopted and followed, that are not found in the *Shaster*, and are to be looked upon as valid.' This exposition was considered at the time as reconciling their opinion with that of Kasheenauth and the other Benares pandits, who stated 'that the adoption of an only son is one of those acts which is tolerated by usage, although it incurs guilt according to the *Shaster*.' These testimonies corroborating the opinions of the Tanjore pandits, transmitted by the widow of the Rajah Tulsajee, and those received through the Government of Fort St. George, decided the Supreme Government that the objection that Serfojee was an only son was not sufficiently founded to invalidate his adoption and succession."

Only son may be adopted.

§ 134. In his second volume Sir Thomas Strange gives the opinions of pandits declaring that neither an only, nor an elder, son can be adopted. These are accompanied by

European opinions.

remarks of Mr. Colebrooke, who says that a valid adoption of an only son cannot be made, except in the case of a brother's son, who performs the offices of a son to both natural and adoptive father, the absolute gift being forbidden; and of Mr. Ellis, who says that if the act be duly completed it cannot be reversed (*m*). In the text he reiterates the opinion, already expressed from the Bench, that the prohibitions respecting an eldest and only son are only directory, and an adoption of either, however blameable in the giver, would nevertheless for every legal purpose be good (*n*).

Pandits.

§ 135. In a Madras case in 1817 the question was whether a man was bound to adopt the son of his elder brother, being an only son, in preference to the son of his uncle. The pandits answered: "It is not lawful for a man to give his only son in adoption to another. It is not lawful for a man to receive in adoption the only son of another, therefore it is not lawful, and consequently not incumbent, on a man to adopt the only son of his elder brother in preference to the youngest son of his uncle. But if such an adoption as aforesaid should take place, although the giver and receiver in adoption have thereby committed sin, the adoption is valid" (*o*). Here the pandits seem to have overlooked the distinction between the only son of a brother and of a stranger. In other respects they agree with Sir T. Strange.

Madras decisions.

Eldest son.

In 1851 a case came before the Sudr Udalut in which an uncle had adopted the eldest son of his brother. The pandits, after having referred to an opinion they had given in 1848 declaring the adoption of an eldest son to be invalid, repeated their opinion that as a general rule it would be so, but not in this case where the person adopted

(*m*) 2 Stra. H. L. 87, 106, 107. Proceedings of the Sudr Udalut of Madras to the same effect appear to have been passed in 1824 and 1825. See Stra. Man. § 99.

(*n*) 1 Stra. H. L. 87.

(*o*) *Arnachellum* v. *Iyasamy*, 1 Mad. Dec. 154.

was a brother's son. The Court, citing this opinion and also the opinion of Sir Thomas Strange, say, "In the present instance the adoption was by a paternal uncle, and having thus taken place, though a thing to have been avoided, it must be held to be valid." (*p*).

In 1854 the same question as to an eldest son arose, but in this case without the circumstance of his being a brother's son. The Sudder Pandits again pronounced the adoption invalid, and on the strength of their opinion the Civil Judge rejected his claim. The Sudder Court reversed the decision, solely on the ground that the adoption had been made good by acquiescence and lapse of time. They did not notice the finding as to invalidity in law (*q*).

The case came on for a direct decision in the Madras High Court in 1862, and it was decided, on a review of the previous cases, that the adoption of an only son was valid (*r*). A similar conclusion has lately been arrived at by the majority of the Judges of the High Court of Allahabad, *Turner*, J., dissenting (*s*). Allahabad.

§ 136. In Bombay there is a conflict of authority. It is stated by Mr. Steele that an only son should not be given in adoption, except to his uncle, or with the concurrence of both parties, by which I suppose he means as a *dwyamushyayana* (*t*). But in a case where a man who had only two sons gave them both away in adoption, the pandits said the adoptions were valid, as the sin lies with the giver, and not with the receiver (*u*). And in 1862 and 1867 the High Court expressly decided that the adoption of an only son was valid, if accomplished, though improper (*v*). On Bombay.

(*p*) *Permaul Naicken* v. *Pottee Ammall*, Mad. Dec. of 1851, p. 234.
(*q*) *Chocummal* v. *Surathy*, Mad. Dec. of 1854, p. 31.
(*r*) *Chinna Gaundan* v. *Kumara*, 1 Mad. H. C. 54. Followed in *Narayanasami* v. *Kuppusami*, 11 Mad. 43.
(*s*) *Hanuman* v. *Chirai*, 2 All. 164, (F. B.) Doubted by *Straight* and *Mahmood*, JJ., 12 All. 331—337.
(*t*) Steele. 45, 183. (*u*) *Huebut Rao* v. *Govindrao*, 2 Bor. 75, 86 [83].
(*v*) *Mhalsabai* v. *Vithoba*, 7 Bom. H. C. Appx. 26; *Raje Nimbalkar* v. *Jayavantrav*, 4 Bom. H. C. (A. C. J.) 191.

the other hand, in a later case the High Court spoke of "the general rule of Hindu law that an only son cannot be the subject of adoption, a rule recently re-affirmed and illustrated by a judgment of the Calcutta High Court" (*w*). The remark, of course, was merely *obiter dictum*. In 1877 the objection that the boy adopted was an only son was taken in the High Court, but abandoned as untenable (*x*). In 1875, a question arose whether the giving by a widow of an only son in adoption was valid or invalid. The only question necessary to be decided was, whether the authority of the deceased husband could be presumed. For this purpose it was necessary to consider the propriety of the act. The whole law, and all the precedents upon the point were minutely examined by *Westropp*, C. J. The only point actually decided was, that the giving or receiving of an only son was so improper that the consent of the husband could not be presumed. The Chief Justice, however, expressed himself most unfavourably to the validity of such an adoption, though he admitted that such cases had been recognised as legal under the old Sudder Court. This ruling was followed in an exactly similar case in 1882 (*y*). In 1883, the validity of the adoption of an eldest son was in question. The High Court, while holding that the prohibition against such an adoption was only admonitory, contrasted it with the prohibition against the adoption of an only son, which it treated as unqualified and absolute. This again was only *obiter dictum* (*z*). The opinion of the authors of West and Bühler's Digest is that such adoptions are invalid in Bombay. In addition to the above authorities they refer to two unreported cases, in one of which the adoption of an only son in the Linghait caste was held to be invalid, while in the other the general principle seems to have been laid down that such adoptions could only be valid by virtue of a special custom (*a*). Finally in

(*w*) *Bhasker Trimbak* v. *Mahadev Ramji*, 6 Bom. H. C. (O. C. J.) 4.

(*x*) *Rangubai* v. *Bhaghirthibai*, 2 Bom. at p. 379.

(*y*) *Lakshmappa* v. *Ramappa*, 12 Bom. H. C. 364; *Somasekhara* v. *Subhadramaji*, 6 Bom. 524.

(*z*) *Kashibai* v. *Tatia*, 7 Bom. 221.

(*a*) W. & B. 909, 912, 1040.

1889 the same Court, in a Full Bench decision, decided that the adoption of an only son was absolutely invalid. They held that the Full Bench had already decided in the Linghait case that under Hindu law a gift of an only son in adoption was invalid, and could not be made good by the doctrine of *Factum valet* (*b*). This of course finally closes the discussion in Bombay.

§ 137. In Bengal the authorities are nearly all opposed to the validity of the adoption of an only son. Sir F. MacNaghten and Mr. Sutherland both declare unhesitatingly against it (*c*), and the younger MacNaghten cites numerous futwahs in accordance with that view, the only exception being where the adoption was of the *dwyamushyayana* character (*d*). The decisions are to the same effect.

Bengal: only son may not be adopted.

§ 138. In the case of *Shumshere Mull* v. *Dilraj Konwur* (*e*), the plaintiff rested his case on an adoption which was void as being made by a widow without her husband's authority. The Sudder Court, however, with reference to the claims of other parties, one of whom, named Tej Mull, was an only son who had been taken in adoption, asked the pandits whether such an adoption was valid. They replied that the validity of the adoption of Tej Mull, and his right to the estate, depended upon whether he had been delivered to, and accepted by, the adopting parent on the condition that he should belong as a son to both. If not so delivered, the adoption would be illegal, and carry with it no title to the estate. No decision upon the point was required, or given. In a later case, the plaintiff, who was an only son, claimed as adopted. His adoption was declared illegal on this ground, and his suit was dismissed. This decision was confirmed on review. After the case had been submitted to a new pandit, he gave an equally unqualified opinion with his

(*b*) *Waman Raghupati* v. *Krishnaji*, 14 Bom. (F. B.) 249.
(*c*) F. MacN. 123, 147, 150; Suth. Syn. 665.
(*d*) 2 W. MacN. 178, 179, 192, 195.
(*e*) 2 S. D. 189 (216).

Bengal: decisions as to only son.

predecessor. One of the Judges thought that the adoption, though improper, was not invalid; but two other Judges disagreed with him, and the former decision was confirmed (*f*). The same decision was given in another case, where the defendant in possession was an only son, whose title rested on the validity of his adoption. The pandits pronounced "that the fact of his being an only son was sufficient to invalidate the adoption, as such a person was forbidden to be adopted; and the violation of this law was a criminal act on the part of both giver and receiver." It was then alleged that he had been given as *dwyamushyayana*. But it appeared that he had been given by his mother after his father's death, and the pandits said that a widow could not give away her son in this manner without express authority from her husband, which she had not received. He was, therefore, turned out of possession by the Court (*g*). On the other hand, in a case in the Bengal Supreme Court, the Court said: "The adoption of an only son is no doubt blameable by Hindu law, but when done it is valid." They went on, however, to say that rather than treat it as invalid they would assume an agreement between the natural and adoptive father that the boy was to be the son of both, which, of course, got over the difficulty (*h*). Finally, the point came before the Bengal High Court in 1868, when the title of the plaintiff rested on the validity of his adoption, he being an only son. The Madras case and others were cited, but it was held by the Court that the adoption was absolutely invalid. *Mitter*, J. said, "One of the essential requisites of a valid adoption is that the gift should be made by a competent person, and the Hindu law distinctly says that the father of an only son has no such absolute dominion over that son as to make him the subject of a sale

(*f*) *Nundram* v. *Kashee Pande*, 3 S. D 232 (310) S. C. 1 Mor. 17; 4 S. D. 70 (89). This case is erroneously cited by *Scotland*, C. J., as an authority the other way in *Chinna Gaundan* v. *Kumara*, 1 Mad. H. C. 57.

(*g*) *Debee Dial* v. *Hur Hor Singh*, 4 S. D. 320 (407).

(*h*) *Joymony* v. *Sibosoondry*, Fulton, 75. In one case in Bengal an adoption was held valid where it was admitted that the boy at the time of his adoption was an only son, his elder brother having predeceased. No discussion on the point is recorded in the report. *Mt. Dullabh* v. *Manu*, 5 S. D. 50 (61).

or gift (D. M. iv. 5). Such a gift, therefore, would be as much invalid as a gift made by the mother of a child, without the consent of the father. It is to be borne in mind that the prohibition in question is applicable to the giver as well as to the receiver, and both parties are threatened with the offence of 'extinction of lineage' in case of violation. Now the perpetuation of lineage is the chief object of adoption under the Hindu law, and if the adoptive father incurs the offence of 'extinction of lineage,' by adopting a child who is the only son of his father, the object of the adoption necessarily fails" (*i*). In 1878 the whole subject was again elaborately discussed by the High Court of Bengal, and it was decided that according to the law of that province the adoption of an only son was illegal, and that the prohibition applied to Sudras as well as to the higher classes (*k*). It may therefore be taken that on this point the law of Bengal differs from that of Madras.

Two persons cannot adopt same boy.

§ 139. Two persons cannot adopt the same boy, even if the persons adopting are brothers. It is, however, suggested by the author of the Dattaka Mimamsa that two brothers may jointly adopt the son of a third brother, so that he may be the *dwyamushyayana*, or son of both. Mr. W. MacNaghten expresses a strong opinion against the legality of such a proceeding (*l*).

Ritual.

§ 140. FOURTH, THE CEREMONIES NECESSARY TO AN ADOPTION are stated by Vasishtha as follows : "A person being about to adopt a son, should take an unremote kinsman, or the near relation of a kinsman, having convened his kindred,

---

(*i*) *Upendra Lal* v. *Rani Prasanna Mayi*, 1 B. L. R. (A. C. J.) 221 ; S. C. 10 Suth. 347, *Sub nomine*, *Opendur Lall* v. *Bromo Moyee* ; approved, *Janokee* v. *Gopaul*, 2 Cal. 365, and by Bombay H. Ct., *Bhaskar Trimbak* v. *Mahadev Ramji*, 6 Bom. H. C. (O. C. J.) 4. See *obiter dictum* of Jud. Committee, *Nilmadhub* v. *Bishumber*, 13 M. I. A. 100. S. C. 12 Suth. (P. C.) 29 ; S. C. 3 B. L. R. (P. C.) 27. In a later case a man had three sons, one of whom died leaving a widow, who had adopted to her deceased husband. The High Court held that under these circumstances there was no objection to the adoption of the two surviving sons. *Manik Chand* v. *Jagat Sattani*, 17 Cal. 518, 536.

(*k*) *Manick Chunder* v. *Bhuggobutty*, 3 Cal. 443.

(*l*) Dattaka Mimamsa, i. § 30, ii. § 40—47 ; 1 W. MacN. 77.

and announced his intention to the king, and having offered a burnt offering, with recitation of the holy words in the middle of his dwelling" (*m*). A fuller ritual, which, however, is merely an enlargement of the above, is given by Çaunaka and Baudhayana, in passages which are referred to by writers as the leading authorities upon the subject (*n*). In these much stress is laid upon the giving and receiving of the boy. Upon this Baudhayana says, "Then having performed the ceremonies beginning with drawing the lines on the altar, and ending with the placing of the water vessels, he should go to the giver of the child, and ask him, saying, Give me thy son. The other answers, I give him. He receives him with these words, I take thee for the fulfilment of my religious duties. I take thee to continue the line of my ancestors" (*o*). "The expression 'king' in these texts has been explained by commentators to signify the chief of the town, or village. They seem, however, agreed that the notice enjoined, and the invitation of kinsmen are no legal essentials to the validity of the adoption, being merely intended to give greater publicity to the act, and to obviate litigation and doubt regarding the succession" (*p*).

Notice to officials.

Giving and receiving.

§ 141. The giving and receiving are absolutely necessary; they are the operative part of the ceremony, being that part of it which transfers the boy from one family into another (*q*). According to some authorities nothing else is so essential, that the want of it will absolutely invalidate an adoption. Even the *datta homam*, or oblation to fire, though a most important part of the rite in the case of the three higher classes, has been held to be a mere matter of unessential ceremonial (*r*). On this point, however, there

Datta homam.

(*m*) Mitakshara, i. 11, § 13.

(*n*) V. May., iv. 5, § 8, 36—42; Dattaka Mimamsa, v. § 2, 42; Dattaka Chandrika, ii. See, too, 2 Stra. H. L. 218; Steele, 45.

(*o*) Baudhayana, ii. § 7—9; Journ. As. Soc. Bengal, 1866, art. *Çaunaka Smriti.*

(*p*) Suth. Syn. 667, 675; 1 N. C. 117; as to assent of Government, *ante*, § 122.

(*q*) *Mahashoya Shosinath* v. *Srimati Krishna*, 7 I. A. 250, S. C., 6 Cal. 381; *Ranganayakamma* v. *Alwar Setti*, 13 Mad. 214.

(*r*) *Veerapermall* v. *Narrain Pillay*, 1 N. C. 91, 117; 1 Stra. H. L. 95; 3 Dig. 244, 248; *Singamma* v. *Venkatacharlu*, 4 M. H. C. 165; *per cur. Sootrogun*

is a conflict of authority. The Dattaka Mimamsa, after reciting the ritual prescribed by Vasishtha and Çaunaka, both of which include the oblation to fire, says, "Therefore the filial relation of these five sons proceeds from adoption only with observance of the forms of either Vasishtha or Çaunaka; not otherwise" (*s*). And he winds up the chapter on the mode of adoption by saying, "It is, therefore, established that the filial relation of adopted sons is occasioned only by the (proper) ceremonies. Of gift, acceptance, a burnt sacrament, and so forth, should either be wanting, the filial relation even fails" (*t*). So the Dattaka Chandrika, after giving the ritual of Baudhayana for the followers of the Taittiri Veda, which also includes the *datta homam*, says, "In case no form, as propounded, should be observed, it will be declared that the adopted son is entitled to assets sufficient for his marriage" (*u*). A Madras Pandit says, *datta homam* is essential to Brahmans, but not to the other classes; and his opinion is stated to be correct by Mr. Colebrooke and Mr. Ellis (*v*). So Mr. Steele says, "Sudras cannot perform any ceremonies requiring *Muntras* from the Vedas" (*w*). Judging from these passages, it would certainly seem that the sacrifice to fire was essential to those classes for whom it was prescribed, and probable that it was not prescribed for the Sudras.

No religious ceremonies for Sudras.

§ 142. After a good deal of conflict of decisions, it appears to be now settled that for Sudras, at all events, no religious ceremony is necessary; whether this applies to the superior classes seems to be still unsettled. In 1834 the Judicial Committee said, "Although neither written acknowledgments, nor the performance of any religious ceremonials, are essential to the validity of adoptions, such acknowledgments are usually given, and such ceremonies observed, and notices given of the times when adoptions are to take place,

---

v. *Sabitra*, 2 Kn. 290; 2 W. MacN. 199; 1 Gib. 93. See the native authorities cited, Jolly, § 159.

(*s*) Dattaka Mimamsa, v. 50.

(*t*) Dattaka-Mimamsa, v. 56.

(*u*) Dattaka Chandrika, ii. 16, 17, vi. 3; 2 W. MacN., 198.

(*v*) 2 Stra. H. L. 87—89.

(*w*) Steele, 46.

in all families of distinction, as those of Zemindars or opulent Brahmans; so that wherever these have been omitted, it behoves the Court to regard with extreme suspicion the proof offered in support of an adoption" (*x*). It appears from the report of the case in Bengal that the parties were Brahmans. It was admitted that no religious ceremonies were performed. But both in the Sudder Court and in the Privy Council their absence was treated as merely a matter of evidence, and not as in itself invalidating the adoption. As a matter of fact both Courts found that the adoption had not taken place. In a much later case before the Privy Council, where a Sudra adoption was concerned, the High Court of Bengal had treated it as an open question whether or not a Sudra could be adopted without the performance of religious ceremonies, *viz.*, the offering of burnt sacrifice and the like. On appeal, the Judicial Committee said, "In the case of *Streemutty Joymonee* v. *Streemutty Sibosoonderee* (Fult. 75), it was held by the Supreme Court in Calcutta that amongst Sudras no religious ceremony, except in the case of marriage, is necessary" (*y*). In the view taken of the case by their Lordships the point did not arise, and was not decided. The next time the point arose in Bengal between Sudras the High Court decided, on the authority of a passage in the Dattaka Nirnaya, cited in the Vayavastha Darpana, that the performance of the *datta homam* was essential to an adoption even amongst Sudras, and as no such ceremony had been performed in the particular case, held the adoption invalid (*z*). In a later case, however, which was also between Sudras, the Court professed to treat this decision as having gone upon the special facts, which it certainly had not done; and drew a further distinction between the two cases, on the ground that "in the

Case of Sudras.

(*x*) *Sootroqun* v. *Sabitra*, 2 Kn. 287, 290; S. C in the Sudder Adawlut, *Sub nomine*, *Sabitreea* v. *Sutur Ghun*, 2 S. D. 21 (26).

(*y*) *Sreenarain Mitter* v. *Sreemutty Kishen*, 11 B. L. R. (P. C.) 171, 187; S. C. 19 Suth. 133; S. C. I. A. Sup. Vol. 149: in the High Court, 2 B. L. R. (A. C. J.) 279; S. C. 11 Suth. 196.

(*z*) *Bhairabnath* v. *Maheschandra*, 4 B. L. R. (A. C. J.) 162; S. C. 13 Suth. 168 cited and approved, *Sayamalal* v. *Saudamini*, 5 B. L. R. 366.

present case, the adopted son is a brother's son, a member of the same family, in regard to whom the mere giving and taking may be sufficient to give validity to the adoption" (*a*). Finally, the express point was referred to a Full Bench. It was then found that the passage in the Dattaka Nirnaya, which had formerly been relied upon as showing that a Sudra should adopt with the *datta homam*, proved exactly the opposite; an essential part of the passage having been omitted. The Court accordingly answered the question put by saying, "Amongst Sudras in Bengal no ceremonies are necessary in addition to the giving and taking of the child in adoption" (*b*).

Case of superior classes.

§ 143. Whether the same rule holds good in the three superior classes is, of course, a different question. In Madras, it has been expressly decided that even among Brahmans the *datta homam*, or any other religious ceremony, is unnecessary (*c*). The same rule is certainly implied in the case in Knapp., cited in the last section, though not decided, and the opinion of Jagannatha is to the same effect (*d*). The ruling in the Madras case was affirmed in a later decision, where the parties were Kshatrias (*e*). In a still later case, where the parties were Brahmans, the same Court doubted the authority of the ruling; but affirmed the adoption on the ground that the *datta homam* had in fact been performed, though at an interval of five years after the giving and receiving (*f*). In that case it would appear that the giving and receiving had been made with reference to a formal adoption to take place afterwards. This adoption, when it took place, was duly

---

(*a*) *Nittianand* v. *Kishna Dyal*, 7 B. L. R. 1; S. C. 15 Suth. 300. As to the last point suggested, see *ante*, § 129.

(*b*) *Behari Lal* v. *Indramani*, 13 B. L. R. 401; S. C. 21 Suth. 285 *affd.* in P. C. *Sub nomine*, *Indromoni* v. *Behari Lall*, 7 I. A. 24; S. C. 5 Cal. 770, *acc.* *Dyamoyee* v. *Rasbeharee*, S. D. of 1852, 1001; *Perkash Chunder* v. *Dhunmonnee*, S. D. of 1853, 96; *Alwar* v. *Ramasamy*, 2 Mad. Dec. 67; *Thangathanni* v. *Ramu Mudali*, 5 Mad. 358.

(*c*) *Singamma* v. *Venkatacharlu*, 4 Mad. H. C. 165; 1 Stra. H. L. 96; *contra*, 2 Stra. H. L. 131.

(*d*) 3 Dig. 244, 248.

(*e*) *Chandramala* v. *Muktamala*, 6 Mad. 20.

(*f*) *Venkata* v. *Subhadra*, 7 Mad. 548. See however the cases in § 144.

accompanied by the *datta homam*. It may be a question whether the decision would have been the same if the adoption had been completed without performing or intending to perform the *datta homam*, and that ceremony had been appended at a later period, *pro majori cautelâ*. In 1884 a case arose in which a Brahman had adopted a boy of the same *gotra* as himself without the *homam* ceremony. The Court seemed to treat the case of *Singamma* v. *Venkatacharlu* as of little weight, pointing out that it was not argued on both sides, and that Jagannatha, who was cited, was no authority in Southern India. They held that in this case the adoption was good, because both parties were of the same *gotra*, relying upon the authority of Mr. Ellis in 2 Strange's Hindu Law, p. 155 (*g*). Both in this case and in the later one of *Ranganayakamma* v. *Alwar Setti* (*h*) the Judges relied on the dictum of the Judicial Committee in *Mahashoya Shosinath* v. *Srimati Krishna* (*i*), where their Lordships say, "All that has been decided is that amongst Sudras no ceremonies are necessary in addition to the giving and taking of the child in adoption. The mode of giving and taking a child in adoption continues to stand as Hindu law and usage, and it is perfectly clear that amongst the twice-born classes there could be no such adoption by deed, because certain religious ceremonies, the *datta homam* in particular, are in their case requisite." So the pandits in two Bengal cases seem to have laid down that the *datta homam* was essential in the case of an adoption among the three superior classes (*k*), and the same statement was made very recently by Mr. Justice *Mitter* (*l*). It seems also to have been assumed that this was the general rule in a Bombay case. There it had been omitted in the case of an adoption of a brother's son. The pandits held the adoption nevertheless valid under a special text of

(*g*) *Govindayyar* v. *Dorasami*, 11 Mad. 5.

(*h*) 13 Mad. 214, 219.

(*i*) 7 I. A. 250, p. (256).

(*k*) *Alank Manjari* v. *Fakir Chand*, 5 S. D. 356 (418); *Bullubakant* v. *Kishenprea*, 6 S. D. 219 (270).

(*l*) *Luchmun* v. *Mohun*, 16 Suth. 179; see, too, *Thakoor Oomrao* v. *Thakoorance*, N. W. P., H. C. 1868, 103.

Yama. "It is not expressly required that burnt sacrifice and other ceremonies should be performed on adopting the son of a daughter, or of a brother, for it is accomplished in those cases by word of mouth alone" (*m*). In Allahabad, where a similar case arose among Dakhani Brahmans, the inclination of some of the members of the Court seems to have been to hold that no religious ceremonies were necessary. The decision, however, was limited to holding that when the boy was the son of a daughter or of a brother, a gift and acceptance was sufficient (*n*).

So far as it is possible to reconcile these conflicting decisions, they seem to point to the conclusion that, among the twice-born classes, the *datta homam* is necessary, unless the adopted boy is of the same *gotra* as his adopter, or unless a usage to the contrary can be established. In Madras there is also high authority for limiting the application of the rule to Brahmans.

§ 144. In any case it is quite clear that if the omission of the ceremonies has been intentional, with a view to leaving the adoption absolutely unfinished; or, if from death, or any other cause, a ceremony which had been intended has not been carried out, no change of condition will take place, even though the ceremonies which have been omitted might lawfully have been left out. Because the mutual assent, which is necessary to a valid and completed adoption, has never taken place (*o*). And even in cases where giving and receiving are sufficient, there must be an actual giving and receiving. A mere symbolical transfer by the exchange of deeds would not be sufficient (*p*). Intentional omission.

(*m*) *Huebut Rao* v. *Govindrao*, 2 Bor. 75, 87 [83]; Steele, 45. This is in accordance with many authorities cited by Dr. Jolly, § 159. See W. & B. 923, 1083. In *Ravji Vinayakrav* v. *Lakshmibai*, 11 Bom. 381, (393), the Court while not deciding the point, expressed a strong opinion that the *datta homam* was essential among Brahmans.

(*n*) *Ayma Ram* v. *Madho Rao*, 6 All. 276.

(*o*) 2 W. MacN. 197; *Isserchunder* v. *Rasbeharee*, S. D. of 1852, 1001; *Banee Pershad* v. *Moonshee Syud*, 25 Suth. 192.

(*p*) *Sreenarain Mitter* v. *Sreemutty Kishen*, 2 B. L. R. (A. C. J.) 279; S. C. 11 Suth. 196; *Mahashoya Shosinath* v. *Srimati Krishna*, 7 I. A. 250; S. C. 6 Cal. 381.

Punjab.

Ceylon.

In the Punjab and among the Jains, no ceremonial whatever is required, the transaction being purely a matter of civil contract (*q*). Among the Moodelliars of Northern Ceylon the only ceremonial appears to be the drinking of saffron water by the adopting person (*r*).

Doctrine of *Factum valet.*

§ 144A. In many of the cases previously discussed, where it is necessary to admit that an adoption has been made in violation of a rule laid down by ancient authorities, an attempt has been made to support the adoption on the principle of *Factum valet quod fieri non debuit.* The existence of this rule in other districts than that of Bengal has been expressly affirmed by the Privy Council (*s*). The limits within which the rule can be applied have been much discussed in several cases in Bombay and in Allahabad. In the former Presidency it has been said of this rule "That its proper application must be limited to cases in which there is neither want of authority to give nor to accept, nor imperative interdiction of adoption. In cases in which the Shastra is merely directory and not mandatory, or only indicates particular persons as more eligible for adoption than others, the maxim may be usefully and properly applied, if the moral precept or recommended preference be disregarded" (*t*).

In an Allahabad case (*u*) where all the previous decisions were reviewed by *Mahmood,* J., he said, "In the case of adoption there are, of course, questions of formalities, ceremonies, preference, in the matter of selection, and other points which amount to moral and religious suggestions. Such matters, speaking generally, are dealt with in the texts in a directory manner, relating to what I may perhaps call the *modus operandi* of adoption. To such

---

(*q*) Punjab Customs, 82. Punjab Customary Law, III, 82. *Lakmi Chand* v. *Gatto Bai*, 8 All. 319.

(*r*) Thesawaleme, ii.

(*s*) *Uma Deyi* v. *Gokoolanund*, 5 I. A., p. 53. S. C. 3 Cal. p. 601.

(*t*) *Lakshmappa* v. *Ramava*, 12 Bom. H. Ct., p. 398, approved and followed; *per curiam*, 3 Bom. 293; 10 Bom., p. 86.

(*u*) *Ganga Sahai* v. *Lekhraj Singh*, 9 All. 253, pp. 296, 297.

matters, which do not affect the essence of the adoption, the doctrine of *factum valet* would undoubtedly apply upon general grounds of justice, equity and good conscience, and irrespective of the authority of any text in the Hindu law itself. There may, indeed be codes where the express letter of the texts renders that which in other systems be regarded as a matter of form, a matter of imperative mandate or prohibition affecting the very essence of the transaction." "Adoption under the Hindu law being in the nature of gift, three main matters constitute its elements apart from questions of form. The capacity to give, the capacity to take, and the capacity to be the subject of adoption, seem to me to be matters essential to the validity of the transaction, and, as such, beyond the province of the doctrine of *factum valet*.

Application of these rules.

§ 144B. In accordance with these rules, the principle of *factum valet* has been held to be ineffectual where the son was given or received by a mother who was destitute of the necessary authority (*v*), or where the boy taken in adoption was one whose mother could not have been married by the adopting father (*w*). It has been held to be effectual where a preferential relation has been passed over in favour of the son of a stranger (*x*), or where the limit of age fixed by the Dattaka Mimamsa has been exceeded (*y*). On the other hand the above principles give no help in a case where it is possible to hold different views on the question, whether a particular direction is, or is not so imperative as to be of the essence of an adoption. For instance, not only different Courts, but the same Court at different times, have disagreed as to the applicability of the doctrine of *factum valet* in cases of the adoption of an only son (*z*), or of a member of the superior classes, where

(*v*) *Rangabai* v. *Bhagirthibai*, 2 Bom. 377 ; *Narayan Babaji* v. *Nana Manohar*, 7 Bom. H. C., A. C. 153.
(*w*) *Gopal Narhar* v. *Hanmant Ganesh*, 3 Bom. 273.
(*x*) *Uma Deyi* v. *Gokoolanund*, 5 I. A. 40 ; S. C. 3 Cal. 587.
(*y*) *Ganga Sahai* v. *Lekhraj Singh*, 9 All. 254. (*z*) *Ante* §§ 131—138.

the prescribed religious ceremonies were omitted (*a*). Of course completely different considerations arise where a direct prohibition has been worn away by conflicting usage. Probably no Court except one governed by the authority of the Mayukha, and of the practices recognised by it, would give effect to the adoption of a married Brahman (*b*).

Presumption as to adoption.

§ 145. FIFTH, THE EVIDENCE OF AN ADOPTION.—There is no particular evidence required to prove an adoption. Those who rely on it must establish it like any other fact, whether they are plaintiffs, or defendants (*c*). In one respect they are in a favourable position; that is in consequence of the peculiar religious views of Hindus. The probability is that a sonless Hindu will contemplate adoption; and this probability is increased if he is advanced in years, or sickly; if he has property to leave behind, as regards which he would naturally wish for a lineal successor; and still more if, from family dissensions, the person who would otherwise be his successor is a person whom he would not be likely to desire. In countries governed by the Mitakshara law the further circumstance would arise that his widow, supposing him to leave one, would be dependent for her maintenance on a collateral, perhaps a distant, member of the family. If, therefore, he was on affectionate terms with her, he would naturally wish to leave her in the more advantageous position of mother and guardian of an adopted son (*d*). Similarly, an opposite state of things, such as the youth of the adopting father, the probability of his having issue by his wife, or the like, would render the fact of the adoption unlikely (*e*). No writing is necessary; though, of course,

Writing.

(*a*) *Ante* § 143. (*b*) *Dharma Dagu* v. *Ramkrishna Chimnaji*, 10 Bom. 80.

(*c*) *Tarini Charan* v *Saroda Sundari*. 3 B. L. R. (A. C. J.) 146; S. C. 11 Suth. 468; *Hur Dyal Nag* v. *Roy Krishto*, 24 Suth. 107.

(*d*) 1 Hyde, 249; *Huradhun* v. *Muthoranath*, 4 M. I. A. 414; S. C. 7 Suth. (P. C.) 71; where the P. C. reversed concurrent decisions of the Lower Courts, finding against the adoption; *Soondur Koomaree* v. *Gudadhur*, 7 M. I. A. 64; S. C. 4 Suth. (P. C.) 116; *Raghunadha* v. *Broso Kishoro*, 3 I. A. 177; S. C. 1 Mad. 69; S. C. 25 Suth. 291. See as to force of presumption in favour of adoption, *per Mitter*, J., *Rajendro Narain* v. *Saroda*, 15 Suth. 548. *Harman Chull Singh* v. *Koomar Gunsheam*, 2 Kn., p. 220.

(*e*) *Mt. Sabitreea* v. *Sutur Ghun*, 2 S. D. 21 (26); affirmed, 2 Kn. 287.

in case of a large property, or of a person of high position, the absence of a writing would be a circumstance which would call for strict scrutiny, and for strong evidence of the actual fact (*f*). Nor is it even in all cases necessary to produce direct evidence of the fact of the adoption; where it has taken place long since, and where the adopted son has been treated as such by the members of the family and in public transactions, every presumption will be made that every circumstance has taken place which is necessary to account for such a state of things as is proved, or admitted, to exist (*g*).

§ 146. It has been held that a decision in favour of an adoption, in a suit in which it was in dispute, is *primâ facie* evidence of the fact of the adoption, even as against persons who were no parties to the suit (*h*). It has even been held that a valid regular judgment of a competent Court upon the status of an alleged adopted son is a judgment *in rem*, which is binding and conclusive as against the whole world, unless fraud, or collusion, can be made out; and that a summary adjudication of the same nature, though not conclusive, is *primâ facie* evidence of the facts adjudicated upon, sufficient to throw the burthen of disproving the same upon the opposite party (*i*). But this doctrine is now over-ruled. The binding character of judgments of the Courts of India upon questions of personal status was exhaustively examined by Mr. Justice *Holloway* in a Madras case, where a decree upon a question of division was relied upon as a judgment *in rem* (*k*), and later in a Bengal case, where the point decided in 3 Suth. 14, was referred to a Full Bench. It had been held upon the authority of that decision, where a

Effect of res judicata.

Not a judgment in rem.

(*f*) 2 Kn. 290; *Ondy Kadaron* v. *Aroonachella*, Mad. Dec. of 1857, p. 53.

(*g*) *Perkash Chunder* v. *Dhunmonnee*, S. D. of 1853, 96; *Nittianand* v. *Krishna Dyal*, 7 B. L. R. 1; S. C. 15 Suth, 300; *Rajendro Nath*, v. *Jogendro Nath*, 14 M. I. A. 67; S. C. 15 Suth. (P. C.) 41; *Hur Dyal* v. *Roy Krishto*, 24 Suth. 107; *Sabo Bewa* v. *Nuboghun*, 11 Suth. 380; S. C. 2 B. L. R. Appx. 51.

(*h*) *Seetaram* v. *Juggobundoo*, 2 Suth. 168.

(*i*) *Kistomonee* v. *Coll. of Moorshedabad*, S. D. of 1859, 550; *Rajkristo* v. *Kishoree*, 3 Suth. 14.

(*k*) *Yarakalumma* v. *Anakala*, 2 Mad. H. C. 276. See also *Gopalayyan* v. *Raghupati Aiyyan*, 3 Mad. H. C. 217.

reversioner had brought a suit against a widow as heiress, to set aside alienations by her, and to establish his title as reversioner, and the Court had found that her husband had been adopted, and therefore that the plaintiff was next heir, that this finding was conclusive against a person who was no party to that suit, and who denied the adoption. *Peacock*, C. J., after referring to Mr. Justice *Holloway's* judgment, said, "I concur with him entirely in the conclusion at which he arrived; *viz.*, that a decision by a competent Court that a Hindu family was joint and undivided, or upon a question of legitimacy, adoption, partibility of property, rule of descent in a particular family, or upon any other question of the same nature in a suit *inter partes*, or, more properly speaking, in an action in *personam*, is not a judgment *in rem* or binding upon strangers, or, in other words, upon persons who were neither parties to the suit nor privies. I would go further, and say that a decree in such a case is not, and ought not to be, admissible at all as evidence against strangers" (*l*).

Important as evidence.

But though the decree itself might neither be conclusive, nor admissible, as evidence, the proceeding in which the decree took place might be very important. For instance, when the fact of any adoption at all having taken place was in dispute, it would be most important to show that the alleged adopted son had put forward his title as owner of, or interested in, the property, by preferring or defending suits, or proceedings in the revenue or Magisterial Courts, relating to the property; just as his failing to do so would be important the other way. Again if those who now denied his title were shown to have been cognisant of, or to have joined him in, such transactions, the evidence would be still stronger in his favour.

(*l*) *Kanhya* v. *Radha Churn*, 7 Suth. 338; S. C. B. L. R. Sup. Vol. 662; followed in *Jogendro Deb* v. *Funindro*, 14 M. I. A. 367; S. C. 11 B. L. R. 244; S. C. 17 Suth. 104; *Katama Nachiar* v. *Rajah of Shivagunga*, 9 M. I. A. 539; S. C. 2 Suth (P. C.) 31; *Jumoona Dassya* v. *Bamasoonderai*, 3 I. A. 72, 84; S. C. 1 Cal. 289.

§ 147. Lapse of time may operate in two ways. *First,* as strengthening the probability of an adoption. *Secondly,* as barring any attempt to set it aside. In the first case it goes to show that the adoption was valid; in the second case, it prevents the results which would follow from holding that it was invalid.

Lapse of time as evidence.

First, it is evident that where a length of time has elapsed since an alleged adoption, and that adoption has been treated by the family, and by the society in which the family moves, as a valid and subsisting one, this is in itself strong evidence of the opinion of those acquainted with the facts that everything had taken place necessary to a valid adoption. It is like that repute which is always so much relied on in cases of disputed marriage, or legitimacy (*m*). But it is evident that the force of the testimony lies in repute prevailing through a long period of time, not upon the time itself. If, therefore, it appears that the adoption was kept a secret, or that being asserted on one side it was simply ignored on the other, and that no action was ever taken upon it, nor any course of treatment pursued in respect to the alleged adopted son, different from that which would have prevailed if no adoption had been set up, then there is no repute, and the longer the time during which such a state of things lasts the greater is the evidence against the adoption.

Where adoption admittedly invalid.

Secondly, such repute can have no effect whatever when the admitted facts show that there has been no valid adoption; *e.g.*, in the case of the adoption of a sister's son by a Brahman, or of a son by a man who had one living. But there might be facts, or a course of dealing which, though they could not render the adoption valid, would prevent certain persons from disputing it. A bar of this sort would arise in two ways: 1, by way of estoppel; 2, by way of the Statute of Limitations.

(*m*) *Rajendro Nath* v. *Jojendro Nath*, 14 M. I. A. 67; S. C. 15 Suth. (P. C.) 41; S. C. 7 B. L. R. 216; *Anandrav Sivaji* v. *Ganesh Eshvant*, 7 Bom. H. C. Appx. 33.

Effect of acquiescence.

§ 148. First.—A merely passive acquiescence by one person in an infringement of his rights by another person, or in an assertion of an adverse right by another person, will not prevent the former from afterwards maintaining his own strictly legal right in a Court of law, provided he does so within the period of limitation fixed by the law. The reason is that the law gives him a specified period during which he may, if he choose, submit with impunity to an encroachment on his rights, and there is nothing inequitable in his availing himself of this period. But it is different if his acquiescence amounts to an active consent to conduct on the part of another of which he might justly complain. If by his own behaviour he encourages another to believe that he has not the right which he really possesses, or that he has waived that right; or if by representations, or acts, he induces another to enter upon a course which he would not otherwise have entered on, or leads him to believe that he may enter on that course with safety, then he will not afterwards be allowed to assert any rights which are inconsistent with, or infringed upon by, that new state of things which he himself has been influential in bringing about. And this is equally so whether the right he is asserting is a legal, or an equitable, right. For it would be unjust that after he had by his own conduct induced another to alter his position, he should afterwards be allowed to complain of the very thing which he had himself brought about (*n*). This doctrine has been applied in India to cases of invalid adoption. In one, the adoption, being that of a sister's son by a Brahman, was held to be absolutely invalid. In another, in Western India, being the case of a Brahman adopted after *upanayana* and marriage, the Court declined to decide the question of invalidity. In both cases they were of opinion that the objecting

(*n*) *Rama Rau* v. *Raja Rau*, 2 Mad. H. C. 114; *Peddamuthulaty* v. *N. Timma Reddy*, *ib.* 270; *Rajan* v. *Basura Chetti*, *ib.* 428, where the English cases are examined, and the distinction between legal and equitable rights and the mode in which they are barred, is pointed out; *Taruck Chunder* v. *Huro Sunkur*, 22 Suth. 267. Indian Evidence Act, § 115.

party was estopped from disputing the adoption, since he had himself not only acquiesced in it, but in one case had encouraged it, and concurred in it, at the time it took place; and in another had, by treating the adopted son as a member of the family, induced him to abandon the right in his natural family which he might otherwise have claimed (*o*). In a later case, however, the High Court of Madras, while admitting the general principle, limited its application to instances where one party had knowingly and intentionally produced upon the mind of the other a false belief as to some definite fact. Where all parties erroneously believed a particular adoption to be valid, no estoppel arose which would prevent a person claiming under the adopter from impugning its validity (*p*). The application of this doctrine when so limited is peculiarly just in cases of adoption. Even if the invalidity of the adoption was such that the person adopted was not legally excluded from his natural family, he would necessarily be driven to legal proceedings to effect his return into it; he might be met by the Statute of Limitations, and so completely defeated; or might find that from change of circumstances his position, when restored to his natural family, was very different from what it would have been if he had never left it (*q*). It must, however, be remembered that estoppel is purely personal, and that it cannot affect any one who claims by an independent title, and who is not bound by the acts of the person estopped (*r*).

§ 149. SECONDLY.—The Statute of Limitations will also

Statute of Limitations:

(*o*) *Gopalayyan* v. *Raghupatiayyan*, 7 Mad. H. C. 250; *Sadashiv* v. *Hari Moreshvar*, 11 Bom. H. C. 190; *Ravji Venayakrav* v. *Lakshmibai*, 11 Bom. 381, 396; *Pillari Setti* v. *Rama Lakshmama*, Mad Dec. of 1860, 92; *Appuaiyan* v. *Rama Subbaiyan*, Mad. Dec. of 1860, 54. See *Sukhbasi* v. *Guman*, 2 All. 366; where it is not clear whether the Court meant to lay down that a valid adoption once made could not be cancelled, or that a person, who had once deliberately made an adoption, was estopped from asserting that it was originally invalid.

(*p*) *Vishnu* v. *Krishnan*, 7 Mad. 3.

(*q*) See *per cur.*, *Rajendro Nath* v. *Jojendro Nath*, 14 M. I. A. 77; S. C. 15 Suth. (P. C.) 41; S. C. 7 B. L. R. 216.

(*r*) *Lala Parbhu Lal* v. *Mylne*, 14 Cal. 401.

be a bar in some cases to an attempt to set aside a disputed adoption; that is, it will bar a suit to recover property held under colour of an adoption. The important question here will be, from what time does the statute run? The answer will be, from the time the party seeking to set it aside is injuriously affected by it. Where a person would be entitled to immediate possession, but for the intervention of one claiming as adopted son, of course the statute must run at the very latest from the time at which the title to possession accrues; because from this time, at all events, the possession of the adopted son must be adverse. But there are cases of greater difficulty, where an adopted son is in possession, but the person whose rights would be affected by the adoption is a reversioner, who is not entitled to immediate possession. An instance of this sort is the case of an adoption by a widow who is in as heir to her husband.

time from which it runs.

§ 150. On this point there was a direct conflict of authority. In several cases previous to 1869 it was held that the statute ran from the time at which the adopted son was put in possession as such, with the cognisance of those whose rights would be affected by his adoption, and in such a public manner as to call upon them to defend their rights (s). The whole series of authorities, however, was reviewed in a case which was referred to the decision of the Full Bench of the High Court of Bengal. There the ancestor died leaving a widow, who adopted in 1824, and survived him till 1861. In 1866 the suit was commenced by the daughter's son of the ancestor, who claimed the property, alleging that the adoption was invalid. It was admitted that the adopted son and his son, the then defendant, had been in possession by virtue of the adoption since 1824. The plaintiff's suit was dismissed as barred by limitation. But this decision was reversed by the Full Bench, who held that the statute did not begin to run till the death of the

(s) *Bhyrub Chunder* v. *Kalee Kishwur*, S. D. of 1850, 369, followed in various other cases which were examined in the one next cited.

widow (*t*). That decision was given under the Limitation Act XIV of 1859. Act IX of 1871, Sched. II, contained the following provision Art. 129 : "To establish or set aside an adoption—twelve years from the date of the adoption, or (at the option of the plaintiff) the date of the death of the adoptive father." A suit was brought to recover property held adversely to the claimant by a person who had been admittedly adopted by the widow of the last male holder. Much more than 12 years had elapsed since the death of the husband, or since the adoption, but much less since the death of the widow. The adopted son had admittedly been placed in open adverse possession more than 12 years before suit and had been recognized by the plaintiffs themselves as legally in possession in such capacity. The plaintiffs contended that they were entitled to sue for possession within 12 years of the death of the widow, exactly as if she had made an alienation to the defendant. The latter contended that the suit was barred under Art. 129, inasmuch as the plaintiff could not recover without setting aside the adoption, and in fact the only issue recorded was as to its validity. The Judicial Committee, reversing the judgment of the Bengal High Court, held that the suit was barred, as the expression to "set aside an adoption" had been for many years applied in the ordinary language of Indian lawyers to proceedings which bring the validity of an alleged adoption under question, and applied indiscriminately to suits for possession of land and to suits of a declaratory nature. The present Limitation Act XV of 1877, § 118 provides a period of six years for a suit "to obtain a declaration that an alleged adoption is invalid, or never in fact took place," the statute to run from the time "when the alleged adoption became known to the plaintiff." Their Lordships declined to say whether the alteration of language in the later Act denoted a change of policy, or how much change of law it affected. They proceeded, however, to express themselves strongly

---

(*t*) *Srinath Gangopadhya* v. *Mahes Chandra*, 4 B. L. R. (F. B.) 3 S. C. 12 Suth. (F. B.) 14 *Sub Nomine, Sreenath Gangooly* v. *Mohesh Chunder*.

against the probability that the same statute would apply two different periods of limitation for a suit declaring the invalidity of an adoption, and a suit to recover possession of land founded on such invalidity. Should the same question arise under the new statute, the argument that a similar construction is to be placed upon it will be at least a plausible one (u). The Allahabad High Court, however, has recently expressed its opinion that § 118 of Act XV of 1877 only applied to suits for a declaration of right, and that suits for possession of property were governed by a different period of limitation (v), and a similar decision has been still more recently given by the High Court of Calcutta (w).

Creates rights not status.

§ 151. It may be necessary to remark that neither the law of Estoppel nor the Statute of Limitations can make a person an adopted son if he is not one. They can secure him in the possession of certain rights, which would be his if he were adopted, by shutting the mouths of particular people, if they propose to deny his adoption; or, by stopping short any suit which might be brought to eject him from his position as adopted. But if it becomes necessary for the person who alleges himself to have been adopted, to prefer a suit to enforce rights of which he is not in possession, he would be compelled strictly to prove the validity of his adoption, as against all persons but the special individuals who were precluded from disputing it.

Results of adoption.

§ 152. SIXTH.—THE RESULT OF ADOPTION may be stated generally to be, that it transfers the adopted son out of his natural family into the adopting family, so far as regards all rights of inheritance, and the duties and obligations connected therewith. But it does not obliterate the tie of blood, or the disabilities arising from it. Therefore, an adopted son is just as much incapacitated from marrying

(u) *Jagadamba Chowdhrani* v. *Dakhina Mohun*, 13 I. A. 84, 94,—explaining *Raj Bahadur* v. *Achumbit Lal*, 6 I. A. 110; *per curiam*, 11 Bom. p. 396.
(v) *Basdeo* v. *Gopal*, 8 All. 644.
(w) *Lala Parbhu Lal* v. *Mylne*, 14 Cal. 401.

in his natural family as if he had never left it. Nor can he himself adopt a person out of his natural family, whom he could not have adopted if he had remained in it.

Questions of inheritance arise, *first ;* where there is only an adopted son : *secondly ;* where there is also legitimate issue of the adoptive father. Under the first head, succession is either to the paternal line, lineally or collaterally, or to the maternal line.

Lineal succession.

§ 153. Where there is only an adopted son, properly constituted, he is beyond all doubt entitled to inherit to his adoptive father, and to the father and grandfather and other more distant lineal ancestors, of such adoptive father, just as if he was his natural-born son (*x*). But there has been considerable discussion as to whether he was entitled to inherit to collaterals.

Collateral succession.

A reference to the table of sonship (*y*) will show that eight of the fourteen authorities referred to place the adopted son beyond the sixth in number. Now, all of these say that the first six sons inherit to the father, and to collaterals ; the last six only to the father. From this it is argued by those who rely on the eight, that he only succeeds lineally ; by those who rely on the remaining six, that he inherits collaterally also. The real fact, of course, is that the two sets of authorities represent different historical periods of the law of adoption ; the former relating to a period when the adopted son had not obtained the full rights which he was recognized as possessing at a later period. The Dattaka Chandrikâ as usual tries to make all the passages harmonise by saying : "In the same manner the doctrine of one holy saint that the son given is an heir to kinsmen—and that of another that he is not such heir—are to be reconciled by referring to the distinction of his being endowed with good qualities

(*x*) Dattaka Mimamsa, vi. § 3, 8 ; Dattaka Chandrika, v. § 25, iii. § 20 ; *Gourbullub* v. *Juggenoth*, F. MacN. 159. *Mokundo* v. *Bykunt*, 6 Cal. 289. Sir F. MacNaghten was of opinion that an adopted son in Bengal was even in a better position than a natural-born son, as having an indefeasible right to his father's estate, which a natural-born son would not have. F. MacN. 157, 228. *Sed quære ?*

(*y*) *Ante*, § 66.

or otherwise," and concludes the controversy by saying, that wherever a legitimate son would succeed to the estate of a brother or other kinsmen, the adopted son will succeed in the absence of such legitimate son (*z*). The Mitakshara follows Manu, who places the adopted among the first class of sons, and, of course, makes him a general and not merely a special heir, while it explains away the conflicting texts as being founded on the difference of good and bad qualities (*a*). The Daya Bhaga on the other hand follows Devala, who has been supposed to make the adopted son only heir to his father, and not to collaterals (*b*). But it seems that is a misapprehension. Devala no doubt enumerates the different sons so as to bring in the adopted son as ninth. But then he goes on, "These twelve sons have been propounded for the purpose of offspring, being sons begotten by a man himself, or procreated by another man, or received for adoption, or voluntarily given. Among these the first six are heirs of kinsmen, and the other six inherit only from the father." Now, if the words "the first six" refer, not to the original enumeration, but to the new arrangement by classes, the adopted son comes within the first six (*c*) Jagannatha, after appearing to rest the claim of an adopted son to collateral succession upon endowment with transcendant good qualities, finally states the present practice to be "for a son given in adoption, who performs the acts prescribed to his class, to take the inheritance of his paternal uncles and the rest" (*d*). This is also the opinion of Sir F. MacNaghten, of Mr. W. MacNaghten, of Sir Thomas Strange, and of Mr. Sutherland (*e*). The right has also been affirmed by express decision. In two cases, the right of an adopted son to succeed to another adopted son was declared (*f*). In other cases, the adopted son was held en-

---

(*z*) Dattaka Chandrika, v. § 22—24.

(*a*) Mitakshara, i. 11, § 30—34.

(*b*) Daya Bhaga, x. § 7, 8.

(*c*) See D. Bh. x. 7, note, *per curiam; Puddo Kumaree* v. *Juggut Kishore*, 5 Cal. 630.

(*d*) 3 Dig. 270, 272; F. MacN. 162.

(*e*) F. MacN. 128, 132; 1 W. MacN. 78; 2 W. MacN. 187; 1 Stra. H. L. 97; 2 Stra. H. L. 116; Suth. Syn. 668, 677.

(*f*) *Shamchunder* v. *Narayni*, 1 S. D. 209 (279); affirmed 3 Kn. 55. (So much of this decision as allowed a second adoption to take place during the life

titled to share an estate of his adoptive father's brother (*g*). In a later case, the adoptive son was held entitled to share in the property of one who was first cousin to his grandfather by adoption. And he takes exactly the same share as a legitimate son, when he is sharing with all other heirs than the legitimate son of his adoptive father (*h*). And so do his descendants, whether male or female (*i*). In the latest case upon the point, the right of an adopted son was maintained to succeed to all his adoptive father's sapindas, whether the latter were related to the former through males only or through females (*k*).

Succession *ex parte maternâ*.

§ 154. Another question as to which there was, till lately, a singular conflict of opinion, is as to the right of an adopted son to succeed to the family of his adoptive father's wife, or wives. *Primâ facie* one would imagine that he must necessarily do so. The theory of adoption is that it makes the son adopted to all intents and purposes the son of his father, as completely as if he had begotten him in lawful wedlock. The lawful son of a father is the son of all his wives, and would, therefore, I presume, be the heir of all or any of them (*l*). And so it has been laid down that a son adopted by one wife becomes the son of all, and succeeds to the property of all (*m*). The same result must follow where the son is adopted, not by the wife, but by the man himself.

Native writers.

The authors of the Dattaka Chandrika and Dattaka Mimamsa seems to lay the point down with the most perfect clearness. The former states that "where there may be a diversity of

---

of the first adopted son must be taken as bad. But a note states that it was considered as settling the right of an adopted son to inherit from the collaterals of his adoptive father.) *Gourhurree* v. *Mt. Rutnasuree*, 6 S. D. 203 (250); *Joy Chundro* v. *Bhyrub Chundro*, S. D. of 1849, 461. See also the Judgment of *Hobhouse*, J., in the Full Bench case of *Guru Gobind* v. *Anand Lal*, 5 B. L. R. 15; S. C. 13 Suth. (F. B.) 49.

(*g*) *Lokenath* v. *Shamasoonduree*, S. D. of 1858, 1863; *Kishenath* v. *Hurreegobind*, S. D. of 1859, 18; *Gooroopershad* v. *Rasbehary*, S. D. of 1860, i. 411.

(*h*) *Taramohun* v. *Kripa Moyee*, 9 Suth. 423.

(*i*) S. D. of 1858, 1863; of 1859, 18.

(*k*) *Puddo Kumaree* v. *Juggut Kishore*, 5 Cal. 615 affd. *Sub nomine Pudma Coomari* v. *Ct. of Wards*, in P. C. 8 I. A. 229.

(*l*) Manu, ix. § 183; Dattaka Mimamsa, ii. § 69; Dáttaka Chandrika, i. § 23—26.

(*m*) *Teencowree* v. *Dinonath*, 3 Suth. 49.

mothers, the sires of the natural mothers are first designated by a son, who is son to two fathers, at the funeral repast in honour of the maternal grandsires; subsequently the sires of her who is the adoptive mother. But the absolutely adopted son presents oblations to the father and to the other ancestors of his adoptive mother only; for he is capable of performing the funeral rites of that mother only" (*n*). And the latter says, "The forefathers of the adoptive mother only are also the maternal grandsires of sons given and the rest; for the rule regarding the paternal is equally applicable to the maternal grandsires of adopted sons (*o*); and in an earlier chapter (I. § 22) Nanda Pandita says, "In consequence of the superiority of the husband, by his mere act of adoption, the filiation of the adopted, as son of the wife, is complete in the same manner as her property in any other thing accepted by her husband." So Mr. Sutherland states as the effect of these passages that—"He likewise represents the real legitimate son in relationship to his adoptive mother, whose ancestors are his maternal grandsires" (*p*). To the same effect is a futwah recorded by Mr. MacNaghten, where the adopted son of a sister was held to be an heir to that sister's brother, that is to say, he inherited to his adoptive mother's family (*q*). On the other hand Mr. W. MacNaghten himself decides against the right of an adopted son to succeed to property, which the wife of the adopting father had received from her relations. For this he refers to a case in Bengal, where he says the point was determined (*r*). This, however, was a mistake, as has been repeatedly pointed out. There was no decision of the Sudder Court such as Mr. MacNaghten supposed, but there was an unnecessary opinion of the pandits, which itself rested only upon an irrelevant text of the Daya Bhaga. Upon this supposed decision, however, two express rulings, negativing the right of the adopted son to succeed to property *ex parte maternâ*, were subse-

Decisions.

(*n*) Dattaka Chandrika, iii. § 16, 17.
(*o*) Dattaka Mimamsa, vi. § 50—52.
(*p*) Suth. Syn. 668.
(*q*) 2 W. MacN. 88.
(*r*) 1 W. MacN. 78, citing *Gunga Mya* v. *Kishen Kishore*, 3 S. D. 128 (170).

quently given in Bengal and in Madras (*s*). Yet, in direct conflict with the only principle which could have justified such a decision, it was settled that the next-of-kin of an adoptive mother would be the heirs of her adopted son (*t*), and that an adopted son would succeed to the *stridhanum* of his adoptive mother (*u*). Finally it was decided by the Allahabad High Court, that an adopted son had all the rights of a natural-born son in the maternal line as well as in the paternal line, and would therefore succeed to property which his adoptive mother had inherited from her father (*v*). This decision was followed by the High Court of Bengal in a case where the plaintiff claimed property which had devolved upon the son of A, by virtue of his adoption by the daughter of A. In their judgment the former Bengal decision and that which followed it in Madras were formally over-ruled, and the general principle laid down by the Allahabad High Court was approved and adopted to the fullest extent. This ruling was supported on appeal by the Judicial Committee, and has finally settled a controversy which had lasted for upwards of eighty years (*w*). In conformity with it, the adopted son of a daughter has been held to share equally with the natural-born son of another daughter the inheritance left by his maternal grandfather (*x*).

After-born legitimate son.

§ 155. Cases where a legitimate and an adopted son exist together can only occur lawfully where a legitimate son has been born after an adoption. The adoption of a son by one who had male issue would be absolutely invalid (§ 97), and the son so adopted would be entitled to no share whatever. It may be suggested, on the authority of a text ascribed to Manu, that he would be entitled to have his marriage ceremony performed, which I suppose includes maintenance

(*s*) *Marun Moee* v. *Bejoy*, Suth. Sp. No. 121; *Chinna Ramakristna* v. *Minatchi*, 7 Mad. H. C. 245.
(*t*) *Gunga Persad* v. *Brojessaree*, S. D. of 1859, 1091.
(*u*) *Teen Cowrie* v. *Dinonath*, 3 Suth. 49, and so laid down by the Pandits in Bombay, W. & B. 513.
(*v*) *Sham Kuar* v. *Gaya*, 1 All. 256.
(*w*) *Uma Sunker* v. *Kali Komul*, 6 Cal. 256. *Affd.* 10 I. A. 138, S. C. 10 Cal. 232.
(*x*) *Surjokant Nundi* v. *Mohesh Chunder*, 9 Cal. 70.

also. But the text, if in force at all at present, seems to me to relate rather to informal than to wholly invalid adoptions, which would create no change of status (*y*). Where, however, a legitimate son is born after an adoption, which was valid when it took place, the latter is entitled to share along with the legitimate son, taking a portion which is sometimes spoken of as being one-fourth, and sometimes as being one-third of that of the after-born-son (*z*). Dr. Wilson says that the variance is only apparent, and that all the texts mean the same thing, *viz.*, that the property should be divided into four shares, of which the adopted son gets one. That is to say, he gets one-fourth of the whole, or one-third of the portion of the natural-born son (*a*). Whatever may have been the original meaning of the texts, a difference of usage seems to have sprung up, according to which the adopted son takes one-third of the whole in Bengal, and one-fourth of the whole in other Provinces which follow Benares law (*b*). The Madras High Court, however, have decided on the authority of the Sarasvati-Vilasa, that the fourth which he is to take is not a fourth of the whole, but a fourth of the share taken by the legitimate son. Consequently, the estate would be divided into five shares, of which he would take one, and the legitimate son the remainder. A similar construction has been put upon the texts in Bombay (*c*). Nanda Pandita suggests a further explanation, that he is to take a quarter share; *i.e.*, a fourth of what he would have taken as a legitimate son, that is to say a fourth of one-half, or one-eighth (*d*). Where there are several after-born sons, of course the shares will vary according to the principle adopted. Supposing there were two legitimate sons, then, upon the principle laid down by Mr. MacNaghten, the estate would be divided into seven shares in Benares, and into five

Share of adopted son.

Madras.

Bombay.

(*y*) Dattaka Mimamsa, vi. § 1, 2; Dattaka Chandrika, vi. § 3.

(*z*) Dattaka Mimamsa, x. § 1; Dattaka Chandrika, v. § 16, 17; Mitakshara, i. 11, § 24, 25; Daya Bhaga, x. § 9; 3 Dig. 154, 179, 290; V. May., iv. 5, § 25; 2 W. MacN. 184.

(*a*) Wilson's Works, v. 52.

(*b*) D. K. S. vii. § 23; 1 W. MacN. 70; 2 W. MacN. 184; F. MacN. 137; *Taramohun* v. *Kripa Moyee*, 9 Suth. 423; 1 Stra. H. L. 99.

(*c*) *Ayyavu* v. *Niladatchi*, 1 Mad. H. C. 45; W. & B. 373.

(*d*) Dattaka Mimamsa, v. § 40; Suth. Syn. 678.

shares in Bengal. According to the Sarasvati-Vilasa it would be divided into nine shares, the adopted son taking one share in each case. According to Nanda Pandita he would take one-twelfth (*e*). Among various castes in Western India the rights of the adopted son vary from one-half, one-third, and one-fourth, to next to nothing, the adoptive father being at liberty, on the birth of a legitimate son, to give him a present and turn him adrift (*f*).

Sudras.

According to a text of Vriddha Gautama, an adopted and an after-born son share equally. This text is said in the Dattaka Chandrika to apply only to Sudras, and in the Dattaka Mimamsa it is explained away altogether, as referring to an after-born son destitute of good qualities. The High Court of Madras, following Mr. W. MacNaghten and Sir Thomas. Strange, say it is in force among all Sudras in Southern India, and M. Gibelin says it is the rule among all classes in Pondicherry. It is the rule still in Northern Ceylon. Baboo Shamachurn says that in Bengal this rule only applies to the lower class of Sudras (*g*).

Rights of adopted son on partition with collaterals.

§ 156. A curious question, as to which there has been a decision in Calcutta (*h*), is, whether the inferiority of an adopted son for purposes of inheritance is limited to the case of the subsequent birth of natural sons to the adopting father, or whether it applies also for the benefit of the brothers of such adopting father and their issue. In the particular case the pedigree was as follows:—

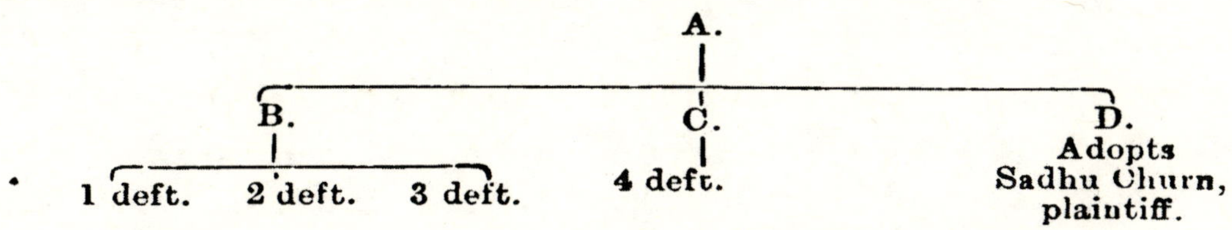

The family was governed by Mitakshara law. The

(*e*) F. MacN. 151; 1 MacN. 70; Jolly, Lect. 182. (*f*) Steele, 47, 186.

(*g*) Dattaka Mimamsa, v. § 43; Dattaka Chandrika, v. § 32; 1 Stra. H. L. 99; 1 W. MacN. 70, n.; 1 Gib. 82; Thesawaleme, ii. § 2; V. Darp., 979. *Raja* v. *Subbaraya*, 7 Mad. 253. A son-in-law affiliated in the *Illátom* form, which is in use in some of the Telugu-speaking districts of Madras takes an equal share with a natural-born son. *Hanumantamma* v. *Rami Reddi*, 4 Mad. 272.

(*h*) *Raghubanand Doss* v. *Sadhu Churn*, 4 Cal. 425.

plaintiff sued for a partition after the deaths of A, B, C, and D. In the Original and Appellate Courts the only points taken were to establish that he was not entitled to any share. The defendants being defeated in this contention urged an appeal to the High Court that his share would not be one-third but one-sixth. The High Court affirmed this view, relying upon the Datta Chandrika V. 24 & 25. *Markby*, J., pointed out that Mr. Sutherland's translation of § 24 omitted some lines, and that the two sections really ran as follows :—" 24. 'Therefore by the same relationship of brother and so forth, in virtue of which the real legitimate son would succeed to the estate of a brother or other kinsman, *the adopted son of the same description obtains his due share. And in the event of the ancestor having other sons, a grandson by adoption whose father is dead obtains the share of an adopted son.* Where such son may not exist, the adopted son takes the whole estate even.' The words in italics are omitted by Mr. Sutherland.

" There is no dispute between the parties to this appeal that this emendation of Mr. Sutherland's translation ought to be made.

" Paragraph 25 is as follows :—' Since it is a restrictive rule that a grandson succeeds to the appropriate share of his own father, the son given, where his adopter is the real legitimate son of the paternal grandfather, is entitled to an equal share even with a paternal uncle, who is also such description of son : therefore a grandson who is an adopted son may (in all cases) inherit an equal share even with an uncle. This must not be alleged (as a general rule). For there would be this discrepancy where the father of the grandson were an adopted son, he would receive a fourth share : but the grandson, if he were such son (of him) would receive an equal share (with an uncle in the heritage of the grandfather) and accordingly, whatever share may be established by law for a father of the same description as himself, to such appropriate share of his father does the individual in question (*viz.*, the adopted son of one adopted) succeed. Thus, what had been advanced only is correct. The same rule is to be applied by inference to the great-grandson also.' The words, *viz.*, 'the adopted son of one adopted' do not occur in the original. But even if we strike out these words, and take the two paragraphs according to their more correct version, they clearly enunciate that, upon partition, an adopted son and the adopted son of a natural son stand exactly in the same position, and that each takes only the share proper for an adopted son,—*i.e.*, half of the share which he would have taken had he been a natural son."

The learned Judge then proceeded to deal with the objection, that under Mitakshara law the plaintiff's adoptive father D acquired by birth a vested interest in one-third of the estate, and that the whole of this interest descended to the plaintiff by right of representation. This he answered by pointing out (p. 430), that under Mitakshara law no definite share vested in any member of the family so long as it remained joint, and that the share of each must be determined by the state of the family, and the position of each individual member at the time of partition. If then the sole adopted son of a natural-born son was only entitled to half the share that a natural-born son of the same father would have been entitled to, it made no difference that his father, if he had sought for a partition earlier, would have obtained twice that share, and that the whole share so obtained would have descended to him. It came back again to the same question, what were his own personal rights at the time of partition.

§ 157. The text of Vasishtha upon which all the authorities rely is as follows (XV. 9) "when a son has been adopted, if a legitimate son be afterwards born, the given son shares a fourth part." To which the author of the Dattaka Mimamsa adds (X. 1) "on the default of him Case discussed.

he is entitled to the whole." That is to say, to the whole of the property of his adoptive parent. This is quite intelligible. An adopted son is a substitute for a natural-son, and cannot come legally into existence if there is a natural son. But a man may adopt under the belief that he will never have a natural son, and find himself mistaken. Then justice is done by giving a larger share to the natural son, and a smaller to the son who would never have been adopted, if it could have been foreseen how matters would really have turned out. But is there anything in the wording or principle of the rule to suggest that a person who has become by adoption the sole son of his adopter shall have his rights in the family diminished, because other legitimate sons have been born, not to his adopter but to the brothers of that adopter? It is admitted that no authority can be found for such a position in the text of Vasishtha itself, or in any commentary except that of the Datta Chandrika as cited. But the latter seems to me to bear a very different interpretation. The clauses 24 and 25 relate to the general rights of all adopted sons, not to the special position of an adopted son where there are after-born legitimate sons of his adoptive parent. The author is commenting not only on the text of Vasishtha, but on texts of Manu and others, some of which lay down that an adopted son only inherits to lineals, others that he inherits to lineals and collaterals also. He reconciles these by the usual formula that a son with good qualities is meant in the latter case (§ 153). It seems to me that § 24 merely states the general principle that, however distant from the common ancestor, an adopted son has the full rights of an adopted son as such; not merely of an adopted son who is driven to share with legitimate sons. The commencement of § 25 lays down explicitly that the adopted son of one natural son inherits equally with the natural born brother of such son. Then the author meets the question whether every grandson by adoption would inherit in the same manner. To this he answers, not necessarily. If an adopted son himself adopted, then his son could take no more than himself; *i.e.*, if there were legitimate sons along with the first adopted son he himself would only take one-fourth, and therefore his son by adoption could take no more. Or as the Smriti Chandrika expresses it "the individual in question (an assumed grandson by adoption) will only take whatever share may be established for a father of the same description as himself" (a son by adoption). What share that is would depend upon whether legitimate sons were afterwards born to the first adopting father or common ancestor. If there were he would only take one-fourth, and his son, whether natural or adopted, could take no more.

Survivorship.

§ 158. When the legitimate and adopted son survive the father, and then the legitimate son dies without issue, it has been held in Madras that the adopted son takes the whole property by survivorship (*i*). Of course, it would be different in Bengal, if the legitimate son left a widow, daughter, &c.

Removal from natural family.

§ 159. By adoption the boy is completely removed from his natural family as regards all civil rights or obligations. He ceases to perform funeral ceremonies for those of his family for whom he would otherwise have offered oblations, and he loses all rights of inheritance as completely as if he had never been born (*k*). And, conversely, his natural family cannot inherit from him (*l*), nor is he liable for their debts (*m*). Of course, however, if the adopter was already a relation of the adoptee, the latter by adoption would simply alter his degree of relationship, and, as the son of his

---

(*i*) 1 Mad. H. C. 49, note.

(*k*) Manu, ix. 142; Dattaka Mimamsa, vi. § 6—8; Dattaka Chandrika, ii. § 18—20; Mitakshara, i. 11, § 32; V. May., iv. 5, § 21. See *contra*, 1 Gib. 95, as to Pondicherry. In parts of the Punjab the rights of the adopted son in his natural family take effect if his natural father dies without leaving legitimate sons. Punjab Customary Law, III. 83. A son-in-law, affiliated by the Custom of *Illatom* which prevails among some classes of Sudras in Madras, does not lose his rights in his natural family. *Balarami* v. *Pera*, 6 Mad. 267; *Hanumantamma* v. *Rami Reddi*, 4 Mad. 272.

(*l*) 1 W. MacN. 69; *Rayan* v. *Kuppanayyangar*, 1 Mad. H. C. 180.

(*m*) *Pranvullubh* v. *Deocristin*, Bom. Sel. Rep. 4; *Kasheepershad* v. *Bunseedhur*, 4 N.-W P. (S. D.) 343.

adopting father, would become the relative of his natural parents, and in this way mutual rights of inheritance might still exist. The rule is merely that he loses the rights which he possessed, *quâ* natural son. And the tie of blood, with its attendant disabilities, is never extinguished. Therefore, he cannot after adoption marry any one whom he could not have married before adoption (*n*). Nor can he adopt out of his own natural family a person whom, by reason of relationship, he could not have adopted had he remained in it (*o*). He is equally incompetent to marry within his adoptive family within the forbidden degrees (*p*).

Case of son of two fathers.

§ 160. An exception to the rule that adoption severs a son from his natural family exists in the case of what is called a *dwyamushyayana,* or son of two fathers. This term has a two-fold acceptation. Originally it appears to have been applied to a son who was begotten by one man upon the wife of another, but for and on behalf of that other. He was held to be entitled to inherit in both families, and was bound to perform the funeral oblations of both his actual and his fictitious fathers (*q*). This is the meaning in which the term is used in the Mitakshara, but sons of this class are now obsolete (*r*). Another meaning is that of a son who has been adopted with an express or implied understanding that he is to be the son of both fathers. This again seems to take place under different circumstances. One is what is called the *Anitya,* or temporary adoption, where the boy is taken from a different *gotra,* after the tonsure has been performed in his natural family. He performs the ceremonies of both fathers, and inherits in both families, but *his* son returns to his original gotra (*s*). This form of adoption seems now to be obsolete. At all

(*n*) Dattaka Mimamsa, vi. § 10; Dattaka Chandrika, iv. § 8; V. May., iv. 5, § 30.

(*o*) *Moottia Moodelly* v. *Uppon*, Mad. Dec. of 1858, p. 117.

(*p*) Dattaka Mimamsa, vi. § 25, 38.

(*q*) Baudhayana, ii. 2, § 12; Narada, 13, § 23; Dattaka Chandrika, ii § 35.

(*r*) Mitakshara, i. 10; 2 Stra. H. L. 82, 118.

(*s*) 2 Stra. H. L. 120; 1 W. MacN. 71. See futwah of Pandits in *Shumshere* v. *Dilraj*, 2 S. D. 169 (216); Dattaka Mimamsa, vi. § 41—43; Dattaka Chandrika, ii. § 37.

events I know of no decided case affirming its existence. Another case is that of an adoption by one brother of the son of another brother. He is already for certain purpose considered to be the son of his uncle. When he is the only son, the law appears to reconcile the conflicting principles that a man should not give away his only son, and that a brother's son should be adopted, by allowing the adoption, but requiring the boy so adopted to perform the ceremonies of both fathers, and admitting him to inherit to both in the absence of legitimate issue. It is stated by Mr. *Strange* in his Manual that the *dwyamushyayana* in this sense also is obsolete. And so it was laid down in one Madras case. But the weight of authority in opposition to that statement seems to be overwhelming (*t*). Among the Nambudri Brahmans of the West Coast (§ 42) the *dwyamushyayana* form prevails generally without any special circumstances, as the ordinary incident of an adoption (*u*)

§ 161. Where a legitimate son is born to the natural father of a *dwyamushyayana*, subsequently to the adoption, the latter takes half the share of the former; if, however, the legitimate son is born to the adopting father, the adopted son takes half the share which is prescribed by law for an adopted son, exclusively related to his adoptive father, where legitimate issue may be subsequently born to that person (*v*), that is half of one-fourth or one-third, according to the doctrines of different schools (§ 155). The Mayukha, however, seems only to allow him to inherit in the adoptive family, if there are legitimate sons subsequently born in both, and then gives him the share usual in such a case where the adoption has been in the ordinary form, that is, one-fourth or one-third (*w*). It lays down no After-born son.

(*t*) Stra. Man. § 99; Mad. Dec. of 1859, p. 81; Dattaka Chandrika, v. § 33; V. May., iv. 5, § 22, 25; Dattaka Mimamsa, vi. § 34—36. 47, 48. And see authorities cited *ante*, § 132. Mr. V. N. Mandlik says that whatever the theory may be, such adoptions are in practice obsolete, p. 506. In the N.-W. Provinces adoptions of this character are said to be very common, Jolly, Lect. 166.

(*u*) 11 Mad. 167, 178.

(*v*) Dattaka Chandrika, v. § 33, 34.

(*w*) V. May., iv. 5, § 25.

rule for the case of legitimate sons arising in one family only.

Origin of rule.

§ 162. It is probable that the rule which deprived an adopted son of the right to inherit in his natural family, originated, not from any fiction of a change of paternity, but simply from an equitable idea, that one who had been sent to seek his fortunes in another family, and whose services were lost to the family in which he was born, ought not to inherit in both. This is the view taken of the matter in the Punjab, where it is said that if the natural father dies without heirs, the village custom would be in favour of the child's double succession (*x*). In Pondicherry, a boy, notwithstanding adoption, preserves his rights of inheritance in his natural family, if he has not found a sufficient fortune in his acquired family, and in all cases if his natural father and brothers have died without issue. This doctrine, however, is based not upon any special usage, but upon the view which the French jurists have taken of the Hindu texts (*y*). The *Thesawaleme* merely states that "an adopted child, being thus brought up and instituted as an heir, loses all claim to the inheritance of his own parents, as he is no longer considered to belong to that family, so that he may not inherit from them." It is not stated whether his right would revive if there were no heirs in his natural family. But he only forfeits rights to the extent to which he acquires others; therefore, if his adoption is only by the husband, he continues to inherit to his natural mother; if it is only by the wife, he continues to inherit to his natural father (*z*).

Effect of an invalid adoption.

§ 163. A question of very great importance, which seems plain enough in theory, but which appears to be still unsettled, is as to the effect of an invalid adoption. *Primâ facie* one would imagine that it would confer no rights in the adoptive family, and take away no rights in the natural

(*x*) Punjab Cust., 81. Punjab Customary Law, III. 83.
(*y*) 1 Gib. 95, citing Dattaka Mimamsa, i. § 31, 32; vi. § 9; Mitakshara, i. 10, § 1 note, § 32, note.
(*z*) Thesawaleme, ii. § 2.

family. The claim to enforce rights in the former family, or to resist them in the latter, must depend upon a change of *status*, and if the adoption, upon which such change depended, were invalid, it would seem as if no change could have taken place. But there certainly is much authority the other way. I have already (§ 126) noticed the texts which award maintenance to a son adopted out of an inferior class, and suggested that they are merely a survival from a time when such adoptions were in fact valid, though less efficacious than others (*a*). A text is also ascribed to Manu which lays down that "He who adopts a son without observing the rules ordained, should make him a participator of the rites of marriage, not a sharer of wealth." This text seems to be interpreted as applying to a person who makes an adoption without observing the proper forms (*b*). Sir *Thomas Strange* cites these texts, as establishing that a person may be adopted under circumstances which will deprive him of his rights in one family, without entitling him to more than maintenance in the other. But he questions the proposition in a note, and refers to Mr. Sutherland as being of opinion that if the adoption were void the natural rights would remain (*c*). In one old case the pandits of the Sudr Court of Madras laid it down, that an adoption of a married man over thirty years of age, and with three children, was invalid, but that he was entitled to maintenance in the family of his adopting father. The proposition was cited before the High Court, and approved of. The approval, however, was extra-judicial, as the High Court considered that, they were bound by former decrees to treat the adoption as valid, and actually awarded the plaintiff his full rights as adopted son (*d*). In a later case, where a boy had been adopted by a widow without any authority, it was held that the adoption was wholly invalid, and gave the boy no right to maintenance. The Court said: "in reason and

Madras.

(*a*) See *per cur. Bawani* v. *Ambabay*, 1 Mad. H. C. 367.
(*b*) Dattaka Mimamsa, v. § 45; Dattaka Chandrika, ii. § 17; vi. § 8.
(*c*) 1 Stra. H. L. 82.
(*d*) *Ayyavu* v. *Niladatchi*, 1 Mad. H. C. 45.

good sense it would hardly seem a matter of doubt that where no valid adoption, in others words, no adoption, has taken place, no claim of right in respect of the legal relationship of adoption can properly be enforced at law." The Court also expressed their opinion that the natural rights of the plaintiff remained quite unaffected (*e*).

Bengal.

§ 164. In Bengal the case has twice arisen incidentally, though in neither instance in such a manner as to require a decision. In the first case, which was before the Supreme Court, *Colvile*, C.J., said, "It has been said on one side and denied on the other (neither side producing either evidence or authority in support of their contention) that a *Dattaka*, or son given, would forfeit the right to inherit to his natural father, even though he might not, for want of sufficient power, have been duly adopted into the other family. This proposition seems to be contrary to reason, but for all that may be very good Hindu law. But from the enquiries we have made, we believe the true state of the law on the subject to be this. There may undoubtedly be cases in which a person, whose adoption proves invalid, may have forfeited his right to be regarded as a member of his natural family. In such a case some of the old texts speak of him as a slave, entitled only to maintenance in the family into which he was imperfectly adopted. But one very learned person has assured me, that the impossibility of returning to his natural family depends, not on the mere gift or even acceptance of a son, but on the degree in which the ceremonies of adoption have been performed; and that there is a difference in this respect between Brahmans and Sudras. A Brahman being unable to return to his natural family if he has received the Brahmanical thread in the other family; the Sudra, if not validly adopted, being able to return to his natural family at any time before his marriage in the other family.

Depends on performance of ceremonies.

(*e*) *Bawani* v. *Ambabay*, 1 Mad. H. C. 363. Approved by *Westropp*, C. J. *Lakshmappa* v. *Ramava*, 12 Bom. H. C., p. 397.

Even if it be granted that a person, merely because he is a *Dattaka*, or son given, apart from the performance of any further ceremony, becomes incapable of returning to his natural family, that rule would not govern the case of an adoption that was invalid because the widow had not power to adopt. For to constitute a *Dattaka*, there must be both gift and acceptance. A widow cannot accept a son for her husband unless she is duly empowered to do so, and, therefore, her want of authority, if it invalidates the adoption, also invalidates the gift" (*f*).

§ 165. In the above passage, the words "ceremonies *after* adoption" ought apparently to be substituted for the words "ceremonies *of* adoption." The principle of the rule suggested seems to be, that a man cannot take his place in his natural family unless the essential ceremonies have been performed in it, and that if performed in a wrong family, they cannot be performed over again in the right one. But that where no such ceremonies have followed upon the adoption, he can return, if there has not been a valid giving and receiving. Where there has been a valid giving and receiving, then, apparently, he could not return, even though, in consequence of some other defect, the adoption may have been so far invalid, as not to invest the person taken with the full privileges of an adopted son. Rule suggested.

§ 166. In the other Bengal case, the Court refused to enforce specific performance of a contract to give a boy in adoption in consideration of an annuity. They said that this would be a *Kritaka* adoption which is now invalid, therefore that the contract, "if it were capable of being carried out, and were recognized by the Court, would involve an injury to the person and property of the adopted son, inasmuch as if it could be proved that the boy was purchased and not given, it is very probable that the adoption would be set aside; and if such adoption were set aside,

(*f*) *Sreemutty Rajcoomaree* v. *Nobocoomar*, 1 Boul., 137; S. C. Sevest., 641, note.

he would not only lose his status in the family of his adopting father, but also lose his right of inheritance to his natural parents" (*g*). In this case there would have been a complete giving and acceptance. But if the mode of doing so had ceased to be lawful, it is difficult to see how there could be a valid giving and acceptance, any more than if the son had been a self-given or a castaway. It may be suggested whether the whole theory of imperfect adoptions is not a relic of the times when some sorts of adoption were falling into disfavour, though still practised and permitted. The view taken by the Madras High Court, that an adoption must either be effectual for all purposes, or a nullity, has the merit of being practical and intelligible, while doing substantial justice to all parties.

Validity of gift to a person whose adoption is invalid.

§ 167. The validity of an adoption often becomes material as determining the validity of a gift or of a bequest. Suppose a gift made to a person who is believed to be an adopted son, but whose adoption turns out to be invalid; is the gift to fail or to stand good? The answer to this question does not depend upon any special doctrine of Hindu law, but upon general principles applicable to all similar cases. Where a gift is bestowed upon a person who is described as possessing a particular character or relationship, the gift may be to him absolutely as an individual, the addition of his supposed character or relationship being simply a matter of description. In this case, if the identification is complete the gift prevails, though the description is incorrect. For instance a bequest to Charles Millar Standen and Caroline Elizabeth Standen, legitimate son and daughter of Charles Standen. It appeared that they were really illegitimate, but their claim was supported (*h*). So where a will was to this effect, "I declare that I give my property to *Koibullo* whom I have adopted. My wives shall perform the ceremonies according to the Shastras and

(*g*) *Eshan Kishor* v. *Haris Chandra*, 13 B. L. R., *Appx.* 42; S. C. 21 Suth. 381.
(*h*) *Standen* v. *Standen*, 2 Ves. Jun 589.

bring him up." Then followed a clause showing that no other adoption was to be made till after his death. It was held in the Privy Council that even if the widows never performed the contemplated ceremonies, or performed them ineffectually, the bequest was valid (*i*). So a foster child, that is, one who has been taken into the family of another, nurtured, educated, married and put forward in life as his son, but without the performance of an actual adoption, does not obtain any rights of inheritance thereby (*k*). But a gift made to such a person by his foster-father, if in other respects valid, will not be made void, merely because he was under the mistaken belief that the foster-son would be able to perform his funeral obsequies (*l*).

Gift to a supposed relation, as such.

§ 168. Again a gift may be made to a person who is supposed to possess some special relationship, in such a manner that the existence of the relationship is a condition precedent to the coming into operation of the gift, or is an essential limitation as determining the person who is to benefit by it. Here if the relationship does not exist the gift cannot take effect. A Hindu made an adoption under circumstances which were held not to justify him in making any adoption. At the same time he executed in favour of the boy so adopted an *angikar-patra*, which, after reciting the adoption, provided as follows : "I authorize you by this *angikar-patra* to offer oblations of water and pinda to me and my ancestors after my death, by virtue of your being my adopted son. Moreover you shall become the proprietor of all the movable and immovable properties which I own and which I may leave behind." The Judicial Committee held that the gift failed with the adoption, as it was evidently the intention of the donor to give his property to the boy as his adopted son, capable of inheriting by the adoption (*m*). So where a testator left an annuity to his

(*i*) *Nidhoomoni Debya* v. *Saroda Pershad*, 3 I. A. 253; S. C. 26 Suth. 91.
(*k*) 2 Stra. H. L. 111. 113; Steele, 184; *Bhimana* v. *Tayappa*, Mad. Dec. of 1861, 124.
(*l*) *Abhachari* v. *Ramachendrayya*, 1 Mad. H. C. 393.
(*m*) *Fanindra Deb* v. *Rajeswar Dass*, 12 I. A. 72; S. C. 11 Cal. 463; *Doorga*

wife, "So long as she shall continue my widow and unmarried." After the date of the will, and before his death she obtained a divorce *ab initio* on the ground of nullity of marriage. It was held that she could not take the annuity, as it was only capable of being held by a person who occupied the position of widow of the testator (*n*).

Where relationship is a motive, but not the essence of the gift.

§ 169. An intermediate state of things is where the supposed character of the donee is the motive, but not necessarily the only motive, for the disposition in his favour. If a man makes a gift to one whom he erroneously supposes to be his son or his wife, he does so, partly because it is his duty to provide for such near relations, partly because feelings of affection have arisen in reference to them. Here the gift will be valid though the relationship never existed; *à fortiori* if the relationship had existed at the time the gift was made, though it had ceased before the gift came into effect (*o*). Where however "a legacy is given to a person under a particular character which he has falsely assumed, and which alone can be assumed to be the motive for the bounty, the law will not permit him to avail himself of it, and therefore he cannot demand the legacy." Hence a bequest to a person who had fraudulently induced the testator to contract a bigamous marriage with him or her, the testator being ignorant of the facts, is invalid (*p*).

Adoption by widow:

§ 170. The case of an adoption made by a widow to her husband, after her husband's death, raises special considerations, owing to the double fact that the person adopted has in general a better title than the person in possession, while on the other hand the title of the person so in pos-

---

Sundari v. *Surendra Keshav*, 12 Cal. 686. *Karsandas* v. *Ladkavahu*, 12 Bom. 185. *Shamavahoo* v. *Dwarkadas*, ib. 202; *Patel Vandravan Jekisan* v. *Manilal*, 15 Bom. p. 573.

(*n*) In re *Boddington*, 22 Ch. D. 597, *affd.*, 25 Ch. D. 685.

(*o*) Re *Boddington* ub. sup. *Bullnore* v. *Wynter*, 22 Ch. D. 619; *Wilkinson* v. *Joughin*, 2 Eq. 319. See however, re Morrisson, 40 Ch. D. 30.

(*p*) Per Lord Cottenham, 5 Myl. & Cr. 150, following *Kennel* v. *Abbott*, 4 Ves. 802; *Wilkinson* v. *Joughin*, ub. sup.

session has been a perfectly valid title up to the date of adoption. Questions of this sort arise in two ways. *First,* with regard to title to an estate; *secondly,* with regard to the validity of acts done between the date of the husband's death and the date of adoption.

§ 171. It has already been pointed out (*q*) that a widow with authority to adopt cannot be compelled to act upon it unless she likes. Consequently, the vesting of the inheritance cannot be suspended until she exercises her right. Immediately upon her husband's death it passes to the next heir, whether that heir be herself or some other person, and that heir takes with as full rights as if no such power to adopt existed, subject only to the possibility of his estate being devested by the exercise of that power. But as soon as the power is exercised, the adopted son stands exactly in the same position as if he had been born to his adoptive father, and his title relates back to the death of his father to this extent, that he will devest the estate of any person in possession of the property of that father to whom he would have had a preferable title, if he had been in existence at his adoptive father's death. One of the most common cases is an adoption by a widow, who is herself heir to her husband. The result of such an adoption is that her limited estate as widow at once ceases. The adopted son at once becomes full heir to the property; the widow's rights are reduced to a claim for maintenance; and if, as would generally happen, the adopted son is a minor, she will continue to hold as his guardian in trust for him (*r*). Where there are several widows, holding jointly, one who has authority from her husband to adopt would, of course, by exercising it, devest both her own estate and that of her co-widows. And in the Mahratta country, where no authority is required,

its effect.

Devests estate of widow;

(*q*) *Ante*, § 107.

(*r*) *Dhurm Das Pandey* v. *Mt. Shama Soondri*, 3 M. I. A. 229; S. C. 6 Suth. (P. C.) 43. Of course, the adopted son does not take any of the property which is held by the widow as her *Stridhana*, W. & B. 1174. The Court in awarding the property to the adopted son will take all necessary steps for determining and securing the maintenance of the widow. *Vrandivandas* v. *Yamunabai*, 12 Bom. H. C. 229; *Jamnabai* v. *Raychand*, 12 Bom. 225.

it is held that the elder widow may of her own accord adopt, and thereby destroy the estate of the younger widow, without obtaining her consent. The Court said, "It would seem to be unjust to allow the elder widow to defeat the interest of the younger by an adoption against her wish. But, on the other hand, if the adoption is regarded as the performance of a religious duty and a meritorious act, to which the assent of the husband is to be implied wherever he has not forbidden it, it would seem that the younger widow is bound to give her consent, being entitled to a due provision for her maintenance, and if she refuses, the elder widow may adopt without it" (*s*). It was not decided, but it seems to be an inference from the language of the Court, that they did not think the junior widow would have had the same right. Of course, an adoption would *à fortiori* devest all estates which follow that of the widow, such as the right of a daughter, or a daughter's son (*t*).

or of inferior heir.

§ 172. An adoption will equally devest the estate of one who takes before the widow, provided he would take after the son. For instance, where, in the Madras Presidency, an undivided brother succeeded to an impartible Zemindary in Berhampore, on the decease of his brother, the last holder, it was held that his estate was devested by an adoption made by the widow of the latter after his death, and under his authority (*u*). On the other hand, if the estate has once vested in a person who would have had a preferable title to that of a natural-born son, an adoption will not defeat his title or that of his successor, whether male

Estate of preferable heir not devested.

(*s*) *Rakhmabai* v. *Radhabai*, 5 Bom. H. C. (A. C. J.) 181, 192. *Per curiam*, 18 Cal. p. 74. See *post*, § 177.

(*t*) *Ramkishen* v. *Mt. Sri Mutee*, 3 S. D. 367 (489).

(*u*) *Raghunadha* v. *Brozo Kishoro*, 3 I. A. 154; S. C. 1 Mad. 69; S. C. 25 Suth. 291. The facts of this case seem to have been misunderstood by the High Court of Bengal, in *Kally Prosonno* v. *Gocool Chunder*, *post*, § 179, where they say (2 Cal. 309), "The property in dispute in that case was not a joint family property, and the surviving members of the joint family unjustly took possession of it, by excluding the widow of the owner, who was entitled by the Mitakshara law to succeed to it." The property was joint though impartible, and it was admitted that, as the brothers were undivided, the widow had no right to anything beyond maintenance. *Surendra Nandan* v. *Sailaja*, 18 Cal. 385, p. 393; *Mondakini* v. *Adinath Dey*, *ib.* 69; *Chandra* v. *Gojrabai*, 14 Bom. 468.

or female, unless the successor be herself the widow who makes the adoption. Both branches of this rule are illustrated by decisions of the Privy Council. In the first case, Gour Kishore, a Zemindar in Bengal, died leaving a widow Chundrabullee, and a son, Bhowanee. Previous to his death he executed a document whereby he directed his wife to adopt a son in the event of failure of her own issue. Bhowanee succeeded to the Zemindary, married, came to full age and died, leaving no issue, but a widow, Bhoobun Moyee. Chundrabullee then adopted Ram Kishore under her authority. He sued the widow of Bhowanee for the estate. It will be remembered that under the law of Bengal a widow is the heir of her husband, dying without issue, even though he has an undivided brother. The Judicial Committee held that the plaintiff's suit must be dismissed, since his adoption gave him no title that was valid against Bhowanee's widow. They said, "In this case Bhowanee Kishore had lived to an age which enabled him to perform, and it is to be presumed that he had performed, all the religious services which a son could perform for a father. He had succeeded to the ancestral property as heir: he had full power of disposition over it; he might have alienated it: he might have adopted a son to succeed to it if he had no male issue of his body. He could have defeated every intention which his father entertained with respect to the property. On the death of Bhowanee Kishore, his wife succeeded as heir to him, and would have equally succeeded in that character in exclusion of his brothers, if he had had any. She took a vested estate, as his widow, in the whole of his property. It would be singular if a brother of Bhowanee Kishore, made such by adoption, could take from his widow the whole of his property when a natural-born brother could have taken no part. If Ram Kishore is to take any of the ancestral property, he must take all he takes by substitution for the natural-born son, and not jointly with him. Whether under his testamentary power of disposition Gour Kishore could have restricted the interest of Bhowanee in his estate to a

Chundrabullee's case.

life interest, or could have limited it over (if his son left no issue male, or such issue male failed) to an adopted son of his own, it is not necessary to consider; it is sufficient to say that he has neither done, nor attempted to do, this. The question is, whether, the estate of his son being unlimited, and that son having married and left a widow his heir, and that heir having acquired a vested estate in her husband's property as widow, a new heir can be substituted by adoption, who is to defeat that estate, and take as an adopted son what a legitimate son of Gour Kishore would not have taken. This seems contrary to all reason, and to all the principles of Hindu law, as far as we can collect them. It must be recollected that the adopted son, as such, takes by inheritance and not by devise. Now the rule of Hindu law is, that in the case of inheritance, the person to succeed must be the heir of the last full owner. In this case Bhowanee Kishore was the last full owner, and his wife succeeds, as his heir, to a widow's estate. On her death the person to succeed will again be the heir at the death of Bhowanee Kishore. If Bhowanee Kishore had died unmarried, his mother, Chundrabullee, would have been his heir, and the question of adoption would have stood on quite different grounds. By exercising the power of adoption, she would have devested no estate but her own, and this would have brought the case within the ordinary rule; but no case has been produced, no decision has been cited from the text books, and no principle has been stated, to show that by the mere gift of a power of adoption to a widow, the estate of the heir of a deceased son, vested in possession, can be defeated or devested" (*v*).

Unless heiress is adopting widow.

§ 173. The case suggested by their Lordships at the close of the above quotation, was the case which actually came before them for decision in 1876. There a Zemindar in Guntur in the Madras Presidency died, leaving a widow, an infant son, and daughters. The son was placed in

Guntur case.

(*v*) *Bhoobun Moyee* v. *Ram Kishore*, 10 M. I. A. 279, 310; S. C. Suth. (P. C.) 15.

possession, but died a minor, and unmarried. His mother was then placed in possession, and adopted a son, without any authority from her deceased husband, but with the consent of all the husband's sapindas. This was before the decision in the *Ramnaad* case (§ 109), and the Government refused to recognize the adoption, and the adopted son was never put in possession. On the death of the mother, the Collector placed the daughters in possession, apparently treating the heirship as one which had still to be traced to their father, the last full-aged Zemindar. The Madras High Court treated the adoption as invalid, on grounds which have been already discussed. On appeal, the Privy Council maintained the adoption, and the right of the adopted son to take as heir. They held that in the Madras Presidency the consent of the sapindas was as efficacious for the purpose of enabling a widow to adopt in lieu of a son who had died without issue, as it admittedly was where there never had been issue at all. As to the effect of the adoption they proceeded to say, "If, then, there had been a written authority to the widow to adopt, the fact of the descent being cast would have made no difference, unless the case fell within the authority of that of Chundrabullee, reported in 10 Moore, in which it was decided, that the son having died leaving a widow in whom the inheritance had vested, the mother could not defeat the estate which had so become vested by making an adoption, though in pursuance of a written authority from her husband. That authority does not govern the present case, in which the adoption is made in derogation of the adoptive mother's estates; and indeed expressly recognizes the distinction" (*w*).

Whether an adoption by a mother devests her estate?

§ 174. Both in Chundrabullee's case and in the Guntur case just cited, it seems to have been assumed by the Judicial Committee, that an adoption made by a woman on

(*w*) *Vellanki* v. *Venkata Rama*, 4 I. A. 1; S. C. 1 Mad. 174; S. C. 26 Suth. 21. *Boicunt Money* v. *Kishen Soonder*, 7 Suth. 392.

behalf of her deceased husband would always devest her own estate, whether she held as widow of the person to whom she adopted, or as mother of the son of that person. But in a more recent appeal before the Privy Council, it was suggested that there might be a difference in that respect between the two cases. In the former case, the adoption produces a son who takes as heir to his own father, and as such heir is prior to the widow. But in the latter case the adoption produces a son who is brother to the last male holder, and it is to the last male holder that descent is traced. Now a mother ranks before a brother as heir to her own son. Why then should he destroy her estate? If the adoption could be treated as relating back to the life of the deceased, then it would have given him an undivided brother, who would take by survivorship in preference to the mother. But it would seem that no such fiction is now admitted, (§ 181). In the particular instance it was unnecessary to decide the point, but it is well worthy of attention (*x*). When the adoption in Chundrabullee's case came again before the High Court of Bengal, the Judges seemed to think that the son so adopted would only take in his proper place and order after the mother (*y*). In a still later case the High Court of Bombay treated the Guntur case as evidencing the opinion of the Judicial Committee, that an adoption by a mother would devest her estate, and ruled in accordance with that opinion (*z*).

Principle of above cases.

§ 175. It will be observed that in both the Madras cases, in which the right of the adopted son was affirmed by the Privy Council, the property had descended lineally from the person to whom the adoption was made. In the Berhampore case (§ 172), the last male holder was the person to whom the adoption was made. In the Guntur case (§ 173), there had been an intermediate descent to his own

Cases in which estate will not be devested.

(*x*) *Ramasawmy* v. *Venkatramien*, 6 I. A. 196, 208.
(*y*) *Puddo Kumaree* v. *Juggut Kishore*, 5 Cal. 615, 644; reversed on another point, 8 I. A. 229.
(*z*) *Jamnabai* v. *Raychand*, 7 Bom. 225; followed, *Ravji Vinayakrav* v. *Lakshmibai*, 11 Bom. 381, 397.

son, and on his death without issue the Zemindary had reverted to the person making the adoption, who was at once his mother and his father's widow. Two different cases, however, have arisen. *First,* where the property has descended to A. the son of B. to whom the adoption is made, as in the Guntur case, but has passed at his death to a person different from the widow who makes the adoption. *Secondly,* where the property has descended from A., and the adoption has been made to B., a collateral relation of A. Let it be assumed that the adopted son of B. would in each case have been the heir to A., if he had been adopted previously to the death of A. The question arises, whether, if he is adopted subsequently to the death, he will devest the estate of the person who has taken as heir of A. It has been held that he will not.

§ 176. The first point was decided in a Madras case. **Madras decision.** There N. had died, leaving a widow the first defendant, and a son, Sitappah, by another wife. Sitappah died unmarried, and thereupon his stepmother, the first defendant, adopted Munisawmy, who was the son of one Bali. Bali sued as guardian of his son to establish the adoption. Its validity was conceded by the High Court. It seems to have been admitted in argument that the first defendant, as stepmother, was not the heir of Sitappah, and that Bali was his heir. Upon this the High Court held that the adoption conveyed no title to the property. They said, "Even if it be considered that N.'s widow possessed or acquired in 1870 (the date of Sitappah's death) power to adopt a son to her husband, it has to be determined whether, according to Hindu law, any adoption could then be lawfully made by her. The principle of the decision of the Privy Council in the case reported in 10 Moore's Indian Appeals, 279, (*ante,* § 172) appears to us to govern this case, and show that it could not. Chinna Sitappah had inherited his father's property; "He had full power of disposition over it; he might have alienated it; he might have adopted a son to succeed to it, if he had no male issue of his body. He could have defeated every intention which his father entertained with respect to the property." On the death of Chinna Sitappah, the next heir, it is here admitted, was Bali Reddy, who is the natural father of the minor plaintiff, and who has also other sons. The inheritance having passed in 1870 to Bali Reddy, still remains in him; and we must hold upon the authority cited, that the estate of the deceased son, thus vested in possession, cannot be defeated and devested" (*a*)

Bombay decision.

§ 177. The second point arose both in Bombay and in Bengal. In the Bombay case the facts were as follows :—

A.

Anandram = Sarjabai, adopts Badridas. — Sobharam = Rakhmabai.

Anandram and Sobharam were undivided brothers, who died leaving widows but no male issue. Anandram died first, therefore his whole interest passed to Sobharam, and on the death of the latter the entire property vested in his widow Rakhmabai. After the death of Sobharam, Sarjabai, widow of Anandram, adopted a son. Thereupon a creditor raised the question, whether he took the estate of Sobharam. It was argued that the case in 10 M. I. A. 279 (*ante*, § 172) established that an adoption can never be held valid, which has the effect of devesting an estate once vested. Upon that however *Melvill*, J. remarked, "In that case A claimed, by virtue of adoption, an estate which B. had inherited from C. Even if A had been a natural-born son, B. and not A. would have been the heir of C.; and it was held that under such circumstances A. could not defeat B.'s estate. There would seem to be no room for doubt on this point, and the decision in that case certainly does not

(*a*) *Annamah* v. *Mabbu Bali Reddy*, 8 Mad. H. C., 108; followed, *Doobomoyee* v. *Shama Churn*, 12 Cal. 246; *Keshar Ramkrishna* v. *Govind Ganesh*, 9 Bom. 94; *Chandra* v. *Gojrabai*, 14 Bom. 463.

support the argument (which is moreover at variance with the decision in *Rakhmabai* v. *Radhabai*) (*b*), that an adoption can in no case operate to defeat an interest once vested." The same Judge, however, expressed a strong opinion that the adoption would not be valid on the ground suggested by the Judicial Committee in the *Ramnaad* case (*c*). He summarised their views as follows:—"In other words, when the estate is vested in the widow, she may adopt without the consent of reversioners, but when the estate is vested in persons other than the widow, and the immediate effect of an adoption would be to defeat the interest of those persons, then justice requires that their consent should be obtained. This proposition seems very reasonable and just." He distinguished the case from that of *Rakhmabai* v. *Radhabai* by saying: "The two widows being equally bound to take the measures necessary to secure their husbands' future beatitude, the younger widow, who by withholding her consent, ignores the religious obligation imposed upon her, has no right to complain of injustice if the adoption be made by the elder without her consent. But it does not follow that the plea of injustice is to be equally disregarded where it is put forward by a person who is under no such religious obligation. In *Rakhmabai* v. *Radhabai* it was certainly laid down in the broadest terms that in the Mahratta country a Hindu widow may, without the consent of her husband's kindred, adopt a son to him, if the act is done by her in the proper and *bonâ fide* performance of a religious duty, and neither capriciously nor from a corrupt motive. But the Judges by whom that case was decided were not dealing with an adoption which would have had the effect of devesting an estate vested in a relative other than a widow, nor in any of the decided cases on which they relied was the validity of such an adoption in issue. It does not appear to me that the authorities quoted would be

Rupchand *v.* Rakhmabai:

(*b*) 5 Bom. H. C. (A. C. J.) 181, *ante*, § 171.

(*c*) *Collector of Madura* v. *Moottoo Ramalinga*, 12 M. I. A. 397; S. C. 1 B. L. R. (P. C) 1; S. C. 10 Suth. (P. C.) 17, *ante*, § 110.

sufficient to support the validity of an adoption working such manifest injustice" (*d*).

differs from Madras ruling.

§ 178. As a matter of fact, the Court found that Sobharam's widow had given her consent to the adoption, so the whole of the above discussion was extra-judicial. It will, of course, be observed that the Madras and the Bombay Courts went upon different grounds. The Madras Court considered that the question was decided by the authority of the Privy Council. But there was this difference between the two cases, that in *Chundrabullee's* case, the adopted son, if natural-born, would not have been heir to the property he claimed. In the Madras case he certainly would have been. This was pointed out by the Bombay High Court (*e*). Their judgment proceeded upon the ground that the adoption itself was invalid. No objection of that sort could be taken in the Bengal case, and there the judgment went upon different grounds from those taken in either of the cases last cited. The facts of it were as follows :—

Bengal decision.

§ 179. R. and B. named in the annexed table were undivided brothers, who held their property in the quasi-severalty of the Bengal law. P. by his will bequeathed his

A dies 1825.

P. dies 1851 = B. D. dies 1864, | daughter dies childless after her father and before her mother.	B. dies 1845 | K. dies 1855 = Bamasoondery who in 1876 adopts KALLY PROSONNO, *the plaintiff.*

share to his widow B. D. for life, and after her to the sons of his daughter, if any, subject to trusts, legacies and annuities. The daughter died without issue during the widow's

(*d*) *Rupchand* v. *Rakhmabai*, 8 Bom. H. C. (A. C. J.) 114. This reasoning was followed in the case of *Ramji* v. *Ghaman*, 6 Bom. 498; *Dinker* v. *Ganesh*, ib. 505; *Patel Vandravan Jekisan* v. *Manilal*, 15 Bom. 565.

(*e*) See also the remarks made upon it by the Bengal High Court in *Ram Soondur* v. *Surbanee Dossee*, 22 Suth. 121.

life, and at her death the widow made a will, bequeathing the property to the defendant as executor, for religious purposes. K. died in 1855, leaving to his widow authority to adopt. If she had exercised that authority prior to the death of B. D., there can be no doubt that the son adopted to K. would have been the heir of his grand-uncle P., and would have been entitled to set aside the will of B. D., and to claim the property of P., so far as he had not disposed of it by his will. But the power was not exercised till 1876. When the suit was brought by the adopted son, the Court held that he could not succeed. At the death of B. D. the whole property of P. must have vested in some one who was then the heir of P.; or if there was no such heir in existence, it must have passed to Government by escheat. The Court held, upon a review of all the cases, that there was no authority for holding that an estate, which had once vested in a person as heir of the last full owner, could be subsequently devested by the adoption of a person who would have been a nearer heir, had his adoption taken place previously to the death. They considered that the inheritance could not remain in a sort of latent abeyance, subject to be changed from one heir to another, on the happening of an event which might never take place, or only at some indefinite future time (*f*). Some passages in the judgment are more broadly expressed than they would have been if the Court had not misconceived the facts of the case in the Privy Council from Berhampore (*g*). But the decision itself, coupled with the other cases cited, seems to lead to the following conclusions: ***First,*** where an adoption is made to the last male holder, the adopted son will devest the estate of any person, whose title would have been inferior to his, if he had been adopted prior to the death. *Secondly,* where the adoption is not made to the last male holder, **Rules.**

(*f*) *Kally Prosonno* v. *Gocool Chunder*, 2 Cal. 295, followed in a later case when it was held that it made no difference that the delay in adoption had arisen from the fraud of the person who took the estate in default of adoption. *Nilcomul* v. *Jotendro*, 7 Cal. 178. Affd. *Bhubaneswari* v. *Nilkomul*, 12 I. A. 137, S. C. 12 Cal. 18.

(*g*) See *ante*, § 172, note.

but is made by the widow of any previous holder, it will perhaps devest her estate, subject, however, to the doubt suggested in § 174. *Thirdly*, under no other circumstances will an adoption made to one person devest the estate of any one who has taken that estate as heir of another person. All these rules seem to be consistent with natural justice. In the first case, the object of an adoption is to supply an heir to the deceased. That heir, when created, properly takes precedence over any one who is a less remote heir. Further, the services which he renders to the deceased are fitly rewarded by the estate. In the second case, the widow who makes the adoption exercises a discretion which may be intended to produce a preferable heir to herself. Naturally she takes the consequences. But in the third case, there can be no reason why an adoption which is intended to benefit A. should disturb the succession to the estate of B., who receives no benefit from it, and who has not been consulted upon it, or been instrumental in bringing it about. (*h*).

Son's estate postponed.

§ 180. In Bengal, where a father has the absolute power of disposing of his property, he may couple with his authority to the widow to adopt, a direction that the estate of the widow shall not be interfered with during her life, or indeed any other condition derogating from the interest which would otherwise be taken by the adopted son (*i*). In provinces governed by the Mitakshara law, where a son obtains a vested interest in his father's property by birth, a person who has once made a complete and unconditional adoption could not derogate from its operation either by deed during his lifetime or by will. But where a man made a disposition of part of his property which was valid when made, and as part of the same transaction took a boy in adoption, the father of the adopted boy being aware of the provisions of the will, and

(*h*) Approved and followed *per curiam*, 18 Cal. 74, 398.
(*i*) *Radhamonee* v. *Jadubnarain*, S. D. of 1855, 139; *Prosunnomoyee* v. *Ramsoonder*, S. D. of 1859, 162; *Bepin Behari* v. *Brojonath Mookhopadya*, 8 Cal. 357.

assenting to them, and knowing that the testator would not have made the adoption without such assent, it was held that the will was valid against the adopted son (*k*). If, however, a will disposed of the whole of the testator's property, making no provision for an adopted son, it would probably be held that a subsequent adoption operated as a revocation of the will (*l*). It has been held in Bombay, that if the parent of the boy, when giving him in adoption, expressly agree with the widow that she shall remain in possession of the property during her lifetime, and she only accepts the boy on those terms, the agreement will bind him, as being made by his natural guardian, and within the powers given to such guardian by law (*m*). In a later case, however, before the Privy Council the effect of a similar agreement was much discussed, and not determined. The Committee refused to decide more than that such an agreement was not absolutely void, and therefore might be ratified by the youth on arriving at full age (*n*). *A fortiori*, an agreement by the adopted son himself when of full age, waiving his rights in favour of the widow, would be valid (*o*). And he may after adoption renounce all rights in his adopted family, but this will not restore him to the position he has abandoned in his natural family. Upon his renunciation the next heir will succeed (*p*).

Son's rights date from adoption.

§ 181. The second question which arises in the case of an adoption by a widow after her husband's death, is as to the date at which the rights of the adopted son arise. It has been suggested that a son so adopted must be considered

(*k*) *Lakshmi* v. *Subramanya*, 12 Mad. 490; *Narayanasami* v. *Ramasami*, 14 Mad. 172; *Vinayek Narayan* v. *Govindrav Chintaman*, 6 Bom. H. Ct., A. C. 224.

(*l*) Per *Couch*, C. J., 6 Bom. H. Ct. A. C., p. 230, citing *futwah* of a pundit; 6 M. I. A., p. 320.

(*m*) *Chitko Raghunath* v. *Janaki*, 11 Bom. H. C. 199; followed *Ravji Vinayakrav* v. *Laksmibai*, 11 Bom. 381, p. 398.

(*n*) *Ramasawmi* v. *Vencataramaiyan*, 6 I. A. 196; S. C. 2 Mad. 91. The Madras High Court subsequently expressed a strong opinion that such an agreement by the father of the boy would not bind him; *Laksmana Rau* v. *Lakshmi Ammal*, 4 Mad. 160; *Narainah* v. *Savoobhady*, Mad. Dec. of 1854, 117; and see *per curiam*, 16 I. A. 59.

(*o*) *Mt. Tara Munee* v. *Dev Narayun*, 3 S. D. 387 (516); 2 W. MacN. 183; *Mt. Bhugobutty* v. *Chowdhry Bholanath*, 15 Suth. 63.

(*p*) *Ruvee Bhudr* v. *Roopshunker*, 2 Bor. 656, 662, 665, [713].

as a posthumous son, and that his rights would relate back to the death of the father when he ought to be considered as having been born, or even to the date of the authority to adopt, when he ought to be considered as having been conceived. The whole of the authorities on the point were examined in an elaborate judgment of the Sudder Court of Bengal, which was appealed against, and adopted in its entirety by the Privy Council, and which may be considered as having settled the question (q). The point for decision in the case was, whether a widow, who had received an authority to adopt, was thereby debarred from suing for her husband's estates in her own right. It was argued that she must be considered as a pregnant widow, and could only sue on behalf of the son whom she was about to bring forth. The Court refused to act upon any such fanciful analogy, and laid it down that although a son, when adopted, entered at once into the full rights of a natural-born son, his rights could not relate back to any earlier period. Till he was adopted, it might happen that he never would be adopted; and when he was adopted, his fictitious birth into his new family could not be ante-dated. It must not, however, be supposed that an adopted son would necessarily have to acquiesce in all the dealings with the estate between the death of his adoptive father and his own adoption. The validity of those acts would have to be judged of with reference to their own character, and the nature of the estate held by the person whom he supersedes. Where that person, as frequently happens, is a female, either a widow, a daughter, or a mother, her estate is limited by the usual restrictions which fetter an estate which descends by inheritance from a man to a woman. These restrictions exist quite independently of the adoption. The only effect of the adoption is that the person who can question them springs into existence at once, whereas in the absence of an adoption he

How far he may dispute previous acts of widow.

(q) *Bamundoss* v. *Mt. Tarinee*, S. D. of 1850, 533; 7 M. I. A. 169. See cases collected, 3 M. Dig. 186; *Narain Mal* v. *Kooer Narain*, 5 Cal. 251; *Rambhat* v. *Lakshman*, 5 Bom. 630.

would not be ascertained till the death of the woman. If she has created any incumbrances, or made any alienations which go beyond her legal powers, the son can set them aside at once. If they are within her powers, he is as much bound by them as any other reversioner would be (*r*). And he is also bound, even though they were not fully within her powers, provided she obtained the consent of the persons who, at the time of the alienation, were the next heirs, and competent to give validity to the transaction (*s*). One case goes a good deal beyond this. A widow adopted a son under the authority of her husband. She succeeded him as his heir, and made an alienation, and then adopted another son. The Court held that the alienation was good as against the second adopted son (*t*). The decision was given without any inquiry as to the propriety of the alienation, and was rested on the authority of *Chundrabullee's* case (*u*). It does not seem to have occurred to the Court that a mother had no more than a limited estate, which, upon the authority of the case cited, was devested by the adoption. The son then came in for all rights which had not been lawfully disposed of, or barred, during the continuance of that estate (*v*).

Acts of previous male holder.

§ 182. I am not aware of any case which has raised the same question, where the person whose estate was devested by adoption, was a male, and therefore a full owner. But I conceive the same rule would apply. Until adoption has taken place he is lawfully in possession, holding an estate which gives him the ordinary powers of alienation of a Hindu proprietor. No doubt he is liable to be superseded ;

(*r*) *Kishenmunnee* v. *Oodwunt*, 3 S. D. 220 (304) ; *Ramkishen* v. *Mt. Strimutee*, 3 S. D. 367 (489), explained, 7 M. I. A. 178 ; *Doorga Soonduree* v. *Goureepersad*, S. D. of 1856, 170 ; *Sreenath Roy* v. *Ruttunmulla*, S. D. of 1859, 421 ; *Manikmulla* v. *Parbuttee*, ib. 515 ; *Lakshmana Rau* v. *Lakshmi Ammal*, 4 Mad. 160 ; *per curiam*, 8 M. I. A., p. 443 ; *Lakshman Bhau* v. *Radhabai*, 11 Bom. 609.

(*s*) *Rajkristo* v. *Kishoree*, 3 Suth. 14.

(*t*) *Gobindonath* v. *Ramkanay*, 24 Suth. 183, approved *per cur.*, *Kally Prosonno* v. *Gocool Chunder*, 2 Cal. 307. See *per curiam*, 11 Bom. 614.

(*u*) *Bhoobum Moyee* v. *Ram Kishore*, 10 M. I. A. 279 ; S. C. 3 Suth. (P. C.) 15 ; *ante*, § 172.

(*v*) See as to the effect of acts done during the estate of a woman, *post*, § 578 ; as to the effect of a decree passed against a widow before the adoption, see *Hari Saran Moitra* v. *Bhubaneswari*, 15 I. A. 195 ; S. C. 16 Cal. 40.

but on the other hand he never may be superseded. It would be intolerable that he should be prevented from dealing with his own, on account of a contingency which may never happen. When the contingency has happened, it would be most inequitable that the purchaser should be deprived of rights which he obtained from one who, at the time, was perfectly competent to grant them. Accordingly, where the brother of the last holder of a Zemindary was placed in possession in 1869, and subsequently ousted by an adoption to the late Zemindar, the Privy Council held that he could not be made accountable for mesne profits from the former date. Their Lordships said, "At that time Raghunada was, in default of a son of Adikonda, natural or adopted, unquestionably entitled to the Zemindary. The adoption took place on the 20th November, 1870, and the plaint states that the cause of action then accrued to the plaintiff. The plaint itself was filed on the 15th December, 1870, and there is no proof of a previous demand of possession. Their Lordships are of opinion that the account of mesne profits should run only from the commencement of the suit" (*w*).

Widow cannot adopt to herself.

§ 183. It is hardly necessary to say that as under the ordinary Hindu law an adoption by a widow must always be to her husband, and for his benefit, an adoption made by her to herself alone would not give the adopted child any right, even after her death, to property inherited by her from her husband (*x*). Nor, indeed, to her own property, however acquired, such an adoption being nowhere recognized as creating any new *status*, except in Mithila, under the *Kritrima* system.

Dancing girls.

But among dancing girls it is customary in Madras and Western India to adopt girls to follow their adoptive mother's profession, and the girls so adopted succeed to their property. No particular ceremonies

---

(*w*) *Raghunadha* v. *Brozo Kishoro*, 3 I. A. 154, 193; S. C. 1 Mad. 69; S. C. 25 Suth. 291. As to alienations by the father himself, see *post*, § 317.

(*x*) *Chowdhry Pudum* v. *Koer Oodey*, 12 M. I. A. 350: S. C. 12 Suth. (P. C.) 1: S. C. 2 B. L. R. (P C.) 101.

are necessary, recognition alone being sufficient (*y*). In Calcutta and Bombay, however, such adoptions have been held illegal (*z*). A recent attempt by a Brahman in Poona to adopt a daughter who should take the place of a natural-born daughter, was held to be invalid by general law, and not sanctioned by local usage (*a*).

§ 184. Kritrima adoption.—According to the *Dattaka Mimamsa,* the *Kritrima* form is still recognized by the general Hindu law, since the modern rule which refuses to recognize any sons except the legitimate son and the son given includes the *Kritrima* under the latter term (*b*). But the better opinion seems to be that this form is now obsolete, except in the Mithila country, where it is the prevalent species (*c*), and among the Nambudri Brahmans of the West Coast where it exists along with the usual form (*d*). The cause of its continuance in Mithila is attributed by Mr. MacNaghten to the rule which exists there, which forbids an adoption by a widow even with her husband's authority. As the tendency of man is to defer an adoption until the last moment, the form which could be most rapidly and suddenly carried out, naturally found most favour (*e*). This cannot be the reason for the existence of this form among the Nambudri Brahmans, who allow a widow to adopt without her husband's consent (*f*). Probably in each case the *Kritrima* has maintained a successful competition with the *dattaka* form as being laxer in its rules, and therefore easier of application. **Prevails in Mithila.**

§ 185. The *Kritrima* son is thus described by Manu (*g*): **Described.**

(*y*) *Venkatachellum* v. *Venkatasawmy*, Mad. Dec. of 1856, 65; Stra. Man. § 98, 99; Steele, 185, 186. In the absence of a special custom, and on the analogy of an ordinary adoption, only one girl can be adopted, *Venku* v. *Mahalinga*, 11 Mad. 393; *Muttukannu* v. *Paramasami*, 12 Mad. 214.

(*z*) *Hencower* v. *Hanscower*, 2 M. Dig. 133; *Mathura* v. *Esu*, 4 Bom. 545; but see *Tara Naikin* v. *Nana Lakshman*, 14 Bom. 90.

(*a*) *Gangabai* v. *Anant*, 13 Bom. 690.

(*b*) Dattaka Mimamsa, ii. § 65.

(*c*) Suth. Syn. 663, 674; 3 Dig. 276; 2 Stra. H. L. 202; note to *Sutputtee* v. *Indranund*, 2 S. D. 173 (221); Madhaviya, § 32. Mr. Sarvadhikari says (526) that this form of adoption is still practised in Behar, Benares and other places, citing the note to *Srikant Sarma* v. *Radhakant*, 1 S. D. A. 15 (19.)

(*d*) 11 Mad. 174, 176, *ante* § 42.

(*e*) 1 W. MacN. 97.

(*f*) 11 Mad. 174, 176.

(*g*) Man., ix. § 169.

"He is considered as a son made (or adopted) whom a man takes as his own son, the boy being equal in class, endued with filial virtues, acquainted with (the) merit (of performing obsequies to his adopter) and with (the) sin (of omitting them)." The Mitakshara adds the further definition "being enticed by the show of money or land, and being an orphan without father or mother; for, if they be living, he is subject to their control" (*h*).

Only adult.

§ 186. The consent of the adoptee is necessary to an adoption in this form (*i*), and the consent must be given in the lifetime of the adopting father (*k*). This involves the adoptee being an adult. Consequently there appears to be no limit of age. The initiatory rites need not be performed in the family of the adopter, and the fact that those rites, including the *upanâyana*, have already been performed in the natural family is no obstacle (*l*). Even marriage can be no obstacle, for it is stated by *Keshuba Misra* in treating of this species of adoption that a man may even adopt his own father (*m*).

No restrictions on choice.

§ 187. The great distinction between this species of adoption and the *dattaka*, appears to be that the fiction of a new birth into the adoptive family, with the limitations consequent upon that fiction, do not exist. A *Kritrima* son "does not lose his claim to his own family, nor assume the surname of his adoptive father; he merely performs obsequies, and takes the inheritance" (*n*). Hence any person may be adopted who is of the same tribe as his adopter, even a father as above stated, or a brother. In one case, from the Mithila district, it was stated by the Pandits and held by the Court that an adoption of an elder brother by

(*h*) Mitakshara, i. 11, § 17.

(*i*) Suth. Syn. 673; Baudhayana, ii. 2, 14; 2 W. MacN. 196.

(*k*) *Sutputtee* v. *Indranund*, 2 S. D. 173 (221); *Durgopal* v. *Roopun*, 6 S. D. 271 (340); *Luchman* v. *Mohun*, 16 Suth. 179.

(*l*) 2 Stra. H. L. 204; 2 W. MacN. 196; *Shibo Koeree* v. *Joogun*, 8 Suth. 155, S. C. 4 Wym. 121.

(*m*) 1 W. MacN. 76; *Chowdree* v. *Hunooman*, 6 S. D. 192 (235); *Ooman Dut* v. *Kunhia*, 3 S. D. 145 (192).

(*n*) 3 Dig. 276, n.; 1 W. MacN. 76.

the younger was invalid (*o*). But Mr. MacNaghten points out that the authorities relied upon in that case related exclusively to the *dattaka* form. A daughter's son may be adopted, and so may the son of a sister (*p*). For the same reason, the prohibition against adopting an only or an eldest son does not apply to a Kritrima adoption (*q*). It has been held in the case last cited, that where a brother's son exists, no other can be adopted. But the opinion of the Pandits was principally founded upon texts applying to the *dattaka* form, and which, with reference to that form, have been long since held to be no longer in force. It is probable, therefore, that they would be held inapplicable to the *Kritrima* form, which is so much laxer in its rules.

Results of adoption.

§ 188. As regards succession, the *Kritrima* son loses no rights of inheritance in his natural family. He becomes the son of two fathers to this extent, that he takes the inheritance of his adoptive father, but not of that father's father, or other collateral relations, nor of the wife of his adoptive father, or her relations (*r*). Nor do his sons, &c., take any interest in the property of the adoptive father, the relationship between adopter and adoptee being limited to the contracting parties themselves, and not extending further on either side (*s*). Among the Nambudri Brahmans (*ante*, § 42) where it is desired to perpetuate the line of the adopter, the adopted son receives a special appointment to marry and raise up issue for the *illam* or line of the adopter (*t*).

Female may adopt to herself.

§ 189. It has already been stated that in Mithila a woman cannot adopt to her husband, after his death, whether she has obtained his permission or not. But she is at liberty to

(*o*) *Runjeet Singh* v. *Obhya*, 2 S. D. 245 (315). See 1 W. MacN. 76, n.

(*p*) *Ooman Dut* v. *Kunhia*, 3 S. D. 144 (192); *Chowdree* v. *Hunooman*, 6 S. D. 192 (235).

(*q*) *Ooman Dut* v. *Kunhia*, 3 S. D. (197); 2 W. MacN. 197, where however the opinion of the pandits was based upon the fact that the adoptor was the uncle of the adoptee.

(*r*) See note to *Srinath Serma* v. *Radhakaunt*, 1 S. D. 15 (19); 1 W. MacN. 76; *Deepoo* v. *Gowreeshunker*, 3 S. D. 307 (410); *Sreenarain Rai* v *Bhya Jha*, 2 S. D. 23 (29, 34); *Shibo Koeree* v. *Jugun*, 8 Suth. 155; S. C. 4 Wym. 121.

(*s*) *Juswant Doolee*, 25 Suth. 255.

(*t*) 11 Mad. 158, 175, 179.

do in Mithila, what she can do nowhere else, *viz.*, adopt a son to herself, and this she may do either during her husband's life, or after his death. And husband and wife may jointly adopt a son, or each may adopt separately. "If a woman appoint an adopted son, he stands in the relation to her of a son, offers to her funeral oblations, and is heir to her estate; but he does not become the adopted son of her husband, nor offer to him funeral oblations, nor succeed to his property. If a husband and wife jointly appoint an adopted son, he stands in the relation of son to both, and is heir to the estate of both. If the husband appoint one, and the wife another adopted son, they stand in the relation of sons to each of them respectively, and do not perform the ceremony of offering funeral oblations, nor succeed to the estate of the husband and wife jointly" (*u*).

Ceremonies.

§ 190. No ceremonies or sacrifices are necessary to the validity of a *Kritrima* adoption. "The form to be observed is this. At an auspicious time, the adopter of a son having bathed, addressing the person to be adopted, who has also bathed, and to whom he has given some acceptable chattel, says, "Be my son." He replies, "I am become thy son." The giving of some chattel to him arises merely from custom. It is not necessary to the adoption. The consent of both parties is the only requisite; and a set form of speech is not essential" (*v*).

Similar form practised in Jaffna.

It is a curious thing that this form of adoption, which now only exists in Mithila and among the Nambudris of Western India is almost identical in its leading features with that at present practised in Jaffna. There is the same absence of religious ceremonies, the same absence of any assumed new birth, and the same right of adoption both by husband and wife, followed by the same results of heirship

---

(*u*) Futwah of pandits, *Sree Narain Rai* v. *Bhya Jha*, 2 S. D. 28 (29, 34); 1 W. MacN. 101; *Collector of Tirhoot* v. *Huropershad*, 7 Suth. 500; *Shibo Koeree* v. *Jugun*, 8 Suth. 155; S. C. 4 Wym. 121.

(*v*) *Rudradhara*, cited note to *Mitakshara*, i. 11, § 17; 1 W. MacN. 98; *Kullean* v. *Kirpa*, 1 S. D. 9 (11); *Durgopal* v. *Roopun*, 6 S. D. 271 (340).

only to the adopter (*w*). The explanation given by Mr. MacNaghten (§ 184) may account for the survival of the *Kritrima* adoption : but it does not explain its origin. It seems plain that both the Mithila and the Ceylon form arose from purely secular motives, and existed anterior to, and independent of, Brahmanical theories. The growth of these put the *Kritrima* form out of fashion. But the similar type continued to flourish in Ceylon, where no such influence prevailed. An enquiry into the usages of the Tamil races in Southern India would probably disclose the existence of analogous customs.

Illatam adoption.

§ 190A. A custom known as that of *Illatam* adoption prevails among the *Reddi* caste in the Madras Presidency. It consists in the affiliation of a son-in-law, in consideration of assistance in the management of the family property. No religious significance appears to attach to the act. It seems uncertain whether such an affiliation can take place where there is already a son, or whether the person so affiliated can claim a partition during the life of his adopting father. After the death of the adopter he is entitled to the full rights of a son, even as against natural sons subsequently born (*x*). As between himself and his own descendants he takes the property as self-acquisition, and therefore free from all restraints upon alienation (*y*). The property so taken descends to his relations, not to the heirs of the adopter (*z*), while he himself loses no rights of inheritance in his natural family (*a*).

(*w*) Thesawaleme, ii. (*x*) *Hanumantamma* v. *Rami Reddi*, 4 Mad. 272.
(*y*) *Chella Papi* v. *Chella Koti*, 7 Mad. H. C. 25.
(*z*) *Ramakristna* v. *Subbakka*, 12 Mad. 442.
(*a*) *Balarami* v. *Pera*, 6 Mad. 267.

CHAPTER VI.

FAMILY RELATIONS.

Minority and Guardianship.

Period of minority.

§ 191. MINORITY under Hindu law terminates at the age of sixteen. There was, however, a difference of opinion as to whether this age was attained at the beginning, or at the end, of the sixteenth year. The Hindu writers seem to take the former view (*a*), and this was always held to be the law in Bengal (*b*). The latter limit is stated to be the rule in Mithila and Benares, and was followed in Southern India and apparently in Bombay (*c*). Different periods were also fixed for special purposes by statutes, which it does not come within the scope of this work to discuss. These variances will soon loose all importance in consequence of Act IX of 1875, which lays down as a general rule for all persons domiciled in British India or the Allied States, that in the case of every minor of whose person or property a guardian has been, or shall be, appointed by any Court of Justice, and of every minor under the jurisdiction of any Court of Wards, minority terminates at the completion of the twenty-first year; in all other cases, at the completion of the eighteenth year (*d*). Where a guardian has once been appointed by a Court of Justice,

---

(*a*) 1 Dig. 293; 2 Dig. 115; Mitakshara on Loans, cited V. Darp., 770; Daya Bhaga, iii. 1, § 17, note; Dattaka Mimamsa, iv. § 47.

(*b*) 1 W. MacN. 103; 2 W. MacN. 220, 288, note; *Callychurn* v. *Bhuggobutty*, 10 B. L. R. 231; S. C. 19 Suth. 110; *Mothoor Mohun* v. *Surendro*, 1 Cal. 108.

(*c*) W. MacN. *ubi sup.*; 1 Stra. H. L. 72; 2 Stra. H. L. 76, 77; *Lachman* v. *Rupchand*, 5 S. D. 114 (136); *Shivji* v. *Datu*, 12 Bom. H. C. 281, 290.

(*d*) *Khwahish* v. *Surju*, 3 All. 598; *Reade* v. *Krishna*, 9 Mad. 391. As to whether the appointment is complete until a certificate has actually been issued, see under Bombay Minors Act XX of 1864, *Yeknath* v. *Warubai*, 13 Bom. 285; under Bengal Act XL of 1858, *Mungniram* v. *Mohunt Gursahai*, 16 I. A. 195, S. C. 17 Cal. 347. A Collector appointed under Act XL of 1858, s. 7 is a guardian within the meaning of Act IX of 1575, s. 8, but one appointed under s. 12 is not. 17 Cal. p. 948.

minority will last till 21, whether the guardian so appointed continues to act or not, or has, or has not taken out a certificate (*e*). But where the Court of Wards has assumed jurisdiction, the disability of minority only continues so long as the Court of Wards, retains charge of the minor's property, and no longer (*f*). The Act is not to affect any person in respect of marriage, dower, divorce, or adoption.

Order of guardianship.

§ 192. GUARDIANSHIP.—The Hindu law vests the guardianship of the minor in the sovereign as *parens patriæ*. Necessarily this duty is delegated to the child's relations. Of these the father, and next to him the mother, is his natural guardian. In default of her, or if she is unfit to exercise the trust, his nearest male kinsmen should be appointed, the paternal kindred having the preference over the maternal (*g*). Of course, in an undivided family, governed by Mitakshara law, the management of the whole property, including the minor's share, would be vested in the nearest male, and not in the mother. It would be otherwise where the family was divided (*h*). But this would not interfere with her right to the custody of the child itself (*i*). The husband's relations, if any exist within the degree of a sapinda, are the guardians of a minor widow, in preference to her father and his relations (*k*). A mother loses her right by a second marriage (*l*), and a father loses

(*e*) *Rudra Prokash* v. *Bholanath Mukherjee*, 12 Cal. 612; *Girish Chunder* v. *Abdul Selam*, 14 Cal. 55.

(*f*) *Birjmohun Lal* v. *Rudra Perkash*, 17 Cal. 944.

(*g*) Manu, viii. § 27; ix. § 146, 190, 191; 3 Dig. 542—544; F. MacN. 25; 1 Stra. H. L. 71; 2 Stra. H. L 72—75; *Gungama* v. *Chendrappa*, Mad. Dec. of 1859, 100; 1 W. MacN. 103; *Mooddookrishna* v. *Tandavaroy*, Mad. Dec. of 1852, 105; *Muhtaboo* v. *Gunesh*, S. D. of 1854, 329. Under Mithila law, however, it has been held that the mother is entitled to be guardian of the person of her minor son in perference to the father. *Jussoda* v. *Lallah Nettya*, 5 Cal. 43. As to the claim of the step-mother, see *Lukmee* v. *Umurchund*, 2 Bor. 144 [163]; *Ram Bunsee* v. *Soobh Koonwaree*, 7 Suth. 321; S. C. 3 Wym. 219; S. C. 2 In. Jur. 193, *Baee Sheo* v. *Ruttonjee*, Morris, Pt. 1. 103. As to the Punjab, see Punjab Customary Law, II. 133.

(*h*) *Alimelammal* v. *Arunachellam*, 3 Mad. H. C. 69; *Bissonauth* v. *Doorgapersad*, 2 M. Dig. 49; *Gourahkoeri* v. *Gujadhur*, 5 Cal. 219. But she can sue on his behalf if the proper guardian refuses to do so, *Mokrund Deb* v. *Ranee Bissessuree*, S. D. of 1853, 159.

(*i*) *Kooldeep* v. *Bajbunsee*, S. D. of 1847, 557.

(*k*) *Khudiram Mookerjee* v. *Bonwari*, 16 Cal. 584.

(*l*) *Baee Sheo* v. *Ruttonjee*, Morris, Pt. I. 103.

his right by giving his son in adoption (*m*). And, of course, any guardian, however appointed, may be removed for proper cause (*n*). Little is to be found on the subject of guardianship in works on Hindu law. The matter is principally regulated by statute (*o*).

Right of guardian to custody of minor.

§ 193. The right of the guardian to the possession of the infant is an absolute right, of which he cannot be deprived, even by the desire of the minor himself, except upon sufficient grounds. In the case of parents, especially, it is obvious that the custody of their child is a matter of greater moment to them than the custody of any article of property. Cases, however, have frequently occurred in the Indian Courts, where the right of a parent to recover his child has been contested, on the ground that the parent had changed his religion, and was therefore no longer a fit guardian for his child; or that the child had changed its religion, and was no longer willing to live with its parent. On the former point it has been decided, that the fact that a father has changed his religion, whether the change be one to Christianity or from Christianity, is of itself no reason for depriving him of the custody of his children. It would be different, of course, if the change were attended with circumstances of immorality, which showed that his home was no longer fit for the residence of the child (*p*). But the case of a change of religion by the mother might be different. The religion of the father settles the law which governs

Change of religion by parent;

(*m*) *Lakshmibai* v. *Shridar*, 3 Bom. 1.

(*n*) *Alimelammal* v. *Arunachellam*, 3 Mad. H.C. 69; *Gourmonee* v. *Bamasoonderee*, S. D. of 1860, i. 532; *Skinner* v. *Orde*, 14 M. I. A. 309; S. C. 10 B. L. R. 125; S. C. 17 Suth. 77; *Kanahi* v. *Biddya*, 1 All. 549; *Abasi* v. *Dunne*, 1 All. 598.

(*o*) See Ct. of Wards Acts, Beng. Reg. XXVI of 1793, LII of 1803, VI of 1822; Mad. Reg. V of 1804; Act XX of 1864; Bengal Act, IV of 1870. Minors not under Court of Wards, Acts XL of 1858, IV of 1872. Education and marriage of minors, Acts XXVI of 1854, XXI of 1855, XIV of 1858. *Ram Bunsee* v. *Soobh Koonwaree*, 7 Suth. 321; S. C. 3 Wym. 219; S. C. 2 In. Jur. 193; *Ramchunder* v. *Brojonath*, 4 Cal. 929. See as to Procedure, Act IX of 1861; Guardian and Ward Act, XIII of 1874, VIII of 1890. Where the Law requires the appointment of a guardian under any statute, no greater powers can be exercised by a guardian *de facto* than would have been vested in him by statute, if he had been duly appointed. *Abhassi Begam* v. *Rajroop Koonwar*, 4 Cal. 33.

(*p*) R. v. *Bezonji*, Perry, O. C. 91.

himself, his family, and his property. "From the very necessity of the case, a child in India, under ordinary circumstances, must be presumed to have his father's religion, and his corresponding civil and social *status*; and it is, therefore, ordinarily, and in the absence of controlling circumstances, the duty of a guardian to train his infant ward in such religion." Therefore, where a change of religion on the part of the mother would have the effect of changing the religion, and therefore the legal *status* of the infant, the Court would remove her from her position as guardian. And the asserted wish of the minor, also, to change his religion, in conformity with that of the mother, would not necessarily alter the case; unless, perhaps, where the advanced age of the minor, and the settled character of his religious convictions would render it improper, or impossible, to attempt to restore him to his former position (*q*). The rights of a father to direct the religion in which his children shall be brought up is so inseparable from his character as parent that he cannot be bound by an agreement renouncing the rights, even though the agreement is made before marriage and was a *sine quâ nòn* to the marriage taking place (*r*). But where the father has allowed his agreement to be acted on during his life, and has died without expressing any contrary wish, these circumstances will be taken into consideration as showing that he had abandoned any desire that his children should be brought up in his own religion, especially if it appears that it would be for their temporal benefit to continue in the religion of their mother (*s*).

§ 194. The case of a child voluntarily leaving its parents has frequently occurred where there has been a conversion to Christianity. It seems at one time to have been the practice of the Courts of Calcutta and Madras to allow the by infant.

(*q*) *Skinner* v. *Orde*, 14 M. I. A. 309; S. C. 10 B. L. R. 125; S. C. 17 Suth. 77.

(*r*) *Re Agar Ellis*, 10 Ch. D. 49. This right of the father continues in England till the child is 21. *Re Agar Ellis*, 24 Ch. D. 317.

(*s*) *Re Clarke*, 21 Ch. D. 817; *Re Violet Nevin*, 2 Ch. (1891) 299.

child to exercise his discretion, if, upon a personal examination, they were satisfied that his wish was to remain away from his parents, and that he was capable of exercising an intelligent judgment upon the point. The contrary rule was for the first time laid down by the Supreme Court of Bombay, when they directed a boy of twelve years old to be given back to his father, and refused to examine him as to his capacity and knowledge of the Christian religion, or as to his wish to remain with his Christian instructors (*t*). This course was approved by Mr. Justice *Patteson,* to whom Sir Erskine Perry referred the point (*u*). That decision was followed in the Supreme Court of Madras in 1858, in the case of *Culloor Narrainsawmy* (*v*), when Sir *Christopher Rawlinson* and Sir *Adam Bittleston* decided that a Hindu youth of the age of fourteen, who had gone to the Scottish missionaries, should be given up to his father, though he had become a convert to Christianity, and was most anxious to remain with his new protectors. A similar decision was given in Calcutta in 1863, by Sir *Mordaunt Wells,* where a boy of fifteen years and two months had voluntarily gone to reside with the missionaries (*w*). All these cases were lately examined and affirmed by the Madras High Court, which held that under Act IX of 1875 the period of parental control and custody lasted until 18 (*x*). It may also be observed, that it is a criminal offence under the Indian Penal Code, to entice from the keeping of its lawful guardian a male minor under the age of fourteen, or a female minor under the age of sixteen (*y*).

Illegitimate child.

§ 195. The mother is the natural guardian of an illegitimate child. But where she has allowed the child to be

---

(*t*) *R.* v. *Nesbitt,* Perry, O. C. 103. (*u*) *Ib.*, p. 109.

(*v*) Not reported. I was counsel for the missionaries in the case.—J. D. M.

(*w*) *Re Himnauth Bose,* 1 Hyde, 111.

(*x*) *Reade* v. *Krishna,* 9 Mad. 391. No agreement by which a parent surrenders to another the right to the custody of the child is binding, and in this respect the mother of an illegitimate child is in the same position as the father of one that is legitimate. *Reg.* v. *Barnardo,* A. C. (1891) 388.

(*y*) I. P. C. § 361, 363. The consent, or wish, of the minor is quite immaterial. See cases cited *sub loco.* Mayne's Commentaries on the Indian Penal Code.

separated from her and brought up by the father, or by persons appointed by him, the Court will not allow her to enforce her rights. Especially if the result would be disadvantageous to the child, by depriving it of the advantages of a higher mode of life and education (*z*). Her own continued immorality would of itself be a sufficient reason against handing over to her a child which was otherwise properly provided for (*a*).

Effect of contracts.

§ 196. Contracts made by a minor himself are, at the utmost voidable, not void. If made for any necessary purpose they are absolutely binding upon him, and they can always be ratified by him after he attains full age, either expressly, or impliedly by acquiescence, and taking the benefit of them (*b*). He will also be bound by the act of his guardian, in the management of his estate, when *bonâ fide* and for his interest, and when it is such as the infant might reasonably and prudently have done for himself, if he had been of full age (*c*). But not where the act appears not to have been for his benefit (*d*), unless he has ratified

---

(*z*) *R.* v. *Fletcher*, Perry, O. C. 109; *Mittibhayi* v. *Kottekarati*, Mad. Dec. of 1860, 154; *Lal Das* v. *Nekunjo*, 4 Cal. 374.

(*a*) *Venkamma* v. *Savitramma*, 12 Mad. 67.

(*b*) *Rennie* v. *Gunganarain*, 3 Suth. 10; *Boiddonath* v. *Ramkishore*, 13 Suth. 166; *Doorga Churn* v. *Ram Narain*, *ib.* 172.

(*c*) *Cauminany* v. *Perumma*, Mad. Dec. of 1855, 99: *Temmakal* v. *Subbammal*, 2 Mad. H. C. 47; *Manishankar* v. *Bai Muli*, 12 Bom. 686; *Nathuram* v. *Shoma Chhagan*, 14 Bom. 562; *Kumurooddeen* v. *Shaikh Bhadoo*, 11 Suth. 134; *Makbul* v. *Srimati Masnad*, 3 B. L. R. (A. C. J.) 54; S. C. 11 Suth. 396; *Gooroopersad* v. *Muddun*, S. D. of 1856, 980; *Soonder Narain* v. *Bennud Ram*, 4 Cal. 76; *Roshan Singh* v. *Har Kishan*, 3 All. 535; *Sikher Chund* v. *Dulputty*, 5 Cal. 363; *Nirvanaya* v. *Nirvanaya*, 9 Bom. 365. See as to a guardian's power of leasing, *Nubokishen* v. *Kaleepersad*, S. D. of 1859, 607; *Gopeenath* v. *Ramjeewun*, *ib.* 913; *Beebee Sowlutoonisa* v. *Robt. Savi*, *ib.* 1575. See also as to contracts requiring statutory sanction, *Debi Dutt* v. *Subodra*, 2 Cal. 283. *Manji Ram* v. *Tara Singh*, 3 All. 852; *Doorga Persad* v. *Kesho Persad*, 9 I. A. 27. S. C. 8 Cal. 656; *Rai Balkrishna* v. *Mt. Masuma Bibi*, 9 I. A. 182; S. C. 5 All. 142; *Dunput Singh* v. *Shoobudra*, 8 Cal. 620; *Harendra Narain* v. *Moran*, 15 Cal. 40; *Bhupendro Narayan* v. *Nemye Chand*, 15 Cal. 627; *Girraj Baksh* v. *Kasi Hamid*, 9 All. 340. Documents executed by a Hindu widow who described herself as "mother of A, minor," were held in the absence of evidence to the contrary, to be executed by her in her capacity as guardian of the infant, *Watson* v. *Sham Lal Mitter*, 14 I. A. 178, S. C. 15. Cal. 8.

(*d*) *Sambasivien* v. *Kristnien*, Mad. Dec. of 1858, 252; *Nawab Syud Ashrufooddeen* v. *Mt. Shama Soonderee*, S. D. of 1853, 531; *Nubokishen* v. *Kaleepersad*, S. D. of 1859, 607; *Lalla Bunseedhur* v. *Koonwur Bindeseree*, 10 M. I. A. 454. A guardian may pay debts barred by statute if fairly due, *Chowdhry Chuttersal* v. *Government*, 3 Suth. 57.

it on reaching his majority (*e*). And where the act is done by a person who is not his guardian, but who is the manager of the estate in which he has an interest, he will equally be bound, if under the circumstances the step taken was necessary, proper, or prudent (*f*). In all cases the power of the guardian or manager is limited to the disposal of the estate with which he is entrusted. He cannot bind the minor by any purely personal covenant. For instance, a guardian in order to pay off a charge upon the estate sold part of it, and was held to have acted properly in so doing. The part was sold as free of all Government claim for revenue, and naturally fetched a higher price on that account. The conveyance contained a covenant binding the minor and his heirs to indemnify the purchaser against any claims for revenue which the Government might make at any future time, and provided that the amount of such indemnity should be a charge upon the unsold portion of the estate, and should also be payable personally by the vendor and his heirs. After the termination of the minority Government assessed the land, and an action was brought upon the covenant by the purchaser. The Privy Council held that the personal covenant was not binding on the minor after he attained majority, such a covenant being beyond the guardian's powers. They thought that possibly it might bind the land, as the result of the covenant was to save part of the land which would otherwise have to be sold. It was unnecessary to decide this point, as under a special statute the land was made free from incumbrance (*g*).

Where the act is done by a person in possession of

(*e*) *Chetty Colum* v. *Rajah Rungasawmy*, 8 M. I. A. 319; S. C. 4. Suth. (P. C.) 71. *Golaub Koonwurree* v. *Eshan Chunder*, 8 M. I. A. 447; S. C. 2 Suth. (P. C.) 47. *Kumuroodddeen* v. *Shaikh Bhadoo*, 11 Suth. 134; *Bhobanny* v. *Teerpurachurn*, 2 M. Dig. 100; *Mongooney* v. *Gooroopersad*, *ib*. 188. See as to carrying out, after the removal of a personal disability, a contract which was agreed upon while the disability lasted, *Gregson* v. *Aditya Deb*, 16 I. A. 221. S. C. 17 Cal. 228. A ratification will be of no effect, if the property has already passed away from the person who ratifies the transaction, *Lallah Kawuth* v. *Chadee*, S. D. of 1858, 312.

(*f*) *Hunoomanpersaud* v. *Mt. Babooee*, 6 M. I. A. 393.

(*g*) *Waghela Raj Sanji* v. *Shekh Masludin*, 14 I. A. 89; 11 Bom. 551.

property, who does not profess to be acting on behalf of the minor, but who claims to be independent owner, and to be acting on his own behalf, it will not bind the infant who is really entitled (*h*).

Of course the objection to an act on the ground of minority must be taken by the minor himself. Those who deal with him are always bound, though he may not be (*i*).

Equities on setting aside.

Where a minor on coming of age sues to set a sale aside, he is bound to refund the purchase money, when his estate has benefited by it, or to hold the property charged with the amount of debt from which it has been freed by the sale (*k*).

Decrees.

§ 197. A minor, who is properly represented in a suit, will be bound by its result, whether that result is arrived at by hostile decree, or by compromise or by withdrawal (*l*). But the Court will not make a decree by consent without ascertaining whether it is for the benefit of the infant. Without such approval by the Court, the compromise will not bind the infant, and the decree passed in accordance therewith will be set aside at his instance (*m*). Where a decree binding on a minor has once been obtained, the creditor will not be deprived of the benefit of his decree, because he has by mistake taken out execution against the guardian

---

(*h*) *Bahur Ali* v. *Sookeea*, 13 Suth. 63.

(*i*) *Canaka* v. *Cottarappah*, Mad. Dec. of 1855, 184. *Hanmant Lakshman* v. *Jayarao*, 12 Bom. 50; *Mahamed Arif* v. *Saraswati Debya*, 18 Cal. 259.

(*k*) *Bukshun* v. *Doolhin*, 12 Suth. 337; S. C. 3 B. L. R. (A. C. J.) 423; *Paran Chandra* v. *Karunamayi*, 7 B. L. R. 90; S. C. 15 Suth. 268; *Bai Kesar* v. *Bai Ganga*, 8 Bom. H. C. (A. C. J.) 81; *Mirza Pana* v. *Saiad Sadik*, 7 N.-W. P. 201; *Kuvarji* v. *Moti Haridas*, 3 Bom. 234; and see *Gadgeppa* v. *Apaji*, 3 Bom. 237.

(*l*) *Kamaraju* v. *Secretary of State*, 11 Mad. 309; *Chengal Reddi* v. *Venkata Reddi*, 12 Mad. 483; *Tarinee Churn* v. *Watson*, 12 Suth. 414; S. C. 3 B. L. R. (A. C. J.) 437; *Modhoo Soodun* v. *Prithee Bullub*, 16 Suth. 231; *Jungee Lall* v. *Sham Lall*, 20 Suth. 120; *Lekraj* v. *Mahtab*, 14 M. I. A. 393; S. C. 10 B. L. R. 35; S. C. 17 Suth. 117; *Mrinamoyi* v. *Jogo Dishuri*, 5 Cal. 450. And the guardian may equally compromise claims before suit; *Gopeenath* v. *Ramjeewun*, S. D. of 1859, 913. As to effect of withdrawal of suit, *Eshan Chunder* v. *Nundamoni*, 10 Cal. 357.

(*m*) *Ram Churn* v. *Mungul*, 16 Suth. 232. Civil Procedure Code, Act XIV of 1882, § 462; *Rajagopal* v. *Muttupalem*, 3 Mad. 103; *Karmali* v. *Rahimbhoy*, 13 Bom. 137.

by name instead of against the minor as represented by the guardian (*n*). And the mere fact that a proceeding was partly conducted through the intervention of a Civil Court —as for instance, a decree on a foreclosure—does not give it any additional validity against a minor, unless he is properly made a party to the proceeding at a stage when he can question it on its merits (*o*). Of course a compromise or a decree can always be set aside if obtained by fraud (*p*). Cases might arise in which a guardian by mere carelessness, amounting to gross neglect of duty but without fraud, failed properly to support the interests of his ward, and thereby failed in a suit which he ought to have won. Whether the ward in attaining full age might set aside the decree against him is a point which has been raised, but not decided (*q*).

The natural father of an adopted son is not his guardian, unless specially so appointed, so as to bind him by his conduct of a suit in his behalf (*r*). And although the minor may properly be represented by the manager of the undivided family, the mere fact that the suit is conducted or defended by the manager is not in itself sufficient to show that the minor is adequately represented (*s*). If, however, the Court has in fact given permission to any one to represent the minor, his acts will not be invalid for want of a certificate under Act XL of 1858, though the absence of such certificate may, if not rebutted, be evidence that there never has been such a permission (*t*). A mere want of form in the mode of describing the minors will not affect

(*n*) *Hari* v. *Narayan*, 12 Bom. 427.

(*o*) *Buzrung* v. *Mt. Mautora*, 22 Suth. 119.

(*p*) *Lekraj* v. *Mahtab*, 14 M. I. A. 393; S. C. 10 B. L. R. 35; S. C. 17 Suth. 117; *Bibee Solomon* v. *Abdul Azeez*, 6 Cal. 687; *Eshan Chunder* v. *Nundamoni*, 10 Cal. 357; *Raghubar Dyal* v. *Bhikya Lall*, 12 Cal. 69.

(*q*) *Mungniram* v. *Mohunt Gursahai*, 16 I. A., p. 204, S. C. 17 Cal. p. 361.

(*r*) *Srinarain Mitter* v. *Sreemutty Kishen*, 11 B. L. R. 171. (P. C.)

(*s*) *Padmakar Vinayek* v. *Mahadev Krishna*, 10 Bom. 21. Doubting *Gan Savant* v. *Narayen Dhond*, 7 Bom. 467; *Vishnu Keshav* v. *Ramchandra*, 11 Bom. 130.

(*t*) *Jgoi Singh* v. *Behari Singh*, 11 Cal. 509; *Alim Buksh* v. *Jhalo Bibi*, 12 Cal. 48; *Durgopershad* v. *Kesho Pershad*, 9 I. A. 27; S. C. 8 Cal. 656; *Suresh Chunder* v. *Jugat Chunder*, 14 Cal. 204; *Parmeshar Das* v. *Bela*, 9 All. 508. As to suits brought on behalf of a minor without the sanction of the Court of Wards, see *Dinesh Chunder* v. *Golam Mostapha*, 16 Cal. 89.

the validity of the decree, if they have been really represented and sued (*u*).

A decree in a suit in which a minor is properly represented may be liable to set aside for fraud or other reasons, but till set aside it binds him, and proceedings to get rid of it must be commenced within a year from the date of the decree or from the termination of the minority (*v*). Where the minor has not been properly represented the decree is a nullity, as far as he is concerned. He need take no notice of it, and may proceed to enforce his rights within the period of limitation which would be applicable if no decree had been passed (*w*).

Suits against guardian.

A guardian is liable to be sued by his ward for damages arising from his fraudulent or illegal acts (*x*). For debts due by the ward, the guardian of course is only liable to the extent of the funds which have reached his hands (*y*).

(*u*) *Jogi Singh* v. *Behari Singh*, *ub sup.*, *Bhaba Pershad* v. *Secretary of State*, 14 Cal. 159; *Suresh Chunder* v. *Jugat Chunder*, 14 Cal. 204; *Natesvayyan* v. *Narasimmayyar*, 13 Mad. 480; *Hari Saran Moitra* v. *Bhubaneswari Debi*, 15 I. A. 195. S. C. 16 Cal. 40.

(*v*) Act XV of 1877, Sched. II, Art. 12. *Mungniram Marwari* v. *Mohunt Gursahai*, 16 I. A. 203. S. C. 17 Cal. 347. As to the mode of setting aside such a decree, see *Mirali Rahimbhoy* v. *Rehmoobhoy*, 15 Bom. 594.

(*w*) *Daji Himat* v. *Dhirajram*, 12 Bom. 18.

(*x*) *Issur Chunder* v. *Ragab*, S. D. of 1860, 1, 349.

(*y*) *Sheikh Azeemooddeen* v. *Moonshee Athur*, 3 Suth. 137.

CHAPTER VII.

EARLY LAW OF PROPERTY.

Misleading effect of English analogies.

§ 198. THE student who wishes to understand the Hindu system of property, must begin by freeing his mind from all previous notions drawn from English law. They would not only be useless, but misleading. In England ownership, as a rule, is single, independent, and unrestricted. It may be joint, but the presumption will be to the contrary. It may be restricted, but only in special instances, and under special provisions. In India, on the contrary, joint ownership is the rule, and will be presumed to exist in each individual case until the contrary is proved. If an individual holds property in severalty, it will, in the next generation, relapse into a state of joint tenancy. Absolute, unrestricted ownership, such as enables the owner to do anything he likes with his property, is the exception. The father is restrained by his sons, the brother by his brothers, the woman by her successors. If property is free in the hands of its acquirer, it will resume its fetters in the hands of his heirs. Individual property is the rule in the West. Corporate property is the rule in the East. And yet, although the difference between the two systems can now only be expressed in terms of direct antithesis, it is pretty certain that both had a common origin (*a*). But in India the past and the present are continuous. In England they are separated by a wide gulf. Of the bridge by which they were formerly connected, a few planks, only visible to the eye of the antiquarian, are all that now remain.

(*a*) See Maine, Village Communities, 82.

§ 199. Three forms of the corporate system of property exist in India; the Patriarchal Family, the Joint Family and the Village Community. The two former, in one shape or other, may be said to prevail throughout the length and breadth of India. The last still flourishes in the north-west of Hindostan. It is traceable, though dying out, in Southern India. It has disappeared, though we may be sure it formerly existed, in Bengal and the upper part of the peninsula. In some regions, such as among the Hill tribes and the Nairs of the Western Coast, it appears never to have arisen at all. The analogy between the two latter forms is complete. The Village Community is a corporate body, of which the members are families. The Joint Family is a corporate body, of which the members are individuals. The process of change which has been undergone both by Village Communities and Families is similar, and the causes of this change are generally identical. It seems a tempting generalisation to lay down, that one must have sprung from the other; that the Village Community has grown out of the extension of the Joint Family, or that the Joint Family has resulted from the dissolving of the larger body into its component parts. But such a generalisation would be unsafe. The same causes have no doubt produced the Village system and the Family system. But it is certain that there are many Villages which have never sprung from the same Family, and many places where the Family system has shown no tendency to grow into the Village system.

Different forms of corporate property.

§ 200. The Village system of India may be studied with most advantage in the Punjab, as it is there that we find it in its most perfect, as well as in its transitional, forms. It presents three marked phases, which exactly correspond to the changes in an undivided family. The closest form of union is that which is known as the *Communal Zemindari* village. Under this system "the land is so held that all the village co-sharers have each their proportionate share in it as common property, without any possession of, or title to, distinct portions of it; and the measure of each proprietor's

Village communities in the Punjab.

interest is his share as fixed by the customary law of inheritance. The rents paid by the cultivators are thrown into a common stock, with all other profits from the village lands, and after deduction of the expenses the balance is divided among the proprietors according to their shares" (*b*). This corresponds to the undivided family in its purest state. The second stage is called the *pattidari* village. In it the holdings are all in severalty, and each sharer manages his own portion of land. But the extent of the share is determined by ancestral right, and is capable of being modified from time to time upon this principle (*c*). This corresponds to the state of an undivided family in Bengal. The transitional stage between joint holdings and holdings in severalty is to be found in the system of re-distribution, which is still practised in the Pathan communities of Peshawur. According to that practice, the holdings were originally allotted to the individual families on the principle of strict equality. But as time introduced inequalities with reference to the numbers settled on each holding, a periodical transfer and re-distribution of holdings took place (*d*). This practice naturally dies out as the sense of individual property strengthens, and as the habit of dealing with the shares by mortgage and sale is introduced. The share of each family then becomes its own. The third and final stage is known as the *bhaiachari* village. It agrees with the *pattidari* form, inasmuch as each owner holds his share in severalty. But it differs from it, inasmuch as the extent of the holding is strictly defined by the amount actually held in possession. All reference to ancestral right has disappeared, and no change in the number of the co-sharers can entitle any member to have his share enlarged. His rights have become absolute instead of relative, and have ceased to be measured by any reference to the extent of the whole village, and the

Punjab.

(*b*) Punjab Customs, 105, 161. This stage is the same as that described by Sir H. S. Maine, as existing in Servia and the adjoining districts. Ancient Law, 267. See Evans, Bosnia, 44.

(*c*) Punjab Customs, 106, 156.

(*d*) Punjab Customs, 125, 170. See Corresponding Customs, Maine, Anc. Law, 267; Village Communities, 81; Lavaleye, ch. vi.; Wallace, Russia, i. 189.

numbers of those by whom it is held (*e*). This is exactly the state of a family after its members have come to a partition.

§ 201. The same causes which have broken up the Joint Family of Bengal have led to the disappearance of the Village system in that province. In Western and Central India, the wars and devastations of Muhammedans, Mahrattas, and Pindarries swept away the Village institutions, as well as almost every other form of ancient proprietary right (*f*). But in Southern India, among the Tamil races, we find traces of similar communities (*g*). The Village landholders are there represented by a class known as *Mirasidars,* the extent and nature of whose rights are far from being clearly ascertained. It is certain, however, that they have a preferential right over other inhabitants to be accepted as tenants by the Government, a right which they do not even lose by neglecting to avail themselves of it at each fresh settlement (*h*). They are jointly entitled to receive certain fees and perquisites from the occupying tenants, and to share in the common lands (*i*). Some villages are even at the present time held in shares by a body of proprietors who claim to represent the original owners, and a practice of exchanging and re-distributing these shares is known still to exist, though it is fast dying out (*k*). In Madras the Government claim is made upon each occupant separately, not upon the whole village, as in the Punjab; but the contrary usage must once have existed.

Southern India.

(*e*) Punjab Customs, 106, 161.

(*f*) See speech of Sir J. Lawrence, cited Punjab Customs, 138.

(*g*) Elphinstone, India, 66, 249.

(*h*) *Ramanooja* v. *Peetayen*, Mad. Dec. of 1850, 121; *Alagappa* v. *Ramasamy*, Mad. Dec. of 1859, 101; 5th Report House of Commons, cited *Mootoopermall* v. *Tondaven*, 1 N. C. 320. [275]. See *Fakir Muhammad* v. *Tiramalu Chariar*, 1 Mad. 205.

(*i*) *Mootoopermall* v. *Tondaven*, 1 Stra. N. C 300. [260] *Koomarasawmy* v. *Ragava*, Mad. Dec. of 1852, 33; *Viswanadha* v. *Moottoo Moodely*, Mad. Dec. of 1854, 141; *Muniappa* v. *Kasturi*, Mad. Dec. of 1862, 50. In the Punjab this right may be retained by a co-sharer, though he has ceased to possess any land in the village. Punjab Customs, 108.

(*k*) Madura Manual, Pt. V. 12; *Venkatasvami* v. *Subba Rau*, 2 Mad. H. C. 1, 5; *Anandayyan* v. *Devarajayyan*, ib. 17; *Saminathaiyan* v. *Saminthaiyan*, 4 Mad. H. C. 159; *Sittiaramiyer* v. *Alagiri*, 3 Mad. Rev. Reg. 189.

Sir G. Campbell mentions an instance in which the Government supposed that they were receiving their revenue as usual, from the individual ryots. It was ascertained that the village had really taken the matter into its own hands, and regularly re-distributed the burthen according to ancient practice among the several occupants (*l*).

Tradition of common descent.

§ 202. The co-sharers in many of these Village Communities are persons who are actually descended from a common ancestor. In many other cases they profess a common descent, for which there is probably no foundation (*m*). In some cases it is quite certain there can be no common descent, as they are of different castes, or even of different religions (*n*). But it is well known that in India the mere fact of association produces a belief in a common origin, unless there are circumstances which make such an identity plainly impossible. I have often heard a witness say of another man that he was his relation, and then upon cross-examination explain that he was of the same caste. The ideas presented themselves to his mind, not as two but as one. An instance is given by Sir H. S. Maine, in which some missionaries planted in villages converts collected from all sorts of different regions. They rapidly adopted the language and habits of a brotherhood, and will no doubt before long frame a pedigree to account for their juxta-position (*o*). It is evident that an actual community of descent must depend upon mere accident. If a family settled in an unoccupied district, it might spread out till it formed one community, or several Village Communities. The same result might happen if a family became sufficiently powerful to turn out its neighbours, or to reduce them to submission. Where the country was more thickly peopled, several families would have to unite from the first for

(*l*) Land Tenures, Cobden Club, 197.
(*m*) Punjab Customs, 136, 164; Maine, Vill. Com. 12, 175; Early Instit. 1, 64; Lyall, Asiatic Studies, ch. vii; Hunter's Orissa, ii. 72; McLennan, 214. It must be remembered that the co-sharers of a village are a much smaller body than the inhabitants.
(*n*) Maine, Vill. Com. 176; *Muniappa* v. *Kasturi*, Mad. Dec. of 1862, 50.
(*o*) Maine, Early Instit. 238.

mutual protection, and would in time begin to account in the usual way for the fact that they found themselves united in interest. Families which settled, or sprung up, in regions that were fully occupied never could form new communities based on the possession of land.

Joint families do not always expand into village communities.

§ 203. As it is certain that Village Communities have not always sprung from a single Joint Family, so it is equally certain that a Joint Family does not necessarily tend to expand into a Village Community. For instance, the Nairs, whose domestic system presents the most perfect form of the Joint Family now existing, never have formed Village Communities. Each *tarwad* lives in its own mansion, nestling among its palm trees, and surrounded by its rice lands, but apart from, and independent of, its neighbours. This arises from the peculiar structure of the family, which traces its origin in each generation to females, who live on in the same ancestral house, and not to males, who would naturally radiate from it, as separate but kindred branches of the same tree. In a lesser degree the same thing may be said of the Kandhs. Among them the Patriarchal Family is found in its sternest type. But though the families live together in septs and tribes, tracing from a common ancestor, and acknowledging a common head, and although their hamlets have a deceptive similarity to a Hindu village, they want the one element of union—there is no unity of authority, and no community of rights. Each family holds its property in severalty, and never held it in any other way. It is absolute owner of the land it occupies; and it ceases to have any interest in the land which it abandons. The chieftain has influence, but not authority. The families live in proximity, but not in cohesion. They are not branches of one tree, but a collection of twigs (*p*). This, again, seems to arise from the circumstances of their position. With them land is so abundant, and their wants so few, that it has never been

Kandhs.

(*p*) Hunter's Orissa, ii. 72, 204.

necessary to restrain the individual for the benefit of the community. Where the common stock is limited, it is necessary to make rules for its enjoyment; but where all can have as much as they want, no one would take the trouble to make rules, and no one would submit to them if made.

Arrested expansion of the Patriarchal Family.

§ 204. The same causes which have prevented the Joint Family from extending into the Village Community, appear also to check the Patriarchal Family at the stage at which it would naturally expand into the Joint Family. For instance, among the Kandhs, at the death of the father, the family union, which previously was absolute, appears to dissolve. The property is divided, and each son sets up for himself as a new head of a family (*q*). Among the Hill Tribes of the Nilgiris, and among the Kols, the same practice prevails (*r*).

§ 205. It would appear, therefore, that in tracing society backwards to its cradle, one of the earliest, if not the earliest, unit, is the Patriarchal Family. In the language of Sir H. S. Maine (*s*), "Thus all the branches of human society may, or may not, have been developed from joint families which arose out of an original Patriarchal cell; but, wherever the Joint Family is an institution of an Aryan race (*t*), we see it springing from such a cell, and, when it dissolves, we see it dissolving into a number of such cells."

Its origin and nature.

§ 206. The Patriarchal Family may be defined as "a group of natural, or adoptive, descendants held together by subjection to the eldest living ascendant, father, grand-

(*q*) Hunter's Orissa, ii. 79.

(*r*) Breeks, Primitive Tribes of the Nilgiris, 9, 39, 42, 68.

(*s*) Early Institutions, 118. I have retained the following pages unaltered, notwithstanding the attack lately made upon Sir H. S. Maine's views by Mr. McLennan Patriarchal Theory, 1885. For a reply to that work, so far as it affects Hindu Law, see an article by the present author in the Law Quarterly Review, I. 485. For a general reply, see the London Quarterly Review, Jan. 1886.

(*t*) This qualification was no doubt intended to exclude cases where the Joint Family is of a polyandrous type.

father, or great-grandfather. Whatever be the formal prescription of the law, the head of such a group is always in practice despotic; and he is the object of a respect, if not always of an affection, which is probably seated deeper than any positive institution" (*u*). The absolute authority over his family possessed by the Roman father in virtue of this position is well known. A very similar authority was once possessed by the Hindu father. Manu says, "Three persons, a wife, a son, and a slave, are declared by law to have in general no wealth exclusively their own; the wealth which they may earn is regularly acquired for the man to whom they belong" (*v*). And so Narada says of a son, "he is of age and independent, in case his parents be dead; during their lifetime he is dependent, even though he be grown old" (*w*). But this doctrine was not peculiar to the Aryan races. Among the Kandhs it is stated that "in each family the absolute authority rests with the house father. Thus, the sons have no property during their father's lifetime; and all the male children, with their wives and descendants, continue to share the father's meal, prepared by the common mother" (*x*). An indication of a similar usage still exists among the Tamil inhabitants of Jaffna, where all acquisitions made by the sons while unmarried, except mere presents given to them, fall into the common stock (*y*). As soon as they are married, it would appear that each becomes the head of a new family.

Origin of Joint Family.

§ 207. The transition from the Patriarchal to the Joint Family arises (where it does arise) at the death of the common ancestor, or head of the house. If the family choose to continue united, the eldest son would be the natural head (*z*). But it is evident that his position would be very different from that of the deceased Patriarch. The former

Difference between Patri-

(*u*) Early Institutions, 116; Ancient Law, 133. Here seems to be the origin of the great Hindu canon of inheritance, that the funeral cake stops at the third in descent. See *post*, § 474.

(*v*) Manu, viii. § 416; Narada, v. § 39; Sancha & Lich., 2 Dig. 526.

(*w*) Narada, iii. § 38. See too Sancha & Lich., 2 Dig. 533.

(*x*) Hunter's Orissa, ii. 72.

(*y*) Thesawaleme, iv. 5.

(*z*) Manu, ix. § 105.

archal and Joint Family.

was head of the family by a natural authority. The latter can only be so by a delegated authority. He is *primus* but *inter pares*. Therefore, in the first place, he is head by choice, or by natural selection, and not by right. The eldest is the most natural, but not the necessary head, and he may be set aside in favour of one who is better suited for the post. Hence Narada says (*a*), "Let the eldest brother, by consent, support the rest like a father; or let a younger brother, who is capable, do so; the prosperity of the family depends on ability." And so the old Toda, when asked which of his sons would take his place, replied, "the wisest (*b*)." In the next place the extent of his authority is altered. He is no longer looked upon as the owner of the property, but as its manager (*c*). He may be an autocrat as regards his own wife and children, but as regards collaterals he is no more than the president of a republic. Even as regards his own descendants, it is evident that his power will tend gradually to become weaker. The property which he manages is property in which they have the same interest as the other members of the family. The restrictions which fetter him in dealings with the property as against collaterals, will, by degrees, attach to his dealings with it as against his own children. They also will come to look upon him as the manager, and not as the father. The apparent conflict between many of the texts of Hindu sages as to the authority of the father, may, perhaps, be traced to this source. Those which refer to the father as head of the Patriarchal Family will attribute to him higher powers than those which refer to him as head of a Joint Family.

Not in necessary sequence.

§ 208. We have already seen (*d*) that the step from the Patriarchal to the Joint Family is one which, in some states of society, never takes place. Conversely the Joint Family is by no means necessarily preceded by the Patriarchal Family. For instance, the Nair system absolutely excludes

(*a*) Narada, xiii. § 5.
(*b*) Breeks, Primitive Tribes, 9.
(*c*) See Maine, Early Institutions, 116.
(*d*) *Ante*, § 204.

the Patriarchal idea. Its essence is the tracing of kinship through females, and not through males. Mr. McLennan considers that the Nair system was the necessary antecedent of the patriarchal form of relationship. According to his view, the loose relation between the sexes in early ages first settled into polyandry. Where it existed in its rudest shape, in which a woman associated with men unrelated to each other, the only family group that could be formed would be that of the mother and her children, and the children of such of them as were females. This is the Nair type, and still exists in the Canarese and Malabar *tarwâds*. Here kinship by females was alone possible. When the woman passed into the possession of several males of the same family, the circle of possible paternity became narrowed. The wife then lived in the house of her husbands, and the children were born in their home as well as hers. They could be identified as the offspring of some one of the husbands, though not with certainty as the offspring of any particular one. This was the first dawning of kinship through males. It is the species of polyandry that exists in Thibet, Ceylon, among the Todas on the Nilghiri Hills and elsewhere. Where the woman was the wife of several brothers, the eldest, to whom she was first married, would naturally have a special claim upon her, and could be ascertained to be the father of the children who were first born. By degrees this special claim would change into an exclusive claim, and so a system of absolute monandry would arise, and the Patriarchal Family become possible (*e*). Substantially the same view is put forward by Dr. Mayr in a less elaborate form (*f*). Now, as the

Polyandrous origin of family system.

(*e*) McLennan, Studies in Ancient History. Patriarchal Theory. See further discussion on the same subject in Spencer's Principles of Sociology, I, chaps. iii—viii. ; Fortnightly Review, May and June, 1877 ; and in Mr. Morgan's "Ancient Society," Part III. Mr. C. Staniland Wake, "The development of marriage and kinship," chapters ii, viii, ix, x. Mr. Edward Westermarck, "The History of Human Marriage," chapters iv, v.. Maxime Kovalevsky, "Tableu des Origines et de l : Evolution de la Famille et de la Propriete," Lecons i—v.

(*f*) Ind. Erbrecht, pp. 72—76. He appears not to have been acquainted with Mr. McLennan's work on Primitive Marriage, and bases his theory on the cruder speculations of Sir J. Lubbock, as to the early prevalence of what the latter terms "Communal Marriage." Lubbock, Origin of Civilisation, chap. iii.

tenure of property always moulds itself to the family relations of the persons by whom it is held, the result would be that property would first be held by the entire tribe; next by those who claimed relationship to a common mother; and next by a family, tracing either from several males, or from a single male. According to this theory, the Patriarchal Family would always be evolved from a wider Joint Family, instead of the reverse.

Theory discussed.

§ 209. It seems to me that the fallacy of these speculations consists in assuming that a cause, which is sufficient to produce a particular result, is the cause which has invariably produced that result. It is certain that polyandry, and the female-group system of property, has a tendency to change into monandry, and individual property. We have seen the process going on among the Kandyan chiefs of Ceylon, and the Todas evince the same tendency (*g*). I have been told that fidelity to a single husband is becoming common among the Nair woman of the better class (*h*). And it is certain that the Malabar *tarwâds* would long since have broken up into families, each headed by a male, if our Courts had allowed them to do so. It is equally certain that the Patriarchal Family is capable of expanding, and has a tendency to expand into the wider Joint Family, for we see instances of it every day. Every Hindu who starts with nothing, and makes a self-acquired fortune, is a pure and irresponsible patriarch. But we know that in a couple of generations his offspring have ramified into a Joint Family, exactly, to use Mr. McLennan's simile, like a banian tree which has started with a single shoot. It may possibly be that the Village Communities and undivided families of Southern India have originated among polyandrous tribes,

(*g*) McLennan, 195; Breeks, Primitive Tribes, 9. Mr. Lewis H. Morgan gives numerous instances of the same transition among the American Indian tribes.

(*h*) Mr. Wigram in his work on Malabar Law and Custom, Introduction iii, says, "But polyandry may now be said to be dead, and although the issue of a Nair marriage are still children of their mother rather than of their father, marriage may be defined as a contract based on mutual consent and dissoluble at will. It has been well said that nowhere is the marriage tie, albeit informal, more rigidly observed or respected than it is in Malabar; nowhere is it more jealously guarded, or its neglect more savagely avenged."

for we have evidence of the recent existence of polyandry among the Dravidian races (§ 59). But it is difficult to attribute to the same cause the existence of similar organizations among the Aryan races of Northern India. We know that the village and family system in these races must be of enormous antiquity, because we find an exactly similar system existing among the kindred races which branched off from them before history commenced. It is impossible to say that the ancestors of the common race were not polyandrous, but it is almost certain that their descendants neither are nor have been so during any period known to tradition (§ 60). It is difficult therefore to imagine that polyandry could have been the necessary antecedent of a system of property, which is able to flourish in every part of the world under exactly opposite conditions.

§ 210. The following suggestions seem to me capable of accounting for all the known facts, and are equally applicable to any families, however formed.

I assume that an original tribe, finding themselves in any tract of country, would consider that tract to be the property of the tribe; that is to say, they would consider that the tribe, as a body, had a right to the enjoyment of the whole of the tract, in the sense of excluding any similar body from a similar enjoyment (*i*). It would never occur to them that any individual member of the tribe had a right to exclude any other member permanently from any part of it; they would hunt over it and graze over it in common. When they came to cultivate the land, each would cultivate the portion he required. The produce would go to support himself and his family, but the land would be the common property of all. So long as the ratio between population and land was such as to enable any one to occupy as much as he liked, and when the land was exhausted, to throw it up and exhaust another patch, the community would have Tribal rights.

(*i*) This is the sort of right which the Red Indians are always asserting against the Americans.

no motive for restraining him in so doing. His rights would appear to be unlimited, merely because no one had an interest in limiting them. The same cause would produce the continual break-up of families. They might cling together for mutual protection; but as soon as each fraction grew strong enough to protect itself, it would wander apart to seek fresh pasturage for its flocks, or virgin soil for its crops (*k*). This is the condition of the hill tribes of India at present. But it would be different when population began to press upon subsistence, either from the increase of the original tribe, or from the closing in of adjoining tribes. Then the unlimited use of the land by one would be a limitation of its use by another. An individual or a family might be sufficiently strong to enforce an exclusive possession, but every one could not encroach upon every one else. The community would assert its right to put each of its members upon an allowance. That allowance would be apportioned on principles of equality, giving to each family according to its wants. The mode of apportionment might be, either by throwing all the produce into a common stock, and then re-distributing it, as in a communal Zemindari village; or by allotting separate portions of land to each family, with reference to the number of its members, as in a *pattidari* village. In the latter case equality would probably be from time to time restored by an exchange and re-distribution of shares, as in the Russian Mir, and the Pathan communities. In time this periodical dislocation of society would cease: it would tend to die out when the members began to improve their own shares. In the Punjab it is found that community has died out in spots whose cultivation depends entirely upon wells (*l*). Gradually the shares would come to be looked upon as private property. The idea of community would be limited to a joint interest in the village waste, and a joint responsibility for the claims of Government. This is the *bhaiacharry* village. If Government chose to settle with each individual instead of with the

Growth of restrictions.

Private property.

(*k*) See the separation of Abraham and Lot, in Genesis, xiii.
(*l*) Punjab Customs, 128.

village, the members would be exactly in the same position as the Mirasidars of Southern India.

§ 211. During the whole of this time the family system might be going through a series of analogous changes. The same causes which led to the compression or disruption of the tribe would lead to the compression or disruption of the family. The same feeling of common ownership which caused the tribe to look upon the whole district as their joint property, would cause the family to look upon their allotment in the same way. The same sense of individual property which led to the break-up of the village into shares, would lead to the break-up of the family by partition. But as the motives for union are stronger in a family than in a village, the union of the family would be more durable than that of the village. And this, in fact, we find to be the case. Progress of the family.

§ 212. The ancient Hindu writers give us little information as to the earlier stages of the law of property. So far as property consisted in land, they found a system in force which had probably existed long before their ancestors entered the country, and they make little mention of it, unless upon points as to which they witnessed, or were attempting innovations. No allusion to the village coparcenary is found in any passage that I have met. Manu refers to the common pasturage, and to the mode of settling boundary disputes between villages, but seems to speak of a state of things when property was already held in severalty (*m*). But we do find scattered texts which evidence the continuance of the village system, by showing that the rights of a family in their property were limited by the rights of others outside the family. For instance, as long as the land held by a family was only portioned out by the community for their use, it is evident that they could not dispose of it to a stranger without the consent of the general body. This is probably the real import of two anonymous texts cited in the Mitakshara: "Land passes by six form- Early Hindu writers. Limitation of family rights.

(*m*) Manu, viii. § 237—265. Jolly, Lect. 88.

alities; by consent of townsmen, of kinsmen, of neighbours and of heirs, and by gift of gold and water." "In regard to the immoveable estate, sale is not allowed; it may be mortgaged by consent of parties interested" (*n*). This would also explain the text of Vrihaspati, cited Mitakshara, i., 1, § 30. "Separated kinsmen, as those who are unseparated, are equal in respect of immoveables, for one has not power over the whole, to make a gift, sale or mortgage." It is evident that partition would put an end to further rights within the family, but would not affect the rights which the divided members, in common with the rest of the village sharers, might possess as ultimate reversioners. Consequently they would retain the right to forbid acts by which that reversion might be affected. And this is the law in the Punjab to the present day (*o*). Perhaps the text of Uçanas, who states that land was "indivisible among kinsmen even to the thousandth degree" (*p*), may be referred to the same cause.

Right of pre-emption.

§ 213. A further extension of the rights of co-sharers took place, when each sub-division was saleable, but the members of the community had a right of pre-emption, so as to keep the land within their own body. This right exists, and is recognized at present by statute, in the Punjab (*q*). The existence of an exactly similar right among the Tamil inhabitants of Northern Ceylon is recorded in the Thesawaleme (*r*).

§ 214. With the exception of these scattered and doubtful hints, the Sanskrit writers take up the history of the

---

(*n*) Mitakshara, i. 1, § 31, 32; see too Vivada Chintamani, p. 309. It will be observed that here, as in other cases, Vijnaneswara gives the texts an explanation which makes them harmonize with the law as known to him. But it is more probable that they were once literal statements of a law which in his time had ceased to exist. See Mayr, 24, 30.

(*o*) Punjab Customs, 73. (*p*) Mitakshara, i. 4, § 26. See Mayr, 81.

(*q*) Punjab Customs, 186; Act XII of 1878, § 2.

(*r*) Thesawaleme, vii. § 1, 2. The right of pre-emption is there said to extend to the vendor's "heirs or partners, and to such of his neighbours whose grounds are adjacent to his land, and who might have the same in mortgage, should they have been mortgaged."

family at a period when it had become an independent unit, unrestrained by any rights external to itself. As regards the rights of the members, *inter se*, their statements are very meagre. The *status* of the undivided family was, apparently, too familiar to every one to require discussion. They only notice those new conditions which were destined to bring about the dissolution of the family itself. These were *Self-Acquisition*, *Partition* and *Alienation*.

Origin of self-acquired property.

§ 215. SELF-ACQUIRED PROPERTY in the earliest state of Indian society did not exist (*s*). So where the family was of the purely Patriarchal type, the whole of the property was owned by the father, and all acquisitions made by the members of the family were made for him, and fell into the common stock (*t*). When the Joint Family arose, self-acquisition became possible, but was gradual in its rise. While the family lived together in a single house, supported by the produce of the common land, there could be no room for separate acquisition. The labour of all went to the common stock, and if one possessed any special aptitude for making clothes or implements of husbandry, his skill was exercised for the common benefit, and was rewarded by an interchange of similar good offices, or by the improvement of the family property, and the increased comfort of the family home. But as civilization advanced, and commerce arose, new modes of industry were discovered, which had no application to the joint property. As the family had only a claim upon its members for their assistance in the cultivation of the land, and the ordinary labours of the household, they could not compel the exertion of any special form of skill, unless it was to meet with a special reward. It was recognized that a member, who chose to abandon his claims upon the family property, might do so, and thenceforward pursue his own special occupation for his own exclusive profit (*u*). But it might be for the advantage of all to keep

(*s*) See Mayr, 28. (*t*) Manu, viii. § 416; *ante*, § 206.
(*u*) Manu, ix. § 207; Yajnavalkya, ii. § 116; Mayr, 29, 43.

the specially gifted member in the community by allowing him to retain for himself the fruits of his special industry. On the other hand, an injury would be done to the family, if, while living at its expense, he did not contribute his fair share of labour to its support, or if he used any appreciable portion of the family property for the purpose of producing that which he afterwards claimed as exclusively his own. The doctrine of self-acquired property sprung from a desire to reconcile these conflicting interests.

Its earliest forms.

§ 216. The earliest forms of self-acquisition appear to have been the gains of science and valour, peculiar to the Brahman and the Kshatriya. Wealth acquired with a wife, gifts from relations or friends, and ancestral property, lost to the family, and recovered by the independent exertions of a single member, were also included in the list; and Manu laid down the general rule, "What a brother has acquired by labour or skill, without using the patrimony, he shall not give up without his assent, for it was gained by his own exertion" (*v*). But we can see that self-acquisi-

Not favoured.

tions were at first not favoured, and that Manu's formula was rather strained against the acquirer than for him. Katyayana and Vrihaspati refuse to recognize the gains of science as self-acquisition, when they were earned by means of instruction imparted at the expense of the family (*w*); and Vyasa similarly limits the gains of valour, if they were obtained with supplies from the common estate, such as a vehicle, a weapon, or the like, only allowing the acquirer to retain a double share (*x*). It would also seem doubtful whether the acquirer was originally entitled to the exclusive possession of the whole of his acquisitions. Vasishtha says, "If any of the brothers has gained something by his own efforts, he receives a double share." This text is supposed by Dr. Mayr to mark a stage at which the only benefit obtained by the acquirer was a right to retain, on partition,

(*v*) Manu, ix. § 206—209; Gautama, xxviii, § 27, 28; Narada, xiii. § 6, 10, 11; Vyasa, 3 Dig. 333.

(*w*) 3 Dig. 333, 340.

(*x*) 3 Dig. 71; V. May, iv. 7, § 12.

an extra portion of the fruits of his special industry (*y*). If that be the correct explanation, the text of Vyasa just quoted shows a further step in advance. He restricts the rights of the acquirer, only in cases where assistance, however slight, has been obtained from the family funds; as where a warrior has won spoil in battle, by using the family sword or chariot. In later times all trace of such a restriction had passed away. The text of Vasishtha had lost its original meaning, and was explained as extending Manu's rule, not as restricting it; and as establishing that a member of a family, who made use of the patrimony to obtain special gains, was entitled to a double portion as his reward (*z*). This is evidently opposed both to the spirit and the letter of the ancient law. It has, however, come to be the present rule in Bengal, as we shall see hereafter (§ 264).

Right over self-acquisitions.

§ 217. It does not appear that an acquirer had from the first an absolute property in his acquisition, to the extent of disposing of it in any way he thought fit. Originally the benefit which he derived from a special acquisition seems to have come to him in the form of a special share at the time of partition (*a*). While the family remained undivided, he would be entitled to the exclusive use of his separate gains. If he died undivided, they would probably fall into the common stock (*b*). Probably he was only allowed to alienate, where such alienation was the proper mode of enjoying the use of the property. This would account for the distinction which is drawn between self-acquired movables and immovables. The right to alienate the former is universally admitted by the commentators, but the Mitakshara cites with approval a text, which states that, "Though immova-

(*y*) Vasishtha, xvii. § 51; Mayr, 29, 30; Dr. Burnell's translation of Varadrajah (p. 31) renders it, "If any of them have self-acquired property, let him take two shares." The text seems to be similarly interpreted by Jimuta Vahana. Daya Bhaga, ii § 41. See *post*, 265.

(*z*) Mitakshara, i. 4, § 29; Daya Bhaga, vi. 1, § 24—29.

(*a*) Vishnu, xvii. § 1; Yajnavalkya, ii. 118—120, and texts referred to at note (*v*).

(*b*) This is at present the case with the Nambudri Brahmans of the West Coast (11 Mad. 162), as to whom, see *ante*, § 42.

bles or bipeds have been acquired by a man himself, a gift or sale of them should not be made without convening all the sons" (c). According to the existing Malabar law, a member of a *tarwâd* may make separate acquisitions, and dispose of them as he pleases during his life; but anything that remains undisposed of at his death becomes part of the family property (d). According to the Thesawaleme a member of an undivided family appears to have more power of disposal over self-acquired than he has over ancestral property, but not an absolute power (e).

Originally unknown.

§ 218. PARTITION of family property, so far as that property consisted of land, could not arise until the land possessed by each family had come to be considered the absolute property of the family, free from all claims upon it by the community. Nor would there be any very strong reason for partition, as long as the bulk of the property consisted of land. It would furnish a better means of subsistence to the members when it remained in a mass, than when it was broken up into fragments. The influence of the head of the family, and the strong spirit of union which is characteristic of Eastern races, would tend to preserve the family coparcenary, long after the looser village bond had been dissolved. In Malabar and Canara, at the present day, no right of partition exists. In some cases, where the family has become very numerous, and owns property in different districts, the different branches have split into distinct *tarwâds*, and become permanently separated in estate. But this can only be done by common consent. No one

(c) Mitakshara, i. 1, § 27. This text is ascribed by Mr. Colebrooke to Vyasa. In the Vivada Chintamani, p. 309, it is attributed to Prakasha, while Jagannatha quotes it as from Yajnavalkya. 2 Dig. 110. How far this is still the law n Southern India appears unsettled. See *post*, § 318. The Viramitrodaya treats the consent of the sons to the alienation of self-acquired and immovable property, like that of separated members to the alienation of separated immovable property as being desirable for purposes of evidence, but not necessary as a matter of law. Viramit., p. 87, § 22.

(d) *Kallati* v. *Palat*, 2 Mad. H. C. 162; *Vira Rayen* v. *Valia Rani*, 3 Mad. 141; *Ryrappen Numbiar* v. *Kelu Kurup*, 4 Mad. 150. By the Alya Santana law of South Canara such acquisitions pass to the personal representatives of the acquirer. *Antamma* v. *Kaveri*, 7 Mad. 575.

(e) Thesawaleme, ii. § 1.

member, nor even all but one, can enforce a division upon any who object (*f*). The text of Uçanas, already quoted (*g*), which forbids the division of land among kinsmen, seems to evidence a time when the Hindu joint family was as indivisible as the Malabar *tarwâd* (*h*).

Its origin.

§ 219. Partition would begin to be desired, when self-acquisitions became common and secure. A man who found that he was earning wealth more rapidly than the other members of his family, would naturally desire to get rid of their claims upon his industry, and to transmit his fortune entire to his own descendants. This is one of the commonest motives which brings about divisions at present. But the family feeling against partition is so strong (*i*), since what one gains all the others lose, that it is probable the usage would have had a painful struggle for existence, if it had not been supported by the strongest external influence, *viz.*, that of the Brahmans. This support it certainly had. As long as a family remained joint, all its religious ceremonies were performed by the head. But as soon as it broke up, a multiplication of ceremonies took place, in exact ratio to the number of fractions into which it was resolved. Hence a proportionate increase of employment and emolument for the Brahmans. The Sanskrit writers are perfectly frank in advocating partition on this very ground. Manu says (*k*). "Either let them live together, or if they desire religious rites, let them live apart; since religious duties are multiplied in separate houses, their separation is therefore legal,"—to which Kulluka adds, in a gloss, "*and even laudable!*" And so Gautama says (*l*), "If a division takes place, more spiritual merit is acquired."

Stimulated by Brahmanism.

(*f*) *Munda Chetty* v. *Timmaju*, 1 Mad. H. C. 380; *Timmappa* v. *Mahalinga*, 4 Mad. H. C 28. The same rule applies in the case of the Nambudri Brahmans who are governed by Hindu law of a primitive character, 11 Mad. 162; *ante*, § 42.

(*g*) *Ante*, § 212.

(*h*) See Mayr, 31, 43.

(*i*) I have been assured that even in Bengal, where the family tie is so loose, no one can enforce a division except at the cost of all natural love and harmony. In Madras I have invariably found that a family feud was either the cause, or the consequence, of a suit for partition.

(*k*) ix. § 111.

(*l*) xxviii. § 4.

Its development.

§ 220. It was, however, by very slow steps that the right to a partition reached its present form. At first it is possible that a member who insisted on leaving the family for his own purposes, went out with only a nominal share, or such an amount as the other members were willing to part with (*m*). This is the more probable, since, so long as the family retained its Patriarchal form, the son could certainly not have compelled his father to give him a share at all, or any larger portion than he chose. The doctrine that property was by birth—in the sense that each son was the equal of his father—had then no existence. The son was a mere appendage to his father, and had no rights of property as opposed to him (*n*). The family was then in the same condition as a Malabar *tarwâd* is now. There the property is vested in the head of the family, not merely as agent or principal partner, but almost as an absolute ruler. The right of the other members is only a right to be maintained in the family house, so long as that house is capable of holding them. The scale of expenditure to be adopted, and its distribution among the different members, is a matter wholly within the discretion of the *karnaven*. No junior member can claim an account, or call for an appropriation to himself of any special share of the income. Partition, as we have already seen, can never be demanded (*o*). It is quite certain that in the earlier period of Hindu law, no son could compel his father to come to a partition with him. Manu speaks only of a division after the death of the father, and says expressly that the brothers have no power over the property while the parents live. Kulluka Bhatta adds in a gloss, "unless the father chooses

Malabar tarwâd.

Originally subject to consent of father.

(*m*) *Ante*, § 215, note (*u*). See *Peddayya* v. *Ramalingam*, 11 Mad. 406.

(*n*) Manu, viii. § 416; *ante*, § 206.

(*o*) *Kunigaratu* v. *Arrangaden*, 2 Mad. H. C. 12; *Subbu Hegadi* v. *Tongu*, 4 Mad. H. C. 196; *ante*, § 218, note (*f*); *Varanakot* v. *Varanakot*, 2 Mad. 328. As to separate Maintenance, see *Peru Nayar* v. *Ayyappan*, *ib.* 282. *Narayani* v. *Govinda*, 7 Mad. 352. As to power of removing the Karnaven for imprudent management, see *Ponambilath Kunhamod* v. *Ponambilath Kuttiath*, 3 Mad. 169. As to cases where a tarwâd is split up into several taverais, or sub-divisions, see *Chalayil Kandotha* v. *Chathu*, 4 Mad. 169; *Mammali* v. *Pakki*, 7 Mad. 428. As to one member having separate property, as affecting his right to maintenance, see *Thaya* v. *Shungunni*, 5 Mad. 71.

to distribute it" (*p*). This was no doubt added because the actual or mythical Manu did himself divide his property among his sons, or was alleged by the Veda to have done so, and the fact is put forward by the sages as an authority for such a division (*q*). The consent of the father is also stated by Baudhayana, Gautama, and Devala to be indispensable to a partition of ancestral property (*r*), and Sancha and Lichita even make his consent necessary where the sons desire to have a partition of their own self-acquired property (*s*). Subsequently a partition was allowed even without the father's wish, if he was old, disturbed in intellect, or diseased; that is, if he was no longer fit to exercise his paternal authority (*t*). A final step was taken when it was acknowledged that father and son had equal ownership in ancestral property; that is to say, when the Patriarchal Family had changed into the Joint Family (*u*). It then became the rule that the sons could require a division of the ancestral property, but not of the acquired property (*v*). The joint family then ceased to be a corporation with perpetual succession, and became a mere partnership, terminable at will.

Growth of son's right.

Partition deferred till death of mother.

§ 221. The above sequence of rights is perfectly intelligible. It is more difficult to account for the early limitations upon partition with reference to the mother. There seems to be no doubt that originally the right of brothers to divide the family estate was deferred till after the death, not only of the father, but of the mother (*w*). Gautama, Narada and Vrihaspati allow of partition during the

(*p*) Manu, ix. § 104; see also Vasishtha, xvii. § 23—29. A text of Manu (ix. § 209) is, however, cited in the Mitakshara, (i. 6, § 11) as evidencing the right of sons to compel a partition of the ancestral property held by their father. The translation given by Sir W. Jones (*brethren* for *sons*) is incorrect, see 2 W. & B. xxiv. 1st ed. The text itself refers, not to partition, but to self-acquisition. It contemplates the continuance of the coparcenary, not its dissolution, and points out what property falls into the common stock, and what does not.

(*q*) Apastamba, xiv. § 11; Baudhayana, ii. 2, § 1.

(*r*) Baudhayana, ii. 2, § 4; Gautama, xxviii. 2; Devala, 2 Dig. 522.

(*s*) 2 Dig. 526, 533.

(*t*) Sankha, or Harita, cited Mitakshara, i. 2, § 7.

(*u*) See *ante*, § 207; *post*, § 229.

(*v*) Vyasa, 3 Dig. 35; Vishnu, xvii. § 1, 2.

(*w*) Manu, ix. § 104; Sancha & Lichita, 2 Dig. 533; Yajnavalkya, ii. § 117; Mitakshara i. 3, § 1—3; Daya Bhaga, iii. § 1.

mother's life, but make it an essential that she should have become incapable of child bearing, or that cohabitation on the part of the father should have ceased (*x*). The latter limitation, which is also the later, may be explained as intended to protect the interests of after-born children (*y*). It would operate as forbidding partition until after possibility of further issue was extinct. But why extend the prohibition to the death of the mother when the father was already dead? It might be suggested that this prohibition was necessary at a time when a widow was authorized to raise up issue by a relation. But it seems to me that it may evidence a time when the widow had a life estate in her husband's property, even though he left issue. It has often been said that the ground on which a widow's right of inheritance is rested, *viz.*, that she is the surviving half of her husband, would be a reason for her inheriting before her sons, instead of after them (*z*). Now according to the Thesawaleme this is actually the rule. Where the father dies leaving children, the mother takes all the property and gives the daughters their dowry, but the sons may not, demand anything as long as she lives (*a*). An indication of such a state of things having once existed may perhaps be found in the text of Sancha and Lichita (*b*), which, after forbidding partition without the father's consent, goes on to say, "Sons who have parents living are not independent, nor even after the death of their father while their mother lives." And similarly Narada makes the dependence of sons, however old, last during the life of both parents; and, in default of the father, places the authority of the mother before that of her first-born (*c*).

(*x*) Gautama, xxviii. § 2; Narada, xiii. § 3; 3 Dig. 48.

(*y*) Daya Bhaga, i. § 45. The Sarasvati Vilasa, p. 12, § 61 treats it as introduced in the father's interest, so as to secure him against a compulsory partition, so long as he might wish to marry again.

(*z*) See 3 Dig. 79.

(*a*) Thesawaleme, i. § 9.

(*b*) 2 Dig. 533.

(*c*) Narada, iii. § 38, 40: "He is of age and independent in case his parents be dead. During their lifetime he is dependent, even though he be grown old. Of the two parents the father has the greater authority, since the seed is worth more than the field; in default of the father, the mother; in her default, the first-born. These are never subject to any control from dependent persons; they are fully entitled to give orders, and make gifts or sales."

§ 222. When we come to the commentators who wrote at a time when all these restrictions had passed away, we find that the above passages had lost all meaning for them. But no Hindu lawyer admits that any sacred text can conflict with existing law. As usual, they attempt to reconcile the irreconcilable, either by forced explanations, or by simple collocation of contradictory passages, without any effort to explain their bearing upon each other. The Mitakshara, in dealing with the time of partition, quotes several of the texts just cited, as establishing that partition, during the father's lifetime, can only be made in three cases, *viz.*, first, when he himself desires it; or secondly, even against his will, when both parents are incapable of producing issue; or thirdly, when the father is addicted to vice, or afflicted with mental or bodily disease (*d*). And so he quotes, without any objection or explanation, the passage which directs partition to take place after the death of both parents (*e*). But in treating of the rights of father and son to ancestral property, he explains these texts as referring only to the self-acquired property of the father, and concludes that "while the mother is capable of bearing more sons, and the father retains his worldly affections, and does not desire partition, a distribution of the grandfather's estate does nevertheless take place by the will of the son" (*f*).

Restrictions become obsolete.

Mitakshara.

§ 223. The *Smriti Chandrika* explains the passage of Manu, ix. § 104, which defers partition till after the death of both parents, as meaning that the property of each parent can only be divided after his or her decease (*g*). But the result of an involved disquisition as to the right of sons to exact partition during the father's life, appears to be, that as long as the father is competent to beget children, and to manage the family affairs, the sons have not such inde-

Smriti Chandrika.

(*d*) Mitakshara, i. 2, § 7. The Viramitrodaya only recognises the 1st and 3rd cases, (p. 49, § 4).
(*e*) Mitakshara, i. 3, § 1, 2.
(*f*) Mitakshara, i. 6, § 5, 7, 8, 11. To the same effect is the Mayukha, iv. § 1—4.
(*g*) Smriti Chandrika, i. § 12—17.

pendent power as entitles them to compel him to proceed to a division (*h*).

It will be seen hereafter (*i*), that, until quite lately, the point was still open to discussion in Southern India.

Bengal writers.

§ 224. The writers of the Bengal school had to perform an exactly opposite feat of interpretation to that accomplished by those of the Benares school. The latter considered the sons to be joint owners with their father, and had to explain away the texts which restricted or delayed their right to a partition. The former considered that the father was the exclusive owner, and had to explain away the other texts which authorised a partition. The mode in which they attained this result will be found in the first chapter of the Daya Bhaga. Jimuta Vahana takes up all the texts which assert that sons cannot compel a partition during the father's lifetime, as supporting his view that property in the sons arises not by birth, but by the death of the father. Consequently, even in the case of ancestral property, there can be no partition during the father's life, without his consent. Upon his death, whether actual or civil, the property of the sons arises for the first time, and with it their right to a division (*k*).

Rights of mother.

§ 225. The condition that the mother should be past child-bearing, is taken by the writers of this school to be a limitation upon the father's power to make a partition, where the property is ancestral, on the ground, that if the ancestral estate were divided while the mother was still productive, the after-born children would be deprived of subsistence (*l*). They also interpret literally the prohibition against partition even after the father's death, while the mother is still alive, and repudiate the explanation that this prohibition

(*h*) Smriti Chandrika, i. § 19—23, 28—38. (*i*) *Post*, § 430.

(*k*) Daya Bhaga, i. § 11—31, 38—44, 50; ii. § 8. Raghunandana, i. 5—14; ii. 26, 34, 35. This appears to be the rule in the Punjab. See Punjab Customary Law, II. 168, III. 122.

(*l*) Daya Bhaga, i. § 45; D. K. S. vi. § 1.

relates to the separate property of the mother (*m*). Later commentators, however, do not allow that the rule is still in force, or get out of it, by the usual Bengal formula, that it is morally wrong but legally valid. In practice neither the mother's death nor consent is now required (*n*).

Results.

§ 226. The result of this long history is, that the right to a partition at any time, between co-sharers, is now admitted universally. But the writers of the Bengal school do not allow that sons are co-sharers with their father. Elsewhere all members of a Joint Family are considered to be co-sharers, whether they are related to each other lineally or collaterally.

Development of right to alienate.

§ 227. THE RIGHT OF ALIENATION of course proceeds *pari passu* with the development of property from its communal to its individual form. As each new phase of property arose, there was a transitional period before it absolutely escaped from the fetters which had ceased to be properly binding upon it. We have already seen reason to believe, that there was a time when the shares of separated kinsmen in land were not absolutely at their own disposal. But all such restrictions had passed away before the time of Narada (*o*). So it would appear that at first sons were not at liberty to dispose of their own self-acquired property, and it is still an unsettled point whether, under Mitakshara law, a father has absolute control over self-acquired land (*p*). Conversely, a relic of the supreme power of the father, as head of the family, may, perhaps, be found in his asserted right to dispose of ancestral movables at pleasure (*q*). Possibly the absolute obligation of the sons to pay his debts may be traceable to the same source (*r*).

Joint property.

§ 228. As regards joint property, it necessarily followed, from the very essence of the idea, that no one owner could

(*m*) Daya Bhaga, iii. § 1—11; D. K. S. vii. § 1. See F. MacN. 37, 57; 1 W. MacN. 49.
(*n*) 3 Dig. 78; 1 W. MacN. 50.
(*o*) *Ante*, § 212; Narada, xiii. § 43.
(*p*) *Ante*, § 206; *post*, § 233.
(*q*) *Post*, § 231.
(*r*) *Post*, § 278.

dispose of that which belonged to others along with himself, unless with their consent, or under circumstances of necessity, from which their assent might be implied (*s*). But a most important difference of opinion arose, as to who were joint owners in property, and as to the power of disposal each joint owner had over his own share.

Power of father.

The former point arose with reference to the position of a father in regard to his sons. Where the Joint Family was an enlargement of the Patriarchal Family, the power of the head would necessarily be different, according as he was looked upon as the father of his children, or merely as the manager of a partnership (*t*). The texts which had their origin in the former stage of the family, would necessarily ascribe to him wider powers than those which originated in its later stage. For instance, when Narada says, "women, sons, slaves, and attendants are dependent; but the head of a family is subject to no control in disposing of his hereditary property" (*u*);—he is evidently quoting a text which had once been true of the father as a domestic despot, but which had long since ceased to be true of him as the head of a Joint Family. At each stage of the transition, the original writers, who spoke merely with reference to the facts which were under their own eyes, would speak clearly and unhesitatingly. When the era of commentators arrived, who had to weave a consistent theory out of conflicting texts, all of which they were bound to consider as equally holy and equally true, controversy would begin. Those who wished to diminish the father's authority would quote the later texts. Those who wished to enlarge his authority would quote the earlier texts. This is exactly what took place.

Mitakshara.

§ 229. The author of the Mitakshara enters into an elaborate disquisition, as to whether property in the son arises for the first time by partition, or the death of the previous

(*s*) Vyasa, 1 Dig. 455; 2 Dig. 189. (*t*) *Ante*, § 207.
(*u*) Narada, iii. § 36.

owner, or exists previously by birth (*v*). He quotes two anonymous texts, "The father is master of the gems, pearls, coral, and of all other (movable property), but neither the father nor the grandfather is of the whole immovable estate;" and this other passage, "By favour of the father, clothes and ornaments are used, but immovable property may not be consumed even with the father's indulgence" (*w*). He sums up his views in § 27, 28, as follows:—"Therefore it is a settled point that property in the paternal or ancestral estate is by birth, although the father have independent power in the disposal of effects other than immovables for indispensable acts of duty, and for purposes prescribed by texts of law, as gifts through affection, support of the family, relief from distress, and so forth; but he is subject to the control of his sons and the rest in regard to the immovable estate, whether acquired by himself or inherited from his father or other predecessor; since it is ordained, 'though immovables or bipeds have been acquired by a man himself, a gift or sale of them should not be made without convening all the sons. They who are born, and they who are yet unbegotten, and they who are still in the womb, require the means of support. No gift or sale should therefore be made.'" An exception to it follows: "Even a single individual may conclude a donation, mortgage, or sale of immovable property during a season of distress, for the sake of the family, and especially for pious purposes."

Property is by birth.

§ 230. The opinion of Vijnanesvara that sons had by birth an equal ownership with the father in respect of ancestral immovable property, is followed by all writers except those of the Bengal school, and is now quite beyond dispute (*x*). But upon the other points, *viz.*, as to the extent

(*v*) Mitakshara, i. 1, § 17—27. Viramit., ch. i.

(*w*) Mitakshara, i. 1, § 21. The former of these texts is cited by Jimuta Vahana, ii. § 22, as from Yajnavalkya, but cannot be found in the existing text. It is also opposed to Yajnavalkya, ii. § 121, quoted *post*, § 232.

(*x*) Smriti Chandrika, viii. § 17—20; Madhaviya, § 15, 16; Varadrajah, pp 4—6; V. May., iv. 1, § 3, 4; Vivada Chintamani, 309. As to whether land purchased with ancestral movable property possesses incidents of ancestral immovable, see § 251.

of the father's power over ancestral movables, and the limitation upon his power over self-acquired land, there is no such harmony, and his own views appear to have been in a state of flux upon the subject.

Father's power over movables.

§ 231. As regards movables, it is evident that the head of the family, whether in his capacity as father or as manager, must necessarily have a very large control over them. Money and articles produced to be sold or bartered, he must have the power to dispose of, in the ordinary management of the property. Clothes, jewels, and the like he would apportion to and reclaim from the various members of the family at his discretion. Household utensils, and implements of trade or husbandry, he would buy, exchange and dispose of as the occasion arose. Now, in early times, movable property would be limited to such articles. Even at the present day, not one Hindu family in a thousand possesses any other species of chattel property. The very instance adduced by the text—gems, pearls and corals—points to things over which the father would necessarily have a special control. And the Mayukha says of this very text, "it means the father's independence only in the wearing and other use of ear-rings, rings, &c., but not so far as gift or other alienation. Neither is it with a view to the cessation of the cause of his ownership in the production of a son. This very meaning is made manifest also by the text noticing only gems and such things as are not injured by use" (*y*).

§ 232. In another portion of the Mitakshara (*z*) he quotes without comment a text of Yajnavalkya (ii. § 121). "The ownership of father and son is the same in land which was acquired by the grandfather, or in a corrody (or settled income), or in chattels which belonged to him." This evidently contradicts the idea that the father had any absolute power of disposal over ancestral movables. Further,

(*y*) V. May., iv. 1, § 5.

(*z*) Mitakshara, i. 5, § 3.

although in ch. i. 1, § 24, he lays down the general principle, that "the father has power, under the same text, to give away such effects, though acquired by his father;" in § 27, already quoted, he seems to limit this power to the right of disposing of movables for such necessary or suitable purposes as would come within the ordinary powers of the head of a household. It is evidently one thing to bestow a rupee on a beggar, and another to give away the balance at the bank. Lastly, it is important to observe, that none of the later writers in Southern India, who follow the Mitakshara, make any such distinction. They quote the above text of Yajnavalkya, and a similar one from Vrihaspati, which place ancestral movables and immovables on exactly the same footing as regards the son's right by birth (*a*).

Over self-acquired land.

§ 233. As regards the second point, *viz.*, the restriction upon a father's power to dispose of his own self-acquired land, Vijnanesvara is equally at variance with himself. He asserts the restriction in the most unqualified terms in the passage already quoted. He denies it in equally unqualified terms in later passage (*b*). "The grandson has a right of prohibition, if his unseparated father is making a donation, or a sale of effects inherited from the grandfather; but he has no right of interference, if the effects were acquired by the father. On the contrary, he must acquiesce, because he is dependent. Consequently the difference is this: although he have a right by birth in his father's and in his grandfather's property, still, since he is dependent on his father in regard to the paternal estate, and since the father has a predominant interest, as it was acquired by himself, the son must acquiesce in the father's disposal of his own acquired property; but since both have indiscri-

Mitakshara.

(*a*) Smriti Chandrika, viii. § 17—20; Madhaviya, § 15, 16; Varadrajah, § 4—6. Exactly a similar conflict of opinion to that which is found in the Mitakshara as regards the father's power of disposal over movable property appears in the Viramitrodaya, at p. 6, § 9; p. 74, § 17, and p. 16, § 30. See the modern decisions on this point, *post*, § 310.

(*b*) Mitakshara, i. 5, § 9, 10, 11.

minately a right in the grandfather's estate, the son has a power of interdiction." And in the next paragraph he quotes Manu, ix. § 209, as showing that the father was not compelled to share self-acquired wealth with his sons. The Smriti Chandrika is explicit on the point that as regards all self-acquired property, without any exception, the father has independent power, to the extent of giving it away at his pleasure, or enjoying it himself, and he cites texts of Katyayana and Vrihaspati, which state this to be the rule, as plainly as can be (*c*). On the other hand, the Vivada Chintamani, which always maintains the rights of the family in their strictest form, cites with approval the same text as that which is relied on by the Mitakshara, as restraining the dealings of the father with self-acquired land (*d*). But in an earlier chapter the author states the unqualified rule, "Self-acquired property can be given by its owner at his pleasure" (p. 76), and at p. 229 he repeats the same rule expressly as to a father.

Smriti Chandrika.

Vivada Chintamani.

Explanation of text.

§ 234. It is probable that the text which is relied on both by the Mitakshara and the Vivada Chintamani, was one of a class of texts which forbid the alienation by a man of his entire property, so as to leave his family destitute (*e*). To our ideas such a prohibition would seem to be unnecessary. But in India, where generosity to Brahmans was inculcated as the first of virtues, and a life of asceticism and mendicancy was pointed out as the fitting termination of a virtuous career (*f*), a direction that a man should be just before he was generous, might not have been uncalled for. Whether the direction, so far as it regards self-acquired land, is anything more than a moral precept, is a point which cannot be treated as absolutely settled even now (*g*).

(*c*) Smriti Chandrika, viii. § 22—28. Mr. Colebrooke refers to both the Smriti Chandrika and the Madhaviya as laying down exactly the opposite doctrine (2 Stra. H. L. 439, 441). I suppose the passages he refers to are in portions which have not yet been translated. I have been unable to find them.

(*d*) Vivada Chintamani, p. 309.

(*e*) See Narada, iv. § 4, 5; Vrihaspati, 2 Dig. 98; Daksha, 2 Dig. 110; Viramit., p. 89.

(*f*) Manu, vi.

(*g*) See the modern decisions, *post*, § 318.

The Daya Bhaga.

§ 235. When we come to Jimuta Vahana, we find that by a little dexterous juggling he arrives at exactly the opposite conclusion from that of the Mitakshara, out of precisely the same premises. He, too, discusses the origin of a son's right in property, with the same elaborate subtlety as Vijnanesvara, and announces as the result of the texts, "That sons have not a right of ownership in the wealth of the living parents, but in the estate of both when deceased" (*h*). The process he adopts is as follows. He relies on the texts of Manu and Devala which prohibit partition in the father's lifetime, without his consent, as showing that the father was the absolute owner of the property (*i*). He then grapples with the text—"The father is master of the gems, pearls and corals, and of all other (movable property), but neither the father nor the grandfather is so of the whole immovable estate." From this he argues, 1. That since the grandfather is mentioned, the text must relate to his effects, *viz.*, to ancestral property; 2. That with regard to such property, "the father has authority to make a gift or other similar disposition of all effects other than land, &c., but not of immovables, a corrody, and chattels, (*i.e.*, slaves);" 3. That even as to land "the prohibition is not against a donation or other transfer of a small part not incompatible with the support of the family. For the insertion of the word 'whole' would be unmeaning (if the gift of even a small part were forbidden)." The other texts which forbid a transfer by one of several joint owners, or even the sale by a father of his own self-acquisitions without the consent of his sons, he dismisses with the simple remark, that they only show a moral offence: "Therefore, since it is denied that a gift or sale should be made, the precept is infringed by making one. But the gift or transfer is not null, for a fact cannot be altered by a hundred texts" (*k*).

Attempt to reconcile usage with texts.

§ 236. Of course this argument is opposed to the first

(*h*) Daya Bhaga, i. § 30; D. K. S. vi. § 18. Raghunandana, i. 5—14; ii. 26.
(*i*) Daya Bhaga, i. § 12—34.
(*k*) Daya Bhaga, ii. § 22—30; D. K. S. vi. § 18—20.

principles both of historical and legal reasoning. Manu and Devala forbid compulsory partition at the will of the sons, in order to prevent the family corporation being broken up. The whole object of the prohibition would be frustrated if the father was at liberty to dispose of its property, in whole or in part, at his own pleasure. Not a suggestion is to be found in any writer earlier than Jimuta Vahana himself, that he possessed such a right, or anything approaching to it (*l*). Every authority which speaks of alienation, directly negatives the existence of such a right. It might with equal logic be argued, that the karnaven of a Malabar tarwâd at the present day is absolute owner of its property, because none of the junior members can demand a share. The indissoluble character of the property would furnish as complete an answer to the former claim as it does to the latter. As to the suggestion that what is forbidden may still be valid, Mr. W. MacNaghten points out, that there is a distinction between an improper but legal mode of dealing with a man's self-acquisition, which is wholly his own, and an improper and illegal manner of dealing with ancestral land which is only shared by him with his sons. He was of opinion that, as to the former, the father could dispose of it as he liked, while as to the latter he could only dispose of his own share (*m*). But the badness of the reasoning arose from the fact that Jimuta Vahana considered it necessary to reconcile the usage which had sprung up in Bengal, with the letter of texts which applied to a state of things that had ceased to exist. He was the apologist of a revolution which must have been completed long before he wrote. But from his writings that revolution derived the stability due to a supposed accordance with tradition. If no law-books of a later tone than the Mitakshara had been in existence when our Courts

---

(*l*) The only exception is the text of Narada, cited *ante*, § 228, which, even if it is to be taken literally, plainly refers to a time anterior to that of the Joint Family.

(*m*) 1 W. MacN. Pref., vi. 2—15. See *per East*, C. J., 2 M. Dig. 200—204; *per Peacock*, C. J., *Mangala* v. *Dinanath*, 4 B. L. R. (O. C. J.) 78; S. C. 12 Suth. (A. O. J.) 35. As to the modern decisions, see *post*, § 346.

were established, there can be little doubt that the conscientious logic of English judges would have refused to recognize that the revolution had ever taken place.

Suggested explanation of Bengal doctrines.

§ 237. There are probably no materials in existence which would enable us to trace the causes of that change in popular feeling, and family law, which is marked by the difference between the Mitakshara and the Daya Bhaga. Much was of course due to the natural progress of society. A race so full of commercial activity as the Hindus who were settled along the lower course of the Ganges, would find their growth cramped by the Procrustean bed of ancient tradition. As soon as land came to be looked on as an object of mortgage and sale, the restraints upon alienation imposed by the early law would be found insufferable. But I imagine that the Brahmanical influence helped most strongly in the same direction. Sir H. S. Maine, while discussing a similar transition in Celtic law, says, "When this writer affirms that, under certain circumstances, a tribesman may grant or contract away tribal land, his ecclesiastical leaning constantly suggests a doubt as to his legal doctrine. Does he mean to lay down that the land may be parted with generally, or only that it may be alienated in favour of the Church? This difficulty of construction has an interest of its own. I am myself persuaded that the influence of the Christian Church on law has been very generally sought for in a wrong quarter, and that historians of law have too much overlooked its share in diffusing the conceptions of free contract, individual property, and testamentary succession, through the regions beyond the Roman Empire, which were peopled by communities held together by the primitive tie of consanguinity. It is generally agreed among scholars that churchmen introduced these races to wills and bequests. The Brehon tracts suggest to me at least that, along with the sacredness of bequests, they insisted upon the sacredness of contracts; and it is well known that, in the Germanic countries, their ecclesiastical societies were among the earliest and largest grantees of public or 'folk' land. The Will, the Contract, and the Separate Ownership, were in fact indispensable to the church as the donee of pious gifts" (*n*).

Influence of Brahmans.

§ 238. It seems to me that every word of this passage is applicable to the effect caused by Brahmanical influence upon Hindu law. The moral law, as promulgated by Manu, might be described as a law of gifts to Brahmans. Every step of a man's life, from his birth to his death, required gifts to Brahmans. Every sin which he committed might be expiated by gifts to Brahmans. The huge endowments for religious purposes which are found in every part of India show that these precepts were not a dead letter. Every day's experience of present Indian life shows the practical belief in the efficacy of such gifts. Naturally, every rule of law which threw an impediment in their way would be swept aside as far as possible. And, when we remember that the Brahman was the King's minister in his Cabinet, the King's judge in his Court, it is obvious that it was a mere question of the means that would be adopted to secure the end. Even the earlier writers had led the way, by mingling pious gifts with the necessary purposes which would justify an alienation of family property (*o*). It was a further step to emancipate the holder of the estate from all control whatever. This was effected in Bengal by the doctrine that a father was absolute owner of the property; and by its further extension, that every collateral member held his share as tenant in common, and not as joint tenant. The favour shown to women, who are always the pets of the priesthood, by allowing them to inherit and to enforce partition in an undivided family, seems to me an additional stage in the same direction. The validity attributed to death-bed gifts for religious objects, which gradually ripened into a complete system of devise (*p*), completed the downfall of the common law of property in India.

(*n*) Maine, Early Instit., 104.
(*o*) Katyayana, 2 Dig. 96; Mitakshara, i. 1, § 28; Daya Bhaga, xi. 1, § 63.
(*p*) See *post*, § 368.

§ 239. There can be no doubt that Brahmanism was rampant among the law writers of Bengal. I think it can be shown that it was this influence which completely remodelled the law of inheritance in that Province, by applying tests of religious efficacy which were of absolutely modern introduction (*q*). We can easily see why this influence was more powerful in Bengal than in Southern and Western India, where the Brahmans had never been so numerous; and than it was in the Punjab, where Brahmanism seems from the first to have been a failure (*r*). But it is difficult to see why a similar system should never have been developed in Benares, which is the very hot-bed of Brahmanism. Much may, perhaps, have been due to the personal character and influence of Jimuta Vahana. It has been supposed that the Daya Bhaga was written under the influence of one of the Hindu sovereigns of Bengal, and perhaps even received his name, much as the great work of Tribonian came to bear the name of Justinian (*s*). It would be unphilosophical to suppose that he originated the changes we have referred to. But if he had had the acuteness to see that these changes actually had taken place, the wisdom to adopt them, and the courage to avow that adoption, it is obvious that a work written under such inspiration would take precisely the form of the Daya Bhaga. It would be based upon the new system as a fact, while its arguments would be directed to show that the new system was the old one. Its authority would necessarily be accepted as absolute throughout the kingdom, and it would become a fresh starting point for all subsequent treatises on law. On the other hand, the Benares jurists, in consequence of the very strength of their Brahmanism, would continue slavishly to reproduce their old law books, without caring, or daring, to consider

Powerful in Bengal.

Personal influence of Jimuta Vahana.

(*q*) See *post*, § 468, *et seq*. (*r*) See 2 Muir, S. T. 482; *ante*, § 8.

(*s*) See Colebrooke's Introduction to the Daya Bhaga. Dr. Jolly, however, states that the fabulous character of the supposed monarch is now established. Lect. 22. He suggests that the difference between the doctrines of the Daya Bhaga and the Mitakshara may arise from the fact that Jimuta Vahana followed the views of commentators earlier than Vijnaneswara. *Ibid.* 25. It seems to me difficult to account for the uniformly progressive character of his doctrines by any such supposition.

how far they had ceased to correspond with facts; just as we find comparatively modern works discussing elaborately the twelve sorts of sons, long after any but two had ceased to be recognized. Conversely, of course, the treatises themselves, both in Bengal and Benares, would alter the current of usage, by affecting the opinion of Pandits and Judges upon any concrete case that was presented for their decision. If any writer of equal authority with Jimuta Vahana had arisen in Southern India, had represented plainly the usages which he found in force, and painted up the picture with a plausible colouring of texts, we should probably find the Mitakshara as obsolete in Madras as it is in Bengal.

Power of father to distribute.

§ 240. When Jimuta Vahana had established to his own satisfaction that a father was the absolute owner of property, and that the sons had no right in it till his death, it would seem to follow, as a necessary consequence, that if the father chose to make a partition, he might distribute his estate among his sons exactly as he liked. But this conclusion he declined to draw. Nothing can show the artificial character of his reasoning more strongly than this fact. In the very chapter in which he lays down that the absolute ownership of the father enables him to deal with his ancestral property as he likes, he also lays down that if he chooses to distribute it, he must do so upon general principles of equality, and cannot, even for himself, reserve more than a double share (*t*). He affirms for one purpose the very ownership by birth which he denies for another. The reason probably was, that unequal distributions of a man's property during his life had not become common, and that there was no particular motive for encouraging them. The result, however, possibly was to preserve the family union in many cases in which it would otherwise have been broken up.

Interest of coparcener in his share.

§ 241. The second point upon which Jimuta Vahana

(*t*) Daya Bhaga, ii. § 15—20, 47, 56—82. See the whole subject discussed, *post*, § 449, 451.

differed from the earlier writers, was as to the nature of the interest which each person who was admitted to be a co-sharer, had in the joint property. The point will have to be fully discussed hereafter (*u*). It is enough to say here that the Mitakshara, and those who follow its authority, consider that no coparcener has such an ascertained share, prior to partition, as admits of being dealt with by himself, apart from his fellow sharers (*v*). They look upon every co-sharer as having a proprietary right in the whole estate, subject to a similar right on the part of all the others. Jimuta Vahana, on the other hand, denies the existence of such a general right, and says that their property consists in unascertained portions of the aggregate (*w*). Hence he argues that the text of Vyasa which prohibits sale, gift or mortgage by one of several coparceners, cannot be taken literally, for each has a property consisting in the power of disposal at pleasure (*x*).

Rights of women.

§ 242. Another feature of Bengal law which must have helped much to break up the family union, was the favour with which it regarded the rights of women. According to the Benares school, a widow could never inherit unless her husband had been a sole or a separated owner (*y*). This resulted from the nature of his interest in the property. So long as he was undivided, he had not a share but a right to obtain a share by partition. If he died without exercising this right, his interest merged, and went to enlarge the possible shares of the survivors. But according to the Daya Bhaga, a widow inherits to an issueless husband whether he dies divided or undivided. This would have been a logical result of holding that each coparcener during his lifetime held a definite though unascertained share. But though Jimuta Vahana relies upon this as an answer to his opponents, he grounds the right itself upon the texts of

---

(*u*) See *post*, § 348.

(*v*) See Vyasa, 1 Dig. 455.

(*w*) Daya Bhaga, xi. 1, § 26.

(*x*) Daya Bhaga, ii. § 27; 2 Dig. 99—105, 189; D. K. S. xi.

(*y*) Mitakshara, ii. 1, § 30.

early sages. It is probable that in this respect he may have been really reviving the old law (z). Certainly he was so in allowing the mother a right to obtain a share. But the result is, that in Bengal property falls far more frequently under female control than it does in other parts of India, and we may be certain, with proportionate advantage to the Brahmans.

Wills. § 243. I have now traced the changes which the law of property underwent in India, up to the time when its administration fell into English hands. I have not touched upon the subject of wills. The fruitful germ of a system of bequest can be seen in very early writers, but all the evidences of its growth are to be found in the records of the British Courts.

The succeeding chapters will be devoted to a fuller examination of this law, as it has been developed and applied by our tribunals.

(z) Daya Bhaga, xi. 1, § 1—26; see *ante*, § 221.

CHAPTER VIII.

THE JOINT FAMILY.

§ 244. In discussing the Joint Family or coparcenary which forms the subject of this chapter, we shall have to consider—*first,* who are its members; *secondly,* what is coparcenary property; *thirdly,* self-acquisition, and the burthen of proof when it is set up; *fourthly,* the mode in which the joint property is enjoyed. The historical discussion contained in the previous chapter has shown that originally every Hindu family, and all its property, was not only joint but indivisible. This state of things ceased when partition broke up the family, and when property came to be held in severalty, either as being the share of a divided member, or as being the separate acquisition of one who was still living in a state of union. But the presumption still continues, that the members of a Hindu family are living in a state of union, unless the contrary is established. "The strength of the presumption necessarily varies in every case. The presumption of union is stronger in the case of brothers than in the case of cousins, and the farther you go from the founder of the family, the presumption becomes weaker and weaker" (*a*). Even where separation, either of person or estate, is established, it can never be more than temporary. The man who has severed his union with his brothers, if he has children, becomes the head of a new joint family, composed of himself and his children, and their issue. And so property, which was the self-acquisition of the first owner, as soon as it descends to his heirs, becomes

Division of subject.

Presumption of union.

(*a*) *Moro Visvanath* v. *Ganesh,* 10 Bom. H. C. 444, 468; 2 Stra. H. L. 347.

their joint property, with all the incidents of that condition (*b*).

Its members

§ 245. It is evident that there can be no limit to the number of persons of whom a Hindu joint family consists, or to the remoteness of their descent from the common ancestor, and consequently to the distance of their relationship from each other. But the Hindu coparcenary, properly so called, constitutes a much narrower body. When we speak of a Hindu joint family as constituting a coparcenary, we refer not to the entire number of persons who can trace from a common ancestor, and amongst whom no partition has ever taken place; we include only those persons who, by virtue of relationship, have the right to enjoy and hold the joint property, to restrain the acts of each other in respect of it, to burthen it with their debts, and at their pleasure to enforce its partition. Outside this body there is a fringe of persons who possess inferior rights such as that of maintenance, or who may, under certain contingencies, hope to enter into the coparcenary. In defining the coparcenary, therefore, it will be necessary somewhat to anticipate matters which have to be more fully treated of hereafter.

§ 246. The Hindu lawyers always treat partition and inheritance as part of the same subject (*c*). The reason of this is that the normal state of the property with which they have to deal is to be joint property, and that they can only explain the amount of interest which each member has in the property, by pointing out what share he would be entitled to in the event of a partition.

do not succeed to each other.

There is no such thing as succession, properly so called, in an undivided Hindu family (*d*). The whole body of such

---

(*b*) *Ram Narain Singh* v. *Pertum Singh*, 11 B. L. R. 397; S. C. 20 Suth. 189.

(*c*) The works of Jimuta Vahana and Madhaviya are known by names (Daya-Bhaga and Daya-vibhaga) which mean simply partition of heritage. See *Bhimul Doss* v. *Choonee Lall*, 2 Cal. 379, where the right of a nephew to share in the property with his uncles was argued as if he was claiming to succeed to the property before his uncles.

(*d*) Coparcenary and survivorship are incidents of Hindu law, which are

a family, consisting of males and females, constitutes a sort of corporation, some of the members of which are coparceners, that is, persons who on partition would be entitled to demand a share, while others are only entitled to maintenance. In Malabar and Canara, where partition is not allowed, the idea of heirship would never present itself to the mind of any member of the family. Each person is simply entitled to reside and be maintained in the family house, and to enjoy that amount of affluence and consideration which arises from his belonging to a family possessed of greater or less wealth (§ 220). As he dies out his claims cease, and as others are born their claims arise. But the claims of each spring from the mere fact of their entrance into the family, not from their taking the place of any particular individual. Deaths may enlarge the beneficial interest of the survivors, by diminishing the number who have a claim upon the common fund, just as births may diminish their interests by increasing the number of claimants. But although the fact that A. is the child of B. introduces him into the family, it does not give him any definite share of the property, for B. himself has none. Nor upon the death of B. does he succeed to anything, for B. has left nothing behind to succeed to. Now in the rest of India the position of an undivided family is exactly the same, except that within certain limits each male member has, and in Bengal some females have, a right to claim a partition, if they like. But until they elect to do so, the property continues to devolve upon the members of the family for the time being by survivorship and not by succession. The position of any particular person as son, grandson, or the like, or as one of many sons or grandsons, will be very important when the time for partition arrives, because it will determine the share to which he is then entitled. But until that time arrives he can never say, I am entitled to such a definite portion of the property; because next year the proportion he would

Rights arise by birth:

are ascertained by partition.

---

repealed by the Succession Act, except as to rights previously vested, in the case of Native Christians. *Tellis* v. *Saldanha*, 10 Mad. 69.

have a right to claim on a division might be much smaller, and the year after much larger, as births or death supervene. For instance, suppose a family to consist only of A.

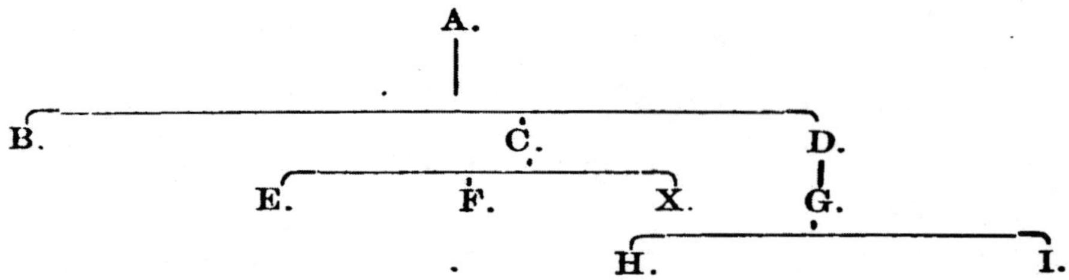

and his sons B. and C., on a partition each would take one-third. But if D. was born while the family remained joint, each would take one-fourth. Supposing the family still to remain undivided, on the death of A., the possible shares of the three sons would be enlarged to one-third; and if B. were subsequently to die without issue, they would again be enlarged to one-half. As C. and D. married, their sons E.,

Mitakshara. F. and G. would enter into the family and acquire an interest in the property. But that interest again would be a shifting interest, depending on the state of the family. If C. were to die, leaving only two sons E. and F., and they claimed a partition, each would take one-half of one-half. But if X. had previously been born, each would only take one-third of one-half. If they put off their claim for a division till D., G., H. and I. had all died, they would each take one-third of the whole. It is common to say that in an undivided family each member transmits to his issue his own share in the joint property, and that such issue takes *per capita inter se*, but *per stirpes* as regards the issue of other members. But it must always be remembered that this is only a statement of what would be their rights on a partition. Until a partition their rights consist merely in a common enjoyment of the common property, to which is further added, in Provinces governed by Mitakshara, the right of male issue to forbid alienations, made by their direct ancestors (*e*). These observations, however, require modifica-

(*e*) See this subject discussed, *Appovier* v. *Rama Subbaiyan*, 11 M. I. A. 75; S. C. 8 Suth. (P. C.) 1; *Sadabart Prasad* v. *Foolbash Koer*, 8 B. L. R. (F. B.) 31; S. C. 14 Suth. 340; *Ram Narain* v. *Pertum Singh*, 20 Suth. 189; S. C. 11

tion in Bengal. There, "admitting the family to have been joint, and the sons joint in estate, the right of any one of the co-sharers would not, under the Hindu law, pass over, upon his death, to the other co-sharers. It would be part of the estate of the deceased co-sharer, and would devolve upon his legatees or natural heirs" (*f*). The share of an undivided brother will pass to his widow, daughter and daughter's son, and may thus vest in a family completely different from his own (§ 486). Bengal.

§ 247. Now it is at this point that we see one of the most important distinctions between the coparcenary and the general body of the undivided family. Suppose the property to have all descended from one ancestor, who is still alive, with five generations of descendants. It by no means follows that on a partition every one of these five generations will be entitled to a share. And if the common ancestor dies, so that the property descends a step, it by no means follows that it will go by survivorship to all these generations. It may go to the representatives of one or more branches, or even to the widow of the survivor of several branches, to the total exclusion of the representatives of other branches. The question in each case will be, who are the persons who have taken an interest in the property by birth (*g*). The answer will be, that they are the persons who offer the funeral cake to the owner of the property. That is to say, the three generations next to the owner in unbroken male descent (*h*). Therefore, if a man has living, sons, grandsons, and great-grandsons, all of these constitute a single coparcenary with himself. Every

The coparcenary limited to those who partake in the funeral cake.

B.L.R. 397; *Rajnarain* v. *Heeralal*, 5 Cal. 142; *Bhimul Doss* v. *Choonee Lall*, 2 Cal. 379; *Debi Parshad* v. *Thakur Dial*, 1 All. 105; *Raol Gorain* v. *Teza Gorain*, 4 B. L. R. Appx. 90.

(*f*) *Per Turner*, L. J. *Soorjeemoney Dossee* v. *Denobundo*, 6 M. I. A. 553; S. C. 4 Suth. (P. C.) 114. This seems also to have been the view of Apararka. Partition, he says, does not create a new right; it has but the effect to render visible the right of each of the former joint owners to his share of the estate. Jolly Lect. 87, 114, n.

(*g*) This principle will not apply in Bengal, where sons take no interest by birth in their father's property. See *ante*, § 235.

(*h*) Manu, ix. § 186; Viramit., p. 72, § 16, *post*, § 460.

one of these descendants is entitled to offer the funeral cake to him, and therefore every one of them obtains by birth an interest in his property. But the son of one of the great-grandsons would not offer the cake to him, and therefore is out of the coparcenary, so long as the common ancestor is alive. But while fresh links are continually being added to the chain of descendants by birth, so earlier links are being constantly removed from the upper end of the chain by death. So long as the principle of survivorship continues to operate, the right to the property will devolve from those who are higher in the line to those who are lower down. As each fresh member takes a share, his descendants to the third generation below him take an interest in that share by birth. So the coparcenary may go on widening and extending, until its members may include persons who are removed by indefinite distances from the common ancestor. But this is always subject to the condition that no person who claims to take a share is more than three steps removed from a direct ascendant who has taken a share. Whenever a break of more than three degrees occurs between any holder of property and the person who claims to take next after that holder, the line ceases in that direction, and the survivorship is confined to those collaterals and descendants who are within the limit of three degrees. This was laid down in two cases in Bombay and Madras.

Coparcenery not limited to three degrees from common ancestor.

§ 248. In the former case the claim to partition was resisted, on the ground that the plaintiff was beyond the fourth degree from the acquirer of the property in dispute, the defendant being within that degree. It was argued that the analogy of the law of inheritance prevented a lineal descendant, beyond the great-grandson, from claiming partition at the hands of those who are legally in possession, as descendants from the original sole owner of the family property or any part of it (*i*). *West*, J., said, "The Hindu

---

(*i*) *Moro Vishvanath* v. *Genesh*, 10 Bom. H. C. 444, 449.

law does not contemplate a partition as absolutely necessary at any stage of the descent from a common ancestor; yet the result of the construction pressed on us would be to force the great-grandson in every case to divide from his coparceners, unless he desired his own offspring to be left destitute. Where two great-grandsons lived together as a united family, the son of each would, according to the Mitakshara law, acquire by birth a co-ownership with his father in the ancestral estate; yet if the argument is sound, this co-ownership would pass altogether from the son of A. or B., as either happened to die before the other. If a coparcener should die, leaving no nearer descendant than a great-great-grandson, then the latter would no doubt be excluded at once from inheritance and from partition by any nearer heirs of the deceased, as, for instance, brothers and their sons; but where there has not been such an interval as to cause a break in the course of lineal succession, neither has there been an extinguishment of the right to a partition of the property in which the deceased was a co-sharer in actual possession and enjoyment (*k*). Each descendant in succession becomes co-owner with his father of the latter's share, and there is never such a gap in the series as to prevent the next from fully representing the preceding one in the succession." The same principles were illustrated in detail by Mr. Justice *Nanabhai Haridas*. He said (*l*), "Take, for instance, the following case. A., the original owner of the property in dispute, dies, leaving a son B. and a grandson C., both members of an undivided family. B. dies, leaving C. and D., son and grandson respectively; and C. dies, leaving a son D. and two grandsons by him, E. and F. No partition of the family property has taken place, and D., E., and F. are living in a state of union. Can E. and F. compel

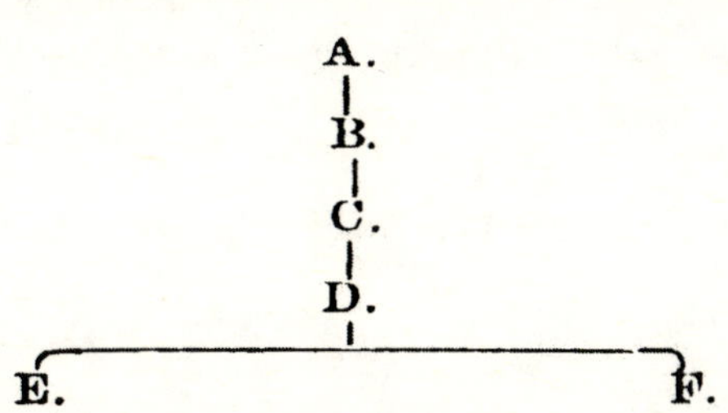

(*k*) See *per* Jagannatha, 3 Dig. 446—450.

(*l*) 10 Bom. H. C. 463.

D. to make over to them their share of the ancestral property? According to the law prevailing on this side of India they can, sons being equally interested with their father in ancestral property (*m*). In the same way, suppose B. and C. die, leaving A. and D. members of an undivided family, and then A. dies, whereupon the whole of this property

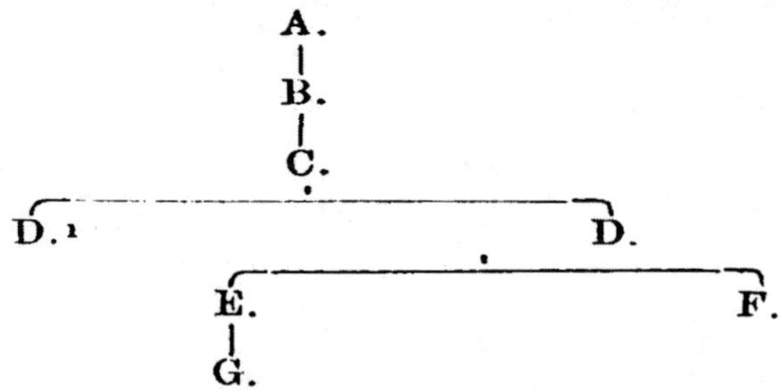

devolves upon D., who thereafter has two sons, E. and F. They, or either of them, can likewise sue their father D. for partition of the said property, it being ancestral. Now suppose B. and C. die, leaving A., D., and D.¹, members of an undivided family, after which A. dies, whereupon the whole of his property devolves upon D. and D.¹ jointly, and that D. thereafter has two sons, E. and F., leaving whom D. dies. A suit against D.¹ for partition of the joint ancestral property of the family would be perfectly open to E. and F., or even to G. and F., if E. died before the suit. It would be a suit against D.¹ by a deceased brother's sons, or son and grandson (*n*). But E. and F. are both fifth, and G. sixth in descent from the original owner of the property, whereas D. and D.¹ are only fourth. Suppose, however, that A. dies after D. leaving a great-grandson, D.¹ and the two sons of D., E. and F. In this case E. and F. could not sue D.¹ for partition of property descending from A., because it is inherited by D.¹ alone, since E. and F., being sons of a great-grandson, are excluded by D.¹, A.'s surviving great-grandson, the right of representation extending no further (*o*).
Rule The rule, then, which I deduce from the autho-

(*m*) 1 Stra. H. L. 177; 2 ibid. 316; Mitakshara, i. 1, § 27, i. 5, § 3, 5, 8, 11; V. May., iv. 6, § 13.
(*n*) V. May., iv. 4, § 21.
(*o*) See Jagannatha's Comment, on text, ccclxx.; 3 Dig. 388; 1 Nort. L. C. 292; Stra. Man § 323; 2 Stra. H. L. 327.

rities on this subject is, not that a partition cannot be demanded by one more than four degrees removed from the acquirer or *original owner* of the property sought to be divided, but that it cannot be demanded by one more than four degrees removed from the last owner, however remote he may be from the original owner thereof."

applied to impartible Zemindary.

§ 249. This principle was also affirmed by the Madras High Court, and its application put to a more violent test. The question was as to the right of succession to an impartible Zemindary. The original owner and common ancestor of the claimant was A. The Zemindary had descended throughout in the line of H., and was last held by N., who

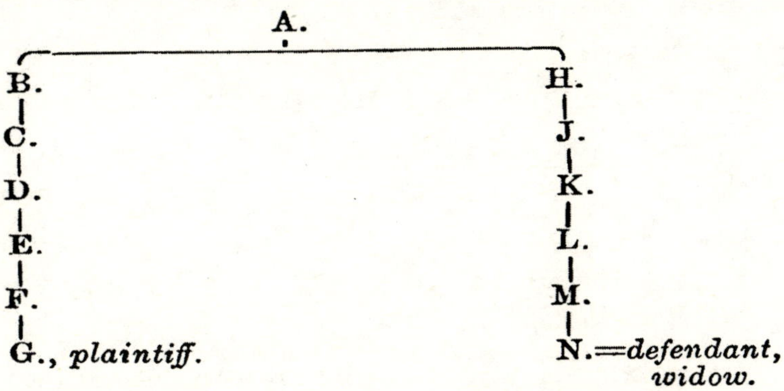

died without issue, leaving a widow, the defendant. The plaintiff was G., who was admittedly the nearest male of kin to N. The family was undivided. It was conceded that according to the law of the Mitakshara, an undivided coparcener would take before the widow. But it was contended on her behalf, "that only those of the unseparated kinsmen were coheirs, who by birth had acquired a proprietary interest in the estate in common with the deceased; his coparceners, who, on a division in his lifetime, would have been sharers of the estate, and that such a coparcenership can exist only between kindred who are near sapindas (*i.e.*, not beyond the fourth degree), and consequently, that the respondent (plaintiff) was not a coheir of the deceased." The Court assented to the first branch of the argument, but denied the second. They held that the Zemindary, though impartible, was still coparcenary property, and that the members of the undivided family acquired the same right to it by birth, as they would have done to any other property, subject only to the limitation of the enjoyment to one. Then as to who were coparceners, they said: "It appears to us equally certain that the limit of the coheirs must be held to include undivided collateral relations, who are descendants in the male line of one who was a coparcener with an ancestor of the last possessor. For, in the undivided coparcenary interest which vested in such coparcener, his near sapindas were coheirs, and when on his death, the interest vested in his sons, or son, or other near sapinda in the male line, the near sapindas of such descendants or descendant became in like manner coheirs with them or him, and so on, the coheirship became extended through the new sapindas down to the last descendant. Obviously, therefore, as long as the *status* of non-division continues, the members of the family who have, in this way, succeeded to a coparcenary interest, are coheirs with their kindred who possess the other undivided interests of the entire estate, and one of such kindred and his near sapindas in the male line cannot be the only coheirs, until by the death of all the others without descendants in the male line to the third degree, he has, or he and they have, by survivorship acquired the entire right to the heritage, as effectually as if the estate had passed upon an actual partition with the coheirs." The Court, therefore, held that the plaintiff, as undivided coparcener, would succeed before the widow (*p*). In this case it will be observed the plaintiff was sixth in descent from the common ancestor, the defendant's husband being equally distant.

Definition of coparceners.

Obstructed and unobstructed property.

§ 250. The same principle, *viz.*, that property vests in certain relations by birth, and not in other relations, gives rise to a division of property into two classes, which are spoken of by Hindu lawyers as *Apratibandha* and *Saprati-*

(*p*) *Yenumula* v. *Ramandora*, 6 Mad. H. C. 94, 106. See also in Bengal, *Girwurdharee* v. *Kulahul*, 4, S. D. 9 (12), where property was divided among persons four, five, and six degrees removed from the common ancestor.

bandha; terms which have been translated, not very happily, *unobstructed* and *obstructed*, or liable to obstruction. These terms are thus explained in the Mitakshara (*q*), "The wealth of the father or of the paternal grandfather becomes the property of his sons or of his grandsons, in right of their being his sons or his grandsons; and that is an inheritance not liable to obstruction. But property devolves on parents or uncles, brothers, or the rest, upon the demise of the owner, if there be no male issue; and thus the actual existence of a son, and the survival of the owner are impediments to the succession; and on their ceasing, the property devolves on the successor in right of his being uncle or brother. This is an inheritance subject to obstruction." The distinction is the same as that which is present to the mind of an English lawyer, when he speaks of estates as being vested or contingent, or of an heir as being the heir-at-law, or the heir presumptive. The unobstructed, or rather the unobstructible, estate is that in which the future heir has already an interest by the mere fact of his existence. If he lives long enough he must necessarily succeed to the inheritance, unless his rights are defeated by alienation or devise; and if he dies, his rights will pass on to his son, unless he is himself in the last rank of sapindas, in which case his son is out of the line of unobstructed heirs. On the other hand, the person who is next in apparent succession to an obstructed, or rather an obstructible estate, may at any moment find himself cut out by the interposition of a prior heir, as for instance a son, widow or the like. His rights will accrue for the first time at the death of the actual holder, and will be judged of according to the existing state of the family at that time. Any nearer heir who may then be in existence will completely exclude him; and if he should die before the succession opens, even though he would have succeeded, had he survived, his heirs will not

---

(*q*) Mitakshara, i. 1, § 3; Viramit., p. 3, V. May., iv. 2, § 2. See *per curiam*, *Nund Coomar Lall* v. *Ruzziooddeen*, 10 B. L. R. 191; S. C. 18 Suth. 477; *Debi Parshad* v. *Thakur Dial*, 1 All. 112. These terms are not used by the writers of the Bengal or Mithila School. V. N. Mandlik, 359. Jolly, Lect. 176.

take at all, unless they happen themselves to be the next heirs to the deceased. In other words, he cannot transmit to others rights which had not arisen in himself. (*r*)

Ancestral property

§ 251. The second question is as to the coparcenary property. The first species of coparcenary property is that which is known as ancestral property. The meaning of this phrase might be taken to be, property which descended upon another from an ancestor, however remote, or of whatever sex. Where property so descended upon several persons simultaneously, and with equal rights both of possession and enjoyment, as for instance upon several brothers, sons, grandsons, nephews or the like, it would certainly be joint property, by the very hypothesis. But this is not what is generally known as ancestral property. That term, in its technical sense, is applied to property which descends upon one person in such a manner that his issue (*s*) acquire certain rights in it as against him. For instance, if a father under Mitakshara law is attempting to dispose of property, we enquire whether it is ancestral property. The answer to this question is, that property is ancestral property if it has been inherited as unobstructed property, that it is not ancestral if it has been inherited as obstructed property (§ 250). The reason of this distinction is, that in the former case the heir had an actual vested interest in the property, before the inheritance fell in, and therefore his own issue acquired by birth an interest in that interest. Hence, when the property actually devolved upon him, he took it subject to the interest they had already acquired. But in the latter case, he had no interest whatever in the property, before the descent took place; there-

is unobstructed property.

(*r*) The High Court of Bengal has lately stated the rule of the Mitakshara law to be "that the principle of survivorship is limited to two descriptions of property, namely (1) what is taken as unobstructed inheritance and property acquired by means of it; and (2) what forms the joint property of re-united coparceners; and that property obtained in the ordinary course of inheritance (*e.g.*, by several daughter's sons) is not subject to that incident. *Jasoda Koer v. Sheo Pershad*, 17 Cal. 33.

(*s*) I may as well state, once for all, that the word "issue" will be used throughout this work as embracing son, grandson, and great-grandson. *Post*, § 498.

fore, when that event occurred, he received the property free of all claims upon it by his issue, and *à fortiori*, by any other person. Hence all property which a man inherits from a direct male ancestor, not exceeding three degrees higher than himself, is ancestral property, and is at once held by himself in coparcenary with his own issue. But where he has inherited from a collateral relation, as for instance from a brother, nephew, cousin or uncle, it is not ancestral property (*t*); consequently his own descendants are not coparceners in it with him. They cannot restrain him in dealing with it, nor compel him to give them a share of it (*u*). On the same principle, property which a man inherits from a female, or through a female, as for instance a daughter's son, or which he has taken from an ancestor more remote than three degrees, or which he has taken as heir to a priest or a fellow-student, would not be ancestral property (*v*). And that which is ancestral, and therefore coparcenary property, as regards a man's own issue, is not so as regards his collaterals. For they have no interest in it by birth (*w*). On the other hand, property is not the less ancestral because it was the separate or self-acquired property of the ancestor from whom it came (*x*). When it

Ancestral property.

(*t*) It is hardly necessary to remark that I am speaking of inheritance, not of survivorship. The enlarged share which accrues to the remaining brothers on the death of an undivided brother is ancestral property, and subject to all its incidents. *Gungoo Mull* v. *Bunseedhur*, 1 N. W. P. 170.

(*u*) *Rayadur Nallatambi* v. *Mukunda*, 3 Mad. H. C. 455; *Nund Coomar Lall* v. *Ruzziooddeen*, 10 B. L. R. 183; S. C. 18 Suth. 477; *Jawahir* v. *Guyan*, 3 Agra H. C. 78; *Lochun* v. *Nemdharee*, 20 Suth. 170; *Pitam* v. *Ujagar*, 1 All. 652. Jolly, Lect. 121.

(*v*) 3 Dig. 61; W. & B. 710, approved *per cur.* 10 B. L. R. 192 *supra*. The High Court of Madras has held that property which descended to a man from his maternal grandfather was ancestral property, which he could not alienate to the detriment of his son. None of the above authorities were referred to. The decision was reversed by the P. C. on another point (*Muthayan Chetti* v. *Sangili*, 3 Mad. 370. 9 I. A. 128. *Sivagunga* v. *Lakshmana*, 9 Mad. 188, 190). When the case arises again it will be material to remember that property only becomes joint property by reason of being ancestral property, where the ancestor from whom it was derived was a paternal ancestor. See Mit., i. 1, § 3, 5, 21, 24, 27, 33; i. 5, § 2, 3, 5, 9—11; *Per Mitter*, J., *Gunga Prosad* v. *Ajudhia Pershad*, 8 Cal. 131, p. 134; *per curiam*, *Jasoda Koer* v. *Sheo Pershad*, 17 Cal., p. 38; *Nanabhai* v. *Achratbai*, 12 Bom., p. 133; *post*, § 252.

(*w*) *Ajoodhia* v. *Kashee Gir*, 4 N. W. P. 31; *Gopal Singh* v. *Bheekunlal*, S. D. of 1859, 294; *Gopal Dutt* v. *Gopal Lall*, *Ibid*. 1314.

(*x*) *Ram Narain* v. *Pertum Singh*, 20 Suth. 189; S. C. 11 B. L. R. 397, *per curiam*, 9 Bom. 450.

has once made a descent, its origin is immaterial as regards those persons to whom it has descended. It is very material, however, as regards those who have not taken it by descent. A father with two sons A and B had self-acquired property. A died in his lifetime leaving a widow, and upon his death B took the property. A's widow claimed maintenance out of it as ancestral property. The Court admitted that in any question between B and his sons it would be ancestral property. But it was not so as regards A. During his life the property was absolutely at the disposal of the father. As regards A it was neither ancestral nor coparcenary property, and on his death his widow had no higher claim over it than her husband. Her rights were not enlarged by its change of character when it reached the hands of B (*y*). All savings made out of ancestral property, and all purchases or profits made from the income or sale of ancestral property, would follow the character of the fund from which they proceeded (*z*). On the same principle accretions to a riparian village are ancestral property, if the village itself was such (*a*).

Divided property.

§ 252. Where ancestral property has been divided between several joint owners, there can be no doubt that if any of them have issue living at the time of the partition,

(*y*) *Janki* v. *Nandram*, 11 All. F. B. 194, p. 198.

(*z*) *Shudanund* v. *Bonomalee*, 6 Suth. 256; S. C. on review; *Sub nomine*, *Sudanund* v. *Soorjo Monee*, 8 Suth. 455; S. C. 11 Suth. 436, reversed on another point in P. C.; *Sub nomine*, *Soorjomonee* v. *Suddanund*, 12 B. L. R. 304; S.C. 20 Suth. 377; S. C. 8 Mad. Jur. 466; *Ghansham* v. *Govind*, 5 S. D. 202 (240); *Umrithnath* v. *Goureenath*, 13 M. I. A. 542; S. C. 15. Suth. (P. C.) 10; *Kristnappa* v. *Ramasawmy*, 8 Mad. H. C. 25. *Jugmohundas* v. *Mungaldas*, 10 Bom. 529. In the case of *Gunga Prosad* v. *Ajudhia Pershad*, the High Court of Bengal treated it as a point still unsettled, whether property purchased out of the income of ancestral property before the birth of a son was ancestral property vested in the after-born son. Mr. Justice *Mitter* was strongly of opinion that it was not. It was admitted that it would be otherwise as to property so purchased after his birth, 8 Cal. 131; S. C. 9 C. L. R. 417. In Madras it has been held that property purchased from the income of ancestral is ancestral property which cannot be given to a stranger in derogation of the right of a son who was *in gremio matris* at the time of the gift. The Court refused to follow the dictum of *Mitter*, J. cited above, *Ramanna* v. *Venkata*, 11 Mad. 246. As to savings from income of impartible Zemindary, or purchases made out of such savings, see *post*, § 262. *Semble*, that movable property which has made a descent, and is then converted into land, possesses all the incidents of ancestral immovable property. *Sham Narain* v. *Raghoobur*, 3 Cal. 508.

(*a*) *Ramprasad* v. *Radha Prasad*, 7 All. 402.

the share which falls to him will continue to be ancestral property in his hands, as regards his issue, for their rights had already attached upon it, and the partition only cuts off the claims of the dividing members. The father and his issue still remain joint (*b*). But it is not so clearly settled whether the same rule would apply where the partition had been made before the birth of issue. In a case in Calcutta it was held that where a father by various deeds of gift had distributed his property among his sons, the portion obtained by each was ancestral property as regards his issue. It does not appear whether the issue had been in existence at the time of the gift. But the son contended that it was by the gift his self-acquired property. This the Court refused to admit. After a full examination of the Hindu authorities, they said, "We think that according to the Mitakshara, landed property acquired by a grandfather and distributed by him amongst his sons, does not by such gift become the self-acquired property of the sons so as to enable them to dispose of it by gift or sale without the consent, and to the prejudice of, the grandsons. The property cannot be said to have been acquired without detriment to the father's (*i.e.*, ancestral) estate, because it was not only given out of that estate, but in substitution for the undivided share of that estate to which the father appears to have been entitled. It cannot therefore be taken to have been given simply by the favour of the father, but upon consideration of the father surrendering some interest or right to share in the grandfather's estate, which he did by the acceptance of this separate parcel. We think that the father took it with the incidents to which the undivided share for which it was substituted would have been subject" (*c*). This reasoning would appear to apply equally

Property obtained from ancestor by gift

(*b*) *Lakshmibai* v. *Ganpat Moroba*, 5 Bom. H. C. (O. C. J.) 129. *Chatterbhooj* v. *Dharamsi*, 9 Bom. 438. The same point was very lately decided in Calcutta. The report does not state whether the son was born before or after the partition, but I think the latter seems to have been the case. *Adurmoni* v. *Chowdhry*, 3 Cal. 1.

(*c*) *Muddun Gopal* v. *Ram Buksh*, 6 Suth. 71, 73; followed *Nanomi Babuasin* v. *Modun Mohun*, 13 I. A. 5. In *Mohabeer Kooer* v. *Joobha*, 16 Suth. 221; S. C. 8 B. L. R. 38, a contrary opinion seems to have been expressed by *Jackson*, J.

in favour of issue unborn at the time of the gift. Similarly it was held in Madras, that a father did not take his share of the estate as self-acquired property, in consequence of having received it under the will of his own father. The Court said, "It seems to us that there is no reason whatever in the contention that its quality was changed by his choosing to accept it, apparently under the terms of his father's will. Still less ground would there be for the contention that his acquiescence in that mode of receiving it would vest in himself a larger interest than he would have taken by descent" (*d*). In Bombay it has been recently decided, after a review of all the cases, that where a grandfather bequeathes his self-acquired property to a son, who has at the time male issue, in terms showing an intention that the devisee should take an absolute estate, the property so devised does not vest in the issue as ancestral estate, so as to entitle them to sue their father for a partition (*e*). The same principle was followed in a case under Mitakshara law, where a father bequeathed his self-acquired property to his widow and his three sons jointly. Two of the sons separated. The third continued to live in union with his mother, and on her death took her share by survivorship. The Court, after reviewing the above decisions, held that the share of the widow which came to the son must be considered in his hands as ancestral property, since it had originally formed part of his father's estate. (*f*) Whatever the nature of the widow's interest may have been, its descent was governed by the incidents attaching to the source from which it arose. Where a man had obtained a share of family property on partition, which was mortgaged to its full value, and which he had subsequently cleared from the mortgage by his own self-acquisitions, it was held that the unencumbered property was ancestral property in his hands (*g*).

or by will.

But in that case the property appears not to have been ancestral at all. See as to what is "a gift through affection," *Lakshman* v. *Ramchandra*, 1 Bom. 561.

(*d*) *Tara Chand* v. *Reeb Ram*, 3 Mad. H. C. 50, 55.

(*e*) *Jugmohundas* v. *Mangaldas*, 10 Bom. 528.

(*f*) *Nanabhai* v. *Achratbai*, 12 Bom. 122, p. 133.

(*g*) *Visalatchy* v. *Annasamy*, 5 Mad. H. C. 150.

Property jointly acquired

§ 253. *Secondly*, property may be joint property without having been ancestral. Where the members of a Joint Family acquire property by or with the assistance of joint funds, or by their joint labour, such property is the joint property of the persons who have acquired it, whether it is an increment to ancestral property, or whether it has arisen without any nucleus of descended property (*h*). Whether the issue of such joint acquirers would by birth alone acquire an interest in such property, without evidence that they had in any way contributed to it, is a question which, as far as I know, has never arisen. If a single individual acquired a fortune by his own exertions, without any assistance from ancestral property, his issue would certainly take no interest in it. If several brothers did the same, the property would be joint as between themselves. It would certainly be self-acquired as regard all collaterals, and it is difficult to see why it should not be the same as regards their issue, unless they chose voluntarily to admit the latter to a share of it. This seems to have been the view taken by the High Court of Bombay in a case where property had been acquired by trade. They said, "There is no evidence to show that the parties were members of an ordinary trade partnership resting on contract. If the sons had a joint interest with their father in the piece-goods business, it was apparently because they were members of an undivided family carrying on business jointly in that capacity. If the property of the family firm had been acquired by the equal exertions of the three members, without the aid of any nucleus of property other than acquired by themselves, then, no doubt, the property of the firm with its accumulations would be self-acquired property even

---

(*h*) Manu, ix. § 215; Yajnavalkya, ii. 120; Mitakshara, i. 4, § 15; 3 Dig. 386; F. MacN. 351, 362; *Ramasheshaiya* v. *Bhagavat*, 4 Mad. H. C. 5; *Rampershad* v. *Sheochurn*, 10 M. I. A. 490; *Radhabai* v. *Nanarav*, 3 Bom. 151. By § 45 of the Transfer of Property Act (IV of 1882) persons who purchase immovable property out of a common fund are, in the absence of any contract to the contrary, entitled to hold it in shares proportioned to their interest in the common funds; and similarly where a joint purchase is made by several with their separate funds.

though it was owned jointly. And on a partition such property would apparently remain self-acquired property in the hands of the several members, even though one of them was the father of the other two" (*i*).

or thrown into common stock.

§ 254. *Thirdly*, property which was originally self-acquired, may become joint property, if it has been voluntarily thrown by the owner into the joint stock, with the intention of abandoning all separate claims upon it. This doctrine has been repeatedly recognized by the Privy Council. Perhaps the strongest case was one, where the owner had actually obtained a statutory title to the property under the Oudh Talukdars Act I of 1869. He was held by his conduct to have restored it to the condition of ancestral property (*k*). To create such a new title, however, a clear intention to waive the separate rights of the owner must be established, and will not be inferred from acts which may have been done out of kindness and affection. A younger brother who was insane from birth, had for many years been treated by his elder brother as if he was under no incapacity. His name was entered in the revenue records as joint owner, and documents were issued and taken in his name. It appeared that for many years his case had been treated by the family as one that might be cured. Finally a family arrangement was entered into by which he was set aside as incapacitated. The Privy Council held that the previous course of conduct could not be treated as amounting to a fresh grant of rights which the youth was incapable of taking by inheritance (*l*).

Impartible property may be joint.

§ 255. Liability to partition is one of the commonest incidents of joint property, but it must not be supposed that

---

(*i*) *Chatterbhooj* v. *Dharamsi*, 9 Bom. 438, p. 445.

(*k*) *Hurpurshad* v. *Sheo Dyal*, 3 I. A. 259; S. C. 26 Suth. 55; *Shankar Baksh* v. *Hardeo Baksh*, 16 I. A. 71; S. C. 16 Cal. 397; *per cur.*, *Rampershad* v. *Sheochurn*, 10 M. I. A. 506; *Chellayamal* v. *Mutialamal*, 6 Mad. Jur. P. C. 108; *Sham Narain* v. *Ct. of Wards*, 20 Suth. 197; *Gopalasami* v. *Chinnasami*, 7 Mad. 458; *per curiam*, 15 Bom. p. 39; 10 Cal. pp. 392, 398, 401; *Madhavrav Manohar* v. *Atmaram*, 15 Bom. 519.

(*l*) *Lala Muddun Gopal* v. *Khikhinda Koer*, 18 I. A. 9; S. C. 18 Cal. 341.

joint property and partible property are mutually convertible terms. If it were so, an impartible Zemindary could never be joint property. The reverse, however, is the case. The mode of its enjoyment necessarily cuts down to a very small point the rights of the other members of the family with respect to it. But there are two particulars in which its joint character becomes material—first, with reference to the order of succession; and, secondly, as to the powers of alienation possessed by each successive holder. Now as to the first point, it has been repeatedly held by the Privy Council that the order of succession to a Zemindary depended upon whether " though impartible it was part of the common family property," or was the separate or self-acquired property of the holder (*m*). As to the second point, the Courts of Madras, till very lately, ruled that the holder of an impartible Zemindary under Mitakshara law would be under the same restrictions as to alienation in regard to it as to any other ancestral property. This course of decisions has, however, been interrupted in consequence of a recent ruling of the Privy Council. The subject will have to be discussed more fully hereafter (*n*).

Coparceners may hold property separately.

§ 256. An examination into the property of the joint family would not be complete without pointing out what property may be held by the individual members which is not joint property. Property which is not joint must be either separate property or self-acquired, or property which has devolved upon another in such a manner as to be held by him free of all claims by members of the same undivided family. The last of the three cases has already been discussed (§ 251, 252). Separate property, *ex vi termini*, assumes that the holder of it has ceased to be in union

---

(*m*) *Katama Natchier* v. *Rajah of Shivagunga*, 9 M. I. A. 539, 589, 610; S. C. 2 Suth. (P. C.) 31; *Yanumula* v. *Boochia*, 13 M. I. A. 333, 336; S. C. 13 Suth. (P. C.) 21; *Chowdhry Chintamun* v. *Nowlukho*, 2 I. A. 263; S. C. 24 Suth. 255; *Yenumala* v. *Ramandora*, 6 Mad. H. C. 93, 103; *Periasamy* v. *Periasamy*, 5 I. A. 61; S. C. 1 Mad. 312; *Runganayakamma* v. *Bulli Ramaya*, P. C. 5th July 1879.

(*n*) See *post*, § 314.

with those in reference to whom the property is separate. But a man is very commonly separated from one set of persons, as, for instance, his brothers, while he is in union with others, as, for instance, his own issue. As regards the former, his property is separate; as regards the latter, it is joint (§ 252). Self-acquisition, on the other hand, may be made by any one while still in a state of union, and when made will be effective against the whole world. I have already (§ 215—217) pointed out the early history of this branch of the law. The following remarks will show how it has been dealt with by modern decisions.

Self-acquisition.

§ 257. The whole doctrine of self-acquisition is briefly stated by Yajnavalkya as follows:—"Whatever is acquired by the coparcener himself, without detriment to the father's estate, as a present from a friend, or a gift at nuptials, does not appertain to the coheirs (*o*). Nor shall he who recovers hereditary property which has been taken away give it up to the coparceners; nor what has been gained by science" (*p*). Upon this the Smriti Chandrika remarks that the estate of the father means the estate of any undivided coheir (*q*). While the Mitakshara adds, that the words "without detriment to the father's estate" must be connected with each member of the sentence. "Consequently what is obtained from a friend as the return of an obligation conferred at the charge of the patrimony; What is received at a marriage concluded in the form Asura or the like (*r*); What is recovered of the hereditary estate by the expenditure of the father's goods; What is earned by science acquired at the expense of ancestral wealth; all that must be shared with the whole of the brethren and the father" (*s*). The author of the Mitakshara enlarges the text of Yajnavalkya by

(*o*) See as to presents from relations or friends, Manu, ix. § 206; Narada, xiii. § 6, 7; *Muddun Gopal* v. *Ram Buksh*, 6 Suth. 71; *ante*, § 252; Mitakshara, i. 5, § 9.

(*p*) Yajnavalkya, ii § 118, 119; Mitakshara, i. 4, § 1. See D a Bhaga, vi. 1 D. K. S. iv. 2, § 1—12; V. May., iv. 7, § 1—14; *Raghunandana*, v. 1—12.

(*q*) Smriti Chandrika, vii. § 28.

(*r*) *Sheo Gobind* v. *Sham Narain*, 7 N. W. P. 75.

(*s*) Mitakshara, i. 4, § 6.

defining self-acquisition as "that which had been acquired by the coparcener himself without any detriment to the goods of his father *or mother*." Hence the Madras High Court has recently decided that property inherited by a man from his mother's father is not his self-acquisition, and this ruling has been affirmed by the Privy Council (*t*). The whole contest in each instance is to show that the gain has been without "detriment to the estate." In early times the slightest assistance from the joint patrimony, however indirect, was considered to be such a detriment, and the possession of any joint property was considered as conclusively proving that there had been such an assistance. The Madras Court has always leant very strongly against self-acquisition. But the recent tendency of decisions seems to be towards a more sensible view of the law, following out its spirit rather than its letter.

§ 258. For instance, the gains of science or valour, which seem to have been the earliest forms of self-acquisition, were held to be joint property, if the learning had been imparted at the expense of the Joint Family, or if the warrior had used his father's sword (§ 216). The law upon this point was examined with great fulness in a case where the adoptive mother of a dancing girl claimed her property, on the ground that it had been acquired by skill imparted at the mother's expense. The High Court of Madras, overruling a very elaborate judgment of the Civil Judge, decided that if these gains were to be considered the gains of science, they were joint property of the acquirer and her mother (*u*). It would admittedly have been otherwise if her gains had merely been the result of prostitution, unaided by any special education (*v*). In a later case the gains of a Vakil were held to be divisible, on the ground that they had been

Gains of science.

(*t*) Mit., i. 4, § 2; acc. *Raghunandana*, v. 5; *Muttayan Chetty* v. *Sangili*, 9 I. A. 127, 3 Mad. 370, 1882. The Privy Council declined to commit itself to the consequence drawn by the Madras High Court that property so inherited became the joint property of the taker and his son. See *ante*, § 251.

(*u*) *Chalakonda* v. *Ratnachalam*, 2 Mad. H. C. 56. See 2 W. MacN. 167.

(*v*) *Boologam* v. *Swornam*, 4 Mad. 330.

obtained by education imparted at the family expense, although it was found that he had received from his father nothing more than a general education. *Holloway*, J., referring to the dancing girl's case, said, "I fully adhere to the judgment of the High Court, for which I am responsible, and especially to the statement that the ordinary gains of science by one who has received a family maintenance are certainly partible" (*w*). The decisions in the above cases were adopted in general terms by the Chief Justice in Bombay in another case of a Vakil. There, however, the point really did not arise, as it appeared that he united the business of money-lender with that of Vakil, and that there was joint family property of which he had the use (*x*).

Effect of education in family.

§ 259. It is, however, difficult to see why a person who has made gains by science, after having been educated or maintained at the family expense, should be in a worse position than any other person who has been so educated, or maintained, and who has afterwards made self-acquisitions. Jimuta Vahana lays it down, that where it is attempted to reduce a separate acquisition into common property on the ground that it was obtained with the aid of common property, it must be shown that the joint stock was used for the express purpose of gain. "It becomes not common merely because property may have been used for food or other necessaries, since that is similar to the sucking of the mother's breast" (*y*). This seems to be good sense. If a member of a Hindu family were sent to England at the joint expense, to be educated for the Bar or the Civil Service, it seems fair enough that his extra gains should fall into the common stock, as a recompense for the extra outlay incurred. It might be assumed that when the outlay was incurred the reimbursement was contemplated. But it is different where all start on exactly

(*w*) *Gungadharudu* v. *Narasammah*, 7 Mad. H. C. 47.
(*x*) *Bai Manchha* v. *Narotamdas*, 6 Bom. H. C. (A. C. J.) 1, 6.
(*y*) Daya Bhaga, vi. 1, § 44—50; 1 Stra. H. L. 214; 2 Stra. H. L. 374.

the same level, with nothing but the ordinary maintenance and education which is common to persons of that class of life. Accordingly, in a Madras case, where a Hindu had made a large mercantile fortune, his claim to hold it as self-acquired was allowed, though he had admittedly been maintained in his earlier years, educated and married out of patrimonial means (*z*). So in a Bengal case, where self-acquisition was set up, and the defendant had been maintained at the family expense, but it was proved that in acquiring his property he did not use any funds which belonged to the joint family, his gains apparently being derived from some lucrative employment, it was held that the plea was made out. *Mitter*, J., said, "The plaintiff's case in the Court below was that the defendant received his education from the joint estate, and that he is consequently entitled to participate in every property that has been acquired by the defendant by the aid of such education. But this contention is nowhere sanctioned by the Hindu law, and I see nothing in justice to recommend it" (*a*). This case was approved by the Privy Council in an appeal where it had been contended that the property acquired by a successful merchant was joint property, because he had been educated out of the joint funds. The fact was negatived, upon which the Committee observed, "This being their Lordships' view, it does not become necessary to consider whether the somewhat startling proposition of law put forward by the appellant, which, stated in plain terms, amounts to this—that if a member of a joint Hindu family receives any education whatever from the joint funds, he becomes for ever after incapable of acquiring by his own skill and industry any separate property—is or is not maintainable. Very strong and clear authority would be required to support such a proposition. For the reasons that they have given, it does not appear to them necessary to review the text-books or the authorities which

Maintenance and education in family.

(*z*) *Chellaperoomall* v. *Veeraperoomal*, 4 Mad. Jur. 54, affd. on appeal, *ib.*, 240.
(*a*) *Dhunookdaree* v. *Gunput*, 11 B. L. R. 201, note; S. C. 10 Suth. 122.

have been cited on this subject. It may be enough to say, that according to their Lordships' view, no texts which have been cited go to the full extent of the proposition contended." Then, after referring with approval to the Bengal case as laying the law down less broadly than those in Madras and Bombay, the judgment concluded by saying, "It may hereafter possibly become necessary for this Board to consider, whether or not the more limited and guarded expression of the law upon this subject of the Courts of Bengal, is not more correct than what appears to be the doctrine of the Courts of Madras" (*b*).

The science must have been specially taught at the family expense.

§ 260. All of the above cases were recently examined by the High Court of Bombay (*c*). They said, "It certainly appears to us that the dictum of *Mitter*, J., that the proposition which we are considering 'is no where sanctioned by Hindu law,' is not strictly accurate. The texts which have been cited to us do, in our opinion, establish it as a rule of Hindu law that the ordinary gains of science are divisible, when such science has been imparted at the family expense, and acquired while receiving a family maintenance, but that it is otherwise when the science has been imparted at the expense of persons who are not members of the student's family. But the question still remains, whether the term 'Science' as used in the texts, is, in modern days, to be construed as meaning a mere general education, and not rather a special training for a particular profession. The words 'any education whatever' in the judgment of the Judicial Committee in *Pauliem* v. *Pauliem*, as well as an observation of one of their Lordships in the course of the argument, that the Madras case of the dancing girl was a case of a special training, and not necessarily applicable to a case of general training, may seem to indicate that, if the question again comes before their Lordships, it will be considered chiefly with reference to the nature and extent of the educa-

(*b*) *Pauliem Valoo* v. *Pauliem Sooryah*, 4 I. A. 109, 117; S. C. 1 Mad. 252.

(*c*) *Lakshman* v. *Jamnabai*, 6 Bom. 225, p. 242. Approved and followed *Krishnaji Mahadev* v. *Moro Mahadev*, 15 Bom. 32.

tion imparted at the family expense." The Court, after citing with approval the remarks at the beginning of the preceding paragraph, proceed to say: "We think that we shall be doing no violence to the Hindu texts, but shall be only adapting them to the condition of modern society, if we hold, that, when they speak of the gains of science which has been imparted at the family expense, they intend the special branch of science which is the immediate source of the gains, and not the elementary education which is the necessary stepping stone to the acquisition of all science."

Possession of joint funds not conclusive.

§ 261. On the same principle, although the admitted possession or existence of joint funds will throw upon the self-acquirer the onus of proving that such funds did not form the nucleus of his fortune (*d*), the fact itself is not conclusive. In a case in the Supreme Court of Bengal, *Grant*, J., said, "Where the property descended is incapable of being considered as the germ whose improvement has constituted the wealth subsequently possessed, this wealth must evidently be deemed acquired. An ancestral cottage never converted, or capable of conversion to an available amount into money, in which the maker of the wealth had the trifling benefit of residing with the rest of the family when he commenced turning his industry to profit,—so of other things of a trifling nature" (*e*). Of course the contrary would be held, if it appeared that the income of the joint property was large enough to leave a surplus, after discharging the necessary expenses of the family, out of which the acquisitions might have been made (*f*). And purchases made with money borrowed on the security of the common property will belong to the Joint Family, the members of which will be jointly liable for the debt (*g*).

(*d*) *Shib Pershad* v. *Gungamonee*, 16 Suth. 291; *Pran Kristo* v. *Bhageerutee*, 20 Suth. 158; *Subbayya* v. *Surayya*, 10 Mad. 251.

(*e*) *Gooroochurn* v. *Goluckmoney*, Fulton, 165, 181; *per curiam*, *Meenatchee* v. *Chetumbra*, Mad. Dec. of 1853, 63; *Jadoomonee* v. *Gungadur*, 1 Bouln. 600; V. Darp. 521; *Ahmedbhoy* v. *Cassumbhoy*, 13 Bom. 534; 10 M. I. A., p. 505.

(*f*) *Sudanund* v. *Soorjo Monee*, 11 Suth. 436.

(*g*) *Sheopershad* v. *Kulunder*, 1 S. D. 76 (101).

But it would be otherwise if the loan was made on the sole credit of the borrower, or even if the loan was made out of the common fund, under a special agreement that it was to be at the sole risk of the borrower, and for his sole benefit (*h*).

Government grants.

§ 262. Estates conferred by Government in the exercise of their sovereign power, become the self-acquired property of the donee, whether such gifts are absolutely new grants, or only the restoration to one member of the family of property previously held by another, but confiscated (*i*). But where one member of a family forcibly dispossesses another who is in possession of an ancestral Zemindary, and there is no legal forfeiture, nor any fresh grant by a person competent to confer a legal title, the new occupant takes, not by self-acquisition, but in continuation of the former title (*k*). And where a confiscation made by Government was subsequently annulled, and no grant to any third person was ever made, it was held that the old title revived, for the benefit of all persons capable of claiming under it (*l*). So a grant made by Government to the holder of an estate, which merely operates as an ascertainment of the State claim for revenue, and a release of the reversionary right of the crown, is a mere continuance of the old estate (*m*).

Savings from impartible property.

A point which has only recently been decided is, whether the savings made by the holder of an impartible estate

---

(*h*) *Rai Nursingh* v. *Rai Narain*, 3 N. W. P. 218.

(*i*) *Katama Natchiar* v. *Rajah of Shivaganga*, 9 M. I. A. 606; S. C. 2 Suth. (P. C.) 31; *Beer Pertab* v. *Maharajah Rajender*, 12 M. I. A. 1, (Hunsapore Case); S. C. 2 Suth. (P. C.) 31. As to grants in Oudh after the Confiscation of 1858, and under Act I of 1869 (Oudh Estate Act); see *Thakurain Sookraj* v. *The Government*, 14 M. I. A. 112. *Hurpurshad* v. *Sheo Dyal*, 3 I. A. 259; S. C. 26 Suth. 55; *Hardeo Bux* v. *Jawahir*, 4 I. A. 178; 6 I. A. 161. *Brijindar* v. *Janki Koer*, 5 I. A. 1; *Thakur Shere* v. *Thakurain*, 3 Cal. 645; *Gouri Shunker* v. *Maharajah of Bulrampore*, 6 I. A. 1; S. C. 4 Cal. 839; *Mulka Jahan* v. *Deputy Commissioner of Lucknow*, ib. 63; *Mirza Jehan* v. *Nawab Afsur Bahu*, ib. 76; S. C. 4 Cal. 727; *Seth Jaidial* v. *Seth Siteeram*, 8 I. A. 215; *Ramanund* v. *Raghunath*, 9 I. A. 41; S. C. 8 Cal. 769. *Pirthi Pal* v. *Jewahir Singh*, 14 I. A. 37. A grant of a jaghire is presumably only for life. *Gulabdas* v. *Collector of Surat*, 6 I. A. 54; S. C. 3 Bom. 186.

(*k*) *Yanumula* v. *Boochia*, 13 M. I. A. 333; S. C. 13 Suth. (P. C.) 21.

(*l*) *Mirza Jehan* v. *Badshoo Bahoo*, 12 I. A. 124; S. C. 12 Cal. 1.

(*m*) *Narayana* v. *Chengalamma*, 10 Mad. 1.

under Mitakshara law, are his self-acquired property, or not. It is quite settled that, although an impartible Zemindary may be joint property, in the sense that all the family have a joint and vested interest in the reversion (§ 255), its annual income, and the accumulations of such income, are the absolute and exclusive property of the possessor of the Zemindary for the time being. None of his kindred can claim an account of the mode in which he has spent his income, nor a share in the profits annually accruing or laid by. He may spend as much or as little of his income as he likes. If he spends it all, it is not waste, and whatever he invests is absolutely at his own disposal during his life (*n*). There could therefore be no coparcenary in such savings, and therefore no survivorship (*o*). If, therefore, a Zemindar in Madras left no issue, it seems to me that his widow would take his savings before his brothers, or their issue, and if he left issue, they would take exclusively. This appears to have been the view of the Madras High Court in one of the two cases quoted above, where they say, "Whether regarded as the separately acquired funds of the Zemindar, or as it really is, his acquisition derived from ancestral property owned by him solely, it is equally divisible family property as between his sons" (*p*). Accordingly when a Poligar died leaving debts which would not bind the family, but also leaving property which had been purchased out of the savings of his income, it was held that such purchases were his separate property, to which his creditors would be entitled in discharge of their debts (*q*). Of course savings handed down from previous Zemindars would follow a different rule; they would become the joint property of his descendants, of whom the succeeding Zemindar was only one, his brothers and their issue being the others.

(*n*) *Maharajulungaru* v. *Rajah Row Pantalu*, 5 Mad. H. C. 31, 41; *Lutchmana Row* v. *Terimul Row*, 4 Mad. Jur. 241.

(*o*) See *Neelkisto Deb* v. *Beerchunder*, 12 M. I. A. 540; S. C. 3 B. L. R. (P. C.) 13; S. C. 12 Suth. (P. C.) 21 (Tipperah Case).

(*p*) 5 Mad. H. C. 41, *Supra*, note (n).

(*q*) *Kotta Ramasami* v. *Bangari*, 3 Mad. 145. Both Judges agreed that this would be the case with a *de jure* Poligar, but they differed as to the law where the Poligar was one *de facto* but not *de jure*. See pp. 155, 165.

Recovery of ancestral property.

§ 263. Another mode of self-acquisition, which is not very likely to arise now, is where one coparcener unaided by the others, or by the family funds, recovers, with the acquiescence of his co-heirs, ancestral property, which had been seized by others, and which his family had been unable to recover (*r*). In order to bring a case within this rule, the property must have passed into the possession of strangers, and be held by them adversely to the family. It is not sufficient that it should be held by a person claiming title to hold it as a member of the family, or by a stranger claiming under the family, as for instance by mortgage. So also the recovery by one co-heir for his own special benefit is only permissible where "the neglect of the coparceners to assert their title had been such as to show that they had no intention to seek to recover the property, or were at least indifferent as to its recovery, and thus tacitly assented to the recoverer using his means and exertions for that purpose, or upon an express understanding with the recoverer's coparceners." "The recovery, if not made with the privity of the co-heirs, must at least have been *bonâ fide*, and not in fraud of their title, or by anticipating them in their intention of recovering the lost property." Finally, it must be an actual recovery of possession, and not merely the obtaining of a decree for possession (*s*).

Result to recoverer.

As to the result of such a recovery, there seems to be a conflict in the Mitakshara. At ch. i. 5, § 11, the author, referring to Manu, ix. § 209, makes the property which has been recovered belong exclusively to the recoverer. At ch. i. 4, § 11, he quotes a text of Sankha as establishing that, "if it be land, he takes the fourth part, and the remainder is equally shared among all the brethren." Dr. Mayr reconciles the discrepancy by supposing that the former

---

(*r*) Manu, ix. § 209; Mitakshara, i. 4, § 2, 6; Daya Bhaga, vi. 2, § 31—37; D. K. S. iv. 2, § 6—9; Raghunandana, v. 29—31.

(*s*) *Visalatchy* v. *Annasamy*, 5 Mad. H. C. 150; *Bisheswar* v. *Shitul*, 8 Suth. 13; S. C. Confirmed on review; *Sub nomine*, *Bissessur* v. *Seetul*, 9 Suth. 69; *Bolakee* v. *Ct. of Wards*, 14 Suth. 34; *Jugmohundas* v. *Mangaldas*, 10 Bom. 528; *Muttu Vadhuganadha* v. *Dorasinga*, 8 I. A. 99; S. C. 8 Mad. 300; *Naraganti* v. *Venkatachalapati*, 4 Mad. p. 259.

text refers to the case of a recovery by the father, while the latter refers to one of several brethren or other coparceners, who all stand on the same level (*t*). The Bengal authorities, however, take the latter rule as applying to every recoverer, but only in the case of land (*u*). It is to be observed that the recoverer takes one-fourth first, and then shares equally with the others in the residue (*v*).

Acquisitions aided by joint funds.

§ 264. An intermediate case between self-acquired and joint property is the case, resting upon a text of Vasishtha, in which property acquired by a single coparcener, at the expense of the patrimony, is said to be subject to partition, the acquirer being entitled to a double share (*w*). It has already been suggested (§ 216) that this text probably applied originally to self-acquisition properly so called, and that it cut down the rights of a self-acquirer, instead of enlarging the rights of one who has made use of common property. The Smriti Chandrika and Madhaviya both restrict the text to the gains of learning, when considered to be partible in consequence of the education from which they sprung, having been imparted at the expense of the family (*x*). The general principles laid down by Vijnanesvara seem to exclude the idea that any special and exclusive benefit can be obtained to any co-heir by a use of the family property (*y*). Mr. W. MacNaghten states that under Benares law no such benefit can be obtained, whatever may have been the personal exertions of any individual, but that the rule does exist in Bengal (*z*). There is no doubt that in that province the rule has been repeatedly

---

(*t*) Mayr, 25; Vrihaspati, 3 Dig. 32.
(*u*) Daya Bhaga, vi. 2, § 36—39; D. K. S. iv. 2, § 7, 8; 1 W. MacN. 52; 2 W. MacN. 157.
(*v*) D. K. S. iv. 2, § 9; 3 Dig. 365.
(*w*) "And if one of the brothers has gained something by his own effort, he shall receive a double share." Vasishtha, xvii. 51; Mitakshara, i. 4, § 29; Daya Bhaga, vi. 1, § 27—29; Raghunandana, i. 20, v. 18.
(*x*) Smriti Chandrika, vii. § 9; Madhaviya, p. 49, and see futwah, 2 W. MacN. 167.
(*y*) Mitakshara, i. 4, § 1—6.
(*z*) 1 W. MacN. 52; 2 W. MacN. 7, n., 158, 160, n., 162, n.

laid down (*a*), but little attempt has been made to define its extent, or the cases to which it applies. In a case before the Supreme Court of Bengal, Sir *Lawrence Peel*, C. J., laid down the law as follows: "The authorities establish, and the uniform course of practice in this Court is conformable to them, that the sole manager of the joint stock is thereby entitled to no increased share, and that skill and labour contributed by one joint sharer alone in the augmentation or improvement of the common stock, establishes no right to a larger share; that the acquisition of a distinct property without aid of the joint funds or joint labour gives a separate right, and creates a separate estate; that the acquisition of a *distinct* property, with the aid of joint funds, or of joint labour, gives the acquirer a right to a double share, and prevents the character of separate estate from attaching to such an acquisition; and lastly, that the union with the common stock of that which might otherwise have been held in severalty, gives it the character of a joint and not of a separate property." *Grant*, J., held to the same effect, adding that in this respect the law of Bengal and the Mitakshara coincide, and that to entitle the acquirer to a double share, he must only be "aided by means drawn from the joint funds of little consideration" (*b*). This decision is cited with approval by the Supreme Court of Bengal (*c*) as laying down both the rule and the exception as to joint and separate acquisitions. The first principle laid down by Sir *Lawrence Peel*, that in order to entitle the acquirer to a double share, the property acquired must be a distinct one, is in accordance with the Mitakshara, which, after citing Vasishtha's text, proceeds, "The author (Yajnavalkya) propounds an exception to that maxim. But if the common stock be improved, an equal division is ordained;" and says

---

(*a*) *Gudadhur* v. *Ajodhearam*, 1 S. D. 6 (7); *Koshul* v. *Radhanath*, 1 S. D. 336 (448); *Doorputtee* v. *Haradhun*, 3 S. D 98; *Kripa Sindhu* v. *Kanhaya*, 5 S. D. 335 (393); *per curiam*, *Uma Sundari* v. *Dwarkanath*, 2 B. L. R. (A. O. J.) 287.

(*b*) *Gooroochurn* v. *Goluckmoney*, Fulton, 165.

(*c*) *Soorjeemoney Dossee* v. *Denobundo*, 6 M. I. A. 539; S. C. 4 Suth. (P.C.) 114; *post*, § 268.

that in such a case, a double share is not allotted to the acquirer (*d*). The second principle laid down by *Grant*, J., that the assistance derived from the joint funds must be of little consideration, seems also to be in accordance with the Daya Bhaga. It will be seen that Jimuta Vahana rests the doctrine of the double share of the acquirer, not upon the text of Vasishtha, which he seems to take as applying to self-acquisition, properly so called, but upon a text of Vyasa. "The brethren participate in that wealth, which one of them gains by valour or the like, using any common property, either a weapon or a vehicle" (*e*). Here the meritorious cause of the acquisition is the brother himself, the assistance derived from the joint funds being insignificant. This view is in accordance with the futwah of the Pandits in *Purtab Bahaudur* v. *Tilukdharee* (*f*), "of several brothers living together in family partnership, should one acquire property by means of funds common to the whole, the property so acquired belongs jointly to all the brothers. Should, however, the means of acquisition, drawn from the joint funds, be of little consideration, and the personal exertions considerable, two shares belong to the acquirer, and one to each of the other brothers." Both points have been affirmed by later decisions of the Bengal High Court (*g*).

Burthen of proof.

§ 265. There is a good deal of conflict, probably more apparent than real, between the decisions of the High Court of Bengal as to the question upon whom lies the onus of proof, where property is claimed by one person as being joint property, and withheld by another as being self-acquired, or *vice versâ*. The general principle undoubtedly is, that as every Hindu family is supposed to be joint unless the contrary is proved, so if nothing appears upon the case except that a member of a family, admittedly or presumably joint, is in possession of property, if he alleges that it is his

(*d*) Mitakshara, i. 4, § 30, 31. (*e*) Daya Bhaga, ii. § 41, vi. 1, § 28, 14.
(*f*) 1 S. D. 179 (236).
(*g*) *Sree Narain* v. *Gooro Pershad*, 6 Suth. 219; *Sheo Dyal* v. *Judoonath*, 9 Suth. 61; and *per Colvile*, C. J., *Jadoomonee* v. *Gangadhur*, 1 Bouln., 600; V. Darp., 521.

own self-acquisition, he is alleging something which is an exception to the general rule, and it lies upon him to prove the exception (*h*). But on the other hand, the case of a plaintiff who seeks to establish a claim to Joint Family property is no exception to the rule, that the plaintiff must make out his case. He starts with a presumption in his favour. But this presumption must be taken along with the other facts, proved or admitted, and those facts may so far remove the presumption arising from the ordinary condition of a Hindu family, as to throw back the burthen of proof on the other side (*i*). What, then, is the extent of the presumption as to the condition of a Hindu family? "The normal state of every Hindu family is joint. Presumably every such family is joint in food, worship, and estate. In the absence of proof of division, such is the legal presumption. But the members of the family may sever in all or any of these three things" (*k*). Of course there is no presumption that a family, because it is joint, possesses joint property, or any property. But where it is proved or admitted that a Joint Family possesses some joint property, and the property in dispute has been acquired, or is held in a manner, consistent with that character, "the presumption of law is that all the property they were possessed of was joint property, until it was shown by evidence that one member of the family was possessed of separate property." And this presumption is not rebutted merely by showing "that it was purchased in the name of one member of the family, and that there are receipts in his name respecting it; for all that is perfectly consistent with the notion of its having been joint property, and even if it had been joint property, it still would have been treated in exactly the same manner" (*l*). The difference of opinion seems to arise as to the degree to

Presumption as to union.

(*h*) *Luximon Row* v. *Mullar Row*, 2 Kn., 60, 63.

(*i*) *Bholanath* v. *Ajoodhia*, 12 B. L. R. 336; S. C. 20 Suth. 65; *Bodh Singh* v. *Gunesh*, 12 B. L. R. (P. C.) 317; S. C. 19 Suth. 356; *per curiam*, 12 Bom. pp. 131, 309, 13 Bom. p. 66.

(*k*) *Per curiam*, *Neelkisto Deb* v. *Beerchunder*, (Tipperah case) 12 M. I. A. 540; S. C. 3 B. L. R. (P. C.) 13; S. C. 12 Suth. (P. C.) 21; *Naraguntу* v. *Vengama*, 9 M. I. A. 92; S. C. 1 Suth. (P. C.) 30.

(*l*) *Dhurm Das* v. *Mt. Shama Soondri*, 3 M. I. A. 229, 240; S. C. 6 Suth. (P.

which the presumption is to be pushed, where the family is joint, but where no nucleus of joint property is either admitted or proved, and where some property is held by one or more members in a manner, as regards either origin or enjoyment, apparently, though not necessarily, inconsistent with the idea of a joint interest.

§ 266. The law upon this point was laid down as follows by the Sudder Court of Bengal. "Where, by the plaintiff's own admission, the properties in dispute were not acquired by the use of patrimonial funds, and the defendants never acknowledged that they were acquired by the joint exertions and aid of the plaintiff and his father, it was for the plaintiff to prove his own allegations as to the original joint interest in the purchase of the property. The mere circumstance of the parties having been united in food, raises no such sufficient presumption of a joint interest as to relieve the plaintiffs from the onus of proof" (*m*). And the Bengal High Court said, "To render it joint property, the consideration for its purchase must have proceeded either out of ancestral funds, or have been produced out of the joint property, or by joint labour. But neither of these alternatives is matter of legal presumption. It can only be brought to the cognizance of a Court of justice in the same way as any other fact, *viz.*, by evidence. Consequently, whoever's interest it is to establish it, he must be able to produce the evidence. The plaintiff coming into Court to claim a share in property as being Joint Family property, must lay some foundation before he can succeed in his suit. He must, at least, show that the defendants whom he sues constitute a Joint Family, and that the property in question became joint property when acquired, or that at some period since its acquisition it has been enjoyed jointly by the family. It will be sufficient for this purpose for him to show that the family, of

Burthen of proof.

C.) 43; *Umrithnath* v. *Goureenath*, 13 M. I. A. 542; S. C. 15 Suth. (P. C.) 10; *Rampershad* v. *Sheochurn*, 10 M. I. A. 490, 505.

(*m*) *Kishoree* v. *Chummun*, S. D. of 1852, 111, citing 2 W. MacN. 152—156; F. MacN. 60, approved; *Soobhedur* v. *Boloram*, Suth. Sp. No. 57.

which the defendants came, was at some antecedent period, not unreasonably great, living joint in estate; and that the property in question was either a portion of the patrimonial estate, so enjoyed by the family, or that it has been since acquired by joint funds. In this case the Principal Sudr Amin has found that the plaintiff has given no proof of the family being joint, beyond the admitted fact of the three persons being brothers and the plaintiff has also given no sort of proof that these brothers ever were living in the joint enjoyment of any property, still less that this property was acquired by the use and employment of any joint funds. It seems to us that he was entirely right, on this finding, to dismiss the plaintiff's suit without looking further into the case" (n). The principles laid down in this case as to *onus probandi* were, however, denied to be law by the Chief Justice, Sir *Richard Couch*, in *Taruck Chunder* v. *Jodeshur* (o). He laid down the rule to be that, "as the presumption of law is that all the property the family is in possession of is joint property, the rule that the possession of one of the joint owners is the possession of all would apply to this extent, that if one of them was found to be in possession of any property, the family being presumed to be joint in estate, the presumption would be, not that he was in possession of it as separate property acquired by him, but as a member of the Joint Family." This ruling, however, was considered and differed from by other Judges of the High Court in two subsequent cases (p), and was again considered by the High Court and affirmed by two later cases. One of these was the decision of a Court of Appeal, and in the second a single Judge refused to refer the point to a full bench as being conclusively settled (q).

Conflict of opinion.

(n) *Shiu Golam* v. *Baran*, 1 B. L. R. (A. C. J.) 164; S. C. 10 Suth. 198; *Sub nomine*, *Sheo Golam* v. *Burra*.

(o) 11 B. L. R. 193; S. C. 19 Suth, 178; acc. *Annundo Mohun* v. *Lamb*, 1 Marsh. 169; *Hait Singh* v. *Dabee Singh*, 2 N. W. P. 308; *Nursingh Das* v. *Narain Das*, 3 N. W. P. 217; *Sidapa* v. *Pooneakooty*, Morris, 100.

(p) *Bholanath* v. *Ajoodhia*, 12 B. L. R. 336; S. C. 20 Suth. 65; *Denonath* v. *Hurrynarrain*, 12 B. L. R. 349.

(q) *Gobind Chunder* v. *Doorgapersad*, 14 B. L. R. 337; S. C. 22 Suth. 248; *Shushee Mohun* v. *Aukhil*, 25 Suth. 232; *Vedavalli* v. *Narayana*, 2 Mad. 19.

§ 267. It seems to me that the difficulty arises from attempting to lay down an abstract proposition of law which will govern every case, however different in its facts. It is correct to say that a Hindu family is presumed to be joint. It is merely equivalent to saying, that, where nothing else is known of a family, the probability is that its members have never entered into a partition with each other. It is a definite statement as to the probability of a single fact. But to say generally of any piece of property in the possession of any member of the family, that it is presumably joint estate, is to assert one or other of a great many different propositions. Either that in its present condition it was ancestral property, or that it was acquired by means or with the assistance of ancestral property, or by means of joint labour, or joint funds, or both, or that it was acquired by a single member without aid from other funds, or from other members, and then thrown into the common stock. Now, these propositions are each different in their probability, and different in the facts which would establish them. The very statement of the plaintiff's case, or his evidence, may negative some of them, just as the defendant's case may admit some of them. It seems impossible to say what the presumption is, until it is known what proposition the plaintiff and defendant respectively put forward. This seems to be all that is laid down by the Bengal cases, which go most strongly against the rights of undivided family. The Judges say, "Tell us what your case is: when we find how much of it is admitted by the other side, we will then be able to say whether you are relieved of the necessity of proving any part of your case, and how much of it." For instance, if the plaintiff's case was that the property was ancestral, and the defendant admitted that it was purchased with his father's money, but alleged that the purchase was made in his own name, and for his own exclusive benefit, the burthen of proof would lie on him (*r*). Again, if the case was that the property was purchased out of the proceeds

Suggested solution.

Burthen of proof varies.

(*r*) *Gopeekrist* v. *Gungapersaud*, 6 M. I. A. 53; *Bissessur* v. *Luchmessur*, 6 I. A. 233; S. C. 5 C. L. R. 477.

of the family estate, and it was admitted that there was family property, of which the defendant was manager, the *onus* would also lie on him to show a separate acquisition (*s*). And so it would be where the property was acquired by any member, if the family was joint, and there was an admitted nucleus of family property (*t*). If it was denied that there ever had been any family property, or admitted that the defendant was not the person in possession of it, the plaintiff would, I imagine, fail if he offered no evidence whatever. The amount of evidence necessary to shift upon the other side the burthen of displacing it might be very small, but would necessarily vary according to the facts of each case. On the other hand, if the property was admitted to be originally self-acquisition, but stated to have been thrown into the common stock, this would be a very good case, if made out (§ 254), but the *onus* of proving it would be heavily on the party asserting it. And so it would be if the property were admitted to have been acquired by one member without the use of family funds, but the plaintiff asserted that he had rendered such assistance as made it joint property. Even where it appeared that the family had ancestral property in their joint possession, but that some of the family acquired separate property from their own funds, and dealt with it as their own without reference to the other members of the family, the Privy Council held "that such a state of things may be fairly held to weaken, if not altogether to rebut, the ordinary presumption of Hindu law as to property in the name of one member of a Joint Family, and to throw upon those who claim as joint property that of which they have allowed their coparcener, trading and incurring liabilities on his separate account to appear to be the sole owner, the obligation of establishing their title by clear and cogent reasons" (*u*). *A fortiori*,

(*s*) *Luximon Row* v. *Mullar Row*, 2 Kn. 60; *Pedru* v. *Domingo*, Mad. Dec. of 1869, 8; *Janokee* v. *Kisto*, Marsh, 1.

(*t*) *Prankristo* v. *Bhagerutee*, 20 Suth. 158; *Moolji Lilla* v. *Gokuldas*, 8 Bom. 154; *Lakshman* v. *Jamnabai*, 6 Bom. 225.

(*u*) *Bodh Singh* v. *Gunesh*, 12 B. L. R. 317, 327; S. C. 19 Suth. 356; *Murari Vithoji* v. *Mukund Shivaji*, 15 Bom. 201.

where there had been admitted self-acquisitions, and an actual partition, if one of the members sued subsequently for a share of property left in the hands of one of the members as his self-acquired property, alleging that it was really joint property; or if a member of the family admitted a partition among some of the members, but asserted that the others had remained undivided, the *onus* would lie upon him to make out such a case (*v*).

§ 268. The fourth subject of examination relates to the mode in which the Joint Family property is to be enjoyed by the coparceners. This must necessarily vary according to the view taken of the nature of the family corporation. In Malabar and Canara, where the property is indissoluble, the members of the family may be said rather to have rights out of the property than rights to the property. The head of the family is entitled to its entire possession, and is absolute in its management. The junior members have only a right to maintenance and residence. They cannot call for an account, except as incident to a prayer for the removal of the manager for misconduct, nor claim any specific share of the income, nor even require that their maintenance or the family outlay should be in proportion to the income. An absolute discretion in this respect is vested in the manager (*w*). A family governed by Mitakshara law is in a very similar position, except as to their right to a partition, and to an account as incident to that right. In a judgment which is constantly referred to, Lord *Westbury* said, "According to the true notion of an undivided family in Hindu law, no individual member of that family while it remains undivided, can predicate of the joint and undivided property that he, that particular member, has a certain

Enjoyment of family property.

Malabar.

Mitakshara.

(*v*) *Badul* v. *Chutterdharee*, 9 Suth. 558; *Bannoo* v. *Kashee Ram*, (P. C.) 3 Cal. 315; *Radha Churn* v. *Kripa*, 5 Cal. 474; *Obhoy Churn* v. *Gobind Chunder*, 9 Cal. 237; *Upendra Narain* v. *Gopanath*, *ibid.* 817; *Bata Krishna* v. *Chintamani*, 12 Cal. 262. In the two latter cases it was held, that the mere fact that one member of the family had separated from the joint stock, raised no presumption that the other members had separated *inter se*. See the converse case, *Kristnappa* v. *Ramasawmy*, 8 Mad. H. C. 25.

(*w*) § 220. *Tod* v. *Kunhamod*, 3 Mad. 175.

definite share. No individual member of an undivided family could go to the place of the receipt of rent, and claim to take from the collector or receiver of the rents a certain definite share. The proceeds of undivided property must be brought, according to the theory of an undivided family, to the common chest or purse, and there dealt with according to the modes of enjoyment by the members of an undivided family" (*x*). The position of a Joint Family under

Bengal. Bengal law is in some respects less favourable, and in other respects, apparently, more favourable than that of a family under Mitakshara law. Where property is held by a father as head of an undivided family, his issue have no legal claim upon him or the property, except for their maintenance. He can dispose of it as he pleases, and they cannot require a partition (§ 224). Consequently they can neither control, nor call for an account of his management. But as soon as it has made a descent, the brothers or other co-heirs hold their shares in a sort of quasi-severalty, which admits of the interest of each, while still undivided, passing on to his own representatives, male or females, or even to his assignees (*y*). How far this principle enlarges the rights of the co-sharers *inter se* is a matter of some obscurity. *Primâ facie* one would imagine that it would entitle each coparcener under Bengal law to do what, according to Lord *Westbury*, no coparcener can do under Benares law, *viz.*, "to predicate of the joint and undivided family property that he, that particular member, has a certain definite share." But this seems hardly to be admitted by the Supreme Court of Bengal, in a passage where they laid down the following propositions as setting forth the characteristics of joint property held by an undivided family in Bengal. "*First*, each of the coparceners has a right to call for a partition, but until such partition takes place, and even an inchoate partition does not

(*x*) *Appovier* v. *Rama Subba Aiyan*, 11 M. I. A. 89; S. C. 8 Suth. (P. C.) 1.

(*y*) *Per Turner*, L. J., *Soorjeemoney Dossee* v. *Denobundo*, 6 M. I. A. 553; S. C. 4 Suth. (P. C.) 114; Daya Bhaga, ii. § 28, note, xi. 1, § 25, 26; D. K. S. xi. § 2, 3, 7; 2 Dig. 104; *ante*, § 241. Raghunandana, however, lays down most strongly the doctrine that each undivided coparcener has an equal right over the whole and every portion of the undivided property, i. 21—29.

seem to vary the rights of the co-sharers, the whole remains common stock; the co-sharers being equally interested in every part of it. *Second,* on the death of an original co-sharer his heirs stand in his place, and succeed to his rights as they stood at his death; his rights may also in his life-time pass to strangers, either by alienation, or as in the case of creditors, by operation of law; but in all cases those who come in, in the place of the original co-sharer, by inheritance, assignment or operation of law, can take only his rights as they stand, including of course the right to call for a partition. *Third,* whatever increment is made to the common stock whilst the estate continues joint, falls into and becomes part of that stock. On a partition it is divisible equally, no matter by what application of the common funds, or by whose exertions it may have been made; the single exception to the rule being, that on the acquisition by one co-sharer of a distinct property, with the aid only of the joint funds, the acquirer may take a double share in that property. The increment arising from the accumulations of undrawn income is obviously within the general rule" (*z*).

§ 269. So long as the manager of the Joint Family administers it for the purposes of the family, he is not under the same obligation to economise or to save, as would be the case with a paid agent or trustee. For instance, where the family concern is being wound up on a partition, the accounts must be taken upon the footing of what has been spent, and what remains, and not upon the footing of what might have been spent, if frugality and skill had been employed (*a*). The reason, of course, is that the manager is dealing with his own property, and if he chooses to live expensively, the remedy of the others is to come to a partition. On the other hand "he is certainly liable to make good to them their shares of all sums which he has actually

Position of manager;

(*z*) *Soorjeemoney Dossee* v. *Denobundo*, 6 M. I. A. 526, 539; S. C. 4 Suth. (P. C.) 114, reversed by the P. C. upon the construction of a will, but these propositions were not disputed. See too *Chuckun* v. *Poran*, 9 Suth. 483.

(*a*) *Tara Chand* v. *Reeb Ram*, 3 Mad. H. C. 177; *Choonee* v. *Prosunno*, Sev. 231; *Jugmohundas* v. *Mangaldas*, 10 Bom. 528.

of ordinary member of family.

mis-appropriated, or which he has spent for purposes other than those in which the Joint Family was interested. Of course, no member of a joint Hindu family is liable to his coparceners for anything which might have been actually consumed by him in consequence of his having a larger family to support, or of his being subject to greater expenses than the others; but this is simply because all such expenses are justly considered to be the legitimate expenses of the whole family. Thus, for instance, one member of a joint Hindu family may have a larger number of daughters to marry than the others. The marriage of each of these daughters to a suitable bridegroom is an obligation incumbent upon the whole family, so long as they continue to be joint, and the expenses incurred on account of such marriages must be necessarily borne by all the members, without any reference whatever to respective interests in the family estate" (*b*). Observations to the same effect were made by the Supreme Court of Bengal in the case from which I have already quoted, and they add, "We apprehend that at the present day, when personal luxury has increased, and the change of manners has somewhat modified the relations of the members of a Joint Family, it is by no means unusual that in the common *Khatta* book an account of the separate expenditure of each member is opened and kept against him; and that on a partition, even in the absence of fraud or exclusion, those accounts enter into the general account on which the final partition and allotment are made" (*c*).

Right to an account.

§ 270. The right of each member of an undivided Hindu family to require an account of the management, has been both affirmed and denied in decisions which are not very easy to reconcile. Possibly, however, the apparent conflict may be explained, by considering the various purposes for which an account may be demanded. It is of course quite clear, that every member of the coparcenary, who is entitled

(*b*) *Per Mitter*, J., *Abhaychandra* v. *Pyari*, 5 B. L. R. 347, 349.

(*c*) *Soorjeemoney Dossee* v. *Denobundo*, 6 M. I. A. 540; S. C. 4 Suth. (P. C.) 114.

to demand a partition, is also entitled to an account, as a necessary preliminary to such partition. A different question arises, where the account is sought by a member who desires to remain undivided. A claim by a continuing coparcener to have a statement furnished to him of the amount standing to his separate account, with a view to having that amount or any portion of it paid over to him, or carried over to a fresh account, as in the case of an ordinary partnership, would, in a family governed by Mitakshara law, be wholly inadmissible. The answer to such a demand would be, "You have no separate account. Your claim is limited to the use of the family property, and everything that has not been specifically set apart for you belongs to the family and not to its members." It was a claim to an account of this sort to which *Jackson*, J., referred, when he said, "It appears to be admitted that, although a son has a joint interest in the ancestral estate with his father, he cannot, as long as that estate remains joint, call upon his father for an account of his management of that estate; that he, for instance, could not sue his father for mesne profits for years during which it was under his father's management" (*d*). But it would be very different if he said, "I wish to know how the affairs of the corporation to which I belong are being managed." It certainly seems a matter of natural justice that such a demand should be complied with. The remedy which any coparcener has against mismanagement of the family property, is his right to a partition. But he cannot know whether it would be wise to exercise this right, unless he can be informed as to the state of the affairs of the family. Yet even a right to an account of this nature has in some cases been denied. The Supreme Court of Bengal in the case already referred to (*e*) say, "the right to demand such an account, when it exists, is incident to the right to require partition; the liability to account can only be enforced upon a partition." In one case of a Bengal

Right to an account.

(*d*) *Shudanund* v. *Bonomalee*, 6 Suth. 256, 259.

(*e*) *Soorjeemoney Dossee* v. *Denobundo*, 6 M. I. A. 540; S. C. 4 Suth. (P. C.) 114.

family, *Phear*, J., drew a distinction as to the liability to account between the case of a management on behalf of a minor and on behalf of one of full years. In the former case he considered that the manager was strictly a trustee, and was bound when his trust came to an end, that is at the end of the minority, to account for the manner in which he had discharged it. But as regards adult members, he said, "the manager is merely the chairman of a committee, of which the family were the members. They manage the property together, and the '*karta*' is but the mouthpiece of the body, chosen and capable of being changed by themselves. Therefore, unless something is shown to the contrary, every adult member of an undivided Joint Family, living in commensality with the '*karta*,' must be taken, as between himself and the '*karta*,' to be a participator in, and authoriser of, all that is from time to time done in the management of the joint property to this extent, namely, that he cannot, without further cause, call the '*karta*' to account for it. Of course, it may, as a matter of fact, be the case in a given family that the '*karta*' is the agent of, or stands in a fiduciary and accountable relation to, one or more of the members. It would be easy to imagine a state of things under which he had become the trustee of the property relative to his adult coparcener, or in which, by reason of his fraud or other behaviour, they, some or one of them, had acquired an equity to call upon him for an account. All that I desire to say is, that, in my judgment, he does not wear this character of accountability, merely because he occupies the position of '*karta*'" (*f*). In this case, the plaintiff sought for the account, not merely for information, but as incidental to a claim for his share of the surpluses which such an account would show that the manager had received. The suit was not one for partition, as is evident from the fact that the entire suit was dismissed. Had he sued for a partition he would of course have been

(*f*) *Chuckun* v. *Poran*, 9 Suth. 483. See this case explained by *Phear*, J., *Abhaychandra* v. *Pyari*, 5 B. L. R. 354; S. C. *Sub nomine*, *Obhoy Chunder* v. *Pearee*, 13 Suth. (F. B.) 75.

entitled to it, though on different terms as to accounting from those which he tried to impose.

§ 271. This decision was relied on in a later case, where a widow (in Bengal) sued for a partition of the property, and, as incidental thereto, for the dissolution of a banking partnership, and that the defendant, the manager, should render an account of the estate of the common ancestor, and of the banking business (*g*). *Markby*, J., said, "I am clearly of opinion that, in the ordinary case of a joint Hindu family, the manager of the whole, or any portion of the family property, is not, by reason of his occupying that position, bound to render any accounts whatever to the members of the family." He granted an account in the special case on the ground that the banking business was carried on, not as a common family business in the strict sense, the profits of which were all to sink into the common family fund, but rather on the footing of a partnership, the profits of which, when realised, were to be divided among the individual members in certain proportions. This decision however was directly overruled by the Full Bench, in a case where the following questions were referred for decision:—1. Whether the managing member of a joint Hindu family can be sued by the other members for an account, and (it appearing that one of the plaintiffs was a minor) 2. Whether such a suit would not lie, even if the parties suing were minors, during the period for which the accounts were asked. Mr. Justice *Mitter* in making the reference said, "suppose, for instance, that one of the members of a Joint Family, with a view to separate from the others, asks the manager what portion of the family income has been actually saved by him during the period of his managership. If the manager chooses to say that nothing has been saved, but at the same time refuses to give any account of the receipts and disbursements, which were

Full Bench decision.

Right to an account.

(*g*) *Ranganmani* v. *Kasinath*, 3 B. L. R., (O. C. J.) 1; S. C. 13 Suth. (F. B.) 75, note.

entirely under his control, how is the member, who is desirous of separation, to know what funds are actually available for partition? And according to what principle of law or justice can it be said that he is bound to accept the *ipse dixit* of the manager as a correct representation of the actual state of things?" Both questions accordingly were answered in the affirmative. The previous decision was overruled, and that of *Chuckun* v. *Poran* was reconciled and explained, as meaning only that joint managers must be taken to have authorized each other's acts, and, therefore, could not after a lapse of years call for an account by one of themselves of dealings which were in fact their own (*h*).

Relief incidental to account.

§ 272. The decision upon the two questions referred is no doubt perfectly sound. But I cannot understand the framework of the suit. The plaint alleged that there was real and personal property, the management of which was taken by the defendant in 1863; that although the profits were large, yet the plaintiffs had not been properly maintained; that the elder plaintiff had taken upon himself, in 1866, the management of the one-third share belonging to himself and his minor brother; he prayed for recovery of one-third share of the profits during the defendant's management from 1863 to 1866, and also for one-third share of the *personal* property. No share of the real property was asked for. The account was asked for as incidental to this claim. The defendant pleaded a partition in 1849 which was found against. The original Court gave a decree for the plaintiff for a share of the profits of the real and personal property, but not for a share of the *corpus*. This decree seems to have been in principle affirmed on appeal. It would appear then that the claim made by the plaintiff was, that a separate account should be kept in the name of each co-sharer, in which he should be credited with an aliquot share of the savings, and debited with the amount

(*h*) *Abhaychandra* v. *Pyari*, 5 B. L. R. 347; S. C. 13 Suth. (F. B.) 75; *Sub nomine*, *Obhoy Chunder* v. *Pearee*.

actually expended on himself, and that the balance should be paid over to him annually, or as it accumulated, whenever he chose to ask for it. It is evident that if this principle were carried out, no additions could ever be made to the family property. If the entire family chose to live up to their income, of course they could do so. But would any one member of the family have a right to insist upon living upon a scale higher than was thought suitable by the other members? Would he have a right to withdraw his own share of the income annually from the family system of management or trade, and to deal with it on his own account? If he did so, would the accumulations of such annual withdrawals, and the profits made by means of them, be his own separate property, or would they continue to be joint property? Either supposition involves a contradiction. If they became separate property, that would be in conflict with the rule that the savings of joint property, and acquisitions made solely by means of joint property, continue to be joint. If they became separate, it would follow that a member of an undivided family might accumulate large separate acquisitions by simply investing portions of the family property. On the other hand, if such accumulations remained joint property, the absurdity would arise that A. might sue B. and get a decree for a thousand rupees, and B. might sue A. the very next week, to enforce a partition of that sum and recover a moiety of it.

§ 273. It is, however, quite possible that the plaint was based upon a system of family management, which is by no means uncommon, when the family continues undivided, but each member holds a portion of the property separately, and applies the income arising from it to his own use. Of course, if the portion appropriated to A. was placed in charge of B., the income would be held by him for the use of A., and he would be entitled to an account of its application, and to payment over of the balance, But this would be, not by virtue of the general usage of an undivided Hindu family, but in opposition to that usage, by virtue of

Special family arrangement.

a special arrangement for the apportionment of the income among the individual branches. It must be owned, however, that the language of *Couch*, C. J., looks as if he took a different view. He says (*i*), "It appears to me that the principle upon which the right to call for an account rests is not, as has been supposed, the existence of a direct agency, or of a partnership where the managing partner may be considered as the agent for his co-partners. It depends upon the right which the members of a joint Hindu family have to a share of the property; and where there is a joint interest in the property, and one party receives all the profits, he is bound to account to the other parties who have an interest in it, for the profits of their respective shares, after making such deductions as he may have the right to make." If by this the learned Chief Justice meant that he was bound to account for these profits, in the sense of paying them over, or holding them at the disposal of the individual members, the opinion must be founded upon a distinction between the rights of co-sharers under Bengal and Mitakshara law. It must proceed upon the idea that the entire share of each member, and therefore its entire income, is appropriated to him, free of all claims by the others, and therefore that the manager only receives it as his agent and trustee. Such a view is certainly the logical result of Jimuta Vahana's theory of joint-ownership. But it is opposed to many of the judicial *dicta* already quoted.

Necessity for joint action.

§ 274. A necessary consequence of the corporate character of the family holding is, that wherever any transaction affects that property all the members must be privy to it, and whatever is done must be done for the benefit of all, and not of any single individual. For instance, a single member cannot sue, or proceed by way of execution (*k*), to recover a particular portion of the family property for himself, whether his claim is preferred against a stranger

(*i*) *Abhaychandra* v. *Pyari*, 5 B. L. R. 353; S. C. *Sub nomine, Obhoy Chunder* v. *Pearee*, 13 Suth. (F. B.) 75.
(*k*) *Banarsi Das* v. *Maharani Kuar*, 5 All. 27.

who is asserted to be wrongfully in possession, or against his coparceners. If the former, all the members must join, and the suit must be brought to recover the whole property for the benefit of all. And this, whether the stranger is in possession without a shadow of title, or by the act of one of the sharers, in excess of his power (*l*). If any of the members refuse to join as plaintiffs, or are colluding with the defendant, they should be made co-defendants, so that the interests of all may be bound (*m*). If from any cause, such as lapse of time, the other members cannot be joined as plaintiffs, the whole suit will fail (*n*). If the suit is against the coparceners, it is vicious at its root. The only remedy by one member against his co-sharer is by a suit for partition, as until then he has no right to the exclusive possession of any part of the property (*o*). The same rule forbids one of several sharers to sue alone for the ejectment of a tenant (*p*), unless, perhaps, in a case where by arrangement with his coparceners the plaintiff has been placed in the exclusive possession of the whole (*q*); or for enhancement of rent (*r*) or for his share of the rent (*s*), unless where the defendants

Suits by one co-sharer.

(*l*) *Sheo Churn* v. *Chukraree*, 15 Suth. 436; *Cheyt Narain* v. *Bunwaree*, 23 Suth 395; *Parooma* v. *Valayooda*, Mad. Dec. of 1853, 35; *Rajaram Tewari* v. *Lachman*, 4 B L. R. (A. C J.) 118; S. C. 12 Suth, 478 approved in *Phoolbas Koonwur* v. *Lalla Jogeshur*, 3 I. A. at p. 26; S. C. 1 Cal. 226; S. C. 25 Suth. 285; *Biswanath* v. *Collector of Mymensing*, 7 B. L. R. Appx. 42; S. C. 21 Suth. 69, note; affirmed by F. B. *Unnoda* v. *Erskine*, 12 B. L. R. 370; S. C. 21 Suth. 68; *Dewakur* v. *Naroo*, Bom. Sel. Rep. 190; *Nundun* v. *Lloyd*, 22 Suth. 74; *Teeluk* v. *Ramjus*, 5 N. W. P. 182; *Nathuni* v. *Manraj*, 2 Cal. 149. *Arunachela* v. *Vythialinga*, 6 Mad. 27. The joinder of all necessary parties is the right not only of the plaintiff but of the defendant, as it is his interest that the decree should bind the whole family. *Harigopal* v. *Gokaldas*, 12 Bom. 158.

(*m*) *Rajaram Tewari* v. *Lachman*, *ub sup*; *Juggodumba* v. *Haran*, 10 Suth. 109; *Gokool* v. *Etwaree*, 20 Suth. 138; *Kattusheri* v. *Vallotil*, 3 Mad. 234; *Bechu Lal* v. *Oliullah*, 11 Cal. 338; *Kalichandra* v. *Raj Kishore*, *ib*. 615; *Dwarkanath Mitter* v. *Tara Prosunno*, 17 Cal. 160.

(*n*) *Kalidas Kevaldas* v. *Nathu Bhagvan*, 7 Bom. 217.

(*o*) *Phoolbas Koonwur* v. *Lalla Jogeshur*, 3 I. A. 7; S. C. 1 Cal. 226; S. C. 25 Suth. 285; *Dadjee* v. *Wittal*, Bom. Sel. Rep. 151; *Trimbak* v. *Narayan*, 11 Bom. H. C. 69; *Gobind Chunder* v. *Ram Coomar*, 24 Suth. 393. *Ramanuja* v. *Virappa*, 6 Mad. 90.

(*p*) *Sree Chand* v. *Nim Chand*, 13 Suth. 337; S. C. 5 B. L. R. Appx. 25; *Alum* v. *Ashad*, 16 Suth. 138; *Hulodhur* v. *Gooroo*, 20 Suth. 126; *Krishnarav* v. *Govind*, 12 Bom. H. C. 85; *Sobharam* v. *Gunga*, 2 N. W. P. 260; *Balaji* v. *Gopal*, 3 Bom 23; *Reasut* v. *Chorwar*, 7 Cal. 470. See also *Gopal* v. *MacNaghten*, 7 Cal. 751.

(*q*) *Amir Singh* v. *Moazzim*, 7 N. W. P. 58.

(*r*) *Jogendro* v. *Nobin Chunder*, 8 Cal. 353.

(*s*) *Indromonee* v. *Suroop*, 15 Suth. 395; S. C. 12 B. L. R. 291 (note); *Hur*

40 *in*.

have paid their rent to him separately, or agreed to do so, in which case they at all events could not raise the objection. Even in such a case, however, it would clearly be open to any of the other sharers to intervene, if they considered that their rights were being endangered (*t*). And so where one member of a Joint Family has laid out money upon any portion of the joint estate, he cannot sue his co-sharers for repayment, unless there has been an express agreement that he should be repaid. Otherwise his outlay is only a matter to be taken into account on a partition (*u*).

On the other hand, where the act of a third party with respect to the joint property has caused any personal and special loss to one of the co-sharers, which does not affect the others, he can sue for it separately, and they need not be joined (*v*). And it would seem that one co-sharer may sue to eject a mere trespasser, when his object is to remove an intruder from the joint property, without at the same time claiming any special portion of it for himself (*w*). *A fortiori*, a member, of a Joint Family who has contracted in his own name for the benefit of the family, may sue upon the contract in their behalf, without joining the others (*x*).

Rights of coparceners *inter se*.

§ 275. The rights of shareholders *inter se* depend upon the view taken by the law which governs them of their interest in the property. In the early conception of a

---

Kishore v. *Joogul*, 16 Suth. 281; S. C. 12 B. L. R. 293 (note); *Bhyrub* v. *Gogaram*, 17 Suth. 408; S. C. 12 B. L. R. 290 (note); *Annoda* v. *Kall Coomar*, 4 Cal. 88. *Manohar Das* v. *Manzar Ali*, 5 All. 40. As to cases where the other co-sharers are colluding with the defaulting tenant, *Cf. Jadu* v. *Sutherland*, 4. Cal. 556; and *Jadoo* v. *Kadumbinee*, 7 Cal. 150.

(*t*) *Ganga* v. *Saroda*, 3 B. L. R. (A. C. J.) 230; S. C. 12 Suth 50; *Haradhun* v. *Ram Newaz*, 17 Suth. 414; *Saleehoonissa* v. *Mohesh*, *ib.* 452; *Sree Misser* v. *Crowdy*, 15 Suth. 243; *Dinobundhoo* v. *Dinonath*, 19 Suth. 168; by F. B., *Doorga* v. *Jampa*, 12 B. L. R 289; S. C. 21 Suth. 46; *Rakhal* v. *Muhtab*, 25 Suth. 221. Of course the co-sharers might agree that the tenant should pay each of them a portion of the rent, and would then be entitled to sue separately for their respective portions. *Guni* v. *Moran*, 4 Cal. 96; *Lootfulhuck* v. *Gopee*, 5 Cal. 941.

(*u*) *Nubkoomar* v. *Jye Deo*, 2 S. D. 247 (317); *Jalaluddaula* v. *Sumsamuddaula*, Mad. Dec. of 1860, 161; *Muttusvami* v. *Subbiramaniya*, 1 Mad. H. C. 309.

(*v*) *Gopee* v. *Ryland*, 9 Suth. 279; *Chundee* v. *MacNaghten*, 23 Suth. 386.

(*w*) *Radha Proshad* v. *Esuf*, 7 Cal. 414.

(*x*) *Bungsee* v. *Soodist*, 7 Cal. 789.

Hindu family the right of any member consisted simply in a general right to have the property fairly managed in such a manner as to enable himself and his family to be suitably maintained out of its proceeds. The duties which he was to perform, and the profits which he was to receive, would be regulated by the discretion of the head of the family. This is at present the case in a Malabar *tarwad* (*y*). Except so far as it is varied by special agreement or usage, the members of a family governed by Mitakshara law are still in much the same position (*z*). In Bengal, where the members hold rather as tenants in common than as joint tenants, a greater degree of independence is possessed by each (*a*). There, each member is entitled to a full and complete enjoyment of his undivided share, in any proper and reasonable manner, which is not inconsistent with a similar enjoyment by the other members, and which does not infringe upon their right to an equal disposal and management of the property (*b*). But he cannot, without permission, do anything which alters the nature of the property; as, for instance, build upon it. Where such an act is an injury to his coparceners the Court will, as a matter of discretion, though not as a matter of absolute right, direct the removal of the building (*c*). In exercising this discretion it is material to consider, whether the defendant is building on land in excess of that which would come to him on a partition, and

---

(*y*) *Kunigaratu* v. *Arrangaden*, 2 Mad. H. C. 12; *Subbu Hegadi* v. *Tongu*, 4 Mad. H. C. 196.

(*z*) See *per* Lord *Westbury*, *Apporier* v. *Rama Subbaiyan*, 11 M. I. A., p. 89; S. C. 8 Suth. (P. C.) 1; *ante*, § 268.

(*a*) See *per Phear*, J., *Chuckun* v. *Poran*, 9 Suth. 483; *ante*, § 270.

(*b*) *Eshan Chunder* v. *Nund Coomar*, 8 Suth. 239; *Gopee Kishen* v. *Hemchunder*, 13 Suth. 322; *Nundun* v. *Lloyd*, 22 Suth. 74; *Stalkartt* v. *Gopal*, 12 B. L. R. 197; S. C 20 Suth. 168; *Watson* v. *Ram Chand Dutt*, 17 I. A. 110. And he may lease out his share, *Ramdebul* v. *Mitterjeet*, 17 Suth. 420.

(*c*) *Jankee* v. *Bukhooree*, S. D. of 1856, 761; *Inderdeonarain* v. *Toolseenarain*, S. D. of 1857, 765; *Guru Dass* v. *Bijaya*, 1 B. L. R. (A. O. J.) 108; S. C. *Sub nomine*, *Goroodoss* v. *Bejoy*, 10 Suth. 171; *Sheopersad* v. *Leela*, 12 B. L. R. 188; S. C. 20 Suth. 160; (see *Lala Bishwambhar* v. *Rajaram*, 3 B. L. R. Appx. 67; S. C 16 Suth. 140 (note), where such a decree was refused, and *Nobin Chunder* v. *Mohesh Chunder*, 12 Suth 69); *Holloway* v. *Mahomed*, 16 Suth. 140; S. C. 12 B. L. R. 191 (note) *Sub nomine*, *Holloway* v. *Sheik Wahed*; (see apparently *contra*, *Dwarkanath* v. *Gopeenath*, 16 Suth. 10; S. C. 12 B. L. R. 189 note). *Mehdee* v. *Anjud*, 6 N. W. P. 259; *Rajendro* v. *Shama Churn*, 5 Cal. 188.

whether on a partition the plaintiff could be adequately compensated (*d*). And the same rule has been applied where an entire change of crops has been introduced, where the produce would be valueless unless followed up by manufacture (*e*).

Coparcener may be tenant.

§ 276. There is nothing to prevent one co-sharer being the tenant of all the others, and paying rent to them as such. But the mere fact that one member of the family holds exclusive occupation of any part of the property, carries with it no undertaking to pay rent, in the absence of some agreement to that effect, either express or implied (*f*).

(*d*) *Paras Ram* v. *Sherjit*, 9 All. 661; *Shaik* v. *Dorup Singh*, 12 All. (F. B.) 436.

(*e*) *Crowdee* v. *Bhekdari*, 8 B. L. R. Appx. 45; S. C. 16 Suth. 41.

(*f*) *Alladinee* v. *Sreenath*, 20 Suth. 258; *Gobind Chunder* v. *Ram Coomar*, 24 Suth. 393.

CHAPTER IX.

DEBTS.

§ 277. I HAVE thought it well to treat the subject of Debts, as affecting property, before that of voluntary alienations, as it illustrates a principle which is constantly recurring in Hindu law, *viz.*, that moral obligations take precedence of legal rights; or, to put the same idea in different words, that legal rights are taken subject to the discharge of moral obligations.

Three sources of liability.

The liability of one person to pay debts contracted by another arises from three completely different sources, which must be carefully distinguished. These are—*first*, the religious duty of discharging the debtor from the sin of his debts:—*secondly*, the moral duty of paying a debt contracted by one whose assets have passed into the possession of another:—*thirdly*, the legal duty of paying a debt contracted by one person as the agent, express or implied, of another. Cases may often occur in which more than one of these grounds of liability are found co-existing; but any one is sufficient.

Debts of father:

§ 278. The first ground of liability only arises in the case of a debtor and his own sons and grandsons. In the view of Hindu lawyers, a debt is not merely an obligation but a sin, the consequences of which follow the debtor into the next world. Vrihaspati says, "He who having received a sum lent or the like, does not repay it to the owner, will be born hereafter in his creditor's house, a slave, a servant, a woman, or a quadruped" (*a*). And Narada says, "when a

(*a*) 1 Dig. 334.

Liability of son independent of assets.

devotee, or a man who maintained a sacrificial fire, dies without having discharged his debt, the whole merit of his devotions, or of his perpetual fire, belongs to his creditors" (*b*). The duty of relieving the debtor from these evil consequences falls on his male descendants, to the second generation, and was originally quite independent of the receipts of assets. Narada says, "The grandsons shall pay the debt of their grandfather, which having been legitimately inherited by the sons has not been paid by them; the obligation ceases with the fourth descendant (*c*). Fathers desire offspring for their own sake, reflecting, 'this son will redeem me from every debt whatsoever due to superior and inferior beings.' Therefore a son begotten by him should relinquish his own property, and assiduously redeem his father from debt, lest he fall into a region of torment" (*d*). Vrihaspati states a further distinction as to the degrees of liability which attached to the descendants. "The father's debt must be first paid, and next a debt contracted by the man himself; but the debt of the paternal grandfather must even be paid before either of these. The sons must pay the debt of their father, when proved, as if it were their own, or with interest; the son's son must pay the debt of his grandfather, but without interest; and his son shall not be compelled to discharge it;" to which the gloss is added, "unless he be heir and have assets" (*e*). Finally Yajnavalkya adds an exception to these rules: that the son is not liable to pay if the father's estate is actually held by another; as, for instance, if he is from any cause incapacitated from succession (*f*).

(*b*) Narada, iii. § 10. The text of Manu, xi. § 66, which Jagannatha cites (1 Dig. 267) as referring to a money debt, seems to refer to the three debts which are elsewhere spoken of, *viz.*, reading the Vedas, begetting a son, and performing sacrifices. See Manu, vi. § 36, 37, ix. § 106; Vishnu, xv. § 45.

(*c*) This is counted inclusive of the debtor, 1 Dig. 302; Yajnavalkya, ii. § 90.

(*d*) Narada, iii. § 4—6. According to the Thesawaleme (i. § 7), sons were also bound to pay their father's debts, even without assets.

(*e*) 1 Dig. 265; Katyayana, 1 Dig. 301; V. May., v. 4, § 17.

(*f*) 1 Dig. 270; V. May., v. 4, § 16; Katyayana, 1 Dig. 278. It has been held that this principle of Hindu law does not apply to the Nambudri Brahmans of Malabar, who are governed by a combination of Hindu and Marumakatayem law, *Nilakandan* v. *Madharan*, 10 Mad. 9. See as to their usages. *Vishnu* v. *Krishnan*, 7 Mad. 15; *Vasudevan* v. *Secretary of State*, 11 Mad. 157.

Obligation is religious.

§ 279. The liability to pay the father's debt arises from the moral and religious obligation to rescue him from the penalties arising from the non-payment of his debts. And this obligation equally compels the son to carry out what the ancestor has promised for religious purposes (*g*). It follows, then, that when the debt creates no such moral obligation the son is not bound to repay it, even though he possess assets. This arises in two cases, 1*st*, when the debt is of an immoral character; 2*nd*, when it is of a ready-money character.

Cases in which it does not arise.

"The sons are not compellable to pay sums due by their father for spirituous liquors, for losses at play, for promises made without any consideration, or under the influence of lust or of wrath; or sums for which he was a surety (except in the cases before mentioned), or a fine or a toll, or the balance of either," nor generally, "any debt for a cause repugnant to good morals" (*h*). Jagannatha denies that a son is not liable for the debts of his father as surety, and says with much reason, that if by a toll is meant one payable at a wharf or the like, that is a cause consistent with usage and good morals and it ought to be paid (*i*). Another meaning of the word "*Çulka*," translated toll, is a nuptial present, given as the price of a bride, and this has been determined not to be repayable by the son, apparently on

(*g*) Katyayana, 1 Dig. 299.

(*h*) Vrihaspati, Gautama, 1 Dig. 305; Vyasa, *ib.* 305; Yajnavalkya, *ib.* 311; Katyayana, *ib.* 300, 309; 2 W. MacN. 210. As to what are immoral, debts, see *Budree Lall* v. *Kantee*, 23 Suth. 260; *Wajed Hossein* v. *Nankoo*, 25 Suth. 311; *Luchmi* v. *Asman*, 2 Cal. 213; S. C. 25 Suth. 421; *Suraj Bunsi Koer* v. *Sheo Proshad*, 6 I. A. 88; S. C. 5 Cal. 148; *Sitaram* v. *Zalim Singh*, 8 All. 231. A decree against a father for money which he had criminally misappropriated does not bind his son's estate as being a debt which they were bound to pay. *Mahabir Prasad* v. *Basdeo Singh*, 6 All. 234. The onus of proving that the debt was contracted for an immoral or illegal purpose lies upon those who allege it, and the onus is not discharged by showing that the father lived an extravagant or immoral life. *Bhagbut Pershad* v. *Girja Koer*, 15 I. A. 99; S. C. 15 Cal. 717; *Chintamanrav* v. *Kashinath*, 14 Bom. 320.

(*i*) 1 Dig. 305, *acc.* Manu, viii. § 159, 160. As regards suretyship, the son's liability has been expressly affirmed. *Moolchund* v. *Krishna*, Bellasis, 54. *Sitaramayya* v. *Venkatramanna*, 11 Mad. 83. As regards fines, the reason is given "that a son is not liable for a penalty incurred by his father in expiation of an offence; for neither sins nor the expiation of them are hereditary." *Nhanee* v. *Hureeram*, 1 Bor. 90 [101] analogous to the principle of English Law that an action for a tort does not survive.

the ground that it constitutes the essence of one of the unlawful forms of marriage (*k*). Sir *Thomas Strange* takes the term in its natural signification, and explains the non-liability on the ground that such payments are of a ready-money character, for which no credit is, or at all events ought to be given (*l*).

Debt need not be beneficial.

It also follows that the obligation of the son to pay the debt is not founded on any assumed benefit to himself, or to the estate, arising from the origin of the debt; still less is that obligation affected by the nature of the estate, which has descended to the son, as being ancestral, or self-acquired. "Unless the debt was of such a nature that it was not the duty of the son to pay it, the discharge of it, even though it affected ancestral estate, would still be an act of pious duty in the son. By the Hindu law, the freedom of the son from the obligation to discharge the father's debt has reference to the nature of the debt, and not to the nature of the estate, whether ancestral or acquired by the creator of the debt" (*m*).

Ancestral estate equally liable.

Now limited to assets.

§ 280. The law as administered in our Courts, in all the provinces except Bombay, has for many years held that the heir is only liable to the extent of the assets he has inherited from the person whose debts he is called on to pay (*n*). But as soon as the property is inherited a liability *pro tanto* arises, and is not removed by the subsequent loss or destruction of the property, and still less, of course, by the fact that the heir has not chosen to possess himself of it, or has alienated it after the death (*o*). In Bombay, however,

---

(*k*) *Keshow Rao* v. *Naro*, 2 Bor. 194 [215]. (*l*) 1 Stra. H. L. 166.

(*m*) *Hunoomanpersaud* v. *Mt. Babooee*, 6 M. I. A. 421; S. C. 18 Suth. 81, (note); *Girdharee Lall* v. *Kantoo Lall*, 1 I. A. 321; S. C. 14 B. L. R. 187; S. C. 22 Suth. 56; *Suraj Bunsi Koer* v. *Sheo Proshad*, 6 I. A. 88; S. C. 5 Cal. 148; *Muttayan Chetty* v. *Sangili*, 9 I. A. 128; *Narayanasami* v. *Samidas*, 6 Mad. 293; *Bhagbut Pershad* v. *Girja Koer*, 15 I. A. 99; S. C. 15 Cal. 717.

(*n*) *Rayappa* v. *Ali Sahib*, 2 Mad. H. C. 336; *Karuppan* v. *Veriyal*, 4 Mad. H. C. 1; *Aga Hajee* v. *Juggut*, Montr. 272; *Jamoonah* v. *Mudden*, *ib.* 227; *Dyamonee* v. *Brindabun*, S. D. of 1856, 97; *Kunhya* v. *Bukhtawar*, 1 N. W. P. (S. D.) 3; *Ponnappa* v. *Pappuvayyangar*, 4 Mad. pp. 9, 21, 45; S. C. 5 Ind. Jur. Supplement.

(*o*) *Kasi* v. *Buchireddi*, Mad. Dec. of 1860, 78; *Unnopoorna* v. *Gunga*, 2 Suth. 296; *Keval Bhaghvan* v. *Ganpati*, 8 Bom. 220; *Girdharlal* v. *Bai Shiv*, *ibid.* 309.

the stricter rule was applied, that a son was liable to pay his father's debts with interest, and a grandson those of his grandfather without interest, even though no assets had been inherited; but the Courts held that the rights of the creditor could only be enforced against the property of the descendant, and not against his person (*p*). But in that presidency, also, the law has, by legislation, been brought into conformity with the more equitable rule observed elsewhere. (*q*).

Evidence of assets.

§ 281. As regards the onus of proof that assets have come to the hands of the heir, it has been ruled by the Madras High Court, that the plaintiff must in the first instance give such evidence as would *primâ facie* afford reasonable grounds for an inference that assets had, or ought to have, come to the hands of the defendant. But when the plaintiff has laid this foundation for his case, it will then lie on the defendant to show that the amount of the assets is not sufficient to satisfy the plaintiff's claim, or that they were of such a nature that the plaintiff was not entitled to be satisfied out of them, (*r*) or that there never were any assets, or that they have been duly administered and disposed of in satisfaction of other claims. The mere fact of a certificate having been taken out was held not to be even *primâ facie* evidence of the possession of assets. But the Court refused to offer any opinion whether the same rule would apply since the Stamp Act, which made it necessary that the amount of assets to be administered under the certificate should be apparent from it (*s*). As to the doubt expressed by the High Court as to the effect of the stamp, it is probable that

---

(*p*) *Pranvullubh* v. *Deocristin*, Bom. Sel. Rep. 4; *Hurbojee* v. *Hurgovind*, Bellasis, 76; *Narasimharav* v. *Antaji*, 2 Bom. H. C. 64.

(*q*) Bombay Act VII of 1866 [Hindus liability for ancestor's debts]. *Sakharam* v. *Govind*, 10 Bom. H. C. 361; *Udaram* v. *Ranu*, 11 Bom. H. C. 76. In Bombay the Courts appear still to hold that the creditor is entitled to obtain a decree with costs against the son as legal representative of the father for the debts of the latter, though the decree cannot be enforced without proof of assets. *Lallu Bhagvan* v. *Tribhuvan Motiram*, 13 Bom. 653. It seems hard, however, that the son should be put to the cost of proving a merely worthless claim.

(*r*) *Krishnaya* v. *Chinnaya*, 7 Mad. 597.

(*s*) *Kottala* v. *Shangara*, 3 Mad. H. C. 161; *Joogul* v. *Kalee*, 25 Suth. 224.

they would have given the same decision had it been necessary to decide the point. The primary object of a certificate is to collect debts, and the stamp would be assessed on the value of these. But this would be no evidence that the assets had been realised.

Assets include the whole joint property.

§ 282. Another very important question which has lately been much discussed is this; where property has descended from father to son, is the whole, or any lesser part, of such property to be treated as assets which are liable to be taken in payment of the father's debts? In Bengal no such question could arise, as the rights of the son come into existence for the first time on the father's death. He takes the ancestor's property strictly as heir, and all that he so takes is necessarily assets of him from whom it descends (§ 235). But it is different in districts governed by the Mitakshara. There each son takes at his birth a co-ordinate interest with his father in all ancestral property held by the latter, and on the death of the father the son takes, not as his heir, but by survivorship, the father's interest simply lapsing, and so enlarging the shares of his descendants (§ 229, 246). It is evident then that three views might be taken of the son's liability. *First*; that it only attached to the separate, or self-acquired, property of the father, which the son strictly took as his heir. *Secondly*; that it attached to that share of the joint property which, according to the rulings in Madras and Bombay (§ 330—335), a father can dispose of in his lifetime. *Thirdly*; that it applied to the whole property in the hands of the father as representing the Joint Family. After some conflict of decisions the last view has recently been decided to be the correct one, in a case where the property was of the ordinary partible character (*t*); and the same rule was applied by the Privy Council where the estate was an ancient impartible polliem of the nature of a Raj (*u*).

(*t*) *Ponnappa* v *Pappuvayyangar*, 4 Mad. 1; S. C. 5 Ind. Jur. Supplement; *Sheo Proshad* v. *Jung Bahadur*, 9 Cal. 389.

(*u*) *Muttayan Chetti* v. *Sangili*, 9 I. A. 128, reversing S. C. 3 Mad. 370; *Sivagiri* v. *Tiruvengada*, 7 Mad. 339.

Liability arises after father's death.

§ 283. The liability of the son is stated by the old writers to arise not only after the actual death of the father, but after his civil death, as when he has become an anchoret, or when he has been twenty years abroad, in which case his death may be presumed, or when he is wholly immersed in vice, which is explained by Jagannatha as indicating a state of combined insolvency and insolence, in which the father being devoted to sensual gratifications, gives up all attempts to satisfy his creditors, and sets them at defiance (*v*). And so when the father is suffering from some incurable disease, or is mad, or is extremely aged (*w*). But I imagine that no suit could now be brought directly against sons, based solely on their liability to pay the debt of their father, until he was either actually or civilly dead, so that the estate had legally vested in the sons. In a Madras case where a son, living apart from his father, was sued for his father's debt during the life of the latter, the Pandits being questioned as to his liability replied, "The Hindu law-books, Vijnanesvareyum, etc., do not declare that the debt contracted by a person shall be discharged by his wife and son, while the said person is alive, is residing in his own village, and is still capable of carrying on business" (*x*). And in a later case, where the plaintiff sought to recover from the wife and brothers of the obligor of a bond, not on the ground of any personal liability, but as the representatives of the obligor, who was supposed to be dead, the Court held that no suit could be maintained before the lapse of the time which raised the legal presumption of the death of the obligor, unless there was proof of special circumstances which warranted the inference of the death within a shorter period (*y*). In Bombay a son had taken a share of the ancestral property by partition with his father, and held it as separate property for twenty years. A suit was brought against the son

---

(*v*) Vishnu, 1 Dig. 266; Yajnavalkya, *ib.* 268; 2 Stra. H. L. 277; 2 W. MacN. 282.

(*w*) Katyayana; Vrihaspati, 1 Dig. 277, 278.

(*x*) *Chennapah* v. *Chellamanah*, Mad. Dec. of 1851, p. 33.

(*y*) *Karuppan* v. *Veriyal*, 4 Mad. H. C. 1. Here, however, the supposed liability rested on possession of the estate.

during his father's life to compel him to pay a debt of his father out of his share. The Poona Shastri gave his opinion that the son was liable, on the ground that "the expression 'incurable disease' is to be understood as referring to disease either mental or bodily, and a father having the anxiety of his debts in his mind may be considered as suffering from mental disease, and therefore it is binding on his son to discharge them." On appeal the Shastri of the Sudr Adawlut stated in his futwah "that if a son has taken possession of his share of the ancestral property, and a release has been passed, and if his father be free from any incurable disease, the father's debt cannot be recovered from the share allotted to his son," also, "that during the father's lifetime, his son is not obliged to liquidate his father's debts." This futwah was accepted by the Sudr Adawlut, and a decision was passed exempting the property of the son from liability (*z*).

Son's liability not limited to father's interest in property.

§ 284. Where the son is sued after his father's death for the payment of his father's debts, it is, as already observed, utterly immaterial whether the debts had been contracted for the benefit of the family, or for the sole use of the father, provided, in the latter case, they were not of an immoral character (*a*). The Madras Court for some time struggled against the full application of this doctrine, on the ground that it would enable the father indirectly to make the family property liable to a greater extent than that to which he could have affected it by any direct act in his lifetime. Their views were, however, overruled by the Judicial Committee. The facts of the case were as follows: the holder of an impartible estate in Madras contracted certain debts for necessary purposes previous to the birth of his son. Subsequently he contracted other debts which were found by both Courts to be neither necessary nor

(*z*) *Amrut* v. *Trimbuck*, Bom. Sel. Rep. 218. See *Ponnappa* v. *Pappuvayyangar*, 4 Mad. pp. 13, 18, 26; *Gurusami* v. *Chinna Mannar*, 5 Mad. 37, p. 46. W. & B. 643.

(*a*) *Ante*, § 279; *Udaram* v. *Ranu*, 11 Bom. H. C. 76, 83; *Goburdhon* v. *Singessur*, 7 Cal. 52.

beneficial to the family. For these he was sued in 1867, and to satisfy the decree he entered into an arrangement for payments by instalments, hypothecating part of his Zemindary as security for the debt. Upon default of payment this portion of the Zemindary was attached during his life. Upon his death the Court released the attchment. The creditor then sued the son and successor of his original debtor for the double purpose of restoring the attachment, and of making the entire property liable for payment of his debt. The High Court held that the estate was liable for so much of the debt as was contracted for necessary purposes, but refused to make it liable to any extent for the remainder of the debt contracted subsequent to the birth of the son, and not for the benefit of the family. On appeal the Privy Council refused to restore the attachment upon the portion of the estate which was specifically pledged, but held that the whole estate was liable in the hands of the heir for all the debts, which though neither necessary nor beneficial to him were free from any taint of immorality (*b*).

Father may alienate family property to satisfy his own debts.

§ 285. The principle of these decisions has recently received a considerable extension by its application by the Privy Council to cases where the father has mortgaged or sold the family property to liquidate his private debts, or where it has been sold in execution of decrees against him for such debts. Where such transactions affect a larger share of the property than his own interest in it, the result evidently is that the sons are compelled indirectly to discharge during the father's life an obligation which in strictness only attaches upon them at his death. The body of law deducible from the rulings of the Judicial Committee seems to rest upon a series of exceptions to a

---

(*b*) *Muttayan Chetti* v. *Sangili*, 3 Mad. 370; S. C. on appeal, 9 I. A. 128, following *Girdharee Lall* v. *Kantoo Lall*, 1 I. A. 321; S. C. 14 B. L. R. 187; S. C. 22 Suth. 56; *Suraj Bunsi Koer* v. *Sheo Proshad*, 6 I. A. 88; S. C. 5 Cal. 148; and affirming *Ponnappa* v. *Pappuvayyangar*, 4 Mad. 1. Where the father's property has fallen to the son by survivorship, the liability of the latter must be enforced by fresh suit, and not by execution of the decree against the father, unless it had been enforced by attachment during his life, in which case it becomes a charge upon the estate. *Venkatarama* v. *Senthivelu*, 13 Mad. 265.

general rule. The general rule is that no member of an undivided family can by any process appropriate to his own benefit a larger portion of the family property than the share he would obtain on partition. The exception is, that where the father has incurred a debt which would bind his son, the creditor can obtain satisfaction of the debt, either by conveyance from the father, or by a decree of Court, to the extent of even the whole family property. And this is subject to a further exception, that a creditor who wishes to enforce his claim against the interests of the sons, must show that he intended to do so by his proceedings in execution, or that he believed he was doing so by the form of the conveyance which he received. The first branch of these special rules was decided by the Privy Council under the following circumstances. Certain property descended from Kunhya Lall to his two sons, Bhikaree and Bhujrung. The former of the two had a son, Kantoo. The family was governed by Mithila law, and therefore, the property being ancestral, Kantoo acquired an interest in it by his birth. Subsequently to his birth Bhikaree executed a bond, upon which judgment was obtained, and his share of the property was attached. To pay off this judgment a portion of the property was sold by both brothers. It does not appear that Bhikaree's bond was in any respect for the benefit of the family, or that the sale of the property was for the family benefit, except in so far as it went to satisfy the decree, and except as to a small portion which was applied in payment of Government revenue. Kantoo Lall sued to set aside the sale, as not having been made for his benefit or with his consent. A similar suit was brought by Mahabeer, the son of Bhujrung. The High Court dismissed Mahabeer's suit, on the ground that he was not born at the time the deed of sale was executed, but awarded to Kantoo Lall one-half of his father's share. The Privy Council reversed this decree. They remarked in their judgment, "It is said that they (Bhikaree and Bhujrung) could not sell the property, because before the deed of sale was executed, Kantoo Lall was born, and by reason of his birth, under the

Girdharee Lall v. Kantoo Lall.

Mithila law, he had acquired an interest in that property. Now it is important to consider what was the interest which Kantoo Lall acquired. Did he gain such an interest in this property as prevented it from being liable to pay a debt which his father had contracted? If his father had died, and had left him as his heir, and the property had come into his hands, could he have said that because this was ancestral property which descended to his father from his grandfather, it was not liable at all to pay his father's debts?" They then quoted the passage above referred to (6 M. I. A. 421, § 279) and proceeded, "that is an authority to show that ancestral property which descended to a father under the Mitakshara law is not exempted from liability to pay his debts because a son is born to him. It would be a pious duty on the part of the son to pay his father's debts, and it being the pious duty to pay his father's debts, the ancestral property, in which the son, as the son of his father, acquires an interest by birth, is liable to the father's debts. The rule is, as stated by Lord Justice *Knight Bruce*, "the freedom of the son from the obligation to discharge the father's debt has respect to the nature of the debt, and not to the nature of the estate, whether ancestral or acquired by the creator of the debt." It is necessary, therefore, to see what was the nature of the debt for the payment of which it was necessary to raise money by the sale of the property in question. If the debt of the father had been contracted for an immoral purpose, the son might not have been under any pious obligation to pay it; and he might possibly object to those estates which had come to the father as ancestral property being made liable to the debt. That was not the case here. It was not shown that the bond upon which the decree was obtained was given for an immoral purpose: it was a bond given apparently for an advance of money, upon which an action was brought. The bond had been substantiated in a Court of Justice; there was nothing to show that it was given for an immoral purpose; and the holder recovered a decree upon it. There is no suggestion either that the bond, or the decree, was obtained *benamee* for the benefit of the father, or merely for the purpose of enabling the father to sell the family property, and raise money for his own purpose. On the contrary, it was proved that the purchase-money for the estate was paid into the bankers of the father, and credit was given to them with the bankers for the amount, and that the money was applied partly to pay off the decree, partly to pay off a balance which was due from the father to the bankers, and partly to pay Government revenue; and then there was some small portion of which the application was not accounted for. But it is not because a small portion is unaccounted for that the son has a right to turn out the *bonâ fide* purchaser who gave value for the estate, and to recover possession of it with mesne profits. Even if there was no necessity to raise the whole purchase-money, the sale would not be wholly void" (*c*).

Bengal rulings in regard to minors and adults.

§ 286. This decision has been followed in numerous cases from all the Presidencies, where sales or mortgages by a father for the purpose of satisfying antecedent debts of his own, which were neither immoral on the one hand, nor beneficial to the family on the other, have been held to bind the sons' and grandsons' share in the property as well as the father's share (*d*). The Bengal Court, however, takes a distinction which seems to be peculiar to itself. They hold that such a transaction is valid against the other members of the family as being "an alienation for the performance of indispensable duties within the meaning of parà. 29, Chap. I, § 1 of the Mitakshara." But they also hold that even such an alienation, though it binds minors, cannot

(*c*) *Girdharee Lall* v. *Kantoo Lall*, 1 I. A. 321, 330; S. C. 14 B. L. R. 187; S. C. 22 Suth. 56; *Suraj Bunsi Koer* v. *Sheo Proshad*, 6 I. A. 88; S. C. 5 Cal. 148. See these cases discussed. W. & B. 646.

(*d*) *Muddun Gopal* v. *Mt. Gowrunbutty*, 15 B. L. R. 264; S. C. 23 Suth. 365; *Adurmoni* v. *Chowdhry*, 3 Cal. 1; *Ponnappa* v. *Pappuvayyangar*, 4 Mad. 1; *Gangulu* v. *Ancha*, 4 Mad. 73; *Narayana* v. *Narso*, 1 Bom. 262; *per curiam*, *Lakshman* v. *Satyabhamabai*, 2 Bom. 498; *Kastur* v. *Appa*, 5 Bom. 622; *Darsu* v. *Bikarmajit*, 3 All. 125; *Sadashiv Dinkar* v. *Dinkar Narayan*, 6 Bom. 520; *Ramphul Singh* v. *Deg Narain*, 8 Cal. 517; S. C. 10 C. L. R. 489; *Velliyammal* v. *Katha Chetty*, 5 Mad. 61; *Fakirchand* v. *Motichand*, 7 Bom. 438; *Trimbak Balkrishna* v. *Narayan Damodar*, 8 Bom. 481; *Ponnappa* v. *Pappuvayyangar*, 9 Mad. 343; *Koer Hasmal* v. *Sunder Das*, 11 Cal. 396.

bind adults without their consent express or implied. Consequently, that a sale or mortgage by a father to satisfy his antecedent debt cannot *per se* bind his adult sons, though it would bind any who were minors at the time (*e*). Practically, however, the Court seems to get rid of its own distinction by holding that even in such a case, "the property would be bound; not indeed by virtue of the mortgage but by virtue of the father's debt antecedent to the suit being enforceable against the joint ancestral estate and therefore against the mortgaged property as part of it. Strictly speaking, perhaps, the suit should be in the form of a suit upon the mortgage as against the father, and upon the debt as an antecedent debt as against the interests of the sons in the joint ancestral estate. But this would be merely matter of form (*f*)." Similarly, though the Bengal Court holds that the rule laid down by *Girdharee Lall* v. *Kantoo Lall* only applies where the sale or mortgage was made in consideration of a debt antecedent to the transaction purporting to deal with the property (*g*), they practically arrive at the same result in cases where there has been no antecedent debt, by holding that the money, which is the consideration for the sale or mortgage, constitutes a debt to the purchaser or mortgagee, which, in a suit properly framed against the son, might be enforced by a decree directing the debt to be raised out of the whole ancestral estate, including the mortgaged property, and this whether the son was a minor or an adult at the time of the transaction (*h*).

Sales in execution of decrees enforcing a mortgage.

§ 287. Where a father has sold or mortgaged the family property for an antecedent debt, not of an immoral or illegal character, it seems now quite settled that a sale

---

(*e*) *Upooroop* v. *Lalla Bandhjee*, 6 Cal. 749, 753; see *Muthoora* v. *Bootun*, 13 Suth. 30; contra, *Phulchand* v. *Mansingh*, 4 All. 309.

(*f*) *Laljee* v. *Fakeer*, 6 Cal. 135, 138. See *Baso Kooer* v. *Hurry Dass*, 9 Cal. 495.

(*g*) *Supra* (note *f*) 6 Cal. 138; *Hanuman Kamat* v. *Dowlut Munder*, 10 Cal. 528; *Lal Singh* v. *Deo Narain*, 8 All. 279; *Arunachela* v. *Munisawmy*, 7 Mad. 39.

(*h*) *Luchman* v. *Giridhur*, 5 Cal. 855, (F. B.); *Gunga Prosad* v. *Ajudhia*, 8 Cal. 131; *Contra*, *Jamna* v. *Nain Sukh*, 9 All. 493.

under a decree against him enforcing such a transaction will bind his sons, even though they have not been made parties to the suit (*i*). The reason for this appears to be that the right of the purchaser or mortgagee was complete by means of the transfer made to him by the father, and did not require the decree to give it validity against his sons. The only effect of the decree is to give the stamp of genuineness to the demand, and to direct the mode in which the transaction is to be carried out. Where the Court enforces a mortgage by directing a sale of "the right title and interest" of the mortgagor, these words may "include the entire interest which he had authority to mortgage at the time he executed the deed of mortgage, as distinguished from the share of the judgment debtor which was available to creditors generally at the date of the attachment" (*k*). Hence where the decree would deprive the sons of any right which they would possess, not inconsistent with the validity of the mortgage, as for instance the right to redeem, the Madras High Court holds that this right is not taken away from them by a decree to which they are not a party (*l*). The High Court of Bombay had occasion to consider the same question in a case where there had been a partition between father and sons after the mortgage and before suit. They refrained from deciding the general question as to the effect of such a decree against the father alone in binding the sons. They considered it quite clear that after the partition the father could not be treated as representing the interests of his sons in the suit, and that, therefore, their right to redeem was unaffected by the decree (*m*).

(*i*) *Suraj Bunsi Koer* v. *Sheo Pershad Singh*, 6 I. A. 88; S. C. 5 Cal. 148; *Ponnappa* v. *Pappuvayyangar*, 4 Mad. 1; 9 Mad. 343; *Srinavasa* v. *Yelaya*, 5 Mad. 251; *Ramphul Singh* v. *Deg. Narain*, 8 Cal. 517; *Krishnamma* v. *Perumal*, 8 Mad. 388; *Sadashiv Dinkar* v. *Dinkar Narayan*, 6 Bom. 520; *Hurdey Narain* v. *Rooder Perkash*, 11 I. A. 26, 28; S. C. 10 Cal. 626; *Basamal* v. *Maharaj Singh*, 8 All. 205; *Sundraraja* v. *Jagannada*, 4 Mad. 111. The decisions of the Privy Council in *Simbhu Nath* v. *Golab Singh*, and *Pettachi Chetty* v. *Sivagiri Zemindar*, 14 I. A. 77, 84, rested on grounds which are stated, *post*, § 294, 295.

(*k*) *Per curiam*, 8 Bom. p. 486, 4 Mad. p. 65, 17 I. A. p. 16.

(*l*) *Ponnappa* v. *Pappuvayyangar*, 4 Mad. 1, 69. The High Court of Bengal appears to have taken the same view in *Ramphul Singh* v. *Deg Narain*, 8 Cal. p. 525.

(*m*) *Trimbak Balkrishna* v. *Narayan Damodar*, 8 Bom. 481.

§ 288. After much conflict of decision in the Indian Courts, arising from a misunderstanding of certain cases which will be referred to hereafter, it is now settled that the sons may be bound by proper proceedings taken by the creditor against the father to enforce a mere money debt due by him, although the sons are not made parties to the suit. The leading case upon this point is that of *Muddun Thakoor* v. *Kantoo Lall* (*n*). The facts of that case were as follows. Kunhya Lall died in 1843 leaving two sons Bhikaree and Bujrung. Kantoo Lall, the son of Bhikaree, was born in 1844. In 1855 Bhikaree and Bujrung borrowed Rs. 3,540 from Mt. Asmutanissa and others, and executed a bond for the amount, in which they hypothecated certain specified Mousahs of the joint family property. In 1857 the bondholders obtained a decree against Bhikaree and Bujrung in these terms: "Plaintiffs sue defendants for the recovery of Rs. 3,540 under a bond duly registered, and Rs. 1,189 interest thereon from date of bond to date of suit at one per cent. aggregating Rs. 4,729." An acknowledgment by defendants was recited, and it was "ORDERED that this suit be decreed to plaintiffs according to acknowledgment filed by defendants. The plaintiffs do recover from defendants the money claimed with costs and interests from the date of suit to that of realisation." It is evident that though the plaintiffs might have sued to enforce the hypothecation as such, they chose to treat the bond as a mere money claim, upon which they sought a simple decree for money. Kantoo Lall who was then of full age was not made a party to the suit, nor was Mahabeer, an infant son of Bujrung, who was born after 1856. In 1859 the right, title and interest of the judgment debtors in certain specified properties was sold in execution of the decree, and was purchased by a benamidar for Muddun Thakoor. Judging from the names of the properties it would appear, that although most of those which were hypothecated in

Muddun Thakoor v. Kantoo Lall.

(*n*) 1 I. A. 321, 333; S. C. 14 B. L. R. 187; S. C. 22 Suth. 56. The facts of the case are not set out in the report, but are fully stated by the Chief Justice of Madras (9 Mad. 347) from a personal examination of the original record.

1855 were sold under the execution, yet some which were hypothecated were not sold, and some which were sold had not been hypothecated. The whole execution appears to have proceeded upon the footing of an ordinary money decree, and not of a mortgage. Kantoo Lall sued Muddun Thakoor to recover the whole property, a relief to which he would have been entitled if his share had been improperly sold (§ 340). The High Court of Bengal awarded him the share to which he would have been entitled on partition. This decree was reversed by the Judicial Committee. The judgment followed that in Girdhar Lall's case (§ 285) of which it formed part. It rested on the principle laid down in that case that, "It would be a pious duty on the part of the son to pay his father's debts and it being the pious duty of the son to pay his father's debts, the ancestral property, in which the son, as the son of his father, acquires an interest by birth, is liable to the father's debts." It applied that principle to the particular case by saying. "It has already been shown that if the decree was a proper one, the interest of the sons as well as the interest of the fathers in the property, although it was ancestral, were liable for the payment of the father's debts." Their Lordships were of opinion that in favour of the auction purchaser the propriety of the sale must be assumed. It has been suggested (*o*) that the decree in Muddun Thakoor's case was given on the footing of a mortgage, or at all events that the Privy Council acted on that view. I think it is quite clear that such a supposition would have been a mistake, and that there is no reason to suppose that their Lordships were under any misapprehension.

Affirmed by Privy Council. § 289. This case again has been approved and followed to its full extent by the Judicial Committee in more recent cases. In the case of *Suraj Bunsi* v. *Sheo Pershad,* their Lordships quote *Muddun Thakoor's* case with approval, and cite it as establishing "that where joint ancestral property

(*o*) By Kernan, Offg. C. J., 9 Mad. 196.

has passed out of a joint family, either under a conveyance executed by a father, in consideration of an antecedent debt, or in order to raise money to pay off an antecedent debt, or under a sale in execution of a decree for the father's debt, his sons, by reason of their duty to pay their father's debts, cannot recover that property unless they show that the debts were contracted for immoral purposes, and that the purchasers had notice they were so contracted" (*p*).

§ 290. These rules are subject, as already stated (§ 285) to a further exception, of which the first branch is that the creditor, who wishes to enforce his claim against the interests of the sons, must show that he intended to do so by his proceedings in execution. The leading case upon this point is that of *Deendyal* v. *Jugdeep Narain* (*q*). There *Toofani Singh*, the father of the respondent, being indebted to the appellant to the amount of Rs. 5,000, executed to him a Bengali mortgage bond for securing the repayment of that sum with interest. The appellant afterwards put that bond in suit, and obtained a decree against Toofani Singh for Rs. 6,328. The decree was an ordinary decree for money, and no proceedings were taken to enforce it against the property specially hypothecated. So far the case seems identical with that of *Muddun Thakoor*. Six years after decree, the appellant caused "the rights and proprietary and Mokurruri title and share of Toofani the judgment debtor," in the joint family property to be sold for the amount then alleged to be due, and bought it himself and got into possession of the whole. The son then sued to recover the whole property, on the ground that being under Mitakshara law the joint property of his father and himself, it could not be sold for his father's debts, which were incurred without any

(*p*) 6 I. A. 88, p. 106; S. C. 5 Cal. 148, p. 171; followed *Bhagbut Pershad* v. *Girja Koer*, 15 I. A. 99; S. C. 15 Cal. 717; *Meenakshi Naidoo* v. *Immudikanaka*, 16 I. A. 1; S. C. 12 Mad. 142.

(*q*) 4 I A. 247; S. C. 3 Cal 198. Some of the facts of this case are more fully set out by Mr. Justice Mitter in 8 Cal. p. 903 than they are in the Privy Council report. See also *Jugdeep* v. *Deendyal*, 12 B. L. R. 100, the case appealed from.

necessity. An issue was recorded as to whether Toofani Singh borrowed from the defendant under a legal necessity or not. No special issue was recorded as to whether the debt was of an immoral character, though evidence to that effect was given as bearing on the question of necessity. The Original Court appears to have considered that it could not go behind the order of sale, and that as that purported only to deal with the interests of Toofani Singh, the son was entitled to possession of the other moiety. The Zillah Judge dismissed the suit, being of opinion that a legal necessity was made out, that therefore the debt was binding on the son, and his share as well as the father's was liable for the debt. This finding of fact was binding on the High Court on special appeal. It held, however, upon the construction of the sale proceedings that the purchaser could get nothing more than what was put up to sale, *viz.*, the rights and share of Toofani Singh. They further were of opinion that such an interest was not saleable under Mitakshara law (§ 329) and therefore decreed for the plaintiff. This was treated by the Judicial Committee as "the first and principal question," and after an elaborate examination of the authorities they decided that the father's interest could be sold, so as to enable the purchaser at the execution sale to compel such a partition as the debtor might have compelled, if no sale had taken place. In dealing with the conclusive finding of the Zillah Judge that the debt was contracted under a legal necessity, the Judicial Committee say :—" This issue, however, seems to their Lordships to be immaterial to the present suit, because whatever may have been the nature of the debt, the appellant cannot be taken to have acquired by the execution sale more than the right, title and interest of the judgment debtor. If he had sought to go further, and to enforce the debt against the whole property, and the co-sharers therein who were not parties to the bond, he ought to have framed his suit accordingly, and have made those co-sharers parties to it. By the proceedings which he took he could not get more than what was seized and sold in execution, *viz.*, the right, title and interest of the father. If any authority be required for this proposition, it is sufficient to refer to the cases of *Nugender Chunder Ghose* v. *Srimutty Kaminee Dossee*, and *Baijun Doobey* v. *Brij Bhookun Lall* (r)." The result was that the son was held entitled to recover the whole property, subject to a declaration that the purchaser had acquired the share of *Toofani Singh*, and was entitled to have that share ascertained by partition (s).

Hurdey Narain v. Rooder Perkash.

§ 291. This case was followed in the Privy Council by that of *Hurdey Narain* v. *Rooder Perkash* (t). The facts there were exactly the same as in *Deendyal's* case; *viz.*, a decree for a money debt against the father followed by execution against "whatever rights and interests the said judgment debtor had" in the property sold. Here the Judicial Committee, agreeing with the High Court, held on the authority of *Deendyal* v. *Jugdeep Narain* that the interest purchased by the creditor was only "the right which the father, the debtor, would have to a partition, and what would come to him upon the partition." The cases of *Girdharee Lall* v. *Kantoo Lall*, and of *Suraj Bunsi* v. *Sheo Pershad* were cited in argument, but not in the judgment. No doubt it was in reference to them that their Lordships said, "the decree was the ordinary one for the payment of the money, and this case is distinguishable from the cases where the father, being a member of a joint family governed by the Mitakshara law, had mortgaged the family property to secure a debt, and the decree had been obtained upon the mortgage, and for a realisation of the debt by means of the sale of the mortgaged property." No such distiuction existed as to the case of *Muddun Thakoor* v. *Kantoo Lall*, which does not seem to have been referred to.

Explanation of these cases.

§ 292. These cases were for some time taken by the Courts in India as, to a certain extent, over-ruling *Muddun*

(r) 11 M. I. A. 241; 2 I. A. 275.

(s) As to this last point, see also *Hurdey Narain* v. *Rooder Perkash*, 11 I. A. 26; S. C. 10 Cal. 626; *Maruti Narayan* v. *Lilachand*, 6 Bom. 564.

(t) 11 I. A. 26; S. C. 10 Cal. 626.

Thakoor's case, and as laying down the general principle, that where a decree has been obtained against a father on a mere money debt it could not be executed so as to bind the rights of the sons, unless they were parties to the decree. It is abundantly clear, however, that the Judicial Committee did not intend to over-rule that decision. It was never referred to from beginning to end of *Deendyal's* decision. It never seems to have occurred to any one that it had any bearing upon the decision. Both the original Court and the High Court had accepted as an undisputed fact that the judgment creditor chose, for reasons of his own, to sell only the right, title and interest of the father, (*u*). The Privy Council adopted this finding and acted upon it. Between the hearing of *Deendyal's* case and that of *Hurdey Narain* the decision in *Suraj Bunsi* v. *Sheo Prasad* (§ 289) had been given, in which the rulings in *Muddun Thakoor's* case had been fully adopted. Yet in *Hurdey Narain's* case neither *Muddun Thakoor* nor *Suraj Bunsi* were noticed in the judgment as being at all in point. In a much later case, in which the Privy Council over-ruled a decision of the Madras High Court founded on this mistake, they say, "The High Court seems to have acted on the rule of law so laid down as a rigid rule of law apparently applicable to this particular case. But the distinction is obvious. In *Hurdey Narain's* case, all the documents shew that the Court intended to sell, and that it did sell nothing but the father's share—the share and interest that he would take on partition, and nothing beyond it—and this tribunal in that case puts it entirely upon the ground that every thing showed that the thing sold was "whatever rights and interests the said judgment debtor had in the premises and nothing else" (*v*). Accordingly in the case in which those observations were made, and also in a previous one (*w*), the Privy Council affirmed sales under a money decree against

(*u*) See 12 B. L. R., pp. 101, 103.

(*v*) *Minakshi Naidu* v. *Immudi Kanaka*, 16 I. A. 1, p. 5; S. C. 12 Mad. 142, p. 147.

(*w*) *Bhagbut Pershad* v. *Girja Koer*, 15 I. A. 99; S. C. 15 Cal. 717.

the father to which the sons were no parties, being of opinion that the creditor and the Court both intended to put up for sale the entirety of the family property (*x*.)

§ 293. A further branch of the same exception (§ 285) in that the purchaser of family property for the debt of the father, whether he takes by a conveyance direct from the father, or by a sale at Court auction, must be intended to take, and must believe that he is taking the entire estate, and not merely the father's interest in it. This was laid down in several cases before the Privy Council, the first of which was that of *Nanomi Babuasin* v. *Modun Mohun* (*y*). There a father with minor sons was manager of an ancestral estate. In an ejectment suit against the father the plaintiff obtained a decree for mesne profits. The High Court stated the execution proceedings which ensued as follows. "In the petition for execution an inventory of the judgment debtor's property was given, which described it as 'The share of 8 annas 11 gundahs out of the entire 16 annas, right and interest of the judgment debtor in Mouzah Rampore,' and prayed that this might be attached and sold. The proceeding confirming the sale, and the certificate of sale are to the same effect, *viz.*, describing the property as 8 annas 11 gundahs share, and stating it to be the right and interest of the judgment debtor in the whole estate. This language might be regarded as specifically stating the object of the sale, *viz.*, an 8 annas 11 gundahs share, and the statement as to its being the right and interest of the creditor as mere description. Section 249 of the Civil Procedure Code, however, provides that the proclamation of sale shall declare that the sale extends only to the right, title, and interest of the judgment debtor in the property specified, and it may be contended that, read in the light

Nanomi Babuasin v. Modun Mohun.

(*x*) In considering this question it is not sufficient to examine the decree without also considering the proceedings in execution. *Kagal Ganpaya* v. *Manjappa*, 12 Bom. 691.

(*y*) 13 I. A. 1; S. C. 13 Cal. 21; followed, *Daulet Ram* v. *Mehr Chand*, 14 I. A. 187; S. C. 15 Cal. 70; *Mahabir Pershad* v. *Moheswar Nath*, 17 I. A. 11; S. C. 17 Cal. 584.

of this section this was the proper meaning of the petition and certificate. This is the view taken by the original Court." The High Court then proceeded to state that in its opinion the intention of all parties was to bring the whole property to sale, and in this view the Privy Council agreed. They said, (z) "It appears to their Lordships that sufficient care has not always been taken to distinguish between the question, how far the entirety of the estate is liable to answer the father's debt, and the question how far the sons can be precluded by proceedings taken by or against the father alone from disputing that liability. Destructive as it may be of the principle of independent coparcenary rights in the sons, the decisions have for some time established the principle, that the sons cannot set up their rights against their father's alienation for an antecedent debt, or against his creditors remedies for their debts, if not tainted with immorality. On this important question of the liability of the joint estate their Lordships think that there is now no conflict of authority. The circumstances of the present case do not call for any enquiry as to the exact extent to which sons are precluded by a decree against their father from calling into question the validity of the sale, on the ground that the debt which formed the foundation of it was incurred for immoral purposes, or was merely illusory and fictitious. Their Lordships do not think that the authority of *Deendyal's* case bound the Court to hold that nothing but Girdhari's (the father's) coparcenary interest passed by the sale. If his debt was of a nature to support a sale of the entirety, he might legally have sold it without suit, or the creditor might legally procure a sale of it by suit. All the sons can claim is, that not being parties to the sale or execution proceedings, they ought not to be barred from trying the fact or the nature of the debt in a suit of their own. Assuming they have such a right, it will avail them nothing unless they can prove that the debt was not such as to justify the sale. If the expressions by which the estate is conveyed

(z) 13 I. A. p. 17; 13 Cal. 85.

to the purchaser are susceptible of application either to the entirety, or to the father's coparcenary interest alone, (and in *Deendyal's* case there certainly was an ambiguity of that kind) the absence of the sons from the proceedings may be one material consideration. But if the fact be that the purchaser has bargained and paid for the entirety, he may clearly defend his title to it upon any ground which would have justified a sale if the sons had been brought in to oppose the execution proceedings." The Committee then pronounced its opinion that the debt for which the property had been sold was a joint family debt, adding, "If it is a joint family debt, a sale to answer if effected either by Girdhari himself, or in a suit against him cannot be successfully impeached." Finally they agreed with the Courts below "that the execution and sale proceedings was such that the purchaser must have thought that he was buying the entirety. It is equally clear that all parties thought the same. The purchaser therefore has succeeded in showing that he bought the entirety of the estate which could lawfully be sold to him, and the suit fails upon its merits." (*a*).

Simbhu Nath v. Golab Singh.

§ 294. Two later decisions of the Judicial Committee are in accordance with the view of the law stated in the last case. In one (*b*) Luchmun who had four sons was sued for a money debt by one Bhichook. The suit was terminated by a decree for a specified sum, to secure which the debtor mortgaged "his right and interest in Mouzah Kindwar." The sons assented to this arrangement. Upon default execution was taken out upon the decree; and the property was sold to Bhichook, who received a certificate stating that "whatever right, title, and interest the said judgment debtor had in the said property, being extinguished from the date of the sale, is transferred to Bhichook." The purchaser got into possession of the entire family property in

---

(*a*) See the construction put upon this case by the Madras High Court in *Narasanna* v. *Gurappa*, 9 Mad. 424.

(*b*) *Simbhu Nath* v. *Golab Singh*, 14 I. A. 77, 14 Cal., 572; *Sakharam Shet* v. *Sitaram Shet*, 11 Bom. 42.

the Mouzah. The sons sued to recover their shares. The Subordinate Judge held, upon the authority of *Upooroop Tewary* v. *Lalla Bandajee,* (c) that the mortgage by Luchmun with his sons' assent bound the whole family property. This decision was reversed by the High Court, and their reversal was affirmed by the Judicial Committee in the following judgment.

"Their Lordships cannot agree with the Subordinate Judge. Whatever part any of the sons may have taken in negotiating between Luchmun and Bhichook, there is no evidence whatever of their proposing to mortgage their own interests. The sons may have assented to what was done, but the question is, what was done? That must be answered by the documents.

"Moreover if Bhichook relied on assent by the sons he should have taken care to make them parties to the execution proceedings. In *Deendyal's* case, where the expressions used by the mortgagor were much more favourable to the conveyance of the entirety than they are here, the creditor's omission of the sons from the proceedings was made a material circumstance against him. And in *Nanomi Babuasin's* case, where the decision was in favour of the purchaser, the same circumstance was recognized as being material when the expressions by which the estate is conveyed to the purchaser are susceptible of application either to the entirety or to the father's coparcenary interest alone.

"In the case of *Upooroop Tewary,* Mr. Justice Mitter thought that the words "my proprietary share" in a Mouzah were calculated to describe the entirety of the family property in dispute; and he distinguished them from the expression "right, title, and interest." In *Hurdey Narain's* case, 11 Ind. App., 26, there was no conveyance, but a sale on a money decree. The only description was "whatever

---

(c) 6 Cal. 749.

"rights and interests the said judgment debtor had in the "property," these were purchased by Hurdey Narain. The High Court held that nothing passed beyond the debtor's interest which gave him a right to partition, and which perhaps may for brevity be called his personal interest, and this Committee affirmed the decision. Each case must depend on its own circumstances. It appears to their Lordships that in all the cases, at least the recent cases, the inquiry has been what the parties contracted about if there was a conveyance, or what the purchaser had reason to think he was buying if there was no conveyance, but only a sale in execution of a money decree.

"Their Lordships are sorry that they cannot follow the learned Judges of the High Court into their examination of the vernacular petition. But they find quite enough ground in the decree to express a clear agreement with them. They conceive that when a man conveys his right and interest and nothing more, he does not *primâ facie* intend to convey away also rights and interests presently vested in others, even though the law may give him the power to do so. Nor do they think that a purchaser who is bargaining for the entire family estate would be satisfied with a document purporting to convey only the right and interest of the father. It is true that the language of the certificate is influenced by that of the Procedure Code. But it is the instrument which confers title on the purchaser. Its language, like that of the certificate in *Hurdey Narain's* case, is calculated to express only the personal interest of Luchmun. It exactly accords with the expressions used in the decree of August 1869, founded on Luchmun's own vernacular expressions, which the High Court construe as pointing to his personal interest alone. The other circumstances of the case aid the *primâ facie* conclusion instead of counteracting it. For the creditor took no steps to bind the other members of the family, and the Rs. 625 which he got for his purchase appears to be nearer the value of one-sixth than of the entirety."

Pettachi Chetty v. Sivagiri Zemindar.

§ 295. In a later case (*d*), from Madras the Sivagiri Zemindar had contracted numerous debts to different creditors, in respect of the majority of which he had consented to decrees by which specific portions of his impartible Zemindary were hypothecated as security for payment. The debts in question were neither illegal nor immoral, but were not shown to be necessary or beneficial to the family. He had one son who was born before these decrees commenced. During the life of the judgment debtor his whole Zemindary was attached and ordered to be sold at the demand of 13 creditors, of whom all but two held specific mortgages on the Zemindary. The sale did not take place till after his death. There can be little doubt that, if proper steps had been taken, it would have been possible to sell the Zemindary in such a manner as absolutely to bind the son's interest. But during the whole course of the execution proceedings the Civil Judge, acting upon the view of the law which was taken by the High Court previous to the decision in *Muttayen Chetty* v. *Sangili* (*e*), announced his opinion that the sale could only bind the father's life-interest, and that it would only pass to the purchaser the rents in arrear at his death. The son was made a party to the suit after his father's death as his legal representative. Upon these facts both the Indian Courts were of opinion that nothing was intended to pass, and therefore that nothing did pass, to the auction purchaser except the father's life-interest, and this opinion was affirmed on appeal by the Privy Council.

Execution proceedings liberally construed.

§ 296. Lastly, there is a class of cases which has an indirect, though important, bearing upon the present question, in which the Privy Council has laid down the rule "that in execution proceedings the Court will look at the substance of the transaction, and will not be disposed to set aside an execution upon mere technical grounds, when

(*d*) *Pettachi Chetty* v. *Sangili Vira*, 14 I. A 84, 10 Mad. 241.
(*e*) 9 I. A. 128; S. C. 6 Mad. 1.

they find that it is substantially right." Where therefore a defendant possesses both an individual and a representative character, and where he has been sued for a debt which would bind the whole family which he represents, and where execution is taken out against him under the decree, the Court is at liberty to look at the judgment to see what was intended to be sold under his right, title, and interest, and may treat the decree as binding the whole family which is represented by the defendant, and as properly executed against the joint family property (*f*).

§ 296A. It appears to me that the above decisions lay down the following rules : **Suggested summary of decisions.**

I. That in cases governed by Mitakshara law a father may sell or mortgage not only his own share, but his sons' shares in family property, in order to satisfy an antecedent debt of his own, not being of an illegal or immoral character, and that such transaction may be enforced against his sons by a suit and by proceedings in execution to which they are no parties (*g*).

II. That the mere fact that the father might have transferred his sons' interest, affords no presumption that he has done so, and that those who assert that he has done so must make out, not only that the words in the conveyance are capable of passing the larger interest, but that they are such words as a purchaser, who intended to bargain for such a larger interest, might be reasonably expected to require (*h*).

III. That a creditor may enforce payment of the personal debt of a father, not being illegal or immoral, by seizure

(*f*) *Bissessur Lall* v. *Luchmessur Singh*, 6 I. A. 233 ; S. C. 5 C. L. R. 477 ; *Darbhunga* v. *Coomar*, 14 M. I. A. 605 ; *Jugol Kishore* v. *Jotindra Mohun*, 11 I. A. 66 ; S. C. 10 Cal. 985 ; *Jairan Babaja Shet* v. *Joma Kondia*, 11 Bom. 361 ; *Lala Parbhu Lal* v. *Mylne*, 14 Cal. 401 ; *Hari Saran Moitra* v. *Bhubaneswari*, 15 I. A. 195 ; S. C. 16 Cal. 40.

(*g*) *Girdhari Lall* v. *Kantoo Lall*, *ante*, § 285.

(*h*) *Simbhu Nath* v. *Golab Singh*, *ante*, § 294.

and sale of the entire interest of father and sons in the family property, and that it is not absolutely necessary that the sons should be a party either to the suit itself or to the proceedings in execution (*i*).

IV. That it will not be assumed that a creditor intends to exact payment for a personal debt of the father by execution against the interest of the sons, unless such intention appears from the form of the suit, or of the execution proceedings, or from the description of the property put up for sale; and the fact that the sons have not been made parties to the proceedings in execution is a material element in considering whether the creditor aimed at the larger, or was willing to limit himself to the minor remedy (*k*).

V. That the words "right, title, and interest of the judgment debtor" are ambiguous words, which may either mean the share which he would have obtained on a partition, or the amount which he might have sold to satisfy his debt (*l*).

VI. That it is in each case a mixed question of law and fact to determine what the Court intended to sell at public auction, and what the purchasers expected to buy. That the Court cannot sell more than the law allows. If it appears as a fact that the Court intended to sell less than it might have sold, or even less than it ought to have sold, and that this was known to the purchasers, no more will pass than what was in fact offered for sale (*m*).

Can sons set up immorality of debt against purchaser under decree?

§ 297. Another very important point which does not appear to be quite settled is this. Assuming that a decree against a father alone for a debt not immoral or illegal can be enforced against the whole family property, is it open

(*i*) *Muddun Thakoor* v. *Kantoo Lall, ante*, § 289; *Nanomi Babuasin* v. *Modun Mohun, ante*, § 293.

(*k*) *Deendyal* v. *Jugdeep Narain, ante*, § 290; *Hurdey Narain* v. *Rooder Perkash, ante*, § 292; *Nanomi Babuasin* v. *Modun Mohun, ante*, § 293.

(*l*) Same cases *et per curiam*, 17 I. A. p. 16; S. C. 17 Cal. p. 589; 8 Bom. p. 486; 4 Mad. p. 65.

(*m*) *Nanomi Babuasin* v. *Modun Mohun, ante*, § 293; *Simbhu Nath* v. *Golab Singh, ante*, § 294; *Pettachi Chetty* v. *Sangili Vira, ante*, § 295; *Muhammad Abdul* v. *Kutul Husain*, 9 All. 185.

to the sons to set up such immorality or illegality against the auction purchaser ? Upon this point there have been three very important decisions of the Prviy Council.

Muddun Thakoor v. *Kantoo Lall.*

In the first case a son sought to set aside a sale made under a decree of Court against his father, the debt not being for the family benefit on one hand, nor immoral on the other. The Judicial Committee held that he had no such right. They said, "It appears that *Muddun Mohun Thakoor* purchased at a sale under an execution of a decree against the two fathers. He found that a suit had been brought against two fathers; that a Court of Justice had given a decree against them in favour of a creditor; that the Court had given an order for this particular property to be put up for sale under the execution; and therefore it appears to their Lordships that he was perfectly justified, within the principle of the case which has already been referred to in 6th Moore's Indian appeal cases, p. 423 (*n*), in purchasing the property, and paying the purchase money *bonâ fide* for the purchase of the estate. The same rule has been applied in the case of a purchaser of joint ancestral property. A purchaser under an execution is surely not bound to go back beyond the decree to ascertain whether the Court was right in giving the decree, or, having given it, in putting up the property for sale under an execution upon it. It has already been shewn that if the decree was a proper one, the interest of the sons, as well as the interest of the fathers, in the property, although it was ancestral, were liable for the payment of the father's debts. The purchaser under that execution, it appears to their Lordships, was not bound to go further back than to see that there was a decree against those two gentlemen; that the property was property liable to satisfy the decree, if the decree had been properly given against them; and, having inquired into that, and having *bonâ fide* purchased the estate under the execution, and *bonâ fide* paid a valuable

Purchaser need not enquire beyond decree.

(*n*) *Hunoomanpersaud* v. *Mt. Babooee*; S. C. 18 Suth. 81 (note).

44 *in.*

consideration for the property, the plaintiffs are not entitled to come in, and to set aside all that has been done under the decree and execution, and recover back the estate from the defendant." (*o*)

§ 298. It is evident that the general principle laid down in this judgment went very much beyond the necessities of the case. Even if the son had been allowed to rip up the decree, it appears that the evidence showed the debt to have been one which he was liable to pay, at all events after his father's death, and therefore the sale to satisfy it came within the ruling in *Girdharee Lall* v. *Kantoo Lall.* But it might happen that the debt was contracted for purposes which would prevent its binding the son. These circumstances might fail to afford any defence to an action against the father, or they might not be set up by the father. In either case the decree would have been a proper one as against the father, and properly enforced against his interest in the property. But when the creditor tried to enforce it against the son's interest also, would the son be allowed to show that although the decree was properly given against the debtor, the property, that is the son's interest in it, was not property liable to satisfy the decree? In other words, can he show that the facts do not exist which would entitle the creditor to seize the property of B in execution of a personal decree against A? A later decision of the Judicial Committee seems to show that he cannot do even this as against a *bonâ fide* purchaser at the execution sale, who has no notice of the original taint affecting the debt. In that case the sons sued to set aside a sale of joint property made to the defendant in execution of decree against the father. The lower Courts found that the debt was not for the benefit of the family, and that the money borrowed was spent by the father for immoral purposes. The High Court upon these findings held that although the original creditor could not have enforced his claim against the sons, the pur-

Effect of notice that debt was immoral.

Suraj Bunsi Koer v. *Sheo Proshad.*

(*o*) *Muddun Thakoor* v. *Kantoo Lall*, 1 I. A. 321, 333; S. C. 14 B. L. R. 187; S. C. 22 Suth. 56.

chaser at the sale, having purchased *bonâ fide* for value without notice, was entitled to hold the property free of all claims by the sons. For this view they relied upon the decision last cited. The Judicial Committee quoted the passage already set out, remarking that they desired to say nothing which could be taken to affect the authority of *Muddun Thakoor's* case, or of the cases which might have since been decided in India in conformity with it. They summarised the judgments in that case and in the kindred case of *Girdharee Lall* v. *Kantoo Lall* as being "undoubtedly an authority for these propositions; 1*st*, that where joint ancestral property has passed out of a Joint family, either under a conveyance executed by a father in consideration of an antecedent debt, or in order to raise money to pay off an antecedent debt, or under a sale in execution of a decree for the father's debt, his sons, by reason of their duty to pay their father's debts, cannot recover that property, unless they show that the debts were contracted for immoral purposes, and that the purchasers had notice that they were so contracted; and 2*ndly*, that the purchasers at an execution sale, being strangers to the suit, if they have not notice that the debts were so contracted, are not bound to make inquiry beyond what appears on the face of the proceedings." Their Lordships, however, proceeded to distinguish the case before them from that of *Muddun Thakoor*, on the ground of notice, actual or constructive, of the plaintiff's objections before the sale, by virtue of which the respondents must be held to have purchased with knowledge of the plaintiff's claim, and subject to the result of the suit to which the plaintiffs had been referred. It followed, therefore, that as against them, as well as against the original creditor, the plaintiffs had established that by reason of the nature of the debt neither they nor their interests in the joint ancestral estate were liable to satisfy their father's debt (*p*).

(*p*) *Suraj Bunsi Koer* v. *Sheo Proshad*, 6 I. A. 88, 106, 108; S. C. 5 Cal. 148; *Krishnaji Lakshman* v. *Vithal Ravji*, 12 Bom. 625.

§ 299. It certainly does appear singular that a purchaser under a decree should be entitled, as against third parties, to assume the existence of a state of facts which was not, and perhaps could not have been, adjudicated upon in the suit which led to the decree. The primary effect of a personal decree against a father is to bind his interest alone. It might be imagined that a purchaser under such a decree, who claimed to extend its operation to the interests of others, would have to make out such facts as would warrant its extension. Even if it were held that he started with a presumption in his favour, it might have been thought that the presumption would have been rebuttable. In the case before the Privy Council, which has already been cited at length (§ 293), their Lordships treated this point as still open to argument. They said "all the sons can claim is, that not being parties to the sale or execution proceedings, they ought not to be barred from trying the fact or the nature of the debt in a suit of their own" (*q*). This of course is all they could desire. In some later cases the Judicial Committee appears to have laid down in general terms, and without any reference to the necessity of notice, that sons could successfully impeach a sale merely by proof of the immorality of the debt (*r*). But in all these cases, as in that of *Nanomi Babuasin,* the fact of immorality had been disproved, so that the question of notice could not have arisen. Where the execution creditor is himself the purchaser at the auction, he cannot protect himself under the plea of being a purchaser without notice, if there is any flaw in the nature of the debt (*s*). Where the purchaser was the son of the execution creditor, it was considered to be a question of fact, whether he was such a stranger to the suit as to be entitled to rely upon the decree without further enquiry (*t*).

Nanomi Babuasin v. Modun Mohun.

(*q*) 13 I. A., p. 18; *Jagabhai* v. *Vijbhookundas*, 11 Bom. 37.

(*r*) *Bhagbut Pershad* v. *Girja Koer*, 15 I. A. 99; S. C. 15 Cal. 717; *Minakshi Naidu* v. *Immudi Kanaka*, 16 I. A. 1; S. C. 12 Mad. 142; *Mahabir Pershad* v. *Moheswar Nath*, 17 I. A. 11; S. C. 17 Cal. 584.

(*s*) *Luchmun Dass* v. *Giridhur Chowdhry*, 5 Cal. 855; *Ramphul Singh* v. *Deg Narain*, 8 Cal. 517, p. 522.

(*t*) *Trimbak Balkrishna* v. *Narayan Domodar*, 8 Bom. 481.

§ 300. Even if the strictest view should ultimately be taken of the rights of the purchaser under an execution, it must be remembered that under the Civil Procedure Code the sons have ample opportunity of protecting themselves. When property is about to be sold for a money decree it is always attached before sale. The proper course is for the sons to come in under § 278, and object to the sale of their interests on the ground that the debt was immoral or illegal. The party against whom the order is made will then, under § 283, be entitled to bring a suit in which the whole question can be determined (*u*). Where the property is put up for sale under a decree enforcing a mortgage no attachment need take place (*v*), but the sale is always notified beforehand by proclamation. By giving public notice at the time of sale to all intending purchasers, the sons will obtain the benefit of the ruling in their favour in Suraj Bunsi's case, as stated above (§ 298). It has been held by the Allahabad High Court that the decree must be read with the plaint, and that where the latter contains express statements showing that the debt is one which could not bind the sons,—in the particular instance, a claim for the refund of money criminally misappropriated by the father,—this is in itself a constructive notice to the purchaser, which brings his case within that of Suraj Bunsi (*w*). **Remedies under Civil Procedure Code.**

§ 301. A father's debts are a first charge upon the inheritance, and must be paid in full before there can be any surplus for division (*x*). As between the parceners themselves, the burthen of the debts is to be shared in the same proportion as the benefit of the inheritance. But, except by special arrangement with the creditors, the whole property, and all the heirs are liable jointly and severally (*y*). Where, how- **Mode of adjustment.**

(*u*) *Umamaheswara* v. *Singaperumal*, 8 Mad. 376.
(*v*) *Krishnamma* v. *Perumal*, 8 Mad. 388.
(*w*) *Mahabir Prasad* v. *Basdeo Singh*, 6 All. 234.
(*x*) Narada, xiii. § 32; Daya Bhaga, i. § 47, 48; V. May., iv. § 6; *Tarachand* v. *Reeb Ram*, 3 Mad. H. C. 177, 181.
(*y*) Katyayana, 1 Dig. 291; Narada, iii. § 2; Vishnu, 1 Dig. 288; D. K. S.

ever, a father has separated from his sons, the whole of his property will descend at his death to an after-born son. Therefore all debts contracted by him subsequent to the partition will, in the first instance, be payable by that son. But Jagannatha is of opinion that even in such a case, if the after-born son has not property sufficient to pay the debts, they should be discharged by the separated sons (*z*). This would certainly have been the case under the old law, when the possession of assets was not necessary in order to render the sons liable. But it is probable that a different view would be taken now, when the creditor must show that the son's estate has been enlarged by the death, to the full extent of the liability attempted to be imposed.

Obligation arising from possession of assets.

§ 302. *Secondly,* the obligation to pay the debts of the person whose estate a man has taken is declared with equal positiveness. It does not rest, as in the case of sons, upon any duty to relieve the deceased at any cost, but upon the broad equity that he who takes the benefit should take the burthen also (*a*). And it is evident that this obligation attached whether the property devolved upon an heir by operation of law, or whether it was taken by him voluntarily, as an executor *de son tort* as an English lawyer would say; for the liability is said to arise equally whether a man takes possession of the estate of another or only of his wife. As Narada says, "He who takes the wife of a poor and sonless dead man becomes liable for his debts, for the wife is con-

---

vii. § 26—28; 2 Stra. H. L. 283. The case of *Doorga Pershad* v. *Kesho Pershad*, 9 I. A. 27; S. C. 8 Cal. 656, which seems to contradict the proposition in the text must, I think, depend on the special circumstances of the case. Certain minors had been decreed to pay money in a suit in which they were not really represented. The High Court, however, apparently to prevent a fresh suit, held them liable for so much of the decree as represented their father's debt. That debt originally due by himself and other members of the joint family to a stranger, had been apportioned at a partition. As between the father and his sons the sum so allotted to him was the only debt they could be equitably bound to pay.

(*z*) Vrihaspati, 1 Dig. 279; D. K. S. v. § 16—18.

(*a*) "He who has received the estate of a proprietor leaving no son, must pay the debts of the estate, or, on failure of him, the person who takes the wife of the deceased." Yajnavalkya, 1 Dig. 270; Katyayana, ib. 278, 330; Vrihaspati, ib. 274. "Of the successor to the estate, the guardian of the widow, or the son, he who takes the estate becomes liable for the debts." Narada, iii. § 18, 25; Gautama, cited 2 W. MacN. 284; 1 Dig. 314.

sidered as the dead man's property" (*b*). Even the widow is not bound to pay her husband's debts, unless she is his heir, or has promised to pay them, or has been a joint contractor with him (*c*).

§ 303. "Assets are to be pursued into whatever hands. See Narada, cited by Jagannatha, 1 Dig. 272. And innumerable other authorities may be cited were it requisite in so plain a case." This is the remark of Mr. Colebrooke, approving of a Madras pandit's *futwah,* that where uncle and nephew were undivided members, and the nephew borrowed money and died, leaving his property in the hands of the uncle's widow, she might be sued for the debt (*d*). So in Bombay, a suit was maintained on an account current with a deceased debtor against his widow and three other persons, strangers by family, on the ground that they had taken possession of his property, but they were held only liable to the extent to which they became possessed of the property (*e*). Similarly in Madras, where a suit was brought against the representatives of two deceased codebtors to recover a debt incurred for family purposes, it was decided that the son-in-law of one of the deceased codebtors and his brothers were properly joined as defendants, on the ground that they in collusion with the widow of the deceased, had, as volunteers, intermeddled with, and substantially possessed themselves of, the whole property of the family of the deceased co-debtor (*f*). In each of these cases the person in possession of the property held it without any title or consideration, like an executor *de son tort* in England. On the other hand, in a Madras case, where the plaintiff sued on a bond by the first defendant's husband, and joined the second defendant, his son-in-law, as being in possession

---

(*b*) Narada, iii. § 21—26; *ante*, § 71.
(*c*) Narada, iii. § 17; Yajnavalkya, Vishnu, 1 Dig. 313; Katyayana, 1 Dig. 315; 2 W. MacN. 283, 286.
(*d*) 2 Stra. H. L. 282.
(*e*) *Kupurchund* v. *Dadabhoy*, Morris, Pt. II. 126.
(*f*) *Magaluri* v. *Narayana*, 3 Mad. 359; *Kanakamma* v. *Venkataratnam*, 7 Mad. 586.

of the property, and judgment was given against both, the Sudr Court reversed the decision against the second defendant, observing, "that he is not in the line of the first defendant's husband's heirs, and that although property derived by him from the deceased debtor may in execution be made liable for the debt, his possession of the property does not render him personally responsible" (*g*). Now, if a decree had been obtained during his lifetime against the debtor, it might, of course, have been executed against his property in the hands of the son-in-law. But it is difficult to see in what way the property could have been got at in the hands of the second defendant, except by a suit to which he was a party (*h*). In a suit against the widow she could only have been made liable to the extent of the assets she had received. According to English law, an administratrix might also be made liable to the extent of the assets which, but for her wilful default, she might have received, and if she chose to leave them in the hands of her son-in-law, this would be a wilful default. But I doubt whether a Hindu widow is bound to bring suits against third parties to recover assets for the benefit of creditors (*i*). It seems to me that the son-in-law was properly joined in order to enable him to show that he had no property of the deceased, or that he held the property for value. And so in Calcutta, where the half-brother of the deceased was sued jointly with his sons for a debt, the Court held that he could not be liable as heir, which he manifestly was not, but that he would have been liable if it had been shown that he had possessed himself of any of the property of the deceased (*k*).

Liability is personal.

§ 304. In some early cases this principle was pushed so far that it was even held that an heir could not alienate property which had descended to him, while the debts of the

(*g*) *Amanchi* v. *Manchiraz*, Mad. Dec. of 1861, 78.
(*h*) See *post*, § 596.
(*i*) See 2 W. MacN. 286, where a man left a widow, who was clearly his heir, but his father and brothers appropriated his property. The pandit said that they and not the widow were bound to pay his debts.
(*k*) *Rampertab* v. *Gopeekishen*, Sev. 101.

Debts are not a charge upon the estate.

deceased were unpaid. That is, that a simple debt immediately on death acquired all the force of a specific mortgage (*l*). But this veiw has been denounced by more recent decisions, and it is now held, "that the property of a deceased Hindu is not so hypothecated for his debt as to prevent his heir from disposing of it to a third party, or to allow a creditor to follow it, and take it out of the hands of a third party, who has purchased in good faith and for valuable consideration. The creditor may hold the heir personally liable for the debt, if he have alienated the property, but he cannot follow the property" (*m*). The same ruling has been applied by the High Court of Bengal, in a case where it was attempted to make a devisee liable for the debts of the testator, in respect of his possession of part of the estate. The Court held that no such liability attached, whether his possession had commenced before the death as by gift, or after the death as by bequest (*n*). The case was argued purely upon principles of English law, which, of course, had little bearing upon the point. It has, however, been held in Madras, that a voluntary transfer of property by way of gift, if made *bonâ fide,* and not with the intention of defrauding creditors, is valid against creditors (*o*). What the deceased could have done during his life, it would probably be held, he could also do by will, unless a specific lien had attached to the property. And so a gift by the heir would probably also be held valid in favour of the donee, though, of course, such a gift would in no degree lessen his own liability to the creditors (§ 279). The Bombay High Court,

---

(*l*) *Luggah* v. *Trimbuck*, Bom. Sel. Rep. 33 ; *Kishundass* v. *Keshoo Wulud*, Morris, Pt. II. 108.

(*m*) *Unnopoorna* v. *Gunga*, 2 Suth. 296 ; *Jamiyatram* v. *Parbhudas*, 9 Bom. H. C. 116 ; *Lakshman* v. *Sarasvatibai*, 12 Bom. H. C. 78. As to what circumstances will negative good faith, see *Greender* v. *Mackintosh*, 4 Cal 897.

(*n*) *Ram Oottum* v. *Oomesh*, 21 Suth. 155. A contrary opinion, also founded upon arguments drawn from English statutes, was expressed by *Pontifex*, J., in *Greender* v. *Mackintosh*, 4 Cal. 897. The case was ultimately decided upon the law of Limitation.

(*o*) *Gnanabhai* v. *Srinivasa*, 4 Mad. H. C. 84 ; *Raibishen Chand* v. *Asmaida Koer*, 11 I. A. 164 ; S. C. 6 All. 560. By the Transfer of Property Act (IV of 1882) a person who takes by gift the whole property of another is liable for all the debts due by the donor at the time of the gift to the extent of the property received, § 128.

in *Jamiyatram* v. *Parbhudas* (*p*), says that Mr. Colebrooke laid the proposition down too broadly that the assets of the debtor may be pursued into whatsoever hands they may come, and they rather indicate an opinion that this rule only applies to those who take the inheritance as heirs. The case before them, however, was one of a purchaser for value. There is nothing to show that they would have exonerated a person who took the estate after the death by his own voluntary act, and without a title derived either from the deceased, or from the representatives of the deceased.

Liability of coparcener taking by survivorship.

§ 305. Another question arises, how far the liability to pay debts out of assets prevails against the right of survivorship, in cases where the debtor does not stand in the relation of paternal ancestor to the heir. In this case the moral and religious obligation has vanished, and it is a mere conflict of two legal rights. It will be seen hereafter (§ 331) that in cases under the Mitakshara law there is a strong body of authority in favour of the view, that an undivided coparcener cannot dispose of his share of the joint property, unless in a case of necessity, without the consent of his coparceners. But it may now be taken as settled by the Privy Council, that even if this be so, still a creditor who has obtained a judgment against him for his separate debt may enforce it during his life by seizure and sale of his undivided interest in the joint property (*q*). But that decision left open the further question, whether the creditor loses his rights against the undivided share of the debtor, if the latter dies before judgment against him, and seizure in satisfaction of it? In other words, do those who take by survivorship take subject to the equities existing between their deceased co-sharer and his creditors? I say *equities*, because it is quite clear that a debt is not a lien, but only a cause of action which may be enforced by way of execution.

This question after being decided against the creditor by

(*p*) 9 Bom. H. C. 116.

(*q*) *Deendyal* v. *Jugdeep*, 4 I. A. 247; S. C. 3 Cal. 198. As to the mode of enforcing such a decree, see *post*, 329.

the High Courts of Bombay, Madras, and the North-West Provinces, has now been definitely settled in the same way by the Privy Council.

§ 306. The first case in which the point arose directly for decision was in the North-west Provinces (*r*). There the share of Mahadev in a house, which was undivided family property, was attached in his lifetime, under a decree obtained against him for his separate bond. He died before any sale under the attachment. The High Court affirmed the ruling of the Courts below, which discharged the attachment on the ground that Mahadev at his death "left no right at all in the house, and that there was nothing, therefore, in connection with it which was liable to be sold" for the purpose of satisfying the plaintiff's claim. The principle of this decision was followed in Bombay in the case of *Udaram* v. *Ranu* (*s*). There a father and son were in possession of a shop which was ancestral property. The son contracted a separate debt and died, and the creditor obtained a decree against the father and widow for payment of the debt "out of the property and effects" of the deceased son, and then sued the father for a declaration that the son's share of the shop was liable in the father's hands for the son's debt. The High Court held that no such declaration could be made. After reviewing and approving of the cases which decided that an undivided Hindu might sell his share, and that it might be seized in execution during his lifetime, and admitting that the divided or separate estate of a Hindu would be liable to be sold after his death in execution of a decree against his heir, they noticed the doctrine that, except in certain special cases, the whole of the undivided family estate would be, when in the hands of the sons or grandsons, liable to the debts of the father or Cases in India.

(*r*) *Goor Pershad* v. *Sheodeen*, 4 N.-W. P. 137.

(*s*) 11 Bom. H. C. 76 followed in *Narsimbhat* v. *Chenapa*, 2 Bom. 479; *Balbhadar* v. *Bisheshar*, 8 All. 495; *Jaganath Prasad* v. *Sitaram*, 11 All. 302. See also *per Peacock*, C. J., in *Sadabart Prasad* v. *Foolbash Koer*, 3 B. L. R. (F. B.) 34—37; S. C. 12 Suth. (F. B.) 1; and *per Mitter*, J., *Goburdhon* v. *Singessur*, 7 Cal. 52, 54.

grandfather. They then pointed out that "there is not any authority for the converse of that proposition, *viz.*, that the father or grandfather is responsible for the debts of the son or grandson independently of the receipt of assets." Finally, they held that the son's interest in the shop could not be held to be assets in the hands of the father, since "the right of the son to share in it, as being ancestral property, had come into existence at his birth and it died with him." The Madras case was intermediate between the above two. There a decree had been obtained against a member of a Joint Family for his separate debt. He died before execution, and a suit was then brought by the decree holder, against his undivided cousin, to enforce the decree against the share of the property to which the deceased had been entitled. The decisions in the North-West Provinces and Bombay were cited, and the plaintiff's suit dismissed. The Chief Justice said, "I am not aware that it can be contended that the undivided interest of a coparcener, which passes by survivorship to the other coparceners by his death, can be proceeded against in execution. A distinction must be made between a specific charge on the land, and a general decree which is merely personal. Every debt which a man incurs is not necessarily a charge upon the estate, and there is no reason for saying that a man who has obtained judgment against an undivided member of a Joint Family, has established a charge upon the property" (*t*). The result is that if the deceased debtor is an ordinary coparcener, who has left neither separate nor self-acquired property, the creditor who has not attached his share before his death, is absolutely without a remedy. If he stood in the relation of father to the survivors, his liability can only be enforced by a separate suit against the sons (*u*). If, however, the estate of a coparcener has vested in the Official Assignee under an insolvency, that estate would continue after his death, and would not be defeated by survivorship (*v*).

(*t*) *Koopookonan* v. *Chinnayan*, 1 Mad. Law Reporter, 63.

(*u*) *Sivagiri* v. *Alwar Ayyangar*, 3 Mad. 42; *Karnataka Hanumantha* v. *Hanumayya*, 5 Mad. 232.

(*v*) *Fakirchand* v. *Motichand*, 7 Bom. 438.

§ 307. Most of the above cases were reviewed, and, except as to one point, affirmed by the Privy Council in the case of *Suraj Bunsi Koer* v. *Sheo Proshad* (*w*), already referred to. There the Court held that the father's debt as being of an immoral character, was not binding upon the sons and that the purchaser under the decree was affected with notice of the fact, so that he could claim no protection under the decree. The result was that the special liability of the sons for their father's debt was swept away, and depended solely upon their possession of assets. On the other hand, the case agreed with that in the North-West Provinces, and differed from those in Madras and Bombay in this respect, that the sale after the father's death had taken place in pursuance of an attachment and order for sale during his life. Upon this state of facts their Lordships said, "The question remains, whether they (the purchasers) are entitled to any and what relief as regards the father's share in this suit? It seems to be clear upon the authorities, that if the debt had been a mere bond debt, not binding on the sons by virtue of their liability to pay their father's debts, and no sufficient proceedings had been taken to enforce it in the father's lifetime, his interest in the property would have survived on his death to his sons, so that it could not afterwards be reached by the creditor in their hands. On the other hand, if the law of the Presidency of Fort William were identical with that of Madras, the mortgage executed by *Adit Sahai* (the father) in his lifetime, as a security for the debt, might operate after his death as a valid charge upon Mouzah *Bissumbhurpore* to the extent of his own then share. The difficulty is that, so far as the decisions have yet gone, the law, as understood in Bengal, does not recognise the validity of such an alienation. Their Lordships are of opinion that it is not necessary in this case to determine that vexed question, which their former decisions have hitherto left open. They think that, at the time of *Adit*

Privy Council decision.

Attachment binds estate.

(*w*) 6 I. A. 88, 108; S. C. 5 Cal. 148; *ante*, § 279, 284.

Sahai's death, the execution proceedings under which the Mouzah had been attached and ordered to be sold had gone so far as to constitute, in favour of the judgment creditor, a valid charge upon the land, to the extent of *Adit Sahai's* undivided share and interest therein, which could not be defeated by his death before the actual sale. They are aware that this opinion is opposed to that of the High Court of the North-West Provinces (*x*), already referred to. But it is to be observed that the Court by which that decision was passed does not seem to have recognised the seizable character of an undivided share in joint property, which has since been established by the before mentioned decision of this tribunal in the case of *Deendyal* (*y*). If this be so, the effect of the execution sale was to transfer to the respondents the undivided share in the Mouzah, which had formerly belonged to *Adit Sahai* in his lifetime; and their Lordships are of opinion that, notwithstanding his death, the respondents are entitled to work out the rights which they have thus acquired by means of a partition." (*z*)

Cases of agency.

§ 308. The *third*, and only remaining, ground of liability is that of agency, express or implied. Mere relationship, however close, creates no obligation. Parents are not bound to pay the debts of their son, nor a son the debt of his mother. A husband is not bound to pay the debts of his wife, nor the wife the debts of her husband (*a*). Still less, of course, can any member of a family be bound to pay the debts of a divided member, contracted after partition, for such a state of things wholly negatives the idea of agency (*b*). It would be different if he had become the heir of the debtor, or taken possession of his assets. On

(*x*) *Goor Pershad* v. *Sheodeen*, 4 N.-W. P. 137.

(*y*) 4 I. A. 247; S. C. 3 Cal. 198.

(*z*) See this decision followed in the converse case, where the property of the son after attachment had vested in the father. *Rai Balkishen* v. *Sitaram*, 7 All. 731; *Bailur Krishna* v. *Lakshmana*, 4 Mad. 302.

(*a*) Narada, iii. § 11, 17, 19; Yajnavalkya, Vishnu, 1 Dig. 313; Vrihaspati, 1 Dig. 316; Katyayana, 1 Dig. 317; *Mootoocoomarappa* v. *Hinnoo*, Mad. Dec. of 1855, 183.

(*b*) *Narayana* v. *Rayappa*, Mad. Dec. of 1860, 51.

the other hand, all the members of the family, and therefore all their property, divided or undivided, will be liable for debts which have been contracted on behalf of the family by one who was authorised to contract them (*c*). The most common case is that of debts created by the manager of the family. He is, *ex-officio*, the accredited agent of the family, and authorised to bind them for all proper and necessary purposes, within the scope of his agency (*d*). But the liability of the family is not limited to contracts made, or debts incurred by him. "The householder is liable for whatever has been spent for the benefit of the family by the pupil, apprentice, slave, wife, agent, or commissioned servant" (*e*). Of course, this implies that the persons referred to have acted either with an express authority, or under circumstances of such pressing necessity that an authority may be implied. Narada says, "Debts contracted by the wife never fall upon the husband, unless they were contracted for necessaries at a time of distress, for the household expenses have to be defrayed by the man" (*f*). *A fortiori* the husband is liable for any debts contracted by a wife in a business which he has assigned to her to manage (*g*). And on the same principle it has been stated "that persons carrying on a family business, in the profits of which all the members of the family would participate, must have authority to pledge the Joint Family property and credit for the ordinary purposes of the business. And, therefore, that debts honestly incurred in carrying on such business must over-ride the rights of all members of the Joint Family in property acquired with funds derived from the joint business" (*h*).

(*c*) Manu, viii. § 166; Raghunandana, v. 33—36. I presume that as in the case of partnership debts, the joint property would be primarily liable, and the separate property only in case it proved insufficient.

(*d*) What are such necessary purposes will be examined fully in the next chapter, § 320.

(*e*) Narada, iii § 12, 13; Vishnu, 1 Dig. 295; Manu, viii. § 167; Yajnavalkya, 1 Dig. 313; Katyayana, 1 Dig. 296, 319; 1 W. MacN. 286. See as to the liability of the heir for debts *bonâ fide* incurred by executors acting under a will which was afterwards set aside, or by an adopted son whose adoption was afterwards held invalid. *Fanindro Deb* v. *Jugudishwari*, 14 Cal. 316.

(*f*) Narada, iii. § 19.

(*g*) Yajnavalkya, Vrihaspati, 1 Dig. 317, 318; 2 W. MacN. 278, 281.

(*h*) *Per Pontifex*, J., *Johurra Bibee* v. *Strigopal*, 1 Cal. 475.

Similarly a mortgage of family property by the managers of a family trade partnership for the purposes of the partnership binds all the other members of the family, and if the property is sold under a decree obtained against the mortgagors alone, the sale cannot be set aside by the other members merely on the ground that they were not parties to the suit (*i*). In Bombay, however, it is held that a decree against the managers of a Joint Family for a mere money debt only binds their share of the family property, although they were sued as managers and the debt was incurred for family purposes (*k*). Debts contracted or conveyances executed by any individual member of a Joint Family, for his own personal benefit, will not bind the interests of the other members (*l*). It is said, however, that a subsequent promise by one member of a family to pay the individual debt of another member, previously contracted, would bind him (*m*). But such a promise would now be held invalid for want of consideration (*n*).

(*i*) *Daulat Ram* v. *Mehr Chand*, 14 I. A. 187; S. C. 15 Cal. 70.

(*k*) *Maruti Narayan* v. *Lilachand*, 6 Bom. 564; *Lakshman Venkatesh* v. *Kashinath*, 11 Bom. 700.

(*l*) *Venkatasami* v. *Kuppaiyan*, 1 Mad. 354; *Guruvappa* v. *Thimma*, 10 Mad. 316.

(*m*) Narada, iii. § 17; Vrihaspati, Katyayana, 1 Dig. 316, 317.

(*n*) Indian Contract Act (IX of 1872), § 25.

CHAPTER X.

ALIENATIONS.

§ 309. The law of alienation falls naturally into two branches, according as the property in question is joint or several. Further distinctions arise under each head with respect to the nature of the property, as being movable or immovable. Again; under the first branch, the person who makes the alienation may do so, in his capacity of father of the family, or manager of the corporation, or merely as a private member of the corporation. Again; the act in dispute may purport to dispose of more than the alienor's share in the entire property, or of a portion equal to, or less than, his share. Finally; in each particular instance the validity of the transaction will vary, according as it is decided by the law of the Mitakshara or of the Daya Bhaga. I shall first examine the position of the father of the family under Mitakshara law.

Division of subject.

§ 310. I have already explained the process by which the father descended from being the head of the Patriarchal Family to be the manager of a Joint Family, in which the sons acquired by birth rights almost equal to his own (*a*). But in respect of movables he was still asserted by Vijnanesvara to possess a larger power of disposition, even though they were ancestral. The texts upon which he founds this opinion may either be a survival from the period when the father actually possessed a higher power than belongs to him at present, or, more probably, merely indicate the authority which the manager of a family would necessarily

Power of father over movables.

(*a*) See *ante*, § 207, 229.

possess over the class of articles which would come under the head of movables in early times (*b*). In fact Vijnanesvara himself does not claim for the father an absolute power of disposing of movables at his own pleasure, but only an "independent power in the disposal of them for indispensable acts of duty, and for purposes prescribed by texts of law, as gifts through affection, support of the family, relief from distress and so forth," and this is the view taken by Sir *Thomas Strange* and Dr. Mayr (*c*). Mr. Colebrooke and Mr. MacNaghten, however, appear to lay it down, that in regard to ancestral movables the power of the father is only limited by his own discretion, and by a sense of spiritual responsibility (*d*). The point has arisen incidentally in several cases, but until recently has never received a full discussion. In a case in the High Court of Bengal, it was said, "By the Mitakshara law the son has a vested right of inheritance in the ancestral immovable property; on the other hand, the father has it in his power to dispose as he likes of all acquired and all personal property" (*e*). This latter remark, however, was merely *obiter dictum*. In Madras a son sued his father for a partition of property, partly house property and partly jewels. As regards the latter, *Bittleston*, J., quoted the texts of the Mitakshara (I. i. § 21, 24) as showing that "it does not follow that the plaintiff has any right to complain of his father having made an unjust and partial distribution of them" (*f*). What the father was said by the plaintiff himself to have done was, that he gave the bulk of the jewels to the daughters of the family, only giving one to the wife of his son. Possibly

Power over ancestral movables.

(*b*) See *ante*, § 231, 232.

(*c*) Mitakshara, i. 1, § 27; Viramit., p. 16, § 30; 1 Stra. H. L. 20, 261; Mayr, p. 40. In the Punjab a father is said to be at liberty to make gifts of ancestral movable property without the consent of his male heirs, but not of immovable property, whether ancestral or self-acquired. Punjab Customary Law, ii. 102, 163, 178.

(*d*) 2 Stra. H. L. 9, 436, 441; 1 W. MacN. 3. The latter passage was cited with approval by the P. C., in *Gopeekrist* v. *Gungapersaud*, 6 M. I. A. 77, but this point was not then before them. M. Gibelin states the law with the same generality. 1 Gib. 126; 2 Gib. 14; and Dr. Wilson, Works, v. 69.

(*e*) *Sudanund* v. *Bonomallee*, Marsh. 320; S. C. 2 Hay, 205.

(*f*) *Nallatambi* v. *Mukunda*, 3 Mad. H. C. 455. See too *per Turner*, C. J., *Ponnappa* v. *Pappuvayyangar*, 4 Mad. 47.

Power over ancestral movables.

this was only the sort of family arrangement which the Mayukha intimates as being within the powers of the head of the family (*g*). In any case the remark was extra-judicial, as the learned Judge went on to decide that none of the property sued for was ancestral. In a later Madras case, a son had sued for a declaration of his right to succeed to the whole of the ancestral property, movable and immovable, in his father's possession, and for an injunction against waste. The original and appellate Courts decreed in his favour as regards the immovable, but not as regards the movable, property, "on the ground that the defendant had the absolute right to dispose of such portion." The High Court dismissed the suit, considering that the plaintiff was claiming a right to the whole property, which he did not possess. They did not notice the distinction taken below between movables and immovables, simply observing, "As only son he has a present proprietory interest in one undivided moiety of the property, and nothing more. Consequently, the suit for the establishment of an existing reversionary right in him as heir to the whole property on the death of the defendant, and the decrees declaring such rights, are groundless" (*h*). In the North-West Provinces the point has been spoken of as being "the subject of much discussion." The question then before the Court was whether ancestral movables were chargeable with maintenance. This it was held that they were, since whatever might be the father's power of disposal, they were not the subject of such separate ownership by him as to be free from the ordinary charges affecting Hindu inheritance (*i*). In one case in the Privy Council, where the extent of a father's power of disposal *inter vivos* became material, as determining his testamentary power, the Judicial Committee said that in cases under the Mitakshara law, "a Hindu without male descendants may dispose by will of his separate and self-acquired property, whether movable or

(*g*) V. May. iv. 1 § 5; *ante*, 231.
(*h*) *Rayacharlu* v. *Venkataramaniah*, 4 Mad. H. C. 60.
(*i*) *Shib Dayee* v. *Doorga Pershad*, 4 N.-W. P. 63.

Power over ancestral movables.

immovable; and that one having male descendants may so dispose of self-acquired property, if movable, subject perhaps to the restriction that he cannot wholly disinherit any one of such descendants" (*k*). Here it is not suggested that he had any such power over movables, when not self-acquired but ancestral. A case of exactly that nature was recently before the Privy Council on appeal from Madras. There it was attempted to set aside a will by which the testator left only about one-eleventh of his whole property to his only son, bequeathing the rest to his divided brother. The property was all movable (*l*). The lower Court found that the property was self-acquired, and *therefore* held the will valid. On appeal the entire argument before the Judicial Committee was directed to overthrow, or support, this finding. It was never contended on behalf of the respondent in any of the Courts that the father would have had an absolute power of disposition over the property, as being movable, even if it was ancestral—though such an argument, if well founded, would have been a complete answer to the contention of the appellant (*m*). Of course this is only a negative inference. But considering the experience of the counsel who appeared for the respondent, it seems deserving of much weight. The point was raised in a somewhat similar case in Bombay, and decided. There a Hindu under the Mitakshara law died possessed of a large amount of ancestral movable property, and with two undivided sons. By his will he bequeathed to one of his sons nearly the whole of the property. The Court, after reviewing the provisions of the Mitakshara and Mayukha, and the *dicta* in Marshall and 12 Moore I. A already quoted (*ante*, notes (*e. k.*)), set aside the will. They held that it could not be valid either as a gift or a partition. They said, "It would be impossible to hold a gift of the great bulk of the

---

(*k*) *Beer Pertab* v. *Maharajah Rajender*, (Hunsapore) 12 M. I. A. 38; S. C. 9 Suth. (P. C.) 15.

(*l*) It is not so stated in the report, probably because no argument was directed to the point, but the fact was so. It was all in Government paper, except two or three houses of trifling value.—J. D. M.

(*m*) *Pauliem Valloo* v. *Pauliem Sooryah*, 4 I. A. 109; S. C. 1 Mad. 252.

family property to one son, to the exclusion of the other, to be a gift prescribed by texts of law; for the texts which we next quote distinctly prohibit such an unequal distribution" (*n*). That is to say, the Court adopted the opinion of Sir *Thomas Strange*, that the father has a special power of dealing with ancestral movable property, but only for certain very special purposes, specified by the Mitakshara. Whenever the case arises again, the contention probably will be to bring the alienation within those purposes.

Power over ancestral movables.

§ 311. Except in this instance, and in regard to the liability for his debts (§ 284), there is under Mitakshara law no distinction between a father and his sons. They are simply coparceners (*o*). So long as he is capable, the father is the head and manager of the family. He is entitled to the possession of the joint property. He directs the concerns of the family within itself, and represents it to the world (*p*). But as regards substantial proprietorship, he has no greater interest in the joint property than any of his sons. If the property is ancestral, each by birth acquires an interest equal to his own. If it is acquired by joint labour or joint funds, then, from the very nature of the case, all stand on the same footing. And in the same manner his grandsons and great-grandsons severally take an interest on their respective births in the rights of their fathers who represent them, and therefore in unascertained shares of the entire property (§ 247). It is, therefore, an established rule that a father can make no disposition of the joint property which will prejudice his issue, unless he obtains their assent, if they are able to give it, or unless there is some established necessity, or moral, or religious,

Authority of father

restricted by rights of issue.

(*n*) *Lakshman* v. *Ramchandra*, 1 Bom. 561, *affd.* 7 I. A. 181; practically overruling the previous decision in *Ramchandra* v. *Mahadev*, 1 Bom. H. C. Appx. 76 (2nd ed.) *acc.* *Chatturbhooj* v. *Dharamsi*, 9 Bom. 438. See also *per curiam*, 10 Bom. p. 545; *Baba* v. *Timma*, 7 Mad. 357.

(*o*) See *per curiam*, *Suraj Bunsi* v. *Sheo Prashad*, 6 I. A. p. 100; *Palanivelappa* v. *Mannaru*, 2 Mad. H. C. 417; *Rayacharlu* v. *Venkataramaniah*, 4 Mad. H. C. 61; *Shudanund* v. *Bonomalee*, 6 Suth. 256; *Lalti Kuar* v. *Ganga*, 7 N.-W. P. 279.

(*p*) *Buldeo* v. *Sham Lal*, 1 All. 77.

obligation to justify the transaction. Where his acts are questioned, he has not even the benefit of a presumption in his favour that they were necessary or justifiable (*q*). And it makes not the least difference whether the disposition is in favour of a stranger, or one of the family themselves. The test is, whether it is an infringement upon their vested rights (*r*). For instance, where the father had given a lease of land to the family dewan as a reward for faithful services, during the minority, and therefore without the consent, of his sons, the lease was set aside (*s*). On the same principle, it has been held that one of several coparceners has a right to forbid the common property being dealt with in any way that alters its character; as, for instance, by building upon it (*t*); or that places any part of it in the exclusive possession of one, so as to bar the joint rights of the others (*u*). Of course, it would be otherwise if such acts were done in the ordinary course of management, as by building on building-land, or leasing out houses held as an investment.

Life estates.

§ 312. In some cases property is vested in its holder only for life, or during good behaviour, as remuneration for services to be rendered from time to time to the Government, the village or the like. For instance, lands held on *Ghatwali* tenure in Bengal, or on *Vatan* tenure in Bombay, or by Karnams in Madras. Here, from the nature of the tenure, the land is neither alienable by the holder, nor capable of being seized in execution of a decree against him. If upon his death it passes to his heir as successor, the latter takes it as successor, and not as heir. Consequently,

(*q*) *Gurusawmi* v. *Ganapathia*, 5 Mad. 337; *Subramaniya* v. *Sadasiva*, 8 Mad. 75; *Chinnaya* v. *Perumal*, 13 Mad. 51.

(*r*) *Sham Singh* v. *Mt. Umraotee*, 2 S. D. 75 (92); *Motee Lall* v. *Mitterjeet*, 6 S. D. 71 (82); *Rajaram Tewari* v. *Lachman*, 8 Suth. 15; *Ganga Bisheshar* v. *Pirthi*, 2 All. 635.

(*s*) *Pratabnarayan* v. *Court of Wards*, 3 B. L. R. (A. C. J.) 21; S. C. *Sub nomine*, *Protap Narain* v. *Court of Wards*, 11 Suth. 343; *Muttumaran* v. *Lakshmi*, Mad. Dec of 1860, 227.

(*t*) *Jankee* v. *Bukhooree*, S. D. of 1856, 761; *Indurdeonarain* v. *Toolseenarain*, S. D. of 1857, 765; *Guru Das* v. *Bijaya*, 1 B. L. R. (A. C. J.) 108; S. C. 10 Suth. 171; *Sheopersad* v. *Leela*, 12 B. L. R. 188; S. C. 20 Suth. 160.

(*u*) *Stalkartt* v. *Gopal*, 12 B. L. R. 197; S. C. 20 Suth. 168.

it is not liable in his hands as assets for payment of the debts of the last holder (*v*).

Rights of the holder of an impartible estate under Mitakshara law.

§ 313. Until very lately it was the settled usage of those provinces of India which administer Mitakshara law that the holder of an ancestral impartible estate could not alien or encumber it beyond his own life, so as to bind his coparceners, except for purposes beneficial to the family and not merely to himself. It is very possible that a usage to this effect may have sprung up quite independently of the Mitakshara or any other law. The leading examples of estates of this class were in the nature of Royalties, whose owners did pretty much what they pleased under Native rule. A grant by one of these feudal sovereigns to a subject, not too powerful to be affronted with impunity, would naturally be set aside by his successor; not on any refined considerations of law, but simply because the power to grant could not rank higher than the power to revoke. When these estates came under the control of British tribunals, the exercise of such a right had to be placed upon a legal basis. The decisions of the Madras Sudr Court, in the early part of the century, while uniformly maintaining the substantive doctrine, varied from time to time in the grounds upon which it was supported. Ultimately, in the case of Hindus, it was rested upon the general principles by which the Mitakshara law restrains the head of a family in his dealings with the joint property. Where the impartible estate was ancestral it became the property, not only of each successive holder, but of him and of those who in respect of partible property would be his coparceners. It was true that they could not claim a share of either the *corpus* or the annual income, but it was contended that they had a vested interest in the

(*v*) *Nilmoni Singh* v. *Bakranath*, 9 I. A. 104; *Jagjivandas* v. *Imdad*, 6 Bom. 211; *Anundo Rai* v. *Kali Prosad*, 10 Cal. 677; *Muppidi Papaya* v. *Ramaya*, 7 Mad. 85 See as to the result of an abolition of the services. *Radhabai* v. *Anantrav*, 9 Bom. 198; *Appaji Bapuji* v. *Keshav Shumrav*, 15 Bom. 13. Akharagpore Ghatwali, which is held under a Zemindar and not under the Government, is alienable absolutely, and not merely for the life of the Ghatwal, *Tekait Kali* v. *Anund Roy*, 15 I. A. 18; S. C. 15 Cal. 471.

succession which the holder for the time being could not defeat at his pleasure. It was held that these conflicting rights could be reconciled by allowing each holder to alienate for his own life, but not longer, unless for purposes of family necessity. In support of this view it was pointed out that the Privy Council had frequently treated an ancestral impartible estate as joint property when questions of succession arose, and that it might with equal propriety be treated as such for purposes of alienation (*w*). A doctrine which was in this way removed from the basis of usage, and rested upon certain definite propositions of law, naturally became open to attack. The first assault upon it was delivered by *Couch*, C. J., in a case before the High Court of Bengal. There, an impartible estate, which descended by the law of primogeniture, was held during the mutiny by a rebel. He was sentenced to death, and his estate confiscated under Act XXV of 1857. (Native Army, Forfeiture for Mutiny). The family was governed by Mitakshara law. The son of the rebel claimed the estate, on the ground that by birth a joint interest in the estate vested in him, and that the confiscation could only apply to the life interest of his father. This contention was overruled. The Chief Justice said, "The question appears to be reduced to this:—Is the law of Mitakshara, by which each son has by birth a property in the paternal or ancestral estate (ch. i. s. 1, v. 27) consistent with the custom that the estate is impartible, and descends to the eldest son? The property by birth gives to each son a right to compel the father to divide the estate, which is inconsistent with the estate being impartible. On the father's death the whole estate goes to the eldest son, and the property by birth in the others has no effect. Property by birth in such an estate is a right which can never be enjoyed by the younger sons.

Effect of a forfeiture.

Right of son to impartible property denied.

(*w*) I have not thought it necessary to set out again the series of decisions in the Madras Presidency which established the practice above referred to. They will be found in §§ 312 and 313 of the 4th ed. of this work. See as to the effect of a long course of judicial decisions which are subsequently held to have been erroneous. 13 M. I. A. 500; 2 I. A. 250.

It is not only not necessary to secure the estate to the eldest son, but if it had effect in respect to the younger sons, it would prevent it. This part of the Mitakshara law cannot be reconciled with the custom, and we think we should hold it is not applicable to this estate." "The plaintiff's case, in truth, is that only the eldest son becomes a co-owner with his father, which is not the law of the Mitakshara. Either all the sons must become so, or none of them do, and the right of the eldest is only to inherit on his father's death" (*x*).

§ 314. The same question arose again in the case of the Patkoom Raj in Chota Nagpore (*y*), where upon the death of one Rajah his successor claimed the right to set aside grants which had been made by the deceased for the maintenance of the junior members. No question of Mitakshara law arose, and it appears to have been assumed that the case was governed by Bengal law, so far as that law was applicable to the case. The argument appears to have been that "the very nature of the grant which created a raj of this description, only gave each successive owner of the grant restricted rights." No evidence was adduced of any special terms annexed to the original grant, and it appeared that similar alienations had been customary in the family. The Court rejected the suits, saying, "The estate is an impartible one, but the effect of impartibility does not seem to interfere with the ordinary law as to rights beyond this, that it makes the estate pass to the eldest son. His right to alienate under the ordinary law can only be restrained by some family custom, which has the effect of overriding and controlling the general law." This of course would be so under Bengal law. This decision was affirmed on appeal. The Judicial Committee referred to a former decision of their own in the case of the Pacheet **Effects of grants for maintenance.**

(*x*) *Thakoor Kapilnauth* v. *The Government*, 13 B. L. R. 445, 458, 460; S. C. 22 Suth. 17. The Court in fact found that the suit was barred by limitation.

(*y*) *Uddoy Adittya Deb* v. *Jadublal*, 5 Cal. 113. See as to the law which governed the family, p. 116.

Raj, as showing that the mere impartibility of an estate did not render it inalienable, but that inalienability depended upon family custom which would require to be proved (z). Here again the case was under Bengal law. In a later case a dispute arose between several members of a Mitakshara priestly family, to whom a grant had been made by the Rajah of Chota Nagpore of a nature known as *putro putrodik*, which was said to be an hereditary grant, in which all the members of a Mitakshara family would share, and which would descend from father to son like any other ancestral property. One of the members asserted that a succeeding Rajah had revoked the joint grant, and conferred the whole property upon himself. The High Court held that such a revocation was unlawful. *Garth*, C. J. said "The fact that the Raj is impartible does not prevent the Maharajah for the time being from making grants of the land in perpetuity" (a). Here again it does not appear that the Raj of Chota Nagpore was governed by any law but that of Bengal. From the remarks of Mr. Justice *Mitter* in the previous case (b) that is the law which seems to govern the district in question.

§ 315. In 1888, however, a decision was given by the Privy Council in a case governed by the Mitakshara law, which struck at the root of all the previous rulings (c). The Rajah of Maholi in the North-Western Provinces had alienated seventeen of the most valuable villages of his estate in perpetuity in favour of his junior wife. His son sued for a declaration that the Rajah had according to Hindu law no right "under any circumstances except to enjoy possession of the estate during his lifetime," and had no power to alien any part of it. This claim of course was stated too widely to be correct, but the proposition really contended

(z) *Uditya Deb* v. *Jadub Lal*, 8 I. A. 248, citing *Anund Lal* v. *Maharajah Dheraj Gurrood*, 5 M. I. A. 82.
(a) *Narain Khootia* v. *Lokenath*, 7 Cal. 461.
(b) 5 Cal. p. 116.
(c) *Rani Sartaj Kuari* v. *Rani Deoraj*, 15 I. A. 51.

for was rightly laid down by the Court as follows: "In other words the plaintiff claims that, except in so far as from the nature of the estate they are inapplicable, his case must be determined according to the principles of the Hindu law, which govern joint families and their property." After examining the previous decisions of the Judicial Committee, the Court said; "If we have correctly held that the Maholi Raj estate is joint family property, then, save for urgent or necessary expenses of the family, no one member, even though he stands in the position of father, or manager, can alienate it, or any part of it, without the consent of all. Such at least is the view of the Hindu law that has been always recognised by this Court in a long, and as far as we know, unbroken series of decisions from which we should hesitate to depart." On appeal the attention of the Judicial Committee was not called to the Madras decisions, which of course added nothing to the argument relied on by the Allahabad High Court, and were only important as showing the wide extent and persistency of a course of decisions, now held to be erroneous. Their Lordships said, "The property in the paternal or ancestral estate acquired by birth under the Mitakshara law is, in their Lordships' opinion, so connected with the right to a partition, that it does not exist where there is no right to it. In the Hansapore case (*d*) there was a right to have babaana allowances as there is in this case, but that was not thought to create a community of interest which would be a restraint upon alienation. By the custom or usage the eldest son succeeds to the whole estate on the death of the father, as he would if the property were held in severalty. It is difficult to reconcile this mode of succession with the rights of a Joint Family, and to hold that there is a joint ownership which is a restraint upon alienation. It is not so difficult where the holder of the estate has no son, and it is necessary to decide who is to succeed." "If, as their Lordships are of opinion, the eldest son, where the

(*d*) 12 M. I. A. 1. There the Raj was the self-acquired property of the alienor (p. 34) and therefore, even under Mitakshara law, was absolutely at his disposal.

Mitakshara law prevails, and there is the custom of primogeniture, does not become a co-sharer with his father in the estate, the inalienability of the estate depends upon custom, which must be proved, or, it may be in some cases, upon the nature of the tenure." "The absence of evidence of an alienation without any evidence of facts which would make it probable that an alienation would have been made, cannot be accepted as proof of a custom of inalienability."

Followed in Madras.

This decision was, of course, followed, though reluctantly, by the Madras High Court. The son of the Shivagunga Zemindar sued to set aside a mining lease for 20 years granted by his late father. The High Court found "that the transaction was not one which the manager of a Joint Hindu Family, acting with ordinary care and prudence, in the exercise of his qualified power of dealing with family property should conclude." They said in reference to the recent decisions of the Privy Council: "These decisions are in direct conflict with the principle upon which the whole series of decisions in this Presidency as to the right of a zemindar to alienate depends. It has been invariably held that acts and alienations by the holder of an impartible Zemindary made to enure beyond his lifetime will, if otherwise than *bonâ fide*, and if prejudicial to the family, be set aside." Yielding, however, to the authority of the Judicial Committee, they directed an issue to enquire whether any family custom to restrain alienation could be made out. Of course none such could be established, and the plaintiff's suit was dismissed (*e*).

Right to object.

§ 316. Dispositions of property by a father can, of course, only be objected to by those who have a joint interest with him in the property, either by joint acquisition, or by birth. Where the objection is based on the latter ground, it is necessary to show that such an interest vested in the objector at his birth, or by his birth. Therefore, a son cannot object to

Interest by birth.

(*e*) *Beresford* v. *Rama Subba*, 18 Mad. 197.

alienations validly made by his father before he was born or begotten, because he could only by birth obtain an interest in property which was then existing in his ancestor. Hence, if at the time of the alienation there had been no one in existence whose assent was necessary, or if those who were then in existence had consented, he could not afterwards object on the ground that there was no necessity for the transaction (*f*). On the other hand, if the alienation was made by a father without necessity, and without the consent of sons then living, it would not only be invalid against them, but also against any son born before they had ratified the transaction; and no consent given by them after his birth would render it binding upon him (*g*). In one case the pandits advised the Madras Sudr Court that the rule as to the rights of sons extended so far, that a man "had not the power to dispose of all his property so long as he was able to beget children, but that he might alienate a small portion of the same, if by so doing he did not deprive his issue then born, or that might be born to him, of the means of support" (*h*). This futwah evidently rested on a text of *Vyasa* cited in the Mitakshara (I i. § 27): "They who are born, and they who are yet unbegotten, and they who are still in the womb, require the means of support. No gift or sale should therefore be made." But this text, so far as it applies to sons yet unbegotten, was treated by the Madras High Court as merely a moral precept, and they held that the rights of an unborn son only extended to the case of one who was in the womb at the time of the transaction complained of (*i*). Whether a son could defeat an alienation for value made when he was *in gremio matris*,

---

(*f*) *Jado* v. *Mt Ranee*, 5 N.-W. P. 113; *Raja Ram Tewary* v. *Luchmun*, 8 Suth. 16, 21; *Girdharee Lall* v. *Kantoo Lall*, 1 I. A. 321; S. C. 15 B. L. R. 187; S. C. 22 Suth. 56. A mere right to bring a suit, or to make a representation to Government for the enlargement of a grant, on the ground of fraud, is not such a right as vests in a son by birth. *Chaudhri Ujagar* v. *Chaudhri Pitam*, 8 I. A. 190; S. C. *sub nomine*, *Ujagar* v. *Pitam*, 4 All. 120.

(*g*) *Hurodoot* v. *Beer Narain*, 11 Suth. 480.

(*h*) *Soobbaputten* v. *Jungameeah*, Mad. Dec. of 1851, 3.

(*i*) *Yekeyamian* v. *Agniswarian*, 4 Mad. H. C. 307. See *Parichat* v. *Zalim*, 4 I. A. 159, where the P. C. declined to pronounce upon the point.

as he could a gift or devise, was a point which the same Court left undecided (*k*).

Adopted son.

§ 317. An adopted son stands in exactly the same position as a natural-born son, and has the same right to object to his father's alienations. In two cases pandits have relied on the above text of *Vyasa*, as enabling a son who had been adopted under an authority from the father to set aside alienations made by the father himself, before the adoption but after the authority; the ground being, that the possession of an authority to adopt by the widow was equivalent to a pregnancy (*l*). But this principle must now be taken as being overruled (*m*), and there can be no doubt that the interest of an adopted son arise for the first time on his adoption, and that he cannot after his adoption set aside any transaction which was valid when it took place, at all events as against his adopting father (*n*).

Alienation after authority.

Separate property.

§ 318. A father who is separated from his sons can, of course, dispose at pleasure, not only of his share, but of all property acquired after partition; since as to the former the sons have relinquished the rights they obtained by birth, and as to the latter they never had any such rights (*o*). *Primâ facie* one would imagine the same rule must apply as to self-acquisition, and on the same grounds. Self-acquisition *ex vi termini* does not belong to the co-heirs (*p*), and in one passage *Vijnanesvara* expressly states that "the son must acquiesce in the father's disposal of his own self-acquired property" (*q*). In an earlier passage, however, he states that the father "is subject to the control of his sons

Self-acquisitions.

(*k*) *Minakshi* v. *Virappa*, 8 Mad. 89.

(*l*) *Ram Kishen* v. *Mt. Stri Muttee*, 3 S. D 367 (489, 495); *Nagalutchmee* v. *Gopoo*, 6 M. I. A. 320, and *per curiam*, *Durma* v. *Coomara*, Mad. Dec. of 1852, 117.

(*m*) See *ante*, § 181, 182.

(*n*) *Sudanund* v. *Soorjoomonee*, 11 Suth. 436; *Rambhat* v. *Lakshman*, 5 Bom. 630.

(*o*) Narada, xiii. § 43; Vivada Chintamani, 314; Mitakshara, i. 1, § 30; *Juvar* v. *Jaki*, Mad Dec. of 1862, 1. See as to the early law, *ante*, § 212.

(*p*) Mitakshara, i. 4, § 1, 2.

(*q*) Mitakshara, i. 5, § 10.

Self-acquired immovable property.

and the rest, in regard to the immovable estate, whether acquired by himself, or inherited from his father or other predecessor," citing as an authority the text of *Vyasa* above quoted (*r*). Hence, a conflict of decision has arisen as to whether self-acquired immovables are absolutely at the father's disposal, or not. In Madras it has been held that they are not, and in this opinion Mr. Colebrooke and Sir *Thomas Strange* concur (*s*). There is also a decision of the High Court of the North-West Provinces to the same effect (*t*), and the Judicial Committee, when stating the power of disposition possessed by a Hindu under Mitakshara law, say that "if without descendants he may dispose by will of his separate and self-acquired property, whether movable or immovable; and that one having male descendants may so dispose of self-acquired property, if movable, subject perhaps to the restriction that he cannot wholly disinherit any one of such relations" (*u*). On the other hand, Mr. W. MacNaghten says, in speaking of a father's powers, "with respect to real property acquired or recovered by the occupant, he is at liberty to make any alienation or distribution which he may think fit, subject only to spiritual responsibility" (*v*). And this was expressly determined to be the law by the High Court of Bengal on a full examination of all the native texts. They said that "the apparent conflict between the passages of the Mitakshara is reconciled, if the right of the sons in the self-acquired property of the father is treated as an imperfect right incapable of being enforced" (*w*). The Vivada Chintamani, which is

---

(*r*) Mitakshara, i. 1, § 27. See the earlier law discussed *ante*, § 233, 234.

(*s*) 1 Stra. H. L. 261; 2 Stra. H. L. 436—441, 450; *Muttumaran* v. *Lakshmi*, Mad. Dec. of 1860, 227; *Komala* v. *Gangadhera*, Mad. Dec. of 1862, 41. See *Meenatchee* v. *Chetumbra*, Mad. Dec. of 1853, 61; *per curiam*, *Tara Chand* v. *Reeb Ram*, 3 Mad. H. C. 55.

(*t*) *Madhasookh* v. *Budree*, 1 N.-W. P. 153.

(*u*) *Beer Pertab* v. *Maharajah Rajendar*, 12 M. I. A. 38; S. C. 9 Suth. (P. C.) 15.

(*v*) 1 W. MacN. 2, cited with approval in the P. C., but as to a different point; *Gopeekrist* v. *Gungapersaud*, 6 M. I. A. 77. See too *Rungama* v. *Atchama*, 4 M. I. A. 1, 103; S. C. 7 Suth. (P. C.) 57.

(*w*) *Muddun Gopal* v. *Ram Buksh*, 6 Suth. 71; *Ojoodhya* v. *Ramsarun*, *ib.* 77; *Rajaram Tewary* v. *Luchmun*, 8 Suth. 15; *Sudanund* v. *Soorjo Monee*, 11 Suth. 436.

the ruling authority in the Mithila, but which is really little more than a compendium of the Mitakshara, states without any exception that a father may dispose of his self-acquired property at his pleasure, and this has been affirmed to be the law of that district by the Privy Council (*x*). The same rule has been laid down by the High Courts of Bombay, Allahabad and Madras (*y*), and M. Gibelin states that the understanding in Pondicherry is to the same effect (*z*). And similarly a man is at perfect liberty to dispose of property which he has inherited collaterally, or in such a mode that his descendants do not by birth acquire an interest in it (*a*). And whatever be the nature of the property, or the mode in which it has been acquired, a man without issue may dispose of it at his pleasure, as against his wife, or daughters, or his remote descendants, or his collateral relations (*b*). Of course, as regards collaterals it is assumed that it has not been acquired by him in such a way as to make them coparceners with him in respect of it (*c*).

Persons who have no interest by birth.

Consent.

§ 319. Any want of capacity on the part of the father to alienate the family property, may be supplied by the consent of the coparceners. Such consent may either be express, or implied from their conduct at or after the time of the transaction (*d*). Where the property is invested in trade, or in any other mercantile business, the manager of the property will be assumed to possess the authority usually exercised by persons carrying on such business (*e*). And,

(*x*) Vivada Chintamani, 76, 229, but see p. 309; *Bishen Perkash* v. *Bawa*, (P. C.) 12 B. L. R. 430; S. C. 20 Suth. 137; affirming the decision of the lower Court, 10 Suth. 287, from which it appears that the property in dispute was immovable. See too *Nana Nurain* v. *Huree Punth*, 9 M. I. A. 96, 121.

(*y*) *Gangabai* v. *Vamanaji*, 2 Bom. H. C. 318; *Sital* v. *Madho*, 1 All. 394; *Subbayya* v. *Surayya*, 10 Mad. 251.

(*z*) 1 Gib. 14.

(*a*) See *ante*, § 251. *Jugmohundas* v. *Mungaldas*, 10 Bom. 528.

(*b*) *Mulraz* v. *Chalekany*, 2 M. I. A. 54; *Nagalutchmee* v. *Gopee*, 6 M. I. A. 309; *Narottam* v. *Narsandas*, 3 Bom. H. C. (A. C. J.) 6; *Ajoodhia* v. *Kashee*, 4 N.-W. P. 31. These were all cases of wills, which of course are less favoured than alienations *inter vivos*.

(*c*) *Tayumana* v. *Perumal*, 1 Mad. H. C. 51.

(*d*) *Arumuga* v. *Ramasami*, Mad. Dec. of 1860, 258; *Vittal* v. *Ananta*, Mad. Dec. of 1861, 37; *Virasami* v. *Varada*, *ib.* 146; *Miller* v. *Runganath*, 12 Cal. 389.

(*e*) *Bemola* v. *Mohun*, 5 Cal. 792; *Samalbhai* v. *Someshvar*, 5 Bom. 38; *In re Haroon Mahomed*, 14 Bom. 189, p. 194.

of course, ratification will supply the want of an original consent; such a ratification will be inferred where a son, with full knowledge of all the facts, takes possession of, and retains that which has been purchased with the proceeds of the property disposed of (*f*). Whether the consent of all the coparceners is necessary will depend upon the question, which will be discussed hereafter, as to the power of one of several to dispose of his share (§ 327). If it is the law that he can do so, then, of course, the consent of some would bind their own shares, though not the shares of the dissenting members. If the contrary is the law, then the consent of all would be required to give any validity to the transaction. Where a grandfather alienates with the consent of his son, that consent binds an after-born grandson. But where the grandson is already in existence, and has taken a vested interest, his father's consent would not of itself bind him (*g*).

§ 320. Circumstances of necessity will also justify a father, as head of the family, in disposing of any part of the family property. In the Mitakshara the explanation which follows the text of *Vyasa*—"Even a single individual may conclude a donation, mortgage, or sale of immovable property, during a season of distress, for the sake of the family, and especially for pious purposes"—seems to limit this authority to cases where the other coparceners are minors and incapable of giving their consent (*h*). And it has been held in Bengal that the consent of those who are of age cannot be dispensed with, even where the transaction is for the benefit of the family (*i*). The contrary, however, was held in other cases, and seems to have been Mr. Colebrooke's opinion (*k*). The whole current of authorities appears to support the view that Necessity.

(*f*) *Gangabai* v. *Vamanaji*, 2 Bom. H. C. 318; *per curiam*, *Modhoo Dyal* v. *Kolbur*, B. L. R. Sup. Vol. 1020; S. C. 9 Suth. 511.

(*g*) *Buraik* v. *Greedharee*, 9 Suth. 337, where the second proposition seems to follow from the statement that the grandson, if alive at the alienation, would have had a cause of action, notwithstanding his father's consent.

(*h*) Mitakshara, i. 1; § 28, 29.

(*i*) *Muthoora* v. *Bootun*, 13 Suth. 30, acc. 1 Stra. H. L. 20; *ante*, 286.

(*k*) *Juggurnath* v. *Doobo*, 14 Suth. 80; 2 Stra. H. L. 340, 348; *Bishambhur* v. *Sudasheeb*, 1 Suth. 96, *per Muttusawmy Iyer*, J., *Ponnappa* v. *Pappuvayyangar*, 4 Mad. p. 18.

the manager of the family property has an implied authority to do whatever is best for all concerned, and that no individual can defeat this power merely by withholding his consent. The powers of the manager of a Hindu estate were very fully considered by the Privy Council in a case which is always referred to as settling the law on the subject (*l*). That was the case of a mother managing as guardian for an infant heir. Of course, a father, and head of the family, might have greater powers, but could not have less, and it has been repeatedly held that the principles laid down in that judgment apply equally to fathers, or other joint owners, when managing property governed by the Mitakshara law (*m*). Their Lordships said (p. 423): "The power of the manager for an infant heir to charge an estate not his own, is, under the Hindu law, a limited and qualified power. It can only be exercised rightly in case of need, or for the benefit of the estate. But where, in the particular instance, the charge is one that a prudent owner would make, in order to benefit the estate, the *bonâ fide* lender is not affected by the precedent mismanagement of the estate. The actual pressure on the estate, the danger to be averted, or the benefit to be conferred upon it, in the particular instance, is the thing to be regarded (*n*). But, of course, if that danger arises, or has arisen, from any misconduct to which the lender is or has been a party, he cannot take advantage of his own wrong, to support a charge in his own favour against the heir, grounded on a necessity which his wrong has helped to cause, therefore the lender in this

Hunoomanpersaud's case.

(*l*) *Hunoomanpersaud* v. *Mt. Babooee*, 6 M. I. A. 393; S. C. 18 Suth. 81; note. The same rules apply to the case of one who is *de facto* though not *de jure* manager, *ibid.* 413. See as to the position of one who deals with the holder of an impartible estate *ante*, § 314.

(*m*) *Deotaree* v. *Damoodhur*, S. D. of 1859, 1643; *Tandavaraya* v. *Valli*, 1 Mad. H. C. 398; *Soorendra* v. *Nundun*, 21 Suth. 196; *Kameswar* v. *Run Bahadoor*, 8 I. A. 8, *ante*, § 297; *Chotiram* v. *Narayandas*, 11 Bom. 605. As to alienations by manager for idol, see *post*, § 397; by female heirs, *post*, § 586. The manager for a lunatic has the same power. *Goureenath* v. *Collector of Monghyr*, 7 Suth. 5.

(*n*) See *Deotaree* v. *Damoodhur*, *ubi sup*. A mere manager cannot revive or pay time barred debts, and *a fortiori* could not pledge or sell the estate on their account. *Chinnaya* v. *Gurunatham*, 5 Mad. 169. But it is said that a widow may do so as regards debts of her husband, *post*, § 587.

case, unless he is shown to have acted *malâ fide*, will not be affected, though it be shewn that, with better management, the estate might have been kept free from debt. Their Lordships think that the lender is bound to enquire into the necessities for the loan, and to satisfy himself as well as he can, with reference to the parties with whom he is dealing, that the manager is acting in the particular instance for the benefit of the estate (*o*). But they think that if he does so enquire, and acts honestly, the real existence of an alleged sufficient and reasonably credited necessity is not a condition precedent to the validity of his charge (*p*), and they do not think that under such circumstance he is bound to see to the application of the money (*q*). It is obvious that money to be secured on any estate is likely to be obtained upon easier terms than a loan which rest on mere personal security, and that, therefore, the mere creation of a charge securing a proper debt, cannot be viewed as improvident management; the purposes for which a loan is wanted are often future, as respects the actual application, and a lender can rarely have, unless he enters on the management, the means of controlling and directing the actual application. Their Lordships do not think that a *bonâ fide* creditor should suffer when he has acted honestly and with due caution, but is himself deceived."

§ 321. The case before the Privy Council was one of mortgage and not of sale. But it is evident that the same principles would apply in either case. A prudent manager should, of course, where it is possible, pay off a debt from

Necessity justifying sale.

(*o*) See *Nowrutton* v. *Baboo Gouree*, 6 Suth. 193; *Pertab Bahadur* v. *Chitpal Singh*, 19 I. A. 33; *Lala Amarnath* v. *Achan Kuar*, 19 I. A. He is not bound to inquire into the causes which produced the necessity. *Mohabeer* v. *Joobha*, 16 Suth. 221; S. C. 8 B. L. R. 38; *Sheoraj* v. *Nukchedee*, 14 Suth. 72. A stranger purchasing from a guardian who sells or mortgages under the authority of the Court, given under Act XL of 1858, § 18, (Bengal—Minors) is protected unless he himself has been guilty of actual fraud. *Sikher Chund* v. *Dulputty*, 5 Cal. 363. And see Act V of 1881, § 90, (Probate and Administration) as to the powers of alienation of an executor by leave of the Court.

(*p*) See *Soorendro* v. *Nundun*, 21 Suth. 196; *Ratnam* v. *Govindarajulu*, 2 Mad. 339.

(*q*) See *Sundarayan* v. *Sitaramayan*, Mad. Dec. of 1861, 1, where the head of the family misappropriated the money which he had raised.

savings rather than by a sale of part of the estate (*r*), and it might be more prudent to raise money by mortgage than by sale. On the other hand, where the mortgage was at high interest, it might be more prudent to sell than to renew (*s*). In every case the question is one of fact, whether the transaction was one which a prudent owner, acting for his own benefit, would enter into. A sale of part of the property in order to raise money to pay off debts which bound the family, or to discharge the claims of Government upon the land, or to maintain the family, or to perform the necessary funeral or marriage or family ceremonies, would be proper if it was prudent or necessary (*t*). And where there are binding debts, which cannot otherwise be met, a sale will be justifiable to pay them off, even though there was no actual pressure at the time in the shape of suits by the creditors (*u*). For the manager is not bound, and indeed ought not, to put the estate to the expense of actions. *A fortiori*, of course, such dealings will be justified where there are decrees in existence, whether, *ex parte* or otherwise, which could at any moment be enforced against the property (*v*). And the same circumstances which would justify the sale of part, might justify the sale of the whole property, though, of course, a very strong case would have to be made out.

Ancestral debts. § 322. It must be owned that the principle of the Mitakshara that sons have a right to control their father in the alienation of the family property, is almost nullified by the other principle that they are bound after his death to pay his debts, even though contracted without necessity; and

(*r*) *Bukshun* v. *Doolhin*, 3 B. L. R. (A. C. J.) 423; S. C. 12 Suth. 337.

(*s*) *Muthoora* v. *Bootun*, 13 Suth 30. Whether there is a necessity for borrowing at an unusually high rate of interest is itself a matter to which the lender should apply his mind, and the Court may reduce the interest while affirming the loan. *Hurronath Roy* v. *Rundhir Singh*, 18 I. A. 1; S. C. 18 Cal. 311.

(*t*) *Bishambhur* v. *Sudasheeb*, 1 Suth. 96; *Sacaram* v. *Luxumabai*, Perry, O. C. 129; *Saravana* v. *Muttayi*, 6 Mad. H. C. 371; *Babaji* v. *Krishnaji*, 2 Bom. 666. See *Kullar* v. *Modho Dhyal*, 5 Wym. 28, where it is said the transaction must be necessary, and not merely advantageous.

(*u*) *Kaihav* v. *Roop Singh*, 3 N.-W. P. 4.

(*v*) *Purmessur* v. *Mt. Goolbee*, 11 Suth. 446; *Sheoraj* v. *Nukchedee*, 14 Suth. 72.

binding character to debts which were contracted by the official head and representative of the family, while the religious obligation would assume greater prominence in proportion as the secular obligation was weakened. The tendency would be to reconcile a conflict of rights, which was becoming important, by allowing the sons to restrain their father in his dealings with the property before they matured into transactions which conferred rights upon others. Where such rights had been created, it might fairly be held, if a struggle ensued between the interest of a son in the paternal property and the interest of a creditor or a purchaser claiming by virtue of the father's acts, that the latter interest should prevail, as being the older, and enforced by a double sanction. Where the rival interest was that of a collateral coparcener, who was under no religious obligation to discharge the liabilities of the debtor, a contrary decision would result (*x*).

Pious gifts.

Another ground upon which alienations are valid, though made without necessity, is in the case of pious gifts. These, no doubt, were looked upon by the Brahmans as being of general benefit to the family from the store of religious merit which they procured. The subject will be treated fully in the chapter on religious endowments (§ 393).

Burthen of proof of necessity.

§ 323. Those who deal with a person who has only a limited interest in property, and who professes to dispose of a larger interest, are *primâ facie* bound to make out the facts which authorise such a disposition. But the nature and extent of the proof which they must offer will vary according to the facts of the case. In *Hunoomanpersaud's* case, it was contended that the burthen was discharged by showing an advance to the manager, and the *factum* of a deed by him, and in support of this a *dictum* of the Agra Sudder Court was quoted. Upon this the Judicial Committee remarked, "It might be a very correct course to

Proof of necessity varies.

(*x*) See *per Muthusawmy Iyer*, J., *Ponnappa* v. *Cappuvayyangar*, 4 Mad. p. 33, and *per Turner*, C. J., *ibid.* pp. 41 *et seq.*

binding character to debts which were contracted by the official head and representative of the family, while the religious obligation would assume greater prominence in proportion as the secular obligation was weakened. The tendency would be to reconcile a conflict of rights, which was becoming important, by allowing the sons to restrain their father in his dealings with the property before they matured into transactions which conferred rights upon others. Where such rights had been created, it might fairly be held, if a struggle ensued between the interest of a son in the paternal property and the interest of a creditor or a purchaser claiming by virtue of the father's acts, that the latter interest should prevail, as being the older, and enforced by a double sanction. Where the rival interest was that of a collateral coparcener, who was under no religious obligation to discharge the liabilities of the debtor, a contrary decision would result (*x*).

Pious gifts.

Another ground upon which alienations are valid, though made without necessity, is in the case of pious gifts. These, no doubt, were looked upon by the Brahmans as being of general benefit to the family from the store of religious merit which they procured. The subject will be treated fully in the chapter on religious endowments (§ 393).

Burthen of proof of necessity.

§ 323. Those who deal with a person who has only a limited interest in property, and who professes to dispose of a larger interest, are *primâ facie* bound to make out the facts which authorise such a disposition. But the nature and extent of the proof which they must offer will vary according to the facts of the case. In *Hunoomanpersaud's* case, it was contended that the burthen was discharged by showing an advance to the manager, and the *factum* of a deed by him, and in support of this a *dictum* of the Agra Sudder Court was quoted. Upon this the Judicial Committee remarked, "It might be a very correct course to

Proof of necessity varies.

(*x*) See *per Muthusawmy Iyer*, J., *Ponnappa* v. *Cappuwayyangar*, 4 Mad. p. 33, and *per Turner*, C. J., *ibid.* pp. 41 *et seq.*

adopt with reference to suits of that particular character, which was one where the sons of a living father were, with his suspected collusion, attempting, in a suit against a creditor, to get rid of the charge on an ancestral estate created by the father, on the ground of the alleged misconduct of the father in extravagant waste of the estate. Now, it is to be observed, that a lender of money may reasonably be expected to prove the circumstances connected with his own particular loan, but cannot reasonably be expected to know, or come prepared with proof of, the antecedent economy and good conduct of the owner of an ancestral estate, whilst the antecedents of their father's career would be more likely to be in the knowledge of the sons, members of the same family, than of a stranger; consequently this *dictum* may perhaps be supported on the general principle that the allegation and proof of facts, presumably in his better knowledge, is to be looked for from the party who possesses that better knowledge, as well as on the obvious ground in such suits of the danger of collusion between father and sons in fraud of the creditor of the former. Their Lordships think that the question on whom does the *onus* of proof lie in such suits as the present is one not capable of a general and inflexible answer. The presumption proper to be made will vary with circumstances, and must be regulated by and dependent on them. Thus, where the mortgagee himself, with whom the transaction took place, is setting up a charge in his favour made by one whose title to alienate he necessarily knew to be limited and qualified, he may be reasonably expected to allege and prove facts presumably better known to him than to the infant heir, namely, those facts which embody the representations made to him of the alleged needs of the estate, and the motives influencing his immediate loan. It is to be observed that the representations by the manager accompanying the loan as part of the *res gestæ*, and as the contemporaneous declarations of an agent, though not actually selected by the principal, have been held to be evidence against the heir; and as their Lordships are informed that such *primâ facie* proof has been generally required in the Supreme Court of Calcutta, between the lender and the heir, where the lender is enforcing his security against the heir, they think it reasonable and right that it should be required. It is obvious, however, that it might be unreasonable to require such proof from one not an original party, after a lapse of time and enjoyment, and apparent acquiescence; consequently, if, as is the case here as to part of the charge, it be created by substitution of a new security for an older one, where the consideration for the older one was an old precedent debt of an ancestor not previously questioned, a presumption of the kind contended for by the appellant would be reasonable" (*y*). It appears to have been the intention of the Legislature to summarise the above rulings in § 38 of the Transfer of Property Act IV of 1882. "Where any person, authorised only under circumstances in their nature variable to dispose of immoveable property, transfers such property for consideration, alleging the existence of such circumstances, they shall, as between the transferee on the one part and the transferor and other persons (if any) affected by the transfer on the other part, be deemed to have existed, if the transferee, after using reasonable care to ascertain the existence of such circumstances, has acted in good faith."

Burthen of proof

in case of decrees.

§ 324. One point as to which there seems at first to be a conflict of decisions, is as to the amount of proof incumbent upon a purchaser under a decree, or upon one who lends money to the manager of an estate to pay off a decree, or who purchases a part of an estate from the manager to

(*y*) *Hunoomanpersaud* v. *Mt. Babooee*, 6 M. I. A. pp. 418—420; S. C. 18 Suth. 81, note; *Tandavaraya* v. *Valli*, 1 Mad. H. C. 398; *Vadali* v. *Manda*, 2 Mad. H. C. 407; *Saravana* v. *Muttayi*, 6 Mad. H. C. 371; *Lalla Bunseedhur* v. *Koonwur Bindeserree*, 10 M. I. A. 454; *Syud Tasoowar* v. *Koonj Beharee*, 3 N.-W. P. 8; *Chowdhry* v. *Brojo Soondur*, 18 Suth. 77; *Sikher Chund* v. *Dulputty*, 5 Cal. 363; *Makundi* v. *Sarabsukh*, 6 All. 417; *Lal Singh* v. *Deo Narain*, 8 All. 279; *Gurasawmi* v. *Ganapathia*, 5 Mad. 337. Where a son attempts to defeat an alienation by his father, or to escape from his debts by alleging immorality or illegality, the burthen of establishing such a state of things rests upon him. *Subramaniya* v. *Sadasiva*, 8 Mad. 75.

supply him with funds for that purpose. Is the production of a *bonâ fide* decree sufficient of itself to establish a case of necessity; or is it incumbent upon the purchaser or creditor to go further, and to show that the decree was passed for a purpose which would bind the estate? The result of the decisions appears to be, that the party who relies on the decree is entitled to assume that it was properly passed, and that everything done under it was properly done. But the extent to which this will benefit him depends upon the nature of the decree, and the person against whom it was given, and upon the form of the proceedings taken in execution of the decree. It is evident that a decree may be one which upon its face, and by the mere fact that it was passed, binds the person against whom it is enforced. Or it may be one which will not bind him unless something was proved in the course of the case, and that something may or may not have been proved. Again; the form of the decree, and of the proceedings taken under it, may show that the creditor, while only suing his debtor by name, sued him as the representative of the family, in order to bind its property. Or, conversely, it may appear that although the creditor had a remedy, which he might have enforced, against the whole family and its property, he chose to restrict his claim to his original debtor and the interests of that debtor. Where the decree is against a father, it conclusively establishes that there was a debt due by him, and as against his issue nothing more is necessary. It is not, as we have seen, necessary to show that the debt was for the benefit of the family. Where property is sold under such a decree, "the purchaser is not bound to go back beyond the decree to ascertain whether the Court was right in giving the decree, or having given it, in putting up the property for sale under an execution upon it" (*z*). And, of course, the same rule would apply where

---

(*z*) *Per curiam*, *Muddun Thakoor* v. *Kantoo Lall*, 1 I. A. 321, 334; S. C. 14 B. L. R. 187; S. C. 22 Suth. 56; *ante*, §§ 289, 297; *Bhagbut Pershad* v. *Mt. Girja Koer*, 15 I. A. 99; S. C. 15 Cal. 317. See numerous cases following this decision; *Bhowna* v. *Roopkishore*, 5 N.-W. P. 89; *Budree* v. *Kantee*, 23 Suth. 260; *Kooldeep* v. *Runjeet*, 24 Suth. 231; *Sheo Pershad* v. *Soorjbunsee*, *ib.* 281; *Burtoo* v. *Ram Purmessur*, *ib.* 364; *Anooragee* v. *Bhugobutty*, 25 Suth. 148;

Transactions founded on decrees.

a minor sought to set aside a sale made by his guardian in order to pay off a decree against the minor himself (*a*); or where the transaction was disputed by an heir, not being a coparcener, for he is bound to pay the debts of the person whose estate he takes (§ 302). But it would be otherwise where the decree was given against a simple coparcener. It would be a perfectly valid decree against him, and might during his life be enforced by execution and sale of his interest in the property (§ 305). But as his debt would not bind his coparceners or their sh r in the property, unless it was contracted by their consent or for their benefit (§ 308), so a decree against him can create no higher liability. It ascertains his debt, but does no more. If it is intended to procure payment of the debt, directly or indirectly, out of the shares of the other members, the creditor must show that the debts themselves were such as to be properly binding upon those who have not personally incurred them (*b*). This proof must be given in a suit to which the joint members of the family are parties, and in which they can resist the allegations made against them. If the managing member of the family executes a document which would bind the other members, the proper course is to sue them all. If the creditor chooses, he may only sue the person who executed the document. But if he adopts this course, his execution will only take effect upon the share of the execution debtor. He cannot enforce it against the other members (not being the sons of the debtor) merely by proving that the transaction was entered into for the benefit of the family. This only shows that he had a larger

---

Ramsahoy v. *Mohabeer*, *ib.* 185; *Wajed Hossein* v. *Nankoo*, *ib.* 311; *Luchmi* v. *Asman*, 2 Cal. 213; S. C. 25 Suth. 421; *Sivasankara* v. *Parvati*, 4 Mad. 96. As to how far it is necessary to make the sons parties to suits against a father to enforce his sales or mortgages or to recover debts due by him, see *ante*, §§ 285—296A. As to the extent to which decrees are conclusive against the sons, see *ante*, §§ 297—299.

(*a*) *Sheoraj* v. *Nukchedee*, 14 Suth. 72.

(*b*) *Saravana* v. *Muttayi*, 6 Mad. H. C. 371; *Pareyasami* v. *Saluckai*, 8 Mad. H. C. 157; *Reotee* v. *Ramjeet*, 2 N.-W. P. 50; *Venkatasami* v. *Kuppaiyan*, 1 Mad. 354; *Venkataramayyan* v. *Venkatasubramania*, *ib.* 358; *Loki* v. *Aghoree*, 5 Cal. 144; *Gangulu* v. *Ancha*, 4 Mad. 73.

remedy, of which he did not avail himself (c). Finally there is a class of cases in which it has been held that a suit against one member of the family must be taken as a proceeding against the family represented by him, so that the decree binds them, and may be enforced by execution against the shares of all (d). In a case where several brothers were jointly interested in a tenure, but the manager alone was registered as the owner, and he was sued for arrears of rent, and his right, title, and interest was sold in execution, it was held that the whole tenure passed to the purchaser. *Garth*, C. J., said: "Where it is clear from the proceedings, that what is sold, and intended to be sold, is the interest of the judgment debtor only, the sale must be confined to that interest, although the decree holder might have sold the whole tenure if he had taken proper steps to do so, or although the purchaser may have obtained possession of the whole tenure under the sale. But if, on the other hand, it appears that the judgment debtor has been sued as representing the ownership of the entire tenure, and that the sale, although purporting to be of the right and interest of the judgment debtor only, was intended to be, and in justice and equity ought to operate, as a sale of the tenure, the whole tenure then must be considered as having passed by the sale. And if the question is a doubtful one on the face of the proceedings, or one part of the proceedings may appear inconsistent with another, the Court must look to the substance of the matter, and not the form or language of the proceedings" (e).

(c) *Deendyal* v. *Jugdeep Narain*, 4 I. A. 247; S. C. 3 Cal. 198, *ante*, § 290; *Armugum* v. *Sabapathy*, 5 Mad. 12; *Subramanien* v. *Subramanien*, *ib.* 125; *Dorasawmy* v. *Atiratra*, 7 Mad. 136; *Viraragavamma* v. *Samudrala*, 8 Mad. 208; *Guruvappa* v. *Thimma*, 10 Mad. 316; *Abilak Roy* v. *Rubbi Roy*, 11 Cal. 293; *Maruti Narayan* v. *Lilachand*, 6 Bom. 564; *Kisansing* v. *Moreshwar*, 7 Bom. 91; *Doolar Chand* v. *Lalla Chabul*, 6 I. A. 47.

(d) *Bissessur* v. *Luchmessur*, 6 I. A. 233; 5 C. L. R. 477; *Deva* v. *Ram Manohur*, 2 All. 746; *Ram Sevak* v. *Ragnubar*, 3 All. 72; *Radha Kishen* v. *Bachhaman*, *ibid.* 118; *Gaya* v. *Rajbansi*, *ibid.* 191; *Ramnarain* v. *Bhawani*, F. B. *ibid.* 443; *Hari Saran Moitra* v. *Bhubaneswari Debi*, 15 I. A. 195; S. C. 16 Cal. 40.

(e) *Jeo Lal Singh* v. *Gunga Pershad*, 10 Cal. 996, 1001; *Kombi* v. *Lakshmi*, 5 Mad. 201, 205.

Where other funds are available.

§ 325. It has been said that where a debt is ancestral, and property is sold to meet it, the purchaser is not bound to enquire whether the debt could have been met from other sources (*f*). But, I imagine, this can only apply where there is at all events an apparent necessity for the sale. In the case where the rule was laid down, the Court went on to say, "Nor is it indicated from what sources it would have been met." In a Bengal case, the Sudder Court laid down nearly the opposite principle. They said, "It may be shown that the ostensible object of the loan was to pay off Government revenue, but, to render such a loan binding upon those who had reversionary interests upon the property, it must also be satisfactorily proved that such loan was absolutely necessary from failure of the resources of the estate itself, and was not raised through the caprice or extravagance of the proprietor" (*g*). Here the law seems to be laid down rather too strictly. The person who deals with the manager of a joint family property has to consider the propriety and necessity of the transaction in which he is engaged, not merely the propriety and necessity of paying the debt which is the pretext for the transaction. If the debt is improper or unnecessary, and known to be so by the lender, the transaction is, of course, invalid. If the payment of the debt is proper and necessary, the transaction will still be invalid, unless the lender has reasonable ground for supposing that it cannot be met without his assistance. The caprice or extravagance of the proprietor is only material as showing, either that the object of the transaction was an improper one, or that the necessity for it was non-existent.

Extravagances of manager.

Proof of payment.

Where it is once established that there was a debt which ought to be paid, and which could not be paid without a loan or sale, if the validity of the transaction is disputed on the ground that the debt had previously been discharged

(*f*) *Ajey* v. *Girdharee*, 4 N.-W. P. 110.
(*g*) *Damoodhur* v. *Birjo Mohapattur*, S. D. of 1858, 802.

or diminished, the burthen of making out this case rests upon the person who sets it up. Payment is an affirmative fact which cannot be assumed, merely on account of the antiquity of the debt (*h*).

§ 326. The powers of the manager of a joint family property who is not the father are governed by exactly the same principles as those already laid down (*i*). Of course, his personal debts are not binding upon his coparceners, as those of a father are upon his sons, and therefore alienations made by him to pay such debts would not bind them. In his case, too, there could be no suggestion that he had any greater power over movables than over immovables, except so far as arose from their own nature, and the mode in which they would usually be dealt with. Nor, of course, could his coparceners claim any interest in his self-acquired land. **Powers of manager.**

§ 327. So far we have been considering dispositions of the family property by which one member professed to bind the others, by selling or encumbering their shares as well as his own. We have now to examine the right of one member of a family governed by Mitakshara law to dispose of his own share. To an English lawyer the existence of such a right would seem obvious. Under the early Hindu law it is equally certain that no such right existed. It has become thoroughly established in Bengal, as will be seen hereafter; but in the other provinces there is a complete variance as to its existence, and the extent to which it may be exercised. The theory of the Mitakshara law is clearly against such a right. I have already pointed out (§ 246) that under that law all the coparceners are joint owners of the property, but only as members of a corporation in which **Right of coparcener to dispose of his share.**

(*h*) *Cavaly Vencata* v. *Collector of Masulipatam*, 11 M. I. A. 619, 633; S. C. 2 Suth. (P. C.) 61.

(*i*) A son does not by the mere absence of his father acquire the powers of alienation or mortgage vested in the managing member. *Patil Hari* v. *Hakamchand*, 10 Bom. 363. See as to the powers of alienation possessed by the Karnaven of a Malabar Tarwaad. *Kombi* v. *Lakshmi*, 5 Mad. 201; *Kalliyani* v. *Narayana*, 9 Mad. 266.

there are shareholders, but no shares. The family corporation remains unchanged, but its members are in a continual state of flux. No one has any share until partition, because until then it is impossible to say what the share of each may be. It will be larger one day, when a member dies; smaller the next, when a member is born (*k*). The right of the members to a partition has been slowly and reluctantly admitted. But this right carries with it the consequence of being cut off from the benefits of sharing in the family property, and participating in its future gains. If any member were allowed, from time to time, to sell his share in the joint family property, without severing himself from the family by partition, he would be securing the advantages of a division without submitting to its inconveniences. He would be benefiting himself by the exclusive appropriation of a part of the property which had never become his. He would be injuring the family by diminishing their estate, and, at the same time, he would be retaining the right to profit by the future gains of their industry. No doubt the amount so disposed of might be taken into account in the event of a subsequent partition. But the rules of Hindu law contemplate the continuance of the family union, not its disruption. Until a partition took place he would have been in a position of exceptional advantage. It would be like the case of a partner who claimed the right to withdraw his capital from the concern at pleasure, without withdrawing himself. Even before partition such alienations would be subversive of the family system. That system assumes that each member of the family is supplied out of its funds in proportion to his requirements, as often as they arise, the unspent balance of each year being carried over to the capital for the benefit of all. There is no such thing as a system of individual accounting, with a ledger opened in the name of each member, and a debiting to him of his expenses, and a crediting of his proportion of the

---

(*k*) See *per curiam*, *Sadabart Prasad* v. *Foolbash Kooer*, 3 B. L. R. (F. B.) 44; S. C. 12 Suth. (F. B.) 1.

income. But if any member were allowed to dispose of his share, such a system would be necessary; and upon taking the annual account, it might turn out that the amount of income to which he was entitled was not sufficient to defray his expenses. The anomaly would then arise, that a member of the undivided family would either not be entitled to be maintained at all, or would be maintained as a matter of charity, and not of right. Finally, the permission to alienate without a partition would necessarily have the effect of introducing strangers into the coparcenary, without the consent of its members, and defeating the right of survivorship, which they would otherwise possess.

Rights of coparcener in joint property.

His power of alienation.

§ 328. Of course, nothing is to be found in the earlier writers upon the subject. They did not notice the point, because such an occurrence did not present itself to their minds at all. An alienation of family property, even with the consent of all, was probably a very rare event. But as property began more frequently to pass from hand to hand, the circumstances which would justify an alienation began to be defined. *Vyasa* says, "A single parcener ought not, without the consent of his coparceners, to sell or give away immovable property of any sort, which the family hold in coparcenary. But at a time of distress, for the support of his household, and particularly for the performance of religious duties, even a single coparcener may give, mortgage or sell the immovable estate" (*l*). Not, be it observed, his own share for his own private benefit. So *Narada* mentions joint property among the eight kinds of things that may not be given, though he expressly authorizes divided brothers to dispose of their shares as they like (*m*). And the author of the *Vivada Chintamani*, while commenting on, and approving, these texts, gives as his reason, "for none has any right over them according to common sense." He adds in another passage: "What belongs to many may be

(*l*) 1 Dig. 455; 2 Dig. 189.

(*m*) Narada, Pt. II. iv. § 4, 5; xiii. § 42—43; acc. Vrihaspati, 2 Dig. 98; Dacsha, *ib*. 110.

given with their assent. Joint ancestral property may be given with the assent of all the heirs" (*n*). Probably all

Power to dispose of share.

these passages referred to the powers of the father or manager. The Mitakshara and Mayukha in laying down the right of alienation are evidently dealing with the case of the father as representing the entire family (*o*). The idea of any individual acting solely on his own account does not seem to have occurred to them. The same view is laid down unhesitatingly by Mr. W. MacNaghten. He says, "A coparcener is prohibited from disposing of his own share of joint ancestral property; and such an act where the doctrine of the Mitakshara prevails (which does not recognize any several right until after partition, or the principle of *factum valet*), would unquestionably be both illegal and invalid" (*p*). On the other hand, Mr. Ellis, writing of the Madras Presidency, thought a sale would be valid to the extent of the alienor's own share (*q*). Mr. Colebrooke seems to have been in much uncertainty upon the point. The result of his various opinions appears to be, that a gift by one co-heir of his own share would be certainly invalid, and that a sale or mortgage would in strictness be also illegal; but that in the latter case "equity would require redress to be afforded to the purchaser, by enforcing partition of the whole or of a sufficient portion of it, so as to make amends to the purchaser out of the vendor's share" (*r*). This opinion was adopted by Sir *Thomas Strange* in his book, and acted on by him from the Bench (*s*).

§ 329. It is probable that the first inroad upon the strict law took place in enforcing debts by way of execution. In strict logic, of course, what a man cannot do directly by way of sale, he ought not to be allowed to do indirectly through the intervention of a decree-holder. But we have already

(*n*) Vivada Chintamani, pp. 72, 77.
(*o*) Mitakshara, i. 1, § 27—32; V. May., iv. 1, § 3—5.
(*p*) 1 W. MacN. 5. (*q*) 2 Stra. H. L. 350.
(*r*) 2 Stra. H. L. 344, 349, 433, 439.
(*s*) 1 Stra. H. L. 200—202; *Sashachella v. Ramasamy*, 2 N. C. 234 [74]; *post*, § 331.

seen that the Hindu law ascribed great sanctity to the obligation of a debt, and, in the case of a father, enabled him to defeat the rights of his sons, through the medium of his creditors, though it denied him the power to do so by an express alienation (§ 278). It would be a natural transition to extend this principle to all coparceners, so far as to allow a creditor to seize the interest of any one in the joint property as a satisfaction of his separate debt. There are decisions in which it has been held that even this cannot be allowed in cases under the Mitakshara law (*t*). But the contrary rule has been repeatedly laid down in all the Presidencies, and has been recently affirmed by the Privy Council. It may be taken as settled that under a decree against any individual coparcener, for his separate debt, a creditor may during the life of the debtor seize and sell his undivided interest in the family property (*u*). The decisions which show that this cannot be done after the death of the debtor have been already stated (§ 305). There may be greater difficulty in determining how the right of the purchaser at the sale under the decree is actually to be enforced. In Bengal, where the coparceners hold in quasi-severalty, each member has a right before partition to mark out his own share, and to hold it to the exclusion of the others. Accordingly, it has been held that the purchaser at a Court sale of the rights of one member is entitled to be put into physical possession even of a part of the family house; the only remedy of the other members being to purchase the rights of the debtor at the auction sale (*v*). But it is other-

Share may be seized in execution.

Right of purchaser.

(*t*) *Nana Tooljaram* v. *Wulubdas*, Morris, 40; *Bhyro Pershad* v. *Basisto*, 16 Suth. 31.

(*u*) *Valayooda* v. *Chedumbara*, Mad. Dec. of 1855, 234; *Subbarayudu* v. *Gopavajjulu*, Mad. Dec. of 1860, 247; *Virasvami* v. *Ayyasvami*, 1 Mad. H. C. 471; *Vasudev* v. *Venkatesh*, 10 Bom. H. C. 139; *Pandurang* v. *Bhaskar*, 11 Bom. H. C. 72; *Udaram* v. *Ranu*, *ib.* 76; *Gour Pershad* v. *Sheodeen*, 4 N.-W. P. 137; *Deendyal* v. *Jugdeep*, 4 I. A. 247; S. C. 3 Cal 198; overruling *Jugdeep* v. *Deendial*, 12 B. L. R. 100; S. C. 20 Suth. 174; *Venkataramayyan* v. *Venkatasubramania*, 1 Mad. 358; *Suraj Bunsi Koer* v. *Sheo Proshad*, 6 I. A. 88; S.C. 5 Cal. 148; *Jallidar* v. *Ramlal*, 4 Cal. 723; *Rai Narain* v. *Nownit*, 4 Cal. 809. The purchaser does not become a coparcener whose assent is required to any future dealings with the property by the remaining members; *Ballabh* v. *Sunder*, 1 All. 429; *Ganraj* v. *Sheozore*, 2 All. 898.

(*v*) *Ramtonoo* v. *Ishurchunder*, S. D. of 1857, 1585; *Koonwur* v. *Shama Sooonduree*, 2 Suth. (Mis.) 30; *Eshan Chunder* v. *Nund Coomar*, 8 Suth. 239.

wise in cases under Mitakshara law, where no member has a right, without express agreement, to say that any specific portion is exclusively his. Consequently, the purchaser at a Court auction cannot claim to be put into possession of any definite piece of property (*w*). As the Judicial Committee said in one case, "No doubt can be entertained that such a share is property, and that a decree-holder can reap it. It is specific, existing and definite ; but it is not properly the subject of seizure under this particular process, but rather by process direct against the owner of it, by seizure, or sequestration, or appointment of a receiver" (*x*). In cases which have occurred in Bombay, the High Court has held that the only mode in which the execution purchaser can enforce his rights is by a suit for a partition of the debtor's share in the whole estate, to which, of course, he must make all the members of the family parties. In carrying out the decree for partition, the Court will, as far as they can with regard to the interests of others, try to award to the purchaser any specific portion which the debtor may have originally pledged, mortgaged, or sold. The purchaser cannot sue for a partition of part of the property only, because an account of the whole estate must be taken, in order to see what interest, if any, the debtor possesses (*y*). On the other hand, even prior to partition, the purchaser of the interests of one coparcener is a tenant in common with the others. Therefore, if he has got into possession of what was formerly enjoyed by the debtor, the other members cannot treat him as a mere trespasser. If they are willing to continue the tenancy in common, they may compel him so to enjoy his share as not to interfere with a similar enjoyment by themselves. If they object to the tenancy in common, they must sue for a partition (*z*).

Right of execution creditor.

(*w*) *Kalee* v. *Choitun*, 22 Suth. 214 ; *Kallapa* v. *Venkatesh*, 2 Bom. 676.
(*x*) *Syud Tuffuzzool* v. *Rughoonath*, 14 M. I. A. 50.
(*y*) *Pandurang* v. *Bhaskar*, 11 Bom. H. C. 72 ; *Udaram* v. *Ranu*, *ib.* 76 ; *acc.* *Lall Jha* v. *Juma*, 22 Suth. 116 ; *Jallidar* v. *Ramlal*, 4 Cal. 723 ; *Maruti* v. *Lilachand*, 6 Bom. 564 ; *Venkatarama* v. *Meera Labai*, 13 Mad. 275.
(*z*) *Mahabalaya* v. *Timaya*, 12 Bom. H. C. 138 ; *Babaji* v. *Vasudev*, 1 Bom. 95 ; *Kallapa* v. *Venkatesh*, 2 Bom. 676 ; *Patil Hari* v. *Hakamchand*, 10 Bom. 363. See *post*, § 452.

§ 330. The step from holding that the share of one member can be sold under a decree, to holding that he can sell it himself, is such an easy one, that it is surprising that those who admit the former right should deny the other. Yet it will be found that it is denied by the High Courts of Bengal and the North-West Provinces, while it is admitted by the High Courts of Madras and Bombay. The reason appears to be that in Bengal the right of even an execution creditor was originally not admitted. It was denied in 1871 in a decision which was not appealed against (*a*), and was only finally established by the Privy Council in an appeal which reversed a later decision of 1873 (*b*). Consequently, an unbroken current of decisions maintained a practice in conformity with the theory. In Madras and Bombay the earlier decisions negatived the right of a coparcener to alien his share. But the right of the execution creditor was admitted, and therefore the analogous right of the coparcener was ultimately recognized. As the question may still be treated as uncertain, it will be advisable to show rather fully what the state of the authorities really is.

Conflict of authority as to voluntary alienation.

Bengal.

§ 331. The earliest case actually decided in Madras was one before Sir *Thomas Strange* in 1813. There, one of two undivided brothers had mortgaged family property for his private purposes. A suit was first brought by the other brother to declare that the mortgage was not binding upon his share of the property. In this suit an account and partition was decreed. A cross suit was brought by the mortgagee against both brothers for payment and sale of the property mortgaged. The decree was that the suit should be dismissed against the second brother, that the share of the mortgagor should be held bound for payment of whatever was due upon the mortgage, but that no part of the property comprised in the bond and mortgage should be sold, until the account and partition directed under the original decree

Madras.

(*a*) *Bhyro Pershad* v. *Basisto*, 16 Suth. 31.
(*b*) *Deendyal* v. *Jugdeep*, 4 I. A. 247 ; S. C. 3 Cal. 198.

was completed. These proceedings were submitted to Mr. Colebrooke, and were approved of by him, subject to a doubt whether the charge was valid even for the share of the alienor (c). In a case in 1853 the Madras Sudr Court appears to have held a sale by one of several members to be valid for his share, even without a partition (d). On the other hand, the opinion of a pandit of the Tellicherry Court is recorded, which supports the doubt expressed by Mr. Colebrooke. In reply to a question, "Can one of an undivided family, consisting of two only, dispose of half the property, leaving his coparcener's moiety undisturbed?" he answered: "It is stated in the text of *Narada* that it is necessary that a division should be previously made, with the concurrence of all the members; wherefore the disposing to the extent of one's share at discretion is not legal" (e). This principle was followed by the Sudr Court in three cases in 1859 and 1860, when they held that a sale by an undivided member was not valid, even within the limits of his individual share, unless made under emergent circumstances (f).

Alienation of share.

Sanction by High Court of Madras.

§ 332. In this state of things the question came before the High Court of Madras. One of two brothers, members of an undivided family, had mortgaged one of two houses which formed part of the family property, for his own personal debt. He was then sued in an action for damages for a tort, and judgment was recovered against him. The judgment creditor took out execution, and, under a writ of *fi. fa.*, the Sheriff seized and sold the debtor's interest in the mortgaged house and also in another. The purchaser sued both brothers to recover possession. *Scotland*, C. J., decided that both the mortgage and the execution stood on the same footing; that each was valid to the extent of the alienor's share, and that "What the purchaser or execution creditor of the copar-

(c) *Ramasamy* v. *Sashachella*, 5 N. C. 234, 240 [74].
(d) *Chinnapiel* v. *Chocken*, Mad. Dec. 1853, 220.
(e) 2 Stra. H. L. 451.
(f) *Ramakutti* v. *Kallaturaiyan*, Mad. Dec. of 1859, 270; *Kanakasabhaiya* v. *Seshachala*, Mad. Dec. of 1860, 17; *Sundara* v. *Tegaraja*, *ib.* 67.

cener is entitled to is the share to which, if a partition took place, the coparcener himself would be individually entitled, the amount of such share, of course, depending upon the state of the family" (*g*). This decision has since been treated as the ruling authority in Madras, and has been repeatedly followed (*h*). And the Court enjoined a father against alienating more than his share of the undivided property, but refused to interfere with alienations which appeared to be within his share (*i*). In all these cases the transaction was enforced during the life of the alienor, and the principle was stated to be, that as the alienor could himself have obtained a partition, the Court would compel him "to give to his creditor all the remedies to which he would himself be entitled as against the object matter of his agreement" (*k*). The same ruling was applied where a partition had become impossible by death. There, a father had given a portion of the property which was less than half of the whole to his wife, by a registered deed followed by possession. After his death, his only son sued to set it aside. The Court refused even to listen to discussion as to the father's power to make such a gift; "because the law is quite settled that a Hindu can make a gift to the extent of his power, and in this case the deceased has done no more than that" (*l*). This case has, however, been recently overruled on the principle that the equity to enforce a partition which exists in favour of a purchaser for value cannot arise in favour of a mere donee (*m*). On the other hand, the High Court held that no coparcener could give his alienee a title to any

Extent of power.

(*g*) *Virasvami* v. *Ayyasvami*, 1 Mad. H. C. 471, *acc.* Transfer of Property Act, (IV of 1882) § 44, but if the transferee of a share of a dwelling-house belonging to an undivided family is a stranger, he will not be entitled to any joint possession or enjoyment of such house.

(*h*) *Peddamuthulaty* v. *Timma Reddy*, 2 Mad. H. C. 270; *Palanivelappa* v. *Mannaru*, *ib.* 416; *Rayacharlu* v. *Venkataramaniah*, 4 Mad. H. C. 60. For instance one of several coparceners may renounce his share in favour of another. *Peddayya* v. *Ramalingam*, 11 Mad. 406. No such right of alienation exists under Malabar law, where no partition is allowed. *Byari* v. *Puttanna*, 14 Mad. 38.

(*i*) *Kanukurty* v. *Vencataramdass*, 4 Mad. Jur. 251.

(*k*) 2 Mad. H. C. 417; *ante*, note (*h*).

(*l*) *Vencatapathy* v. *Lutchmee*, 6 Mad. Jur. 215.

(*m*) *Baba* v. *Timma*, 7 Mad. 357; *Ponnusami* v. *Thatha*, 9 Mad. 273; *Ramanna* v. *Venkata*, 11 Mad. 246.

specific portion of the joint property, even though such portion was less than his share. Each coparcener had an undivided share in every part of the property, and all that any member could sell was his interest in that part (*n*).

Devise of undivided share invalid.

§ 333. The above decisions were all passed before that given by the Full Bench in Bengal, which will be mentioned hereafter (§ 337). The same point, however, arose again after that decision. The question was, whether a devise by a father of ancestral immovable property was valid as against his only son. It was contended; *first*, that the father could, during his life, have given away his share of the family property; *secondly*, that his devise was valid to the same extent as his gift would have been. The Court admitted the first proposition, but denied the second. After referring to the view taken by the High Court of Bengal that no one could assign his share until it was ascertained by a partition, the Court said, "If by the word 'share' is intended specific share, the argument is, of course, valid, that a coparcener cannot, before partition, convey his share to another, because before partition it cannot be ascertained what it is. It is equally the law in Madras that a coparcener cannot, before partition, convey away, as his interest, any specific portion of the joint property. Considered in this light, the difficulties which have influenced the Calcutta High Court disappear. The person in whose favour a conveyance is made of a coparcener's interest takes what may, on a partition, be found to be the interest of the coparcener. What he so takes is, at the moment of taking, and until ascertained and severed, subject to the same fluctuations as it would be subject to, if it continued to subsist as the interest of the coparcener. But it can, at the proper period, be ascertained without difficulty, and there appears to be no reason, either derived from the Hindu law current in this Presidency, or founded upon general principles, for saying that such an interest is inalienable. With regard to the

(*n*) *Venkatachella* v. *Chinnaiya*, 5 Mad. H. C. 166.

third question we are of opiuion that the will in the case referred to cannot take effect. At the moment of death, the right of survivorship is in conflict with the right by devise. Then the title by survivorship, being the prior title, takes precedence to the exclusion of that by devise (*o*)."

Bombay decisions.

§ 334. In Bombay the decisions have taken very much the same course as in Madras. The earlier cases appear to be opposed to the right of alienation by a coparcener, and it has been laid down that a sale or mortgage by one of two undivided brothers was invalid, even for his own share of the undivided property (*p*). "In subsequent cases it appears that the Bombay Sudder Adawlut, although holding that the purchaser of the share of a parcener in Hindu family property cannot before partition sue for possession of any particular part of that property, or predicate that it belongs to him exclusively, yet was of opinion that he may maintain a suit for partition, and thus obtain the share which he has purchased" (*q*). The Supreme Court, and subsequently the High Court, recognized the right of an undivided member to sell or mortgage his undivided share, and the usage that he should do so. The whole of the previous cases are collected in an elaborate judgment pronounced by *Westropp*, C. J., in 1873 (*r*). He admitted that the strict law of the Mitakshara, and the usage following it in Mithila and Benares, was in accordance with the law laid down by the Full Court of Bengal, but stated that the opposite practice had prevailed in Western India. He concluded his review of the authorities by saying, "On the principle *stare decisis*, which induced Sir *Barnes Peacock* and his colleagues strictly to adhere to the anti-alienation doctrine of the Mitakshara in the provinces subject to their jurisdiction where the

Coheir may sell his share,

(*o*) *Vitla Butten* v. *Yamenamma*, 8 Mad. H. C. 6.

(*p*) *Ballojee* v. *Venkapa*, Bom. Sel. Rep. 216; *Bajee* v. *Pandurang*, Morris, Pt. II. 93. But see the *futwah* in Bom. Sel. Rep. 42, which seems to admit the right.

(*q*) *Per curiam*, *Vasudev* v. *Venkatesh*, 10 Bom. H. C., p. 156, where the cases are cited.

(*r*) *Vasudev* v. *Venkatesh*, 10 Bom. H. C. 139, followed *Fakirapa* v. *Chanapa*, *ib.* 162, (F. B.)

authority of that treatise prevails, we at this side of India find ourselves compelled to depart from that doctrine, so far as it denies the right of a Hindu parcener, for valuable consideration, to sell, incumber, or otherwise alien his share in undivided family property. The foregoing authorities lead us to the conclusion that it must be regarded as the settled law of this Presidency, not only that one of several coparceners in a Hindu family may, before partition, and without the assent of his coparceners, sell, mortgage, or otherwise alien, for valuable consideration, his share in the undivided family estate, movable or immovable, but also that such a share may be taken in execution under a judgment against him at the suit of his personal creditor. Were we to hold otherwise, we should undermine many titles which rest upon the course of decision, that, for a long period of time, the Courts at this side of India have steadily taken. Stability of decision is, in our estimation, of far greater importance than a deviation from the special doctrine of the Mitakshara upon the right of alienation."

The mode in which the Bombay Court enforces this right is by a decree for an account and partition, as already stated (*s*).

but not give or devise it.

§ 335. The Bombay High Court, however, while favouring the rights of a purchaser for value, show no indulgence to a volunteer; they hold that an undivided coparcener cannot make a gift of his share, or dispose of it by will (*t*). In both points they agree with the High Court of Madras, no doubt on the ground, that in the case of a gift there is no equity upon which a decree for partition would depend. The High Court, however, put their decision upon the simple ground that they were not disposed to carry the assignability of the share of a coparcener in undivided family property

---

(*s*) *Ante*, § 329.

(*t*) *Gangubai* v. *Ramanna*, 3 Bom. H. C. (A. C. J.) 66; *Tukaram* v. *Ramchandra*, 6 Bom. H. C. (A. C. J.) 249; *Udaram* v. *Ranu*, 11 Bom. H. C. 76; *Vrandavandas* v. *Yamuna*, 12 Bom. H. C. 229.

any father than they felt compelled to do by the precedents referred to, and by the traditions of the Supreme Court and Sudder Adawlut in the Bombay Presidency (*u*). No decision has as yet been given by the Privy Council as to the validity of a gift of his share by a coparcener, though the leaning of their Lordships' minds seems rather to be against it (*v*).

Extent of share how ascertained.

§ 336. If, as the Courts of Madras and Bombay lay down, the rights of a purchaser from a coparcener can only be worked out by means of a partition, a further question arises, what date must be taken as fixing the amount of interest he possesses in the family property? For instance, suppose one of two brothers grants a mortgage upon the family property for his own private benefit, and the transaction runs on until after three more brothers are born, and the father is dead, and then the creditor sues to enforce his claim—has he a lien upon one-third of the property, which was the interest of his debtor at the time of the mortgage, or only upon one-fifth, which is his interest at the time of suit? The latter view has been recently taken by the Madras High Court (*w*). Again, how is the claim to be dealt with, where his share has wholly lapsed by survivorship, and partition has become impossible—as in the case of one of several brothers dying without issue? In the present state of the authorities it would be useless to do more than indicate these difficulties.

Contrary doctrine in Bengal and N.-W. Provinces.

§ 337. When we come to the Bengal Courts, and that of the North-West Provinces, there is a complete unanimity in affirming the early doctrine. In a Mithila case which was twice referred to the Pandits, on account of a suspicion of the integrity of one of them, they pronounced, "that a gift of joint undivided property, whether real or personal, was not valid, even to the extent of the donor's share; for property cannot be sold or given away until it is defined and

---

(*u*) 12 Bom. H. C. 231; *supra*, note (*a*).
(*v*) See *per curiam*, *Lakshman* v. *Ramchandra*, 7 I. A. 195; S. C. 5 Bom. 48.
(*w*) *Rangasami* v. *Krishnayan*, 14 Mad. 408.

ascertained, which cannot be done without a division" (*x*). The same point was expressly decided in other cases from the same district (*y*). And exactly the same rule was acted on in cases from other districts, which were governed by the Mitakshara (*z*). In 1869 the question was referred to a Full Bench of the High Court of Bengal in consequence of some conflicting decisions of the High Courts of Madras and Bombay. The whole of the previous decisions and the Native texts were elaborately examined, and the Court replied that in cases governed by Mitakshara law, one sharer had no authority, without the consent of his co-sharers, to dispose of his undivided share, in order to raise money on his own account, and not for the benefit of the family. The Court stated that an opposite conclusion could only be arrived at, "by over-ruling that current of authorities by which, for nearly half a century, the law appears to have been settled, and in accordance with the principles of which it appears to have been generally understood and acted upon" (*a*). This ruling has, of course, given the law ever since within the jurisdiction of the High Court of Bengal, and would, no doubt, be regarded in the North-West Provinces as the highest confirmation of the previous decisions of that Court (*b*).

(*x*) *Nundram* v. *Kashee*, 3 S. D. 232 (310); S. C. 1 Mor. 17; confirmed, 4 S. D. 70 (89).

(*y*) *Sheo Churn* v. *Jummun*, 6 S. D. 176 (214); *Sheo Suhaye* v. *Sreekishen*, 7 S. D. 105 (123); *Mt. Roopna* v. *Ray Reotee*, S. D. of 1853, 344; *Jivan* v. *Ram Govind*, 5 S. D. 163 (193).

(*z*) *Sheo Surrun* v. *Sheo Sohai*, 4 S. D. 158 (201), see note; *Cosserat* v. *Sudaburt*, 3 Suth. 210. See decisions of the Court of the N.-W. P. cited, *Sadabart Prasad* v. *Foolbash Koer*, 3 B. L. R. (F. B.) p. 42; S. C. 12 Suth. (F. B.) 1; and *Lalti Kuar* v. *Ganga*, 7 N.-W. P. 277. These decisions have been recently approved and followed by the Allahabad High Court. *Chamaili* v. *Ram Prasad*, 2 All. 267; *Ramanand* v. *Gobind Singh*, 5 All. 384. That Court, however, seems to hold that a member of the family who has alienated his own interest cannot object to a similar alienation by another member. *Ganraj* v. *Sheozore*, 2 All. 898.

(*a*) *Sadabart Prasad* v. *Foolbash Kooer*, 3 B. L. R. (F. B.) 31; S. C. 12 Suth. (F. B.) 1.

(*b*) *Nathu* v. *Chadi*, 4 B. L. R. (A. C. J.) 15; S. C. 12 Suth. 447; *Sub nomine*, *Nuthoo* v. *Chedce*; *Haunman* v. *Baboo Kishen*, 8 B. L. R. 358; S. C. 15 Suth. (F. B.) 6; *Sub nomine*, *Honooman* v. *Bhagbut*; *Phoolbas Kooer* v. *Lall Juggessur*, 14 Suth. 340; S. C. on review, 18 Suth. 48; reversed on another point, 8 I. A. 7; S. C. 1 Cal. 226; S. C. 25 Suth. 285; *Bunsee Lall* v. *Shaikh Aoladh*, 22 Suth. 552; *Chunder Coomar* v. *Hurbuns Sahai*, 16 Cal. 137.

§ 338. Even in Bengal, however, and since the Full Bench decision, the Court has dealt with the equities of the parties in a manner which, under certain circumstances, brings about exactly the same result as is worked out by the Madras and Bombay doctrine (c). In that case, the second defendant, who was father and manager of a family governed by the Mitakshara, mortgaged the family property to the first defendant for a purpose not legally justifiable. The elder son sued on his own behalf, and on that of a minor son, to set aside the deed. The Court found that the plaintiff had assented to the transaction, consequently, only the interest of the minor was concerned. It did not appear that he had been in any way benefited. The Court, after observing that the result of setting aside the sale unconditionally would be "that the property, on going back, will come to be enjoyed by the joint family as it was before the mortgage and sale; and of necessity, by virtue of the provisions of the Mitakshara law, will return to the management of the very man (second defendant) who obtained Rs. 3,000 from the first defendant on the pretended security afforded by the mortgage, which did not seem to accord very well with equity and good conscience;" also that the Full Bench decision, which settled (3 B. L. R. (F. B.) 31; S. C. 12 Suth. (F. B.) 1) that such a deed might be set aside, refrained from saying on what terms such relief was to be granted, proceeded to point out that the father might, at any moment, claim a partition. "And plainly the first defendant is in equity entitled as against the father to insist upon his calling his share into being, and realising it for their benefit. He obtained their money by representing that he had a power to charge the joint family property, which he knew at the time he did

Equities in favour of alienee,

enforced by partition.

(c) *Mahabeer Persad* v. *Ramyad*, 12 B. L. R. 90; S. C. 20 Suth. 192. See *Udaram* v. *Ranu*, 11 Bom. H. C. 76. In no case can any right to set aside a sale upon any terms be enforced, where the member who claims the right is under any disability which would be a bar to a suit by himself for partition. *Ram Sahye* v. *Lalla Laljee*, 8 Cal. 149; *Ram Soonder* v. *Ram Sahye*, *ibid.* 919. Such a right is personal, and does not survive in favour of the heir of a person who has commenced a suit to set aside an alienation, and then died. *Padarath Singh* v. *Rajaram*, 4 All. 235.

not possess: he is, therefore, at least bound to make good to them that representation, so far as he can, by the exercise of such proprietary right over the same property as he individually possesses. Substantially the same reasoning applies to the eldest son (plaintiff), who aided his father in effecting the mortgage. On the whole, then, we are of opinion that a decree ought to be given to the plaintiffs to the effect that the property be recovered by the plaintiffs for the joint family, but that this decree must be accompanied by a declaration that on recovery, the property be held and enjoyed by the family in defined shares *viz.*, one-third belonging to the father (second defendant), one-third to the eldest son (the plaintiff), and one third to the second son, a minor; and that it be also declared that the shares of the father and of the eldest son be jointly and severally subject to the lien thereon of the first defendant for the repayment of the sum of Rs. 3,000 advanced by the first defendant to the second defendant, and interest thereon at six per cent. from the date of the loan until repayment."

Judicial Committee. Upon this decision the Judicial Committee remarked (*d*), "There appears to be little substantially different between the law thus enunciated and that which has been established at Madras and Bombay; except that the application of the former may depend upon the view the Judges may take of the equities of the particular case; whereas the latter establishes a broad and general rule defining the right of the creditor." In no case, however, can such an equity be enforced where the coparcener, who made the alienation is dead. Immediately on this event his share passes by survivorship to persons who are not liable for the debts and obligations of the deceased (*e*).

§ 339. The question now discussed has never come before the Privy Council in such a form as to require decision after formal argument. In the case of *Bhugwandeen* v.

(*d*) *Deendyal* v. *Jugdeep*, 4 I. A. 255; S. C. 3 Cal. 198.
(*e*) *Madho Pershad* v. *Mehrban Singh*, 17 I. A. 194; S. C. 18 Cal. 157.

Myna Baee (*f*), there is a *dictum* that "between coparceners there can be no alienation by one without the consent of the others." In another case, where one of several joint proprietors had mortgaged his share, the Court said, "The sharers, however, do not appear to have been members of a joint and undivided Hindu family, but to have enjoyed their respective shares in severalty. It is, therefore, clear that the mortgagor had power to pledge his own undivided share in these villages" (*g*). On the other hand, in cases where the point was directly taken, but unnecessary to be decided, the Judicial Committee treated it as still doubtful (*h*). In a later case where the point arose the Judicial Committee appear to treat the law in Madras and Bombay as being settled in the manner above stated, while they treated the contrary ruling of the Bengal Courts as a matter still open to doubt in cases within their jurisdiction (*i*). Still more recently the Committee accepted the view of the Bengal and N.-W. Provinces Courts in a case in which it was conceded that their decisions were binding in the districts governed by them (*k*).

Remedies against alienation.

§ 340. The remedies possessed by one member of a family against alienations made by another member, depend, of course, upon the view taken by the Courts of the validity of such alienations. According to the law administered in Madras and Bombay, such alienations, whatever they may profess to convey, are valid to the extent of the alienor's own interest in the property. Hence, no suit could be maintained for the absolute cancelment of such an alienation, still less for recovery of the whole property, on the ground that the illegal alienation by the father or other member had given the plaintiff the right to seek possession for him-

(*f*) 11 M. I. A at p. 516; S. C. 9 Suth. (P. C.) 23.
(*g*) *Byjnath* v. *Ramoodeen*, 1 I. A. at p. 119; S. C. 21 Suth. 233.
(*h*) *Girdharee Lall* v. *Kantoo Lall*, 1 I. A. at p. 329; S. C. 14 B. L. R. 187; S. C. 22 Suth. 56; *Phoolbas Koonwur* v. *Lalla Jogeshur*, 3 I. A. at p. 27; S. C. 1 Cal. 226; S. C. 25 Suth. 285; *Deendyal* v. *Jugdeep*, 4 I. A. at p. 252; S. C. 3 Cal. 198.
(*i*) *Suraj Bunsi Koer* v. *Sheo Proshad*, 6 I. A. 88; S. C. 5 Cal. 148.
(*k*) *Madho Pershad* v. *Mehrban Singh*, 17 I. A. 194; S. C. 18 Cal. 157.

self. But when the alienee takes exclusive possession of any specific portion of the joint property, he will be liable to be turned out at the suit of the other coparceners; for till partition each has an undivided interest in the whole, and, of course, the vendee, claiming under one co-sharer, cannot be in a better position than the person under whom he claims (*l*). And even where there has been no dispossession; if one member of an undivided family has, by gift, mortgage, alienation, or devise, disposed of the family property to a greater extent than the law entitles him to do, the other members have a right to have the transaction declared illegal, and set aside so far as it is illegal (*m*). And in such a suit the alienation would be set aside, wholly or in part, according as the doctrine of Bengal or Madras and Bombay was held to govern the case. *A fortiori*, a sale which was an absolute fraud upon the family, and known by the purchaser to be such, would be rescinded by all the Courts, as the equity by means of which it can be worked out, would absolutely fail (*n*).

Not forfeiture. Even according to the rules laid down by the Bengal Courts, a son is not entitled upon proof of alienation by his father, to apply to have his own name substituted on the registry in place of his father's name, and to have his own exclusive possession and ownership decreed, in place of that previously existing in the head of the family (*o*). But he is entitled to sue for possession of the whole property on behalf of the undivided family, although that whole includes the share of the person who makes the alienation, leaving the purchaser to take proceedings to ascertain that share by partition (*p*).

(*l*) *Venkatachella* v. *Chinnaiya*, 5 Mad. H. C. 166; *ante*, § 275.

(*m*) *Kanukurty* v. *Vencataramdass*, 4 Mad. Jur. 251; *Kanth Narain* v. *Prem Lal*, 3 Suth. 102; *Raja Ram Tewary* v. *Luchmun*, 8 Suth. 16; *Retoo* v. *Lalljee*, 24 Suth. 399; *Chinna Sunyasi* v. *Suriya*, 5 Mad. 196. As to declaratory decrees, see *Dorasinga* v. *Katama Nachiar*, 2 I. A. 169; S. C. 15 B. L. R. 83; S. C. 23 Suth. 314. As to the period of limitation, see Act XV of 1877, Sched. II. § 126; *Raja Ram Tewary* v. *Luchmun Pershad*, *ub. sup.*

(*n*) *Ravji* v. *Gangadharbhat*, 4 Bom. 29; *Sadashiv* v. *Dhakubai*, 5 Bom. 450.

(*o*) *Chutter* v. *Bikaoo*, S. D of 1850, 282; *Kanth Narain* v. *Prem Lall*, 3 Suth. 102. See cases in N.-W. P. cited, *Lalti Kuar* v. *Ganga*, 7 N.-W. P. 277.

(*p*) *Haunman* v. *Baboo Kishen*, 8 B. L. R. 358; S. C. 15 Suth. (F. B.) 6;

§ 341. It does not, however, follow that any member of the family can set aside such alienations unconditionally. The rule is that the party setting aside the sale must make good to the purchaser the amount he has paid, so far as that amount has benefited himself, either by entering into the joint assets, or from having been applied in paying off charges upon the property which would have been a lien upon it in his hands. In the leading case in Bengal (*q*) the following question was referred to a Full Bench Court, "Whether under the Mitakshara law, a son who recovers his ancestral estate from a purchaser from the father, on proof that there was no such necessity as would legalise the sale, and that he never acquiesced in the alienation, is bound in equity to refund the purchase money before recovering possession of the alienated property?" *Peacock*, C. J., replied that "in the absence of proof of circumstances which would give the purchaser an equitable right to compel a refund from the son, the latter would be entitled to recover without refunding the purchase money or any part of it. We ought to add that if it is proved to the satisfaction of the Court that the purchase money was carried to the assets of the joint estate, and that the son had the benefit of his share of it, he could not recover his share of the estate without refunding his share of the purchase money; so if it should be proved that the sale was effected for the purpose of paying off a valid incumbrance on the estate which was binding upon the son, and the purchase money was employed in freeing the estate from the incumbrance, the purchaser would be entitled to stand in the place of the incumbrancer, notwithstanding the incumbrance might be such that the incumbrancer could not have compelled the immediate discharge of it, and that the decree for the

Equities on setting aside alienation.

Deendial v. *Jugdeep Narain*, 4 I. A. 247; S. C. 3 Cal. 198; *Hurdey Narain* v. *Rooder Perkash*, 11 I. A. 26; S. C. 10 Cal. 626. See as to the right of any one to sue in respect of his own share, *Phoolbas Kooer* v. *Lalla Juggessur*, 18 Suth. 48.

(*q*) *Modhoo* v. *Kolbur*, B. L. R. Sup. Vol. 1018; S. C. 9 Suth. 511, followed in *Haunman* v. *Baboo Kishen*, 8 B. L. R. 358; S. C. 15 Suth. (F. B.) 6; *Makundi* v. *Sarabsukh*, 6 All. 417; *Ajit Singh* v. *Bijai Bahadur*, 11 I. A. 211; cf. *Wenlock* v. *River*, Dec. Co., 19 Q. B. D. 155.

Equities on setting aside alienation

recovery by the son of the ancestral property, or of his share of it, as the case might be, would be good; but should be subject to such right of the purchaser to stand in the place of the incumbrancer. It appears to me, however, that the *onus* lies upon the defendant to show that the purchase money was so applied. I do not concur with the decision which has been referred to (*r*), in which it is said that "in the absence of evidence to the contrary, it must be assumed that the price received by the father became a part of the assets of the joint family." If the father was not entitled to raise the money by sale of the estate, and the son is entitled to set aside that sale, the *onus* lies on the person who contends that the son is bound to refund the purchase money before he can recover the estate, to show that the son had the benefit of his share of that purchase money. If it should appear that he consented to take the benefit of the purchase money with a knowledge of the facts, it would be evidence of his acquiescence in the sale" (*s*).

§ 342. The doctrine laid down by the High Court of Bengal in the above case is still good law where the alienation is made by a coparcener other than a father, and is complained of by coparceners who are not his sons. But under the actual facts of that case, and since the decision in *Girdhari Lall* v. *Kantoo Lall*, (§ 285) the ruling to be applied would now be different. If the alienation were made for an antecedent debt, it would be absolutely binding on the sons. If it were not made for an antecedent debt the sons could only set it aside on paying the full purchase money, this being a debt for which their father would be liable to the purchaser as for failure of consideration on the sale being cancelled, and for which in consequence they and their share of the property would be ultimately responsible. If the property sold was not more than would fall to the father on partition, it would be open to the

(*r*) *Muddun Gopal* v. *Ram Buksh*, 6 Suth. 71.
(*s*) Acc. *Gangabai* v. *Vamanaji*, 2 Bom. H. C. 318.

Court to award it at once to the purchaser as his share, free of all claims and equities from the sons (*t*)

§ 343. When the sale was made to discharge the personal debt of the alienor, it was considered that there was no equity to refund the purchase money, on setting aside the sale. Nor did it make any difference that the defendant was an innocent purchaser for value at an auction. He had every opportunity of making enquiry, and must have known the extreme danger of purchasing an interest which had been originally bought from a single member of a joint undivided family living under the Mitakshara law (*u*). So, the value of improvements made by one who has purchased with knowledge of fraud, or after such fraud has come to his knowledge, cannot be recovered. But I apprehend it would be different where the sale was merely set aside as being beyond the powers of the vendor (*v*).

for personal debt of coheir

§ 344. An intermediate case is where the sale of the whole property is not justifiable, but a sale of part would have been justifiable, or where part of the consideration was applied to purposes so beneficial to the family, that in respect of it an equity arises in favour of the purchaser as against a member of the family seeking to set aside the transaction. In one case (*w*) the suit was by a son to set aside a conditional deed of sale executed by his father and his father's brother, so far as it affected his father's moiety of the property. It appeared that the deed was executed upon a loan of money, part of which was properly borrowed on grounds of legal necessity, while the remainder was not. The principal Sudr Amin treated the deed as valid in respect of a portion of the land in proportion to that part of the consideration money which was borrowed for and spent in a matter of legal necessity,

where sale partly justifiable.

Equities on setting aside.

(*t*) *Koer Hasmat* v. *Sunder Das*, 11 Cal. 396.
(*u*) *Nathu* v. *Chadi*, 4 B. L. R. (A. C. J.) 15; S. C. *Sub nomine*, *Nuthoo* v. *Chedee*, 12 Suth. 447.
(*v*) *Sadashiv* v. *Dhakubai*, 5 Bom. 450.
(*w*) *Rajaram Tewar* v. *Luchmun*, 4 B. L. R. (A. C. J.) 118—125; S. C. 12 Suth. 478.

and void as to the residue of the land conveyed. Sir *Barnes Peacock*, C. J., considered the correctness of this principle to be very doubtful, and intimated that in such a case the more reasonable course would be, that upon the defendant's establishing the necessity for part of the loan, the Court should decree that the deed should be set aside, and the plaintiff recover possession upon his paying the amount which was legally taken up for necessary purposes recognized by law, or that the deed should be set aside in proportion. No decision was given, however, as no relief could be given for want of necessary parties. In some later cases the course adopted was to set aside the deed on payment of so much of the consideration money as was a proper charge upon the estate (*x*).

Laches.

So also, even though the charge has not been created for family purposes, if there are circumstances of laches or acquiescence which would render it inequitable that the deed should be set aside unconditionally, the Court will compel a refund of the purchase money (*y*).

Necessity for offer to refund.

§ 345. In some cases where the Court considered that the plaintiff should have offered to refund the purchase money, and the plaint contained no such offer, the suit was dismissed, the plaintiff being at liberty to bring a fresh suit differently framed (*z*). This seems to be a mere question of pleading. If, as Sir *Barnes Peacock* said (*a*), the *onus* lies on the defendant to allege and establish circumstances which entitle him to such repayment, one would imagine that the proper course would be for the plaintiff to claim to have the deed set aside, as not being for a matter of legal necessity or with the consent of the family, and for the defendant to

(*x*) *Shurrut* v. *Bholanath*, 15 B. L. R. 350; S. C. *Sub nomine*, *Surat* v. *Ashootosh*, 24 Suth. 46. See, too, the analogous cases of alienations by a widow, *Phoolchund* v. *Rughoobuns*, 9 Suth. 108; *Mutteeram* v. *Gopaul*, 11 B. L. R. 416; S. C. 20 Suth. 187; *Konwur* v. *Ram Chunder*, 4 I. A. 52, 66; S. C. 2 Cal. 341; *Sadashiv* v. *Dhakubai*, 5 Bom. 450; *Subramania* v. *Ponnusami*, 8 Mad. 92.

(*y*) *Surub* v. *Shew Gobind*, 11 B. L. R. Appx. 29.

(*z*) *Supra*, note (*x*) 11 B. L. R. 416; *ib.*, Appx. 29; *Supra*, note (*y*). See *Durga Prasad* v. *Nawazish*, 1 All. 591.

(*a*) *Modhoo* v. *Kolbur*, B. L. R. Sup. Vol. 1018; S. C. 9 Suth. 511

get rid of this case, wholly or in part, by showing the circumstances which made out his equity to repayment. Where the plaintiff deliberately elected to rest his case upon an allegation of wasteful and extravagant borrowing, and failed to make out that case, the Court refused to allow him to repay the purchase money, and have the deed cancelled (*b*).

§ 346. When we come to Bengal law, as laid down by Jimuta Vahana, the whole of the above distinctions at once vanish. I have already (§ 235) pointed out the process by which he got rid of the principle which pervades the Benares law, that property in a son is by birth, and established the opposite principle, that a son is simply heir presumptive to his father, and entitled to nothing more than his father chooses to leave him. This doctrine, in which an admission that alienations by a father of ancestral property were immoral was coupled with an assertion that they were valid, naturally exercised the minds of English lawyers a good deal. They would have accepted the assertion as a matter of course, but they were perplexed by the admission. Accordingly, we find that Mr. W. MacNaghten laid down the law in a way which was really nothing more than the Mitakshara over again, and Sir *Hyde East* in 1819 took very much the same view (§ 236). The *Futwahs* of the pandits were persistently given in accordance with the doctrines of Jimuta Vahana. But these futwahs appeared to be contradictory, because they were applied to two different states of fact, *viz.*, alienations and distributions. To an English lawyer it seemed obvious, that if a man could give his property to strangers, he could also give it to his sons; and that if he could give everything to one son, to the exclusion of the others, *à fortiori* he could give it to all of them in any proportions he wished. But a Hindu pandit treated one proceeding as an alienation and the other as a partition. He produced one set of texts from Jimuta

Principles of Bengal law.

Apparent contradiction.

(*b*) *Muddun Gopal* v. *Ram Buksh*, 6 Suth. 74.

Vahana to show that the former proceeding was valid, and another set of texts, also from Jimuta Vahana, to show that the latter was invalid. It is not surprising that there was a good deal of confusion before the law was finally settled. As regards the right of a father in Bengal to make an unequal partition among his sons, it can hardly be said that the law is satisfactorily settled even now.

Alienations by father.

§ 347. The earliest reported case is in 1792, when a bequest (*c*) by the Zemindar of Nuddea of his entire ancestral Zemindary to his eldest son was supported. The document recited that the Zemindary was impartible, in which case, of course, it was unnecessary. The opinions of numerous pandits in different parts of the country are said to have been taken, and the majority of them declared, that whether the Zemindary had been previously exempt from division or not, the gift settling the Zemindary on the eldest son with a provision for the younger ones, was valid. This view was affirmed by the Sudr Court. Mr. Colebrooke appends a note to the case in which he agrees with the pandits' opinion, as being in accordance with the doctrines of Jimuta Vahana. He ends by saying, "No opinion was taken from the law officers of the Sudr Court in this case. But it has been received as a precedent which settles the question of a father's power to make an actual disposition of his property, even contrary to the injunctions of the law, whether by gift or by will, or by distribution of shares" (*d*). This decision was followed in 1800 by the Supreme Court, which affirmed the validity of the wills of *Rajah Nobkissen* and *Nemy Churn Mullick*, by which ancestral immovable property had been disposed of, in the former case at all events, to the prejudice of the testator's sons (*e*). And in 1812 the Sudr Court, after consulting their pandits, held that a gift by a father of his whole estate,

(*c*) The document is sometimes spoken of as a will, sometimes as a deed of gift; it seems really to have been the former.

(*d*) *Eshanchund* v. *Eshorchund*, 1 S. D. 2. The judgment of the Sudr Court will be found in 2 Stra. H. L. 447.

(*e*) F. MacN. 356, 340.

real and personal, ancestral and otherwise, to a younger son during the life of the elder was valid, though immoral, the gift of the whole ancestral landed property being forbidden (*f*). In 1816, however, the law was unsettled again by the case of *Bhowanny Churn* v. *The Heirs of Ramkaunt* (*g*). That case will be discussed more fully hereafter (§ 450), but it is sufficient here to point out, that it was a case where a father had made an unequal partition among his sons. The pandits practically found, that as a partition, it was invalid from its inequality, and that it could not be supported as a gift, because there had been no delivery of possession. The result was that the partition was set aside. The case is followed by an elaborate note in which the opinions of the pandits in this and the two previous cases in the Sudr Court are examined, and the writer intimates that those cases had probably been incorrectly decided, so far as they respect the ancestral immovable estate (*h*). It is evident, however, that the pandits would not have agreed in this view, for we find that in 1821 they pronounced opinions affirming a gift by a father of an ancestral taluq to one of his eleven sons (*i*), and in 1829 they supported a sale by a Zemindar of an ancestral taluq during the life of his son. They laid down the broad principle, "The law as current in Bengal recognizes no proprietary right in the son, so long as that of the father is existent; and therefore in the case stated, as *Ram Shunker's* (the father's) right in the soil, was existent, *Mohun Chund* (the son) could have no claim upon it" (*k*). Finally, in 1831, the same question arose again in the Supreme Court of Bengal, and was referred to the Judges of the Sudr Dewanny, who returned the following certificate: "On

Rights of sons.

(*f*) *Ramkoomar* v. *Kishenkunker*, 2 S. D. 42 (52); F. MacN. 277.
(*g*) 2 S. D. 202 (259); F. MacN. 283, 294.
(*h*) These conflicting opinions were probably before Sir *Hyde East* in 1820, when he pronounced his judgment in *Cossinaut Bysack* v. *Hurroosoondry* (2 M. Dig. 198), where he balances against each other two conflicting sets of texts, with an evident consciousness that he had got into a labyrinth to which he did not possess the clue.
(*i*) *Raujkrisno* v. *Taraneychurn*, F. MacN. 265, Appx. viii.
(*k*) *Kumla* v. *Gooroo*, 4 S. D. 322 (410).

mature consideration of the points referred to us, we are unanimously of opinion that the only doctrine that can be held by the Sudr Dewanny Adalut, consistently with the decisions of the Court, and the customs and usages of the people, is, that a Hindu, who has sons, can sell, give, or pledge, without their consent, immovable ancestral property, situated in the province of Bengal; and that without the consent of the sons, he can, by will, prevent, alter or affect their succession to such property" (*l*). This certificate has ever since been accepted as settling the law in Bengal, on the points to which it refers (*m*), and it makes no difference that the property is impartible, and descends by the rule of primogeniture (*n*). Of course there never was any doubt as to the right of a Bengal proprietor to dispose of his property to the prejudice of relations other than his own issue (*o*), as for instance to deprive his widow of her share on a partition (*p*).

Rights of coparceners.

§ 348. As regards those who are coparceners in Bengal, that is brothers, cousins, or the like, who have taken property jointly by descent, or who have acquired it jointly, there is also no difficulty. In Bengal the right of every coparcener is to a definite share, though to an unascertained portion of the whole property (§ 241). This right passes by inheritance to female or other relations, just as if it were already divided, and it may be disposed of by each male proprietor just as if it were separate or self-acquired property. And such alienations will be taken into account as part of his share in the event of a partition. But, of course, no one can dispose of more than his share, unless by consent

(*l*) *Juggomohun* v. *Neemoo*, Morton, 90; *Motee Lal* v. *Mitterjeet*, 6 S. D. 73 (85). A note follows that this certificate overrules the case of *Bhowanny Churn*. It really did nothing of the sort.

(*m*) See *per curiam*, *Ramkishore* v. *Bhoobunmoyee*, S. D. of 1859, 250; S. C. *affd.* on review, S. D. of 1860. i. 489.

(*n*) *Uddoy* v. *Jadublal*, 5 Cal. 113; *Narain* v. *Lokenath*, 7 Cal. 461.

(*o*) F. MacN. 360; *Bhowanee* v. *Mt. Taramunee*, 3 S. D. 138 (184); *Sheodas* v. *Kunwul*, 3 S. D. 234 (313), *Tarnee Churn* v. *Mt. Dasee*, 3 S. D. 397 (530). As to the rights of an adopted son, see *ante*, § 153 and note.

(*p*) *Debendra Coomar* v. *Brojendracoomar*, 17 Cal. 886.

of the others, or for necessary purposes (*q*). And so an undivided coparcener may in Bengal lease out his own share, and put his lessee in possession (*r*). But as a son has no interest in his father's property during the father's life, a sale of such property by him during the father's life would be wholly void, and it has been ruled that if the purchaser had got into possession, the son himself might recover the property from him when his own title as heir accrued. The purchaser, however, would have a right to recover the purchase-money (*s*).

§ 349. It has been held in the Allahabad High Court that an agreement by one coparcener not to alienate his share to any one except his coparcener is valid, and may be enforced, and that an alienation to a stranger made in violation of such an agreement may be set aside at the suit of the other coparceners (*t*). The former part of the ruling is, of course, beyond doubt. But it may be questioned whether the latter part would be followed by those Courts which recognize the right of a coparcener to dispose of his share. Can an agreement by a member of a family not to exercise his ordinary rights of property be enforced against a stranger, who has dealt with him in ignorance of such an agreement? In other words, can the agreement operate as anything more than a trust in favour of the other members of the family, which is ineffectual against a purchaser for value without notice of the trust? (*u*).

§ 350. Throughout the preceding paragraphs no distinc- **Cases of gift.**

(*q*) *Rajbulubh* v. *Mt. Buneta*, 1 S. D. 44 (59) ; *Prannath* v. *Calishunkur*, 1 S. D. 45 (60) ; *Anundchund* v. *Kishen*, 1 S. D. 115 (152), where, see Mr. Colebrooke's notes. *Ramkunhaee* v. *Bung Chund*, 3 S. D. 17 (22) ; *Kounla* v. *Ram Huree*, 4 S. D. 196 (247) ; *Sakhawat* v. *Trilok*, 5 S. D. 338 (397) ; 2 W. MacN. 291, 294, 296, 306 n., 313.

(*r*) *Ram Debul* v. *Miterjeet*, 17 Suth. 420 ; *Macdonald* v. *Lalla Shib*, 21 Suth. 17.

(*s*) *Gunganarain* v. *Bulram*, 2 M. Dig. 152.

(*t*) *Lakhmi* v. *Tori*, 1 All. 618. See *Lachmin* v. *Koteshar*, 2 All. 826. See *post*, §§ 387, 445.

(*u*) See *Kanna Pisharodi* v. *Kombi Achen*, 8 Mad. 381 ; *Ali Hasan* v. *Dhirja*, 4 All. 518.

tion has been drawn between gifts and transfers for valuable consideration. The High Courts of Madras and Bombay it will be remembered, allow a coparcener to alien his undivided share for value, but not by way of gift (§§ 332, 335), and according to the view taken by the High Court of Bengal, equities would arise in favour of a purchaser for value which would not exist in favour of a donee. Where a transaction can only be supported on the plea of necessity, of course a gift could never be valid. An exception may

Gifts.

exist, perhaps, in favour of gifts of a certain part of the property for pious purposes. These will be treated of at length in Chapter XII on Religious Endowments. Where property is absolutely at the disposal of its owner, as being the property of a father under Bengal law, or the separate or self-acquired property of any person, he may give it away as freely as he may sell or mortgage it (*v*), subject to a certain extent to the claims of those who are entitled to be maintained by him (*w*). And where a gift is valid it

Conditional.

may be accompanied with conditions, such as that the donor should be maintained by the donee during his lifetime, and that his exequial ceremonies should be performed after his death in consideration of the gift (*x*); that the donee should forego claims against the donor, and should defray expenses of the worship of the idol (*y*); that the property should pass to another in a particular event (*z*). So a *donatio mortis causâ*, revocable if the donor should recover from an

Invalid.

illness, is valid (*a*). But a gift will be invalid which creates any estate unknown to, or forbidden by, Hindu law (*b*). Provisions which are repugnant to the nature of the grant, such as a restraint upon alienation or partition are inva-

---

(*v*) *Saminadien* v. *Durmarajien*, Mad. Dec. of 1853, 291; and see authorities cited *ante*, § 348, note (*q*), 2 Dig. 159.

(*w*) As to the extent to which this limitation applies, see *post*, § 418.

(*x*) *Ram Narayun* v. *Mt. Sut Bunsee*, 3 S. D. 377 (503); see note.

(*y*) *Madhubchunder* v. *Bamasoondree*, S. D. of 1853, 103; *Gokool Nath* v. *Issur Lochun*, 14 Cal. 222.

(*z*) *Soorjeemoney Dossee* v. *Denobundo*, 9 M. I. A. 123, 135; *per curiam*; *Tagore* v. *Tagore*, 4 B. L. R. (O. C. J.) 192.

(*a*) *Visalatchmi* v. *Subbu*, 6 Mad. H. C. 270.

(*b*) *Tagore* v. *Tagore*, 4 B. L. R. (O. C. J.) 103; S. C. 9 B. L. R. (P. C.) 377; S. C. 18 Suth. 359.

lid (*c*). So are all conditions which are immoral or illegal. Where the gift is in itself good, conditions which are repugnant, or illegal, or immoral are ineffectual, but the gift itself remains good. Where the illegal condition is the consideration for the gift, and therefore forms an essential part of it, both will fail (*d*). Where a gift is already complete so that the property has completely passed from the donor to the donee, any conditions that may be subsequently added are absolutely void, since the person who attempts to impose them has ceased to have any right to do so (*e*). Where a gift to A for life is followed by a gift of the remainder of the estate to B, if the gift to A is void, the estate of B is accelerated, and takes effect at once (*f*). A gift to A with a condition postponing his enjoyment to a period beyond majority is good but the condition is bad, unless there is an intermediate disposition in favour of some other person (*g*). And of course the same principles apply to a transfer for value.

§ 351. Few propositions have been laid down with more confidence than the doctrine that under Hindu law a gift is invalid without possession. Yet Hindu law, properly so called, appears to lay little stress on any such rule as specially applicable to gifts. Gifts have been always favoured by the Brahman lawyers, for the obvious reason that they were generally made to Brahmans. The early sages discuss the **Possession.**

(*c*) See *post*, § 387; F. MacN. 327; *Venkatramanna* v. *Brammanna*, 4 Mad. H. C. 345; *Amiruddaula* v. *Nateri*, 6 Mad. H. C. 356; *Thakoor Kapilnauth* v. *Government*, 13 B. L. R. 445, 457; S. C. 22 Suth. 17; *Anantha* v. *Nagamuthu*, 4 Mad. 200; *Gokool Nath* v. *Issur Lochun*, 14 Cal. 222; *Ali Hasan* v. *Dhirja*, 4 All. 518; *Narayanan* v. *Kannan*, 7 Mad. 315; *Bhairo* v. *Parmeshri*, 7 All. 516. Transfer of Property Act (IV of 1882), §§ 10, 12. See as to such conditions in a lease, *Vyankatroya* v. *Shivrambat*, 7 Bom. 256; *Nil Madhab* v. *Narattam*, 17 Cal. 826, in a mortgage *Mukkanni* v. *Manan Bhatta*, 5 Mad. 186. See *per curiam*, *Tagore* v. *Tagore*, 9 B. L. R. (P. C.) 395, 406; S. C. 18 Suth. 359; and *Renaud*, v. *Tourangeau*, L. R. 2 P. C. 4. As to agreements between coparceners not to divide, see *post*, § 445.

(*d*) *Ram Sarup* v. *Mt. Bela*, 11 I. A. 44; S. C. 6 All. 313. Transfer of Property Act (IV of 1882), §§ 25, 18; re *Dugdale*, 38 Ch. D. 176, re *Moore*, 39 Ch. D. 116.

(*e*) *Ram Sarup* v. *Mt. Bela*, *ub. sup.*

(*f*) *Ajudhia Buksh* v. *Mt. Rukmin Kuar*, 11 I. A. 1. Transfer of Property Act (IV of 1882), § 27. See also for a case where the subsequent estate fails, § 16.

(*g*) *Gosavi Shivgar* v. *Rivett-Carnac*, 13 Bom. 463.

law of gifts with special reference to their liability to resumption. This depends on the purpose of the gift or the special circumstances of the giver. Vrihaspati says, "Things once delivered on the following eight accounts cannot be resumed; for the pleasure of hearing poets, musicians or the like, as the price of goods sold, as a nuptial gift to a bride or her family, as an acknowledgment to a benefactor, as a present to a worthy man, from natural affection, or from friendship. What is given by a person in wrath or excessive joy, or through inadvertence, or during disease, minority or madness, or under the influence of terror, or by one intoxicated, or extremely old, or by an outcast or an idiot, or by a man afflicted with grief or with pain, or what is given in sport; all this is declared ungiven or void. If any thing be given for a consideration unperformed, or to a bad man mistaken for a good one, or for any illegal act, the owner may take it back" (*h*). Katyayana says, that "He who delivers not a present which he has promised to a priest, shall be compelled to pay it as a debt, and incurs the first amercement;" and Harita lays it down broadly that "a promise legally made in words, but not performed in deed, is a debt of conscience both in this world and the next" (*i*). In one case reported by Mr. MacNaghten (*k*) where the facts placed before the pundit stated, "It does not clearly appear that the donee ever took possession of the property given;" his futwah asserted that the gift could not be resumed, quoting as authority a text of Manu "once is the partition of an inheritance made; once is a damsel given in marriage; and once does a man say, "I give." These three are by good men done once for all and irrevocably." No doubt the pundit also answered that even without a gift the donee was entitled to the property as being adopted in the *Kritrima*

(*h*) 2 Dig. 174, 197; Narada, Pt. II. ch. iv. Katyayana, 2 Dig. 197; Manu, viii. §§ 212, 213; Gotama, 2 Dig. 172. See as to revocation of gifts the Transfer of Property Act (IV of 1882), § 126.

(*i*) 2 Dig 170, 171.

(*k*) 2 W. MacN. 249; case xlii. See also case xxxv, p. 243.

form. The necessity for acceptance is put more prominently forward by Yajnavalkya (*l*), who says, "The acceptance of a gift should be public, especially of immovable property. Whatever may be lawfully given and is contracted to be given, shall not after gift be resumed." So far as this text makes possession necessary to give validity to a gift, Yajnavalkya seems to treat it as standing on the same footing with other modes of transfer. In an earlier passage (*m*), he says, "Acquisition by title is stronger than possession, unless this has come down from ancestors. But acquisition by title is of no avail without possession for a short time." The whole subject is discussed at considerable length by the author of the Mitakshara under two headings, of possession without a title and of a title without possession (*n*). As regards gift he says, "gift consists in the relinquishment of one's own right, and the creation of the right of another; and the creation of another man's right is completed on that other's acceptance of the gift but not otherwise. Acceptance is made by three means, mental, verbal or corporeal. Mental acceptance is the determination to appropriate; verbal acceptance is the utterance of the expression, this is mine or the like; corporeal acceptance is manifold, as by touching" (*o*). "In the case of land, as there can be no corporeal acceptance without enjoyment of the produce, it must be accompanied by some little possession; otherwise the gift, sale, or other transfer is not complete. A title, therefore, without corporeal acceptance, consisting of the enjoyment of the produce, is weaker than a title accompanied by it or with such corporeal acceptance. But such is the case only, where of

---

(*l*) II. 176. (*m*) II. 27.

(*n*) Mit. iii. §§ 5 and 6, translated by Mr. William MacNaghten, 1 W. MacN. 212, 217.

(*o*) Under English law the acceptance of a gift by a donee is to be presumed until his dissent is signified, even though the donee is not aware of it, and the presumption has even been held to apply to a gift which the donor desired to revoke before the donee knew that it had been made. *Per Lindley*, L. J., 21 Q. B. D., p. 541. Where, however, delivery is necessary, as in the case of a parol gift of a chattel capable of gift, mere words of giving and acceptance, communicated by the donor to the donee, and by the donee to the donor, do not pass the property without delivery. *Cochrane* v. *Moore*, 25 Q. B. D. 57.

these two the priority is undistinguishable; but when it is ascertained which is first in point of date, and which posterior, then the simple prior title affords the stronger evidence. Or the interpretation may be as follows: "Evidence is said to consist of documents, possession, and witnesses." This having been premised as the general rule, the text "a title is more powerful than possession unaccompanied by hereditary succession," and "where there is not the least possession, there a title is not sufficient," have been propounded to point out to which the superiority belongs, where the three descriptions of evidence meet." Apparently, in the view of Vijnaneswara, acceptance was necessary to complete a gift because according to a Hindu lawyer property can never be in abeyance. It cannot pass out of one till it is received by another. The very nature of a mortgage or sale, which is necessarily a bilateral proceeding, assumes acceptance. No such assumption exists in the case of a gift. But as regards actual corporeal acceptance, or as he calls it "some little possession," he appears to put a gift on the same footing with a sale or other transfer. As to all three evidence of possession is material in order to determine priorities between conflicting claims, where any such dispute exists. Where no such dispute exists, then the general rule applies "In the case of a pledge, a gift, or a sale, the prior contract has the greater force" (*p*).

§ 352. It is probable that the rule that actual possession is necessary to give validity to a gift arose, not from any special doctrine of Hindu law, but from the general principle common to all systems of law, that a voluntary promise cannot be enforced, though the voluntary act, when completed is irrevocable (*q*). To this extent the doctrine received very early recognition in our Courts, and has long since been enforced (*r*). Whether the English doctrine of Equity

(*p*) Mit. iii. 2, § 5; 1 W. MacN. 200.
(*q*) See *per curiam*, 11 I. A., p. 233; *Standing* v. *Bowring*, 31 Ch. D. 282.
(*r*) 2 Stra. H. L. 426; 2 W. MacN. 248, case xxxvi; *Kishto Soondery* v. *Kishto Motee*, Marshall, 367; *Sham Singh* v. *Mt. Umraotee*, 2 S. D. 75 (92); *Harji-*

that a declaration of trust, not amounting to a legal transfer, can be enforced in favour of the object of the trust would be extended to cases governed by Hindu law is undecided (*s*). It is quite certain that no promise to confer a future benefit upon a priest, however holy, would be enforced by the secular Courts (*t*). Where, however, the donor has done every thing in his power to complete the gift, and the resistance to his attempts to give it full effect arises from a third person, the fact that possession has not been given is no answer to a suit by the donee against the obstructing party (*u*).

What amounts to possession.

§ 353. To complete a gift there must be a transfer of the apparent evidences of ownership from the donor to the donee. It is, however, sufficient if the change of possession is such as the nature of the case admits of. Therefore, where the gift is of land, which is in the possession of tenants, receipt of rent by the donee is enough, even though it is received through a person who received it formerly as agent for the donor; or delivery to the donee of the deed of gift, and of the counterpart lease executed to the donor by the tenants (*v*). So a gift may be made to an absent person, if his acceptance of it is certain, but if it is unknown whether he will accept or not, the right of the donor continues (*w*). And it was stated by a pandit in Bengal that a

---

van v. *Naran Haribai*, 4 Bom. H. C. (A. C. J.) 31; *Vasudev* v. *Narayan*, 7 Bom. 131. The Transfer of Property Act (IV of 1882), § 122 only requires an acceptance of the gift by or on behalf of the donee, which acceptance must be made during the lifetime of the donor, and while he is still capable of giving. If the donee dies before acceptance, the gift is void. But by § 129 nothing in the above provisions would affect any rule of Hindu law.

(*s*) *Venkatachella* v. *Thathammal*, 4 Mad. H. C. 460; *Hirbai* v. *Jan Mahomed*, 7 Bom. 229.

(*t*) *Manjanadhaya* v. *Tangamma*, Mad. Dec. of 1861, 24; *Nursing* v. *Mohunt*, S. D. of 1857, 1000.

(*u*) *Kalidas* v. *Kanhya Lall*, 11 I. A. 218; S. C. 11 Cal. 121. See the facts of this case stated, *post*, § 359; followed in cases under Muhammedan law. *Mahomed Buksh* v. *Hosseini Bibi*, 15 I. A. 81; S. C. 15 Cal. 684; *Sheikh Muhummed* v. *Zubaida Jan*, 16 I. A. 205; S. C. 11 All. 460.

(*v*) *Bank of Hindustan* v. *Premchand*, 5 Bom. H. C. (O. C. J.) 83; *Wannathan* v. *Keyakadath*, 6 Mad. H. C. 194; *Harjivan* v. *Naran*, 4 Bom. H. C. (A. C. J.) 31; *Man Bhari* v. *Naunidh*, 4 All. 40; *Kallyani* v. *Narayana*, 9 Mad. 267.

(*w*) Srikrishna, cited with approval by *Macpherson*, J., *Krishnaramani* v. *Ananda*, 4 B. L. R. (O. C. J.) 291.

gift would be valid, even though the donor retained possession, if it was expressly stated in the deed that he was holding the property as a loan from the donee (*x*). So it has been held, that where the donee is incapable of taking possession, as being a minor or a lunatic, the possession of the donor is enough, if it is expressly asserted to be in trust for the donee (*y*). And when the donee was in possession either alone, or jointly with the donor, before the gift, the continuance of his possession is sufficient, without any new delivery (*z*). So where one of several donees is already in possession, a declaration of gift to him on behalf of all, assented to by himself and the other donees is sufficient, without putting them in possession (*a*). The gift of an incorporeal right will be sufficient if it is made in such a manner as would suffice for the transfer of choses in action (*b*). It follows from the above principles, that whether the gift be *in præsenti* or *in futuro* the donee must be a person in existence, and capable of accepting the gift at the time it takes effect (*c*). The only exceptions are the cases of an infant in the womb, or a person adopted after the death of the husband under an authority from him. Such persons are by a fiction of law considered to have been in existence at the time of the death (*d*).

Donee must be in existence.

Gift to a class of whom some are incapable of taking.

§ 354. The principle last stated has given rise to a class of cases as to which there appears to be some conflict of authority. In England it is well settled that where a gift or bequest is made to a class of persons, some of whom are

(*x*) *Sheodas* v. *Kuhwul*, 3 S. D. 234 (313).

(*y*) Punjab Cust., 75 ; 2 W. MacN. 243.

(*z*) *Meyajee* v. *Metha*, Bom. Sel. Rep. 80, 89 ; *Sheik Ibrahim* v. *Sheik Suleman*, 9 Bom. 146. This, and the previous case, were decided under Muhammedan law, which in this respect agrees with the Hindu law.

(*a*) *Bai Kushal* v. *Lakhma Mana*, 7 Bom. 452.

(*b*) *Chellamamma* v. *Subamma*, 7 Mad. 23 ; *Khursadji* v. *Pestonji*, 12 Bom. 573.

(*c*) This is the actual time of giving, that is the date of the gift, if *inter vivos*, or the death of the testator, if by will ; not the possible time of receiving. See *Tagore* v. *Tagore*, 9 B. L. R. 399 ; S. C. 18 Suth. 359 ; *Soudaminey* v. *Jogesh*, 2 Cal. 265 ; *Kherodemoney* v. *Doorgamoney*, 4 Cal. 455 ; *Bai Mamubai* v. *Dossa Moraji*, 15 Bom. 443 ; *post*, § 386.

(*d*) *Tagore* v. *Tagore*, 4 B. L. R. (O. C. J.) 103 ; S. C. on appeal in the P. C. 9 B. L. R. 377, 397, 400, 404 ; S. C. 18 Suth. 359.

incapable of taking, the disposition fails as to all. This rests not upon any technicality of English law, but upon the ground that the intention of the donor was to benefit all equally, and that it is impossible to know what shape his wishes would have taken, if he had been informed that they could not be carried out as he intended (*e*). This rule has been applied in several cases in India, where it has been held that a disposition in favour of a class of persons, as to some of whom the gift is void for remoteness, or some of whom are or may be incapable of taking as being unborn at the time when the gift should take effect, is void as to all. And the rule applies even though all the members of the class are in fact born before the gift or bequest takes effect, if it was antecedently possible that they might not have been so born, since "it is an invariable rule that regard is had to possible not actual events, and the fact that the gift might have included objects too remote, is fatal to its validity irrespective of the event" (*f*). The existence of such a rule as properly applicable to India appears to have been recognised by the Judicial Committee in one case, though they were of opinion that upon the true construction of the instrument the disposition did not come within the rule (*g*). The rule itself is expressly made applicable by the Legislature to transfers which are invalid as offending against the doctrine of perpetuity, or where an attempt is made to create a series of limited interests in favour of persons not in existence at the date of the transfer, after the termination of a previous vested estate (*h*). Whether

---

(*e*) *Leake* v. *Robinson*, 2 Mer. 363, 390; *Pearks* v. *Moseley*, 5 App. Ca. 714.

(*f*) *Brahmamayi* v. *Jages Chandra*, 8 B. L. R. 400; *Soudaminey* v. *Jogesh*, 2 Cal. 262; *Kherodemoney* v. *Doorgamoney*, 4 Cal. 455; *Jairam* v. *Ruverbai*, 9 Bom. 491, 508; *Javerbai* v. *Kablibai*, 15 Bom. 326; 1 Jarman on Wills, 4th ed., 266 Where the invalidity of any disposition of property turns on the possibility that a particular person might have children, evidence is not admissible to show that from advanced age the birth of future children is impossible re *Dawson*, 39 Ch. D. 155. The same rule would, no doubt, apply to any other physical incapacity.

(*g*) *Kumar Tarakeswar* v. *Kumar Shoshi*, 10 I. A. at p. 60; S. C. 9 Cal. at p. 960.

(*h*) Transfer of Property Act (IV of 1882), § 15; Succession Act (X of 1865), § 102. Nothing in these sections alters any principle of Hindu law. Act IV of 1882, § 2; Act XXI of 1870, § 3. *Alangamonjori* v. *Sonamoni*, 8 Cal. 637.

it was intended to exclude the application of the rule in all other cases is matter of argument or inference.

§ 354A. A class within the meaning of this rule has been defined as follows by Mr. Jarman (*i*). "A number of persons are popularly said to form a class when they can be designated by some general term, as children, grand-children, nephews, but in legal language the question whether a gift is one to a class depends not upon those considerations, but upon the mode of gift itself, *viz.*, that it is a gift of an aggregate sum to a body of persons uncertain in number at the time of the gift, to be ascertained at a future time, and who are to take in equal or in some other definite proportions, the share of each being dependent for its amount upon the ultimate number of persons." The rule does not apply where all the individuals are named, as then the intention of the donor as to each is defined. In such a case, if they are to take as tenants in common, and the gift fails as to some, the others take their appointed shares (*k*). If they are to take jointly, those who are capable of taking are entitled to the whole (*l*). Nor does it apply where the nature of the benefit conferred—such as residence in a family house—is not dependent on the number of persons who may ultimately prove that they have a right to share (*m*). Where there are independent and alternative gifts, of which one is good at the time the document takes effect, and the other is void, the former will take effect, and the latter will be disregarded (*n*).

Recent decisions. § 355. Recent decisions throw some doubt upon the above doctrine as of universal application in India. The first case is a decision of the Judicial Committee which of course is conclusive as to whatever it lays down (*o*). In that case

(*i*) Jarman. Wills, I. 266 (4th ed.)
(*k*) *James* v. *Lord Wynford*, 1 Sm. & Giff. p. 59.
(*l*) *Nandi Singh* v. *Sitaram*, 1 I. A. 44; S. C. 16 Cal. 677.
(*m*) *Krishanath* v. *Atmaram*, 15 Bom. 543.
(*n*) Re *Harvey*, 39 Ch. D. 289; *Raikishori* v. *Debendranath*, 15 I. A. 37; S. C. 15 Cal. 409.
(*o*) *Rai Bishen Chand* v. *Mt. Asmaida Koer*, 11 I. A. 164; S. C. 6 All. 560.

there were alive as members of an undivided family governed by Mitakshara law, Mata Dyal, his son Udey Narrain, and Satrujit the only son of Udey Narrain. To protect the estate against the profligacy of Udey Narrain, Mata Dyal, with the consent of Udey Narrain to whom a sum of Rs. 5,000 was paid, transferred the estate to Satrujit Narrain and his own brothers who are born or may be born hereafter. The validity of this gift was objected to, amongst other reasons, on the ground that as the unborn sons of Udey could not take, the gift to Satrujit himself as a member of the class of Udey's sons, was invalid. In support of this view reference was made to § 102 of the Succession Act (X of 1865). As to this the Committee replied that the gift in question did not come within the terms of the section (*p*). Upon the general question their Lordships held that the gift was not made to a class of whom Satrujit was one, but that it was made to Satrujit as a person in whose favour it was intended to operate at once, for a purpose which would be absolutely frustrated if it did not so operate. The further intention that his younger brothers, if he ever had any, should share in the benefit of the gift, could not be carried out, but that was no reason for holding the whole transaction to be void. They said (*q*) "Cases are not rare in which a Court of construction, finding that the whole plan of a donor of property cannot be carried into effect, will yet give effect to part of it, rather than hold that it shall fail entirely. In the present case, there is every reason for holding that, if Satrujit's possible brothers are not able to take by virtue of the gift, he shall take the whole. He is there present and able to receive the gift. He is an individual designated in the deed. If the deed stood alone, it is a question in each case whether a designated person who is coupled with a class described in general terms is

---

(*p*) It seems very doubtful whether under the saving clause of the Hindu Wills Act, § 102 of Act X of 1865 has any application to Hindu Wills. See *per Wilson*, J., 12 Cal. p. 669. It has no application whatever to gifts or transfers *inter vivos*.

(*q*) 10 I. A., p. 178; S. C. 6 All., p. 573.

merged into that class or not. But the deed does not stand alone. It is followed by actions of a kind which, even without a deed, may work a transfer of property in India. Satrujit is entered in the Collector's books as the sole possessor of the property, and his guardian takes possession, first in his name and afterwards as his successor. Their Lordships hold that the circumstance that the parties wished to do something beyond their legal power, and that they have used unskilful language in the deed of gift, ought not to invalidate that important part of their plan which is consistent with one construction of the deed, and is clearly proved from the transfer of the property in fact."

§ 356. This decision was followed in a very similar case in Calcutta (*r*), where a man by deed of gift gave certain property to Ramlal and Shamlal the two existing infant sons of his son Madhub, with a direction that they and their uterine brothers who should be born hereafter should divide the same amongst them in equal shares. He then proceeded to provide that the two grandsons so named should be placed in possession and have their names registered. But the rights of the uterine brothers to be born in future were not to be extinguished by this possession. The Court held on the authority of the Privy Council case that the gift was good to the persons so designated, though ineffectual as to those who might be born hereafter. *Wilson*, J., however, upon an elaborate examination of all the Indian and English authorities, arrived at the conclusion (p. 681) that the rule in *Leake* v. *Robinson* was only applied in England to gifts to a class tainted with the vice of remoteness, and that the Indian Succession Act, § 102, and the Transfer of Property Act, § 15 marked the intention that the rule should only be extended to India in similar cases. He then expressed his opinion that the decision in Rai Bishen Chand's case was inconsistent with the rulings in Soudamoney's and Kherodemoney's cases, and ended by saying (p. 685) "For these reasons I should be prepared, if necessary, to dissent wholly

(*r*) *Ramlal Sett* v. *Kanai Lal*, 12 Cal. 663.

from the doctrine laid down in those cases, and to hold, as the general rule, that where there is a gift to a class, some of whom are or may be incapacitated from taking, because not born at the date of gift or the death of the testator as the case may be, and where there is no other objection to the gift, it should enure for the benefit of those members of the class who are capable of taking."

The latter part of the judgment was, of course, merely *obiter dictum*. The views there laid down have, however, been followed to their full extent by the High Courts of Madras and Bombay. Property was granted to a man for his life, and at his death to persons (in the Madras case his brothers, in the Bombay case his children) forming a class, whose description would equally embrace persons born during and after the life of the testator or settlor. In each case the person who claimed the property had been in fact born before the document took effect, and no one had been born after that date. The Court held that he was entitled to take in accordance with the Calcutta judgment (*s*). The Bombay High Court further supported its opinion by a reference to the language of *Jessel*, M. R., (*t*) where he said: "I think there is a convenient mode of interpreting this testator's intention, and it is this: The testator may be considered to have a primary and a secondary intention. His primary intention is that all members of the class shall take, and his secondary intention is that if all cannot take, those who can shall do so." In the case before *Jessel*, M. R., the testator had given certain property to "the children of my late brother Joseph Coleman who shall survive me or who shall have died in my lifetime leaving issue living at my death in equal shares." Four children of Joseph were living at the testator's death, and one had died leaving issue living at the death of the testator. The Master of the Rolls said that he intended

(*s*) *Manjamma* v. *Padmanabhayya*, 12 Mad. 393; *Mangaldas* v. *Tribhoovandas*, 15 Bom. 562.
(*t*) In re *Coleman*, 4 Ch. D., p. 169.

somehow to provide for a child who died leaving issue, but did not know how to do it. That part of the gift therefore failed; but the supposed secondary intention was carried out by holding that the four children took the share among them. The doctrine of *Leake* v. *Robinson* had no application to the case, which was decided on completely different principles as regards the child who had predeceased the testator.

Valid against creditors.

§ 357. A gift once completed by delivery or its equivalent is binding upon the donor himself, and upon his representatives, and is valid even against his creditors; provided it was made *bonâ fide*, that is with the honest intention of passing the property, and not merely as a fraudulent contrivance to conceal the real ownership (*u*).

Necessity for delivery where transfer is for consideration.

§ 358. Another question which has given rise to numerous and conflicting decisions, is as to the necessity for delivery of possession where the transfer is not by way of gift, but by way of mortgage or sale of land. Such a transaction, even without possession, would, of course, be valid and enforceable as against the transferor. But the importance of the question would arise where the rights of third parties were concerned. For instance, where the same property was mortgaged or sold twice, and possession given to the last transferee. If the first transfer was valid without possession, the first transferee could bring ejectment for the land. If it required possession, his only remedy would be against his transferor by suit for specific performance or for damages. There is a good deal in the passages from the native writers quoted above (§ 351) which might have been interpreted as intimating that an actual delivery of possession was necessary in order to give effect to any

(*u*) *Sabapaty* v. *Panyandy*, Mad. Dec. of 1858, 61; *Abhachari* v. *Ramachendrayya*, 1 Mad. H. C. 393; *Gnanabhai* v. *Srinavasa*, 4 Mad. H. C. 84; *Nasir* v. *Mata*, 2 All. 891; *Rai Bishen Chand* v. *Asmaida Koer*, 11 I. A. 164; S. C. 6 All. 560. Of course it may be set aside for any ground which shows that it was void *ab initio* against the donor, as from fraud practised on him or defective knowledge on his part as to its effect. *Bai Munigavri* v. *Narondas*, 15 Bom. 549.

species of transfer. But the more natural explanation appears to be that they refer to two different matters, *viz.*, the effect of possession as evidencing a right, and the effect of possession as destroying a right. For instance, *Narada* says, "Written proof, witnesses and possession, these are the three kinds of evidence on which the right of property rests, (and by means of which) a creditor may recover a loan. A document remains always evidence, witnesses as long as they live, and possession after a lapse of time. What a man is not possessed of, that is not his own, even though there be written proof, and even though witnesses be living; this is especially the case with immovables." But in the next verse he shows that he is speaking of what we would call the law of limitations, as he fixes periods after which possession shall destroy the right to recover; and further on he says, "Where possession exists, but no title whatever exists, there a title but not possession (alone) can confer proprietary rights. A title having been substantiated, the possession becomes valid; it remains invalid without a proved title." He winds up by saying, "In all business transactions the latest act shall prevail; but in the case of a gift, a pledge, or a purchase, the prior act has the greater force." In a subsequent text he says, "What a man possesses without a title, he must not alienate" (*v*) Vijnaneswara in commenting on the same rule, *viz.*, that "in the case of a pledge, a gift, or a sale, the prior contract has the greater force" expressly points out that this applies to the case where a person who has sold or mortgaged to one, afterwards, through delusion or avarice, makes a similar sale or mortgage to another (*w*). These texts and many others are reviewed by Professor Wilson, in an article on Sir F. MacNaghten's considerations on Hindu Law, and this article with further texts was examined by the Madras High Court in reference to a question of inchoate partition. Dr. Wilson states his view as follows, "It is therefore in

(*v*) Narada, iv. §§ 2—13, 17. See also 18—23, 27.

(*w*) Mit. iii. 2, § 6; 1 W. MacN. 200. The Transfer of Property Act (IV of 1882), § 48 lays down the same rule.

our estimation quite clear that the Hindu Law and common sense go hand in hand. A man may forego his rights if he pleases, and any capricious abandonment of them for an unreasonable time is to be punished by their forfeiture. But he is not to be deprived of what is legally his, because legal proceedings, interested opposition, accident, distance or disease debar him from taking possession of it when it first becomes his due." To which the Madras High Court adds, "This seems to us precisely the doctrine derivable from the text writers" (*x*).

Decisions in Madras.

§ 359. The Madras Courts have always held that a sale by the owner without delivery of possession is valid as against a subsequent sale by the original owner followed by possession, and that the first vendee may bring ejectment both against the vendor and the second vendee, "on the simple principle, that after the conveyance to the first vendee the owner of the land had nothing whatever to convey" (*y*). Two cases in the Privy Council (*z*) were for some time supposed to have laid down the rule that a sale will be invalid, *first,* if the vendor cannot give possession, and *secondly,* if he does not give possession. In earlier editions of this work I had suggested that neither of those cases decided that a document, intended to operate as a transfer *in præsenti* of a specific piece of land, would be invalid because possession was not given under it. In both cases the Judicial Committee held that the document was not intended so to operate. In both cases, too, the sale was not of a specific piece of property, but of a share in something afterwards to be recovered. Something remained to be done between the parties before the purchaser could say

Privy Council decisions.

(*x*) Wilson's works, v. 88; *Lakshmy* v. *Narasimha*, 3 Mad. H. C. 40, 46, *affirmed;* 13 M. I. A. 113; S. C. 12 Suth. (P. C.) 40.

(*y*) *Velayuda* v. *Sivarama*, Mad. Dec. of 1860, 277; *Virabadra* v. *Hari Rama* 3 Mad. H. C. 38; *Vasudeva Bhatlu* v. *Narasamma*, 5 Mad. 6; *Ramasami* v. *Marimuttu*, 6 Mad. 404.

(*z*) *Perhlad Sein* v. *Baboo Budhoo*, 12 M. I. A. 300, 306—309; S. C. 2 B. L. R. (P. C.) 111; S. C. 12 Suth. (P. C.) 6; *Bhobosundree* v. *Issurchunder*, 11 B. L. R. 36; S. C. 18 Suth. 140; *compare Kamala* v. *Pitchoocooty*, 10 M. I. A. 386, 395.

that he had a claim to any definite field or house. This view was taken by the Privy Council in a later case when the same question arose (*a*). There Romasundari gave to Ruttonmoni an estate for an interest which was ultimately decided to be only good for Ruttonmoni's life, and placed her in possession. In 1864 Ruttonmoni's interest was sold in execution, and purchased by Kanhya Lall, who also got into possession. She died in 1867. In 1876 Romasundari by gift bestowed the same estate upon the wife of Kalidas. Neither Romasundari nor her second donee ever regained possession from Kanhya Lall. The suit to recover possession was brought by the executor of the second donee against the purchaser from the first donee, the donor being joined as defendant. It was contended that the second deed of gift was utterly invalid, inasmuch as the donor was out of possession, and no possession was ever given to the donee. The Judicial Committee decided against this contention. After citing the two decisions above referred to they say (p. 232), "Neither of these decisions is applicable to the present case. The ground of them is that the plaintiff was not entitled under the terms of the contract of sale to possession. In this case the appellant is under the terms of the gift entitled to possession, and their Lordships see no reason why a gift or contract of sale of property, whether movable or immovable, if it is not of a nature which makes the giving effect to it contrary to public policy, should not operate to give to the donee or purchaser a right to obtain possession. This appears to be consistent with Hindu Law. On the principle contended for by the respondent, so long as he prevents the true owner from taking possession, however violently or wrongfully, that owner cannot make any title to a grantee."

§ 360. During the period which elapsed between these decisions there was naturally a good deal of conflict in the Decisions in Calcutta.

(a) *Kalidas* v. *Kanhya Lall*, 11 I. A. 218; S. C. 11 Cal 121; followed *Mahomed Buksh* v. *Hosseini Bibi*, 15 I. A. 81; S. C. 15 Cal. 684.

rulings of the Courts of Calcutta and Bombay. The former Court always leant against the doctrine that possession was necessary to complete a transfer for consideration. In cases decided before the earlier Privy Council cases, it was held by the Sudder Court, and by the High Court of Bengal that a person out of possession, but who had a right to possession, might convey his title to a third party, and that the latter might bring ejectment upon that title against any one who had an inferior title (*b*). The same point again came before the High Court after the Privy Council decisions, and they ruled that the *dicta* of the Judicial Committee must be taken subject to the facts of the particular cases. Where the vendor had been in peaceable possession, and then been dispossessed, they ruled that a sale of his title carried with it the right to eject (*c*). The same decision was given in still later cases, in which it was stated that the vendor was out of possession, but it does not appear whether he had previously been in possession (*d*). In 1882, in consequence of a recent decision to the contrary, the question was referred to a Full Bench (*e*), which stated unhesitatingly its opinion "that delivery of possession is not under the Hindu law, essential to complete the title of a purchaser for value." A sale by a person who is out of possession by reason of the adverse holding of hostile claimants is not a sale of an actionable claim within the meaning of § 135 of the Transfer of Property Act (IV of 1882) (*f*). Other cases in which the High Court of Bengal professed to follow the early decisions in the Privy Council in holding that transfers by a person out of possession were invalid, were no doubt rightly decided according to the true meaning of those decisions. They were not actual sales

---

(*b*) *Surbonarrain* v *Maharaj*, S. D. of 1858, 601; *Prankrishna* v. *Biswambhar*, 2 B. L. R. (A. C. J.) 207, over-ruling *Dinomonee* v. *Gyrutoollah*, 2 Suth. 188; *Kumrooddeen* v. *Shaikh Bhadro*, 11 Suth. 134.

(*c*) *Bikan* v. *Mt. Parbutty*, 22 Suth. 99; *Gungahurry* v. *Raghubram*, 14 B. L. R. 307; S. C. 23 Suth. 131; *Nittyanund* v. *Shama Churn*, 23 Suth 163.

(*d*) *Aulock* v. *Aulock*, 25 Suth. 48; *Bissessur* v. *Joykishore*, *ibid.* 223.

(*e*) *Narain Chunder* v. *Dataram*, 8 Cal. 597, 610, over-ruling *Dinonath* v. *Aulockmonee*, 7 Cal. 753.

(*f*) *Modun Mohun* v. *Futturunnissa*, 13 Cal. 297.

of specific pieces of land, but agreements for the division of property then under litigation, and were clearly opposed to public policy (*g*). In another case in which a similar decision was given, nothing appears except that the assignor never at any time had had possession of the property which he assigned (*h*).

Decisions in Bombay.

§ 361. In Bombay both usage and the course of decisions have been in favour of requiring possession, in order to give validity to all sorts of transfer as against subsequent purchasers for value without notice. Some of the later decisions rested on the supposed authority of the two Privy Council cases above referred to (*i*). But the same ruling prevailed anterior to and independent of those *dicta*. The whole law upon the subject was reviewed by the High Court, in a case where the owner of land had sold it by deed of sale to a party who paid a portion of the price, and on the same day sold it by a second deed to another party who paid the whole price and was put into possession. The suit was brought by the first vendee against the vendor and the second vendee. The Privy Council decisions were referred to but apparently little relied on. After an elaborate examination of the native authorities and the decisions in the Presidency Courts, judgment was given in favour of the defendant, on the broad ground, that the sale without possession was invalid as against a subsequent purchaser without notice of it (*k*). In a later case *Westropp*, C. J., said, " Our Bombay reports from their commencement contain cases from which, taken in the aggregate, it may safely be laid down as a general, but not an invariable rule, that possession in the grantor or assignee is deemed essential amongst Hindus and Mahomedans to the complete transfer

---

(*g*) *Tarasoondaree* v. *Collector of Mymensingh*, 13 B. L. R. 495; S. C. 20 Suth. 446; *Boodhun* v. *Mt. Latecfan*, 22 Suth. 535; *Bishonath* v. *Chunder*, 33 Suth. 165.

(*h*) *Ram Khelawun* v. *Mt. Oudh*, 21 Suth. 101.

(*i*) *Ante*, § 359; *Girdhar* v. *Daji*, 7 Bom. H. C. (A. C. J.) 4; *Kachu* v. *Kachoba*, 10 Bom. H. C. 491.

(*k*) *Lalubhai* v. *Bai Amrit*, 2 Bom. 299; *Hasha* v. *Ragho*, 6 Bom. 165.

of immoveable property either by gift, sale or mortgage." Among the exceptions to the above general rule the Chief Justice enumerated cases arising between the transferor or volunteers claiming under him and the transferee; cases in which the second transferee became such with actual notice of the earlier transfer without possession; or in which he had implied notice by the fact that the earlier transfer was registered under any of the Acts XVI of 1861, XX of 1866, VIII of 1871, or III of 1877 prior to the execution of the second instrument. In adopting the principle that registration was an implied notice the Chief Justice admitted that he was following the American in preference to the English or Irish decisions, "*6thly*. It has been held that possession by a judgment debtor having a good title is not necessary to validate a judicial sale of his lands: *7thly*. It appears to have been held that possession by the vendee, who became such at a judicial sale, is not necessary to validate the sale to him as against subsequent attaching creditors under money decrees, or as against purchasers at the sales under such decrees: *8thly*. The purchaser at a judicial sale may re-sell without previously taking possession"(*l*). A purchaser at a judicial sale is not a purchaser without notice, as he only buys such an interest as the execution debtor could equitably sell to him (*m*).

As regards persons other than purchasers for value without notice, the Bombay High Court laid down the rule, that a Hindu whose estate was in the possession of a trespasser or mortgagee, might sell his right of entry, as such, or his equity of redemption, as such, and that the purchaser might thereupon sue to eject the trespasser, or to redeem the mortgage. But if he professed to sell the estate itself, of which he was out of possession, the plaintiff who proceeded to sue as the owner of the estate, would be defeated, on the

(*l*) *Lakshmandas* v. *Dasrat*, 6 Bom. 168, F. B., pp. 175—177, 184—187; *Shivram* v. *Genu*, 6 Bom. 515; *Dundaya* v. *Chenbasapa*, 9 Bom. 427.

(*m*) *Sobhagchund* v. *Bhaichand*, 6 Bom. 93; *Chintaman* v. *Shivram*, 9 Bom. H. C. 304; *Ramaraia* v. *Arunachella*, 7 Mad. 248.

ground that the conveyance to him was ineffectual (*n*). This was very much like a distinction without a difference. Accordingly after the case of *Kalidas* v. *Kanhya Lall* (*o*), the Bombay High Court decided that no such distinction could be maintained, and that it was no objection to an ejectment on the plaintiff's title as absolute owner, that his vendor had been kept out of possession by adverse claim up to the time of his conveyance (*p*).

Cases of mortgage.

§ 362. The case of mortgages creates greater difficulty, as the mortgagor still retains an assignable interest in himself. Distinctions would also arise according as the mortgagor had transferred his property in the land, reserving only a right to redeem, or had retained the property, merely creating a lien upon it in favour of the creditor; in the language of English law, according as the mortgage was legal or equitable. Questions of notice, negligence, &c., would also largely affect the decision of each case. I do not propose to enter into these matters, which are beyond the scope of this work, and have been fully treated by Mr. Macpherson in his book on Mortgages. I shall briefly point out the state of the authorities on the one point of possession. It is evident that the effect of want of possession will depend largely upon whether such non-possession was in accordance with the terms of the contract, or opposed to it. *Narada* says broadly, "Pledges are declared to be of two sorts, movable and immovable. Both are valid when there is actual enjoyment, and not otherwise" (*q*).

Mortgage without possession.

It is possible he may be referring to cases in which possession ought to follow the pledge, as it would do naturally in regard to movables. In Madras it is quite settled that a mere hypothecation of land, neither followed nor intended to be followed by possession, creates a lien upon it, which may be enforced against a subsequent purchaser (*r*). The

(*n*) *Bai Suraj* v. *Dalpatram*, 6 Bom. 380; *Vasudev Hari* v. *Tatia Narayan*, *ibid.* 387.

(*o*) 11 I. A. 218; S. C. 11 Cal. 121, *ante*, § 359.

(*p*) *Ugarchand* v. *Madapa Somana*, 9 Bom. 324.

(*q*) Narada, iv. § 64.

(*r*) *Varden* v. *Luckpathy*, 9 M. I. A. 303; *Kadarsa* v. *Raviah*, 2 Mad. H. C. 108; *Golla* v. *Kali*, 4 Mad. H. C. 434; *Sadagopah* v. *Ruthna*, 6 Mad. Jur. 175.

same point has been decided in Bengal by the Supreme Court, after taking the opinion of the Judges of the Sudder Court (*s*). In Bombay the Courts, in dealing with the rights of a mortgagee against subsequent mortgagees or purchasers, proceed upon the doctrine of the position of a purchaser for value without notice. Except as regards mortgages in Guzerat they hold that a mere mortgage without possession cannot prevail against a subsequent mortgagee or purchaser who has obtained possession without notice (*t*). A purchaser with express notice of a previous mortgage takes subject to it, and either possession under a previous mortgage, or registration of it prior to the execution of the subsequent transfer, is equivalent to notice (*u*). The general principle that possession is not necessary to give validity to a mortgage as against the mortgagor was affirmed by the Bombay High Court in a very elaborate judgment, where all the previous cases were reviewed (*v*); and it has also been held that such a mortgagee may maintain his claim against third persons who are wrongfully in possession (*w*); or against purchasers at a Court sale, who only take the right, title, and interest of the debtor (*x*).

Priority between registered and unregistered documents.

§ 363. Another point as to which there is a conflict of decisions is as to priority between two documents, the former of which is unregistered, and the latter is registered. Where the former document is one of which registration is compulsory, no question can arise. The unregistered document creates no rights, and is inadmissible in evidence (*y*). But

---

(*s*) *Collydoss* v. *Sibchunder*, Morton, 111; *Sibchunder* v. *Russick*, Fulton, 36. These cases over-rule contrary decisions in Montriou, 278, and Morton 105. See *Nanack* v. *Teluckdye*, 5 Cal. 265.

(*t*) *Parmaya* v. *Sonde*, 4 Bom. 459, 461; *Bapuji Balal* v. *Satyabhamabai*, 6 Bom. 490; *per Westropp*, C. J., 6 Bom., p. 176. See as to the early Sudder decisions, *Tooljaram* v. *Meean*, 2 Bor. 180, (147); *Kundoojee* v. *Ballajee*, Bellasis, 5; *Dondee* v. *Suntram*, Morris, 56.

(*u*) See cases in last note, also *Gopal* v. *Kristnappa*, 7 Bom. H. C. (A. C. J.) 69; *Hari* v. *Mahadaji*, 8 Bom. H. C. (A. C. J.) 50; *Balaji* v. *Ramchandra*, 11 Bom. H. C. 37. See as to possession being notice, Act I of 1877, § 27.

(*v*) *Jivandas* v. *Framji*, 7 Bom H. C. (O. C. J.) 45.

(*w*) *Krishnaji* v. *Govind*, 9 Bom. H. C. 275.

(*x*) *Chintaman* v. *Shivram*, 9 Bom. H. C 304. See upon the whole of this subject the judgment in *Lakshmandas* v. *Dasrat*, 6 Bom. 168.

(*y*) Act III of 1877, § 49.

it has been the policy of the Legislature to allow a certain class of documents, evidencing transactions of a small value, to be registered or not at the option of the holders. Under the Registration Acts XVI of 1864, XX of 1866, and VIII of 1871 there was no competition in respect of registration between a document compulsorily registrable and a document which, being optionally registrable, was in fact not registered (z). But under the existing Registration Act, III of 1877, § 50, every document of which registration is compulsory and certain classes of documents of which registration is optional, "shall, if duly registered, take effect as regards the property comprised therein, against every unregistered document relating to the same property, and not being a decree or order, whether such unregistered document be of the same nature as the registered document or not." An *Explanation* to this section makes it apply retrospectively in favour of a document registered under Act III of 1877 against documents whose registration was optional under the previous Acts (a). Upon this section the Madras High Court holds, that the subsequent registered document must, in all cases, take effect against a previous document dealing with the same property which, being optionally registrable, has in fact not been registered, and that neither express notice of the previous instrument, nor possession under it, operating as implied notice, can make any difference in the case (b), unless the second document is merely fraudulent and collusive (c), or unless the second transaction has been expressly made subject to the first, so that both documents may have full operation; as for instance, where property is sold by a registered instrument subject to the claims of a previous mortgagee under an un-

(z) See *per Westropp*, C. J., 6 Bom. 190, and cases cited.

(a) *Lakshman Das* v. *Dipchand*, 2 All. 851; *Gungaram* v. *Kallipodo*, 11 Cal. 661; *Muthana* v. *Alibeg*, 6 Mad. 174; but this explanation has not the effect of giving registration under any of the former Acts a priority over an unregistered document under any of the same Acts which it did not possess under those Acts. *Rupchand* v. *Davlatrav*, 6 Bom 495; *Shivram* v. *Saya*, 13 Bom. 229; *Sriram* v. *Bhagirath*, 4 All. 227.

(b) *Nalliappa Gounden* v. *Ibraim*, 5 Mad. 73; *Kondayya* v. *Guruvappa*, 5 Mad. 139.

(c) *Narasimulu* v. *Somanna*, 8 Mad. 167.

registered instrument (*d*). A mortgage for an optional amount, was made in 1872, and was not registered. In 1878 the property was purchased with full notice of the mortgage, and the deed was registered. In 1879 a suit was brought against the mortgagor to enforce the mortgage, and the land was attached in execution of his decree. It was held that the decree and attachment were ineffectual, as before the date of the suit the second document had put an end to the operation of the first as far as the purchaser was concerned. It would have been different if the decree had been before the purchase. Then the unregistered document would have been merged in and superseded by the decree prior to the execution of the registered document. The competition would have been between the decree and the registered document, and a decree relating to land, though unregistered, is by § 50 unaffected by a subsequent registered document, (*e*). On the other hand the Calcutta, Bombay, and Allahabad Courts hold that express notice of an unregistered document, deprives a purchaser under a registered instrument of the priority to which he would otherwise be entitled (*f*). The High Court of Bombay lays it down with equal distinctness that possession under an optionally unregistered document is notice to a subsequent purchaser by a registered document, which of itself deprives him of the benefits of registration (*g*). The contrary doctrine was expressly laid down by the High Court of Calcutta in one case, in which they overruled various decisions of their own Court in which an opposite view had been

---

(*d*) *Ramachandra* v. *Krishna*, 9 Mad. 495.

(*e*) *Madar Saheb* v. *Subbarayulu*, 6 Mad. 88, citing and distinguishing *Kolluri Nagabhushanum* v. *Ammanna*, 8 Mad. 71 ; *Contra Balinath* v. *Lachman Das*, 7 All. 888 ; *acc. Himalaya Bank* v. *Simla Bank*, 8 All. 23.

(*f*) *Ram Autar* v. *Dhanauri*, 8 All. 540 ; *Fazludeen Khan* v. *Fakir Mahomed*, 5 Cal. 336 ; *Chundernath* v. *Bhoyrub Chunder*, 10 Cal. 250 ; *Abool Hossein* v. *Raghunath*, 13 Cal. 70 ; *Shivram* v. *Genu*, 6 Bom. 515 ; *Moreshwar* v. *Dattu*, 12 Bom. 569. But see *Bamasunderi* v. *Krishna Chandra*, 10 Cal. 424, in which the Court seemed to treat the point as yet open to question. As to the amount of notice necessary, see *Bhalu Roy* v. *Jakhu Roy*, 11 Cal. 667 ; *Churaman* v. *Balli*, 9 All. 591. Act IV of 1882, § 3.

(*g*) *Dundaya* v. *Chenbasapa*, 9 Bom. 427 ; *Hathi Sing* v. *Kuverji*, 10 Bom. 105. The possession must be such as is inconsistent with the title on which the second purchaser relies. *Moreshwar* v. *Dattu*, 12 Bom. 569.

taken (*h*). In later cases the same Court appears to have treated possession under an unregistered deed as a fact from which notice of its existence might, but need not necessarily be inferred (*i*). In one of these cases *Garth*, C. J., intimated his opinion that under § 54 of the Transfer of Property Act (IV of 1882), which requires either a registered instrument or delivery of possession in the case of all sales of immovable property, optional registration was virtually abolished, every written instrument requiring to be registered (*k*). Possibly the Act may be read merely as depriving an unregistered instrument of any operation if not followed by possession. If possession is equivalent to notice, and if notice takes away the benefit of registration, the result would be that wherever an unregistered document had any effect it would rank before a registered document of later date.

Oral agreements or declarations.

§ 364. By § 48 of the Registration Act III of 1877, "All non-testamentary documents duly registered under the Act, and relating to any property whether movable or immovable, shall take effect against any oral agreement or declaration relating to such property, unless where the agreement or declaration has been followed by delivery of possession." A deposit of title deeds under a verbal arrangement to secure a debt, has been held not to be an oral agreement or declaration relating to property within the meaning of this section (*l*). Whatever view the Courts take as to the effect of notice under § 50 would apparently be taken as to this section also (*m*).

Form of transfer

§ 365. Writing is not necessary, under Hindu law, to the validity of any transaction whatever (*n*). Nor is there any

(*h*) *Fazludeen Khan* v. *Fakir Mahomed*, 5 Cal. 336.
(*i*) *Narain Chunder* v. *Dataram*, 8 Cal. 597; *Nani Dibee* v. *Hafizullah*, 10 Cal. 1073.
(*k*) 8 Cal., p. 612; *Contra Knatu* v. *Madhuram*, 16 Cal. 622.
(*l*) *Coggan* v. *Pogose*, 11 Cal. 158.
(*m*) *Chunder Nath* v. *Bhoyrub Chunder*, 10 Cal. 250.
(*n*) *Srinivasammal* v. *Vijayammal*, 2 Mad. H. C. 37; *Krishna* v. *Rayappa*, 4 Mad. H. C. 98; *per curiam*, *Jivandas* v. *Framji*, 7 Bom. H. C. (O. C. J.) 51;

distinction between movable and immovable property as to the mode of granting it (*o*). Nor are any technical words necessary, provided the intention of the grantor can be made out. Hence, an estate of inheritance will be conferred by words which imperfectly describe such an estate, if an intention to create such an estate appears; and if an estate is given to a man simply without express words of inheritance, it would, in the absence of a conflicting context, carry by Hindu law an estate of inheritance (*p*). So, the grant of an estate to a man and his children and grandchildren, or from generation to generation, or to a woman and the generations born of her womb, have been held to confer an absolute estate (*q*). A grant for years to a particular person enures to the benefit of that person's heirs after his death (*r*). A bequest to A for life, with unlimited powers of willing away or appointing to the property, has been treated as a gift of an absolute estate (*s*). So a grant from a husband to his widow was held absolute, where it stated that she was to take all his rights without exception, and that neither he nor his heirs were to have any claim to the estate (*t*). A similar intention will be inferred where the object of the grant, *e.g.*, for building, would be frustrated by a limited possession (*u*). Such an intention would be negatived when the grantor himself had only a limited estate, and it appeared that the grant was intended to endure so long as that interest lasted, but no longer (*v*). Or where from the nature of the thing conveyed, an intention to

---

Rookho v. *Madho*, 1 N.-W. P. 59; *Hurpurshad* v. *Sheo Dhyal*, 3 I. A 259; S. C. 26 Suth. 55. Transfer of Property Act (IV of 1882) § 9.

(*o*) *Per Peel*, C. J., *Seebkisto* v. *East India Co.*, 6 M. I. A. 278.

(*p*) *Per Willes*, J., *Tagore* v. *Tagore*, 9 B. L. R. 395; S. C. 18 Suth. 359; *Lekhraj* v. *Kunhya*, 4 I. A. 223; S. C. 3 Cal. 210; *Churaman* v. *Balli*, 9 All. 591. Transfer of Property Act (IV of 1882) § 8.

(*q*) *Bhoobun* v. *Hurrish*, 5 I. A. 138; S. C. 4 Cal. 23; *Ram Lal* v. *Secy. of State*, 8 I. A. 46; S. C. 7 Cal. 304; *Harihar* v. *Uman Pershad*, 14 I. A. 7; S. C. 14 Cal. 296.

(*r*) *Tej Chund* v. *Srikanth Ghose*, 3 M. I. A. 261; *Gobind Lal* v. *Hemendra*, 17 Cal. (P. C.) 686.

(*s*) *Bai Mamubai* v. *Dosa Morarji*, 15 Bom. 443; *Javerbai* v. *Kablibai*, 15 Bom. 326.

(*t*) *Ram Narain* v. *Pearay Bhugut*, 9 Cal. 830; See *post*, § 584

(*u*) *Gungadhur* v. *Ayimuddin*, 8 Cal. 960.

(*v*) *Lekhraj* v. *Kunhya*, 4 I. A. 223; S. C. 3 Cal. 210.

grant only for the life of the grantee ought to be presumed, as in the case of a jaghire, unless distinct words of inheritance are used (*w*), or an office (*x*), or a gift for maintenance (*y*). Or where the object of the grant was to enable the grantee to perform certain special services, in regard to which the grantor reposed a special confidence in him (*z*). In the case of leases, where no term is fixed, perpetuity cannot be assumed, even where the word "*Mokurruri*" is used, unless there are other circumstances from which such an intention can be inferred (*a*).

Statutory provisions as to alienation.

§ 366. The Transfer of Property Act (IV of 1882) contains various provisions as to the form of alienation which will modify the Hindu law as to all transactions subsequent to the 1st July 1882.

Sales.

By § 54 A transfer by way of sale "in the case of tangible immovable property of the value of one hundred rupees and upwards, or in the case of a reversion or other intangible thing, can be made only by a registered instrument. In the case of tangible immovable property of a value less than one hundred rupees, such transfer may be made either by a registered instrument or by delivery of the property."

Mortgages.

By § 59 "Where the principal money secured is one hundred rupees or upwards, a mortgage can be effected only by a registered instrument, signed by the mortgagor and attested by at least two witnesses. Where the principal money secured is less than one hundred rupees, a mortgage may be effected either by an instrument signed and attested

---

(*w*) *Gulabdas* v. *Collector of Surat*, 6 I. A. 54; S. C. 3 Bom. 186; *Ramchandra* v. *Venkatrao*, 6 Bom. 598; *affd.* 18 I. A. 22; S. C. 15 Bom. 222; *Dosibai* v. *Ishwardas*, 9 Bom. 561.

(*x*) *Daudsha* v. *Ismalsha*, 3 Bom. 72.

(*y*) See *post*, § 425.

(*z*) *Kalidas* v. *Kanhya Lall*, 11 I. A. 218; 11 Cal. 121; *Moulvi Muhammad* v. *Mt. Fatima Bibi*, 12 I. A. 159; S. C. 8 All. 39.

(*a*) *Sheo Pershad* v. *Kally Dass*, 5 Cal. 543; *affd. Bilasmoni* v. *Sheo Pershad* 9 I. A. 33; S. C. 8 Cal. 664; *Toolshi Pershad* v. *Ramnarrain Singh*, 12 I. A. 205; S. C. 12 Cal. 117; *Parmeswar Pertab* v. *Padmanand Singh*, 15 Cal. (P. C.) 342.

as aforesaid or (except in the case of a simple mortgage, *i.e.*, hypothecation) by delivery of the property. Nothing in this section shall be deemed to render invalid mortgages, made in the towns of Calcutta, Madras, Bombay, Karachi, and Rangoon, by delivery to a creditor or his agent of documents of title to immovable property, with intent to create a security thereon."

Leases. By § 107 "A lease of immovable property from year to year, or for any term exceeding one year, or reserving a yearly rent, can be made only by a registered instrument. All other leases of immovable property may be made either by an instrument or by oral agreement."

Gifts. By § 123 "For the purpose of making a gift of immovable property, the transfer must be effected by a registered instrument signed by or on behalf of the donor, and attested by at least two witnesses. For the purpose of making a gift of movable property, the transfer may be effected either by a registered instrument signed as aforesaid or by delivery. Such delivery may be made in the same way as goods sold are delivered." (*b*)

In cases under the old law of gifts it was held that registration of the deed of gift did not amount to, or make up for the want of possession (*c*). Does the present section dispense with possession? It certainly does not dispense with acceptance of the gift, which is essential under § 122. If then there can be no valid acceptance under Hindu law without possession, actual or symbolical, then § 122 does not alter the Hindu law. But if there can be a sufficient acceptance without possession so as to satisfy § 122, then a registered gift of movable property would be valid under § 123 if accepted, even though Hindu law required delivery

---

(*b*) As to gifts by Taluqdars of Oudh, see Act I of 1869, § 13 and cases 11 I. A. 1, 121.

(*c*) *Vasudev* v. *Narayan*, 7 Bom. 131; *Dagai Dabee* v. *Mothura Nath*, 9 Cal. 854.

of possession by the donor, as well as acceptance of the gift by the donee. It will be seen by § 129 that § 122 is not to affect any rule of Hindu law, but that § 123 will not be invalid even though it should do so. The Calcutta High Court has held that delivery of possession of property, whether movable or immovable, is unnecessary, where the deed of gift has been registered (*d*).

(*d*) *Dharmodas* v. *Nistarini*, 14 Cal. 446.

CHAPTER XI.

WILLS.

Wills unknown to Hindu law.

§ 367. THE origin and growth of the testamentary power among Hindus has always been a perplexity to lawyers. It is admitted that the idea of a will is wholly unknown to Hindu law, and that the native languages do not even possess a word to express the idea (*a*). In early times, when the family property was vested in the family corporation, and when the members had nothing more than a right of usufruct, the idea that any individual could exercise a power of disposal to commence after his own death, would have been a contradiction in terms. Even in later times, when a greater freedom of disposition had arisen, the principle that a gift could only take effect by possession would seem to oppose an absolute bar to devises. Yet there can be no doubt that from the earliest period of our acquaintance with India we find traces of a struggling towards the testamentary power, often checked, but constantly renewed. It has been common to ascribe this to the influence of English lawyers in the Supreme Courts; but this explanation seems to me untenable. It is very probable that in the Presidency Towns, the example of Englishmen making wills may have stimulated the natives in the same direction, but the King's Judges appear to have been quite neutral in the matter. They were conscious of their ignorance of native law, and anxiously sought the advice of their own pandits (§ 38), and of the Judges of the Company's Courts, and others who were experts in the unknown science. So far were they from grasping at jurisdiction, that they

---

(*a*) 2 Dig: 516, n.; 2 Stra. H. L. 418, 220, 431.

absolutely disclaimed it. In 1776 the Supreme Court of Calcutta, after taking time to consider, granted administration to the goods of a Hindu, but on the terms that the administrator should administer according to Hindu law. In 1791 they reconsidered the matter, and decided that probate of the will, or administration of the goods of a Hindu or Muhammedan, could not be granted. It was not till July 1832 that a contrary rule was laid down, and from that date the practice of granting probate and administration to the property of natives was fully established (*b*). A similar alteration of practice is recorded by Sir *Thomas Strange* as having taken place at Madras (*c*). The earliest known will of a native is that of the celebrated Omichund. It is dated 1758, a time when the English arms were more in the ascendant than the English Courts (*d*). **Early instances in Supreme Courts.**

§ 368. It seems to me that the true origin of the testamentary power is to be sought for in that Brahmanical influence, the working of which I have already traced in the law of partition and alienation (*e*). It displayed itself, especially, in the sanctity attributed to religious gifts, that is gifts to religious men, or Brahmans. These were considered valid where even transfers for value would have been set aside. In other countries gifts try to clothe themselves with the semblance of a sale. Under Hindu law, sales claimed protection by assuming the appearance of a gift (*f*). It is obvious that a man is never more disposed to pious generosity than in his last days, when the approach of death furnishes him with the strongest motives for investing in the next world that wealth which he can no longer **Origin of wills in religious influence.**

(*b*) *Re Commula*, Morton, 1; *Goods of Hadjee Mustapha, ib.* 74; *Goods of Beebee Muttra, ib.* 75.

(*c*) 1 Stra. H. L. 267.

(*d*) This will was discussed in a case which came before the Supreme Court of Calcutta in 1793. See Montriou, 321; *per Phear*, J., *Tagore* v. *Tagore*, 4 B. L. R (O. C. J.) 138; Beng. Reg. 11. (Collectors and Board of Revenue) and XXXVI of 1793, (Registry for Wills and Deeds) cited by *Macpherson*, J. *Krishnaramani* v. *Ananda*, 4 B. L. R (O. C. J.) 288; *per Norman*, J., *Tagore* v. *Tagore*, 4 B. L. R. (O. C. J.) 217.

(*e*) *Ante*, §§ 219, 237, 238. See particularly the passage from Sir H. S. Maine, cited § 237.

(*f*) See Mitakshara, i. 1, § 32; *Raghunandana*, v. 25.

enjoy in the present. The acuteness of the Brahman would have readily discovered and utilised this fact. Nothing is more remarkable in the earliest Bengal wills than the enormous amounts which they bestow for religious purposes. The same thing was remarked by Sir *Thomas Strange* in all the wills made by Hindus in Madras, and he observes somewhat cynically, that "the proportion is commonly in the ratio of the iniquity with which the property has been acquired, or of the sensuality and corruption to which it has been devoted" (*g*). It is probable that such bequests would often take the form of a *donatio mortis causâ,* revocable if the grantor survived, or that they were effected by death-bed dispositions, followed up by immediate delivery of possession. But there are texts of the Hindu sages which contain the actual germ of a will, and which were capable of being developed into a complete testamentary system. *Katyayana* says, "What a man has promised in health or in sickness, for a religious purpose, must be given; and if he die without giving it, his son shall doubtless be compelled to deliver it." And again, "After delivering what is due as a friendly gift (promised by the father), let the remainder be divided among the heirs." And so *Harita* says: "A promise made in words, but not performed in deed, is a debt of conscience both in this world and the next" (*h*). Such promises, being treated as debts, would be enforced against the heir in exactly the same manner as an ordinary secular debt. At first they would be treated as a moral obligation, and then, by analogy, as a legal obligation. It is significant that the principle seems first to have been applied in favour of pious gifts. But it would rapidly extend to all dispositions of property, to the extent of a man's power of disposing of it. In case of separate and self-acquired property the right would naturally be admitted with little hesitation. It would afterwards be

Early history of wills.

(*g*) 2 Stra. H. L. 453.

(*h*) 2 Dig. 96; 3 Dig. 388; 2 Dig. 171. The only writer, as far as I know, who has remarked the bearing of these texts upon the present question is M. Gibelin. See a very interesting discussion (Vol. ii. Titre. vii), in which he points out that the Hindu will was a native and not an European invention.

applied to the undivided share of a co-heir, or to ancestral property in the hands of a father or sole owner. In each province the rapidity and extent of the growth of the testamentary power would depend upon the degree to which the control of the testator over his property was admitted. This is exactly what took place.

§ 369. The law of devise was, as might be expected, first settled in Bengal, where the power of alienation was most widely extended. The reported cases commence in 1786, and the first two related to divided and self-acquired property, as to which, after reference to the Pandits, the wills were maintained (*i*). In 1792 the Nuddea case, (*k*) which has already been stated (§ 347), was decided in the Sudder Court, and it was followed next year in the Supreme Court by the case of *Dialchund* v. *Kissory* (*l*), where the property appears to have been self-acquired. In both these cases the Pandits affirmed the right of a father to devise property, whether ancestral or self-acquired, and the former of the two is stated by Mr. Colebrooke to have been accepted as establishing the point. Mr. Sutherland, however, to whom the latter case was referred for his opinion, stated that the will would be only valid as against sons, "provided no part of the property conferred by it were real ancestral property" (*m*). This view was evidently not taken by the profession, for in 1800 a most important case arising out of the *Rajah Nobkissen's* will was litigated in the Supreme Court, where the Rajah, who had a natural-born and an adopted son, bequeathed an ancestral taluq to his adopted son, and the four brothers of such son, thereby depriving his natural son of all interest in the taluq, and his adopted son of four-fifths of his interest. The validity of the will was admitted without dispute, though the adoption was

Cases in Bengal.

(*i*) *Munnoo* v. *Gopee*, Montr. 290; *Russick* v. *Choitun*, *ib.* 304; 2 M. Dig. 220.
(*k*) *Eshanchund* v. *Eshorchund*, 1 S. D. 2.
(*l*) Montr. 371; F. MacN. 357.
(*m*) 2 Stra. H. L. 429. See Mr. Colebrooke's own opinions, 2 Stra. H. L. 431, 435, 437.

contested (*n*). In 1808 the will of *Nemychurn Mullick* was contested in the Supreme Court, and the decree declared "that by the Hindu law Nemychurn Mullick might and could dispose by will of all his property, as well movable as immovable, and as well ancestorial as otherwise." This case went on appeal upon another point to the Privy Council, but the finding as to the validity of the will was never disputed (*o*). Accordingly, the will of a brother of Nemychurn, who died possessed of great wealth, ancestral and self-acquired, was never contested, although by it he almost completely disinherited one of his sons (*p*). In 1812 the Sudder Pandits, when consulted as to the validity of an alleged devise by a widow, laid down the general principle, that "the same rule applies to bequests as to gifts; every person who has authority, while in health, to transfer property to another, possesses the same authority of bequeathing it (*q*)." Finally, after the period of doubt caused by the decision in *Bhowanny Churn's* case, the matter was set at rest for ever, as far as Bengal is concerned, by the certificate of the Sudder Court in 1831, which has already been set out (§ 347). It is now beyond dispute that in Bengal a father, as regards all his property, and a co-heir, as regards his share, may dispose of it by will as he likes, whatever may be its nature (*r*).

Their validity established in Bengal.

Minor. Married woman.

§ 370. A minor has been held in Bengal to be incapable of making a will (*s*). A married woman may make a will of her *stridhana* or any other property which is absolutely at her own disposal. But she cannot devise property inherited from males, since her interest in it ceases at her death (*t*).

(*n*) *Gopee* v. *Rajkristna*, Montr. 381; S. C. F. MacN. 356.
(*o*) *Ramtoonoo* v. *Ramgopaul*, F. MacN. 336; S. C. 1 Kn. 245.
(*p*) F. MacN. 350.
(*q*) *Sreenarain* v. *Bhya Jha*, 2 S. D. 23 (29, 37).
(*r*) *Per Ld. Kingsdown*, *Nagalutchmee* v. *Gopoo*, 6 M. I. A. 344; *per Peacock*, C. J., *Tagore* v. *Tagore*, 4 B. L. R. (O. C. J.) 159; *per Willes*, J., *Tagore* v. *Tagore*, 9 B. L. R. 396; S C. 18 Suth. 359
(*s*) *Cossinaut Bysack* v. *Hurroosoondry*, F. MacN. 81; 2 M. Dig. 198, note.
(*t*) *Teencowree* v. *Dinonath*, 3 Suth. 49; *Chooneelal* v. *Jussoo*, 1 Bor. 55 [60]; *Dhoolubh* v. *Jeevee*, *ib.* 67 [75]; *Umroot* v. *Kulyandas*, *ib.* 284 [314]; *Venkata Rama* v. *Venkata Suriya*, 2 Mad. (P. C.) 333.

Both the above points are now affirmed by statute as regards Hindus (*u*).

Wills in Southern India.

§ 371. In Southern India wills had a much more chequered career, as might be anticipated from the stricter views entertained as to the family union. During the time Sir *Thomas Strange* was on the Bench no question as to wills arose in such a form as to require a decision. He evidently considered them a mere innovation, though, after consultation with Mr. Colebrooke, he was disposed to think that they might be allowed to the same extent to which a gift *inter vivos* would have been valid (*v*). He cites several futwahs of Madras pandits in which they seem to take the same view. These are all commented upon by Mr. Ellis, whose authority on Madras law and usage ranked very high. He asserted with confidence that no Hindu could make a will which would turn his property after his death into a different course from that which it would have taken by Hindu law. He intimated a very strong doubt whether the Pandits understood what was meant when they were questioned as to the operation of a will (*w*). It is quite certain that in the case which ultimately settled the law, they thought they were being consulted as to the effect of a gift (*x*). The course of decisions in Madras for many years was certainly in accordance with his view. The only case litigated in the Supreme Court was one where a testator had bequeathed part of his self-acquired property for the performance of religious ceremonies (*y*). This would clearly have been valid under the text of Katyayana already cited (§ 368). In the Sudder Court, however, there were numerous decisions. The first was in 1817, but as the devise was in favour of an adopted son, the first question was as to the validity of the

Early instances doubtful.

(*u*) Act X. of 1865, § 46 [Succession] extended to Hindus by Act XXI of 1870, § 2, and see § 3 [Hindu Wills] and Act V of 1881, § 149 [Probate and Administration].

(*v*) *Veerapermall* v. *Narrain*, 1 N. C. 91; 1 Stra. H. L. 267.

(*w*) 2 Stra. H. L. 217—228.

(*x*) See *post*, § 374. It must be remembered that the Pandits did not speak English, and that their language contained no equivalent for will.

(*y*) *Narrainsamy* v. *Arnachella*, 1 Stra. H. L. 268, note; *Vallinayagam* v. *Pachche*, 1 Mad. H. C. 336.

adoption, and as its validity was established, that of the will never arose (*z*). The next cases arose in 1824 and 1828, and gave rise to much litigation, extending ultimately to the Privy Council. In these a widow sued to set aside two alienations, made by her deceased husband to distant relations, of property which would have otherwise come to her as his heir. In the first case the document is spoken of as a will, but was in terms a deed of gift, and recited that possession had been given. This, however, appears not to have been done. The decision was in favour of the widow, but upon the ground that upon the proper construction of the will the devisee only took as manager for the heir, and was now dead. In their judgment the Court stated as their opinion "that under the Hindu law a man is authorised to dispose of his property by will, which under the same law he could have alienated during his survivorship by any other instrument" (*a*). This, of course, was purely *obiter dictum*.

Dictum of Sudder Court.

Early instances doubtful.

In the second case, possession under the gift was established. The property was self-acquired, and the question was correctly put to the pandits, whether a gift of self-acquired property made by a man without male issue was valid as against a widow, who was left an heir to other property to a large extent. The pandits answered that the gift was valid, and the Court so decided. This case was confirmed by the Privy Council. There, too, though the document is spoken of as a will, the transaction is treated as an alienation, and its validity is rested on the opinion of the Hindu law officers, who had dealt with it purely as such (*b*). In an intermediate case the question was whether a will would be valid if it left the whole of a partible zemindary to one of two sons. The Court decided that the document really left it to the two sons as joint heirs. But they said, "The Court have repeatedly decided that the will of a Hindu is of no validity or effect whatever, except so far as it may be con-

(*z*) *Arnachellum* v. *Iyasamy*, 1 Mad. Dec. 154.
(*a*) *Mulrauze Vencata* v. *Mulrauze Lutchmiah*, 1 Mad. Dec. 438, 449.
(*b*) *Mulrauze* v. *Chellakany*, 2 Mad. Dec. 12, *affirmed*, 2 M. I. A. 54.

sistent with Hindu law (*c*)." Later still the same Court treated a will, by which a grandfather was asserted to have left landed property to his wife to the prejudice of his sons, as being absolutely invalid as against their sons, *i.e.*, his own grandsons (*d*).

Tendency of opinion.

§ 372. So far there really had been no actual decisions, but the tendency of the Sudder Judges had certainly been to accept the opinions of Sir *Thomas Strange*, Mr. Colebrooke, and the pandits, that the legality of a will must be tried by the same tests as that of a gift; for instance, that it would be valid if made to the prejudice of a widow, invalid if made to the prejudice of male issue. At this time Madras Reg. V of 1829 (Hindu Wills) was passed. It recited that wills were instruments unknown, and had been made so as to be totally repugnant, to the authorities prevailing in Madras; it then repealed a former regulation which had authorised the executors of the will of a Hindu to take charge of his property, and enacted that for the future Hindu wills should have no legal force whatever, except so far as they were in conformity with Hindu law, according to authorities prevalent in the Madras Presidency. This regulation appears to have induced the Judges to regard wills as being wholly inoperative. Wills were not only set aside where they prejudiced the issue, as by an unequal distribution of ancestral property between the sons (*e*); but the Court also laid down that where a man without issue bequeathed his property away from his widow and daughters, such a will would be absolutely illegal and void, unless they had assented to it (*f*). These decisions would appear to have put wills completely out of Court. But in the very next year a case was decided which ultimately proved to be the commencement of a complete revolution on the point. The circum-

Reg. V of 1829.

Validity of wills denied.

(*c*) *Sooranany* v. *Sooranany*, 1 Mad. Dec. 495.
(*d*) *Yejnamoorty* v. *Chavaly*, 2 Mad. Dec. 16.
(*e*) *Moottoovengada* v. *Toombayasamy*, Mad. Dec. of 1849, 27.
(*f*) *Tullapragadah* v. *Crovedy*, 2 Mad. Dec. 79; *Sevacawmy* v. *Vaneyummal*, Mad. Dec. of 1850, 50.

stances attending it were so singular as to merit a little detail.

Current reversed.

§ 373. The suit was by a widow to recover her husband's estate, which consisted in part of ancestral immovable property. The defendants set up a will executed by the deceased, by which he constituted them executors and managers of his estate, and, after providing for his wife and daughters, left the rest of his property to religious and charitable uses, with a proviso that if his wife, then pregnant, bore a son, the estate should revert to him on his coming of age. The will was found to be genuine, but the widow set up an authority to adopt a son in the event of a daughter being born. The Civil Judge consulted the Sudder Pandits, and asked whether the will was valid, and if so, whether it would be invalidated by the authority to adopt, if actually given. The Pandits answered, "The will referred to in the question is valid under the Hindu law, the testator having thereby bequeathed a portion of his estate for the maintenance of his wife, and other members of his family, whom he was bound to protect, and directed the remainder to be appropriated to charitable purposes in the event of his wife, who was then pregnant, not being delivered of a son. If the testator had really given his wife verbal instructions to adopt a son in the event of her not bearing male issue, her compliance with those instructions would, of course, invalidate the will according to the Hindu law, it being incompetent for the testator who authorised the adoption of a son to alienate the whole of his estate, and thereby injure the means of the maintenance of his would-be heir." The Civil Judge found against the alleged authority to adopt, and decided in favour of the will. His decision was given in 1849, before the decision of the Sudder Court last quoted. In appeal to the Sudder Udalut, the widow urged that under Reg. V of 1829 (Hindu Wills) the will was void. The case was heard by a single Judge, who affirmed the decree of the lower Court. In regard to the validity of the will, he said, "The third objection taken by the appel-

Nagalutchmy v. Nadaraja.

lant is that the will is illegal, because the widow is the party to whom the law gives the estate. The Court have referred to all the authorities quoted by the appellant in support of this position, and find that although the opinions regarding wills of Hindus generally are conflicting, yet that the majority of them are against the argument of the appellant. It is unnecessary to cite all the opinions given on the subject, and the Court will content itself with referring to the case of *Ramtoonoo Mullick* v. *Ramgopaul Mullick* (Morl. Dig., p. 39, Nos. 3 & 4), in which it was held that a Hindu might, and could, dispose by will of all his property, movable and immovable, and as well ancestral as otherwise, and this decision was affirmed on appeal by the Judicial Committee of the Privy Council. Questions, however, regarding the legality of the will now under discussion were referred to the law officers of the Court, to whom the legislature have assigned the duty of declaring the law on such matters, and they distinctly stated their opinion, that it is a valid and good instrument. The arguments, therefore, of the appellant that it is not recognizable under the provisions of Reg. V of 1829, cannot be sustained" (*g*).

§ 374. Upon this decision, Mr. *Strange*, lately a Judge of the Madras Sudder and High Courts, remarks (*h*), "This decision was passed by a single Judge, confessedly ignorant of the law. He sought to guide himself by authorities, but found them conflicting. Supporting himself by the opinion of the Pandits, and a judgment by the Calcutta Supreme Court, affirmed by the Privy Council, he upheld the will then in issue, which appointed trustees to the testator's property, to the prejudice of his widow. The Pandits then applied to, are the same who have since declared that no Hindu can make a will, and they explain that they gave the opinion rested on in the above case under the idea that they were called upon to test the will by the power the testator had to

Criticised by Mr. Strange.

(*g*) *Nagalutchmy* v. *Nadaraja*, Mad. Dec. of 1851, 226.
(*h*) Stra. Man. § 176.

deal with the property during his lifetime, in the manner he had done by will." Certainly no particular authority can be allowed to the decision of the Sudder Court. It is impossible to imagine where the learned Judge could have found the conflicting decisions he referred to, unless among the Bengal reports, and the case of *Ramtoonoo* v. *Ramgopaul* was, of course, upon this point of no authority whatever in Madras. The only Madras authority he could have found was the *dictum* in *Mulrauze Vencata* v. *Mulrauze Lutchmiah*, (1 Mad. Dec. 449,) which laid down the broad principle that whatever a man may do by act *inter vivos*, he may do by will. Probably this principle accounts for the mode in which the question appears to have been put to the Pandits, and for their misapprehension as to the point on which their opinion was required. That there must have been some misapprehension appears, not only from Mr. *Strange's* statement, made after personal consultation with them, but from a subsequent *futwah* of theirs, in which the very distinction is taken between a gift and a will. In 1852 they pronounced that "A man may in his lifetime alienate his property to the prejudice of his widow, leaving her the means of maintenance; but he cannot make arrangements that such arrangement shall take place after his death, since his widow would be entitled to what he died possessed of (*i*)."

Founded on mistake of Pandits.

Confirmed on appeal.

Privy Council decision.

§ 375. However, the case went, on appeal, to the Privy Council, and was there affirmed. Their Lordships said (*k*), "It may be allowed that in the ancient Hindu law, as it was understood through the whole of Hindustan, testamentary instruments, in the sense affixed by English lawyers to that expression, were unknown; and it is stated by a writer of authority (Sir *Thomas Strange*) that the Hindu language has no term to express what we mean by a will. But it does not necessarily follow that what in effect, though not in form, are testamentary instruments, which are only to

(*i*) Sudder Pandits, 19th July, 1852; Stra. Man. § 178.
(*k*) *Nagalutchmee* v. *Gopoo*, 6 M. I. A. 309, 344. See too *per* Ld. *Kingsdown*, *Bhoobum Moyee* v. *Ram Kishore*, 10 M. I. A. 308; S. C. 3 Suth. (P. C.) 15.

come into operation, and affect property, after the death of the maker of the instrument, were equally unknown. However this may be, the strictness of the ancient law has long since been relaxed, and throughout Bengal a man who is the absolute owner of property may now dispose of it by will as he pleases, whether it be ancestral or not. This point was resolved several years ago by the concurrence of all the judicial authorities in Calcutta, as well of the Supreme as of the Sudder Court (*l*). No doubt the law of Madras differs in some respects, and amongst others with respect to wills, from that of Bengal. But even in Madras it is settled that a will of property, not ancestral, may be good. A decision to this effect has been recognized and acted upon by the Judicial Committee (*m*), and, indeed, the rule of law to that extent is not disputed in this case. If, then, the will does not affect ancestral property, it must be, not because an owner of property by the Madras law cannot make a will, but because, by some peculiarity of ancestral property, it is withdrawn from the testamentary power. It was very ingeniously argued by the respondent's counsel, that in all cases where a man is able to dispose of his property by act *inter vivos,* he may do so by will; that he cannot do so when he has a son, because the son, immediately on his birth, becomes coparcener with his father; that the objection to bequeathing ancestral property is founded on the Hindu notion of an undivided family; but that where there are no males in the family the liberty of bequeathing is unlimited. It is not necessary for their Lordships to lay down so broad a proposition, as they think it safer to confine themselves to the particular case before them. Under the circumstances of testator's family when he made his will and codicil, and having regard to the instruments themselves, the Pandits

(*l*) This evidently refers to the certificate of the Sudder Judges to the Supreme Court in 1831. See *ante*, § 347.

(*m*) See the case of *Mulraz* v. *Chalekany*, 2 M. I. A. 54, and the two cases in the Sudder Court, *Mulrauze Vencata* v. *Mulrauze Lutchmiah*, 1 Mad. Dec. 438, and *Mulrauze* v. *Chellakany*, 2 Mad. Dec. 12, *ante*, § 371, where it is shown that both were cases of gift; the one which was affirmed in the P. C. having undoubtedly been followed by possession given to the donee in the life of the donor.

to whom this question was properly referred by the Court—the Pandits of the Sudder Dewanny Udalut—have declared their opinion that these instruments are sufficient to dispose of ancestral estate; that opinion has been affirmed by two Judges successively, of whom it is but justice to say that they appear to have examined the subject very carefully, and after much consideration to have pronounced very satisfactory judgments, though in one or two incidental observations which have fallen from them their Lordships may not entirely concur."

Change effected by it.

§ 376. This decision undoubtedly gave a new direction to the law of Madras as regards wills. Being a decision of the Court of final appeal, it ought to have been impossible ever again to lay down the principle, that a will could have no operation, and must be treated as wholly invalid, if its directions were opposed to the rules of succession which would have prevailed in its absence. The decision, no doubt, was expressly based upon the opinion of the Pandits, and the judgments of two Judges. The former appears to have been founded on a misconception, and the latter upon the erroneous application of decisions given under one system of law, to a case which ought to have been governed by a wholly different system. But there can be little doubt that the decision was in unconscious conformity to the popular feeling, a feeling which aimed at increased liberty in regard to property, and which showed itself by attempts to alienate it in ways unknown to the law of the *Mitakshara*. In fact, the people of Southern India were trying, perhaps without knowing what they did, to take upon themselves the powers which *Jimuta Vahana* and his disciples had conferred upon the Hindus of Bengal. But beyond the fact that their Lordships, as it were, gave vitality to wills, the actual effect of the decision was very narrow. It carefully refrained from asserting that the power of bequest was co-extensive with that of alienation *inter vivos*. It laid down that a man, who had in other ways provided for his wife and daughters, might devise ancestral immovable property as he pleased to their prejudice. It seemed to assume that he could not do so as against male descendants. It neither affirmed, nor denied, the further doctrine of the Pandits, that, if he had given authority to adopt, his devise would be invalid as against a son adopted in pursuance of such authority (*n*).

Later decisions.

§ 377. The decree of the Judicial Committee was pronounced in 1856, and in 1852 and subsequent years several decisions of the Madras Sudder Court are recorded, which seem to have been passed in perfect unconsciousness of their own decree in 1851. In the first case (*o*) a person who is described as the son of the cousin-german of the testator, sued to set aside a will by the deceased in favour of the foster son. The property in this case was certainly not ancestral. It had come to the testator from his brother, to whom it had been bequeathed by his maternal grandmother. He might therefore have disposed of it by gift at his pleasure (§ 318). The Sudder Pandits said, "As the Hindu law does not recognize a foster son, it was not legal that F. (the testator) should constitute H. (the special appellant) his foster son, and make a will accordingly, nor is it consistent with the Shaster that H. should perform F.'s funeral rites. Such performance on his part is legally ineffectual, and cannot entitle him to the property of F., which must go to F.'s sapinda kinsmen, who are included in the order of succession to the property of a person who died leaving no male issue." The Sudder Court affirmed the correctness of this exposition, but dismissed the suit on the ground that the plaintiff was not the testator's heir. In 1855 and 1859 the Sudder Court again broadly laid down the rule that a will was of no effect unless it took effect by possession during the donor's lifetime; that as a mere will

Sudder Court refuse to act on Privy Council decision.

(*n*) See F. MacN. 151, 228; *Durma* v. *Coomara*, Mad. Dec. of 1852, p. 111.
(*o*) *Samy Josyen* v. *Ramien*, Mad. Dec. of 1852, p. 60.

it created no title, and could not affect the inheritance (*p*). In 1861 there were three cases, in all of which the wills were set aside as being opposed to Hindu law. In two of these cases the will was made to the prejudice of the testator's widow, as in the Privy Council case. The latest case is said to have been exactly similar to that of *Nagalutchmy* v. *Nadaraja;* but the Sudder Court refused to be bound by that decision, holding that it had been based upon an opinion of the Pandits, which was given under a misapprehension, and which the law officers had afterwards retracted (*q*).

Harmony restored by

§ 378. In 1862 the High Court was constituted in Madras, and the question shortly came again before a tribunal which was more willing to be bound by the decisions of the Privy Council than its predecessor. Here the testator, who had no male issue, had bequeathed the bulk of his property, movable and immovable, to a distant relation, allotting what was admitted to be a sufficient maintenance to his legal representative, his widow. No possession had been given, and confessedly the disposition could only operate as a will. There was no finding whether the property was ancestral or self-acquired, but the Chief Justice said it must be assumed to be the former. The Court reviewed all the previous decisions, and affirmed the will. They said, "It is not necessary for us here to consider and lay down any general rule as to how far, or under what circumstances the law gives to a Hindu the power of disposal by will. But we may observe, that now that the legal right to make a will is settled, there seems nothing in principle or reason opposed to the exercise of the power being allowed co-extensively (as stated in some of the cases, and forcibly urged in *Nagalutchmy* v. *Nadaraja*) with the independent right of gift or

High Court decision.

(*p*) Stra. Man. § 177; *Chocalinga* v. *Iyah*, Mad. Dec. of 1859, 35; *Kasale* v. *Palaniayi*, *ib.* 247. See, too, *Bogaraz* v. *Tanjore Venkatarav*, Mad. Dec. of 1860, 115.

(*q*) *Muttu* v. *Annavaiyangar*, Mad. Dec. of 1861, 67; *Virakumara* v. *Gopalu*, *ib.* 147; *Vallinayagam* v. *Pachche*, 1 Mad. H. C. 338, note.

other disposal by act *inter vivos*, which by law or established usage, or custom having the force of law, a native now possesses in Madras. To this extent the power of disposition can reasonably be considered to be in conformity with the respective proprietary rights of the possessor of property, and of heirs and coparceners, as provided and secured by the provisions of Hindu law" (*r*). This decision, of course, put an end to all discussion as to the capacity of a testator in Madras to make a binding will. The extent of that capacity will be considered further on (§ 380).

Wills originally not recognised in Bombay.

§ 379. The same silent revolution appears to have taken place in the Bombay Presidency. In a very early case in which the pandits were consulted they said, "There is no mention of wills in our Shasters, and therefore they ought not to be made;" and proceeded to point out that the owner of property could only dispose of it in a manner, and to the persons, directed by law (*s*). Accordingly, the Shastries declared wills to be invalid by which a man devised property away from his wife and daughters, though he provided for their maintenance, putting it on the general principle that the wife was heir, and therefore the will was ineffectual (*t*). And, similarly, where the will was in favour of one of two sisters' sons, to the exclusion of a third sister, and the second son of the second sister (*u*). In all these cases, it will be observed, a gift would have been perfectly valid. These decisions ranged from 1806 to 1820. When the current changed I am unable to state; but in 1866 *Westropp*, J., said, "In the Supreme Court the wills of Hindus have been always recognized, and also in the High Court, at the original side. Whatever questions there may formerly have

Validity of wills in Bombay.

(*r*) *Vallinayagam* v. *Pachche*, 1 Mad. H. C. 326, 339; *Ashutosh* v. *Doorga Churn*, 6 I. A. 182; S. C. 5 Cal. 438; S. C. 5 C. L. R. 296.

(*s*) 2 Stra. H. L. 449.

(*t*) *Deo Baee* v. *Wan Baee*, 1 Bor. 27 [29]; *Goolab* v. *Phool*, *ib.* 154 [178]; *Gungaram* v. *Tappee*, *ib.* 372 [412].

(*u*) *Ichharam* v. *Prumanund*, 2 Bor. 471 [515]. For cases where the persons disinherited may possibly have been coparceners; see *Tooljaram* v. *Nurbheram*, 1 Bor. 380 [421]; *Hureewulubh* v. *Keshowram*, 2 Bor. 6 [7]; and *Man Baee* v. *Krishnee*, *ib.* 124 [141].

been as to the right of a Hindu to make a will relating to his property in the Mofussil, or as to the recognition of wills by the Hindu law, there can be no doubt that testamentary writings are, as returns made within the last few years from the Zillahs show, made in all parts of the Mofussil of this Presidency; but, as might have been expected, much more frequently in some districts than in others, and this Court at its appellate side, has, on several occasions, recognized and acted on such documents (*v*)."

Extent of the testamentary power.

§ 380. The extent of the testamentary power, after being subject to much discussion, has at length been finally settled by decisions, and by express legislation. Whatever property is so completely under the control of the testator that he may give it away during his lifetime, he may also devise by will. Hence, a man may bequeath his separate, or his self-acquired, property; and one who, by the extinction of coparceners, holds all his property in severalty, may devise it, even in Malabar, so as to defeat the claims of remote heirs (*w*). So, a woman may dispose by will of such parts of her *stridhanum* as are during her life absolutely under her own control (*x*). She cannot dispose of property which she has inherited from a male, and as to which her estate is limited by the usual restrictions (*y*). A member of an undivided family cannot bequeath even his own share of the joint property, because "at the moment of death, the right by survivorship is at conflict with the right by devise. Then the title by survivorship, being the prior title, takes precedence to the exclusion of that by devise" (*z*).

(*v*) *Narottam* v. *Narsandás*, 3 Bom. H. C. (A. C. J.) 8.

(*w*) *Beer Pertab* v. *Maharajah Rajender*, 12 M. I. A. 38; S. C. 9 Suth. (P. C.) 15; *Narottam* v. *Narsandás*, 3 Bom. H. C. (A. C. J.) 6; *Alami* v. *Komu*, 12 Mad. 126. The same rule appears to prevail in the Punjab. Punjab customs, 34, 68. Punjab Customary law, III. 94.

(*x*) *Venkata Rama* v. *Venkata Suriya*, 2 Mad. (P. C.) 333.

(*y*) *Bai Devkore* v. *Amritram*, 10 Bom. 372.

(*z*) *Per curiam*, *Vitla Butten* v. *Yamenamma*, 8 Mad. H. C. 6; *Gooroova* v. *Narrainsawmy*, *ib.* 13; *Narottam* v. *Narsandás*, 3 Bom. H. C. (A. C. J.) 6; *Gangubai* v. *Ramanna*, 3 Bom. H. C. (A. C. J.) 66; *Udaram* v. *Ranu*, 11 Bom. H. C. 76; *Lakshman* v. *Ramchandra*, 7 I. A. 181; S. C. 5 Bom. 48. This rule applies in favour of a son *in gremio matris* as much as it does in the case of a son *in esse*. *Hanmant Ramchandra* v. *Bhimacharya*, 12 Bom. 105.

And on the same principle, a devise by one of several widows of property to which she is entitled jointly with her co-widows, is invalid (a). The cases which decide this latter point are all from Madras and Bombay. But they would, of course, have been followed by the Bengal Courts in cases under the Mitakshara law, since they do not admit the right of a coparcener even by sale, much less by gift, to dispose of his own undivided share during his lifetime, without the consent of those jointly interested in it (§ 337). The same result is arrived at by legislation. Act XXI of 1870 (Hindu Wills) extends to Hindus, Jains, Sikhs and Buddhists various provisions of the Succession Act, X of 1865, which relate to wills; but § 3 provides "that nothing herein contained shall authorise a testator to bequeath property which he could not have alienated *inter viros*, or to deprive any persons of any right of maintenance of which, but for § 2 (the extending section) he could not deprive them by will; and that nothing herein contained shall affect any law of adoption or intestate succession." The probate and administration Act V of 1881, which also applies to Hindus, provides by § 4, that "nothing herein contained shall vest in an executor or administrator any property of a deceased person which would otherwise have passed by survivorship to some other person."

Estate must be one allowed by Hindu law.

§ 381. So far we have been treating of the testator's power to devise as it relates to the persons to whom he may devise, that is, his power to alter the order of succession as it would arise in the event of intestacy. But a completely different question arises as to his power to alter the nature of the estate which will vest in his devisee, that is, to create an estate of a different species from that to which the law would give rise. As to this, the rule is that, so far as he has the power of bequest at all, he may not only direct who shall take the estate, but may also direct what quantity of estate they shall take, both as regards the object

(a) *Gurivi Reddi* v. *Chinnamma*, 7 Mad. 93.

matter to be taken, and the duration of time for which it is to be held, and he may also arrange, so that on the termination of an estate in one person, the estate shall pass over, wholly or in part, to another person. But this liberty is shackled by the condition that no one limitation, either as regards the person who is to take, or the estate that is to be taken, shall violate any of the fundamental principles of the Hindu law (*b*). Therefore the person who is to take must be capable of taking, and the estate which he is given must be an estate recognized by the Hindu law, and not encompassed with limitations or restrictions opposed to the nature of the estate given. And though trustees may be employed to facilitate a legal form of bequest, they cannot be made use of so as to carry out indirectly what the law does not allow to be done directly.

Shifting estate. § 382. The first point was laid down by implication in the case of *Soorjeemoney Dossee* v. *Denobundo Mullick* (*c*), and expressly in the case of *Tagore* v. *Tagore* (*d*). In the former case the testator, a Hindu resident in Calcutta, by the 5th clause of his will left his property to his five sons in such a manner as would, if there had been nothing more, have made them absolute owners. By the 11th clause he declared that if any of his five sons should die without male issue, his share should pass over to the sons then living or their sons, and that neither his widow nor his daughter, nor his daughter's son, should get any share out of his share. The event which he contemplated took place. One of the sons died, leaving no male issue. Under the law of Bengal the widow would inherit his share, and she claimed it, notwithstanding the will, on the ground that the bequest to the son was absolute, and the gift over invalid. The claim was rejected in the Supreme Court, and on appeal the Lord

(*b*) See *per Turner*, L. J., *Sonatun Bysack* v. *Juggutsoondree*, 8 M. I. A. 85.
(*c*) 6 M. I. A. 526; S. C. 4 Suth. (P. C.) 114; 9 M. I. A. 123.
(*d*) 4 B. L. R. (O. C. J.) 103, on appeal in the (P. C.) 9 B. L. R. 377; S. C. 18 Suth. 359; I. A. Supp. Vol. 47.

Justice *Knight Bruce* said (*e*), "Whatever may have formerly been considered the state of that law as to the testamentary power of Hindoos over their property, that power has now long been recognized, and must be considered as completely established. This being so, we are to say, whether there is anything against public convenience, anything generally mischievous, or anything against the general principles of Hindoo law, in allowing a testator to give property, whether by way of remainder, or by way of executory bequest upon an event which is to happen, if at all, immediately on the close of a life in being.

Devise with gift over.

Their Lordships think that there is not; that there would be great general inconvenience and public mischief in denying such power, and that it is their duty to advise Her Majesty that such a power does exist." The bequest above cited was in fact exactly the arrangement which the Mitakshara law would have made for the devolution of the testator's property. If the effect of his will had been permanently to impress upon his property, in the hands of all its successive holders, the law of inheritance prescribed by the Mitakshara in place of that of the Daya Bhaga which governed the family, the will would undoubtedly have been invalid according to the doctrines laid down in the Tagore case. But the case which arose for decision was simply that of a gift to a person in existence, with a proviso that in a certain event the property should pass over to another person also in existence. This was the ordinary case of a gift made with a condition annexed fixing its duration (*f*). A bequest absolute in one event, for life in another. It is, however, undecided whether the Hindu law allows an estate to be given subject to conditions subsequent, upon the happening of any of which an estate, which has once vested, would be divested. And whether the gift over of an estate

(*e*) 9 M. I. A. 135.

(*f*) See the case explained, 4 B. L. R. (O. C. J.) 192, and 9 B. L. R. 399; S. C. 18 Suth. 359; see, also, *Bhoobum Moyee* v. *Ram Kishore*, 10 M. I. A. 279, 308, 311; S. C. 3 Suth. (P. C.) 15; *Bhoobun* v. *Hurrish*, 5 I. A. 138; S. C. 4 Cal. 23; *Kumar Tarakeswar* v. *Kumar Shoshi*, 10 I. A. 51; S. C. 10 Cal. 952; *Kristoromoney* v. *Narendro*, 16 I. A. 29; S. C. 16 Cal. 383.

on events which may happen not upon the close of a life in being, but at some uncertain time during its continuance, would not also be void (*g*).

Executory bequest.

§ 383. The language of the Judicial Committee which might be taken as laying down the general rule that an executory bequest would always be valid by Hindu law where it would be valid by the law of England, was much relied on in a subsequent case of great importance, where an attempt was made to push the right of bequest to an extent greater than would be allowed even in England. This was the case of *Jatindra Mohun Tagore* v. *Ganendra Mohun Tagore* (*h*). There the testator, who had property, ancestral and self-acquired, real and personal, producing an income of 2½ lacs, commenced his will by reciting that he had already provided for his only son, and that he was to take nothing whatever under his will. He then vested the whole of his estate in trustees with provisions for their number being constantly maintained. After providing for numerous legacies he proceeded to direct the course in which the *corpus* of the property should devolve. The key to this was to be found in his express wish that the bulk of the property should neither be diminished nor divided. To effect this he directed that the legacies and annuities should be paid gradually out of the income; and while this process was going on, the trustees were to hold the property, paying only the balance of the yearly income to "the person entitled to the beneficial enjoyment of the real property." As soon as all charges upon the estate were paid off, the trustees were to convey the real estate to the use of the person who should, under the limitations of the will, be entitled to it, subject to the limitations therein expressed, so far as the then condition of circumstances would permit, and so far only as such limitations could be introduced into a deed of conveyance or settlement without infringing

Tagore case.

(*g*) *Ram Lal* v. *Secy. of State*, 8 I. A. 46, 63; S. C. 7 Cal. 804.

(*h*) 4 B. L. R, (O. C. J.) 103, on appeal in the (P. C.) 9 B. L. R. 377; S. C. 18 Suth. 359; S. C. I. A. Supp. Vol. 47.

upon any law against perpetuities which might then be in force. The person beneficially interested in the real estate was to be ascertained by reference to the following limitations :— Tagore case.

1. To the defendant Jatindra for life.
2. To his eldest son, born during the testator's life time, for life.
3. In strict settlement upon the first and other sons of such eldest son in tail male.
4. Similar limitations for life and in tail male upon the other sons of Jatindra, born in the testator's life time, and their sons successively.
5. Limitations in tail male upon the sons of Jatindra born after the testator's death.
6. "After the failure or determination of the uses and estates hereinbefore limited to the defendant Surendra for life."
7. Like limitations for his sons and their sons.
8. Upon failure or determination of that estate, like limitations in favour of the sons of Lalit Mohun, who was dead at the making of the will, and their sons. The will expressly adopted primogeniture in the male line through males, and excluded women and their descendants, and all rights of provision or maintenance of either man or woman. It also forbade the application of any rule of English law whereby entails might be barred, showing an intent that each tenant, though of inheritance, should be prohibited from alienation. The personalty was practically to pass under similar limitations to the person who would from time to time be entitled to the realty.

The only provision made by the testator for the plaintiff, his son, consisted of property producing Rs. 7,000 per annum, settled upon him at his marriage. His being disinherited arose from his having subsequently become a Christian. Of course under Act XXI of 1850 (Freedom of Religion) this circumstance was no bar to his claim as heir.

At the time of the testator's death, Jatindra, the head of the first series of estates, had no son, nor had he any during the suit.

Surendra, the head of the second series of estates, had a son, Promoth Kumar, who was born in the life time of the testator.

Lalit Mohun, the head of the third series, was dead at the making of the will, but left a grandson, Suttendra, born during the life time of the testator, and capable of taking under the will. These were the only persons beneficially interested under the limitations of the real estate.

Objections raised.

The son, as might have been expected, sued to set aside this will, except as to the legacies; contending, 1*st*, that it was wholly void as to the ancestral estate; 2*nd*, that in any case the father was bound to provide him with an adequate maintenance, the adequacy being estimated, not with reference to his own actual wants, but to the magnitude of the estate; 3*rd*, that the whole framework of the will, resting as it did on a devise to trustees, was void, since the Hindu law recognized no distinction between legal and equitable estates; 4*th*, that the life estate to Jatindra was void, since a Hindu testator could bequeath nothing less than what was termed "his whole bundle of rights;" 5*th*, that at all events the estates following upon this life estate were void, as infringing the law against perpetuities; and 6*th*, that as to everything after the life estate there was an intestacy, and the plaintiff was entitled as heir-at-law, notwithstanding the express words of the will that he was to take nothing under it.

Tagore case.

§ 384. The first four points were disposed of with little difficulty. The original and appeal Courts were of opinion that the power of a father in Bengal to bequeath all his property, of every sort, was beyond discussion, and that it went so far as to exclude the son even from maintenance (*i*). The Privy Council did not enter upon this question, being of opinion that in any case the maintenance actually allotted to the son was adequate (*k*). The 3*rd* objection was also set aside (*l*). The Judicial Committee said (*m*), "The anomalous law which has grown up in England of a legal estate which is paramount in one set of Courts, and an equitable ownership which is paramount in Courts of Equity, does not exist in, and ought not to be introduced into, Hindu law. But it is obvious that property, whether movable or immovable, must for many purposes be vested more or less absolutely in some person or persons for the benefit of other persons, and trusts of various kinds have been recognized and acted on in India in many cases (*n*). The distinction between 'legal' and 'equitable' represents only the accident of falling under diverse jurisdictions, and not the essential characteristic of a possession in one for the convenience and benefit of another." As to the 4*th* objection, the Courts dismissed it also. *Peacock*, C. J., referring to a doubtful expression of the Judicial Committee in *Bhoobum Moyee's* case (*o*), and the express decision in *Rewun Persad* v. *Radha Beeby* (*p*), said, "If a testator can disinherit his son by devising the whole of his estate to a stranger, there seems to be no reason why he should not be able to divide his estate by giving particular and limited interests in the whole of the property to different persons in existence, or who may come into existence during his

Father's power of devise

may be exercised through trustees.

Estate may be divided by limitations.

(*i*) 4 B. L. R. (O. C. J.) 132, 159.
(*k*) 9 B. L. R. 413; S. C. 18 Suth. 359.
(*l*) 4 B. L. R. (O. C. J.) 134, 161; *Krishnaramani* v. *Ananda*, 4 B. L. R. (O. C. J.) 278, 284, explaining the remarks of the C. J., in *Kumara Asima* v. *Kumara Krishna*, 2 B. L. R. (O. C. J.) 36.
(*m*) 9 B. L. R. 401; S. C. 18 Suth. 359. See *Seedee Nazeer* v. *Ojoodhya*, 8 Suth. 399; *Peddamuthulaty* v. *Timma Reddy*, 2 Mad. H. C. 272.
(*n*) See *Gopeekrist* v. *Gungapersaud*, 6 M. I. A. 53.
(*o*) 10 M. I. A. 311; S. C. 3 Suth. (P. C.) 15.
(*p*) 4 M. I. A. 137; S. C. 7 Suth. (P. C.) 35.

life time, to be taken in succession, as well as by giving his whole interest or bundle of rights in particular portions of land included in his estate to different persons (*q*).

Devise must conform to ordinary law of property.

385. The 5*th* point was decided in favour of the plaintiff, not upon any application of the English doctrine of perpetuities, which was held to be founded upon special considerations which had no place in Hindu law (*r*), but upon the general principle that the kind of estate tail which the testator wished to create was one wholly unknown and repugnant to Hindu law (*s*). That he was in fact trying to introduce a new law of inheritance, which should make all the subsequent holders of the estate take it in an order, and with restrictions and exemptions, wholly opposed to the principles of law which governed the testator and his family. Their Lordships of the Privy Council observed (*t*) : "The power of parting with property once acquired, so as to confer the same property upon another, must take place either by inheritance or transfer, each according to law. Inheritance does not depend on the will of the individual owner ; transfer does. Inheritance is a rule laid down (or, in the case of custom, recognized) by the State, not merely for the benefit of individuals, but for reasons of public policy. Domat., 2413. It follows directly from this that a private individual who attempts by gift or will to make property inheritable otherwise than the law directs, is assuming to legislate, and that the gift must fail, and the inheritance take place as the law directs. This was well expressed by Lord Justice *Turner* in *Soorjeemoney Dossee* v. *Denobundo Mullick* (*u*) : 'A man

(*q*) 4 B. L. R. (O. C. J.) 166 ; on appeal in the (P. C.) 9 B. L. R. 405 ; S. C. 18 Suth. 359.

(*r*) *Tagore* v. *Tagore*, 4 B. L. R. (O. C. J.) 167 ; *Goberdhun* v. *Shamchand*, Bourke, 282 ; *Kumara Asima* v. *Kumara Krishna*, 2 B. L. R. (O. C. J.) 11, 32. As to religious perpetuities, see *post*, § 395.

(*s*) 4 B. L. R. (O. C. J.) 171, 212.

(*t*) 9 B. L. R. 394, 396 ; S. C. 18 Suth. 359. See *Sonatun Bysack* v. *Juggut Soondree*, 8 M. I. A. 78 ; *Shoshi* v. *Tarokessur*, 6 Cal. 421 ; *affd. Kumar Tarakeswar* v. *Kumar Shoshi*, 10 I. A. 51 ; S. C. 10 Cal. 952 ; *Surya Row* v. *Gungadhara*, 13 I. A. 97 ; *Shookmoy* v. *Monohari*, 7 Cal. 269 ; *affd.* 12 I. A. 103 ; S. C. 11 Cal. 684. *Kristoromoney* v. *Narendro*, 16 I. A. 29 ; S. C. 16 Cal. 383.

(*u*) 6 M. I. A. 555, *sic.* ; S. C. 4 Suth. (P. C.) 114. But these words are not to be found in the judgment referred to. *Cf.* 8 M. I. A., p. 420.

cannot create a new form of estate, or alter the line of succession allowed by law, for the purpose of carrying out his own wishes or policy.' . . . . It follows that all estates of inheritance created by gift or will, so far as they are inconsistent with the general law of inheritance, are void as such, and that by Hindu law no person can succeed thereunder as heir to estates described in the terms which in English law would designate estates tail."

Tagore case.

Estate tail invalid.

§ 386. The result, therefore, was that the life estate to Jatindra was valid, but the estates to successive holders would be void if they must be held as coming in as heirs in tail. It was, however, contended that successive persons might be regarded as successive donees for life, having the power and subject to the restrictions sought to be imposed by the will upon the successive heirs in tail (*v*). If so, they also would defeat the rights of the plaintiff as heir-at-law.

These donees fell into two classes: 1*st*, those not in existence at the death of the testator, but who might come into existence before the first life estate fell in; 2*nd*, those who were in existence at his death.

Jatindra had no sons alive at the death of the testator. But, of course, he might have sons, and in default of natural-born sons might adopt, as under the will each successive taker was authorized to do. The second and third series of estates were also represented by persons living at the testator's death.

Donee must be in existence at death.

It was held that none of these could take. Not the possible issue of Jatindra; because the donee must be a person capable of taking at the time when the gift takes effect, and must either in fact, or in contemplation of law (*w*), be in existence at the death of the testator (*x*). Not the existing

---

(*v*) 9 B. L. R. 396; S. C. 18 Suth. 359.

(*w*) That is when in embryo at the death, or adopted subsequently to death, under authority given before it. 9 B. L. R. (P. C.) 397; S. C. 18. Suth. 359.

(*x*) 4 B. L. R. (O. C. J.) 188, 191, 221; S. C. on appeal in the P. C.; 9 B. L. R. 396—400; S. C. 18 Suth. 359; *Krishnaramani* v. *Ananda*, 4 B. L. R.

representatives of the 2nd and 3rd series of estates, because they were only to take "after the failure or determination" of the previous series, and these words were held to mean the actual exhaustion of the line of Jatindra in conformity with the will, and not its incapacity to succeed by reason of the illegality of the will. Consequently, the event on which they were to take had never arisen and never could arise (*y*). Finally, it was held that all the bequests must be looked on as if they had been made directly to the persons who were the subjects of them, and that the intervention of trustees made no difference, since that which could not be done directly, could not be done indirectly by the medium of a trust (*z*). The result was that the plaintiff, the heir-at-law, was held entitled to the whole estate after the life of Jatindra, subject to the payment of legacies and annuities.

Trust for illegal purpose invalid.

Directions for accumulation.

§ 387. This case has been cited at great length on account of the numerous points decided by it, and also as establishing in the most authoritative manner that the power of devise by a Hindu is limited, as to the objects and subjects of the bequest, by the general purposes of Hindu law. On this ground, wills directing an estate to go in an order of succession which should exclude female heirs, or heirs by adoption, (*a*) or wills containing trust to accumulate the proceeds of the property have been held invalid. In one will, the trust was to accumulate for ninety-nine years, and no direction was given as to the appropriation of the fund at the end of the time (*b*). In another, the fund was to accumulate till it reached three lakhs, and was then to be divid-

(O. C. J.) 231, 279, over-ruling *Arumugam* v. *Ammi Ammal*, 1 M. H. C. 400; *Bramamayi* v. *Jages*, 8 B. L. R 400; *Ramguttee* v. *Kristo*, 20 Suth. 472; *Soudaminey* v. *Jagesh*, 2 Cal. 262; *Mangaldas* v. *Krishnabai*, 6 Bom. 38; *Chundi Churn* v. *Rani Sidheswari*, 15 I. A. 149; S. C. 16 Cal. 71. Succession Act X of 1865, § 92—98.

(*y*) 9 B. L. R. 409; S. C. 18 Suth. 359.

(*z*) 4 B. L. R. (O. C. J.) 162, 195; on appeal 9 B. L. R. 402; S. C. 18 Suth. 359; *Kumara Asima* v. *Kumara Krishna*, 2 B. L R. (O. C. J.) 11; *Krishnaramani* v. *Ananda*, 4 B. L. R. (O. C. J.) 274; *Rajender* v. *Sham Chund*, 6 Cal. 106.

(*a*) *Kumar Tarakeswar* v. *Kumar Shoshi*, 10 I. A. 51; S. C. 10 Cal. 952; *Surya Rao* v. *Gungadhara*, 13 I. A. 97; S. C. 9 Mad. 499.

(*b*) *Kumara Asima* v. *Kumara Krishna*, 2 B. L. R. (O. C. J.) 11.

ed, and the process of accumulation to recommence (*c*). Such provisions not only create an estate held in a manner, and for purposes, foreign to Hindu law, but are also repugnant to the very nature of property, as forbidding its enjoyment by the owner, or, indeed, putting property in a position to have no owner at all. As Mr. Justice *Norman* remarked in the former case (*d*), "A testator cannot, in giving his property by will, impose conditions in contravention of the objects for which property exists, or contrary to the policy of the law. For instance, suppose an estate were given to a man on condition that it should be allowed to relapse into a jungle, or never be cultivated, no one could doubt that such a condition would be void." So, a will would be invalid which forbade alienation within the limits incidental to the estate created (*e*), or prohibited partition by the persons entitled to divide (*f*), or attempted to free property from any of the burthens incident to it by law, such as liability to debts, or maintenance of those whose support is a burthen upon the estate (*g*). So, it has been held in Madras by Mr. Justice *Holloway* that a clause in a will whereby the enjoyment of the property by the son, who was heir-at-law, was postponed beyond the period of minority was invalid, on the ground that this was, *protanto,* taking away from the son a right of property which the law of the Mitakshara vested in him (*h*). A similar decision was given upon a Bengal will, where the testator had attempted to postpone the enjoyment of the shares of his grandchildren until they had attained twenty-one, on the ground that by

Illegal conditions.

Ineffectual provisions.

(*c*) *Krishnaramani* v. *Ananda*, 4 B. L. R. (O. C. J.) 231; *Shookmoy* v. *Monohari*, 7 Cal. 269; *affd.* 12 I. A. 103; S. C. 11 Cal. 684.

(*d*) 2 B. L. R. (O. C. J.) 25.

(*e*) 2 B. L. R. (O. C. J.) 25; *Nitai Charan* v. *Ganga*, 4 B. L. R. (O. C. J.) 265, note; *Promotho* v. *Radhika*, 14 B. L. R. 175; *Ashutosh* v. *Doorga Churn*, 6 I. A. 182; S. C. 5 Cal. 438; S. C. 5 C. L. R. 296; *Gokool Nath* v. *Issur Lochun*, 14 Cal. 222. Act IV of 1882, § 10, 11, (Transfer of Property).

(*f*) *Nubkissen* v. *Hurrishchunder*, F. MacN. 323; *Mokoondo* v. *Gonesh*, 1 Cal. 104; *Rajender* v. *Shamchund*, 6 Cal. 106.

(*g*) *Sonatun Bysack* v. *Sreemutty Juggutsoondree*, 8 M. I. A. 66, 76. See *post*, § 424. The doctrine of election applies to wills in India. *Mangaldas* v. *Ranchhoddas*, 14 Bom. 438.

(*h*) *Devaraja* v. *Venayaga* and *Cunniah Chetty* v. *Lutchmenarasoo*, both decided in the Original Court, May 23, 1867, MS. See, too, *Mokoondo* v. *Gonesh*, 1 Cal. 104; *Gosling* v. *Gosling*, John., 265.

Hindu law an estate cannot remain in suspense, or without an owner (*i*). But, of course, a father in Bengal could delay, just as he could defeat, the rights of his issue, by interposing a valid estate previous to theirs (*k*).

Form of will immaterial.

§ 388. As regards form, the will of a Hindu may be oral, though, of course, in such a case the strictest proof will be required of its terms (*l*). So, a paper drawn up in accordance with the instructions of the testator, and assented to by him, will be a good will, though not signed (*m*). And if a paper contains the testamentary wishes of the deceased, its form is immaterial. For instance, petitions addressed to officials, or answers to official enquiries, have been held to amount to a will (*n*). Even a statement in a deed executed by a widow in pursuance of the instructions of her late husband and containing an assertion of his last wishes as to the devolution of his property has been held to be good evidence of a nuncupative will by the husband (*o*). And a will may be revoked orally, or in any other manner by which it might have been made (*p*). Nor are technical words necessary. The single rule of construction in a Hindu, as in an English, will, is to try and find out the meaning of the testator, taking the whole of the document together, and to give effect to this meaning. In applying this principle, special care must be taken not to judge the language used by a Hindu according to the artificial rules which have been applied to the language of Englishmen, who live under a different system of law and in a different state of society (*q*). A devise in general terms, without

Intention is the guide of interpretation.

(*i*) *Bramamayi* v. *Jages*, 8 B. L. R. 400; *Callynauth* v. *Chundernath*, 8 Cal. 378; S. C. 10 C. L. R. 207.

(*k*) *Hurrosoondery* v. *Cowar*, Fulton, 393.

(*l*) *Beer Pertab* v. *Maharajah Rajender*, 12 M. I. A. 2; S. C. 9 Suth. (P. C.) 15; *ante*, § 365. See now the Hindu Wills Act, XXI of 1870, which applies to Hindus in Bengal, and the towns of Madras and Bombay.

(*m*) *Tara Chand* v. *Nobin Chunder*, 8 Suth. 138; *Radhabai* v. *Ganesh*, 3 Bom. 7.

(*n*) *Shumshul* v. *Shewukram*, 2 I. A. 7; S. C. 14 B. L. R. 226; *Hurpurshad* v. *Sheo Dhyal*, 3 I. A. 259; S. C. 26 Suth. 55; *Kalian* v. *Sanwal*, 7 All. 163; *Haidar Ali* v. *Tasadduk*, 17 I. A. 82; S. C. 18 Cal. 1.

(*o*) *Chintaman* v. *Moro Lakshman*, 11 Bom. 89.

(*p*) *Pertab* v. *Subhao*, 4 I. A. 228; S. C. 3 Cal. 426.

(*q*) See *per* *Turner*, L. J., *Soorjeemoney* v. *Denobundo*, 6 M. I. A. 550; S. C.

words of inheritance, or with words imperfectly describing an estate of inheritance, will pass the entire estate of the testator, unless a contrary intention appears from the context (*r*). On the other hand, stronger words, and a more evident intention, would be required to pass an absolute estate, where the bequest was to a woman, and especially where it would operate to the prejudice of the testator's issue (*s*). But although every effort will be made to carry out the wishes of the testator, where they are ascertainable and legal, the Court cannot make a new will for them. Therefore, a will must fail if its terms are so vaguely expressed that it is impossible to ascertain what are the testator's objects (*t*). And if the intention of the testator is obviously to do something that is illegal, the Court will not put a non-natural construction upon his language, so as to turn an illegal into a legal arrangement (*u*). The result, of course, will be an intestacy as to so much of the property as has been ineffectually disposed of, and the residue will go to the heir-at-law, however positive the expression of the testator's wish may have been that he should not take. The estate must go to somebody, and there is no one to whom it can go except the heir-at-law. As *Peacock*, C. J., said in the Tagore case, "A mere-

where vague, or illegal.

---

4 Suth. (P. C.) 114; *per Ld. Kingsdown*, *Bhoobum Moyee* v. *Ram Kishore*, 10 M. I. A. 308; S. C. 3 Suth. (P. C.) 15; *Lakshmibai* v. *Ganpat*, 4 Bom. H. C. (O. C. J.) 151; *Lallubai* v. *Mankuvarbai*, 2 Bom. 408.

(*r*) *Per Willes*, J., *Tagore* v. *Tagore*, 9 B. L. R. 395; S. C. 18 Suth. 359; *Sursutty* v. *Poorno*, 4 Suth. 55; *Broughton* v. *Pogose*, 12 B. L. R. 74; S. C. 19 Suth. 181; *Vullubhdas* v. *Thucker Gordhandas*, 14 Bom. 360. Succession Act X of 1865, § 82.

(*s*) *Rabutty* v. *Sibchunder*, 6 M. I. A. 1; *Lukhee* v. *Gokool*, 13 M. I. A. 209; S. C. 3 B. L. R. (P. C.) 57; S. C. 12 Suth. (P. C.) 47; *Shumshul* v. *Shewukram*, 2 I. A. 7, 14; S. C. 14 B. L. R. 226; *Bhagbutti* v. *Chowdry*, 2 I. A. 256; S. C. 24 Suth. 168; *Lakshmibai* v. *Hirabai*, 11 Bom. 69; *affd.* p. 573; *Prosunno* v. *Tarrucknath*, 10 B. L. R. 267; S. C. *Sub nomine*, *Tarucknath* v. *Prosono*, 19 Suth. 48; *Kollany* v. *Luchmee*, 24 Suth. 395; *Jeewun* v. *Mt. Sona*, 1 N.-W. P. 66; *Punchoomoney* v. *Troyluckoo*, 10 Cal. 342.

(*t*) *Sandial* v. *Maitland*, Fulton, 475. See *Kumara Asima* v. *Kumara Krishna*, 2 B. L. R. (O. C. J.) 38; *Tagore* v. *Tagore*, 4 B. L. R. (O. C. J.) 198; *Jarman's Estate*, 8 Ch. D. 584.

(*u*) *Tagore* v. *Tagore*, 9 B. L R. 407; S. C. 18 Suth. 359; *per Lord Selborne*, 5 App. Ca. p. 719. See as to the proper interpretation to be put upon wills, where questions of remoteness arise, *Arumugam* v. *Ammi Ammall*, 1 Mad. H. C. 400; *Bramamayi* v. *Jages*, 8 B. L. R. 400; *Soudaminey* v. *Jogesh*, 2 Cal. 262; *Kherodomoney* v. *Doorgamoney*, 4 Cal. 455; *Ram Lall Sett* v. *Kanai Lal*, 12 Cal. 663, *ante*, § 356.

Disinheritance.

expression in a will that the heir-at-law shall not take any part of the testator's estate is not sufficient to disinherit him, without a valid gift of the estate to some one else. He will take by descent, and by his right of inheritance, whatever is not validly disposed of by the will, and given to some other person (*v*)." On the other hand, it is not necessary that a will should contain an express declaration of a testator's desire or intention to disinherit his heirs, if there is an actual and complete gift to some other person capable of taking under it (*w*).

A devise which cannot take effect at all is as if it had never been made. Consequently the property devised passes to the heir. The rule of the English Common law that an undisposed of residue vests in the executor beneficially, does not apply in case of a Hindu will (*x*). The case of a devise to a class of persons, which fails as to some, has already been discussed (§§ 354—356). Where a testator leaves a legacy absolutely as regards his estate, but restricts the mode of the legatee's enjoyment to secure certain objects for the benefit of the legatee, if the objects fail, the absolute gift prevails (*y*).

Possession.

§ 389. As possession under a devise is not necessary to its validity, so neither is it necessary that the legatee should be capable of assenting to it. Therefore, a bequest in favour of an idiot or an infant will be valid. And so it will be in any other case, although the legatee would have been incapable of inheriting from some personal disability (*z*).

The Hindu Wills Act.

§ 390. Under the combined operation of the Hindu Wills Act (XXI of 1870) § 2, and the Probate and Administration

---

(*v*) 4 B. L. R. (O. C. J.) 187; S. C. on appeal, 9 B. L. R. 402; S. C. 18 Suth. 359; *Promotho* v. *Radhika*, 14 B. L. R. 175; *Lallubhai* v. *Mankuvarbai*, 2 Bom. 488.

(*w*) *Prossunno* v. *Tarrucknath*, 10 B. L. R. 267; S. C. 19 Suth. 48, disapproving of *Rooploll* v. *Mohima*, *ib.* 271, note.

(*x*) *Ante*, § 386. *Lallubhai* v. *Mankuvarbai*, 2 Bom. 388.

(*y*) *Administrator-General of Bengal* v. *Apcar*, 3 Cal. 553.

(*z*) *Kooldebnarain* v. *Mt. Wooma*, Marsh, 357.

Act (V of 1881) § 154, numerous sections of the Indian Succession Act (X of 1865) (*a*), are extended to all wills and codicils made by any Hindu, Jain, Sikh or Buddhist, on or after the 1st day of September 1870, within the territories subject to the Lieutenant-Governor of Bengal, or the local limits of the ordinary original civil jurisdiction of the High Courts at Madras and Bombay, and to all such wills and codicils made outside those territories and limits, so far as relates to immovable property situate within such territories or limits. The primary result is to abolish all forms of wills except those written and attested as prescribed by the Succession Act. To guard against the dangers which might arise from the application to persons under one law of a complicated series of provisions intended for persons governed by a wholly different law, § 3 provides that nothing in the Act shall authorise a testator to bequeath property which he could not have alienated *inter vivos*, or to deprive any persons of any right of maintenance of which, but for § 2 of the Act, he could not deprive them by will, or shall affect any law of adoption or intestate succession, or shall authorise any Hindu, &c., to create in property any interest which he could not have created before the first of September 1870. Under this last clause it has been held that notwithstanding the express words of § 99 of the Succession Act, which is one of those extended by the Wills Act, a Hindu cannot make a bequest to a person unborn at the death, but born between that date and the termination of a previous estate after which his interest is to take effect (*b*).

Saving clause.

(*a*) The sections so extended are the following: 46, 49, capacity to make, revoke or alter a will; 48, effect of fraud, &c.; 50, 51, mode of execution; 57—60, or revocation or revival; 55, witness not disqualified by interest; 61—67, 82, 83, 85, 88—98, construction of will; 99—103, void bequests; 106—108, vesting of legacies; 109, 110, onerous; 111, 112, contingent; and 113—124, conditional bequests; 125—127, bequests with directions as to application or enjoyment; 128, bequests to executor; 129—136, specific; and 137, 138, demonstrative legacies; 139—153, ademption; 154—157, liabilities attaching to legacies; 158, general bequests; 159, bequests of interest or produce; and 160—163, of annuities; 164—166, legacies to creditors or portioners; 167—177, election; 187, necessity of probate for executor or legatee. See also as to the Registration and Deposit of Wills Act III of 1877, § 40—46.

(*b*) *Alangamonjori* v. *Sonamoni*, 8 Cal. 687.

Act I of 1869, § 13 also contains a provision requiring wills made by taluqdars in Oudh in certain cases to be executed and attested three months before the death of the testator and registered within one month after execution (*c*).

Probate and Administration Act.

§ 391. The Probate and Administration Act (V of 1881) applies to all Hindus (*d*) and persons exempted under § 332 of the Succession Act, no matter when they died, but does not render invalid any transfer of property duly made before the 1st of April 1881; but, except in cases to which the Hindu Wills Act applies, no Court beyond the limits of the towns of Calcutta, Madras and Bombay, and the territories of British Burmah shall receive applications for probate or letters of administration unless authorised by the Local Government with the sanction of the Governor-General. By § 149 it is provided that nothing in the Act shall validate any testamentary disposition which would otherwise have been invalid; invalidate any such disposition which would otherwise have been valid; deprive any person of any right of maintenance to which he would otherwise have been entitled; or affect the Administrator-General of Bengal, Madras or Bombay.

§ 392. Previous to the Hindu Wills Act, it was held that the executors of a Hindu did not, in the character merely of executors, take any estate properly so called, in the property of the deceased;—or in other words, that the mere nomination of executors, though followed by probate, did not of itself confer any estate on the executor, further than the estate he might have by the express words of the will, or as heir of the testator. The grant of probate or letters of administration to a Hindu took effect only for the purpose of recovering debts and securing debtors paying the same, except so far as was otherwise provided by Act XXVII

(*c*) See as to this section *Ajudhia Buksh* v. *Mt. Rukmin Kuar*, 11 I. A. 1; *Haji Abdul* v. *Munshi Amir Haidar*, 11 I. A. 121; Act X of 1885.

(*d*) This term includes Jains, *Bachebi* v. *Makhan*, 3 All. 55.

of 1860 (*e*). The Hindu Wills Act incorporated § 179 of Act X of 1865 which provided that "the executor or administrator, as the case may be, of a deceased person, is his legal representative for all purposes, and all the property of the deceased vests in him." Also § 187 which provides that no right as executor or legatee can be established in any Court of Justice unless probate or letters of administration shall have been granted (*f*). The Act V of 1881 repeals § 179 as part of Act XXI of 1870 but re-enacts it as part of itself. The result is that in all cases coming within the Hindu Wills Act or the Probate Act, the executor or administrator as such is the legal representative of the deceased, and statutory owner of his property, except such as would otherwise have passed by survivorship to some other person (*g*).

(*e*) *Shaik Moosa* v. *Sheik Essa*, 8 Bom. 241, p. 252; *Ardesir* v. *Hirabai*, ibid. 474, p. 479; *Lallubhai* v. *Mankuverbai*, 2 Bom., p. 406.

(*f*) This section is not incorporated in Act V of 1881. Therefore as regards Hindu Wills prior to 1st September 1870 though probate may be granted, it is not necessary. *Krishna Kinkur* v. *Panchuram*, 17 Cal. 272. Probate cannot be refused on the ground that the will is illegal or void. *Hormusji* v. *Dhanbaiji*, 12 Bom. 164.

(*g*) Act V of 1881, § 4. As to whether a creditor can apply for revocation of probate, see *Nilmoni* v. *Umanath*, 10 I. A. 80. As to wills made before 1st September 1870, see *Krishna Kinkur* v. *Rai Mohun*, 14 Cal. 37.

CHAPTER XII.

RELIGIOUS AND CHARITABLE ENDOWMENTS.

Religious gifts favoured.

§ 393. GIFTS for religious and charitable purposes were naturally favoured by the Brahmans, as they are everywhere by the priestly class. Sancha lays down the general principle that "wealth was conferred for the sake of defraying sacrifices" (*a*). Gifts for religious purposes are made by Katyayana an exception to the rule that gifts are void when made by a man who is afflicted with disease and the like, and he says that if the donor dies without giving effect to his intention, his son shall be compelled to deliver it (*b*). This is an exception to the rule that a gift is invalid without delivery of possession. The Bengal pandits state that this principle applies even against a son under the Mitakshara law, though his assent would be indispensable if the gift was for a secular object; they seem, however, to limit the application of the rule to a gift of a small portion of the land (*c*). Similarly in the N.-W. Provinces the Court affirmed the right of a father, even without his son's consent, to make a permanent alienation of part of the ancestral property as provision for a family idol, provided the grant was made *bonâ fide*, and not with an intention to injure the son (*d*). In Western India grants of this nature have been held valid; even when made by a widow, of land which descended to her from her husband, and to the prejudice of her husband's

---

(*a*) 3 Dig. 484.
(*b*) 2 Dig. 96. See Manu, ix. 323; Vyasa, 2 Dig. 189; Mitakshara, i. 1, § 27, 32.
(*c*) See futwah, *Gopal Chand* v. *Babu Kunwar*, 5 S. D. 24 (29); Mitakshara, i. 1, § 28.
(*d*) *Raghunath* v. *Gobind*, 8 All. 76.

male heirs (*e*). And so a grant by a man to his family priests, to take effect after the life estate of his widow, was decided to be good (*f*).

§ 394. The principle that such gifts can be enforced against the donor's heirs, would naturally slide into a practice of making them by will (§ 368). It is probable that as Brahmanical acuteness favoured family partition as a means of multiplying family ceremonies, so it fostered the testamentary power as a mode of directing property to religious uses, at a time when the owner was becoming indifferent to its secular application. Many of the wills held valid in the Supreme Court of Calcutta have been remarkable for the large amounts they disposed of for religious purposes (*g*). In one case arising out of *Gokulchunder Corformah's* will, where practically the whole property had been assigned for the use of an idol, the Court declared the will proved, but wholly inoperative, except as regards a legacy to the stepmother of the testator (*h*). Sir F. MacNaghten suggests that the will might properly have been cancelled, as, upon its face, the production of a madman. No reason can be offered why such a will should be set aside in Bengal, merely because the whole property was devoted to religious objects. In the case of *Radhabullubh Tagore* v. *Gopeemohun Tagore,* which was decided in Calcutta the very next year (1811), the right of a Hindu so to apply the whole of his property, seems to have been admitted (*i*).

Effected by will.

§ 395. The English law, which forbids bequests for superstitious uses, does not apply to grants of this character

Superstitious uses not forbidden,

(*e*) *Jugjeevun* v. *Deosunkur*, 1 Bor. 394 [436]; *Kupoor* v. *Sevukram*, *ib.* 405 [448]; but see *Umbashunker* v. *Tooljaram*, 1 Bor. 400 [442]; *Muhalukmee* v. *Kripashookul*, 2 Bor. 510 [557]; *Ramanund* v. *Ramkissen*, 2 M. Dig. futwah, at p. 117. See too, *post*, § 586.

(*f*) *Keshoor* v. *Mt. Ramkoonwar*, 2 Bor. 314 [345.]

(*g*) F. MacN. 323, 331, 336—347, 349, 350, 371; *Ramtonoo* v. *Ramgopal*, 1 Kn. 245. The same thing was remarked by Sir *Thomas Strange* as a feature in the wills made by Hindus in Madras. 2 Stra. H. L. 453.

(*h*) F. MacN. 320, App. 58.

(*i*) F. MacN. 335.

in India, even in the Presidency Towns (*k*), and such grants have been repeatedly enforced by the Privy Council (*l*). Nor are they invalid for transgressing against the rule which forbids the creation of perpetuities. "It being assumed to be a principle of Hindu law that a gift can be made to an idol, which is a *caput mortuum*, and incapable of alienating, you cannot break in upon that principle by engrafting upon it the English law of perpetuities (*m*)." In fact both the cases in which the Bengal High Court in 1869 set aside the will as creating secular estates of a perpetual nature, contained devises of an equally perpetual nature in favour of idols, which were supported (*n*). But where a will, under the form of a devise for religious purposes, really gives the beneficial interest to the devisees, subject merely to a trust for the performance of the religious purposes, it will be governed by the ordinary Hindu law. Any provisions for perpetual descent, and for restraining alienation, will, therefore, be void. The result will be to set aside the will, as regards the descent of the property, leaving the heirs-at-law liable to keep up the idols, and defray the proper expenses of the worship (*o*). *A fortiori* will this rule apply, where the estate created is in its nature secular, though the motive for creating it is religious (*p*).

nor perpetuities.

Colourable religious endowment.

Tenure in trustee.

§ 396. As an idol cannot itself hold lands, the practice is to vest the lands in a trustee for the religious purpose, or to impose upon the holder of the lands a trust to defray

(*k*) *Das Merces* v. *Cones*, 2 Hyde, 65; *Andrews* v. *Joakim*, 2. B. L. R. (O. C. J.) 148; *Judah* v. *Judah*, 5 B. L. R. 433; *Khusalchand* v. *Mahadevgiri*, 12 Bom. H. C. 214. *Rupa Jagshet* v. *Krishnaji*, 9 Bom. 169.

(*l*) *Ramtonoo* v. *Ramgopal*, 1 Kn. 245; *Jewun* v. *Shah Kubeerood-deen*, 2 M. I. A. 390; S. C. 6 Suth. (P. C.) 3; *Sonatun Bysack* v. *Juggutsoondree*, 8 M. I. A. 66; *Juggutmohini* v. *Mt. Sokheemoney*, 14 M. I. A. 289; S. C. 10 B. L. R. 19; S. C. 17 Suth. 41.

(*m*) *Per* Markby, J., *Kumara Asema* v. *Kumara Krishna*, 2 B. L. R. (O. C. J.) p. 47. See as to the application of the rule to cases not under Hindu Law, *Fatma Bibi* v. *Advocate-General, Bombay*, 6 Bom. 42; *Limji* v. *Bapuji*, 11 Bom. 441.

(*n*) *Tagore* v. *Tagore*, 4 B. L. R. (O. C. J.) 103, in the P. C., 9 B. L. R. 377; S. C. 18 Suth. 359; *Krishnaramani* v. *Ananda*, 4 B. L. R. (O. C. J.) 231; *Brojosoondery* v. *Luchmee Koonwaree*, 15 B. L. R. (P. C.) 176 note.

(*o*) *Promotho* v. *Radhika*, 14 B. L. R. 175; *Phate* v. *Damoodar*, 3 Bom. 84.

(*p*) *Anantha* v. *Nagamuthu*, 4 Mad. 200.

the expenses of the worship (*q*). Sometimes the donor is himself the trustee. Such a trust is, of course, valid, if perfectly created, though, being voluntary, the donor cannot be compelled to carry it out if he has left it imperfect (*r*). But the effect of the transaction will differ materially, according as the property is absolutely given for the religious object, or merely burthened with a trust for its support. And there will be a further difference where the trust is only an apparent, and not a real one, and where it creates no rights in any one except the holder of the fund. (*s*)

§ 397. The last case arises where the founder applies his own property to the creation of a pagoda, or any other religious or charitable foundation, keeping the property itself, and the control over it, absolutely in his own hands. The community may be greatly benefited by this arrangement, so long as it lasts, but its continuance is entirely at his own pleasure. It is like a private chapel in a gentleman's park, and the fact that the public have been permitted to resort to it, will not prevent its being closed, or pulled down, provided there has been no dedication of it to the public. It will pass equally unencumbered to his heirs, or to his assignees in insolvency. He may diminish the funds so appropriated at pleasure, or absolutely cease to apply them to the purpose at all (*t*). In short, the character of the property will remain unchanged, and its application will be at his own discretion. Trust imperfect.

Another state of things arises where land or other property is held in beneficial ownership, subject merely to a Property held under trust.

(*q*) See futwah in *Kounla Kant* v. *Ram Huree*, 4 S. D. 196, (247). It is said, however, that a trust is not required for this purpose. *Manohur Ganesh* v. *Lakhmiram*, 12 Bom. p. 263. (*r*) See Lewin, Trusts, p. 61.

(*s*) *Acc. per curiam*, 11 All. p. 22-27.

(*t*) *Howard* v. *Pestonji*, Perry, O. C. 535; *Venkatachellamiah* v. *P. Narainapah*, Mad. Dec. of 1853, 104; S. C. Mad. Dec. 1854, 100; *Chemmanthatti* v. *Meyene*, Mad. Dec. of 1862, 90; 2 W. MacN. 103; *Brojosoondery* v. *Luchmee Koonwaree*, in the P. C., 15 B. L. R. 176, (note); S. C 20 Suth. 95; *Delroos* v. *Nawab Syud*, 15 B. L. R. 167, affirmed in P. C. 3 Cal. 324; *Sub nomine*, *Ashgar* v. *Delroos*.

trust as to part of the income, for the support of some religious endowment. Here again the land descends and is alienable, and partible (*u*), in the ordinary way, the only difference being that it passes with the charge upon it (*v*). The same rule would apply where the owner retained the property in himself, but granted the community or part of the community an easement over it for certain specified purposes (*w*).

Absolute dedication of property.

The remaining case is the one first named, where the whole property is devoted, absolutely and in perpetuity, to the religious purposes. Here, of course, the trustee has no beneficial interest in the property, beyond what he is given by the express terms of the trust. He cannot encumber or dispose of it for his own personal benefit, nor can it be taken in execution for his personal debt. But he may do any act which is necessary or beneficial, in the same manner and to the same degree as would be allowable in the case of the manager of an infant heir.

Powers of trustee.

He may, within those limits, incur debts, mortgage and alien the property, and bind it by judgments properly obtained against him (*x*). And he may lease out the property in the usual manner, but he cannot create any other than proper derivative tenures and estates conformable to usage; nor can he make a lease, or any other arrangement which will bind his successor, unless the necessity for the transaction is completely established (*y*).

(*u*) *Ram Coomar* v. *Jogender*, 4 Cal. 56. *Suppammal* v. *Collector of Tanjore*, 12 Mad. 387, p. 391.

(*v*) *Mahatab* v. *Mirdad*, 5 S. D. 268 (313), approved by P. C., 15 B. L. R. p. 178; *sup.* note (*t*) *Futtoo* v. *Bhurrut*, 10 Suth. 299; *Basoo* v. *Kishen*, 13 Suth. 200; *Sonatun Bysack* v. *Juggutsoondree*, 8 M. I. A. 66. *Sheikh Mahomed* v. *Amarchand*; 17 I. A. 28; S. C. 17 Cal. 498.

(*w*) *Jaggamoni* v. *Nilmoni*, 9 Cal. 75.

(*x*) *Prosunno* v. *Golab*, 2 I. A. 145; S. C. 14 B. L. R. 450; *Konwur* v. *Ramchunder*, 4 I. A. 52; S. C. 2 Cal. 341; *Kalee Churn* v. *Bungshee*, 15 Suth. 339; *Khusalchand* v. *Mahadevgiri*, 12 Bom. H. C. 214; *Fegredo* v. *Mahomed*, 15 Suth. 75; *Shankar Bharati* v. *Venkapa Naik*, 9 Bom. 422. *Bishen Chand* v. *Syed Nadir*, 15 I. A. 1; S. C. 15 Cal. 329. In Bombay it has been held that although the rents of a religious endowment may be alienated, the *corpus* of the property is absolutely inalienable; *Narayan* v. *Chintaman*, 5 Bom 393; *Collector of Thana* v. *Hari*, 6 Bom. 546. *Shri Ganesh* v. *Keshavrav*, 15 Bom. 625 This is no doubt the general rule, but see *per curiam*, 4 I. A., p. 62.

(*y*) *Radhabullabh* v. *Juggutchunder*, 4 S. D. 151 (192); *Shibessouree* v.

§ 398. The devolution of the trust, upon the death or default of each trustee, depends upon the terms upon which it was created, or the usage of each particular institution, where no express trust-deed exists (*z*). Where nothing is said in the grant as to the succession, the right of management passes by inheritance to the natural heirs of the donee, according to the rule, that a grant without words of limitation conveys an estate of inheritance (*a*). The property passes with the office, and neither it nor the management is divisible among the members of the family (*b*). Where no other arrangement or usage exists, the management may be held in turns by the several heirs (*c*). Sometimes the constitution of the body vests the management in several, as representing different interests, or as a check upon each other, and any act which alters such a constitution would be invalid (*d*). Where the head of a religious institution is bound to celibacy, it is frequently the usage that he nominates his successor by appointment during his own lifetime, or by will (*e*). Sometimes this nomination requires con-

Devolution of trust.

Mothooranath, 13 M. I. A. 270; S. C. 13 Suth. (P. C.) 18; *Juggessur* v. *Roodro*, 12 Suth. 299; *Tahboonissa* v. *Koomar*, 15 Suth. 228; *Arruth* v. *Juggurnath*, 18 Suth. 439; *Mohunt Burm* v. *Khashee*, 20 Suth. 471; *Bunwaree* v. *Mudden*, 21 Suth 41. Where an unlawful alienation has been made by a trustee of a religious endowment the statute of limitation begins to run from the appointments of his successor. *Mahomed* v. *Ganapati*, 13 Mad. 277; *Vedapurath* v. *Vallabha*, *ib.* 402.

(*z*) *Greedharee* v. *Nundkishore*, Marsh. 573; affd., 11 M. I. A. 428; S. C. 8 Suth. (P. C.) 25; *Muttu Ramalinga* v. *Perianayagum*. 1 I. A. 209; *Janoki* v. *Gopal*, 10 I. A. 32; S. C. 9 Cal. 766; *Genda* v. *Chatur*, 13 I. A. 100, 9. All. 1; *Appasami* v. *Naguppa*, 7 Mad. 499; *Rangachariar* v. *Yegna Dikshatur*, 13 Mad. 524.

(*a*) *Chutter Sein's case*, 1 S. D. 180 (239); *Venkatachellamiah* v. *P. Narainapah*, Mad. Dec. of 1853, 104. See *Tagore case*, 4 B. L. R. (O. C. J.) 182 9 B. L. R. (P. C.) 395; S. C 18 Suth. 359; *per curiam*, 9 Cal., p. 79. *Nanabhai* v. *Shriman Goswami*, 12 Bom. 331.

(*b*) *Jaafar* v. *Aji*, 2 Mad. H. C. 19; *Kumarasami* v. *Ramalinga*, Mad. Dec. of 1860, 261.

(*c*) *Nubkissen* v. *Hurrischunder*, 2 M. Dig. 146. See *Anundmoyee* v. *Boykantnath*, 8 Suth. 193; *Ramsoondur* v. *Taruck*, 19 Suth. 28; *Mitta Kunth* v. *Neerunjun*, 14 B. L. R. 166; S. C. 22 Suth. 437; *Mancharam* v. *Pranshankar*, 6 Bom. 298. There is nothing to prevent a female being manager. See *Moottoo Meenatchy* v. *Villoo*, Mad. Dec. of 1858, 136; *Joy Deb Surmah* v. *Huroputty*, 16 Suth. 282. See *Hussain Beebee* v. *Hussain Sherif*, 4 Mad. H. C. 23; Punjab Customs, 88; unless the actual discharge of spiritual duties is required; *Mujavar* v. *Hussain*, 3 Mad. 93. Special custom is necessary, *Janokee* v. *Gopaul*, 2 Cal. 365; *affd.*, 10 I. A. 32; S. C. 9 Cal. 766.

(*d*) *Rajah Vurmah* v. *Ravi Vurmah*, 4 I. A. 76; S. C. 1 Mad. 235. See *Teramath* v. *Lakshmi*, 6 Mad. 270.

(*e*) *Hoogly* v. *Kishnanund*, S. D. of 1848, 253; *Soobramaneya* v. *Aroomooga*,

firmation by the members of the religious body. Sometimes the right of election is vested in them (*f*). In no case can the trustee sell or lease the right of management, though coupled with the obligation to manage in conformity with the trusts annexed thereto (*g*), nor is the right saleable in execution under a decree (*h*). It has, however, been held in Bombay that there is no objection to an alienation of a religious office, made in favour of a person standing in the line of succession, and not disqualified by personal unfitness. Such an alienation is in fact little more than a renunciation of the right to hold the office (*i*). But, I imagine, that even in such a case, the Court might refuse to ratify the transaction, if it appeared to have been actuated by improper motives. The same rule applies to the sale of religious offices (*k*). It has been decided in Calcutta that a private endowment of a family idol may be transferred to another family, the idol being a part of the gift and the property continuing to be appropriated to its benefit as before (*l*).

Founder's rights.

§ 399. Unless the founder has reserved to himself some special powers of supervision, removal, or nomination, neither he nor his heirs have any greater power in this respect than any other person who is interested in the trust (*m*). And such powers, when reserved, must be strictly followed (*n*). But where the succession to the office of trustee has wholly failed, it has been held that the right of management reverts

---

Mad. Dec. of 1858, 33; *Greedharee* v. *Nundkishore*, 11 M. I. A. 405; S. C. 8 Suth. (P. C.) 25; *Trimbakpuri* v. *Gangabai*, 11 Bom. 514.

(*f*) *Mohunt Gopal* v. *Kerparam*, S. D. of 1850, 250; *Narain* v. *Brindabun*, 2 S. D. 151 (192); *Gossain* v. *Bissessur*, 19 Suth. 215; *Madho* v. *Kamta*, 1 All. 539.

(*g*) *Rajah Vurmah* v. *Ravi Vurmah*, 4 I. A. 76; S. C. 1 Mad. 235, overruling *Ragunada* v. *Chinnappa*, 4 Mad. Rev. Reg. 109; *Rama Varma* v. *Raman Nair*, 5 Mad. 89; *Kannan* v. *Nilakundan*, 7 Mad. 337.

(*h*) *Durga* v. *Chanchal*, 4 All. 81.

(*i*) *Sitarambhal* v. *Sitaram*, 6 Bom. H. C. (A. C. J.) 250; *Mancharam* v. *Pranshankar*, 6 Bom. 298.

(*k*) *Kuppa* v. *Dorasami*, 6 Mad. 76; *Narasimma* v. *Anantha*, 4 Mad. 391; *Juggernath Roy* v. *Pershad Surmah*, 7 Suth. 266; *Dubo Misser* v. *Srinivas*, 5 B. L. R. 617; *Narayana* v. *Ranga*, 15 Mad. 183.

(*l*) *Khettur Chunder* v. *Hari Das*, 17 Cal. 557.

(*m*) *Teertaruppa* v. *Soonderajien*, Mad. Dec. of 1851, 57; *Lutchmee* v. *Rookmanee*, Mad. Dec. of 1857, 152; 2 W. MacN. 102.

(*n*) *Advocate-General* v. *Fatima*, 9 Bom. H. C. 19.

to the heirs of the founder (*o*). Where no trust has been created, the law will vest the trust in the founder and his heirs, unless there has been some usage or course of dealing which points to a different mode of devolution (*p*).

Trust irrevocable.

A trust for religious purposes, if once lawfully and completely created, is of course irrevocable (*q*). The beneficial ownership cannot, under any circumstances, revert to the founder or his family. If any failure in the objects of the trusts takes place, the only suit which he can bring is to have the funds applied to their original purpose, or to one of a similar character (*r*).

(*o*) *Jai Bansi* v. *Chattar*, 5 B. L. R. 181 ; S. C. 13 Suth. 396 ; *Sub nomine, Peet Koonwar* v. *Chuttur* : but see Act XX of 1863, (Native Religious Endowments), *Phate* v. *Damodar*, 3 Bom. 84 ; *Hori Dasi* v. *Secy. of State*, 5 Cal. 228.

(*p*) *Gossamee* v. *Ruman Lolljee*, 16 I. A. 137 ; S. C. 17 Cal. 3.

(*q*) *Juggutmohini* v. *Sokheemoney*, 14 M. I. A. 289 ; S. C. 10 B. L. R. 19 ; S. C. 17. Suth. 41 ; Pubjáb Customs, 92.

(*r*) *Mohesh Chunder* v. *Koylash*, 11 Suth. 443 ; *Reasut* v. *Abbott*, 12 Suth. 182 ; *Nam Narain* v. *Ramoon*, 23 Suth. 76 ; *Atty-Genl.* v. *Brodie*, 4 M. I. A. 190 ; *Mayor of Lyons* v. *Adv-Genl. of Bengal*, 3 I. A. 32 ; S. C. 26 Suth. 1. See Act XX of 1863, *Panchcowrie* v. *Chumsoolall*, 3 Cal. 563. *Brojomohun* v. *Hurrolall*, 5 Cal. 700 ; *Hemangini* v. *Nobin Chand*, 8 Cal. 788 ; see as to suits by devotees or others interested in Religious trust ; *Radhabai* v. *Chimnaji*, 3 Bom. 27 ; *Dhadphale* v. *Gurav*, 6 Bom. 122. As to suits by or with the permission of the Advocate-General, see Civil Pro. Code X of 1877, § 539 ; XIV of 1882, § 539. As to suits for the removal of the trustee on the ground of improper conduct, see *Mohun* v. *Lutchmun*, 6 Cal. 11.

CHAPTER XIII.

BENAMI TRANSACTIONS.

Origin of Benami.

§ 400. **There** probably is no country in the world except India, where it would be necessary to write a chapter "On the practice of putting property into a false name." Yet this is the literal explanation of a Benami transaction, and such transactions are so common as to have given rise to a very considerable body of decisions. Sir George Campbell says of the Benami system, "The most respectable man feels that if he has not need to cheat any one at present, he may some day have occasion to do so, and it is the custom of the country. So he puts his estate in the name of his wife's grandmother, under a secret trust. If he is pressed by creditors or by opposing suitors, it is not his. If his wife's grandmother plays him false, he brings a suit to declare the trust (*a*)." In many cases, however, the object of masking the real ownership was not to prepare the means of future fraud, but to avoid personal annoyance and oppression by providing an ostensible owner who might appear in Court, and before the Government officials, to represent the estate. In some instances the practice can only be accounted for by that mysterious desire which exists in the native mind, to make every transaction seem different from what it really is. Whatever be the origin of it, the custom of vesting property in a fictitious owner, known as the Benamidar, has been long since recognized by the Courts of India, and by the Privy Council. Even the familiar principle that a tenant cannot dispute his landlord's title has been made to yield to its influence. A tenant,

---

(*a*) Systems of Land Tenure, 181.

when sued for rent due to his lessor, has been allowed to prove that the person from whom, nominally, he accepted a lease, was only a Benamidar for a third person, to whom the rent was really due (*b*). And conversely, where a landlord had accepted rent continuously from persons in whose name a lease had been taken for the benefit of their husbands, when the Benamidars were unable to pay, he was allowed to sue the persons really interested in the lease (*c*).

Tenancy no estoppel.

Principles of Benami.

§ 401. Of course, the law of Benami is in no sense a branch of Hindu law. It is merely a deduction from the well-known principle of equity, that where there is a purchase by A. in the name of B., there is a resulting trust of the whole to A.; and that where there is a voluntary conveyance by A. to B., and no trust is declared, or only a trust as to part, there is a similar resulting trust in favour of the grantor as to the whole, or as to the residue, as the case may be, unless it can be made out that an actual gift was intended (*d*). In the English Courts an exception is made to this rule, where the person in whose name the conveyance is taken or made is a child of the real owner, when the transaction is presumed to have been made by way of advancement to him. But this exception has not been admitted in India. There the rule is well established, that in all cases of asserted Benami the true criterion is to ascertain from whose funds the purchase-money proceeded. Whether the nominal owner be a child or a stranger, a purchase made with the money of another is *primâ facie* assumed to be made for the benefit of that other (*e*). It has been suggested, that where a conveyance was taken by a Hindu in the name of a daughter, the probability that it was intended as an advancement would be much stronger

---

(*b*) *Donzelle* v. *Kedarnath*, 7 B. L. R. 720; S. C. 16 Suth. 186.
(*c*) *Debnath* v. *Gudadhur*, 18 Suth. 132.
(*d*) Lewin, Trusts, 127, 144. *Standing* v. *Bowring*, 31 Ch. D. 282. Act II of 1882, § 81, 82 [Trusts].
(*e*) *Gopeekrist* v. *Gungapersaud*, 6 M. I. A. 53; *Moulvie Sayyud* v. *Mt. Bebee*, 13 M. I. A. 232; S. C. 13 Suth. (P. C.) 1; *Bissessur* v. *Luchmessur*, 6 I. A. 233; S. C. 5 C. L. R. 477; *Naginbhai* v. *Abdulla*, 6 Bom. 717; *Ashabai* v. *Haji Tyeb*, 9 Bom. 115.

than if it were taken in the name of a son; "for in a Hindu joint-family the son's holdings would always remain part of the common stock, whereas the daughters would, on their marriage, necessarily be separated" (*f*). But the existence of any distinction of this sort was denied in a much later case by Mr. Justice *Mitter*. He said, "So far as the ordinary and usual course of things is concerned, the practice of making benami purchases in the names of female members of joint undivided Hindu families is just as much rife in this country, as that of making such purchases in the names of male members" (*g*). It has been lately held that, in the absence of evidence as to the origin of the purchase money, there is no presumption either way as to whether property purchased in the name of a Hindu wife was her husband's property or her own. (*h*). But, I imagine, it could hardly be said there was an absence of evidence as to the origin of the purchase money, unless there was evidence that both wife and husband possessed funds from which the purchase might have been made. The decision was reversed upon the evidence by the Privy Council, which found that the purchase was Benami (*i*).

Strict proof. Of course, the assertion that a transaction is not really what it professes to be, is one that will be regarded by the Courts with great suspicion, and must be strictly made out by evidence (*k*). But when the origin of the purchase-money is once made out, the subsequent acts done in the name of the nominal owner will be explained by reference to the real nature of the transaction. The same motive

(*f*) *Obhoy Churn* v. *Punchanun*, Marsh. 564.

(*g*) *Chunder Nath* v. *Kristo*, 15 Suth. 357; *Nobin Chunder* v. *Dokhobala*, 10 Cal. 686

(*h*) *Chowdrani* v. *Tariny*, 8 Cal. 545; disapproving of *Bindoo* v. *Pearee*, 6 Suth 312; *Narayana* v. *Krishna*, 8 Mad. 214

(*i*) *Dharani Kant* v. *Kristo Kumari*, 13 I. A. 70; S. C. 13 Cal. 181; cf. Mt. *Thakro* v. *Ganga Pershad*, 15 I. A. 29; S. C. 10 All. 197.

(*k*) *Sreemanchunder* v. *Gopaulchunder*, 11 M. I. A. 28; S. C. 7 Suth. (P. C.) 10; *Azimut* v. *Hurdwaree*, 13 M. I. A. 395; S. C. 14 Suth. (P. C.) 14; *Faez Buksh* v. *Fukeeroodeen*, 14 M. I. A. 234; S. C. 9 B. L. R. 456; *Uman Pershad* v. *Gandharp Singh*, 14 I. A. 127; S. C. 15 Cal 20. Oral evidence is sufficient, *Palaniyappa* v. *Arumugam*, 2 Mad. H. C. 26; *Taramonee* v. *Shibnath*, 6 Suth. 191; *Kumara* v. *Srinivasa*, 11 Mad. 218.

which dictated an ostensible ownership, would naturally dictate an apparent course of dealing in accordance with such ownership (*l*).

Effect given to real title.

§ 402. Where a transaction is once made out to be Benami, the Courts of India, which are bound to decide according to equity and good conscience, will deal with it in the same manner as it would be treated by an English Court of Equity (*m*). The principle is that effect will be given to the real and not to the nominal title, unless the result of doing so would be to violate the provisions of a statute, or to work a fraud upon innocent persons. For instance, the real may sue the ostensible owner to establish his title, or to recover possession (*n*); and conversely, if the benamidar attempts to enforce his apparent title against the beneficial owner, the latter may establish the real nature of the transaction by way of defence (*o*). Similarly, creditors who are enforcing their claims against the property of the real owner, will have exactly the same rights against his property held benami as if it were in his real name (*p*); and conversely, if they seize this estate in execution of a decree against the benamidar, the real owner will be entitled to set aside the execution (*q*). On the other hand, there are various statutes which provide that in sales under a decree of Court, or for arrears of revenue, the certified purchaser shall be conclusively deemed to be the real purchaser, and shall not be liable to be ousted on the ground that his purchase was really made on behalf of another (*r*). Such acts, of course, bar the equitable jurisdiction of the Courts,

Violation of statute.

(*l*) *Beebee Nyamut* v. *Fuzl Hossein*, S. D. of 1859, 139; *Rohee* v. *Dindyal*, 21 Suth. 257.

(*m*) *Exparte Kahundas*, 5 Bom. 154.

(*n*) *Thukrain* v. *Government*, 14 M. I. A. 112.

(*o*) *Ramanugra* v. *Mahasundur*, in the P. C., 12 B. L. R. 433.

(*p*) *Musadee* v. *Meerza*, 6 M. I. A. 27; *Hemanginee* v. *Jogendro*, 12 Suth. 236; *Gopi* v. *Markande*, 3 Bom. 30; *Abdool Hye* v. *Mir Mahomed*, 11 I. A. 10; S. C. 10 Cal. 616.

(*q*) *Tara Soonduree* v. *Oojul*, 14 Suth. 111.

(*r*) See Act VIII of 1859, § 260 (Old Civil Procedure Code); X of 1877, § 317 (Ditto); Act XIV of 1882, § 317 (New Civil Procedure Code); Act I of 1845, § 21 (Bengal—Revenue Sale); Act XI of 1859, § 36 (Bengal—Zemindary Revenue Sale).

but they will be strictly construed. Therefore if the real owner is actually and honestly in possession, and the benamidar attempts to oust him by virtue of his nominal title, the statute will not prevent the Courts from recognizing the unreal character of his claim (*s*). And a purchase made by the manager of a Hindu family in his own name, as is usual, would not be considered as coming within the meaning of such statutes (*t*). It has also been held that these provisions are only intended to prevent the real owner disputing the title of the certified purchaser, and that they do not preclude a third party from enforcing a claim against the true owner in respect of the property purchased as *benami* (*u*).

Fraud on third parties.

§ 403. Even independently of statute, the Courts will not enforce the rights of a real owner where they would operate to defraud innocent persons. One familiar instance occurs, where the benamidar has sold or mortgaged the property of which he is the ostensible owner, for value, to persons who had no knowledge that he was not the real owner. In such a case the Judicial Committee said, "It is a principle of natural equity, which must be of universal application, that where one man allows another to hold himself out as the owner of an estate, and a third person purchases it for value from the apparent owner in the belief that he is the real owner, the man who so allows the other to hold himself out shall not be permitted to recover upon his secret title, unless he can overthrow that of the purchaser, by showing either that he had direct notice, or something which amounts to constructive notice of the real title, or that there were circumstances which ought to have put him upon an enquiry that, if prosecuted, would have led to a discovery of it" (*v*). But, of course, notice of the

(*s*) *Buhuns* v. *Lalla Buhooree*, 14 M. I. A. 496; S. C. 18 Suth. 157; *Lokhee* v. *Kalypuddo*, 2 I. A. 154.

(*t*) See *Tundun* v. *Pokh Narain*, 5 B. L. R. 546; S. C. 13 Suth. 347; *Bodh Singh* v. *Gunesh*, in P. C. 12 B. L R. 317; S. C. 19 Suth. 356.

(*u*) *Chundra Kaminey* v. *Ramrutton*, 12 Cal. 302.

(*v*) *Ramcoomar* v. *McQueen*, 11 B. L. R. (P. C.) 46, at p. 52; *Luchmun Chunder* v. *Kalli Churn*, 19 Suth. (P. C.) 292. See too per *Phear*, J., *Bhugwan*

trust may be implied as well as express, and if a man deals with another who is not in possession, or who is unable to produce the proper documents of title, these facts may amount to notice which will make his transaction be subject to the real state of the title of the person with whom he deals (*w*). In such cases there is no deliberate intention on the part of the real owner to commit a fraud upon any one. But if he deliberately places all the means of committing a fraud in the hands of his benamidar, Equity will not allow him to assert his title to the detriment of a person who has actually been defrauded.

Frauds upon creditors.

§ 404. A still stronger case is that in which property has been placed in a false name, for the express purpose of shielding it from creditors. As against them, of course, the transaction is wholly invalid (§ 402). But a very common form of proceeding is for the real owner to sue the benamidar, or to resist an action by the benamidar, alleging, or the evidence making out, that the sale was a merely colourable one, made for the express purpose of defrauding creditors. In other words, the party admits that he has apparently transferred his property to another to effect a fraud, but asks to have his act undone, now that the object of the fraud is carried out. The rule was for some time considered to be, that where this state of things was made out, the Court would invariably refuse relief, and would leave the parties to the consequences of their own misconduct; dismissing the plaint, when the suit was brought by the real owner to get back possession of his property (*x*), and refus-

---

v. *Upooch*, 10 Suth. 185. See numerous cases, *Rackhaldoss* v. *Bindoo*, Marsh. 293; *Obhoy* v. *Panchanun*, *ib.*, 564; *Kally Doss* v. *Gobind*, *ib.*, 569; *Rennie* v. *Gunganarain*, 3 Suth. 10; *Nundun* v. *Tayler*, 5 Suth. 37; *Brojonath* v. *Koylash*, 9 Suth. 593; *Nidhee* v. *Bisso*, 24 Suth. 79; *Chunder Coomar* v. *Hurbuns Sahai*, 16 Cal. 137; cf. *Sarat Chunder* v. *Gopal Chunder*, ibid. 148, where it was held, that the mere fact of a benami transfer did not amount to a representation which bound the real owner or his heirs as against a purchaser from the benamidar.

(*w*) *Hakeem* v. *Beejoy*, 22 Suth. 8; *Mancharji* v. *Kongseoo*, 6 Bom. H. C. (O. C. J.) 59; *Imambandi* v. *Kumleswari*, 13 I. A. 160, p. 165; S. C. 14 Cal. 109.

(*x*) *Ramindur* v. *Roopnarain*, 2 S. D. 118 (149); *Roushun* v. *Collector of Mymensingh*, S. D. of 1846, 120; *Brimho* v. *Ram Dolub*, S. D. of 1849, 276; *Rajnarain* v. *Jugunnath*, S. D. of 1851, 774; *Koonjee* v. *Jankee*, S. D. of 1852,

ing to listen to the defence, when he set it up in opposition to the person whom he had invested with the legal title (*y*). And persons who take under the real owner, whether as heirs or as purchasers, were treated in exactly the same manner as he was (*z*). On the other hand, a contrary doctrine was laid down in more recent cases. In the first of these the plaintiff claimed registration of title as vendee of certain parties, whom the defendant asserted to have been merely benamidars for her, she being actually in possession. The sale by the benamidars was found to be without consideration. It appeared, however, that in a former suit, to which the defendant and the benamidars were all parties, she had maintained that the latter were the real owners. It was also found that the property had been placed in the name of the benamidars by the defendant's late husband for the purpose of defrauding his creditors. On these two grounds the Judge held that the defendant could not now rely on the real state of the title. The High Court of Bengal reversed his judgment on both points. On the latter point, *Couch*, C. J., said: "In many of these cases, the object of a benami transaction is to obtain what may be called a shield against a creditor; but notwithstanding this the parties are not precluded from showing that it was not intended that the property should pass by the instrument creating the benami, and that in truth it still remained in the person who professed to part with it." He then referred to English decisions, and proceeded, "Although, no doubt, it is improper that transactions of this kind should be entered into for the purpose of defeating creditors, yet the real nature of the transaction is what is to be discovered,

Frauds upon creditors.

838; *Bhowanny* v. *Purem*, S. D. of 1853, 639; *Ramsoonder* v. *Anundnath*, S. D. of 1856, 542; *Hurry Sunker* v. *Kali*, Suth. for 1864, 265; *Aloksoondry* v. *Horo*, 6 Suth 287; *Keshub* v. *Vyasmonee*, 7 Suth. 118; *per curiam*, *Azimut* v. *Hurdwaree*, 13 M I. A. 402; S. C. 14 Suth. (P C.) 14; *Sukhimani* v. *Mahendranath*, 4 B. L. R. (P. C.) 28, 29; S. C. 13 Suth. (P. C.) 14.

(*y*) *Obhoychurn* v. *Treelochun*, S. D. of 1859, 1639; *Ram Lall* v. *Kishen*, S D. of 1860, i. 436; *per curiam*, *Ramanurga* v. *Mahasundur*, 12 B. L. R. (P. C.) 438.

(*z*) *Luckhee* v. *Taramonee*, 3 Suth. 92; *Purikheet* v. *Radha Kishen*, *ib.* 221; *Kaleenath* v. *Doyal Kristo*, 13 Suth. 87.

the real rights of the parties. If the Courts were to hold that persons were concluded under such circumstances, they would be assisting in a fraud, for they would be giving the estate to a person when it was never intended that he should have it" (*a*).

Principle of decision.

§ 405. Possibly the real rule is something intermediate between that which was laid down broadly in this last case, and in those which it appears to over-rule. Where a transaction is once made out to be a mere benami, it is evident that the benamidar absolutely disappears from the title. His name is simply an *alias* for that of the person beneficially interested. The fact that A. has assumed the name of B. in order to cheat X., can be no reason whatever why a Court should assist or permit B. to cheat A. But if A. requires the help of the Court to get the estate back into his own possession, or to get the title into his own name, it may be very material to consider whether A. has actually cheated X. or not. If he has done so by means of his *alias*, then it has ceased to be a mere mask, and has become a reality. It may be very proper for a Court to say that it will not allow him to resume the individuality, which he has once cast off in order to defraud others. If, however, he has not defrauded any one, there can be no reason why the Court should punish his intention by giving his estate away to B., whose roguery is even more complicated than his own. This appears to be the principle of the English decisions. For instance, persons have been allowed to recover property which they had assigned away in order to confer a parliamentary qualification upon a friend, who never sat in parliament; or in order to avoid serving in the office of a sheriff, where they ultimately paid the fine, instead of pleading that they had no property in the country; or where they had intended to defraud creditors, who in fact were never

Has fraud gone beyond intention.

(*a*) *Sreemutty Debia* v. *Bimola*, 21 Suth. 422, followed *Gopeenath* v. *Jadoo*, 23 Suth. 42; *Bykunt* v. *Goboollah*, 24 Suth. 391. See, too, *Birj Mohun* v. *Ram Nursingh*, 4 S. D. 341, (435); *Param* v. *Lalji*, 1 All. 403.

injured (*b*); or in order to avoid the effects of a conviction for a felony, which the grantor supposed he had committed, but which in fact he had not, and could not have committed (*c*). But where the fraudulent or illegal purpose has actually been effected by means of the colourable grant, then the maxim applies, "*In pari delicto potior est conditio possidentis.*" The Court will help neither party. "Let the estate lie where it falls" (*d*). But it was suggested by Lord *Eldon* that perhaps this rule would not be enforced in case of one who claimed under the settlor, but was himself not a party to the illegality or fraud (*e*). And in order to enable the grantee to retain the property, he must expressly set up the illegality of the object, and admit that he is holding for a different purpose from that for which he took the property (*f*). Even when the case is one in which the Court would not have relieved as matters stood originally, if fresh dealings have taken place between the real owner and the benamidar inconsistent with the ostensible character of the transaction, the former may be precluded from relying on his apparent title (*g*).

Original purchase made as benami.

§ 406. Even before the recent decisions, it was held in Bengal that there was nothing to prevent a man enforcing his rights against a benamidar, where he had made a new purchase, taking the conveyance in the name of a stranger, even though he had done so for the purpose of preventing the property from being seized by creditors. The Court, after referring to the cases already cited, said, "In this case the plaintiff does not seek to render void an act done by him

(*b*) *Birch* v. *Blagrave*, Amb. 264; *Cottington* v. *Fletcher*, 2 Atk. 156; *Platamone* v. *Staple*, G. Coop. 250; *Young* v. *Peachey*, 2 Atk. 254; *Symes* v. *Hughes*, L. R. 9 Eq. 475; *per Lord Westbury*, *Tennent* v. *Tennent*, L. R. 2 Sc. & D 9; *Cecil* v. *Butcher*, 2 Jac. & W 565.

(*c*) *Davies* v. *Otty*, 35 Beav. 208; *Manning* v. *Gill*, L. R. 13 Eq. 485. See *Great Berlin Steamboat Co.*, 26 Ch. D. 616.

(*d*) *Duke of Bedford* v. *Coke*, 2 Ves. Sen. 116; *Muckleston* v. *Brown*, 6 Ves. 68; *Chaplin* v. *Chaplin*, 3 P. W. 233; *Brackenbury* v. *Brackenbury* 2 Jac. & W. 391; *Doe* v. *Roberts*, 2 B. & Ald. 367; Lewin, 93; Story, Eq. Jur. § 298. This seems to be the effect of the Indian Trusts Act, II of 1882, § 84. *Chennvirappa* v. *Puttappa*, 11 Bom. 708.

(*e*) Lewin, 93; 6 Ves. 68.

(*f*) *Haigh* v. *Kaye*, L. R. 7 Ch. 469.

(*g*) *Mahadaji* v. *Vittil Vallal*, 7 Bom. 78.

in fraud, or, in other words, to be relieved from the effect of his own fraudulent act. He simply sues to have a legal act enforced, an act legal in itself, though in the present instance done with a motive of keeping the property out of the reach of his creditors" (*h*). It may also be well to remember that the rules which govern benami transactions have no application to the case of gifts made in contemplation of insolvency, and with the intention of defrauding creditors (*i*). Nor to cases in which property has been sold or handed over to one creditor, in order to defeat an expected execution by another creditor (*k*). If the transfer is really intended to operate, and is not colourable, it is not a benami transaction. Whether it is valid or not, depends upon other considerations.

Insolvency

Effect of decrees.

§ 407. Decrees are conclusive between the parties both as to the rights declared, and as to the character in which they sue. It is allowable for a third person, who was not on the record, to come in and show that a suit was really carried on for his benefit (*l*). So, it is allowable for a person who is on the record, to show that a suit was carried on really against a person who was not a party to it. But where judgment is given in an apparently hostile suit, it is not allowable for either party to come in and assert that the fight was all a sham, and for the defendant on the record to show, that so far from being really a defendant he was the plaintiff, and that so far from judgment having been recovered against him, he had really recovered judgment (*m*). Hence as a general rule it is desirable, if not necessary, that the benamidar should be a party to all suits which affect the property of which he is the nominal owner. But this is not necessary when there is no dispute as to his title being only apparent (*n*). In the absence of any evi-

Benamidar should be a party.

..., *Suboodra* v. *Bikromadit*, S. D. of 1858, 543, 548.
(*i*) See *Gnanabhai* v. *Srinavasa*, 4 Mad. H. C. 84.
(*k*) *Sankarappa* v. *Kamayya*, 3 Mad. H. C. 231; *Pullen* v. *Ramalinga*, 5 Mad. H. C 368; *Tillakchand* v. *Jitamal*, 10 Bom H C. 206.
(*l*) *Lachman* v. *Patniram*, 1 All. 510.
(*m*) *Bhowabul* v. *Rajendro*, 13 Suth. 157; *Chenvirappa* v. *Puttappa*, 11 Bom. 708.
(*n*) *Kurreemonissa* v. *Mohabut*, S. D. of 1851, 356.

dence to the contrary, it is to be presumed that a suit brought by a benamidar has been instituted with the full authority of the beneficial owner, and if this is so, any decision come to in his presence would be as much binding upon the real owner, as if the suit had been brought by the real owner himself (*o*). Where, however, a suit is brought to establish the plaintiff's right to land and for possession, if it appears that he is only benamidar his suit must be dismissed, and it will make no difference that the real owner is a defendant, and gave evidence disclaiming title (*p*).

(*o*) *Gopinath* v. *Bhugwat*, 10 Cal. 697, p. 705.
(*p*) *Hari Gobind* v. *Akhoy Kumar*, 16 Cal. 364.

CHAPTER XIV.

MAINTENANCE.

§ 408. THE importance and extent of the right of maintenance necessarily arises from the theory of an undivided family. Originally, no doubt, no individual member of the family had a right to anything but maintenance. This is still the law of Malabar (*a*), and the case is much the same in an ordinary Hindu family under Mitakshara law prior to partition (§ 268). The head of the undivided family is bound to maintain its members, their wives and their children; to perform their ceremonies, and to defray the expenses of their marriages (*b*). In other words, those who would be entitled to share in the bulk of the property, are entitled to have all their necessary expenses paid out of its income. But the right of maintenance goes farther than this. Those who would be sharers, but for some personal disqualification, are also similarly entitled for themselves and their sons, for their wives, if chaste, and for their daughters. As for instance, those who from some mental or bodily defect are unable to inherit (*c*); illegitimate sons, when not entitled as heirs, even though the connection from which they sprung may have been adulterous (*d*); persons taken in adoption whose adoption has proved invalid, or who have been

Persons who are entitled.

(*a*) *Ante*, § 220. As to the rights of the male members of a Malabar Tarwaad to maintenance, see *Bappan* v. *Makki*, 6 Mad. 259; *Parvati* v. *Kamaran*, *ibid.* 341; *Kunhammata* v. *Kunhikutti*, 7 Mad. 233. *Kesava* v. *Unikkanda*, 11 Mad. 307; *Chandu* v. *Raman*, *ib.* 378; *Chekkutti* v. *Pakki*, 12 Mad. 305.

(*b*) Manu, ix, § 108; Narada, xiii. § 26—28, 33. This right is not founded on contract; and, therefore, a suit for maintenance, where there is no special contract, is not cognizable by a Small Cause Court. *Sidlingapa* v. *Sidava*, 2 Bom. 624; *Apaji* v. *Gangabi*, *ib.* 632.

(*c*) Mitakshara, ii. 10; Daya Bhaga, v. § 10, 11; D. K. S. iii. § 7—17; V. May., iv 11, § 1—9; W. & B. 751.

(*d*) Mitakshara, i. 12, § 3; *Muttusamy* v. *Venkatasubha*, (Yetteyapooram Zemindary) 2 Mad. H. C. 293; *affirmed* 12 M. I. A. 203; S. C. 2 B. L. R.

63 *in.*

deprived of their full rights by the subsequent birth of a legitimate son (*e*). Whether the same privilege extended to outcasts and their offspring, is a point upon which the authorities differ (*f*). Since Act XXI of 1850 (Freedom of Religion) it has ceased to be a point of any practical importance. Concubines also are entitled to be maintained, even though the connection with them is an adulterous one (*g*). But this liability only exists where the connection was of a permanent nature, analogous to that of the female slaves who in former times were recognized members of a man's family (*h*). *A fortiori* the widows of the members of the family are so entitled, provided they are chaste, and so long as they lead a virtuous life (*i*); and the parents, including the step-mother, and mother-in-law (*k*). The sister, or step-sister, is entitled to maintenance until her marriage, and to have her marriage expenses defrayed. After marriage, her maintenance is a charge upon her husband's family; but, if they are unable to support her, she must be provided for by the family of her father (*l*).

(P. C.) 15; S. C. 11 Suth. (P. C.) 6; *Chuoturya* v. *Sahub Purhulad*, 7 M. I. A. 18; S. C. 4 Suth. (P. C.) 132; *Rahi* v. *Govind*, 1 Bom. 97; *Viraramuthi* v. *Singaravelu*, 1 Mad. 306. *Kuppa* v. *Singaravelu*, 8 Mad. 325; *Hargobind* v. *Dharam*, 6 All. 329.

(*e*) Mitakshara, i, 11, § 28; Datta Chandrika, i. § 15. See *ante*, § 163—165.

(*f*) Mitakshara. ii. 10, § 1; Daya Bhaga, v. § 11, 12; D. K. S. iii. § 14—16; V. May., iv. 11, § 10.

(*g*) Mitakshara, ii. 1, § 28; Daya Bhaga, xi. 1, § 48; V. May, iv. 8, § 5; 1 Stra. H. L. 174; 2 W. MacN. 119; W. & B. 164; *Khemkor* v. *Umiashankar*, 10 Bom. H. C. 381; *Vrandavandas* v. *Yamuna*, 12 Bom. H. C. 229.

(*h*) *Sikki* v. *Vencatasamy*, 8 Mad. H. C. 144.

(*i*) "Let them allow a maintenance to his woman for life, provided these preserve unsullied the bed of their lords. But if they behave otherwise, the brethren may resume that allowance" (Narada, xiii. § 26). This text is said by Jimuta Vahana to apply to women actually espoused who have not the rank of wives, but another passage of Narada (cited Smriti Chandrika, xi. 1, § 34) is open to no such objection. "Whichever wife (*patnî*) becomes a widow and continues virtuous, she is entitled to be provided with food and raiment." See, too, Smriti Chandrika, xi. 1, § 47; 2 W. MacN. 112; *Muttammal* v. *Kamakshy*, 2 Mad. H. C. 337; *per curiam*, *Sinthayee* v. *Thanakapudayen*, 4 Mad. H. C. 185; *Kery Kolitany* v. *Moneeram*, 13 B. L. R. 72, 88; S. C. 19 Suth. 367, 7 I. A. p. 151. But see *Honamma* v. *Timannabhat*, 1 Bom. 559, where it was held that subsequent unchastity did not deprive a widow of a mere starving maintenance awarded by decree, *post*, § 414. See too *Roma Nath* v. *Rajonimoni*, 17 Cal. 674

(*k*) 2 W. MacN. 113, 118; W. & B., 234; *per Norman, J.*, *Khetramani* v. *Kashinath*, 2 B. L. R. (A. C. J.) 15; S. C. 10 Suth. (F. B.) 93; *Cooppummal* v. *Rookmany*, Mad. Dec. of 1855, 238. *Per curiam Savitribai* v. *Luximibai*, 2 Bom. 597.

(*l*) 2 W. MacN. 118; W. & B., 245, 437.

Misbehaviour, or ex-communication from caste on the ground of misbehaviour, does not of itself disentitle the offender to maintenance (*m*).

§ 409. There is some difference of opinion as to whether the right of maintenance is an absolute obligation, which attaches itself upon certain persons by virtue of their relationship to the destitute individual, or whether it is merely a claim upon the property of those who hold it, by virtue of their possession of the property. It is stated in a text ascribed to Manu, that "A mother and a father in their old age, a virtuous wife, and an infant son, must be maintained, even though doing an hundred times that which ought not to be done" (*n*). So the Mitakshara lays down that "Where there may be no property but what has been self-acquired, the only persons whose maintenance out of such property is imperative are aged parents, wife, and minor children" (*o*). The Smriti Chandrika also expressly states that the obligation to maintain widows is dependent on taking the property of the deceased (*p*). This rule is followed in Madras, where suits for maintenance have been dismissed when brought by a widow against her brothers-in-law, or her father-in-law, who held no ancestral property, or where the only property out of which maintenance could be given was a salary (*q*). So, it has been held in Bengal that the widow of a separated brother is not entitled to be main-

How enforced.

Nature and extent of obligation.

(*m*) *Putanvitil Seyan* v. *Putanvitil Ragavan*, 4 Mad. 171; *R.* v. *Marimuttu*, *ibid.* 243.

(*n*) 3 Dig. 406. The last clause is cited in another chapter as meaning that these relations must be maintained even by crime. See *per curiam*, *Savitribai* v. *Luximibai*, 2 Bom. 597.

(*o*) Mitakshara on Subtraction of Gift, cited Stra. Man. § 209; *Subbarayana* v. *Subbakka*, 8 Mad. 236. A step son is not bound to support his step-mother unless he has family property. *Bai Daya* v. *Natha Govindlal*, 9 Bom. 279; *Kedar Nath* v. *Hemangini*, 13 Cal. 336.

(*p*) Smriti Chandrika, xi. 1. § 34. "In order to maintain the widow, the elder brother or any of the others above mentioned must have taken the property of the deceased; the duty of maintaining the widow being dependent on taking the property." It is immaterial whether the property is movable or real. *Kamini Dassee* v. *Chandra Pode*, 17 Cal. 373.

(*q*) *Vudda* v. *Venkummah*, Mad. Dec. of 1858, 225; *Comarasawmy* v. *Sellummaul*, Mad. Dec. of 1859, 5; *Virabadrachari* v. *Kuppammal*, ib. 265; *Brahmavarapu* v. *Venkamma*, ib. 272; *Ammakannu* v. *Appu*, 11 Mad. 191. See *Visalatchy* v. *Annasami*, 5 Mad. H. C. 150, where the point had been left undecided.

tained by the family of her father-in-law, and the same opinion was given by the Bombay High Court, in a case where a deserted wife claimed maintenance from her husband's brothers. Their liability was stated to depend upon their having in their hands any of her husband's property (*r*). In a case under the Mitakshara law in Bengal, *Kemp*, J., said, "The question to be decided is, whether the father and son were joint in estate, and whether any joint estate was left which was burthened with the payment of proper maintenance to the plaintiff, the defendant's daughter-in-law" (*s*). The question was recently examined with great fulness and care by the Courts of the North-West Provinces and of Bengal. In the former the widow of a deceased member of a joint family claimed maintenance from her father-in-law and brothers-in-law. There was admittedly joint ancestral property, but it was contended that the widow could only be maintained out of her husband's property, and that he left none, his interest in it passing to his coparceners. The Court affirmed her claim. They rested it on the ground that the share which her husband had in the property had passed to the defendants, that she could not be in a worse position than the wife of a disqualified heir, who would be admittedly entitled to maintenance; that she might be looked upon as one who, though interested in the property, was disqualified from inheriting it by sex; and that where her husband had an interest in property, out of which she would be maintained during his life, the obligation to maintain her out of that property continued after his death, whether it passed by inheritance or by survivorship (*t*). It will be observed that it was assumed that there would have been no such obligation if there had been no joint property, or if it had not passed into the hands of the defendants, and the judgments relied much on the passage in the Smriti Chandrika (xi. 1, § 34), in which this rule is

Widow of deceased coparcener.

(*r*) *Kumulmoney* v. *Bodhnarain*, 2 W. MacN. 119; *Ramabai* v. *Trimbak*, 9 Bom. H. C. 283.

(*s*) *Hema Kooeree* v. *Ajoodhya*, 24 Suth. 474.

(*t*) *Lalti Kuar* v. *Ganga*, 7 N.-W. P. 261.

laid down. The principle that a widow of a son has no legal claim for maintenance against the separate or self-acquired property of her father-in-law was affirmed by a Full Bench of the Allahabad High Court. They held, however, that the father-in-law was under a moral obligation to provide for the widow out of this property, and that when, upon his death, the property devolved upon his other sons they came under a legal obligation to carry out this moral obligation, and could be compelled to do so (*u*).

Not entitled to independent allowance,

§ 410. The Bengal decision was given on appeal from a judgment of a Full Bench under the following circumstances (*v*) : The plaintiff was the widow of the defendant's son. There was no joint family property, and the son left no property of his own. The only property possessed by the father-in-law was a monthly pension. After her husband's death, the widow went to reside in her own father's house. The suit was brought by her to have a fixed money payment made to her. It was admitted that the defendant was willing to support her in his own house, and that she had not been driven from his house by any ill-treatment. It was held by eleven out of thirteen Judges (*diss. Loch* and *Kemp*, JJ.) that her claim could not be supported. For the purpose of this ruling, however, it was not necessary to decide whether the father-in-law was under an obligation to give his daughter-in-law lodging, food and raiment. It was only necessary to decide that where she practically refused to accept these, she was not entitled to a fixed monthly allowance. It was admitted by all the Judges that where a person took property, either by inheritance or survivorship, he would be legally bound to maintain those whose maintenance was a charge upon it in the hands of the last holder. But where there was no such property, *Peacock*, C. J., *Macpherson*, *Bayley*, *Glover*, JJ., were of opinion that there was no legal obligation whatever to

where no property.

Whether maintenance of widow depends

(*u*) *Janki* v. *Nand Ram*, 11 All. 194. This case was approved and followed by the High Court of Bengal, *Kamini Dassee* v. *Chandra Pode*, 17 Cal. 373.

(*v*) *Khetramani* v. *Kashinath*, 2 B. L. R. (A. C. J.) 15 ; S. C. 10 Suth. (F. B.) 89 ; *Ramcoomar* v. *Ichamoyi*, 6 Cal. 36.

on possession of property.

maintain the daughter at law, and that the precepts which seemed to enjoin upon relations the duty of maintaining the widows of deceased members were of merely moral obligation. On the other hand, several of the other Judges stated that they offered no opinion as to the right of a dependent widow to receive necessary subsistence in the house of the head of the family. If he allowed her to continue in his house as a member of the family, and if she were an infant, or otherwise unable to maintain herself, it was intimated by *Norman*, J., that such a state of things would carry with it a legal obligation on the part of the father-in-law, who had taken upon himself the care of her person, and the charge of entertaining her as a member of his family, and on whose protection she was dependent, to provide her with food and the actual necessaries of life. But the Civil Courts would have no jurisdiction to interfere with his discretion in determining the manner in which this obligation should be discharged (*w*).

Bombay

§ 411. In Bombay, it was formerly laid down that where a widow of one of the near members of the family, such as a father, son, or brother, is actually destitute, she has a legal right to be maintained by the other members, even though they were separated from her late husband, and possess no assets upon which he or she ever had a claim (*x*). These cases were, however, examined and over-ruled in a later decision, in which a widow, who was living apart from her husband's family, sued his paternal uncle, the nearest surviving male relation of her husband, for a money allowance as maintenance. The Court, after an exhaustive review of the whole law upon the subject, held that the suit must fail for two reasons, either of which would be fatal to her claim; *first*, that the defendant was separated in estate from the plaintiff's husband at the time of his death; and

(*w*) 2 B. L. R. (A. C. J.) p. 48; S. C. 10 Suth. (F. B.), p. 95.

(*x*) *Baee* v. *Lukmeedass*, 1 Bom. H. C. 13; *Chandrabhagabai* v. *Kashinath*, 2 Bom. H. C. 341; *Timmappa* v. *Parmeshriamma*, 5 Bom. H. C. (A. C. J.) 130; *Udaram* v. *Sonkaboi*, 10 Bom. H. C. 483.

secondly, that at the institution of the suit there was not in the possession, or subject to the disposition, of the defendant, any ancestral estate, or estate of the plaintiff's husband, or of his father (*y*).

§ 412. The obligation to maintain a son appears to be limited to the case of his being an infant (*z*), in which case the law of every nation imposes an obligation upon the parent to maintain him, or of his being a co-sharer in the property of which his father is the manager. The mere relationship of father and son imposes no such obligation, where the son has reached an age at which he can support himself. Whether the case might be different if a permanent incapacity to support himself were made out is not clear. A temporary incapacity would certainly entail no such duty (*a*). Where, however, the whole of the family property is impartible, and subject to the law of primogeniture, an adult son is entitled to maintenance, since this is the only mode in which he can obtain any benefit from the ancestral estate (*b*). Rights of son.

§ 413. The maintenance of a wife by her husband is, of course, a matter of personal obligation, arising from the very existence of the relation, and independent of the possession of any property (*c*). And this obligation attaches from the moment of marriage. Where the wife is immature it is the custom that she should reside with her parents, and they maintain her as a matter of affection, but not of obligation. If from inability, unwillingness, or any other cause, they choose to demand her maintenance from her husband, he is bound to pay it (*d*). And, conversely, her Wife to be maintained by husband.

(*y*) *Savitribai* v. *Luximibai*, 2 Bom. 573; *Apaji* v. *Gangabai*, *ib.* 632; *Kalu* v. *Kashibai*, 7 Bom. 127; *Bai Kanku* v. *Bai Jadav*, 8 Bom. 15; *Adibai* v. *Cursandas*, 11 Bom. 199.

(*z*) *Ante*, § 409. *Amma Kannu* v. *Appu*, 11 Mad. 91.

(*a*) *Premchand* v. *Hulashchand*, 4 B. L. R. Appx. 23; S. C. 12 Suth. 494. So as to grandson, *Mon Mohinee* v. *Baluck*, 8 B. L. R. 22; S. C. 15 Suth. 498; or adult illegitimate son, *Nilmoney* v. *Baneshur*, 4 Cal. 91.

(*b*) *Himmat* v. *Ganpat*, 12 Bom. H. C. 94; *Ramchandra* v. *Sakharam*, 2 Bom. 346; *post*, § 416.

(*c*) *Ante*, § 409. (*d*) *Ramien* v. *Condummal*, Mad Dec. of 1858, 154.

husband is alone liable. No other member of the family, whether joint or separate, can properly be made a party to the suit, unless, perhaps, in cases where he has abandoned her, and his property is in the possession of some other relation. (*e*).

Bound to reside with him.

§ 414. As soon as the wife is mature, her home is necessarily in her husband's house (*f*). He is bound to maintain her in it while she is willing to reside with him, and to perform her duties. If she quits him of her own accord, either without cause, or on account of such ordinary quarrels as are incidental to married life in general, she can set up no claim to a separate maintenance (*g*). Nothing will justify her in leaving her home except such violence as renders it unsafe for her to continue there, or such continued ill-usage as would be termed cruelty in an English matrimonial Court (*h*). For instance, where a Hindu husband kept a Mahomedan woman, the Court considered that this was such conduct as rendered it impossible for the wife to live with him any longer, consistently with her self-respect and religious feelings (*i*). But I doubt whether the same rule would be applied to the mere keeping of a concubine, which is a matter of familiar usage among Hindus, especially of the higher ranks (*k*). And the circumstance of a man's taking another wife, even without any of the reasons which are stated as justifying such a course (*l*), does not entitle a

Wife leaving her home.

(*e*) *Iyagaree* v. *Sashamma*, Mad. Dec. of 1856, 22; *Rangaiyan* v. *Kaliyan*; Mad. Dec. of 1860, 86; *Gudimella* v. *Venkamma*, Mad. Dec. of 1861, 12; *Ramabai* v. *Trimbak*, 9 Bom. H. C. 283.

(*f*) See the whole subject discussed in *Dadaji* v. *Rukmabai*, 9 Bom. 529, reversed 10 Bom. 301, where a wife of mature years, whose marriage had never been consummated, refused to take up her residence with her husband, and it was held that a suit would lie to compel her to do so.

(*g*) 2 W. MacN. 109; *Kullyanessuree* v. *Dwarkanath*, 6 Suth. 116; S. C. 2 Wym. 123; *Sidlingapa* v. *Sidava*, 2 Bom. 634.

(*h*) *Pudmanabiah* v. *Moonemmah*, Mad. Dec. of 1857, 138; *Vejayah* v. *Anjalummaul*, Mad. Dec. of 1853, 223; *Matangini* v. *Jogendro*, 19 Cal. 84.

(*i*) *Lalla Gobind* v. *Dowlut*, 6 B. L. R. Appx. 85; S. C. 14 Suth. 451. As to cases where either party becomes a convert and is therefore repudiated by the other, see Act XXI of 1866, (Native Converts Marriage Dissolution).

(*k*) Yajnavalkya says (V. May., xx. § 2), "Let the bidding of their husbands be performed by wives; this is the chief duty of a woman. Even if he be accused of deadly sin, yet let her wait until he be purified from it."

(*l*) See as to these, Manu, ix. § 77—82.

wife to leave her home, so long as her husband is willing to keep her there (*m*). For such a step on his part is one of the incidents of Hindu married life. Of course, a wife who leaves her home for purposes of adultery cannot claim to be maintained out of it, nor to be taken back (*n*) Whether an unchaste wife can be turned out of doors by her husband without any provision whatever seems unsettled. It is stated generally that an unchaste woman may be turned out of doors without any maintenance (*o*). But the passages upon which this *dictum* rests refer to the maintenance either of the wives of disqualified heirs, or of the widows of deceased coparceners (*p*). Vasishtha treats even adultery on the part of a wife as an expiable offence, and states the particular penances by which she is rendered pure again. He adds, "But these four wives must be abandoned, one who yields herself to her husband's pupil or guru, and especially one who attempts the life of her lord, or who commits adultery with a man of a degraded caste." In another passage he says, "A wife though tainted by sin, whether she be quarrelsome, or have left the house, or have suffered criminal force, or have fallen into the hands of thieves, must not be abandoned; to forsake her is not prescribed by the sacred law." "Those versed in the sacred law state that there are three acts only which make women outcastes, the murder of the husband, slaying a learned Brahman, and the destruction of the fruit of their womb" (*q*). It appears pretty certain that no one except her husband, or perhaps her son, is bound to keep an unchaste woman alive. But there are contradictory opinions as to whether her husband is not liable to furnish her with a bare subsistence. The obligation, if it exists, is dependent on the

When unchaste.

(*m*) Manu, ix. § 83; *Virasvami* v. *Appasvami*, 1 Mad. H. C. 375; *Rajah Row Boochee* v. *Vencata Neeladry*, 1 Mad Dec. 366.

(*n*) 2 W. MacN. 109; *Ilata* v. *Narayanan*, 1 Mad. H. C. 372.

(*o*) V. May., iv. 11, § 12; Smriti Chandrika, v. § 43.

(*p*) See Narada, xiii. § 25, 26; Mitakshara, ii, 1, § 7; Viramit., p. 174; Daya Bhaga, xi. 1, § 48, and *per* P. C. *Moniram* v. *Kerry Kolitany*, 7 I. A. 151; S. C. 5 Cal. 776.

(*q*) Vasishtha, xxi. 7—10; xxviii. 2—7.

woman abandoning her course of vice (r). Where a decree has been given awarding a bare maintenance to a woman, it has been held that she does not forfeit it by subsequent unchastity. Though it might be different if the maintenance awarded were on the full scale (s). This ruling was dissented from in a later case where a widow was declared not entitled even to a starving maintenance on account of her incontinence. There, however, the property out of which she claimed to be maintained had been bequeathed by her father-in-law to her mother-in-law, by whom the action was brought to recover it, and the Court intimated that possibly her husband or her son would be bound to keep her from absolute destitution (t). This decision was again followed in a case very similar to that of *Honamma* v. *Timannabhat,* the widow having obtained a decree for maintenance before her misconduct. The Court held that her subsequent unchastity might be used either as a defence to an action by her to enforce the decree, or as a ground for setting it aside. They relied on the text of Narada referred to in the Daya Bhaga (XI. 1, § 48) :—" Let them (the husband's relations) allow a maintenance to his women for life, provided they keep unsullied the bed of their lord; but if they behave otherwise, the brother may resume that allowance." This text is pointed out by the Privy Council in *Moniram* v. *Kerry Kolitany* (u), as clearly showing that the right was one liable to resumption or forfeiture as distinguished from the case of a widow's estate by succession (v).

For a lawful purpose.

When a wife leaves her husband's home by his consent, he

(r) *Bussunt* v. *Kummul,* 7 S. D. 144 (168); 1 Stra. H. L. 172; 2 Stra. H. L. 39, 309; Stra. Man. § 206; *Muthammal* v. *Kamakshy Ammal,* 2 Mad. H. C. 337. And consider remarks of H. Ct. *Lakshman* v. *Ramchandra,* 1 Bom. 560. See texts. 2 Dig. 422—425; Narada, xii. § 91; Yajnavalkya, i. § 70; Viramit., p. 153; *per curiam,* 17 Cal. p. 679.

(s) *Honamma* v. *Timannabhat,* 1 Bom. 559. But see *per curiam, Sinthayee* v. *Thanakapudayen,* 4 Mad. H. C. 185.

(t) *Valu* v. *Gunga,* 7 Bom. 84. (u) 7 I. A. p. 151.

(v) *Vishnu Shambhog* v. *Manjamma,* 9 Bom. 108. The rule applies *a fortiori* in the case of a concubine of a deceased coparcener. *Yashvantrav* v. *Kashibai,* 12 Bom. 26.

is, of course, bound to receive her again when she is desirous to return, and if he refuses to do so, she will be entitled to maintenance just as if he had turned her out (*w*).

A wife who is unlawfully excluded from her own home, or refused proper maintenance in it, has the same right to pledge her husband's credit, as a wife in England. But the *onus* lies heavily on those who deal with her to establish that she is in such a position (*x*).

Widow not bound to reside with husband's family.

§ 415. The same reasons which require a wife to remain under her husband's roof do not apply where she has become a widow. No doubt the family house of her husband's relations is a proper, but not necessarily the most proper, place for her continued residence (*y*). Where she is young, and is surrounded by young men, it may even be more prudent and decorous for her to return to her father's care, and it may, under many circumstances, be not only a safer but a happier home. At all events it is now settled by decisions of the highest tribunal that "all that is required of her is, that she is not to leave her husband's house for improper or unchaste purposes, and she is entitled to retain her maintenance, unless she is guilty of unchastity, or other disreputable practices, after she leaves that residence" (*z*). It does not, however, follow, that the right to choose a separate residence and a money maintenance rests absolutely with the widow, merely for her own pleasure. The Bombay High Court, after a review of all the previous decisions, appears to be of opinion that the Courts have a discretion, "which should be exercised so as not to throw upon the deceased husband's family a needless or oppressive burden at the caprice of the widow or her family." They cited with approval, as containing the true principle

Widow residing apart.

(*w*) *Nitye* v. *Soondaree*, 9 Suth. 475.

(*x*) *Virasvami* v. *Appasvami*, 1 Mad. H. C. 375. (*y*) 2 Dig. 450.

(*z*) *Pirthee Singh* v. *Rani Rajkooer*, 12 B. L. R. (P. C.) 238; S. C. 20 Suth. 21, where most of the previous cases are cited; *Visalatchi* v. *Annasamy*, 5 Mad. H. C. 150; *Kasturbai* v. *Shivajiram*, 3 Bom. 372, dissenting from *Rango Vinayak* v. *Yamunabai*, 3 Bom. 44; *per curiam*, 6 Mad. p. 85; *Gokibai* v. *Lakhmidas*, 14 Bom. 490.

of law, the statement by Colebrooke (2 Stra. H. L. 401) "She does not lose her right of maintenance by visiting her own relations; but a widow is not entirely her own mistress, being subject to the control of her husband's family, who might require her to return to live in her husband's house (*a*)." If the husband chose by his will to make it a condition, that his widow should reside in his family house, such a direction would be binding, and the continuance of her maintenance would depend upon her obedience (*b*). A widow cannot insist on residing in any particular house. If she elects to live with her husband's family, she must accept such arrangements for her residence as they make for her (*c*). In Madras it has been laid down that a widow who, without any special cause, elects to live away from her husband's relations, is not entitled to as liberal an allowance as she would be if, from any fault of theirs, she was unable to live with them (*d*). But I imagine that her election to live apart from them cannot be visited with anything in the way of a penalty, or forfeiture of her proper rights (*e*). Under Bengal Law, where a partition takes place between the sons and stepsons of a widowed mother, her claim for maintenance attaches upon the share of her own sons, not upon the whole estate. So long as the estate is undivided the maintenance of all the mothers is a charge upon the whole estate (*f*).

All heirs bound. § 416. A female heir is under exactly the same obligations to maintain dependent members of the family as a male heir would have been under by virtue of succeeding to the same estate (*g*). The obligation extends even to the

(*a*) *Rango Vinayak* v. *Yamunabai*, 8 Bom. 44; *Ramchandra* v. *Sagunabai*, 4 Bom. 261.

(*b*) *Bamasunderi* v. *Puddomonee*, S. D. of 1859, 457; *Cunjhunnee* v. *Gopee*, F. MacN. 62; *per curiam*, *Pirthee Singh* v. *Rani Rajkooer*, 12 B. L. R. 247; S. C. 20 Suth 21. *Mulji Baishanker* v. *Bai Ujam*, 18 Bom. 218; *Girianna* v. *Honamma*, 15 Bom. 236.

(*c*) *Mohun Geer* v. *Mt. Tota*, 4 N.-W. P. 158.

(*d*) *Anantaiya* v. *Savitramma*, Mad. Dec. of 1861, 59.

(*e*) See cases cited, note (z); *Nittokissoree* v. *Jogendor*, 5 A. I. 55.

(*f*) *Hemangini Dasi* v. *Kedarnath*, 16 I. A. 115; S. C. 16 Cal. 758.

(*g*) *Gunga* v. *Jeevee*, 1 Bor. 384 [426]; 3 Dig. 460.

King when he takes the estate by escheat, or by forfeiture (*h*). And where the claim to maintenance is based upon the possession of family property, it equally exists though the property is impartible, as being in the nature of a Raj, or a Zemindary in Southern India (*i*). In Bombay it has been held that where a member of an ordinary undivided Hindu family is in a position to sue for a share of the property, he cannot sue for maintenance (*k*). But it is difficult to see why a coparcener, who is willing to continue as a member of an undivided family, should be driven out of it by what must be wrongful conduct on the part of the manager, in refusing him his proper support out of the family funds. Such suits are, of course, very rare, as maintenance would never be refused to a coparcener unless his right as such was denied, in which case he would naturally test his right by suing for a partition. **Right of coparcener tc**

§ 417. In cases where a man forsakes his wife without any fault on her part, it is said that he is bound to give her one-third of his property, provided that would be sufficient for her maintenance (*l*). In other cases no rule is, or can be, laid down as to the amount which ought to be awarded. In any particular instance the first question would be, what would be the fair wants of a person in the position and rank of life of the claimant? The wealth of the family would be a proper element in determining this question. A member of a family who had been brought up in affluence would naturally have more numerous and more expensive wants than one who had been brought up in poverty. The extent of the property would be material in deciding whether these **Amount.** **How determined.**

(*h*) Narada, xiii. § 52; *Golab Koonwur* v. *Collector of Benares*, 4 M. I. A. 246; S. C. 7 Suth. (P. C.) 47.

(*i*) *Muttusawmy* v. *Vencataswara*, 12 M. I. A 203; S. C. 2 B. L. R. (P. C.) 15; S. C. 11 Suth. (P. C.) 6; *Katchekaleyana* v. *Kachivijaya*, *ib.* 495; S. C. 2 B. L. R. (P. C) 72; S. C. 11 Suth. (P. C.) 33; *ante*, § 412. In the case of the *Pachete* Raj the Court held that there was no law, or custom, which entitled any one but a son or daughter of the deceased Rajah to receive maintenance. *Nilmony Singh* v. *Hingoo*, 5 Cal. 256.

(*k*) *Himmat Sing* v. *Ganpat Sing*, 12 Bom. H. C. 96, note.

(*l*) V. May., xx. § 1; *Huree Bhaee* v. *Nathoo*, 1 Bor. 63 [69]; *Ramabai* v. *Trimbak*, 9 Bom. H. C. 283.

wants could be provided for, consistently with justice to the other members (*m*). The extent of the property is not, however, a criterion of the sufficiency of the maintenance, in the sense that any ratio had existed between one and the other. Otherwise, as the Judicial Committee remarked (*n*), "a son not provided for might compel a frugal father, who had acquired large means by his own exertions, to allow a larger maintenance than he himself was satisfied to live upon, and than children living as part of his family must be content with." Every case must be determined upon its own peculiar facts. As regards widows, since they are only entitled to be maintained by persons who hold assets over which their deceased husbands had a claim, (§ 409—411) the High Court of Bombay has ruled that it follows as a corollary, "that the widow is not, at the utmost, entitled to a larger portion of the annual produce of the family property than the annual proceeds of the share to which her husband would have been entitled on partition were he now living" (*o*).

Where widow has property.

In calculating the amount of maintenance to be awarded to a female, her own *stridhana* is not be taken into account, if it is of an unproductive character, such as clothes and jewels. For she has a right to retain these, and also to be supported, if necessary, by her husband's family. But if her property produces an income, this is to be taken into consideration. For her right is to be maintained, and, so far as she is already maintained out of her own property, that right is satisfied (*p*). And it would seem that a member of the family, who has once received a sufficient allotment for maintenance, and who has dissipated it, cannot bring a suit either for a money allowance, or for subsistence out of the

(*m*) *Baisni* v. *Rup Singh*, 12 All. 558.

(*n*) *Tagore* v. *Tagore*, 9 B. L. R. p. 413; S. C. 18 Suth 359; *Bhugwan* v. *Bindoo*, 6 Suth. 286; *Nittokissoree* v. *Jogendro*, 5 I. A. 55.

(*o*) *Madhavrav* v. *Gangabai*, 2 Bom. 639; *Adibai* v. *Cursandas*, 11 Bom. 199.

(*p*) 1 Stra. H. L. 171; 2 Stra. H. L. 307; *Shib Dayee* v. *Doorga Pershad*, 4 N.-W. P. 63; *Chandrabhagabai* v. *Kashinath*, 2 Bom. H. C. 341; *per curiam*, *Savitribai* v. *Luximibai*, 2 Bom. at p. 584. A mere right of action to recover property under a will is not a legitimate ground for reducing maintenance. *Gokebai* v. *Lakhmidas*. 14 Bom. 490.

family property (*q*). On the other hand, an allowance fixed in reference to a particular state of the family property may be diminished by order of the Court if the assets are afterwards reduced (*r*), provided the reduction has not arisen from the voluntary act of the person liable for maintenance (*s*). And on the same principle, no doubt, the allowance might be raised, if the property increased.

Arrears of maintenance used to be refused by the Madras Sudder Court. But this view has now been over-ruled, and it is settled that such arrears may be awarded, at all events from the date of demand (*t*). Such an award is, however at the discretion of the Court, and arrears may properly be refused where a widow has chosen to live apart from her husband's relations without any sufficient cause, and has then sued not only for a declaration of her right to future maintenance, but for a lump sum as arrears for the period during which she resided with her own family (*u*). The Bombay High Court has lately ruled that, even without a precedent demand, a widow may recover arrears of maintenance for any period, subject to the operation of the law of limitation. That is to say, that a demand and refusal may limit her right to arrears, but is not required to create it (*v*). Arrears.

§ 418. Another question is, whether the claim for maintenance is merely a liability which ought, in the first place, to be satisfied out of the family property, or whether it is an actual charge upon that property, which binds it in the hands of the holders of the property? How far a charge upon the property.

(*q*) *Savitribai* v. *Luximibai*, 2 Bom 573.
(*r*) *Rukabai* v. *Gandabai*, 1 All. 594.
(*s*) *Vijaya* v. *Sripathi*, 8 Mad. 94.
(*t*) *Venkopadhyaya* v. *Kavari*, 2 Mad. H. C. 36; *Sakwarbai* v. *Bhavanjee*, 1 Bom. H. C. 194; *Abalady* v. *Mt. Lukhymonee*, 2 Wym. 49; *Pirthee Singh* v. *Ranee Raj Kooer*, 2 N.-W. P. 170; *affirmed*, 12 B. L. R. (P. C.) 238; S C. 20 Suth. 21; *Jadumani* v. *Kheytra Mohan*, V. Darp. 884; *Narbadabai* v. *Mahadev*, 5 Bom. 99.
(*u*) *Rango Vinayak* v. *Yamunabai*, 3 Bom. 44.
(*v*) *Jivi* v. *Ramji*, 3 Bom. 207. See as to the effect of limitation upon a decree awarding maintenance, *Lakshmibai* v. *Bapuji*, 12 Bom. 65. A merely declaratory decree for maintenance cannot be enforced, *Venkanna* v. *Aitamma*, 12 Mad. 183. Otherwise where the decree specifically awards future maintenance. *Ashutosh Bannerjee* v. *Lukhimoni*, 19 Cal. 139.

How far a charge upon the property.

There are several texts which prohibit the gift of property to such an extent as to deprive a man's family of the means of subsistence. *Vrihaspati* says (*w*), "A man may give what remains after the food and clothing of his family; the giver of more (who leaves his family naked and unfed) may taste honey at first, but shall afterwards find it poison. If what is acquired by marriage, what has descended from an ancestor, or what has been gained by valor, be given with the assent of the wife, or the co-heirs, or of the King, the gift is valid." "*Katyayana* declares what may and may not be given. Except his whole estate and his dwelling-house, what remains after the food and clothing of his family a man may give away, whatever it be (whether fixed or movable); otherwise it may not be given" (*x*). *Vyasa* says (*y*), "They who are born and they who are yet unbegotten, and they who are actually in the womb, all require the means of support, and the dissipation of their hereditary maintenance is censured." So a passage ascribed to *Manu* (*z*) declares, "The support of persons who should be maintained is the approved means of attaining heaven. But hell is the man's portion if they suffer. Therefore let a master of a family carefully maintain them." This *Jimuta Vahana* explains by saying, "The prohibition is not against a donation or other transfer of a small part not in compatible with the support of the family."

Upon these passages, however, it is to be observed: *First*, that they all refer to cases of gift or dissipation, where no consideration exists for the transfer. The same prohibition would not apply to a sale, either for a family necessity, or for value, where the purchase-money would take the place of that which was disposed of. *Secondly*, the penalties suggested seem to be rather of a religious nature, punishing the act, than of a civil nature, invalidating it. *Thirdly*, the very authors who cite these texts treat them as merely

(*w*) 2 Dig. 131. (*x*) 2 Dig. 133; 3 Dig. 581. (*y*) Daya Bhaga, i. § 45.
(*z*) Daya Bhaga, ii. § 23, 24, not to be found in the Institutes.

moral prohibitions, and *Jagannatha* points out, acutely enough, as to one text, that the gift cannot be invalid, if the immediate result of it is to taste as honey in the mouth of the donor (*a*).

§ 419. The question has arisen frequently for decision within the last few years, though it can hardly be said that every point that can be suggested has been set at rest. It seems to be now settled that the claim even of a widow for maintenance is not such a lien upon the estate as binds it in the hands of a *bonâ fide* purchaser for value without notice of the claim (*b*). As *Phear*, J., said (*c*), "When the property passes into the hands of a *bonâ fide* purchaser without notice, it cannot be affected by any thing short of an existing proprietary right; it cannot be subject to that which is not already a specific charge, or which does not contain all the elements necessary to its ripening into a specific charge. And obviously, the consideration received by the heir for the sale of the deceased's property will, so far as the widow's right of recourse to it is concerned, take the place of the property sold." It was also pointed out by the Bombay High Court (*d*) that the texts which are relied on as making the maintenance a charge upon the inheritance are exactly similar to those which charge it with the payment of debts, the expenses of marriage and funeral ceremonies, and the charges of initiation of younger members. But these charges would admittedly not be payable by a purchaser for value, whether with or without notice of their existence. They also pointed out that such a doctrine would equally invalidate a sale made by the husband himself, as a wife's maintenance is even a stronger obligation than that of maintaining a widow. In fact the Madras Sudder Court did carry out the principle to that full extent, by holding that a sale of property made by a

Does not bind purchaser without notice.

(*a*) 2 Dig. 132; Daya Bhaga, ii. § 28.
(*b*) *Bhagabati* v. *Kanailal*, 8 B L. R. 225; S C. 17 Suth. 433 note; *Adhiranee* v. *Shona Malee*, 1 Cal. 365; *Lakshman* v. *Sarasvatibai*, 12 Bom. H. C. 69; *Lakshman* v. *Satyabhamabai*, 2 Bom. 494.
(*c*) 8 B. L. R. 229. (*d*) 12 Bom. H. C. p. 77.

husband was invalid, where nothing was left for the maintenance of his wife (*e*.)

Where right has become fixed.

§ 420. Supposing this to be established, it would follow that the purchaser must have notice, not merely of the existence of a right to maintenance—that is, of the existence of persons who did or might require to be maintained—but of the existence of a charge actually created and binding the estate. Otherwise, it is evident that an estate never could be purchased as long as there was any person living whose maintenance was, or might become, a charge upon the property. A decree actually settling the amount of maintenance, and making it a lien upon the property, would, of course, be a valid charge; but not, apparently, a merely personal decree against the holder of the property (*f*). So, if the property was bequeathed by will, and the widow's maintenance was fixed and charged upon the estate by the same will (*g*); or, if by an agreement between the widow and the holder of the estate, her maintenance was settled and made payable out of the estate (*h*), a purchaser taking with notice of the charge would be bound to satisfy it. And the charge, where it exists, is a charge upon every part of the property, and may be made the ground of a suit against any one who holds any part of it (*i*). In a case already quoted, *Phear*, J., seemed to think that notice of a widow having set up a claim for maintenance against the heir would be sufficient (*k*). But if nothing binds the

Effect of notice.

(*e*) *Lachchanna* v. *Bapanamma*, Mad. Dec. of 1860, 230.

(*f*) *Per West*, J., *Lakshman* v. *Satyabhamabai*, 2 Bom. p. 524; *Adhiranee* v. *Shona Malee*, 1 Cal. 365; *Saminatha* v. *Rangathammal*, 12 Mad. 285. Nor would a decree against a member of a joint family in her individual capacity bind the joint family property as against its representative, or other members, not parties to the suit. *Muttia* v. *Virammal*, 10 Mad. 283.

(*g*) *Prosonno* v. *Barbosa*, 6 Suth. 253.

(*h*) *Heera Lall* v. *Mt. Kousillah*, 2 Agra, 42. See this case explained, 12 Bom. H. C. 75; *Abadi* v. *Asa*, 2 All. 162.

(*i*) *Ramchandra* v. *Savitribai*, 4 Bom. H. C. (A. C. J.) 73. See it explained, *Nistarini* v. *Makhanlal*, 9 B. L. R. 27; S. C. 17 Suth. 432; 12 Bom. H. C. 73. If the holder of part of the property pays the whole maintenance, his remedy is by a suit for contribution, 4 Bom. H. C. (A. C. J.) 73.

(*k*) 8 B. L. R. p. 229; S. C. 17 Suth. 433, note; *West*, J., says "We should rather substitute 'notice of the existence of a claim likely to be unjustly impaired by the proposed transaction,'" 2 Bom. p. 517.

estate except a charge, actually created, it is difficult to see how a purchaser could be affected by notice that a widow had a claim which had not matured into a lien. And in a later case *Couch*, C. J., said, "Whatever may be the rights of the younger members of a family, where the estate is inherited by the eldest member, until the maintenance has become a specific charge upon the property, which it might be by a decree of a Court making provision for the payment of the maintenance, and declaring that a part of the property should be a security for it, or by a contract between the parties charging the property with a certain sum for maintenance, we do not see how it can be a charge upon the estate in the hands of a *bonâ fide* purchaser for consideration" (*l*). Even express notice at an execution sale under the decree that a widow had a claim for maintenance upon the estate, has been held not to affect the rights of the purchaser (*m*). In a case in which the Crown had confiscated property out of which a widow was being maintained, it does not appear that any charge in the above sense had ever been created. But the decree affirming the maintenance against the Crown was submitted to without opposition (*n*). **Escheat.**

§ 421. The whole of this subject was lately examined by *West*, J., in Bombay, in a judgment which collects all the authorities bearing upon the matter. He points out that mere notice of a claim for maintenance, which contains all the elements necessary for its ripening into a specific charge, cannot be sufficient to bind a purchaser, because in the case of a widow under Mitakshara law her claim would always contain such elements. Nor could the rights of the purchaser depend solely upon the question, whether after the sale there was enough property left in the hands of the heir to satisfy her claim? What was honestly purchased was

(*l*) *Juggernath* v. *Odhiranee*, 20 Suth. 126. See *Goluck* v. *Ohilla*, 25 Suth. 100; *Sham Lal* v. *Banna*, 4 All. 296.

(*m*) *Soorja Koer* v. *Natha Baksh*, 11 Cal. 102.

(*n*) *Golab Koonwar* v. *Collector of Benares*, 4 M. I. A. 246; S. C. 7 Suth. (P. C.) 47. See *Adhiranee* v. *Shona Malee*, 1 Cal. 373.

free from her claim for ever, and no new right could spring up in the widow by virtue of any subsequent exhaustion of the family funds. His view, apparently, is, that the question will always be, *first,* was the vendor acting in fraud of the widow's claim to maintenance; *secondly,* was the purchaser acting with notice, not merely of her claim, but of the fraud which was being practised upon her claim? He says "If the heir sought to defraud her, he could not by any device in the way of parting with the estate, or changing its form, get rid of the liability which had come to him along with the advantage derived from his survivorship; and the purchaser—taking from him with reason to suppose that the transaction was one originating not in an honest desire to pay off debts, or satisfy claims for which the estate was justly liable, and which it could not otherwise well meet, but in a desire to shuffle off a moral and legal liability,—would, as sharing in the proposed fraud, be prevented from gaining by it; but if, though he knew of the widow's existence and her claim, he bought upon a rational and honest opinion that the sale was one that could be effected without any furtherance of wrong, he has, as against the plaintiff, acquired a title free from the claim which still subsists in full force as against the recipient of the purchase-money" (*o*).

Transfer of Property Act.

This is substantially the effect of the recent Transfer of Property Act (IV of 1882) § 39. "Where a third person has a right to receive maintenance, or a provision for advancement or marriage, from the profits of immovable property, and such property is transferred with the intention of defeating such right, the right may be enforced against the transferee, if he has notice of such intention, or if the transfer is gratuitous; but not against a transferee for consideration and without notice of the right, nor against such property in his hands." Where a transferee is liable, he ceases to be so when the property passes out of his hands (*p*).

(*o*) *Lukshman* v. *Satyabhamabai*, 2 Bom. 494, 524; *Kalpagathachi* v. *Ganapathi*, 3 Mad. 184; *Mahalakshmamma* v. *Venkataratnamma*, 6 Mad. 83.

(*p*) *Dharam Chand* v. *Janki*, 5 All. 389.

Priority of debts.

§ 422. Debts contracted by a Hindu take precedence over maintenance as a charge upon the estate. Therefore, a purchaser of property sold to discharge debts has a better title than a widow who seeks to charge the estate with her maintenance. And this would be especially so where the property has been acquired in trade, and is held for trading purposes, and seized for the trading debts (*q*). It has been held in Allahabad that a sale to satisfy debts would even take precedence over a charge for maintenance actually and *bonâ fide* created before sale or seizure (*r*). Where a husband under Mitakshara law dies leaving separate property and also joint property, which passes to his coparceners, the widow's claim to maintenance must be met first out of the separate estate, and she cannot come upon the joint property till the separate property is proved insufficient (*s*). Where there is family property which has been partly alienated, it does not appear to be settled whether the widow is bound to sue those of the family who are still in possession of the remainder of the property before she comes upon the purchasers (*t*).

Property liable.

Widow's claim on family house.

§ 423. It has been laid down that there is a distinction between the right of a widow to continue to live in the ancestral family house, and her right over other parts of the property. Accordingly, where a man died leaving a widow and a son, and the son immediately on his coming of age sold the family house, and the purchaser proceeded to evict the widow, the High Court of Bengal dismissed his suit. *Peacock*, C. J., held that the text of *Katyayana* (*u*) was restrictive, and not merely directory, and that the son

---

(*q*) *Natchiarammal* v. *Gopalakrishna*, 2 Mad. 126; *Adhiranee* v. *Shona Malee*, 1 Cal. 365; *Johurra* v. *Sreegopal*, *ib.* 470; *Lakshman* v. *Satyabhamabai*, 2 Bom. 494.

(*r*) *Sham Lal* v. *Banna*, 4 All. 296; *Gur Dial* v *Kaunsila*, 5 All. 367. In neither of these cases, however, does it appear from the report that there was any actual charge created as distinct from the general lien.

(*s*) *Shib Dayee* v. *Doorga Pershad*, 4 N.-W. P. 63.

(*t*) See *Goluck* v. *Ohilla*, 25 Suth. 100; *Adhiranee* v. *Shona Malee*, 1 Cal. 365; *Ram Churun* v. *Mt. Jasooda*, 2 Agra, H. C. 134: doubted *per curiam*, *Lakshman* v. *Sarasvatibai*, 12 Bom. H. C. 76.

(*u*) 2 Dig. 133; *ante*, § 418.

could not turn his father's widow out of the family dwelling-house himself, or authorize a purchaser to do so, at all events until he had provided for her some other suitable residence (*v*). And the same has been held in the North-West Provinces, where the son of the survivor of two brothers sold the dwelling-house, in part of which the widow of his uncle was living. The Court held that she could not be ousted by the purchaser of her nephew's rights (*w*). Where, however, a Hindu mortgaged his ancestral dwelling-house, and then died, and his mother and widow were made parties to a suit to enforce the mortgage, the Court held, that the fact that they were dwelling in the house was no objection to a decree for its sale. They appear to have left it an open question whether the purchaser at the sale would be entitled to turn them out of possession (*x*). In a similar case in Madras and Bombay the Court held that the sale must be made subject to the widow's right of residence (*y*), unless the sale was made for a debt binding upon the family, and therefore upon the widow (*z*).

Right of widow to family house.

Against volunteer in possession of property.

§ 424. So far we have been discussing the case of a purchaser for value. *Phear, J.*, in the judgment so often referred to, said, "As against one who has taken the property as heir, the widow has a right to have a proper sum for her maintenance ascertained and made a charge upon the property in his hands. She may also doubtless follow the property for this purpose into the hands of any one who takes it as a volunteer, or with notice of her having set up a claim for maintenance against the heir" (*a*). Both these points have been settled by express decisions. In Madras, where a testator devised all his property by will, without making any provision for his widow, the will was held valid, except

(*v*) *Mangala* v. *Dinanath*, 4 B. L. R. (O. C. J.) 72; S. C. 12 Suth. (O. C. J.) 35; *folld. Bai Devkore* v. *Sanmukhram*, 13 Bom. 101.
(*w*) *Gauri* v. *Chandramani*, 1 All. 262; *Talemand* v. *Rukmina*, 3 All. 353.
(*x*) *Bhikham* v. *Pura*, 2 All. 141.
(*y*) *Venkatammal* v. *Andyappa*, 6 Mad. 130; *Dalsukhram* v. *Lallubhai*, 7 Bom. 282.
(*z*) *Ramanaden* v. *Rangammal*, 12 Mad. 260.
(*a*) *Bhagabati* v. *Kanailal*, 8 B. L. R. 228; S. C. 17 Suth. 433, note.

as to her claim for maintenance, and a reference was directed to ascertain what amount should be set aside for that purpose (*b*). And so in Bengal, Sir F. MacNaghten, while admitting that a husband can, by will, deprive his widow of her share in the estate, adds, " It cannot be doubted but that her right to maintenance remains in full force—and, if it had been asked for on reasonable grounds, I take for granted that the Court would in this case (as it had in a similar one) have ordered funds sufficient for the purpose of maintaining her, to be set apart out of the whole of her husband's estate" (*c*). This view was followed by the Supreme Court in a later case, where a Hindu in Bengal left all his property to his three sons, not mentioning his widow. A decree was made for partition in three equal shares between them. The Court held the decree erroneous, as it ought to have awarded a share to the mother for her maintenance. *Grant*, J., said " Her legal right was not excluded by her husband's will, since her name was not mentioned in his will, and rights so much the favoured object of the Hindu law as that of a widow to maintenance could not be excluded by implication. And so, we are informed by Sir F. MacNaghten, the Court thought, and, if not excluded, they must have subsisted such as the law declared them" (*d*). And, I imagine, the ruling would be the same even though the testator expressly, and by name, declared that his widow or daughter should not receive maintenance. It has, no doubt, been decided that a father in Bengal may by will deprive his son of any right to maintenance (*e*). But that is because an adult son has no right whatever to maintenance (*f*). His only right is as an heir expectant, and that right may be wholly defeated by sale, gift or devise. But the right of a widow to her maintenance arises by marriage,

(*b*) S. A. 634 of 1871, *per Morgan*, C. J., and *Holloway*, J., 8 Mar. 1872, not reported. Acc. *Rasabai* v. *Sadu*, 8 Bom. (A. C. J.) 98.

(*c*) F. MacN. 92.

(*d*) *Comulmoney* v. *Rammanath*, Fulton, 189; *Joytara* v. *Ramhari*, 10 Cal. 638.

(*e*) *Tagore* v. *Tagore*, 4 B. L. R. (O. C. J.) 132, 159.

[illegible], § 409, 412.

and that of a daughter by birth; it exists during the life of the father, and continues after his death. It is a legal obligation attaching upon himself personally, and upon his property. He cannot free himself from it during his lifetime, and it attaches upon the inheritance immediately after his death. It seems, therefore, contrary to principle to hold that by devising the property to another, he could authorize that other to hold it free from claims which neither he himself nor his heir could have resisted (*g*).

The same principle has been affirmed as against donees. In a case from Allahabad, a husband, during his life, made a gift of his entire estate, without reserving maintenance to his widow, and it was held that the donee took subject to the liability to maintain her (*h*). The same decision was given in Bombay, where a husband had, by gift to his undivided sons by his first and second wives, assigned the whole of his self-acquired immovable property, without making provision for his third wife who was left absolutely destitute. It was held that she was entitled to have her maintenance charged upon this property in the hands of her step-sons, and that this right was not affected by any agreement made by her with her husband during his life (*i*).

Maintenance for life.

§ 425. As a general rule, property allotted for maintenance is resumable at the death of the grantee, the presumption being that the income only was granted, and not the body of the fund (*k*). But, of course, there is nothing to prevent an owner making over a sum of money or landed property

---

(*g*) The High Court of Bengal has held that under Bengal law a husband may dispose of his property by will so as to deprive his widow of her share as partition; *Debendra* v. *Brojendra Coomar*, 17 Cal. 886, following *Bhoobunmoyee* v. *Ramkissore*, S. D. of 1860, i. p. 489, where the Court said, "In Bengal a widow has no indefeasible vested right in the property left by her husband, though she has by virtue of her marriage a right, if all the property be willed away, to maintenance." See also *Sonatun Bysack* v. *Juggutsoondree*, 8 M. I. A. 66. The side note there is erroneous What the widow claimed and obtained was her share, and not merely maintenance. See per *Muttasami Aiyar*, 12 Mad. p. 267.

(*h*) *Jamna* v. *Machul*, 2 All. 315.

(*i*) *Narbadabai* v. *Mahadeo*, 5 Bom. 99.

(*k*) *Woodoyaditto* v. *Mukoond*, 22 Suth. 225; *Bhavanamma* v. *Ramasami*, 4 Mad. 193; *Uddoy* v. *Jadublal*, 5 Cal. 113; *Kachwain* v. *Sarup Chand*, 10 All. 462.

absolutely, in full discharge of all claims for maintenance. And a grant so made would be absolutely at the disposal of the person to whom it was given (*l*). The validity of such a grant would depend upon the capacity of the person who made it. On the other hand there may be circumstances evidencing that a grant for maintenance was resumable at the pleasure of the grantor (*m*).

(*l*) *Nursing Deb* v. *Roy Koylasnath*, 9 M. I. A. 55. Long uninterrupted enjoyment for successive generations [illegible] would warrant a presumption that [illegible] *Salur Zemindar* v. *Pedda Pakir Raju*, [illegible]

(*m*) *Najban* v. *Chand Bibi*, 10 I. A. 133.

CHAPTER XV.

PARTITION.

Division of subject.

§ 426. I HAVE already (§ 218—226) discussed the early history of the law of partition. The modern law may be divided into four heads. *First*, the property to be divided; *secondly*, the persons who are to share (§ 430); *thirdly*, the mode of division (§ 447); *fourthly*, what constitutes a partition (§ 453). A few words will have to be added on the subject of re-union. In treating of THE JOINT FAMILY (Chapter VIII.), I have anticipated much that is usually placed under the Law of Partition.

Coparcenary property alone divisible.

First.—The property to be divided is *ex vi termini* the property which has been previously held as joint property in coparcenary (*a*). Therefore a man's self-acquisition is indivisible (*b*), and so is any property which he has inherited collaterally, or from such a source that the persons claiming a share obtained no interest in it on its devolution to him (§ 251). Property allotted on a previous partition is of course indivisible as between the separated members or their representatives; but it would be divisible as between those members and their own descendants, unless at the time of partition the father had cut himself off from his own issue, as well as from his collateral relations (§ 252). And as soon as such property has descended a step, it loses its

(*a*) As to what is coparcenary property, see *ante*, § 251, *et seq*.

(*b*) Mitakshara, i. 4; Daya Bhaga, vi., 1; V. May., iv. 7. In Bengal, where a division is made in the life of the father, the father has a moiety of the goods acquired by his son at the charge of the estate; the son who made the acquisition has two shares, and the rest take one apiece. But if the father's estate has not been used, he has two shares, the acquirer as many, and the rest are excluded from participation. Daya Bhaga, ii. § 7; *per Peacock*, C. J., *Uma Sundari* v. *Dwarkanath*, 2 B. L. R. (A. C. J.) 287; S. C. 11 Suth. 72.

character of impartibility, and becomes ancestral and joint property in the hands of those who take it. It retains its original character as regards collaterals. For instance, if A. and B. are undivided brothers, and A. makes a separate

Coparcenary property is divisible.

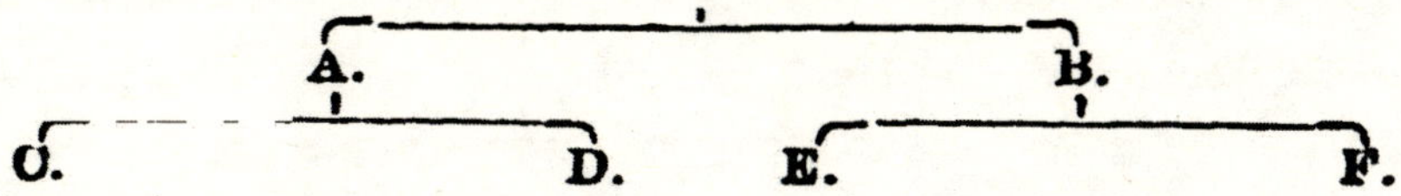

acquisition, it descends to his two sons exclusively. In their hands it is ancestral property, and divisible. But it does not become the property of the coparcenary of which they are members with E and F. Consequently, neither the two latter, nor their descendants, will ever be entitled to share in it, so long as the direct heirs of A. are in existence (*c*). In one case the Bombay High Court decided that even ancestral movable property was so completely at the disposal of the father, that his own sons could not claim a partition of it. But this decision appears to have been overruled by implication in a later case (*d*). The whole doctrine on which it rests has been already discussed (§ 310).

Property indivisible from its nature.

§ 427. Other matters were originally declared to be indivisible from their nature, such as apparel, carriages, riding-horses, ornaments, dressed food, water, pasture ground and roads, female slaves, houses or gardens, utensils, necessary implements of learning or of art, and documents evidencing a title to property (*e*). The ground of the exception seems to have been that they were things which could not be divided *in specie*, that they were originally of small value, and specially appropriated to the individual members of the family; consequently, that if each were left in possession of his own, the value held by one would be balanced by a corresponding value in the hands of another. But as

---

(*c*) *Katama Natchiar* v. *Rajah of Shivaganga*, 9 M. I. A. 539; S. C. 2 Suth. (P. C.) 81; *Periasami* v. *Periasami*, 5 I. A. 61; S. C. 1 Mad. 312.

(*d*) *Ramchandra Dada Naik* v. *Dada Mahadev*, 1 Bom. H. C. Appx. 76 (2nd ed.), *contra*, *Lakshman* v. *Ramchandra*, 1 Bom. 561; affd. 7 I. A. 181; S. C. 5 Bom. 48; *ante*, § 310.

(*e*) Mitakshara, i. 4, § 16—27; Daya Bhaga, vi. 2, § 23—30; V. May., v. 7, § 23.

property of this sort increased in value, the strict letter of the texts was explained away, and it was established that where things were indivisible by their nature, they must either be enjoyed by the heirs in turns or jointly, as a well or a bridge; or sold, and their value distributed, or retained by one co-sharer exclusively, while the value of what he retained was adjusted by the appropriation of corresponding values to the others (*f*). Where part of the property consists of idols and places of worship, which are valuable from their endowments, or from the respect attaching to their possessor, the members will be decreed to hold them by turns, the period of tenure being in proportion to their shares in the *corpus* of the property (§ 398). A partition of a dwelling-house will be decreed if insisted on (*g*), but the Court will, if possible, try to effect such an arrangement as will leave it entire in the hands of one or more of the coparceners (*h*). In a later case the Court said "the principle in these cases of partition is, that if a property can be partitioned without destroying the intrinsic value of the whole property, or of the shares, such partition ought to be made. If, on the contrary, no partition can be made without destroying the intrinsic value, then a money compensation should be given instead of the share which would fall to the plaintiff by partition (*i*).

Impartible property.

§ 428. Another class of estates which are indivisible, without being either separate or self-acquired, are those which by a special law or custom descend to one member of the family (generally the eldest), to the exclusion of the other members. The most common instance of this is in the case of ancient Zemindaries, which are in the nature of a Raj or Sovereignty, or which descend to a single member by special family custom (*k*), or royal grants of revenue for

(*f*) Viramit., p. 8; 3 Dig. 376—385.
(*g*) *Hullodhur* v. *Ramnauth*, Marsh. 35.
(*h*) *Rajcoomaree* v. *Gopal*, 8 Cal. 514.
(*i*) *Ashinullah* v. *Kali Kinkur*, 10 Cal. 675.
(*k*) See *ante*, § 50, 51.

services, such as jaghirs or Saranjams in Bombay (*l*). But an estate which is not in the nature of a Raj is not impartible, and does not descend to a single heir, merely because it is a Zemindary, in the absence of a special and binding family custom (*m*). Another case in which property is *primâ facie* impartible, is where it is allotted by the State to a person in consideration of the discharge of particular duties, or as payment for an office, even though the duties or office may become hereditary in a particular family. An instance of the sort is to be found in the case of lands held under ghatwali tenure in Beerbhoom, which are hereditary but impartible (*n*). So in Madras, where the office of curnum, or village accountant, has become hereditary, the land attached to the office is not liable to division (*o*). In Bombay, however, there are numerous revenue and village offices, such as *deshmuk, despandya desai* and *patel*, which are similarly remunerated by lands originally granted by the State. These lands have, by lapse of time, come to be considered as purely private property of the family which holds the office, though they are subject to the obligation of discharging its duties, and defraying all necessary expenses. Land of this character is so frequently, though not invariably, partible that it has been decided that in a suit for partition of such property, its nature raises no presumption that it is indivisible. Consequently, the holder of the office and of the land attached to it must rebut the claim for partition by evidence of a local or family usage that the land should be held exclusively by the holder of the office (*p*).

(*l*) *Ramchandra* v. *Venkatrao*, 6 Bom. 598; *Narayan Jagannath* v. *Vasudev*, 15 Bom. 247. A Saranjam may have been originally partible, or made so by family usage; *Madhavrav Manohar* v. *Atmaram*, 15 Bom. 519.

(*m*) *Venkatapetty* v. *Ramachendra*, 1 Mad. Dec. 495; *Mootoovengada* v. *Toombayasamy*, Mad. Dec. of 1849, 27; *Jagunnadha* v. *Konda*, *ib.* 112; *Moottoovencata* v. *Munarsawmy*, Mad. Dec. of 1853, 217; *Koernarain* v. *Dhorinidhur*, S. D. of 1858, 1132. See as to estates confiscated, and re-granted, *ante*, § 51.

(*n*) *Hurlall* v. *Jorawun*, 6 S. D. 169 (204) approved by P. C., *Lelanund* v. *Govt of Bengal*, 6 M. I. A. 125; S. C. 1 Suth. (P. C.) 20; *Nilmoni* v. *Bakranath*, 9 I. A. 104; S. C.

(*o*) *Alymalummaul* v. *Vencatoovien*, 2 Mad. Dec. 85; *Bada* v. *Hussa Bhai*, 7 Mad. 236.

(*p*) Steele, 203, 210, 229. *Shidhojirav* v. *Naikojirav*, 10 Bom. H. C. 228;

On partition a portion of the property will be set aside sufficient to provide for the discharge of the duties, and the rest will become private property free from all obligations to the State (*q*). The discontinuance of services attached to an impartible estate does not alter the nature of the estate, and render it partible (*r*). So, an estate which has been allotted by Government to a man of rank for the maintenance of his rank is indivisible, as otherwise the purpose of the grant would be frustrated. But where it is allotted for the maintenance of the family, then it is divisible among the direct descendants of the family, as the special object is to benefit all equally, not to maintain a special degree of state for one (*s*). And where an estate is impartible, its income is impartible, and the savings of such income, and the purchases made out of such savings are equally impartible, so long as they remain in the hands of the person out of whose income they proceeded. But as soon as they pass from him to a successor, they become divisible and ancestral property (*t*).

Raj taken in partition.

Although a Raj or Zemindary may be itself indivisible, there is no reason why it should not be taken into a division, as property allotted to a separating member. The result would be that its descent would be governed by the rules which relate to separate property (*u*). Therefore, in a family governed by the Mitakshara law, it would pass to female heirs in preference to male collaterals (*v*).

Mode of taking account.

§ 429. Having ascertained what property there is to

Adrishappa v. *Gurushidappa*, 7 I. A. 162 ; S. C. 4 Bom. 494 ; *Ramrao* v. *Yeshvantrao*, 10 Bom. 327 ; *Gopalrav* v. *Trimbakrav*, *ib.* 598.

(*q*) Act XI of 1843, § 13 (Hereditary Officers) ; *Adrishappa* v. *Gurushidappa*, *ub sup.*

(*r*) *Ramrao* v. *Yeshvantrao*, *ub sup.*

(*s*) *Viswanadha* v. *Bungaroo*, Mad. Dec. of 1851, 87, 94, 95 ; *Booloka* v. *Comarasawmy*, Mad. Dec. of 1858, 74 ; *Bodhrao* v. *Nursing Rao*, 6 M. I. A 426 ; *Panchanadayen* v. *Nilakandayan*, 7 Mad. 191. See Indian Pensions Act XXIII of 1871.

(*t*) See *ante*, § 262, and cases in last note.

(*u*) An instance of the sort occurred in the case of *Runganayakamma* v. *Bull Ramaya*, P. C. 5th July 1879.

(*v*) *Per curiam*, *Katama Natchiar* v. *Rajah of Shivagunga*, 9 M. I. A. 589 S. C. 2 Suth. (P. C.) 81 ; *Tekaet* v. *Tekaetnee*, 20 Suth. 154.

divide, the next step is to ascertain its amount. For this purpose it is necessary first to deduct all claims against the united family for debts due by it (*w*), or for charges on account of maintenance, marriages or family ceremonies, which it would have had to provide for, if it remained united (*x*). When these are set aside, an account must be taken of the entire family property in the hands of all the different members. In general this account is simply an enquiry into the existing assets (*y*). No member can have any claim to mesne profits previous to partition, because it is assumed that all surplus profits have, from time to time, been applied for the family benefit, or added to the family property. No charge is to be made against any member of the family, because he has received a larger share of the family income than another, provided he has received it for legitimate family purposes. Nor can the manager be charged with gains which he might have made, or savings which he might have effected, nor even with extravagance or waste which he has committed, unless it amounts to actual misappropriation. But, of course, advances made to any member for a special private purpose, for which he would have no right to call upon the family purse, or to discharge his own personal debts, contracted without the authority of the other members, or alienations of the family property made by an individual for his own benefit, would be properly debited against him in estimating his share (*z*). And, conversely, money laid out by one member of the family upon the improvement or repair of the property, or for any other object of common benefit, in general constitutes no debt to him from the rest of the family. The money which he expends is probably in itself part of the joint

(*w*) Under this head come all the complicated questions discussed, *ante*, § 285, 310, *et seq* as to whether transactions entered into by one member of the family bind the whole.

(*x*) *Ante*, § 301; Yajnavalkya, ii. § 124; Mitakshara, i. 7, § 3—5; Daya Bhaga, i. § 47, iii. 2 § 38—42; V. May., iv. 4, § 4, iv. 6, § 1, 2, v. 4, § 14; 3 Dig. 73, 96, 389; W. & B. 786—792. See as to the eight ceremonies, 3 Dig. 104.

(*y*) *Jugmohundas* v. *Mangaldas*, 10 Bom. 529.

(*z*) *Ante*. § 269; *Lakshman* v. *Ramchandra*, 1 Bom. 561; *Konerrav* v. *Gurrav*, 5 Bom. 589; *per curiam*, 11 Mad. p. 248.

property, so that he is merely returning to the family its own. But this presumption might be rebutted. If the funds which he had expended were advanced out of his own self-acquired property, or out of the income of property which by mutual agreement had been set aside for his exclusive enjoyment, an arrangement with his coparceners by which he was to lay out money from his separate funds, and they were to reimburse his outlay, would be valid (*a*).

Mesne profits.

Mesne profits may be allowed on partition, where one member of the family has been entirely excluded from the enjoyment of the property, or where it has been held by a member of the family who claimed a right to treat it as impartible, and therefore exclusively his own (*b*). Such a claim, however reasonable and *bonâ fide*, negatives the ordinary presumption that the annually accruing profits have been applied for the benefit of the family, and that the savings have been carried into the family treasury. The same rule applies, where, by family arrangement, the property is held in specific and definite shares, the enjoyment of which has been disturbed (*c*).

Coparceners.

§ 430. SECONDLY, AS TO THE PERSONS WHO SHARE.—Any coparcener may sue for a partition, and every coparcener is entitled to a share upon partition (*d*). But some persons are entitled to a share upon a partition who cannot sue for it themselves. Upon these points there are many distinctions between the early and the existing law, and also between the law of Bengal and of the other provinces.

Son during life of father.

In Bengal the son has no right to demand a partition of property held by his father during the life of the latter (§ 224). The Mitakshara, on the other hand, expressly

---

(*a*) *Muttusvamy* v. *Subbiramaniya*, 1 Mad. H. C. 309.

(*b*) *Per curiam*, *Konnerav* v. *Gurrav*, 5 Bom. p. 595; *Venkata* v. *Narayy* 7 I. A. 38, 51; S. C. 2 Mad. 128; *Venkata* v. *Rajagopala*, 9 I. A. 125; S. C. Mad. 236; *Krishna* v. *Subbanna*, 7 Mad. 564.

(*c*) *Shankar Baksh* v. *Hardeo Baksh*, 16 I. A. 71; S. C. 16 Cal. 397.

(*d*) As to the persons who are coparceners, see *ante*, § 248.

asserts the right (§ 222). Yet it is remarkable how slowly the right came to be recognized in practice. Sir *Thomas Strange* discusses the subject with an evident leaning against the right (*e*). Mr. *Strange*, in his Manual, treats the right as existing, but as one which, until very recent times, was opposed to public opinion, unless under exceptional circumstances (*f*). Several of the *futwahs* quoted by West and Bühler affirm that the right only arises where the father is old, diseased or wasteful (*g*). The High Court of Bombay, in a case already cited, held that as regards movable property at all events the son could not enforce a partition against his father's consent; and in the argument it was stated that no bill for such a purpose had ever been filed in the Supreme Court (*h*). The right both of a son and a grandson under Mitakshara law to a partition of movable and immovable property in the possession of a father, against his consent, has now, however, been settled by express decisions in Madras, Bengal, the North-West Provinces, and Bombay (*i*). In the Privy Council the right of the son to compel his father to make a partition of ancestral immovable property has also been recognised as the settled law of all the Presidencies (*k*). The right of the great-grandson to a division is not expressly stated in any of the early Hindu law-books, but it rests on the same grounds as that of the son, *viz.*, equality of right by birth (*l*).

Grandson.

Great-grandson.

Afterborn sons.

§ 431. The rights even of unborn sons were originally so

(*e*) 1 Stra. H. L. 179. (*f*) Preface, viii.
(*g*) W. & B. 364, 402, (2nd ed.)
(*h*) *Ramchandra* v. *Mahadev*, 1 Bom. H. C. Appx. 76 (2nd ed.)
(*i*) *Nagalinga* v. *Subbiramaniya*, 1 Mad. H. C. 77; *Nagalinga* v. *Vellusamy*, 1 Mad. Law Rep. 76; *Laljeet* v. *Rajcoomar*, 12 B. L. R. 373; S. C. 20 Suth. 336; *Kaliparshad* v. *Ramcharan*, 1 All. 159; *Jogul Kishore* v. *Shib Sahai*, 5 All. 430. See futwahs, Bom. Sel. Rep. 41, 42; W. & B. 365, 370, 373, (2nd ed); *per curiam*, *Moro Vishvanath* v. *Ganesh*, 10 Bom. H. C. 463; *Jugmohundas* v. *Mangaldas*, 10 Bom. 529, 578. This rule has been extended to Khoja Muhammadans, as being governed by Hindu Law; *Cassumbhoy* v. *Ahmedbhoy*, 12 Bom. 280, 294
(*k*) *Suraj Bunsi* v. *Sheo Pershad*, 6 I. A., p 100.
(*l*) W. & B. 672; Daya Bhaga, xi. 1, § 31—43; Raghunandana, ii. 24; Smriti Chandrika, viii. § 11; Vivada Chintamani, 239; Manu, ix. § 137; Viramit., p. 90, § 23*a*; Sarasvati Vilasa, § 221; Sarvadhikari, 561; Jolly, Lect., 170.

much respected, that when a son was born after a partition had taken place between a father and his sons, the partition was opened up again, in order to give him the share which he would have had if he had then been alive (*m*). And *Jimuta Vahana* was of opinion that the rule was still applicable where the property to be distributed was inherited from the grandfather, because distribution of such property was illegal so long as the mother was capable of bearing children. Consequently, the rights of an after-born child could not be prejudiced by the illegal act (*n*). Other writers, however, stated that a son born after a partition could only take his father's share, representing him to the exclusion of the previously divided brethren (*o*). The Mitakshara reconciles the conflict by saying that the latter texts lay down the general rule, while the former are limited to the case of a son who was in his mother's womb at the time of partition. *Jimuta Vahana* takes the same view in cases where the partition is made by the father of his self-acquired property. Therefore, in all cases where the birth of a son would add to the number of sharers, if the pregnancy is known at the time, the distribution should be deferred till its result is ascertained. If it is not known, and a son is afterwards born, a redistribution must take place of the estate as it then stands (*p*). If the father had divided the whole property among his sons, retaining no share for himself, it is said that the sons, with whom partition has been made, must allot from their shares a portion equal to their own to an after-born son (*q*).

Right of representation

§ 432. Under Mitakshara law, the right to a share passes

(*m*) Vishnu, xvii. § 3; Yajnavalkya, ii. 122; *per curiam*, 11 I. A. p. 179; S. C. 6 All p. 574. See the subject discussed, *Krishna* v. *Sami*, 9 Mad. 64, p. 70, 77.

(*n*) Daya Bhaga, i. § 45, vii. § 10; Raghunandana, ii. 30, 31, 36. This restriction however is no longer in force, *ante*, § 225.

(*o*) Manu, ix. § 216; Gautama, xxviii. § 26; Narada, xiii. § 44; Vrihaspati, 3 Dig. 49, 435; *Nawal* v. *Bhagwan*, 4 All 427.

(*p*) Mitakshara, i. 6, § 1—12; Daya Bhaga, vii. § 4; V. May, iv. 4, § 35—37; Viramit, p. 92, § 24; *Yekeyamian* v. *Agniswarian*, 4 Mad. H. C. 307; *Peacock*, C. J., *Kalidas* v. *Krishan*, 2 B. L. R. (F. B.) pp. 118—121.

(*q*) 1 W. MacN. 47.

by survivorship among the remaining coparceners, subject to the rule that where any deceased coparcener leaves male issue they represent the rights of their ancestor to a partition (*r*). For instance, suppose A. dies, leaving a son B., two grandsons E. and F., three great-grandsons H., I., J., and one great-great-grandson Z. The last named will take nothing, being beyond the fourth degree of descent (§ 247). The share of his ancestor W. will pass by survivorship to the other brothers, B., C., D., and their descendants, and enlarge their interests accordingly. Hence B., C., and D. will each be entitled to one-third, E. and F. will take the

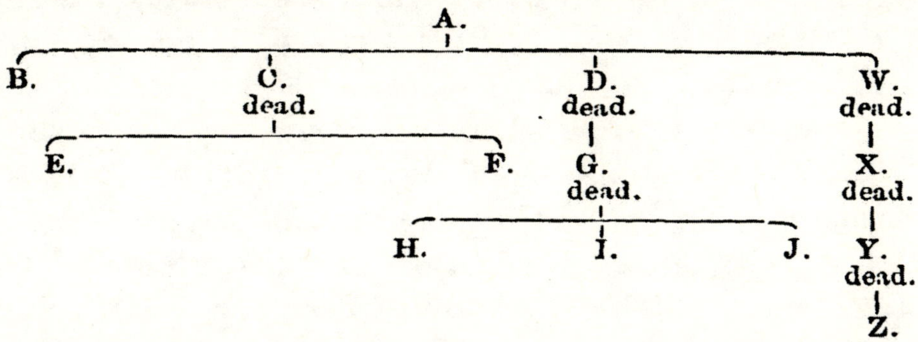

third belonging to C., and H., I., J., will take D.'s third. Each class will take *per stirpes* as regards every other class, but the members of the class take *per capita* as regards each other. This rule applies equally whether the sons are all by the same wife, or by different wives (*s*). But if W. had effected a partition with A., then, on his death, his fourth would have passed at once to Z., supposing X. and Y. to have predeceased. The right of any descendant, or set of descendants, to a partition assumes, however, that the ancestors above him or them are dead. C. can compel a partition with

Representation arises on death of ancestor.

(*r*) It must always be remembered that what passes is not a share, as in Bengal, but the right to have a share on partition, *ante*, § 246.

(*s*) Mitakshara, i. 5, § 1; V. May., iv. 4, § 20—22; Smriti Chandrika, viii. § 1—16; Katyayana, 3 Dig. 7; Devala, *ib.* 9, 10, 446, 448; Narada, xiii. § 25; 2 Dig. 572, 575, 576; 1 Stra. H. L. 205; 2 Stra. H. L. 351—357; *Moottoovengada* v. *Toombayasamy*, Mad. Dec. of 1849, 27; *Poovathay* v. *Paroomal*, Mad. Dec. of 1856, 5; *Manjanatha* v. *Narayana*, 5 Mad. 362. In some families, however, a custom called *Patnt-bhaga* prevails of dividing according to mothers; so that if A had two sons by his wife B., and three sons by C., the property would be divided into moieties, one going to the sons by B., and the other to the sons by C. *Sumrun* v. *Khedun*, 2 S. D. 116 (147). This practice prevails locally in Oudh, as evidenced by numerous *Wajib-ul-arz* which I have seen in cases under appeal to the Privy Council. J. D. M.

A., but E. and F. cannot compel a partition during the life of C. Their right arises for the first time, when, by the death of C., his interest in the estates descends upon them. It is evident that they cannot have their own share apportioned without a previous apportionment of the share of C. But the sons or grandsons of C. cannot compel him to proceed to a partition unless he wishes it (*t*).

Bengal law. § 433. These principles require some modification where the case arises in Bengal. A son can never demand a partition of property held by his father, but as soon as A., in the above diagram, died, his property would descend to his sons and their descendants, and would be divisible among them in the same manner as above stated. If any coparcener dies without male issue, but leaving a widow, a daughter, or daughter's sons, his share will descend to them, and will not lapse into the shares of the other members as it would do under the Mitakshara law (*u*). The principles of this line of succession will be discussed hereafter. It is sufficient here to say that representation does not extend beyond daughters. Daughters of the same class inherit to their father, *per stirpes*. But daughters' sons do not take as heirs to their mother, but as heirs to their grandfather. Consequently no daughter's son takes at all, until all the eligible daughters are dead; and such sons, where they do inherit, take *per capita* and not *per stirpes*. That is to say, if a man has two daughters, A. and B., of whom A. has one son, and B. has five, on the death of the last daughter the six sons will take equally (*v*).

(*t*) Mitakshara, i. 5, § 3; W. & B. 658; 1 W. MacN. 50; 2 W. MacN. 150; 3 Dig. 9, 38, 388; *ante*, § 248; Daya Bhaga, iii. 1, § 19, xi. 6, § 29, Raghunandana, ii. 23, 24; *per curiam*, 11 I. A. p. 179; S. C. 6 All. p. 574; *Apaji Narhav* v. *Ramchandra*, 16 Bom. (F. B.) 29. The Viramitrodaya appears to be of a contrary opinion. Viramit., p. 90, § 23*a*. The High Court of Allahabad has held that the grandson, even during the life of his father and grandfather, has a vested interest in the ancestral property which can be realised by a partition, and is saleable under a decree. *Jogul Kishore* v. *Shib Sahai*, F. B. 5 All. 430, considered and disagreed with by the majority of the Bombay Full Bench, 10 Bom. 29.

(*u*) Daya Bhaga, xi. 1, § 47, 59, 65; 1 W. MacN. 19, 22; *post*, § 438.

(*v*) See *post*, § 519, 520.

Illegitimate sons.

§ 434. Illegitimate sons of the three higher classes are entitled to nothing but maintenance (*w*). As regards the illegitimate son of a Sudra there is greater difficulty. It is said that if a partition is made by the father, he may be allotted a share at the father's choice, and that if the partition is made after the father's death, the brethren should make him a partaker of the moiety of a share. The Bengal writers say that where the partition is made by the father himself, or after his death in pursuance of his directions, the share of such an illegitimate son may be equal to that of a legitimate son. This would be natural enough, considering the power which a father in Bengal has in the disposition of his property. *Vijnanesvara* lays down no rule upon the point, but speaks vaguely of "a share." Where there are no legitimate sons, but there are daughters or daughters' sons, the Mitakshara says that he is entitled to half a share only; the Daya Bhaga and Daya-krahma-sangraha say that he shares equally with the daughter's son (*x*): while the author of the Datta Chandrika considers that where there is no legitimate male issue, the illegitimate son of a Sudra shares equally with the whole series of heirs down to the daughter's son (*y*). In a Bombay case, where however the point did not arise, it seems to have been the opinion of *Nanabhai Haridas*, J., that an illegitimate son could enforce a partition as against his brothers, but not as against his father, "seeing that his right to take a share during his father's lifetime is expressly made to depend on the father's choice" (*z*). In Madras it is held that the illegitimate son of a Sudra may enforce a partition against his legitimate brothers, but not against his father, or his father's copar-

---

(*w*) Mitakshara, i. 12, § 3; Daya Bhaga, ix. § 28; V. May., iv. § 29—31; Viramit., p. 121, § 17; *Chuoturya* v. *Sahub Purhalad*, 7 M. I. A. 18; S. C. 4 Suth. (P. C.) 132; *Gajapathy* v. *Gajapathy*, 2. Mad. H. C. 369, reversed on a different point, 13 M. I. A. 497; S. C. 6 B. L. R. 202; S. C. 14 Suth. (P. C.) 33. The same rule prevails among the Punjab tribes. Punjab Customary Law, II. 161.

(*x*) Yajuavalkya, ii. § 133, 134; Mitakshara, i. 12, § 1, 2; Daya Bhaga, ix. § 29, 30; D. K. S. vi. § 32—34; 3 Dig. 143; V. May., iv. 4, § 32; Raghunandana, ii, 39, 40. As to the meaning of the half-share, see *post*, § 504. As to the persons entitled under these texts, *post*, § 501, 502.

(*y*) Datta Chandrika, v. § 30, 31. See *post*, § 503.

(*z*) *Sadu* v. *Baiza*, 4 Bom. pp. 44, 45; *acc. per curiam*, 11 Cal. 714.

ceners, as for instance, his father's brothers, or their sons (*a*). In Khandesk a legitimate daughter and an illegitimate son divide the property (*b*).

Minority not a bar.

§ 435. The legality of a partition during the minority of some of the coparceners is recognized by *Baudhayana*, who says that "the shares of sons who are minors, together with the interest, should be placed under good protection until the majority of the owners" (*c*). One text of *Katyayana* appears to prohibit partition while there is a minor entitled to share (*d*). But it is quite evident that if such a rule existed, a partition could hardly ever take place. It is now quite settled that a partition made during the minority of one of the members will be valid, and if just and legal will bind him. Of course, his interests ought to be represented by his guardian, or some one acting on his behalf, though I imagine that the fact of his not being so represented would be no ground for opening up the partition, if a proper one in other respects (*e*). When he arrives at full age he may apply to have the division set aside as regards himself, if it can be shown to have been illegal or fraudulent (*f*), or even if it was made in such an informal manner that there are no means of testing its validity (*g*). But a suit cannot be brought by, or on behalf of, a minor to enforce partition, unless on the ground of malversation, or some other circumstances, which make it for his interest that his share should be set aside and secured for him (*h*). Otherwise he might be thrust out of the family at the very time when he was least able to protect himself.

Minority.

(*a*) *Thangam Pillai* v. *Suppa Pillai*, 12 Mad. 401.
(*b*) Steele, 180. (*c*) Baudhayana, ii § 2. (*d*) 3 Dig 544.
(*e*) 2 Stra. H. L. 362; 2 W. MacN. 14; *Deowanti* v. *Dwarkanath*, 8 B. L. R. 363, note; S. C. *Sub nomine*, *Deo Bansee* v. *Dwarkanath*, 10 Suth. 273.
(*f*) *Nallappa* v. *Balammal*, 2 Mad. H. C. 182; *per curiam*, *Lakshmibai* v. *Ganpat*, 4 Bom. H. C. (O. C. J.) 159; *Deowanti* v. *Dwarkanath*, 8 B. L. R. 363, note; *supra*, note (*e*).
(*g*) *Kalee Sunkur* v. *Denendro*, 23 Suth. 68.
(*h*) 1 Stra. H. L. 206; *Svamiyar* v. *Chokkalingam*, 1 Mad. H. C. 105; *Alimelammal* v. *Arunachellam*, 3 Mad. H. C. 69; *Kamakshi* v. *Chidambara*, ib. 94; *Damoodur* v. *Senabatty*, 8 Cal. 537; *Thangam Pillai*, v. *Suppa Pillai*, 12 Mad. 401.

Absent members. An absent coparcener stands on the same footing as a minor. The mere fact of his absence does not prevent partition. But it throws upon those who effect it the obligation to show that it was fair, and legally conducted, and the duty of keeping the share until the return of the absent member (*i*). The right to receive a share of property divided in a man's absence is laid down as extending to his descendants to the seventh degree. But, of course, it would now be regulated by the law of limitation (*k*).

Wife. § 436. A wife can never demand a partition during the life of her husband, since, from the time of marriage, she and he are united in religious ceremonies (*l*). But in former times, where a partition took place at the will of others, the interests of the women of the family, whether wives, widows, mothers, or daughters, were much better provided for than they are at present. **Right of wife,** Where the partition was made in the father's lifetime, the furniture in the house and the wife's ornaments were set aside for the wife, and where the allotments of the males were equal, and the wives had no separate property, shares equal to those of the sons were set apart for the wives for their lives (*m*). According to *Harinatha*, however, this right to a share did not arise where the husband reserved two or more shares to himself, as he was entitled to do, as the extra shares were a sufficient provision for his wives (*n*). And so, where the partition took place after the father's death, the mother and the grandmother were each entitled to a share equal to that of the sons, **mother, and daughter.** and the unmarried daughters each to the fourth of a share (*o*). If the sons chose to remain undivided they had a right to do

---

(*i*) 1 Stra. H. L. 206; 2 Stra. H. L. 341; 3 Dig. 544.

(*k*) Daya Bhaga, viii.; D. K. S. ix. See Act XV of 1877, Sched. ii. § 123; 127, 144.

(*l*) Apastamba, xiv. § 16.

(*m*) Yajnavalkya, ii. § 115; Mitakshara, i. 2, § 8—10; Daya Bhaga, iii. 2, § 31; D. K. S. vi. § 22—31; Raghunandana, ii. 13, 14, 18; V. May., iv. 6, § 15. Viramit., p. 57, § 10.

(*n*) 1 W. MacN. 47. See, too, D. K. S. vi. § 27.

(*o*) Vyasa, Vrihaspati, 3 Dig. 12; Vishnu, 3 Dig. 15; Manu, ix. § 118; Mitakshara, i. 7; Daya Bhaga, iii. 2, § 29, 34; V. May., iv. 4, § 18, 39, 40. Viramit., p. 79, § 19.

so. The women of the family could never compel a division, and were entitled to no more than a maintenance. This is still the law universally where the father leaves male issue (*p*). But where he leaves no male issue there is, as already observed, a difference between the law of the Mitakshara and that of the Daya Bhaga. Under the former system females never succeed to the share of an undivided member so long as there are male coparceners in existence; under the latter system they do. But according to the doctrines of *Jimuta Vahana*, the shares even of an undivided member are held in a sort of quasi-severalty (§ 348), so that the right of the female heirs to obtain possession of this share is rather a branch of the law of inheritance than of the law of partition (*q*).

Obsolete in Southern India.

§ 437. In Southern India the practice of allotting a share upon partition to wives, widows, or mothers has long since become obsolete. The Smriti Chandrika, which admits the right of an aged father, when making a partition with his sons, to reserve a double share for himself, says that if he does not avail himself of this right, he ought to take, on account of each of his wives, a share equal to that taken by himself (*r*). But the right of a father to reserve an extra share for himself in regard to ancestral property is now obsolete (§ 447), and the corresponding practice of reserving a share for wives has also disappeared. The pandits of the Madras Sudr Court, in a case where a man had made a deed of division allotting a share to his son, and another to his wife and daughter, declared that such a division was

Rights of women in Southern India.

(*p*) 2 W. MacN. 65, n.; F. MacN. 45, 57.

(*q*) See the remarks of Jagannatha, 3 Dig. 9. "The right of partition consists in the relation of son to the original possessor and the like. Even the son of the daughter of a man who leaves no male issue, and the son of a mother's sister, are not intended by the term 'undivided,' since they belong to other families." A daughter's son in Bengal would certainly be entitled to have his grandfather's share ascertained and delivered to him (§ 433). But his suit would be more in the nature of an ejectment than of a partition, which implies previous membership in a joint family.

(*r*) Smriti Chandrika, iv. § 26—39. This appears also to be the opinion of the author of the Sarasvati Vilasa, who cites Apararka in support of it, §§ 77, 111—117.

illegal by Hindu law, "inasmuch as a wife and daughter, who have no right to property while a son is alive, are not capable of participating in the property while he is alive" (*s*). The practice in Madras, as far as my experience goes, is that in making a division during a father's life, no notice is taken of his wife or wives, their rights being included in his, and provided for out of his share. As regards the mother, where partition is made after the death of her husband, the Smriti Chandrika, after discussing the texts already cited, points out that a widowed mother with male issue cannot be entitled to a partition of the heritage, as she is not an heir, but only to a portion sufficient for her maintenance and her religious duties. Consequently, that where she is stated to be entitled to a share equal to that of a son, this must mean such a portion as is necessary for her wants, and which can never exceed a son's share, but which is subject to be diminished, if the property is so large that the share of a son would be greater than she needs, or where she is already in possession of separate property (*t*). This is in accordance with existing practice. The plaint in a suit for partition in Madras always sets out the names of such widows as are chargeable upon the property, and asks that the amount necessary for their maintenance may be ascertained and set aside for them. This amount, though of course in some degree estimated with reference to the magnitude of the property (§ 417), is never considered to be equal to, or to bear any definite proportion to, the share of sons. Mr. W. MacNaghten states that this exclusion of mothers from a distinct share on partition is peculiar to the Smriti Chandrika, and that according to the Mitakshara and other works current in Benares and the Southern Provinces, not only mothers, but also childless wives are entitled to shares, the term *mâtâ* being interpreted to signify both mother and stepmother (*u*). The Viramitro- Benares law.

(*s*) *Meenatchee* v. *Chetumbra*, Mad. Dec of 1853, 61.

(*t*) Smriti Chandrika, iv. § 4—17; 2 Stra. H. L. 309; *Venkatammal* v. *Andyappa*, 6 Mad. 130; *per curiam*, 8 Mad. at p 123.

(*u*) 1 W. MacN. 50. Vyasa expressly lays down that "the wives of the father who have no sons are entitled to equal shares (with the sons of other wives);

daya admits sonless wives to a share when partition is made by the father, but excludes them from a partition made after his death. The ground of the distinction is, that in the former case they take as wives, while in the latter case they can only take as mothers. He seems however to admit that the Mitakshara and the Madanaratna recognise the right of stepmothers to a partition with their sons (v). I have been informed on high authority that the usage as regards allotting maintenance instead of shares to mothers,

Bombay.

when a partition takes place in Bombay, is the same as that which prevails in Madras. But the futwahs of the pandits lay it down that she is entitled to a share equal to that of a son, and the same view is stated by Mr. Justice *West* in a well considered judgment in a recent case (w). I know of no express decision upon the point in Bombay. The High Court of Bengal has on several occasions decided that, under Mitakshara law, a mother is entitled when a partition takes place to have a share equal to that of a son set apart for her, either by way of maintenance or as a portion of the inheritance, even though the partition takes place in the lifetime of the father (x). The same view is taken by the High Court of the North-West Provinces which holds that a Hindu widow, entitled by the Mitakshara to a proportionate share with her sons upon partition, can claim such share, not only *quoad* the sons, but as against an auction purchaser at a sale in execution of the right title and interest of one of the sons before partition (y).

Rights of women in Bengal.

§ 438. Under the law of Bengal the rights of females stand much higher than they do in the other provinces.

---

and so are all the wives of the paternal grandfather." 3 Dig. 12; V. May., iv. 4, § 19, says this includes step-grandmothers also. So also the Mithila school D. K. S. vii. § 7. See 3 Dig. 13; *Damoodur* v *Senabutty*, 8 Cal. 537.

(v) Viramit, p. 79, § 19.

(w) *Madhowrao* v. *Yuswuda*, 2 Bor. 454 [468]; W. & B., 2nd ed., 91, 92, 97, 100, 306, 390; *Lakshman* v. *Satyabhamabai*, 2 Bom. 494, 504.

(x) *Judoonath* v. *Bishonath*, 9 Suth. 61; *Mahabeer* v. *Ramyad*, 12 B. L. R. 90; S. C. 20 Suth. 192; *Laljeet* v. *Rajcoomar*, *ib.* 378; S. C. 20 Suth. 336; *Pursid* v. *Honooman*, 5 Cal. 845; *Sumrun* v. *Chundar Mun*, 8 Cal. 17; *Krishori* v. *Moni Mohun*, 12 Cal. 165.

(y) *Bilaso* v. *Dina Nath*, 3 All. 88.

Partition during the life of a father is so uncommon in Bengal, that I can find no authority as to setting aside shares for the wives. The Daya-krama-sangraha seems to limit the right of wives to have such shares to cases where the father makes a partition of his self-acquired property. In such a case, if peculiar property has been already given to one wife, the other wives, whether childless or otherwise, are entitled to have their shares made up to an equal amount. If they have had no peculiar property, then they are to have shares equal to those of sons (*z*). After the death of the father, the right of the widow depends upon whether the father has left male issue or not, and whether she is a mother or a childless wife. That is to say, she may either be a coparcener before partition, or only entitled to a share in the event of a partition, or entitled in no case to more than maintenance.

Right of widow in Bengal.

1. If the father dies leaving no male issue, his widow becomes his heir, whether he is divided or not. She is in the strictest sense a coparcener. She became a member of the same *gotra* with her husband on her marriage, and is the surviving half of his body, as well as his heir (*a*). She can herself sue for a partition, and need not wait for her share until a partition is brought about by the act of others (*b*). The Calcutta High Court, however, has laid it down that owing to the special nature of a woman's estate, it would be the duty of a Court, before decreeing partition in favour of a widow, to see that the interests of the presumptive heir be not affected by the decree. The Court ought to be satisfied that it is a *bonâ fide* claim arising from

Where no issue.

(*z*) D. K. S. vi. § 22—26.

(*a*) W. & B. 129; Vrihaspati, 3 Dig. 458; Daya Bhaga, xi. 1, § 14 note, 43, 46, 54; D. K. S. ii. 2, § 41.

(*b*) F. MacN. 39, 59; 1 W. MacN. 49; *Dhurm Das* v. *Mt. Shama Soondri*, 3 M. I. A. 229, 241; S. C. 6 Suth. (P. C.) 43; *Shib Pershad* v. *Gunga Monee*, 16 Suth. 291; *Soudaminey* v. *Jogesh*, 2 Cal. 262. Even before partition the widow has an alienable interest which may be enforced by partition by her assignee. *Janoki Nath* v. *Mothura Nath*, 9 Cal. 580. As to the rights of several widows *inter se*, *post*, § 510. As to the right of widows among the Jains to demand a partition of their husband's share, see *Sheo Singh* v. *Mt. Dakho*, 6 N.-W. P. 406, affd. 5 I. A. 87; S. C. 1 All. 688.

such necessities as render partition desirable between two joint owners, and that she would properly represent the interest of the estate, including that of the person who would come after her (*c*).

Stepmother.

2. If the father dies leaving issue, and a widow who is not the mother of such issue, she is never entitled to more than maintenance. The writers of the Bengal school differ in this respect from those of the other provinces, since they exclude a stepmother from the operation of the texts which speak of the share of a mother. And this exclusion equally applies, whether the widow was originally childless, or was the mother of daughters only, or was the mother of sons whose line has become extinct before partition (*d*).

Mother.

3. If the father dies leaving male issue, and also a widow who is the mother of such issue, she is only entitled to maintenance until partition, and she can never herself require a partition. But if a partition takes place by the act of others, she will be entitled to receive a share, if the effect of that partition is to break up or diminish the estate out of which she would otherwise be maintained (*e*). Hence her claim to a share is limited to the two following cases: *first*, when the partition takes place between her own descendants, upon whose property her maintenance is a charge. *Secondly*, when it takes place in respect of property in which her husband had an interest.

Right of mother in Bengal.

§ 439. *First*. If a widowed mother has only one son, she can never claim a share from him, and if he comes to a partition with his brothers by another mother, her claim for maintenance is a charge upon his share and not upon the whole estate (*f*). But if he dies, and his sons come to a division,

(*c*) *Mohadeay* v. *Haruk Narain*, 9 Cal. 244, 250.

(*d*) F. MacN. 41, 57; 1 W. MacN. 50; 3 Dig. 13; D. K. S. vii. § 3, 5, 6; Daya Bhaga, iii. 2, § 30; Raghunanda, ii. 17; *ante*, § 437.

(*e*) 2 W. MacN. 65, *n.*; F. MacN. 45, 57, 59; *Bilaso* v. *Dinanath*, 3 All. 88. Hence until partition she has no alienable interest. See *Judoonath* v. *Bishonath*, 9 Suth. 61.

(*f*) *Hemangini Dasi* v. *Kedarnath*, 16 I. A. 115; S. C. 16 Cal. 758.

then she would be entitled to share with them as grandmother. Similarly, if a man dies leaving three widows, each of whom has one son, and these three sons come to a division, none of the mothers would have a right to a share; because each of them retains her claim intact upon her own son. . But if the sons of one son divide among themselves, their grandmother will be entitled to a share. If the grandsons of all three widows divide, all the grandmothers will be entitled (*g*). In each case the share of the widow will be equal to the share of the persons who effect the partition. If it takes place between her sons, she will take the share of a son; if between her grandsons, she will take the share of a grandson (*h*). If a mother has three sons, one of whom dies leaving grandsons, and a partition takes place between the two surviving sons and the grandsons, the mother will be entitled to the same share as if the division had been effected between three sons; that is to say, the property will be divided into four shares, of which the mother will take one, each surviving son will take another, and the grandsons will take the fourth (*i*). Where the partition takes place between grandsons by different fathers, the matter becomes more complicated. For instance, suppose A.

Grandmother.

Grandmother in Bengal.

A.

B.	C.	D.
2 grandsons.	3 grandsons.	4 grandsons.

to have died leaving a widow and three sons, and these sons to die, leaving respectively two, three, and four grandsons, and that these grandsons come to a division. If their grandmother was dead, the property would be divided into three portions, *per stirpes*, which would again be divided into two, three, and four parts, *per capita* (§ 432). But if the grand-

F. MacN. 39, 41, 54; *Sibbosoondery* v. *Bussomutty*, 7 Cal. 191.

D K. S. vii. § 2, 4; Raghunandana, ii. 19. If she has already been provided for to the extent to which she would be entitled on partition, she takes no more; if to a less extent, she takes as much more as will make up her share. *Jodoonath* v. *Brojonath*, 12 B. L. R. 385.

(*i*) *Prawnkissen* v. *Muttoosoondery*, Fulton, 389; *Gooroopersaud* v. *Seebchunder*, F. MacN. 29, 52.

mother is alive, she will be entitled to the same share as *a grandson*. But it is evident that the grandsons by B. take a larger share than those by C., and these again a larger share than those by D. The mode of division, therefore, is stated to be, that the whole property is divided into ten shares, of which the grandmother will take one, the two sons of B. will take three, the three sons of C. will take three, and the four sons of D. will take three. If the widows of B., C. and D. were also living, they would be entitled to shares also. Each widow would take the same as her son. But in order to arrive at this share, a fresh division would have to be made. The three-tenths taken by the sons of B. would be divided into three parts, of which his widow would take one. Similarly, the three-tenths taken by the sons of C. would be divided into four parts, and the three-tenths taken by the sons of D. would be divided into five parts, of which one would go to the respective widows of C. and D., the remainder being divisible among their sons (*k*). The same widow may take in different capacities, as heir of one branch of the family, and as mother or grandmother in another branch. A very complicated instance of this sort is recorded by Sir F. MacNaghten as having been decided in the Supreme Court at Calcutta (*l*).

In one case in Bengal, where a partition was made after the death of all the sons by their widows, it was held that the grandmother had no right to a share. No counsel appeared for the grandmother, and, as might be expected, no precedents were cited. The decision can hardly be looked upon as of much weight, in the face of the direct authority on the other side (*m*).

(*k*) F. MacN. 52—54.

(*l*) *Sree Motee Jeemoney* v. *Attaram*, F. MacN. 64; *Callychurn* v. *Jonava*, 1 Ind. Jur. N. S. 284; *Jugomohan* v. *Sarodamoyee*, 3 Cal. 149; *Torit* v. *Taraprosonno*, 4 Cal. 756; *Kristo Bhabiney* v. *Ashutosh*, 13 Cal. 39.

(*m*) *Rayee* v. *Puddum*, 12 Suth, 409, affirmed on review, 13 Suth. 66; *contra*, *Sibbosoondery* v. *Bussoomutty*, 7 Cal. 193; *Bhadri Roy* v. *Bhugwat*, 8 Cal. 649, S. C. 11 C. L. R. 186 See Vyasa and Vrihaspati, 3 Dig. 12, where the right of the grandmother to a share is expressly asserted; and so Jagannatha says, 3 Dig. 27.

Where a partition takes place among great-grandsons only, it is said that the great-grandmother has no right to a share (*n*). But if a son be one of the partitioning parties with great-grandsons by another son, she would take a son's share. And if a grandson and great-grandson divide, she would take a grandson's share (*o*). **Great-grand-mother.**

§ 440. *Secondly.* "Partition, to entitle a mother to the share, must be made of ancestral property, or of property acquired by ancestral wealth. Therefore, if the property had been acquired by A., the father of B. and C., and B. and C. come to a division of it, their mother (the widow of A.) shall, but their grandmother shall not, take a share of it. And if the estate shall have been acquired by B. and C. themselves, neither their mother nor grandmother will be entitled to a share upon partition" (*p*). **Wife only shares in husband's property.**

§ 441. Where a partition takes place during the life of the father, the daughter has no right to any special apportionment. She continues under his protection till her marriage; he is bound to maintain her and to pay her marriage expenses, and the expenditure he is to incur is wholly at his discretion (*q*). But where the division takes place after the death of the father, the same texts which direct that the mother should receive a share equal to that of a son, direct that the daughter should receive a fourth share (*r*). It is evident, however, that there was much less need to set apart a permanent provision for a daughter than for a widow. The expenses of her marriage, and her maintenance for the very few years that she could remain in her father's family, constituted the only charge that had to be met in respect of her. Hence it was very early considered that the mention of a definite fourth only meant that **Rights of daughter.** **Daughter.**

3 Dig. 27; F. MacN. 28, 51, doubted by Dr. Wilson, Works, v. 25.
F. MacN. 52.
F. MacN. 51, 54; *Isree Pershad* v. *Nasib Kooer*, 10 Cal. 1017.
Mitakshara, i. 7, § 14.
(*r*) Yajnavalkya, ii. § 124: see *ante*, § 436. As to the mode of calculating the fourth, see Mitakshara, i. 7, § 5—10; 3 Dig. 93, 94; Smriti Chandrika, iv. § 34; Wilson, Works, v.

a sufficient amount must be allotted to each daughter to defray her nuptials. This view is combated by *Vijnanesvara,* who maintains that the letter of the law must be respected. The Smriti Chandrika, however, evidently inclined to the modern doctrine, as it states that the full fourth is only to be given where the estate is inconsiderable. And it is expressly asserted by the Madhaviya and the Bengal writers, and those of the Mithila school (*s*). The practice at present is in conformity with this opinion (*t*).

Where daughters take as joint-heirs, the effect of partition between them comes under the law of succession, and will be discussed hereafter (§ 515).

Strangers.

§ 442. A stranger cannot compel a partition, in the sense of compelling any or all of the members of a family to assume the *status* of divided members, with the legal consequences following upon that *status*. But he may acquire such rights over the property of any coparcener as to compel him to separate the whole or part of his interest in the joint property, and so sever the coparcenary in respect of it. This may be effected either by actual assignment, or by operation of law, as by insolvency, or upon a sale in execution of a decree (*u*). How far a member of an undivided family under Mitakshara law can, by his own voluntary act, transfer his rights in the joint property to a stranger, is a matter upon which there is much difference of opinion, and which has already been examined (*v*). But

(*s*) Mitakshara, i. 7, § 11 ; Smriti Chandrika, iv. § 18, 19 ; Madhaviya, § 25, where he misrepresents the opinion of Vijnanesvara : Daya Bhaga, iii. 2, § 39 : D. K. S. vii. § 9, 10 ; Raghunandana, iii. 19, 20 ; 3 Dig. 90—94. The Viramitrodaya argues for the view adopted by the Mitakshara, but sets out the conflicting opinions, Viramit., p. 81, § 21. The Sarasvati Vilasa sets out both views, but states the modern doctrine, which is that of Apararka, last, though without offering any opinion of his own, § 119—133.

(*t*) F. MacN. 55, 98 ; 1 W. MacN. 50. Daughters have no right to claim a share of their mother's property during her life, in cases in which they would be her heirs ; *Mathura* v *Esu*, 4 Bom. 545.

(*u*) *Per curiam*, *Soorjeemoney Dossee* v. *Denobundoo*, 6 M. I. A. 539 S. C. 4 Suth. (P. C.) 114 ; *Deendyal* v. *Jugdeep*, 4 I. A. 247 ; S. C. 3 Cal.

(*v*) *Ante*, § 327, *et seq.*

so far as the right of transfer is recognized it will be enforced, either by putting the purchaser in possession of an undivided interest, or by compelling the owner of the undivided interest to proceed to, or permit a partition, by means of which the hostile right can be satisfied (*w*).

Disqualified heirs.

§ 443. Persons who labour under any defect which disqualifies them from inheriting, are equally disentitled to a share on partition (*x*). But except in the case of degradation, which has now been practically abolished by Act XXI of 1850, (Freedom of religion) such incapacity is purely personal, and does not attach to their legitimate issue (*y*). **Disqualification is personal.** Its effect is to let in the next heir, precisely as if the incapacitated person were then dead. But that heir must claim upon his own merits, and does not step into his father's place. For instance, suppose the dividing parties were C. and F., and that E. were incapacitated but alive, his son F.

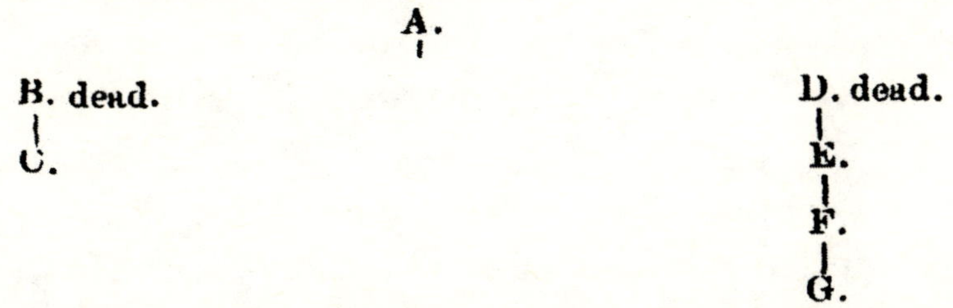

would be entitled to claim half of the property. But if F. was the incapacitated person, and D., and E. were dead, G. would have no claim, being beyond the limits of the coparcenary (*z*). On the other hand, such disqualification only operates if it arose before the division of the property. One already separated from his coheirs is not deprived of his **Result of its removal.**

(*w*) *Anand* v. *Prankisto*, 3 B. L. R. (O. C. J.) 14; *Rughoonath* v. *Luckhun*, 18 Suth. 23; *Muddun Gopal* v. *Mt. Gowrbutty*, 21 Suth. 190; *Lall Jha* v. *Shaikh Juma*, 22 Suth. 116; *Jhubboo* v. *Khoob Lall*, *ib* 294; *Alamalu* v. *Rungasami*, 7 Mad. 588; *Janokinath* v. *Mothuranath*, 9 Cal. 580; *Rajani Kanth* v. *Ram Nath*, 10 Cal 244; *Bepin Behari* v. *Lal Mohun*, 12 Cal. 209.

(*x*) Mitakshara, ii. 10; V. May., iv. 11; Daya Bhaga, v.; D. K. S. iii. See *post*, chap. xix, *Ramsahye* v. *Lalla Laljee*, 8 Cal. 149.

(*y*) Mitakshara, ii. 10, § 9—11; Daya Bhaga, v. § 17—19. As to adopted sons, see *ante*, § 99.

(*z*) 2 W. MacN. 42; *Bodhnarain* v. *Omrao*, 13 M. I. A. 519; S. C. 6 B. L. R. 509; *per* Peacock, C. J., *Kalidas* v. *Krishan*, 2 B. L. R. (F. B.) 115;

Removal of disability.

allotment (*a*). And if the defect be removed at a period subsequent to partition, the right to share arises in the same manner as, or upon the analogy of, a son born after partition (*b*). How this analogy is to be worked out is not so clear. If the removal of the defect is to be treated as a new birth at the time of such removal, then the principles previously laid down would apply (*c*). If the partition took place during the life of the father, and one of the sons were then incapable, he would take no share. But if his defect were afterwards removed, he would inherit his father's share. If, however the partition took place after the father's death, and one of the brothers was excluded as being incapable, and was afterwards cured, his cure could only be treated as a new birth, so as to give him any practical rights, by the further fiction that he was in his mother's womb at the time of the partition. If this analogy could be applied, he would be entitled to have the division opened up again, and a new distribution made for his benefit. But that would be rather a violent fiction to introduce, in a case where the incapacity was removed, possibly many years after new rights had been created by the division, and acted upon. Suppose, however, that the incapable heir was never cured, but had a son who was capable of inheriting. If the son was actually born, or was in the womb, at the time of the partition, he would be entitled to a share, if sufficiently near of kin. But if he was neither born nor conceived at that time, he could not claim to have the partition re-opened. He could only claim to succeed as heir to the share taken by his grandfather; and if the partition took place between the brothers, he could claim nothing more than maintenance (*d*).

Effect of fraud.

§ 444. It has been suggested that a coparcener, other-

(*a*) Mitakshara, ii. 10, § 6; *Sevachetumbara* v. *Parasucty*, Mad. Dec. of 1857, 210.

(*b*) Mitakshara, ii. 10, § 7; V. May., iv. 11, § 2.

(*c*) *Ante*, § 431.

(*d*) See this subject discussed by *Peacock*, C. J., *Kalidas* v. *Krishan*, 2 B. L. R. (F. B.) 118—121, and in *Krishna* v. *Sami*, 9 Mad. 64. Of course all diffi-

wise entitled, may lose his right to a share if he has been guilty of defrauding his coheirs. This view rests upon a text of Manu (*e*): "Any eldest brother who from avarice shall defraud his younger brother, shall forfeit his primogeniture, be deprived of his share, and pay a fine to the king." This text is explained by *Kalluka Bhatta* and *Jagannatha* as meaning, that the eldest brother by such fraudulent conduct forfeits his right to the special share to which in early times he was entitled by seniority (*f*). *Yajnavalkya* and *Katyayana* merely say, that property wrongly kept back by one of the co-sharers shall be divided equally among all the sharers when it is discovered (*g*). This excludes the idea that the fraudulent person is to forfeit his whole share, or even his share in the property so secreted. The Mitakshara discusses the act with reference only to the question of criminality. The author decides that the act is criminal, but does not assert that it is to be followed by forfeiture, and seems to assume that the only result will be that the partition will be opened up, and a fresh distribution made of the property wrongly withheld (*h*). The other commentators of the Benares school either follow the Mitakshara, or pass the point over without special notice (*i*). On the other hand, the Bengal writers are of opinion, that the act of one coparcener, in withholding part of the property which is common to all, is not technically theft, and is not to be punished by any forfeiture (*k*). The Madras Sudder Court in one case followed the literal meaning of the text of Manu, and held that it was a complete answer to a suit for partition by a brother, that he had committed a theft of part of the paternal property. In this decision they set aside the opinion of their senior pandit, who was of opinion that the

Fraud of coparcener.

culty would be removed, if the earlier doctrine were sustained which appears to allow a partition to be opened up at any distance of time in favour of an after-born son.

(*e*) ix. § 213. (*f*) 2 Dig. 564. (*g*) Yajnavalkya, ii. § 126; 3 Dig. 398.

(*h*) Mitakshara, i. 9. This chapter seems to have been differently understood by Sir Thomas and Mr. Strange, 1 Stra. H. L. 232; Stra. Man. § 278. Messrs. West and Bühler take the view stated in the text, W. & B. 679.

(*i*) Smriti Chandrika, xiv. § 4—6; Madhaviya, § 54; V. May., iv. 6, § 3; Viramitrodaya, p 245, § 1, 2.

(*k*) Daya Bhaga, xiii. § 2, 8—15; D. K. S. viii.; 3 Dig. 397, 400.

embezzler of common property incurred no forfeiture thereby. The junior pandit had first stated generally, that the person who had embezzled part of the common property forfeited all claim to share in the estate. On giving in his written opinion, he modified this view by limiting the forfeiture to a prohibition of sharing in the portion actually embezzled. This opinion also the Court set aside, preferring that first given (*l*). The Court of the North-West Provinces has arrived at an exactly opposite conclusion, and has laid down that the wrongful appropriation by one brother of part of the joint estate, which the others might have recovered by an action at law, was no bar to a suit by him for partition (*m*). This certainly appears to me to be the sounder view.

Partition prohibited.

direction in a will prohibiting a partition, or postponing the period for partition, is invalid, as it forbids the exercise of a right which is essential to the full enjoyment of family property by Hindu law (*n*). On the other hand, an agreement between the members of a Hindu family not to come to a partition might be binding upon themselves. But unless the agreement also contained a condition against alienation, it would not prevent any of the parties to it from selling his share, and would be no bar to a suit by the vendee to compel a partition (*o*). Nor could such an agreement ever bind the descendants of the parties to it (*p*). In Bombay it has been held that it would not even bind the parties themselves (*q*).

Lapse of time.

§ 446. As Hindu law contemplates union and not partition as the normal state of the family, it follows that lapse

(*l*) *Canacumma* v. *Narasimmah*, Mad. Dec. of 1858, 118.
(*m*) *Kalka* v. *Budree*, 3 N.-W. P. 267. Jolly, Lect. 142.
(*n*) *Nubkissen* v. *Hurris Chunder*, F. MacN. 323 ; *Mokoondo* v. *Gonesh*, 1 Cal. 104 ; *Jeebun* v. *Romanath*, 23 Suth. 297 ; Act IV of 1882, § 10, 11. (Transfer of Property).
(*o*) *Rhamdhone* v. *Anund*, 2 Hyde, 97 ; *Anand* v. *Prankisto*, 3 B. L. R. (O. C. J.) 14 ; *Anath* v. *Mackintosh*, 8 B. L. R. 60 ; *Rajender* v. *Sham Chund*, 6 Cal. 107.
(*p*) See *Venkataramanna* v. *Bramanna*, 4 Mad. H. C. 345.
(*q*) *Ramlinga* v. *Virupakshi*, 7 Bom.

of time is never in itself a bar to a partition. But the Statute of Limitations will operate from the time that a plaintiff is excluded from his share, and that such exclusion becomes known to him (*r*).

§ 447. THIRD, THE MODE OF DIVISION.—The principle of Hindu law is equality of division, but this was formerly subject to many exceptions, which have almost, if not altogether, disappeared. One of these exceptions was in favour of the eldest son, who was originally entitled to a special share on partition, either a tenth or a twentieth in excess of the others, or some special chattel, or an extra portion of the flocks (*s*). Sir H. S. Maine suggests that this extra share was given as the reward, or the security, for impartial distribution; and refers to the fact that such extra privileges were sometimes awarded to younger sons (*t*), or to the father, as a proof that the right was unconnected with the rule of primogeniture (*u*). It seems to me probable that the double share which the father was allowed to retain for himself (*v*), was the inducement given to him to consent to a partition, at the time when his consent was indispensable (§ 220,) and perhaps also was intended to enable him to support the female members of the family, who would naturally remain under his care. Among the Hill tribes, when a division takes place, the family house sometimes passes to the youngest, sometimes to the eldest, son; but invariably the son who takes the house takes with it the burthen of supporting the females of the family (*w*). The practice of allotting a larger share to the father would naturally survive, though to a lesser degree, in favour of

Special shares formerly allowed.

Special shares

(*r*) *Thakur Durriao* v. *Thakur Dari*, 1 I. A. 1; *Kali* v *Dhununjoy*, 3 Cal. 228; Act XV of 1877, sched. ii. § 127.

(*s*) Apastamba, xiii. § 13; Baudhayana, ii. 2, § 2—5; Gautama, xxviii. § 11, 12; Vasishtha, xvii. § 23; Manu, ix. § 112, 114, 156; Narada, xiii. § 13; Devala, 2 Dig. 553; Vrihaspati, *ib.* 556; Harita, *ib.* 558; Yajnavalkya, ii. § 114; Viramit., p 53, § 9.

(*t*) Gautama, xxviii. § 6, 7; Vasistha, xvii. § 23; Manu, ix. § 112.

(*u*) Early Institutions, 197.

(*v*) Narada, xiii. § 12; Vrihaspati, 3 Dig 44; Katyayana, *ib.* 53; Sancha & Lichita, 2 Dig. 555.

Breeks, Primitive Tribes, 9, 39, 42, 68.

the eldest son as head of the family. Under the law of the Mitakshara the practice of giving an extra share to the father is now said either to be a relic of a former age, or only to apply to a partition by the father of his own self-acquired property (x). As between brothers or other relations absolute equality is now the invariable rule in all the provinces (y), unless, perhaps, where some special family custom to the contrary is made out (z); and this rule equally applies whether the partition is made by the father, or after his death (a).

now obsolete.

Other grounds of preference arose in regard to sons of different rank; that is to say, sons by mothers of different caste, or sons of the ten supplementary species. These shared in different proportions, or some absolutely to the exclusion of others (b). But these different sorts of sons are long since obsolete (§ 75, 85). The right of a person who has made acquisitions, in which he has been slightly assisted by the joint property, to reserve to himself a double share, has already been fully considered (§ 264).

Where property is self-acquired.

§ 448. Hitherto we have been considering the case of joint property, as to which partition was a matter of right and not of favour. There is greater uncertainty where the partition was of property which was divisible as a matter of favour and not of right. Under Mitakshara law this case could only arise where the father chose to divide his self-acquired property among his sons. It is quite clear that

(x) Mitakshara, i. 6, § 7: Madhaviya, § 16; V. May., iv. 6. § 12. 13; Viramit., p. 65, § 13. See Smriti Chandrika, ii. 1, § 28—32, 41, where it is said to be allowable on a partition made by an aged parent.

(y) Mitakshara, i. 2, § 6. i. 3, § 1—7; Smriti Chandrika, ii. 2, § 2, ii. 3, § 16—24; Madhaviya, § 9: V. May., iv. 6, § 8—11, 14. 17: Daya Bhaga, iii. 2. § 27; D. K. S., vii. § 12, 13: Viramit., p. 60, § 11, p. 70, § 14. The case of an adopted son, where natural born sons afterwards come into existence, has been discussed, *ante*, § 155.

(z) *Sheo Buksh* v. *Futteh*, 2 S. D. 265 (340); 2 W. MacN. 16. As to agreements to divide in particular shares, see *Ram Nirunjun* v. *Prayag*, 8 Cal. 138.

(a) *Bhyrochund* v. *Russomunee*, 1 S. D 28 (36); *Neelkuunt* v. *Munee*, *ib.* 58 (77); *Taliwar* v. *Puhlwand*, 3 S. D. 301 (402); *Lakshman* v. *Ramchandra*, 1 Bom. 561.

(b) Mitakshara, i. 8, 11; Daya Bhaga, ix. § 12; D. K. S., vii. § 19; V. May., iv. 4, § 27.

the father might give away this property to any one he chose (§ 350), and it would seem to follow that he might distribute it among his family at his own pleasure. *Vishnu* says, "If a father make a partition with his sons, he does so in regard to his own self-acquired property by his own pleasure" (*c*). This, of course, may refer to his right of withholding such property absolutely from distribution. Other texts which seem to leave the father a discretion as to allowing larger or smaller shares to his sons, may refer to the practice of giving extra shares to an elder son, an acquirer or the like (*d*). The interpretation put upon these texts by the Hindu commentators was, that even in regard to self-acquired property, the right of the father to make an unequal distribution could only exist where there was either a legal reason, as in case of an elder son's share, or a moral reason, such as the necessitous state of one of the sons, and that it could never exist where the act emanated from mere partiality or vicious preference (*e*). The author of the Smriti Chandrika sums up his argument upon the point by saying, "It is hence settled that unequal distribution made by the father, even of his own self-acquired property, according to his whims, without regard to the restrictions contained in the *shastras*, is not maintainable, where sons are dissatisfied with such distribution" (*f*). In a Madras case, where a man had made a division of his self-acquired property, giving about a tenth to his son, and the rest to his wife and daughter, the Sudder Pandits said that such a disposition would be valid as regards the personalty, but not as regards the realty (*g*). In the Punjab it is held that a man may distribute his self-acquisitions at his own pleasure (*h*). If the rule is anything more than a moral precept, it must depend upon the distinction, which I will notice presently, between a partition, which

---

(*c*) xvii. § 1.
(*d*) Yajnavalkya, ii. § 114, 116; Narada, xiii. § 15, 16.
(*e*) 3 Dig. 540, 541, 546; Mitakshara, i. 2, § 6, 13, 14.
(*f*) Smriti Chandrika, ii. 1, § 17—24; Varadrajah, p 8; 1 Stra. H. L. 194; 2 W. MacN. 147, note.
(*g*) *Meenatchee* v. *Chetumbra*, Mad Dec. of 1853, 61.
(*h*) Punjab Cust. 35.

may be effected by mere agreement, and a gift, which requires delivery of possession.

Bengal law.

§ 449. In Bengal the peculiar doctrines of the Daya Bhaga leave a father practically at liberty to dispose of all his property, no matter of what sort, or how acquired, at his own free pleasure, in favour of any one upon whom he chooses to bestow it. One would expect, therefore, to find that, when he chose to distribute it among his sons, he would be at liberty to do so to whatever extent, and in whatever proportions he liked. This, however, is by no means so. *Jimuta Vahana* draws the distinction between self-acquired and ancestral property, saying that in the former case the father may give his sons greater or lesser allotments at his pleasure, but in the latter case his discretion is limited. He cannot reserve more for himself than his double share (*i*) With regard to his sons, he is also under restrictions. If the partition is made at the request of his sons, he is bound to give each an equal share, the legal deduction in favour of the eldest being alone allowed (*k*). If, however, he makes the partition of his own accord, he may make a partial or a total division. The former seems not to come under the rules which govern a legal division. The father appears still to remain the head of the family, and to retain a certain control over the whole property, but allots small portions of it to his sons, retaining the right to take these portions back, if he becomes indigent (*l*). Where, however, the partition is a total one, the same distinction exists between his rights over the ancestral and self-acquired property. As regards the former, the distribution must be equal or uniform, in the sense of not being arbitrary; that is, any inequality in the shares of the sons must be an inequality prescribed, or at least permitted, by the law, as arising from the superior age or merit of the son whom he

By father in Bengal

(*i*) Daya Bhaga, ii. § 15—20, 35, 47, 56, 73; D. K. S. vi. § 16; Raghunandana, ii. 2—6, 26—29.

(*k*) Daya Bhaga, ii. § 86.

(*l*) Daya Bhaga, ii. § 57; 2 W. MacN. 148; D. K. S. vi. § 8.

prefers (*m*). But as regards the self-acquired property, he may make a distribution according to his own free will, though even in this case the preference must arise from motives recognized by the law, on account of the good qualities or piety of the one who is preferred, or his incapacity, numerous family, or the like (*n*). Whether such reasons are sufficient to authorize an unequal distribution of ancestral property also, does not seem clear. In commenting on the text of *Narada* (xiii. 4), the father, "being advanced in years, may himself separate his sons, either dismissing the eldest with the best share, or in any manner, as his inclination may prompt." *Jimuta Vahana* says that this last clause means something different from the giving of an extra share to the first-born, but that the discretion so allowed is again restrained by the subsequent text (xiii. 16), which forbids a distribution made under improper influences, or contrary to the directions of law (*o*). If these passages apply also to ancestral property, the result would be that the power of distribution, both of ancestral and self-acquired property, would stand on the same footing. The father might divide either sort unequally, if he could find any justifying pretext in the superior qualities, or greater necessities, of the son whom he preferred. The Daya-krahma-sangraha, however, limits the right of making an unequal distribution among sons, in consequence of their superior qualifications or greater necessities, to the case of self-acquired property, or ancestral movable property, such as gems, pearls, corals, gold, and other effects (*p*). As regards ancestral landed property, the only inequality it appears to sanction is the special share for the elder son (*q*). In the case of a man's own self-acquired property, he may allot it as he chooses, subject as before to the necessity of showing some

(*m*) Daya Bhaga, ii. § 50, 76, 79. See as to extra shares, *ib.* § 37, 42, 74.
(*n*) Daya Bhaga, ii. § 74, 76, 82; Raghunandana, ii. 4
(*o*) Daya Bhaga, ii. § 81—85.
(*p*) D. K. S. vi. § 13, 18—20; acc. Jagannatha, 3 Dig. 39, 42, and pandits in *Bhowanny Churn* v. *Ramkaunt*, 2 S. D. 202 (259); 2 W. MacN. 2, 16.
(*q*) *Ib.* § 21.

proper ground of preference, and an absence of improper motive (*r*).

§ 450. It is, of course, obvious that where a father is allowed to prefer one son to another on the ground of superior piety or moral qualifications, and is himself constituted as the sole judge of such qualifications, it is merely another way of saying that he may distribute the property as he chooses. A little hypocrisy is all that is needed in order to convert illegality into legality (*s*). But even as regards ancestral immovable property, the Bengal pandits appear in two cases to have taken the view which is suggested by *Jimuta Vahana,* rather than that which is expressed by the Daya-krama-sangraha, and to lay it down that grounds of personal preference, actually existing, will justify a father in preferring one son over another (*t*). The only question that arises is, whether the pandits in the two last cases were not speaking of a gift, and not of a partition. I think they were. I have already quoted the series of decisions in Bengal which practically affirm the right of a father to do what he wishes with his property. They seem in complete conflict with the opinions of the pandits in the case of *Bhowanny Churn* v. *Ramkaunt* (*u*). Now it will be observed that throughout the opinions of the pandits in the latter case, they directed their attention exclusively to the law of partition, and only cited texts bearing upon that law. In the opinions cited in the other cases, and referred to in the remarks on *Bhowanny Churn's* case, they directed their attention as exclusively to the law of gifts, and only cited texts showing the power of an owner of property to dispose of it during his lifetime. The fact is, the two sets of texts

(*r*) D. K. S. vi. § 8—15. See F. MacN. 242—268. In the Punjab a father appears to have the right to divide the family property among his sons in any proportions which seem fit to him, but if the division is thoroughly unequal, a fresh apportionment will be made after his death. Punjab Customary Law, II 168, 171, 180, 222, 261.

(*s*) See the opinions of Pandits, quoted F. MacN. 260; 3 Dig. 1.

(*t*) F. MacN. 260, 265.

(*u*) 2 S. D. 202 (259); *ante*, § 347. See this case discussed by Sir F. MacN. p. 288; *per curiam*, *Lakshmy* v. *Narasimha*, 3 Mad. H. C. 42, 48; Wilson's Works, v. 76, 8<.

are quite irreconcilable. They mark different periods of law. The former are a survival from the time when the power of a father over property was as restricted in Bengal as it is now in the provinces governed by the Mitakshara. These texts probably remained unexplained away, because unequal distributions of a mans's whole property continued to be unusual. The texts which forbid alienations of particular portions of it were explained away, because such alienations became common. *Jagannatha* tries to reconcile the two principles which allow a gift to one in preference to another, but forbid a distribution which gives more to one than another (*v*). His reasoning, so far as I am able to follow it, appears to be, that, where a father proceeds to a partition with his sons, he divests himself of his property, with a view to its vesting again in those who are entitled to share it by virtue of their affinity to him. That being so, it can only vest in such persons, and in such proportions, as the law of partition directs. But when he divests himself of his property in order to make a gift, he immediately vests it again in the person, be it a stranger or otherwise, to whom he delivers the possession. The transaction is valid if it conforms to the law of gifts. Now this is really all that was decided by the case of *Bhowanny Churn* v. *Ramkaunt*. The pandits were unanimous that as a partition the transaction was bad. In this they were apparently right. They differed as to whether it would have been invalid for want of possession, if, as a partition, it had been legal. As to this it may now be taken that their doubts were unfounded, and that actual possession is not necessary in order to make a partition final and binding (§ 454). The Judges of the Sudder Court accepted their finding that the distribution was illegal. If so, it could only take effect as a series of gifts. But viewed in this light it was inoperative, because there had been no delivery of possession (§ 353). The result would be, that a father under Mitakshara law, in dealing with his self-acquired property,

Bhowanny Churn's case.

Result of cases.

(*v*) 3 Dig. 5, 47.

or any other property in which his sons take no interest by birth, and a father under Bengal law in dealing with any property, may distribute it as he likes. If he conforms to the rules of partition, the transaction will be valid by mutual agreement, without actual apportionment followed by possession; but if he does not conform to those rules, then he must deliver the share to each of the sharers, so as to make a valid gift to each.

Where only some divide.

§ 451. A partition may be partial either as regards the persons making it, or the property divided. Any one coparcener may separate from the others, but no coparcener, except perhaps the father, can compel the others to become separate among themselves. A father may separate from all or from some of his sons, remaining joint with the other sons, or leaving them to continue a joint family with each other (*w*). It was stated in two Bengal cases, that where one brother separates from the others, and these continue to live as a joint family, it must be presumed that there has been a complete separation of all the brothers, but that those who continue joint have re-united (*x*). But that seems to be merely a question of fact. If nothing appeared but that one brother had taken his share, and left the family, while the other brothers continued exactly as before, it seems to me the proper presumption would be, that there never had been any severance in their interests (*y*). It has been suggested by Messrs. West and Bühler that one Bombay decision (of which they disapprove) lays down that a grandfather can, by his will, enforce a state of division among his grandsons. The case referred to appears to me only to decide, that property may be devised in such a way that the persons to whom it is bequeathed, if they take it under the will, will take it in severalty and not as joint tenants (*z*).

Division directed.

(*w*) Mitakshara, i. 2, § 2; W. & B. 665.

(*x*) *Judub Chunder* v. *Benodbeharry*, 1 Hyde, 214; *Petambur* v. *Hurish Chunder*, 15 Suth. 200; *Kesabram* v. *Nand Kishore*, 3 B. L. R. (A. C. J.) 7; S. C. 11 Suth. 308.

(*y*) *Upendra Narrain* v. *Gopeenath*, 9 Cal. 817.

(*z*) W. & B. 195, 666; *Lakshmibai* v. *Ganpat Morobu*, 4 Bom. H. C. (O. C. J. 150; S. C. on appeal, 5 Bom. H. C. (A. C. J.) 128.

Such a state of things would be quite consistent with their remaining undivided in other respects. Whether a grandfather could so bequeath property would depend upon the nature of his interest in it. If it was his own exclusive property, of course, he could devise it on any terms he liked. But if it was ancestral property, which would by law descend to his grandsons as coparceners, I doubt whether he could by his will compel them to accept it with the incidents of separate property. The death which severed his interest, would also, as I imagine, terminate his power over the property (§ 380). A different case recently occurred in Madras. A father with three sons by one wife, and two sons by another, executed a document in his last illness, directing the property to be divided into three-fifths, and two-fifths shares, with a small reservation for himself. The Court found that the document was intended to operate from its date as an actual severance, *first*, of the interest of his sons by one wife from that of his sons by another; *secondly*, of the interest of all his sons from his own during his life. Neither his eldest son, who was of age, nor the guardian of his infant sons, were parties to the suit. It was held by the Court that the transaction was a partition which altered the status of the sons though without their consent, by virtue of the special authority of the father. *Muthusawmy Aiyer*, J., upon a review of the native authorities, said, "According to the Hindu law it is competent to a father to make a partition during his life, and the partition so made by him binds his sons, not because the sons are consenting parties to the arrangement, but because it is the result of a power conferred on him, though subject to certain restrictions imposed in the interest of the family. In cases like this the question is not whether such partition is a contract, like a partition made among brothers after their father's decease, but whether it is a legal transaction, concluded in conformity to the Hindu law" (*a*).

All must be parties to suit.

Even where the division is only between certain members

(*a*) *Kandasami* v. *Doraisami*, 2 Mad. 317, 321.

of the family, it is necessary, unless in such a case as that just cited, that all the members should be parties to it, as the interests of all are necessarily affected by the separation of any. And if the partition is effected by decree of Court, all the members must be brought before the Court, either as plaintiffs or defendants (*b*).

Partition should be complete.

§ 452. Every suit for a partition should embrace all the joint family property (*c*), unless different portions of it lie in different jurisdictions, in which case suits may be brought in the different Courts to which the property is subject (*d*); or unless some portion of it is at the time incapable of partition as for instance from being in the possession of a mortgagee (*e*); or is from its nature impartible, as a Zemindary governed by the law of primogeniture (*f*). And if a member sues for partition of property in the hands of the defendant, he must bring into hotchpot any undivided property held by himself, even though it is out of the jurisdiction of the Court, and thus make a complete and final partition (*g*). Hence, where there has been a partition at all, the presumption is that it was a complete one, and that it embraced the whole of the family property. Therefore, if property is afterwards found in the exclusive possession of one member of the family, and it is alleged that such property is still undivided and divisible, the proof of such an allegation rests upon the party making it (*h*). But there

Partition presumed to be complete; may be partial.

(*b*) *Narsimha* v. *Ramchendra*, 1 Mad. Dec. 52; *Pahaludh* v. *Mt. Luchmunbutty*, 12 Suth. 256.

(*c*) Manu, ix. § 47; *Dadjee* v. *Wittal*, Bom. Sel. Rep. 151; *Dasari* v. *Dasari*, Mad. Dec. of 1861, 86; *Ruttun Monee* v. *Brojo Mohun*, 22 Suth. 333; *Nanabhai* v. *Nathabhai*, 7 Bom. H. C. (A. C. J. 46); *per curiam*. *Narayan* v. *Nana Manohar*, *ib*. 178, affirming 2 W. & B Introd. 17, 2nd ed.; *Trimbak* v. *Narayan*, 11 Bom. H. C. 71. See *per Phear*, J., *Padmamani* v. *Jagadamba*, 6 B. L. R. 140, *sed qy.?* *Haridas* v. *Pran Nath*, 12 Cal. 566; *Jogendro Nath*. v. *Jugobundhu*, 14 Cal. 122.

(*d*) *Lutchmana Row* v. *Terimul Row*, 4 Mad. Jur. 241; *Subba Rau* v. *Rama Rau*, 3 Mad. H. C. 376. See *Jairam* v. *Atmaram*, 4 Bom. 482; *Radha Churn*, v. *Kripa*, 5 Cal. 474; *Punchanun Mullick* v. *Sib Chunder*, 14 Cal. 835.

(*e*) *Pattaravy* v. *Audimula*, 5 Mad. H. C. 419; *Narayan* v. *Pandurang*, 12 Bom. H. C. 148.

(*f*) *Parvati* v. *Tirumalai*, 10 Mad. 334.

(*g*) *Ram Lochun* v. *Rughoobur*, 15 Suth. 111; *Lalljeet* v. *Rajcoomar*, 25 Suth. 353; *Hari Narayan* v. *Ganpatrav*, 7 Bom. 272.

(*h*) *Narayan* v. *Nana Manohar*, 7 Bom. H. C. (A. O. J.) 153.

may be a partial division, of such a nature that the coparcenary ceases as to some of the property, and continues as to the rest (*i*). Where such a state of things exists, the rights of inheritance, alienation, &c., differ, according as the property in question belongs to the members in their divided, or in their undivided, capacity (*k*); or, there may be such a partition as amounts to an absolute severance of the coparcenary between the members, although the whole or part of the property is for convenience, or other reasons, left still unapportioned, and in joint enjoyment. In that case, the interest of each member is divided, though the property is undivided. That interest, therefore, will descend, and may be dealt with, as separate property (*l*). Or, lastly, there may be a partition and distribution which is intended to be final, but some part of the family property may have been overlooked, or fraudulently kept out of sight. In such a case, when the property is discovered it will be the subject of a fresh distribution, being divided among the persons who were parties to the original partition, or their representatives; that is, among the persons to whom each portion would have descended as separate property (*m*). But the former distribution will not be opened up again (*n*). Where, however, the whole scheme of distribution is fraudulent, and especially where it is in fraud of a minor, it will be absolutely set aside, unless the person injured has acquiesced in it, after full knowledge that it was made in violation of his rights (*o*).

or imperfect.

or mistaken.

Case of fraud.

(*i*) *Acc. Kandasami* v. *Doraisami*, 2 Mad 324; *per curiam*, 4 M. I. A. 168. The High Court of Bengal seems to think that a partial division may be effected by arrangement, but not by suit. *Radha Churn* v. *Kripa*, 5 Cal. 474.

(*k*) *Patni Mal* v. *Ray Manohar*, 5 S. D. 349 (410); *Maccundas* v. *Ganpatrao*, Perry's O. C. 143; W. & B. 344, 345, 702; F. MacN. 46; 2 Stra. H. L 387; 1 W. MacN. 53.

(*l*) *Appovier* v. *Rama Subbaiyan*, 11 M. I. A. 75; S. C. 8 Suth. (P. C.) 1; *Rewun Persad* v. *Radha Beeby*, 4 M. I. A. 137, 168; S. C. 7 Suth. (P C.) 35; *Narayan* v. *Lakshmi Ammal*, 3 Mad. H. C. 289.

(*m*) Manu, ix. § 218; Mitakshara, i. 9, § 1—3; Daya Bhaga, xiii. § 1—3; V. May., iv. 6, § 3; *Lachman* v. *Sanwal*, 1 All. 543; *ante*, § 444. See as to enlargement of share, where a coparcener dies after decree and pending appeal. *Sakharam* v. *Hari Krishna*, 6 Bom. 118.

(*n*) Daya Bhaga, xiii. § 6; 3 Dig. 400.

(*o*) Vrihaspati, 3 Dig. 399; Manu, ix. § 47; Daya Bhaga, xiii. § 5; Mad. Dec of 1859, 84; *Moro Vishvanath* v. *Ganesh*, 10 Bom. H. C. 444

Suit for partition by or against a stranger.

§ 453. Where a stranger to the family acquires a title to a portion of the family property, by purchase or under an execution, he is entitled to be placed in possession jointly with the other members. If he is not satisfied with joint possession, and desires the exclusive possession of a particular portion of the property, his remedy is by suit to compel his vendor to come to a partition, and so give him an absolute title. But he cannot demand a partition merely as to the portion over which he has a claim. The vendor must have a complete and final partition, so that all the family accounts may be taken against him, and all the other members of the family must be made parties to the suit (§ 329). Where the suit for partition is brought by other members of the family, in order to get rid of the joint possession of the stranger, it has been held by the Madras High Court that the suit may be limited to their share in the particular parcel of family property which had been sold (*p*). On the other hand the Calcutta High Court has ruled that in this case, as in all others, the suit must be one for a complete partition, and that this is not a mere technical objection, because on partition of the whole of the joint family property, the whole land so alienated by a single member might fall entirely to the share of the alienor (*q*).

How effected.

§ 454. FOURTH.—As to what constitutes a partition, it is undisputed that it may be effected without any instrument in writing (*r*). Numerous circumstances are set out by the native writers as being more or less conclusive of a partition having taken place, such as separate food, dwelling, or worship; separate enjoyment of the property; separate income and expenditure; business transactions with each other, and the like (*s*). But all these circumstances are

---

(*p*) *Chinna Sannyasi* v. *Surya*, 5 Mad. 196.

(*q*) *Koer Hasmat* v. *Sunder Das*, 11 Cal. 396.

(*r*) *Per curiam*, *Rewun Persad* v. *Radha Beeby*, 4 M. I. A. 168; S. C. 7 Suth. (P. C.) 35. See as to unregistered deeds of partition in Madras, Act II of 1884.

(*s*) Narada, xiii. § 36—43; Mitakshara, ii. 12; Daya Bhaga, xiv.; 3 Dig. 407—429; 2 W. MacN. 170, n. See *Hurish Chunder* v. *Mokhoda*, 17 Suth. 564. *Murari Vithoji* v. *Mukund Shivaji*, 15 Bom. 201; *Ram Lall* v. *Debi Dat*, 10 All. 490.

merely evidence, and not conclusive evidence, of the fact of partition. Partition is a new *status*, which can only arise where persons, who have hitherto lived in coparcenary, intend that their condition as coparceners shall cease. It is not sufficient that they should alter the mode of holding their property. They must alter, and intend to alter, their title to it. They must cease to become joint owners, and become separate owners (*t*). And as, on the one hand, the mere cesser of commensality and joint worship, the existence of separate transactions (*u*), the division of income (*v*), or the holding of land in separate portions (*w*), do not establish partition, unless such a condition was adopted with a view to partition (*x*); so, on the other hand, if the members of the family have once agreed to become separate in title, it is not necessary that they should proceed to a physical separation of the particular pieces of their property. "If there be a conversion of the joint tenancy of an undivided family into a tenancy in common of the members of that undivided family, the undivided family becomes a divided family with reference to the property that is the subject of that agreement, and that is a separation in interest and in right, although not immediately followed by a *de facto* actual division of the subject-matter. This may, at any time, be claimed by virtue of the separate right" (*y*). And in provinces governed by the Mitakshara, if a brother so divided

Intention essential.

Apportionment unnecessary.

As to the effect of separate performance of religious rites, see Goldstücker, Administration of Hindu law, 53.

(*t*) Mere petitions or declarations of intention are not sufficient. *Mookta Keshee* v. *Oomabutty*, 14 Suth. 31; S. C. 8 B. L. R. 396, note.

(*u*) *Rewun Persad* v. *Radha Beeby*, 4 M. I. A 168; S. C. 7 Suth. (P. C.) 35; *Neelkisto Deb* v. *Beerchunder*, 12 M. I. A. 540; S. C. 3 B. L. R (P. C.) 13; S. C. 12 Suth. (P. C.) 21; *Anundee* v. *Khedoo*, 14 M. I. A. 412; S. C. 18 Suth. 69; *Chhabila* v. *Jadavbai*, 3 Bom. H. C. (O. C. J.) 87; *Narraina* v. *Veeraraghava*, Mad. Dec. of 1855, 230; *Garikapati* v. *Sudam*, Mad. Dec. of 1861, 101; *Kristnappa* v. *Ramasawmy*, 8 Mad. H. C. 25.

(*v*) *Sonatun Bysack* v. *Juggutsoondree*, 8 M. I. A. 66.

(*w*) *Runjeet* v. *Kooer*, 1 I. A. 9; *Ambika* v. *Sukhmani*, 1 All. 437.

(*x*) *Ram Kissen* v. *Sheonundun*, (P. C.) 23 Suth. 412.

(*y*) *Appovier* v. *Rama Subbaiyan*, 11 M. I. A. 75; S. C. 8 Suth. (P. C.) 1; *Suraneni* v. *Suraneni*, 13 M. I. A. 113; S. C. 12 Suth. (P. C.) 40; *Doorga Pershad* v. *Mt. Kundun*, 1 I. A. 55; S. C. 13 B. L. R. 235; S. C. 21 Suth. 214; *Babaji* v. *Kashibai*, 4 Bom. 157; *Ashabai* v. *Haji Tyeb*, 9 Bom. 111; *Tej Protap* v. *Champakalle*, 12 Cal. 96; *Adi Deo* v. *Dukharan*, 5 All. 532; *Anant Balacharya* v. *Damodhar Makund*, 13 Bom. 25.

should die before actual separation of the property, his widow would succeed to his share (*z*). On the same principle a decree for a partition dissolves the joint tenure from its date; and it does so equally, although the suit was not in terms a suit for partition, provided the relief given is inconsistent with the continuance of the joint interest (*a*). And any arrangement by which one member of the family abandons his rights to a share amounts to a partition in respect to the property so abandoned, even though he takes no specific portion in its place (*b*).

Rarity of reunion.

§ 455. Reunion among coparceners, though provided for by the text-books, is of very rare occurrence. Sir F. MacNaghten states that the Pandits of the Supreme Court of Bengal told him that no instance of the sort had ever fallen within their knowledge, nor had he himself ever met with a case (*c*). It is obvious that the same reasons which make partitions more frequent will tend to remove all motives for reunion.

Who may reunite.

The leading text on this subject is that of *Vrihaspati*. "He who being once separated dwells again through affection with his father, brother, or paternal uncle, is termed reunited." This text is interpreted literally by the Mitakshara, and the authorities of Southern India and Bengal, as excluding reunion with other relations, such as a nephew, cousin, or the like (*d*). The writers of the Mithila school, take these words, not as importing a limitation, but as offering an example. *Vachespati* says, "The first principle of

---

(*z*) *Gajapathi* v. *Gajapathi*, 13 M. I. A. 497; S. C. 6 B. L. R. 202; 14 Suth. (P. C.) 33.

(*a*) *Joy Narain* v. *Grish Chunder*, 5 I. A. 228; S. C. 4 Cal. 434; *Chidambaram* v. *Gouri*, 6 I. A. 177; S. C. 2 Mad. 83. The Bombay High Court holds that a decree for partition does not operate as a severance so long as it remains under appeal. *Sakharam* v. *Hari Krishna*, 6 Bom. 113.

(*b*) *Balkrishna* v. *Savitribai*, 3 Bom. 54; *Periasami* v. *Periasami* 5 I. A. 61; S. C. 1 Mad. 312; but see *Appa Pillay* v. *Runga Pillay*, 6 Mad. 71, where a renunciation by one member of all his interests in the family property was held not to be a partition, and to be invalid as a contract.

(*c*) F. MacN. 107.

(*d*) Mitakshara, ii. 9, § 3; Smriti Chandrika, xii. § 1; Daya Bhaga, xii. § 3, 4; D. K. S. v. § 4.

reunion is the common consent of both the parties; and it may either be with the coheirs or with a stranger after the partition of wealth (*e*)." The Mayukha agrees with him so far as to hold that other persons besides those named by *Vrihaspati* may reunite; for instance, "a wife, a paternal grandfather, a brother's grandson, a paternal uncle's son, and the rest also." But it restricts the reunion to the persons who made the first partition (*f*). This view is followed in Bombay, where it has been held "that the meaning of the passage of *Vrihaspati* which is the foundation of the law, is, that the reunion must be made by the parties, or some of them, who made the separation. If any of their descendants think fit to unite, they may do so; but such a union is not a reunion in the sense of the Hindu law, and does not affect the inheritance" (*g*). No such limitation is to be found in any of the other early writers, who only mention reunion with reference to the law of inheritance. Dr. Mayr looks upon it as an innovation, which grew out of a feeling that it was unjust that a man, by reunion with distant relations, should disappoint the claims of those who would otherwise have succeeded to him, in the event of his dying without issue (*h*).

§ 456. As the presumption is in favour of union until a partition is made out, so after a partition the presumption would be against a reunion. To establish it, it is necessary to show, not only that the parties already divided lived or traded together, but that they did so with the intention of thereby altering their *status*, and of forming a joint estate with all its usual incidents (*i*). The circumstance that one of the dividing parties, being a minor, continued to live on in apparent union with his father, would not be conclusive, Evidence.

(*e*) Vivada Chintamani, 301; D. K. S. v. § 5.
(*f*) V. May., iv. 9 § 1.
(*g*) *Vishvanath* v. *Krishnaji*, 3 Bom. H. C. (A. C. J.) 69; *Lakshmibai* v. *Ganpat Moroba*, 4 Bom. H. C. (O. C. J.) 166.
(*h*) Mayr, 130.
(*i*) 3 Dig. 512; Smriti Chandrika, xii. § 2; *Prankishen* v. *Mothooramohun*, 10 M. I. A. 403; S. C. 4 Suth. (P. C.) 11; *Gopal* v. *Kenaram*, 7 Suth. 35; *Ram Huree* v. *Trihee Ram*, 7 B. L. R. 336; S. C. 15 Suth. 442.

or I should imagine, even *primâ facie* evidence of a reunion (*k*).

Its effect.

The effect of a reunion is simply to replace the re-uniting coparceners in the same position as they would have been in if no partition had taken place. But with regard to rights of inheritance, there seems to be some distinction between coparceners in a state of original union, and of reunion. These will be discussed hereafter (§ 542).

(*k*) *Kuta Bully* v. *Kuta Chudappa*, 2 Mad. H. C. 235.

CHAPTER XVI.

INHERITANCE.

Principles of Succession in Case of Males.

Inheritance assumes separate property.

§ 457. We have now reached that point in the development of Hindu law in which Inheritance, properly so called, becomes possible. So long as the joint family continued in its original purity, its property passed into the hands of successive owners, but no recipient was in any sense the heir of the previous possessor (§ 246). The Bengal law made considerable inroads upon this system by allowing the share of each member to pass to his own direct heirs or assignees, and in this manner even to pass out of the family (*a*). But the rule of survivorship still governed the devolution of the share where a coparcener left no near heirs, and determined its amount. When, however, property came to belong exclusively to its possessor, either as being his own self-acquisition, or in consequence of his having separated himself from all his coparceners, or having become the last of the coparcenary, then it passed to his heir properly so-called. It must always be remembered, that the law of Inheritance applies exclusively to property which was held in absolute severalty by its last male owner. His heir is the person who is entitled to the property, whether he takes it at once, or after the interposition of another estate. If the next heir to the property of a male is himself a male, then he becomes the head of the family, and holds the property either in severalty or in coparcenary (§ 244) as the case may be. At his death the devolution of the property is traced from him. But if the

(*a*) *Ante* § 433, 438.

property of a male descends to a female, she does not, except in Bombay, become a fresh stock of descent. At her death it passes not to her heirs, but to the heirs of the last male holder. And if that heir is also a female, at her death, it reverts again to the heir of the same male, until it ultimately falls upon a male who can himself become the starting point for a fresh line of inheritance (*b*).

Succession never in abeyance.

§ 458. The right of succession under Hindu law is a right which vests immediately on the death of the owner of the property (*c*). It cannot under any circumstances remain in abeyance in expectation of the birth of a preferable heir, not conceived at the time of the owner's death. A child who is in the mother's womb at the time of the death is, in contemplation of law, actually existing, and will, on his birth, devest the estate of any person with a title inferior to his own, who has taken in the meantime (*d*). So, under certain circumstances, will a son who is adopted after the death (*e*). But in no other case will an estate be devested by the subsequent birth of a person who would have been a preferable heir if he had been alive at the time of the death (*f*). And the rightful heir is the person who is himself the next of kin at that time. No one can claim through or under any other person who has not himself taken. Nor is he disentitled because his ancestor could not have claimed. For instance, under certain circumstances a daughter's son would be heir, and would transmit the whole estate to his issue. But if he died before his grandfather, his son would never take. So, again, a sister's son

(*b*) See this subject discussed, *post*, § 665, *et seq*.

(*c*) Retirement into a religious life, when absolute, amounts to civil death; 1 Stra. H. L. 185; 2 Dig. 525; V. Darp. 10. As to the presumption that death has taken place, see Act I of 1872, § 107, 108 [Evidence.]

(*d*) *Per curiam*, *Tagore* v. *Tagore*, 9 B. L. R. 397; S. C. 18 Suth. 359; *Lakhi* v. *Bhairab*, 5 S. D. 315 (369); *Beroguh* v. *Nubokissen*, Sev. 238.

(*e*) *Ante*, § 171—179.

(*f*) *Aulim* v. *Bejai*, 6 S. D. 224 (278); *Kesub* v. *Bishnopersaud*, S. D. of 1860, ii. 340; *Bamasoondury* v. *Anund*, 1 Suth. 353: *Kalidas* v. *Krishan*, 2 B. L. R (F. B.) 103. These cases must be taken, as overruling others which will be found at 2 W. MacN. 84, 98; *Mt. Solukhna* v. *Ramdolal*, 1 S. D. 324 (434); *Pran Nath* v. *Rajah Govind*, 5 S. D. 46 (50); *Sumbochunder* v. *Gunga*, 6 S. D. 234 (291), and note. See however *Krishna* v. *Sami*, 9 Mad. 64, *post*, § 555.

will inherit in certain events, though his mother would never inherit. And the son of a leper or a lunatic, or of a son who has been disinherited for some lawful cause, will inherit, though his father could not (*g*).

Principle of religious efficacy.

§ 459. The principle upon which one person succeeds to another is generally stated to depend on his capacity for benefiting that person by the offering of funeral oblations. As the Judicial Committee remarked in one case, "There is in the Hindu law so close a connection between their religion and their succession to property that the preferable right to perform the *Shradh* is commonly viewed as governing also the preferable right to succession of property; and as a general rule they would be expected to be found in union (*h*)." I have already (§ 9) suggested that this principle, while universally true in Bengal, is by no means such an infallible guide elsewhere. The question is not only most interesting as a matter of history, but most important as determining practical rights. I shall, therefore, proceed to examine the principles which determine the order of succession both under the Daya Bhaga and the Mitakshara. In this enquiry I shall reverse the usual order, and examine first the modern, or Bengal, system (*i*). When we have seen what is the logical result of the doctrine of religious efficacy, it will be easier to ascertain how far that doctrine can be applicable under a system where no such results are admitted.

(*g*) See *per Holloway*, J., *Chelikani* v. *Suraneni*, 6 Mad. H. C. 287, 288; *Balkrishna* v. *Savitribai*, 3 Bom. 54; and *post*, § 491, 520, 581, 555.

(*h*) *Soorendronath* v. *Mt. Heeramonee*, 12 M. I. A. 96; S. C. 1 B. L. R. (P. C.) 26; S. C. 10 Suth. (P. C.) 35; see too *per curiam*, *Katama Natchiar* v. *Rajah of Shivagunga*, 9 M. I. A. 610; S. C. 2 Suth. (P. C.) 31; *Neelkisto Deb* v. *Beerchunder*, 12 M. I. A. 541; S. C. 3 B. L. R. (P. C.) 13; S. C. 12 Suth. (P. C.) 21; *Tagore* v. *Tagore*, 9 B. L. R. 394; S. C. 18 Suth. 359.

(*i*) The whole doctrine of religious efficacy has been most elaborately discussed, especially by the late Mr. Justice *Dwarkanauth Mitter*, in some decisions of the Bengal High Court, to which I shall frequently refer. *Amrita* v. *Lakhinarayan*, 2 B. L. R. (F. B.) 28; S. C. *sub nomine Omrit* v. *Luckhee Narain*, 10 Suth. (F. B.) 76; *Guru* v. *Anand*, 5 B. L. R. 15; S. C. 13 Suth. (F.B.) 49; *Gobind* v. *Mohesh*, 15 B. L. R. 35; S. C. 23 Suth. 117; see also V. N. Mandlik, Introduction, xxxvi. and p. 345. A very full account of the whole system of *Shradhs* will be found in Mr. Rajkumar Sarvadhikari's Lectures, pp. 73—128.

Funeral offerings.

§ 460. A Hindu may present three distinct sorts of offering to his deceased ancestors; either the entire funeral cake, which is called an undivided oblation, or the fragments of that cake which remain on his hands, and are wiped off it, which is called a divided oblation, or a mere libation of water. The entire cake is offered to the three immediate paternal ancestors, *i.e.*, father, grandfather, and great-grandfather. The wipings, or *lepa*, are offered to the three paternal ancestors next above those who receive the cake, *i.e.*, the persons who stands to him in the fourth, fifth, and sixth degree of remoteness. The libations of water are offered to paternal ancestors ranging seven degrees beyond those who receive the *lepa*, or fourteen degrees in all from the offerer; some say as far as the family name can be traced.

Sapinda Sakulya. Samanodaka.

The generic name of *sapinda* is sometimes applied to the offerer and his six immediate ancestors, as he and all of these are connected by the same cake, or *pinda*. But it is more usual to limit the term *sapinda* to the offerer and the three who received the entire cake (*k*). He is called the *sakulya* of those to whom he offers the fragments, and the *samanodaka* of those to whom he presents mere libations of water (*l*). Now, upon first reading this statement, one would suppose the theory of descent to be this: that a deceased owner was related in a primary and special degree to persons in the three grades of descent next below himself; in a secondary, and less special degree, to persons in the three grades below the former three; and in a still more remote manner to a third class of persons extending to the fourteenth degree of

(*k*) This narrower signification seems to be unknown to the Mitakshara, see *post*, § 469, note. This distinction is expressly stated by Baudhayana, (i. 5, 11, § 9, 10,) as follows: "The great-grandfather, the grandfather, the father, oneself, the uterine brothers, the son by a wife of equal rank, the grandson and the great-grandson—these they call sapindas, but not the great-grandson's son—and amongst these a son and a son's son together with their father are sharers of an undivided oblation. The sharers of divided oblations they call Sakulyas." Raghunandana after explaining this passage, says, that "this relationship of Sapinda (extending no further than the fourth degree) as well as that of Sakulyas, is propounded relatively to inheritance. But relatively to mourning, marriage, and the like, those too that partake of the remnants of oblations are denominated Sapindas," xi. 8.

(*l*) Manu. iii. § 122—125, 215, 216; v. § 60; ix § 186, 187; Baudhayana, i. 5, § 1; Daya Bhaga, xi. 1. § 37—42; Viramit., p. 154, § 11; Colebrooke, Essays (ed. 1858), 90, 101—117.

descent. But the actual theory is much more complicated. In the first place, sapindaship is mutual. He who receives offerings is the sapinda of those who present them to him, and he who presents offerings is the sapinda of the person who receives them. Therefore, every man stands as the centre of seven persons, six of whom are his sapindas, though not all the sapindas of each other. He is equally the sapinda of the three above, and of the three below him. Further, a deceased Hindu does not merely benefit by oblations which are offered to himself. He also shares in the benefit of oblations which are not offered to him at all, provided they are presented to persons to whom he was himself bound to offer them while he was alive. As Mr. Justice *Mitter* said, "If two Hindus are bound during the respective terms of their natural life to offer funeral oblations to a common ancestor or ancestors, either of them would be entitled after his death to participate in the oblations offered by the survivor to that ancestor or ancestors; and hence it is that the person who offers those oblations, the person to whom they are offered, and the person who participates in them, are recognized as sapindas of each other" (*m*). Theory relationship.

§ 461. The sapindas just described are all *agnates*, that is persons connected with each other by an unbroken line of male descent. But there are other sapindas who are *cognates*, or connected by the female line. The only definition of the cognate, or *bandhu* (if it may be called one), in the Mitakshara, is contained in ii. 5, § 3, last clause: "For *bhinna-gotra sapindas* are indicated by the term *bandhu*," or as Mr. Colebrooke translates it, "For kinsmen sprung from a different family, but connected by funeral oblations (*n*), are indicated by the term cognate." The defini- Agnates. Cognates. Bandhus.

(*m*) *Guru* v. *Anand*, 5 B. L. R. 39; S. C. 13 Suth. (F. B.) 49, citing Daya Bhaga, xi. 1, § 38. See too the Nirnaya Sindhu, cited *Amrita* v. *Lakhinarayan*, 2 B. L. R. (F. B.) 34; S. C. 10 Suth. (F. B.) 76, and *per Mitter*, J., in S. C. 2 B. L. R. (F. B.) 32; 3 Dig. 453.

(*n*) It will be seen hereafter that it is more than doubtful whether Vijnanesvara in using the term *sapinda* intended to refer to funeral oblations at all. See *post*, § 469—472.

tion given by Jimuta Vahana is fuller:—"Therefore a kinsman, whether sprung from the family of the deceased, though of different male descent, as his own daughter's son, or his father's daughter's son, or sprung from a different family, as his maternal uncle or the like, being allied by a common funeral cake, on account of their presenting, offerings to three ancestors in the paternal and the maternal family of the deceased owner, is a sapinda" (*o*). Now, the mode in which cognates come to be connected with the agnates by funeral oblations is by means of that ceremony which is called the *Parvana Shradh*, and which is one of the principal of the series of offerings to the dead. "This ceremony consists in the presentation of a certain number of oblations, namely, one to each of the first three ancestors in the paternal line and maternal lines respectively; or, in other words, to the father, the grandfather, and the great-grandfather in the one line, and the maternal grandfather, the maternal great-grandfather, and the maternal great-great-grandfather in the other" (*p*). This would give one explanation of the texts which state that sapindaship does not extend on the side of the father beyond the seventh degree, and on the mother's side beyond the fifth (*q*). The sapinda who offers a cake as *bandhu* is the fifth in descent from the most distant maternal ancestor to whom he offers it. Now, on the principle of participation already stated, any bandhu who offers a cake to his maternal ancestors will be the sapinda, not only of those ancestors, but of all other persons whose duty it was to offer cakes to the same ancestors. But the maternal ancestors of A. may be the paternal or maternal ancestors of B., and in this manner A. will be the

Parvana Shradh.

(*o*) D. Bh. xi. 6, § 19; translated by Mr. J. Mitter, 6 Cal. 268.

(*p*) Per Mr. Justice *Mitter*, *Guru* v. *Anand*, 5 B. L. R. 40; S. C. 13 Suth. (F. B.) 49; Daya Bhaga, xi. 6. § 13, 19; Manu, ix. § 182; 3 Dig. 165, note by Colebrooke. It will be observed that the paternal ancestors are counted inclusive of the father; the maternal exclusive of the mother. See too Dattaka Mimamsa, iv. § 72, note by Sutherland.

(*q*) Vrihat Manu, cited Dattaka Mimamsa, vi. § 9; Gautama, *ib.* § 11; Yajnavalkya, i. § 53. It is more probable, however, that the original texts simply stated an arbitrary rule as to the degree of affinity which excluded intermarriage. See *post*, § 469.

bandhu, or *bhinna-gotra sapinda* of B., both being under an obligation to offer to the same persons (r).

Relationship to females.

Females.

§ 462. *Lastly.*—Although here I am anticipating the next chapter, a man is the sapinda of his mother, grandmother, and great-grandmother for a double reason; *first*, because they become part of the body of their respective husbands, and *next*, because the cakes which are offered to a man's male ancestors are also shared in by their respective wives (s). And so the wife is the sapinda of her husband; both as being the surviving half of his body, and because in the absence of male issue she performs the funeral obsequies

Tables of descent.

Hence the table of descents will stand as follows:—

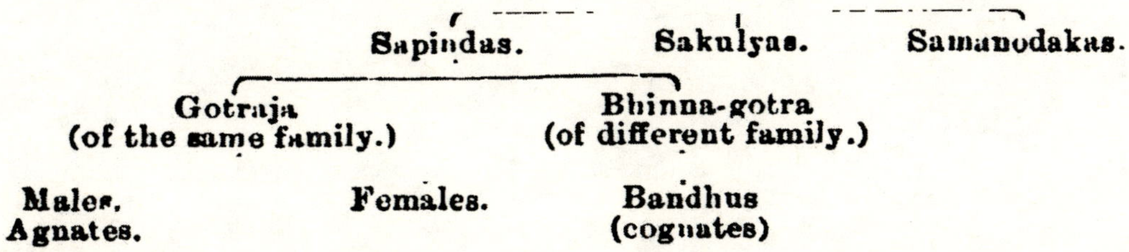

Gotraja Sapindas.

§ 463. This will all be made clearer by reference to the accompanying diagrams. The OWNER, who is called in the Daya Bhaga the middlemost of seven, is the *sapinda* of his

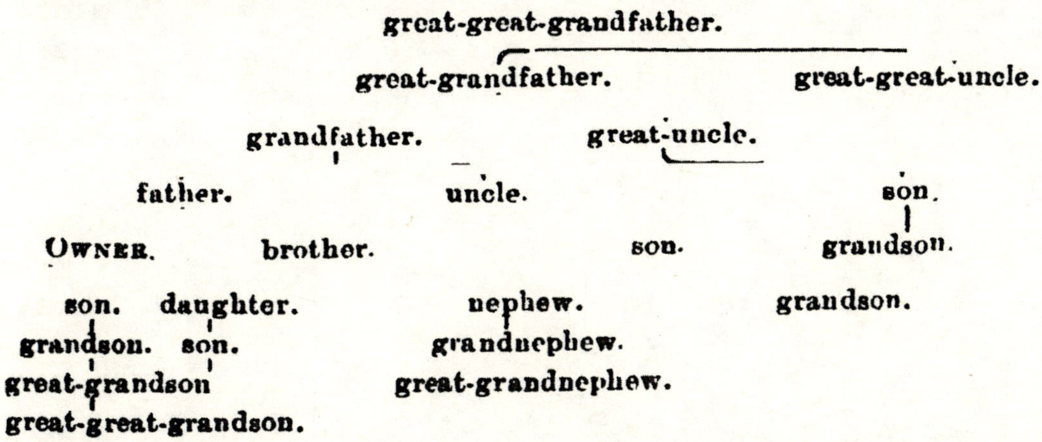

own son, grandson, and great-grandson, because they offer the

(r) For instance the daughter's son of A's grandson is a *bhinna-gotra sapinda* of the great-great-grandson of the same A. *Manik Chand* v. *Jagat Sattani*, 17 Cal. 518.

(s) Manu, ix. § 45; Daya Bhaga, xi. 6, § 3; 3 Dig. 519, 598, 625; Colebrooke, Essays, 116; *Lallubhai* v. *Mankuvarbai*, 2 Bom. 420, 440, 445.

(t) Mitakshara, ii. 1, § 5, 6; Vivada Chintamani, 290.

NO. I.
BANDHUS EX PARTE PATERNÂ.

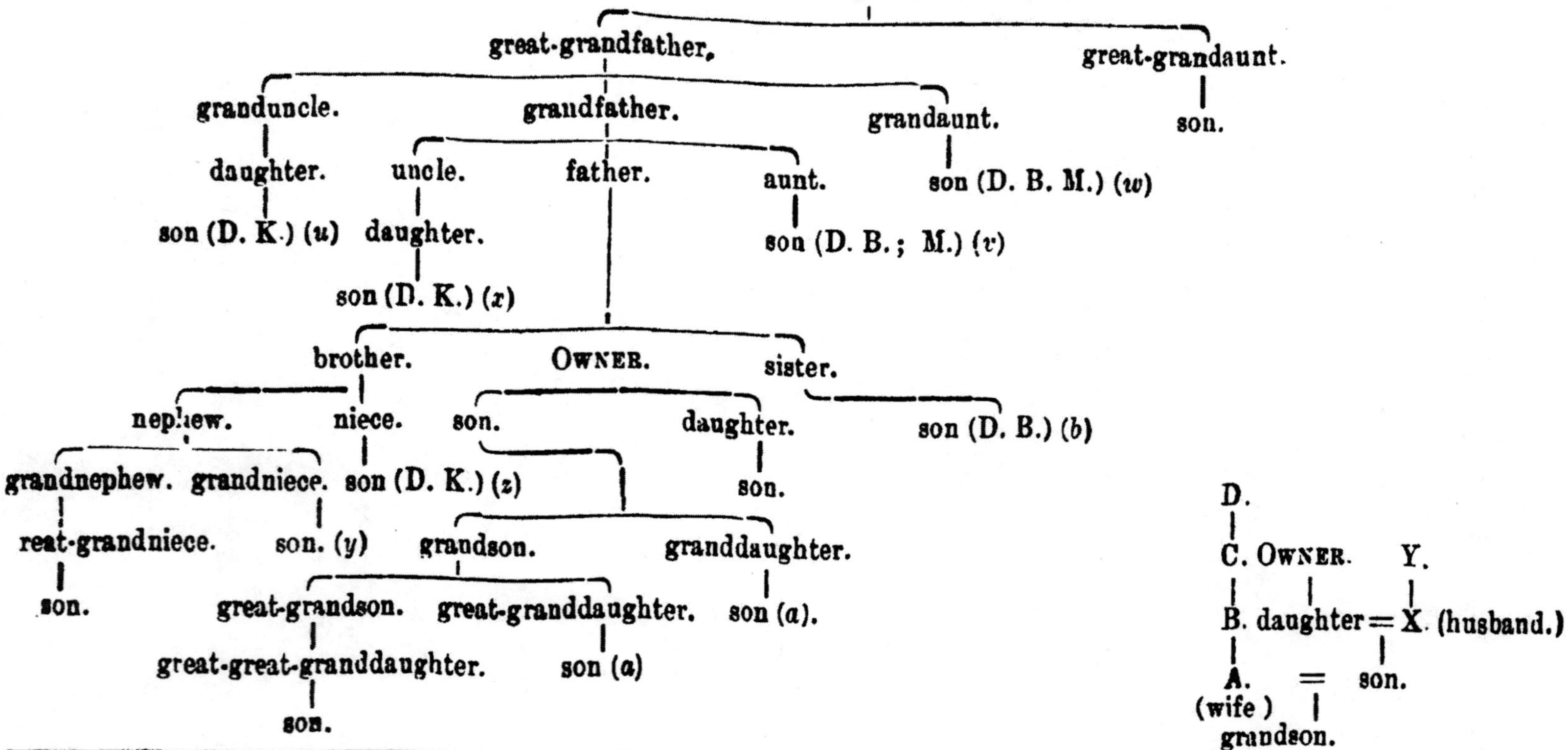

(u) *Kissen* v. *Javallah*, 3 Mad. H. C. 346; *post*, § 534.
(v) 2 W. MacM. 93; W. & B. 204; *Bamasoondree* v. *Rajkrishto*, Sev. 742.
(w) *Gosaien* v. *Mt. Kishenmunnee*, 6 S. D. 77 (90).
(x) *Guru* v. *Anand*, 5 B. L. R. 15; S. C. 13 Suth. (F. B.) 49.
(y) 3 Dig. 530; *Gopal Chunder* v. *Haridas*, 11 Cal. 343; *Prannath* v. *Surrut*, 8 Cal. 460; S. C. 10 C. L. R. 484.
(z) *Doorga Bibee* v. *Janak*, 10 B. L R. 341; S. C. 18 Suth. 331; *Gobind* v. *Mohesh*, 15 B. L. R. 35; S. C. 23 Suth. 117; *Digamber* v. *Moti Lal*, 9 Cal. 563; *Huri Das Bundopadhya* v. *Bama Churn*, 15 Cal. 780.
(a) 3. Dig. 530.
(b) See *post*, § 531, takes before mother's sister's son. *Gunesh* v. *Nil Komul*, 22 Suth. 264.

cake to him, and they are his *sapindas*, as he receives it from them. But his great-great-grandson is only his *sakulya*. So also he is the *sapinda* of his own father, grandfather, and great-grandfather, because he offers the cake to them, and they are his *sapindas*, because they receive it from him. But he and his great-great-grandfather are only *sakulyas* to each other. Next as regards collaterals. The owner receives no cake from his own brother, but he participates in the benefit of the cakes which the brother offers to his own three direct ancestors, who are also the three ancestors to whom the owner is bound to make offerings. So the nephew offers cake to his own three ancestors, two of whom are the father and grandfather of the owner; and the grandnephew to his three ancestors, one of whom is the father of the owner. All of these, therefore, are the *sapindas* of the owner, though they vary in religious efficacy in the ratio of three, two, and one. But the highest ancestor to whom the great-grandnephew offers cakes is the brother of the owner. He is therefore not a *sapinda*; but he is a *sakulya*, because he presents divided offerings to the owner's three immediate ancestors. Similarly the owner's uncle and great-uncle present cakes to two and one respectively of the ancestors to whom the owner is bound to present them. They are therefore his *sapindas*. But the great-great-uncle is not a sapinda, since he is himself the son of a *sakulya*, and presents cakes to persons all of whom stand in the relation of *sakulya* to the owner. Sapindas and sakulyas.

§ 464. We now come to the *bandhus*, whose relationship is more complicated. There are two classes of bandhus referred to by the Bengal writers, and who alone can be brought within the doctrine of religious efficacy (*c*); those *ex parte paternâ* and *ex parte maternâ*. The first class will be found in the accompanying pedigree. Their sapindaship arises from the fact that they offer cakes to their maternal ancestors, who are also the paternal ancestors of the owner. Bandhus.

(c) Daya Bhaga, xi. 6, § 8—20; D. K. S. i. 10, § 1—20. As to other bandhus, see *post*, § 472.

For instance, the sister's son, in addition to the oblations which he presents to his own father, &c., presents oblations to the three ancestors of his own mother, who are also the three ancestors of the owner. The aunt's son presents them to two, and the grandaunt's son to one of his three ancestors. These persons, therefore, all come within the definition of *bandhus*, as being persons of a different family, connected by funeral oblations, though with different degrees of religious merit. But the great-grandaunt's son is not a *bandhu*, because the ancestors to whom he presents cakes are the *sakulyas* only of the owner. Following out the same principle, it will be seen that the grandsons by the female line of the uncle and the granduncle, of the brother and the nephew, are all *bandhus*. But the son of the grandnephew's daughter is not a *bandhu*. Similarly in the descending line, the sons of the owner's daughter, granddaughter, and great-granddaughter are *bandhus*, as they all present cakes to himself. But the offerings made by the son of his great-great-granddaughter do not reach as far as the owner, and therefore he is not a *bandhu*. It will be observed that the above pedigree always stops with the son of the female relation. The reason of this will be seen on referring to the smaller pedigree in the same sheet. The grandson of the owner's daughter will present cakes to his own paternal ancestors, that is to the owner's grandson, and to X. and Y., and also to his own maternal ancestors, that is to B., C., and D. But none of these are persons to whom the owner is bound to make oblations, and five of them are complete strangers to him. And so, of course, it is in every other similar case.

Bandhus ex parte paternâ

Bandhus ex parte maternâ.

§ 465. The *bandhus ex parte maternâ* will be found in the next pedigree. They differ from those just described in being connected with the owner through his maternal ancestors instead of his paternal ancestors. Those on the left side of the pedigree are the agnates of these maternal ancestors, while those on the right side are cognates, and are, therefore, removed from the owner by a double descent in

NO. II.

BANDHUS EX PARTE MATERNÂ.

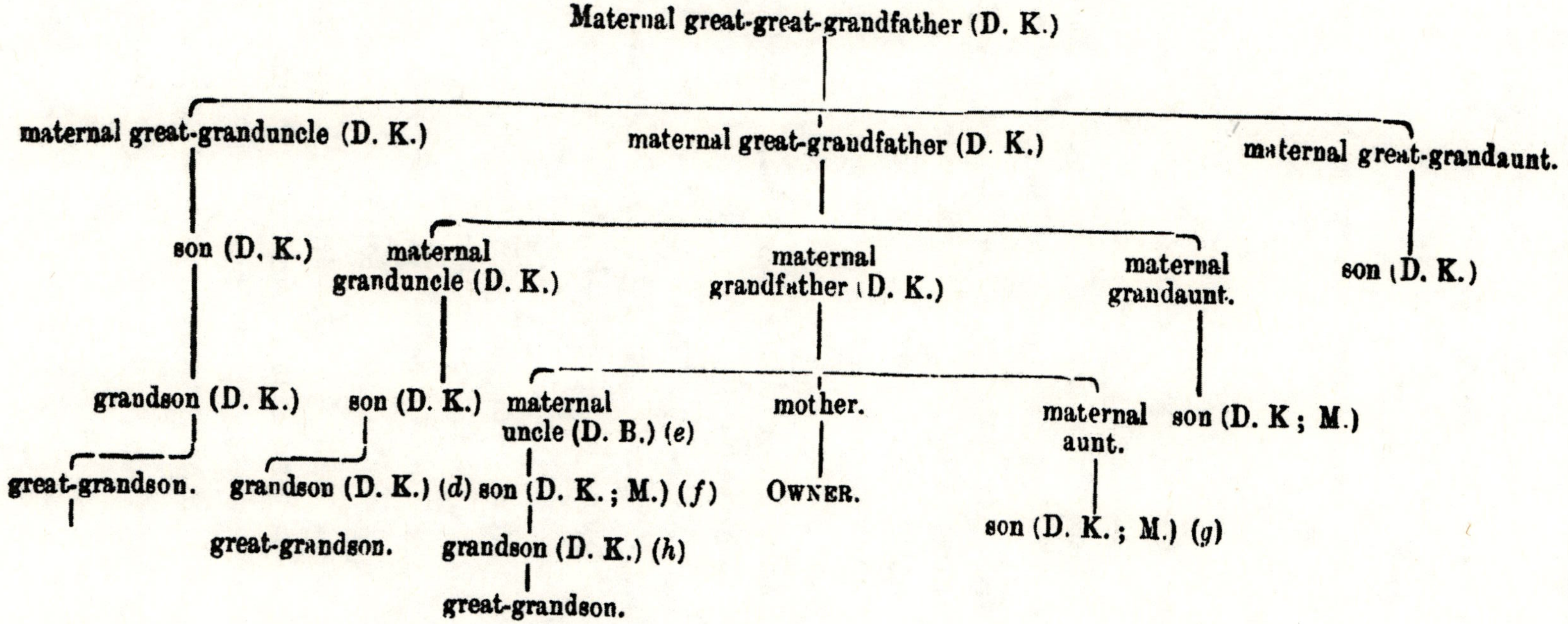

(d) *Brajakishor* v. *Radha Govind*, 3 B. L. R. (A. C. J.) 435; S. C. 12 Suth. 339.

(e) *Gridhari* v. *Bengal Government*, 12 M. I. A. 448; S. C. 1 B. L. R. (P. C.) 44; S. C. 10 Suth. (P. C.) 32. He succeeds before the maternal aunt's son. *Mohandas* v. *Krishnabai*, 5 Bom. 597.

(f) *Roopchurn* v. *Anund*, 2 S. D. 35 (45); *Srimuty Dibeah* v. *Rany Koond*, 4 M. I. A. 292; S. C. 7 Suth. (P. C) 44; *Kassee* v. *Goluckchunder*, S. D. of 1848, 28.

(g) *Deyanath* v. *Muthoor*, 6 S. D. 27 (30); *Rutcheputty* v. *Rajunder*, 2 M. I. A. 132.

(h) *Ratna Subbu* v. *Ponnappa Chetit*, 5 Mad. 69.

the female line. The explanations already given will render it unnecessary to go through the table in detail. The owner is bound to offer cakes to his own maternal grandfather, great-grandfather, and great-great-grandfather, and therefore the other persons who make similar offerings to them, or to any of them, are his *bandhus*. All the males in the table except the great-grandsons on the left are such *bandhus*.

Enumeration is not exhaustive.

§ 466. The letters D. B., D. K. and M., attached to the steps in the above pedigrees, point out which of the persons there described are specifically enumerated by the Daya Bhaga, Daya-krahma-sangraha and Mitakshara. It will be observed that very few are set out by *Vijnanesvara*; that many unnoticed by him are named by the Daya Bhaga, and still more which are omitted by the Daya Bhaga are supplied by the Daya-krahma-sangraha; but that in table No. I many are wholly passed over who yet come within the definition of *bandhu*, and are even more nearly related than those who are expressly mentioned. The daughter's son is really only a *bandhu*, though he is always placed in a distinct category on grounds which will be stated hereafter (§ 518). But the sons of the granddaughter and great-granddaughter offer oblations direct to the owner himself, which no other *bandhu* does except the daughter's son. Obviously, therefore, they should rank before *bandhus* who only offer to the owner's ancestors. So the son of the grandniece is omitted, though he stands in exactly the same relation to the son of the niece, who is included, as the grandnephew does to the nephew (*i*). At one time it was supposed that no *bandhu* could be recognized who was not expressly named in the authorities which governed each province. On this ground the sister's son (*k*), and the granduncle's daughter's son were rejected in Madras (*l*); and the sons of the grand-

(*i*) His title has been expressly affirmed, *Kashee Mohun* v. *Raj Gobind*, 24 Suth. 229.
(*k*) See *post*, § 531.
(*l*) *Kissen* v. *Javallah*, 3 Mad. H. C. 346.

daughter and great-granddaughter (*m*), and the son of the uncle's daughter in Bengal (*n*). But it is now settled, after an unusually full discussion of the whole subject, that the examples given in the different commentaries are illustrative and not exhaustive, (*o*) and that if any one comes within the definition of a *bandhu*, he is entitled to succeed as such, although he is nowhere specifically named (*p*).

§ 467. I have now pointed out the manner in which the principle of religious efficacy applies to the different male heirs who are recognized by Bengal law. As to the grounds upon which one heir is preferred to another, the following rules may be laid down.

Principles of precedence.

1. Each class of heirs taken before, and excludes the whole of, the succeeding class. "The *sapindas* are allowed to come in before the *sakulyas*, because undivided oblations are considered to be of higher spiritual value than divided ones; and the *sakulyas* are in their turn preferred to the *samanodakas*, because divided oblations are considered to be more valuable than libations of water" (*q*).

2. The offering of a cake to any individual constitutes a superior claim to the acceptance of a cake from him, or the participation in cakes offered by him. On this ground the male issue, widow, and daughter's son rank above the ascendants, or the brothers who offer exactly the same number of cakes as the deceased (*r*).

(*m*) 2 W. MacN. 81; *contra*, 3 Dig. 530.

(*n*) *Gobindo* v. *Woomesh* Suth. Sp. No. 176, overruled by *Guru* v. *Anand* 5 B. L. R. 15; S. C. 13 Suth. (F. B.) 49.

(*o*) Apararka says that *bandhus* are the sons of the father's sister, mother's sister, and maternal uncle's son, and similar kinsmen. Sarvadhikari, 428.

(*p*) *Gridhari* v. *Bengal Government*, 12 M. I. A. 448; S. C. 1 B. L. R. (P. C.) 44; S. C. 10 Suth. (P. C.) 32; *Amrita* v. *Lakhinarayan*, 2 B. L. R. (F. B.) 28; S. C. 10 Suth. (F. B.) 76; *Guru* v. *Anand*, 5 B. L. R. 15; S. C. 13 Suth. (F. B.) 49; *Ratna Subbu* v. *Ponnappa*, 5 Mad. 69.

(*q*) *Per Mitter*, J., *Guru* v. *Anand*, 5 B. L. R. 38; S. C. 13 Suth. (F. B.) 49; approved, *Gobind* v. *Mohesh*, 15 B. L. R. 47; S. C. 23 Suth. 117; *Degumber* v. *Moti Lal*, 9 Cal. 563.

(*r*) 3 Dig. 499, 503; Daya Bhaga, xi. 1, § 32—40, 43; xi. 2, § 1, 2; xi. 5, § 3.

3. Those who offer oblations to both paternal and maternal ancestors are superior to those who offer only to the paternal. Hence the preference of the whole to the half-blood (*s*).

4. "Those who are competent to offer funeral cakes to the paternal ancestors of the deceased proprietor, are invariably preferred to those who are competent to offer such cakes to his maternal ancestors only; and the reason assigned for the distinction is, that the first kind of cakes are of superior religious efficacy in comparison to the second." And this rule extends so far as to give a preference to one who offers a smaller number of the superior oblations over one who offers a larger number of the inferior sort (*t*).

5. "Similarly, those who offer larger numbers of cakes of a particular description are invariably preferred to those who offer a less number of cakes of the same description; and where the number of such cakes is equal, those that are offered to nearer ancestors are always preferred to those offered to more distant ones."

"The same remarks are equally applicable to the *sakulyas* and *samanodakas*" (*u*).

Cognates not postponed to Agnates

The result of these rules in Bengal is, that not only do all the *bandhus* come in before any of the *sakulyas* or *samanodakas*, but that the *bandhus* themselves are sifted in and out among the agnates, heirs in the female line frequently taking before very near sapindas in the direct male line, on the principle of superior religious efficacy (*v*). In

(*s*) 3 Dig. 480, 519; Daga Bhaga, xi. 5, § 12.

(*t*) *Per Mitter*, J., 5 B. L. R. 89; *supra* note (*q*); *Gobind* v. *Mohesh*, 15 B. L. R. 35; S. C. 23 Suth. 117. See this case, *post*, § 587.

(*u*) *Per Mitter*, J., 5 B. L. R. 39; approved, 15 B. L. R. 47; *ante*, note (*q*); *Khettur* v. *Poorno*, 15 Suth. 482. A person who offers one oblation to the father of the deceased owner is preferred to another who offers two oblations to the grandfather and great-grandfather. Hence the grandnephew ranks before the paternal uncle, and the nephew's daughter's son before the uncle's daughter's son. Daya Bhaga, xi. 6, § 5, 6; *Prannath* v. *Surrut*, 8 Cal. 460.

(*v*) Daya Bhaga, xi. 6; D. K. S. i. 10; 3 Dig. 528, 529. See *post*, § 536.

fact, if the test of religious efficacy is once admitted, no other arrangement would be logically possible.

Religious principle not the rule of the Mitakshara.

§ 468. When we go a stage back to the Mitakshara, and still more to the actual usage of those districts where Brahmanical influence was less felt, the whole doctrine of religious efficacy seems to disappear. In the chapters which treat of succession, the Daya Bhaga and the Daya-Krahma-Sangraha appeal to that doctrine at every step, testing the claims of rival heirs by the numbers and nature of their respective offerings. The Mitakshara never once alludes to such a test. No doubt it refers to the distinction between *sapindas* and *samanodakas*, and states that the former succeed before the latter, and that the former offer the funeral cake, while the latter offer libations of water only. But this distinction is stated, not as evidencing different degrees of religious merit, but as marking different degrees of propinquity. The claims of rival heirs are determined by the latter test, not by the former. Persons who confer high religious benefits are postponed to persons who confer hardly any. Persons who confer none whatever are admitted as heirs, for no other reason than that of affinity.

Meaning of 'sapinda.'

§ 469. Throughout the Mitakshara Mr. Colebrooke invariably translates the word *sapinda* by the phrase "connected by funeral oblations," and this gives the appearance of a continued reference by the author to religious rites. But there is every reason to suppose that, in using the word *sapinda*, *Vijnanesvara* was thinking of propinquity, and not of religious offerings. In another part of his work, which has not been translated (*w*), where he is commenting on the text of *Yajnavalkya* (i. § 5) which forbids a man to marry his *sapinda*, he defines sapindaship solely as a matter of affinity, without any reference to the capacity to offer

(*w*) It will be found in W. & B. 120. It is also referred to by Mr. Justice *Mitter*, *Amrita* v. *Lakhinarayan*, 2 B. L. R. (F. B.) 33; S. C. 10 Suth. (F. B.) 76; and by Mr. Justice *West Vijiarangam* v. *Lakshuman*, 8 Bom. H. C. (O. C. J.) 262, and by *Westropp*, C. J., in *Lallubhai* v. *Mankuvarbai*, 2 Bom. 428.

gious oblations, and so as to include cases where no such capacity exists. He says, "*sapinda* relationship arises between two people through their being connected by particles of the one body." Hence he states that a man is the sapinda of his paternal and maternal ancestors, and his paternal and maternal uncles and aunts. "So also the wife and the husband, because they together beget one body. In like manner brothers' wives are sapinda relations to each other, because they produce one body (the son) with those who have sprung from one body." He then observes that this principle, if carried to its extreme limits, would make the whole world akin, and proceeds to comment on the text of *Yajnavalkya* (*x*) as follows:—

Sapinda denotes affinity.

"On the mother's side, in the mother's line, after the fifth, on the father's side, in the father's line, after the seventh (ancestor), (*y*) the *sapinda* relationship ceases, and therefore the word *sapinda*, which on account of its etymological import (connected by having in common particles of one body) (*z*), would apply to all men, is restricted in its signification; and thus the six ascendants, beginning with the father, and the six descendants, beginning with the son, and one's-self (counted) as the seventh (in each case), are *sapinda* relations. In case of a division of the line also, one ought to count up to the seventh (ancestor), including him with whom the division begins (*e.g.*, two collaterals, A. and B., are sapindas, if the common ancestor is not further removed from either of them than six degrees), and thus must the counting of the sapinda relationship be made in every case" (*a*).

Yajnavalkya, i. § 52, 53, "A man should marry a wife who is not his *sapinda*, one who is further removed from him than five degrees on the side of the mother, and seven degrees on the side of the father."

(*y*) The narrow signification of *Sapinda* as limited to those who are connected by offerings of the entire cake, and therefore extending only to three degrees on either side of the owner, seems to be unknown to the Mitakshara.

(*z*) *Sapinda* is compounded from *sa* for *samana*, like, equal or the same, and *pinda*, ball or lump. As applied to funeral rites the *pinda* is the ball or lump into which the funeral cake was made up. I am informed by very high Sanskrit authorities that the application of the word *sapinda* in the text is peculiar to *Vijnanesvara*.

(*a*) It is no doubt in reference to this passage that the Samskara Mayukha,

§ 470. It will be remarked that in this passage the author does not notice the distinction between those who offer undivided oblations, and those who offered divided oblations. Nor does he in the corresponding part of his treatise on inheritance (*b*), where he divides the *Gotraja*, or Gentiles, into two classes only—those connected by funeral oblations of food, extending to seven degrees, and those connected by libations of water, extending to the fourteenth degree, or even further.

Includes sakulyas.

Theory of relationship according to the Mitakshara.

From this passage Messrs. West and Bühler draw the conclusions that, "1, *Vijnanesvara* supposes the *sapinda* relationship to be based, not on the presentation of funeral oblations, but on descent from a common ancestor, and, in the case of females, also on marriage with descendants from a common ancestor; 2, That all blood-relations within six degrees, together with the wives of the males amongst them, are *sapinda* relations to each other (*c*)." And with reference to his definition of *bandhu* (Mitakshara, ii. 5, § 3), they say, "It would seem that *Vijnanesvara* interpreted *Yajnavalkya's* term *bandhu* as meaning relations, within the sixth degree who belong to a different family;" or at least that all such persons who come under the term *sapinda*, according to the definition given in the *Acharakanda*, are included in the term *bandhu* (*d*).

§ 471. This preference of consanguinity, or family relationship, to efficacy of religious offerings, is further shown by the rule laid down in the Mitakshara, and the works which follow its authority, according to which the *bandhus*, or relations through a female, never take until the direct male line, down to and including the last *samanodaka*, has been

Agnates exclude cognates.

---

in a passage cited in *Lallubhai* v. *Mankuvarbai*, 2 Bom. 425, says "Hence *Vijnanesvara* and others abandoned the theory of connexion through the rice-ball offering, and accepted the theory of transmission of constituent atoms."

(*b*) Mitakshara, ii. 5.

(*c*) W. & B. 123. See too Dattaka Mimamsa, vi. § 10, 32, where the relation of *sapinda* is said to rest on two grounds, consanguinity and the offering of funeral oblations.

(*d*) W. & B. 136, 489.

exhausted (*e*). A stronger instance than this could not be imagined, since, as has been already shown, many of the *bandhus* are not only *sapindas,* but very close *sapindas,* while the fourteenth from a common ancestor is scarcely a relation at all, and certainly possesses religious efficacy of the most attenuated character. And so, whether the Mitakshara agrees with the Daya Bhaga, or disagrees with it, the reasons offered always show that the governing idea in the author's mind was that propinquity, not religious merit, was the test of heirship. For instance, *Jimuta Vahana* prefers the father to the mother, because he presents two oblations in which the deceased son participates, while the mother presents none (*f*). *Vijnanesvara* takes exactly the opposite view, on the ground that, "since her propinquity is greatest, it is fit that she should take the estate in the first instance, conformably with the text 'to the nearest sapinda the inheritance next belongs.'" And he goes on to say, "Nor is the claim in virtue of propinquity restricted to *sapindas,* but, on the contrary, it appears from this very text that the rule of propinquity is effectual, without any exception, in the case of *samanodakas,* as well as other relatives, when they appear to have a claim to the succession" (*g*). So he agrees with *Jimuta Vahana* in preferring the whole blood, among brothers, to the half. But he rests his preference on the same text "to the nearest *sapinda,* &c.," saying, very truly, that "those of the half-blood are

Propinquity, not offerings, the test of heirship.

Narada, xiii. § 51; Mitakshara. ii. 5 and 6; Vivada Chintamani, 297—299; V. May., iv. 8, § 22; *Rutcheputty* v. *Rajunder*. 2 M. I A. 132; *Srimuti Dibeah* v. *Rany Koond*, 4 M. I. A 292; S. C. 7 Suth. (P. C.) 44; *Bhyah Ram* v. *Bhyah Ugur*, 13 M. I. A. 373; S. C. 14 Suth. (P. C.) 1; *Thakoor Jeebnath* v. *Court of Wards*, 2 I. A 163; S. C. 23 Suth. 409: *Naraini Kuar* v. *Chandi Din*, 9 All. 467. See also cases in the N. W. P., cited in the last case, in the Court below, 5 B. L. R. 449; S. C. 14 Suth. 117. Mr. Rajkumar Sarvadhikari, (p. 865,) explains the preference given by the Mitakshara to agnates over cognates, as arising from the principle of religious efficacy, the oblations given by agnate kinsmen being of superior efficacy to those offered by cognate kinsmen This of course is so, when the offerings of near agnates are contrasted with those of near cognates. It certainly is not so where the offerings of near cognates are contrasted with those of distant agnates, unless some doctrine of religious efficacy is assumed completely different from that elaborated by the Bengal lawyers. Nor is this the principle which determines the preference of agnates to cognates in the Punjab, or among the Jains where the theory of religious efficacy is unknown (§ 475).

(*f*) Daya Bhaga, xi. 3, § 3.

(*g*) Mitakshara, ii. 3, § 3, 4.

remote through the difference of mothers;" while the Daya Bhaga grounds it on the religious principle, that the brother of the whole-blood offers twice as many oblations in which the deceased participates, as the brother of the half-blood (*h*). So the right of a daughter to succeed, is rested by *Jimuta Vahana* upon the funeral oblations which may be hoped for from her son, and the exclusion of widowed, or barren, or sonless daughters, is the natural result (*i*). The Mitakshara follows *Vrihaspati* in basing her claim upon simple consanguinity. "As a son, so does the daughter of a man proceed from his several limbs. How then should any other person take her father's wealth?" And he excludes neither the widowed nor the barren daughter, but prefers one to another, according as she is unmarried or married, poor or rich; that is, according as she has the best natural claim to be provided for (*k*).

Bandhus.

§ 472. When we come to the enumeration of *bandhus*, in Mitakshara, ii. 6, it appears pretty clear that they do not depend upon any such principle of community in religious offerings, as is supposed to be laid down in the definition at Mitakshara, ii. 5, § 3 (*l*). It is said, "Cognates are of three kinds; related to the person himself, to his father, or to his mother, as is declared by the following text:—'The sons of his own father's sister, the sons of his own mother's sister, and the sons of his maternal uncle, must be considered as his own cognate kindred. The sons of his father's paternal aunt, the sons of his father's maternal aunt, and the sons of his father's maternal uncle, must be deemed his father's cognate kindred. The sons of his mother's paternal aunt, the sons of his mother's maternal aunt, and the sons of his mother's maternal uncles, must be reckoned his mother's cognate kindred (*m*). Here, by reason of near affinity, the

Bandhus do not depend on religious merit.

(*h*) Mitakshara, ii. 4, § 5; Daya Bhaga, xi. 5, § 12.
(*i*) Daya Bhaga, xi. 2, § 1—3, 17.
(*k*) Mitakshara, ii. 2, § 2—4; Viramit., p. 176, § 1.
(*l*) See *ante*, § 461, 470.
(*m*) This is the correct translation of the text. See 2 W. MacN. 96; Smriti Chandrika, xi. 5, § 14; *Amrita* v. *Lakhinarayan*, 2 B. L. R. (F. B.) 37; S. C.

cognate kindred of the deceased himself are his successors in the first instance; on failure of them, his father's cognate kindred, or, if there be none, his mother's cognate kindred. This must be understood to be the order of succession here intended." Now, if we look back to the pedigrees already given (§ 464, 465), we shall find that the sons of the father's sister, and the sons of the father's paternal aunt, come in among the *bandhus ex parte paternâ* of the Bengal scheme, and are indicated by the letter M. So, the sons of his mother's sister, and of his maternal uncle, and of his mother's paternal aunt, come in among the *bandhus ex parte maternâ* and are similarly indicated. The others named by the Mitakshara do not occur in those lists, and are nowhere referred to by any Bengal authority. The accompanying diagrams will show that they could not pos-

Cognates through father's mother.

A.

X.		paternal grandmother.	father's maternal aunt.	father's maternal uncle.
mother	=	father	son (M.)	son (M.)
		OWNER.		

sibly be brought within any system which depends on religious merit (*n*). Here it will be seen that the sons of the father's maternal aunt, and of the father's maternal uncle, that is the father's cognate kindred on his mother's side, are only connected with the owner through his paternal grandmother. Now, neither of these persons presents

10 Suth. (F. B.) 76. In Mr. Colebrooke's translation the first clause obviously is incorrectly given.

(*n*) Mr. Rajkumar Sarvadhikari says, in reference to this passage (p. 870) "We at once admit that the father's and the mother's bandhus" could not possibly be brought within any system which depends upon religious merits "accruing from parvana rites alone." But they could surely be brought within a system which lays down that "any benefit whatsoever is a sufficient title to inherit." He then points to tables (p. 860) which show that these persons are competent to perform the *ekodishta* or individual rites of the deceased. But so are strangers, such as a pupil, a friend or the king; that is to say, any one who takes the inheritance is bound, and therefore entitled to perform the personal rites connected with the funeral ceremonies of the deceased. and extending to those held on the anniversary of his death (Raj Sarvadhikari, p. 84). The *bandhus* in question take the inheritance because they are near relations, and having taken it they perform these special rites. But when we come to the Bengal system of succession, which is really founded on the theory of religious benefits, these bandhus are excluded. So in Madras the grandson of a paternal

offerings to any one to whom the owner presents them. Their offerings are presented to A. and his ancestors. Those of the owner are presented to his father's line, and to his mother's line, that is, the line of X. (*o*). Consequently, their offerings are neither shared in by the owner, nor do they operate in discharge of any duty which he is bound to perform. Similarly, the sons of the mother's maternal uncle and aunt, that is the mother's cognate kindred, on

A.

X. = maternal grandmother. — mother's maternal uncle. — mother's maternal aunt.

Y. = mother. — son (M.) — son (M.).

OWNER.

Cognates through mother's mother.

her mother's side, are only connected with the owner through his maternal grandmother. The same observation as before applies to them. Their offerings are presented to A. and his line. Those of the owner are presented to the lines of Y. and X., that is, to his own male ancestors, and those of his mother. Here again there is no conceivable community of religious benefit. On the other hand, when we apply "the reason of near affinity," on which *Vijnanesvara* himself bases the heirship, the whole thing is as simple as possible. The first of the three classes contains the owner's first cousins; the second contains his father's first cousins, and the third contains his mother's first cousins. All of these are postponed to the *samanodakas*, because they are connected through a female, and are therefore members of a different family from that of the owner. But when they are admitted, they are brought in upon natural principles (*p*.) No other explanation can be required, except by those who persist in distorting the plain meaning of the Mitak-

great-aunt of the deceased inherits to him as a *bandhu*; *Sethurama* v. *Ponnammal*, 12 Mad. 155, though he would be excluded in Bengal, *ante*, § 464.

(*o*) This is not only clear on principle (§ 461), but I have ascertained by inquiry from very learned natives both in Bengal and Madras, that a man is under no obligation to present any offerings to his grandmother's ancestors. See too Jagannatha, 3 Dig. 602.

(*p*) The Viramitrodaya (p. 200, § 5) distinctly states that the cognates in in the above order "by reason of greater propinquity."

shara, in order to find in it something which never was there. The Bombay authorities even go farther than the letter of the Mitakshara, as they include under the term *bandhu* females such as the daughters of a brother or of a sister, who can make no offerings at all (*q*).

Early principles of succession.

§ 473. Let us now go a stage further back, and try to find out what was the original law as to religious obligations, and how far it was connected with the right of succession. I have already suggested that the practice of offerings to the dead was connected with that Ancestor worship, which was common to all the leading Aryan races (§ 60). Those offerings would necessarily be made by the direct male descendants of the deceased in the order of their nearness. The character of those offerings, and the strictness of the obligation to make them, would naturally vary according to the remoteness of the offerer from the ancestor. The rule, as we have seen (§ 460), was in accordance with what might have been expected. The devolution of the property would naturally be in exactly the same line, partly because the whole organization of the family would be broken up if its property were allowed to pass through females to persons of a different family or tribe (*r*); and partly because the direct males had a double claim, as being not only the descendants, but the worshippers of the deceased. Collateral relations through females who belonged to a different family, with a different line of ancestors, would be under no obligation to make offerings, and would have no right to inherit. Now this seems to be exactly what is laid down in the early

(*q*) W. & B. 125, 137. See *post*, § 541. I have retained from the first edition (1378) the whole of the reasoning in the preceding paragraphs, which were written at a time when I was not aware that the doctrine which they advocate had been the subject of express decision. The principle that succession under the Mitakshara law depends upon propinquity and not upon religious efficacy has now, however, been settled by distinct rulings. The rule was first laid down in Bombay by the case of *Lallubhai* v. *Mankuvarbai*, 2 Bom. 388, *affd.* by the P. C. *Lulloobhai* v. *Cassibai*, 7 I. A. 212; S. C. 5 Bom. 110. The same rule has been applied by the High Court of Bengal to cases in that Presidency governed by the Mitakshara; *Umaid* v. *Udoi*, 6 Cal. 119; *Ananda Bibee* v. *Nownit Lal*, 9 Cal. 315, p. 318. See, however, *per Mahmood*, J., 11 All. p. 212.

(*r*) See Maine, Ancient Law, 149; Punjab Customs, 11, 16, 25, 37, 48, 51.

treatises. The obligation to offer cakes, divided oblations and libations of water, is set out, and it is also said that the inheritance goes in order to the *sapindas, sakulyas,* and *samanodakas*. Immediately after these it passes to strangers, such as the spiritual preceptor, the pupil, learned Brahmans, or the king (*s*). The only person of a different family who is ever stated to be under an obligation to perform funeral rites, or to have a right to inherit, is the daughter's son (*t*). But he is always treated as being in an exceptional position, the reasons for which will be discussed hereafter (§ 518); he does not take as a *bandhu,* which in strictness he is, but very high up in the line of agnates. It would appear then that a man did not inherit because he performed funeral rites, or made religious offerings. He inherited because he was the nearest of kin to the deceased, and he made religious offerings for exactly the same reason. In the majority of cases the heir to the estate would also be a person who was bound to offer the funeral cake. But the mere fact of succession to the estate would carry with it the obligation to perform all rites which were needed for the repose of the deceased, just as it entailed the duty of discharging his debts (*u*). Accordingly, when a pupil is heir, he performs the funeral rites, and it is stated generally, "He who takes the estate shall perform the obsequies" (*v*). Accordingly, Mr. Colebrooke says, "It is not a maxim of the law that he who performs the obsequies is heir, but that he who succeeds to the property must perform them" (*w*). And in a remark appended by him to the case of *Duttnaraen* v. *Ajeet* (*x*), he says, in reference to the texts just quoted,

Religious duty the result, not the cause, of inheritance.

(*s*) Manu, ix. § 185—189; Apastamba, ii. 14, § 2—5; Baudhayana, i. 5, § 1—8; Gautama, xxviii. § 18; Vasishtha, xvii. § 29—31; Vishnu, xvii. § 4—16; Narada, xiii. § 51. The word *bandhavas* in the last two authorities is translated by Mr. Colebrooke remoter kinsmen, and appears to refer to persons of the same family.

(*t*) Manu, ix. § 127—133, 139, 140.

(*u*) The due performance of sacrifices was one of the three debts. Manu, v. § 35, 36. Raj. Sarvadhikari, 871.

(*v*) Vrihaspati Smriti, 3 Dig. 545; Vishnu, *ib.* 546; Satatapa, *ib.* 625; Goldstücker, 13; *per curiam, Bhyah Ram* v. *Bhayh Ugur,* 13 M. I. A. 390; S. C. 14 Suth. (P. C. 1; Smriti Chandrika, xi. 5, § 10; note (2); but see *per Mitter,* J., *Guru* v. *Anand,* 5 B. L. R. 38; S. C. 13 Suth. (F. B.) 49.

(*w*) 2 Stra. H. L. 242. (*x*) 1 S. D. 20 (26.)

"These passages do not imply that the mere act of celebrating the funeral rites gives a title to the succession, but that the successor is bound to the due performance of the last rites for the person whose wealth has devolved on him." This is also the view taken by Dr. Mayr (*y*). He says, "The descent of the inheritance was not regulated by the offerings to the dead, as *Gans* supposes. Those offerings, and the whole system of ancestor-worship, date from a period at which the idea of a partition had not arisen. In later times, however, when partition was resorted to, it became necessary to define who should offer the funeral cake, and to whom it should be offered. Naturally this duty fell upon those who took the inheritance (*z*). In earlier times it would have been impossible to mark out any particular individual, because each succeeding generation stood in the relation of descendant to the whole generation which preceded it, and not any particular person to any other particular person. But when we find in a text of Manu that the great-grandson must offer the cake, we may infer that this duty resulted from the fact that he inherited."

Great-grandson the last direct heir.

§ 474. The fact that the line of direct descent stopped short at the great-grandson, and then ascended, is generally looked upon as a crucial proof that the Hindu law of inheritance was founded on the principle of religious efficacy. The reason offered for this by the Bengal lawyers is, that those who are more remote in descent present offerings of less religious efficacy. But it seems to me that the matter is capable of a very different explanation. When property no longer passed exclusively by survivorship, the rule of inheritance would naturally be framed upon the analogy of the original system. The right of succession would be limited to the same persons who formerly took by survivorship, but they would take by distinct steps, instead of

(*y*) Ind Erbrecht, 85

(*z*) See Goldstücker, 36 *et seq.*, where he points out that all ceremonies involving expense must be performed by the head of the family, who is in possession of the property.

simultaneously as one body. Now, the persons upon whom the property fell by survivorship were the persons who lived together in the same house, or, at all events, who were so closely connected as to be under the control of one head. It was almost impossible that a single family could ever contain more than four generations in direct descent. If such were in existence, they would probably have quitted the family house. In any case the more remote would be looked upon as less nearly akin to the patriarch than his own brothers, nephews, or grandnephews. These last would be more closely united to him in affection, and more likely to interest themselves in the performance of his obsequies, where such performance was considered a matter of moment. It was natural, therefore, that the inheritance should be kept within the family, first passing to its lower extremity, and then rising again. This is really all that *Manu* says, "For three is the funeral cake ordained. The fourth is the giver. But the fifth has no concern. To the nearest after him in the third degree the inheritance belongs" (*a*). In the Punjab, where, as I have often remarked, the doctrine of religious efficacy is unknown, the line of direct descent stops short in the same way, and those beyond the third generation from the common ancestor are considered to have no interest in the property which entitles them to object to its alienation (*b*). That is, they are practically considered to be outside the family. Mr. McLennan has drawn attention to the early Irish law, which appears in a somewhat similar manner to have limited the right of participation in the ancestral property to the fourth generation (*c*).

Punjab.

Succession of cognates.

§ 475. I have no information which would enable me to state whether the practice of making offerings to maternal

---

(*a*) Manu, ix. § 187. Mr. Rajkumar Sarvadhikari (pp. 284, 286) points to this text as marking two conflicting theories of succession, propinquity and religious benefits. To me it seems to contain no reference to any principle but propinquity. Those who offered the funeral cakes were the three nearest to the deceased.

(*b*) Punjab Cust., 32.

(*c*) McLennan, 471, 496.

ancestors always existed, or whether it was an innovation, springing from the Brahmanical desire to multiply religious ceremonies, and from the principle that "wealth was produced for the sake of solemn sacrifices" (*d*). If it existed as a ceremonial usage, the absence of all reference to it in the law writers shows that it had no legal significance. One thing is quite clear, that it carried with it no right to inheritance, since the persons who presented such offerings could never inherit under the old system of law, until the extinction of the last male in the direct line of descent (§ 471). The Bengal notion of weighing the merits of an offering made by a cognate against an offering made by an agnate, and giving the inheritance accordingly, is an absolute innovation. The theory arose from treating the offering of oblations, and the succession to the estate as cause and effect, instead of antecedent and consequent. The offering of sacrifices to the deceased was really a duty. It grew to be considered the evidence of a right. When this idea became fixed, it was readily applied to all persons who presented such offerings, whatever might be the reason for their presentation. Those principles, which were applied in testing the title of persons who really were heirs, were applied to create a title in persons who were out of the line of heirs. An agnate who presented three cakes to the owner was necessarily nearer than an agnate who only presented one, and was therefore a preferable heir. It came to be assumed that this principle was not limited to agnates, but afforded a means of comparison between agnates and cognates. The application of this principle is the simple distinction between the Mitakshara and the Daya Bhaga. The Mitakshara recognized the difference between the offerings which A. and B. were bound to make to X., but it used the difference in order to ascertain which of the two was nearer to X. in a direct line. The Daya Bhaga considered the directness of

Origin of Bengal theory.

(*d*) Mitakshara, ii. 1, § 14. See *ante*, § 219.

the line as immaterial, if the difference between the offerings was established.

In the Punjab, and among the Sikhs and Jains, the rules of descent appear to be in the main those of the Mitakshara, but the doctrine of religious efficacy is wholly unknown (*e*).

(*e*) Punjab Cust., 11; *ante*, § 44; Punjab Customary Law, II. 100, 137, 142, 175.

CHAPTER XVII.

INHERITANCE.

Principles of Succession in case of Females.

Early position of women.

§ 476. THE right of women to possess and inherit the family property would necessarily depend upon the organization of the family to which they belonged. Among polyandrous tribes of the promiscuous or Nair type, the head and visible centre of the family was not the father, who was unknown, nor the wife, who had not begun to exist, but the mother (§ 208). The home was the home of the woman and her children. There she was visited by the man who might or might not be the father of her children. His home was in the circle to which his mother belonged. He inherited in one family and his children in another. In Canara, where this system is maintained in its most archaic form, the actual management of the property formerly was, and even now generally is, vested in females. In Malabar the manager is always the eldest male of the family, though succession is traced through females (*a*). Exactly the reverse would take place in the ordinary undivided family of the Aryan type. The whole property would vest in the males, and be managed by the head of the family for the time being. The women would be mere dependents upon their husbands and fathers. So long as there were any males in the family, no woman could possibly set up a claim to inherit. It is to this period that the texts must be referred which represent women as absolutely without independent rights. "Three persons, a

(*a*) Stra. Man. § 400—404; *Munda Chetty* v. *Timmaju*, 1 Mad. H. C. 380; *Timmappa* v. *Mahalinga*, 4 Mad. H. C. 28; *Devu* v. *Deyi*, 8 Mad. 353; *Mahalinga* v. *Mariammah*, 12 Mad. 462. See Teulon, 25, where he gives an exactly similar description of the ancient Carians.

wife, a son, and a slave, are declared by law to have no wealth exclusively their own; the wealth which they may earn is regularly acquired for the man to whom they belong" (*b*). "The father protects a woman in her childhood, the husband during her youth, the son in old age; a woman has no right to independence" (*c*). *Baudhayana* and *Vasishtha* mention no females in their list of heirs, and the former expressly states, on the authority of a text of the Vedas, that women have no right to inherit (*d*). The text on which *Baudhayana* relies may, it would appear, be so interpreted as to give no support to his assertion (*e*); but, of course, this does not detract from the weight to be given to his statement as evidence of the then prevailing usage. His authority is still so far respected, that the schools of Bengal and Benares consider that women can only inherit under some express text (*f*). In this respect, as it will be seen hereafter, the western lawyers differ (§ 488, 490.)

Women originally without rights.

§ 477. The same causes which led to the break up of the family union would introduce women to the possession of the family property. When partition took place, the fund out of which the women had been maintained would be split into fragments. The natural course would be, either to give an extra share to any member of the family who would make himself responsible for their support, or to allot to them shares out of which they could maintain themselves. This appears to have been what actually took place (*g*). Similarly, upon the death without issue of a male owner who was the last survivor of the coparcenary, or who had been separated

Growth of their right to property.

(*b*) Manu, viii. § 416.
(*c*) Baudhayana, ii. 2, § 27; Manu, ix. § 3. See Sancha & Lichita, Dig. 484; and text quoted Madhaviya, § 44; Varada, p. 39.
(*d*) Baudhayana, i. 5. 11, § 1—14, ii. 2, 3, § 44—46; Vasishtha, xvii.
(*e*) W. & B. 126; Madhaviya, § 44.
(*f*) W. & B. 126; Daya Bhaga, xi. 6, § 11; Smriti Chandrika, xi. 5, § 2, 3, 6. Viramitrodaya, pp. 174—197; *per Mitter*, J., *Guru* v. *Anand*, 5 B. L. R., 37; S. C. 13 Suth. (F. B.) 49; *per Westropp*, C. J., *Lallubhai* v. *Mankuvarbai*, 2 Bom. 418, 428, 438; S. C. on appeal, *Lulloobhoy* v. *Cassibai*; *per curiam*, 7 I. A. 231; S. C. 5 Bom. 110; *Gauri* v. *Rukko*, 3 All. 45; *Jagat Narain* v. *Sheodas*, 5 All. 311; *per curiam*. 9 Cal. 322. V. N. Mandlik, 357, 364. The Madras Court appears in recent decisions rather to doubt the universal application of this rule;—See 5 Mad. p. 249; 8 Mad. pp. 117, 127, 129.
(*g*) See *ante*, § 436, 447.

from the other members, or whose property had been self-acquired, it would be more natural that his property should remain in the possession of the women of his family for their support, than that they should be handed over with the property to distant members of the family, who might be utter strangers. In this way their right as heirs, properly so called, and not merely as sharers, would arise. But that right would not extend beyond the reason for it, *viz.*, their claim to a personal maintenance. The old preference for the male line over the female (§§ 471, 473) would limit the right, so as to prevent the property passing absolutely out of the family into the hands of male strangers. The woman would not be allowed to become a new stock of descent, so as to transmit the inheritance to her heirs. This is no doubt the foundation of that rule which is assumed in all the works on inheritance, that where a woman inherits to a male, his heirs and not hers take at her death (§ 565).

Only for maintenance.

§ 478. The women who were the actual members of a man's family, and as such entitled to support, would always stand to him in the position of daughter, mother, wife, or sister, taking in under these terms more distant relations of the same class, such as grandmother and the like. The daughter and the mother appear to have been the first to obtain a recognized right to inherit.

Right of daughter.

Manu allows a daughter to inherit after her father. But it seems very doubtful whether he did not limit this right to the case of the daughter, specially appointed to raise up a son for him. I have already suggested that a daughter so appointed remained in her father's family, so that her son was his son, and not the son of his actual father (*h*). Naturally such a daughter would be specially favoured, as the descent of property to her would not take it out of the family. Now, the text of *Manu* which states her right of inheritance follows after three texts which relate to the

(*h*) See *ante*, § 78; *post*, § 518.

appointed daughter solely. It then proceeds, "The son of a man is even as himself, and as the son such is the daughter (thus appointed). How then (if he have no son) can any inherit his property but a daughter who is closely united with his own soul?" (*i*). The words in brackets are the gloss of *Kalluka Bhatta,* who evidently understood the text as I do. The same view was taken of it by *Daraiswara, Davaswamy,* and *Davarata,* as stated by the Smriti Chandrika (*k*). It is remarkable that in the texts where Manu states the order of succession to a man who has left no issue, he makes no reference to a daughter as an heir (*l*). The texts would harmonize, if we suppose that in the former passage he was speaking only of a daughter who, by virtue of her special appointment, became his son, as she is stated to be by *Vasishtha* (*m*). This also accords with the position given to her by *Narada,* who places her after the son, upon the ground that "she continues the lineage. A son and a daughter equally continue the race of their father" (*n*). This could be strictly true only of an appointed daughter; for the son of any other daughter would be of a different family and a different name, like any other *bandhu.* But when the practice of making an appointed daughter became obsolete (§ 75), the daughter not appointed would naturally fall into the same position, or rather would retain the position which usage had made familiar. Her right would then rest on the simple ground of consanguinity. This is the ground on which it is based by *Vrihaspati* and the Mitakshara: "As a son, so does the daughter of a man proceed from his several limbs. How then should any other person take her father's wealth?" (*o*).

Appointed daughter.

479. No distinction is to be found in the earlier sages as to the capacity of one daughter to inherit in preference to another. *Devala* says, "To unmarried daughters a nuptial portion must be given out of the estate of the father;

Grounds of precedence between daughters.

(*i*) Manu, ix. § 127—130.
(*k*) Smriti Chandrika, xi. 2, § 16.
(*l*) Manu, ix. § 185, 217.
(*m*) *Ante,* § 73.
(*n*) Narada, xiii. § 50.
(*o*) Mitakshara, ii. 2, § 2.

and his own daughter, lawfully begotten, shall take, like a son, the estate of him who leaves no male issue" (*p*). This suggests the idea that the daughter's right of inheritance arose from the obligation to endow her. Hence *Katyayana* says, "Let the widow succeed to her husband's wealth, and in default of her the daughter inherits, if unmarried or unprovided" (*q*). *Parasara* enlarges the rule as follows (*r*). "The unmarried daughter shall take the inheritance of the deceased, who left no male issue, and on failure of her the married daughter." So far, at all events, there is no idea of religious merit. The object of the dowry is to facilitate marriage, and to benefit the daughter (*s*). Naturally, the daughter who is already set up in the world has a claim inferior to that of one who has her fortune to seek. And similarly, in a competition between married daughters, the preference was given to the poor daughter over the rich one (*t*). None of the writers of the Benares school, except the Smriti Chandrika, absolutely exclude any daughter, or suggest any reason for her inheriting except the simple one of consanguinity (*u*). The Bengal writers for the first time introduce the idea of religious efficacy. A daughter of course could offer no religious oblations herself, but her right was put upon the ground that she produced sons who could present oblations (*v*). A reference to Manu will show, as might have been expected, that the daughter's son, whose power of offering funeral cakes was considered to be equal to that of a son's son, was the son of the appointed daughter (*w*). *Jimuta Vahana*, however, laid down that no daughter could inherit unless she had, or was capable of having, male

Benares.

Bengal law.

(*p*) 3 Dig. 491. See too Yajnavalkya, ii. § 135; Mitakshara, ii. 1, § 2.
(*q*) Cited Smriti Chandrika, xi. 2, § 20; Mitakshara, ii. 2, § 2.
(*r*) 3 Dig. 490.
(*s*) See Vasishtha, cited Daya Bhaga, xi. 2, § 6. Also Teulon, 12, note 2, where he points out, that as the degradation of woman consisted in her being a mere object of purchase, so the first step towards her elevation was taken, when the dowry made it no longer necessary that she should be sold.
(*t*) Mitakshara, ii. 2, § 4; Smriti Chandrika, xi. 2, § 21; V. May., iv. 8, § 11, 12; Viramit, p. 181.
(*u*) Vivada Chintamani, 291, 292; V. May., iv. 8, § 10; Madhaviya, § 36; Varadrajah, 34; Viramit., pp. 176—182.
(*v*) See *per Mitter*, J., *Gunga* v. *Shumbhoonath*, 22 Suth. 393; *per Jagannatha*, 3 Dig. 194.
(*w*) Manu, ix. § 131—140. See *post*, § 518.

issue, and the natural result was the exclusion of daughters who were widows, or barren, or who appeared to have an incapacity for bringing any but daughters into the world (*x*). This principle is also adopted by the author of the Smriti Chandrika, who necessarily excludes barren daughters (*y*). It will be seen that his authority in this respect has not been accepted in Southern India (§ 514). The mode in which these various principles operate will be examined in the next chapter, upon THE ORDER OF SUCCESSION (§ 514).

Right of mother;

§ 480. The mother is of course not mentioned as an heir by *Baudhayana*, who excludes all women (*z*), nor by *Apastamba, Gautama*, or *Vasishtha ; Narada* states her right to a share on partition by the sons after the death of their father, but does not refer to her as an heir (*a*). Her claim, however, and that of the grandmother, are expressly stated by *Manu* (*b*) : "Of a son dying childless (and leaving no widow) the (father and) mother shall take the estate : and the mother also being dead, the paternal (grandfather and) grandmother shall take the heritage (on failure of brothers and nephews)." The gloss of Kulluka as contained in brackets marks the changes in the law since the time of *Manu*. *Vishnu* also inserts the mother in the list of heirs next after the father (*c*), and *Yajnavalkya* places both parents after the daughters (*d*). Her claim is also mentioned by *Vrihaspati* and *Katyayana*, of whom the former places her after wife and male issue, while the latter brings her in after male issue, father or brother (*e*).

its origin.

As to the ground of her claim, the mother as well as the grandmother and great-grandmother, are certainly sapindas, as sharing with their husbands the cakes which are offered to them by the male issue (*f*). But her claim, and indeed

Daya Bhaga, xi. 2, § 1—3 ; D K. S. i. 3, § 5.
(*y*) Smriti Chandrika, xi. 2, § 10, 21. See *post*, § 514.
(*z*) *Ante*, § 476. (*a*) Narada, xiii. § 12.
(*b*) Manu, ix. § 217 ; cf. § 185, where Manu makes the father and then the brothers take.
(*c*) Vishnu, xvii. § 7. (*d*) Yajnavalkya, ii. § 136. (*e*) 3 Dig. 502, 506.
(*f*) *Ante*, § 471. Subodhini extends the right of female ascendants to the

that of the father too, is always placed on the ground of consanguinity, and of the merit she possesses in reference to her son, from having conceived and nurtured him in her womb. And by many commentators she is preferred to the father, upon considerations derived from a comparison of the respective degrees in which mother and father share in the composition of the son (*g*), while the Mitakshara prefers her on the ground of greater propinquity (*h*). When we come to *Jimuta Vahana*, however, we find the religious doctrine introduced for the first time. He prefers the father to the mother, because the father offers oblations in which the son participates; and he prefers the mother, who offers none, to the brothers, who offer three, "because she confers benefits on him by the birth of other sons who may offer funeral oblations in which he will participate" (*i*). An argument which obviously would never apply as regards the mother of an only son, or of a son whose brothers had died before him without leaving issue.

Right of widow;

§ 481. The growth of a widow's right of succession is much more complicated than that of mother or daughter. Originally of course she shared in the general incapacity for inheritance which affected all women. But her right was recognized later than that of other females who now take after her. Neither *Manu*, *Apastamba*, *Vasishtha* nor *Narada* recognize her right as heir; though they do acknowledge that of the daughter and mother (*k*). *Vishnu*, however, assigns to her a place after male issue (*l*). *Vriddha Manu*, *Vrihaspati*, *Sancha* and *Lichita* and *Devala* all make her

mother and grandmother of the paternal great-grandfather, and says that the same analogy holds good among the *Samanodakas*. Mitakshara, ii. 5, § 5. Colebrooke's note; *Lullubhai* v. *Mankuvarbai*, 2 Bom. 433.

(*g*) 3 Dig. 504; Mitakshara, ii. 3; Smriti Chandrika, xi. 3, § 3; Daya Bhaga, xi. 4, § 2; Vivada Chintamani, 293.

(*h*) Mitakshara, ii. 3, § 3; *ante*, § 471.

(*i*) Daya Bhaga, xi. 4, § 2; D. K. S. i. 6, § 2.

(*k*) See Manu, ix. § 185, 212, 217, where Kalluka inserts a gloss in favour of the widow, whose rights are not recognized in the original. See the explanation of Mitakshara, xi. 1, § 35.

(*l*) Vishnu, xvii § 4.

heir (*m*). So, of course, does *Yajnavalkya* (*n*), who is followed by his commentator *Vijnanesvara*.

The following account of the manner in which the rights of a widow arose, is taken almost exclusively from Dr. Mayr's dissertation upon the subject (*o*).

its origin and growth.

§ 482. From the very earliest times the widow was entitled to be maintained by her husband's heirs. When a brother died without issue, or entered a religious order the other brothers were to divide his wealth, except the wife's separate property, and to allow a maintenance to his women for life. But even this maintenance depended upon their living a life of chastity. If they behaved otherwise, it might be resumed (*p*). So *Narada* says (*q*), "when the husband is deceased, his kin are the guardians of his childless widow; in disposing of her, and in the care of her, as well as in her maintenance, they have full power." Even as against the king, when he took by escheat, the widow did not inherit, but he was bound to give a maintenance to the women of such persons (*r*). These passages of *Narada* are of special importance, because, as his work was professedly based upon *Manu*, they show that nothing in *Manu* was then understood as countenancing the right of a widow to inherit.

Origin and growth of widow's rights.

§ 483. The next step would naturally be that the amount necessary for the maintenance should be set apart for it, and left at her own disposal. In the case of an escheat the text of *Katyayana* cited above seems to indicate that this was done. And the same course was adopted in case of a parti-

---

(*m*) 3 Dig. 458, 473, 474, 478; Katyayana, Mitakshara, ii. 1, § 6.

(*n*) Yajnavalkya, ii. 135.

(*o*) Mayr, 179, *et seq.* See too *per curiam*, *Bhau Nanaji* v. *Sundrabai*, 11 Bom. H. C. 273.

(*p*) Narada, xiii. § 25, 26. Vijnanesvara explains these texts as applying to the case of a reunited parcener, Mitakshara, ii. 1, § 20; but, as Mayr observes, his case had been provided for by the preceding text, § 24.

(*q*) Narada, xiii. § 28. See too Sancha, 3 Dig. 482.

(*r*) Narada, xiii. § 52; Katyayana, cited Mitakshara, ii. 1, § 27; Vijnanesvara remarks upon these passages that the words used for women, "stri" and "yoshit," apply to concubines, which, as Mayr remarks (184), is opposed to innumerable passages.

tion (*s*). Where the property was very small in amount, the whole would often be handed over to the widow. And so *srikara* and others were of opinion that a widow's right of succession was limited to the case of a small property (*t*). No such explanation can be given to the texts of *Yajnavalkya* and others, which expressly state a woman's right of succession, since they all put her succession on exactly the same footing as that of sons (*u*). But the view of *Srikara* and those who thought with him, is valuable, from a historical point of view, as showing what the usage was, before the widow's right was firmly established. When it had once become customary to hand over the whole of a small property to a widow, the decision whether a property was sufficiently small would become difficult and invidious. The more wealthy the husband had been, the larger would be the scale of maintenance suitable to his widow, especially when it came to be expected that she should perform her husband's *Shradhs* and discharge the charities to which he had been accustomed (*v*). Where the relations were themselves adequately provided for, there would often be a strong feeling in favour of leaving the whole property to the widow for her life, and this feeling would naturally exist among all relations of the husband other than the next in succession. They might benefit by the property in the hands of a widow, while they would not do so to the same extent if it fell into the hands of the next male heir.

Influence of *niyoga*.

§ 484. The practice of the *niyoga* would also help in the same direction. A passage of *Gautama* (*w*) is by some translated so as to indicate that a widow was only entitled to succeed if she raised up issue for her husband, in which case her right would be not personal but as guardian for her son. The author of the Mitakshara explains the passage, not as making the raising up of issue a condition precedent

(*s*) *Ante*, § 436.
(*t*) Mitakshara, ii. 1, § 31. So among the Sutlej chiefs, Punjab Customs, 25.
(*u*) Mitakshara, ii. 1, § 36; Daya Bhaga, xi. 1, § 6.
(*v*) Vrihaspati, 3 Dig. 458.
(*w*) Gautama, xxviii. § 18, 19. See Mitakshara, *ii.* 1, § 8.

to inheritance, but as offering her an alternative. In either view it is clear that she had the alternative. The male relations would have a strong interest in inducing the widow to refrain from exercising her right, and she would have a specially strong interest in availing herself of it, if she at once became the manager of the property. An obvious compromise would be to allow her to succeed at once to a life-estate in the property, provided she waived the privilege of producing a new and absolute owner. Hence the condition of chastity which the Brahman lawyers engrafted upon her right of succession, a condition which is wholly unsupported by the early texts of the Vedas (*x*).

Widow only takes separate estate.

§ 485. It is impossible now to ascertain when the widow's right of inheritance was first established. *Yajnavalkya* and others already referred to, lay it down absolutely; but the author of the Mitakshara (*y*) still thought it necessary to enter into an elaborate discussion of the whole subject, as if it were even in his time an open question. The conclusion he arrives at is, that the widow is entitled to inherit to her husband, if he died separated and not reunited, and leaving no male issue. And this rule is now adopted universally, except where the authority of *Jimuta Vahana* prevails (*z*). The rule seems necessarily to follow from the view taken by the Mitakshara of the rights of undivided members. While the husband lived, his wife had only a right to be maintained by him in a suitable manner; after

Widow is heir but not coparcener,

(*x*) Mayr, 181; *ante*, § 88.

(*y*) Mitakshara, ii. 1.

(*z*) Mitakshara, ii. 1, § 19, 30; ii. 9, § 4; Smriti Chandrika, xi. 1, § 24, 25, 53, 54; xii. § 9; Varadraja, 34; Madhaviya, § 34, 35, says nothing as to division; Viramit., p. 181, ch. iii; *Katama Natchiar* v. *Rajah of Shivagunga*, 9 M. I. A. 539; S. C 2 Suth. (P. C.) 31. As to Benares: 2 W. MacN. 21; *Hiranath* v. *Baboo Ram Narayan*, 9 B. L. R. 274; S. C. 17 Suth. 316; *Chowdhry Chintamun* v. *Mt. Nowlukho*, 2 I. A. 263; S. C. 24 Suth. 255; *Rup Singh* v. *Baisni*, 11 I. A. 149; Mithila, Vivada Chintamani, 290; *Pudmavati* v *Baboo Doolar*, 4 M. I. A. 259, 264; S. C. 7 Suth. (P. C.) 41; *Anundee* v. *Khedoo*, 14 M. I. A. 416; S. C. 18 Suth. 69. Bombay: V. May., iv. 8, § 6; *Goolab* v. *Phool*, 1 Bor. 154 [178]; *Govinddas* v. *Muhalukshumee*, *ib.*, 241 [267]; *Mankoonwur* v. *Bhugoo*, 2 Bor. 139 [157]; *Gun Joshee* v. *Sugoona*, 2 Bor. 401 [440]; W. & B. 68. In some cases in the Punjab and among the Jains a widow appears to succeed to her husband's estate, even though undivided. But the general practice seems to follow the Mitakshara; Punjab Customs, 56; *Sheo Singh* v. *Mt. Dakho*, 6 N. W. P. 406.

his death, his rights all lapse to his surviving coparceners, and she can have no higher right against them than she had against her husband. The question of heirship for the first time arises in case of a divided member, as it is only in regard to divided property that there can be an heir, properly so called. In other words, the widow can take by succession as heir, but cannot take by survivorship as coparcener (*a*).

except in Bengal.

§ 486. Of course the very foundation of this reasoning fails as regards *Jimuta Vahana,* for he denies the premise, *viz.,* that all the undivided members of the family hold each an unascertained interest in every part of the whole, and that at the death of each that interest passes to the survivors. On the contrary he considers that each has a separate right to an unascertained portion of the aggregate, that is, that each holds as a tenant in common, and not as a joint tenant. That being so, of course, there is no reason to restrain the express words of texts which state the right of a widow to succeed to her husband, by limiting them to the case of a divided member. It is therefore equally settled in Bengal, that a widow succeeds to her husband's share when he is undivided, just as she would to the entire property of one who held as separated (*b*). But this does not apply in case of the widow of a son who dies before his father, undivided, and leaving no separate property (*c*) ; because in Bengal the son is not a co-sharer with his father, and therefore has no interest which can pass to his widow.

She takes self-acquired property.

§ 487. Even under the Mitakshara, if a man dies undivided, but leaving property, part of which is his self-acquisition, his widow will succeed to that part, though the rest of his property passes by survivorship to his coparceners.

(*a*) This exclusion of the widow does not take place where the property is that of an ordinary mercantile partnership, and not that of an undivided Hindu family; *Rampershad* v. *Sheochurn*, 10 M. I. A. 490.

(*b*) Daya Bhaga, xi. 1, § 25, 26, 27; D. K. S. ii. 2, § 41; F. MacN. 5. See cases 1 M. Dig. 316; 3 Dig. 476, 485; *per West J., Lakshman* v. *Satyabhamabai*, 2 Bom 508.

(*c*) F. MacN. 1.

This had been already laid down by the pandits in Bombay, and in a case under the Mithila law, and was finally settled by the Judicial Committee in the Shivagunga case (*d*). And so where the *status* of division has been established by agreement, but no actual apportionment has taken place, or where part has been apportioned, and not the remainder, in either case the widow inherits as the heir of a divided member, instead of being only entitled to maintenance (*e*).

Partition not completed.

Lastly, a widow will always succeed to the estate of her husband, where that estate does not pass on his death to any other male by survivorship. Therefore, where several daughter's sons take by descent from their maternal grandfather, the widow of each succeeds to her husband, as they take definite, though unascertained shares and not as coparceners with survivorship (*f*).

Reasons for widow's succession.

§ 488. When the right of a widow was once established, the Hindu lawyers were at no loss for reasons to show that it had always existed. According to *Manu,* upon conception by a wife the husband himself was born again in her, and became one person with her (*g*). And so *Vrihaspati* says, "Of him whose wife is not deceased, half the body survives. How should another take the property while half the body of the owner lives? (*h*)." It is obvious that this metaphor has the fault of many other metaphors. It proves too much. If the husband still survives, the sons cannot take. If the widow is looked upon as the continuation of

(*d*) W. & B., 2nd ed , 81, 127 ; 2 W. MacN. 92 ; *Katama Natchiar* v. *Rajah of Shivagunga*, 9 M. I. A. 539 ; S. C. 2 Suth. (P. C.) 31 ; *Periasamy* v. *Periasamy*. 5 I. A. 61 ; S. C. 1 Mad. 312 ; followed *Tekait* v. *Tekaitni*, 5 I. A. 160 ; S. C. 4 Cal. 190.

(*e*) *Suraneni* v. *Suraneni*, 13 M. I. A. 113 ; S. C. 12 Suth. (P. C.) 40 ; *Gajapathi* v. *Gajapathi*, *ib.*, 497 ; S. C. 6 B. L. R. 202 ; S. C. 14 Suth. (P. C.) 33 ; *ante*, § 454 ; *Narayan* v. *Lakshmi*, 3 Mad. H. C. 289 ; *Patni Mal* v. *Ray Manohur*, 5 S. D. 349 (410) ; *Rewun Persad* v. *Mt. Radha Beeby*, 4 M. I. A. 137, 148, 152 ; S. C. 7 Suth. (P. C.) 35 ; *Timmi Reddy* v. *Achamma*, 2 Mad. H. C. 325.

(*f*) *Jasoda Koer* v *Sheo Pershad*, 17 Cal. 33.

(*g*) Manu, ix. § 8, 45.

(*h*) 3 Dig. 458. See Smriti Chandrika, xi. 1, § 6 ; *Katama Natchiar* v. *Rajah of Shivagunga*, 9 M. I. A. 610 ; S. C. 2 Suth. (P. C.) 31 ; *Tamburatti Valia* v. *Vira Rayyan*, 1 Mad. 228.

her husbands' existence, she ought to take even before male issue (*i*). But the widow had also another ground of merit, as offering funeral oblations to her husband. In respect of these *Jimuta Vahana* points out that she was inferior to her sons, as she only performed acts spiritually beneficial to him from the date of her widowhood, while they did so from the date of their birth (*k*). In any point of view it will be seen

Only takes husband's property.

that the merits of the widow were purely personal, as between herself and her husband. As a mother she has claims on her descendants; but as a widow her claim for anything beyond maintenance is only against her husband. Therefore if her marriage with him has been legally dissolved, or if in consequence of his having become an outcaste, she has exercised the right of abandoning him recognised by Hindu law, her claim to inherit from him is lost (*l*). So also, she can only succeed to his property or rights, that is, to the property which was actually vested in him, either in title or in possession, at the time of his death (*m*).

Widow is only heir to husband,

She must take at once at his death, or not at all. No fresh right can accrue to her as widow in consequence of the subsequent death of some one to whom he would have been heir if he had lived. Hence, no claim as heir can be set up on behalf of the widow of a son (*n*), or of a grandson (*o*), or of a daughter's son (*p*), or of a father (*q*), or of a

(*i*) See *ante*, § 221, where it is suggested that at one time the mother's life-estate may have been interposed before full enjoyment by the sons.

(*k*) 3 Dig. 456, 458; Daya Bhaga, xi. 1, § 43.

(*l*) *Sinammal* v. *Administrator-General*, 8 Mad. 169.

(*m*) Viramit., p 164. § 13, p. 197, § 2. If his title was vested, though his enjoyment postponed, she will equally take. *Rewun Persad* v. *Radha Beeby*, 4 M. I. A. 137, 176; S. C. 7 Suth. (P. C.) 85; *Hurrosoondery* v. *Rajessuree*, 2 Suth. 321.

(*n*) 2 W. MacN. 48, 75, 104; 2 Stra. H. L. 233, 234; *Ayabuttee* v. *Rajkissen*, 3 S. D 28 (38); *Rai Sham Bullubh* v. *Prankishen*, *ib.*, 33 (44); *Himulta* v. *Mt. Pudo Monee*, 4 S. D. 19 (25); *Monee Mohun* v. *Dhun Monee*. S. D. of 1858, 910; *Raj Kishore* v. *Hurrosoondery*, S. D. of 1858, 825; *Ananda Bibee* v. *Nownit*, 9 Cal. 315; *Bai Amrit* v. *Bai Manik*, 12 Bom. H. C. 79; Punjab Custom., 64. The claim of a daughter-in-law is supported by Nanda Pandita and by Balambhatta, but by no other authorities. Jolly Lect. 199.

(*o*) *Ambawow* v. *Rutton*, Bom. Sel. Rep. 132.

(*p*) 2 W. MacN. 47.

(*q*) *Vencata* v. *Venkummal*, 1 Mad. Dec. 210; *Vadrevu* v. *Wuppuluri*, Mad. Dec. of 1861, 125; *Ram Koonwar* v. *Ummur*, 1 Bor. 415 [458]; *Bhyrobee* v. [illegible], 6 S. D. 53 (61).

brother (*r*), or of an uncle (*s*), or of a cousin (*t*). In all of the above cases the contest was between the widow and some other heir, who was held to have a preferential title. In some of the recent cases, however, the widow was excluded under Benares law on the general principle that she did not come within the line of heirs at all (*u*). In the latest case it was held that the Crown would take by escheat in preference to her (*v*). This is undoubtedly the law of Bengal, Benares and Madras (*w*). It is now, however, settled that the law in Bombay is different. The subject is discussed by Messrs. West and Bühler, and their views have been fully adopted by the High Court of Bombay in the case of *Lallubhai* v. *Mankuvarbai* (*x*). The process of reasoning of the Western lawyers seems to be as follows. They accept the general principle that succession goes in the order of sapindaship, taking the text of *Manu* (ix. § 187) with the gloss of *Kulluka*, so that it runs :—"To the nearest *sapinda*, male or female, after him in the third degree, the inheritance next belongs." Then they interpret sapindaship as meaning connection by blood, in the manner explained by *Vijnanesvara* (§ 469), which makes even the wives of brothers be sapinda to each other, because they produce one body with those who have sprung from one body. On the same principle they make the daughter-in-law a sapinda (*y*). Hence "They prefer the sister-in-law to the sister's son, and to a male cousin, and more distant male *sagotra-sapindas*, the paternal uncle's

except in Bombay.

Western India.

(*r*) 2 W. MacN. 78; 2 Stra. H. L. 231; *Yetiraj* v. *Tayammal*, Mad. Dec. of 1854, 184; *Peddamuttu* v. *Appu Rau*, 2 Mad. H. C. 117; *Jymunee* v. *Ramjoy*, 3 S. D. 289 (385).

(*s*) *Upendra* v. *Thanda*, 3 B. L. R. (A. C. J.) 349; S. C. *Sub nomine*, *Wopendro* v. *Thanda*, 12 Suth. 263; *Gauri* v. *Rukko*, 3 All. 45.

(*t*) *Soorendronath* v. *Mt. Heeramonee*, 12 M. I. A. 81; S. C. 1 B. L. R. (P. C.) 26; S. C. 10 Suth. (P. C.) 35.

(*u*) *Gauri* v. *Rukko*, 3 All. 45; *Ananda Bibee* v. *Nownit*, 9 Cal. 315.

(*v*) *Jogdamba Koer* v. *Secretary of State*, 16 Cal. 367.

(*w*) *Per curiam*, *Lulloobhoy* v. *Cassibai*, 7 I. A. 230; S. C. 5 Bom. 110; *Vithaldas* v. *Jeshubai*, 4 Bom. 221; *Per West*, J., 11 Bom. p. 293; *per Muthisami Iyer*, J., 8 Mad. pp. 119, 129.

(*x*) W. & B. 129; 2 Bom. 388; *affd.* 7 I. A. 212; S. C. 5 Bom. 110; following and affirming *Lakshmibai* v. *Jayram*, 6 Bom. H. C. (A. C. J.) 52; *Vithaldas* v. *Jeshubai*, 4 Bom. 219.

(*y*) W. & B. 481—486.

widow to the sister, the maternal uncle, and the paternal grandfather's brother, and they allow a daughter-in-law, and a distant gotrajasapinda's widow to inherit." The learned editors remark, "It is however sometimes impossible to bring the authorities which they quote into harmony with their answers (z)." It may be added, that it is equally difficult to bring their answers into harmony with each other. I have given up in despair the attempt to reconcile the futwahs and rulings from Bombay, already cited in this paragraph, with those which will be found below (a). The result of this doctrine is, that "the members of the compact series of heirs specifically enumerated take in the order in which they are enumerated (V. M. iv. 8, § 18) preferably to those lower in the list and to the widows of any relatives, whether near or remote, though where the group of specified heirs has been exhausted the right of the widow is recognised to take her husband's place in competition with the representative of a remoter line (b)." This rule of succession is stated by the Bombay High Court to be deduced, or rather to be deducible, from the Mitakshara, though they admit that the foundation afforded for it by that work is slender, inasmuch as "no widow of a collateral is expressly provided for; the only wife of an ascendant expressly admitted, is one for whom there is an express text." Under the Mayukha, according to Mr. Justice *West*, such a right "may be called almost shadowy (c)." Yet, curiously enough, in Southern India such a rule admittedly does not exist, while in Western India its acceptation in practice is beyond doubt. It certainly seems to me that this is one of those cases in which usages, which sprung up without any reference to the Sanskrit law books, are now supported by torturing those books so as to draw from them conclusions of which their

---

(z) W. & B., 2nd ed., 181, 195—199.

(a) *Muhalukmee* v. *Kripashookul*, 2 Bor. 510 [557]; *Jethee* v. *Mt. Sheo*, *ib.*, 588 [640]; *Baee Umrut* v. *Baee Koosul*, Morris, 5.

(b) *Nahalchand* v. *Hemchand*, 9 Bom. 31 at p. 34; *Lallubhai* v. *Mankuvarbai*, 2 Bom. at p. 445.

(c) *Lallubhai* v. *Mankuvarbai*, 2 Bom. at p. 447.

authors had no idea (*d*). In the Punjab, on the other hand, special family customs exist under which widows are not allowed even to succeed to their husband's estate, or only to a small portion of it (*e*). Punjab.

§ 489. The relations whom we have been considering have all had express texts asserting their title as heirs. The widow and mother are also *gotraja sapindas,* both in the meaning of the Mitakshara, as being connected with the deceased owner by affinity, and in the meaning of the Daya Bhaga, as being connected with him by funeral oblations (§ 462). The daughter is a *sapinda,* though not a *gotraja sapinda,* according to the view of *Vijnanesvara,* and although she neither presents nor participates in oblations, she is fitted into the scheme of *Jimuta Vahana* by her capacity for producing a presenter of offerings. The sister stands in a different position from all these. She has no religious efficacy whatever, as she is in no way connected with the funeral offerings to her brother. She is a sapinda, as regards affinity, but she is not a *gotraja sapinda,* according to the Benares writers, as she passes into a strange *gotra* immediately upon her marriage. As regards the authority of texts, the matter stands in this way. The sister is stated to take a share, either upon an original partition, or after a reunion (*f*), but this is a different thing from taking as heiress. A passage from *Sancha* and *Lichita* (*g*). "The daughter shall take the female property, and she alone is heir to the wealth of her mother's son who leaves no male issue," would certainly seem to be a direct affirmation of the right of a sister to succeed to her brother. *Jagannatha* explains the latter part of the text as referring to an appointed daughter. The text itself is not cited in any commentary that I am aware of as an authority for her right

Sister.

Text.

Text relating to sister.

(*d*) The Privy Council in affirming the decision in *Lulloobhoy* v. *Cassibai,* expressly rest the right of the widow "on the ground of positive acceptance and usage," 7 I. A. p. 237; S. C. 5 Bom. 110.

(*e*) Punjab Customs, 25, 48; Punjab Customary Law, II. 142, 237.

(*f*) Manu, ix. § 118, 212; Vrihaspati, 3 Dig. 476; *ante,* § 436; *post,* § 542.

(*g*) 3 Dig. 187.

as an heir, even by the Mayukha, which admits that right. Possibly it may refer to *stridhanum* which had passed from the mother to the son, which, as will be seen hereafter, is sometimes the case (§ 622). *Nanda Pandita*, and *Balambhatta*, interpret the text of the Mitakshara which gives the inheritance to *brethren*, as including sisters, so that the brothers take first, and then the sisters (*h*). But this order of succession is opposed to the whole spirit of the Benares law. It is not accepted even by the Mayukha, which makes the sister come in after the grandmother, under a different text (*i*), and the interpretation has been rejected by the Judicial Committee (*k*). It may be taken, therefore, and it appears always to be assumed, that there is no text which in express terms asserts the right of a sister to succeed to her brother. In Bombay, however, her right is now beyond dispute. In Bengal and Benares it seems clear that she has no right at all. In Madras her right has been recently affirmed, by a decision which is certainly opposed to the entire current of authority in Southern India. This will render it necessary to examine the law upon the subject at greater length than the importance of the point would seem to require.

Her right admitted in Bombay.

§ 490. The mode in which the sister's title is made out in Western India, appears to be as follows. She is considered a *sapinda*, as already stated, by virtue of her affinity to her brother (§ 488). She is also considered a *gotraja sapinda*, on the ground that this term is satisfied by her having been born in her brother's family, and that she does not lose her position as a *gotraja* by being born again in her husband's *gotra*, upon her marriage. That being so, her place among the *gotrajas* is determined by nearness of kin, and is settled to be between the grandmother and the

(*h*) Mitakshara, ii. 4, § 1, note. This interpretation is accepted by the Bombay High Court as one ground for admitting a sister to succeed, though they do not follow it to its logical conclusion as fixing her position in the line of heirs. *Kesserbai* v. *Valab*, 4 Bom. 188, 204.

(*i*) V. May., iv. 8, § 19; *post*, § 541.

(*k*) *Thakoorain* v. *Mohun*, 11 M. I. A. 386, 402; S. C. 7 Suth. (P. C.) 25.

grandfather (*l*). It is probable that the whole of this reasoning is a mere contrivance to bring a succession, which was established by immemorial usage, into apparent conformity with Sanskrit law. The usage itself is established beyond doubt, and has received the sanction of the Privy Council. And half-sisters succeed as well as sisters of the whole blood, though they come in after whole sisters (*m*). Sisters take equally *inter se,* without any such preference for the unendowed over the endowed, as exists in the case of daughters (*n*).

Not an heir in Bengal.

§ 491. In Bengal it is equally clear, both on principle and authority, that the sister is not an heir. She possesses no spiritual efficacy, and comes under the general text of *Baudhayana* which excludes all females, without being rescued from it by any special text in her favour (*o*). *Jagannatha* says of her, "It is nowhere seen that sisters inherit the property of their brothers" (*p*). And her exclusion is treated as quite undisputed by both the MacNaghtens and Sir *Thomas Strange* (*q*). There is also a uniform current of decisions to the same effect, extending from 1816 to 1870 (*r*). In one case a *futwah* was given by the Pandits declaring that a sister, though not herself an heir, was entitled to enter upon and hold the estate in trust for a son whom she might afterwards produce, where such a son would be the next heir (*s*). But this decision has been expressly declared not to be law, on the well-established principle that a Hindu estate can never be in abeyance, but must always

(*l*) V. May., iv. 8, § 18—20; W. & B. 131, 463; *per West*, J., *Lallubhai* v. *Mankuvarbai*, 2 Bom. p. 445; *Westropp*, C. J., prefers resting her right upon her affinity as *sapinda* even though not a *gotraja*, and upon the express authority of Vrihaspati and Nilakantha, *ib.* 421.

(*m*) W. & B. 469—470; *Vinayek* v. *Luxumeebaee*, 1 Bom. H. C. 118; affirmed 9 M. I. A. 516; S. C. 3 Suth. (P. C.) 41; *Sakharam* v. *Sitabai*, 3 Bom. 353; *Dhondu* v. *Gangabai*, *ib.*, 369; *Kesserbai* v. *Valab*, 4 Bom. 188, 198.

(*n*) *Bhagirthibai* v. *Baya*, 5 Bom. 264.

(*o*) Daya Bhaga, xi. 6, § 11.

(*p*) 3 Dig. 517.

(*q*) F. MacN. 4, 7; 1 W. MacN. 35, note; 1 Stra. H. L. 146.

(*r*) 2 W. MacN. 68, 80, 81, 85, 97, 98; *Koonwaree* v. *Damoodhur*, 7 S. D. 192 (226); *Bamasoondree* v. *Rajkrishto*, Sev. 742; *Kalee Pershad* v. *Bhoirabee*, 2 Suth. 180; *Anund Chunder* v. *Teetoram*, 5 Suth. 215; *Rukkini* v. *Kadarnath*, 5 B. L. R. Appx. 87.

(*s*) *Karuna* v. *Jai Chandra*, 5 S. D. 46 (50).

vest at once in the person who is, at the time of descent cast, the next heir (*t*).

Nor under Benares law.

Sister not recognized by Benares authorities.

§ 492. As regards the provinces which follow the Mitakshara, both principle and authority seem also to exclude the sister. She is not named in the line of heirs by the Mitakshara or the Viramitrodaya (*u*), nor by the Smriti Chandrika, the Madhaviya, the Varadrajah or the Sarasvati Vilasa, none of which even refers to her, except as being entitled to a share upon partition or after reunion. She cannot come in as a *gotraja sapinda* within the meaning of *Vijnanesvara*, because the Hindu law never contemplates a female as remaining unmarried after the period of puberty, and as soon as she does marry, she passes into a different *gotra* (*v*). Nor is there any text in her favour, which is as much required by the Benares school as by that of Bengal (§ 476). I have already noticed the construction of the text of the Mitakshara, which would bring in the sister as included in the term brethren. This has not been approved of by the writers of any school (§ 489). *Nanda Pandita* also proposes to bring in the sister on another principle as being the daughter of the father (*w*). The reasoning would be, a man's own daughter succeeds, as bringing forth the daughter's son. It is now settled that the sister's son—that is, the son of the father's daughter—also succeeds (§ 531). Therefore the father's daughter herself should succeed as bringing him forth. The answer would be, that a man's own daughter succeeds, both because she is his own offspring, and because she produces a son who is of such importance to him, that he is the next male who takes after his own issue. Neither ground would apply to a sister. Not the first of course; nor the second, because, although the sister's son is an heir, he only comes in under the Mitakshara as a *bandhu* after the

(*t*) *Kesub Chunder* v. *Bishnopersaud*, S. D. of 1860, ii. 840; *ante*, § 458.
(*u*) Mitakshara, ii. 5, § 5, note.
(*v*) Daya Bhaga, xi. 2, § 6; W. & B. 129. See too Daya Bhaga, xi. 6, § 10, where Jimuta Vahana says that Yajnavalkya uses the term *Gotraja* to exclude females related as *sapindas*, and Smriti Chandrika, xi, *Lallubhai* v. *Mankuvarbai*, 2 Bom. 438.
(*w*) Mitakshara, ii. 5, § 5, note.

last of the *samanodakas*. Further, the fact that the sister's son is an heir does not involve any assumption that his mother must have been an heir also. He takes by his own independent merit, not through her (*x*). Accordingly we find that the son of an uncle's daughter is an heir to the nephew, though the uncle's daughter is not an heir (*y*); the son of a brother's daughter is, but the brother's daughter is not, an heir (*z*); the son of a nephew's daughter is, but the nephew's daughter is not, an heir (*a*).

Adverse decisions.

§ 493. The weight of authority seems also to be against the sister's claim. The opinions of both the MacNaghtens, of Mr. Colebrooke, Mr. Sutherland, and Sir *Thomas Strange*, were opposed to her claim; and a futwah by a Madras Pandit to the same effect is cited by the latter author (*b*). In 1858 a case came before the Madras Sudder Court, in which a sister claimed as heir to her brother, relying on the texts of *Manu* and the authority of *Nanda Pandita* and *Balambhatta*. The Court said, "The Judges of the Sudder Udalut, while admitting that the arguments of the special appellant have much force, and that the texts relative to division after reunion show that under such circumstances a sister has a right of inheritance, from which a presumption might perhaps be drawn that the spirit of the law may possibly not have originally contemplated the exclusion which now prevails, are of opinion that the law is not only too ill defined to admit of such construction, in opposition to existing usage, but must even, if speaking more clearly, be regarded as obsolete and virtually changed, and modified by practice prevailing beyond memory, and acquiesced in by all parties concerned" (*c*). The same claim was set

(*x*) See *per Holloway*, J., *Chelikani* v. *Suraneni*, 6 Mad. H. C. 288.

(*y*) *Guru* v. *Anand*, 5 B. L. R. 15; S. C. 13 Suth. (F. B.) 49; *Gosaien* v. *Mt. Kishenmunnee*, 6 S. D. 77 (90).

(*z*) *Gobind* v. *Mohesh*, 15 B. L. R. 35; S. C. 23 Suth. 117; *Jogmurut* v. *Seetulpersaud*, Sev. 433.

(*a*) *Kashee Mohun* v. *Rajgobind*, 24 Suth. 229; *Radha Pearee* v. *Doorga Monee*, 5 Suth. 131.

(*b*) 1 Stra. H. L. 146; 2 Stra. H. L. 243—246; F. MacN. 4, 7; 1 W. MacN. 35, n. See *per Holloway*, J., *Chelikani* v. *Suraneni*, 6 Mad. H. C. 288.

(*c*) *Chinnasamien* v. *Koottoor*, Mad. Dec. of 1858, 175.

up, with the same arguments and the same result, before the High Court of Bengal in 1863, in a case governed by Mitakshara law. The Court, after referring to *Manu*, ix., § 187, 217, Mitakshara, ii., 4 and 5, 1 Stra. H. L. 146; 1 W. MacN. 35, and a Bengal case, proceed to say, "On the whole, then, we are clearly of opinion that the Vayavastha of the Pandit cannot be set up successfully against the text of the Mitakshara, or the general principles of Hindu law, which exclude sisters, or against the marked omission from our precedents of any decision in favour of such a claim, for more than sixty years" (*d*). This opinion was reiterated by the Bengal High Court after a fresh discussion of the authorities in 1882 (*e*). The same decision was given in 1880 by the Allahabad High Court, also in a case under Mitakshara law, the Court referring to a previous ruling which laid down that according to Mitakshara law none but females expressly named can inherit (*f*).

Sister's right

In the Punjab, among the Sikh Jats, the sister is also excluded by long-established and recorded usage, which was affirmed by express decision in 1870 (*g*).

The title of a sister was raised for the first time on appeal to the Privy Council in a case from the North-West Provinces in 1871, but the Judicial Committee refused to enter upon the question (*h*); it was also referred to, but without any expression of opinion, by the Committee in 1876 (*i*).

recently admitted in Madras.

§ 494. On the other hand, a sister was for the first time decided to be an heir to her brother in a recent case in the Madras High Court (*k*). Property had devolved on a son, upon whose death it was taken by his mother. She alienated portions of it to strangers, and then died. The

---

(*d*) *Guman* v. *Srikant*, Sev. 460. (*e*) *Jullessur* v. *Uggur Roy*, 9 Cal. 725.
(*f*) *Jagat Narain* v. *Sheodas*, 5 All. 311. (*g*) Punjab Custom, 17.
(*h*) *Kooer Goolab* v. *Rao Kurun*, 14 M. I. A. 176; S. C. 10 B. L. R. 19.
(*i*) *Vellanki* v. *Venkata Rama*, 4 I. A. 1, 8; S. C. 1 Mad. 174; S. C. 26 Suth. 21.
(*k*) *Kutti Ammal* v. *Radakristna*, 8 Mad. H. C. 88.

plaintiff, who was one of three sisters, sued to set aside the alienations. These were admittedly invalid beyond the life of the mother. The only question, therefore, was, whether the sister had any title which would support her suit. The Court held that she had. They first declared that she was not a *sapinda,* setting aside the construction put upon the word "brethren" by *Balambhatta.* They then proceeded to say, "Whether the sister is entitled to succeed as a relative of deceased more remote than a *sapinda* is another question. Since the decision of the Judicial Committee in *Gridhari* v. *The Government of Bengal* (*l*), the High Court of Madras, following that decision, and the decision of the High Court of Bengal in *Amrita* v. *Lakhinarayan* (*m*), of which the Judicial Committee approved, have held (*n*) that a sister's son is entitled to succeed as a *bandhu,* and that the text and commentary in chap. ii., § 6, of the Mitakshara do not restrict the limit of *Bandhus* to the cognate kindred there mentioned, but are to be read as merely offering illustrations of the degree of Bandhus in their order of succession. In § 3 of chap. ii. of the Mitakshara, § 4, it is said, "Nor is the claim in virtue of propinquity restricted to kinsmen allied by funeral oblations, but on the contrary, it appears from this very text (*o*) that the rule of propinquity is effectual without any exception in the case of (*samanodakas*) kindred connected by oblations of water, as well as other relations, where they appear to have a claim on the succession." And it is afterwards said in § 7, "If there be no relatives of the deceased, the preceptor, &c., according to the text of *Apastamba,* 'If there be no male issue, the nearest kinsman inherits, or in default of kindred, the preceptor.'" It follows from the above, not only that, in regard to cognates, is there no intention expressed in the law or to be inferred from it, of limiting the right of inheritance to certain specified relationships of that nature, but that, in

Madras High Court decision.

(*l*) 12 M. I. A. 448; S. C. 1 B. L. R. (P. C.) 44; S. C. 10 Suth. (P. C.) 32.
(*m*) 2 B. L. R. (F. B.); 28; S. C. 10 Suth (F. B.) 76.
(*n*) *Chelikani* v. *Suraneni,* 6 Mad. H. C. 278. (*o*) Manu, ix. § 187.

regard to other relationships also, there is free admission in the order of succession, prescribed by law for the several classes; and that all relatives, however remote, must be exhausted, before the estate can fall to persons who have no connection with the family. In this view plaintiff must be regarded as a relative entitled to succeed on an equal footing with her sisters, who are relatives of the same degree."

Madras decision discussed.

§ 495. This decision will, of course, settle the law in Madras unless reversed. But as it will not be a binding authority upon Mitakshara law in other parts of India, it may be as well to examine its reasoning more closely. The three cases quoted have, of course, no application. They merely decide that male relations, who come within the definition of a bandhu in the Mitakshara (*p*) are not excluded from the mere fact that they are not specifically enumerated in the next section. But if that definition means, as those cases held that it did mean, a person connected by funeral oblations with the deceased, then a sister does not come within the definition, not being "connected by funeral oblations" (*q*). It is also to be remarked that the enumeration in Mitakshara, ii. 6, though not exhaustive as to the individuals, includes none but males, and is, therefore, strong evidence that none but males were supposed capable of satisfying the definition. And the cases cited show that none but

(*p*) Mitakshara, ii. 5, § 3.

(*q*) According to the *Dharma Sindhu Sara* of Kasinatha, a work of the highest authority in the Benares School, among the persons who are competent to perform the funeral rites to a deceased kinsman it is stated that, "on failure of the daughter, and the nephew, the father, the mother, the daughter-in-law and the sister claim the right in succession. In case there are both uterine and stepsisters, the same rules apply to them as to uterine and stepbrothers. On failure of sisters their sons are entitled to this right." Raj. Sarvadhikari, 111. This right to perform ceremonies certainly does not carry with it any right under Benares law to inherit. See as to a daughter-in-law, *ante*, § 488 and as to a sister, *ante*, § 493. Mr. Rajkumar Sarvadhikari, after pointing out that the views of Balambhatta and Nanda Pandita in favour of a sister have met with no acceptance, says (p. 665), "According to the doctrines of the Benares School, then, the married and unmarried daughters of *gotraja-sapindas* are not entitled to inherit." The funeral rites which these females are competent to perform are only the *ekoddishta* or funeral ceremonies of the individual, ending with the first year's anniversary rites. They are not competent to perform the *parvana* rites, which are the most important of all, and upon the punctual observance of which the peace of the disembodied spirit depends (Raj. Sarvadhikari, 860, 84, 74.)

males could satisfy the definition, as there understood. The judgment, however, goes on to cite two texts as showing (apparently) that other relatives who are neither *gentiles* nor *bandhus* may inherit by virtue of mere propinquity. In the first passage (*r*), *Vijnanesvara* is weighing the comparative merits of the father and the mother, both of whom are gotraja sapindas. He decides in favour of the latter on the ground of propinquity, and proceeds, in the text cited by the High Court, to remark that this principle of propinquity applies not only to *sapindas*, but to *samanodakas*, "as well as other relatives, when they appear to have a claim to the succession." That is to say, given a rivalry between two persons, both entitled to inherit, the one who is nearest in blood shall take. The text does not attempt to lay down who have a claim to succession. On the contrary, it seems to assume that there may be relatives who would not "appear to have a claim to the succession." It does not define the class of heirs—that, as will be shown immediately, had been done already—but lays down a rule by which one member of the class is to be preferred to another. The word which is translated by Mr. Colebrooke "as well as other relatives," is simply *adi* appended to *samanodakas*, and means the like, or *et cetera* (*s*). It would be contrary to the ordinary principles of construction to interpret such a word as introducing a completely different genus. The next text proves exactly the opposite of what it is cited for by the High Court. To understand it we must go back a little. The first seven sections of the Mitakshara, cap. ii., are merely a commentary on the text of *Yajnavalkya* (*t*), "The wife, and the daughters also, both parents, brothers likewise and their sons, gentiles, *cognates* (*u*), a pupil and a fellow-student; on failure of the first among these, the next in order is indeed heir to the estate of one who departed for heaven, leaving no male issue. This rule extends to all

Madras decision discussed.

(*r*) Mitakshara, ii. 3, § 3, 4.
(*s*) See as to the use of this *adi*, Burnell's Preface to Varadraja.
(*t*) Yajnavalkya, ii. § 135; cited Mitakshara, ii. 1, § 2.
(*u*) Bandhu, see Goldstücker, 26.

(persons and) classes." This text recognizes no relatives coming after nephews who are not either gentiles (*gotraja*) or *bandhus*. Sections 1—4 treat of relations up to and including nephews. Section 5, § 1 defines *gotraja*, and § 3 defines *bandhus*. The remainder of section 5 illustrates the succession of gentiles or *gotrajas*. Section 6 illustrates the succession of *bandhus*. It is now settled that these illustrations are not exhaustive, but that any one who comes within the definition may inherit (§ 471). Then comes § 7, which treats of the succession of those who are not relatives at all. It commences, "If there be no relations of the deceased, the preceptor, or on failure of him the pupil, inherits, by the text of *Apastamba*. 'If there be no male issue, the nearest kinsman inherits, or in default of kindred the preceptor, or, failing him, the disciple.'" The Court infers from this "that in regard to other relationships also" (meaning, apparently, relationships which do not come under the head of cognates) "there is free admittance to the inheritance in the order of succession prescribed by law for the several classes, and that all relatives, however remote, must be exhausted before the estate can fall to persons who have no connection with the family." That is to say, the Court seems to think that the words, "If there be no relations of the deceased," let in a new class of relations, who are neither gentiles nor cognates, but who are connected with the deceased by propinquity. It would be rather remarkable if a section which is devoted to strangers should have this effect, and should, by a side wind as it were, bring in an entirely new set of heirs, who are not defined, and of whose very existence there is no previous hint. But the fact is that the word which Mr. Colebrooke has translated "relations" is *bandhu* (*v*). This makes everything consistent. Section 5 treats of *gotrajas*. Section 6 treats of *bandhus*. Section 7 of those who come in when there are no *bandhu*. There is no third class of persons who, being neither *gotraja* nor *bandhu*, are still relations. In the passage of *Apastamba*,

(*v*) Goldstücker, 26; *per curiam*, 16 Cal. p. 879.

clusion. That the Madras decisions are opposed to usage and authority in that Presidency, and that in Bombay, where a sister's right is undoubted, it is rested, not upon any conclusions derivable from the Mitakshara, but upon long custom and the express authority of the Mayukha.

Even in Madras a step-sister is not an heir (*c*).

(*c*) *Kumara Velu* v. *Virana*, 5 Mad. 29.

shara, to run counter to that which appears to them to be the current of modern authority" (z).

Later Madras decision.

§ 497. The case of *Kutti Ammal* v. *Radakrishna,* as well as the above observations upon it, were very fully considered by the Madras High Court in a later case (*a*), where a conflict arose between a sister and a sister's son, each claiming as heir to the deceased. It was not necessary to decide whether a sister could be heir to her brother, since, assuming that she could be, the Court was of opinion that the male claimant was a preferential heir. Had it been necessary to decide the point, the Court intimated that the criticism in the previous sections would have induced them to remit the point for decision to a Full Bench. They, however, suggested that the decision was right, on the ground that the term *bhinnagotra sapinda* as used by Vijnanesvara meant no more than a person connected by consanguinity, but belonging to a different family, either by birth or by marriage. They seemed disposed to doubt whether the Mitakshara had accepted the doctrine that females could only inherit under an express text, and they appeared to accept the authority of Sancha and Lichita as supplying such a text if one were necessary. Such a view is of course thoroughly intelligible and arguable, and is probably the line that would be followed with most chance of success if the case came before the final Court of Appeal. The principle so laid down has been followed by the Madras Court in later cases, while they have held that a father's sister, and a son's daughter, were within the line of possible heirs under the Mitakshara, although they would be postponed to male heirs more remotely connected with the deceased owner (*b*). It would be urged in reply with much force, that every other Court which professes to administer the Mitakshara law has come to a different con-

---

(z) *Supra*, 11 M. I. A. 403; *Kooer Goolab* v. *Rao Kurun*, 14 M. I. A. 196; S. C. 10 B. L. R. 1; *Chotay* v. *Chunno*, 6 I. A. 32; S. C. 4 Cal. 744.

(*a*) *Lakshmanammal* v. *Tiruvengada Mudali*, 5 Mad. 241.

(*b*) *Narasimma* v. *Mangammal*, 13 Mad. 10; *Nallanna* v. *Pounal*, 14 Mad. 149.

clusion. That the Madras decisions are opposed to usage and authority in that Presidency, and that in Bombay, where a sister's right is undoubted, it is rested, not upon any conclusions derivable from the Mitakshara, but upon long custom and the express authority of the Mayukha.

Even in Madras a step-sister is not an heir (*c*).

(*c*) *Kumara Velu* v. *Virana*, 5 Mad. 29.

CHAPTER XVIII.

INHERITANCE.

Order of Succession.

§ 498. We now proceed to examine the order of succession under Hindu law, always remembering that it only applies to estates held in severalty, unless in cases governed by Bengal law, where quasi-severalty is the normal condition of each sharer (§ 457). Each of the successive classes takes in default of the preceding. If the estate has once vested in any male he becomes a fresh stock, and on his death the descent is governed by the law of survivorship or of inheritance, according as he has left undivided coparceners or not. Where the estate has vested in a female, or in any number of females in succession to each other, on the death of the last descent is again traced from the last male holder, unless in certain cases under Bombay law, hereafter discussed (§ 565).

Issue

Issue.—If a man has become divided from his sons, and subsequently has one or more sons born, he or they take his property exclusively (§ 431). If he is undivided from them, his property passes to the whole of his male issue, which term includes his legitimate sons, grandsons, and great-grandsons (*a*). All of these take at once as a single heir, either directly or by way of representation. Suppose, for instance, a man has had three sons, and dies leaving his

---

(*a*) Baudhayana, i. 5, 11, § 9; Manu, ix. § 137, 185; Mitakshara, i. 1, § 3, ii. 8, § 1; Apararka cited Sarvadhikari, 649, 9 Cal. 320; Daya Bhaga, iii. 1, § 18, xi. 1, § 31—34; V. May., iv. 4, § 20—22; Viramit., p. 154, § 11; Vivada Chintamani, 295; per curiam, *Rutcheputty* v. *Rajunder*, 2 M. I. A. 156; *Bhyah Ram* v. *Bhyah Ugur*, 13 M. I. A. 378; S. C. 14 Suth. (P. C.) 1.

eldest son A., and B. the son of A.; two grandsons, C.[1] and C.[2], by his second son, and three great-grandsons, D[1], D.[2], and D.[3], by his third son; A. takes for himself and B., C.[1] and C.[2] take for themselves, and D.[1], D.[2], and D.[3] take for themselves, and these three lines all take at once, and not in succession to each other. The mode in which they take *inter se*, and the nature of the interests which they take, have been discussed already (*b*). This seems to be an exception to the general rule, that among heirs of different degrees, the nearer always excludes the more remote (*c*). It really is no exception. It is merely an illustration of the rule that property, which is held as separate is one generation, always becomes joint in the next generation (§ 244). If it is held by a father who is himself the head of a coparcenary, it passes at his death to the whole coparcenary, and not to any single member of it, all of them having under the Mitakshara equal rights by birth. The Daya Bhaga puts forward the same view from its religious aspect. According to it, the son, grandson, and great-grandson, all present religious offerings to the deceased, and all with equal efficacy. There is, therefore, no reason why one should be preferred to the other. But as the grandson presents no offerings while his own father is alive, B. does not take directly, but C. and D. do (*d*).

take simultaneously.

Right of issue.

§ 499. Property which is in its nature impartible, as a Raj or ancient Zemindary, can, of course, only descend to one of the issue; which that one is to be will depend upon the custom of the family (§ 51). In general, such estates descend by the law of primogeniture (*e*). In that case the eldest son is the son who was born first, not the first-born son of a senior, or even of the first married, wife (*f*).

Primogeniture.

(*b*) See *ante* § 422. (*c*) *Khettur* v. *Poorno*, 15 Suth. 482.

(*d*) Daya Bhaga, iii. 1, § 18, 19.

(*e*) This presumption of course may be displaced by evidence showing that some other rule prevailed such as selection of the successor. *Ishri Singh* v. *Baldeo Singh*, 11 I. A. 135. See also *Achal Ram* v. *Udai Pertab*, *post* § 501.

(*f*) Manu, ix. § 125, 126; *Rughonath* v. *Hurrehur*, 7 S. D. 126 (146); *Bhujangrav* v. *Malojirav*, 5 Bom. H. C. (A. C. J.) 161; *Ramalakshmi* v. *Sivanan-*

Primogeniture. So long as the line of the eldest son continued in possession, the estate would pass in that line (*g*). That is to say, on the death of an eldest son, leaving sons, it would pass to his eldest son and not his brother. But there is a singular want of authority as to the rule to be adopted where an eldest son, who has never taken the estate, has died, leaving younger brothers, and also sons. The point has been twice argued very lately before the Privy Council, but in neither case was it necessary to decide the question. The only cases that I am aware of in which the point was actually decided, were in Madras. The earlier cases arose in the same family, as will appear from the following pedigree. It only shows so much of the relationship as will render the litigation intelligible.

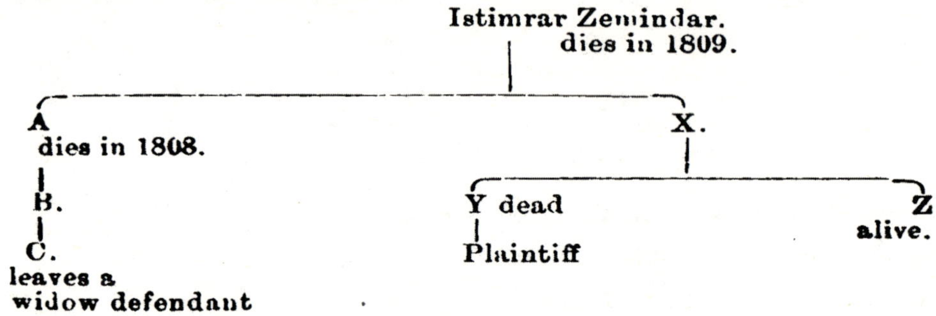

Here it will be seen that at the death of the Zemindar he left a grandson, B., by an elder son, and a younger son X. The latter got possession of the Zemindary, but B. brought a suit against him, and ultimately recovered possession. There were circumstances in the case which might have justified the decree on other grounds, but on the whole it must be taken that the Provincial Court, which tried the case, went on the broad principle that the son of a predeceased elder son was entitled to the Zemindary in preference to a surviving younger son. No appeal was preferred against the decree. The estate then passed to C., at whose death it was claimed by the plaintiff, as son of Y., the

---

tha, 14 M. I. A. 570; S. C. 12 B. L. R. 396; S. C. 17 Suth. 553; *Pedda Ramappa* v. *Bangari*, 8 I. A. 1; S. C. 2 Mad. 286. See as to the old law, *ante*, § 87.

(*g*) See pedigree in *Yenumula* v. *Ramandora*, 6 Mad. H. C. 93; *Naraganti* v. *Venkatachelapati*, 4 Mad. 250.

deceased elder brother of Z. The original Court held, amongst other grounds for dismissing the claim, that Z. was a nearer heir than the plaintiff. This decision was reversed by the Madras High Court, which held that by the ordinary law of primogeniture, applicable to impartible estates, the plaintiff represented the eldest line. It will be seen that there was an important distinction between the two disputed successions. In the first case B. was the grandson of the last male holder, and therefore, in an ordinary case of succession, would have as good a claim as his uncle X.; a son and a grandson being considered equally near, and equally efficacious (§ 498). But in the second case the plaintiff and Z. were cousins, and in an ordinary case of collateral succession the nearer takes before the more remote, as for instance, a brother before a nephew (§ 525, 526). This was the view submitted to the Judicial Committee. On the other hand it was argued that the property, though impartible, was still joint family property, and therefore passed by survivorship, in which case Y. was the heir expectant during his life, and at his death his rights passed on to the plaintiff who represented him. The Judicial Committee, however, found that there had been a partition of the whole property during the life of B., under which he took the Zemindary as separate estate. Consequently, the widow of C. was the heir, and it was unnecessary to decide between the claims of the plaintiff and Z (*h*). Upon principle it would seem, that at the death of each holder the estate would go to the eldest member of the class of persons who, at that time, were his nearest heirs. If so, Z. was certainly nearer to C. than the plaintiff. This seems to have been the ground of the decision of the Judicial Committee, in a case relating to the Tipperah Raj, where

Primogeniture.

(*h*) *Runganayakamma* v. *Ramaya*, P. C. 5th July 1879. In the case of *Periasami* v. *Periasami*, 5 I. A. 61; S. C. 1 Mad. 312, the same point was argued but not decided. There the converse question arose. The Zemindary had been awarded to a person standing in the same position as Z., and the widow, who was defendant, urged that the real heir was a person who stood in the same position as the plaintiff, and whose rights had not been noticed by the High Court.

Whole and half-blood.

the question was, whether an elder brother by the half blood, or a younger brother by the full blood, would be the next heir to a Raj. They were pressed with the argument that on the death of the previous holder, who was the father both of the deceased Rajah and of the claimants, the Raj had vested in all the brothers jointly, though of course it could only be held by one. If so, of course, all the brothers were equally near to the father, and on the death of one it would survive to the eldest. But the Committee held that in the case of an impartible estate survivorship cannot exist, as being an incident of joint ownership, which is inconsistent with the separate ownership of the Rajah. Therefore, title by survivorship, where it varies from the ordinary rule of heirship, cannot, in the absence of custom, furnish the rule to ascertain the heir to a property which is solely owned and enjoyed, and which passes by inheritance to a single heir. Then, upon the double ground of nearness of kin and religious efficacy, the whole blood was entitled in preference to the half blood (*i*); that is to say, they held that nothing vested in any member of the family until the death of the last holder, and that at his death the heir was the person who was nearest to him. Some of the language used by their Lordships in their judgment seems inconsistent with the Shivagunga case, and those cases which have followed it (§ 487), but the decrees themselves, and the *ratio decidendi* in each, are perfectly in harmony. The Shivagunga case settled that where an impartible Zemindary was joint property, the heir to it must be sought among the male coparcenary. That is to say, no female nor separated member could succeed. The Tipperah case decided, that amongst these coparceners the person to succeed was the one who was nearest the last male holder at the time of his death, and that the principle of survivorship could not be applied so as to give the succession to a person who was not the nearest heir.

(*i*) *Neelkisto Deb v. Beerchunder*, 12 M. I. A. 523, 540; S. C. 3 B. L. R. (P. C.) 13; S. C. 12 Suth. (P. C.) 21.

§ 500. In a later case, where the succession to one of the Chittur Polliems was disputed, the Madras High Court followed its own decision in *Runganayakamma v. Ramaya*, and refused to be bound by the principle laid down in the Tipperah case. The state of the family is shown by the diagram. On the death of a distant collateral relation,

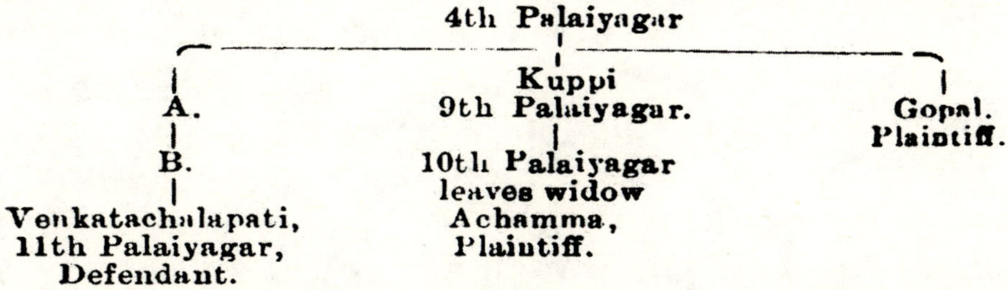

Kuppi succeeded as 9th Palaiyagar by an arrangement with his elder brother A. The High Court found that the effect of this arrangement was, that the elder consented to resign his immediate right of succession and that of his descendants in favour of Kuppi and his descendants, but that any rights which A. and his line might have on failure of Kuppi and his line were preserved intact. Kuppi was succeeded by his son, who died leaving no issue, a widow Achamma, his uncle Gopal, and his cousin Venkatachalapati. The Government gave the Polliem to the last named person, and he was sued by both the widow and Gopal. The claim of the widow was dismissed on the ground that the family was undivided, and that of Gopal on the ground that the defendant was the nearest heir. The Court held that the ruling in the Tipperah case that co-ownership, and therefore survivorship, did not exist in impartible property, was opposed to the doctrine of the Shivagunga case, and to the ordinary law of Southern India and Benares, respecting the impartible property of a joint family. They laid down the canon that " when impartible property passes by survivorship from one line to another, it devolves not necessarily on the coparcener nearest in blood, but on the nearest coparcener of the senior line" (*k*).

(*k*) *Naraganti* v. *Venkatachalapati*, 4 Mad 250, 265.

Lineal and ordinary primogeniture.

§ 501. In a later case the Judicial Committee drew a distinction between lineal and ordinary primogeniture, which may perhaps reconcile the apparent conflict of cases (*l*). The estate was one of the Oudh taluks. Under Act I of 1869 which governs such estates it is provided that each taluq is to be entered in one or other of certain lists, which regulate its mode of devolution. The estate in question was entered in the second list, which is a list of the taluqdars whose estates, according to the custom of the family before 1856, ordinarily devolved upon a single heir. It was not entered in the third list, which included estates regulated by the rule of primogeniture. The plaintiff was the eldest surviving male of the eldest branch of the family of Pirthi Pal from whom descent was to be traced, but there were in existence other males of junior branches of the same family who were nearer of kin to Pirthi Pal than he was. The defendant admittedly had no title. Both Courts found that the estate went by the rule of primogeniture; by which apparently they only meant, that, as between several persons of the same class, the eldest would be entitled to succeed. Both Courts found in favour of the plaintiff, but the Judicial Commissioner seems to have thought that his decision only went in favour of the family as against the defendant, and that the rights of the respective members of the family, *inter se*, would be still open to discussion. The Privy Council reversed the decree of the lower Courts. They pointed out that the plaintiff in ejectment must make out an absolute title in himself. It was necessary therefore for the plaintiff to make out that the estate descended according to the rules of lineal primogeniture as distinguished from descent to a single heir amongst several in equal degree. That when a taluqdar's name was entered in the second list and not in the third, the estate although it is to descend to a single heir, is not to be considered as an estate passing according to the rules of lineal primogeniture. Consequently that the plaintiff had not established a title

(*l*) *Achal Ram* v. *Udai Pertab*, 11 I. A. 51.

which would enable him to evict a defendant in actual possession.

§ 502. Possibly the following rules may be found to reconcile all the cases : Suggested rules.

1. When an estate descends to a single heir, the presumption is that it will be held by the eldest member of the class of persons, who would hold it jointly if the estate were partible.

2. In the absence of evidence to the contrary, the heir will be the eldest member of those persons who are nearer of kin to the last owner than any other class, and who are equally near to him as between themselves.

3. Special evidence will be required to establish a descent by lineal primogeniture, that is by continual descent to the eldest member of the eldest branch, in exclusion of nearer members of younger branches.

4. The presumption as to primogeniture of either sort may be rebutted by showing a usage that the heir should be chosen on some other ground of preference

§ 503. Illegitimate sons in the three higher classes never take as heirs, but are only entitled to maintenance (§ 434). It is said that by a special usage they may inherit, but in the only cases in which such a special usage was set up it was negatived (*m*). The illegitimate son of a Sudra may, however, under certain circumstances, inherit either jointly or solely. His rights have already been referred to under the head of Partition (§ 434), but it will be necessary to go a little more fully into them here. His position rest upon two texts. *Manu* says (*n*), "A son begotten by a man of Illegitimate sons.

(*m*) *Mohun* v. *Chumun*, 1 S. D. 28 (37); *Pershad* v. *Muhesree*, 3 S. D 132 (176); *Bhaoni* v. *Maharaj*, 3 All. 738.

(*n*) ix. § 179. The words 'by the other sons' in Sir W. Jones' translation are taken from the gloss of Kullaka Bhatta. Dr. Bühler translates the same text,

the servile class on his female slave, or on the female slave of his male slave, may take a share of the heritage, if permitted (by the other sons)." *Yajnavalkya* enlarges the rule as follows : "Even a son begotten by a Sudra on a female slave may take a share by the father's choice. But, if the father be dead, the brethren should make him partaker of the moiety of a share; and one who has no brothers may inherit the whole property in default of daughters' sons" (*o*). The first question that arises upon these texts is as to the nature of the connection out of which the illegitimate son contemplated by them must issue. Are the texts to be taken literally, as denoting that the mother must be the slave of the father, or do they denote a son born from a concubine, or the offspring of a merely temporary intercourse? On this point there is a direct conflict of authority.

Illegitimate son of a Sudra.

Whether his mother must have been a slave.

Meaning of slave.

§ 504. *Jimuta Vahana,* as translated by Mr. Colebrooke, takes the less strict view. He says in reference to *Manu,* "The son of a Sudra by a female slave, *or other unmarried woman,* may share, &c.;" and he paraphrases the text of *Yajnavalkya* by the words "begotten *on an unmarried* woman, and having no brother, &c." (*p*). In a case which arose in Calcutta, Mr. Justice *Mitter* stated that the above passages of the Daya Bhaga were incorrectly translated, and that the first passage should run, "The son of a Sudra by an unmarried female slave, &c.;" and that the second passage should begin, "Having no other brother begotten on a married woman, he may take the whole property." The Court, therefore, held that the words "son of a female slave" must be literally interpreted, so far as the districts governed by Bengal law were concerned, and that an illegitimate son whose mother was not a slave could not inherit (*q*). Now, there seems to be no ground for suppos-

"if permitted (by his father)." This agrees with the rule laid down by Yajnavalkya.

(*o*) Yajnavalkya, ii. § 133, 134; Mitakshara, i. 12, § 1.

(*p*) Daya Bhaga, ix. § 29, 31; 3 Dig. 143.

(*q*) *Narain* v. *Rakhal*, 1 Cal. 1; S. C. 23 Suth. 334, citing 1 W. MacN. 18; 2 W. MacN. 15, n.; Dattaka Chandrika, v. § 30, followed, after an examination of the Madras and Bombay cases, in *Kirpal Narain* v. *Sukurmoni*, 19 Cal. 91.

ing that there is any difference in this point between the law of Bengal and the other provinces, as all the authorities rely upon the same texts. As slavery was abolished by Act V of 1843, it follows, if the above construction is sound, that the inheritance of the illegitimate son of a Sudra, born after that date, has now become impossible. On the other hand, the Bombay High Court in an equally recent case, give a literal translation of the text of *Jimuta Vahana,* which exactly corresponds with Mr. Colebrooke's translation (*r*). So, *Mahesvara* renders the same text: "He being born of an unmarried woman, and having no brother born of a wedded wife," &c. (*s*). Prosonno Coomar Tagore renders the corresponding passage by *Vachespati Misra:* "A son of a Sudra by an unmarried woman," (*t*) and the same rendering is given by Mr. Borradaile of the passage in the Mayukha (*u*). If, however, the proper translation of the passage in the Daya Bhaga be that which is given by Mr. Juttice *Mitter,* then the question would be narrowed to this: What is meant by the term *Dasi,* or female slave? The Dattaka Mimamsa, in describing the slave's son (*Dasi putra*), says, "A female purchased by price, who is enjoyed, is a slave. The son who is born on her is considered a slave son" (*v*). **Meaning of slave.** The point is discussed by the Bombay High Court, apparently without any knowledge of the Calcutta case, and they arrive at the conclusion that the word does not necessarily mean anything more than an unmarried Sudra woman kept as a concubine (*w*). In Madras it has frequently been held that the illegitimate son of a Sudra will inherit, and, although it has not been necessary to decide the point, it has been stated, or assumed, that the mother need not be a slave in the strict sense of that term. In Southern India, at all events, the word *Dasi* is invariably applied to a dancing girl

(*r*) *Rahi* v. *Govind*, 1 Bom. 110. (*s*) Daya Bhaga, ix. § 31, note.
(*t*) Vivada Chintamani, 274.
(*u*) V. May, iv. 4, § 32. The Mitakshara, i. 12, § 2, and the Dattaka Chandrika, v. § 30, only use the term "female slave."
(*v*) Dattaka Mimamsa, iv. § 75, 76.
(*w*) *Rahi* v. *Govind*, 1 Bom. 97, followed *Sadu* v. *Baiza*, 4 Bom. 37, 44.

in a pagoda (*x*). Finally upon a review of all the authorities, the Madras High Court has ruled that "although the primary meaning of the word *Dasi* was a slave, it included also a concubine, or a woman of the servile class in a secondary sense, and there is reason to hold upon the texts that an unmarried Sudra woman kept as a continuous concubine came within its scope" (*y*). And the Judicial Committee has also stated, though without reference to this point, that "they are satisfied that in the Sudra caste illegitimate children may inherit" (*z*). Throughout the *futwahs* recorded by Messrs. West and Bühler, the term slave girl, or *Dasi*, and concubine, appear to be treated as convertible terms (*a*). The Allahabad High Court follows the Madras and Bombay ruling in preference to that of the Calcutta Judges (*b*).

Connection must be continuous, and lawful.

§ 505. Probably in former times the permanent concubine was always a slave, that is, a person purchased, or born in the house, and incapable of leaving it at her own free will. But the principle of the rule seems to have been, that as the marriage tie was less strict among Sudras than among the higher classes, so the issue of women who were permanently kept by Sudras, though not actually married to them, was regarded as something between a legitimate son and the mere bastard offspring of a promiscuous, or illegal, intercourse. Accordingly, it has been held that the son born of an absolutely prohibited union, such as an incestuous, or adulterous, connection, could not inherit, even to a Sudra; and it was suggested, though not absolutely decided,

---

(*x*) *Chendrabhan* v. *Chingooram*, Mad. Dec. of 1849, 50; *Pandaiya* v. *Puli*, 1 Mad. H. C. 478, affirmed; *Sub nomine*, *Inderun* v. *Ramasawmy*, 13 M. I. A. 141; S. C. 3 B. L. R. (P. C.) 1; S. C. 12 Suth. (P. C.) 41; S. C. 4 Mad. Jur. 328; *Muttusamy* v. *Venkatasubha*, 2 Mad. H. C. 293; S. C. on appeal, 12 M. I. A. 203; S. C. 2 B. L. R. (P. C.) 15; S. C. 11 Suth. (P. C.) 6; *Datti Parisi* v. *Datti Bangaru*, 4 Mad. H. C. 204; S. C. 4 Mad Jur. 136; *Krishnamma* v. *Papa*, *ib* 234; S. C. 4 Mad. Jur. 130. See too *per* Mr. Colebrooke, 2 Stra. H. L. 68.

(*y*) *Krishnayan* v. *Muttusami*, 7 Mad. 407, p. 412; *Brindavana* v. *Radhamani*, 12 Mad. p. 86

(*z*) *Per* Giffard, L. J., *Inderun* v. *Ramasawmy*, 13 M. I. A. 159; *supra*, note (*x*).

(*a*) W. & B. 375—385.

(*b*) *Sarasuti* v. *Mannu*, 2 All. 134; *Hargobind* v. *Dharam Singh*, 6 All. 329.

that "the intercourse between the parents must have been a continuous one; there must have been an established concubinage, or, in other words, the woman must have been one exclusively kept by the man" (c). In Bombay it is said by the High Court, that the condition that the Sudra woman should never have been married, has in practice been disregarded. But the cases referred to by the Court are all cases in which the subsequent connection with the previously married woman was not an adulterous one, but was sanctioned by usage having the force of law (d).

§ 506. Supposing an illegitimate Sudra to be entitled, the next question would be as to his rights. Upon this the Mitakshara says in explanation of the texts of *Manu* and *Yajnavalkya* (§ 503), "The son begotten by a Sudra on a female slave, obtains a share by the father's choice, or at his pleasure. But after the demise of the father, if there be sons of a wedded wife, let these brothers allow the son of the female slave to participate for half a share, that is, let them give him half as much as the amount of one brother's allotment; however, should there be no sons of a wedded wife, the son of the female slave takes the whole estate, provided there be no daughters of a wife, nor sons of daughters. But if there be such, the son of the female slave participates for half a share only" (e). The Bengal authorities are to the same effect, but say nothing of his right to share with the daughters (f). The only writer who refers to his right where there is a widow, is the author of the *Dattaka Chandrika.* He says, "If any, even in the series of heirs down to the daughter's son, exist, the son by a female slave does not take the whole estate, but on the contrary shares equally

Share of illegitimate son.

(c) *Datti Parisi* v. *Datti Bangaru*, 4 Mad. H. C., 204, 215; S. C. 4 Mad. Jur. 136; *Vencatachella* v. *Parvatham*, 8 Mad. H. C. 134; *Rahi* v. *Govind*, 1 Bom. 97; *Kuppa* v. *Singaravelu*, 8 Mad. 325; *Dalip* v. *Ganpat*, 8 All. 387. See *ante*, § 72.

(d) *Rahi* v. *Govind*, 1 Bom. 113.

(e) Mitakshara, i. 12, § 2.

(f) Daya Bhaga, ix. § 29–31; D. K. S. vi. § 32—35; 3 Dig. 143; Viramit., p. 130, § 22.

His share

with such heir" (*g*). This is also the opinion of a pandit whose futwah is given in West and Bühler 383. On the other hand, the editors, in a remark appended to that futwah, say, "The illegitimate son would inherit the whole estate of his father, even though a widow of the latter might be living." This remark is adopted by the High Court of Bombay, and they state that the illegitimate son will also share the property with the daughter and the daughter's son, while there is a widow in existence, subject, of course, to the charge of maintaining the widow (*h*). The rule was affirmed in a later case also in Bombay (*i*). There *Manaji*, a Sudra, died leaving a legitimate son *Mahadev*, an illegitimate son *Sadu*, two widows *Baiza* and *Savitri*, and a legitimate daughter *Daryabai*. *Mahadev* and *Sadu* entered into joint possession of the estate, and then *Mahadev* died without issue. It was held that if *Mahadev* had died before his father, *Sadu* would have been entitled to only half a share, *i.e.*, one-third of the property, and the remaining two-thirds would have vested in *Darya* as the legitimate daughter of *Manaji*, and *Baiza* and *Savitri* would have been entitled to maintenance. But that under the actual facts of the case *Mahadev* and *Sadu* took the whole, subject to the maintenance and marriage expenses of the widows and daughter, and that, on the death of *Mahadev*, *Sadu* took the whole by survivorship. The result would be, that wherever there was an illegitimate son, the widow would be entitled to no more than maintenance. Also, that a daughter and a daughter's son would, in such a case, inherit to the exclusion of the widow, and maintain her, though it is a first principle that neither can ever take, except in default of her.

where there is a widow.

§ 507. It certainly would require very strong authority to establish such an abnormal state of things. Yet there is absolutely no original authority for it, except the remark of Messrs. West and Bühler, which itself rests upon

---

(*g*) Dattaka Chandrika, v. § 30, 31. (*h*) *Rahi* v. *Govind*, 1 Bom. 97, 104.
(*i*) *Sadu* v. *Baiza*, 4 Bom. 37, 52.

nothing (*k*). The chapters of the Hindu law-books, which treat of a widow's estate, nowhere suggest such a limitation of her rights. No text writer, no decision, alludes to such a possibility. The passages which discuss the position of an illegitimate son do not even mention the widow, and seem to me not to involve the doctrine of the Bombay High Court, by necessary, or even by probable, implication. Suppose we try a perfectly literal interpretation of the texts upon the subject. *Yajnavalkya* says that an illegitimate son without brothers may inherit the whole estate in default of daughters' sons. The obvious meaning is that until the line, which terminates with a daughter's son, is exhausted, he cannot take the whole estate, but is only entitled to a part of it. *Vijnanesvara* makes this even clearer, by saying that a daughter also excludes him from the whole estate, leaving him still entitled to part. He does not think it necessary to say the same as to the widow, who ranks before the daughter. Then, as to the intermediate period, he is to have a share, which is to be half the share for a son. The literal meaning of this is, that in each given instance you are to ascertain what share he would take if he were legitimate, and then give him half of it. Suppose there is a legitimate son, then, if he also were legitimate, the estate would be divided into moieties, of which each would take one. Being illegitimate, he only takes half of the moiety, leaving the remaining three-quarters to his brother (*l*). Suppose there is no legitimate son, but a widow, daughter, or daughter's son; now, if he were legitimate, he would take the whole. Being illegitimate,

Share of illegitimate Sudra.

(*k*) There is a futwah quoted at W. & B. 380, in which illegitimate sons are made to exclude a widow. But the widow in question was one who had been married twice. Such a widow appears not to be entitled to the full rights of a widow married as a virgin. See W. & B. 386.

(*l*) This is the view taken by one Shastry, W. & B. 382. But according to others the meaning is that the division is to be made so that the legitimate son shall have double the share of the illegitimate, that is, in the case put, the former would have two-thirds and the latter one-third; W. & B. 381, 384; *per curiam*, *Sadu* v *Baiza*, 4 Bom. 52. A similar difference exists as to the mode in which the fourth share to be received by a daughter on partition was to be calculated, *ante*, § 441, or by an adopted son in the case of the subsequent birth of a legitimate son; *ante*, § 155.

he takes only half, the other half going to the widow, daughter, or daughter's son, respectively. If there are none of these, or upon the extinction of all, he takes the whole. Now this is exactly what *Devanda Bhatta* says in the passage above referred to (*m*). And the same is substantially the view taken by the Bombay Shastries quoted in West and Bühler, though they differ as to the exact proportions taken, and by Mr. W. MacNaghten and *Jagannatha* (*n*). In the first Bombay case the whole discussion was *obiter dictum*, as the Court decided that the claimant did not come within the terms of the texts at all. In the second case the illegitimate had actually taken along with the legitimate son, so as to let in the principle of survivorship. The Madras High Court appears to take the view of the widow's rights which has been suggested above in cases where the property is partible (*o*), and gives the widow the preference over the illegitimate son, where the property is impartible (*p*). In a recent case in Bombay, *Sargent*, C. J. seems to have adopted the view of the above texts which is stated in this paragraph (*q*).

Bastards inherit to each other.

§ 508. Illegitimate sons can only take to their father's estate. They have no claim to inherit to collaterals (*r*). It has also been held by the Madras High Court that they have no claim by survivorship against the undivided coparceners of the father, and therefore cannot sue his brothers and their sons for a partition after his death (*s*). The principle is, that as against the father the illegitimate son can only take by his choice, and therefore is not a joint heir with him, until he has actually been made such by some paternal act (*t*). In the absence of such an act he can

(*m*) Dattaka Chandrika, v. § 30, 31.
(*n*) W. & B. 381—386; acc. 1 W. MacN. 18; 3 Dig. 143.
(*o*) 8 Mad. 561. (*p*) *Parvati* v. *Thirumalai*, 10 Mad. 334.
(*q*) *Sheagiri* v. *Girewa*, 14 Bom. 282. In Khandeish a legitimate daughter and an illegitimate son share together. Steele, 180.
(*r*) 2 W. MacN. 15, n.; *Nissar* v. *Kowar*, Marsh, 609.
(*s*) *Krishnayan* v. *Muttusami*, 7 Mad. 407; *Kanoji* v. *Kandoji*, 8 Mad. 557; approved 12 Mad. p. 403.
(*t*) *Sadu* v. *Baizu*, 4 Bom. 37; *per curiam*, 11 Cal. 714.

only take as heir, and survivorship will intercept his claim in that capacity, just as it does that of the widow, daughter, or daughter's son, with whom he would share. If, however, the father leaves legitimate and illegitimate sons, then the legitimate takes in preference to all other heirs and the illegitimate share with him. When they have once taken jointly, on the death of the legitimate son without issue, the illegitimate takes the whole by survivorship, and in this way supersedes the right of the widow (*u*). It is also to be remembered that, as the English rule which prevents bastards tracing to their father has no existence in Hindu law, so the fact of illegitimacy does not prevent bastard brothers claiming to each other. Accordingly, where two take jointly, the estate passes by survivorship in the ordinary way. Still less is there any absence of heritable blood as between bastards and their mother (*v*).

Several widows.

§ 509. WIDOW.—In default of male issue, joint with, or separate from, their father, the next heir is the widow (*w*). Where there are several widows, all inherit jointly, according to a text of the Mitakshara, which should come in at the end of ii. 1, § 5, but which has been omitted in Mr. Colebrooke's translation: "The singular number, 'wife,' in the text of *Yajnavalkya*, signifies the kind. Hence, if there are several wives belonging to the same, or different classes, they divide, and take it (*x*)" All the wives take together as a single heir with survivorship, and no part of the hus-

(*u*) *Sadu* v. *Baiza*, *ub. sup*; *Jogendro* v. *Nittyanund*, 11 Cal. 702, *affd.* 17 I. A. 128; S. C. 18 Cal. 151, where it was held that the same rule applied to an impartible Raj.

(*v*) *Venkataram* v. *Venkata Lutchmee*, 2 N. C. 304; *Pandaiya* v. *Puli*, 1 Mad. H. C. 478; *Mayna Bai* v. *Uttaram*, 2 Mad. H. C. 197; *Myna Boyee* v. *Ootaram*, 8 M. I. A. 400; S. C 2 Suth. (P. C.) 4; W. & B. 455. 11 Mad. p. 397; *Sivasangu* v. *Minal*, 12 Mad. 277; *Narasanna* v. *Gangu*, 13 Mad. 133; *per curiam*, 11 Cal. p. 714; *Tara Munnee* v. *Motee Buneanee*, 7 S. D. 278 (325).

(*w*) Mitakshara, ii. 1; Daya Bhaga, xi. 1, § 43; V. May., iv. 8, § 1—7, Viramit., p. 131, ch. iii. *Ramappa* v. *Sithammal*, 2 Mad. 182; *Balkrishna* v. *Savitribai*, 3 Bom. 54. See *ante*, § 481, *et. seq.* So the widow succeeds at once on renunciation of his rights by the prior heir. *Ruvee* v. *Roopshunker*, 2 Bor. 656, 665 [713]; *Ram Kannye* v. *Meernomoyee*, 2 Suth. 49.

(*x*) See as to the omission, Goldstücker, 15; Smriti Chandrika, xi. 1, § note 2; *Tara Chand* v. *Reeb Ram*, 3 Mad. H. C. 51; Viramit., p. 153.

Several widows. band's property passes to any more distant relation till all are dead (*y*). Where the property is impartible, as being a Raj or ancient Zemindary, of course it can only be held by one, and then the senior widow is entitled to hold it, subject to the right of the others to maintenance (*z*). In other cases the senior widow would, as in the case of an ordinary coparcenership, have a preferable right to the care and management of the joint property. But she would hold it as manager for all, with equality of rights, not merely on her own account, with an obligation to maintain the others (*a*).

§ 510. Where several widows hold an estate jointly, or where one holds as manager for the others, each has a right to her proportionate share of the produce of the property, and of the benefits derivable from its enjoyment. And the widows may be placed in possession of separate portions of the property, either by agreement among themselves, or by decree of Court, where from the nature of the property, or from the conduct of the co-widows, such a separate possession appears to be the only effectual mode of securing to each the full enjoyment of her rights. But no partition can be effected between them, whether by consent or by adverse decree, which would convert the joint estate into an estate in severalty, and put an end to the right of survivorship. In the case of *Rindamma* v. *Venkataramappa* cited below, it was suggested that the widows might possibly enter into such an agreement as would bind each to an absolute surrender of all interest in the share of the other, so as to let in the next heirs of the husband after the death of that other (*b*). It is difficult, however, to see how such an

(*y*) 1 W. MacN. 20; 2 W. MacN. 37; F. MacN. 6; *Berjessory* v. *Ramconny*, 2 M. Dig. 80; *Rumea* v. *Bhagee*, 1 Bom. H. C. 66; *Jijoyiamba* v. *Kamakshi*, 3 Mad. H. C. 424; *Bhugwandeen* v. *Myna Baee*, 11 M. I. A. 487; S. C. 9 Suth. (P. C.) 23; *Nilamani* v. *Radhamani*, 4 I. A. 212; S. C. 1 Mad. 290; *Bulakidas* v. *Keshavlal*, 6 Bom. 85. The contrary opinion of Jimuta Vahana is not now law; Daya Bhaga, xi. 1, § 15, 47.

(*z*) *Vutsavoy* v. *Vutsavoy*, 1 Mad. Dec. 453; *Seenevullala* v. *Tungama*, 2 Mad Dec. 40.

(*a*) *Jijoyiamba* v. *Kamakshi*, *ub. sup.*

(*b*) *Jijoyiamba* v. *Kamakshi*, *Bhugwandeen* v. *Myna Baee*. *Nilamani* v. *Radhamani*, *ub. sup.*, note (*y*); See however *Mt. Sundar* v. *Mt. Parbati*, 16 I. A. 186. S. C. 12 All. 51; *Rindamma* v. *Venkataramappa*, 8 Mad. H. C. 268; *Rampiyari* v. *Mulchand*, 7 All. 114.

agreement could bind the surviving widow, for the benefit of any heir of the husband who was not a party to the contract. On the same principle of joint tenancy with survivorship, no alienation by one widow can have any validity against the rights of the others without their consent, or an established necessity arising under circumstances which rendered it impossible to seek for consent (c). It has, however, been held that a widow can alienate her life interest as against her co-widows, just as she can against the reversioners, and that such alienation can be enforced by partition against them, without prejudice to their rights of survivorship (d).

Effect of want of chastity.

§ 511. Whatever may have been the ancient law on the subject (§ 88), it is quite clear now that chastity is a condition precedent to the taking by the widow of her husband's estate (e). But a question upon which there has been much conflict of authority arises, whether the incontinence of a widow is like any other ground of disability, which only prevents the inheritance from vesting, or whether it will devest her estate when she has once become entitled to it in possession. The weight of authority in earlier times seems certainly to have been in favour of the latter view, upon the principle, no doubt, that the widow only received her husband's estate for the purpose of providing for his spiritual necessities, and that she would be unable to do so if she were living in a state of guilt. In later times, however, the more secular view prevailed, that a widow's estate was in this respect not different from that of any other limited owner, and could not be defeated by any ground of incapacity intervening after it had once

(c) *Bhugwandeen* v. *Myna Baee*, *ub. sup*; *Vasudeva Singaro* v. *Vizianagram Rani*, 19 I. A. See *post*, Chap. XX.

(d) *Janokinath* v *Mothuranath*, (F. B.) 9 Cal. 580, disagreeing with *Kathaperumal* v. *Venkabai*, 2 Mad. 174; *Ariyaputri* v. *Alamelu*, 11 Mad. 304.

(e) Mitakshara, ii. 1, § 37—39; Smriti Chandrika, xi. 1, § 12—21; Vivada Chintamani, 289—91; V. May., iv. 8, § 2, 6, 8, 9; Daya Bhaga, xi. 1, § 47, 48, 56. See all the cases discussed, *Kery Kolitany* v. *Moneeram*, 13 B. L. R. 1; S. C. 19 Suth. 367.

vested in possession. The whole law upon the subject was elaborately discussed and examined in a case before the Bengal High Court, in which the latter doctrine was maintained, and this decision was affirmed by the Privy Council. The same ruling had previously been laid down by the Courts of Bombay, the North-West Provinces and the Punjab, and it may be assumed, therefore, to be the general law of India (*f*).

Second marriage.

§ 512. The second marriage of a widow was formerly unlawful, except where it was sanctioned by local custom (§ 89), consequently it entailed the forfeiture of a widow's estate, either as being a signal instance of incontinence, or as necessarily involving degradation from caste (*g*). Even where second marriages were allowed in Bombay, the wife was compelled to give up the property she had inherited from her first husband (*h*). This seems also to have been the custom among the Tamil tribes, upon the evidence of the Thesawaleme (*i*), and the same principle has been recently applied by the High Court of Madras in the case of a second marriage of a Maraver woman, and of a Lingait Gounden in the Wynaad (*k*). In the case of the Maraver woman they proceeded upon the ground that the Maravers were governed by the general body of Hindu law, except in so far as it could be shown that exceptional usages prevailed. Therefore, that the special usage which allowed a Maraver widow to re-marry, did not prevail over the general principle that a widow could only retain the property of her husband so long as she continued to be the surviving portion of the deceased. In the case of the *Lingait Gounden*

Act authorising widow marriage.

(*f*) *Kery Kolitany* v. *Moneeram*, 13 B. L. R. 1; S. C. 19 Suth. 367; *affd.* 7 I. A. 115; S. C. 5 Cal. 776; *Parvati* v. *Bhiku*, 4 Bom. H. C. (A. C. J.) 25; *Nehalo* v. *Kishen*, 2 All. 150; *Bhawani* v. *Mahtab*, *ib.*, 171; Punjab customs, 61. See as to the effect of Act XXI of 1850 (Freedom of Religion) upon the unchastity of a widow. *Rajkoonwaree* v. *Golabee*, S. D. of 1858, 1891.

(*g*) 1 Stra. H. L. 242; W. & B. 110; *Kery Kolitany* v. *Mooneeram*, 13 B. L. R. 75; S. C. 19 Suth. 367.

(*h*) *Hurkoonwur* v. *Ruttun Baee*, 1 Bor. 431 [475]; *Treekumjee* v. *Mt. Laroo*, 2 Bor. 361 [397]; Steele, 26, 159, 168.

(*i*) Thesawaleme, i. § 10.

(*k*) *Murugayi* v. *Viramakali*, 1 Mad. 226; *Koduthi* v. *Madu*, 7 Mad. 321.

they found a special usage that the widow on her re-marriage ceased to inherit her husband's estate. In an Allahabad case a widow of the Sweeper caste had re-married, and it was found as a fact "that she did what in her caste never had been and was not prohibited by the law to which she was subject, and her marriage was a good and valid marriage." The Court held that she did not forfeit her interest in her husband's property, since the Act of 1856 was passed for the purpose of enabling persons to marry who could not re-marry before the Act and § 2 only applies to such persons (*l*). In this case no special usage entailing forfeiture was suggested, and no very strong presumption could arise as to the rigorous application of Hindu law to such outcastes as sweepers. The marriage of widows is now legalised in all cases. But the Act which permits it provides that "All rights and interests which any widow may have in her deceased husband's property, by way of maintenance, or by inheritance to her husband or to his lineal successors, or by virtue of any will or testamentary provision conferring upon her, without express permission to re-marry, only a limited interest in such property, with no power of alienating the same, shall, upon her re-marriage, cease and determine as if she had then died; and the next heirs of her deceased husband, or other persons entitled to the property on her death, shall thereupon succeed to the same" (*m*). It has been held that this section only operates as a forfeiture of existing rights, and creates no disability to take future interests in the family of the widow's late husband. Therefore, that she may succeed as heir to the estate of her son by a first marriage, who had died after her second marriage (*n*). There has been a conflict of decisions in Calcutta, as to whether the disabling section applies to a Hindu widow, who had ceased to be a Hindu at the time of her second

(*l*) *Har Saran Das* v. *Nandi*, 11 All. 330.

(*m*) Act XV of 1856, § 2 (Hindu Widow Marriage). This Act does not render illegal proceedings of a caste nature, such as exclusion from a temple, founded upon the Act of re-marriage. *Venkatachalapati* v. *Subbarayadu*, 13 Mad. 293.

(*n*) *Akora* v. *Boreani*, 2 B. L. R. (A. C. J.) 199; S. C. 11 Suth. 82; *Rupan* v. *Hukmi*, Punjab Customs, 99.

marriage. It has been lately decided by a Full Bench that it does (*o*). There a Hindu widow, who had inherited the estate of her deceased husband, married a second husband who was not a Hindu, in the form provided by Act III of 1872, having previously made a declaration under § 10 of that Act that she was not a Hindu. The Chief Justice stated the opinion of the Full Bench as follows (p. 299),— "Section 1 no doubt relates to marriages between Hindus, but § 2 includes all widows who are within the scope of the Act, that is to say, all persons who being Hindus become widows, and it must follow from this, that if any such widow marries, she is deprived by the section of the estate which she inherited from her deceased husband."

This decision leaves untouched the questions decided by the Madras Court in the *Lingait Gounden* case, and by the Allahabad Court in the Sweeper case. *Wilson*, J. who was one of the referring Judges in the Calcutta case, pointed out that the Act of 1856, as explained by its preamble, applied "to all Hindu widows other than those referred to under the words 'with certain exceptions' who could without the aid of the Act marry according to the custom of their caste. He would, therefore, have agreed with the Allahabad Court that neither the enabling nor the disabling clauses (§§ 1 and 2) of that Act applied to such exceptional persons. On the other hand, both he and *Banerji*, J. agreed that it was of the essence of a Hindu widow's estate that it should only continue while held by her as a widow, and that no act of hers could enlarge this estate (*p*). In the case, therefore, of a widow who could re-marry without the assistance of the Act, the question would still remain, was her estate restricted, either by general law or local usage to the period of her widowhood. If it was, the legality of her second marriage would not prevent the determination of her estate.

(*o*) *Matangini Gupta* v. *Ram Rutton Roy*, 19 Cal. 289, over-ruling *Gopal Singh* v. *Dhungasee*, 3 Suth. 206.
(*p*) 19 Cal. pp. 292, 293, 295.

It has been laid down in the North-West Provinces that a widow, having minor children, who has re-married is not their mother within the meaning of Act XV of 1856, § 3, so as to entitle her to be made guardian by virtue of her relationship, in the absence of an express appointment by the late husband (*q*).

Daughter,

§ 513. THE DAUGHTER comes next to the widow, taking after her or in default of her (*r*), except where by some special local or family custom she is excluded (*s*). It has been held in Bengal that she is under the same obligation to chastity as a widow; therefore, as the law is now settled, incontinence will prevent her taking the estate, but will not deprive her of it if she has once taken it (*t*). In Bombay, however, it has been held after a full examination of all the authorities bearing on the point, that, under the law prevailing in Western India, a widow is the only female heir who is excluded from inheritance, by incontinence, and the opinion of the Allahabad High Court seems to be in the same direction, though the point has not required an express decision (*u*). It will be observed that the Daya Bhaga and the Daya Krama Sangraha, which are the leading Bengal authorities, both quote in support of the daughter's right of succession, a text ascribed to *Vrihaspati* which states that she must be virtuous (*v*). The same text is also relied on in the passages in the Viramitrodaya and the Smriti Chandrika which refer to a daughter's right, while no mention of the qualification is contained in the correspond-

how far she is bound to chastity

(*q*) *Khushali* v. *Rani*, 4 All. 95.

(*r*) Mitakshara, ii. 2; Smriti Chandrika, xi. 2; V. May., iv. 8, § 10; Vivada Chintamani, 292; Daya Bhaga, xi. 2, § 1, 30; Viramit., pp. 137, 140.

(*s*) See as to such customs, Perry, O. C. 117; *Bhan Nanaji* v. *Sundrabai*, 11 Bom. H. C. 249; *Russic* v. *Purush*, S. D. of 1847, 205; *Hiranath* v. *Ram Narayan*, 9 B. L. R. 274; S. C. 17 Suth. 316; *Chowdhry Chintamun* v. *Mt. Nowlukho*, 2 I. A. 263; S. C. 24 Suth. 255; *Prasijivan* v. *Bai Reva*, 5 Bom. 482; Punjab Customs, 16, 25, 37, 47.

(*t*) 2 W. MacN. 182; *per Mitter*, J., *Kery Kolitany* v. *Moneeram*, 13 B. L. R. 48; S. C. 19 Suth. 367; *ante*, § 511; *Ramnath* v. *Durga*, 4 Cal. 550.

(*u*) *Advyapa* v. *Rudrava*, 4 Bom. 104; *Deokee* v. *Sookhdeo*, 2 N.-W. P. p. 363; *Ganga* v. *Ghasita*, 1 All. 46; followed as regards a mother in *Kojiyadu* v. *Lakshmi*, 5 Mad. 149.

(*v*) 3 Dig. 186; Daya Bhaga, xi. 2, § 8; Daya Krama Sangraha, i. 3, § 4.

ing passages of the Mitakshara and Mayukha (*w*). This is the more remarkable in the case of the Mitakshara, since the author borrows part of the text of *Vrihaspati*, omitting the clause which requires virtue in the daughter. It may, therefore, well be that in the Bengal school chastity may be essential to a daughter's right to inherit, while it may be unnecessary in Western India. Further, in Bengal there is the authority of *Rughunandana* that the word, 'wife,' in passages relating to the rules of succession, is only illustrative, and applies to females generally. This he expressly states to be the case as to the obligation to chastity (*x*). In considering the question in the Northern parts of India which are governed by the Mitakshara, it will be important to ascertain what weight is to be given to the opinion of the Viramitrodaya, while in Southern India similar reference will have to be made to the Smriti Chandrika. It will be seen in the next paragraph that the Smriti Chandrika appears to base its views as to the rights of daughters upon religious principles, which have failed to secure acceptance in Madras. There seems to be no doubt that a daughter will be excluded by incurable blindness or any other ground of disability, such as would disqualify a male (*y*). It must be remembered that a daughter can only inherit to her own father. The daughter of the brother, the uncle, or the nephew is not an heir (§ 491). If a son dies before his father, leaving a daughter, and then the father dies, also leaving a daughter, the inheritance will pass to the daughter of the father (*z*). And so, if one of two undivided brothers under Mitakshara law dies first, leaving a daughter, and afterwards the surviving brother dies childless, the estate will pass to his collateral relations, not to the daughter of the first brother (*a*). Of course, in Bengal the daughter would at once have taken the share of her deceased father.

only inherits to her own father,

(*w*) Viramit., p. 179, § 3; Smriti Chandrika, xi. 2, § 26; Mitakshara, ii. 1, § 2; V. May., iv. 8, § 10—12. See *per Westropp*, C. J., 4 Bom. p. 110, *supra*.
(*x*) See *Ramnath* v. *Durga*, 4 Cal. p. 554.
(*y*) *Bakubai* v. *Manchhabai*, 2 Bom. H. C. 5.
(*z*) *Sooranamy* v. *Vencataroyen*, Mad. Dec. of 1853, 157; 2 W. MacN. 176.
(*a*) *Soobba Moodelly* v. *Auchalay*, Mad. Dec. of 1854, 158.

except in Bombay.

The case of the father's daughter, claiming as sister, has already been discussed (§ 489). In Bombay, a granddaughter, a brother's daughter, and a sister's daughter are held capable of inheriting, on the principle which prevails in Western India, that females born in the family are *gotraja sapindas* (*b*). They come in, however, not as daughters but as distant kindred.

Precedence.

§ 514. The mode in which daughters inherit *inter se* depends upon the school of law which governs the case. The different principles which prevail upon this point in Bengal and the other provinces have been stated already (§ 479). Mr. W. MacNaghten states the order of precedence in the different provinces as follows (*c*).

Bengal.

"According to the doctrine of the Bengal school the unmarried daughter is first entitled to the succession; if there be no maiden daughter, then the daughter who has, and the daughter who is likely to have male issue are together entitled to the succession, and on failure of either of them, the other takes the heritage. Under no circumstances can the daughters who are either barren, or widows destitute of male issue, or the mothers of daughters only, inherit the property (*d*).

Precedence.

Benares.

But there is a difference in the law as it obtains in Benares on this point; that school holding that a maiden is in the first instance entitled to the property; failing her, that the succession devolves on the married daughters who are indigent, to the exclusion of the wealthy daughters; that in default of indigent daughters, the wealthy daughters are competent to inherit; but no preference is given to a daughter who has, or is likely to have male issue, over a

(*b*) W. & B. 495—498. See *ante*, § 488.

(*c*) 1 W. MacN. 22.

(*d*) See also 2 W. MacN. 39, 44, 46, 49, 58; V. Darp, 166, 172; Anon, 2 M. Dig. 17; *Rajchunder* v. *Mt. Dhunmunee*, 3 S. D. 862 (482); *Binode* v. *Purdhan*, 2 Suth. 176. But since a widow may now re-marry (§ 512) and have male issue, it has been held that even in Bengal widowhood is not *per se* an absolute ground of exclusion. *Bimola* v. *Dangoo*, 19 Suth. 189. A widowed daughter who, at the time the succession opens, has a son who is dumb, but not shown to be incurably so, may inherit. It was not decided whether she would have been excluded, if it could be shown that the defect was congenital and incurable. *Chara Chunder* v. *Nobo Sundari*, 18 Cal. [illegible]

daughter who is barren or a childless widow (*e*). According to the law of Mithila, an unmarried daughter is preferred to one who is married; failing her, married daughters are entitled to the inheritance. But there is no distinction made among the married daughters; and one who is married, and has, or is likely to have male issue, is not preferred to one who is widowed or barren. Nor is there any distinction made between indigence and wealth." The law of the Mitakshara has been also stated in accordance with this view by Mr. Colebrooke and the High Courts of Bengal, Bombay and the North-West Provinces, and by the Privy Council (*f*).

Mithila.

Smriti Chandrika.

I have already observed (§ 479), that the *Smriti Chandrika* follows the doctrine of religious efficacy so far as to exclude barren daughters, and Madras pandits have stated in accordance with it, that a daughter with male issue excludes a sonless daughter (*g*). The High Court of Madras, however, upon a full examination of all the authorities, has declined to follow the Smriti Chandrika upon this point in preference to the Mitakshara (*h*).

Several daughters.

Succession of several daughters.

§ 515. Where daughters of the same class exist, they all, except in Bombay, take jointly in the same manner as widows (§ 509) with survivorship (*i*). If they choose to divide the property for the greater convenience of enjoyment they can do so, but they cannot thereby create estates of severalty, which would be alienable or descendible in any different manner (*k*). If at the death of the last survivor another class of daughters exists, who have been previously exclud-

---

(*e*) Indigence is an absolute term, and is not limited to cases where a daughter, otherwise well off, has received no provision from her father; *Danno* v. *Darbo*, 4 All. 243. As to Bombay law, acc. *Bakubai* v. *Manchhabai*, 2 Bom. H. C. 5; *Poli* v. *Narotum*, 6 Bom. H. C. (A. C. J.) 183; *Jamnabai* v. *Khimji*, 14 Bom. p. 12.

(*f*) 2 Stra. H. L. 242; 2 Suth. 176, *supra*; *Uma Deyi* v. *Gokoolanund*, 5 I. A. 46; S. C. 3 Cal. 587; *Audh Kumari* v. *Chandra*, 2 All. 561; *Jamnabai* v. *Khimji*, 14 Bom. p. 4.

(*g*) Smriti Chandrika, xi. 2, § 21; Stra. Man. § 328; *Doorasamy* v. *Ramamaul*, Mad. Dec of 1852, 177. Semb., *Gocoolanund* v. *Wooma Daee*, 15 B. L. R. 405; S. C. 23 Suth. 340; *affd.* 5 I. A. 46; S. C. 3 Cal. 587.

(*h*) *Simmani* v. *Muttammal*, 3 Mad. 265.

(*i*) Daya Bhaga, xi. 2, § 15, 30; V. May., iv. 8, § 10; *Kattama Nachiar* v. *Dorasinga Tevar*, 6 Mad. H. C. 310.

(*k*) F. MacN. 55; *per curiam*, *Sengamalathammal* v. *Valayuda*, 3 Mad. H. C. 317.

ed, they will come in as next heirs, if admissible (*l*). And although according to Bengal law a childless, or barren, widow cannot inherit originally, still if she has already taken as one of a class of sisters, that which would have been an original disqualification will not prevent her taking the whole by survivorship on the death of her co-heiresses (*m*). Where property is impartible, the eldest daughter of all the sisters, or of the class which takes precedence, is the heir (*n*).

Bombay. In Bombay the text of the Mayukha (iv. 8, § 10) "if there be more daughters than one they are to divide (the estate) and take (each a share)" has been held to support the view that daughters take not only absolute but several estates, which, in the absence of issue, they may dispose of during their lives or by will. Of course where this doctrine prevails there can be neither a joint holding nor survivorship (*o*).

Exception to rule. § 516. It was at one time supposed that an exception to the right of any daughter (otherwise admissible) to succeed before a daughter's son, existed in Bengal. Mr. MacNaghten says: "If one of several daughters who had, as maidens, succeeded to their father's property, die leaving sons, and sisters, or sister's sons, then, according to the law of Bengal, the sons alone take the share to which their mother was entitled, to the exclusion of the sisters, or sisters' sons" (*p*). This exception rests on the authority of *Srikrishna Tarkalankara* alone. In the corresponding passage of the Daya Bhaga, the case of the maiden daughter is made no exception to the general rule, that on the death of any daughter the estate which was hers becomes the property of those persons,

(*l*) *Dowlut Kooer* v. *Burma Deo*, 14 B. L. R. 246 (note); S. C. 22 Suth. 55.
(*m*) *Aumirtolall* v. *Rajonee Kant*, 2 I. A. 113; S. C. 15 B. L. R. 10; S. C. 23 Suth. 214.
(*n*) *Kattama Nachiar* v. *Dorasinga Tevar*, 6 Mad. H. C. 310.
(*o*) *Bulakhidas* v. *Keshavlal*, 6 Bom. 85. See *post*, § 570.
(*p*) 1 W. MacN. 24; D. K. S. i. 3, § 3; *Bijia Debia* v. *Mt. Unnapoorna*, 8 S. D. 26 (35); *per curiam*, *Dowlut Kooer* v. *Burma Deo*, 14 B. L. R. 246 (note); S. C. 22 Suth. 55; *Kattama Nachiar* v. *Dorasinga Tevar*, 6 Mad. H. C. 332.

a married daughter or others, who would regularly succeed if she had never existed (*q*). There seems to be no reason for the alleged rule, and the High Court of Bengal has finally decided that the alleged exception does not exist (*r*).

Exclusion of daughters and their issue in Punjab.

§ 517. In Northern India the principle of agnation prevails in its strictest form. Not only are agnates preferred to cognates, but in many tribes of the Punjab cognates are absolutely excluded from succession, so that the landed property of the family may not pass out of the gotra. Even such near relations as daughters and their sons are debarred from inheritance (*s*). In numerous cases from Oudh which have come under my notice in appeal to the Privy Council, the village *wajib-ul-arz* states that whether the property be ancestral or self-acquired, daughters and daughter's children have no right of inheritance. A circular of the Chief Commissioner of Oudh, 42 of 1864, lays down the same rule as regards the great Chattri families of that province.

Position of daughter's son.

§ 518. The Daughter's Son, though a *sapinda,* is not a *gotraja sapinda*. He is nearer in degree, but exactly similar in class, to a sister's son or an aunt's son, who only come in as *bandhus* (*t*). Yet, according to all systems, even those which prefer the *gotraja sapinda* as far as the seventh degree, and the Samanodakas as far as the fourteenth degree, to the *bandhus,* he comes in before brothers and other more remote sapindas. The cause of this peculiar favour is to be found in the old practice of appointing a daughter to raise up issue for a man who had none. The daughter so appointed was herself considered as equal to a son. Naturally her son was equivalent to a grandson, and as the merits of son and grandson are equal, he ranked as as a son (*u*). Consequently, we find him enumerated among

Origin of his right.

(*q*) Daya Bhaga, xi. 2, § 30.
(*r*) *Timmoni* v. *Nibarun*, 9 Cal. 154.
(*s*) Punjab Customs, 72; Punjab Customary Law, II. 80; III. 48.
(*t*) *Ante* § 464. Apararka treats the daughter's son as a mere bandhu, and as such postpones him to the gotraja sapindas. Sarvadhikari, 791.
(*u*) Manu, ix. § 127—136; Vasishtha, xvii. § 12; *ante*, § 478.

the subsidiary sons, and taking a very high rank among them, generally second or third (*v*). Subsequently the appointment of a daughter to raise up issue for her father became obsolete (*w*). But the fact of the nearness of daughter and daughter's son remained, and their natural claim to succession on the ground of mere consanguinity recommended itself for general acceptance. The daughter's son ceased to rank as son, but he retained his place next in succession to the daughter, or where there was no daughter (*x*). In some parts of Northern India he is excluded by special custom (*y*).

The daughter's son is not enumerated in the list of heirs by *Yajnavalkya* (*z*), and from this it was at one time suggested by some commentators that his right did not accrue till all those who were enumerated had been exhausted (*a*). Mr. W. MacNaghten also states that he is not recognized as an heir by the Mithila school (*b*). But this seems to be incorrect, even as regards the Vivada Chintamani, which appears to admit him after both parents (*c*). It is now settled, however, after an elaborate examination of all the Mithila authorities, that the daughter's son is admitted by them after the daughter just as elsewhere (*d*). **Mithila.**

§ 519. A daughter's son can never succeed to the estate of his grandfather, so long as there is in existence any daughter who is entitled to take, either as heir or by survivorship to her other sisters (*e*). The reason is that he takes, **He succeeds after all daughters.**

(*v*) See table, *ante*, § 64.
(*w*) Smriti Chandrika, x. § 5, 6. See question whether this is so raised, but not decided. *Thakoor Joobnath* v. *Court of Wards*, 2 I. A. 163; S. C. 15 B. L. R. 190; S. C. 23 Suth. 409.
(*x*) Mitakshara, ii. 2, § 6; Smriti Chandrika, xi, 2, § 28; V. May., iv. 8, § 18; Daya Bhaga, xi. 2, § 17—29; D. K. S. i. 4; Vivada Chintamani, 294.
(*y*) Punjab Customs, 16, 37; *ante*, § 517.
(*z*) Yajnavalkya, ii. § 135, 136.
(*a*) Daya Bhaga, xi. 2, § 27; D. K. S. i. 4, § 3.
(*b*) 1 W. MacN. 23; and so the pandits, *Pokhnarain* v. *Mt. Seesphool*, 3 S. D. 114 (152).
(*c*) Vivada Chintamani, 294.
(*d*) *Surja Kumari* v. *Gandhrap*, 6 S. D. 140 (168).
(*e*) *Aumirtolall* v. *Rajoneekant*, 2 I. A. 113; S. C. 15 B. L. R. 10; S. C. 23 Suth. 214; *Sastri* v. *Vengu Ammal*, Mad. Dec. of 1861, 137; 1 W. MacN. 24;

not as heir to any daughter who may have died, but as heir to his own grandfather, and, of course, cannot take at all so long as there is a nearer heir in existence. For the same reason, sons by different daughters all take *per capita* not *per stirpes;* that is to say, if there are two daughters, one of whom has three sons, and the other has four sons, on the death of the first daughter, the whole property passes to the second, and on her death, it passes to the seven sons in equal shares (*f*). And on the same principle, where the estate is impartible, it passes at the death of the last daughter to the eldest of all the grandsons then living, and not to the eldest son of the last daughter who held the estate (*g*). Daughter's sons do not take as coparceners with right of survivorship. Such survivorship only exists where the property has been taken as unobstructed heritage. It is obvious that such a coparcenary could not exist in the cases of sons who might all belong to families differing in gotra from such other, and from that of their maternal grandfather (*h*). It was laid down by the Bengal pandits in one case, that if property passes to daughter's sons, any such sons born afterwards will also take shares, in reduction of the shares already taken (*i*). But this assumes that a daughter capable of producing sons is still alive. If so, the grandsons could not take at all.

Takes *per capita*.

Is full owner.

§ 520. A daughter's son, on whom the inheritance has once actually fallen, takes it as full owner, and thereupon he becomes a new stock of descent, and on his death the succession passes to his heir, and not back again to the heir

2 W. MacN. 44, 57; *Ramdan* v. *Beharee*, 1 N. W. P. 200; *Baijnath* v. *Mahabir*, 1 All. 608; *Jamiyatram* v. *Bai Jamna*, 2 Bom. H. C. 10, *contra* is now overruled. See *Lakshmebai* v. *Ganpat Moroba*, 5 Bom. H. C. (O C. J.) 139; *Sibchunder* v. *Sreemutty Treepoorah*, Fulton, 98; *Sant Kumar* v. *Deo Saran*, 8 All. 365.

(*f*) 1 W. MacN. 24; 1 Stra. H. L. 139; 3 Dig. 501; *Ramdhun* v. *Kishenkanth*, 3 S. D. 100 (133).

(*g*) *Kattama Nachiar* v. *Dorasinga Tevar*, 6 Mad. H. C. 310; *Muttu Vaduganadha* v. *Dorasinga Tevar*, 8 I. A. 99; S. C. 3 Mad. 290. The doctrine stated in the Sarasvati Vilasa (§ 632, 655) that property as soon as it passes to a daughter vests at once in that daughter's son and in his son, cannot be now maintained.

(*h*) *Jasoda Koer* v. *Sheo Pershad*, 17 Cal. 33; *Gopalasami* v. *Chinnasami*, 7 Mad. 458.

(*i*) *Mt. Solukna* v. *Ramdolal*, 1 S. D. 324 (434).

of his grandfather (*k*). But until the death of the last daughter capable of being an heiress, he takes no interest whatever, and therefore can transmit none. Therefore, if he should die before the last of such daughters leaving a son, that son would not succeed, because he belongs to a completely different family, and he would offer no oblation to the maternal grandfather of his own father (*l*). Nor can the daughter's daughter ever succeed, except in Bombay, whether her mother has taken or not, because she confers no benefits on her maternal grandfather, and is estranged from his lineage (*m*).

Daughter's son has no vested right

Daughter's daughter.

§ 521. PARENTS.—The line of descent from the owner being now exhausted, the next to inherit are his parents. And here, for the first time, there is a variance between the different schools of law as to the order in which they take. The right of the mother as an heir was very early recognized (§ 480), but her precedence as regards the father, who was also stated to be an heir, was left uncertain. The Mitakshara gives the preference to the mother on the ground of propinquity, and is followed in Mithila by the Vivada Chintamani; and this is stated by Mr. W. MacNaghten to be the law of Benares and Mithila (*n*). The Smriti Chandrika prefers the father, upon the authority of a text of *Bhrat Vishnu* (*o*). The Madhaviya leaves the point undecided, and *Varadrajah,* apparently following *Srikrishna,* seems to make both inherit together (*p*). *Sambhu* says that the point is immaterial, as whichever of the two takes will take

Precedence.

(*k*) 3 Dig. 494, 502; *Ramjoy* v. *Tarrachund,* 2 M. Dig. 79; *Sibta* v. *Badri,* 8 All. 134.

(*l*) Daya Bhaga, xi. 2, § 2; iv. 3, § 34; *Ilias* v. *Agund Rai,* 3 S. D. 37 (50); *Senkul* v. *Aurulananda,* Mad. Dec. of 1862, 27; *Dharap Nath* v. *Gobind Saran,* 8 All. 614; *Strinavasa* v. *Dandayudapani,* 12 Mad. 411. See to the contrary, but I think erroneously, *Sheo Sehai* v. *Omed,* 6 S. D. 301 (378); *Doe* v. *Ganpat,* Perry, O. C. 133. The son of a daughter's son may take in the absence of other heirs as a bhandu. *Krishnaya* v. *Pichamma,* 11 Mad. 287.

(*m*) Daya Bhaga, xi. 2, § 2; F. MacN. 6; W. & B. 477, 496.

(*n*) Mitakshara, ii. 3. See Notes by Colebrooke. Vivada Chintamani, 293, 294; 2 W. MacN. 55, n.; *ante,* § 471. The Sarasvati Vilasa also follows the rule of the Mitakshara in preference to that of the Smriti Chandrika. § 566—572.

(*o*) Smriti Chandrika, xi. 3, § 9. So also Apararka, Sarvadhikari, 427.

(*p*) Madhaviya, § 38; Varadrajah, 36. See 3 Dig. 480.

for the benefit of the other (*q*). The Viramitrodaya, while giving a general preference to the doctrine of the Mitakshara, reconciles it with the conflictng text of *Bhrat Vishnu* by making the precedence of father or mother depend on personal merit, which again he appears to test by pecuniary rather than by moral considerations (*r*). In Bengal it is quite settled that the father takes before the mother, both on the express authority of *Vishnu*, and upon principles of religious efficacy (*s*). The Mayukha takes the same view, and a futwah to the same effect is recorded from Poonah. But Messrs. West and Bühler adopt the opposite order on the authority of the Mitakshara and their opinion has been recently confirmed by the High Court (*t*). In Guzerat the father is preferred to the mother on the authority of the Mayukha (*u*).

Stepmother.

§ 522. According to Bengal law a stepmother does not succeed to her stepson. This would necessarily be so upon the principles of *Jimuta-Vahana*, as she does not participate in the oblations offered by such stepson (*v*). The Mitakshara does not notice the point, but the reasons given by *Vijnanesvara* for allowing the mother to inherit, *viz.*, her close relationship to her son, seem to show that he could only have had the natural mother in view (*w*). The Bengal pandits have, on several occasions, asserted that the word *mata* in the Mitakshara includes a stepmother, and, in accordance with that view, it was decided that a woman in Orissa would inherit to her stepson (*x*). These opinions, however, were reviewed by the Full Bench of the Bengal High Court in a case from Mithila, and it was decided that

---

(*q*) Smriti Chandrika, xi. 3, § 8. (*r*) Viramit., pp. 185—191.

(*s*) Vishnu, xvii. § 6, 7; Daya Bhaga, xi. 3; D. K. S. i. 5; 3 Dig. 502—505; 2 W. MacN. 54; *Hemluta* v. *Goluck Chunder*, 7 S. D. 108 (127).

(*t*) V. May., iv. 8, § 14; W. & B. 110, 448; V. N. Mandlik, 360, 378; *Balkrishna* v. *Lakshman*, 14 Bom. 605.

(*u*) *Khodabai* v. *Bahdar*, 6 Bom 541

(*v*) Daya Bhaga, iii. 2, § 30; xi. 6, § 3; D. K. S. vi. § 23; vii. § 3; 2 W. MacN. 62; *Lakhi* v. *Bhairab*, 5 S. D. 315 (369); *Bhyrobee* v. *Nubkissen*, 6 S. D. 53 (61); *Alhadmoni* v. *Gokulmoni*, S. D. of 1852, 563.

(*w*) Mitakshara, ii. 3; *acc.* 1 Stra. H. L 144; *Kesserbai* v. *Valab*, 4 Bom. 208.

(*x*) 2 W. MacN. 63; *Bishenpiria* v. *Soogunda*, 1 S. D. 37 (49); *Narainee* v. *Hirkishor*, *ib.* 39 (52).

a stepmother was equally excluded by the Mitakshara and the Daya Bhaga. The same rule applies *à fortiori* to higher ascendants, such as a grandmother (*y*). In Bombay it has been decided that a stepmother cannot be introduced as an heir under the word "mother," but that she is a more distant heir as the wife of a *gotraja sapinda*, and, therefore, herself a *gotraja sapinda*, according to the doctrines of that Presidency. Her place in the line of heirs has not yet been settled (*z*). In Madras also it has been decided that a stepmother cannot succeed in competition with a sapinda of the deceased (*a*).

Disability arising from unchastity.

In Bengal it has been held that the rule which incapacitates an unchaste wife from succession, applies also to a mother. This is based not upon any express text relating to mothers, but upon the authority of *Rughunandan*, who lays it down that the passages in the Daya Bhaga which refer to a wife have a general application to all female heirs. He expressly asserts that in the text of *Katyayana*, "the wife who is chaste takes the wealth of her husband," the word "wife" is illustrative (*b*). On the other hand in Bombay and Madras it has been decided that the condition as to chastity only applies to a widow, and the inclination of the Court of the North-West Provinces seems to be in the same direction (*c*). It is admitted that an estate, once taken by a mother, will not be divested on the ground of unchastity (*d*). Since Act XV of 1856 (Hindu Widow Marriage) a mother will not lose her rights as heiress to her son, by reason of a second marriage previous to his death (*e*).

Brothers.

§ 523. BROTHERS.—Next to parents come brothers. There

(*y*) *Lala Joti* v. *Mt. Durani*, B. L. R. Sup. Vol. 67; S. C. Suth. Sp. No. 173.
(*z*) *Kesserbai* v. *Valab*, 4 Bom. 188.
(*a*) *Kumaravelu* v. *Virana*, 5 Mad. 29; *Muttammal* v. *Vengalakshmi*, *ib.* 32; *Mari* v. *Chinnammal*, 8 Mad. 107.
(*b*) *Ramnath* v. *Durga*, 4 Cal. 550.
(*c*) *Advyapa* v. *Rudrava*, 4 Bom. 104; *Kojiyadu* v. *Lakshmi*, 5 Mad. 149; *Deokee* v. *Sookhdeo*, 2 N.-W. P. p. 363; *Ganga* v. *Ghasita*, 1 All. 46; *ante*, § 513.
(*d*) See cases in two preceding notes.
(*e*) *Akora* v. *Boreani*, 2 B. L. R. (A. O. J.) 199; S. C. 11 Suth. 82; *ante*, § 512.

are texts which show that at one time their position in the line of heirs was unsettled, the brother being by some preferred to the parents, while according to others even the grandmother was preferred (*f*). From a religious point of view the claim of the brother would seem to preponderate over that of the father, as he offers exactly the same three oblations as were incumbent on the deceased, while the father receives one and offers two, *viz.*, to his own father and grandfather. But the principle of propinquity in this, as in other cases, turned the scale (*g*).

Whole before half-blood.

Among brothers, those of the whole blood succeed before those of the half-blood. The Mitakshara prefers them on the natural ground of closer relationship, and the Bengal authorities on the ground that the former offer oblations to the ancestors of the deceased both on the male and female side, while the latter offer oblations in the male line only. If there are no brothers of the whole blood, then those of the half-blood are entitled, according to the law of Benares and Bengal, and the Punjab, and that which prevails in those parts of the Bombay Presidency which follow the Mitakshara. The Mayukha, however, prefers nephews of the whole to brothers of the half-blood, and its authority is paramount in Guzerat, and the island of Bombay (*h*).

Supposed exception in Bengal,

§ 524. Until very lately it was supposed, that the preference of the whole to the half-blood in succession between brothers was subject to an exception in Bengal where the property was undivided. The point could never arise out of Bengal, for under Mitakshara law, where the property is undivided, it passes by survivorship, and not by inheritance

---

(*f*) Smriti Chandrika, xi. 6, § 4—16, 24.

(*g*) Mitakshara, ii. 4; Vivada Chintamani, 295; V. May., iv. 8, § 16; Daya Bhaga, xi. 5; D. K. S. i. 7.

(*h*) Mitakshara, ii. 4, § 5, 6; Vivada Chintamani, 296; Daya Bhaga, xi. 4, § 9—12; D. K. S. i. 7, § 1—3; Viramit., p. 193, § 2; 3 Dig. 509, 528; *Neelkisto Deb* v. *Beerchunder*, 12 M. I. A. 523; S. C. 3 B. L. R. (P. C.) 13; S. C. 12 Suth. (P. C.) 21; *Krishnaji* v. *Pandurang*, 12 Bom. H. C. 65; V. May., iv. 8, § 16; W. & B. 455, 458; Punjab Customs, 26—28.

But in Bengal the share of an undivided coparcener does not lapse into the entire property, but passes to his own heirs, of whom, in the absence of nearer relations, his brother is one (§ 246). *Jagannatha* quotes a text of *Yama*: —"Immovable undivided property shall be the heritage of all the brothers (be their mothers the same or different), but immovable property, when divided, shall on no account be inherited by the sons of the same father only." This he explains by saying, "If any immovable property of divided heirs, common to brothers by different mothers, have remained undivided, being held in coparcenary, the half-brothers shall have equal shares with the rest. But the uterine brother has the sole right to divided property, movable or immovable" (*i*). And in various cases it was decided that where the brothers were undivided, those of the half-blood were entitled to come in as heirs equally with those of the whole blood (*k*). If this distinction really existed, it would merely show that the Bengal lawyers did not push the doctrine, that undivided brothers hold their shares in quasi-severalty, to its logical consequences. If brothers of the whole and half-blood are to succeed equally in a system which is governed by the principle of religious efficacy, it can only be by treating the property of the deceased as undivided family property, which is to be dealt with according to the rules of partition, and not as several property, to be dealt with according to the rules of inheritance. Of course, on the former principle the brothers would all share equally, as being equally related to their common father (§ 432). The whole law on the point was, however, subsequently examined by a Full Bench of the High Court of Bengal, and it was decided that no such distinction existed, and that brothers of the half could never take along with brothers of the whole blood, unless the former were undivided, and the latter divided (*l*).

where brothers undivided,

held not to exist.

(*i*) 3 Dig. 517, 518.

(*k*) 2 W. MacN. 66; *Tilock* v. *Ram Luckhee*, 2 Suth. 41; *Kylash* v. *Gooroo*, 3 Suth. 43; *Shibnarain* v. *Ram Nidhee*, 9 Suth. 87.

(*l*) *Rajkishore* v. *Gobind Chunder*, 1 Cal. 27; S. C. 24 Suth. 234; affirmed *Sheo Soondary* v. *Pirthee*, 4 I. A 147.

Undivided before divided.

Where no preference exists on the ground of blood an undivided brother always takes to the exclusion of a divided brother, whether the former has re-united with the deceased, or has never severed his union (*m*).

Illegitimate brothers may succeed to each other (§ 508).

Nephews.

§ 525. Nephews.—In default of all brothers, of the whole or half-blood, the sons of brothers, or nephews, succeed. To this, as I have already observed, the Mayukha appears to make an exception. It allows the sons of a brother of the full blood to succeed before a half-brother, and it appears also to allow the sons of a brother who is dead to share along with surviving brothers (*n*). But, according to the Benares and Bengal schools, no nephew can succeed as long as there is any brother capable of taking, the rule being universal that, except in the case of a man's own male issue, the nearer sapinda always excludes the more remote (*o*). If, however, a brother has once inherited to his brother, and then dies leaving sons, they will take along with the other brothers. Because an interest in the estate and actually vested in their own father, and that interest passes on to them as his heirs. But it must be remembered that the brother must live until the estate has actually vested in him. That is, he must not only survive his own brother, but survive any other persons, such as the widow, daughter, mother, &c., who would take before him (*p*).

Precedence.

There is the same order of precedence between sons of brothers of whole and of half-blood, and between divided and re-united nephews, as prevails between brothers (*q*).

(*m*) *Judubchunder* v. *Benodbenharry*, 1 Hyde, 214; *Kesabram* v. *Nandkishor*, 3 B. L. R. (A. C. J.) 7; S. C. 11 Suth. 308.

(*n*) V. May., iv. 8, § 16, 17.

(*o*) Manu, ix. § 187; Mitakshara, ii. 4, § 7, 8; Smriti Chandrika, xi. 4, § 22, 23; Daya Bhaga, xi. 5, § 2, 3; xi. 6, § 1; D. K. S. i. 8, § 1; Vivada Chintamani, 295; 3 Dig. 518; 1 W. MacN. 26; *Rooder* v. *Sumboo*, 3 S. D. 106 (142); *Jymunee* v. *Ramjoy*, 3 S. D. 289 (385); *Prithee* v. *Court of Wards*, 23 Suth. 272.

(*p*) Mitakshara, ii. 4. § 9; *Burham* v. *Punchoo*, 2 Suth. 123.

(*q*) Daya Bhaga, xi. 6, § 2; D. K. S. i. 8; Smriti Chandrika, xi. 4, § 26; Mitakshara, ii. 4, § 7, note; Viramit., p. 195, § 2; 3 Dig. 524; 2 W. MacN. 72; *Kylash* v. *Gooroo*, 3 Suth. 43; affirmed 6 Suth. 93.

§ 526. Where nephews succeed as the issue of a brother on whom the property has actually devolved, they, of course, take his share, that is, they take *per stirpes* with their uncles if any. For instance, suppose at a man's death he leaves two brothers, A. and B., of whom A. has two sons, and immediately afterwards A. dies; then, as the estate had already vested in A., his sons take half, and B. takes the other half: but if he left at his death two nephews by a deceased brother A., and three nephews by another deceased brother B., the five would take in equal shares, or *per capita*, because they take directly to the deceased, just as daughter's sons do, and not through their fathers (*r*).

They take *per capita*.

On the same principle, *viz.*, that nephews take no interest by birth, but merely from the fact of their being the nearest heirs at the time the inheritance falls in, it follows that a nephew can only take, if he is alive when the succession opens. A nephew subsequently born will neither take a share with nephews who have already succeeded, nor will the inheritance taken by others, to whom he would have been preferred if then alive, be taken from them for his benefit. But if on any subsequent descent he should happen to be the nearest heir, it will be no impediment to his succession that he was born after the death of the uncle to whose property he lays claim (*s*). Of course, the adopted son of a brother succeeds exactly as he would have done if he had been the natural-born son of that brother (*t*).

Nephew has not a vested interest.

§ 527. The brother's grandson, or grandnephew, is not mentioned by the Mitakshara, unless he may be included in the term brother's sons. He is, however, expressly mentioned by the Bengal text books as coming next to the nephew, and is evidently entitled as a sapinda, since he

Grandnephew.

(*r*) 1 W. MacN. 27; 1 Stra. H. L. 145; Mitakshara, ii. 4, § 7, note; *Brojo* v. *Gouree*, 15 Suth. 70; *Gooroo* v. *Kylash*, 6 Suth. 93; *Brojo* v. *Streenath Bose*, 9 Suth. 463.

(*s*) *Bidhoomookhi* v. *Echamoee*, Sev. 182; *Banymadhob* v. *Juggodumba*, Sev. 248.

(*t*) 2 W. MacN. 74.

offers an oblation to the father of the deceased owner (*u*). On the same principle the brother's great-grandson is excluded as a sapinda, though he comes in later as a sakulya. The same distinction as to whole and half-blood prevails as in the case of brothers (*v*). Of course, he cannot succeed so long as any nephew is alive, except by special custom (*w*).

Said to be excluded by Benares law.

Mr. W. MacNaghten states that the brother's grandson is excluded by the authorities of the Benares and Mithila school (*x*). But he is included by *Varadrajah,* and perhaps by the Madhaviya, and it has been decided by the Bengal High Court that under the Mitakshara system he is an heir, though it was not decided, and was not necessary to decide, whether he came in next after nephews (*y*). If he succeeds as one of the brother's sons, in the wide meaning usually given to that term, his place would be next after the nephew. That this is his place has been held to be the law in a case from Mithila (*z*). And in Western India the grandnephew has been decided to be an heir, though his position is not exactly defined (*a*). In Madras it has been held upon a very full discussion of the authorities, that the word 'sons' in Mitakshara, ii. 4, § 7 and ii. 5, 1, does not include grandsons, and that the son of the paternal uncle succeeds before a brother's grandson (*b*).

Grandnephew.

Father's line.

§ 528. On referring to the tables given at § 463 and § 464 it will be seen that, in the first place, the descendants of the owner himself, down to and including his great-grandson and his daughter's son, have been exhausted.

(*u*) See *Parasara* v. *Rangaraja*, 2 Mad. 202.

(*v*) Daya Bhaga, xi. 6, § 6, 7; D. K. S. i. 9, 3 Dig. 525; *Degumber Roy* v. *Moti Lal*, 9 Cal. 563.

(*w*) 2 W. MacN. 67. In the Punjab, nephews and grandnephews succeed together. Punjab Customs, 12.

(*x*) 1 W. MacN. 28, *acc.* Smriti Chandrika, xi. 5.

(*y*) Varadrajah, 36; Madhaviya, § 40; *Kureem* v. *Oodung*, 6 Suth. 158; *Oorhya Kooer* v. *Rajoo Nye*, 14 Suth. 208.

(*z*) *Sumbhoodutt* v. *Jhotee*, S. D. of 1855, 382, and so Varadrajah, 36.

(*a*) W. & B. 480.

(*b*) *Suraya Bhukta* v. *Lakshminarasamma*, 5 Mad. 291.

The line then ascended a step higher, *viz.*, to his parents, and then descended, exhausting all the male descendants of the father who are also sapindas of the owner. Now, the sister and sister's son of the owner, are merely the daughter and daughter's son of the owner's father. Similarly, his niece and his son are the daughter and daughter's son of his brother. His female first cousin and her son are the daughter and daughter's son of his uncle. His aunt and her son are the daughter and daughter's son of his grandfather. All these sons, as will be seen, are the *sapindas* of the owner; but they are not *gotraja* sapindas. Therefore, upon the principles of all the schools which are not based upon the Daya Bhaga, none of them can succeed until all the *sapindas*, *sakulyas*, and *samanodakas* in an unbroken male line have been exhausted. We shall, therefore, first examine the order of descent as laid down by the Benares and Mithila schools, which in this, as in most other respects, are identical, and point out the different order of devolution adopted in Bengal and Western India. **Bhinna-gotra sapindas.**

§ 529. GRANDFATHERS' AND GREAT-GRANDFATHERS' LINE.— **Precedence.** On the exhaustion of the male descendants in the line of the owner's father, a similar course is adopted with regard to the line of his grandfather and great-grandfather. In each case, according to the Mitakshara, the grandmother and great-grandmother take before the grandfather and great-grandfather. Then come their issue to the third degree inclusive. That is to say, so far as the issue of each ancestor are his *sapindas*, they are also the *sapindas* of the owner, with whom they are connected through that ancestor (*c*), In these more distant relationships there is no preference of whole-blood over half-blood, in cases governed by the Mitakshara and Mayukha. Priority on this ground is limited

(*c*) Mitakshara, ii. 5, § 1—6; Madhaviya, § 41, only includes sons and grandsons, but there can be no reason for excluding the great-grandson. His title was affirmed, *Gobind* v. *Mohesh*, 15 B. L. R. 35; S. C. 23 Suth. 117; W. & B. 481; *Mahoda* v. *Kuleani*, 1 S. D. 67 (82); V. Darp., 224, and see *Rutcheputty* v. *Rajunder*, 2 M. I. A. 157; W. & B. 118; V. N. Mandlik, 361, 378.

to the cases of brothers and their issue (*d*). It would probably be different in Bengal. The author of the Smriti Chandrika gives a completely different line of descent. He makes each line of descent end with the grandson; he makes the son and grandson in each line take before the father, and then brings in the father of one series as the son in the next ascending series (*e*). This arrangement, however, seems not to have been followed by any other author.

Smriti Chandrika.

§ 530. SAKULYAS AND SAMANODAKAS.—The above order, as will be seen, exhausts all the *gotraja sapindas* of the nearer class. Then follow the *sakulyas,* or persons connected by divided oblations, and the *samanodakas,* or kindred connected by libations of water. The former extend to three degrees, both in ascent and descent, beyond the sapindas, and the latter to seven degrees beyond the sakulyas or even further, so long as the pedigree can be traced (*f*). Little is to be found as to the order in which they succeed. The Bengal writers make those in the descending line take first, and then those in the successive ascending lines with their descendants (*g*). This arrangement follows the analogy of succession among sapindas, where those who offer oblations take first, and then those who participate in them (*h*). In the table of succession given by Prosonno Coomar Tagore in his translation of the Vivada Chintamani, no mention is made of any descendants beyond the three generations below the owner. He makes the *sakulya* ascendants follow in regular order after the last of the collateral *Sapindas,* and after them the *samanodaka* ascendants. Clearly, however, the *sakulyas* and *samanodakas* in the descending line are entitled equally with the ascendants, if not in priority to them. The Mitakshara gives no

Order of their succession.

Precedence of ascendants or descendants.

(*d*) *Samat* v. *Amra*, 6 Bom. 394. (*e*) Smriti Chandrika, xi. 5, § 8—12.

(*f*) Mitakshara, ii. 5, § 6; V. May., iv. 8; *Bai Devkore* v. *Ambitram*, 10 Bom. 272.

(*g*) 1 W. MacN. 30; Daya Bhaga, xi. 6, § 22, note; Recapitulation, at § 36, note; V. Darp., 305; Saravadhikari, 826.

(*h*) This is also the order of succession in the list of heirs compiled by Rama Rao, which will be found in Cunningham's Digest.

instances of succession for either *sakulyas* or *samanodakas*. After it has exhausted the near sapindas it merely says, "In this manner must be understood the succession of kindred belonging to the same general family and connected by funeral oblations," (*samanagotra sapinda*) *i.e.*, *sakulyas*. "If there be none such, the succession devolves on kindred connected by libations of water," *i.e.*, *samanodakas* (*i*). But *Subodhini* in his commentary carries on the enumeration two steps further, on the same principle as Prosonno Coomar Tagore, making the *sakulyas* in the ascending line and their issue follow next after the collateral sapindas. Messrs. West and Bühler suggest two arrangements: either that the fourth, fifth, and sixth, in the owner's own line should take first; next the remoter descendants in the lines of the father, grandfather, &c., successively, and so on; or that those in the different lines should take jointly in the order of nearness, instead of one line excluding the other (*k*). I am not aware of any case in which a conflict between heirs in the ascending and descending lines has arisen. It is obvious that a case could very seldom arise in which remote relations in the ascending and in the descending lines would be simultaneously in existence. The question of priority is therefore practically unimportant.

Who are entitled as bandhus.

§ 531. BANDHUS.—After all the *samanodakas* are exhausted, the *bandhus* succeed according to Benares and Mithila law (§ 471). I have already discussed the meaning of this term, and pointed out that none of the enumerations of *bandhus* in the law-books are to be considered exhaustive (*l*). In the tables annexed to § 464, 465, will be found references to the decisions which have affirmed the right as *bandhus* of the various persons there named.

Sister's son.

Among those *bandhus* who are omitted by the Mitakshara, the sister's son has had the severest struggle for

(*i*) Mitakshara, ii. 5, § 5, 6, note.
(*k*) W. & B. 114, 124. See futwah, *Umroot*, v. *Kulyandas*, 1 Bor. 292 [322].
(*l*) See *ante*, § 461—466.

existence, having even run the gauntlet of an adverse decision of the Privy Council. His right has always been recognized under Bengal law, as he is expressly named by the Daya Bhaga (*m*). But in the provinces governed by the Mitakshara (not including Western India) it was supposed that he had no claim, and this view was put forward almost unanimously by text writers, pandits, and Judges (*n*). The case came on for the decision of the Privy Council in an appeal from the North-West Provinces, which are governed by the Benares law. There, a sister's son sued to set aside an adoption made by the widow of his deceased uncle. The objection was taken that he was not in the line of heirs at all, and as such had no interest, vested or contingent, which would entitle him to maintain the suit. Of course, this was the strongest possible form in which the question of his right could arise. It was not a question of precedence, but of absolute exclusion. It went the full length of saying, that if there were no other heir in existence, the estate would escheat rather than pass to him. Yet the doctrine of the inability of the sister's son to inherit was accepted by the Judicial Committee to this full extent, and the suit was dismissed on the preliminary objection that he had no interest whatever in the subject-matter (*o*). In ordinary cases such a decision would have set the matter at rest for ever. But the case itself was rather an extraordinary one. The plaintiff's counsel chose to make an express admission that his client could not inherit as a *bandhu*, not being mentioned as such in the Mitakshara. He asserted that he was really a *gotraja sapinda*. This claim he rested, partly on the authority of the Mayukha, and partly on the views of *Balambhatta* and *Nanda Pandita*, who consider

Right of sister's son under Mitakshara,

denied by Judicial Committee.

(*m*) Daya Bhaga, xi. 6, § 8. He has also been recognized as an heir in Lahore. Punjab Customs, 22.

(*n*) 1 Stra. H. L. 147; Stra. Man. § 341; 2 W. MacN. 85, 87, 88; *contra*, 2 W. MacN. 91; *Rajchunder* v. *Goculchund*, 1 S. D. 45 (56); *Jowahir* v. *Mt. Kailassoo*, 1 Suth. 74; *Guman* v. *Srikant Neogi*, Sev. 460; *Nagalinga* v. *Vaidilinga*, Mad. Dec. of 1860, 246, where the pandits differed from the Judges; *Kullammal* v. *Kuppu*, 1 Mad. H. C. 85; *Moonea* v. *Dhurma*, N.-W. P. 1866, cited *Thakoorain* v. *Mohun*, 11 M. I. A. 393.

(*o*) *Thakoorain* v. *Mohun*, 11 M. I. A. 386.

their attention appear to have been called to the Full Bench ruling on the point in Bengal.

On the whole, however, it may probably be considered that the rights of the sister's son, and of all others similarly situated, are now settled beyond dispute.

Granduncle's daughter's son.

§ 534. The right of the granduncle's daughter's son has also been discussed in Madras, and decided against (v). But this decision rested upon the supposition, that as he was not named by the Mitakshara, he was excluded. The Court admitted that on general principles he would inherit, but pointed out that he stood on exactly the same footing as the sister's son, who at the date of the decision was supposed not to be in the line of heirs. As the right of the latter is now established, the reasoning put forward by the Judges for shutting out the son of the granduncle's daughter, would apply directly in favour of letting him in.

Precedence rests on affinity under the Mitakshara.

§ 535. The order of succession among *bandhus* under Mitakshara law is very obscure. Nothing is to be found upon the subject either among text-writers or in precedents, and the principle upon which any case is to be decided is far from clear (w). If the text of the Mitakshara in which the *bandhus* are enumerated is to be taken as indicating the order of succession, it will be seen that proximity, and not religious efficacy, is the ground of preference; the first of the three classes contains the man's own first cousins, the second contains his father's first cousins, and the third contains his mother's first cousins (§ 472). This is corroborated by the next verse (x), where the author says, "By reason of near affinity, the cognate kindred of the deceased are his successors in the first instance, on failure of them the father's cognate kindred, or if there be none, the mother's cognate kindred. This must be understood to be the order of suc-

(v) *Kissen* v. *Javalla*, 3 Mad. H. C. 346.

(w) A very elaborate and ingenious discussion on the subject will be found in Mr. Rajkumar Sarvadhikari's Lectures, pp. 687—735.

(x) Mitakshara, ii. 6, § 2.

cession here intended." This is the view taken by the author of the Viramitrodaya. It has also been adopted by the Courts of Bengal and Bombay as the principle upon which they have preferred the sister's son to the aunt's son, and the maternal uncle to the son of the maternal aunt (*y*). In the accompanying table the letter M. affixed to any relation shows that he is expressly named in the Mitakshara as a *bandhu*, and the Roman numeral following shows the order in which he is named. From this it will be seen that the order followed is strictly that of propinquity, but that as regards two sets of persons, equally near, those on the father's side always take precedence of those on the mother's side, and those on the paternal grandfather's side precede those on the paternal grandmother's side. This preference of the father's kindred to that of the mother is in accordance with the general preference of the male line to the female, (§ 471). It has already been stated that the enumeration of *bandhus* in the Mitakshara is illustrative not exhaustive, (§ 466). In fact the object of the author seems to have been to name only the most unlikely heirs. For instance, he does not mention any in the descending line, nor the sister's son, who are nearer than any of the enumerated relations. He mentions the uncle's son, but not the uncle who is nearer than him. He mentions two in the mother's maternal line (viii. and ix.), and only three (ii., iii., vii.) in the more numerous body of the mother's paternal line. It will be observed that in each case where an aunt's and an uncle's son stand on the same line, the aunt's son is named first. This seems to violate the ordinary rule by which male descent ranks before female. Probably the order of enumeration is not intended to convey any right of precedence. The annexed table contains in one view all the bandhus *exparte paternâ* and *maternâ* already referred to. Those under the lines A. and B. contained in a circle are named in the Mitakshara but

---

(*y*) Viramit., p. 200, § 5; *Gunesh* v. *Nilkomul*, 22 Suth. 264; *Mohandas* v. *Krishnabai*, 5 Bom. 597.

Exparte maternâ.

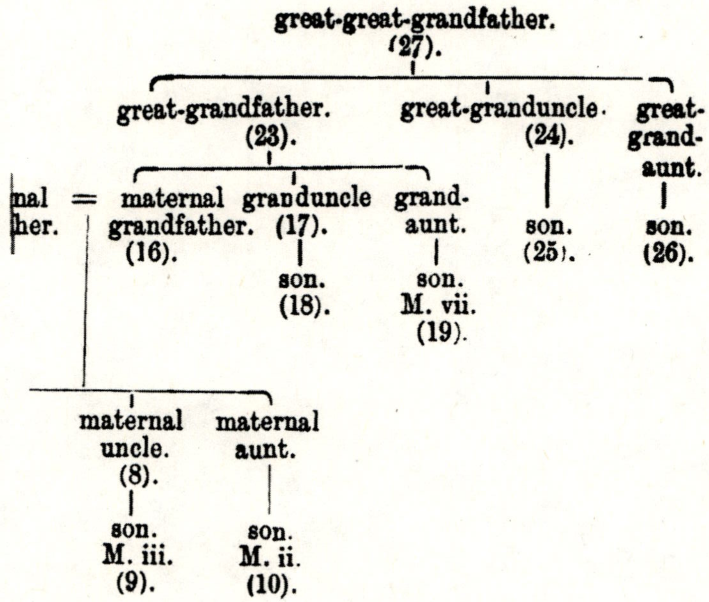

N. B. Should the claims of the sister and the grand daughter ultimately prevail, they would according to the view of the Madras High Court, which alone is inclined to admit them, come in after all male heirs (§ 497).

cannot be brought into the Bengal system (§ 472). The Arabic numerals attached to each relation mark the order in which I suggest they should rank *inter se,* on the analogy of those expressly named. All of the persons so marked come within Vijnanesvara's definition as being persons who being of a different family are still *sapindas;* the relationship of *sapindas* among cognates only extending to the fifth in descent from the common ancestor, both inclusive (*z*).

Arrangement under Bengal law.

Order of precedence in Bengal.

§ 536. BENGAL LAW.—The radical difference between the system of the Daya Bhaga and of the Mitakshara is, that the former allows the *bandhus,* that is the *bhinna-gotra sapindas,* to come in along with, instead of after, the *gotraja sapindas* (§ 467), the principle of religious efficacy being the sole test applied in deciding between rival claimants. Upon examining the application of this principle, it will be seen in the first place, that all the *bandhus exparte paternâ* come in before any of those *exparte maternâ.* The reason is that the former present oblations to paternal ancestors, which are of higher efficacy than those presented by the latter to maternal ancestors (*a*). As regards the position *inter se* of the *bandhus exparte paternâ,* it will be seen by a reference to the table (§ 464) that every one of them is a daughter's son in the branch where he occurs. Only three of these are mentioned in the Daya Bhaga—*viz.,* the sons of the daughters of the father, the grandfather, and the great-grandfather respectively; and these are ranked immediately after the male issue of those ancestors, that is, they come in before the males of the branch next above them. Just as the daughter's son of the owner comes in before his father, brothers, nephews, and grandnephews (*b*).

(*z*) Yajn., i. 53.

(*a*) Daya Bhaga, xi. 6, § 12, 20; D. K. S. i. 10, § 14; 3 Dig. 529; *ante,* § 467, rule 4.

(*b*) Daya Bhaga, xi. 6, § 8—12; 3 Dig. 528; V. Darp., 224. Accordingly the sister's son has been held to take before paternal uncles (2 W. MacN. 84); *Sumbochunder* v. *Gunga,* 6 S. D. 234 (291), and their issue (1 W. MacN. 28); *Rajchunder* v. *Goculchund,* 1 S. D. 43 (56); 2 W. MacN. 85, 87; *Karuna* v. *Jai Chandra,* 5 S. D. 46 (50); *Kishen* v. *Tarini, ib.* 55 (66); *Lakhi* v. *Bhairab,*

The Daya-krama-sangraha introduces a new series of bandhus, *viz.*, those who occupy the position of sons of the nieces of the father, grandfather, and great-grandfather. It follows the Daya Bhaga in making the daughter's son succeed the male issue of each branch, and places the niece's sons immediately after the daughter's son (*c*). It does not mention the sons of the grandniece in each branch, but their title is exactly of a similar nature, and has been affirmed to exist (*d*). Now, this order of succession would be the natural one if proximity alone was regarded, the agnates in each branch being preferred to the cognates, but the cognates in each branch being preferred to the agnates in the more distant branch. It would also be the proper course if the mere number of oblations were regarded. The daughter's son in each line presents exactly the same number of oblations as the son in the same line, and presents them to the same persons. So, the sons of the niece and of the grandniece present the same number of oblations, and to the same persons, as the nephew and grandnephew. Each of these presents a greater number of oblations than the son in the line above him. But then comes in the principle, that oblations presented to paternal ancestors are more efficacious than those presented to maternal ancestors (*e*). If this principle goes to the extent, that a man who presents a greater number of oblations to persons who are his maternal ancestors, is inferior to one who presents a lesser number to persons who are his paternal ancestors, then the principle is undoubtedly disregarded both by the Daya Bhaga and the Daya-krama-sangraha. If, however, it only goes to this extent, that where the number is equal, those

Precedence under Bengal system.

---

ib. 315 (369); W. & B. 474; *Duneshwur* v. *Deoshunker*, Morris, Pt. II. 63; *Brojo* v. *Sreenath Bose*, 9 Suth. 463. *A fortiori* before the issue of the great-grandfather (2 W. MacN. 89, 90). But he takes after the son of a half-brother (2 W. MacN. 68, 82); and he will take equally whether he is alive at the death of the last male holder, or of any female who takes by inheritance from such male (*Seeta Ram* v. *Fukeer*, 15 Suth. 433.)

(*c*) D. K. S. i. 10, § 1, 2; 8, 9; 12, 13.

(*d*) *Kashee Mohun* v. *Raj Gobind*, 24 Suth. 229.

(*e*) 3 Dig. 530; *per Mitter*, J., *Guru* v. *Anand Lal*, 5 B. L. R. at p. 39; S. C. 13 Suth. (F. B.) 49.

who present offerings to paternal ancestors are preferred to those who present them to maternal ancestors, then the whole course of descent is logical and consistent.

Son of a niece.

§ 537. This question arose in Bengal under the following circumstances. In 1864 the High Court had held that the son of a brother's daughter was not an heir at all, and that the passage in the Daya-krama-sangraha which stated that he was an heir was an interpolation (*f*). In 1870 this decision was reversed by the Full Bench, in an elaborate judgment by Mr. Justice *Mitter*. His judgment was based entirely upon general considerations as to the nature of the relationship of *bandhus*, and the grounds upon which they were entitled. The decision did not refer to, still less affirm the genuineness of the disputed text of the Daya-krama-sangraha (*g*). No question was then raised as to the position which such a *bandhu* would take in the line of heirs. Finally, this last question arose in 1874. The relationship of the conflicting parties is shown in the annexed pedigree.

Postponed to distant agnate.

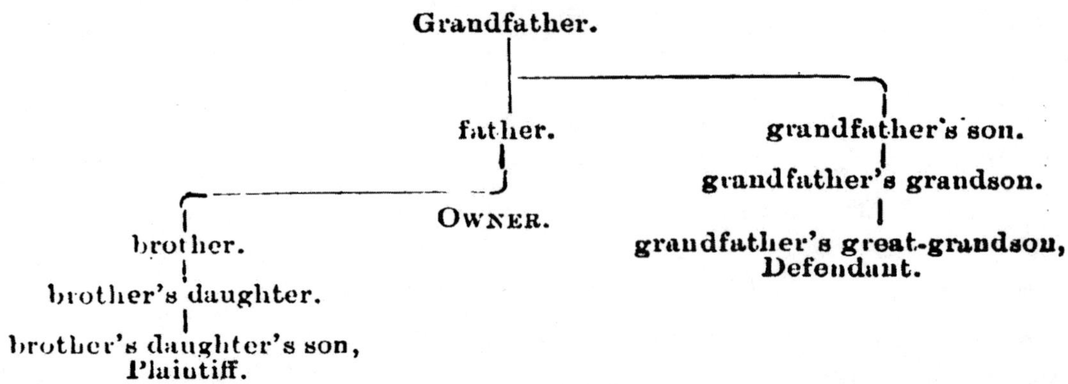

The plaintiff was son of the owner's niece. The defendants were what we should call first cousins once removed, in the male line. Both the Lower Courts decided in favour of the plaintiff. It is evident that he offered oblations to the owner's father, while the defendant only offered to the

(*f*) *Gobindo* v. *Woomesh*, Suth. Sp. 176, referring to D. K. S. i. 10, § 2.

(*g*) *Guru* v. *Anand*, 5 B. L. R. 15; S. C. 13 Suth. (F. B.) 49. It may be observed that the decision in the over-ruled case had been obtained by the argument of Mr. Justice *Mitter* himself when at the bar. This may account for the fact that no notice was taken of the D. K. S. in the over-ruling judgment.

grandfather. On appeal, however, this decision was reversed. The Court admitted the plaintiff's right as a *bandhu*, but held that he must come in after the defendant, on the ground that they who offer to maternal ancestors, are inferior in religious efficacy to those who offer a lesser number of cakes to paternal ancestors. The text of the Daya-krama-sangraha, which makes him succeed after the son of the father's daughter, and before the grandfather, was treated, on the authority of the case in 1864, as being of too doubtful authenticity to weigh against the infringement of first principles which it was supposed to contain (*h*).

§ 538. It may be remarked upon this decision, that if § 2 of the Daya-krama-sangraha, ch. i., § 10, is to be rejected as spurious, § 9 and 13 must go with it, for all three lay down exactly the same rule, and rest upon the same principle. If this principle is erroneous, it is difficult to see how the Daya Bhaga (xi. 6, § 8—12) can be maintained, for it places the daughter's son of the branches above the owner, before the males of the next higher branch. The Court deals with this by saying, that the special reason given by *Jimuta Vahana* for that arrangement does not apply to the others. The special reason is, that "his father's or grandfather's daughter's son, like his own daughter's son, transports his *manes* over the abyss by offering oblations of which he may partake." But the brother's daughter's son offers oblations of exactly the same character. The only remaining supposition is, that the daughter's sons of the direct lineal ancestors have an efficacy of a different character from that possessed by the daughter's sons of the collateral branches. If so the Daya-krama-sangraha would be wrong, the Daya Bhaga and the High Court of Bengal right. The arrangement would then be, that the daughter's sons of collaterals should come in one after the other, at the end of the nearer sapindas, and before the sakulyas.

Decision discussed.

(*h*) *Gobind* v. *Mohesh*, 15 B. L. R. 85; S. C. 23 Suth. 117; followed in *Oodoychurn's* case, 4 Cal. 411.

Sakulya preferred to a bandhu.

§ 539. The principle of the above decision was carried out in a later case, to the extent of preferring a male, who was not a sapinda at all, to an undoubted bandhu (*i*). The last male holder of the property in dispute, named Bharut, was the third son of the common ancestor. He was succeeded by his daughter, on whose death the conflict arose between plaintiff and defendant. Their relationship to him appears in the accompanying pedigree. It was admitted that defendant was only a sakulya. On the other hand,

Ancestor.

son. 1	son. 2	OWNER, Bharut. 3
grandson.	grandson.	granddaughter (last holder) Bejoye Dibia.
great-grandson, Kashee Nath.	great-granddaughter, Joy Doorga.	
great-great-grandson, Defendant.	great-great-grandson, Plaintiff.	

the plaintiff offered cakes to his three maternal ancestors, one of whom was the common ancestor. Of course, the question would have been exactly the same if the last holder had been the ancestor himself. It certainly does seem anomalous, that where two claimants are equally distant, a case can arise, in which the one who claims through a female is actually preferred to one who claims through an unbroken line of males. Under Mitakshara law, of course, no such preference could ever be asserted. Yet, upon the ground of religious efficacy, it seems clear that on Bengal principles the plaintiff had a superiority over the defendant, unless it can be laid down, that a divided oblation offered to 'the father of the deceased owner by A. must be more meritorious than an undivided oblation offered to him by B., wherever such father is the paternal ancestor of A. and only the maternal ancestor of B.' The ground upon which the Court proceeded was as follows: "It is quite clear that going back a generation to the time when

(*i*) *Kashee Mohun* v. *Raj Gobind*, 24 Suth. 229.

Kashee Nath represented one generation and Joy Doorga the other, Kashee Nath was the preferential heir. He alone could have performed the *parbana shradh*, and not Joy Doorga. Consequently, it seems to us that the son of Kashee Nath would have a necessarily preferential right over, and would exclude the son of Joy Doorga."

Contrary rule now laid down.

In former editions the soundness of this decision was questioned. It has now been expressly over-ruled by a Full Bench of the Bengal High Court (*k*). In the later case the contest was between the brother's daughter's son of the deceased, and the great-great-great-grandson of the great-great-great-grandfather. The exact form of the pedigree is not given, but the following diagram appears to represent it.

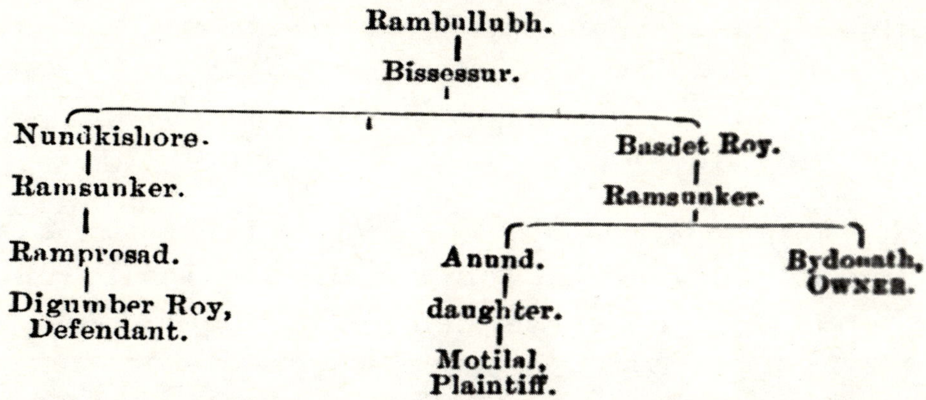

The High Court decided in favour of the plaintiff upon the broad principle that he was a *sapinda* of the deceased, as he offered undivided oblations to his own three maternal ancestors, two of whom were the paternal ancestors of the OWNER, in which therefore the latter participated. On the other hand the defendant offered only divided oblations to Bissessur and Rambullubh, who were also the ancestors of the OWNER. The competition therefore was between a cognate who was a *sapinda*, and an agnate who was a *sakulya*. According to the Daya Bhaga (xv. 6, § 20, 21) it did not admit of any doubt that a *sapinda* though a cognate was a preferable heir to a *sakulya* agnate.

(*k*) *Digumber Roy* v. *Moti Lal*, 9 Cal. 563, 566. See also *Deyanath* v. *Muthoor*, 6 S. D. 27 (30), where the son of the maternal aunt was held entitled in preference to any lineal descendant from a common ancestor beyond the third degree.

Bandhus ex-parte maternâ.

§ 540. *Jimuta Vahana* hardly notices the ***bandhus exparte maternâ,*** merely alluding to them as "the maternal uncle and the rest," who come in "on failure of any lineal descendant of the paternal great-grandfather, down to the daughter's son." He seems to attempt to reconcile his order of succession with that of *Yajnavalkya,* by assuming that the term *bandhu,* as used by the latter, only referred to those on the mother's side (*l*). *Srikrishna,* however, sets out their order very fully, adopting the same principle as he had done in regard to the other sapindas. He gives the property first to the mother's father, and his issue, that is the maternal uncle, his son, and grandson, then to the daughter's son of the mother's father, then to the line of the mother's grandfather, and great-grandfather, in similar manner, and, on failure of all these, to the *sakulyas* and *samanodakas* (*m*). These, as already stated, take first in the descending line, and then in the ascending (*n*).

Admission of females.

§ 541. BOMBAY LAW.—The distinctive feature of the law which prevails in Western India, is the laxity with which it admits females to the succession. The doctrine of *Baudhayana,* which asserts the general incapacity of women for inheritance, and its corollary, that women can only inherit under a special text, appears never to have been accepted by the Western lawyers. They take the word *sapinda,* in the widest sense, as importing mere affinity, and without the limitation of the Mitakshara, that female sapindas can only inherit when they are also *gotrajas,* that is, persons who continue in the family to which they claim as heirs (*o*). The most prominent instance of this doctrine is the introduction of the sister into the line of succession. She is brought in by the Mayukha after the paternal grandmother, and before the paternal grandfather, under that serviceable text of *Manu,* "To the nearest sapinda (male or female) after him in the third degree the inheritance next belongs" (*p*).

Sister.

(*l*) Daya Bhaga, xi 6, § 12—14. (*m*) D. K. S. i. 10, § 14—21.
(*n*) Daya Bhaga. xi. 6, § 22; D. K. S. i. 10, 22—25.
(*o*) W. & B. 125—132. (*p*) Manu, ix. § 187.

Nilakantha applies this text by saying, "In case of the non-existence of that (the paternal grandmother) the sister (texts) according to the *dictum* of *Manu*, 'that whoever is the nearest *sapinda* his should be the property'; and according to the text of *Vrihaspati*, that where there are many *jnati, sakulyas*, and *bandhavas*, among them whoever is the nearest, he should take the property of the childless; she the sister also being born in the brother's *gotra*, and so there being no difference of *gotrajatva* (the state of being born in the *gotra*). But (says an objector) there is no *sagotrata* (state of being in the same *gotra*). True, but neither is that stated here as a reason for taking property" (*q*). And not only full sisters, but stepsisters, inherit (*r*). Another instance is the rule which allows widows of persons who would have been heirs to inherit after their husbands. The other schools of law never allow a widow, *as such*, to inherit to any one but her own husband. In Bombay the widows of *gotraja sapindas* stand in the same place as their husbands, if living, would respectively have occupied, subject to the right of any person whose place is specially fixed as a sister, mother or the like (*s*). The stepmother heads the list of non-specified female heirs, and takes place after the paternal grandmother, and before the widow of the half-brother (*t*). So, daughters of descendants and collaterals within six degrees inherit; for instance, both a brother's daughter, and a sister's daughter (*u*). Also "descendants of a person's own daughters, and of those persons expressly mentioned within four degrees of such persons respectively, *e. g.*, a granddaughter's grandson, but not the great-grandson, since sapinda relationship through females is restricted to four degrees" (*v*). I can offer no

Widows.

Daughters.

(*q*) V. May, iv. 8, § 19; translated in *Lallubhai* v. *Mankuvarbai*, 2 Bom. 421; *ante*, § 490.

(*r*) W. & B. 469; *Kesserbai* v. *Valab*, 4 Bom. 188.

(*s*) W. & B. 131, 481; *Lakshmibai* v. *Jayram*, 6 Bom. H. C. (A. C. J.) 152; *Lallubhai* v. *Mankuvarbai*, 2 Bom. 388; *affd. Lulloobhoy* v. *Cassibai*, 7 I. A. 212; S. C. 5 Bom 110; see *per curiam*, 4 Bom. p. 209; *Vithaldas* v. *Jesubhai*, 4 Bom. 219; *Nahalchand* v. *Hemchand*, 9 Bom. 31.

(*t*) *Rukhmabai* v. *Tukharam*, 11 Bom. 47.

(*u*) W. & B. 137, 496—498.

(*v*) W. & B. 137.

Their precedence.

opinion whatever as to the order in which such persons take. Messrs. West and Bühler suggest that they would come in after the nine *bandhus* who are expressly named in the Mitakshara, on the principle stated by the Mayukha, that incidental persons are placed last, and that, as between each other, nearness of kin to the deceased is the only guide (*w*).

Tables of descent.

Tables of descent, professing to give all possible heirs in the order of succession, for the different provinces, will be found in the works referred to below (*x*). I have not attempted to compile any such list. I doubt the possibility of preparing one that should be at once exhaustive and accurate. It would certainly be beyond my powers. Wherever a conflict arises between any two specific claimants, I believe that the principles already stated, will, in general, be sufficient to decide their priority.

Succession after a reunion.

§ 542. Before passing from this part of the subject, it may be well to refer to the rare case of succession after a reunion. *Manu*, after speaking of a second partition after a reunion, says, "Should the eldest or youngest of several brothers be deprived of his share (by a civil death on his entrance into the fourth order), or should any one of them die, his (vested interest in a) share shall not wholly be lost. But (if he leave neither son nor wife, nor daughter, nor father, nor mother), his uterine brothers and sisters, and such brothers as were reunited after a separation, shall assemble, and divide his share equally" (*y*). Now it will be remembered that *Manu* requires a share to be given to a sister on a partition (§ 436), but nowhere refers to her as an heir. It is probable, therefore, that this text refers to a case where

(*w*) W. & B. 491; V. May., iv. 8, § 18. See *per curiam*, *Mohandas* v. *Krishnabai*, 5 Bom. 602; *Rukhmabai* v. *Tukharam*, 11 Bom. 47.

(*x*) V. Darp., 266—271; Daya Bhaga, xi. 6, § 36; Smriti Chandrika, p. 221; Stra. Man., § 315; Cunningham's Digest, § 249; Prosonno Coomar Tagore's Vivada Chintamani; Sarvadhikari, 510 *a*—*j*.

(*y*) *Manu*, ix. § 210—212. The words in brackets are the gloss of Kalluka Bhatta. See also a similar text by Vrihaspati, 3 Dig. 476, where there is a various reading of *daughters* for sister. V. May., iv. 9, § 23; Smriti Chandrika, xii. § 25; Madhaviya, § 47; Varadrajah, 55.

a partition had already commenced, but had not been concluded, and merely directs that in such a case his share shall not pass by inheritance, but shall be thrown into the property, and divided again. The sisters would then be entitled to their shares (z). This seems the more probable, as no allusion is made to the sister in the passage of *Yajnavalkya,* which treats of the descent of the share of a reunited coparcener. That passage, as translated by Mr. Colebrooke (a), is as follows:—"A reunited (brother) shall keep the share of his reunited (co-heir) who is deceased, or shall deliver it to (a son subsequently) born. But an uterine (or whole) brother shall thus retain or deliver the allotment of his uterine relation. A half-brother, being again associated, may take the succession; not a half-brother, though not reunited; but one united (by blood, though not by coparcenary) may obtain the property, and not (exclusively) the son of a different mother." The meaning of this unusually obscure passage is, that if a reunited coparcener dies, leaving issue actually born, or then in the womb, such issue takes his share. If however, he only leaves brothers, there may have been a reunion of all the brothers, or only of the uterine brothers, or only of the half-brothers. In such events the rule already stated (§ 523), that the whole is preferred to the half-blood, remains in force. But reunion gives the reunited brother a claim which is not possessed by the divided brother. Therefore where two brothers are in the same position as to whole or half-blood, the reunited brother has a preference over the divided brother. But where they are in a different position, the one who is inferior in blood, if reunited, is raised to a level with the one who is superior in blood, but divided. The result, therefore, is, if all the surviving brothers are divided, or if all are reunited, those of the whole blood take before the half-blood. If some are divided, and some are reunited, the reunited brothers take to the exclusion

Succession after a reunion.

Whole and half-blood.

(z) Raghunandana says that the right of the sister extends only to so much as is required for her marriage, xi. 48.

(a) Yajnavalkya, ii. § 138, 139; Mitakshara, ii. 9.

of the divided brothers, provided they are both of equal merits as to blood. Where the reunited brothers are of the half-blood, and the divided brothers are of the whole blood, both take equally. Of course, if the cases were reversed, the reunited brothers of the whole blood would take before divided brothers of the half-blood (*b*).

After reunion under Benares law.

§ 543. The above rule of succession is perfectly clear and logical on the principles of the Bengal school. But on the principles of the Benares school one would suppose, that the property of reunited members stood on exactly the same footing as that of members who had always been undivided. In that case, upon the death of any one member of the undivided family, his share would pass by survivorship to the remaining members, and could by no possibility get into the hands of any divided member, so long as there were undivided members in existence. The difficulty was seen by the author of the Smriti Chandrika. His explanation is, in substance, that there is a difference between the interest in property held by an originally undivided member, and by one who has reunited after partition. In the former case there has been no ascertainment of his share. In the latter case his share has been ascertained, and continues so ascertained after reunion. The reunion only destroys the exclusive right which he acquired by partition in the property which had fallen to his share (*c*). That is, as I understand him, that he was a joint tenant before partition, a sole tenant after partition, a tenant in common after reunion. After reunion his share is held in quasi-severalty, and at his death passes by descent, and not by survivorship, in the same manner as that of an undivided brother in Bengal.

In default of reunited brothers of the half-blood, or of

(*b*) V. May., iv. 9, § 5—13; Vivada Chintamani, 308; V. Darp., 204; Mitakshara, ii. 9, § 4—13; Daya Bhaga, xi. 5, § 13—39; D. K. S. i. 7, § 3—6, v. § 8, 9; Viramit., p. 205, § 4—8; 3 Dig. 507—517, 554; *Rajkishore* v. *Gobind*, 1 Cal. 27; F. MacN. 110; *Tarachand* v. *Pudum*, 5 Suth. 249; *Gopal* v. *Kenaram*, 7 Suth. 35; *Sham Narain* v. *Court of Wards*, 20 Suth. 197.

(*c*) Smriti Chandrika, xii. § 9.

any brothers of the whole blood, the succession passes in order to the father, or paternal uncle, if reunited; to the half-brother not reunited, to the father not reunited; in default of any of them, then successively to the mother, the widow and the sister. If none of these exist then to the nearest sapindas or samanodakas as in the case of ordinary property (*d*). Of this line of succession the author of the Viramitrodaya says very truly. "In this order there is no principle; hence this order rests entirely upon the authority of the texts of law."

§ 544. STRANGERS.—Where there are no relations of the deceased (*e*), the preceptor, or, on failure of him, the pupil, the fellow-student, or a learned and venerable priest, should take the property of a Brahman, or, in default of such a one, any Brahman (*f*). The Daya Bhaga interposes persons bearing the same family name between the fellow-student and the priest (*g*). In case of traders who die in a foreign country, leaving no heirs of their own family, the fellow trader is authorised to take (*h*). Finally, in default of all these, the king takes by escheat, except the property of a Brahman, which it is said can never fall to the Crown (*i*). Ulterior heirs. Strangers. King.

§ 545. I know of no instance in which a claim has ever been set up by a preceptor, or pupil, to the property of a person dying without heirs, and it is clear that the claims of all the other possible successors above named are too indefinite to be maintained. The direction that the king can never take the estate of a Brahman, has also been overthrown in the only case in which the exemption was set up (*k*) There the Crown claimed by escheat as against the alienee Escheat.

(*d*) Smriti Chandrika, xii. § 23—39; Viramit., p. 214, § 9—11.
(*e*) The word here translated relations is *bandhus*, Goldstücker, 26.
(*f*) Mitakshara, ii. 7, § 1—4. See V. Darp., 307.
(*g*) Daya Bhaga, xi. 6, § 26.
(*h*) See a passage in the Mitakshara, not translated by Mr. Colebrooke, cited in *Gridhari* v. *Bengal Govt.*, 12 M. I. A. 457, 465; S. C. 1 B. L. R. (P. C.) 44; S. C. 10 Suth. (P. C.) 32.
(*i*) Daya Bhaga, xi. 6, § 27; Mitakshara, ii. 7, § 5, 6.
(*k*) *Collector of Masulipatam* v. *Caraly Vencata*, 8 M. I. A. 500; S. C. 2 Suth. (P. C.) 59.

of a Brahman widow, whose husband had left no heirs. It was held that the claim must prevail, notwithstanding the rule relied on; either on the ground, that the rule itself assumed that the king must take the estate for a time, in order to pass it on to a Brahman; or on the ground, that where the last owner died without heirs, there ceased to be any personal law governing the case of Brahmans, which could settle the further devolution of the property. In the former case the title of the Crown to hold was complete, subject only to the question whether the Crown held absolutely, or in trust. In the latter case, in the absence of any personal law, the general prerogative of the Crown as to heirless property must prevail.

Its effect.

Where the Crown claims by escheat, it must make out affirmatively that there are no heirs (*l*). When it has taken, its title prevails against all unauthorised alienations by the last owner, as for instance by a widow, but is subject to any trust or charge properly created (*m*).

Escheat is only to Crown.

The principle of escheat does not apply in favour of Zemindars who have carved out a subordinate, but absolute and alienable interest, from their own estate. On failure of heirs of the subordinate holder, the estate will pass to the Crown, and will not revert to the Zemindar (*n*).

Property of ascetic.

§ 546. Special rules are also propounded for succession to the property of a hermit, an ascetic, or a professed student (*o*). Practically, however, such a case seldom arises. When a hermit has any property which is not of secular origin, he generally holds it as the head of some Mutt or religious endowment, and succession to such property is

(*l*) *Gridhari* v. *Government of Bengal*, 12 M. I. A. 448; S. C. 1 B. L. R. (P. C.) 44; S. C. 10 Suth. (P. C.) 32.

(*m*) *Collector of Masulipatam* v. *Cavaly Vencata*, 8 M. I. A. 500, 529; S. C. 2 Suth. (P. C.) 59; *Cavaly Vencata* v. *Collector of Masulipatam*, 11 M. I. A. 619; S. C. 2 Suth. (P. C.) 61.

(*n*) *Sonet* v. *Mirza*, 3 I. A. 92; S. C. 25 Suth. 239.

(*o*) Yajnavalkya, ii. 137; Mitakshara, ii. 8; Daya Bhaga, xi. 6, § 35, 36; 2 Stra. H. L. 248; W. & B. 490, 555; 3 Dig. 546; Smriti Chandrika, xi. 7; Viramit., p. 202; V. Darp., 312; See *Khuggender* v. *Sharupgir*, 4 Cal. 543.

regulated by the special custom of the foundation (§ 398). No one can come under the above heads, for the purpose of introducing a new rule of inheritance, unless he has absolutely retired from all earthly interests, and, in fact, become dead to the world. In such a case all property then vested in him passes to his legal heirs, who succeed to it at once. If his retirement is of a less complete character, the mere fact that he has assumed a religious title, and has even entered into a monastery, will not devest him of his property, or prevent his secular heirs from succeeding to any secular property which may have remained in his possession (*p*).

(*p*) 2 W. MacN. 101; *Mudhoobun* v. *Huri*, S. D. of 1852, 1089; *Ameena* v. *Radhabinode*, S. D. of 1856, 596; *Khoodeeram* v. *Rookhinee*, 15 Suth. 197; *Jagannath* v. *Bidyanand*, 1 B. L. R. (A. C. J.) 114; S. C. 10 Suth. 172; *Dukharam* v. *Luchmun*, 4 Cal. 954.

CHAPTER XIX.

EXCLUSION FROM INHERITANCE.

Principle of exclusion.

§ 547. The Brahmanical theory of wealth is, that it is conferred for the sake of defraying the expense of sacrifices (*a*). The theory of inheritance is, that it descends upon the heir to enable him to rescue the deceased from eternal misery. Consequently, one who is unable or unwilling to perform the necessary sacrifices is incapable of inheriting (*b*). The son who neglects the duty of redeeming his father, is compared by *Vrihaspati* to a cow, which neither affords milk nor becomes pregnant. He has no claim to the paternal estate. It must devolve on those learned priests who offer the funeral cake to the deceased (*c*). Such a theory was likely to meet with a good deal of extension from the priestly lawyers. Accordingly we find that not only congenital defects, such as impotence, idiocy, being born blind, deaf or dumb, without a limb or a sense, were grounds of exclusion, but the same penalty befel those who were afflicted with madness, or an obstinate or agonising disease (*d*), or who were addicted to vice (*e*), or who were hypocrites or impostors (*f*), or even persons who might be held not to possess sacred knowledge, or courage, or industry, or devotion, or liberality, or who failed to observe immemorial good customs (*g*). Naturally, degradation from caste, the highest penalty for sin, was itself accompanied with forfeiture of inheritance (*h*).

(*a*) 3 Dig. 317.

(*b*) 3 Dig. 298; Vivada Chintamani, 243; Ind. Wisd. 159, 275, 281. These principles of the Hindu law do not apply to the Alya Santana law. *Chandu* v. *Subba*, 13 Mad. 209.

(*c*) 3 Dig. 301. (*d*) 3 Dig. 303, 309. (*e*) 3 Dig. 299.

(*f*) 3 Dig. 304. The same phrase however is elsewhere translated as having assumed the garb or profession of a beggar or ascetic.

(*g*) 3 Dig. 301.

(*h*) 3 Dig. 300. See generally, Mitakshara, ii. 10; V. May., iv. 11; Daya

§ 548. Of course, such a system could never have been practically enforced, even if the Brahmans had possessed all the power which they claimed. The substantial part of it probably consisted in the parallel theory of expiation, which at once rendered it profitable to the priestly class, and endurable by the rest of the community. Just as the Romish Church created an elaborate system of restraints on marriage, and then proceeded straightway to dispense with them for a consideration. Various maladies were noted as the specific penalties of sins committed in the present or in former states of existence, and thus brought within the sphere of religious discipline (*i*). Minute classifications of crime and disease were framed, and the penalties accruing in respect of some of these were expiable, wholly or in part, whereas in respect of others, the sin could be removed, but not the forfeiture of right resulting from it (*k*). I imagine that secular Courts could only take notice of the last-named grounds of disability. If it appeared that a particular sort of disability was in fact removeable by penance, a Judge could hardly be called on to decide whether the penance had been properly performed, and if not, why not (*l*). The result seems to be that the causes entailing civil disability are reduced to those originally stated by *Manu* with the addition of lunacy and idiocy (*m*). "Eunuchs and outcasts, persons born blind or deaf, the dumb, and such as have lost the use of a limb, are excluded from heritage." To this enumeration *Yajnavalkya* adds, "And a person

Mitigated by expiation.

Bhaga. v.; D. K. S. iii.; V. Darp., 995. There is nothing in these rules to prevent a person who is disqualified as an heir from taking by gift. *Ganga v. Hira*, 2 All. 809. *Lala Muddun Gopal v. Mt. Khikhinda*, 18 I. A. 9 S. C., 18 Cal. 341.

(*i*) 3 Dig., 314, 314; Manu, xi. § 48—53.

(*k*) V. Darp., 999 *et seq.*, 1005; 1 Stra. H. L. 155; *Sheo Nath v. Mt. Dayamyee*, 2 S. D. 108; (137); Manu, xi. § 47, 54, 183—188, 240, 248, &c., from which it appears that every sin however great was expiable.

(*l*) Acc. V. Darp., 1007, where it is said that in cases where the disability is removable by penance, persons are seen to take the inheritance even without performing the penance. 1 Stra. H. L. 159. But see *Bhola Nath v. Mt. Sabitra*, 6 S. D. 62 (71); *Bhoobunessuree v. Gouree Doss*, 11 Suth. 535, where a claim to inheritance was dismissed on the ground of disabilities which appear to have been expiable, but were not in fact expiated.

(*m*) Manu, ix. § 201.

afflicted with an incurable disease" (*n*), which again seems now to be limited to the worst form of leprosy.

Loss of caste now relieved.

§ 549. Outcasts are now relieved by Act XXI of 1850 (Freedom of Religion). "So much of any law or usage now in force within the territories subject to the government of the E. I. Co. as inflicts on any person forfeiture of rights or property, or may be held in any way to impair or affect any right of inheritance, by reason of his or her renouncing, or having been excluded from the communion of any religion, or being deprived of caste, shall cease to be enforced as law." The effect of this section is that degradation or exclusion of caste, from whatever cause it may arise, is absolutely immaterial in all cases where, except for the Act, it would have debarred a person from enforcing or exercising a right (*o*). But where there are circumstances which, independent of all considerations of caste, create a disability under Hindu law, the fact that degradation from caste follows upon the disability, leaves it just where it was before. The disability is not removed, because the degradation is inoperative. For instance, the incontinence of a Hindu widow is a bar to her claiming the estate of her husband (*p*). If her incontinence is of a very aggravated character—as, for instance, the union of a Brahmani with a Sudra man, it would involve loss of caste. But that circumstance would not be an element in deciding whether her rights of inheritance were lost. It would not enhance the effect of her unchastity. Nor would the fact that the loss of caste was cured by Act XXI of 1850 remove the effect of the antecedent incontinence (*q*).

I am only aware of two cases in which a claim to an inheritance has been set up under this Act, after a change of

(*n*) Mitakshara, ii. 10, § 1.
(*o*) *Bhujjun* v. *Gya*, 2 N.-W. P. 446; *Honamma* v. *Timmannabhat*, 1 Bom. 559.
(*p*) *Ante*, § 511.
(*q*) *Matangini* v. *Jaykali*, 5 B. L. R. 466; *Kery Kolitany* v. *Moneeram*, 13 B. L. R. 1, 25, 75; S. C. 19 Suth. 367; affd. on appeal, 7 I. A. pp. 115, 156; S. C. 5 Cal. 776.

religion. In one a Hindu who had become a Muhammedan in 1839 sued for his inheritance after 1850. The Madras Sudder Court rejected his claim, holding that Act XXI of 1850 was not retrospective (*r*). In Allahabad the son of a Hindu who had turned Muhammedan, and who was himself a Muhammedan was held entitled to succeed as heir to his Hindu uncle, after the death of that uncle's widow (*s*). Even with the aid of the Statute it seems difficult to see how a purely personal law, such as the Hindu or Muhammedan law, can be applied in favour of a person who has renounced it.

§ 550. Where it is sought to exclude an heir on the ground that he is blind, deaf or dumb, it is necessary to show that these defects are incurable and congenital (*t*). As to mental infirmity, it has been held, that the degree of incapacity which amounts to idiocy is not utter mental darkness. It is sufficient if the person is, and has been from his birth, of such an unsound and imbecile mind as to be incapable of instruction or of discriminating between right and wrong. He must in short be one whom it would be impossible to describe as a reasoning being. Mere want of sound, or even ordinary, intelligence is not sufficient (*u*).

What defects must be congenital.

Mental infirmity

There is a difference of opinion as to whether insanity also need be congenital. The texts and cases are all collected and discussed in a judgment of the High Court of Bombay. The question for decision was only as to blindness, but the Court expressed a strong opinion that mad-

Whether it must be congenital.

(*r*) *Naugammah* v. *Karebbasappah*, Mad. Dec of 1858, 250.

(*s*) *Bhagwant Singh* v. *Kallu*, 11 All. 100.

(*t*) *Mohesh Chunder* v. *Chunder Mohun*, 14 B. L. R. 273; S. C. 23 Suth. 78; *Murarji* v. *Parvatibai*, 1 Bom. 177 (blindness); *Paroshmani* v. *Dinanath*, 1 B. L. R. (A. C. J.) 117; *Balgovind* v. *Pertab*, S. D. of 1860, i. 661; *Hira Singh* v. *Ganga Sahai*, 6 All. 322, (deaf and dumb); *Vallabhram* v. *Bai Hariganga*, 4 Bom. H. C. (A. C. J.) 135, (dumb); *Umabai* v. *Bhavu*, 1 Bom. 557; *Chara Chunder* v. *Nobo Sunderi*, 18 Cal. 327; *Ran Bijai* v. *Jagatpal Singh*, 18 Cal. (P. C.) 111. In the last case an alleged insanity, founded chiefly on incapacity for speech due to paralysis, was held by the Privy Council not to be a ground for exclusion.

(*u*) *Tirumamagal* v. *Ramasvami*, 1 Mad. H. C. 214; *Surti* v. *Narain Das*, 12 All. 530.

ness as well as blindness must be shown to have existed from birth (*v*). It may, however, be doubted whether the texts which go to this extent do not refer to the case of idiocy, which is always congenital, while madness, as distinguished from idiocy, is rather a disease than an incapacity of the mind (*w*). Cases of disability from lunacy have come at least twice before the Privy Council. In one (*x*) it was admitted that the lunacy was not congenital, and it was assumed that the only question was whether the insanity had existed at the time the succession opened. In the second (*y*) no question was raised as to the date of the lunacy. From the fact that the lunatic was a married man and a father, it is most probable that he had not been born so. On the other hand, in Bengal and Allahabad it has been expressly held that insanity at the time the inheritance falls in is sufficient to exclude; and in the second of the two cases cited below it was further held that the insanity itself need not be incurable. If it was sufficient to prevent the claimant from offering the proper funeral oblations he was an unfit person to succeed (*z*). The same principle was applied where a person, who had become insane since his birth, brought a suit which assumed a right to claim a partition. It was held that his insanity would have been a bar to a claim as heir, and therefore would equally preclude a suit as coparcener for a share (*a*).

Leprosy. § 551. Leprosy of course need not be congenital. Its

---

(*v*) *Murarji* v. *Parvatibai*, 1 Bom. 177, 182. See too *Ananta* v. *Ramabai*, 1 Bom. 554.

(*w*) See Narada, 3 Dig. 303. Other translations of the same text omit any reference to birth. W. & B. 576; Madhaviya, § 49. Sir *Thos. Strange* (1 Stra. H. L. 153) says that all the disabilities must be coeval with birth, though Jagannatha seems to make the case of the madman an exception. The latter certainly says so in one passage (3 Dig. 314), though he interprets the texts of Narada and Devala as limited to congenital madness, (*ib.* 304). See too futwah, W. & B. 579; Sarasvati Vilasa, § 148. *Contra* Smriti Chandrika, v. § 9.

(*x*) *Bodhnarain* v. *Omrao*, 13 M. I. A. 519; S. C. 6 B. L. R. 509.

(*y*) *Kooer Goolab* v. *Rao Kurun*, 14 M. I. A. 176; S. C. 10 B. L. R. (P. C.) 1.

(*z*) *Braja Bhukan* v. *Bichan*, 9 B. L. R. 204, n.; S. C. 14 Suth. 329; *Dwarkanath* v. *Mahendranath*, 9 B. L. R. 198; S. C. *sub nomine*, *Dwarkanath* v. *Denobundoo*, 18 Suth. 305; *Woma Pershad* v. *Grish Chunder*, 10 Cal. 68; *Deo Kishen* v. *Budh Prakash*, 5 All. (F. B). 509.

(*a*) *Ram Sahye* v. *Lalla Laljee*, 8 Cal. 149.

occurrence is looked upon as the punishment of sin, either in a present or a past existence (*b*), and produces an incapacity for inheritance from the moment it is exhibited until it is removed by expiation (*c*). Some cases of leprosy are of a mild and curable form, while others are of a virulent and aggravated type, and incurable. It is only the latter form of the malady which causes inability to inherit (*d*). Other agonizing and incurable diseases are also spoken of as causing the same effect, as an example of which atrophy is given (*e*). It is probable, however, that the Courts would be slow to disinherit a man, merely because he was suffering from cancer or consumption, and in any case the strictest proof would be required that the disease was in fact incurable (*f*).

§ 552. Lameness is specifically alleged by *Yajnavalkya* as a ground of disability, and the word is explained by the Mitakshara as meaning "deprived of the use of his feet (*g*)." Lameness.

The corresponding word in *Manu*, *nirindriya* (*h*), is translated by Sir W. Jones and by Prosunno Comar Tagore, "such as have lost the use of a limb." And the commentary of *Vachespati Misra* upon the text is, "*Those who have lost the use of a limb* signifies those who have been deprived of a hand, a leg, or any other member of the body. Such persons are not competent to perform ceremonies relating to the Vedas and Smriti. They are consequently not entitled to inherit paternal property (*i*)." Colebrooke translates the same word when cited in the Mitakshara, "those who have lost a sense (*or a limb*)," and the explanation of *Vij*- Loss of a limb.

(*b*) 3 Dig. 313, 314.

(*c*) *Sevachetumbara* v. *Parasucti*, Mad. Dec. of 1857, 210; *Lakhi* v. *Bhairab*, 5 S. D. 315 (369). See futwah in *Lakshmi* v. *Tulsi*, 5 S. D. 285 (334).

(*d*) 3 Dig. 309, 311; 1 Stra. H. L. 156; *Muttuvelayudu Pillay* v. *Parasakti*, Mad. Dec. of 1860, 239; followed *Janardhan* v. *Gopal Pandurang*, 5 Bom. A. C. 145; *Ananta* v. *Ramabai*, 1 Bom. 554.

(*e*) 3 Dig. 303, 313.

(*f*) See *Issur Chunder* v. *Ranee Dossee*, 2 Suth. 125. The D. K. S. explains the text of Narada, which refers to a long and painful disease, as meaning a disease from the period of birth. D. K. S. iii. § 11.

(*g*) Mitakshara, ii. 10, § 1, 2.

(*h*) ix. 201.

(*i*) Vivada Chintamani, 242, 243.

nanesvara is, "any person who is deprived of an organ by disease, or any other cause, is said to have lost that sense or limb" (*k*). It would appear from this that lameness arising from illness or accident would operate as a bar to inheritance. I know of no instance in which any such objection has succeeded. In a case reported by West and Bühler the disqualified person is said to have been born lame, and *Jagannatha* seems to think that lameness arising subsequently would be no disability (*l*). In an early case in Bombay a person was asserted to be disqualified as a Pungoo or helpless cripple. It appeared that he could walk a little, and was a married man and a father. The Shastri to whom the point was referred said, "that according to the *Shasters* a Pungoo or helpless cripple was excluded from inheritance; that the term Pungoo was not very clearly defined, but in his opinion a person deprived of the use of his hands or feet was a Pungoo; and that '*Nirindriya,*' or such as were deprived of a sense, were excluded from inheritance. That persons only deformed in a hand did not come under the term '*Narindriya,*' though persons afflicted with an obstinate or incurable disease did." He was of opinion that the claimant was not disqualified from inheritance. Upon this futwah the Appellate Court decided in favour of the claimant. The Sudder Court reversed the decision, but not upon a point affecting the question now in discussion (*m*). It would seem, therefore, that the loss of a sense or organ must be absolute or complete. Not, perhaps, necessarily the absolute want of the limb, but, at all events, a complete incapacity to make any use of it.

Lameness or loss of a limb.

Vice.

§ 553. As to vice, several futwahs from Bombay are to be found, which would practically place the son at the mercy of his father, if he chose to disinherit him for vicious habits, hostility or disobedience (*n*). In a Surat case, a

---

(*k*) Mitakshara, ii. 10, § 3, 4; see *per curiam*, *Murarji* v. *Parvatibai*, 1 Bom. 185.

(*l*) W. & B. 578; 3 Dig. 304.

(*m*) *Dadjee* v. *Wittul*, Bom. Sel. Rep. 151.

(*n*) W. & B. 583—587.

will by which a father disinherited his son for vicious and dissolute habits was affirmed (*o*). But it would rather seem as if the testator's property had been self-acquired. Further, the son had executed an agreement, acknowledging that his debts had been paid off, and admitting his father's right to disinherit him, in case of renewed misconduct. In a case from the North-West Provinces the Court refused to act upon the texts which debarred a son from his share on account of his being addicted to vice, and a professed enemy of his father. They said that "the evidence given of the plaintiff's gambling and licentious propensities was of a vague and general character, and not such as would allow them to conclude that he had disqualified himself by addiction to vice for the performance of obsequies and such like acts of religion." Also, that although the evidence showed that he had quarrelled with and even struck his father, it did not disclose anything like habitual maltreatment, or active and malignant hostility which would authorise them to pronounce him a professed enemy of his father. They further observed that the texts in question were not only inapplicable to the facts, but are understood to have become obsolete in practice (*p*). In the same case they refused to act upon the supposed rule which disqualifies a coparcener from obtaining his own share, where he has attempted to defraud his coparceners of any portion of their rights. In a similar (though certainly a stronger case) the rule had been strictly applied by the Sudder Court of Madras (*q*). I imagine that all such disabilities as the above would come under the head of minor grounds of forfeiture, removable by penance (*r*). In one Bengal case an adopted son, who sued for his inheritance, was met by a plea that he had publicly and falsely

Fraud.

(*o*) *Mihirwanjee* v. *Poonjea*, 1 Bor. 141 [159]. This was a case between Parsis. See *per curiam*, *Advyapa* v. *Rudrava*, 4 Bom. 117.

(*p*) *Kalka* v. *Budree*, 3 N.-W. P. 267. See *Jye Koonwur* v. *Bhikari*, S. D. of 1848, 320, where, being a professed enemy to a father, was treated (under Mithila law) as a possible ground of exclusion, but not made out in fact.

(*q*) *Choondoor* v. *Narasimmah*, Mad. Dec. of 1858, 118; *ante*, § 444.

(*r*) See Manu, xi. § 183—187.

accused his adoptive mother of profligacy. The pandit, when consulted, replied that such an offence could only be expiated by a process of atonement, which would last twelve years, or in lieu thereof, by the gift of 180 milch cows and their calves, or their value, not to the calumniated parent, but to the Brahmans. The Court accordingly dismissed the suit, holding that the claimant could not inherit until he had performed the prescribed penance (*s*). I greatly doubt, however, whether this precedent would be followed in the present day.

Disabilities exclude females

All grounds of disqualification which would exclude males apply equally as against female heirs (*t*).

Disability only personal :

§ 554. Except in the case of degradation, the disability is purely personal, and does not extend to the legitimate issue of the disqualified person (*u*). But their adopted sons will be in no better position as regards ancestral property than themselves, and only entitled to maintenance out of it (*v*). There seems, however, to be no reason why the adopted son of a disqualified person should not succeed to all property which had already vested in his father, or which was acquired by him (*w*). Similarly, the widow of a disqualified heir cannot claim, as widow, to succeed to any property which her husband could not have inherited (*x*). But she would be his heir. And if his son succeeded and then died, she would inherit as mother to such son (*y*).

not a forfeiture.

Property which has once vested in a person, either by inheritance or partition, is not devested by a subsequently arising disability (*z*).

Lets in next heir.

§ 555. The effect of a disability on the part of a person

(*s*) *Bhola Nath* v. *Mt. Sabitra*, 6 S. D. 62 (71).
(*t*) Mitakshara, ii. 10, § 8.
(*u*) Mitakshara, ii. 10, § 9, 10; Daya Bhaga, v. § 17—19.
(*v*) Mitakshara, ii. 10, § 11; Dattaka Chandrika, vi. § 1; *ante*, § 99.
(*w*) Suth. Syn. 671. (*x*) D. K. S. iii. § 17. (*y*) 2 W. MacN. 130.
(*z*) Mitakshara, ii. 10, § 6; *Balgovind* v. *Lal Bahadoor*, S. D. of 1854, 244; *Deo Kishen* v. *Budh Prakash*, 5 All. 509; *Kery Kolitany* v. *Mooneeram*, 7 I. A. 115; 5 Cal. 776. *per curiam*, 14 Mad. p. 294.

who would otherwise have been heir, is at once to let in the next heir. For instance, if a man left an insane son and a daughter, the latter would take at once (*a*). So if he left an insane daughter, and sons by her, the latter would take at once (*b*) that is to say, the effect of the lunacy is, for purposes of succession, exactly the same as if the lunatic was then dead. If the incapacitated person has issue then living, or in *ventre sa mère*, who would, if the father were actually dead, be the next heir, such issue will be entitled to succeed. But he must succeed by his own merits. He will not be allowed to step into his father's place. For instance, if a man dies, leaving a brother, and an insane brother and his son, the brother will take the whole estate; because the nephew cannot inherit while a brother is in existence. So if a man dies leaving a sister's son, who is insane, and the sister's son himself has a son, the latter cannot inherit; because the sister's grandson is not an heir (*c*). And if the estate has in consequence of the incapacity vested in a male, the latter becomes full and absolute owner. If the incapacitated heir has a son, subsequently conceived, that son will not inherit, even though he would have been next heir or a sharer if born, or conceived, when the succession fell in (§ 556).

Afterborn son.

Removal of disability.

§ 556. Where the defect which produces exclusion is subsequently removed, the right to inheritance revives, in the same manner as, or upon the analogy of a son born after partition (*d*). The effect of this rule in cases of partition has been already discussed (§ 443). But the revival of this right will not necessarily place the previously disqualified heir in the same position as if the incapacity had never existed. The Hindu law never allows the inheritance to be in abeyance, and if the claimant is not capable of succeeding at the

---

(*a*) 2 W. MacN. 42.

(*b*) *Bodhnarain* v. *Omrao*, 13 M. I. A. 519; S. C. 6 B. L. R. 509. See too *Kalidas* v. *Krishan*, 2 B. L. R. (F. B.) 115.

(*c*) *Per Peacock*, C. J., *Kalidas* v. *Krishan*, 2 B. L. R. (F. B.) 115. See too ...

(*d*) Mitakshara, ii. 10, § 7; V. May., iv. 11, § 2.

time the descent takes place, the subsequent removal of his incapacity will not enable him to dispossess a person whose title was better than his while the defect existed, though inferior to his own after the defect was removed. For instance, suppose a man has a son who is born blind. If we can imagine the blindness removed before his father's death, he would of course inherit. If it was not removed, and his father died leaving a widow, she would inherit. If the blindness was cured during her life, she would continue to hold the property, but at her death, the son would likewise inherit, because he would be the nearest to her deceased husband. But if, on the father's death, his brother had inherited, and during his life the blind son was cured, and then the brother died leaving a widow, she would inherit, and not the formerly blind son. Because succession would be traced to the last full owner who was the brother, and his heir would be the widow, and not a person who stood to

Removal of disability.

him only in the relation of nephew (*e*). If, however, the brother died, leaving no nearer heir than a nephew, then of course the person who was previously incapacitated as son would now succeed as nephew. These principles were laid down by a Full Bench of the High Court of Bengal under the following circumstances. At the death of A. his son, being blind, was incapable of succeeding, and the estate

passed to the widows of A., of whom the last died in 1849. At her death the estate passed to C., the nephew of A. In 1858 a son was born to the blind man, and he claimed the estate from C. If he had been alive either at the death of A., or of the last widow, he would have been the heir, but it was held that once the estate reached C., he took it with all the rights of a full owner, and could not be deprived of

(*e*) *Bhoobum Moyee* v. *Ramkishore*, 10 M. I. A. 279; S. C. 3 Suth. (P. C.) 15; *ante*, § 172.

it by any subsequent birth (*f*). It was not necessary to decide what would have been the result if the blind man himself had recovered his sight after the property has vested in C. It might be suggested that he would have devested the estate of the nephew, on the analogy of a son born or adopted after the death of the last owner (*g*). But it is difficult to see why these analogies should be applied in his favour, and not in favour of his own son, who was born without any imperfection. The former case is really not analogous at all, as the unborn infant is in contemplation of law actually existent from conception, and is only incapable of taking at once, because it may die before leaving the womb. As to the adopted son, it seems almost sufficient to say, that there can be no reason for applying analogies, drawn from the case of a very highly-favoured heir, to a disqualified heir, who is let in afterwards by special indulgence.

§ 557. The same point arose in Bombay and in Madras, when different decisions were arrived at. In Bombay (*h*) the position of the family was as follows: Conflict of decisions

Bombay.

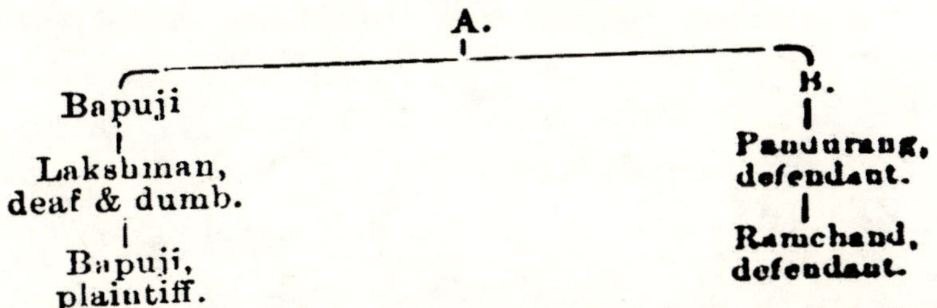

Bapuji the plaintiff's grandfather died, leaving the defendants, his undivided nephew and grandnephew, and a deaf and dumb son. After his death the son married, and the plaintiff was born. The latter sued to recover his share of the family property. The Bombay High Court held that the rule laid down in Bengal applied equally

(*f*) *Kalidas* v. *Krishan*, 2 B. L. R. (F. B.) 103; *Pareshmani* v. *Dinanath*, 1 B. L. R. (A. C. J.) 117; *Deo Kishen* v. *Mudh Prakash*, 5 All. 509.

(*g*) See *per Willes*, J., in *Tagore case*, 9 B. L. R. 397; S. C. 18 Suth. 359; S. C. I. A., Sup. Vol. 47.

(*h*) *Bapuji* v. *Pandurang*, 6 Bom. 616.

in Bombay, and that as the whole property had vested in Pandurang at the death of Bapuji, it could not be devested by the subsequent birth of the plaintiff. In

Madras decision. the case from Madras (*i*), the facts were exactly similar.

A.

- Sami.
  - deaf & dumb son.
    - Sami. plaintiff.
- Venkatasami.
  - Krishna, 1st defendant.
    - 2nd defendant.
    - 3rd defendant.

The plaintiff was born after the death of his grandfather, and it was contended that the whole property vested in the undivided line of Venkatasami. The Madras High Court held that the Bengal decision went on the peculiar doctrines of the Daya Bhaga, whereby the separate interest of A. passed to his widow, and then to his nephew C, who held it as separate property. Under Mitakshara law the lines of Sami and Venkatasami were an undivided coparcenary, liable to be enlarged or diminished by births or deaths. The share of Sami passed to his nephews by survivorship but subject to the possibility that their interest in it might be curtailed by the subsequent birth of a coparcener in Sami's line. Undoubtedly if the plaintiff had been born in his grandfather's life, he would have been at once by birth a joint owner in the family property. The Court considered that it made no difference that he was not born till afterwards. They likened it to the case of a brother who takes an impartible estate by survivorship, but whose estate is devested by a subsequent adoption made by the widow of the deceased (*k*).

Discussion of these cases. § 558. It is obvious that although the Bengal and Madras cases may be reconciled in the way suggested above, there is no way of reconciling the Bombay and Madras cases. Both were governed by Mitakshara law. The

---

(*i*) *Krishna* v. *Sami*, 9 Mad. 64.
(*k*) *Raghunada* v. *Broso Kishore*, 3 I. A. 154; S. C. 1 Mad. 69.

analogy derived from the rights of an adopted son seems also imperfect. His case has always been treated as an anomalous one, and as subject under certain circumstances to the same rules which preserve the rights of an infant in its mother's womb (*l*). Further, this indulgence is only shewn to an adopted son when the adoption is made to the last male holder of the estate (§ 175—179). Again the plaintiff in the Madras case could only become a coparcener by virtue of the rule that a son or a grandson takes by birth an interest in the estate of his father or grandfather. But that estate had passed away to the defendants before his birth, as much as if it had been sold to them. It is difficult to see how he could by his birth enter into a coparcenary which had ceased to exist. On the death of the grandfather the whole estate vested absolutely in the nephew, subject only to the rights of his son. The plaintiff by his birth took no interest whatever in the property of his cousins. Therefore it would appear, with the greatest respect to the learned Judges, as if his birth could have no effect in devesting or diminishing their interests.

§ 559. One who has entered into an order of devotion is also excluded from inheritance, since he has of his own accord abandoned all earthly interests (*m*). The persons who are excluded on this ground come under three heads, *viz.*, the *Vanaprasatha*, or hermit; the *Sanyasi* or *Yati*, or ascetic; and the *Brahmachari*, or perpetual religious student. In order to bring a person under these heads, it is necessary to show an absolute abandonment by them of all secular property, and a complete and final withdrawal from earthly affairs. The mere fact that a person calls himself a *Byragi*, or religious mendicant, or indeed that he is such, does not of itself disentitle him to succeed to property (*n*).

Entrance into religious order.

Must be absolute and final.

(*l*) *Tagore* v. *Tagore*, 9 B. L. R., (P. C.) 377, 397, 400, 404.

(*m*) Yajnavalkya, ii. § 137; Vasishtha, xvii. § 27; Mitakshara, ii. 10, § 3; Daya Bhaga, v. § 11; V. May., iv. 11, § 5.

(*n*) See *ante*, § 546; *Teeluck Chunder* v. *Shama Churn*, 1 Suth. 209.

Non-Aryan races.

I have not been able to find any evidence of the grounds which are held to exclude from inheritance by usage in the Punjab, or among the non-Aryan races of India. It will be seen that the Madras Sudder Court has in several cases applied the Sanskrit rules to Tamil litigants. I should imagine that rules founded so completely upon Brahmanical principles, would require to be applied with great caution to tribes who had not thoroughly accepted those principles. The more so as those principles have no foundation in natural equity or justice.

CHAPTER XX.

WOMAN'S ESTATE.

In Property inherited from Males.

Meaning of Stridhanum.

§ 560. THE term *Stridhanum* (literally woman's estate) is used in two different acceptations by Hindu lawyers. In one sense it denotes that special sort of woman's estate over which she has absolute control, even during the life of her husband (*a*). In another sense it includes all sorts of property of which a woman has become the owner, whatever may be the extent of her rights over it (*b*).

Now, it will be found that property held by a woman is at once divisible into two classes, which have completely different incidents, *viz.*, property which has devolved upon her by inheritance from a male owner, and property which she has obtained in any other way. In speaking of *stridhanum* hereafter I shall wholly exclude from it the former class of property. It is evident that it would only create confusion to apply the same word to estates which are obtained in different ways, and which are held by different tenure.

Limitations on inherited property.

§ 561. The typical form of estate inherited by a woman from a male is the widow's estate. But it may now be considered that the same limitations apply to all estates derived by a female by descent from a male, in whatever capacity she may have inherited them. The only exception is as to the estate of a sister, and possibly of a daughter, in Bombay. The rule upon this point is still open to discussion.

(*a*) Daya Bhaga, iv. 1, § 18.

(*b*) Mitakshara, ii. 11, § 3.

It was at one time common to speak of a widow's estate as being one for life. But this is wholly incorrect. It would be just as untrue to speak of the estate of a father under the Mitakshara law as being one for life. Hindu law knows nothing of estates for life, or in tail, or in fee. It measures estates not by duration but by use. The restrictions upon the use of an estate inherited by a woman are similar in kind to those which limit the powers of a male holder, but different in degree. The distinctive feature of the estate is, that at her death it reverts to the heirs of the last male owner. She never becomes a fresh stock of descent (c).

Not a life estate.

Reverts to heirs of last male holder.

§ 562. It is evident that these two qualities of her estate are connected together. It would be of little use to mark out a line of descent which should keep the estate in the family from which it came, unless the woman was restrained from absolutely disposing of it. On the other hand, the line of descent which is marked out, shows that the estate was given to the woman for a special purpose, which would be satisfied without giving any interest in it to her own immediate heirs. But it is by no means clear, whether the estate reverted to the man's heirs, because the woman was only allowed a special use of it; or whether she was only allowed the special use in order to preserve it for those heirs; or whether both incidents arose from the purpose for which such estates were originally allowed to exist.

Scanty authority.

It is singular how little is to be found on the subject in the Hindu writings. We are told in very early texts that a widow is restrained in dealing with the estate she may inherit from her husband, but we are nowhere told that the same restrictions apply to other female heirs. Again, the course of inheritance laid down in the earlier texts seems to assume that the estate reverts after a widow or a daughter to the heirs of the last male; but until we

(c) *Collector of Masulipatam* v. *Cavaly Vencata*, 8 M. I. A. 529, 550; S. C. 2 Suth. (P. C.) 59; *Kery Kolitany* v. *Moneeram*, 13 B. L. R. 5, 53, 76; S. C. 19 Suth. 367.

come to *Jimuta Vahana* we are nowhere told that it is the rule (*d*). The literal wording of the Mitakshara seems to state that it is not the rule (*e*).

§ 563. As regards the first point, *viz.*, the limited powers of disposal possessed by a female—we must recollect that according to Hindu law restriction was the rule, absolute power the exception. Even the male head of a family was hemmed in by limitations. These were gradually reduced in their application, when separate and self-acquired property was introduced, and at last disappeared entirely in the Bengal system. It would have seemed absurd to a Hindu lawyer that any one should imagine that a female, herself a most subordinate member of the family, could possess higher rights over its property than its head. The earlier writers contented themselves with general statements that a woman was never fit for independence, but must at every stage of her life be under the tutelage of some male protector, the widow being under the control of her husband's family (*f*). As regards the widow, too, the state of asceticism in which she was expected to live was of itself a restriction upon her right to spend the property (*g*). Most of the texts which definitely speak of the restrictions upon a woman's power of dealing with property relate to a widow. *Katyayana* says, "Let the childless widow, preserving unsullied the bed of her lord, and abiding with her venerable protector, enjoy with moderation the property until her death. After her, let the heirs take it. But she has not property therein to the extent of gift, mortgage, or sale (*h*)." The Mahabharata says, "For women the heritage of their husbands is pronounced appli-

Limited power of disposal.

(*d*) Daya Bhaga, xi. 1, § 57—59; xi. 2, § 30, 31; Viramit., p. 140.
(*e*) See *post*, § 566.
(*f*) Manu, viii. § 416; ix. § 2, 3, 104; Baudhayana, ii. 2, § 27; Narada, xiii. § 28—30; Smriti Chandrika, xi. 1, § 35—39.
(*g*) Daya Bhaga, xi. 1, § 61; 2 Dig. 459; *per curiam*, *Collector of Masulipatam v. Cavaly Vencata*, 8 M. I. A. 551; S. C. 2 Suth (P. C.) 59.
(*h*) Daya Bhaga, xi. 1, § 56; V. May., iv. 8, § 4; Virada Chintamani, 292; Vrihaspati, cited Smriti Chandrika, xi. 1, § 28. Viramit., p. 136, § 3.

cable to use. Let not women on any account make waste of their husband's wealth (*i*)." *Narada,* however, lays down the same proposition with greater generality: "Women's business transactions are null and void, except in case of distress, especially the gift, pawning, or sale of a house or field. Women are not entitled to make a gift or sale; a woman can only take a life-interest whilst she is living together with the rest of the family. Such transactions of women are valid where the husband has given his consent, or, in default of the husband, the son, or in default of husband and son, the king (*k*)." If, as I have already suggested (*l*), the widow's inheritance originally commenced as a compendious mode of enabling her to maintain herself, it would naturally follow, both that her right of using the property would be limited, and that after her death, it would revert to the heirs of her husband's family. Probably the same origin may be ascribed to the limitations on the estate of a mother and other female ancestor.

Cause of the restriction.

Daughter's Estate.

§ 564. The same reasoning, however, would not apply to the case of a daughter. She takes the inheritance not by way of maintenance—the obligation to maintain her ending at marriage,—but as beneficial owner. In her case, possibly, the limitation arose originally from the natural dislike to any succession which would carry the property of the family permanently into a different line (*m*). This principle would be strengthened when inheritance came to be looked on as a reward for religious benefits. Under that system, each heir takes the estate *primâ facie* as a means of performing the religious obsequies of the last male. When the heir is himself a male, his own obsequies require to be attended to, therefore at his death, the property passes to those who are bound to make offerings to him, that is, to his own heirs. But where the property is taken by a female,

---

(*i*) Daya Bhaga, xi. 1, § 60. (*k*) Narada, iii. § 27—30.
(*l*) *Ante*, § 483.
(*m*) The rule is thoroughly established by usage in the Punjab as regards both widows, daughters, and mothers. Punjab Customs, 16, 45, 52, 54, 58.

her obsequies are provided for quite independently, *viz.*, in her husband's family, if she is married. The duty which has to be performed to the deceased male still remains, and it can only be discharged by returning the estate to a member of his family, who, as being his heir, is bound to discharge his funeral rites. Now if the female holder is bound to return the property into his family, an obligation would naturally arise to return it intact. She would be considered as holding the property for a special purpose, and bound to pass it on to the next heir, with its capacity for performing that purpose undiminished.

§ 565. Whatever may be the origin of the rule, there can be no doubt now that the rule exists universally (except in Bombay) that where any female takes as heir to a male, she takes a restricted estate, and on her death the property passes not to her heirs, but to the person who would be the next heir of the last full owner. In Bengal the point was always beyond dispute, as it was expressly so laid down by *Jimuta Vahana* (n). It was at one time supposed that a different rule prevailed in Southern India (o). This idea was based on a text of the Mitakshara which appears to class such property as *stridhanum*, which passes to the heirs of the woman. In Madras it will be seen that no weight is any longer attributed to that text. But as it appears to be at the root of a conflicting series of decisions in Bombay, and as the matter is also one of much historical interest, it will be necessary to examine the passage somewhat minutely. Restricted estate applies to all female heirs.

§ 566. The whole discussion turns upon the question, whether the devolution of a woman's property, stated by the Mitakshara at ii. 11, § 8, 9, applies to all the sorts of Supposed exception under Mitakshara.

(n) Daya Bhaga, xi. 1, § 57—59; xi. 2, § 30, 31; 3 Dig. 494, 497; *Hurry-doss* v. *Pungunmoney*, Sev. 657.

(o) 1 Stra. H. L. 139, 248; Stra. Man. § 354; *Gopaula* v. *Narraina*, Mad. Dec. of 1850, p. 76; *Iyavoo* v. *Sengen*, *ib.*, 1856, p. 47; *Jagadunda* v. *Camacheamma*, 1858, p. 244. In Pondicherry the Courts hold that even a widow becomes absolute owner of property inherited by her from her husband, with full powers of disposition. Eyssette, pp. 178, 314, 324, 340, 374, 415; *contra*, p. 310.

property which he had already described at § 2, 3, of the same section, or only to some of those sorts of property. Section 11 is a commentary on the three texts of *Yajnavalkya* (ii. § 143—145) which relate to *stridhanum,* illustrated in the author's usual manner by citations from other writers. He commences (§ 1) by quoting the first of the three texts in a manner which is translated by Mr. Colebrooke as follows :—"What was given to a woman by the father, the mother, the husband or a brother, or received by her at the nuptial fire, or presented to her on her husband's marriage to another wife, as also any other (separate acquisition), is denominated woman's property." Now the word in the original text, which is here rendered *any other,* is *adi* annexed to the preceding term, which really means "and the like," and is so translated elsewhere (*p*). *Primâ facie,* therefore, they only refer to property of the same nature as the foregoing, that is, to special gifts made to a woman by her own family, and to particular gifts made to her as a bride, or a superseded wife. In the next section *Vijnanesvara* repeats and expands this text, adding, "and also property which she may have acquired by inheritance, purchase, partition, seizure of finding, are denominated by *Manu* and the rest 'woman's property.'" Now *Manu* certainly says nothing of the sort. His enumeration (ix. § 194) is contained in the fourth clause of the same section of the Mitakshara. It is so strictly limited to personal gifts, that *Vijnanesvara* and others think it necessary to add, that the six classes of gifts there stated are not exclusive of any other sorts of property. But the general statement which closes § 2 will be found in *Gautama,* cited in the Mitakshara, i. 1, § 8. "An owner is by inheritance, purchase, partition, seizure or finding (*q*)." But this is a definition

Stridhanum defined by Mitakshara,

(*p*) See translation of the text, ii. 143, by Montriou and Roer, and Stenzler; also by Dr. Burnell, Varadrajah, p. 45. See also his remarks, Introd. p. 18; Mayr, 171.

(*q*) And see Manu, x. § 115, where he points out seven virtuous modes of acquiring property, the last three of which at all events are peculiar to men.

of ownership in general, not of woman's property, specially so called. The passage of the Mitakshara, therefore, merely comes to this, that a woman may acquire property, not only by the special modes, which give it peculiar incidents of alienability and succession, as *stridhanum*, strictly so called, but by any other mode by which a male can acquire it. Then at § 3 he makes this quite clear by saying, "The term woman's property conforms in its import with its etymology, and is not technical, for, if the literal sense be admissible, a technical acceptation is improper." That is to say, he gives the reader express notice that, when he uses the word *stridhanum*, he means, not "woman's property" specially and technically so called, but the property of a woman, vested in her by any legal means (*r*). Then at § 8 he says, "A woman's property has been thus described. The author (that is, *Yajnavalkya*) next propounds the distribution of it. 'Her kinsmen take it, if she die without issue.'" The question is, to what sort of property does this rule apply? Does it apply to *stridhanum* in its technical, or in its general, meaning? In other words, does it apply to it as defined by *Yajnavalkya*, or as defined by *Vijnanesvara*? I think it evidently applies to it in its former, or restricted sense. The rule is a citation of the second of the three texts of *Yajnavalkya*. It follows in the original text of *Yajnavalkya* after the definition given by him, and it can only apply to the sorts of property specified by *Yajnavalkya*. It is evidently not an exhaustive statement of the mode in which all property, however acquired by a woman, will devolve, for at clauses 14, 20 and 30, three other modes of

Has no technical meaning.

Text of the Mitakshara discussed.

(*r*) This is directly opposed to the use of the word by Jimuta Vahana. "That alone is her peculiar property which she has power to give, sell, or use, independently of her husband's control." Daya Bhaga, iv. 1, § 18. So Katyayana excludes from the term Stridhanum the earnings of a woman or what she has received from any but the kindred of her husband or parents, 3 Dig. [illegible]. Property inherited by a woman is not included in the definition of Stridhanum by the Smriti Chandrika, ix. 1; the Mayukha, iv. 10; the Vivada Chintamani, 256; the Madhaviya, § 50 or Varadrajah, 45. On the other hand it is included by the Viramitrodaya, 221, § 2 and the Sarasvati Vilasa § 264, both of which follow the definition given in the Mitakshara. Also by Apararka, Kamalakara in the Vivadatandava, Nandapandita in the Vaijayanti, and Viçveçara in the Madavaparijota. See Dr. Jolly, Lectures, pp. 248—251.

descent are mentioned. These modes are different from that specified by *Yajnavalkya*, and apply to property which is not included in his definition. No part of this section of the Mitakshara applies in terms to property which a woman has inherited from a male. But the reason for that obviously is, that the devolution of such property had been exhaustively treated in the former sections of the same chapter. In those sections he explained how a man's property would go to his widow, his daughter, his daughter's son, and, in default of them, to parents and others. But if the section now under consideration applies to property inherited by a woman from a male, the result would be that if a daughter took property it would go to her daughter, or her daughter's son, or her son's son, or to her husband. But this is a line of descent directly opposed to everything in the parts of the Mitakshara which expressly treat of the descent of such property. In short, the view I would submit is this. *Vijnanesvara* includes under the term *stridhanum* property which a woman has acquired in any way whatever. The descent of that which she has derived from a male—that is from a husband, father, or son—is treated of in the earlier sections of chap. ii.; that which she obtained otherwise, is treated of in § 11 (*s*). Its other quality, *viz.*, alienability, he appears nowhere to discuss.

Contrary opinions.

§ 567. This explanation would of course be treated as wholly inadmissible by those who consider not only that the Mitakshara includes in the term *stridhanum* property inherited from a male, but that it declares that such property passes at the death of the female to her heirs, and not to those of the last male owner (*t*). It is also controverted by Dr. Jolly (*u*), on the ground that the respect due to Yajnavalkya makes it impossible to assume that Vijnanesvara admitted that his explanation of the term *stridhanum*,

(*s*) See *per Holloway*, J., *Kattama Nachiar* v. *Dorasinga Tevar*, 6 Mad. H. C. at p. 340. This explanation would deprive the passage of the significance attributed to it by Sir H. S. Maine. Early Institutions, 321.

(*t*) Banerjee, Law of Marriage and Stridhanum, 301—304; W. & B. 146, 323.

(*u*) Lectures, 246.

differed from or extended that of the text which he was explaining. Consequently, that even if the line of devolution stated in § 8, 9 only applies to the *stridhanum* referred to by Yajnavalkya, still that *stridhanum* must be taken with his own explanation of what he supposed Yajnavalkya to have meant. The argument is, that although Yajnavalkya, as Dr. Jolly admits (p. 243), used the word *stridhanum* in its technical sense, as excluding property inherited from a male, Vijnanesvara mistook his meaning, and therefore intended in § 8, 9 to specify the line of descent appropriate to all property acquired by a woman in any manner whatever. But as a matter of fact this was not his intention, because as I have already pointed out (§ 566) he subsequently gives three different lines of descent for different sorts of *stridhanum* in § 14, 20 & 30. If therefore these sorts of property are not included in § 8, why should we assume as a matter of necessary inference that property inherited from a male is so included? It is evident that there are two distinct questions. First, did Vijnanesvara mean to say that property so inherited would pass to a woman's daughters, and the daughters of those daughters? Secondly, how are we to account for the fact that the most influential of the commentators who accept him as an authority, differ from him upon this line of descent? The Viramitrodaya, as already stated, accepts the wide explanation of the Mitakshara as to the meaning of the word *stridhanum,* but when the author comes to the line of descent he expressly states that the heirs of the husband take his property after the death of the widow. For this he refers to the text of Katyayana. "Let the sonless widow, preserving unsullied the bed of her husband, and abiding with her venerable protector, only enjoy her husband's property, being moderate until her death, after her let the heirs or *dayadas* take it." This he explains as meaning "after her let the husband's heirs or dayadas, *i.e.,* those that are entitled to take his undivided property, take also what remains of the estate of a separated brother after the enjoyment thereof by his wife; and not the heirs to the estate of the wife, such as daughters and the like" (*v*). The Mitakshara contains no express statement to this effect, but the line of descent to the separate property of a male given in Ch. ii. 1—3, seems to assume such a rule. This would reconcile those sections with § 11. It would also account for the fact that the commentators who undoubtedly do not allow the property of a male to go to a woman's special heirs, never appear to imagine that they are differing from the Mitakshara.

Cannot apply to widow.

Again, if the passage in the Mitakshara is to be taken as meaning, that all property which a woman takes by inheritance goes to her special heirs, and not to those of the last male, the same rule should apply to every case in which a woman inherits in that way; to a widow or a mother, as much as to a sister or a daughter. Such a devolution in the case of property inherited by a widow is directly opposed to the whole theory of the Mitakshara, and to the usage of every part of India. This very text of the Mitakshara has been, on two occasions at least, pressed upon the Judicial Committee as an argument for holding, that a widow has greater power over property inherited from her husband in provinces governed by that law, than elsewhere. But the argument has always failed, and it is thoroughly settled that a widow takes only a restricted estate, and that at her death it passes to her husband's heirs (*w*). And this is admitted in its fullest sense by the High Court of Bombay (*x*). It is

Held inapplicable to mother.

also admitted by the Courts of all the Presidencies that the

(*v*) Viramitrodaya, 136, 140. *West*, J., says (11 Bom. p 305). "As to Madras, the authority there of the Smriti Chandrika and the Madhaviya, which reject the fundamental notion of the Mitakshara as to women's rights prevent any identity between its law and that of Bombay."

(*w*) *Thakoor* v. *Rai Baluk Ram*, 11 M. I. A. 139, 173; S. C. 10 Suth. (P. C.) 3; *Bhugwandeen* v. *Myna Baee*, *ib.* 487, 509; S. C. 9 Suth. (P. C.) 23; *Collector of Masulipatam* v. *Cavaly Vencata*, 8 M. I. A. 529; S. C. 2 Suth. (P. C.) 59. Vivada Chintamani, 261; *Keerut* v. *Koolahul*, 2 M. I. A. 331; S. C. 5 Suth. (P. C.) 131.

(*x*) *Per curiam*, *Pranjeevandas* v. *Dewcooverbaee*, 1 Bom. H. C. 130; *Jamiyatram* v. *Bai Jamna*, 2 Bom. H. C. 10; *Lakshmibai* v. *Ganpat Moroba*, 4 Bom. (O C. J.) 163; *Bhaskar* v. *Mahadev*, 6 Bom. H. C. (O. C. J.) 1. The same rule has been held to apply to movable property undisposed of at the death of the widow. *Harilal Harjivandas* v. *Pranvalabdas*, 16 Bom. 229. As to her power of disposition, see *post*, § 598.

mother and grandmother, when inheriting from a son or grandson, take an estate similar in all respects to that of a widow (*y*). If so, the presumption is very strong that the passage should be interpreted in the case of other female heirs, so as to admit of a similar application.

Case of daughter.

§ 568. The only other female who can inherit to a male, except in Bombay, is a daughter. That property which she takes as daughter does not pass from her as *stridhanum*, is evident, from the circumstance that where there are several daughters, each of whom has sons, no son takes till all the daughters are dead, and then all take *per capita* (§ 519), that is, they take as direct heirs to the male ancestor, and not as representing their mothers. It has been repeatedly decided by the Bengal Courts, not only in cases under the Daya Bhaga, but also under Mithila and Mitakshara law, that the estate of a daughter exactly corresponds to that of a widow, both in respect to the restricted power of alienation, and to its succession after her death to her father's heirs, and not her own (*z*). The same point has been twice decided in a similar manner by the High Court of Madras, after a full examination of the passage in the Mitakshara, and of the Bombay authorities which have taken a different view (*a*). The rulings of these Courts

Bengal.

Madras.

(*y*) 1 W. MacN. 25; 2 W. MacN. 125, 209; 3 Dig. 505. See as to Bengal, *Bijya* v. *Unpoorna*, 1 S. D. 162 (215); *Nufur* v. *Ram Koomar*, 4 S. D. 310 (393); *Bhyrobee* v. *Nubkissen*, 6 S. D. 53 (61); *Hemlutta* v. *Goluckchunder*, 7 S. D. 108 (127); *Rughober* v. *Mt. Tulashee*, S. D. of 1847, 87. As to Mithila, Vivada Chintamani, 263; *Punchanund* v. *Lalshan*, 3 Suth. 140. As to Madras, *Bachiraju* v. *Venkatappadu*, 2 Mad. H. C. 402; *Kutti* v. *Radakristna*, 8 Mad. H. C. 88; *Vellanki* v. *Venkata*, 4 I. A. 1, 8; S. C. 1 Mad. 174: S. C. 26 Suth. 21. As to Bombay, *Vinayek* v. *Luxumeebaee*, 1 Bom. H. C. 117; *Narsappa* v. *Sakharam*, 6 Bom. H. C. (A. C. J.) 215. As to the N.-W. P., *Phukar* v. *Ranjit*, 1 All. 661; *Sakhram* v. *Sitabai*, 3 Bom. 353; *Dhondu* v. *Gangabai*, *ib.* 369; *per curiam*, *Bharmangavda* v. *Rudrapgavda*, 4 Bom. 187; *Tuljaram* v. *Mathuradas*, 5 Bom. 670.

(*z*) Daya Bhaga, xi. 2, § 30; 1 W. MacN. 21; 2 W. MacN. 224; F. MacN. 7; *Gunga Mya* v. *Kishen Kishore*, 3 S. D. 128 (170); *Gosaien* v. *Mt. Kishen*, 6 S. D. 77 (90), from Bengal, *Gyan* v. *Dookhurn*, 4 S. D. 330 (420); *Deo Pershad* v. *Lujoora*, 20 Suth. 102; S. C. 14 B. L. R. 245 (note), from Mithila, *Chotay* v. *Chunnoo*, 14 B. L. R. 235; S. C. 22 Suth. 496, Benares law; where the Bombay decisions were considered and disapproved. Affirmed in P. C. 6 I. A. 15; S. C. 4 Cal. 744.

(*a*) *Sengamalathammal* v. *Valaynda*, 3 Mad. H. C. 312; *Kattama Nachiar* v. *Dorasinga Tevar*, 6 Mad. H. C. 310; *Muttu Vaduganadha* v. *Dorasinga Tevar*, 290, 8 I. A. 99; S. C. 3 Mad. 290.

have been affirmed by the Privy Council. The law as to daughters may therefore be taken to be the same as that which governs widows and mothers in every part of India except in Bombay.

Rule in Bombay as to nature of estate taken by a female heir.

§ 569. In Bombay the Courts divide female heirs into two classes. Those who by marriage have entered into the *gotra* of the male whom they succeed, take an estate similar to that of a widow. Those who are of a different *gotra*, or who upon their marriage will become of a different *gotra* from the last male owner, take absolutely. Under the former head fall a widow, mother, grandmother, &c., and the widow of a sapinda succeeding under circumstances similar to those under which Mankuvarbai succeeded in the case of *Lallubhai* v. *Mankuvarbai* (*b*). Under the latter head are ranked a daughter, sister, niece, grandniece, and the like (*c*). In examining the cases in which this rule has been applied, one is struck by the uniformity of the decisions in themselves, as contrasted with the weakness of the reasoning on which they rest. The absolute right of the daughter, sister, &c., is rested upon texts of the Mayukha, which seem unable to support the conclusion which is drawn from them, and upon a continued reference to the definition of the word *stridhanum* in the Mitakshara, from which, since the recent decisions of the Privy Council (*d*), no inference can be drawn. It is probable, however, that in this case, as in that of the female sapinda discussed in § 488, the pundits and judges, in their zeal for written authority, have striven to maintain by express texts a practice which could have been sufficiently supported by long established and inveterate usage. In the judgment in which the above rule was laid down, *Westropp*, C. J., expressly relies upon a long course of practice, followed by the High Court in numerous unreported cases, and by the legal profession in advising

(*b*) 2 Bom. 388; *affd. sub nomine*, *Lullubhoy* v. *Cassibai*, 7 I. A. 212; S. C. 5 Bom. 110.

(*c*) *Tuljaram* v. *Mathuradas*, 5 Bom. 662, 670.

(*d*) *Ante*, § 567, 568.

upon titles, any departure from which would cause much confusion and injustice throughout the Presidency (*e*).

§ 570. The leading case as to the rights of daughters, is one known as *Dewcooverbaee's* case (*f*), decided on the Equity side of the Supreme Court, in 1859. There an estate passed first to the widows, and then to the daughters. *Sausse*, C. J., said as to the latter, " What then is the nature of the estate they take? Here again there are differences of opinion, but, dealing with the question according to the three works I have mentioned (Manu, Mitakshara, Mayukha), we find quoted in the Mayukha (iv. 8, § 10) a passage from *Manu*. 'The son of a man is even as himself, and the daughter is equal to a son; how then can any other inherit his property, but a daughter who is as it were himself (*g*).' With reference to this point also I consulted the Shastries, both here and at Poona, and enquired whether daughters could alienate any, and what portion, of the property inherited from a father who died separate? The answer was, that daughters so obtaining property could alienate it at their will and pleasure; and in this the Shastries of both places agreed, both also referring to the above text in the Mayukha as the authority for that position. On reviewing all accessible authorities, I have come to the conclusion that daughters take the immovable property absolutely from their father after their mother's death."

Dewcooverbaee's case.

This ruling as to a daughter's estate has been followed in other cases in the Bombay Courts which are cited below (*h*), and, as will be seen hereafter (§ 572), has received the implied assent of the Judicial Committee. On the other hand, there are early cases, founded upon the opinions of

---

(*e*) 5 Bom. p. 672. See also 11 Bom. p. 312.

(*f*) 1 Bom. H. C. 130; *Vinayeck* v. *Luxumeebaee*, 9 M I. A. 528, note; S. C. 3 Suth. (P. C) 41.

(*g*) Manu, ix. § 130. See this text discussed, *ante*, § 479.

(*h*) *Navalram* v. *Nandkishor*, 1 Bom. H. C. 209; *Vijiarangam* v. *Lakshuman*, 8 Bom. H. C. (O. C. J.) 244; *Haribhat* v. *Damodarbhat*, 3 Bom. 171; *per curiam*, *Bharmangavda* v. *Rudrapgavda*, 4 Bom. 187; *Tuljaram* v. *Mathuradas*, 5 Bom. 670; *Bulakhidas* v. *Keshavlal*, 6 Bom. 85.

the Surat Shastries, in which it has been held that a daughter, inheriting from her father, could not alienate the property without the consent of her son (*i*). In the 3rd edition of West and Bühler's Digest (p. 432) the learned editors after referring to the above decisions say, "But in *Muttuvadaganadha* v. *Dorasinga Tevar* (*k*) the Judicial Committee say definitively that the Mitakshara is not to be construed as conferring on any 'woman taking by inheritance from a male a stridhana estate transmissible to her own heirs.' It would seem, therefore, that the heritage taken by daughters must in future be regarded as but a life-interest, whether with or without the extensions recognised in the case of a widow, except in cases governed by the Vyavahara Mayukha, iv. 10, § 25, 26. See 2 W. MacN. 57." The Bombay High Court in one case signified its approval of this view (*l*); but, on a later and fuller examination of the subject, it reverted to its former conclusion that, in the Bombay Presidency, whether under the Mitakshara or Mayukha, a daughter inheriting from her father takes an absolute and not a life estate (*m*).

Right of sisters.

§ 571. As regards the right of sisters, the only decisions available are from Bombay, since, with the exception of a single case in Madras, their claim is not recognized in other parts of India. The rulings of the Bombay High Court are to the effect that they take an absolute interest.

Vinayek v. *Luxumeebaee.*

In the first case (*n*) Bhugwantrao died, leaving a will by which he bequeathed all his property to Luxumeebaee and his infant son Gujanun, and made his wife sole executrix. Gujanun survived him, and then died an infant. The plain-

---

(*i*) *Poonjea* v. *Prankoonwar*, 1 Bor. 173 [194]; *Krishnaram* v. *Mt. Bheekee*, 2 Bor. 329 [362].

(*k*) 8 I. A. 99, 109.

(*l*) *Dalpat Narotam* v. *Bhagvan Khushal*, 9 Bom. 301, 303.

(*m*) *Bhaghirtibai* v. *Kahnujirav*, 11 Bom. (F. B.) 285; *Jankibai* v. *Sundra*, 14 Bom. 612.

(*n*) *Vinayek* v. *Luxumeebaee*, 1 Bom. H. C. 117; *affrd.*, 9 M. I. A. 516; S. C. 3 Suth. (P. C.) 41; followed *Bhaskar Trimbak* v. *Mahadev*, 6 Bom. H. C. (O. C. J.) 1.

tiffs, nephews of Bhugwantrao, filed their bill against the

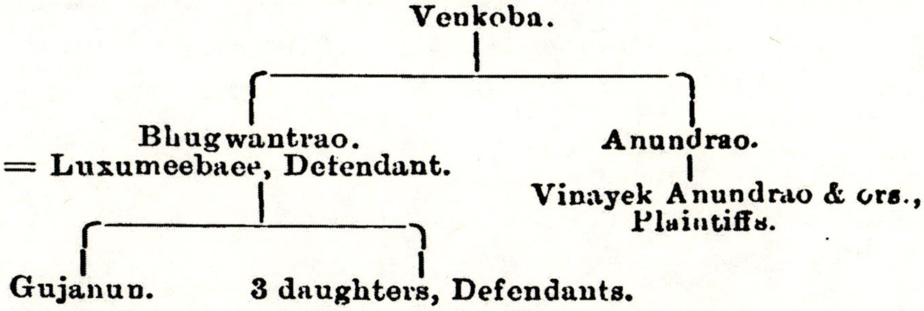

widow and daughters. They prayed for a declaration that the widow was only entitled for life, and that they were entitled as next heirs in remainder. It is stated that the bill set out various acts and omissions amounting to waste, and charged Luxumeebaee with attempting to adopt. It prayed that she should be restrained from selling or disposing of any part of the estate, from committing waste, and from adopting. The bill was demurred to, so that all the allegations contained in it were taken as true.

Sisters said to take absolutely.

The whole argument turned upon the asserted right of the plaintiffs as next heirs after the widow. The Court held that the persons to succeed after Luxumeebaee were the heirs of Gujanun, and that according to the Mayukha those heirs were his sisters, the defendants, and not his cousins, the plaintiffs. This decision was confirmed by the Privy Council. But at the end of their judgment (*o*), the Supreme Court said, that as to the mode in which sisters take it would appear by analogy that they take as daughters. As it had been decided by *Dewcooverbaee's* case that the daughters of a man take absolutely, so therefore do the sisters. In confirming this decision, the Judicial Committee said (*p*). "They consider that in Bombay at least the sisters in such a case as this are the heirs of the brother. The consequence is, that in whatever possible manner the will of the testator is read, the entire interest in the property must, we think, be viewed as vested in the widow and her daughters, or some or one of them, and that, therefore, the appellants

(*o*) 1 Bom. H. C. 124. (*p*) 9 M. I. A. 538.

here, the sons of the brother of the testator, are suing in a matter in which they have not shewn the slightest interest, nor with which they have any concern. The result is, that in their Lordships' opinion the demurrer was rightly allowed, and that the appeal should be dismissed with costs."

§ 572. The force of these decisions consists in the fact that they were given upon demurrer. If, therefore, the bill alleged acts of waste which would have entitled reversioners coming in after the sisters to an injunction, then, inasmuch as the demurrer admitted the allegations in the bill, the decision is conclusive that the estate was vested absolutely in the daughters, after the widow's life estate. In consequence of a suggestion which was made in previous editions of this work, that the general allegation of waste might not have been put in any form which would have supported a decree, *Westropp*, C. J., in a judgment already referred to (*q*), stated that he had sent for the original record of the suit. It appeared from it that, amongst other specific charges of waste committed by *Luxumeebaee*, paragraph 13 of the bill contained the following statement. "The defendant *Luxumeebaee* has sold the said piece of land situate at *Warli*, forming part of the immovable estate of her deceased husband, and is still attempting to sell part of the immovable property of her said husband, with a view of appropriating the money to her own use, although she did not and does not pretend that there was or there is any necessity for the said sale, and several brokers have, during the last year and a half, at her request, gone into the bazar at Bombay, and on several occasions offered the said last mentioned property for sale." Upon this the learned Chief Justice correctly remarks. "This paragraph (the truth of which for the purpose of the demurrer was admitted) was alone quite sufficient to support a decree and injunction, if the plaintiffs had any interest in the property, the subject of the suit.

(*q*) *Tuljaram* v. *Mathuradas*, 5 Bom. p. 671.

The Supreme Court and Privy Council, however, held that the plaintiffs had not any interest, reversionary or otherwise, in the property." It will be observed that the plaintiffs rested their whole case on the assertion that they were next in succession to the widow, and that the sisters were not heirs at all. The question of heirship appears to have been the only one argued, and no point seems to have been made, that the sisters, even if they were heirs, only took a limited estate. The Supreme Court, however, decided that the quality of a sister's estate must be taken to be the same as that of a daughter's estate. They assumed that *Dewcooverbaee's* case had settled that this latter estate was an absolute one. Sir *Michael Westropp* says (*r*), "the appellants in *Vinayek* v. *Luxumeebaee* resorted to her Majesty's Privy Council against the advice given to them by counsel." As he states that the decisions in that case and in *Dewcooverbaee's* case "were in accordance with the pre-existing traditions in that Court and in the legal profession in Bombay," it is probable that counsel in England were instructed that the question of heirship was the only point open to argument. The result is, that there is a tacit recognition by the Privy Council that both daughters and sisters take an absolute estate in property which they inherit from father or brother. Where there are several daughters or sisters they take in severalty and act as joint tenants (*s*).

Descent of property taken absolutely by a female heir.

§ 573. A much more difficult question is as to the line of descent appropriate to property which has been taken as her absolute estate by a female inheriting to a male. In some of the earlier Bombay decisions this question was answered summarily by saying that, as she took the property as her *stridhanum,* it must necessarily pass from her to those persons who, under the texts of the Mitakshara, II, 11, § 8, 9, are the heirs to such property (*t*). A different

(*r*) 5 Bom. 672. (*s*) *Rindabai* v. *Anacharya*, 15 Bom. 206.

(*t*) *Navalram* v. *Nandkishor*, 1 Bom. H. C. 209; *Bhaskar Trimbak* v. *Mahadev Ramji*, 6 Bom. H. C. (O. C. J.) 1.

decision was given by Mr. Justice *West* in the case of *Vijiarangam* v. *Lakshuman* (*u*).

Special descent of inherited stridhanum.

There certain property descended from Vithoba to Bapu,

Vithoba.

Lakshuman. — Bhagirthi, died 1840. = Bapu. died 1843. — Thamabai.

Yesubai, died 1869.

and from him to his daughter Yesubai. At her death Lakshuman, her mother's brother, and Thamabai, her father's sister, each claimed to carry on a suit in which she was engaged in reference to the property. It was decided that Thamabai was entitled. A most elaborate judgment was pronounced by Mr. Justice *West*, in which he naturally took the same view upon the subject of *stridhanum* that had been propounded by the learned editors of West and Bühler's Digest (*v*). He held that the property which had descended to Yesubai from her father was her *stridhanum*. But according to the Mayukha (iv. 10, § 26), inherited property, though it is *stridhanum*, not being one of those kinds of *stridhanum* for which express texts prescribed exceptional modes of descent, goes on the woman's death to her sons and the rest, as if she were a male, and this notwithstanding her having daughters. This being so, the property inherited by Yesubai would, in the absence of descendants, go to her parents, just as if she had been their only son, and failing them to the paternal grandmother and the *sapindas* of the father, the *gotrajas* taking precedence over the *bhinnagotras*. But according to the doctrine of Western India, a female who is born in the family is a *gotraja sapinda*. Therefore Thamabai (though married) was the next heir.

Descent according to Mayukha.

§ 574. This view practically gets rid of the idea that property, inherited by a daughter, would pass to her heirs in the line of descent of *stridhanum* properly so-called. It would

(*u*) 8 Bom. H. C. (O. C. J.) 244. (*v*) W. & B. 2nd ed. 481, 3rd ed. 146, 323.

make it go in a new line of descent, as if she were a male. The same view of the meaning of the Mayukha was adopted in a later case, where a married woman had received a house from a stranger to the family, and had also saved money from her own earnings. It was held that the succession to her must be treated as if she was a male, and therefore that her daughter-in-law would inherit in preference to the daughter of a deceased daughter (*w*).

§ 575. The learned Judge then went on to pronounce his views as to the law of the Mitakshara (*x*). He considered that according to it, property inherited by a woman would pass like *stridhanum*, strictly so-called. In this particular case, as Yesubai's marriage was in the *Asura* form, her *stridhanum* would go to her parents and their next of kin. But as by marriage Bagirthi would pass into the family of her husband, the *sapindas* of Bagirthi and Bapu would be, in the first instance, Bapu's blood relations, of whom, according to Western law, Thamabai was the nearest living. According to either principle of descent, Thamabai was the heir.

According to the Mitakshara.

Mitakshara law.

As the case was necessarily decided by the law of the Mayukha, of course everything said by the learned Judge as to the different system of the Mitakshara was *obiter dictum*. But it is important to observe, that exactly the same result would have been arrived at upon the doctrines laid down in Bengal and Madras. According to them, on the death of Yesubai, the property would go to the person who was next heir to Bapu, the last male holder. But in Western India, his sister was clearly the nearest heir. *Westropp*, C. J., assented to the conclusions of his learned colleague, but gave no opinion as to his reasoning. He merely said, that according to the Mayukha, Thamabai was the heir. This she undoubtedly was on any view of the law.

(*w*) *Bai Narmada* v. *Bhagwantrai*, 12 Bom. 505. See *Dalpat Narotam* v. *Bhugvan Kushal*, 9 Bom. 301.
(*x*) 8 Bom. H. C. (O. C. J.) 261.

Property obtained on partition.

§ 576. Partition is another mode by which the property of a male may come into the hands of a female. This, however, can hardly ever take place except in Bengal. In Southern India women never appear to take upon partition anything more than a life provision for maintenance. And though the contrary rule is asserted as to the other provinces governed by Mitakshara law, the cases seem very rare (*y*). In two early cases which came before the Supreme Court of Calcutta, where a share was decreed to a widow on partition, the Court seems at first to have treated her share as governed by the laws which regulate the right of a woman over property given to her by her husband, and not by those which relate to property inherited from him (*z*). Consequently, in each case their first decree was that she should take the movable property absolutely, and the immovable only for life. But in each case they reviewed their decree, and ordered that she should take the whole to be enjoyed in the manner prescribed by Hindu law; that is, for a widow's estate. The Court Pandits "expressly declared that the mother who took upon partition, and the widow who succeeded to her husband's property, stood upon the same footing with regard to their interests in the estates (*a*)." The Judicial Committee treat it as an open question under Benares law, whether a widow taking a share on partition does not take an absolute interest in that share, though they observe that in a case coming from Lower Bengal, the contrary had been decided by themselves (*b*). Of course it would be different if, by the terms of the partition, the widow or mother took an absolute estate (*c*). *Jagannatha* seems to be of the contrary opinion, so far as it is possible to make

---

(*y*) *Ante* § 437—441; *Gooroobuksh* v. *Lutchmana*, Mad. Dec. of 1850, 61.

(*z*) See as to the distinction, *per curiam*, *Bhugwandeen* v. *Myna Baee*, 11 M. I. A. 510; S. C. 9 Suth. (P. C.) 23.

(*a*) *Cossinaut* v. *Hurrosoondry*, affirmed on appeal to P. C., 2 M. Dig., 198; F. MacN. 79, 85, 88; V. Darp., 97; *Gooroopershad* v. *Seebchunder*, F. MacN. 69, 73; *Kamikhaprasad* v. *Jagadamba*, 5 B. L. R. 508.

(*b*) *Per curiam*. 11 M. I. A. 514, *supra*, referring apparently to *Cossinaut* v. *Hurrosoondry*, *supra*, note (*a*).

(*c*) *Bolye Chund* v. *Khetterpaul*, 11 B. L. R. 459; *Rampershad* v. *Chaineram*, 1 N.-W. P. 10.

out what his opinion is (*d*). But upon analogy there can be no reason why a woman who takes part of a property on partition between her sons, should have a larger interest than if she had taken the whole in the absence of sons. *Apararka* includes the share received by a wife or mother on partition under the head of *stridhanum* (*e*). This of course leads to no necessary inference that she has an absolute power of disposal over it (*f*).

Mother's estate on partition when a widow.

§ 577. The whole of this question was very elaborately discussed in a recent case under Bengal law, where it was necessary to decide how property should devolve which had been allotted to a mother on partition with her sons (*g*). The Court pointed out that "the wife's interest in her husband's estate resolved itself into a right to maintenance, except in the absence of lineal male heirs, in which case she takes the inheritance, and in two cases—one occurring in her husband's life time, the other after his death—in which she takes a share" While her husband lives, he is absolute owner of the estate, and her claim is merely to maintenance. But if he chooses to come to a partition with his sons, and the wife is without male issue, she is allowed a share equal to a son's. So after the husband's death, the whole inheritance vests absolutely in his male issue, and the widow is only entitled to maintenance. But if she has sons, and her sons or grandsons partition among themselves, she is entitled to a share out of the property which comes to them, but not out of that which falls to her stepsons (*h*). In either case the share allotted to her goes back on her death to her husband's family, while during her life her power of alienating is certainly not greater, and apparently not less than that which she possesses over property inherited from her husband. As to the case under

(*d*) 3 Dig., 22.

(*e*) Jolly, Lect. 250. See the subject discussed by *West*, J., 11 Bom. p. 302; W. and B. 780.

(*f*) See Viramit., p. 222. *Ante*, § 567.

(*g*) *Sorolah Dossee* v. *Bhoobun Mohun Neoghy*, 15 Cal. 292, pp. 306, 314.

(*h*) *Strimati Hemangini* v. *Kedar Nath*, 16 I. A. 115, S. C. 16 Cal. 758.

discussion, *viz.*, that of a partition after her husband's death, the Court said—"The conclusion which I draw from the Bengal authorities is that a wife's interest in her husband's estate given to her by marriage ceases upon the death of her husband leaving lenial heirs in the male line; that such heirs take the whole estate; and that the share which a mother takes on a partition among her sons she does not take from her husband, either by inheritance, or by way of survivorship in continuation of any pre-existing interest, but that she takes it from her sons in lieu of, or by way of provision for, that maintenance for which they and their estates are already bound. I think it follows as a necessary inference that, on her death, that share does not descend as if she had inherited it from her husband, but goes back to her sons from whom she had received it." In many cases these sons would be the same persons who would take if the share went back to the heirs of the late husband. But it would not be so if there were sons by different mothers. In such a case, "the rule contended for by the appellant would, on the death of either mother, who had obtained a share on partition among her sons, take her portion, which had been carved out of her own sons' share alone, and divide it rateably among sons and step-sons.

Estate of wife on partition by husband.

§ 577A. Upon these principles it would seem to follow, that where the father made a partition with his sons during his life, the share allotted to the sonless wife would, on her death, revert to the heirs of the husband. The portion is taken out of the estate of the husband in which the sons, under Bengal law, have no interest until his death, unless by partition. The share allotted to her is in lieu of the maintenance which is during the husband's life charged upon the entire share. It intercepts from the whole body of the heirs a certain portion of the estate which would otherwise have devolved upon them, and to a corresponding extent relieves them of the obligation to maintain her. On her death, therefore, her share would devolve, as an undistributed portion of the husband's estate upon his heirs.

Her power of disposal.

§ 578. EXTENT OF A WOMAN'S ESTATE.—The nature of a woman's estate must, as already stated, be described by the restrictions which are placed upon it, and not by terms of duration. It is not a life estate, because under certain circumstances she can give an absolute and complete title. Nor is it in any sense an estate held in trust for reversioners. Within the limits imposed upon her, the female holder has the most absolute power of enjoyment. She is accountable to no one, and fully represents the estate, and so long as she is alive no one has any vested interest in the succession. On the other hand, the limitations upon her estate are the very substance of its nature, and not merely imposed upon her for the benefit of reversioners. They exist as fully if there are absolutely no heirs to take after her, as if there were. Acts which would be unlawful as against heirs expectant, are equally invalid as against the Sovereign claiming by escheat (*i*). The principles which restrict a widow were laid down by the Judicial Committee in the case cited above, as follows: "It is admitted, on all hands, that if there be collateral heirs of the husband, the widow cannot of her own will alien the property except for special purposes. For religious or charitable purposes, or those which are supposed to conduce to the spiritual welfare of her husband, she has a larger power of disposition than that which she possesses for purely worldly purposes. To support an alienation for the last, she must show necessity. On the other hand, it may be taken as established that an alienation by her which would not otherwise be legitimate, may become so if made with the consent

defined by Judicial Committee.

(*i*) *Collector of Masulipatam* v. *Cavaly Venkata*, 8 M. I. A. 529, 550; S. C. 2 Suth. (P. C.) 59; *Hurrydoss* v. *Rungunmoney*, Sev. 657, where the nature of the estate is very fully described by *Peel*, C.J., *Gurunath* v. *Krishnaji*, 4 Bom. 462; *Karuppa Tevan* v. *Alagu*, 4 Mad. 152; *Mohadeay Kooer* v. *Haruk Narain*, 9 Cal. 244; *Dhondo* v. *Balkrishna*, 8 Bom. 190. See as to the position of a widow in possession, where a preferable title has been created by adoption or will, *Mt. Sundar* v. *Parbati*, 16 I. A. 186; S. C. 12 All. 51. The widow of a Nambudri Brahman is governed by the same rules. 11 Mad. pp. 157, 165.

of her husband's kindred. But it surely is not the necessary or logical consequence of this latter proposition, that in the absence of collateral heirs to the husband, or on their failure, the fetter on the widow's power of alienation altogether drops. The exception in favour of alienation with consent may be due to a presumption of law that where that consent is given, the purpose for which the alienation is made must be proper." (*k*)

Full power of enjoyment.

§ 579. It is probable that in early times a widow was morally, if not legally, bound to restrain her personal expenditure within the modest limits which were considered suitable to her bereaved condition (*l*). But whatever may in former times have been the force of the injunctions contained in such passages of the Hindu Shastras, or whatever may now be their effect as religious or moral precepts, they cannot be regarded at the present day as of any legal force, in restricting a widow in the use and enjoyment of her husband's property while she lives. Her absolute right to the fullest benefit of her life-interest appears long to have been recognized (*m*). And, of course, there could be still less reason for imposing any such restrictions upon other female heirs. A woman is in no sense a trustee for those who may come after her. She is not bound to save the income. She is not bound to invest the principal. If she chooses to invest it, she is not bound to prefer one form of investment to another form, as being more likely to protect the interests of the reversioners. She is forbidden to commit waste, or to endanger the property in her possession, but short of that, she may spend the income and manage the principal as

Not a trustee.

(*k*) The position of a widow in the Punjab appears to be exactly the same, except that her powers of disposition are only to be exercised for secular objects, Punjab Customary Law, II. 177, 179, 203, 209.

(*l*) It seems to have been the opinion of *Mitter*, J., that she was still subject to such a restraint. See his remarks, *Kery Kolitany* v. *Moneeram*, 13 B. L. R. 5; S. C. 19 Suth. 367; but see *contra*, *per Glover* and *Kemp*, JJ., *ib.* 53, 76.

(*m*) *Per curiam*, *Kamavadhani* v. *Joysa*, 3 Mad. H. C. 116; *Cossinaut Bysack* v. *Hurrosundry*, 2 M. Dig. 198, 214, affirmed in P. C. Morton, 85; V. Darp., 97; *Gooroobuksh* v. *Lutchmana*, Mad. Dec. of 1850, 61.

she thinks proper (*n*). If she makes savings, she can give them away as she likes during her life. She is not bound to leave anything behind her beyond that which she received (*o*).

Accumulations.

§ 580. The law as to the right of a woman to accumulations from the estate of the last male holder is rather complicated, and appears to be in some respects unsettled. These accumulations may be, 1*st*. Accumulations made by her husband, or other male to whom she succeeds. 2*nd*. Accumulations made after his death, and before the estate was handed over to her. 3*rd*. Accumulations made by herself personally, and either invested, or converted into some different form or else remaining uninvested in her possession.

Her interest in accumulations

made by last holder:

1. Accumulations made by the last male holder would in general be accretions to his estate, and follow it. In such a case, of course, no question could arise. The female would take the whole as an entire estate, subject to the usual restrictions. There might, however, be a special settlement which would cause the *corpus* of the last male holder's estate to pass to a male, and the accumulations to go by heirship to a female. In such a case she would hold these accumulations as a new estate, subject to the restrictions which apply to the property inherited by a female (*p*).

between death and delivery:

2. The same principle is said to apply to accumulations which have been made from the income of the estate after the death, but before it reached the hands of the widow. They are treated as accretions to the body of the fund, and can only be dealt with in the same manner as the bulk of the property (*q*). Perhaps, however, the application of this

(*n*) *Hurrydoss* v. *Uppoornah*, 6 M. I. A. 433; *Biswanath* v. *Khantomani*, 6 B. L. R. 747; *Hurrydoss* v. *Rungunmoney*, Sev. 657.

(*o*) *Chundrabulee* v. *Brody*, 9 Suth. 584; S. C. 5 Wym. 335; *Harendranarayan's goods*, 4 B. L. R. (O. C. J.) 41.

(*p*) *Soorjeemoney* v. *Denobundo*, 6 M. I. A. 526; S. C. 4 Suth. (P. C.) 114; 9 M. I. A. 123.

(*q*) *Per Macpherson*, J., *Grose* v. *Amirtamayi*, 4 B. L. R. (O. C. J.) at p. 41; S. C. 12 Suth. (A. O. J.) 13; *Rabutty* v. *Sibchunder*, 6 M. I. A. at p. 25; *Isri Dut* v. *Hunsbutti*, 10 I. A. at p. 159; S. C. 10 Cal. p. 335.

rule would depend upon the amount of such savings, and the form they had assumed. If a widow was kept out of her estate for some time, and then received it with the ordinary cash balance, and current rents or interest which had accrued since the death, still uninvested, it would be difficult to say that she might not deal with these, exactly as she would have been entitled to do, if she had been let into possession at once. In any case debts or expenses, properly incurred by her while she was kept out of her income, would be a good charge upon such accumulations, just as they would have been upon the corpus (*r*).

by herself. § 581. The third case is the one which has caused the greatest difficulty. It is admitted that a female heir need not make any savings at all. She may spend her whole income every year, either upon herself, or by giving it away at her pleasure (*s*). But suppose she does not choose to spend her whole income, but accumulates the savings, may she dispose of these at her pleasure? If she has invested them, or purchased property with them, does it still remain at her disposal during her life? If she has not disposed of it, does it pass at her death with the rest of the property, or does it pass as her separate property to her own heirs?

Her right in accumulations made by herself, There is one case in the Privy Council where it would seem to have been distinctly laid down, that all the accumulations of a fund which had descended to a widow, from the time the estate vested in her, were absolutely her own, in her own right, as distinct from the fund itself, which she was only entitled to hold and enjoy as a widow (*t*). But in that case no question arose between the heirs of the widow and the reversioner. The point was not discussed, and the Judicial Committee has since refused to consider the ruling "as a conclusive or even a direct authority upon the question" (*u*). On the other hand, it has been decided by the

(*r*) See cases in last note, and *per Jackson*, J., *Puddo Monee* v. *Dwarkanath*, 25 Suth. at p. 341.

(*s*) *Ante*, § 579.

(*t*) *Soorjeemoney Dossee* v. *Denobundo*, 9 M. I. A. 123.

(*u*) *Gonda Kooer* v. *Kooer Oodey*, 14 B. L. R. at p. 165.

High Court of Bengal, that any property which a Hindu widow has purchased out of the income of her husband's estate would be an increment to that estate, would be inalienable by her during life, and would descend at her death to her husband's heirs. To that extent the judgment was affirmed by the Privy Council to be good law (*v*). It has, however, been suggested by the Judicial Committee, that perhaps purchases made by a widow from the income of her husband's estate are not necessarily accretions to it, unless she intended them to be such; and that such intention will be presumed in the absence of proof to the contrary, but might possibly be rebutted by evidence of a direct intention on her part to appropriate to herself, and to sever from the bulk of the estate, such purchases as she had made. It was not necessary, however, to decide the point (*w*). In a later case, upon a review of all the previous authorities, the High Court of Bengal held, that if a widow purchased property out of the current savings, that is out of the year's income, this would not be an irrevocable addition to the *corpus* of the estate, but might be disposed of by her at her pleasure, or sold again, and the proceeds spent as she chose. That the same rule would apply if the widow, "having no present occasion for spending monies, but foreseeing one after the lapse of a year or two, had thought it advisable to invest the money temporarily in land." They offered no opinion as to what might be her power over accumulations properly so called, or over property purchased with such accumulations. But they said,

Accumulations specially reserved for her own use.

Cash balances.

(*v*) *Chowdhry Bholanath* v. *Mt. Bhagabatti*, 7 B. L. R. 93, reversed on another point; *Bhagbutti* v. *Chowdhry Bholanath*, 2 I. A. 256; S. C. 24 Suth. 168; *acc.* as to the descent of such property; *Chundrabulee* v. *Brody*, 9 Suth 584; S. C. 5 Wym. 335; *Hurrydoss* v. *Rungunmoney*, Sev. 657; *Anund Chundra* v. *Nilmoni*, 9 Cal. 758; *Isri Dut* v. *Hunsbutti*, 10 I. A. 150, p. 158; S. C. 10 Cal. 324, p. 334; *acc.* as to the first point; *Kooer Oodey* v. *Phoolchund*, 5 N.-W. P. 197, 201. See too *Bissessur* v. *Ram Joy*, 2 Suth. 327; *Gobind* v. *Dulmeer*, 23 Suth. 125, in which it was assumed that property purchased by a Hindu widow out of the proceeds of her husband's estate, or from a fund obtained by speculating with such proceeds, would pass to *his* heirs. Of course purchases made by her out of her own separate property are her own. But the *onus* of proving they are so rests on those who assert it. *Lamb* v. *Mt. Govindmoney*, S. D. of 1852, 125; 23 Suth. 125, *ub sup.*

(*w*) *Gonda Kooer* v. *Kooer Oodey*, 14 B. L. R. 159.

"What are accumulations in the view of these cases? Not, surely, the accidental balances of one or two years of the widow's income, but a fund distinct and tangible. There is nothing whatever in this case to indicate that any such fund ever had been formed or had existed; and we have no reason to suppose that accumulations had ever arisen, except that the widow may have spent in some years more, in others less, and in that sense the savings of the less costly year might be an accumulation to meet the charges of the next." (*x*).

Isri Dut v. *Hunsbutti.*

§ 582. The whole law upon this subject was again examined by the Bengal High Court and in the Privy Council under the following circumstances (*y*). A husband left two widows, and a daughter by one of them, named Dyji. The widows inherited landed property from their husband, and purchased further property out of the income of what they had inherited. The husband died in 1857, the new property was purchased shortly after, and in 1873 the widows made an absolute gift to the daughter of lands consisting partly of what they had inherited and partly of what they had purchased. The collateral males, who were heirs presumptive after the death of the daughter, sued for a declaration that this gift would not affect their reversionary interest. The Bengal High Court examined the law very fully, but did not decide whether the gift by the widows of the after-acquired property, would be effectual beyond their lives, considering that the case was one in which it was premature to make any declaration of right. The Judicial Committee thought that the heirs were entitled to have a declaration as to the effect of the gift, and decided, that the widows had no greater power over the purchased property than over what had been inherited. They treated

(*x*) *Puddo Monee* v. *Dwarkanath*, 25 Suth. 335. As to purchases made by a widow with money borrowed on her own credit, or on the credit of her husband's estate, see *Kooer Oodey* v. *Phoolchund*, 5 N.-W. P. 97.

(*y*) *Hunsbutti* v. *Isri Dut*, 5 Cal. 512; *Isri Dut* v. *Hunsbutti*, 10 I. A. 150; S. C. 10 Cal. 324; *Sheo Lochun Singh* v. *Babu Saheb Singh*, 14 I. A. 63; S. C. 14 Cal. 387; *Grish Chunder* v. *Broughton*, 14 Cal. 861, affd. *sub nomine*, *Soudamini Dassee* v. *Broughton*, 16 Cal. 574.

it as settled that "a widow's savings from her husband's estate are not her stridhan. If she has made no attempt to dispose of them in her lifetime, there is no dispute but that they follow the estate from which they arose. The dispute arises when the widow, who might have spent the income as it accrued, has in fact saved it, and afterwards attempts to alienate it." They also said that they did not "think it possible to lay down any sharp definition of the line which separates accretions to the husband's estate from income held in suspense in the hands of the widow, as to which she has not determined whether she will spend it or not." They then proceeded to say, "In this case the properties in question consist of shares of lands, in which the husband was a shareholder to a larger extent. They were purchased within a short time after his death in 1857. No attempt to alienate them was made till 1873. The object of the alienation was not the need or the personal benefit of the widows, but a desire to change the succession, and to give the inheritance to the heirs of one of themselves, in preference to their husband's heirs. Neither with respect to this object, nor apparently in any other way, have the widows made any distinction between the original estate and the after purchases. Parts of both are conveyed to Dyji immediately, and parts of both are retained by the widows for life. These are circumstances which, in their Lordship's opinion, clearly establish accretion to the original estate, and make the after purchases inalienable by the widows for any purposes which would not justify alienation of the original estate."

Balance held in suspense.

§ 583. On the other hand a sum of money representing rents accruing during the last year of the widow's life was held to pass to the widow's representatives, not to the reversioner (z). *Sargent*, C.J., said, "In the present case the cash balance in question does not amount to much more than half the yearly payment by K. B. and had not been

(z) *Rivett Carnac* v. *Jivibai*, 10 Bom. 478, p. 483.

separated from the general account so as to form a distinct fund which could be regarded as "savings." There is an entire absence of any outward sign of an intention to accumulate; whilst on the contrary the existence of debts rebuts any such intention, and points to the conclusion that the balance was held in suspense by the widow at the time of her death, to use the language of the Privy Council in *Isri Dut* v. *Hunsbutti*."

Express power of disposal.

§ 584. None of these restrictions apply to property which has passed to a female, not as heir, but by deed or other arrangement which gives her express power to appropriate the profits. The savings of such property, and everything which is purchased out of such savings, belong absolutely to herself. They may be disposed of by herself at her pleasure, and, at her death, they pass to her representatives, and not to the heirs of the last male (*a*). But the mere fact that a Hindu female takes under a will or a deed of gift or arrangement, that to which she is really entitled as heiress, does not necessarily enlarge her powers. The question will still be, what estate did she take? not how did she take it (*b*).

Devise or grant.

Case of manager differs.

§ 585. It will be observed that the right of a Hindu female to acquire a separate estate for herself out of the savings of her limited estate, stands on a completely different footing from that of a Hindu father, under the Mitakshara law, or the managing member of a joint Hindu family. It has been decided in such a case that all purchases made from the profits of the estate form part of it, and follow its

---

(*a*) *Bhagbutti* v. *Chowdhry Bholanath*, 2 I. A. 256; S. C. 24 Suth. 168; *Guru* v. *Nafar*, 3 B. L. R. (A. C. J.) 121; S. C. 11 Suth. 497; *Nellaikumaru* v. *Marakathammal*, 1 Mad. 166.

(*b*) *Moulvie Mahomed* v. *Shewukram*, 2 I. A. 7; S. C. 14 B. L. R. 226; S. C. 22 Suth. 409; see *per curiam*, 2 I. A. 261, explaining decision in *Rabutty* v. *Sibchunder*, 6 M. I. A. 1; *Lakshmibai* v. *Hirabai*, 11 Bom. 69. affd. p. 578, *Ganpat Rao* v. *Ramchander*, 11 All. 296; *Nunnu Meah* v. *Krishnasami*, 14 Mad. 274. There is no rule of Hindu law that a gift to a female should only carry with it the limited nature of a female estate by inheritance. *Kollany* v. *Lutchmee*, 24 Suth. 395; *Pubitra* v. *Damoodur*, *ib.* 397.

character (*c*). But then the entire annual profits of the estate are not the property of the father or manager. The sons in the first instance, and the other members of the family in the second instance, are jointly interested in the income as well as in the principal. But in the case of the female heir the whole annual profits are hers, and until her death no vested interest comes into existence.

Religious purposes.

§ 586. The purposes which authorize a Hindu widow to mortgage or sell her property are summed up by the Judicial Committee in the words already quoted (§ 578) (*d*). The same rules apply to any other female, except perhaps in Bombay. But of course it is only when the property comes to her from her husband that religious benefit to him constitutes a reason for alienation.

The primary religious purpose which a widow is bound to carry out at any expense to the estate, is the performance of the funeral obsequies of her husband, and of all ceremonies incidental to those obsequies. These are absolute necessities. There are other religious benefits procurable for him, which are more of the nature of spiritual luxuries. Pilgrimages by the widow to holy places come under this head. For these it would appear that she may dispose of a part of the estate, but that the expense which is allowable must be limited by a due regard to the entire bulk of the property, and may even be totally inadmissible, where it is not warranted by the circumstances of the family (*e*). She may also alienate the property in order to defray the expenses of ceremonies for other members of the family, such as her husband's mother, provided they were ceremonies which he was bound to perform in his lifetime, and in the benefits of

---

(*c*) *Shudanund* v. *Bonomalee*, 6 Suth. 256; S. C. on review, *sub nomine*, *Sudanund* v. *Soorjo Monee*, 8 Suth. 455; S. C. 11 Suth. 436.

(*d*) See too *Lukhee* v. *Gokool*, 13 M. I. A. 209; S. C. 3 B. L. R. (P. C.) 57; S. C. 12 Suth. (P. C.) 47. See 5 Wilson, 16.

(*e*) *Huromohun* v. *Auluckmonee*, 1 Suth. 252; *Ushruf* v. *Brojessuree*, 11 B. L. R. 118; S. C. 19 Suth. 426; *Mutteeram* v. *Gopaul*, 11 B. L. R. 416; S. C. 20 Suth. 187; *Lukmeeram* v. *Khooshalee*, 1 Bor. 412 [455]; *Rama* v. *Runga*, Mad. 552; *Lakshminarayana* v. *Dasu*, 11 Mad. 288. Punjab Customs, 60.

which he would participate. And it makes no difference that the ceremonies for which the outlay was incurred, would be actually performed by some other member of the family (*f*). But a daughter is not authorized to charge the family property in order to defray the expense of her mother's *Shradh* (*g*). Nor is a widow authorised to sell her husband's property for pious and religious purposes, intended to secure her own spiritual welfare (*h*).

Charities.

Religious purposes are said to include a portion to a daughter, building temples for religious worship, digging tanks and the like (*i*). It has, however, been held that the digging of a tank would not justify a Hindu widow in alienating a portion of the property (*k*). So various cases are found in which gifts to Brahmans or to idols have been supported against reversioners (*l*). But such alienations must be to a small extent, and would hardly be supported if they trenched materially on the property (*m*).

Husband's debts.

§ 587. The obligation of a widow taking her husband's property to pay his debts comes under the head of religious benefit, unless they are contracted for immoral purposes. She is under the same obligation to discharge them as a son would be. Whether they were or were not contracted for the benefit of the estate is immaterial (*n*). It has, however,

Debts barred.

been held that where debts are already barred by lapse of time, she cannot burthen or dispose of the estate for their

(*f*) *Chowdry* v. *Russomoyee*, 11 B. L. R, 418; S. C. 10 Suth. 309; *Ramcoomar* v. *Ichamoyi*, 8 Cal. 36.
(*g*) *Raj Chunder* v. *Sheeshoo*, 7 Suth. 146.
(*h*) *Puran Dai* v. *Jai Narain*, 4 All. 482.
(*i*) Futwah in *Cossinaut* v. *Hurrosundry*, in the P. C., cited V. Darp., 101; 2 M. Dig. 119.
(*k*) *Runjeet* v. *Mahomed Waris*, 21 Suth. 49.
(*l*) *Jugjeevun* v. *Deoshunkur*, 1 Bor. 394 [436]; *Kupoor* v. *Sevukram*, *ib.* 405 [448].
(*m*) *Gopaula* v. *Narraina*, Mad. Dec. of 1850, p. 74; *Choonee Lall* v. *Jussoo*, 1 Bor. 55 [60].
(*n*) *Chetty Colum* v. *Rungasawmy*, 8 M. I. A. 319; S. C. 4 Suth. (P. C.) 71, *Goluck* v. *Mahomed Rohim*, 9 Suth. 316; *Cossinaut* v. *Hurrosoondry*, 2 M. Dig. at p. 204; *Subbaiyan* v. *Akhilandammal*, Mad. Dec. of 1860, p. 15; *per curiam*, *Lakshman* v. *Satyabhamabai*, 2 Bom. 499.

discharge (*o*), and this appears to be certainly the law as regards an ordinary manager of the family property (*p*). This seems sensible enough as a matter of mundane equity, though it may be doubted whether a plea of the statute would be accepted in the Court of the Hindu Rhadamanthus. In more recent cases it has been repeatedly held that a widow's obligation to pay her husband's debts, and her right to alienate property descended from him for that purpose, is not affected by the statute of limitations, or any similar contrivance for getting rid of his obligations (*q*).

Such a payment, however, must be made *bonâ fide* in discharge of the duty of the widow to pay all her husband's debts equally as far as she can. She ought not to prefer one valid claim to another; still less ought she to alienate the estate for the express purpose of giving creditors whose debts were barred by time a preference over those whose debts were valid and subsisting. Such a preference, exercised in the case of an insolvent estate, would be fraudulent and void if the act were that of the insolvent himself, and would be equally invalid both in equity and under the Transfer of Property Act where it is the act of the widow. If she was led to make this preference in ignorance of the fact that the debts were barred, those who profited, by an ignorance which, in dealing with an inexperienced woman, they were bound to remove, would be unable to profit by their own fraud (*r*).

As a female heir is bound to maintain, and perform the marriages and other ceremonies of those who are a burthen on the estate, so she may mortgage or sell the property to procure the necessary funds. *A fortiori*, of course, may she **Maintenance.**

(*o*) *Melgirappa* v. *Shivappa*, 6 Bom. H. C. (A. C. J.) 270. See *Ramchurn* v. *Nunhoo*, 14 Suth. 147

(*p*) *Chinnaya* v. *Gurunathan*, (F. B.) 5 Mad. 169.

(*q*) *Chimnaji* v. *Dinkar*, 11 Bom. 320; *Bhan Babaji* v. *Gopala*, 11 Bom. 325, where the same principle was applied to a widowed daughter-in-law in possession of the estate of her father-in-law. *Kondappa* v. *Subba*, 13 Mad. 189.

(*r*) *Rangilbai* v. *Vinayak*, 11 Bom. 666. Citing Act IV of 1882, § 53, which is not extended to Bombay.

do so to procure maintenance for herself, or to defray the expense of her own religious ceremonies (*s*), but she must wait till the necessity occurs. She must not anticipate her wants by raising money, or contracting for the discharge of such liabilities before they arise (*t*).

Necessity.

§ 588. These are some of the cases specially pointed out as authorising a woman to dispose of her inheritance. Others come under the general head of necessity. It is, of course, impossible to define what is necessity. Every case must be judged upon its own facts. A Hindu female certainly cannot have less power than the manager of a family property, and does not in this respect appear to have more. The principles laid down by the Privy Council in the well-known case of *Hunoomanpersaud* v. *Mt. Babooee* (*u*) will equally apply to her acts. But it must be remembered, that in regard to her alienations it is not a question of absolute but of relative invalidity. She cannot, in the absence of legal necessity, bind the inheritance for her own personal debts or private purposes as against reversioners (*v*), but she can do so for her own life (*w*).

Acts good for her own life.

Government revenue.

§ 589. One very common case of necessity is that of a loan of money, or a mortgage or sale of part of the property, to pay off arrears of Government revenue. In such a case

---

(*s*) *Rajchunder* v. *Bulloram*, Fulton, 133; *Lalla Gunput* v. *Mt. Toorun*, 16 Suth. 52; *Sadashiv* v. *Dhakubai*, 5 Bom. 450.

(*t*) *Mullakkal* v. *Mada Chetty*, 6 Mad. Jur. 261.

(*u*) *Hunoomanpersaud* v. *Mt. Babooee*, 6 M. I. A. 393; S. C. 18 Suth. 81 (note); *ante*, § 320; *Kameswar* v. *Run Bahadoor*, 8 I. A. 8; S. C. 6 Cal. 843.

(*v*) *Muteeoollah* v. *Radhabinodee*, S. D. of 1856, p. 596; *Lalla Byjnath* v. *Bissen*, 19 Suth. 80.

(*w*) This was formerly doubted, on the ground that she had only a right of enjoyment, and that a sale which purported to be absolute, was actually void, as being a sale of that which she never possessed. 1 W. MacN. 19; 3 Dig. 465. *Ramanund* v. *Ram Kissen*, 2 M. Dig. 115, 118; *Gunganarain* v. *Bulram*, 2 M. Dig. 152, 155. But the reverse is now quite settled, on the ground that the woman is absolute owner, though with limited powers. Her acts are therefore valid to the extent of her powers, though they may be exercised in excess of those powers. *Gobindmani* v. *Shamlal*, B. L. R. Sup. Vol. 48; S. C. Suth. Sp. 165; *Periya Gaundan* v. *Trumala*, 1 Mad. H. C. 206; *Bhagavatamma* v. *Pampanna*, 2 Mad. H. C. 393; *Kamavadhani* v. *Joysa*, 3 Mad. H. C. 116; *Melgirappa* v. *Shivappa*, 6 Bom. H C. (A. C. J.) 270; *Ramchandra* v. *Bhimrav*, 1 Bom. 577; *Prag Das* v. *Hari Kishn*, 1 All. 503. And the same rule has been applied, even where the widow held under a condition against alienation. *Bibi Sahodra* v. *Rai Jang*, 8 Cal. 204; S. C. 8 I. A. 310.

it has been several times held by the Bengal Sudder Court, that it is not sufficient to show that the money was borrowed, or even required for such a purpose, without going on to show that the necessity for it arose from circumstances beyond the widow's control (*x*). The result would be, that where the estate fell into arrears through the extravagance or mismanagement of the widow, no one would venture to lend money to pay the Government claim, and the estate would be brought to the hammer. As a sale for Government arrears gives a completely new title, the result would be that not only the widow's estate, but that of the reversioners, would be forfeited (*y*). But the decision in *Hunoomanpersaud's* case shows, that if there is an actually existing necessity for an advance of money, the circumstance that this necessity is brought about by previous mismanagement does not vitiate the loan, unless the lender has himself been a party to the misconduct which has produced the danger (*z*). And this rule has been followed in more recent decisions. Of course it will be necessary to show that there was an actual pressure, such as an outstanding decree or impending sale, and one which the heiress had no funds capable of meeting (*a*). A widow is justified in charging or alienating her husband's property in order to pay the costs properly incurred in defending it, or her own interest in it against attack; but not in a merely speculative suit brought to recover property, not belonging to his estate, but to which she alleged a title (*b*). So a debt incurred for the

---

(*x*) *Muteeoollah* v. *Radhabinodi*, S. D. of 1856, p. 596; *Radhamohun* v. *Girdhareelal*, S. D. of 1857, 460.

(*y*) *Ramchandra* v. *Bhimrav*, 1 Bom. 577; *Douglas* v. *Collector of Benares*, 5 M. I. A. 271; *Nugender* v. *Kaminee*, 11 M. I. A. 241; S. C. 8 Suth. (P. C.) 17. See too sales of under-tenures under Act X of 1859; *Teluck* v. *Muddun*, 12 Suth. 504; S. C. 15 B. L. R. 143 (note); *Anund Moyee* v. *Mohendro*, 15 Suth. 264, approved; *Baijun* v. *Brij Bhookun*, 2 I. A. 281; S. C. 1 Cal. 133, or under Benga Act VIII of 1869; *Mohima* v. *Ram Kishore*, 15 B. L. R. 142; S. C. 23 Suth. 174.

(*z*) 6 M. I. A. p. 423; S. C. 18 Suth. 81 (note).

(*a*) *Sreenath Roy* v. *Ruttunmalla*, S. D. of 1859, 421; *Lalla Byjnath* v. *Bissen*, 19 Suth. 80; *Mata* v. *Bhagheeruthee*, 2 N.-W. P. 78; *Lala Amarnath* v. *Achan Kuar*, 19 I. A. , *Lakhsman Bhau* v. *Radhabai*, 11 Bom. 609.

(*b*) *Amjad Ali* v. *Moniram*, 12 Cal. 52; *Indar Kuar* v. *Lalta Prasad*, 4 All. 532.

necessary repairs of the property will be a charge upon it in the hands of the reversioners (*c*).

She may sell.

Where a case of necessity exists, the heiress is not bound to borrow money, with the hope of paying it off before her death. Nor is she bound to mortgage the estate, and thereby reduce her income for life. She is at liberty, if she thinks fit, absolutely to sell off a part of the estate. And even if a mortgage would have been more beneficial, still if the heiress and the purchaser are both acting honestly, the transaction cannot be set aside at the instance of the next heir (*d*).

Husband's estate not bound by personal obligation of widow.

§ 590. Where a person dealing with a widow wishes to bind the husband's estate in the hands of reversioners, it is necessary to show, not only that the dealing was one in respect of which the widow was authorised to bind the estate, but that she intended to do so, and was supposed to do so. A mortgage by a widow for proper and necessary purpose will bind the estate, though she contracted, not as widow in her own right, but as guardian for a supposed adopted son, whose adoption turned out to be invalid (*e*). On the other hand the Courts of Bombay and Madras have refused to hold reversioners liable to satisfy bonds executed by a widow as security for loans contracted by her, which neither specifically pledged the estate, nor purported to be executed by her as representing the estate, though in each case the object of the loan was one for which the widow might legitimately have bound her successors (*f*). A contrary decision appears to have been arrived at in Calcutta. There a widow had borrowed money for the marriage expenses of a granddaughter. A suit was brought after her death to recover the money from her husband's heirs. The Court held that there was nothing in the cir-

(*c*) *Hurry Mohun* v. *Gonesh Chunder*, 10 Cal. 823.

(*d*) *Phoolchund* v. *Rughoobuns*, 9 Suth. 108; *Nabakumar* v. *Bhabasundari*, 3 B. L. R. (A. O. J.) 375.

(*e*) *Lala Parbhu Lal* v. *Mylne*, 14 Cal. 401.

(*f*) *Gadgeppa* v. *Apaji*, 3 Bom. 237; *Ramasami* v. *Sellattammal*, 4 Mad. 375.

cumstances which constituted the debt a charge upon the estate, but that the estate was, and therefore that the heirs in possession of the estate were, liable to satisfy the debt as being incurred by the deceased Hindu's widow for a proper purpose (*g*). Either of the two views put forward by the Calcutta High Court is intelligible, but it is difficult to see how both can be reconciled.

§ 591. In cases which would not otherwise justify a sale by a female, the transaction will be rendered valid by the consent of the heirs. Either on the ground suggested by the Judicial Committee, that such a consent is itself an evidence of the propriety of the transaction (*h*), or because this consent operates as a release of the claims of those who might otherwise dispute the transaction. But it seems to be by no means clear who are the parties whose consent is required. The Pandits in an early Supreme Court case in Bengal (*i*) stated, that a gift or a sale of the whole estate by the widow would be valid, if made "with the consent of those who are legally entitled to succeed to the estate after her death." In a later case, the Supreme Court held, that where the immediate reversioners abandoned their rights, those who claimed through them were equally bound (*k*). And in a case before the Sudder Court in 1849 the Judges seem to have been of opinion, that where the next heir, a daughter's son, consented to an alienation by a widow, this would bar the right of a more remote heir, such as an uncle's son, not claiming through him (*l*). And so it was ruled by the High Court of Bengal in later cases, in one of which *Markby*, J., said, "To hold otherwise would only necessitate the adding of two or three words to the

Consent of heirs.

(*g*) *Ramcoomar* v. *Ichamoyi Dasi*, 6 Cal. 36.

(*h*) *Ante*, § 578. See *Madhub* v. *Gobind*, 9 Suth. 350, where *Markby*, J., appeared to think that the signature of the next heir was only material as evidence of the necessity for the transaction; *acc. Raj Bullubh* v. *Oomesh*, 5 Cal. 49.

(*i*) *Ramanund* v. *Ram Kissen*, 2 M. Dig. 115, 119.

(*k*) *Kaleechund* v. *Moore*, cited *Muteevollah* v. *Radhabinode*, S. D. of 1856, 604; S. C. *sub nomine*, *Collychund* v. *Moore*, Fulton, 73.

(*l*) *Deep Chund* v. *Hurdeal*, S. D. of 1849, 204.

conveyance, because the widow may at any time surrender the property to the apparent next taker, who will then become absolute owner (*m*). The contrary decision, however, was arrived at in 1812. There the husband left a widow and two sets of heirs; the sons of his maternal uncle, who were the next in succession, and paternal kindred in a more distant degree. It was held, on the opinion of the Pandits, that not only was the consent of all the maternal uncle's sons necessary, but that even if this consent had been given, it would have been further necessary to procure the consent of the paternal kindred. Not as heirs in reversion, but as being the legal guardians and advisers of the widow. Those, however, who did consent would be unable to claim in opposition to the deed (*n*). This ruling was followed by the Bengal Sudder Court in 1856, when they said, "We are of opinion from the authorities cited in the margin (*o*), that in order to render a sale by a Hindu widow valid it must be signed or attested by *all the heirs* of her husband then living; the execution or attestation by the nearest heirs alone is insufficient (*p*)." To the same effect is the language of the High Court of Bombay, in a case where a widow and daughter (the latter of whom in Bombay would take an absolute estate) conveyed to the defendant. It was held that the grant was invalid as against the plaintiff who, on the death of the daughter before her mother, became next heir. The Court said (*q*). "It may be taken as well established that the consent of heirs will render valid an alienation by a widow under circumstances which would not otherwise justify it. But the question, who are the heirs whose consent will

Who must consent.

(*m*) *Behari Lal* v. *Madho Lal*, 19 I. A. 30; *Mohunt Kishen* v. *Busgeet*, 14 Suth. 379; *Raj Bullubh* v. *Oomesh*, 5 Cal. 44. But *quœre* whether such a conveyancing contrivance would be allowed, if the general principle as to consent would be defeated by it.

(*n*) *Mohun* v. *Siroomunnee*, 2 S. D. 32 (40). See Narada, cited Daya Bhaga, xi. 1, § 64; *Sid Dasi* v. *Gur Sahai*, 8 All. 362; *Ramadhin* v. *Mathura Singh*, 10 All. 407.

(*o*) *Nandkomar* v. *Rughoonundun*, 1 S. D. 261 (349); *Bhuwani* v. *Solukhna*, *ib.* 322 (431); *Hemchund* v. *Taramunnee*, *ib.* 359 (481); *Mohun* v. *Siroomunnee*, 2 S. D. 32 (40). Only the last touched the point.

(*p*) *Muteeoollah* v. *Radhabinode*, S. D. of 1856, 596.

(*q*) *Varjivan* v. *Ghelji*, 5 Bom. 563, p. 571.

thus render the alienation indefeasible, has led to much conflict of decision. The principle, however, upon which that question is to be answered has, we apprehend, been laid down by the Privy Council in the case of *Raj Lukhee Dabea* v. *Gokool Chunder Chowdhry* (*r*). Their Lordships say: "They do not mean to impugn the authorities, &c., which lay down that a transaction of this kind may become valid by the consent of the husband's kindred, but the kindred in such cases must generally be understood to be all those who are likely to be interested in disputing the transaction. At all events, there should be such a concurrence of the members of the family as suffices to raise a presumption that the transaction was a fair one, and one justified by Hindu law." In the present case, the plaintiffs, although distant heirs, were the heirs presumptive of the deceased husband at the time of the sale, entitled to succeed in the event of Vakhat dying before her mother without issue, and, as such clearly interested in disputing the sale. Nor can the mere concurrence of Bai Vakhat albeit the nearest in succession, (having regard to the state of dependence in which all women are supposed by Hindu law to have their being) be regarded as affording the slightest presumption that the alienation was a justifiable one." Where, however a sufficient consent has been given, the transaction cannot be questioned by one who subsequently comes into existence either by birth or adoption (*s*).

Who must consent.

§ 592. It must be remembered that where an estate is held by a female, no one has a vested interest in the succession. Of several persons then living, one may be the next heir in the sense that, if he lives, he will take at her death, in preference to any one else then in existence. But his claim may pass away by his own death, or be defeated by the birth or adoption of one who would be nearer than

(*r*) 13 M. I. A. p. 228; S. C. 3 B. L. R. (P. C.) 57; S. C. 12 Suth. (P. C.) 47.
(*s*) *Rajkristo* v. *Kishoree*, 3 Suth. 14; *ante*, § 316.

Who must consent.

himself. It certainly does seem to be common sense, that the person who turns out to be the actual reversioner, should not find his rights signed away by the consent of one who, when he consented, had a preferable title in expectation, but who, in the actual event, proved to have no title at all. Till recently the decisions of the High Court of Bengal were in favour of this view (*t*). The Allahabad High Court went even further. It not only held that the consent of the heir presumptive to an alienation by a widow was not sufficient to defeat the rights of a mere remote reversioner, but that even an assignment by the widow to the heir presumptive had no greater effect in his favour than it would have had if he had been a stranger. That is to say, that it did not accelerate his reversionary interest, so as to rest the whole estate absolutely in him at once, but only conferred upon him the widow's life interest, leaving the contingency still open that he might not be the next heir at her death (*u*). For instance, if the widow assigned or surrendered to the daughter's son, he would upon this view be entitled for her life, and if he survived her would become absolute owner. If, however, he died before her, leaving a son, that son would hold for her life, but not longer, because at her death he would not be the heir of the widow's husband. A contrary conclusion, however, was arrived at by the High Court of Bengal upon a reference to the Full Bench, in which the question referred was, "whether, according to the law current in Bengal, a transfer or conveyance by a widow upon the ostensible ground of legal necessity, such transfer being assented to by the person who at the time is the next reversioner, will conclude another person, not a party thereto, who is the actual reversioner upon the death of the widow, from asserting his title to the property." This question the Court answered in the affirmative (*v*). They considered it as settled beyond

(*t*) *Ramchunder* v. *Haridas*, 9 Cal. 463; *Gopeenath* v. *Kallydoss*, 10 Cal. 225.

(*u*) *Ramphul Rai* v. *Tula Kuari*, 6 All. (F. B.) 116; *Madan Mohun* v. *Puran Mull*, *ibid.* 288.

(*v*) *Nobokishore* v. *Harinath*, 10 Cal. 1102; *Srimati Dibea* v. *Rani Koond*, 4 M. I. A. 292.

all question by a long current of decisions that a widow might surrender her estate to the next reversioner, so as to bring his estate at once into possession, and thereby defeat all subsequent interests. They considered that it followed as a logical consequence, that the widow and the next reversioner might by their joint act convey an indefeasible estate to a stranger, of their own mere will and without any necessity. *Garth*, C. J., yielded to this conclusion with reluctance, but considered that the Court was bound by a series of authorities, on the faith of which many thousands of estates had been bought and sold in Bengal during the last twenty years. If no similar current of authorities exists in the other Presidencies this decision would, of course, have little weight with them. Where the next reversioner is herself a female, who only takes a life estate, her consent will not bind the next reversioner who takes an absolute estate (*w*). The High Court of Bengal has also held that the Full Bench decision above cited only applies where the whole body of persons constituting the next reversion assent to the alienation. For instance, suppose there are four persons equal in degree who would all take simultaneously on the death of the widow. If she alienated to the four, their estate would at once come into possession and her's would cease. But if she alienated to two only, one half of her estate would remain, which the Court held could not be done, except of course for her own life. And the consent of two to an alienation to a stranger would, apparently, be equally ineffectual (*x*).

Who must consent.

Evidence consent.

§ 593. Consent by signature or attestation is spoken of. But, of course, this is only one of many modes by which it is evidenced. Presence at, or knowledge of, the transaction, followed by acquiescence, express or implied, would be just as effective, though less easily proved than consent

(*w*) *Kooer Goolab Singh* v. *Rao Kurun Singh*, 14 M. I. A. 176; S. C. 10 B. L. R. 1; *Bhupal Ram* v. *Lachma Kuar*, 11 All. 253.
(*x*) *Radha Shyan* v. *Joy Ram*, 17 Cal. 896.

given in writing (*y*). In Malabar it has been laid down that consent of all the members of the *tarwad* is necessary to a sale, but no written consent is required. The signature of the chief *anandraven* or member of the family, who is next in seniority to the *karnaven* or manager, is not necessary, but if given it is *primâ facie* evidence of the assent of all who are interested in the property. If they did not in fact consent they are bound to prove their dissent (*z*). More recently, however it has been decided that there is no invariable rule requiring the consent of all the junior members, and "that a factious or capricious dissent of a single anandraven ought not to be allowed to invalidate a sale made in pursuance of the decision of a family conclave, and which was either absolutely necessary, or the most reasonable and prudent arrangement for the protection of the other family property." (*a*).

Onus of proof.

§ 594. In this, as in all other cases, when a person deals with a qualified owner, he must prove the facts, either of purpose or consent, upon which he relies as giving validity to the transaction. But the amount of proof may vary considerably, according as he is the immediate party to the transaction, or only the representative of such party, and according to the lapse of time that has taken place, and other similar circumstances. And if he once proves the existence of a debt, which would justify the transaction, its continuance will be assumed, unless the person who contests the transaction shows sufficient cause for assuming that it was satisfied (*b*). Nor is he bound to prove that the facts were actually as they were represented to him, provided he made *bonâ fide* and proper enquiry, and such facts were represented to him as would, if true, have justified the trans-

---

(*y*) *Muteeoollah* v. *Radhabinode*, S. D. of 1856, 596; *Mohesh* v. *Ugra*, 24 Suth. 127.

(*z*) *Kondi Menon* v. *Sranginreagatta*, 1 Mad. H. C. 248; *Kaipreta* v. *Makkaiyil*, *ib.* 359; *Koyiloth* v. *Puthenpurayil*, 3 Mad. H. C. 294.

(*a*) *Kalliyani* v. *Narayana*, 9 Mad. 266.

(*b*) *Hunoomanpersad's case*, 6 M. I. A 393; *Cavala Vencata* v. *Collector of Masulipatam*, 11 M. I. A. 619; S. C. 2 Suth. (P. C.) 61; *Lukhee* v. *Gokool*, 13 M. I. A. 209; S. C. 3 B. L. R. (P. C.) 57; S. C. 12 Suth. (P. C.) 47; *Rao Kurun* v. *Nawab Mahomed*, 14 M. I. A. 187; S. C. 10 B. L. R. (P. C.) 1.

action (*c*). Nor is he in any case bound to see to the application of the money (*d*). But the mere statement in a document that it was executed for a particular purpose is not sufficient evidence either of the existence of the purpose or of the adequacy of the enquiry (*e*). It is hardly necessary to add that, as between the widow herself and the person dealing with her, the transaction must be absolutely free from fraud, and must be shown to have been entered into after the fullest explanation to her of its nature and consequences (*f*).

§ 595. A sale in execution of a decree against a female heir is merely an involuntary alienation, and will be judged of by the previous principles. Where the suit is founded upon a purely personal debt or contract of her own, the decree can only be against her own person and property, and a sale in execution will only convey her own interest in the property. But even though the foundation of the decree be a liability which might bind the reversioners, that alone is not sufficient. The suit must be so framed as to show that it is not merely a personal demand upon the female in possession, but that it is intended to bind the entire estate, and the interests of all those who come after her. The reason of this is, that although in a suit brought to recover or charge an estate of which a Hindu female is the proprietress, she will, as defendant, represent and protect the estate, as well in respect of her own as of the reversionary interest; still, and on this very account, the plaintiff is bound to give notice that he is seeking so large a remedy, in order to put those who may be ultimately affected upon their guard, and to enable them to protect

Effect of execution for debt of female.

(*c*) *Hunoomanpersad's case, ub sup.*; *Kameswar* v. *Run Bahadoor*, 8 I. A. 8; S. C. 6 Cal. 843; Act IV of 1882, § 38 (Transfer of Property).

(*d*) *Hunoomanpersad's case, ub sup.*; *Ram Pershad* v. *Mt. Nagbungshee*, 9 Suth. 501.

(*e*) *Sunker Lall* v. *Juddoobuns*, 9 Suth. 285. See *ante*, § 323, *et seq.*

(*f*) *Kameswar* v. *Run Bahadoor*, 8 I. A. 8; S. C. 6 Cal. 843; *Sudisht* v. *Mt. Sheobarat*, 8 I. A. 39; *Sadashiv* v. *Dhakubai*, 5 Bom. 450.

themselves (*g*). If, therefore, the suit is framed so as only to claim a personal decree against the heiress, the plaintiff will be relieved from the necessity of proving anything beyond her personal liability. But then the decree can only be executed against the female holder personally, and against her limited interest in the land (*h*).

As representing estate.

Execution for debt of last male holder.

§ 596. A different case is where the proceeding is nominally against the heiress, but is really against her merely as representing the estate, that is, where the debt on which the decree is founded was not her own at all, but was the debt of the last male holder. Here, again, there is a distinction, according as the decree was passed in the life of the male holder, and against him, or not. In the former case, if execution has not been taken out during his life it may be taken out after his death against any property which he may have left behind. No matter into whose hands such property has passed (*i*), the property seized and sold will be described as the property of the deceased, and the entire interest in it will pass by the sale. But if no decree has been passed against him before his death, it is necessary to bring or revive the suit against his representative, whether male or female. "In such cases the representative, and not the deceased, is the defendant; and in the notification of sale, and in the certificate of sale, it ought to be set forth that what is sold is the right title and interest of the representative on the record, and not that of the deceased person. As the whole estate of the deceased vests in his legal representative, the purchaser would be safe if the representative on the record

---

(*g*) See *Nugender* v. *Kaminee*, 11 M. I. A. 267; S. C. 8 Suth. (P. C.) 17; *post*, § 605. The language of the Court here, and in *Mohima* v. *Ram Kishore*, 15 B. L. R. 160; S. C. 23 Suth. 174, would suggest that the reversioners must be parties to a suit framed for this purpose, *sed quære*. They would certainly be entitled to come in and ask to be made parties, and, of course, it would be safer to include them from the first, if ascertainable.

(*h*) *Nugender* v. *Kaminee*, 11 M. I. A. 241; S. C. 8 Suth. (P. C.) 17; *Baijun* v. *Brij Bhookun*, 2 I. A. 275; S. C. 1 Cal. 133; *Mohima* v. *Ram Kishore*, 15 B. L. R. 142; S. C. 23 Suth. 174; *Kisto Moyee* v. *Prosunno*, 6 Suth. 304. See *Venkataramayyan* v. *Venkatasubramania*, 1 Mad. 358; *Siva Bhagiam* v. *Palani Padiachi*, 4 Mad. 401; *Kristo Gobind* v. *Hem Chunder*, 16 Cal. 511.

(*i*) See *ante*, § 304, as to the effect of a gift or devise upon the right of a creditor.

were really the legal representative. But on this point he would be bound to satisfy himself, and must take the consequences if it turned out to be otherwise (*k*)." Therefore, where the deceased was divided, and therefore represented by his widow, but the suit was brought against his divided brother; and, conversely, where the deceased was undivided, and the suit was brought against his widow, and not against his brothers, in each case it was held that nothing passed to the purchaser at an auction sale under the decree (*l*). So where the deceased left a widow and a minor son, and the suit was brought against the widow, decree obtained and execution taken out against her, as representing the estate, the existence of the minor being ignored throughout, it was held that his interests were not affected (*m*). But where the estate is actually represented by a female, and the suit is properly brought against her upon a debt of the last male holder, no liability can possibly attach upon her personally (*n*). The basis of the suit against her is, that the estate which she holds is bound, and that she is compellable to pay, not out of *her* assets, but out of *the* assets. Consequently, any decree against her, and all proceedings in execution of it, will be interpreted so as to give proper effect to the transaction. For instance, a man had given a bond, and died leaving an infant son, and a widow who was guardian of the son. She was sued on the bond, judgment was given against her, and execution was issued. The advertisement stated that the property was hers, and that the rights and interest of the debtor were to be sold. It was held that the estate of the deceased was what was sold, and that the purchaser had a good title against the

Binds estate of deceased.

(*k*) *Per curiam*, *Natha* v. *Jamni*, 8 Bom. H. C. (A. C. J.) 41.

(*l*) *Natha* v. *Jamni*, 8 Bom. H. C. (A. C. J.) 37; *Sadabart Prasad* v. *Foolbash Koer*, 3 B. L. R. (F. B.) 31; S. C. 12 Suth. (F. B.) 1; *Phoolbash Koonwar* v. *Lalla Jogeshur*, 3 I. A. 7; S. C. 1 Cal 220; S. C. 25 Suth. 285; See *Hendry* v. *Mutty Lall*, 2 Cal. 395.

(*m*) *Jatha Naik* v. *Venktapa*, 5 Bom. 14; *Akoba Dada* v. *Sakharam*, 9 Bom. 429; *Subbanna* v. *Venkata Krishnan*, 11 Mad. 408.

(*n*) Personal liability can only attach to a married woman in respect of her *stridhanum*, even though the decree is general in its form: *in re Radhi*, 12 Bom. 228.

son (*o*). This decision was approved and followed by the Privy Council, in a case where a widow was sued for arrears of rent, which accrued due in the time of the husband. The plaintiff had, according to the practice which then existed, obtained a decree in the Civil Court against the husband for the arrears. He then proceeded against the widow in the Collector's Court to enforce payment from the estate. The decree was given against the widow as sole heiress and representative. It was held that the execution of this decree bound all the interests in the property, and not merely that of the widow (*p*). And where the advertisement of sale points to a decree against the husband as that which is being enforced, it is immaterial that it states that what is being sold is the right title and interest of the widow (*q*).

Her power over self-acquisitions.

§ 597. The self-acquired property of a man will descend to his widow where his joint or ancestral property would not do so. But she has no other or greater power over the one than over the other (*r*). A different rule prevails among the Jains. A widow among them is said to have an absolute interest over her husband's self-acquired property. And apparently, if not an absolute, yet a very much larger interest over his ancestral property than an ordinary widow possesses (*s*).

Jains.

(*o*) *Ishan* v. *Buksh Ali*, Marsh., 614; S. C. Suth. (F. B.) 119. See *Alukmonee* v. *Banee Madhub*, 4 Cal. 677. So a decree against a widow binds her subsequently adopted son, and the result of an appeal brought by her, after the adoption, equally binds him, though he is not made a party to it. *Hari Saran Moitra* v. *Bhubaneswari*, 15 I. A. 195; S. C. 16 Cal. 40.

(*p*) *Durbhunga* v. *Coomar*, 14 M. I. A. 605; S. C. 10 B. L. R. 294; S. C. 17 Suth. 459. The effect of this and the preceding decisions has been stated by the Judicial Committee to be "that in execution proceedings, the Court will look at the substance of the transaction, and will not be disposed to set aside the execution upon mere technical grounds when they find that it is substantially right." *Bissessur* v. *Luchmessur*, 6 I. A. 233, 238; S. C. 5 C. L. R. 477; *Ramkishore* v. *Kally Kanto*, 6 Cal. 479; *Jotendro* v. *Jogul*, 7 Cal. 357; *affd.* *Jugol Kishore* v. *Jotendro*, 11 I. A. 66; S. C. 10 Cal. 985; *Hari Vydianathayyan* v. *Minakshi*, 5 Mad. 5.

(*q*) *Mt. Nuzeerum* v. *Moulvie Ameerooddeen*, 24 Suth. 3.

(*r*) Mt. *Thakoor* v. *Rai Baluk Ram*, 11 M. I. A. 139; S. C. 10 Suth. (P. C.) 3.

(*s*) *Sheo Singh* v. *Mt. Dakho*, 6 N.-W. P. 382; S. C. *affd.* on appeal, 5 I. A. 87; S. C. 1 All. 688.

Her power over movables.

§ 598. Another point on which there appears to be much difference of opinion, is whether a widow or other female heir has any larger power of disposition over movable property than over immovable property. It is now finally settled, as regards cases governed by the law of Bengal and Benares, that there is no difference, and that the same restrictions apply in each case (*t*). But in both those decisions, and in that cited above, *Mt. Thakoor* v. *Rai Baluk Ram*, it was admitted by the Judicial Committee that there might be a difference in this respect between the law of those provinces, and that administered in the Mithila and in Western and Southern India. Certainly as regards these latter districts there is a strong current of authority the other way (*u*). It is difficult to ascertain upon what ground these decisions rested. Most of them were given in accordance with *futwahs* which set out no reasons or authority. The Madras High Court has lately decided, though apparently without noticing the decisions of the Sudr Court to the contrary, that the restrictions upon a widow's estate apply to movable as well as to immovable property (*v*). Whenever the question arises for final decision, it will be well to bear in mind the observations of the Judicial Committee in *Bhugwandeen* v. *Myna Baee* (*w*). These show that the texts which authorise a woman to dispose absolutely of movable property given to her by her husband, are different

Power of heiress over movables.

(*t*) D. Bhaga, xi. 1, § 56, 60, 63, 64; D. K. Sangraha, i. 2; *Cossinaut Bysack* v. *Hurrosoondry*, 2 M. Dig. 198; affirmed in P. C. Clarke, Rules, 91; V. Darp., 97; *Bhugwandeen* v. *Myna Baee*, 11 M. I. A. 487; S. C. 9 Suth. (P. C.) 23. This position was doubted as regards Bengal, 7 Bom. 163.

(*u*) See as to the Mithila, Vivada Chintamani, 261—263; *Sreenarain* v. *Bhya Jha*, 2 S. D. 23 (29, 36); *Doorga* v. *Poorun*, 5 Suth. 141; *Birajun Kooer* v. *Luchmi Narain*, 10 Cal. 392. Madras: Madhaviya, § 44; *Ramasashien* v. *Akylandummal*, Mad. Dec. of 1849, 115; *Gooroobuksh* v. *Lutchmana*, ib. 1850, 61; *Gopaula Narraina Putter*, ib. 74; *Cooppa* v. *Sashappien*, ib. 1858, 220. Bombay: V. May., iv. 8, § 3; *Bechur* v. *Baee Lukmee*, 1 Bom. H. C. 56; *Pranjeevandas* v. *Dewcooverbaee*, 1 Bom. H. C. 130; *Jamiyatram* v. *Bai Jamna*, 2 Bom. H. C. 10; *Lakshmibai* v. *Ganpat Moroba*, 4 Bom. H. C. (O. C. J.) 150, 162; *Bhaskar Trimbak* v. *Mahadev Ramji*, 6 Bom. H. C. (O. C. J.) 1, 13; *per curiam*, *Tuljaram* v. *Mathuradas*, 5 Bom. 670; *Damodur* v. *Purmanandas*, 7 Bom. p. 163; *Harilal* v. *Pranvalasdas*, 16 Bom. 229; *Bai Jamna* v. *Bais Nauker*, *ibid.* 233

(*v*) *Narasimma* v. *Venkatadri*, 8 Mad. 290; *Buchi Ramayya* v. *Jagapathi*, *ib.* 805.

(*w*) 11 M. I. A. 510—514; S. C. 9 Suth. (P. C.) 23.

from those which control her disposition of property inherited, and that she may probably have larger powers over the former than over the latter. Also, that reliance can no longer be placed upon the much canvassed text of the Mitakshara (ii. 11, § 2), as raising any analogy between property inherited by a woman and her *stridhanum*, as regards the right to dispose of it.

Remedies.

§ 599. REMEDIES AGAINST THE ACTS OF A FEMALE HEIR.—This part of the subject divides itself into three branches —Who may sue; for what they may sue; and the equities that arise in giving relief.

Persons interested.

WHO MAY SUE.—No one can sue in respect of the acts of the female proprietor, except those who have an interest in the succession, and who would be injured by the acts complained of. It is quite clear that a mere stranger cannot sue. And he is not put into a better position by joining the reversionary heirs as defendants, or even by obtaining their consent (*x*). But the further question arises, who is a mere stranger? The next reversioner, that is the presumptive heir in succession, has only a contingent estate. But it is settled that this estate gives him such an interest as will justify a suit, where that interest is in danger (*y*). On the other hand it seems equally settled that only the immediate reversioners can bring such a suit (*z*), unless the reversioners are themselves fraudulently colluding with the female heir, so that their protection of the estate is in fact

Suit by reversioners.

(*x*) *Brojokishoree* v. *Sreenath Bose*, 9 Suth. 463. Nor can the assignee of a reversioner's right sue, even though he would be the next reversioner after the assignor; *Raicharan* v. *Pyari Mani*, 3 B. L. R. (O. C. J.) 70. *Sed qy*. as to last position? If the assignment was valid he became next reversioner. See *Ammur* v. *Mardun*, 2 N.-W. P. 31.

(*y*) *Lukhee* v. *Gokool*, 13 M. I. A. 209, 224; S. C. 3 B. L. R. (P. C.) 57; S. C. 12 Suth. (P. C.) 47; *Kooer Goolab* v. *Rao Kurun*, 14 M. I. A. 176; S. C. 10 B. L. R. 1; *Jumoona* v. *Bamasoonderai*, 3 I. A. 72; S. C. 1 Cal. 289; *Adi Deo* v. *Dukharam*, 5 All. 532. See § 602, note (*o*).

(*z*) *Gogunchunder* v. *Joy Durga*, S. D. of 1859, 620; *Brojokishoree* v. *Sreenath Bose*, 9 Suth. 463; *Bamasoonduree* v. *Bamasoonduree*, 10 Suth. 301; (but see *Oojulmoney* v. *Sagormoney*, Tayl. & B. 370;) *Raghunath* v. *Thakuri*, 4 All. 16; *Madari* v. *Malki*, 6 All. 428.

withdrawn (*a*), or unless the immediate reversioner is herself only the holder of a life estate (*b*).

§ 600. FOR WHAT THEY MAY SUE.—Of course an action against the heir in possession is only maintainable in respect of some act of hers which is injurious to the reversioner. Such acts are of two classes, *First,* those which diminish the value of the estate; *Second,* those which endanger the title of those next in succession.

To restrain waste.

Waste by heiress in possession.

First.—Under this head come all acts which answer to the description of waste, that is, an improper destruction or deterioration of the substance of the property. The right of those next in reversion to bring a suit to restrain such waste, was established, apparently for the first time, by an elaborate judgment of Sir *Lawrence Peel,* C. J., in 1851 (*c*). What will amount to waste, has never been discussed. Probably no assistance upon this point could be obtained from an examination of the English cases in regard to tenants for life. The female heir is, for all purposes of beneficial enjoyment, full and complete owner. She would, as I conceive, have a full right to cut timber, open mines and the like, provided she did so for the purpose of enjoying the estate, and not of injuring the reversion. As Sir *Lawrence Peel* said (*d*), "The Hindu female is rather in the position of an heir taking by descent until a contingency happens, than an heir or devisee upon a trust by implication. Therefore, a bill filed by the presumptive heir in succession against the immediate heir who has succeeded by inheritance, must show a case approaching to spoliation." She must appear not merely to be

(*a*) *Naikram* v. *Soorujbuns*, S. D. of 1859, 891; *Shama Soonduree* v. *Jumoona*, 24 Suth. 86; *Retoo* v. *Lalljee*, *ib.* 399; *Kooer Goolab* v. *Rao Kurun*, 14 M. I. A. 176; S. C. 10 B. L. R. 1, 193; *Anand* v. *Court of Wards*, 8 I. A. 14; *Balgobind* v. *Ramkumar*, 6 All. 431; *Gauri* v. *Gursahai*, 2 All. 41; *Jhula* v. *Kanta Prasad*, 9 All. 441; *Mahomed* v. *Krishnan*, 11 Mad. 106. See as to misjoinder of causes of action by plaintiff seeking a declaration that alienations to several persons were invalid. *Kachar* v. *Bai Rathore*, 7 Bom. 289.

(*b*) *Kooer Goolab* v. *Rao Kurun*, 14 M. I. A., I. A. 176, *Kandasami* v. *Akkammal*, 13 Mad. 195.

(*c*) *Hurrydoss* v. *Rungunmoney*, Sev, 657.

(*d*) *Hurrydoss* v. *Rungunmoney*, Sev. 661.

using, but to be abusing, her estate. Therefore, specific acts of waste, or of mismanagement, or other misconduct, must be alleged and proved. Unless this is done, the female heir can neither be prevented from getting the property into her possession, nor from retaining it in her hands, nor compelled to give security for it, nor can any orders be given her by anticipation as to the mode in which she is to use or invest it (*e*). But where such a case is made out, the heiress will be restrained from the act complained of. In a very gross case, she may even be deprived of the management of the estate, and a receiver appointed. Not upon the ground that her act operates as a complete forfeiture, which lets in the next estate, and entitles the reversioner to sue for immediate possession, as if she were actually dead (*f*), but upon the ground that she cannot be trusted to deal with the estate in a manner consistent with her limited rights in it (*g*). In such a case the next heirs may be, but need not necessarily be, appointed the receivers, unless they appear to be the fittest persons to manage for the benefit of the estate (*h*); and the Court will, unless perhaps in a case where the female has been guilty of criminal fraud, direct the whole proceeds to be paid over to her, and not merely an allowance for her maintenance (*i*).

Abandonment of right.

In one case the widow had given up the estate to a third party, under threat of legal proceedings, and refused to have anything to do with the assets. It was held that the reversioners might sue the widow and the third party to have the possession restored to the proper custody, and that a manager should be appointed to collect, account for, and pay into Court, the assets, to be

---

(*e*) *Hurrydoss* v. *Uppoornah*, 6 M. I. A. 433; *Bindoo* v. *Bolie*, 1 Suth. 125; *Grose* v. *Amirtamayi*, 4 B. L. R. (O. C. J.) 1; S. C. 12 Suth. (A. O. J.) 13.

(*f*) *Per curiam*, *Rao Kurun* v. *Nawab Mahomed*, 14 M. I. A. 198; S. C. 10 B. L. R. 1; *Kishnee* v. *Khealee*, 2 N.-W. P. 424.

(*g*) *Nundlal* v. *Bolakee*, S. D. of 1854, 351; *Gouree Kanth* v. *Bhugobutty*, S. D. of 1858, 1103.

(*h*) *Golukmonee* v. *Kishenpersad*, S. D. of 1859, 210.

(*i*) *Nundlal* v. *Bolakee*, S. D of 1854, p. 351; S. D. of 1859, 210, *supra*; *Lodhoomona* v. *Gunneschunder*, S. D. of 1859, 436; *Koroonamoyee* v. *Gobindnath*, S. D. of 1859, 944; *Maharani* v. *Nanda Lal*, 1 B. L. R. (A. C. J.) 27; S. C. 10 Suth. 73; *Shama Soonduree* v. *Jumoona*, 24 Suth. 86.

held for the ultimate benefit of the heirs who should be entitled to succeed at the death of the widow (*k*).

Of course the reversioners will be equally entitled to restrain the unlawful acts of persons holding under the female heiress (*l*). But the mere fact that strangers are affecting to deal with the property as their own, without actual dispossession of the intermediate estate, or waste, or injury to it, gives no right of action against them to the reversioner, either for a declaration of title, or otherwise (*m*). **Acts of strangers.**

§ 601. *Second.*—During the lifetime of the heiress no one can bring a suit to have it declared that he will be the next heir at her death. Because as his title must depend upon the state of things existing at her death, a suit before that time would be an unnecessary and useless litigation of a question which may never arise, or may only arise in a different form (*n*). But he may sue to remove that which would be a bar to his title when it vested in possession. **Declaratory suits.**

There are two classes of transactions which would have this effect: *first*, adoptions; *second*, alienations.

§ 602. The Specific Relief Act (I of 1877) § 42 provides that "any person entitled to any legal character, or to any right as to any property, may institute a suit against any person denying, or interested to deny, his title to such character or right, and the Court may in its discretion make therein a declaration that he is so entitled, and the plaintiff need not in such suit ask for any further relief. Provided that no Court shall make any such declaration where the plaintiff, being able to seek further relief than a **Specific Relief Act**

(*k*) *Radha Mohun* v. *Ram Das*, 3 B. L. R. (A. C. J.) 362; S. C. 24 Suth. 86. note. See *Joymooruth* v. *Bulded*, 21 Suth. 444.

(*l*) *Gobindmani* v. *Shamlal*, B. L R. Sup. Vol. 48; S. C. Suth. Sp. 165; *per curiam*, *Kamavadhani* v. *Joysa*, 3 Mad. H. C. 119.

(*m*) *Suraj Bansi Kunwar* v. *Mahipat*, 7 B. L. R. 669; S. C. 16 Suth. 18.

(*n*) *Pranputty* v. *Lallah Futteh*, 2 Hay, 608; S. C. Sev. 638; *Kathama Natchiar* v. *Dorasinga Tever*, 2 I. A. 169; S. C. 15 B. L. R. 83; S. C. 23 Suth. 314; *Greeman* v. *Waheri*, 8 Cal. 12.

mere declaration of title omits to do so" (*o*). The illustrations to this section, amongst which (*e. f.*) are expressly mentioned suits for a declaration that alienations by a widow are void beyond her life, and that her adoption of a son is invalid, seem to show that the Act is intended to reproduce the previous law, as embodied in the following decisions.

Suit to set aside adoptions.

§ 603. It was ruled under the Limitation Act XIV of 1859, that the mere fact of an adoption was no necessary injury to a reversioner, until his right to possession arises, and that the Statute of Limitations ran from the latter date, and not from the date of the adoption. A contrary rule was laid down by the Privy Council as regards the Limitation Act of 1871. It is yet undecided which rule will apply as regards the later Limitation Act XV of 1877, Sched. ii., § 118, 140, 141 (*p*). In any case it was settled that the next reversioner might bring a suit for a declaration that the adoption was invalid, on the ground that he might otherwise lose the evidence which would establish its invalidity, when the occasion arose (*q*). But the granting of merely declaratory decrees is discretionary (*r*), and in one case where the evidence was unsatisfactory, the Court refused to make any declaration (*s*). And no decla-

Declaratory suits.

(*o*) *Bholai* v. *Kali*, 8 All. 70; *Abhoy Churn* v. *Kally Prasad*, 5 Cal. 949. The Calcutta Court has held that a reversioner has not such an estate as would entitle him to sue under this Act. *Greeman Singh* v. *Wahari Lall*, 8 Cal. 12, The Madras Court takes an opposite view. *Gangayya* v. *Mahalakshmi*, 10 Mad. 90.

(*p*) See *ante*, § 150.

(*q*) *Chunder* v. *Dwarkanath*, S. D. of 1859, 1623; *Nobinkishory* v. *Gobind* Sev. 628, note; *per curiam*, *Gangopadhya* v. *Mahesehandra*, 4 B. L. R. (F. B.) 9; S. C. 12 Suth (F. B.) 14; *Brojo* v. *Sreenath Bhose*, 9 Suth. 463; *Mrinmoyee* v. *Bhoobunmoyee*, 15 B. L. R. 1; S. C, 23 Suth. 42; *Siddhessur* v. *Sham Chand*, 15 B. L. R. 9, note; S. C. 23 Suth. 285. (See as to Statute of Limitations in these two last cases). *Kotomarti* v. *Vardhanamma*, 7 Mad. H. C. 351; *Kalova* v. *Padapa*, 1 Bom. 248; *Jumoona* v. *Bamasoonderai*, 3 I. A. 72; S. C. 1 Cal. 289; *Anund* v. *Court of Wards*, 8 I. A. 14; S. C. 6 Cal. 764; *Thayammal* v. *Venkatarama*, 7 Mad. 401.

(*r*) *Sreenarain* v. *Sreemutty*, 11 B. L. R. 171, 190; S. C. 19 Suth. 133; S. C. I. A. Sup. Vol. 149; *Motee Lal* v. *Bhoop Singh*, 8 Suth. 64; *Brojo* v. *Sreenath Bhose*, 9 Suth. 463.

(*s*) *Brohmo Moyee* v. *Anund Lall*, 19 Suth. 419. See as to cases where it was held that the Court had wrongly refused to make a declaration. *Upendra* v. *Gopeenath*, 9 Cal. 817; *Isri Dut* v. *Hunsbutti*, 10 I. A. 150; S. C. 10 Cal. 324.

ration will be made as to merely collateral matters, such as the existence of agreements to give or receive in adoption, where the declaration, when made, would not affect the validity of the adoption (*t*).

§ 604. It was at one time thought that alienations by a widow beyond her powers were absolutely void, and even operated as a forfeiture of her estate. Consequently, that the reversioners might sue to have the estate restored to the widow, or even placed at once in their own possession. It is now, however, settled that this is not the case. Such an alienation will be valid during the widow's lifetime. If not made for a lawful purpose, such as will bind the heirs, it has no effect against them till their title accrues; they may then sue for possession, and the Statute will run from that date (*u*). But here, as in the case of adoptions, the validity of the transaction may depend upon facts the evidence of which would be lost by delay. Therefore, a suit will lie by the reversioner at once, not to set aside the transaction absolutely, but to set aside so much of it as would operate against himself (*v*). But a suit of this character must be founded on specific instances of alienation extending beyond the restricted powers of the heiress. A suit to restrain all alienations would not be maintainable, because the validity of each alienation would depend upon the circumstances under which it was made, and could not be decided upon

to set aside alienations.

When maintainable.

(*t*) *Sreenarain* v. *Sreemutty*, 11 B. L. R. 171, *supra*.

(*u*) Where the suit is during the life of a widow to declare her alienation void beyond her life, the statute runs from the alienation. If after her death for possession, the statute runs from the death. In each case the period is twelve years. Act XV of 1877, Sched. ii. § 125, 141; *Pursut Koer* v. *Palut Roy*, 8 Cal. 442; *Srinath* v. *Prosonno*, 9 Cal. 934.

(*v*) *Gobindmani* v. *Shamlal*, B. L. R. Sup. Vol. 48; S. C. Suth. Sp. 165; *Oodoy* v. *Dhunmonee*, 3 Suth. 183; *Grose* v. *Amirtamayi*, 4 B. L. R. (O. C. J.) 1; S. C. 12 Suth. (A. O. J.) 13; *Shewak* v. *Syad Mohammed*, 3 B. L. R. (A. C. J.) 196; S. C. 12 Suth. 26; *Lalla Chuttur* v. *Mt. Wooma*, 8 Suth. 273; *Bykunt* v. *Grish Chunder*, 15 Suth. 96; *Bistobehari* v. *Lala Baijnath*, 7 B. L. R. 213; S. C. 16 Suth. 49; *Damoodur* v. *Mohee Kant*, 21 Suth. 54. See per *Macpherson*, J., *Prosunno* v. *Tripoora*, 24 Suth. 88, explaining *Brinda* v. *Pearee*, 9 Suth. 460; *Shumsool* v. *Shewukram*. 2 I. A. 7; S. C. 14 B. L. R. 226; S. C. 22 Suth. 409; *Kalian Singh* v. *Sanwal Singh*, 7 All. 163; *Sant Kumar* v. *Sukh Nidhan*, 8 All. 365; *Gopichand* v. *Sujankuar*, 8 All. 646.

beforehand (*w*). Such declarations will not be granted, unless the act complained of is one which, if allowed to stand unchallenged, would be an injury to the estate of the next heir (*x*). And they may be refused, at the discretion of the Court, if it appears that the lapse of time will not render it more difficult for the next heir to establish his right when the succession falls in, for, if this be so, the litigation is premature and unnecessary (*y*).

Effect of declaratory decree.

§ 605. It was formerly unsettled how far a decree in a declaratory suit would bind any but the parties to it. Where a suit is brought by or against a female heiress in possession, in respect of any matter which strikes at the root of her title to the property, it is held that a decree, fairly and properly obtained against her, binds all the reversioners, because she completely represents the estate (*z*). But it is by no means clear that the same result would follow in a suit where she was not defending her own title at all. In one case of an application to set aside an adoption, the Judicial Committee said that they would give no opinion what the effect of a decree in such a suit might be; whether one in favour of the adoption would bind any reversioner except the plaintiff, or whether one adverse to the adoption would bind the adopted son, as between himself and anybody except the plaintiff (*a*). In a later case they refused

(*w*) *Pranputtee* v. *Mt. Poorn*, S. D. of 1856, 494; S. C. on review, *Lalla Futteh* v. *Mt. Pranputtee*, S. D. of 1857, 381.

(*x*) *Sreenarain* v. *Sreemutty*, 11 B. L. R. 171; S. C. 19 Suth. 183; S. C. I. A. Sup. Vol. 149; *Behary* v. *Madho*, 13 B. L. R. 222; S. C. 21 Suth. 430; *Nilmony* v. *Kally Churn*, 2 I. A. 83; S. C. 14 B. L. R. 382; S. C. 23 Suth. 150; *Rampershad* v. *Jokhoo Roy*, 10 Cal. 1003.

(*y*) *Behary* v. *Madho*, ub sup.

(*z*) *Katama Natchiar* v. *Rajah of Shivagunga*, 9 M. I. A. 539, 604; S. C. 2 Suth. (P. C.) 31; *Nobinchunder* v. *Guru Persad*, B. L. R. Sup. Vol. 1008; S. C. 9 Suth. 505; approved, *Aumirtolall* v. *Rajoneekant*, 2 I. A. 121; S. C. 15 B. L. R. 10; S. C. 23 Suth. 214; *Pertab Narain* v. *Trilokinath*, 11 I. A. 197; S. C. 11 Cal. 186. As to effect of Statute of Limitations, see *Natha* v. *Jamni*, 8 Bom. H. C. (A. C. J.) 37; *Babu Valad* v. *Bhikaji*, 14 Bom. 317; *Brammoye* v. *Kristomohun*, 2 Cal. 222; *Nandkumar* v. *Radha Kuari*, 1 All. 282; *Gandharat Singh* v. *Lachman Singh*, 10 All. 485; *Gya Prasad* v. *Heet Narain*, 9 Cal. 93; *Srinati Kuar* v. *Prosonno Kumar*, 9 Cal. (F. B.) 934; *Kokilmoni* v. *Manick Chandra*, 11 Cal. 791; *Drobomoyi Gupta* v. *Davis*, 14 Cal. 323, 344, *ante*, § 595.

(*a*) *Jumoona* v. *Bamasoonderai*, 3 I. A. 72, 84; S. C. 1 Cal. 289. See per

to give any declaration as to the effect of a will upon the rights, if any, of an unborn son, on the ground that no judgment which they could give would affect his rights (*b*). Now, by Act I of 1877, § 43 (Specific Relief) it is provided, that a declaration made under Chap. VI is binding only upon the parties to the suit, persons claiming under them respectively, and, where any of the parties are trustees, on the persons for whom, if in existence at the date of the declaration, such persons would be trustees.

§ 606. EQUITIES.—In general, where a conflict arises between the reversioner and the alienee of the heiress, the question is simply whether her alienation was for a lawful and necessary purpose, or not. If it was, it binds him; if it was not, it does not bind him. In either view no equity can arise between them. And when the sale is valid, the reversioner is not at liberty to treat it as a mere mortgage, and to set it aside on payment of the amount which it was proved that the female in possession had been under a necessity to raise (*c*). In some cases the reversioner is at liberty to set aside the transaction, but only on special terms. For instance, if the heiress sold a larger portion of the estate than was necessary to raise the amount which the law authorized her to raise, the sale would not be absolutely void as against the reversioners, but they could only set it aside (if at all) upon paying the amount which the widow was authorized to raise, with interest from her death, the defendant accounting for rents and profits from the same period (*d*). And it is probable that even this amount of relief would not be granted, unless the circumstances were such as to affect the purchaser with notice that the sale was in excess of the legal requirements of the case (*e*); or

Equities on setting aside her acts.

Excessive sale.

Peacock, C. J., *Brojo* v. *Sreenath Bose*, 9 Suth 465; *per Markby*, J., *Brohmo* v. *Anund*, 13 B. L. R. 225 (note); S. C. 19 Suth. 420.

(*b*) *Ram Lal Mookerjee* v. *Secy. of State*, 8 I. A 46; S. C. 7 Cal. 301.

(*c*) *Sugeeram* v. *Juddoobuns*, 9 Suth. 284.

(*d*) *Phool Chund* v. *Rughoobuns*, 9 Suth. 108; *Mutteeram* v. *Gopaul*, 11. B. L. R. 416; S. C. 20 Suth. 187.

(*e*) *Kamikhaprasad* v. *Jagadamba*, 5 B. L. R. 503.

unless it was shown that he had failed to make proper enquiries upon the point (*f*).

In discharge of mortgage.

§ 607. On the other hand, where the female heiress has sold property in order to pay off a mortgage on the estate, if it appears that her funds were sufficient to have enabled her to satisfy it without alienating the property, the sale will be set aside at the suit of the reversioners. But only on the terms of treating the mortgage as a subsisting debt, and giving the purchaser credit for the amount, which otherwise the heir would have had to meet (*g*). Here, it will be observed, the heiress might, without any breach of duty, have allowed the mortgage to continue, leaving the reversioner to pay it off or not, as he thought best. But I do not imagine the same rule would be applied, if the widow sold the estate, without any necessity, to pay off claims which she herself was bound to meet, such as her husband's debts, or the maintenance or marriages of dependent members of the family; for the result of such a course would be, to shift the burthen of these claims off her own shoulders upon those of the reversioner.

(*f*) *Lulleet* v. *Sreedhur*, 13 Suth. 457.
(*g*) *Shumsool* v. *Shewukram*, 2 I. A. 7; S. C. 14 B. L. R. 226; S. C. 22 Suth. 409; *Sadashiv* v. *Dhakubai*, 5 Bom. 450.

CHAPTER XXI.

WOMAN'S ESTATE.

In Property not inherited from Males.

§ 608. THIS Chapter will be devoted to a discussion of that which is generally spoken of as *stridhanum*, or woman's *peculium*, or property specially so called. But I have preferred the more general heading, so as to avoid disputes as to whether any particular species of property comes within the definitions of *stridhanum* or not. Such an enquiry is frequently no more than a dispute about words (*a*). To the historical or practical lawyer the only question of interest is, what are the incidents of any sort of property. Its name is a matter of indifference, unless so far as that name guides us in ascertaining the incidents. If the name itself has been applied to different things at different times, it is more likely to mislead than to guide (*b*). **Woman's *peculium*.**

§ 609. It is evident that the recognition of any right of property in women must have been of gradual growth. In every race there has been a time when woman herself is no more than a chattel, and incapable of any property except what her owner allows her to possess, and so long as he allows it. Indications of such a state of society have already been pointed out in the Sanskrit texts (§ 70). Dr. Mayr adduces passages from the Veda to show that in early times married women pursued independent occupations, and **Its origin and growth.**

(*a*) *See per Holloway, J., Kattama Nachiar v. Dorasinga Tevar*, 6 Mad. H. C. 340.

(*b*) The whole subject of *stridhanum* is very elaborately discussed by Dr. Mayr (pp. 164—179). I have borrowed much from him throughout this chapter, and not merely in passages where there is a special reference to his work.

acquired gain by them (c), but both *Manu* and *Katyayana* assert that their earnings were absolutely at the disposal of the man to whom they belonged (d). The simplicity of a Hindu household would limit a woman's possessions to her own clothes and ornaments, and perhaps some domestic utensils. Her husband, if he chose, might recognize her right to these, but it would seem that in early times this right ended with his life. That is to say, as soon as he died, the dominion over her passed to others, and with it the power of appropriating her property. *Vishnu* says, "those ornaments which the wives usually wear should not be divided by the heirs, whilst the husbands of such wives are alive." Messrs. West and Bühler add in a note, "But the ornaments of widows may be divided. The latter point is especially mentioned by *Nanda Pandita*" (e). The same text apparently is found in *Manu*, where it is slightly altered, so as to prohibit the husband's heirs from taking the property of a woman even after the husband's death. This is the meaning put upon it in the Mitakshara, and no doubt was a later phase of law (f). In accordance with it is the remark of *Apastamba*, "According to some the share of the wife consists of her ornaments, and the wealth which she may have received from her relations" (g). That is to say, an after usage sprang up of recognizing the right of the woman, by formally allotting her special property to her upon a family division. It would be a still further advance to separate her property completely from that of her husband, by making it pass after her death in a different line of descent.

Her paraphernalia.

The bride-price.

§ 610. Infant marriage is so universal in India that a girl, even in a wealthy family, would seldom possess orna-

(c) Mayr, 162.

(d) Manu, viii. § 416; Daya Bhaga, iv. 1, § 19. In the Punjab villages it is said that such a thing as woman's separate property seldom exists. Punjab customs 115; Punjab Customary law, II 80; III 101, 159.

(e) Vishnu, xvii. § 22, as explained by his commentator Vaijayanti.

(f) Manu, ix. § 200; Mitakshara, ii. 11, § 33; Mayr, 164.

(g) Apastamba, ii. 14, § 9.

ments of any value before betrothal. For her, property would commence at her bridal, in the shape of gifts from her bridegroom and her own family. Gifts of the former kind were probably the earlier in point of time. The bride-price in all its varied forms, as a bribe before marriage, or a reward immediately after it; as a payment to the parents, or a dowry for the wife, is one of the earliest elements in every marriage which has passed beyond the stage of pure capture (*h*). Gifts by the girl's own family pre-suppose that consent, which was only asked for when the parental dominion was recognized (§ 77). But they do not necessarily involve the idea that her right to separate property had yet arisen. Dr. Mayr suggests that when the husband's relations began to make gifts to her, such a separate capacity for property must have been recognized, and therefore that gifts of this class are later in point of origin than the others (*i*). For obvious reasons gifts from strangers, or persons beyond the limit of very close relationship, would not be encouraged, and, if permitted, would pass to the husband. Similarly, any earnings made by the wife could only be made by the permission of the husband, and as a reward for services which she could otherwise be rendering in his family. They also would be his, not hers.

Gifts to wife.

Early texts as to *stridhanum*.

§ 611. The texts in regard to *stridhanum* accord with the above views. The principal definition is that contained in *Manu*, "What was given before the nuptial fire (*adhyagni*), what was given on the bridal procession, what was given in token of love (*dattam priti-karmani*), and what was received from a brother, a mother, or a father, are considered as the six-fold (separate) property of a (married) woman" (*k*). The words "a brother, a mother, or a father,"

(*h*) Maine, Early Instit., 324; Mayr, 168; *ante*, § 73.

(*i*) Mayr, 169.

(*k*) Manu, ix. § 194. Narada gives the same definition (xiii. § 8), substituting for "a token of love," "her husband's donation." The Daya Bhaga, (iv. 1, § 7) observes that this does not include the heritage of her husband. See as to *stridhanum* generally Mitakshara, ii. 11; V. May., iv 10; Smriti Chandrika, ix.; Daya Bhaga, iv. 1; D. K. S ii. 2; Viramitrodaya, p. 220, § 1; Madhaviya, § 50; Varadarajah, 45; Virada Chintamani, 256. The term "given before the nuptial

appear to be given only by way of illustration, for he says in the next verse, "What she received after marriage (*anvadheyam*) from the family of her husband, and what her affectionate lord may have given her, shall be inherited, even if she die in his life-time, by his children" (*l*). *Vishnu* and *Yajnavalkya* give a similar enumeration, but both add, that which a woman receives when her husband takes another wife. *Vishnu* substitutes the term *sulka* or fee for the "gift in token of love;" and *Yajnavalkya* terminates his list with the mysterious *adyam*, or &c., which *Vijnanesvara* expands into, "And also property which she may have acquired by inheritance, purchase, partition, seizure, and finding" (*m*).

Essentials of stridhanum.

§ 612. It will be observed that these various classes of property have all these qualities in common, that they belong to a married woman, that they are given to her in her capacity of bride or wife, and that, except perhaps in the case of purely bridal gifts, they are given by her husband, or by her relations, or by his relations. *Jimuta Vahana* expressly limits gifts presented in the bridal procession, to such as are received from the family of either her father or mother. In this *Jagannatha* differs from him, being of opinion that gifts received from any one would come within the definition, and a *futwah* to the same effect is recorded by Mr. W. MacNaghten (*n*). It is probable that in early times strangers to the family did not take part in family ceremonies.

Sulka.

The *sulka* or fee is variously described, as being a special present to the bride to induce her to go cheerfully to the mansion of her lord (*o*), or as the gratuity for the receipt of which a girl is given in marriage (*p*). *Varadrajah* puts the latter view even more coarsely, when

---

fire," includes all gifts during the continuance of the marriage ceremonies. *Bistoo* v. *Radha Soonder*, 16 Suth. 115.

(*l*) Manu, ix. § 195.

(*m*) Vishnu, xvii. § 18; Yajnavalkya, ii. § 143, 144; Mitakshara, ii. 11, § 2. See also Katyayana, Mitakshara, ii. 11, § 5; Devala, Daya Bhaga, iv. 1, § 15. See *ante*, § 566.

(*n*) Daya Bhaga, iv. 1, § 6; 3 Dig. 559; 2 W. MacN. 122.

(*o*) Vyasa, 3 Dig. 570; Daya Bhaga, iv. 3, § 21.

(*p*) Mitakshara, ii. 11, § 6

he describes it as, "What is given to the possessors of a maiden by way of price for the sale of a maiden" (*q*). In the Viramitrodaya it is stated to be, "the value of household utensils and the like which is taken (by the parents) from the bridegroom, and the rest, in the shape of ornaments for the girl" (*r*). These various meanings probably mark the different steps, by which that which was originally received by the parents for the sale of their daughter, was converted into a dowry for herself (*s*). A still later signification was given to the word, when it was taken to denote special presents given by the husband to the wife for the discharge of extra household duties (*t*), or even presents given to her by strangers for the exercise of her influence with her husband or her family (*u*).

Of course an unmarried woman might have property, either in the shape of ornaments or other presents, given to her by her affianced bridegroom, or by her own family, or property which she had inherited from others than males. The former class of property is expressly recognized as *stridhanum,* and goes in a peculiar course of descent (*v*). And in Bengal, property devised by a father to his daughter before her marriage has been held to be her *stridhanum,* and descendible as such (*w*). Her property inherited will be treated of hereafter (§ 627). Maiden's property.

§ 613. Before quitting this branch of the subject it is necessary to explain two terms which are frequently used in regard to *stridhanum;* that is, *Saudayika* and *Yautaka,* with its negative *Ayautaka.* *Yautaka* refers exclusively to gifts received at the time of the marriage (*x*). *Ayautaka* of course is that which does not come within the term *yautaka.* *Yautaka. Ayautaka.*

(*q*) Varadrajah, 48.
(*r*) W. & B. 2nd. ed. 500; Viramit., p. 223.
(*s*) Mayr, 170; *ante*, § 78.
(*t*) Katyayana, 3 Dig. 563.
(*u*) Daya Bhaga, iv. 3, § 20.
(*v*) Mitakshara, ii. 11, § 30; V. May., iv. 10, § 33.
(*w*) *Judoonath* v. *Bussunt Coomar*, 11 B. L. R. 286; S. C. 19 Suth. 264.
(*x*) Daya Bhaga, iv. 2. § 13—15; Smriti Chandrika, ix. 3, § 13. It is derived from the word 'yu' signifying to unite, in reference to the union by marriage. Raghunandana, x. 14; Viramit, p. 230, § 3.

Saudayika.

Saudayika is translated as "the gift of affectionate kindred." The author of the Smriti Chandrika limits it to wealth "received by a woman from her own parents or persons connected with them in the house of either her father or her husband, from the time of her betrothment to the completion of the ceremony to be performed on the occasion of her entering her lord's house" (*y*). But the same texts of *Katyayana* and *Vyasa,* upon which he places this interpretation, are explained by others as including gifts received by her from her husband, and from others after her marriage (*z*). The modern *futwahs* and decisions take the same view. Provided the gift is made by the husband, or by a relation either of the woman or of her husband, it seems to be immaterial whether it is made before marriage, at marriage, or after marriage; it is equally her *saudayika* (*a*). All savings made by a woman from her *stridhanum,* and all purchases made with it, of course, follow the character of the fund from which they proceeded (*b*). And her arrears of maintenance have also been held to be her *stridhanum,* under a text of *Devala* which speaks of her subsistence, *i.e.,* what remains of that which is given for her food and raiment—as being her separate property (*c*). Whether such arrears are also *saudayika* is a different question. The importance of the distinction arises, when her power of disposition over any particular property, and her independence of marital control, come under consideration.

Saudayika.

Her power of disposition,

§ 614. The Mitakshara, in treating of woman's property, expressly includes under that term all property lawfully obtained by a woman, in its most general sense, and lays

---

(*y*) Smriti Chandrika, ix. 2, § 7.

(*z*) Viramitrodaya, p. 222, § 3; Madhaviya, § 50, p. 42; Varadrajah, 50; Daya Bhaga, iv. 1, § 21.

(*a*) *Gosaien* v. *Mt. Kishenmunnee,* 6 S. D. 77 (90); *Doorga* v. *Mt. Tejoo,* 5 Suth. Mis., 53; *Gangadaraiya* v. *Parameswaramma,* 5 Mad. H. C. 111; *Jeewun* v. *Mt. Sona,* 1 N. W. P. 66; *Kashee* v. *Gour Kishore,* 10 Suth 139; *Radha* v. *Biseshur,* 6 N. W. P. 279; *Hurrymohun* v. *Shonatun,* 1 Cal. 275; *Ramasami* v. *Virasami,* 3 Mad. H. C. 272.

(*b*) *Luchmun* v. *Kalli Churn,* 19 Suth 292 (P. C.); *Venkata* v. *Suriya,* 1 Mad. 281. See *Hurst* v. *Mussoorie Bank,* 1 All. 762.

(*c*) Daya Bhaga, iv. 1, § 15; *Court of Wards* v. *Mohessur,* 16 Suth. 76.

down no rules whatever as to her power of disposal of it (*d*). No inference of course can be drawn that she has the same power over all the species there enumerated. This is a point which *Vijnanesvara* has nowhere discussed. The question is minutely examined in the Smriti Chandrika, and in the Viramitrodaya, where distinctions are drawn as to a woman's power of alienating different sorts of property. *Jimuta Vahana,* however, follows *Katyayana* in limiting the term *stridhanum,* as used by him, to that property "which she has power to give, sell, or use independently of her husband's control" (*e*). But it is evident that a woman may have absolute power over her property, as regards all other persons but her husband, and yet be fettered in her disposal of it by him. Her property, therefore (taking it in its widest sense), falls under three heads: 1*st,* Property over which she has absolute control; 2*nd,* Property as to which her control is limited by her husband, but by him only; 3*rd,* Property which she can only deal with at all for limited purposes.

over her saudayika.

Property over which she has absolute control.

§ 615. First. *Saudayika* of all sorts, whether movable or immovable, which has been given by relations other than the woman's own husband, and *saudayika* of a movable character which has been given by him, are absolutely at a woman's own disposal. She may spend, sell, devise, or give it away at her own pleasure (*f*). The same rule applies to land which a woman has purchased by means of such *saudayika* as was absolutely at her own disposal (*g*). Her husband can neither control her in her dealings with

(*d*) Mitakshara, ii. 11, § 2, 3.

(*e*) Daya Bhaga, iv. 1, § 18, 19; D. K. S. ii. 2, § 24. Raghunandana, ix. 1.

(*f*) Daya Bhaga, iv. 1, § 21—23; D. K. S. ii. 2, § 26, 31, 32; Raghunandana, ix. 3—5; V. May, iv. 10. § 8, 9; Smriti Chandrika, ix. 2, § 1—12; *Luchmun* v. *Kalli Churn*, 19 Suth. 292; *Kullammal* v. *Kuppu*, 1 Mad. H. C. 85; 2 W. MacN. 215; *Wulubhram* v. *Bijlee*, 2 Bor. 440 [481]; *Damodar* v. *Parmanandas*, 7 Bom. 155; *Munia* v. *Puran*, 5 All. 310; *Venkata* v. *Suriya*, 2 Mad 333 (P. C.)

(*g*) *Venkata* v. *Suriya*, 2 Mad. 333. Where a married woman with *stridhanum*, contracts she will be assumed to have intended to satisfy her liability out of her separate property. *Govindji* v. *Lakmidas*, 4 Bom. 318; *Narotam* v. *Nanko*, 6 Bom. 473. If she is unmarried at the time of her contract, she will be liable personally, and not merely to the extent of her *stridhanum*, for payment of her debt ,even though she marries before it is enforced. *Nahalchand* v. *Bai Shiva*, 6 Bom. 470.

it, nor use it himself. But he may take it in case of extreme distress, as in a famine, or for some indispensable duty, or during illness, or while a creditor keeps him in prison. Even then he would appear to be under at least a moral obligation to restore the value of the property when able to do so. What he has taken without necessity he is bound to repay with interest (*h*). This right to take the wife's property is purely a personal one in the husband. If he does not choose to avail himself of it, his creditors cannot (*i*).

Jagannatha states that property which a woman has inherited from a woman is also absolutely at her disposal (*k*). It is clear that where property given by any person to a woman would be her *stridhanum*, it will equally be such if devised (*l*). It has, however, been decided in Bengal that a woman who inherits from a woman only takes a qualified estate, which descends on the death of the taker to the heirs of the woman from whom she took, not to her own heirs (*m*). It has also been decided by the Bengal High Court that, under the law of the Daya Bhaga, property so inherited is subject to the same restrictions as to power of alienation as would apply to it if it had descended from a male (*n*).

Property subject to husband's control.

In other respects absolutely hers.

§ 616. Secondly. *Devala* mentions a woman's gains as part of the separate property, over which she has exclusive control, and which her husband cannot use except in time of distress. But it is probable that he employs the word in the sense of gifts (*o*). *Katyayana* lays down that

---

(*h*) Mitakshara, ii. 11, § 31, 32, Smriti Chandrika, ix. 2, § 13—22; Madhaviya, § 51; V. May., iv. 10, § 10; Daya Bhaga, iv. 1, § 24; D. K. S. ii. 2, § 33.

(*i*) Viramitrodaya, p. 225, § 6; 1 Stra. H. L. 27; 2 Stra. H. L. 23; *Tukaram* v. *Gunaji*, 8 Bom. H. C. (A. C. J.) 129; *Radha* v. *Biseshur*, 6 N.-W. P 279.

(*k*) 3 Dig. 629.

(*l*) *Ramdolal* v. *Joymoney*, 2 M. Dig. 65; *per curiam*, *Judoonath* v. *Bussunt Coomar*, 11 B. L. R. 295; S. C. 19 Suth. 264.

(*m*) *Prankissen* v. *Noyanmoney*, 5 Cal. 222; *Huri Doyal Singh* v. *Grishchunder*, 17 Cal. 911.

(*n*) *Bhoobun Mohun Banerjee* v. *Muddunmohun Shomis*, *Rep.* 8. I only know this case from its citation and approval, *per curam*, 17 Cal. p. 917.

(*o*) Daya Bhaga, iv. 1, § 15. See a different rendering of the same text at 3 Dig. 577, where the word "gains" is translated "wealth received by a woman

"the wealth which is earned by mechanical arts, or which is received through affection from any other (but the kindred), is always subject to the husband's control." And *Jimuta Vahana* adds that he has a right to take it, even though no distress exist (*p*). So, the Smriti Chandrika states that "women possess independent power only over *saudayika,* and their husband's donation, except immovables, and that their power is not independent over other sorts of property, although they may be *stridhanum*" (*q*). But her authority over such property is only subject to her husband's control. He may take it, but nobody else can. Therefore, if she dies before her husband, the property remains in his possession, and passes to his heirs. But if he dies before her, she becomes absolute owner of the property, and at her death it passes to her heirs, not to those of her husband (*r*). And of course the rule would be the same, if the acquisitions were made by a widow (*s*). It has been suggested by the Madras High Court, upon the authority of a remark by Mr. Colebrooke, that even as regards landed property not derived from her husband, a married woman would be incapable of making an alienation without her husband's consent (*t*). There is also a text of *Katyayana,* which implies that the husband has a control over his own donations which are not of an immovable character, and that the woman for the first time acquires complete power of disposal after his death (*u*). There can be no doubt that a husband would always be able to exercise a very strong pressure upon his wife, so as to restrain her from giving away her own private property, just as an

---

(from a kinsman)." The Viramitrodaya, (p. 226, § 7,) explains gains as "what is received from any person who makes the present for the purpose of pleasing a goddess."

(*p*) Daya Bhaga, iv. 1, § 19, 20; D. K. S. ii. 2, § 25, 28, 29; Raghunandana, ix. 1; V. May, iv. 10, § 7; *Ramdolal* v. *Joymoney,* 2 M. Dig. 65.

(*q*) Smriti Chandrika, ix. 2, § 12.

(*r*) *Per* Jagannatha, 3 Dig. 628; *Madavarayya* v. *Tirtha Sami,* 1 Mad. 307.

(*s*) 2 W. MacN. 239. See case of a grant made by Government to a widow, *Brij Indar* v. *Janki,* 5 I. A. 1; S. C. 1 C. L. R. 318.

(*t*) *Dantuluri* v. *Mallapudi,* 2 Mad. H. C. 360.

(*u*) Daya Bhaga, iv. 1, § 8, 9; Smriti Chandrika, ix. 1, § 14, 15; ix. 2, § 3, 4. See too Narada, cited Daya Bhaga, iv. 1, § 23; Viramitrodaya, p. 224, § 5.

English husband would do, if his wife proposed to sell her diamonds. But the texts referred to seem not to convey any more than a moral precept, while those already cited, which assert her absolute power, are express and unqualified.

Restricted property.

§ 617. THIRDLY. Immovable property, when given or devised by a husband to his wife, is never at her disposal, even after his death. It is her *stridhanum* so far that it passes to her heirs, not to his heirs. But as regards her power of alienation, she appears to be under the same restrictions as those which apply to property which she has inherited from a male even though the gift is made in terms which create a heritable estate (*v*). Of course it is different if the gift or devise is coupled with an express power of alienation (*w*).

Succession to maiden's property.

§ 618. The succession to woman's property is a matter of much intricacy, as the lines of succession vary, according as the woman was married or unmarried, according as her marriage was in an approved or an unapproved form, and according to the mode in which the property was obtained. There are also differences between the doctrines of the Benares and the Bengal lawyers on this head. Little is to be found in the Hindu writers in regard to the property of a maiden. So long as she remained in her father's house, the only property she would be likely to possess would be her clothes and her ornaments. If already betrothed, she might also have received gifts in contemplation of marriage from her own family, or from the bridegroom. In some rare cases she might also have inherited property from a female relation. The only text upon the subject is one which

---

(*v*) See anthorities cited, *ante*, § 615, note (*h*) ; Viramitrodaya, p. 224, § 5 ; 2 W. MacN. 35 ; *Gangadaraiya* v. *Parameswaramma*, 5 Mad. H. C. 111 ; *Kotarbasapa* v. *Chanverova*, 10 Bom. H. C. 403 ; *Ruar* v. *Rup Kuar*, 1 All. 784 ; *Bhujanga Rau* v. *Ramayamma*, 7 Mad. 387.

(*w*) *Jeewun* v. *Mt. Sona*, 1 N.-W. P. 66 ; *Koonjbehari* v. *Premchand*, 5 Cal. 684 ; S. C. 5 C. L. R. 684 ; *Prosonno Coomar* v. *Tarrucknath*, 10 B. L. R. 267. *Kanria* v. *Mahilal*, 10 All. 495. See *ante*, § 584 The case of *Seth Mulchand* v. *Bai Mancha*, 7 Bom. 491, so far as it goes beyond the statement in the text has been doubted by the Madras High Court, 7 Mad., p. 389.

is variously ascribed to *Baudhayana* and to *Narada*, but which cannot be found in the existing works of either writer. "Of an unmarried woman deceased the brothers of the whole blood shall take the inheritance; on failure of them it shall go to the mother, or if she be not living, to the father" (*x*). The Mitakshara explains this by saying, "The uterine brothers shall have the ornaments for the head and other gifts which may have been presented to the maiden by her maternal grandfather, or other relations, as well as the property which may have been regularly inherited by her" (*y*). The latter remark clearly applies to property not inherited from a male, as her father is spoken of as still alive. The result, of course, is that her property is kept in her own family. In default of parents the property goes to their nearest relations (*z*). All presents which may have been received from the bridegroom are to be returned to him, after deducting the expenses already incurred on both sides (*a*).

§ 619. Property possessed by a married woman would go in different lines of succession according to its nature and origin. Her bridal gifts, being articles of specially feminine ornament or use, would naturally pass to her own daughters. And as any of her daughters who had married would probably have received a suitable provision when they left their father's home, where there were daughters both married and unmarried, the latter would be the preferable heirs. So among the married, those who were most in need would have the preference (*b*). Her dowry (*Sulka*) had in early times belonged to her parents, and not to herself. It would return to her father's family, instead of passing into the family of her husband (§ 78). When that separation of interest between herself and her husband arose, which

Property of a married woman.

(*x*) Daya Bhaga, iv. 3, § 7; D. K. S. ii. 1, § 1.
(*y*) Mitakshara, ii. 11, § 30; Smriti Chandrika, ix. 3, § 35; Madhaviya, § 50; V. May., iv. 10, § 34.
(*z*) Viramitrodaya, p. 241.
(*a*) Yajnavalkya, ii. § 146; Mitakshara, ii. 11, § 29, 30; Smriti Chandrika, ix. 3, § 34; V. May., iv. 10, § 33; D. K. S. ii. 1, § 2; Mayr, 178.
(*b*) Mayr, 173.

admitted of her acquiring independent property after her marriage, the property so acquired might be of a more general and important character than that obtained at her bridal. No reason would exist for making it pass exclusively to daughters, and sons would be allowed to share as well as daughters (*c*). Hence a separate line of succession would arise for what are called "gifts subsequent," and the husband's donation.

Devolution of *Sulka.*

§ 620. First. The earliest rule as to the devolution of the *Sulka* is to be found in a text of *Gautama,* which has been variously translated. Dr. Bühler renders it, "The sister's fee belongs to her uterine brothers, if her mother be dead. Some say (that it belongs to them even) whilst the mother lives" (*d*). This text in the Daya Bhaga is translated, "The sister's fee belongs to the uterine brothers; after them it goes to the mother, and next to the father. Some say before her." This *Jimuta Vahana* explains by saying that according to some the father takes before the mother, and both after the uterine brothers (*e*). The explanation of *Balambhatta,* which Dr. Mayr prefers, is, that the word mother in this verse refers to the same person who is spoken of in the preceding verse of Gautama, where her other property is said to go to her daughters; that is to say, that it refers to the woman who has received the *Sulka,* not to the mother of that woman. Accordingly Dr. Mayr translates it, "After the death of the mother, her fee passes to her uterine brothers; some think that the sister's fee belongs to them even during her life." If this translation is correct, it would mark two stages of law in regard to the *Sulka*. *First,* when it was considered to be the property of the bride's father, as the price paid to him for her, and accordingly passed to his sons, even during her life. *Secondly,* when it became the property of the girl at once, as her dowry, but on her death passed in the same manner as it had formerly done to her father's heirs (*f*).

Devolution of *Sulka.*

(*c*) Mayr, 174

(*d*) Gautama, xxviii. § 25, 26.

(*e*) Daya Bhaga, iv. 3, § 27, 28.

(*f*) Mayr, 170.

However this may have been in early times, it is quite clear that the writers of the Benares school treat the *Sulka* as an exception to the rule that a woman's property goes to her daughters, and make it pass at once to the brothers, and in default of them to the mother (*g*). *Yajnavalkya*, however, classes the *Sulka* with gifts from her kindred, and gifts subsequent, which only go to the brothers if the sister has died without issue. Accordingly the Bengal authorities treat the text of *Gautama*, not as an exception to the general rule, but only as explaining how this species of property devolves in the absence of nearer heirs (*h*). Its succession, as understood by them, will be treated under the third head (§ 625).

Benares.

Bengal.

§ 621. SECONDLY. *Yautaka*, or property given at the nuptials, always passes first to the woman's daughters or other issue, if she has any. Little is to be found on the subject in the early writers. *Baudhayana* says, "The daughters shall inherit, (of) the mother's ornaments as many as (are worn) according to the custom of the caste" (*i*). *Vasishtha* says, "Let the daughters share the nuptial gifts of their mother" (*k*). The word here used for nuptial gifts, '*parinayyam*,' is the same which is used by *Manu* (ix. § 11), where he says that a wife should be engaged in the superintendence of household utensils (*l*). It apparently refers to articles of domestic use given to a girl on her marriage, like the clocks, teapots, and table ornaments which an English bride receives to adorn her new home. So, among the Kandhs, the personal ornaments and household furniture go to the daughters and not to the sons (*m*). *Gautama* adds a further distinction, "A woman's separate property (*stridhanum*) belongs (in the first instance) to her unmarried

Devolution of *Yautaka*.

***Yautaka*.**

(*g*) Mitakshara, ii. 11, § 14; Smriti Chandrika, ix. 3, § 33; Viramitrodaya, p. 242, § 12; Vivada Chintamani, 270; V. May., iv. 10, § 32; Madhaviya, § 50, p. 45; Varadrajah, 48.

(*h*) Yajnavalkya, ii. § 145; Daya Bhaga, iv. 3, § 10—30; D. K. S. ii. 3, § 15—18; *Judoonath* v. *Bussunt Coomar*, 11 B. L. R. 286, 297; S. C. 19 Suth. 264.

(*i*) Baudhayana, ii. 2, § 27.

(*k*) Vasishtha, xvii. § 24.

(*l*) Mayr, 166; Vivada Chintamani, 268.

(*m*) 2 Hunter's Orissa, 79.

daughters (and on failure of them) to those daughters who are poor" (*n*). None of these authors suggest different lines of descent for the property referred to. This, for the first time, appears in *Manu*. He says, "Property given to the mother on her marriage (*yautaka*) is inherited by her (unmarried) daughter" (*o*). In a later passage he says generally, "On the death of the mother let all the uterine brothers and the uterine sisters (if unmarried) equally divide the maternal estate." This necessarily refers to property different from the *yautaka* which had been stated to go exclusively to the daughters. Then, after describing the six-fold property of a woman (§ 611), he goes on, "What she received after marriage (*anvadeya*) from the family of her husband, and what her affectionate lord may have given her, shall be inherited, even if she die in his lifetime, by her children" (*p*). This seems to be the origin of the different lines of succession, which are here treated of under the second and third heads.

Rule of descent.

§ 622. The authors of the Smriti Chandrika and the Viramitrodaya appear to take the first text of *Manu* literally, as allowing none of a woman's issue except her unmarried daughters to take her *yautaka*. In default of such daughters, they make it pass at once to the husband, or to the parents, according as the marriage was of an approved or an unapproved form (*q*). But this narrow interpretation is not followed by either the Benares or the Bengal school. The rule of descent laid down by *Yajnavalkya* is as follows: "The *stridhanum* of a wife dying without issue, who has been married in one of the four forms of marriage designated *Brahma, &c.*, (§ 76), belongs to the husband; if she have issue, then the *stridhanum* goes to her daughters; should she have been married in another form, then her *stridhanum*

(*n*) Gautama, xxviii. § 21.
(*o*) Manu, ix. § 131; Daya Bhaga, iv. 2, § 13.
(*p*) Manu, ix. § 192, 195; Mayr. 174; *Ashabai* v. *Haji Tyeb*, 9 Bom. 115.
(*q*) Smriti Chandrika, ix. 3, § 12, 15; Viramitrodaya, p. 230, § 2; 235, § 6; 236, § 7.

goes to her parents" (*r*). This rather vague rule is expanded by the Mitakshara. "Hence, if the mother be dead, daughters take her property in the first instance; and here, in the case of competition between married and maiden daughters, the unmarried take the succession; but on failure of them, the married daughters; and here again, in the case of competition between such as are provided and those who are unendowed, the unendowed take the succession first; but, on failure of them, those who are endowed" (*s*). Next to daughters come granddaughters, and then sons of daughters, sons, and grandsons, those in the second generation always taking *per stirpes* (*t*). Step-children are not recognized by the Mitakshara as entitled, except in the single case, which has now become impossible, where the woman who has left the property was a wife of an inferior class, while the children who claim it are by a wife of a higher class (*u*). The Smriti Chandrika, however, allows the step-children to come in if there are no other heirs, such as progeny, husband or the like (*v*). In default of all these, if the marriage was in an approved form, the property passes to the husband, and after him, according to *Vijnanesvara*, to his nearest sapindas (*w*). According to the Mayukha, to those relations who are nearest to him through her in his own family. If the marriage was in an unapproved form it passes to her parents, the mother taking before the father (*x*). *Vijnanesvara* traces the line of descent no further. But other writers of the same school cite a text of *Vrihaspati*, in accordance with which the succession next passes to the son of the mother's sister, of the maternal and paternal

Descent of *Yautaka* by Benares law.

(*r*) Yajnavalkya, ii. § 145.

(*s*) Mitakshara, ii. 11, § 13; V. May., iv. 10, § 17, 18.

(*t*) Mitakshara, ii. 11, § 9, 12, 15—19, 24; V. May., iv. 10, § 20—23. Sons wholly exclude grandsons whose father is dead. *Raghunandana* v. *Gopeenath*, 2 W. MacN. 121; *post*, § 627.

(*u*) Mitakshara, ii. 11, § 22; V. May., iv. 10, § 19. The text of Manu, on which this rule is based, is explained differently in Bengal. *Post*, § 626.

(*v*) Smriti Chandrika, ix. 3, § 38. *Brahmappa* v. *Papanna*, 13 Mad. 348.

(*w*) This has been held to be the Mithila law also. *Bachha Jha* v. *Jugmon Jha*, 12 Cal. 348.

(*x*) Mitakshare, ii. 11, § 11; V. May., iv. § 28 According to the Smriti Chandrika, property given to a woman at the time of a disapproved marriage reverts to the donors; ix. 3, § 31, 32.

uncle's wife, of the father's sister, of the mother-in-law, and of an elder brother's wife, (*y*).

Extended to other cases.

Precisely the above order is laid down by the Smriti Chandrika and the Viramitrodaya in respect of all the mother's property, which is not *yautaka*, or received after marriage or from the husband; that is, which does not come under the two texts of *Manu* already cited (*z*).

Bengal law.

§ 623. The order of succession to *Yautaka*, according to the Bengal authorities, is similar, but not exactly the same. "It goes first to the unaffianced daughters; if there be none such, it devolves on those who are betrothed. In their default it passes to the married daughters" (*a*). *Jimuta Vahana* does not notice barren or widowed daughters, but the Daya-krahma-sangraha states that they succeed in default of married daughters who have, or who are likely to have, male issue. *Srikrishna* also says that these daughters take one after the other, as distinct classes, and not merely in default of each other. For instance, that on the death of a

Bengal law as to *Yautaka*.

daughter who had taken as affianced or married, but who has died without a son, the estate will pass to the next daughter who is capable of taking, and not to the husband of the one who had already succeeded. "For the right of the husband is relative to the 'woman's separate property,' and wealth which has in this way passed from one to another can no longer be considered as the 'woman's separate property' (*b*)." The Bengal writers also differ from those of the Benares school in excluding granddaughters altogether, and bringing in the son before the daughter's son, and the grandson and great-grandson in the male line next after the daughter's

---

(*y*) V. May., iv. 10, § 30; Smriti Chandrika, ix. 3, § 36, 37; Viramitrodaya, p. 248; in Mithila, but not elsewhere, the son of a woman's half sister is her heir. *Sreenarain* v. *Bhya Jah*, 2 S. D. 23 (29, 35.) The husband's kinsmen take before the father's kinsmen, *e. g.*, the husband's brother's son before the sister's son. *Bachha Jha Jugmon*, 12 Cal. 348.

(*z*) Manu, ix. § 131, 195; Smriti Chandrika, ix. 3, § 16—30, 36—41; Viramitrodaya, p. 231, *et seq*.

(*a*) Daya Bhaga, iv. 2, § 13, 22, 23, 26; Raghunandana, x. 12—15, 17—20.

(*b*) D. K. S., ii. 3, § 5, 6. See *post*, § 627.

son (*c*). They also differ in introducing stepsons, as far as the great-grandchildren, next after the great-grandsons of the woman herself. This appears to be upon the authority of a text of *Manu*, which declares that if one of several wives of a man brings forth a male child, they are all by means of that son mothers of male issue (*d*). In default of all these the husband or the parents succeed, according to the form of marriage. But the husband's sapindas do not appear to take as in the Mitakshara. In default of him, the succession passes at once to the brother, mother, or father of the deceased woman (*e*). On the other hand, where the marriage is of a disapproved form, the inheritance passes to the mother, father, and brother, each in default of the other, and if none of them exist, then to the husband (*f*). Last of all come in the ulterior heirs under the text of *Vrihaspati*. But they do not take in the order there stated. They are arranged upon the Bengal principle of religious benefits, as follows: husband's younger brother, husband's brother's son, sister's son, son of husband's sister, brother's son, daughter's husband, father-in-law, and husband's elder brother. In default of all these, sakulyas, learned Brahmans, and the King (*g*).

§ 624. THIRDLY. The succession to that property belonging to a married woman which is neither her *Sulka* nor her *Yautaka* is a matter upon which there is much variance. The texts of *Manu*, which state that her property shall be shared equally by her sons and daughters, and that gifts received by her after marriage from her husband and his family shall go to her children generally, have been already cited (§ 621). Other writers say with equal distinctness, that her property shall be shared equally by sons and unmar- *Devolution of Ayautaka.*

(*c*) Daya Bhaga, iv. 2, § 17—21; D. K. S., ii. 3, § 8—10. The son of the daughter's son never succeeds. Daya Bhaga, iv. 3, § 34; D. K. S., ii. 6, § 2.

(*d*) Daya Bhaga, iv. 3, § 32; D. K. S. ii. 3, § 11—13.

(*e*) D. K. S., ii. 3, § 14—17; *Bistoo* v. *Radha Soondr*, 16 Suth. 115.

(*f*) D. K. S., ii. 3, § 19—21.

(*g*) Daya Bhaga, iv. 3, § 31, 35—37; D. K. S., ii. 6; Raghunandana, x. 23—26 30—39. It is impossible to see upon what principle the husband's father and elder brother come in last.

ried daughters (*h*). *Vijnanesvara* only recognizes one line of descent for the whole of a married woman's property, except her *Sulka, viz.*, that already given for her *Yautaka* (§ 622). He explains the text of *Manu,* not as meaning that brothers and sisters take together, but that the sisters take first and the brothers afterwards, each class sharing equally *inter se;* that is, he brings it in as an illustration of the rule previously stated as to the succession of daughters before sons, and not as an exception to it. And the same view is apparently taken by the Madhaviya (*i*). But the Smriti Chandrika, Viramitrodaya, Vivada Chintamani, Mayukha, and *Varadrajah* all take these texts literally, as prescribing a different course of descent for the two sorts of *stridhanum* there specified, *viz.*, gifts subsequent to marriage, received either from the woman's own family or the family of her husband, and gifts received from her husband. These are shared simultaneously and equally by the woman's sons and daughters being unmarried. Those who are married, and granddaughters, only receive a trifle as a mark of respect, and widows are wholly excluded. But if there are no unmarried daughters, married daughters, whose husbands are living, are also allowed by *Katyayana* to share with their own brothers (*k*). According to the Mayukha it has been held that property received by a married woman from a stranger and her own earnings pass to the person who would be her heir if she were a male (*l*). The writers of the Benares school do not trace the line of descent any further, nor suggest how the property is to go in default of the heirs above named.

Mitakshara.

Benares law.

Bengal law.

§ 625. The Bengal writers also interpret the above texts literally, and take them as applying to all property except

(*h*) Devala, Daya Bhaga, iv. 2, § 6; Sancha and Lichita, 3 D. Dig. 588; Vrihaspati, *ib.*

(*i*) Mitakshara, ii. 11, § 19—21. See Viramitrodaya, p. 232, § 5; Madhaviya, § 50, p. 43.

(*k*) Smriti Chandrika, ix. 3, § 1—11; Viramitrodaya, p. 228, § 1; V. May., iv, 10, § 15, 16; Varadrajah, 47; Vivada Chintamani, 266; *Ashabai* v. *Haji Tyeb*, 9 Bom. 115.

(*l*) *Bai Narmada* v. *Bhagwantrai*, 12 Bom. 505.

the *Yautaka*, and that given by the father of the woman (*m*). The order of succession as laid down by them is as follows: first, son and maiden daughter take together (*n*), and in default of either the other takes the whole; on failure of both, the estate passes to the married daughter who has, or who may have male issue, then to the son's son, the daughter's son, and the son's grandson successively; and in default of all of these, to the male issue of the rival wife, and lastly to barren and widowed daughters (*o*). The further descent depends on the source from which the property was derived. If it comes within the text of *Yajnavalkya*—"that which has been given to her by her kindred, as well as her fee or gratuity, and anything bestowed after marriage, her kinsmen take if she die without issue,"—then the order of succession is first to the whole brothers; if there be none, to the mother; if she be dead, to the father; and on failure of all these to the husband, and the ulterior heirs as already described (*p*). But in this text the words, "given to her by her kindred," signify that which was given to her by her parents in her maiden state, and the word "fee," does not include "a gratuity presented to damsels at marriages, called *Asura*, and the rest (*q*)." If, on the other hand, the property being *Ayautaka* does not come within the terms of the above text, then it devolves in exactly the same manner as the *Yautaka* of a married woman who has left no issue (*r*).

Devolution of *Ayautaka*.

Property given by the father.

§ 626. The text of *Manu* (ix. § 198), "The wealth of a woman, which has been in any manner given to her by her father, let the Brahmani damsel take; or let it belong to her offspring," is explained by the Mitakshara as authoris-

(*m*) Daya Bhaga, iv. 2, § 1—9; Raghunandana, x. 1—10.

(*n*) The word maiden means unbetrothed. *Gangopadhya* v. *Sarbamangala*, 2 B. L. R. (A. C. J.) 144; S. C. 10 Suth. 488

(*o*) Daya Bhaga, iv. 2, § 9—12; D. K. S. ii. 4, § 1—10.

(*p*) Daya Bhaga, ii. 3, § 10, 29—31; *ante*, § 623; *Judoonath* v. *Bussunt Coomar*, 11 B. L. R. 286; S. C. 19 Suth. 264; *Hurrymohun* v. *Shonatun*, 1 Cal. 275.

(*q*) Daya Bhaga, iv. 3, § 15, 23.

(*r*) D. K. S. ii. 4, § 11; *ante*, § 628.

ing step-children of a wife of superior class to inherit (s). The Bengal writers treat the word Brahmani as merely illustrative, and explain the text as establishing an exception to the rule laid down in the last paragraph. According to them, property given by a father to his daughter at any time is never shared by her sons, but goes to her daughters exclusively; the maiden taking first, then the married daughter who has, or is likely to have male issue, and lastly the barren or widowed daughters. After all these come their sons (t). The succession then proceeds, as in the case of *Yautaka*, down to the great-grandson of the co-wife, after which it goes to the brother, mother, father, and husband, under the text of *Yajnavalkya* already cited (u).

Property inherited from a female.

§ 627. The order of succession in the case of property inherited by a female from a female, has not till very lately received any discussion. It has been decided, that even if such property was *stridhanum* in the hands of the last holder, it would not be *stridhanum* for the purpose of descent in the hands of the next heir (v). None of the rules, therefore, which are given for the descent of a woman's separate property by those who use the term in a technical sense, would appear to have any application. *Vijnanesvara* uses the term in its general sense, and declares that all the property included in that term (except *Sulka*) goes in the line of female heirs. As regards a maiden's property, he expressly says that the line marked out by him applies to property which she has inherited (w). I have already offered reasons for supposing that he was not referring to property which she had inherited from males (§ 566) but there is no reason why he should not have included

(s) Mitakshara, ii. 11, § 22.
(t) Daya Bhaga, iv. 2. § 16; D. K. S. ii. 5; Raghunandana, x. 11. 16.
(u) *Judoonath* v. *Bussunt Coomar*, 11 B. L. R. 286, 300; S. C. 19 Suth. 264.
(v) D. K. S. ii 3, § 6; 1 W. MacN. 38; *Prankishen* v. *Mt. Bhagwutee*, 1 S. D. 8, (4); *Gangopadhya* v. *Sarbamangala*, 2 B. L. R (A. C. J.) 144; S. C. *sub nomine*, *Gangooly* v. *Sarbo Mongola*, 10 Suth. 488; *per curiam*, *Sengamalathammal* v. *Valayuda*, 3 Mad. H. C. 314; *Bhaskar Trimbak* v. *Mahadev*, 6 Bom. H. C. (O. C. J.) 18; *Chotay* v. *Chunnoo*, 14 B. L. R. 237; S. C. 22 Suth. 496; *Prankissen* v. *Nayanmoney*, 5 Cal. 225.
(w) Mitakshara, ii. 11, § 8, 30.

property inherited by her from a female. The only other reference to the point by a native writer is in the Daya-krahma-sangraha. The author points out that if property has fallen to a maiden daughter with married sisters, and she dies after marriage, but without sons, the property will not pass to her husband, who would be heir to her separate property, but to the married sisters. This assumes that on her death succession would be traced back again to the last holder. The sister would not be her heir, but would be the heir of the mother from whom she derived the property (*x*). The same principle seems to have been followed in a Bengal case. There, a father gave a taluq to his daughter: she died, upon which the property passed to her daughter; she

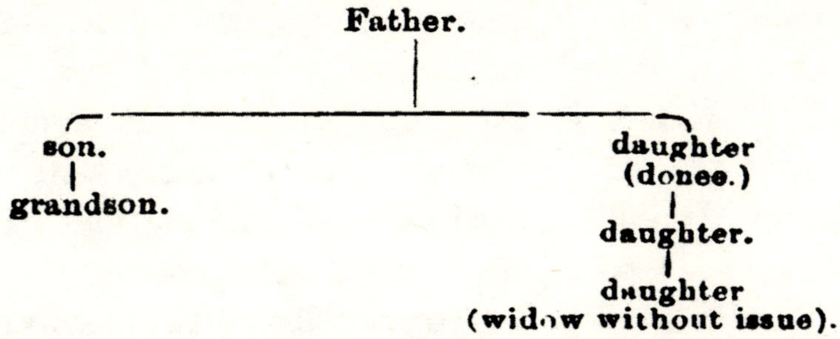

also died, leaving a widowed and issueless daughter. It was held, upon the opinion of the pandits, that the taluq had been the *stridhanum* of the daughter who took by gift, but not of the daughter who took by inheritance. Consequently, that at her death it did not pass to her daughter, but to her mother's brother; if he was not living, to the brother's son (*y*). Now the brother was the heir of the original donee, but he was certainly not the heir of his niece, who took after the donee. This was the view of the case taken, by Mr. Justice *Wilson* in ***Prankissen* v. *Noyanmoney*** (*z*) where the learned Judge referred to it as deciding that a daughter who takes by inheritance from her mother takes a qualified estate, and that on the daughter's death the heir of the mother succeeds. The Mayukha says,

(*x*) D. K. S. ii 3, § 6.
(*y*) *Prankishen* v. *Mt. Bhagwujtee*, 1 S. D. 3 (4); *Sengemalathammal* v. *Valayuda*, 3 Mad H. C. 312.
(*z*) 5 Cal. 222.

"It is clear that although there be daughters, the sons or other heirs still succeed to the mother's estate, as far as it is distinct from the part already described (as subject to the peculiar devolution under texts applicable to particular species of *stridhanum.*)" This Mr. Justice *West* explains as meaning that, where a woman holds property which is not strictly *stridhanum* as described by the early writers, descent is traced from her as if she were a male. (*a*). It is possible that this passage may be explained differently, as meaning that the property would go to such heirs as would have taken it if it had never fallen into the hands of the female; that is, that it would go to the heirs of the last holder. This accords with the view taken in the case last cited. The point was expressly decided by the High Court of Bengal where a daughter had inherited her mother's *stridhanum.* On the death of the daughter it was held that under the law of the Daya Bhaga all property inherited by a woman, whether from a male or a female, was held under the same restrictions as to power of alienation and passed at her death to the heirs of the last holder. Consequently, that in a conflict between the brother and the daughter of the deceased, the brother was entitled to succeed, as being the nearer heir to the mother from whom the property had been inherited (*b*).

Want of chastity.

Chastity has been held not to be an essential, where a female claims as heir to the property of a woman (*c*). I know of no native authority on the point.

(*a*) *Ante,* § 573.
(*b*) *Hari Doyal Singh* v. *Grish Chunder,* 17 Cal. 911.
(*c*) *Ganga* v. *Ghasita,* 1 All. 46.

INDEX.

*** *The references throughout are to paragraphs :*

THE END.

	Rs.	A.
Cash Prices with Postage.		
Gribble & Hehir's Outlines of Medical Jurisprudence for Indian Criminal Courts, 8vo., *3rd edition*, 1892, *revised and enlarged* ...	5	14
Griffith's (W.) Code of Criminal Procedure, Act 10 of 1882 as modified by the Government up to February 1889, with notes thereon and appendices, 8vo., *just published*	6	4
Griffith's Commentaries on the Indian Easements Act	2	12
——— **Transfer of Property Act, 1892,** *just published*	5	13
N.B.—Griffith's other Law Works, apply for list.		
Hindu Law books, The Vyavahara Mayukha, translated by Borra- daile and two original treatises on the Hindu Law of Adoption, the Dattaka Mimansa, and the Dattaka Chandrika, translated by J. C. C. Sutherland with a Synopsis or General summary of Hindu Law of Adoption, with copious Index, *uniform with the latter* ...	9	6
Hindu Law books, Three treatises on the Hindu Law of Inheritance, Dáya-Bhága and Mitákshará, translated by H. T. Colebrooke, Esq., and the Dáya-krama-sangraha, translated by P. M. Wynch, Esq., third edition, with Index, *uniform with the above*	9	6
Houston's Manual of Hindu and Muhammadan Law as administered in British India and adapted to the use of Candidates ...	3	2
Income Tax Act II of 1886, by Prudhomme	0	10
Indian Cantonments Act No. XIII of 1889 (as amended by Act XII of 1891)	0	9
Indian Factories' Act XV of 1881, Amended 1891, with Addendum, 1892	0	9
Indian (The) Companies Act No. 6 of 1882, with amendment Act 6 of 1887, *2nd edition*, 1892	1	12
Indian (The) Contract Act No. 9 of 1872, with Contents and Index...	1	11
Indian (The) Easement Act No. 5 of 1882. (*See Griffith & Michell.*) ...	0	10
Indian (The) Evidence Act No. 1 of 1872, as amended by Act 18 of 1872, and 3 of 1887 with Stephen's Speech, and the Indian Oaths Act No. 10 of 1873, Index, &c., 8vo., *5th edition. See Cunningham*	1	6
Indian (The) Limitation Act No. 15 of 1877, with Index	1	2
Indian (The) Oaths Act No. 10 of 1873, with Schedule	0	5
Indian (The) Penal Code, Act No. 45 of 1860, in which is incorpo- rated the Amendment Acts Nos. 6 of /61, 14 of /70, 27 of /70, 19 of /72, 10 of /73, & 8 of /82, with an elaborate Index, and to which the following have been added Act No. 24 of /55 (Penal Servitude) and Act 6 of /64 (Whipping), *7th ed...*	3	11
Indian (The) Penal Code as originally framed in 1837, with notes, by T. B. Macaulay, J. M. Macleod, G. W. Anderson and F. Millett, and the First and Second Reports thereon, dated 23rd July 1846 and 24th June 1847, by C. H. Cameron and D. Eliot, Indian Law Commissioners. *A Verbatim Reprint*	6	6
Indian (The) Registration Act No. 3 of 1877, together with the Revised Rules, prepared under the provisions of Sections 69 and 78, 26th May 1877 and 20th May 1882 and Index, *in the Press* ...	0	0
Indian (The) Succession Act No. 10 of 1865, and the Parsee Succes- sion Act No. 21 of 1865, with Hindu Will's Act 21 of 1870, as amended by Act 5 of 1881, with Index.	3	4
Indian (The) Trusts Act No. 2 of 1882	0	10
Indian (The) Trusts Act, 1882 (Act 2 of 1882) with a Commentary, by Eyre B. Powell	3	3
Indian (The) Trusts Act, 1882 (Act 2 of 1882) Commentaries on, by W. Griffith, B.A., 8vo.	4	4
Innes' (Mr. Justice) Examination of Nelson's View of Hindu Law...	2	4
Insolvent Act—Rules and Orders and Table of Fees of the Court for the Relief of Insolvent Debtors at Madras	3	4
Land Acquisition Act. Act X of 1870	0	9
Law Student's Manual, containing Prinicipal Legal Maxims, Terms, Phrases, &c., *4th edition*, 1888	2	10

	Cash Prices with Postage.	RS.	A.
Legal Practitioners' Act (The) No. 18 of 1879...		0	9
Lindley's Study of Jurisprudence, reprinted by authority, 1890— *Text Book for the B. L. Examination*		9	6
Macnaghten's Principles and Precedents of Mahomedan Law, new *edition. 7th reprint, with Digest of cases up to* 1889		14	10
Madras High Court Reports, Vol. I, 3 Parts; II, 3; III, 5; IV, 5; V, 4; VI, 5; VII, 5; each Part, *net* 1/10, Vol. 8, 2/4 ... total...		51	0
M. H. C. Reports, Table of Cases in the—Affirmed, Followed, Doubted, Overruled and Reversed, and an Index to the M. H. C. Rulings from Vols. I to VIII...		1	2
The above bound in cloth, Re. 1-8, and in half calf, Rs. 2 extra ℔ vol.			
M. H. C. Reports—Digest of Cases decided in the High Court of Madras, Vols. I to VIII, by H. Wigram, C.S., *3rd ed.*		3	5
M. H. C. Reports—A Digest of the Report of Cases forming a complete Index to Vols. I to VII, by M. Srinivasa Row, with Supplement...		3	14
Madras Salt Act IV of 1889		0	5
Madras Salt, Abkari and Opium Acts		0	9
Madras (The) District Municipalities Act, No. 4 of 1884 ...		1	3
Madras (The) District Municipalities Act, (Tamil)		1	7
If 12 or more copies be taken Re. 1 per copy exclusive of postage.			
Madras (The) Local Boards Act, No. 5 of 1884		0	12
Magistrates' (The Presidency) Act No. 4 of 1877, and Index ...		2	12
Malabar Law and Land Tenure—an Epitome of—with Glossary, by M. Kelu Nambiar, royal 12mo., 52 pages		1	1
Mayne's Commentaries on the Penal Code, 14th edition, adapted to the Criminal P. Code Act 10 of 1882, and Evidence Act No. 1 of 1872, *with registration*		13	10
Mayne's Treatise on Hindu Law and Usage, *5th edition, just published*		18	12
Mayne's Hints on confessions & approvers for the use of the Police ..		0	13
Menu's Institutes—Manava Dharma Sastra, or Institutes of Menu, by Rev. P. Percival, *4th edition*		6	8
Michell's Law of Easements and Licenses in India, 1891 ...		5	4
Michell's (R. B.) Digest of all the Indian Law Reports for 1876, 2nd ed.		3	3
———————— **for 1877** ...		3	3
———————— **for 1880** ...		4	3
Mukherjee's Guardians and Wards Act. Act VII of 1890 ...		1	7
Negotiable (The) Instruments Act No. 26 of 1881		0	10
Negotiable (The) Instruments Act, Act No. 26 of 1881, with notes, by P. D. Shaw, Barrister-at-Law		3	12
Nelson's (J. H.) View of Hindu Law, with Index, 165 pages ...		6	4
Nelson's (J. H.) Letter to Mr. Justice Innes touching his attack on his view of Hindu Law		0	10
Normandy's Digest of the Cases reported in the following Law Reports, Bengal, Vols. 1—15 and Supplemental Vol. of Full Bench Decisions; Madras, Vols. 1—8; Bombay, Vols. 1—12; N.-W. Provinces, Vol. 1—7; up to 1875, new edition, re-arranged, 1,420 pp. double column, royal 8vo., *half bound, reduced to*		10	8
Norton's (J. B.) Topics of Jurisprudence or Aids to the Office of the Indian Judge, 2nd ed., 1870, by J. W. Handley, Barrister-at-Law		5	8
Pleaders' (The) Test-Book containing the following: Regulations XXV of 1802; XXVI of 1802, also IV of 1822. Acts II of 1864; VIII of 1865; IV of 1882; III of 1885; V of 1882; II of 1882; IX of 1872; XXVI of 1881; II of 1885; XIV of 1882; I of 1877; XV of 1877, (as amended by XII of 1879 and VIII of 1880 and V of 1881); XLV of 1860, (as amended); XXVII of 1870; X of 1882, &c., &c., in one octavo vol., *2nd edition, corrected and revised to date* ...		7	10
Prisoners' Testimony Act No. XV of 1869		0	9
Ragoonatha Row's Review of Hindu Law		0	9

Cash Prices with Postage.	RS.	A.
Rent Recovery Act—Madras, No. 8 of 1865, with Preface, Notes, and Index, by John French, *2nd edition, revised and enlarged* ...	1	2
Revenue Law—A selection of Leading Cases in—with notes, by P. Ramanuja Charry, demy 8vo, 560 pp., 1875	4	6
*** The design of the book is similar to that of Smith's and Norton's Leading Cases. The judgments are given, in many instances, *in extenso* and care has been taken to give prominence to the leading points and the latest decisions and orders.		
Revenue Regulations and Acts relating to Revenue Matters revised to March 1890, arranged chronologically with Rules, &c., and Index, compiled by F. J. Dawes, *4th edition*	4	10
Salt and Abkari Test Books.—*Apply for list.*		
Savigny's (Von) System of the Modern Roman Law, translated by W. Holloway, Vol. I	3	5
Shadagopah's Manual of Mahomedan Civil Law, 8th reprint, 1886 ...	2	2
Sloan's Digest of Decisions on Mahomedan Law to 1881, 2nd edition.	3	4
Smruti Chandrika, or the Hindu Law of Inheritance, translated by T. Kristnasawmy Iyer, *2nd edition*	3	7
Small Cause Courts (The Presidency) Act No. 15 of 1882 ...	0	5
——— **(The Provincial) Act IX of 1887**	0	5
Specific (The) Relief Act No. I of 1877, with Index	1	2
Stamp (The) Act No. I of 1879, as amended by Acts IX of 1884, I of 1888 and VI of 1889 together with the Statement of Objects and Reasons, Mr. Cockerell's Speech, Report of the Select Committee, Contents, Schedule, and Rules and Index, 5th ed., revised ...	1	6
Standing Orders of the Board of Revenue, Chapters I—XIV, revised under the orders of Government, by P. Chentsal Rao Pantulu, C.I.E., with Corrigenda et Addenda to December 1891—Glossary of Terms and Index, Royal 8vo., 776 pp. *the latest ed., published under Authority*	5	6
Strange's Hindu Law, vol. 1st, 5th edition, with Introduction, by J. D. Mayne and Digest of Cases, 1875	7	6
Sutherland's Hindoo Law of Adoption, 26 pages	1	1
——— **Digest of the Indian Law Reports and Rulings of the** High Court of Calcutta from 1862, and of the Privy Council from 1831 to 1876, vol. 1	16	0
——— **Digest of the Indian Law Reports and Rulings of the** several High Courts in India, and of the Privy Council from 1876 to 1881, vol. 2 *reduced to*	3	0
——— **Digest of the Judgments of the Privy Council on Appeals** from India, 3 vols....	27	8
Tarrant's Digest of the Decisions of the Privy Council to be found in Moore's, Indian Appeal Cases, Vols. I to XIV, 3rd edition ...	3	4
Teroomal Rows Digest of the Judgments passed by Hon. Privy Council on Appeals from India, with notes from the Acts, Regulations, Hindu and Mahomedan Law	5	4
Thompson's Manual of Hindu Law, 3rd edition, revised and considerably improved, illustrated by the decisions of all the Courts and the Privy Council, with an Index now given for the first time and new cases noted up and added. **The Appendix contains a discussion** of the Shivagungah Case	6	4
Towns (The) Improvement Act, No. 3 of 1871 and Local Funds' Act, No. 4 of 1871, with copious Index	1	6
Transfer (The) of Property Act, No. 4 of 1882	0	14
Vivada Chintamani, a Succinct Commentary on the Hindoo Law prevalent in Mithila, from the original Sanscrit of Vachaspati Misra, by P. C. Tagore, *2nd edition*	3	8
Weirs' Rules Standing Orders and Forms prescribed by the High Court of Judicature Madras (Criminal Rulings) corrected up to **30th September 1887...**	0	18

Cash Prices with Postage.	RS.	A.
Weirs' Law of Offences and Criminal Procedure as expounded by the High Court of Madras from the year 1862 to 30th September 1887, with appendix of orders and forms, compiled and annotated by T. Weir, Esq., M. C. S., *3rd edition, royal 8vo., pages* 1,259 *inclusive of registration*	14	14
The above strongly bound in half calf, holland sides	17	2
Wigram's Malabar Law and Custom, 1882	4	3
Wigram's Selections from the Judgments of the Privy Council recorded in Moore's Indian Appeals, Vols. I to XIV, Sutherland's Privy Council, Law Reports, Madras Appeals, Vols. I to VIII, 8vo., 464 pp., *reduced to*	2	12

INDIAN MISCELLANEOUS PUBLICATIONS.

Cash Prices include Postage. RS. A.

A Blacker Pamphlet, or an attempt to explain the severity of the late Famine at Madras, by H. A. D. Phillips, B.C.S. 1 1
A Chapter on Burmah Ponies, by "Vagrant" 1 1
Ackrill's System of Short-hand 2 2
Agricultural conditions, capabilities and prospects of the Neilgherry and Coimbatore Districts, reports by W. R. Robertson, Esq. ... 2 11
Agriculture in Madras, a lecture by W. R. Robertson, Esq. .. 0 9
Agriculture (Modern) and What modern Agriculture can do for the Indian Farmer, by W. R. Robertson, Esq. 0 9
Agricultural Question papers of Class I of 1876 and Class II of 1878 of the Madras Agricultural College 2 0
A Guide to the City of Madras and its Suburbs, 4th edition ... 2 2
Ainslie's Materia Indica, or account of articles employed by the Hindoos and other Eastern Nations in their Medicine, Arts and Agriculture, 2nd edition, by J. J. Wood, Part I, 104 pages ... 1 2
Anderson's Hand-book of Logic 0 9
Anglo-Indian Race—by T. G. Clarke, 2nd edition, enlarged ... 0 9
Appasawmy Pillay's (C.) Anglo-Tamil Manual or Phrase Book, based on the plan of "*Forbes' Hindustani Manual*," *2nd edition* ... 3 3
Appasawmy's Translation Guide, English and Tamil, *new edition* ... 1 10
Appasawmy Pillay's Manual of Indian Terms used in the Revenue, &c., Departments 1 3
Appasamy's Translation Guide No. I, English and Telugu ... 0 7
Apostolic Succession: (Exclusive Claims to) Refuted by being brought to the test of Holy Scripture, the Ancient Fathers, &c. ... 0 10
Asiatic Journal (Selections) first series, 1816 to 1829, 1 vol., *red. net.* 5 10
Atkinson's Review of the Effect of Low Exchange on the Export Trade of India 1 3
Balfour's (E. G.) Cyclopædia of India, 3rd edition, 3 vols., (apply for Prospectus) reduced to 28 0
Balfour's (E. G.) Eminent Medical Men of Asia, &c., who have ad-vanced Medical science for the use of Students and for the Vydians and Hakims of India 0 5
Balfour's The Vydian and the Hakim; what do they Know of Medi-cine? 3rd edition 0 5
Banting's Letter on Corpulence 0 9
Bayne's Album of Indian Ferns 10 10
Beddome's Hand-book of Indian Ferns 10 8
Beddome's (Lt.-Col. R. H.) The Ferns of Southern India, being de-scriptions and plates of the Ferns of the Madras Presidency, with 270 plates, quarto size, 2nd edition, author of "*Icones Plantarum Indiæ Orientalis*" 25 14

The plates of this work are accurately drawn, and each one has in addition a magnified figure of the frond or distinctive structure.

Bhagavat Gita (The) English and Tamil, by the late Revd. H. Bower, D.D., with life and introduction 2 12
Bidie's Cinchona Culture in British India 1 1
Bidie's Coca, its source, culture, uses, &c., with a plate 0 9
Bidie's Pagoda or Varahara Coins 2 4
Biographical Sketches of Dekkan Poets; being memoirs of the lives of several Eminent Bards, by Cavally Venkata Ramasawmi, *red.* ... 1 10
Boileau's (Col.) Traverse Tables, 4th edition, *carefully revised* ... 4 4
Bower's (Rev. H.) The Chintamani, First book, called Namacal Ilambam with Commentary, notes, &c., in English and Tamil ... 1 4
Brown's Trees, and Herbaceous Plants of Madras 3 4

Cash Prices include Postage.	RS.	A.
Buchanan's Journey through Mysore, Canara and Malabar, 2nd ed., 2 vols., with maps and 37 plates	12	13
Builder's Vocabulary, English and Tamil and English and Telugu, by T. S. Veerasawmy Moodelliar. 2nd edition, improved, *each* ...	2	2
Building (Notes on) and Road-making with Rules for estimating Repairs to tanks and channels, for the use of Surveyors and Overseers, with building data and other Tables, 8th edition, *revised and enlarged*, with 37 plates	5	14
Burmah—Map of Burmah, the Shan States and adjacent countries, showing Railways, 21 × 16, sheet Rs. 1/10, coloured, Rs. 1/14, mounted	2	6
Caldwell's (Bishop R.) Records of the Early History of the Tinnevelly Mission, demy 8vo., 356 pp., cloth, Rs. 5/4; to Catechists ...	4	4
Caldwell's (R. C.) The Chutney Lyrics, 2nd edition, *reprint*, **1889** ...	1	12
Cinchona (Notes on the Propagation and Cultivation of) or Peruvian bark trees on the Nilgiris, by W. G. McIvor	1	2
Civil Engineering College Papers.		
No. I, Conversational Sentences, Tamil and English, 2nd edition	1	11
No. II, Anglo-Telugu Grammar, 2nd edition	1	11
No. IV, Anglo-Tamil Primer, 3rd edition	3	4
No. V, Hydraulics, by Colonel J. Carpendale, 3rd edition ...	1	12
No VII, Anglo-Telugu Primer, 2nd edition	2	4
No. IX, Schoury's Text Book of estimating, 3rd edition, revised, with additional tables, 32 plates	8	10
Coins of Tinnevelly (The) by Rev. E. Loventhal, with 4 photographic plates	2	9
Colebrooke's Miscellaneous Essays, 2 vols., with 7 *fac-similes*, **&c.** ...	12	8
*** A rich assemblage of materials for the history and explanation of the Vedas.		
Connemara's (Lord) Speeches, edited by J. D. Rees, C.I.E.	1	4
Connor's Tables of Products, Quotients, Squares and Roots ...	3	2
Conquest's (Dr.) Outlines of Midwifery, Tamil and English, 2/6; Telugu and English, 2/6; Canarese & English	2	6
Cornish's Under the Southern Cross	3	4
Cotton's (Col. A.) 1,000 Short Colloquial Sentences, composed of 100 common Telugu words, with free translation, 2nd edition ...	1	2
Cotton's (General Sir A. T.) Public Works in India, with an introduction by Major-General J. F. Fischer, R. E.	2	11
Cunningham's (Sir H. S.) British India and its Rulers	8	4
Curtois' (Col. A.) Manual of the Hindustani Language for the use of officers, with Vocabulary and easy stories, pages 150 ...	1	10
Curtois' (Col. A.) Hints to Candidates for Examination by the Higher Standard in Hindustani	0	13
Digby's Famine Campaign in Southern India, 1876-78, 2 vols. ...	10	14
Digby's Forty Years' Citizen Life in Ceylon, 2 vols.	6	8
Drury's Useful Plants of India, 2nd edition	8	8
Supplement to the above	2	4
Drury's Hand-book to the Indian Flora, a guide to all the Flowering Plants indigenous to the continent of India, 3 vols., royal 8vo., cloth.	31	8
DuBois on the People of India, 3rd edition, with notes, corrections and additions, by Dr. G. U. Pope, with Index, 10/8——*Reprint of the original edition*	8	6
DuBois on the People of India, *reprint of the original ed., with Index.*	8	6
Duff's (Lady Grant) Speeches delivered at various Public Institutions and Meetings during 1884-86, half calico, Rs. 1/2, full cloth.	1	10
Dutt's Ancient India—Peoples' Edition, complete in one vol. ...	5	5
Dymock's Vegetable Materia Medica, Parts 1 to 5, *each*	2	4
Dymock's Pharmacographia Indica. A history of the principal drugs in British India. Parts 1—4, *each*	5	
Elliott's Flora Andhrica of Plants met with in the Northern Circars, Part I	1	2

Cash Prices include Postage.	Rs.	A.
English and Tamil Dictionary with the Tamil words romanized for the use of students & colleges, 1 vol., royal 8vo., half bound 1,519 pp with registration...	15	12
English-Tamil Dictionary with abbreviation, by C. P. Anketel ...	1	2
Ephemeris (English, Hindu and Musulman Calendars) 1851—1895	6	6
Extracts from Manuals of the more deadly forms of cattle diseases in India, Messrs. Thacker & Hallen, in English and Tamil ...	1	2
Extracts from Man and Nature or the earth as modified by human action, by Marsh, with notes on Forests and Rain-fall in Madras, by A. J. Stuart, C.S.	1	9
Family washing Book for 2 years	0	13
Fifth Report of the Select Committee on the affairs of the E. I. Company, with Addenda to 1832, with Addenda and Glossary, by Sir C. Wilkins. 2 vols.	22	0
Fifth Report, Vol. I., Bengal (may be had separately)	12	8
—— —— The Addenda with Glossary	2	12
Firminger's Manual of Gardening, 4th edition, *just published* ...	10	13
Foulkes' (Rev.) The Legends of the Shrine of Harihara, in the Pro-vince of Mysore, translated from the Sanskrit, cloth extra ...	2	12
Führers The Sharqi Architecture of Jaunpore, Vol. 1, 1889, *ilstd.*	17	4
Furnell's (Dr.) Lecture on Water, its connection with the Public Health, 3rd edition	0	7
Garrett's Classical Dictionary of India, the Mythology, Philosophy, Literature, Antiquities, Arts. Manners, Customs, &c., of the Hindus, with supplement, 1 vol. 8vo., 960 pages	15	0
The Supplement *separately*, **160 pages**	2	4
Gazetteer (A) of Southern India, with Atlas of Plans of Towns, &c.	5	14
Game, by Hawkeye, 2nd edition, 345 pages	2	4
Geneologie der Malabarishen Gotter, by Ziegenbalg, edited by Dr. W. Germann, *German text*, 4/4; English translation, by Metzger ...	3	4
Ghose's Appeals of the Manipur Princes	1	11
Gough's Philosophy of the Upanishads	7	2
Griffin's Aid-de-Camp or the treatment of Horses in India, by Blunt Spurs, 6th edition, illustrated	6	4
Greenlaw's (Col. *the late*) **Masonic Lectures**	2	8
Guide (A) for Overseers in the D.P.W., interleaved, pocket-book, tuck.	2	11
Hawkes' Diseases of the Elephant and Camel	1	1
Hayes' Racing Reminiscences, *illustrated*	6	10
Hehir's Rudiments of Sanitation for Indian Schools	1	14
Henderson's Elements of the Slide Rule	2	2
Herklot's Quanoon-E-Islam, or the Customs of the Mussulmans of India, 2nd edition, with plates	10	10
Household Expense Book; Tables of Indian Weights, Measures, Reck-oner, Wages &c., Dhoby's accounts, Calendar 1892, Railway time tables, *2nd edition*	2	12
Hygiene of Water and Water Supplies, by Patrick Hehir, M.D. ...	2	2
Income (The) Tax Act 1886 (No. 2 of 1886), with rules, to which is appended a Calculator for facilitating calculations on Incomes and Salaries, and on Government Securities, by E. N. Prudhomme, of the Bank of Madras	0	10
Indian Domestic Economy and Cookery, by Riddell, *reprint*, **1888** ...	7	6
Indian Gardening, by Riddell, 5th edition, edited by Col. Boddam ...	3	4
Indian Grasses, 2nd edition, revised and enlarged, Illustrated with 69 Lithographic plates, by T. J. Symonds, V.S.	3	12
Indian Snakes—An Elementary Treatise on Ophiology, a descriptive catalogue of the Snakes found in India & the adjoining countries, by E. Nicholson, *2nd edition, reprinted*, 1893	7	14
Indian (The) Family Doctor, by G. E. King, Assistant Apothecary...	2	2
Interest Tables, Set of, from 1 Re. to Rs. 100,000 calculated @ 2 to 12 % for 1 to 365 days and for 1 to 12 months, pocket size, 340 pp.	2	10

Cash Prices include Postage. RS. A.

Jaffrey's Hints to the Amateur Gardeners of Southern India, 2nd edition, with chapters on Crotons, Foliage Plants, Palms & Cycads. 2 4
Jenkin's (Rev. E E.) Sermons preached at Madras 1 4
Jones' (J. A.) A Treatise on Switches and Crossings for Railway and Tramway Engineers; calculations for determining spreads and positions with notes on their design and construction, and on the arrangement of Railway Station Yards, with 42 diagrams, royal 8vo.. 2 10
Joss' (Rev. W.) Notes, &c., on Balfour Stewart Physics Primer, with 51 lithographed diagrams, *reduced to* 1 2
Kearns' Kalyana Shatanku, or Marriage Ceremonies of the Natives of S. India 1 12
Keely's Lessons on Domestic Economy 0 9
N.B.—If 25 Copies are ordered at a time @ 6 as. each
Land (The) of the Tamulians and its Missions, by the Rev. E. R. Baierlein, translated from the German, by J. D. B. Gribble ... 4 3
Latin Text Matriculation of 1893 ... ... 1 10
Do. English Translation 1 2
Lay's of Ind, by Alif Cheem 7 12
Macpherson's (James, Gold Medalist) Neilgherry Tea Planter ... 1 2
Madras Cookery Book for the people, 3rd edition, improved, Rs. 1/10; half calico boards; bound in calico 2 2
Madrasiana, by W. T. Munro, Philomath (Rev. Wm. Taylor), 3rd edition, *reprint*, 1889... ... ... 2 2
Malleson's (Col. G. B.) Seringapatam—Past & Present, with 2 plans... 1 2
Map of the city of Madras, 1887, 30 × 18, sheet coloured, 3/2, mounted 4 2
Mathematical Tables for the use of Students in the Civil Engineer-ing College 0 13
McIvor's Our Mountain Ranges, and how to develop them ... 1 12
McMaster's (Col. A. C.) Notes on "Jerdon's Mammals of India," 2nd edition 2 4
Milne's Adjustments of the Dumpy and Y Levels, a reprint with two diagrams 0 9
Mills' Plain Hints on Diseases of Cattle in India 2 2
—— **Indians' Stock owners Manual (Tamil Translation)** ... 2 3
Morgan's (Genl. H. R.) Forestry in S. India, edtd. by John Shortt, M.D. 2 11
Moor's Hindu Pantheon, with plates, edited by Rev. W. O. Simpson. 21 14
Morris' Telugu Selections, 2nd edition, with Vikramarka Tales, 8vo., 607 pp. 6 14
☞ **Test-book for Sub-Judges, Deputy Collectors, &c.**
Mukherji's Art Manufactures of India 3 4
Mullaly's Notes on the Criminal Classes of the Madras Presidency. 3 3
Mullaly's do do half calico boards ... 2 11
Munro's (Sir T.) Selections from his Minutes and other official writ-ings, edited with an Introductory memoir and notes, by Sir A. J. Arbuthnot, K.C.S.I., one thick Vol., 720 pp. reduced to ... 8 12
My Poultry and how I manage them, by an Indian Henwife ... 1 2
Neilgherry Sporting Reminiscences, by an Old Shikari, without photos 5 4
Norton's (George) Rudimentals, a series of discourses addressed to Natives, 2nd edition, with Introduction, by J. B. Norton ... 2 6
Ooty and her Sisters, or our Hill stations in South India ... 1 2
Orme's History of Hindostan, 3 vols., with plates and maps ... 11 0
Ornamental Foliage Plants—Crotons, Foliage Plants, Palms & Cycads 0 9
Percival's (Rev. P.) Tamil Proverbs, with their English translations. 3 5
Peterson's, Shakespeares Merchant of Venice, with notes ... 1 10
Picking's from Old Indian Books, Vol. I 1 11
Planter's (The) Manual, Coffee by Laborie and Cinchona by McIvor, revised edition 2 4

Cash Prices include Postage.	RS.	A.
Pope's First Lessons in Tamil, 5th edition, *revised and enlarged* ...	5	15
Pope's Tamil Primer in the Anglo-Indian character	1	2
Practical Hints on Flower Gardening in Madras, by F. H. L., with chapters on Crotons, Foliage Plants, Palms and Cycads ...	1	2
Ready Reckoner with Tables of Wages, Indian Weights and Measures, Telegraph Tariff, Postal Notes, Rates and Money Orders ...	1	2
Reflections about Russia, by Rajah Sir T. Madhava Row, K.C.S.I. ...	0	5
Rhenius' Tamil Grammar, 4th edition	4	12
Rhodes' (A.) Earth-work Tables, 3rd edition	1	12
Rhodes' Universal Curve Tables for Railways, Canals, &c. ...	2	12
Ricardo's Exchange Remedy, 2nd edition	0	9
Rogers' (Col. H. T.) First Lessons in Telugu	1	10
Ross' Child of the Ocean, A romance of the Andamans	4	0
Rowe and Webb's Hints on the Study of English	3	5
Salt Test-Books,		
Hand-book of Common Salt, by J. J. L. Ratton, 2nd edition, with a chapter on the manufacture and chemistry of Saltpetre ...	6	5
Ratton's Report on the Manufacture of Salt, Madras Presidency, 1872	1	10
Ratton's Additional Chapter on Saltpetre	0	9
Saltpetre, a Brief Account of—its theory, origin, source of supply, methods of manufacture and refining, by W. Kingston ...	0	9
Sankanarayan's English and Telugu Dictionary	4	6
Schmitz's (Dr. L.) Manual of Ancient History, Madras University, F. A. History Text Book, 15th edition	5	14
Set of 10 Classical Maps to accompany above...	1	12
Sell's (Rev. E.) The faith of Islam, sewed, Rs. 2/8, cloth... ...	3	0
Sewell's Archæological Survey of India, Vol. I, 10/12 ; Vol. II ...	8	10
N.B.—*Vol. II, contains the Author's* "SKETCH *of the* DYNASTIES OF SOUTHERN INDIA."		
Sherring's Hindu Tribes and Castes, Vol. 2	12	14
Shortt's (Dr. J.) Autobiographical Memoir	1	7
Shortt's (J., M.D.) *Works.*		
A Manual of Indian Agriculture, with 12 plates, *just out* ...	3	12
Account of Jeypore, in Vizagapatam, descriptive of its feature, climate, people, &c.—The Mahundra Malli—the Yelagary and Jawady Hills—Gallicondah, Part III	1	12
Account of Nundidroog, the Mukh, or Kudar Mookha, the Bábá Búden Hills and Ramandroog in Bellary, with 3 plates, Part IV	2	4
Account of Parts of the Nullamullays, Kurnool District, &c., Part VI	1	12
Account of Thomas' Hill or Kilasa in Vizagapatam. Report on the proposed Sanitarium—Memorandum on Vizagapatam, Harbour & Port—Kondavide in the Kistna District—The Hill Ranges of the Cuddapah District—The Anamally Hills—The Pulni Mountains—North Coimbatore, & Lambton Peak Range, with 3 plates, Part V	2	11
Account of the Tribes & a Geographical and Statistical Memoir of the Neilgherries, by the late Colonel Ouchterlony, Part I ...	2	4
A Manual of Indian cattle & Sheep, their breeds, management, &c., 3rd edition, revised, 1889, with 24 plates	2	12
And Cornish's the Shevaroys, & other Ranges in the Salem Dis-trict, Part II	2	2
Autobiography	1	6
Manual of Family Medicine for India	2	12
On Indigo Culture, Tamil and English	2	4
Sibthorpe's (Dr. C.) Clinical Manual, 3rd ed., enlarged with illus.	3	12
Sketches of Native Life and Character in India, by F. E. W. ...	1	14
Skinner's Description of India and Burman Timbers	2	5

Cash Prices include Postage.	RS.	A.
Staff Corps Officers Companion and Probationers " Vade Mecum", a useful hand-book for all ranks, by Capt. G. J. Shaw, Adjutant, 6th Madras Infantry, 2nd edition, *revised and enlarged*	3	3
Steel's (Vet. Surgeon J. H.) A Manual of the diseases of the camel, *ilstd.*	5	4
Steel and Symond's Materia Medica Veterinaria Indica, colored plates	4	4
Stoddard's (Col.) Hydraulic Rules and Formulæ, 3rd edition ...	2	12
Stoker's, A gold Standard for India, Critically Examined ...	1	1
Strangers Yet. A Tale of three Christmas Morns	1	2
Switches and Crossings for Railway and Tramway Engineers, by J. A. Jones, M.I.C.E., with 42 diagrams, royal 8vo., 57 pp. ...	2	10
Syad Mohammed Latif's History of the Punjab	15	10
Taylor's Hindu Mythology and Philosophy, 2nd edition... ...	1	12
Telugu Selections compiled from the several Test-books in that language, for the use of Officers in the Civil, Military, and Public Works Department, in the Madras Presidency, by order of the Board of Examiners, 2nd edition, 607 pp., demy 8vo.	6	14
Thomas (H. S.) M.C.S. Tank Angling in India, with 17 illustrative plates, Author of the " Rod in India," &c.	5	3
Thurston's History of the Coinage of the East India Company, with plates	2	11
Thurston's Roman Indu-Portuguese and Ceylon Coin (one plate) ...	0	12
Thurston's Catalogue of Frogs, Toads and Cœcilians of Southern India, *illustrated by thirteen plates*	1	12
Thurston's Notes with Pearl and Chank Fisheries and Marine Fauna of the Gulf of Manaar	1	6
Tobacco, its planting and manufacture, in Tamil and English ...	1	2
Tod's Annals and Antiquities of Rajast'han, or the Central and Wes-tern Rajpoot States of India, in 2 vols., with a map, royal 8vo., third reprint, 1880	25	12
Vikramarka Tales in Telegu, revised and reprinted	1	2
Ward on the Hindoos, 5th edition	12	8
Introduction to the above	2	4
What to tell the Cook, or the Native Cook's Assistant, in English and Tamil, 5th edition	2	2
Wheeler's Madras in the Olden Time, new edition, 3 vols. in one ...	6	6
Wheeler's Early Records of British India	12	8
Wickham's (Capt. W.) Military Transport in India	1	9
Wilkins' Hindu Mythology	8	0
Wilkins' Modern Hinduism, an account of the Religion and life of the Hindus in Northern India	8	7
Wilk's Sketches of Southern India, in an attempt to trace the His-tory of Mysore, from the origin of the Hindu Government to the extinction of the Mahomedan Dynasty in 1799—2 vols., royal 8vo., with maps...	12	10
Wilmot's (Capt. H. E.) M.S.C. Manual of Persian Phrases for use in translations	2	10
Wilmot's (Capt. H. E.) M.S.C. Manual of Hindustani Phrases for the L. S. Examination	1	1
Wilmot's (Capt. H. E.) M.S.C. One thousand Hindustani idiomatic Sentences for the use of Candidates for H. S. & H. P. Examinations	2	2
Wilmot's (Capt. H. E) M.S.C. Æsop's Fables in Persian	2	10
Wilson's Descriptive Catalogue of Mackenzie's Oriental Manuscripts	8	6
Woodrow's Gardening in India, 5th edition, 1889 ... *red.*	6	10
"Wyvern's" Furlough Reminiscences, a Potpourri or reflections, observations & Incidents, compiled from the diary of a Happy Holiday in England ... ... *red.*	1	11
"Wyvern's" Sweet Dishes, a little treatise on confectionery and En-tremets Sucrés, 3rd edition, *revised—just published*	3	8
"Wyvern's" Culinary Jottings for Madras, 6th edition... ...	5	6